PRAISE FOR THIS EDITION

T0361246

A remarkable collection of in-depth essays on a vast array of topics relating to Iberian cultures across the ages. Rather than focusing on Spain as an isolated unit, this book encourages readers to view Iberia as a whole—a multifaceted, multicultural entity in which diverse languages, traditions, and histories come into play. Interdisciplinary in concept, it includes essays on politics and art, literature and geography, economics and religion, history and visual culture by acclaimed experts from both sides of the Atlantic. The articles on Irish cultural influences in Spanish are particularly refreshing. The articles on women during different periods of Iberian history help to provide a comprehensive view of Iberian society. Also extremely innovative are the sections on twentieth and twenty-first-century Iberia, which offer not only a new look at the rise of fascism and the civil war, but also groundbreaking work on Spanish film, television and popular literature, including comics. This is a book that all Hispanicists will want to have on their bookshelves.

Professor Barbara Mujica, *Georgetown University*

A timely and engaging exploration of the new mapping of the field. In less than a decade, the debate about the need to shelve monologic and monolithic versions of Hispanism and replace them with a more plural relational approach has taken centre stage. There is growing consensus that the cultural, historical and political complexity of the territory cannot be addressed within traditional disciplinary borders with the old methodological tools. This book is a response to demands to put the reconfiguration of the field into practice. Many of the leading scholars in Iberian Studies have contributed to this monumental collection that demonstrates the justification and rewards of a comparative perspective. It derives some fruitful lessons from the application of the premises of Comparative Literature to the internal differences and tensions in the Peninsula, and to the interaction between forms of cultural production. The most complete picture of the landscape is thus achieved by means of a prismatic composition: the sum of diverse fragments gives us a view of the whole.

Professor Antonio Monegal, *Universitat Pompeu Fabra*

A superbly rich collection of 50 articles by scholars deploying multiple approaches to the diverse cultures of Iberia, medieval to present day. A few samples: a witty history of the Camino de Santiago; articles on translation, medieval, Franco era and present day; on medieval hermeneutics and premodern subjectivity in the *Libro de buen amor*; on Alvar Núñez and sixteenth-century mapping; on blood (im)purity in Iberia and Iberian colonies; on paintings of the *morisco* expulsion; rehearsal scenes and the *comedia* as prompt book for a changing society; on Icarus and Phaethon in Golden Age cultural production; on Enlightenment painting; on women writers – medieval convent voices, Enlightenment Hispano-Irishwomen, Rosalía de Castro, and female detective novels; on the rise and demise of Iberian empires, on civil wars, nation formations, changing political vocabularies, city planning, Basque and Catalán cultures, cinema and graphic novels; and much, much more to savor. In all, an excellent contribution to the several fields of Hispanic studies, and given its interdisciplinary focus, to students and scholars in history, translation studies, art history, theater studies, women's studies, political science and cultural anthropology as well.

Professor Margaret R. Greer, *Duke University*

This impressive book is an essential tool for research in Iberian Studies. The wide range of topics that are dealt with in this *Companion* constitutes a highly comprehensive view of Iberian history, politics and culture together with literature and visual arts. With contributions written by most prestigious scholars, the *Companion* offers a complete exploration of key topics from a systematic and historical perspective, providing a comparative foundation for the understanding of a complex reality. The depth of the articles makes it possible to read each contribution both as a coherent part of a whole and as a single work. The variety of topics guarantees the usefulness of this indispensable volume for all readers and researchers in Iberian culture.

Professor Tomás Albaladejo, *Universidad Autónoma de Madrid*

Following Resina's pioneering call for a more transnational understanding of the Iberian condition, these 50 essays, by scholars of different lands and generations, fully succeed at breaking traditional academic barriers and hierarchies: The *Companion*, organized chronologically from the Middle Ages to the 21st Century, explores, often in comparative fashion, the complex political, cultural – visual/textual – , social and historical tapestry of the Peninsula, unconstrained by language, field, nationality, gender or race. Moreover, the notion of "Iberian Studies," born in the era of globalization, is not here another form of compartmentalization, for it necessarily interacts with other "studies" and their modes of analysis. Media Studies, Afro-Iberian Studies, Visual Studies, and Global studies, among others, become commensurate and indispensable interlocutors. Such equitable dialogue is particularly illuminating when its subjects traverse or confront by definition multiple languages and territories: pilgrimage, nationalism, empire, cartography, emigration/exile and, repeatedly, translation, as much from a "foreign" language as between "national languages."

Professor Luis Fernández Cifuentes, *Harvard University*

THE ROUTLEDGE COMPANION TO IBERIAN STUDIES

The *Routledge Companion to Iberian Studies* takes an important place in the scholarly landscape by bringing together a compelling collection of essays that reflect the evolving ways in which researchers think and write about the Iberian Peninsula.

Features include:

- A comprehensive approach to the different languages and cultural traditions of the Iberian Peninsula;
- Five chronological sections spanning the period from the Middle Ages to the twenty-first century;
- A state-of-the-art account of the field, reaffirming Iberian Studies as a dynamic and evolving discipline with promising areas for future research;
- An array of topics of an interdisciplinary nature (history and politics, language and literature, cultural studies and visual arts), focusing on the cultural distinctiveness of Iberian traditions;
- New perspectives and avenues of inquiry that aim to promote a comparative mode within Iberian Studies and Hispanism.

The fifty authoritative, original essays provide readers with a diverse cross-section of texts that will enrich their knowledge of Iberian Studies from an international perspective.

Contributors: Samuel Amago, Rachel L. Burk, Rodrigo Cacho Casal, Jordi Canal, Isabel Capeloa Gil, Enric Castelló, Manuel Castiñeiras, Jesús Cruz, Frederick A. de Armas, Antonia L. Delgado-Poust, John Edwards, Brad Epps, George Esenwein, Sebastiaan Faber, Javier Fernández Sebastián, Antonio Feros, Robert Folger, Elizabeth Franklin Lewis, Benjamin Fraser, E. Michael Gerli, Richard Gillespie, George D. Greenia, Michelle M. Hamilton, David K. Herzberger, Jonathan Jarrett, María Liñeira, Laura Lonsdale, José Luis Martí, Elisa Martí-López, Kathryn M. Mayers, Raquel Merino-Álvarez, Javier Muñoz-Basols, Micaela Muñoz-Calvo, Rosa Navarro Durán, Mari Jose Olaziregi, Santiago Pérez Isasi, Alexander Ponsen, Ronald Puppo, Richard Rabone, Pamela Radcliff, Helen Rawlings, Joan Ramon Resina, Filipe Ribeiro de Meneses, Cristián H. Ricci, Alberto Romero Ferrer, Teofilo F. Ruiz, Agustín Sánchez Vidal, Julio-César Santoyo, Andrew Schulz, Jonathan Thacker, Lesley K. Twomey and David A. Wacks.

Javier Muñoz-Basols is Senior Instructor in Spanish and Co-ordinator of the Spanish language programme at the University of Oxford.

Laura Lonsdale is Associate Professor of Spanish at the University of Oxford and Fellow of The Queen's College.

Manuel Delgado is Professor of Spanish at Bucknell University.

THE ROUTLEDGE COMPANION TO IBERIAN STUDIES

Edited by Javier Muñoz-Basols,
Laura Lonsdale and Manuel Delgado

LONDON AND NEW YORK

First published 2017
by Routledge

2 Park Square, Milton Park, Abingdon, Oxfordshire OX14 4RN
52 Vanderbilt Avenue, New York, NY 10017

Routledge is an imprint of the Taylor & Francis Group, an informa business

First issued in paperback 2019

British Library Cataloguing-in-Publication Data
A catalogue record for this book is available from the British Library

Library of Congress Cataloging-in-Publication Data
Names: Muñoz-Basols, Javier editor. | Lonsdale, Laura, editor. |
    Delgado, Manuel, 1944– editor.
Title: The Routledge companion to Iberian studies / edited by
    Javier Muñoz-Basols, Laura Lonsdale and Manuel Delgado.
Description: London ; New York : Routledge, 2017. | Includes
    bibliographical references and index.
Identifiers: LCCN 2016039697 | ISBN 9780415722834 (hardback : alk.
    paper) | ISBN 9781315709895 (ebook)
Subjects: LCSH: Iberian Peninsula—Civilization. | Iberian Peninsula—
    Intellectual life. | Spain—Civilization. | Spain—Intellectual life. |
    Portugal—Civilization. | Portugal—Intellectual life. | Iberians.
Classification: LCC DP48 .R68 2017 | DDC 946.00072—dc23
LC record available at https://lccn.loc.gov/2016039697

ISBN: 978-0-415-72283-4 (hbk)
ISBN: 978-0-367-86738-6 (pbk)

Typeset in Times New Roman
by Apex CoVantage, LLC

CONTENTS

Contents

FIGURES

CONTRIBUTORS

Samuel Amago is Professor of Spanish and Associate Chair at The University of North Carolina at Chapel Hill. He teaches courses on modern and contemporary Spanish literary history, cinema, and culture. He is the author of *Spanish Cinema in the Global Context: Film on Film* (2013) and *True Lies: Narrative Self-Consciousness in the Contemporary Spanish Novel* (2006). He is currently working on a study of trash and cinema in democratic Spain.

Rachel L. Burk is Assistant Professor of Spanish at Notre Dame of Maryland University, having taught previously at the University of Pennsylvania, Tulane, and the Universidade de Lisboa, the last as a Fulbright scholar. She is currently completing a book on literary and visual representations of blood purity in early modern Iberia. Rachel holds an A.B. in English from Columbia University and a Ph.D. in Hispanic Studies from the University of Pennsylvania.

Rodrigo Cacho Casal is Reader in Spanish Golden Age and Colonial Studies at the University of Cambridge and a Fellow of Clare College. His research focuses mainly on Renaissance and Baroque cultures and Spanish-American colonial literature. He is currently preparing a monograph on the development of early modern Spanish-American colonial poetry.

Jordi Canal is Maître de conférences at the École des hautes études en sciences sociales in Paris. He has written several books on Carlism and on the history of Catalonia, notably *Banderas blancas, boinas rojas: una historia política del carlismo, 1876–1939* (2006); *La historia es un árbol de historias: historiografía, política, literatura* (2014); and *Historia mínima de Cataluña* (2015), among other works.

Isabel Capeloa Gil is Professor of Cultural Theory at the Universidade Católica Portuguesa, Honorary Fellow at the Institute of Modern Languages Research (University of London), and director of The Lisbon Consortium. She is co-editor of *Landscapes of Memory: Envisaging the Past / Remembering the Future* (2004); editor of *Fleeting, Floating, Flowing: Water Writing and Modernity* (Königshausen & Neumann, 2008); and author of *Literacia Visual. Estudos sobre a Inquietude das Imagens* (2011).

Enric Castelló is Associate Professor at the Department of Communication Studies at the Universitat Rovira i Virgili (Tarragona) and member of the Asterisc Communication Research Group. He was guest researcher at Glasgow Caledonian University. He specializes in media studies, social identities and political conflict, and is founding editor of the *Catalan Journal of Communication and Cultural Studies*.

Manuel Castiñeiras is Associate Professor of Medieval Art History at the Universitat Autònoma de Barcelona (UAB), where he is currently Head of the Department of Art and Musicology. His research focuses primarily on Romanesque imagery, specifically as expressed in panel and wall painting, architectural sculpture and manuscript illumination, as well as on the Pilgrimage to Santiago de Compostela and artistic exchanges in the Mediterranean between the eleventh and fifteenth centuries.

Jesús Cruz is Professor of Iberian History at the University of Delaware. He is the author of *Gentlemen, Bourgeois and Revolutionaries: Political Change and Cultural Persistence among the Spanish Dominant Groups, 1750–1850* (1996); *Los notables de Madrid: las bases sociales de la revolución liberal española* (2000); and *The Rise of Middle-Class Culture in Nineteenth-Century Spain* (2011).

Frederick A. de Armas is Andrew W. Mellon Distinguished Service Professor in Romance Languages and Comparative Literature at the University of Chicago where he served as Chair of Romance Languages. De Armas has been the recipient of several NEH fellowships and has directed NEH Summer Institutes and Seminars. He has also served as President of the Cervantes Society of America. He is the author of some twenty books and edited collections ranging from *The Return of Astraea: An Astral-Imperial Myth in Calderón* (1986) to *Cervantes, Raphael and the Classics* (1998). His most recent monograph, *Don Quixote Among the Saracens: Clashes of Civilizations and Literary Genres* (2011), received the PROSE Award in Literature, honorable mention.

Manuel Delgado is Professor of Spanish at Bucknell University. He is the author of a number of books and articles on the works of Gil Vicente, Lope de Vega, Miguel de Cervantes, Guillén de Castro, Calderón de la Barca, Mira de Amezcua, Ruiz de Alarcón, and Federico García Lorca. In 1991 he received the Lindback Award for Distinguished Teaching at Bucknell University and was awarded the Presidential Professorship in 2007 for his achievements in teaching and research.

Antonia L. Delgado-Poust is Assistant Professor of Spanish at the University of Mary Washington in Fredericksburg, Virginia. Her research addresses themes related to gender violence, identity, motherhood, feminism, and transformation in contemporary Peninsular literature and film. She is currently engaged in a book-length study of feminism, memory, and female ontological insecurity in twenty-first-century narrative.

John Edwards is Modern Languages Research Fellow in Spanish at the University of Oxford. He has published extensively on Spanish religion and society in the late medieval and early modern periods and is currently working on a major study of Spanish religion, at home and abroad, from 1350 to 1600.

Brad Epps is Professor of Spanish and Head of the Department of Spanish and Portuguese at the University of Cambridge. He was Professor of Romance Languages and Literatures and Professor and former Chair of the Committee on Degrees in Studies of Women, Gender, and Sexuality at Harvard University for more than two decades. He has published extensively on modern literature, film, art, architecture, urban theory, queer theory, and immigration from Spain, Latin America, Hispanophone Africa, and Catalonia and has taught as visiting professor or scholar in ten countries in Europe, Latin America, and Asia.

George Esenwein teaches history at the University of Florida (Gainesville). He is the author of *Anarchist Ideology and the Spanish Working-Class Movement, 1868–1898* (1989); *Spain at War: The Spanish Civil War in Context, 1931–1939*, coauthored with Adrian Shubert (1995); and *The Spanish Civil War: A Modern Tragedy* (2005). His latest research and publications focus on the historiography of the Spanish Civil War during the Cold War and beyond.

Sebastiaan Faber is Professor of Hispanic Studies at Oberlin College. He is the author of *Exile and Cultural Hegemony* (2002) and *Anglo-American Hispanists and the Spanish Civil War* (2008), and co-editor of *Contra el olvido. El exilio español en Estados Unidos* (2010), as well as some eighty articles on twentieth- and twenty-first-century Spanish and Latin American literature, history, and culture. He is currently writing about historical memory in Spain.

Javier Fernández Sebastián is Professor of the History of Political Thought at the Universidad del País Vasco (Bilbao). He has published extensively on modern intellectual and conceptual history, focusing in particular on Spain and the Spanish-American world. He currently coordinates an on-going international project called *Iberconceptos*.

Antonio Feros is Associate Professor of History at the University of Pennsylvania and the author of many publications on various aspects of seventeenth-century Spanish history – court politics, art, and political representation, and ideas and images of kingship. He is currently completing a book on views of race and nation in the Spanish world, 1450 to 1820.

Robert Folger is Professor of Romance Literatures at Heidelberg University. He is the author of several monographs and numerous articles on a broad range of topics in Spanish and Latin American literature and cultural history, from the Middle Ages to the present.

Elizabeth Franklin Lewis is Professor of Spanish and Chair of Modern Languages and Literatures at the University of Mary Washington, United States, specializing in women and gender in Spain's Enlightenment period. She is the author of *Women Writers in the Spanish Enlightenment* (2004) and co-editor with Catherine Jaffe of *Eve's Enlightenment: Women's Experience in Spain and Spanish America, 1726–1839* (2009).

Benjamin Fraser is Professor and Chair in the Department of Foreign Languages and Literatures at East Carolina University. Having published twelve single-authored and edited books and some sixty articles in Hispanic Studies and beyond, he is also Founding Editor of the *Journal of Urban Cultural Studies* and Founding Co-editor of the Hispanic Urban Studies book series.

E. Michael Gerli is Commonwealth Professor of Hispanic Studies at the University of Virginia. His research interests include the intellectual and cultural history of the Western Mediterranean from the Middle Ages through early modernity. He is the General Editor of *Medieval Iberia, an Encyclopedia* (2003), one of sixteen books he has authored or edited.

Richard Gillespie is Professor of Politics at the University of Liverpool. He is the author of works on Iberian politics, the foreign and security policy of the EU, and Euro-Mediterranean relations. He is currently directing a research project on 'The Dynamics of Nationalist Evolution in Contemporary Spain,' funded by the ESRC (http://nationalismsinspain.com).

George D. Greenia is Professor of Hispanic Studies, Medieval & Renaissance Studies, and founder of the Institute for Pilgrimage Studies at the College of William & Mary in Virginia. He has published widely on the literature and history of medieval Iberia, its book culture, and the Camino de Santiago.

Michelle M. Hamilton is Professor of Spanish and Portuguese at the University of Minnesota, Twin Cities. Her research focuses on the Romance, Hebrew, and Arabic literatures and cultures of medieval Iberia. Her current project deals with Jewish and *converso* cultural production in fifteenth-century Iberia.

David K. Herzberger is Distinguished Professor of Spanish and Chair of the Department of Hispanic Studies at the University of California, Riverside. He is the author of several books on twentieth and twenty-first-century Spanish literature. His major fields of research are the modern Spanish novel, historiography, and contemporary Spanish theater.

Jonathan Jarrett is Lecturer in Early Medieval History at the University of Leeds. He has taught medieval history at the Universities of Birmingham, Oxford and London and has been Interim Curator of Coins at the Barber Institute of Fine Arts in Birmingham. He has published on numismatics, diplomatics, the digital humanities and especially the early Middle Ages in Western Europe and the Iberian Peninsula. He blogs at http://tenthmedieval.wordpress.com/.

María Liñeira has lectured on Galician and Spanish Studies at the University of Oxford and the University of Exeter. She is currently working on a multidisciplinary project about censorship. Her research areas include emergent literatures, gender, and translation studies.

Laura Lonsdale is Associate Professor of Modern Spanish Literature at the University of Oxford and Fellow of The Queen's College. She works on twentieth-century narrative and theatre, and is currently completing a monograph on literary multilingualism and modernity in the Spanish-speaking world.

José Luis Martí is Associate Professor of Law and Philosophy at Universitat Pompeu Fabra of Barcelona. He has written several books and articles on democratic theory (particularly on the idea of deliberative and participatory democracy), republican political philosophy, philosophy of criminal law, and philosophy of international law. He is currently researching new social movements and their use of new technologies for democratic participation.

Elisa Martí-López is Associate Professor of Spanish at Northwestern University. She has worked on a range of topics including the *folletín*, the translation and imitation of foreign literary models, and processes of cultural production and consumption in the mid-nineteenth century. She is currently engaged in a project on the impact of death and cemeteries on the cultural and literary imagination from the late eighteenth century to the First World War.

Kathryn M. Mayers is Associate Professor of Spanish at Wake Forest University. She is the author of *Visions of Empire in Colonial Spanish American Ekphrastic Writing* (2011), as well as articles on Sor Juana Inés de la Cruz, Hernando Domínguez Camargo, and Álvar Núñez Cabeza de Vaca.

Raquel Merino-Álvarez is Professor of Translation Studies at the Universidad del País Vasco/ Euskal Herriko Unibertsitatea. She has coordinated the TRACE (translation and censorship) Project and she is currently Principal Investigator of the TRALIMA (Translation, Literature and Audio-Visual Media) consolidated research group funded by the Basque Government (www.ehu.es/tralima). Her publications deal with the history of translated theatre in Spain, and translation and censorship.

Javier Muñoz-Basols is Senior Instructor in Spanish at the Faculty of Medieval and Modern Languages at the University of Oxford. He has published on Hispanic literature, translation studies, and applied linguistics. His current research focuses on the interaction between language and culture in various settings, including contemporary graphic literature and humour.

Micaela Muñoz-Calvo is Associate Professor in English Philology at the Department of English and German at the University of Zaragoza, Spain. She teaches scientific English at the Faculty of Sciences and gives doctoral courses on translation studies. Her fields of interest are literary translation, the translation of humour, and translation and culture in contemporary comics and graphic novels.

Rosa Navarro Durán is Professor of Spanish Literature at the University of Barcelona. Her research focuses on the history of Spanish Literature of the Golden Age, the editing of texts of this period, and the theoretical aspects of literary commentary. She has also adapted for children many of the Spanish classics. She is currently engaged in an edition of the continuations of *La Celestina*.

Mari Jose Olaziregi is Associate Professor of Basque Literature at the Universidad del País Vasco/Euskal Herriko Unibertsitatea and former Academic Director of the Etxepare Basque Institute. She has published on topics including the history of Basque literature, postwar Basque fiction, Basque gender studies, and the relationship between literature and politics in the Basque context. She is currently engaged in a collective project on the cultural history of Spanish literature.

Santiago Pérez Isasi is a Post-Doctoral Researcher at the Centro de Estudos Comparatistas (Faculdade de Letras, Universidade de Lisboa). His research interests include Iberian Studies, Literary Historiography, nineteenth- and twentieth-century Spanish narrative, and the Digital Humanities. In 2013 he co-edited the volume *Looking at Iberia: A Comparative European Perspective* (Peter Lang).

Alexander Ponsen is a Ph.D. candidate in History at the University of Pennsylvania. He specializes in the history of the early modern Iberian world and is currently completing a dissertation on imperial sovereignty in remote regions of the Spanish and Portuguese empires during the period of Iberian union.

Ronald Puppo is Associate Professor of English and Translation at the Universitat de Vic. His extensively annotated *Selected Poems of Jacint Verdaguer* (2007) is the first English-language anthology of Verdaguer's poetry, and his full-length, annotated English edition of *Canigó* came out in 2015. He is currently preparing a volume of selected poetry and prose by Joan Maragall.

Richard Rabone is a Junior Research Fellow in Spanish at Merton College, University of Oxford. His research focuses on Golden Age literature, with a particular emphasis on its reception of classical authorities, and he is currently working on a study of the influence of the Aristotelian Golden Mean on early modern Spanish literature. He has also translated the *Libro de Alexandre* and the *Poema de Fernán González* for Aris and Phillips.

Pamela Radcliff is Professor in the Department of History at the University of California, San Diego. She is the author of several books and articles on popular mobilization, gender and women's politics, and civil society in twentieth-century Spain. Her most recent book is *Making Democratic Citizens in Spain: Civil Society and the Popular Origins of the Transition, 1960–1978* (2011).

Helen Rawlings is Senior Lecturer in Spanish at the University of Leicester. She is the author of books on church, religion and society in early modern Spain, the historical legacy of the Spanish Inquisition, and the discourse that has informed the debate on the decline of Spain. She is currently writing a history of the code of *limpieza de sangre*.

Joan Ramon Resina is Professor of Comparative Literature and Iberian Studies at Stanford University. He is the author of books on medieval myth, modernist literature, the concept of the classic, the Avant-Garde, literature and the city, the new ruralism, metadisciplinary theory, and historical memory. He is currently at work on literary journalism, specifically a monograph on Josep Pla.

Filipe Ribeiro de Meneses is Professor of History at the National University of Ireland, Maynooth. He is the author of, among other works, *Portugal 1914–1926: From the First World War to Military Dictatorship* (2004), *Salazar: A Political Biography* (2009) and *Afonso Costa: Portugal* (2010).

Cristián H. Ricci is Professor of Iberian Studies at the University of California, Merced. He is the author of *El espacio urbano en la narrativa del Madrid de la Edad de Plata, 1900–1938* (2009), *Literatura periférica en castellano y catalán: el caso marroquí* (2010) and *¡Hay moros en la costa! Literatura marroquí fronteriza en castellano y catalán* (2014).

Alberto Romero Ferrer is Professor of Spanish Literature at the Universidad de Cádiz. He specialises in Spanish theatre as well as the relationship between politics and literature in the eighteenth to twentieth centuries. He is currently the principal investigator of a research project on the Hispanic imaginary and the literary culture of exile, with a particular focus on drama.

Teofilo F. Ruiz is Distinguished Professor of History and in the Department of Spanish and Portuguese at the University of California at Los Angeles. He has published on the social and cultural history of late medieval and early modern Spain, ranging from festive traditions, the sources of political power, and literature. He is presently completing a book on the western Mediterranean.

Agustín Sánchez Vidal is Professor Emeritus in Cinema and Audiovisual Media in the Department of Art History at the Universidad de Zaragoza, Spain. He is the author of more than sixty books on literature, art and cinema, including *Buñuel, Lorca, Dalí: El enigma sin fin*, awarded the Editorial Planeta's "Espejo de España" prize in 1988.

Julio-César Santoyo is Professor Emeritus of Translation Studies at the Universidad de León, Spain. He has published several books on the theory, history and bibliography of translation, and has translated into Spanish works by Christopher Marlowe, Robert Lewis Stevenson, J.R.R. Tolkien, Jack London, Willa Cather, Edgar Allan Poe, etc. His main interests today include the history of medieval translation on the Iberian Peninsula, self-translation, and pseudo-translations.

Andrew Schulz is Associate Professor of Art History and Associate Dean for Research at the College of Arts and Architecture at The Pennsylvania State University. He is a specialist in the art of Spain and the Spanish world in the eighteenth and early nineteenth centuries. He is particularly interested in the role of visual culture in the construction of national and imperial identity, and in the conditions of artistic production and reception in the age of Enlightenment and Romanticism. He is the author of *Goya's Caprichos: Aesthetics, Perception, and the Body* (2005).

Jonathan Thacker is Professor of Spanish Golden Age Literature at the University of Oxford and Fellow and Tutor in Spanish at Merton College. He is the author of *A Companion to Spanish Golden Age Theatre* (2007) as well as a monograph and articles on early modern Spanish drama. He is currently engaged in research on Golden Age drama in translation and performance.

Lesley K. Twomey is Reader in Hispanic Studies at Northumbria University. She is the author of various monographs about Hispanic literature, such as *The Fabric of Marian Devotion in Isabel de Villena's Vita Christi* (2013). She works on the history of spirituality, on Marian doctrine, and on hagiography.

David A. Wacks is Professor of Spanish in the Department of Romance Languages at the University of Oregon. He is author of *Framing Iberia: Frametales and Maqāmāt in Medieval Spain* (2007) and *Double Diaspora in Sephardic Literature: Jewish Cultural Production before and after 1492* (2015). His research (davidwacks.uoregon.edu) focuses on the literary footprint of the confluence of Christianity, Judaism, and Islam in the Medieval Iberia.

PREFACE

. . . ¿en lugar de hablar de España, no sería mejor hablar de las Españas? El dese-quilibrio profundo que existe entre los diversos países de la Península es camu-flado bajo la ambigüedad genérica de una etiqueta común. La realidad española de Cataluña no es la misma que la de Galicia, ni coincide la de Andalucía con la del País Vasco. En tales condiciones, ¿no es ceder a una simplificación grosera, a una perezosa facilidad, hablar de España en singular, enmascarando así la existencia de unas realidades distintas? La pregunta es pertinente y exigiría una respuesta afirma-tiva. No existe una sola España, sino varias Españas de diferentes niveles económi-cos, sociales y culturales: toda tentativa de reducirlas a un denominador común nos lleva a sacrificar la realidad a la arbitrariedad del método. Mejor que sobre España y los españoles, hubiera sido escribir sobre las Españas y los españoles de cada una de ellas (castellanos, catalanes, vascos, gallegos). El lector tendrá que perdonarnos por no hacerlo: no disponemos de suficiente número de páginas.

Juan Goytisolo, *España y los españoles*

When Goytisolo published his critical study of Spain, *España y los españoles*, in German during the last years of Franco's regime, Américo Castro remarked with a degree of bitter irony that "su libro, por vez primera, sitúa el problema español en el centro de Europa, y es gran cosa que haya salido primero en alemán" (Goytisolo 2002, 12). If it was "gran cosa" in 1969 for the book to highlight the European dimension of Spanish reality, Goytisolo's concern with its Iberian dimension – however briefly elucidated – was an associated challenge to the cultural insularity and nationalistic bravado of Francoism. When the work finally saw the light in Spanish ten years after its publication in German and only a year after the enacting of the Spanish Constitution, Goytisolo appended a final chapter, "De cara al futuro," whose title not only encapsulated the seismic political shift that had taken place in the interim, but also set the tone for a more gradual process of social and cultural change in the years ahead, a process that would be inextricably bound up with the assertion of cultural and linguistic difference.

That process has demanded, in turn, a shift in the study of the languages and cultures of the Iberian Peninsula. Traditionally, Iberian Studies has implied a focus on Spain and Portugal and the respective languages of the two nation-states, Spanish and Portuguese; but as Iberian Stud-ies evolves as a discipline, or, perhaps more accurately, as a project at once academic, cultural, and political, it distinguishes itself from traditional peninsular Hispanism and Lusitanism by seeking to generate a comparative space in which the much greater linguistic and cultural diversity of the Iberian Peninsula is the prime object of interest. For Joan Ramon Resina, champion of the new brand of Iberian Studies, a disciplinary reformulation is necessary for two reasons: firstly, because "the rise of Hispanic studies condemned non-Castilian cultures to the outer darkness," and secondly, because "the period of nation-building, as well as of the rise of Hispanism, resulted in the latter's impoverishing monolingualism and the atomization of Iberian cultures into a number of mutually exclusive national philologies" (2013, 2). Though Resina himself is pessimistic about the prospects of Iberian Studies at a time when Modern Languages and the Humanities are already under pressure in the university, the shift in academic consciousness that he advocates in the essays collected in *Del hispanismo a los estudios ibéricos* (2009) has already gained considerable ground within peninsular Hispanism. Testament to this are not only the essays included in edited volumes devoted to a consideration of the discipline, such as Resina's own *Iberian Modalities* (2013), Mabel Moraña's *Ideologies of Hispanism* (2005), Santiago Pérez Isasi and Ângela Fernandes' *Looking at Iberia* (2013), and the *Comparative History of Literatures in the Iberian Peninsula* (2010, 2016) edited by César Domínguez et al., but also a range of volumes that engage critically with the plural nature of the Iberian literary and cultural context, including *Spain Beyond Spain* (Epps and Fernández Cifuentes 2005), *Reading Iberia* (Buffery et al. 2007), and *New Spain, New Literatures* (Martín-Estudillo and Spadaccini 2010). In addition, many leading research institutions and Hispanic Studies departments worldwide have made curricular changes and even, in some cases, renamed themselves in an attempt to reflect the discipline's changing emphasis. Nonetheless, as Resina himself recognises, the "semantic scope" (2013, blurb) of Iberian Studies remains to be defined, as a more traditional focus on nation-states competes with an increasing attention to (as yet) stateless nations. The Companion therefore takes the temperature of Iberian Studies across a variety of disciplines at a time when different meanings of the term are still in play.

In this already fertile context of growing interest in Iberian Studies, then, *The Routledge Companion to Iberian Studies* takes an important place in the scholarly landscape by bringing together a compelling collection of essays that reflect the evolving ways in which we think and write about the Iberian Peninsula. By drawing on the Peninsula's broad cultural and linguistic base without obscuring its diversity or fragmenting it into isolated pockets, and by offering in the range and scope of its chapters a pluralist and comparative approach to the cultures, languages and histories of the Peninsula, the Companion manifests its engagement with the new contours and dimensions of the discipline. In this way it seeks to open up new perspectives and avenues of inquiry which will not only be fruitful to Iberian Studies, but which may also promote a more comparative mode within Hispanism in particular, which arguably has still to come to terms with the multilingual spaces and histories it occupies. Nonetheless, as one might expect of a volume of this nature and size, it is something of a broad church, seeking to showcase some of the best writing on Iberian subjects rather than to offer a specific theoretical or methodological intervention in the debates currently shaping Iberian Studies.

The aim of this volume is therefore to echo and reflect the evolving nature of Iberian Studies as it is practised today, bringing together established and emerging scholars from across the world in Iberian history, literature, cultural studies and the visual arts, in fifty specially commissioned chapters spanning the Middle Ages to the present day. The volume is structured into five chronological periods: Part I. Medieval Iberia (eighth–fifteenth centuries); Part II. The Iberian Peninsula in the Golden Age (sixteenth and seventeenth centuries); Part III. The Iberian Peninsula in the eighteenth and nineteenth centuries; Part IV. The Iberian Peninsula during the twentieth century; and Part V. Iberian studies in the twenty-first century. Each period is divided into two main sections: History, Politics and Cultural Studies and Literature and Visual Culture, topical clusters that allow for a range of disciplinary and interdisciplinary perspectives on the cultures of the Iberian Peninsula. With a greater number of pages at our disposal than Goytisolo claimed to have at his, the Companion offers a wide range of scholarly perspectives on the Iberian Peninsula, mapping its distinctive linguistic and cultural diversity. The attempt to review and rethink both a national and disciplinary space is captured by the image on the book cover: Equipo Crónica's *La salita* (1970), a Pop Art reinterpretation of Velázquez's *Las Meninas*, the most paradigmatic example of Spanish "classical" painting (Llorens 2015, 20).

The Routledge Companion to Iberian Studies therefore provides a comprehensive, state-of-the-art account of the field, reaffirming Iberian Studies as a dynamic and evolving discipline offering promising areas of future research. This compendium of authoritative, original essays provides readers with a cross-section of varied and interesting texts that will enrich their knowledge of the discipline from the Middle Ages to the present day.

Works cited

Buffery, Helena, Stuart Davis, and Kirsty Hooper. 2007. *Reading Iberia: Theory, History, Identity*. Oxford: Peter Lang.

Cabo Aseguinolaza, Fernando, Anxo Abuín Gonzalez, and César Domínguez. 2010. *A Comparative History of Literatures in the Iberian Peninsula*. vol. 1. Amsterdam: John Benjamins.

Domínguez, César, Anxo Abuín Gonzalez, and Ellen Sapega. 2016. *A Comparative History of Literatures in the Iberian Peninsula*. vol. 2. Amsterdam: John Benjamins.

Epps, Brad and Luis Fernández Cifuentes. 2005. *Spain beyond Spain: Modernity, Literary History, and National Identity*. Lewisburg, PA: Bucknell University Press.

Goytisolo, Juan. 1969. *Spanien und die Spanier*. Lucerne: Verlag C. J. Bucher.

———. 2002. *España y los españoles*. Prologue by Ana Nuño. Barcelona: Lumen.

Llorens, Tomàs. 2015. *Equipo Crónica*. Bilbao: Museo de Bellas Artes de Bilbao/Bilboko Arte Ederren Museoa.

Martín-Estudillo, Luis and Nicholas Spadaccini, eds. 2010. *New Spain, New Literatures*. Nashville, TN: Vanderbilt University Press.

Moraña, Mabel, ed. 2005. *Ideologies of Hispanism*. Nashville, TN: Vanderbilt University Press.

Pérez Isasi, Santiago and Ângela Fernandes, eds. 2013. *Looking at Iberia: A Comparative European Perspective*. Oxford: Peter Lang.

Resina, Joan Ramon. 2009. *Del hispanismo a los estudios ibéricos. Una propuesta federativa para el ámbito cultural*. Madrid: Biblioteca Nueva.

———. 2013. "Iberian Modalities: A Relational Approach to the Study of Culture in the Iberian Peninsula." In *Iberian Modalities*, edited by Joan Ramon Resina, 1–22. Liverpool: Liverpool University Press.

ACKNOWLEDGEMENTS

We thank John Dagenais (UCLA), David Nirenberg (University of Chicago), and Juan-Carlos Conde (University of Oxford) for their suggestions during the planning of the present volume. We are also grateful to the numerous individuals and institutions who have granted us permission to use the images contained in the book: Fundación Bancaja (Juan García Rosell), Cabildo de la Catedral de Girona, Iglesia de San Esteban de Almazorre, Huesca (Antonio García Omedes), Santiago de Turégano, Segovia (Manuel Castiñeiras), Ajuntament d'Anglesola, MNAC–Museu Nacional d'Art de Catalunya, Barcelona (Photographers: Calveras/Mérida/Sagristà), Balliol College, Oxford, Fundación Casa Ducal de Medinaceli, University of Glasgow Library (Special Collections), Museo del Prado, Meadows Museum, Juan Luis Buñuel, Fundación Gala-Salvador Dalí, Astiberri Ediciones (Laureano Domínguez), Guy Delcourt Productions and Paco Roca, El Patito Editorial (Gemma Sesar Ignacio) and Miguelanxo Prado, Norma Editorial (Josefina Blaya) and Isabel Franc and Susanna Martín. We express our gratitude to Fundación Juan March, most especially Manuel Fontán del Junco, to the VEGAP (Visual Entidad de Gestión de Artistas Plásticos), and the artist Manuel Valdés for allowing us to use the image of the work by Equipo Crónica on the cover. Finally, we are grateful to the following people for their help with the editing of the manuscript: First and foremost, Richard Rabone's contribution to the volume has been instrumental both in the editing and translation of a number of chapters. We are also in debt to Pawel Adrjan for his technical know-how and to Meritxell Soler-González for her help with the images. Finally, we are indebted to Agustín Sánchez Vidal for his suggestions on selecting a cover image, to Tina Cottone, Project Manager at Apex CoVantage, for her dedication and superb attention to detail during the typesetting of the volume, and, most especially, to Camille Burns, Editorial Assistant, and to our Editor at Routledge, Samantha Vale Noya, for her guidance, patience and support throughout the development of this project.

PART I

Medieval Iberia
(eighth–fifteenth centuries)

History, politics and cultural studies

1

FESTIVE TRADITIONS IN CASTILE AND ARAGON IN THE LATE MIDDLE AGES

Ceremonies and symbols of power

Teofilo F. Ruiz

The extent (and limits) of royal power throughout medieval and early modern western Europe rested, to a large degree, on the adroit deployment of a variety of rich ideological discourses and symbols of power. These representations of power, whether solemn or festive, were easily identifiable by those in the position to challenge the power of kings and by the population as a whole. Ceremonies and symbols helped create what Joseph R. Strayer, Ernst Kantorowicz, and others have described as "the religion of monarchy." Sometimes, however, such discourses of power failed to impress the Crown's adversaries or worked, in perverse fashion, to undermine or delay the full exercise of regal power. Such was the case in France in the first decades of the fifteenth century when the English (and putative French) king Henry VI (1421–1471), and Charles VII (1403–1461), the so-called king of Bourges, struggled to legitimize their rights to the French throne. While the former king ruled Paris (and was crowned king of France at Westminster Abbey and Notre Dame de Paris) and the latter had an uncertain hold on Bourges and southern France, neither of the two had access to Reims – then in the hands of the Burgundians interested in weakening both rulers. Without Reims there could be no formal crowning and, far more important, no anointment with holy oil which, by the fifteenth century, had become fully associated with Clovis' miraculous baptism in 496. When Charles VII was able to enter Reims and undergo those rituals of monarchy peculiar to France, the claims of Henry VI became defunct.

If I have provided this one lengthy example it is to note – as we begin an examination of ceremonies and festivities in the diverse Iberian realms – that rituals could not only be malleable, as was often the case in Castile, but counterproductive. The example may also serve as a reminder that, while the history of royal ceremonies in northern medieval and early modern Europe has often been presented as normative, their structures and aims are not entirely applicable to parallel rituals of power enacted in the Spanish realms. In that sense, the kingdom of Castile, most of all, and other Iberian realms developed their own festive and ceremonial practices. One should emphasize that, unlike the French and even the English, Iberian ceremonies that marked the ascent to the throne were never so wedded to tradition as to make them indispensable. In fact, Iberian ceremonies often differed greatly from those of the north. Yet, as is the case with every historical event or cultural artifact, context mattered a great deal. It did so then; it does so now.

Late medieval and early modern Spanish rituals of power: divergent models

Without subscribing to a teleological stance that traces modern states to their medieval origins, it is also undeniable that a series of political and cultural developments led to greater centralization of political power in the thirteenth century and beyond. These developments, underlined by the growth of royal bureaucracies, the emergence of borders, new forms of warfare, and, most significantly, taxation, were paralleled by greater emphasis on "public" displays, textual and pictorial representations of royal ceremonies, symbols of power, and festivities. Moreover, from the early fourteenth century onwards the chroniclers' descriptions of these events increased exponentially. What was the meaning of such displays? How effective were they?[1]

In this discussion I wish to focus on a specific genre of ceremonies – regal coronation or royal ascent to the throne – as well as on the symbols of authority and royal power displayed or omitted at these events in the coronation cycles of Castile and the Crown of Aragon. One must begin by dispelling the notion that there was a uniform tradition common to all the Iberian realms. While the different Peninsular kingdoms shared some ritual elements with one another and with other parts of the medieval West, they also had peculiarities that signaled differences among them. For example, depending on the period examined, the Crown of Aragon's ritual ceremonies of royal investiture at times had closer parallels with ceremonies in France and southern Italy than they did with those of Castile. There was no "Spain" in the Middle Ages or in the early modern period in the sense in which such a term could be used in the eighteenth century, when the Bourbons centralized most of the Peninsular kingdoms, following French practice. Yet, strangely enough, neither the Bourbon kings then, nor their descendants now, were ever crowned or bestowed with those symbols of power commonly deployed by their ancestors in France. Following their Castilian and Habsburg predecessors they were neither ritually crowned nor anointed.

Ceremonies and rituals of power in Spain

In Spain's medieval realms, rulers deployed complex rituals of power. These festive events were laden with ideological and symbolic significance, articulating elaborate political discourses. These ceremonies not only differed from realm to realm – though they shared similar purposes and the ritual trappings that had become almost obligatory in royal self-representation – but also often voiced (through imitation and one-upmanship) political antagonisms between the different polities in the Peninsula and internal conflict between the Crown and the high nobility. These ceremonies of power and legitimation rested on the presence and display of a series of symbols – swords, crowns (or the absence of crowns), seals, gestures, knighting, oaths of fidelity, and royal entries – that constituted the ceremonial and symbolic discourse of royalty in the Spanish medieval kingdoms and elsewhere.[2]

Because of space limitations, I have restricted the scope of this paper to two festive cycles. The first encompasses three successive events: the royal entry of Alfonso XI in Seville (1327), the coronation of Alfonso IV in Zaragoza as king of the Crown of Aragon (1328), and the coronation of Alfonso XI in Burgos as king of Castile-Leon (1332). I would argue that all three ceremonies were thematically linked, forming a continuum of political competition between Iberian realms and their rulers. Moreover, though somewhat similar displays and rituals were present, the differences, sometimes subtle and at other times striking, tell us a great deal about the comparative history of festive traditions in both realms. Our second case study examines the ascent to the Castilian throne of Isabella I (1474) and that of her consort, Ferdinand II, to the Crown of Aragon (1479). The second of these cases has been little studied in this context.

A royal entry and two coronations

Elsewhere I have examined in detail Alfonso XI's royal entry into Seville in 1327 for both its festive and symbolic significance (Ruiz 2012, 68–70). Here it is sufficient to note that this royal entry was unprecedented in the festive rituals of the Iberian realms. After restoring order to Castile and bringing rebellious nobles and municipalities into line, Alfonso XI (1312–1350) came to Seville for the first time since reaching his majority. He did so now as the undisputed ruler of the land. Although the chronicle dedicates only a single page to the event in its printed edition, the ritual significance of this entry marks a watershed in the Peninsula's festive traditions. The king was received outside the walls of the city with feigned military equestrian skirmishes (*bohordos*) and knights dressed and riding in the Muslim fashion. Mock battles of barges on the River Guadalquivir re-enacted the Christian conquest of the city in 1248. What was unusual, however, was that the nobles and prominent citizens came to meet the young king outside the gates of Seville, dismounted from their horses, and brought him into the city under a baldachin or *palio*. Although the use of the *palio* will become a permanent fixture in later royal entries, to my knowledge this is the first such occurrence in the Iberian Peninsula for monarchs (Ruiz 2012, 68–70; *Crónica de Alfonso XI* 1953, 204).

The symbolic and ritual pretensions of this entry, allying the king with the sacred and with similar ceremonies that required the use of a baldachin, most of all the Corpus Christi, must not have gone unnoticed in the eastern kingdoms. When Alfonso IV came to the throne after the death of his father Alfonso III, he was, as Bonifacio Palacios Martín showed many years ago, the heir to a well-established tradition of coronation and anointment (see subsequent discussion). Nonetheless, and probably prompted by Alfonso XI's bold claims in Castile, Alfonso IV (1328–1336) made a series of crucial departures from the established traditions or practices of coronation and anointment in the Crown of Aragon. Of course, in Iberia such rituals did not make a king, but were secondary to, and an adornment of, other crucial ceremonies: most importantly, being sworn in by the Crown of Aragon's parliaments. The death of the previous ruler automatically determined the succession to the throne. This was the case even in France with the traditional formula of "*Le roi est mort, vive le roi!.*" Yet while in France a king could not fully be a king until ceremonially crowned and anointed at Reims, in the Crown of Aragon, and far more so in Castile, these rituals of kingship were an added element to an already acknowledged regal authority.

Ramón Muntaner, a Valencian delegate and eyewitness to the festivities, provided a lengthy and vivid description of the rituals surrounding Alfonso IV's accession, to conclude his *Crònica*. Even if one takes into account Muntaner's propensity for exaggeration, there is no question that in 1328 there were substantial additions to the festive programs usually associated with coronations in the Crown of Aragon. It was, in the words of Palacios Martín, a "public spectacle." The ceremonies were held on Easter Sunday, a feast closely associated with renewal and rebirth. After touring his diverse kingdoms and meeting with their respective *Corts* or *Cortes*, the king made his way to Zaragoza. His arrival and the preparations for the coronation took place against the backdrop of endless parades of high nobles and knights through the streets of the city, the knighting of at least 256 lesser nobles, a royal vigil of arms on Good Friday, and, on Easter Saturday, the shedding of mourning clothes and the donning of new and colorful garments. On Easter Sunday, the king placed his sword and crown on the altar. He dressed himself in ceremonial robes, girded the sword unaided, and allowed his brother to place golden spurs on his feet. Raising his sword, the king challenged the enemies of the faith, promising to defend the weak and to give his life to God if necessary. Then, having approached the main altar, he took the crown in his hand and crowned himself, while allowing, afterwards, the bishop to anoint him on the shoulder. (See Muntaner 1999, 610–631; Palacios Martín 1975, 23, 77ff., 204–227.)

If Alfonso IV had been prompted to enhance the ritual and festive aspects of his coronation in response to the symbolic claims made by Alfonso XI in his royal entry into Seville in 1327, the Castilian king was certainly prompted to plan his own coronation in response to that of Alfonso IV. After all, Alfonso XI had been king for twenty years by the time he chose to undertake a coronation and anointment. He had been in firm control of the realm for only slightly less than a decade. The only other reason that may have motivated his coronation was the birth of his legitimate heir, though he had already produced several illegitimate children with his beloved mistress, Leonor de Guzmán. Moreover, there had been no tradition of either coronation or anointment among the kings of Castile for close to two centuries: neither Alfonso XI's father, nor his grandfather, nor his great-grandfather had been crowned. Yet, in the context of Peninsular rivalry and family links – Alfonso XI's sister was Alfonso IV's queen – one may see the reasons for the unexpected ceremonies of 1332.

Alfonso XI traveled to Santiago de Compostela where he was knighted by the mechanical arm of a statue of St. James placed on the main altar. Before that, he had kept vigil over his arms as befitted a soon-to-be-knighted nobleman and as Alfonso IV had done. Surely, for a king who had already led successful campaigns against Granada, knighting was redundant. Furthermore, as Peter Linehan has shown, despite other historians' assertion of its ancient pedigree, the statue of St. James had probably been brought from France for this occasion. As was the case with many Castilian ceremonies including Alfonso XI's crowning, this was another invented tradition. Returning to Burgos to preside over numerous jousts and festivities, the king marched in formal procession to the nearby monastery of Las Huelgas where he crowned himself, crowned his wife, and was anointed on the shoulder, disregarding the *ordo* that had been written for the ceremony. What did all these things have in common? What was the meaning of these rituals (see Linehan 1993, 584–601; Ruiz 1985, 109–144)?

Reading festivals: the malleability of rituals

If we engage in a "thick description" of these three festive events, certain common features and dissimilarities become evident, pointing to the differences in the construction of festive traditions in the two Spanish realms. The first thing to note is the malleable nature of ritual or performative strategies. Rituals depend, as do festivals, on the exact reiteration of certain formulae and gestures to be effective. This is certainly the case of certain rituals such as the elevation of the host in the Mass and transubstantiation. The miracle depends on the exact repetition of the words in a particular order. This was certainly not the case with festive performances. While royal entries, coronations, and the like shared some elements in their basic structure with previous such displays, each particular context allowed for changes, innovations, and subtle differences that addressed particular political needs. Chroniclers and others describing the festivities often sought refuge in such formulae as "as it was done [before] in the kingdom," proclaiming therefore the authority of ancient tradition. This is the case, for example, with Alfonso XI's entry into Seville, even though there is no textual or iconographical evidence that anything similar had ever been done before in the Castilian realm. Yet we know that, in all three of the cases briefly previously described, significant modifications were introduced, and these were pregnant with political symbolism.

In the case of Alfonso XI's entry in 1327, the baldachin or *palio* seems to have been an innovation that advanced political claims which had not been deployed by Castilian kings for five generations or more. The vivid example of Church rituals or a notion (however misguided) of ritual practices associated with the reign of Alfonso VI and Alfonso VII, the last claimants to the imperial title, may have prompted the use of the *palio* and a new understanding of the political role of such sacred symbols in Castile. As we know, the entry into Seville followed upon Alfonso XI's successful restoration of order and an end to the chaos that prevailed during his minority. It preceded his first formal campaign against Muslim rulers. Similarly, as Palacios Martín has noted, Alfonso IV's elaborate coronation rituals in Zaragoza – an event with close chronological links to Alfonso XI's entry but which generally followed Arago-Catalan precedents – aimed at providing something new in terms of coronation rituals. Whether it is simply that Muntaner's lengthy and elaborate description of the event provides us with more details than we have for other coronations in the Crown of Aragon, or whether Alfonso IV truly wished to match the symbolic gestures of his Castilian counterpart, it is clear that at the coronation in Zaragoza new formulae were introduced, and new claims, most of which reflected courtly ideals, were advanced. These new claims, which portrayed Alfonso IV as defender of the faith and righter of wrongs, were either not present before or were not deemed worthy of description in earlier and sparer accounts of coronation rituals.

This ability to try something new, while keeping novelties within the broad structure of coronation rituals, is most evident in the solemn ceremonies for Alfonso XI's coronation in 1332. In fact, no king had been crowned or anointed in Castile since the mid-twelfth century (whether, as Nieto Soria (1998) has argued, they were crowned spiritually by God or not, is inconsequential). The reality is that, without warning, Alfonso XI chose to do something that was far from the norm in Castile. Moreover, after 1332, the Kings of Castile and later Spain abandoned ritual coronation and anointment ceremonies; later medieval kings (except for Henry II, the Trastámara usurper), and their Habsburg and Bourbon descendants, including the present king of Spain, also eschewed this type of ceremony. In the three cases examined previously, which were closely connected politically and chronologically, rituals were summoned out of the past or invented outright while claiming the authority of tradition, performed, and then abandoned once again. What is significant here is that while the high nobility and clergy were most certainly aware of the rituals associated with coronation, anointment, and a royal entry, as far as the audience was concerned – that is, the all-important "public" that by their presence and acclamations gave legitimacy to the performance – these ceremonies were always new. They resembled and reiterated something known while introducing new elements that addressed the political needs of the moment.

Processions, knighting, and symbols

Common also to all three events was the movement from one place to another. Processions, a well-known medieval cultural event that included the peregrination of relics, the Corpus Christi, and other movements of sacred symbols in and out of urban spaces or along established routes within cities, were an important aspect of the festive performance of the royal entry or of the coronations described previously. They were also part of all festive performances in medieval and early modern Europe. In the case of Alfonso XI's entry into Seville in 1327, the king travels to Seville; he is met outside the city and brought into the city in solemn procession, accompanied along the way by equestrian and martial displays; he wends his way through the city of Seville along what must have been a pre-arranged and well-plotted route.

Alfonso XI repeated this performance for his coronation: a pilgrimage to St. James, the return to Burgos, and the formal and hierarchical slow procession from Burgos to the monastery of Las Huelgas in 1332. Alfonso IV would also tour the different capitals of the Crown of Aragon before entering Zaragoza. The movement of people, so vividly described by Ramón Muntaner, is a carefully scripted move from "here to there;" or, to borrow a phrase from Michel de Certeau's *The Writing of History*, from the "known to the unknown." It was a movement from the known world of action, of kings and martial displays, to the unknown and mysterious world of the cathedral and the sacred. Processions, therefore, involved transitions through liminal spaces. They served as markers for important events in the life cycle, and, in this particular case, for the political life of kings. Though the two Alfonsos were kings *before* their coronations or royal entries, the *palio*, the crowns, and the anointments signaled important steps in their respective claims to rule.

Both of the coronations described previously involved knighting, the girding of one's own sword, and other aspects that marked the martial character of kingship in the Iberian kingdoms and elsewhere in the West, as well as the revival of courtly traditions in fourteenth-century western Europe. Similarities abound, but differences too. We already know of the significance of the sword in festive ceremonies. Swords asserted the power of kings and were an important ingredient of royal performance. Both the kings of the Crown of Aragon and those of Castile were punctilious in not allowing anyone to gird their swords. They were equally insistent in bringing many chivalric elements into the act of coronation. In the case of Alfonso XI, as we have already seen, he raised the stakes in 1332 by having a mechanical statue of St. James knight him. This was also an invented tradition and a managing of rituals to advance claims to power. It may have been a unique episode in the history of the Castilian monarchy. The statue, which can be seen in Las Huelgas of Burgos to this very day, does not seem to have been used again in any of the ceremonies accompanying the ascent to power of Castilian kings; at least, there is no textual evidence that it was. The importance of the statue, as Peter Linehan has so powerfully shown, was to give sacred sanction to Alfonso XI's knighting (which in the case of both kings was a prerequisite to the coronation and anointment) without the presence of clergymen. In this the knighting and coronation of 1332 differed from those of 1328, as ecclesiastical participation was kept to a minimum in the former, but was much more significant in the latter (see Linehan 1993, 427, 598–599 and passim).

Finally, there was the question of self-crowning and of the crown itself as a symbol of royal power, central to the ceremonies held at Zaragoza in 1328 and at Burgos in 1332. Both kings crowned themselves, ignoring the bishops present. The studies of Palacios Martín and Percy Schramm make it clear that there was not a well-established tradition of self-crowning before the late thirteenth century in the Crown of Aragon and, as Schramm has shown, crown, sword, scepter, and other symbols played an important role in the representation of regal power. The important example of Frederick II, the Hohenstaufen emperor, who crowned himself, and the connections between the Crown of Aragon and Frederick's Sicily through marriage and rule of the island after the Sicilian Vespers' rebellion against the French created a thread of textual and ritual transmission that explains why Peninsular kings chose not to be crowned by clergy, unlike kings from north of the Pyrenees. In the case of Alfonso XI, this was taken to an extreme, as he not only crowned himself, but crowned his queen as well. A great deal more can be drawn from a close reading of these texts, but for limitations of space this is not the place to press them further (see references at the end of this chapter).

Ascending the throne in late medieval Castile and the crown of Aragon: the Catholic Monarchs

The ascent by Isabella and Ferdinand II to their respective thrones in Castile and the Crown of Aragon in 1474 and 1479 provide ample opportunities for exploring how the process by which new rulers came to power was transformed throughout the Middle Ages. More important to us here is the manner in which claims to power were asserted through ceremonies that, while familiar, also presented new elements that reflected specific political contexts. Moreover, in the particular case of Ferdinand II, the articulation of power in the Mediterranean lands of the Crown of Aragon – Naples and Sicily above all – reflected the peculiar circumstances of each of these realms. If nothing else, the performance of power remained flexible, the rituals malleable. It is very clear that for all their protestations of holding equal power – *tanto monta, monta tanto* – Ferdinand and Isabella ruled over very unequal realms (see Elliott 1963, 73). Moreover, while Isabella sought to unify the Peninsular kingdoms and worked for administrative and legal centralization, Ferdinand II preferred the variety of administrative practices, legal systems, and local privileges so clearly associated with the diverse realms of the Crown of Aragon (see Elliott 1963, 68–72, 96–97 and passim). How did they then articulate their rise to power?

Isabella I and Ferdinand II

As Elliott pointed out long ago, the two members of the royal couple that would, in time, become the Catholic Monarchs reached the throne of their respective realms against long odds and in the midst of severe crises. Isabella's claim to the throne was not straightforward since Juana, also known by her enemies as la Beltraneja, also had rights to the throne regardless of whether she was legitimate or not. Castile had descended into general anarchy, with the nobility engaged in a free-for-all, as they sought to control and take advantage of the monarchy. The Crown of Aragon also suffered from endemic violence in the form of a civil war that pitted the nobility against the peasantry, the so-called war of the *remences*. Catalonia, with Barcelona as the head of the principality, insisted on its ancient privileges and autonomy. The city of Barcelona itself was torn apart by social strife. The situation was hardly a stable one, and this context determined, to a certain extent, the manner in which both rulers would mark their ascent to the throne, Isabella in 1474, and Ferdinand in 1479.

Isabella was in Segovia when she heard of her half-brother King Henry IV's death on December 12, 1474. Ferdinand, her husband for the previous five years, was in Aragon dealing with the mounting problems plaguing the kingdom in the last years of John I's rule. Isabella acted swiftly to establish her claims to the throne. Andrés Bernáldez and other contemporary chroniclers provide details of Isabella's grab for power in what was, surely, a *coup d'état* in which Castile truly became Isabella's realm with Ferdinand as a consort:

> [. . . upon hearing the news] the Princess Doña Isabel covered herself with mourning clothes and cried, as it was to be done, for her brother the king, and she went to the Church of Saint Michael, and there also went the banners of the king Don Enrique [Henry], and those of the city of Segovia, covered in black mourning and carried low, and after enacting all the ceremonies [and prayers] of mourning, masses, and obsequies, they [the people of Segovia] built a stage and they [the magnates and people of Segovia] raised Doña Isabel Queen of Castile and Leon. Then the *mayordomo*

[the king's steward] Cabrera gave the newly named queen the keys to the fortresses [*alcazares*] in the city, the staff of justice, and the treasures of her brother, whose *mayordomo* he was . . .

(My translation of Bernáldez 1953, 576; Ruiz 2007, 198–199)

Hernando del Pulgar's chronicle, always more reliable than Bernáldez's, emphasized the raising of the banners of Castile to the traditional cry of "Castile, Castile for the king Don Fernando and for the queen Doña Isabella, his wife and *ruler of these kingdoms.*" This was followed by other acclamations throughout many cities in northern Castile and by processions of nobles coming to Segovia to kiss Isabella's hand in obeisance (del Pulgar 1953, 253; Ruiz 2007, 198). The emphasis in the quotation is mine and reaffirms John Edwards' (2000, 21) description of Isabella's self-proclamation as queen as a "coup." Similarly, Alfonso de Cartagena described Isabella's procession through Segovia, with the newly invested queen marching behind the sword of justice, which her equerry held high by its point.

Isabella was not crowned or anointed. What legitimized her power were a series of ceremonies that had a long pedigree in Castile, but which were slightly modified for this particular performance. We do not know whether the Queen and her advisers had discussed what to do in the case of Henry IV's death: something that was expected to come sooner rather than later. We do not know either whether her claim to power was scripted on the spot by borrowing from traditional Castilian practices. What we do know is that a series of symbols and ritual performances needed to be enacted as a necessary corollary to her claims to the Castilian crown.

Here once again we are met with processions, this time through the streets of Segovia, which included the donning and discarding of mourning clothes (something that Alfonso IV had done in 1328), and acclamations by the "people," essentially the high nobility allied to Isabella. Other ceremonial elements were also added, for which there were precedents. Yet even though Andrés Bernáldez refers to the formal acclamation of both Ferdinand and Isabella as a coronation, no crowning took place. Moreover, there is no evidence from accounts of previous ascensions to the throne that all these events – processions, acclamations by the people, raising of standards, assuming the keys to the royal fortresses in Segovia, the staff of justice, and Henry IV's treasure – could be undertaken in such a short time span.

The haste of the performances and their order, if we are to take the chroniclers at their word, tell us that the Queen and her advisers understood the need for swift action, owing to both her Castilian rivals and the absence of her husband. What would have been done over the following weeks was carried out in just a day or two – further evidence, once again, of the malleability of rituals within Castile. Yet no other symbol played as powerful a role for the population of Segovia and, ultimately, for the rest of Castile as the sight of the naked sword of justice held aloft in front of the Queen, as she processed through the streets of Segovia. Swords had had special significance in Castile since the glorious sword of Ferdinand III (1217–1252), and were deployed endlessly by Castilian monarchs and regents from Ferdinand III till the late Habsburgs. The messages conveyed by the sword of justice could not have been lost on the population of Segovia and, far more importantly, on the magnates that accompanied the Queen in her ceremonial procession through the city (see Ruiz 2009, 13–48; 2012).

When we turn to Ferdinand II, the story changes dramatically, pointing to the importance of ritual context and traditions in the selection of the appropriate performance for each occasion or locality. One must remember that Ferdinand II became king of Castile in 1474, the moment that Isabella, his wife, became queen. We must also remember that he had earlier been named king of Sicily by his father. Zurita, always an impeccable chronicler, continuously refers to him as king of Sicily. In the turbulent period that followed Isabella's claims to the throne, Ferdinand proved to be a most valuable consort, leading the Castilian armies in subduing rebellious noblemen, meeting the Portuguese invasion, and engaging in a long campaign against Granada. His energies were concentrated on the restoration of order in Castile, but he had also received the homage of many of the great noble houses and ecclesiastical dignities as king of Castile. He spent little time in the eastern kingdoms, despite his father's request for his presence to help deal with the many fierce civil conflicts that plagued the Crown of Aragon. Even though, as Hernando del Pulgar reports, there was some opposition to the female succession and support for King John of Aragon (Ferdinand's father) as the rightful heir to Castile, Ferdinand chose not to press the point (del Pulgar 1953, 255). Instead, del Pulgar's chronicle, like other Castilian accounts of the period, is an endless litany of Ferdinand's martial deeds. In fact, a careful reading of the Castilian and Aragonese chronicles for the late fifteenth century provides a rather sorry portrait of a society besieged by conflict and in search of order. That the Catholic Monarchs managed to restore order after all – though far more in Castile than anywhere else in their realms – is a tribute to their abilities.

We do not hear much about Ferdinand's ascent to the throne in the Crown of Aragon. Upon hearing of his father's death in 1479, Ferdinand undertook a brief visit to the eastern realms to acknowledge his inheritance. After all, Ferdinand had already been sworn in as first born and legitimate heir to the thrones of the Crown of Aragon at the *Cortes* of Calatayud shortly after the death of Alfonso V in 1458 (Zurita 1967, book XVII, chapter XXV). A return visit to Calatayud, Zaragoza, Barcelona, and Valencia in 1481, this time in the company of Queen Isabella and the recently born Infante Don Juan, prompted a new series of exchanges of oaths – the *Cortes* and *Corts* swearing in Ferdinand as rightful king and his young son as heir. This recognition of them as legitimate rulers was given in return for promises to respect the liberties and privileges of each of the realms composing the Crown of Aragon. These ceremonies were accompanied by the usual solemn entries, festivities, and the like, but the exchange of oaths and the reaffirmation of the contractual nature of Aragonese, Catalonian, and Valencian rulership seems to have been the central performance necessary for ascending to the throne.

Even though the kings of the Crown of Aragon had a long tradition of actual coronation and anointment, and even though Ferdinand of Antequera, the new Trastámara king, had followed that tradition with a spectacular coronation feast in 1412, his descendants abandoned such practices in clear imitation of their Castilian relatives and royal counterparts. There was no coronation for Ferdinand II of Aragon as king of the eastern kingdoms. Zurita alerts us to the fact that such ceremonies had been abandoned long before. After a careful description of Ferdinand I's coronation, Zurita comments that: "[this was] the last [such coronation] that there has been until our own times; because the king and his successors [successors of Ferdinand I] were not crowned with that majesty and triumph that was present in the coronation of that prince and as was the custom of his ancestors [Ferdinand I's ancestors]" (MacKay 1987, 2, 949–957; Zurita 1967, book XII, chapter XXXIV).

Ferdinand II did experience the solemnity of kingship by himself after the unexpected death of his son-in-law, Philip the Handsome; the illness of his daughter, Queen Juana; and the unrest brewing in Castile, prompted his return. But it began with his impressive royal entry into Naples, almost a replay (without the breaching of the walls) of that of his uncle Alfonso V. Bernáldez provides an exuberant description of the clothing, the artificial constructions (a bridge between the king's ship and the shore), and, most of all, the rich *palio* under which Ferdinand II entered the city. There was no coronation, but there was pomp and display worthy of a true king. And that royal entry into his Italian possessions served as a prelude to an equally impressive entry into Seville. There he claimed control over Castile, even if it was in his daughter's name, without the very large shadow cast by Isabella (see Bernáldez 1953, 730–731; Ruiz 2012, 86–89).

Conclusion

Several observations are in order as we come to the end of this account. We see that Castile and the Crown of Aragon, though sharing some ritual elements in the acts of coronation – whenever kings were crowned – and most certainly in the festivities that accompanied ascent to the throne, also differed greatly. Those differences tell us a great deal about political culture in the medieval Iberian realms, as well as the importance of context. There was a great deal of competition between Castile and the Crown of Aragon. Most of the differences played out on the battlefield, even if during the fifteenth century both kingdoms were ruled by the same family. Clearly, the events of 1327, 1328, and 1332 were thematically connected. The Castilian king, Alfonso XI, and his Arago-Catalan counterpart, Alfonso IV (or their respective agents and advisers) made concerted efforts to signal ascent to the throne: the use of a baldachin in Seville, the impressive ceremonies of Zaragoza, and the unprecedented coronation and anointment of 1332.

All three events used festive forms – processions, clothing, knighting ceremonies, a willing "public" or audience. In all three cases, there is a flow from the streets of Seville, Zaragoza, or Burgos to the interior spaces of a cathedral or monastery. Each location determined the nature of the audience. On the road to Seville, or in the streets of Zaragoza or Burgos, the expectation was that the inhabitants of the city would line up to witness the king's passage. In these "public" displays important lessons about hierarchy and power were reiterated. They formed part of the manner in which kings displayed their power and sought to gain the allegiance of their people. In the interior spaces, nobles and clergymen were introduced to the mysteries of royal authority, to the forceful acts of self-coronation and knighting, to the sacred elements of anointing. These were rituals that could only be played out by kings or kings to be.

When we turn to the late fifteenth century, there are significant differences. Both Isabella and Ferdinand depended on what was essentially the approbation of important sectors of society, specifically the high nobility and urban representatives. In Castile, this happened right at the moment of ascent, an ad hoc event conjured to fulfil the political needs of an immediate accession to the throne. Oaths taken at the *Cortes* happened much later in Castile where the importance of the *Cortes* declined in the fifteenth century. In Aragon, the process could also occur a long time after the ascent to the throne. Yet it was a more formal affair, and conformed to the contractual nature of rulership in the Crown of Aragon. It required the exchange of oaths, and a promise to abide by the liberties and privileges of each realm. This is worth reiterating. The kings of the Crown of Aragon were anointed and crowned (or self-crowned) until the first of the Trastámaras, Ferdinand I, who was the last to undergo this ceremony. For the rest of the century, Ferdinand I's descendants followed Castilian practices that eschewed formal coronations and anointments. However, unless they were in Sicily or Naples, they could not abandon the traditional ceremonies that legitimized their rule through the approval of each of their kingdoms' *Cortes* or *Corts*. But every ceremony that marked their ascent to power was performed – and performance is the right word here – in the context of feasts that moved from "public" to private and that sought to include all the representatives and people of their realms.

Notes

1 For a discussion of the evolution of festivals in late medieval and early modern Spain see Ruiz (2012, 1–67 and passim).
2 For symbols of royalty see Schramm (1960).

Works cited

Bernáldez, Andrés. 1953. *Historia de los reyes católicos Don Fernando y Doña Isabel. Crónicas de los reyes de Castilla III*. Madrid: Biblioteca de autores españoles.

de Certeau, Michel. 1988. *The Writing of History*. New York: Columbia University Press.

del Pulgar, Hernando. 1953. *Crónica de los señores Reyes Católicos Don Fernando y Doña Isabel de Castilla y Aragón. Crónicas de los reyes de Castilla III*. Madrid: Biblioteca de autores españoles.

Edwards, John. 2000. *The Spain of the Catholic Monarchs*. Oxford: Blackwell.

Elliott, John H. 1963. *Imperial Spain, 1469–1716*. New York: St. Martin's Press.

Linehan, Peter. 1993. *History and Historians of Medieval Spain*. Oxford: Clarendon Press.

MacKay, Angus. 1987. "Don Fernando de Antequera y la Virgen Santa María." In *Homenaje al profesor Juan Torres Fontes*. Murcia: Universidad de Murcia.

Muntaner, Ramón. 1999. *Crònica*. València: Institució Alfons el Magnànim.

Nieto Soria, José Manuel. 1998. *Fundamentos ideológicos del poder real en Castilla (siglos XIII–XVI)*. Madrid: EUDEMA.

Palacios Martín, Bonifacio. 1975. *La coronación de los reyes de Aragón, 1204–1410. Aportación al estudio de las estructuras políticas medievales*. Zaragoza: Universidad de Zaragoza.

———. 2007. *Spain's Centuries of Crisis: 1300–1474*. Oxford: Blackwell.

———. 2009. "The Symbolic Meaning of Sword and Palio in Late Medieval and Early Modern Ritual Entries: The Case of Seville." *Memoria y civilización. Anuario de Historia* 12: 13–48.

———. 2012. *A King Travels. Festive Traditions in Late Medieval and Early Modern Spain*. Princeton, NJ: Princeton University Press.

Schramm, Percy E. 1960. *Las insignias de la realeza en la Edad Media española*. Translated by Luis Vázquez de Parga. Madrid: Instituto de Estudios Políticos.

Zurita, Jerónimo. 1967. *Anales de la Corona de Aragón*, Edited by Angel Canellas López. Zaragoza: Institución Fernando el Católico.

2

FAITH AND FOOTPATHS

Pilgrimage in medieval Iberia

George D. Greenia

Occasionally over the centuries an incident occurs that shifts a center of gravity and draws the attention and energy of formerly disinterested bystanders. In the opening decades of the ninth century, an abandoned Roman mausoleum in remote northwest Spain was proclaimed the resting place of the Apostle St. James the Greater, the only original companion of Jesus buried in Europe other than Peter and Paul in Rome. All three were martyred for the faith, but the celebrated presence of the two greatest princes of the Church in a single city that subsequently became the home of a continuous line of successors to Peter – and interpreters of Paul – had long given Rome the edge.

Yet James was the first to shed his blood, a Son of Thunder whose fame came to muffle some of the official voice booming from central Italy. Pilgrims started arriving in Compostela first from hardscrabble Galicia, then from ambitious Asturias, and soon from all the embattled northern Iberian realms. Eventually they came from the whole of Christendom. Compostela's hillside cemetery prompted its earliest neighboring prelate to relocate his diocesan see in order to hover over his most precious shrine. The freshly repositioned bishopric grew into a metropolitan see that rivaled Toledo and almost deprived that legendary Visigothic capital of its primacy over all Iberia. It was well served by a series of resourceful and well-connected bishops, and succeeded in becoming the most appealing draw of any holy place among the Christian kingdoms of the Peninsula, providing a target for Moorish raiders as well as motivation to counterattack them. It also served as a pretext to levy an homage tribute on all the grateful lands whose byways led to Compostela. Never famous as a destination for cures, apparitions or miracles, the sanctuary of Santiago did trigger wondrous economic growth, a new jostling of disparate cultures among its visitors, and fresh engines of art and architecture that still awe pilgrims today (Ashley and Deegan 2009). The story of Santiago is that of a shrine whose ponderous stature ignited the wrath of Muslims, the envy of neighbors, and the emulation of scattered holy places which could point onward to Compostela. In one way or another, everyone redefined themselves as travelers on the road to St. James.

Finding the tomb

James the Elder, one of Jesus's closest disciples, was beheaded by Herod Agrippa in 44 CE, the first of the Twelve to be martyred according to the Acts of the Apostles. Nothing is reported in

Christian scriptures or even by the earliest Church Fathers as to his remains, but by the ninth century a powerful myth had arisen that would persuade not a few Christians and Muslims that his supposed tomb site was in the far western anchor of the Latin Imperium. As the year 1000 approached, James was invested with apocalyptic significance. The hymns and commentaries of the Asturian monk Beatus de Liebana embraced the Book of Revelation, the last entry in the Christian scriptures and a favorite of believers in times of desperation like those in Muslim-occupied Spain. "Their" James bracketed salvation history for Iberia because after the Resurrection he had come to the ends of the world to preach a good news destined to triumph after savage trials. Northwestern Spain, the forested domain of Celts and Sueves, eventually became a counterweight to distant Jerusalem across the fulcrum that was Rome, and pilgrims surged toward each axis of this fateful spiritual beam (Webb 1999).

The earliest wisps of the Jacobean legend styled him an early missionary to these distant provinces of Imperial Rome in the interval between the crucifixion of Jesus and James's own martyrdom. Accounts which eventually coalesced into the authoritative Vita in the twelfth-century *Codex Calixtinus* (otherwise known as the *Liber Sancti Jacobi*) declared that his erstwhile evangelization was fruitless, and so disheartening that even the apostle needed a consoling apparition by the Virgin Mary to bolster his spirits. A tradition grew that she appeared to him in Zaragoza on a pillar, launching a sizeable cult of its own focused on a jasper pedestal that survives to this day and is still revered by pilgrims to that shrine. James returned to Jerusalem to meet his death, but further legend had it that his disciples gathered the head and body and rather miraculously sailed back to the faraway Iberian Atlantic coast where he was interred and then forgotten.

His posthumous success as an evangelizer began in the 820s or 830s CE when one Pelayo, a pious hermit or monk, saw a play of lights floating above a wooded hillside not far from the port of Padrón and reported his discovery to the local bishop, Theodomir (ca. 819–847 CE). Moved by selfless piety – or sensing an opportunity to reposition his diocese within the only continuous power structure known in Christian Europe – Theodomir validated the discovery as the very tomb containing the remains of St. James and induced king Alfonso II of Asturias to become a patron. The long-abandoned Roman cemetery overgrown by a pine grove was rechristened in the saint's name, as Sanctus Jacobus (Saint Jacob, or James) morphed into Sancti Yagus, Santi Yagüe, and simply Santiago. The Compostela part came shortly afterward, probably from *composita tellus* (groomed plot of land) although the appeal of the folk etymology of *campus stellarum* (field of stars) proved irresistible.

Although there were earlier tomb cults in Iberia such as those of Eulalia of Mérida and Emilianus (Spanish San Millán) of Castile, and collective sites such as the Cámara Santa in Oviedo, Santiago towered above them and served as something of a template and terminus for most of the medieval Iberian sacred circuits whose shrine sites became a rosary of venerated and hospitable stopping points. The rise of pan-European Marian devotions in the thirteenth century prompted the appearance of a torrent of new sightings of the Virgin in Spain as well, often leaving behind iconic images of herself at Nájera, Villalcázar de Sirga, and Ponferrada along the French route, and at Monserrat and other places scattered in territories reconquered from the resident Muslim population. (Not a few historians assume that these apparitions were well-timed wonders that encouraged resettlement of underpopulated frontier towns.) The newer shrines tended to honor Mary's apparitions or merely places of local devotion that sponsored annual feast day treks called *romerías*. Almost none were curative shrines. Santiago de Compostela became something of an antique model of the venerated tomb long after the age of martyrs had passed, and a major goal of long-distance pilgrimage.

The faces of St. James

The image of St. James became ubiquitous. He never lost his canonical representation as a preaching apostle toting a book representing the Gospel proclamation. But he rapidly acquired new attributes as himself a pilgrim with the recognizable attire and equipment of any traveler to Compostela. The earliest (1125–1150 CE) representation of "Santiago peregrino," affixed to the church of Santa Marta de Tera in Zamora, displays the crucial accessories: a walking staff, a traveler's satchel, and the soon-to-be-inescapable scallop shell. The formalities of high Romanesque sculpture are visible in the plaited beard and sheer, almost gauzy drapery, but this James has snapped his head to the left and raises an oddly inflated left hand in apostolic admonition and warning; his eyes are protruding with energy and he even bares his teeth as he speaks. John K. Moore provides the best description of the statue and its message:

> He has the matted hair of a desert prophet, the full but fashionable beard of a court sage, and the paunch of an established authority who knows his throw weight. This is the anti-warrior, armed with his voice, speaking with his arms, head pivoted to take in his audience. The extremities of head and hands are inflated with the mighty bellowing from within. This man is on a mission, something the travel gear underscores, positioning James not on a stage but in motion across a landmass he intends to make echo.
>
> (2014, 35)

The James of Santa Marta is on the cusp of transformation from preacher to pilgrim, urging his devotees onward as both.

Although the Santa Marta statue was produced on-site, it anticipates the French style which esteemed Santiago as the icon for his pilgrimage. All the images of St. James produced in France after the twelfth century, as well as the most influential models in the distinctive French style imported into Spain, are in agreement on the image of the saint those pilgrims sought to visit: a resolute walking sojourner, just like the pilgrims themselves. (See, for example, the image of Santiago Beltza in Puente la Reina, or any one of the dozens now gathered in the Museo das Peregrinacións in Santiago.) These *caminante* (walker) images mostly carved in Spain demonstrate that the cultic representation of St. James, the display figure that invited the observer to prayer, was that of the traveler. Pilgrims prayed to their pilgrim patron, and not to the apostle warrior who came later.

The now definitive representation of James from around the 1180s was completed for the Pórtico de la Gloria as part of the exterior west façade in Santiago itself. The saint is perched on a shallow throne and given unique centrality on the central door column right beneath the matching posture of the Christ risen in glory a few feet above him:

> He is hieratic, elevated, meeting no one's gaze except God's. He holds his attributes with a light touch because they are icons and not serviceable tools. The scroll is too small to contain anything substantive, the staff a dainty symbol of someone already in charge. Most of all he's silent, calm, immobilized by the column against his back.
>
> (Moore 2014, 36)

This is the image that has greeted pilgrims for more than 800 years and is by far the most commonly reproduced likeness of the saint. It became the authoritative model for most of the derivative imagery that radiated back out from Santiago between the thirteenth and fifteenth centuries. The Pórtico de la Gloria is the "Sistine Chapel" of Romanesque statuary and the then polychromed James, head ablaze with a jeweled nimbus, pressed itself into the memory of his devotees.

Celebration and ambition

Bishop Theodomir was the bold visionary who seized on the discovery of the tomb and even moved his diocesan see from Iria Flavia on the Galician coast to that sparsely populated hillside in the interior and launched the first building projects there, first a free-standing chaplaincy, then a small neighboring monastery, then a full architectural structure that served as a sacred envelope for the tomb. The Roman mausoleum above ground was demolished in favor of a superimposed sanctuary with an altar, and century by century laborious construction alternated with even more laborious engineering, earthworks, and the enormous task of taming the heaving shoulders of granite just beneath the Spanish soil (Suárez Otero 2014). And even poor pilgrims played their part. Those without coins to offer or wax candles to light during their night vigils and song fests picked up limestone from Triacastela and carried that burden for a whole week before contributing their gift to help make mortar for the endless edifices commissioned by delirious clerics.

Even at its height in the Middle Ages, there were no more than a few thousand permanent residents in Santiago. Willing pilgrims who donated their muscle and goodwill therefore made up a sizeable portion of the work force that built the vast monuments erected during that period along the endless westward path. Many of those building projects were pilgrim hostels intended for them, and oddly the cathedral in Santiago was too. Those permitted to pray through the night within the church itself could apparently number in the hundreds or even thousands. Italians and Germans and Frenchmen settled in companionable throngs, each in their encampments on the tribune level of the great Romanesque edifice and mustered competing choruses of hymns to St. James in their native tongue. At times those crowds produced unhappy consequences: in the early thirteenth century, for example, some aggressively jostling pilgrims turned violent and committed murder; the cathedral was shuttered by the homicide until it could be rededicated. In the following century, perhaps prompted by successive waves of plague – or at any rate overripe and under-washed travelers – the relentless stream of daily arrivals helped inaugurate the age of the *botafumeiro*, a giant censer attached to the ceiling of the transept in order to symbolize the cloud of prayers arising from the pilgrims, and incidentally mask their odor.

As a site of visitation its success would soon exceed Theodomir's wildest dreams. But it was the more ambitious and internationally savvy diplomat bishop Diego Gelmírez (1069–1149) who drove the cult of St. James, and its potential pilgrim allure, to heights unprecedented in the Latin West. Only Martin of Tours and Thomas Becket in the Middle Ages, and Lourdes and Fatima in the modern era, can compare with Santiago as national shrines with international appeal.

The traditional capital of Visigothic Spain had been Toledo, a centrally located urban complex on a major river and well connected by roadways to the surrounding peninsula. It was retaken from the Moors in 1085, a huge psychological boost for the Christian Reconquest, and once the native Mozarabic liturgy was replaced by the standard Roman rite in 1086, its prelate enjoyed restored status as the Primate of all Catholic Iberia, a decisive reincorporation of the peninsula into Western Christendom and its crusading fervors. But Toledo had no cult that could rival the draw of the tomb of James in the far northwest, no feeder routes lined with attractive secondary shrines, and no relentless stream of foreign visitors with a high sense of agency. And for centuries Toledo sat on the edge of an active war zone.

Diego Gelmírez capitalized on the growing sway of Santiago in church affairs. Already a papal legate and soon the first archbishop of Santiago, Gelmírez saw the pilgrimage route as a potential artery to Rome. He campaigned for his see to become the head of the Spanish church, authoring the major history of his own deeds, the *Historia compostelana* (covering the years 1100–1139, in a fine modern edition by Flaque Rey 1994). Gelmírez also inaugurated the building of the new Romanesque cathedral dedicated posthumously in 1213 which is the unforgettable edifice visitors enter today. Another episcopal diplomat and historian, Rodrigo Jiménez de Rada of Toledo (1170–1247), finally deflected papal validation of Santiago's claim to lead the Spanish Church, but neither he nor mighty Toledo ever managed to eclipse the pull of the bodily remains of an apostle for a relic-crazed medieval Europe (Márquez Villanueva 2004, 255–268; see also the historical surveys of Moralejo and López Alsina 1993, and of Singul 2009).

Tombs and heroes

Tomb cults thrived in the Middle Ages whether the visitor sought saints or epic heroes. French scholars including Gaston Paris (1839–1903) and Joseph Bédier (1864–1938) appreciated the mutual influence of medieval hagiography and epic poetry. Bédier even suggested that epics such as the *Chanson de Roland* were composed as complements to routes that passed by legendary sites of chivalric importance, such as Roland's final battle at Roncesvalles or his supposed burial place at Blaye near Bordeaux. Those landmarks are along well-established pilgrimage routes to Santiago and even if the epics were not composed to promote hero tourism per se, they did reinforce the historic resonance of the trails for both secular as well as sacred history.

The clearest echo of French epic adventure *cum* pilgrimage in Spain is recorded in the twelfth-century Latin *Pseudo-Turpin Chronicle* which recounts a fictional expedition of Charlemagne into Moorish domains to forge a safe path toward Santiago. The earliest surviving version of this fantasy chronicle makes up the central narrative of Book Four of the celebrated *Codex Calixtinus* discussed subsequently. The French emperor is invited by the apostle in a dream to take Spain back from Muslim control as a Crusader *avant la lettre*. His success is accompanied by miracles worked by St. James, but tragedy strikes on Charlemagne's withdrawal over the Pyrenees when the rearguard is ambushed and Roland is slain, a fatal skirmish that actually did take place in 778 CE. The various epic accounts of the adventures of Charlemagne and final misadventure of his kinsman Roland spread throughout Europe in written and oral form, and the fanciful *Pseudo-Turpin Chronicle* was recopied at least 150 times in Latin and another 50 times in various vernacular tongues, so the pious and their pastors were not the only ones indulging in sightseeing. For long centuries the trails of faith promised brushes with adventure both sacred and secular and all Europe looked to Spain as a memorial landscape for belief and heroism.

Dogged travelers

The physical trails themselves deserve their place in the history of European cultural traffic. Santiago de Compostela as a traveler's destination helped define named land routes both inside of and well beyond Iberia, something neither Jerusalem nor Rome could claim. All roads led to Rome and pilgrims simply took to the highways used by merchants and mercenaries, abbots and armies. Visitors to the tombs of Peter and Paul faced a daunting patchwork of diffident principalities and scant infrastructure dedicated to their care.

Overland routes to Jerusalem for their part were often trackless paths through indifferent or hostile wilderness, and the nearly inevitable sea routes were also commercial ones, with pilgrims simply cargo for the merchant marine. Santiago beckoned with well-known highways or *caminos* departing from Paris, Tours, Vézelay, Arles, Le Puy-en-Velay and elsewhere in France; from the Germanic heartland; and from the ports of Ireland, England and the Baltic. Inside the Spanish realms the main route was the "Camino francés" stretching from Roncesvalles westward to Santiago, but there were various others, including the early "Camino primitivo" from Oviedo, the English-Irish-Nordic Route ("Camino inglés") from Ferrol or La Coruña, the Northern or Cantabrian Coastal trail, the "Vía de la Plata" up from Seville, and scores of minor feeder routes that joined the main pathways.

These medieval thoroughfares made good use of surviving Roman roads and when necessary, cattle paths, building an infrastructure that opened up a persistently underpopulated interior and allowed the penetration of international traffic and ideas. A quip long attributed to Goethe pronounced that pilgrimage gave birth to Europe and Christendom was its mother tongue. The core notion at least has clear merit. In an age before citizenship that could be documented by anything other than one's native dialect, being a pilgrim granted a sort of pan-European identity that was itself both membership in a shared community of faith and a universal safe conduct through foreign lands. It also made the pilgrim worthy of charity and shelter, and imposed a stern expectation that locals would provide both to these strangers. Even when pilgrims and their hosts routinely failed to live up to the terms of their idealized relationship, those ideals were universally acknowledged and made borders and frontiers far more porous at every level of society.

Medieval pilgrimage was not always a peaceful affair, and could not be. No cross-country traveler set out across unknown territories naively unarmed against wolves, dogs or thieves. Leaving home was dangerous enough, and the most common feature of the highways of faith after churches, chapels and monasteries were cemeteries. It can only be an educated guess, but perhaps 10% to 15% of all long-distance travelers never made it home again. While some chose to resettle elsewhere, not a few fell victim to misadventures, disease and accident. It was easy enough to die of thirst, hunger or exposure. And the quip is shopworn but true enough that the rich had doctors and the poor had pilgrimage, which meant that setting out for a major shrine entailed surrounding oneself with a concentrated display of human suffering. Pilgrim hostels and hospitals – often nearly interchangeable – were intended as places of charity but ended up more as vectors for disease than as centers of sanitation. The approach to most major towns in medieval Spain and elsewhere was often signaled by a St. Lazarus chapel for lepers (Martínez García 1993).

The majority of pilgrims in Spain were defensively armed, even though officially Spain was considered occupied Christian territory and warriors intent on any combination of faith, valor and plunder qualified as crusaders and therefore armed themselves offensively. But unlike the Holy Land, Spain saw no regular influx of combative foreigners seeking to wrest sacred sites from enemy hands, nor foreign visitors hoping to gain access to holy landmarks sequestered within hostile hands.

Despite this, one of the most persistent, and currently embarrassing depictions of Santiago is as Matamoros, the Moor Slayer (Raulston 2008). Propagandists for military triumphalism, mostly French revisionist historians of the period, turned Santiago into a mounted warrior with attributes of a white horse, a brandished sword, and defeated Muslim foes sprawled before him with their decapitated, turbaned heads scattered on the ground. So embedded did this image become that when conquistadors exported their violent ways to the New World, St. James promptly became a *Mataindios* (Slayer of Indians) and – returning the compliment in the fullness of time – during the wars of Latin American independence he became a *Mataespañoles* (Slayer of Spaniards). The standard reading of these images in more recent centuries affirmed that St. James was reassigned to also be the patron of the Reconquista of Moorish Spain. Francisco Márquez Villanueva rejects this interpretation, showing that the Matamoros that originated in the north along the pilgrim trail only arose well after those avenues were safely contained deep in Christian lands. Santiago was deployed as an icon of a struggle already won for pilgrims and as a patriotic hero, but not an inspiration for the Reconquista itself.

The paths of pilgrimage in medieval Spain – before there was a Spain, of course, when the Iberian lands comprised separate ethnic and dynastic kingdoms – are saturated with pilgrim lore and emblazoned with pilgrim art. The preferred iconography has proven the most durable mark of the travelers who created and canonized these routes, starting with the ubiquitous scallop shell. The humble *vieira* is supposed to represent the trek that takes the traveler all the way to the sea. It may have begun as a pagan fertility symbol suggestive of the *mons veneris*, and scallop shells with perforated flanges clearly intended as wearable emblems of some sort have been found in Iberian pre-Christian burials far from any medieval pilgrimage route. The lucrative sale of scallop shells within Santiago itself was a closed market which admitted no competition with cathedral-sponsored vendors. It was the preferred accessory of all classes of devotees of St. James and deluxe versions appeared in precious metals and carved jet, a type of soft coal which can be polished to a durable luster. Once the association with the journey to Compostela was cemented, however, the scallop shell became the badge worn from the outset of the trip. Utility items such as the dried gourd (used as a canteen) surrendered their identity to the pilgrim user and appear almost nowhere in medieval art except as part of a sacred walker's gear. The shoulder cape, the walking staff, the broad-brimmed felt hat good for rain or sun, and the modest satchel slung from a shoulder strap constituted the most stable costume known in the medieval world except for the monastic habits of those who often never traveled at all (for essays on life in the medieval city of Santiago see Antón Vilasánchez and Tato Castiñeira 2000).

Writing about pilgrimage

Pilgrimage appears relatively rarely in the literary record. The Latin *Codex Calixtinus*, the most celebrated volume on the saint, is a product of clerical encyclopedists at both extremes of the French trails (Márquez Villanueva 2004, 165–179). The components of the *Codex* were assembled in the mid-twelfth century by French propagandists selecting from Spanish raw materials to build a sort of "Summa Jacobea." The given name of the collection comes from the spurious claim that it was authorized by Pope Calixtus II, an assiduous ally of Diego Gelmírez. The editors included an account of the history of the saint's *translatio* and *inventio*, that is, the arrival of James's body in ancient Galicia and its discovery centuries later, followed by complex sermon materials encouraging devotion to the saint. To further excite the faithful, yet another section pulls together an ample collection of miracle stories (Coffey et al. 1996). It is this section that stretches the book's purview back along the trails where James worked his miracles for those approaching his tomb.

The fourth section is the most fanciful, a trumpet blast of Latin prose recounting Charlemagne's mighty exploits in Iberia, apparently designed to tickle the Cluniac monks from France and the laymen who revered them. Both groups were promoting the pilgrimage to St. James as they extended their influence along this soft frontier. The terrain and tribal disputes among Basques, Navarrese, Aragonese, and others may have been irksome to walkers and opportunistic French nobles, but the ecclesiastical avenue was becoming well populated with friendly bishops and abbots who had relocated from north of the Pyrenees. Not to mention thousands of common folk who could count on a friendly welcome from French expatriates who stamped their name on a whole chain of *Villafrancos*, or French Towns, and even christened for themselves a major artery adjacent to the very cathedral in Santiago: the Rúa dos francos, where French influence is just as visible in the 'rúa' part as in the 'francos.'

The fifth book of the *Codex Calixtinus* is an out-and-out first-hand report written by an opinionated French cleric, one Aymari Picaud, writing quite intentionally for his countrymen. The now canonized *Pilgrim's Guide* has become famous as the first true travel guide, describing the various routes that converge on the eponymous French Route in Puente la Reina, Navarre, and then march on to Santiago. He catalogs the journey's dangers, material comforts and opportunities for spiritual satisfactions such as visiting the not-to-be-missed tombs of French saints. There is a haughty disapproval of most natives of Iberia until one reaches Galicia when they start to resemble their Gallic neighbors. This fifth book was unmistakably drafted by a rather diffident Frenchman who carefully elaborated on his successful trek because the most complete description of all is of the cathedral in Santiago with its artistic glories and splendid services. Any Spanish participation in this ambitious travelogue is uncertain because the descriptions are all outsider views, the brochure-worthy hype written for potential visitors and not the report of anyone who made his own unique visit, much less the insider's "peek behind the curtain" that Spanish contributors could have supplied. The numerous hymns spliced into various parts of the *princeps* copy of the *Codex Calixtinus* are meant for Jacobean celebrations either in Compostela itself or in anticipation of arrival there, and not a few of those melodies and lyrics were first composed in France.

Although a number of later copies derived from the earliest *Codex Calixtinus*, which is still zealously treasured in Santiago, are extant, none are as elaborately produced or penetrated much into popular lore. This was an anthology for the clerical elite who could draw on most of its contents for composing their own sermons or for devotional reading in French monastic foundations along the main pilgrimage route (Reilly 1993). As a stand-alone composition, the Pseudo-Turpin history about Charlemagne and Roland was a tremendous literary success, but mostly outside of Spain. The *Pilgrim's Guide* in Book Five has become a classic only in the modern era, imposing itself on contemporary dreams of the Middle Ages and scripting journeys that cannot replicate the idealized composite attributed to Aymari Picaud.

Márquez Villanueva (2004, 165–179) regards the *Codex Calixtinus* as a Trojan horse full of French monks. While Bishop Gelmírez himself may have commissioned components of the collection, it seems to have been given its final editorial stamp sometime before 1173 CE and well north of the Pyrenees. The clerics of Cluny enjoyed a widening sphere of influence among the ruling noble warrior class in central France, and the monks only encountered serious resistance when bartering with Rome. The *Pseudo-Turpin Chronicle* mentioned previously spins an enthusiastic tale of Charlemagne's expedition to establish a safe path through Spain so that foreign travelers could reach the tomb of the apostle. But this account presents a Spain devoid of Spaniards. The Muslim enemy is the only Iberian resident worth talking about, and fighting him is the responsibility of the apparently sole challenger Islam met south of the Pyrenees, namely the French. The Carolingian expeditionary adventure is a wholesale historical fiction – the real Charlemagne barely engaged in skirmishes beyond his southern frontier. The *Pseudo-Turpin* also happily ignores any report of native Christian Spaniards creating and defending their own kingdoms (Barriero Rivas 1997). They do not even merit a footnote as incidental partners to the French. This Trojan horse spills out its agents and its ink over Iberia in the cause of further Frankish incursions, ostensibly as spiritual tourism secured by French feats of arms.

Major works in the Iberian vernaculars, by contrast, reference the Camino de Santiago as part of their native backdrop usually without dwelling on it. When charging Moorish and Christian forces clash in the *Cantar de mio Cid* (probably composed in 1207), "Some shout Mahomat, and others Saint James," but the reference hardly seems religious. The *Poema de Fernán González* (mid-thirteenth century) plays out much of its epic adventure along the vertex of the French Route on either side of Burgos but with no reference to anyone else on the trail other than the boisterous combatants of the plotline. Even Cervantes in his *Don Quixote* (1605 and 1615), a work that loves to recall a lost past, finds little use in summoning pilgrims as extras for his social landscapes. The folk tradition is where pilgrimage really begins to gain traction. Folk sayings allude to the incessant passers-by slogging on towards Santiago, and innumerable legends and ballads recount their chance adventures.

In the plastic arts, devotional objects made for pilgrims are among the most common grave goods found throughout Europe, the treasured possessions of sacred travelers, men and women who wanted to arrive before the heavenly throne dressed in the costume and wearing the physical tokens of their earnest efforts to reach out to God while they were still on earth.

Piety and opportunism

Clerical and folk compositions may also be supplemented with legal texts. Not all pilgrims were saints, and many of those selling them goods and services fleeced the credulous. The early church fathers mistrusted pilgrimage in general because of its multiple external and internal abuses. Not a few greedy bystanders saw how they could profiteer from excesses of piety and misdirected belief, extracting donations and selling false relics. Monumental churches and monasteries were constructed and elaborate decorations ordered. Among the wardens of hospitals and charitable refuges, hospitality fatigue could set in all too quickly. Travelers too, far from the restraints of village life and regular access to their legitimate sex partner, took advantage of the anonymity of foreign settings to sample foreign pleasures. Thousands of pilgrims poured into Spain to fulfill a sentence imposed for violent crimes that outraged a whole community. Condemning an offender to a hazardous journey dampened retaliatory violence between families and clans and transferred punishment from vengeful peers to an inscrutable God. But it also meant that pilgrims as a class could provoke a certain measure of mistrust. And in addition to the truly criminal were unspiritual wanderers, shameless freeloaders, vagabonds, opportunists, and downright flimflam artists (Arribas Briones 1993).

The gamut of motives for pilgrimage is transparent in the totalizing catalogue of pilgrims in the *Liber Sancti Jacobi*. The opening sermon on the Apostle St. James lays out the panorama for us:

> The poor go there, and so do the rich, criminals, knights, princes, rulers, the blind and lame, the mighty, the lords, the scions of great families, bishops and abbots, some barefoot, others penniless, others loaded with irons as a sign of their penance.
> (*Liber Sancti Jacobi*, Book I, Chapter 17)

Yet at times something troubling underlies the motives of certain pilgrims, a presumption of commensurability: that the pilgrimage undertaken will necessarily cancel the offense committed or earn the favor requested. Measuring spiritual matters was one of the most persistent projects of the Church in medieval times, and included not only penances but also benefits such as indulgences earned through the performance of pious acts. Cyrille Vogel's French phrase *pénitence tarifée* ("tariffed penance") aptly conveys the calculations applied to reforming one's life and conduct (Vázquez de Parga 1948). The human decision that selected pilgrimage as a seemly expression of piety has clearly made one attempt at devising appropriate measures of devotion, with the unknown hazards of the road left in the hands of God. This implies the penitential nature of all pilgrimage travel: the inevitable sacrifices, discomforts, vulnerability, inconvenience and indignities that are part of the experience sought and not just incidental to the trip. This sort of computation of grace and expiation also shows a fair measure of calcula-tion on the part of Church authorities who could choose from any number of shrine sites both near and far as the offense warranted. But calibrated schemes for earning grace, or for expia-tion of earthly sins by present suffering, or for gaining indulgences through voluntary pious works would lead to a commodification of grace that proved disastrous for the Church and eventually crippling for the pilgrimage experience. Bartering the temporal for benefits eternal will never find a yardstick to persuade everyone.

By the end of the Middle Ages in Spain and elsewhere, the personalized, psychologi-cal dimensions of pilgrimage were undermined by the steady commodification of diverse forms of civil compensation and remission of sins. Just as murder could be redeemed by payment of *wergeld*, so other crimes normally punished with a judicial pilgrimage could be expiated by a fixed sum of money or by underwriting the costs of a substitute pilgrim who made the trip on commission. The spiritual benefits of a pilgrimage themselves came to be a commodity of transferable value, so a sinner might be required to perform two pilgrimages, one in punishment for a murder, say, and a second trip whose graces were formally reassigned as compensation to the aggrieved family. Thousands of these surro-gate arrangements were apparently made and local records throughout Europe, including faraway northern ranges such as Germany and Scandinavian countries, give witness to the practice and Santiago was a frequently named destination. This practice quickly spread in the fourteenth and fifteenth centuries to testamentary bequests which obliged heirs to perform a pilgrimage for the sake of the soul of the deceased, as a condition of receiving their inheritance. These replacement pilgrims became so common in Iberia itself that a Spanish proverb held that "en vida o muerte, todos han de ir a Santiago" ("In life or in death, everyone ends up going to Santiago").

Movement becomes myth

Pilgrimages of all sorts and to diverse destinations have become firmly embedded in the national Spanish myth. Annual *romerías* help define the cycle of village and even urban life, their colorful traditions a bond for locals and a draw for tourists, whether it be the often raucous parade to the Virgen del Rocío in the province of Huelva or the elaborate hyper-charged piety of the thousands of costumed young people who take part in the Holy Week procession in Seville, and the hundreds of thousands of observers who pour into town to take in the spectacle.

But the most successful and massive of all remnants of medieval pilgrimage in Spain is clearly the Camino de Santiago, reanimated in the late twentieth century and every year attracting more than 300,000 mostly earnest walkers, and millions more respectful visitors to Com-postela. International attention and frank admiration has successfully expanded the Camino's pilgrim catchment across the globe, and it has become not only an economic boon to a strug-gling economy, but also a vehicle for promoting sympathy for Spanish traditions and honoring Spain's capacity for disinterested hospitality. All tourism promises contact with the authentic Other through costumes, food, social practices and demonstrations of belief. The additional attraction of pilgrimage lies in the opportunity which it offers for discovering a more authentic self, and the modern Camino de Santiago seems to fulfill for many the experience sought by centuries of travelers to Compostela.

Works cited

Antón Vilasánchez, María A. and José Luis Tato Castiñeira. 2000. *Santiago de Compostela: ciudad y peregrino. Actas del V Congreso Internacional de Estudios Xacobeos*. Santiago de Compostela: Xunta de Galicia.

Arribas Briones, Pablo. 1993. *Pícaros y picaresca en el camino de Santiago*. Burgos: Ediciones Aldecoa.

Ashley, Kathleen and Marilyn Deegan. 2009. *Being a Pilgrim. Art and Ritual on the Medieval Routes to Santiago*. Burlington, VT: Lund Humphries.

Barriero Rivas, José Luis. 1997. *La función política de los caminos de peregrinación en la Europa medieval. Estudio del Camino de Santiago*. Madrid: Tecnos.

Coffey, Thomas F., Linda Kay Davidson, and Maryjane Dunn, eds. 1996. *The Miracles of Saint James: Translations from the Liber sancti Jacobi*. New York: Italica Press.

Falque Rey, Emma, ed. 1994. *Historia Compostelana*. Madrid: Akal.

Márquez Villanueva, Francisco. 2004. *Santiago: trayectoria de un mito*. Barcelona: Edicions Bellaterra.

Martínez García, Luis. 1993. "La asistencia hospitalaria a los peregrinos en Castilla y León durante la Edad Media." In *Vida y peregrinación*, edited by Reyna Pastor, 57–69. Madrid: Electa.

Moore, John Kitchen, Jr. 2014. "Santiago's Sinister Hand: Hybrid Identity in the Statue of Saint James the Greater at Santa Marta de Tera." *Peregrinations: Journal of Medieval Art & Architecture* 6 (4): 31–62.

Moralejo, Serafín and Fernando López Alsina. 1993. *Santiago, camino de Europa. Culto y cultura en la peregrinación a Santiago de Compostela*. Santiago de Compostela: Xunta de Galicia.

Raulston, Stephen B. 2008. "The Harmony of Staff and Sword: How Medieval Thinkers Saw Santiago Peregrino and Matamoros." *La corónica* 36 (2): 345–368.

Reilly, Bernard F. 1993. *The Medieval Spains*. Cambridge: Cambridge University Press.

Singul, Francisco. 2009. *El Camino de Santiago. Cultura y pensamiento*. A Coruña: Bolanda.

Suárez Otero, José. 2014. "Locus Iacobi. Orígenes de un santuario de peregrinación." PhD diss., Universidad de Santiago.

Vázquez de Parga, Luis. 1948. "Capítulo VII. La peregrinación forzada." In *Las peregrinaciones a Santiago de Compostela*, edited by Luis Vázquez de Parga, José María Lacarra, and Juan Uría Ríu, vol. 1, 155–167. Madrid: Consejo Superior de Investigaciones Científicas.

Webb, Diana. 1999. *Pilgrims and Pilgrimage in the Medieval West*. New York: St. Martin's Press.

3

BEFORE THE RECONQUISTA

Frontier relations in medieval Iberia, 718 to 1031

Jonathan Jarrett

The word "Reconquista" implies a claim by the inhabitants of the northern Iberian Peninsula to a past in which their ancestors had held dominion over the lands to the south, whose recapture would return the Peninsula to Christian control (Menéndez Pidal 1929; cf. Mínguez Fernández 2005).[1] The past to which this claim referred was the Visigothic kingdom that collapsed after defeat at Muslim hands in 711 (Collins 2004). As this view would have it, between then and the era in which conquests were made against the Muslim powers, following the collapse of the Caliphate of Córdoba from 1006 onwards, a spring of righteous resentment and military readiness was being wound in the north by unvarying enmity and conflict. A chronicle written in Oviedo in the early 880s has been held to illustrate this when it describes the Peninsula of its author's day as held by Muslims whom the Christians fight day and night without being able to take it back (Gil Fernández et al. 1985, Albeldense XIV.35). On the other side of the frontier, meanwhile, a historiographic tradition based largely on sources from Córdoba has preserved a picture of a Muslim state founded on enlightened principles of *convivencia* (see e.g. Hillenbrand 1992). For the Christian chronicler, the Muslim enemy was close by and easy to attack; for the Cordoban courtiers, however, the Christians were distant, known mainly by their embassies before the emir or caliph. Neither of these pictures can have been wholly true, and between them, conceptually and geographically, lies a space of many possibilities, some of which this chapter aims to explore (cf. Linehan 2001; Jarrett 2010b).

A political history of the polities vying over this space cannot be attempted here (see instead Reilly 1993). Suffice it to say that after averaging out the shifts of power, the reader of such a history might conclude that the Oviedo chronicler had it more or less right: much micro-scale conflict resulted in little macro-scale difference. They might also conclude that the polities of the north indeed touched Córdoba little. The last generation of work on al-Andalus has stressed how much supposedly Muslim territory actually usually lay beyond the Cordoban emirate's control (Manzano Moreno 1991). This, however, is only to acknowledge that one historiography is focussed on the extreme north and its opposite on the central south, ignoring a vast swathe of the Iberian Peninsula of this time as beyond and other (Manzano Moreno 1999, 32–35).

The inhabitants of this territory have thus fallen between two histories. Less can be known of this zone than of the capitals of north and south where history was literally written, but it also escapes study and recognition because it is part of neither history, not the glory of al-Andalus or the determination of various conquering Kings Alfonso or the cinematically immortalised el Cid (Menéndez Pidal 1929; Reilly 1991; Stalls 2004). El Cid is usually considered a frontier war-lord, yet his world of petty princedoms and distant overlords was of relatively recent origin in the mid-twelfth century, and it is hard to say where in it the frontiers were (Fletcher 1989). Even in the world that preceded his, describing them requires critical reading of the few narratives, exploration of an uneven mass of local documentation and some familiarity with archaeology and art history. Without this, however, our understanding of the Iberian Peninsula's medieval development is marred by a huge gap, in which people lived and things happened. At the edges of this gap, our historiography has set up opposing Others that in theory met in this junction ter-ritory. By confronting them with each other, we can give the few characteristics of that territory which our polarised sources allow us to discern something closer to their full strength.

Dividing al-Andalus in space and time

The beginning of Muslim rule in Iberia has a clear start date, that of the invasion of the Visi-gothic kingdom by the forces of Tarīq ibn Ziyād and his superior Mūsā ibn Nusayr in 711. The history of al-Andalus thereafter is conveniently broken up by major episodes:

- a period of conquest, lasting until 718 in the north-east of the Peninsula and arguably end-ing still later (Collins 1989);
- a period of rule by appointed governors, punctuated by a revolt among troops recruited from Africa in 741 and terminated by the 'Abbasid coup in the Middle East, the flight of the last Umayyad scion to al-Andalus and his takeover there in 756 (Marín 1998);
- the fluctuating fortunes of the new Umayyad emirate until 929 (Kennedy 1998, 30–81);
- and lastly the glory period of the Andalusi caliphate, already running into difficulties by the year 1000 and by 1010 in an irreversible decline marked in 1031 by the final extinc-tion of the Umayyad ruling line (Kennedy 1998, 82–108; Scales 1994).

The only part of this that receives much textbook attention is the Caliphate (e.g. Moran and Gerberding 2004, 206–208), because of the splendour of its material remains and its self-proclaimed political might, and also because its narrative is dramatic and can be told relatively clearly from our Cordoban sources. Its rise and fall is, nonetheless, only a third of our chosen period. That rise also ended a counterbalancing period of ascendancy and expansion among the Christian principalities of the north, its sometime opponents.

Among opponents of the time, however, we should count not just Christians but also Mus-lims. Key figures of that period (756–929) included a convert family of alleged Gothic descent known to us as the Banū Qāsī, from their claimed forebear, one Count Cassius (Fierro 2009). In the mid-ninth century this family could count Huesca, Lleida, Tudela, Zaragoza and several other cities of the north-east of the Andalusi state as theirs. They fought, allied with and mar-ried among Christian princes, as the same Oviedo chronicle of above tells us; another states that their greatest patriarch, Mūsā ibn Mūsā, called himself "the third king of *Hispania*" (Gil Fernández et al. 1985, Alfonso III c. XXV). Certainly at times the Banū Qāsī were loyal serv-ants of the emir, while at others they were effectively uncontrolled, and it was possible for both things to be true as long as no conflict opposed them to the emir. Removing them from this position was only achieved by the slow promotion of a rival lineage to a roughly similar position (Lorenzo Jiménez 2010).

Lords closer to Córdoba could be just as difficult. One of the achievements leading Emir 'Abd al-Rahmān III towards claiming the Caliphate was the conquest in 928 of the citadel of

Bobastro, centre of a rebellion by an alleged apostate to Christianity, 'Umar ibn Hafsūn. The conquest was a notable achievement mostly because this rebellion, 150 km south of Córdoba, had by then been running for forty-six years, during which time Ibn Hafsūn had not just been occasionally recognised as an independent whose army fought alongside the emir's, but had died and been succeeded in his disobedience by his sons (Acién Almansa 1994). Even more surprisingly, it has been calculated that Toledo, the old Visigothic capital and home to a large Christian population but also not far from Córdoba, cumulatively spent a full half of the duration of Umayyad rule in rebellion (Manzano Moreno 1991, 261–310). Was this a territory of al-Andalus in any meaningful way? And if the Emirate's supposed frontier was frequently hardly 300 km away from its capital, how on earth to categorise the areas that lay beyond it but remained attached to the Umayyads (cf. Manzano Moreno 1999, 38–40)? Certainly, defining a single polity with a clear edge must be incorrect for this area however it be done. This situation of al-Andalus in the period of 756 to 929, in which it was occasionally effective outside its territories and always a source of wealth but rarely integrated enough to be threatening to those beyond its control, was an opportunity for those who wished to build rival power bases outside.

The northern redoubts

Few of those who thus set up can have aimed to become "kings of *Hispania*," but it is, naturally enough, those zones where kingdoms or states emerged whose identities persist today that have dominated scholarship, and any history of Spain (though perhaps not of Portugal) will necessarily focus especially on the northern coastline where Christian rule persisted after 718 (Sánchez-Albornoz 1991; Riu i Riu 1999; cf. Linehan 1993, 95–127). While the autonomy and distinctiveness of some of these areas is still a live political issue now, with consequent effects in historical discourse, over the eighth and ninth centuries the sources certainly justify discussion of independent princedoms in at least Galicia, Asturias, Cantabria, Aragon and Navarre, and the tenth century added Castile and at least ten different counties in the modern Catalonia, ruled by a kaleidoscopic succession of counts, several of whose territories are now in modern France. These powers did not exist both autonomously and simultaneously, however. Although sources from their court are naturally keen to assert this, it seems clear that kings in Asturias ruled Cantabria by the end of the ninth century and could usually aspire also to rule Galicia (Escalona Monge 2004). By the early tenth century, however, this nascent kingdom had relocated its capital to León, and though that proved vulnerable, after 924 Asturias never again had its own king (Collins 2012, 52–82). Castile emerged as a county of this new kingdom of León, and only took its "definitive" form by a coincidence of inheritances under Count Fernán González in 931; its autonomy between then and the succession of Count Ferdinand I to the throne of León in 1037 is a matter of highly politicised debate (Mínguez Fernández 2004, 183–199).

The area of modern Catalonia presents further complications for a nationally organised perspective. The territory owes its distinctive political constitution and language to the fact of its having been ruled intermittently by powers across the Pyrenees, before our period as part of the Visigothic kingdom of Toulouse and thereafter as part of a group of counties assembled as a defensive *marca hispanica* by the Carolingian kings of the Franks from 785 onwards (Chandler 2013). Modern Catalonia cannot be identified with the *marca*, however, as that grouping also included Navarre and Aragon, both of which seceded in the 820s.[2] The rump remaining was then diminished by a further coup in 826 whose losses were only recouped half a century later. In what remained, Frankish royal appointments to lay office were made as late as 878 and the groupings of counties thus created proved durable, but this still left four families in charge of them, and while that based in Barcelona was the most powerful, they did not control the others until after our period. Resort to the Frankish king for legal privileges continued until at least 987, when the last Carolingian, Louis V, died (Jarrett 2011). This date has since become inarguable in the local scholarship as the beginning of a "Catalan" independence that no one at the time would have recognised.[3] The only things that then unified all the Catalan counties were their Frankish history and the fact that they were not part of any other polity.

The danger of a teleological perspective on this period will by now be evident. The history of medieval Spain has often been told as the survival and revival of Christian kingship in Asturias, its move to León and takeover by a nascent Castile, with a subplot in which Catalonia is removed from this "national" story and begins the pursuit of its own, joining with Aragon in 1137 to allow the eventual completion of "Spain" in 1492 (e.g. Castro 1948; Sánchez-Albornoz 1956; Barbero and Vigil 1974, otherwise sharply differentiated). This would have been completely unforeseeable in 1031. For one thing, future events in al-Andalus would have been deeply obscure; could Umayyad rule really have been assumed finished after so long? Even if so, the Almoravid and Almohad caliphates would have seemed fantastic. More importantly, however, a Castilian-Aragonese narrative would have been implausible because the supreme kingdom in the Iberian Peninsula in 1031 was actually Navarre. Its ruler, Sancho III the Great, self-proclaimed King of the Spains (*rex hispaniarum*), numbered the Counts of Barcelona, Pallars and indeed Castile among his vassals and ruled León directly (Mínguez Fernández 2004, 123–132). This would not endure, of course: Navarre had no access of its own to expansion into al-Andalus and its later bisection by France has removed it from the main narrative. The point is, however, that this period's importance is not what it led to: its developments frequently "led" nowhere, but they were as life-changing as any later for those involved. The period is in fact a frontier zone itself, between destruction and restoration as one recent work has it (Deswartes 2003), and, like the political frontier we have delineated, it requires examination on its own terms.

The space between and its definitions

The polities on either side of this zone conceptualised it differently. Muslim thinking envisaged a core *dār al-Islam*, domain of Islam, outside which lay the *dār al-harb*, domain of war, although such areas might be placed under tribute without conquest, constituting a *dār al-'ahd*, domain of the pact. Between the *dār al-Islam* and these outer zones lay the *thughūr* (sing. *thaghr*). This Arabic word is usually translated as "frontier," but these frontiers were not barriers but passages, from continuous Muslim rule to uncontrolled spaces (Manzano 1999, 38–42, 45–46). The breach of such a pact would convert *al-'ahd* to *al-harb*, however, and turn the conceptual frontier inside out. This formulation does not fit easily into such categories as "linear," "zonal," "enclosing" or "expanding" frontiers (Berend 1999) but it did and does provide a way to think of most of the Peninsula as being within a Muslim polity despite that polity's faltering central control.

Between the *thughūr* and territory inarguably Christian was still a considerable space. The strongest idea that Christian documents dealing with it expressed was vacancy. For the Count of Barcelona in 973, the old city of Isona was in "the extreme ultimate ends of the Marches," and consequently it was unsurprising that it had been "anciently destroyed by the pagans," although he was garrisoning it anyway and that garrison was apparently being supported by local agriculturalists (Udina Martorell 1951, no. 174). The Barcelona monastery of Sant Cugat del Vallès, when expansion into such areas began to consolidate, was keen to point out that royal concessions of a previous century had allotted them extensive territory in these "places of soli-tude" (Rius Serra 1946, no. 452). Obviously if the places had not been empty the monastery's claim would have been disputable, making all such claims of desertion suspect (Jarrett 2010a). In Asturias this rhetoric was taken to a grander level in the so-called *Chronicle of Alfonso III*, which claimed that most of the lands south of the kingdom were not only long deserted, but so by royal *fiat*, King Alfonso I having moved their occupants north (Gil Fernández et al. 1985, Alfonso III cc. 13–14). The use of such a claim for Alfonso III, striving to bring those areas back under obedience, is evident, and cannot be taken uncritically (Mínguez Fernández 2002).

This language, nevertheless, was often taken literally in the historiography, because of the Arabic sources' similar distancing of their opponents but also because the idea of an empty space into which bold pioneers might rightfully move, but where they might need military protection by the burgeoning state, was mirrored in the fashionable work of Frederick Jack-son Turner on the frontier in the American West.[4] Here as there was an open space, inhabited by no one that mattered to the writers, the occupation of which was the common experience that bound the Iberian kingdoms (except Navarre) together and explained their eventual uni-fication. The power of such a narrative could overwhelm most scruples about exactly how deserted a full third of the Peninsula could have been (Linehan 1993, 95–127).

Inhabiting the frontier

Over the past thirty years, however, historians and archaeologists have become increasingly sure that the frontier zone was not empty. In texts, the hints are evanescent: the evidence is largely transactional documentation that was by definition only generated once a land market existed, unlikely in an autarkic community. As a result, we see areas only as they pass into the normalising structure of government. Nonetheless, differences detectable between groups can expose their deviations from such normalisation (Jarrett 2010b) and, in the later part of the period under discussion, these differences were enshrined in the local law codes known as *fueros*, or in Catalonia *cartes de població* (Manzano Moreno 1994, 94–95). Less program-matic but equally telling hints can be got from place- or personal names displaying antiquity or linguistic mixing between Arabic and Romance languages, although the latter phenom-enon is highly regionalised and imperfectly understood (Aguilar Sebastián and Rodríguez Mediano 1994; Barrios García 1982; Hitchcock 2008, 53–74). Archaeology's contribution has been more recent, and struggles with the difficulty of proving continuity as well as inad-equate publication of many excavations, but enough has been done to show that settlement did not obviously cease in the frontier areas on the Muslim conquest, and that maintenance of churches continued, suggesting the continuing articulation of communities (Gibert Rebull 2006; González García 1995). With this and work on the survival of land boundaries, on the re-use of ancient sites, and on the endurance of local saints' cults (e.g. respectively Bolòs i Masclans 1995; Jarrett 2010b, 99–103; Linage Conde 1971), some generalisations about the circumstances of these almost-invisible populations are possible (cf. Martín Viso 2005).

The most obvious generalisation must be variation, of course. We find settlements both nucleated and dispersed, which has been put down to the origins of such communities but which may in fact have had more basic environmental causes (Mínguez Fernández 1998). We cannot say much about these peoples' origins: while arguments have been made for very deep local continuity from even pre-Roman times in some areas (Barbero and Vigil 1974), population movement cannot be ruled out either, even if sometimes it may have been very short-distance (Jarrett 2010a, 339–341). A charter of 943 recording the occupation of a par-ticular area of the kingdom of León in settlements which included a *villa de cordobeses* and a *villa de asturianos* prevents us from doubting that people were in movement, northwards and southwards, and the Cordobans, at least, could hardly have been relocated by Leonese royal command (Mínguez Fernández 1976, no. 87).

As regards matters of religion, refusal to guess is our only safe position: Christian sources talking of *christiani perversi* in the frontier zones may not have been making doctrinal judgements, but such persons were beyond diocesan structures and Church correction (Jarrett 2010b, 98–99). Similar problems arise with language: later Arabic sources tell us of occasional autochthonous Arabic-speaking populations far beyond Andalusi control (Manzano Moreno 1994, 92, 95), but in certain areas people with Arabic names were frequent occurrences (see Aguilar Sebastián and Rodríguez Mediano 1994; Barrios García 1982; Fernández 2009; Hitchcock 2008, 53–74), the most startling of whom is the scribe of a charter for King Ordoño II of León, a deacon called Muhammad (Sáez 1987, no. 40). On the other hand, Latin documents continued to be issued deep into al-Andalus, although almost none survive (Barrett 2011, citing a charter from Lorvão).

One well-known case in a document from Ribagorza in Aragon brings out the ambiguity of loyalties that we must imagine among the inhabitants of these zones. In it, the villagers of what is now Aguinaliu recorded having settled a boundary dispute with their neighbours in Juseu. These two communities lie about sixty kilometers from the then-new bishopric at Roda d'Isávena, yet rather than resort to either bishop or count of Ribagorza for arbitration they sent much farther afield to Muslim-held Lleida, to a priest called Fortún, "judge of all the Christians in Lleida" (Davies and Fouracre 1986, 255). This was perhaps again the pact at work, but it may also tell us that the villagers wanted to avoid the obligations, like tithe or *censum*, that might be enforced upon them by engagement with the more local powers-that-were. Arguably, the kingdoms of the north expanded by interesting such populations in taking part in the wider polity (Carvajal Castro 2012); if so, in these cases they failed.

Crossing the frontier

Despite such disconnection, there was travel through these areas. Manuscripts made in the south, annotated in the north in hands we can date, silently demonstrate such traffic (Díaz y Díaz 1969). A small number of ecclesiastical travel narratives show us that different standards of travel existed: when relic-seekers from St-Germain-des-Prés went from Paris to Córdoba, their crossing of the frontier was a complex series of escorted transits between jurisdictions (Christys 1998), albeit largely for political reasons (Nelson 2010, 19–20); the unimportant Cordoban cleric Eulogius had no such difficulty while hunting manuscripts in Navarre (Christys 2002b, 55–62). It was not just churchmen who travelled, either. One assumes that a string of Christian emissaries who visited the court of Caliph 'Abd al-Rahmān III in the 940s (Christys 2002b, 109–113), or his Jewish doctor Hasdai ibn Shaprut, sent as diplomat to Catalonia in 940 and León in 941–942, travelled in company and under watchful eyes. There were also fugitives to Córdoba such as the frontier warlord 'Aysūn ibn al-'Arabī, who supposedly escaped from a Frankish prison by guile (Manzano Moreno 1991, 218–222), or the Frankish convert to Judaism, Bodo-Eleazar (Riess 2005).

Movement within the frontier zone can also be seen. A well-studied case is that of 'Abd al-Rahmān ibn Marwān Ibn al-Yillīqī, whose very name suggests a family origin in the *dar al-harb* of *Jillīqīya*, a locution which covered not just modern-day Galicia but also León and Castile. It was in Mérida that he rebelled in 876–877, however, whence he quickly fled north to King Alfonso III of Asturias, governing a frontier castle for him for eight years before returning south to seek reconciliation with the emir, who placed him in charge at Badajoz (Christys

2002a). Although this man had royal lords, it seems that his real loyalties were to a homeland between them. Other such defectors also never quite lost touch with the other 'side' (Collins 1995, 281; Manzano Moreno 1991, 190).

There must also have been trade, but we can hardly see it. In 1018 we have in Barcelona the first documented appearance of a merchant there; he was dealing in cloth, and Andalusi cloths are documented in many a Catalan will, though these may have come by sea rather than across the frontier proper (Wolff 1963). The same might be true of the Caliphal gold mancuses that start appearing as coin of payment in the Catalan counties in the 970s, but it cannot so easily be the case with their occurrences farther west (Balaguer 1988). Coins are not by themselves good evidence of trade, however, especially in a context where tributes were frequently paid (Grierson 1959) and since the historiography is relatively agreed that there was substantial migration, little that is conclusive can be demonstrated yet.

Mozarabism and arabicization

In more traditional historiography, that migration is assumed to have been northwards: the ascendant Christian kingdoms should naturally have called to the Christians of al-Andalus labouring under the Saracen yoke. This is not without support in the evidence. For one thing, the most visible category in the Arabic-named Christian population already mentioned was churchmen, a professional class who could expect employment in the north and might well have felt an increasing pinch in the south as al-Andalus began to tax the Church in its territories more heavily (clear in Samson 1969–1973, II Preface c. 2).[5] The voyages of manuscripts northwards already mentioned tend to confirm such a movement, and this has been used by believers in the magnetism of the new kingdoms to explain those areas' adoption of Andalusi styles of building, decoration and ceramics; all this was supposedly brought by Mozarabs (classically Gómez Moreno 1919; see also Werckmeister 1993).

This term, Mozarabs, is full of problems. It is called upon at once to refer to Christians living in al-Andalus, including those such as the Córdoba martyrs who resisted arabicization, but also Christians outside al-Andalus who were distinctive precisely because of their Andalusi acculturation, thus differing in origins and attitudes almost entirely, as well as those Christians who stuck to the Hispanic liturgy after the Christian takeover of their territories, a different problem that falls beyond our remit here (Hitchcock 2008). This differentiation, however, highlights that aside from the movement of clerics, and hints like the *villa de cordobesos* already mentioned, our evidence for this phenomenon is primarily cultural, and need not mean that the bearers of such culture were born into it. The possibility of northern visitors to the south bringing ideas and books back, for example, is little considered. The belief in Christianity's cultural superiority implicit in such scholarship seems to allow only immigrants to have such cultural uses, immigrants who won admiration for their creativity, but whose styles no native would lastingly adopt. Few if any scholars would outwardly profess such a belief, yet as soon as that assumption is discarded it must be clear that the works themselves could be transmitters of such ideas, that anyone of suitable ability who had seen such things, whatever their origin, could have thus appeared "Mozarab-like," and that we should therefore expect considerable cultural fluidity on both sides of the frontier.

In common and in conflict

A person crossing this space could thus likely not have told from material culture alone when they had left al-Andalus or entered Christian territory. The ceramic record also suggests this:

a coarse grey ware is found almost all over the Peninsula between the tenth and twelfth centuries, despite considerable earlier differentiation, and the only finewares usually recovered are of an Islamic, and even Persian, type (Barceló 1993; Riu-Barrera 1999). Much of the grey ware must have been of local manufacture, and it is probable that more detailed studies will locate more differences than have been identified, but a culture more or less shared across the zone and beyond it seems easiest to suppose even so, however scanty the current evidence.

This should not, of course, be taken to imply that all was harmony in this space. While the vituperations of monastic documents against the bandits who lived in such places, failing to respect the monasteries' unenforceable land claims there, were likely more programmatic than realistic (Jarrett 2010b, 98–99), armies travelled through these zones and the first presence of outside interests often came with fortifications, whose upkeep became the job of the hitherto-ungoverned locals (Benet i Clarà 1991–1992; Escalona Monge 2000–2001, 109–113). At Cardona, on the edges of Catalunya Vella, in 987 the count of Barcelona offered the settlers and citizens many legal privileges to motivate them to stay and defend a fortress that was obviously impossible for him to protect alone: this was the Barcelona family's third attempt to repopulate the city in a century, which shows the problem, but it is that the count undertook to guarantee the citizens' possessions of any lands they could take, from either Muslims or Christians, that shows how few guarantees the area really offered (Galera i Pedrosa 1998, no. 7). Other indications of border warfare and general preparation for conflict are not hard to find, even if fewer in some areas than others (Lourie 1966). This then also needs to be part of our picture of these societies: without wider links of membership of polities, they did not necessarily share friendship either, and in the old adage, no man may have peace longer than his neighbour wishes.[6]

Reconquista and neogothicism

Against this background the idea of a Reconquista, or even as more modern literature would have, a "restoration," seems somewhat strange (cf. Ríos Saloma 2008). The Christians or Muslims of this environment were, while different by profession from each other, not far away and far from alien. The adoption of Andalusi material culture at an élite level demonstrates the lack of commitment to its extinction those élites yet had. Nonetheless, it cannot be denied that at certain times in certain places we find the idea expressed that the Christians ought to fight the Muslims and even that the Visigothic kingdom was to be restored by so doing (Isla Frez 2011). It is easy enough to understand why King Alfonso VII evoked such ideas as he laid siege to Toledo, the old Visigothic capital and Andalusi problem spot, in 1085, but what was the impact of such ideas before then?

The answer seems to be that this was a way for kings whose power rested primarily on military leadership to add symbolic importance to their plundering, often as part of a general campaign of symbolic uplift. We need not, for example, necessarily doubt the *Chronicle of Albelda* when it tells us that King Alfonso II restored the Gothic *ordo* at Oviedo just as it had been in Toledo, even if nobody can have known how correctly he did so (Gil Fernández et al. 1985, Albeldense XVI.9), since we can see his ambitious self-presentation in the building projects he undertook, which included a palace complex in Oviedo (Collins 1995, 280). It is hard to see how anyone who did not already come to the court could have been influenced by such changes, however, and a battle to balance the various factions of the Asturian kingdom probably lies behind this program (Escalona Monge 2004). Alfonso's palace was, after all, supplanted by his successor Ramiro I's probable conversion of what is now Santa Maria de Naranco into a new palace, literally looking down on his predecessor's works from its hill above Oviedo (Collins 1995, 280–281).

It is also easy to see why such Gothicizing efforts were eagerly reported in the reign of Alfonso III, during which the *Chronicle of Albelda* was concluded. The king's name is attached to another chronicle that makes sweeping claims of royal action in the frontier zones (Gil Fernández et al. 1985, Alfonso III). Also produced in his reign was the peculiar *Prophetic Chronicle*, which distorts the Book of Daniel's prophecy concerning Gog and Magog so that it could be taken to refer to the Goths (Gog) being oppressed by the Muslims (Magog) for a fixed period of 170 years, by the author's calculation due to end in a few months with Alfonso III's reconquest (the word does not seem wrong in this context) of the whole of *Hispania* (Gil Fernández et al. 1985, Albeldense XIV–XIX). Although this text must have been proven wrong almost immediately, as Alfonso's successes were not of this order, an audience for it is demonstrated by its travel with the later chronicles, albeit perhaps for the polemical *Life of Muhammad* it also includes (Daniel 1994). Also clear, however, is that Alfonso III's self-representation was also challenged: his reign ended in deposition by his sons and the transfer of the royal capital to more southerly León (Collins 1995, 284).

It is hard to see how any of this would have mattered farther into the frontier. Claims of ancestral defeats of the Muslims presumably did something to strengthen a claim on power, but in both this case and the few Catalan examples of such claims the combats involved were in the past, and often belied by contemporary sources (Jarrett 2011, 15–19). Meanwhile, along the Duero or the Llobregat, what would claims to have succeeded the Gothic kings have meant? If those kings were remembered, it would presumably have been as rulers of Toledo, which still lay in Muslim territory; the north, whence the new claims, was in fact the zone that had given those kings most difficulty of control (Manzano Moreno 1999, 42–43). Ancient tributes or loyalties could not have been called on here; the best that could be expected is that whatever low-level organisation of labour and renders might accrue to the local élites of these zones could somehow be attached to the new structures of rule northern magnates were now extending into the frontier zones (Escalona Monge 2001, 14–54; cf. Carvajal Castro 2012). The performance of the Gothic inheritance was almost certainly effective only closer to home.

The dangers of the frontier

The picture with which we close, then, is one of detachment and disconnection. The sources' claims of desertion or banditry seem more rhetorical than factual and descriptions in terms such as no-man's land (d'Abadal i de Vinyals 1958, 78: "terra de ningú") refer to political possession, not habitation. This land was not so dangerous as to be empty, but it was not safe, and it was certainly not easily governed. Within it we do not find a single "gente de frontera" but many communities and identities with very local reflexes, whose involvement with others would have ebbed and flowed according to need, interest and circumstances. This makes almost any generalisation fraught but the composite of many different possibilities, not all verifiable, that is proffered here ineluctably undermines efforts to extrapolate from territories closer to the developing centres of power.

Another kind of generalisation that is dangerous is one that sees the frontier zone as unchanging over time. As has been stated previously, that its overall state remained similar over much of the period under discussion should not blind us to what we can see of a great many small changes in different places and of different durations. Towards the end of our period, however, even large-scale changes became more durable: under the Caliphate of 'Abd al-Rahmān III and al-Hakam II the fractured polity of al-Andalus was sufficiently bonded that its periphery responded to its centre with unprecedented heed, and Christian rulers who had advanced control into the Islamic borderlands were forced to relinquish it (Kennedy 1998, 82–124). With this situation only slightly relaxed, in the 970s, came the new wars of the Amirids. Every polity in the north now found itself a target for repeated campaigning, yet these were in fact the death throes of a centralised Muslim polity in the Peninsula, unbeknownst either to victims or perpetrators. In the year 1006 civil war broke out and by 1010 the situation had deteriorated so far that Catalan and Castilian troops were called in on opposite sides of a succession struggle for the Caliphate; the Catalans sacked Córdoba itself. With this began the period of raiding and tributes known as *parias*, and in 1031 the last Caliph died and was not replaced, leaving the array of city-states and their rulers known as *taifas* to compete and contest the new and increasing Christian dominance (Wasserstein 1985).

In this changed world the old frontier zones could not remain unattached and disconnected for long, although new disconnections were now in progress throughout the Caliphate. Rather than disappear, therefore, the frontier can be seen as having moved, into the areas where in the twelfth century we find El Cid taking advantage of such larger-scale detachment to form a new principality around Valencia, among others like him. The ways that the polities of the north had developed to advance their control into such disconnected zones in the centuries before would serve such men well, but this does not erase the long period in which that control was not extended and in which the people we have studied made their own ways.

Notes

1 Terminology for this period is difficult. Not every territory had a single ruler in this era, and rulers were not always kings. I have therefore used the terms "polity" and "territory" throughout despite their problems. References could be far more numerous than here attempted: Mínguez Fernández (2004) offers a broader survey from a Castilian perspective, and Sabaté i Curull (1996) a Catalan one. For the period under discussion here, the future Portugal is covered by the Castilian scholarship.
2 The most influential scholarly use of the term *marca hispanica*, De Marca (1688) was sponsored by King Louis XIV of France to undermine the genealogical claim of the kings of Aragon to the area and thus their crown (cf. Abadal 1957–1958)!
3 Much of this scholarship was funded by the Generalitat to celebrate its notional millennium in 1987 and is consequently affirmative. The main dissenting voice from inside, Abadal 1958, despite writing in the time of Franco, managed to retain enough to feel proud of that the book has remained a standard text.
4 The classic example of this historiography is Sánchez-Albornoz (1966); cf. Manzano Moreno (1999), 37–38 and Mínguez Fernández (2002). As Manzano Moreno points out, it is not clear that Sánchez-Albornoz knew Turner's work.
5 Aguilar and Rodríguez (1994, 587–598) take a sample of such persons in the Leonese documents of the Cathedral of León by title where present. Some arithmetic makes it clear that although that is less than a tenth of their total sample (269 of 2,750, from 4,121 documents), the vast majority of them (174) were priests, with other churchmen also common.
6 Although I am sure this is an old adage, I have been unable to locate its source.

Works cited

Acién Almansa, Manuel. 1994. *Entre el feudalismo y el Islam: 'Umar ibn Hafsun en los historiadores, en las fuentes y en la historia.* Jaén: Universidad de Jaén.
Aguilar Sebastián, Víctor and Francisco Rodríguez Mediano. 1994. "Antroponimia de origen árabe en la documentación leonesa (siglos VIII–XIII)." *El Reino de León en la Alta Edad Media* 6: 497–633.
Balaguer, Anna María. 1998. "Parias and Myth of the Mancus." In *Problems of Medieval Coinage in the Iberian Area, 3: A Symposium Held by the Sociedade Numismática Scalabitana and the Instituto de Sintra on 4–8 October*, edited by Mario Gomes Marques and David Michael Metcalf, 499–543. Santarém: Sociedade Numismatica Scalabitana.

Barbero, Abilio and Marcelo Vigil. 1974. *Sobre los orígenes sociales de la Reconquista*. Esplugues de Llobregat: Ariel.

Barceló, Miquel. 1993. "Al Mulk, el verde y el blanco. La vajilla califal omeya de Madinat al-Zahra'." In *La cerámica altomedieval en el sur de al-Andalus: primer encuentro de arqueología y patrimonio*, edited by Antonio Malpica Cuello, 291–299. Granada: Universidad de Granada.

Barrett, Graham. 2011. "Latin Letters under Arab Rule." Paper Presented at the Conference "711: Reassessing the Arab Conquest of Spain in its 1300th Anniversary Year," University of Oxford, July 17.

Barrios García, Ángel. 1982. "Toponomástica e historia. Notas sobre la despoblación en la zona meridional del Duero." In *Estudios en memoria del profesor D. Salvador de Moxó*, edited by Miguel Ángel Ladero Quesada, vol. 2, 115–134. Madrid: Universidad Complutense.

Benet i Clarà, Albert. 1991–1992. "Castells, guàrdies i torres de defensa." In *Symposium internacional sobre els orígens de Catalunya (segles VIII–XI)*, edited by Federico Udina i Martorell, vol. 1, 393–407. Barcelona: Generalitat de Catalunya.

Berend, Nora. 1999. "Medievalists and the Notion of the Frontier." *Medieval History Journal* 2: 55–72.

Bolòs i Masclans, Jordi. 1995. "Onomàstica i poblament a la Catalunya septentrional a l'alta edat mitjana." In *Histoire et archéologie des terres catalanes au moyen âge*, edited by Philippe Sénac, 49–69. Perpignan: Presses universitaires de Perpignan.

Carvajal Castro, Álvaro. 2012. "Superar la frontera: mecanismos de integración territorial entre el Cea y el Pisuerga en el siglo X." *Anuario de Estudios Medievales* 42: 601–628.

Castro, Américo. 1948. *España en su historia: cristianos, moros y judíos*. Buenos Aires: Losada. Revised and translated by Edmund L. King as *The Structure of Spanish History*. Princeton, NJ: Princeton University Press, 1954. Revised and translated by Willard F. King and Selma Margaretten as *The Spaniards: An Introduction to their History*. Berkeley, CA: University of California Press, 1971.

Chandler, Cullen. 2013. "Carolingian Catalonia: The Spanish March and the Franks, c.750–c.1050." *History Compass* 11 (9): 739–750.

Christys, Ann. 1998. "Saint-Germain-des-Prés, St Vincent and the Martyrs of Córdoba." *Early Medieval Europe* 7 (2): 199–216.

———. 2002a. "Crossing the Frontier of Ninth-Century Hispania." In *Medieval Frontiers: Concepts and Practices*, edited by David Abulafia and Nora Berend, 35–53. Cambridge: Cambridge University Press.

———. 2002b. *Christians in al-Andalus 711–1000*. Richmond: Curzon.

Collins, Roger. 1989. *The Arab Conquest of Spain, 710–797*. Oxford: Blackwell.

———. 1995. "Spain: The Northern Kingdoms and the Basques, 711–910." In *The New Cambridge Medieval History, vol. 2: c. 700–c. 900*, edited by Rosamond McKitterick, 272–289. Cambridge: Cambridge University Press.

———. 2004. *Visigothic Spain, 409–711*. Oxford: Blackwell.

———. 2012. *Caliphs and Kings: Spain, 796–1031*. Oxford: Wiley-Blackwell.

d'Abadal i de Vinyals, Ramon. 1957–1958. "El concepte politic i geogràfic de la locució 'marca hispanica'." *Boletín de la Real Academia de Buenas Letras de Barcelona* 27: 157–165.

———. 1958. *Els primers comtes catalans*. Barcelona: Vicens Vives.

Daniel, Norman. 1994. "Spanish Christian Sources of Information about Islam (Ninth-Thirteenth Centuries)." *Al-Qantara: revista de estudios árabes* 15 (2): 365–384.

Davies, Wendy and Paul Fouracre, eds. 1986. *The Settlement of Disputes in Early Medieval Europe*. Cambridge: Cambridge University Press.

De Marca, Petrus. 1688. *Marca Hispanica sive Limes Hispanicus, hoc est geographica & historica descriptio cataloniae, ruscinonis, & circumiacentium populorum*. Edited by Étienne Baluze. Paris: Imprimèrie royale.

Deswartes, Thomas. 2003. *De la destruction à la restauration: L'idéologie du royaume d'Oviedo-León (VIIIe–XIe siècles)*. Turnhout: Brepols.

Díaz y Díaz, Manuel Cecilio. 1969. "La circulation des manuscrits dans la péninsule ibérique du VIIIe au XIe siècle." *Cahiers de Civilisation Médiévale* 12: 219–241, 383–392.

Escalona Monge, Julio. 2000–2001. "Comunidades, territorios y poder condal en la Castilla del Duero en el siglo X." *Studia Historica: historia medieval* 18–19: 85–120.

———. 2001. "De 'señores y campesinos' a 'poderes feudales y comunidades.' Elementos para definir la articulación entre territorio y clases sociales en la alta Edad Media castellana." In *Comunidades locales y poderes feudales en la Edad Media*, edited by Ignacio Álvarez Borge, 117–155. Biblioteca de Investigación 27. [Logroño]: Universidad de la Rioja.

———. 2004. "Family Memories: Inventing Alfonso I of Asturias." In *Building Legitimacy: Political Discourses and Forms of Legitimacy in Medieval Societies*, edited by María I. Alfonso Antón, Hugh Kennedy, and Julio Escalona Monge, 223–262. Leiden: Brill.

Fernández Conde, Javier. 2009. "Los Mozárabes en el Reino de León: siglos VIII–XI." *Studia Historica: historia medieval* 27: 53–69.

Fierro, Maribel. 2009. "El Conde Casio, los Banu Qasi y los linajes godos en al-Andalus." *Studia Historica: historia medieval* 27: 181–189.

Fletcher, Richard. 1989. *The Quest for El Cid*. London: Hutchinson.

Galera i Pedrosa, Antoni, ed. 1998. *Diplomatari de la vila de Cardona, anys 966–1276: Arxiu Parroquial de Sant Miquel i Sant Vicenç de Cardona, Arxiu Abacial de Cardona, Arxiu Històric de Cardona, Arxius Patrimonials de les masies Garriga de Bergus, Pala de Coma i Pinell*. Barcelona: Fundació Noguera.

Gibert Rebull, Jordi. 2006. "Els inicis de l'edat mitjana (segles VIII–IX) al Penedès i el Baix Llobregat: una aproximació arqueològica." *Butlletí de la Societat Catalana d'Estudis Històrics* 17: 65–84.

Gil Fernández, Juan, ed., José L. Moraleja, trans., Juán I. Ruíz de la Peña. 1985. *Crónicas Asturianas: Crónica de Alfonso III (Rotense y "A Sebastián"), Crónica Albeldense y "Profética."* Oviedo: Universidad de Oviedo.

Gómez Moreno, Manuel. 1919. *Iglesias Mozárabes: arte español de los siglos IX à XI*. Madrid: Centro de Estudios Históricos.

González García, J. J. 1995. "Fronteras y fortificaciones en territorio burgalés en la transición de la Antigüedad a la Edad Media." *Cuadernos Burgaleses de Historia Medieval* 2: 7–69.

Grierson, Philip. 1959. "Commerce in the Dark Ages: A Critique of the Evidence." *Transactions of the Royal Historical Society* 5 (9): 123–140.

Hillenbrand, Robert. 1992. "'The Ornament of the World': Medieval Córdoba as a Cultural Centre." In *The Legacy of Muslim Spain*, edited by Salma Jayyusi, 112–135. Leiden: Brill.

Hitchcock, Richard. 2008. *Mozarabs in Medieval and Early Modern Spain*. Aldershot: Ashgate.

Isla Frez, Amancio. 2011. "Identidades y goticismo en época de Alfonso III: las propuestas de la Albeldense." *Territorio, sociedad y poder: revista de estudios medievales* 6: 11–21.

Jarrett, Jonathan. 2010a. "Settling the Kings' Lands: *Aprisio* in Catalonia in Perspective." *Early Medieval Europe* 18 (3): 320–342.

———. 2010b. "Centurions, Alcalas, and *Christiani perversi*: Organisation of Society in the pre-Catalan 'Terra de Ningú'." In *Early Medieval Spain: A Symposium*, edited by Alan Deyermond and Martin Ryan, 97–127. London: Queen Mary.

———. 2011. "Caliph, King, or Grandfather: Strategies of Legitimization on the Spanish March in the Reign of Lothar III." *The Mediaeval Journal* 1 (2): 1–22.

Kennedy, Hugh. 1998. *Muslim Spain and Portugal: A Political History of Al-Andalus*. London: Longman.

Linage Conde, Jesús Antonio. 1971. "La donación de Alfonso VI a Silos del futuro priorato de San Frutos y el problema de la despoblación." *Anuario de Historia del Derecho Español* 41: 973–1012.

Linehan, Peter. 1993. *History and the Historians of Medieval Spain*. Oxford: Clarendon Press.

———. 2001. "At the Spanish Frontier." In *The Medieval World*, edited by Peter Linehan and Janet L. Nelson, 37–59. London: Routledge.

Lorenzo Jiménez, Jesús. 2010. *La Dawla de los Banu Qasi: origen, auge y caída de una dinastía muladí en la frontera superior de al-Andalus*. Madrid: Consejo Superior de Investigaciones Científicas.

Lourie, Elena. 1966. "A Society Organized for War: Medieval Spain." *Past and Present* 35: 54–76.

Manzano Moreno, Eduardo. 1991. *La frontera de al-Ándalus en época de los Omeyas*. Madrid: Consejo Superior de Investigaciones Científicas.

———. 1994. "The Christian-Muslim Frontier in Al-Andalus: Idea and Reality." In *The Arab Influence in Medieval Europe*, edited by Dionisius A. Agius and Richard Hitchcock, 83–96. Reading, IL: Ithaca.

———. 1999. "The Creation of a Medieval Frontier: Islam and Christianity in the Iberian Peninsula, Eighth to Twelfth Centuries." In *Frontiers in Question: Eurasian Borderlands, 700–1700*, edited by Daniel Power and Naomi Standen, 32–52. Basingstoke: Macmillan.

Marín, Manuela, ed. 1998. *The Formation of Al-Andalus, Part 1: History and Society*. Aldershot: Ashgate.

Martín Viso, Iñaki. 2005. "Una frontera casi invisible: los territorios al norte del Sistema Central en la alta edad media (siglos VIII–XI)." *Studia Historica: historia medieval* 23: 89–114.

Menéndez Pidal, Ramon. 1929. *La España del Cid*. Madrid: Plutarco.

Mínguez Fernández, José María, ed. 1976. *Colección diplomática del Monasterio de Sahagún (siglos IX y X)*, vol. 1. León: Centro de Estudios e Investigación San Isidoro.

———. 1998. "Continuidad y ruptura en los orígenes de la sociedad asturleonesa. De la villa a la comunidad campesina." *Studia Historica: historia medieval* 16: 89–127.

———. 2002. "La despoblación del Duero: un tema a debate." In *Homenatge al Profesor M. Riu i Riu*, edited by Salvador Curull, and Antoni Riera, vol. 2, 67–80. *Acta Historica et archaeologica mediaevalia* 20–21 & 22. Barcelona: Universitat de Barcelona.

———. 2004. *La España de los siglos VI al XIII: guerra, expansión y transformaciones*. San Sebastián: Nerea.

———. 2005. *La Reconquista*. Madrid: Alba.

Moran Cruz, Jo Ann and Richard Gerberding. 2004. *Medieval Worlds: An Introduction to European History 300–1492*. New York: Houghton Mifflin.

Nelson, Janet, L. 2010. "'As Ithers See Us': Some Thoughts on Spain and Francia in the Early Middle Ages." In *Early Medieval Spain: A Symposium*, edited by Alan Deyermond and Martin Ryan, 17–23. London: Queen Mary.

Reilly, Bernard F. 1991. *The Kingdom of León-Castilla under King Alfonso VII, 1126–1157*. Philadelphia, PA: University of Pennsylvania Press.

———. 1993. *The Medieval Spains*. Cambridge: Cambridge University Press.

Riess, Frank. 2005. "From Aachen to Al-Andalus: The Journey of Deacon Bodo (823–876)." *Early Medieval Europe* 13 (2): 131–157.

Ríos Saloma, Martín. 2008. "La 'Reconquista': ¿una aspiración peninsular? Estudio comparativo entre dos tradiciones historiográficas." *Le Moyen Âge vu d'ailleurs. Bulletin du Centre d'Études Médiévales* Hors-série 2 : 1–15.

Riu-Barrera, Eduard. 1999. "La cerámica del Mediterráneo noroccidental en los siglos VIII–IX: Cataluña, el país valenciano y las Baleares entre el imperio carolingio y al-Andalus." In *Cataluña en la época carolingia: arte y cultura antes del Románico (siglos IX y X)*, edited by Jordi Camps, 259–263 (English translation 549–551). Barcelona: Museu Nacional d'Art de Catalunya.

Riu i Riu, Manuel, ed. 1999. *La España cristiana de los siglos VIII al XI, 2: los nucleos pirenaicos (718–1035): Navarra, Aragón, Cataluña*, vol. 7.2 of *Historia de España*. Madrid: Espasa-Calpe 1986–1999.

Rius Serra, José. 1946. *Cartulario de "Sant Cugat" del Vallés*, vol. 2. Barcelona: Consejo Superior de Investigaciones Científicas.

Sabaté i Curull, Flocel. 1996. *L'expansió territorial de Catalunya (segles IX–XII): ¿conquesta o reproblació?* Lleida: Universitat de Lleida.

Sáez, Ernesto, ed. 1987. *Colección documental del Archivo de la Catedral de León (775–1230)*, vol. 1. León: Centro de Estudios e Investigación San Isidoro.

Samson of Córdoba. 1969–1973. "Apologeticum contra perfidos." In *Corpvs Scriptorvm Mvzarabicorvm*, edited by Juan Gil, vol. 2, 505–658. Madrid: Emerita.

Sánchez-Albornoz, Claudio. 1956. *España: un enigma histórico*. 2 vols. Buenos Aires: Edhasa. (English translation by Colette Joly Dees and David Sven Reher as *Spain: A Historical Enigma*. 2 vols. Madrid: Fundación Universitaria Española, 1975).

———. 1966. *Despoblación y repoblación del valle del Duero*. Buenos Aires: Instituto de Historia de España.

———. 1991. *La España cristiana de los siglos VIII al XI, 1: El reino astur-leonés (722 a 1037)*, vol. 7.1 of *Historia de España*. Madrid: Espasa-Calpe, 1986–1999.

Scales, Peter C. 1994. *The Fall of the Caliphate of Córdoba: Berbers and Andalusis in Conflict*. Leiden: Brill.

Stalls, W. Clay. 2004. *Possessing the Land: Aragon's Expansion in Islam's Ebro Frontier under Alfonso the Battler, 1104–1134*. Leiden: Brill.

Udina Martorell, Federico. 1951. *El Archivo Condal de Barcelona en los siglos IX–X: estudio crítico de sus fondos*. Madrid: Consejo Superior de Investigaciones Científicas.

Wasserstein, David. 1985. *The Rise and Fall of the Party-Kings: Politics and Society in Islamic Spain, 1002–1086*. Princeton, NJ: Princeton University Press.

Werckmeister, Otto Karl. 1993. "Art of the Frontier: Mozarabic monasticism." In *The Art of Medieval Spain A. D. 500–1200*, edited by John P. O'Neill, Kathleen Howard, and Anne M. Lucke, 121–132. New York: Metropolitan Museum of Art.

Wolff, Philippe. 1963. "Quidam homo nomine Roberto negociatore." *Le Moyen Âge* 69: 123–139.

4

THE FAITHS OF ABRAHAM IN MEDIEVAL IBERIA

John Edwards

Both in academic work and in the general perception fostered, for example, by the tour guides of Córdoba's Mezquita-Catedral, medieval Spain came to be regarded, in late twentieth-century historiography, as the scene of a remarkable and generally peaceful co-existence (*convivencia*) between adherents of the three religious faiths of Abraham: Judaism, Christianity and Islam. Yet in reality the religious history of "the Spains," including Portugal, in the medieval period contained all the contradictions and conflicts which had arisen from the development of the newer faiths, Christianity and Islam, out of Judaism. In the medieval period, in the Iberian Peninsula and elsewhere, none of these religions truly accepted the validity of the others, and although those which possessed political and military power, the Christians and the Muslims, were not always at war, the latent conflict between them was always there to be revived and exploited at any opportune moment. The Iberian Jewish communities, having no political power, were always liable to be exploited and, especially between 1200 and 1500, became a target for attack, particularly in the areas of the Peninsula ruled by Christian princes.

At the time of the ministry of Jesus of Nazareth, and the beginnings of the Christian Church, in the first century CE, Jews were already living in the Roman provinces of Hispania, including the future kingdom of Portugal. It is not entirely clear when the followers of Jesus's "Way," the Christians, began to appear in the Iberian Peninsula, but the fifth-century successor state, ruled by the Germanic Visigoths, was explicitly Christian, though of the Arian persuasion which was eventually condemned as heretical by the "Catholics." Before the Muslim raid across the Straits of Gibraltar in 711, which became an invasion and then a conquest, Iberia's Jewish communities came under ever-increasing pressure to convert to Christianity. It was in this period that much of the Church's teaching, in the form either of papal pronouncements or of the decrees of ecclesiastical councils, put ever-greater pressure on Jews who refused to convert. They were increasingly placed under penal restrictions, and efforts were made to segregate them, geographically and socially, from their Christian neighbours. Although the assertion that Jews welcomed and even militarily assisted the Muslim invasion, which continued to be implicitly believed by most Christian Spaniards and Portuguese in the later Middle Ages and onwards, seems to be false, it is undeniable that pressure on Jews was at least initially reduced in the areas of the Peninsula which were thereafter controlled by Muslims.

Recent historiography has led to an interpretation of Christian-Muslim relations, between the eighth and the fifteenth centuries, that modifies and refines the old account, which simply identified the underlying process in that period as a Christian reconquest (*Reconquista*) of the land that had been "lost" to Islam after 711. Firstly, it now seems clear that the process whereby the existing, largely Christian, population of Iberia, an ethnically diverse mixture of Hispano-Roman and Visigothic German, converted in significant numbers to Islam was slow, erratic and still incomplete by the time of the break-up (*fitna*) of the Caliphate of Córdoba after 1031 (Kennedy 1996, 1–129). Some territories in the far north of the Peninsula, particularly Galicia, Asturias, the Basque country and parts of Catalonia, had never submitted religiously, and, between the eighth and the tenth centuries, these statelets, which would eventually become the medieval Christian kingdoms of León, Castile and Portugal, as well as the principality of Catalunya, launched the earliest of the intermittent military advances southwards, which would eventually lead Isabel and Fernando, the *Reyes Católicos*, to launch a final and successful war of conquest (1482–1492) in what had by then become the Nasrid emirate of Granada. It would be wrong, at least up until that final phase, which indeed might accurately be described as a *Reconquista*, to see the many political and military conflicts which unfolded in the Peninsula as "religious" wars. Although frontier conflicts in the Peninsula, between Muslim and Christian entities, came to be qualified on the Christian side as "crusades" at least until the thirteenth century – and were recognised as such by the Papacy, with the corresponding tax-benefits (the *cruzada*) – they often saw Muslims and Christians fighting on the same side. The epic career of Ruy Díaz de Bivar, "El Cid," symbolises a type of conflict that was neither Christian crusade nor Muslim *jihad* (Michael 1978).

This is not to say that there were no religious and ideological elements in the relations between the Abrahamic faiths in medieval Iberia. Practical co-existence did not mean anything resembling modern notions of tolerance, as a positively relativist concept. The best that could be hoped for was de facto toleration. There were always voices among Christians and Muslims who advocated conversion, often by violence, and Jews were liable to fall prey to the more severe teachings of both the rival faiths, without the possibility of political or military response. The more extreme measures of the Visigoths, which fell into abeyance as a result of the arrival of Muslim rule in the Peninsula, began to be revived in the thirteenth century. By 1200, the Christian kingdom of Portugal had become established, but much of the southern third of the Spanish part of the Peninsula, including Andalusia, remained under the rule of fragmented Muslim states (*taifas*). Up until that point, Christian rulers, in both Spain and Portugal, had advanced irregularly southwards, on more or less parallel fronts and, from 1085, with papal backing as "crusaders." The balance of power between Christian rulers inevitably affected the lives of those who lived on either side of the "frontier." As long as Christians and Muslims were as likely to fight with as against each other, no major territorial advances were to be expected, but in 1212 the battle of Las Navas de Tolosa changed all that. There, Alfonso VIII of Castile, with the help of the Aragonese and Catalans, defeated the Muslim army and opened the gateway to Andalusia. Even then, the traditional pattern repeated itself, and there was no further military advance for more than twenty years. The battle of Las Navas had demonstrated the potential of united force, but the next steps forward were taken separately, by Ferdinand III of Castile and James I of Aragon (Kennedy 1996, 130–272).

The conquest of Córdoba, the former caliphal capital, in 1236, took place more or less by accident. In the Sierra Morena and the Pedroche, to the north of the city, nominally Christian bandits, known as *almogávares*, were making a good living out of the traffic between the Guadalquivir valley and the plains of the central Meseta. In the spring of that year, some of them came down to settle a dispute and discovered the eastern segment of the city, the Ajerquía, undefended. They entered, seized the city, and sent word to King Ferdinand, who later arrived with an army, and gradually incorporated the "kingdom of Córdoba" into the Crown of Castile.

A similar pattern, but with more direct royal involvement, was followed in Seville (1248) and Jaén (1252): only the kingdom, or emirate, of Granada remained in Muslim hands. As far as the religious settlement of western Andalusia was concerned, by the 1260s, the pattern of inter-faith relations in Castilian territory, including Murcia, was largely settled, as it would remain until the reign of Ferdinand and Isabella. Although Muslims and Jews were initially offered religious freedom, subordinated to Christian political and ecclesiastical structures, most urban Muslims quickly departed, either to Granada or to North Africa. In the countryside, Muslims continued to cultivate land that had now been divided, in *repartimientos*, among Christian nobles and churchmen, but, after a major uprising in Andalusia in 1264, most of this rural population departed or was removed as well. Thus the relatively few remaining Jews and Muslims, the latter known as *mudéjares*, mostly lived, under religious and social restriction, in the towns. In parallel to the Castilian enterprise in western Andalusia, the Crown of Aragon expanded, with the capture and resettlement, during the 1230s, of what became the kingdom of Valencia. Here, although, as in Andalusia, most Muslims, including the religious authorities, left the towns; a large *mudéjar* population survived in the countryside, as did Jewish communities in the towns of Aragon, Catalonia and Valencia. A similar situation prevailed in the separate kingdoms of Portugal and Navarre.

Relations among adherents of the three Abrahamic faiths, in the period between the 1260s and the accession of Isabel I of Castile in 1474, and her husband Ferdinand of Aragon five years later, have traditionally been studied and assessed, not only with the inevitable historical hindsight, but also in the light of what happened after the establishment of the new Spanish Inquisition (1478–1480) and the conquest of Granada in 1492. Thus there is still a strong tendency to see the fourteenth and fifteenth centuries, in particular, as a time of steady deterioration in interfaith relations. Increasingly, however, scholars are adding nuances to the picture. Iberian rulers, after 1250, inherited a body of Christian teaching, on relations with other faiths, which had very largely been developed to deal with those Jews who refused to abandon their traditional religion. This meant that royal legislation, notably Alfonso X of Castile's seven-part code (*Siete Partidas*), even though it was not put into full effect until 1348, embodied all the restrictions on Jewish life that popes and Church councils demanded (Carpenter 1986). Although, in the period 1250 to 1450, parallel measures were increasingly adopted by the Peninsular kingdoms to control their remaining *mudéjares*, official thinking on Islam very much followed the restrictive approach that had traditionally been adopted towards Jews. Elsewhere in Europe, what became known as the "First Crusade" to Palestine (1095–1099) had unleashed violence against Europe's Jews, as well as the Muslim rulers of the Christian holy places in the "Holy Land" itself. The twelfth and thirteenth centuries produced not only further violence against Jews, for example in Germany, France and England, but also saw the evolution of Christian "tales" about Jews. Now, they appeared not only as killers and deniers of Jesus Christ, but also as crucifiers of Christian children, who even, in some versions, used their victims' blood to make unleavened bread (*matzos*) for Passover.

Alfonso X's *Partidas* do not explicitly endorse these accusations (to Jews "blood libels"), but they nevertheless re-affirm the old accusations of Christ-killing, and urge the segregation of Jewish communities (*aljamas*) from the Christian majority population. In succeeding reigns in Castile, and with parallels in the Crown of Aragon, while many of these restrictive measures were not enforced, Jews, and in some cases Muslims too, came under a new form of attack. In Iberia, as elsewhere in Western Europe, the period 1250 to 1350 saw a significant expansion of population and strong economic development. Towns grew in size and importance, and increasingly used their representation, by *procuradores* in the various parliaments (*Cortes/Corts*) of the kingdoms, to assert the interests of leading citizens (*caballeros, omes buenos*) against the nobility (*ricos omes, hidalgos*), by influencing the Crown. In this process, which lasted from the late 1280s to the 1340s, taxation became a major issue. Successive Castilian *Cortes* urged kings (Sancho IV, Ferdinand IV, Alfonso XI) to end the farming of royal taxes altogether, and ban nobles, clergy and Jews (in some cases Muslims also) from collecting these taxes (*pechos*) on the Crown's behalf, or acting as tax inspectors. Meanwhile, other Iberian rulers continued to honour, at least in name, the precepts of the Church on Jewish-Christian relations.

The major plague which ravaged much of Europe between 1348 and 1351, and is commonly known as the "Black Death," reached the Iberian Peninsula, through Catalonia and Valencia, in 1349. In March 1350, it killed Alfonso XI of Castile, while he was besieging Gibraltar, thus bringing Pedro I to the throne. His reign, which lasted until 1369, was full of conflict, some of which highlighted the Jewish and Muslim minorities, in the context of war between Castile and Aragon, civil war within Castile itself, and involvement in the long military struggle between France and England, known as the "Hundred Years' War." Pedro's main opponent, his bastard half-brother Enrique, count of Trastámara, not only used as a propaganda weapon the King's supposed favouring of Jews and Muslims, including the emir of Granada, at the expense of Christians and their religion, but also incited violent attacks on Jewish *aljamas*, beginning in Toledo in May 1355. There is no substantial evidence that Pedro in fact pursued policies favouring Jews and Muslims, but, when Enrique seized the throne, by murdering his opponent, he, and the succeeding Trastamaran dynasty, up to Ferdinand and Isabel, faced the same issues as previous Castilian rulers, as well as their Iberian neighbours.

It seems undeniable that social pressure on religious minorities, especially in Spain rather than Portugal, was increasing fairly steadily between 1350 and 1390. This happened even though there is little evidence that Jews were blamed for spreading the "great plague," either in its initial onslaught or in the recurring epidemics which continued well into the fifteenth century. This formed a contrast with events elsewhere in Europe, particularly Germany and France, where many Jews were killed for this supposed reason, or else forced to convert to Christianity. Nevertheless, secular pressure, especially in the larger towns of the Peninsula, remained on rulers, both to enforce the restrictions on Jewish, and to some extent Muslim, life which were enjoined by the Church, and to remove both minorities, especially Jews, from the farming and collection of royal taxes. There was, however, little sign, by 1390, that royal policy was going to change. Jews were so essential to the functioning of the royal administration, particularly in Castile, that there seemed to be no possibility of removing them from the royal service. All this would change with the outbreak of murderous violence against Jews in Seville in June 1391.

Although there had been previous incidents of violence against Jews, some involving forced conversion to Christianity, as well as theft, arson and murder, the events of 1391, involving Spain but not Portugal, were of a different order. While it has been argued that converts, in Castile at least, had been undermining the morale of Jewish communities ever since the civil war of 1366–1369, the scale of the violence from June to August 1391 was unprecedented (Netanyahu 2001, 129–167). It spread from Seville, across Andalusia, then New and Old Castile, and also into Aragon and Catalonia, leading to many deaths, much destruction of property, and a large number of conversions, in that year and subsequently. Thus a new situation was created in Spain, with whole families and groups, instead of individuals, as had been traditional, having access to crucial parts of the majority Christian society, including local governmental offices, the Church, the universities, the professions and guilds. The *converso* phenomenon was thus created, which would affect the history of Spain and, from 1497 onwards, that of Portugal, well into the modern era.

The Christian Church which the Jewish converts joined, between 1390 and about 1420, had developed as part of Western Catholic Christendom, since the conversion of the Visigothic monarchs from the "heresy" of Arianism (an alternative interpretation of the Holy Trinity), in the sixth century. Thanks to the unique history of the Iberian Peninsula, in the context of Western Europe, the late medieval Spanish and Portuguese Church, while organised on lines similar to those of its European neighbours, into dioceses and provinces headed by bishops, and with a parochial structure which covered all areas under Christian rule, had a special role in confronting not only a Jewish minority but also Islam. Against this background, after 1391, the Spanish Church faced two urgent problems, one at home but the other abroad. Firstly, the conversion of tens of thousands of Jews presented the Church with a practical, pastoral problem which had not faced European Church hierarchies since the conversion of the pagan Balts in the thirteenth century. The situation required a systematic programme of instruction in Christian doctrine, not at the level of debate among professional Christian and Jewish scholars but in the context of ordinary Jews who now found themselves in a new religious environment which was at the same time familiar and strange. The second problem was imposed on all Western European Churches by the "Great Schism," the split between rival popes, one in Rome and the other in Avignon, which would rack the Catholic Church between 1378 and 1417. While their colleagues at home proved singularly unsuccessful at integrating the new *converso* population into the established Church, some Spanish churchmen, ironically including some *conversos*, made important contributions to the restoration of a united Roman Papacy, which would have a long future.

The nature of the religious conversion which was experienced by Jews in Spain around 1400, and later in Portugal, has been the subject of an immense amount of controversy ever since. This is not only because of its uniqueness but also because of the shattering events which followed it. In Spain, a significant social movement began in the 1420s, in which it appeared that all the social pressures that had been placed on Jews, in earlier centuries, were transferred to the *conversos*. The converts were accused, fundamentally, of not having made a genuine and complete conversion. In a sense, this appeared even worse than their previous "obstinate" clinging to their Jewish faith. They were now increasingly seen, once many of them began to achieve prominence in mainstream society, as "the enemy within," and thus even more dangerous than they had been before.

Converts from Judaism to Christianity had traditionally been subject to suspicion among those who had always been part of the Christian Church, known in Castilian-speaking Spain as "Old Christians" (*cristianos viejos*). Elsewhere in Europe, in the thirteenth century, for example in England, Dominican friars operated "houses of converts," in which the former Jews were indoctrinated in the Christian faith and kept separate from their former co-religionaries, in case they returned to their former religion. Thus, by the mid-fifteenth century, many *cristianos viejos* in Spain, seeing the *conversos* retaining their links with their Jewish relatives and communities, began to assume that they were still really Jews, and had not truly become "new people" when they received the Christian sacrament of baptism, having instead been guilty of the treachery that was traditionally believed to be characteristic of Jews in general. One of the most distinguished historians of Spanish Jewry, Benzion Netanyahu, powerfully maintained an alternative view, in which the accusations of crypto-Judaism among the *conversos* existed largely, if not entirely, in the highly prejudiced minds of the *cristianos viejos*. For him, the converts and their descendants were sincere Christians, and from this proposition he concluded that the "remedy" for this "problem," proposed and then implemented in Spain from about 1450 onwards, the Inquisition, was predicated on a false perception.

In the Middle Ages, an "inquisition" was a set form of legal inquiry, aimed at arriving at the truth about a particular matter, such as a crime, or the ownership of property. Since the early thirteenth century, this procedure, which derived from Roman law, had been employed in the Catholic Church as a means of identifying incorrect Christian belief and practice. Pope Gregory IX first authorised specialised tribunals, mainly consisting of Dominican friars, to investigate heresy in northern Italy and southern France, and the French activity soon spread into Catalonia. At this stage, the main targets were Christian groups, the Cathars ("Perfect Ones") and Waldensians, who had been declared unorthodox by the Papacy. However, the Catalan and Aragonese inquisitors, based in Barcelona, Valencia and Zaragoza, quickly drew Jews into their net, although non-Christians, such as Jews and Muslims, were not subject to their tribunals' direct jurisdiction. But in the new circumstances of fifteenth-century Castile, where, as in Portugal and Navarre, the earlier tribunals had never functioned, the *conversos*, and therefore Jews, became the primary target (Edwards 2009, 31–84).

The religious identity of the thousands of Jews who converted to Christianity between 1390 and about 1420 remains a deeply controversial subject. The ways in which their beliefs and practices are characterised reveal much of the views and methodologies of the scholars who attempt to analyse them. The approach of the Church to Judaism, set out in the correspondence of popes and in the decrees of Councils, and reflected in secular legislation, in Iberia as elsewhere, was extremely negative. Christianity arose controversially out of Judaism, and left a bitter legacy. On the basis of some texts which came to be included in the official "canon" of the New Testament, the Jews' religion was generally portrayed as hard and legalistic, in contrast to the spiritual freedom which following Christ claimed to offer. In particular, on the basis of a text in Matthew's gospel, Christians came to blame Jews for the crucifixion of Jesus, not only those present at his trials before their own high priests and Pontius Pilate, but all their descendants forever. This belief would, of course, prove highly dangerous to medieval Jews, in Spain and Portugal as well as elsewhere. The conversions around the year 1400 added a new dimension to this ancient anti-Jewish feeling. Because of the violent circumstances in which these baptisms happened, not only in the midst of the 1391 pogroms but also in subsequent years, it could easily be supposed, and often was, that the sacrament was frequently received insincerely, and therefore did not achieve its proper result, by turning the convert into a new person, who had completely abandoned the old, "wicked" religion.

Both the pressure to convert, and suspicion of the sincerity of the conversion, affected all the Spanish Christian kingdoms, though not Portugal, in the first half of the fifteenth century. However, it was in the Crown of Castile that the demand for a new Inquisition developed, while the existing inquisitorial tribunals in Aragon, Catalonia and Valencia, which had originally been set up to deal with "Old" Christian heretics rather than converted Jews, continued to operate on a limited scale. Like the Jews in the fourteenth century, the *conversos* now found themselves being tossed about in the conflicts and confusion of Spanish politics, as kings and aristocracies vied for power, in both Castile and Aragon. It was one such conflict, involving Juan II of Castile and his favourite (*privado*), Don Álvaro de Luna, on one side, and groups of nobles and townsmen on the other, which led to demands for the exclusion from public life of all *conversos*, on the grounds that they were as dangerous to society as Jews. In 1449, a *converso* tax collector in Toledo, Alonso de Cota, was violently attacked and, rather on the model of 1391, the trouble developed into a general assault on the city's *conversos*. Although the king's peace was eventually restored, in the meantime a lawyer working for the city council (*concejo*), Bachiller Marcos, produced a memorandum in which he argued that, because of their innate insincerity and wickedness, converts from Judaism should never be allowed to hold public office in Toledo again. Although the converts were restored (ironically, Jews had temporarily taken over their role in farming and collecting the municipal rents), the issue would not go away, and successive kings and their officials, especially in Castile, were bombarded with demands for a new Inquisition, which would be aimed at establishing whether the *conversos* were in fact sincere Catholic Christians or secret Jews.

Some churchmen took up the cause, the most notable among them being a Franciscan friar, Alonso de Espina who, in his treatise, *Fortalitium fidei* ("Fortress of the Faith") used the anti-Jewish lore of the medieval Church to urge first Juan II and then Enrique IV of Castile to ask the pope for a new Inquisition in Castile. Between 1450 and the accession of Isabel I, in December 1474, Castilian politics were in turmoil, with aristocratic factions fighting for control of the Crown, and many major towns were divided, sometimes militarily, between rival groups. The *conversos*, who were often, by then, the children, or even grandchildren, of those who had actually started their lives as Jews, and then been baptised as Christians, often became the identity mark which defined one seigniorial faction against another. In Córdoba, for instance, where control was being fought over, in the 1460s and 1470s, between two branches of the Fernández de Córdoba family, the Aguilar branch tended to favour *conversos*, whereas the Cabra branch aimed to reduce their influence. In 1473, a major riot broke out in Córdoba, in which *conversos* were attacked, their property was stolen, and some died. Ironically, the city's remaining Jews were not targeted on this occasion, but there, as elsewhere in Andalusia especially, disorder increased, and continued during the first five years of Isabel's reign, with her husband, Fernando of Aragon.

The civil war that broke out in Castile after Isabel's succession, together with an unsuccessful Portuguese invasion on behalf of the rival candidate for the throne, Juana, nicknamed "La Beltraneja," delayed the new queen's programme for strengthening royal authority. Only at the *Cortes* of Toledo, in 1480, was this wide-ranging attempt at reform published and given legal force, but the *converso* question had by then been tackled in a new and significant way. Isabel, in particular, seems to have accepted the argument that the Inquisition was needed in her kingdoms to test the orthodoxy of the converts from Judaism, and she and her husband, Fernando, petitioned Pope Sixtus IV to authorise such a tribunal. He did so on 1 November 1478, and two years later inquisitors began work in Seville. Within five years, other tribunals had begun work in Córdoba and Ciudad Real, the latter soon moving to Toledo. At the same time, Fernando introduced the "new" Inquisition to his Aragonese and Catalan territories, removing and replacing the remaining inquisitors under the original, thirteenth-century foundation (Edwards 2000, 80–99).

It is the work of these tribunals of the "Spanish Inquisition," lasting until the 1830s, which has given the Spanish kingdoms, in particular, a reputation for religious fanaticism and oppression. Although they are far from complete, the surviving archives of the Inquisition (to which the Portuguese Inquisition was added in the sixteenth century) have led scholars to debate the motivation, as well as the methods, of the inquisitors. Until the end of the fifteenth century, the target of the Inquisition was surviving Judaism among the *conversos*, though, after 1492, Muslims were subjected to similar pressures, once the emirate of Granada had been conquered by Isabel and Fernando's armies. There was nothing new in the methodology of the Spanish inquisitors. They retained the traditional view of Jews as hereditary "Christ-killers," who were damned unless they converted, and whose religion, the "Law of Moses," was legalistic, cruel and fundamentally wrong. The surviving trials from Isabel's reign, that is, up to 1504, reveal an approach to the religion of the *conversos* which was equally legalistic. During the 1480s, inquisitors came to believe that they had discovered whole networks of "judaizing" converts ("New Christians"), and this led them to argue that the continuing existence of unconverted Jews in the Spanish kingdoms was preventing the full assimilation of the *conversos* into the Church. Finally, in 1492, in the wake of the conquest of Granada, and shortly before Christopher Columbus was dispatched on his first voyage across the Atlantic, the King and Queen agreed to issue parallel edicts, for Castile and Aragon respectively, whereby Jews were ordered to convert to Christianity in three months, or else leave Spain with only what they could carry. Some converted, a few first left the country and then returned to become Christians, but most, tens of thousands, abandoned Spain for good, going to Portugal (where conversion would be imposed in 1497), North Africa, the Turkish Ottoman empire, and even Rome itself (Edwards 2000, 228–235). The loss of so many industrious Jews inevitably had a negative effect on Spain itself. Yet possibly even more influential, in what would come to be known as Spain's "Golden Age" (*Siglo de Oro*), were the *conversos* and their descendants. Despite the continuing work of the Inquisition, and the ever-growing obsession of Spaniards with genealogy, and "pure" blood, supposedly free of Jewish, Muslim or heretical Christian constituents, in the modern age, Spanish Christianity, and increasingly that of Portugal as well, together with both countries' overseas possessions, continued to show unmistakable signs of influence from these two other faiths of Abraham (Edwards 1996, article VII).

One other vital question needs to be asked about the complex religious history of the Iberian Peninsula in the late Middle Ages. It is basic, and yet often forgotten in the very proper anxiety to get to the real reasons for the inability of the Christian majority, by the time of Isabel and Fernando, to tolerate any longer their Jewish and Muslim neighbours. The question is: What did religion mean to medieval Iberians? On the basis of the documentary sources which are the staple diet of historians, and which tend to be unquestioningly accepted by literary scholars too, "religions" or "faiths" – in the case of Iberia Judaism, Christianity and Islam – are assumed to have consisted of definitions and precepts issued by religious leaders – pope, bishops, imams, rabbis – and reinforced by secular rulers, who also assumed divine authority for themselves. Thus even before the reign of Isabel and Fernando, with its introduction of a new Inquisition to Castile and Aragon, Iberian Christian rulers generally accepted the Church's definition of what should be regarded as correct doctrine, "orthodoxy," and what should be regarded as incorrect or false teaching, "heresy." Such thinking appears to presuppose that "religion" consists of a set of intellectual propositions, which may be assented to or disagreed with, yet much of the surviving evidence for the actual lives of medieval Iberians, of all social classes, suggests a much more practical and down-to-earth approach. The late medieval and early modern Inquisitions in fact combined the intellectual with the practical method. Christian assumptions about the "unspiritual" legalism and ritualism of Judaism, and to a lesser extent Islam, led inquisitors, according to the remaining trial evidence, to spend far more time quizzing suspected "heretics" about details of their domestic lives than about theology. Thus *conversos* were asked if they had a clean tablecloth for the Friday evening meal, as they would have done as Jews for Shabbat, and converted Muslims (*Moriscos*), from the early sixteenth century onwards, were asked about their bathing habits, in case they were still bathing ritually, as they had done before their Islamic prayers (Edwards 1996, article I). In addition, current research is increasingly revealing the extent to which ordinary people, of whichever Abrahamic faith, played fast and loose with their religion, whether intellectually or in their practical daily lives. Also, it is becoming increasingly clear that the old idea of Iberian distinctiveness from the rest of Europe in terms of religion, because of its long period under Islamic rule, has been exaggerated. In fact, the Jewish and Muslim life of late medieval Iberia can validly and usefully be compared with the internal doctrinal, as well as political, disputes of the rest of Catholic Christendom in that period (Edwards 1996, article III).

The religious picture which emerges from this lengthy and complex period in Iberia thus offers two conflicting, but partially truthful, pictures. One was the triumph of a Catholic Christianity, combining Church and State, which by 1500 had largely subjugated both Judaism and Islam in the Peninsula, and soon in Spanish and Portuguese overseas possessions across the world. The second, equally valid and perhaps more attractive to twenty-first-century eyes, shows individuals, in Iberia and in colonies abroad, making daily accommodations in their lives which cut across, and indeed defied, the teachings of priests, rabbis and imams. It was in this diverse and kaleidoscopic way that Iberians entered modernity.

Works cited

Carpenter, Dwayne E. 1986. *Alfonso X and the Jews. An Edition of and Commentary on Siete Partidas 7.24 "De los judíos."* Berkeley, CA: University of California Press.

Edwards, John. 1996. *Religion and Society in Spain, c. 1492.* Aldershot: Variorum.

———. 2000. *The Spain of the Catholic Monarchs, 1474–1520.* Oxford: Blackwell.

———. 2009. *Inquisition.* Stroud: The History Press.

Kennedy, Hugh. 1996. *Muslim Spain and Portugal. A Political History of Al-Andalus.* London and New York: Longman.

Michael, Ian, ed. 1978. *Poema de mio Cid.* Madrid: Castalia.

Netanyahu, Benzion. 2001. *The Origins of the Inquisition in Fifteenth Century Spain.* New York: New York Review of Books.

5

MEDIEVAL IBERIAN CULTURES IN CONTACT

Iberian cultural production as translation and adaptation

Michelle M. Hamilton

Scholars of medieval Iberia have expressed frustration with the perceived limitations of Amé-rico Castro's theory of *convivencia* as a model for explaining the cultural interactions between different religious, ethnic, and linguistic groups in the Iberian Peninsula during the Middle Ages (Catlos 2014b; Ray 2005; Soifer 2009). Brian Catlos (2014a) has argued that the creative and sometimes destructive interactions between Iberians in the Middle Ages are not unique, but reflect the larger Mediterranean world in which Muslims, Jews, and Christians (in addition to Byzantines, North Africans, Romans, Phoenicians, etc.) had been meeting, interacting, and sharing ideas and customs for millennia. While the aforementioned historians are primarily concerned with describing the social, political, and economic exchanges between Iberians (and to a lesser extent their artistic and literary production), scholars of Jewish cultural produc-tion in the medieval Mediterranean have been wrestling with how to explain what they call the Islamic or Arabic nature of Jewish cultural production in the medieval Arabo-Islamic world (including al-Andalus). Charles Manekin (2012), Daniel L. Lasker (2012), Gad Fruedenthal (2012), and Sarah Stroumsa (2012) have nuanced the theory of cultural symbiosis that S. D. Goitein used to describe early medieval Jewish-Islamic thought (1971, 2003). These scholars see the prevalence of philosophical rationalism as key to explaining the nature and types of ideas and cultural production that were both imported (through translation and commentaries), as well as created in original compositions produced throughout the Arabo-Islamic world, and particularly in Iberia. The Peninsula constituted one of the areas in which "polemical exchange between Jews and Christians was rational and relatively free," and where "philosophy and logic were eagerly developed as tools of such exchange" (Goldstein 2012, 9–10).

The present study takes as its point of departure the idea that the free and rational exchange of ideas and theories concerning religious belief – precisely the mechanism that provided the modus operandi of cultural contact and accommodation for medieval Arabized Jews accord-ing to Lasker, Freudenthal, et al. – is central to and a defining element of much medieval Iberian cultural production, even for those works produced after most of the Peninsula was in Christian hands. An examination of all such works is well beyond the scope of the present article. Instead I turn to those Iberian works in which the author-transmitters create a narrative of imaginative fiction to accommodate the Arabo-Andalusi philosophical notion of the active intellect. In the Arabo-Andalusi tradition, philosophic inquiry – whose subjects included the natural world, the cosmos, God, and so on – becomes the way that man can use his intellect, which in turn is considered the uniquely human feature that can, if properly developed, bring man from the world of matter to the celestial realm of the divine (Corbin 1993, 248). Ibn Ṭufayl's *Ḥayy ibn Yaqẓān*, Shem Tov Ibn Falaquera's *Ha-Mebeqqesh* (*The Seeker*), Ramón Llull's *Felix*, and Alfonso de la Torre's *Visión deleitable* all involve the incorporation of translated material into a narrative fictional frame used by the authors to stimulate their readers' intellect/reason and help him/her to achieve knowledge of God. I argue that these fictional narratives are witnesses to the particular form of intellectual openness and free exchange of religious ideas that Stroumsa, Freudenthal, and others have observed in the (Judeo-)Andalusi tradition. Two phenomena related to this intellectual openness and to the imaginative narratives examined herein are the Aristotelian theory of the active intellect, discussed previously, and the translation activity that defines medieval Iberian cultural production.

Translation was a part of intellectual life across the Peninsula from well before the twelfth century (Burnett 1994; Harvey 1977; Márquez Villanueva 1996), and involved many agents, most of whom remain unknown, who facilitated the creation and exchange of translated material. Francisco Márquez Villanueva points out that for medieval Iberia, instead of just thinking of the translators and the works translated in Toledo, we must also consider the libraries, the workshops where books were created, the commercial trade in books, and the various professionals across the Peninsula who provided the infrastructure for this vast cultural phenomenon that was by no means confined to a single city (1996, 24). These lines of exchange and contact – not all of which originated in the Peninsula, and many of which extended beyond the mountains to the north, or the sea to the south and east, continuing even across the Mediterranean to the Levant and beyond – are both real and imagined. Iberian intellectuals of the tenth to sixteenth centuries not only traveled to study and acquire knowledge of close and distant lands and teachers, but they also crafted a series of imaginative fictional texts, such as those studied herein that reflected the very real intellectual journeys of their creators.[1]

The beginnings of this story, as Stroumsa notes, are cloudy, but emerge in the early years of Umayyad rule on the Peninsula, when the caliphs of al-Andalus played important roles in bringing the wisdom of Baghdad to Iberia (2012, 48). While the studies of Burnett (1994), Corbin (1993, 242–52), and Daiber (2012) explore the Arabic translations and commentaries on the work of Greek thinkers such as Aristotle, Plato, and Galen that circulated from al-Andalus into Christian Europe, Rafael Ramón Guerrero notes that the comprehensive study of Andalusi Aristotelianism remains to be written (2013, 403). How the work of Aristotle and his Arab interpreters in the Abbasid realm – Al-Fārābī and Ibn Sīnā (Avicenna) – made their way to the scholars of al-Andalus involves tales that have been lost – those of travelers (scholars, merchants, renegades) who often accompanied the many texts that circulated across the medieval Islamic world and Mediterranean (Stroumsa 2012, 50). However, a few examples do remain, and they provide us with glimpses of how such agents went about their business and how such works were obtained and made accessible.

In *The Ornament of the World*, Maria Rosa Menocal tells the tale of caliph ʿAbd al-Raḥmān II's efforts to find a Greek scholar to translate into Arabic a Greek copy of Dioscorides' *On Medicine* given to him by the Byzantine emperor (2002, 89). It is ʿAbd al-Raḥmān's vizier and personal physician, the Jew Hasdai Ibn Shaprut, who heads the group that carries out the translation for the caliphal library – a group that also includes a Nestorian Christian translator from Constantinople brought to al-Andalus especially for the task. The tale is meant to be emblematic of the process of cultural transmission and translation by which the "great works" of the classical world passed eventually into Western Europe and, according to many scholars, served as catalyst both for the so-called Renaissance of the twelfth century and eventually of the later Renaissance that ushered in our present modernity. Menocal highlights that the tale of Dioscorides in Arabic Córdoba is a tale of a Christian translator, a Jewish courtier and poet (Hasdai ibn Shaprut), and an Andalusi caliph ('Abd al-Raḥmān II) (2002, 48–49); however, Stroumsa further points out that Hasdai Ibn Shaprut's role as creator and patron to the nascent Judeo-Iberian philosophical and literary tradition was contingent upon a network of scholars and texts that in turn depended upon not just rulers and their viziers, but upon merchants, middle men, and even pirates (2012, 50). For both Stroumsa and Menocal this instance of cultural contact was part of a larger process that transcended religious borders.

S. D. Goitein's studies of the Cairo Genizah documents offer glimpses of stories similar to that of Dioscorides' manuscript that Stroumsa and Menocal claim as symbolic of Andalusi cultural contact, with accounts of scholars, soldiers, merchants, and renegades traveling and transporting ideas across the Mediterranean. The Genizah documents reveal that the learned – scribes, teachers, and especially, cantors – often traveled and found work far from where they were born (2003, 279–283). Teachers from Spain were found in small towns, as well as in the larger cities of medieval Egypt (Goitein 1971, 188). In the Genizah there are accounts of books used as valuable trade commodities, collateral for unpaid debts, and communal gifts, as well as coveted objects of study, or even the object of ransom attempts (80, 155, 194, 221). According to Goitein, the portrait of travel and cultural exchange recorded in the Genizah documents can be explained by the fact that "by the injunctions of their religion, Jews (like Muslims) engaged in a lifetime of study" (2003, 269). Houri Touati, in fact, has established travel as a defining characteristic of scholarship and learning in the whole of the medieval Islamic world: "Candidates for learning who hoped to become inscribed within a prestigious genealogy of scholarship were advised to connect themselves to the most renowned masters of their time, those for whom, as the medieval biographical dictionaries put it, 'one packs his bags and loads up the beasts'" (2010, 8). Andalusi scholars such as the ninth-century Baqī ibn Mukhlad of Córdoba, Ibn Ḥabīb, and Abū al-Ṣalt (d. 1126) took up this call (85, 89–90, 235). Their efforts, and the efforts of all those involved in the transmission of ideas, benefited Iberian scholars on the Peninsula, such as Ibn Ḥazm (944–1064), whose works on philosophy and religion show the extent to which the work of Arabic philosophers from Baghdad (including knowledge of Aristotelian philosophy) had been absorbed by eleventh-century scholars on the Peninsula. As Ramón Guerrero points out, Ibn Ḥazm's work shows that Aristotle and works attributed to him had become part of a "*corpus arabicum . . .* which introduced a system of thought that seemed not to contradict the basic tenets of Islam" (2013, 403). This act of accommodating Greek ideas concerning the universe and man's role in it to an Islamic way of seeing that same universe/man becomes the basis for an Arabo-Andalusi narrative of personal enlightenment, Ibn Ṭufayl's *Ḥayy ibn Yaqẓān*, and then subsequently for the Judeo-Iberian and vernacular Christian accounts explored herein.

Ibn Ḥazm is one of a generation of Andalusi scholars and jurists who taught a "rationalist view of religious studies," and, as Avner Ben Zaken points out, "scholarship of philosophy that arose out of it carried its unique stamp in which logic, mathematics, and astronomy took center stage" (2011, 26). These earlier scholars' work is formative in the thinking of Ibn Ṭufayl (1105–1185), who engaged with the ideas of Aristotle, in addition to those of Arabic and Persian theologians. Ibn Ṭufayl penned the influential work *Ḥayy ibn Yaqẓān* (*Ḥayy*), the fictional journey of a wild boy who, although alone on an island, comes to discover the truths of the natural world and of the universe (including the existence of God). For Ibn Ṭufayl, the careful and extended study of the natural world via "exploration and research," as the young Ḥayy does on his island, offered a means of coming to the same truth of God's oneness proposed by Sufi thought and the ideas of al-Ghazālī concerning an intuitive, ecstatic union with God (Ben

Zaken 2011, 27–28). Al-Ghazālī, though, had attacked the Greek and Arab philosophers such as al-Kindī, al-Fārābī, and Avicenna, who in his treatise, the *Tahāfut al-Falāsifa* valued reason and the rational approach to the natural world and metaphysics over intuitive or more faith-based types of argumentation such as revelation (Corbin 1993, 183–184).

Ibn Ṭufayl rejects "the claim that ecstasy is possible without gradual philosophical practice" (Ben Zaken 2011, 18, 22). In *Ḥayy*, "Ibn Tufayl merges Al-Ghazālī's science of practice with the philosophical tradition of al-Andalus that emphasizes logic, mathematics, and astronomy" (22). *Ḥayy* achieves knowledge of God by observing and imitating the movement of the stars and celestial bodies, the beings closest to God in the Aristotelian chain of being (Ben Zaken 2011, 23). Ibn Ṭufayl emphasizes that it is Ḥayy's intellect that ultimately allows him to transcend matter and enter the celestial realm (2009, 173–74). In *Ḥayy* the Aristotelian rational intellect allows such knowledge: "When Ibn Tufayl's Hayy tells the narrator of *Hayy* of the constitution of reality in highly poetic and evocative language . . . he is outlining to the rational intellect why it should make the effort to perfect itself, in terms which an ordinary individual will understand" (Leaman 2009, 99). *Ḥayy* survived in at least six medieval manuscript copies, and, as Ben Zaken points out, was translated and transformed by scholars over the course of the next 700 years (2011, 141n.1, 5–14). For Oliver Leaman, Ḥayy's tale is quintessentially Andalusi (2009, 160). When the learned Absal arrives to the island, Ḥayy sees it as an opportunity for exchange:

> In the philosophical novel by Ibn Tufayl . . . the stranger on the island is greeted enthusiastically by Hayy, and theirs is a genuine dialogue of views and forms of knowledge. Hayy has the confidence of someone who has gone to the source of knowledge, the principles of reason alone, and when someone comes, he is eager to share his knowledge and also to learn from him . . . It is this kind of universalism which had such a radical effect on the West, and which transformed philosophy into a dynamic and revolutionary doctrine . . . [and] produced such a strong reaction, an attempt to throw back the challenging principles of Andalusi thought.
>
> (Leaman 2009, 160)

Ibn Ṭufayl was an agent of the transmission and synthesis of Eastern and Andalusi ideas in the Berber courts of Marrakech and al-Andalus (Ben Zaken 2011, 22). He traveled from his native Guadix to Granada where he served as secretary for the Almohad governor, a position he also held for the governors of Ceuta and Tangier. He was then appointed as court physician for the Almohad ruler Abu Yaʿkūb Yūsuf in Marrakesh (16). It is there that he introduced the young Ibn Rushd to the Almohad ruler Abu Yaʿkūb Yūsuf, for whom the latter penned those works that arguably changed the nature of Western thought (Carra de Vaux 2014).

Perhaps it was this Andalusi thinker, ʾAbū l-Walīd Muḥammad ibnʾAḥmad ibn Rushd, or Averroes (1126–1198), whose ideas were most accommodated by Jewish and Christian thinkers. He was known as "the Commentator" because of his paraphrases and commentaries on the works of Aristotle. In addition to his translations and commentaries of Aristotle, Ibn Rushd composed a work (the *Tahāfut al-Tahāfut* [*Incoherence of the Incoherence*]) defending the use of reason and speculative philosophy to ponder certain theological positions such as the eternity of the universe, the role of God in it, and man's fate in such a cosmos. This work was written in response to al-Ghazālī's attack on the use of philosophy for such purposes (discussed previously).

Born in Córdoba, Ibn Rushd seems to have traveled to Seville to study with Abū Jābir ibn Ḥafṣūn, then to the court of Abū Yaʿkūb Yūsuf in Marrakesh, where Ibn Ṭufayl encouraged him to write his commentaries on Aristotle (the *Organon*) (Goodman 1996, 314). Ibn Rushd's philosophical works spread rapidly across the Iberian Peninsula, revolutionizing thought. They also soon made inroads into Northern Europe where Latin was the *lingua franca* of scholarship:

> By the time Averroes and Maimonides were writing their mature works, at the end of the twelfth century, the "schools" of translation of Toledo and the rest of the network for getting these works out of Arabic and into Latin were so sophisticated and developed that they were being read in the major intellectual centers of Latin Christendom almost as soon as they were available in Arabic.
>
> (Menocal 2005)

The routes and transmitters of Ibn Rushd's version of Aristotelian thought pass through Iberia, and include such figures as Johnannes Hispalense, Dominicus Gundalissalinus, Adelard of Bath, Michael Scot, and several anonymous Arabic-Latin translators working in thirteenth-century Castile (Cruz Hernández 1986; Daiber 2012, 140–141).[2] M. Alonso Alonso (1964) underscores the role of Jewish intellectuals in this process. Taking as an example Qalonymous ben Qalonymous' thirteenth-century Hebrew copy of the *Tahāfut al-Tahāfut*, which was used for the fourteenth-century Latin translation of the work, Alonso Alonso notes the important role that Jewish scholars played in this transmission, and the fact that many other works of the Arabo-Andalusi tradition made their way into Latin via Hebrew.

This is but one example of the many medieval Judeo-Iberian scholars who became experts on and translators into Hebrew of the works of Aristotle and Ibn Rushd's interpretations of them; they also dealt similarly with other important classical works, including those of Plato, Alexander of Aphrodisius, and Plotinus (Freudenthal 2012; Harvey 2003; Zonta 2007). These works had a profound impact on Jewish thought in Iberia and throughout the Mediterranean. The *Moreh Nebukhim*, Maimonides' *Guide of the Perplexed* (*Guide*), which has become one of the most important texts of the Jewish tradition, presents Aristotelian rationalism and the ideas of the Arab philosophers and Christian scholastics in the service of Judaism and the Jewish reader (Frank 2003, 140–144; Stroumsa 2009, 24–52). In the spirit of Ibn Rushd's *Tahāfut al-Tahāfut*, the *Guide* is a defense of philosophical inquiry and a response to those like al-Ghazālī who were opposed to the use of speculative philosophy in the investigation of metaphysics and traditional religious beliefs (Kellner 2006, 11–15, 43–44). In the *Guide*, Maimonides (1138–1204) "insisted that the obligation to understand (i.e., to prove rationally) the tenets of Torah falls upon all Jews. Those who do not or cannot do that fail to earn a share in the world to come" (Kellner 2006, 231). He presents these tenets in a series of principles, including the existence and unity of God, and proceeds to offer rational proofs of the truth of these principles (*Guide* 2.1–2). For the development of the intellect, it is not enough to believe these tenets to be true; the learned must understand why. "Maimonides implicitly adopts a view . . . according to which that which makes us human, and in consequence that which survives our death, is what we know" (Kellner 2006, 220).

The "relative intellectual openness of his world" not only helps explain his thought, but also its legacy (Stroumsa 2009, 6). Maimonides was familiar with the philosophical works of Aristotle, al-Fārābī, Ibn Bājja, and "up to a point, Avicenna" (among others) (Sirat 1985, 162). He was also a practicing medical doctor, familiar with the works of the Arab medical tradition, as well as a religious leader, familiar with the Torah, Mishnah, and Midrash. Stroumsa has noted that Maimonides "is a Mediterranean thinker in the sense that he is more than a Jewish thinker, or more than an Islamic philosopher . . . in modern parlance he could perhaps be called 'cosmopolitan,' that is, a person who belongs to more than one of the subcultures that together form the world in which he lives" (2009, 7).

Within a generation we find the rationalism of the Arabo-Andalusi philosophical tradition that Maimonides defended in his *Guide* become the guiding methodology and the truth sought (and found) by the protagonist of Shem Tov Ibn Falaquera's fictional narrative, *Sefer Ha-Mebaqqesh* (*Book of the Seeker*). In this work, Ibn Falaquera (1225–1290) takes the rhymed prose form of the Hebrew *maqāmāt* and uses it to develop a single linear narrative which features a protagonist who travels in search of knowledge and whose wisdom, gained through encounters with experts in a variety of trades, sciences, and fields of study, accumulates until it is completed in his exchange with the philosopher (Jospe 1988, 46–47).[3] The Seeker is open to learning from all:

> There was once a youth in a certain province, who was tender in years but old in wisdom . . . all those who knew him in those days of the past called him "Mebaqqesh" [Seeker]. He never left the tent of wisdom and sought after all noble qualities . . . Yearning to dwell in the shadow of the wise, he investigated the rightful way. Swift as an eagle, he pursued truth and all those who possessed it. . . . Therefore he set his heart to inquire into and search out men's ways to illumine their actions with the candle of reason and measure them on the scale of wisdom.
>
> (1976, 9–10)

In the *Sefer Ha-Mebeqqesh*, the truths the protagonist finds are culled from the work of Maimonides, Ibn Rushd, Avicenna, and others, put in the mouth of several of the characters he meets. For example, as we would expect, the physician cites Maimonides, Ibn Rushd, Galen, Hippocrates and al-Rāzī (1976, 45). In his exchange with the learned religious scholar, who tells him that his behavior/works are more important than wisdom, the Seeker reacts by telling him that despite his knowledge of Torah, "thou lackest the loftiest quality, which is the quality of reason and science. Inasmuch as thou hast begun to ascend the steps of perfection, and hast mounted some of them, complete thine ascent" (1954, 100). The wise man accepts the Seeker as a pupil, imparting lessons from Aristotle's *Nicomachean Ethics* concerning the nature of moral virtue and the nature of evil. The work offers a fictional account (in the tradition of *Ḥayy*) of how the individual should use his intellect in the pursuit of wisdom, with the goal being knowledge of the divine. The wise man underscores for the Seeker man's obligation to develop his intellect (which, as explored previously, should be done through logic and philosophical speculation): "By virtue of intelligence man has been elevated above all earthly creatures, and God has been with him" (1954, 139).

According to Herschel Levine, it is likely that "Ibn Falaquera derived a partial outline for the first half of the *Seeker* from Maimonides' *Guide* (Book III, Chapter 54) which expands upon a classification of Aristotle and explains the four types of perfections sought by man," although Levine also admits that other scholars have suggested that *Ḥayy* inspired the work (1954, xxx). Ibn Falaquera was born into a rich and powerful family in Tudela in the Kingdom of Navarre. During his youth he wrote poetry, but he then turned to philosophy, composing several paraphrases of the work of Andalusi writers (Ibn Rushd, al-Fārābī, Avicenna, and Ibn Bajja/Avempace) and Classical authors (Aristotle, Plato), as well as one of the first commentaries of Maimonides' *Guide* (Harvey 2003, 266–267; Sirat 1985, 234). As Steven Harvey points out, "his goal was to teach wisdom and science, and this meant . . . Aristotelian science as it was explained by Averroes . . . this offered the Hebrew reader for the first time comprehensive access to the full range of Aristotelian science" (2003, 267). *Ha-Mebeqqesh* reveals not only that the ethos of seeking wisdom remained a central motivator of Iberian cultural production in thirteenth-century Navarre, but also that that production continued to be informed by Ibn Rushd's rationalism (via Maimonides), as well as the thought of Ibn Gabirol, Galen, Aristotle, Plato, and Arabic philosophers and thinkers such as Ḥunayn ibn 'Isḥāq (Levine 1954, xxvii–xxxiv).

Ramón Llull (1232–1315), a contemporary of Ibn Falaquera, shared the latter's desire to impart Andalusi wisdom in his works, and, like such predecessors as Maimonides and Ibn Rushd, Llull similarly martialed the complex Andalusi philosophical tradition in the service of reason and religion. Bonner notes that Llull was born in Mallorca, which "was strategically placed at the center of the commercial wheel of the western Mediterranean," and that "probably only a handful of thirteenth-century European cities were more cosmopolitan" (1985a, 1). Llull himself was a frequent traveler, leaving his home in Mallorca to deliver lectures at the court of Joan I and the University of Paris, and to preach in Tunisia (1–12). Like so many of his Catalan compatriots, past and future, Llull penned treatises reflecting his hybrid, complex cultural formation in a variety of languages, including Latin, Catalan, and Arabic (1–44). Llull cites in his works not only the Talmud and Quran, but several works of Aristotle (15). Logic is central to Llull's thinking and forms an essential part of his Great Universal Art, his combinatory program of "finding truth," based on a "logic which followed the true patterns of the universe" (Johnston 1987, 24; Yates 1954, 117). He produced both an Arabic commentary and a Latin translation of al-Ghazālī's treatise on logic (Johnston 1987; Hasse 2014).

Scholars note, though, that apart from the treatise on al-Ghazālī's logic, much of Llull's knowledge of Muslim philosophy and thought seems to be popular in origin (Garcías Palou 1981, 29–32, 353; Johnston 1987, 11, 32). Llull's exposure to popular forms of Arabo-Andalusi thought – philosophical thought as well as collections of tales – speaks to his origins and life in a region that had until shortly before his birth been in Muslim hands, and where he was exposed to daily interactions with Muslims (Garcías Palou 1981, 25–30). The Arabo-Andalusi connection is perhaps most evident in *Llibre de meravelles/Book of Wonders* or *Felix*, the fictional account of the searcher for truth, which is "the only work in which Llull used identifiable preexisting material," which is "all of oriental origins" (Bonner 1985b, 653). *Felix* offers testimony to the circulation of the Persian philosophical compendium, the *Ikhwān al-safā'*, and to narrative collections such as the *1001 Nights* and *Kalila wa Dimna* (Bonner 1985b, 653). *Felix*, like much of Llull's work, was designed to offer in narrative form an explanation of how reason served religious (Christian) belief. He adapts the imperative to develop the intellect as advocated by Ibn Rushd, Ibn Ṭufayl, Maimonides, and Ibn Falaquera (discussed previously) to the Augustinian triad (in which memory and love/will are added to intellect/understanding to reflect the Christian Trinity).

The work survives in several manuscript copies and fifteenth-century incunabula, as well as medieval translations into French, Spanish, and Italian (Bonner 1985b, 655–658).[4] The work's protagonist, like the Seeker and Ḥayy, is told to travel in search of wisdom. Felix's father, on his death bed, tells his son in the opening scene of the work to "travel through the world" and seek knowledge of God (Llull 1985, 659). Felix is instructed by a hermit who reveals that the laws of the natural world are compatible with Christian truths, offering a Christianized version of the lessons Ḥayy discovered on his own in Ibn Ṭufayl's *Ḥayy*. The work illustrates what Bonner has observed, namely that "it is precisely for theological subjects that Llull uses his logical techniques" (2007, 252). The wise hermit, in response to Felix's question, "What is the purpose of man's life in this world?" replies:

> Man lives in this world so that, by living, he may remember, understand and love
> God; and man lives in this world so that he may live in the next world in everlasting

glory . . . the rational soul is one with a man's life, for what is rational soul, is life; that is to say, that memory, understanding, and will are of the nature of spiritual life, and their life is a being that is the soul, similar to the sun's being, which is to shine with the form and matter of light.

(1985b, 840)

Like Ḥayy and the Seeker, Felix is educated in scientific and moral lessons ("the hermit taught Felix how to wonder and gave him many examples by which he might possess acquired knowledge; for by these examples the soul is uplifted to remember, understand, and will" 1103). One of these *exempla* involves the story of a king whose page brings him a book entitled the *Llibre de plasent visió* (Chapter 57) (865). A hermit had instructed the page to give the king this richly illustrated book, in which "all the philosophers appear, as well as the works of nature, such as men, beasts, birds, fish, and plants; and all of the beasts . . . and all of the mechanical arts" (865). This hermit was a philosopher who made this illustrated encyclopedic work of all he observed over the course of his life. The book changes the king's life, causing him to realize the vanities of this world, after which he builds a monastery and then renounces his throne and becomes a monk, living a life dedicated to contemplating the truths contained in this book (866–867). As in the book in the parable, Llull's encyclopedic *Felix* is meant to direct the reader to the truth of Christianity through philosophical argument.

Felix does not stress the acquisition of traditional Church laws, but of speculative thought – Felix asks about the existence of God, angels, the Aristotelian hierarchy of being, and all aspects of ethics, echoing Llull's belief that "logic and indeed all philosophical discourse must reflect the nature of things" (Johnston 1987, 4). Felix's journey ends in a monastery, where he can impart what he has learned "in matters of science and devotion" to the monks, even taking the habit and becoming one himself (1985, 1103–1104). It is noteworthy that Felix joins the monastic community only at the end of his life, and because the monks seek his wisdom (and not vice versa). Felix seeks out and accrues knowledge as a secular individual, not as a representative of a particular Christian sect. This acquisition of knowledge of the natural world and moral values allows him to die a peaceful death and to live on in the book of the same name that imparts his lessons.

With a title reminiscent of the encyclopedic work of the embedded tale in Llull's *Felix*, the *Llibre de plasent visió*, the fifteenth-century *converso* (whether sincere or not), Alfonso de la Torre crafts his *Visión deleitable* as a self-help guide for the fifteenth-century Iberian's personal use.[5] The work's author, Alfonso de la Torre, studied at the University of Salamanca, served in the court of Carlos de Viana in Navarre, and also spent time in Naples at the court of Alfonso el Magnánimo (Girón Negrón 2001, 16–17). The *Visión* circulated widely and survives in some seventeen Romance manuscript witnesses and eleven early modern print editions, including sixteenth-century copies printed in Frankfurt, Ferrara, Venice, and Amsterdam (García López 1991, 17–34). Adopting the imagined spiritual journey of Ibn Ṭufayl's *Ḥayy*, Ibn Falaquera's *The Seeker*, and Llull's *Felix*, the *Visión* is an encyclopedic work in which verbal descriptions of visual images (reminiscent of the illustrations made by the hermit in Llull's story) complement explicit instruction on the arts, sciences, and moral philosophy. The protagonist, Entendimiento, an allegory for the narrator's intellect, is a seeker for knowledge. Like Ibn Falaquera's *Seeker*, he encounters a series of people who teach him through both explicit instruction and Socratic dialogue on the various fields of knowledge, and, like Ḥayy, he ends up in the celestial realms with the higher celestial beings. Along the way, the reader witnesses as Entendimiento is introduced (either directly or indirectly) to "the authorities and luminaries of each of the sciences he masters, including not only the Liberal Arts in whose homes he encounters Abraham, Moses, Virgil, Aristotle, Boethius, Quintilian, Pythagorus, Hermes Trismegistus, Zoroaster and Euclid, but also, in the palaces of Sabieza, Razón and Natura, the supposed authorities on metaphysics or the science of nature and God, namely Jupiter, Alexander of Aphrodisius, [and] the philosophers of the Andalusi tradition, al-Fārābī, al-Ghazālī, Avicenna, Maimonides, and Ibn Rushd" (Hamilton 2014, 19).[6]

The narrator's intellect is allowed to ascend the mountain of wisdom by mastering one lesson on the natural world after another. At the top of the mountain, Astronomy personified allows him to pass into the celestial realm. Here, Entendimiento receives lessons from the sisters Wisdom, Truth, and Reason. At the core of their lessons on God and man's role in the universe are Maimonides' twenty-six proofs of God's existence from the *Guide* rendered in Castilian translation (Girón Negrón 2001, 59; Wickersham Crawford 1913, 189–195). Subsequent chapters provide paraphrases of Maimonides' proofs regarding the nature and power of God, and the nature of the angels, man, and the chain of being (Wickersham Crawford 1913, 195–209). Entendimiento's journey is an allegorical version of the Arabo-Andalusi conception of the acquired intellect as discussed by Maimonides, and reveals to the reader that man's intellect is capable of "cognition of intelligibles [as] the source of eternal perdurance," that is, the means of achieving immortality/happiness (Tirosh-Samuelson 2003, 382).

However, the work is clear that, even though it adopts ideas (and whole passages) from all the traditions of the Peninsula, including Ibn Rushd, Maimonides, and Isidore, none has a monopoly on the truth.[7] The protagonist, Entendimiento, states, "non me moverá más la verdad dicha por boca de cristiano, que de judío o moro o gentil, sy verdades sean todas, nin negaré menos la falsya dicha por boca de uno que de boca de otro" (1991, 146). Since the twelfth century and the works of ibn Rushd and Maimonides, Iberian thinkers had been willing to accept and engage the opinions of others – the openness that both Stroumsa and Leaman note in prior discussion. As we have seen, the Iberian authors of the narratives examined previously went to great lengths to adopt and "make their own," either through translation or other forms of accommodation within a recognizable "updated" frame, the Arabo-Andalusi legacy of intellectual exchange. Here we find Alfonso de la Torre adopting this ethos in his fifteenth-century Castilian narrative.

The *Visión* clearly shows that the works and ideas of the (Judeo-)Andalusi philosophical tradition with which this brief study opened, survived and continued to shape the form of Iberian cultural production well into the fifteenth century. Alfonso de la Torre's interior journey offers us a topography created out of both the Andalusi and medieval scholastic world of ideas, and shows that Andalusi intellectual openness survived in Iberian fiction, despite the increasing persecution and marginalization of Jews and Muslims and the concurrent rise of imaginative fiction in which heroes such as Tirant lo Blanc and Amadis are portrayed as being divinely inspired to travel to fight "infidels." Such narratives stand in contrast to the narratives of Ibn Ṭufayl, Ibn Rushd, Maimonides, Ramón Llull, and Alfonso de la Torre in which intellectual voyages allow their readers to imaginatively explore and interact with peoples across the globe (and even beyond), and to develop their own critical sense of right and wrong.

I hope to have given a brief overview of a few of the authors and works that helped define a medieval Iberian cultural production marked by knowledge of and reactions to a variety of bodies of knowledge which extended well beyond the geographical borders of the Peninsula and which defy clearly defined categories such as "Arab" or "Jewish" or "Christian." The forementioned Iberian fictional narratives of intellectual development, all of which involve the incorporation of Andalusi material in translation, reveal that the map of medieval Iberian textual transmission encompasses the entire Peninsula and beyond, and that texts were transmitted in a variety of languages (to Latin and Arabic we must add Catalan, Hebrew, French,

Provençal, and Italian when we consider the transmission of those texts beyond the Peninsula). The fact that the imagined narrative of the development of an individual intellect could appeal to Iberians and continue to instruct them from the twelfth to the fifteenth century provides us with compelling evidence that intellectual openness was a defining feature not just of Arabo- or Judeo-Andalusi philosophy, but of medieval Iberian cultural production at large.

Notes

1 On the intellectual journey in Iberian literature, see Haro (1993), Parmley (2013, 2014), and Surtz (1987).
2 Zonta notes that a number of Aristotle's works were known only in the Jewish tradition and have survived only in medieval Hebrew copies (2007, 241).
3 According to Levine, there are two known manuscript copies from the fifteenth century (1954, xxxix–xl).
4 An embedded *exemplum* from the *Llibre des marevelles* circulated independently as the *Llibre de las bestias* (Bonner 1985b, 653).
5 On Alfonso de la Torre's *converso* identity, see Girón Negrón (2001, 18–24).
6 See Torre (1991, 107–137, 150, 211).
7 On the sources of the work, see Girón Negrón (2001, 66–207).

Works cited

Alonso Alonso, Manuel. 1964. "Traducciones arábigos-latinas en el siglo XIV o a fines del siglo XIII." *Estudios Lulianos* 8: 54–66.

Ben Zaken, Avner. 2011. *Reading Hayy Ibn-Yaqzan: A Crosscultural History of Autodidacticism.* Baltimore, MD: Johns Hopkins University Press.

Bonner, Anthony. 1985a. *Doctor Illuminatus: A Ramon Llull Reader.* Princeton, NJ: Princeton University Press.

———. 1985b. "Introduction." In *Felix, or The Book of Wonders*, edited and translated by Anthony Bonner, 649–659. Princeton, NJ: Princeton University Press.

———. 2007. *The Art and Logic of Ramon Llull.* Leiden: Brill.

Burnett, Charles. 1994. "The Translating Activity in Medieval Spain." In *Legacy of Muslim Spain*, edited by Salma Jayussi and Manuela Marín, 1036–1058. Leiden: Brill.

Carra de Vaux, B. 2014. "Ibn Ṭufayl." In *Encyclopaedia of Islam*, edited by P. Bearman, T. Bianquis, C. E. Bosworth, E. van Donzel, and W. P. Heinrichs. Leiden: Brill.

Catlos, Brian. 2014a. "Ethno-Religious Minorities." In *A Companion to Mediterranean History*, edited by Peregrine Horden and Sharon Kinoshita, 361–377. London: Wiley-Blackwell.

———. 2014b. "Christian-Muslim-Jewish Relations, Medieval 'Spain,' and the Mediterranean: An Historiographical Op-Ed." In *In and Of the Mediterranean: Medieval and Early Modern Iberian Studies*, edited by Michelle M. Hamilton and Núria Silleras Fernández, 1–16. Nashville, TN: Vanderbilt University Press.

Corbin, Henry. 1993. *History of Islamic Philosophy.* Translated by Liadain Sherrand. London: Kegan Paul.

Cruz Hernández, Miguel. 1986. *Abu-l-Walid ibn Rusd (Averroes): vida, obra, pensamiento, influencia.* Córdoba: Monte de Piedad y Caja de Ahorros de Córdoba.

Daiber, Hans. 2012. *Islamic Thought in the Dialogue of Cultures: A Historical and Bibliographical Survey.* Leiden: Brill.

Frank, Daniel H. 2003. "Maimonides and Jewish Aristotelianism." In *The Cambridge Companion to Medieval Jewish Philosophy*, edited by Daniel H. Frank and Oliver Leaman, 136–156. Cambridge: Cambridge University Press.

Freudenthal, Gad. 2012. "Arabic into Hebrew: The Emergence of the Translation Movement in Twelfth-Century Provence and Jewish-Christian Polemic." In *Beyond Religious Borders*, edited by D. M. Freidenreich and M. Goldstein, 124–143. Philadelphia, PA: University of Pennsylvania Press.

García López, Jorge. 1991. "Introduction." In *Visión deleytable*, by Alfonso de la Torre, 1: 11–97. Edited by Jorge García López. Salamanca: Universidad de Salamanca.

Garcías Palou, Sebastián. 1981. *Ramon Llull y el Islam*. Palma de Mallorca: Graficas Planisi.

Girón-Negrón, Luis. 2001. *Alfonso de la Torre's Visión Deleytable: Philosophical Rationalism and the Religious Imagination in 15th-Century Spain*. Leiden: Brill.

Goitein, S. D. 1971. *The Community*. vol. 2. of *A Mediterranean Society*. Berkeley, CA: University of California Press.

———. 2003. *A Mediterranean Society: An Abridgment in One Volume*. Edited by Jacob Lassner. Berkeley, CA: University of California Press.

Goldstein, Miriam. 2012. "Introduction." In *Beyond Religious Borders*, edited by D. M. Freidenreich and M. Goldstein, 1–10. Philadelphia, PA: University of Pennsylvania Press.

Goodman, Lenn. 1996. "Ibn Tufayl." In *History of Islamic Philosophy*, edited by Hossein Nasr, Seyyed and Oliver Leaman, 313–329. London and New York: Routledge.

Hamilton, Michelle M. 2014. *Beyond Faith: Belief, Morality and Memory in a Fifteenth-Century Judeo-Iberian Manuscript*. Leiden: Brill.

Haro, Marta. 1993. "El viaje sapiencial en la prosa didáctica castellana de la Edad Media." In *Actas del Primer Congreso Anglo-Hispano*, edited by Alan Deyermond and Ralph Penny, vol. 2, 59–73. Madrid: Castalia.

Harvey, L. P. 1977. "The Alfonsine School of Translators: Translations from Arabic into Castilian Produced under the Patronage of Alfonso the Wise of Castile (1221–1252–1284)." *Journal of the Royal Asiatic Society of Great Britain and Ireland* 1: 109–117.

Harvey, Steven. 2003. "Arabic into Hebrew: The Hebrew Translation Movement and the Influence of Averroes upon Medieval Jewish Thought." In *Medieval Jewish Philosophy*, edited by Daniel H. Frank and Oliver Leaman, 258–280. Cambridge: Cambridge University Press.

Hasse, Dag Nikolaus, 2014. "Influence of Arabic and Islamic Philosophy on the Latin West." In *The Stanford Encyclopedia of Philosophy*, edited by Edward N. Zalta. Stanford, CA: Stanford University, 1997. Accessed November 25, 2014. http://plato.stanford.edu/archives/spr2014/entries/arabic-islamic-influence.Ibn Falaquera, Shem Tob ben Joseph. 1954. "Sefer Ha-Mebaqqesh (The Seeker)." PhD diss., Columbia University.

———. 1976. *The Book of the Seeker (Sefer ha-Mebaqqesh)*. Translated and edited by M. Hershel Levine. New York: Yeshiva University Press.

Ibn Ṭufayl, Muḥammad ibn ʿAbd al-Malik ibn Muḥammad ibn Muḥammad. 2009. *Ibn Tufayl's Ḥayy ibn Yaqẓān: A Philosophical Study*. Edited and translated by Lenn E. Goodman. Chicago: University of Chicago Press.

Johnston, Mark J. 1987. *The Spiritual Logic of Ramon Llull*. Oxford: Clarendon Press.

Jospe, Raphael. 1988. *Torah and Sophia: The Life and Thought of Shem Tov Ibn Falaquera*. Cincinnati: Hebrew Union College Press.

Kellner, Menachem. 2006. *Maimonides' Confrontation with Mysticism*. Portland, OR: Littman Library of Jewish Civilization.

Lasker, Daniel J. 2012. "The Impact of Interreligious Polemic on Medieval Philosophy." In *Beyond Religious Borders*, edited by D. M. Freidenreich and M. Goldstein, 115–123. Philadelphia, PA: University of Pennsylvania Press.

Leaman, Oliver. 2009. *Islamic Philosophy: An Introduction*. Cambridge: Polity.

Levine, M. Herchel. 1954. "A Translation and Edition of Falaquera's *Sefer Ha-Mebaqqesh*, Part 1." PhD diss., Columbia University.

———. 1976. "Introduction." In *The Book of the Seeker*, by Shem Tob ben Joseph Ibn Falaquera, xiii–xlvi. New York: Yeshiva University Press.

Llull, Ramon. 1985. *Felix, or The Book of Wonders. Libre de Maravelles*. Edited and translated by Anthony Bonner, 647–1103. vol. 2 of *Selected Works of Ramon Llull (1232–1316)*. Princeton, NJ: Princeton University Press.

Maimonides, Moses Ben Maimon. 1910. *Guide for the Perplexed*. Translated by M. Friedländer. 1904. Reprinted by George Routledge and Sons. New York: Routledge. Seforim Online. Accessed

November 25, 2014. http://www.teachittome.com/seforim2/seforim/the_guide_for_the_perplexed.
pdf.

Manekin, Charles H. 2012. "Maimonides and the Arabic Aristotelian Tradition of Epistomology." In
Beyond Religious Borders, edited by D. M. Freidenreich and M. Goldstein, 78–95. Philadelphia, PA:
University of Pennsylvania Press.

Márquez Villanueva, Francisco. 1996. "In Lingua Tholetana." In *La escuela de traductores de Toledo*,
edited by J. Samsó, F. Márquez Villanueva, D. Romano, R. Gonzálvez Ruiz, and Á. Sáenz Badillos,
23–34. Toledo: Diputación Provincial de Toledo.

Menocal, Maria Rosa. 2002. *The Ornament of the World: How Muslims, Jews and Christians Created a
Culture of Tolerance in Medieval Spain*. Boston, MA: Little Brown.

———. 2005. "'The Culture of Translation.' Words Without Borders 2003–2013." *The Online Magazine
for International Literature*. Accessed November 25, 2014. http://wordswithoutborders.org/article/
the-culture-of-translation.

Parmley, Nico. 2013. "Imagining the Mediterranean: Disruption and Connectivity in Medieval Iberian
Tales of the Sea." PhD diss., University of Minnesota, Twin Cities.

———. 2014. "Medieval Mediterranean Travel as an Intellectual Journey: Seafaring and Pursuit of
Knowledge in the *Libro de Apolonio*." In *In and of the Mediterranean: Medieval and Early Modern
Iberian Studies*, edited by Michelle M. Hamilton and Núria Silleras Fernández, 49–73. Nashville, TN:
Vanderbilt University Press.

Ramón Guerrero, Rafael. 2013. "Aristotle and Ibn Hazm. On the Logic of the *Taqrīb*." In *Ibn Ḥazm of
Cordoba: The Life and Works of a Controversial Thinker*, edited by Camilla Adang, Maribel Fierro,
and Sabine Schmidtke, 403–416. Leiden: Brill.

Ray, Jonathan. 2005. "Beyond Tolerance and Persecution: Reassessing Our Approach to Medieval Convivencia." *Jewish Social Studies* 11 (2): 1–18.

Sirat, Colette. 1985. *A History of Jewish Philosophy in the Middle Ages*. Great Britain: Cambridge:
Cambridge University Press.

Soifer, Maya. 2009. "Beyond Convivencia: Critical Reflections on the Historiography of Interfaith Relations in Christian Spain." *Journal of Medieval Iberian Studies* 1: 19–35.

Stroumsa, Sarah. 2009. *Maimonides in His World: Portrait of a Mediterranean Thinker*. Princeton, NJ:
Princeton University Press.

———. 2012. "Thinkers of 'This Peninsula': Toward an Integrative Approach to the Study of Philosophy
in al-Andalus." In *Beyond Religious Borders*, edited by D. M. Freidenreich and M. Goldstein, 44–53.
Philadelphia, PA: University of Pennsylvania Press.

Surtz, Ronald E. 1987. "El héroe intelectual en el mester de clerecía." *La Torre: Revista de la Universidad de Puerto Rico* 1 (2): 265–274.

Tirosh-Samuelson, Hava. 2003. *Happiness in Premodern Judaism: Virtue, Knowledge and Well-Being*.
Cincinnati: Hebrew Union College Press.

Torre, Alfonso de la. 1991. *Visión deleytable*. Edited by Jorge García López. Salamanca: Universidad de
Salamanca.

Touati, Houari. 2010. *Islam and Travel in the Middle Ages*. Translated by Lydia G. Cochrane. Chicago:
University of Chicago.

Wickersham Crawford, James P. 1913. "The *Visión Delectable* of Alfonso de la Torre and Maimonides's
Guide of the Perplexed." *PMLA* 28 (2): 188–212.

Yates, Frances A. 1954. "The Art of Ramon Llull." *Journal of the Warburg and Courtauld Institutes* 17:
115–117.

Zonta, Mauro. 2007. "A Note about Two Newly-Discovered Hebrew Quotations of Averroes' Works Lost
in their Original Arabic Texts." In *Studies in Hebrew Language and Jewish Culture*, edited by F. J.
Baasten and Reinier Munk, 241–250. Dordrecht: Springer.

Literature and visual culture

Literature and visual culture

6

COURT AND CONVENT

Senses and spirituality in Hispanic medieval women's writing

Lesley K. Twomey

Vision is the principal sense for medieval people for, through *theoria*, the gaze, it led to knowledge.[1] Christianity based its evangelism on visual testimony, since the disciples saw the risen Christ and the Gospels record their oral testimony. By the late Middle Ages, rituals of seeing (Lentes 2006) reveal a taste for public and private devotions prioritizing the gaze, whether exposition of the Blessed Sacrament or personal devotion to a religious artefact. Seeing something holy with the physical eye or seeing Christ through contemplation in the mind's eye imprint holiness on the seer: "To see was to become similar to the object" (Biernoff 2002, 137; Beresford and Twomey 2013, 103–132). In this chapter, I explore Hildegard of Bingen's theology of the senses, particularly seeing and hearing, aiming to assess seeing and hearing in women's writing.[2] Conventual writers include Teresa de Cartagena (1420/25– ?), who wrote two treatises, one on infirmity and one justifying her writing; Constanza de Castilla (†1478), a Dominican prioress, who wrote liturgy and prayers; and Isabel de Villena (1430–1490), a Franciscan abbess, who wrote a life of Mary and Christ.[3] All are noblewomen: Teresa de Cartagena is from an "upwardly mobile" *converso* family (Seidenspinner-Núñez and Kim 2004, 132), whilst Constanza and Villena had royal blood. I also consider Leonor López de Córdoba's *Memorias*, a treatise justifying her own family's status.

Seeing and authority

Hildegard begins her *Scivias* with a vision of the heavens, whence a divine voice, addressing her as a universal figure, orders her to write: "O homo fragilis, et cinis cineris, et pudredo putredinis, dic et scribe quae vides et audis [O fragile human, ash of ashes and filth of filth! Say and write what you see and hear]."[4] Seeing and hearing lie, therefore, at the heart of *Scivias*. Many women, particularly those from the lower classes, employed mystical vision for the authority to write (Surtz 1995, 19). María de Ajofrín (†1489) recounts her visions to Juan de Corrales, her confessor, who records them (Surtz 1995, 68–84). Similarly, in the early 1500s, the Dominican nun, María de Santo Domingo, narrates her *Revelaciones*, serving as mouthpiece for the crucified Christ (Sanmartín Bastida and Luengo Balbás 2014, citing Mazzoni 2005, 52).

Villena also begins her *Vita Christi* with a vision, the Conception of Mary in the mind of God, although she does not use it to justify writing. López de Córdoba narrates a vision, presented as God's response to prayer, enabling the writer to fashion her own identity. She claims she was vouchsafed the vision, seeing an archway and entering to pick flowers:

> E otro día que no quedaua mas que un día de acauar mi orazión, sáuado, soñaua passando por San Ypólito tocando el alua: bi en la pared de los corrales un arco mui grande e mui alto, e que entraua io por allí y coxíe flores de la Sierra y ueía mui gran zielo. Y, en esto, desperté; e obe esperanza en la Virgen Santa María, que me daría cassa.
>
> (3r–v)

Unlike Hildegard's visions, which are waking visions, Leonor's writes: "*desperté*." The vision, nevertheless, gives her confidence that Mary will give her what she requests, a house for her family. After wandering homeless, she sees a dwelling, symbolizing the restoration of her family's fortunes. It is, however, in religious terms rather self-serving.

Hearing: an author's words made public

For López de Córdoba, hearing is the most natural way of engaging with a written text, disseminating her own words to others: "Y el dolor que a mi corazón llegó, bien lo podéis entender quien esta historia oiere" (López de Córdoba fol. 4r). She repeats how the *Memorias* are read aloud: "y por que quien lo oiere sepan la relación de todos mis hechos, e milagros que la Virgen Santa María me mostró" (fol. 1r). She has written (escríuolo) her story to serve as a model to others:

> Y escríuolo a honrra y alabanza de mi señor Jesuchristo e de la Virgen Santa María, su madre que lo parió, por que todas las criaturas que estubieren en tribulazión sean ziertas que yo espero en su misericordia que, si se encomiendan de corazón a la Virgen Santa María, que Ella las consolará y acorrerá como consoló a mí.
>
> (López de Córdoba fol. 1r)

Yet, a few lines later, she indicates that she had it written: "Y mandelo escreuir assí como vedes" (López de Córdoba, fol. 1r). Her *Memorias* is given physicality in "vedes," whilst its words are repeated: "oiere." The *Memorias'* words are to bring spiritual consolation to all who hear them, assuring them that Mary will bring consolation, "consolará," as she has to the writer.

The ear and the eye of the soul: Hildegard's *Scivias* and Villena's *Vita Christi*

Hildegard differentiates between the inner and outer senses (Emerson 1998, 73), as many medieval authors do. She receives her visions with the mind's eyes and ears: "auribus interioris hominis," the mysterious sixth sense:

> Visiones vero quas vidi: non eas in somnis, nec dormiens, nec in phrenesi, nec corporeis oculis aut auribus exterioris hominis, nec in abditis locis percepi, sed eas vigilans, circumspiciens in pura menteocculis et auribus interioris hominis, in apertis locis secundum voluntatem Dei accepi.
>
> (PL 197, col. 385)

["But the visions I saw I did not perceive in dreams, or sleep, or delirium, or by the eyes of the body, or by the ears of the outer self, or in hidden places; but I received them while awake and seeing with a pure mind and the eyes and ears of the inner self, in open places as God willed it."]

(Hart and Bishop 1990, 60)

She shows her awareness of the nature of dreams and rejects even the highest categories of dream vision in favour of a waking vision mediated by the inner eye and ear. When Villena distinguishes between the inner eye and the eyes of the body, she uses them purposefully. For example, they aid in distinguishing the consecrated body of Christ with its outer elements and its inner reality in the chapter "Com se deu tractar e rebre aquest excel·lent sagrament del cors preciós de Jesus Senyor Nostre." In this way, Isabel de Villena refers to the delights which are unimaginable, having never been seen by the eye nor heard by the ear: "Ço és: 'l'ull no ha vist, ne orella hoït, ne cor de home poria jamés compendre los delits que lo Senyor comunica a aquells que verdaderament l'amen'" (Villena 1916, II, 248, henceforth II, 248). In a similar manner, when she focuses on the Virgin Mary's adoration of the Host, after the Resurrection of Christ, she indicates that the Virgin gazes on the Host with "los ulls de l'ànima:"

e dreçant-se, mirava de fit ab los ulls corporals, a ab los ulls de l'ànima veya e contemplava dins aquella lo fill de Déu ý seu, lo qual ella havia concebut e tengut dins les entràmens sues, e que per mijà de aquell sagrament havia a tornar en sa posada e cubert hon nou mesos era stat. E, levada en pensar aquesta alta e meravellosa obra, posada en èxtasi dins la sua ànima, pujava la altea del cel, super cherubin et seraphin.

(III, 305)

The eyes of the Virgin's soul are able to distinguish within the Host, displayed for her, the flesh and blood human body of Christ, who had been inside her womb. Performing a eucharistic ritual for the Virgin's eyes contributes to the "sacramental institutionalization of grace" (Beckwith 1993, 110), enabling Villena to develop understanding of transubstantiation. It also emphasizes Schaulust, a desire to see the Host but also to see through or see beyond it (Bynum 2006, 232). Discerning this eucharistic mystery leads the Virgin to "èxtasi" (III, 305).

Villena then uses "ulls de l'ànima" for a Resurrection experience. After being raised from the dead, Lazarus pleads with Christ on account of the long bondage in which humankind has been held. Lazarus, returning from limbo, speaks about what he saw with the eye of his soul: "qui ab los propis ulls de l'ànima la he vista" (II, 156).

Villena is also aware how God regards humanity. God is omniscient as his gaze manifests: "totes coses son clares e manifestes *als ulls* de sa clemència" (II, 231). This divine gaze occurs just before Christ washes the feet of his disciples and immediately before he singles out Judas as his betrayer. For Villena, God's gaze may judge. The Virgin reveals this, as she teaches the disciples before Pentecost, using words of penitence: "Creau en mi un cor munde e net e deliure de tota culpa que *als ulls de vostra majestat puga offendre*" (III, 285). Other Vitae Christi do not mention God's gaze. Psalm 51.10 does not either:

God, create in me a clean heart,
Renew within me a resolute spirit
Do not thrust me away from your presence.

Villena writes about eyes on more than a hundred occasions in the *Vita Christi*. These are penitent eyes awash with tears, as well as eyes which bear witness: "ab propis ulls" (ten occasions), eyes which are raised to heaven, seeking heavenly guidance, rather than gazing on the things of the earth. On thirty-one occasions, eyes are raised, to heaven, to God the Father, or to Christ crucified. Eyes are lowered in shame and penitence (nine occasions). God's gaze brings penitential tears to St Peter in the courtyard: "O quin mirar fon aquest de tanta dolçor e pietat que travessà les entràmenes del dexeble, veent-se axí cridat e venia a misericòrdia per aquell qui negat havia" (II, 297). Constanza de Castilla also emphasizes seeing the incarnate Lord, where seeing becomes receiving. She sets her prayer in the context of Simeon's desire to see the Lord: "e desque te vido, con grant reverencia, alegría, et devoción te recibió, diciendo: Nunc dimittis servum tuum, Domine, secundum verbum tuum in pace" (Constanza de Castilla 1998, 5). Her prayer is his. Villena emphasizes "per revelació divina" which encourages him to enter the Temple and bear witness: "que aquell Senyor que vos desijau és a la porta del temple e ara lo veureu ab los propis ulls" (I, 306).

The senses: knowing God

For Hildegard, the senses are not mere bodily functions but connect to "reason and powers of the soul" (Emerson 1998, 86). She "values them and assigns them a role in acquiring knowledge" (Emerson 1998, 83):

> Et altitudo ejus est quinque cubitorum; qui est Excellentia divinarum scientiarum in Scripturis quae propter opus Dei sunt in quinque sensibus qui sunt in homine; quos inspiravit Spiritus Sanctus ad utilitatem hominum, quia homo cum quinque sensibus suis *respicit* ad altitudinem divinitatis, discernens unumquodque, bonum scilicet et malum. (Scivias, Book III, Vision II, PL 197, col. 852) ["The wall is five cubits high, which refers to the virtue of divine knowledge of the Scriptures, which imbue Man's five senses for the sake of the work of God. The Holy Spirit breathed on them for people's good; for with the five senses people can regard the height of Divinity, and discern both good and evil."]
>
> (Hart and Bishop 1990, 336).

The Devil may seduce the senses. They can, however, be cleansed and operate properly:

> Lex ad salutem hominis posita est, et prophetae occulta Dei manifestant: sic et sensus hominis quaeque nociva ab homine depellit et interiora animae denudat. Nam anima sensum spirat. Quomodo? Ipsa hominem vivente facie vivificat, et visu, auditu, gustu, et tactu dotat. Ita quod homo sensu tactus, pervigil in omnibus rebus sit; sensus enim signum omnium virium animae est, sicut et corpus vas animae est. Quomodo? Sensus omnes vires animae claudit. Quid hoc? Homo in facie cognoscitur, occulis videt, auribus audit, os ad loquendum aperit, minibus palpat, pedibus ambulat, at ideo sensus in homine est velut lapides pretiosi, et ut pretiosus thesaurus in vase signatus. Sed ut vas videtur, et thesaurus in eo scitur; ita enim in sensu caeterae vires animae intelliguntur. (Scivias, Book I, Vision IV, PL 197, col. 427–428) [The Law is ordained for human salvation, and the prophets show forth the hidden things of God; so all human senses protect a person from harmful things and lay bare the soul's interior. For the soul emanates the senses. How? It vivifies a person's face and glorifies him with sight, hearing, taste, smell, touch, so that by this touch he becomes watchful

in all things. For the senses are the sign of all the powers of the soul, as the body is the vessel of the soul. What does this mean? A person is recognized by his face, sees with his ears, opens his mouth to speak, feels with his hands, walks with his feet; and so the senses are to a person as precious stones and as a rich treasure sealed in a vase. But as the treasure within is known when the vase is seen, so also the powers of the soul are inferred by the senses.

(Hart and Bishop 1990, 123)

The senses are also treasure in the vessel, *vas*, of the body. Humans regard (respicit) the height of Divinity, discerning good and evil. Hildegard's positive approach to the senses is at variance with their interpretation in medieval moralizing literature and sermons, where they are seen as "dangerous gateways to the vices" (Nordenfalk 1985, 2).[5] Teresa de Cartagena's view of the senses is akin to this. Her spiritual experience centres on the silence she experienced in her convent and more particularly in her cell. On numerous occasions, she writes of how the sounds of the world distract her and prevent her from hearing God's word:

> Ya es puesto silençio por la mano de Dios que me manda callar e yncrepada mi nesçia porfia con aquel dedo que se entiende, demostrándome abiertamente que me conviene del todo callar que quiere decir del todo apartarme de las hablas mundanas y de sus deseos [. . .]. Ca esto solo seria asaz ruydo para que no pudiese entender las bozes; [. . .].

(1967, 43)

In Teresa's Arboleda, the voices of the world are a din, a distraction, and worthless chatter preventing her from discerning what is good. This she indicates through lexical choices such as "palabrear," "ruydo," "conversaçiones del syglo," or "por mucho que el razonador baladre" (1967, 40, 43). According to Covarrubias Horozco (2006, 278), "baladrón" is "El fanfarrón, hablador, vocinglero, rufián, cobarde, que tiene palabras y no manos," and "baladrar" gives a good indication of the deceptive nature of human conversation:

> E asý yo estando enbuelta en el tropel de las fablas mundanas e bien rebuelto e atado mi entendimiento en el cuydado de aquéllos no podia oýr las bozes de la santa Escritura que nos enseña e amonesta.

(1967, 40)

Such a view of human conversation is not unusual. Constanza de Castilla also regards human conversation as more likely to lead astray than to save:

> Señor, por mí tu esclava, *solus et anxiatus* en el monte Oliveti tanto constreñido fueste, yo te suplico, ansí como tú eres vida perpetua, me des graçia que desee morir por tu amor e me arriedre de las conversaçiones dañosas a mi anima e de los negoçios del mundo en que yo me ocupo, como tiraste a sannt Pablo de perseguir tus cristianos.
> (Constanza de Castilla 1998, 8).

Teresa de Cartagena's imagery of "disordering" (tangling and binding) goes further, for she delivers a picture of how physical hearing prevents the soul from discerning and acquiring knowledge. It is generally believed that Teresa, after going deaf, writes the Arboleda as a means of self-consolation, whilst her very disability impelled her towards writing (Deyermond

1976–1977, 22, 29). Writing was transformative for her (Seidenspinner-Núñez and Kim 2004, 123). Deafness, and disability, have been thought to have "exacerbated her loneliness" (Seidenspinner-Núñez 1997, 9), to have created a space for writing (Cammarata 2000), to have deepened her "concienzación de su diferencia frente al 'otro,' es decir frente al conjunto de la sociedad" (Muñoz Pérez 2012, 699), to be the centrepoint of the autobiographical writing she creates (Juárez 2002), and to have led her to create her own salvation in direct partnership with God (Trillia 2007). At the start of the Arboleda, Teresa praises God for stopping the ears of her body, referring to the "claustra de sus santos e graçiosos consejos" (1967, 38), blocking out the sounds around her, because incessant chatter prevented her from hearing God. Later, Teresa affirms that the ear of understanding must strain to hear him:

> Y con el silençio ya dicho, ynclinando la oreja de mi entendimiento, pues la del cuerpo mal me ajuda, parésçeme que oý resonar a aquestas palabras: "Oye, fija, e acata e ynclina tu oreja, oluida el pueblo tuyo y la casa de tu padre."
>
> (1967, 44)

Villena, on the other hand, only occasionally refers to the ear as a principal source of sinful messages. For her, too, the ear can lead astray. Part of the torment of Christ, when he is bound to the column, is the lies and vile words flung at him – which he bears with patience: "E a la porta foren star x saigs, qui ab continues vilanies, escarns e vituperis turmentaren les sues sagrades orelles hoint tanta viltat" (II, 305). Christ endures the jibes without retorting. The implication of this torment is that words were more than sticks and stones but could penetrate into the soul and have a negative effect on it. In Villena's *Vita Christi*, however, the ear can also be a means of conveying secret messages for good or supportive advice. The Virgin goes to the aid of those who are being led astray by what they hear: "e mudaran la vida sua de vicis en virtuts per la intercessió de vostra senyoria, qui continuament los direu a la orella [. . .]" (I, 196). The Virgin intercedes, turning vice into virtue through words "a la orella." Yet even the message whispered focuses on seeing bad examples, and this leads to those bad examples being interiorized:

> Fills meus: si us voleu ben despullar dels vicis que acostumat haveu, fugiu a totes aquelles companies que mal exemple de vida vos poden donar, ca lo veure fer mal mou la persona a desig de fer semblant
>
> (I, 196)

For Villena, seeing evil – as well as hearing wrong things – was a source of distraction for the soul.

The word in the ear of good counsel is a trait which Villena uses six times in the *Vita Christi*, and I could not help but see the whispered word as a feature both of court and convent. The three-year-old Virgin, handed over by St Anne to live in the temple, receives words of encouragement, as she climbs the steps of the temple. She hears she is to pray for human nature from Charity, her handmaid: "dix-li a la orella Senyora, recort-se vostra mercé en aquest pujament de pregar estretament per natura humana" (I, 33); her handmaid "Pietat" counsels her: "Continau" (I, 36). She speaks in the ear of her son at the wedding at Cana, making the first request to launch Christ's public ministry: "e sa senyoria moguda de molta pietat, acostà·se a la orella del amat fill seu" (II, 75). The intimate word in the ear of Mary Magdalene by her sister, Martha, advises her that the Lord is calling her. Villena uses the same words as at Cana, "acostant-se a la orella" (II, 151). It echoes Christ's call. It marks closeness, between sisters, and, earlier, between mother and son. In the Gospel (John 11:28), Martha speaks to her sister in a low voice.

Witness is particularly important in the *Vita Christi*. At the death of Christ, the Virgin asserts she has physically witnessed his sorrows, *a ull*. Seeing has enabled the Virgin to imbibe the sorrows but she has not been able to touch Christ or bring him comfort:

> Jornada és aquesta per a ésser largamente recordada per mi, dolorosa mare, qui *a ull* he vist totes les dolors e penes del meu fill tan amat, e, tenint-lo tan prop en la sua mort, de una set d'aygua no·l he pogut confortar, ne ara, mort, no·l puch tocar!
>
> (III, 65–66)

Seeing can also be a means of spiritual communication in the *Vita Christi*: "e miraven-se mare e fill, parlant més de ulls que de boca" (II, 200). Yet the physical eyes and seeing physically are also valuable. For example, the Virgin expresses her longing to see her baby son about to be born, "desijant-li veure," and this time with the eyes of the body, "ab los ulls corporals" specified:

> E encesa en la sobirana amor del seu Fill, desijant-lo veure ab los ulls corporals, par-lava-li ab sobirana dolçor e deya: O pulcherrimum et dulcissimum Dominum meum, ex toto corde meo te desydero: veni mihi: videam te speciosissime per filiis hominum quia amore langueo et te videre desiderio.
>
> (I, 268)

Both Villena and Teresa de Cartagena seem aware of St Augustine's distinction between three categories of seeing: corporeal vision, which distinguishes the outward form; spiritual vision, which sees an interior image; and, finally, the eyes of the intellect, or the direct perception of unchanging truth (McGinn 2006, 187). This eye is what Teresa calls the intellectual eyes of the soul. However, hearing with the ear of the soul or the interior ear is magnified in importance, as we might expect, in Teresa's writing. Teresa frequently writes of hearing, as expected because of the infirmity from which she suffered, particularly in her Arboleda, yet it is in her *Admiración Operum Dei* where she considers how eyes bring people to understanding (see Howe 1996). In Admiración, Teresa recaps how God blocked her ears to release her from the world's sounds: "Çerró las puertas de mis orejas por donde la muerte entrava al ánima mía" (1967, 137), yet, conversely, he opened the eyes of her understanding: "e abrió los ojos de mi entendimiento e vi e seguí al Saluador" (1967, 137). Teresa considers that the ears of the soul distinguish true knowledge from the word of God. Just as the ears can be blocked by incessant chatter, the dust of sinful desires obscures the eyes:

> ¿E pues cómo se puede apartar del mal el que aun no conosçe el verdadero bien, el qual no se puede ver con los ojos corporals mas con los ynteletuales del alma? E si estos por nuestros pecados se obscuresçen e çiegan con el poluo de las terrenales pecados, en tiniblas estamos.
>
> (1967, 136)

The senses lead humankind astray, preventing sight. The senses blind the discerning mind's eye, whilst the darkness of lifestyle leads humans away from the light and deeper into darkness, whether of sin or separation from God:

> E desta manera e por causa de los sentidos se çiegan los ojos del entendimiento, ca çiego se puede dezir el entendimiento de aquel que vehe la luz accidental del curso

del día e no vehe ni considere las tinieblas de la noche por su escuro beuir las quales le apartan de la Luz verdadera e le lleuan por pasos contados a la eternal tiniebla.

(1967, 135)

She shows how corporeal eyes provide information for the eye of intellect, the "mind's eye." The eye of the body fails "por su escuro beuir" (1967, 135). The Admiración ends on defence of Arboleda. Teresa interprets the blind man cured by Christ on the road to Jericho as a metaphor for her intellect:

E como mi çiego entendimiento sintió por las señales ya dichas qu'el Salvador venía, luego començó a dar secretas boces diziendo: "Ave merçed de mí, Fijo de David." E los que ivan e venían increpavan a este ya dicho çiego entendimiento mío que callase. E sin duda puedo dezir que ivan e venían muchos desvariados cuidados e gran turbamulta de respetos tenporales humanos, de los quales mi entendimiento era increpado e aun costreñido a callar, ca como yo estava en el camino çerca de Jericó, que se entiende puesto todo mi cuidado en la calle d'este mundo, e más çerca mi deseo de las afecçiones humanas que de las espirituales, no era maravilla si los pensamientos que ivan y venían e pasavan por mi entendimiento eran vezinos de Gericó, conviene a saber, más familliares del siglo que no de la religión cuyo nombre usurpava por estonçes. Así que estos ya dichos pensamientos e movimientos umanos increpavan a mi çiego entendimiento que callase, mas él, con el grand deseo que tenía de ver luz, más y más multiplicava sus secretas bozes diziendo: "Ave merçed de mí, Hijo de David."

(1967, 132)

Surtz (1995, 35) argues this is an allegory of how Teresa was cured, enabled to see the light, and, therefore, empowered to write. Nevertheless, she subordinates the blind man's desire to see to hearing, first the jibes of passersby, who are "del siglo," and, then, the words of Christ. Whilst the cacophony distracts the blind man-entendimiento, his "secretas bozes" importune Christ. He pursues the "light" of knowledge, desiring to see. Seeing is the ultimate goal, facilitated by hearing. The way Teresa presents the man surrounded by denigrating voices recalls Villena's words about Christ at the Passion. Teresa, in the guise of the blind man, becomes a Christ-like figure, surrounded by voices calling insults and vile words. Imitatio Christi occurs in Margery Kempe's writing where she becomes an "object of scorn" for others (Beckwith 1993, 82). Teresa emphasizes this near the end of Admiración, when her suffering steps become those of Christ's "cruz de la pasión:"

E quando escreví aquel tractado que trata de aquesta intelectual Luz e sobredicha çiençia, la qual es alabança e conocer a Dios e a mí misma e negar mi voluntad e conformarme con la voluntad suya, e tomar la cruz de la pasión que padesco en las manos del entendimiento interior, e ir en pos del Salvador por pasos de af[l]icçión espiritual, e manificar a Dios por confisión de la lengua, dando loor e alabança al su santo Nonbre, recontando a las gentes la igualanza de la su justiçia,[de] la grandeza de su misericordia, e la manifiçençia e gloria suya.

(1967, 138)

In this part of the text Teresa visualizes herself following Christ and leaping and praising God just as the blind man had. Teresa's text is one of the few occasions on which there is a sense of a woman gazing upon her own salvation.

The female gaze

In medieval love poetry, the beloved woman is generally the object of the male lover's gaze but, very occasionally, a female poet gazes upon something and recounts that gaze:

> Una cosa que desseo
> Trabajo por alcançar,
> péssame quando la veo
> y más quando la posseo:
> ¿de do nasce este pesar?
> > ("Dama," lines 51–55, cited in Deyermond 1978,
> > 1995; Mirrer 1995; Sanmartín Bastida 2007, 40;
> > Snow 1984; Weissberger 2001)

The "dama," directing her question to Diego Nuñez, reflects on longing, looking, striving, and on how possessing a desired object renders it worthless.

Similarly, when Florencia Pinar gazes on caged birds, she sees in them an allegory of suffering and imprisonment:

> Destas aves su nación
> es cantar con alegría,
> y de verlas en prisión
> siento yo grave pasión
> sin sentir nadie la mía.
> > (cited in Weissberger 2001, 42)

The solitude of Pinar rings plaintively from "sin sentir nadie la mía." Whether hers is a sexualized gaze or one expressing entrapment by those around her is elusive.[6]

On rare occasions, a woman may even be the object of her own gaze. Even though it is her lack of hearing which isolates Teresa de Cartagena, describing her suffering when she is among others, she becomes the object of her own gaze: "Cuando en conpañía de otríe *me veo*, yo soy desanparada del todo, ca nin goço de consorçio o fablas de aquéllos, nin de mi mesma me puedo aprouechar" (1967, 39). Teresa observes herself in company from the outside, standing apart, and seeing herself as "other," she is lonely but unable to draw on her own resources:

> Cuando miro esta mi pasión en los temporales negoçios, véola muy penosa y de grandísima angustia, mas quando aparto el pensamiento de la cosas ya dichas, recojéndole a mi proprio seno, y veo la soledat que me haze sentir, apartándome de las negoçiaçiones mundanas, llámola soledat amable.
> > (1967, 40)

The senses purified

Hildegard relates the five senses to the five wounds of Christ, in the Edifice of Salvation in *Scivias* Book III: "The human body and soul by virtue of their strength contain the five senses and purify them through the wounds of Christ and lead them to righteousness of governance from within" (1998, 88). Villena writes of the five wounds as five fountains, from which water and mercy flow to heal sinners:

> Veniu e no dubteu, tots los que de peccats vos trobau carregats, e poareu, ab gran goig, de les aygües dulcíssimes de miséricordia decorrents de aquelles cinch fonts de les sagrades nafres que lo clement Senyor nostre ha pres en la persona sua, stant en lo camp de batalla, de la qual és exit ab victòria, reservant-se los dits senyals per a refugi e repos dels peccadors que a sa magestat acostar se volran.

> (III, 158)

Villena refers to "peccats" washed clean, without matching Christ's wounds to the senses. For Teresa, Christ's wounds are a means of anointing. Anointing can take place either as a cure for sickness or as a commissioning for a given task. In Teresa's case perhaps her writing:

> Qué hago otra cosa syno seguir al Salvador no con pasos corporales mas con los afectos del ánima, corriendo en los olores de los enguentos suyos que son las sus preçiosas llagas.

Yet again it is not with her physical body that Teresa seeks to follow to salvation but with the senses of her soul which not only enable her to see the right path to follow but imbue her with scented unguents, strengthening her to take it.

Conclusion

This chapter assumes that looking at women's writing as a category of literary production which reveals a woman's world view is worthwhile.[7] To group women is the mirror image of what is done constantly in critical approaches to literature, since the canon is an overwhelmingly masculine production in which men's writing is compared constantly. Women's writing is often thought to be plagiarized, copied, or written by someone else.[8] I finish with Jacques Derrida's comments on alterity:

> He says of feminine difference, [. . .] Does it not sketch on the inside of the work, a surfeit of un-said alterity? [. . .]The other as feminine [me] far from being derived or secondary, would become the other of the Saying of the wholly other.

> (2007, 183)

Notes

1 This chapter was presented as a paper at the conference of the Association of Hispanists of Great Britain and Ireland, 14–16 April, National University of Galway, Eire, 2014.
2 Yonsoo Kim (2012, 2) points out that there is no attempt to rescue women's voices in the medieval period which takes account of the lands beyond the Pyrenees. Dronke (1984) considers Perpetua, Dhuoda, Hrotsvitha, Heloise, Hildegard of Bingen, and Marguerite Porete; Chance (2007) studies Hrotsvit, Marie de France, Marguerite Porete, Margery Kempe, and Julian of Norwich. There have, however, been occasional Spanish women included in writings about medieval women writers: Marcelle Thiébaux (1987) translates passages from Egeria (Spain), Amalasuntha (Italy), Radegunda, Caesaria, and Baudonivia (Gaul), Eucheria (Provence), Dhuoda (Carolingian Gaul), Hrotswitha, Anna Comnena (Byzantium), Hildegard of Bingen and Elisabeth of Schönau, Matilda and Julian of Norwich (England), Marie de France and Christine de Pizan (France), as well as a selection of the writings of the French troubadours. Elizabeth Alvilda Petroff (1994) translates the *Memorias* of

Leonor López de Córdoba (1362–c. 1412) (1986, 329–334). Similarly, in their *Women Writing Latin*, Laurie J. Churchill, Phyllis R. Brown, and Jane E. Jeffrey (2002) give their attention to the Spanish writer, Luisa Sigea (1522–1560), whilst Anke Gilleir, Alicia C. Montoya, and Suzan van Dijk (2010, 327–344) include an eighteenth-century Spanish writer, Inés Joyes. Mora (2005) compares Teresa de Cartagena with two Italian religious writers. The picture is not quite so stark as the one Kim (2008) paints, but even where Spanish women merit some attention, they are given far less than women from Italy, England, or France. There have been a number of comparative studies of Iberian women writers, including Calvo (1994), Castro Ponce (1994), Cortés Timoner (2004), Deyermond (1983, 1995), Frieden (2001), Mirrer (1995), Navas Ocaña and de la Torre Castro (2011), Redondo Goicoechea (1992), Rivera-Cordero (2011) and Vicente García (1989).

3 For a biography of Teresa de Cartagena, see Kim (2012), Marimón Llorca (1990, 104–113), Seidenspinner-Núñez (1998, 2004), Seidenspinner-Núñez and Kim (2004) and Surtz (1995, 21–40). For a biography of Isabel de Villena, see the introductions to Hauf's editions (1995, 5–20; 2006); Cantavella (2000, 2005, 2011); de Courcelles (2000, 103–107); Twomey (2013b, especially 1–20). For a study of Costanza de Castilla, see Surtz (1995, 41–67); see also Constance L. Wilkins' edition of *The Book of Devotions* (Constanza de Castilla 1998). For an overview of Iberian "holy women," including all three, see Surtz (2010). For Leonor López de Córdoba, see Estow (1982); Ghassemi (1989); Rivera-Cordero (2011, 180–188).

4 Hildegard uses *Visio* to "designate three related things: her peculiar faculty or capacity of vision; her experience of this faculty; and the content of her experience, all that she sees in her *visio*" (Dronke 1984, 146). The translations from *Scivias* are from Hart and Bishop (1990, 59).

5 For a medieval representation of the five senses, see Mütherich (1955).

6 Being included in the *Cancionero general* suggests that Pinar's poetry was accepted by the majority in court circles and that she was not differentiated from other court poets, as some have sought to argue.

7 Paul Julian Smith also problematizes the validity of a category "women's writing" (1987, 220–222). Women are grouped to discover the nature of their education. Their authority and intellectual ability to write are also a reason for differentiating women: see Castro Ponce (1994), Quispe Agnoli (1997), Seidenspinner-Núñez (1997) and Vicente García (1989).

8 A number of articles explore women's writing in relation to the canon (Navas Ocaña 2009; Ochoa de Eribe 1999; Piera 2003). Huélamo (1992, 154–58) discusses whether Constanza was a copyist, translator, or author. Additionally, Navas Ocaña and de la Torre Castro (2011: 94–102) explore how women's authorship was disputed in the case of three of the women's works, Teresa de Cartagena et al. (2011, 94–102).

Works cited

Beckwith, Sarah. 1993. *Christ's Body: Identity, Culture, and Society in Late Medieval Writings*. London and New York: Routledge.

Beresford, Andrew M. and Lesley K. Twomey. 2013. "Visions of Hagiography: From the Gaze to Spiritual Vision in Medieval Lives of Saints." *La corónica* 42 (1): 103–132.

Biernoff, Suzannah. 2002. *Sight and Embodiment in the Middle Ages*. Houndsmill: Palgrave Macmillan.

Bynum, Caroline Walker. 2006. "Seeing and Seeing Beyond: The Mass of St Gregory in the Fifteenth Century." In *The Mind's Eye: Art and Theological Argument in the Middle Ages*, edited by Jeffrey F. Hamburger and Anne-Marie Bouché, 208–240. Princeton, NJ: Princeton University Press.

Calvo, Yadira F. 1994. "Sor Juana Inés de la Cruz, Teresa de Cartagena, María de Zayas, y la defensa de las mujeres letradas." *Kañina: Revista de Artes y Literatura de la Universidad de Costa Rica* 18: 247–250.

Cammarata, Joan F. 2000. "Teresa de Cartagena: Writing from a Silent Space in a Silent World." *Monographic Review/Revista Monográfica* 16: 38–51.Cantavella, Rosanna. 2000. "Isabel de Villena." In *Breve historia feminista de la literatura española*, edited by Myriam Díaz Diocaretz and Iris M. Zavala, vol. 6, 40–50. Barcelona: Antropos.

———. 2005. "Isabel de Villena (1430–1490)." In *Una altra mirada: deu dones i el cristianisme*, edited by Pere Luis Font, 141–155. Barcelona: Cruïlla.

————. 2011. "Intellectual, Contemplative, Administrator: Isabel de Villena and the Vindication of Women." In *A Companion to Spanish Women's Studies*, edited by Xon de Ros and Geraldine Hazbun, 97–107. Woodbridge: Tamesis.

Cartagena, Teresa de. 1967. *Arboleda de los enfermos. Admiraçión Operum Dey*. Edited by Lewis Joseph Hutton, Boletín de la Real Academia Española, Anejo 16. Madrid: BRAE.

Castilla, Constanza de. 1998. *Book of Devotions/ Libro de devociones y oficios*. Edited by Constance L. Wilkins. Exeter: Exeter University Press.

Castro Ponce, Clara Esther. 1994. "El sí de las hermanas: la escritura y lo intelectual en la obra de Sor Teresa de Cartagena y Sor Juana Inés de la Cruz." *Cincinnati Romance Review* 18: 15–21.

Chance, Jane. 2007. *The Literary Subversions of Medieval Women*. New York: Palgrave Macmillan.

Churchill, Laurie J., Phyllis R. Brown, and Jane E. Jeffrey. 2002. *Women Writing Latin: From Roman Antiquity to Early Modern Europe*. London and New York: Routledge.

Cortés Timoner, María Mar. 2004. "'Poner riquezas en mi entendimiento': Sor Juana Inés de la Cruz y Sor Teresa de Cartagena." *Lectora: Revista de Dones i Textualitat* 10: 377–391.

Courcelles, Dominique de. 2000. "En Mémoire d'elle et en mémoire du sang: la Vita Christi de Sor Isabel de Villena, abbesse des clarisses de Valence au XVe siècle." *Journal de la Renaissance* 1: 103–120.

Covarrubias Orozco, Sebastián de. 2006. *Tesoro de la lengua castellana or española*. Pamplona: University of Navarra Press.

Derrida, Jacques. 2007. *Psyche: Inventions of the Other*. Edited and translated by Peggy Kamuf and Elizabeth Rottenberg. Stanford, CA: Stanford University Press.

Deyermond, Alan. 1976–1977. "'El convento de dolençias': The Works of Teresa de Cartagena." *Journal of Hispanic Philology* 1: 19–29.

————. 1978. "The Worm and the Partridge: Reflections on the Poetry of Florencia Pinar." *Mester* 7: 3–8.

————. 1983. "Spain's First Women Writers." In *Women in Hispanic Literature: Icons and Fallen Idols*, edited by Beth Miller, 27–52. Berkeley, CA: University of California Press.

————. 1995. "Las autoras medievales castellanas a la luz de las últimas investigaciones." In *Medioevo y literatura: Actas del V Congreso de la Asociación Hispánica de Literatura Medieval*, edited by Juan Paredes, vol. 1, 31–52. Granada: Universidad de Granada.

Dronke, Peter. 1984. *Women Writers of the Middle Ages: A Critical Study of Texts from Perpetua (†203) to Marguerite Porete (†1310)*. Cambridge: Cambridge University Press.

Emerson, Jan S. 1998. "A Poetry of Science: Relating Body and Soul in the *Scivias*." In *Hildegard of Bingen: A Book of Essays*, edited by Maud Burnett McInerney, 77–101. New York: Garland.

Estow, Clara. 1982. "Leonor López de Córdoba: Portrait of a Medieval Courtier." *Fifteenth-Century Studies* 5: 23–46.

Frieden, Mary Elizabeth. 2001. "Epistolarity in the Works of Teresa de Cartagena and Leonor López de Córdoba." PhD diss., University of Missouri-Columbia.

Ghassemi, Ruth Lubenow. 1989. "La 'crueldad de los vencidos': un estudio interpretativo de Las memorias de Doña Leonor López de Córdoba." *La corónica* 18 (1):19–32.

Gilleir, Anke, Alicia C. Montoya, and Suzan van Dijk. 2010. *Women Writing Back/Writing Women Back*. Leiden: Brill.

Hart, Mother Columba and Jane Bishop, eds. and trans. 1990. *Hildegard of Bingen: Scivias*. Mahwah, NJ: Paulist Press.

Hauf i Valls, Albert Guillem, eds. 1995. *Vita Christi*. Barcelona: Edicions 62.

————. 2000. *La Vita Christi de Sor Isabel de Villena (s. XV) como arte de meditar: introducción a una lectura contextualizada*. València: Conselleria de Cultura, Educació i Esport.

Howe, Elizabeth. 1996. "Sor Teresa de Cartagena and *entendimiento*." *Romanische Forschungen* 108: 133–145.

Huélamo San José, Ana María. 1992. "El devocionario de la domínica Sor Constanza." *Boletín de la Asociación Española de Archiveros, Bibliotecarios, Museólogos y Documentalistas* 42: 133–147.

————. 1993. "La dominica Sor Constanza, autora religiosa del siglo XV." *Revista de Literatura Medieval* 5: 127–158.

Juárez, Encarnación. 2002. "The Autobiography of the Aching Body in Teresa de Cartagena's Arboleda de los enfermos." In *Disability Studies: Enabling the Humanities*, edited by Sharon L. Snyder, Brenda

Jo Brueggemann, and Rosemarie Garland-Thompson, 131–143. New York: The Modern Language Association of America.

Kim, Yonsoo. 2008. *El saber femenino y el sufrimiento corporal de la temprana Edad Moderna. Arboleda de los enfermos y Admiración Operum Dey de Teresa de Cartagena.* Córdoba: Universidad de Córdoba.

———. 2012. *Between Desire and Passion: Teresa de Cartagena.* Leiden: Brill.

Lentes, Thomas. 2006. "'As Far as the Eye Can See': Rituals of Gazing in the Late Middle Ages." In *The Mind's Eye: Art and Theological Argument in the Middle Ages*, edited by Jeffrey F. Hamburger and Anne-Marie Bouché, 360–373. Princeton, NJ: Princeton University Press.

López de Córdoba, Leonor. *Vida y traxedias de Leonor López de Córdoua. Memorias. Dictadas en Córdoba entre 1401 y 1404.* Edited by María-Milagros Rivera Garretas. Accessed November 24, 2014. http://www.ub.edu/duoda/bvid/obras/Duoda.text.2011.02.0003.html.

Marimón Llorca, Carmen. 1990. *Prosistas castellanas medievales.* Alicante: Publicaciones de la Caja de Ahorros Provincial.

Mazzoni, Cristina. 2005. *The Women in God's Kitchen: Cooking, Eating, and Spiritual Writing.* New York: Continuum.

McGinn, Bernard. 2006. "Theologians as Trinitarian Iconographers." In *The Mind's Eye: Art and Theological Argument in the Middle Ages*, edited by Jeffrey F. Hamburger and Anne-Marie Bouché, 186–207. Princeton, NJ: Princeton University Press.

Mirrer, Louise. 1995. "Género, poder y lengua en los poemas de Florenca Pinar." *Medievalia* 19: 9–15.

Mora, Lisa Catherine. 2005. "The Language(s) of Spirituality in the Writings of Caterina Vigri, Illuminata Bembo, and Teresa de Cartagena." PhD diss., University of California, Los Angeles.

Muñoz Pérez, Laura S. 2012. "Teresa de Cartagena y las estrategias confesionales de la Arboleda de los enfermos." *Bulletin of Hispanic Studies* 89 (7): 697–710.

Mütherich, F. 1955. "An Illustration of the Five Senses in Medieval Art." *Journal of the Warburg and Courtauld Institutes* 18 (1/2): 140–141.

Navas Ocaña, María Isabel. 2009. "The Memoirs of Leonor López de Córdoba and the Canon." *Iberoromania* 67: 61–82.

Navas Ocaña, María Isabel, and José de la Torre Castro. 2011. "Prosistas medievales castellanas: autorías, auditorios, genealogías." *Estudios filológicos* 47: 93–113.

Nordenfalk, Carl. 1985. "The Five Senses in Late Medieval and Renaissance Art." *Journal of the Warburg and Courtauld Institutes* 48: 1–22.

Ochoa de Eribe, Marian. 1999. "El yo polémico de Teresa de Cartagena en la Admiración de las obras de Dios: las argucias del débil por entrar en el canon." *Letras de Deusto* 29 (84): 179–188.

Petroff, Elizabeth Alvilda. 1994. *Essays on Medieval Women and Mysticism.* Oxford: Oxford University Press.

Piera, Montserrat. 2003. "Writing, Auctoritas, and Canon Formation, in Sor Isabel de Villena's Vita Christi." *La corónica* 32 (1): 105–118.

Quispe Agnoli, Rocío. 1997. "'Anse de maravillar que muger haga tratado': defensa y concepción de la escritura en Teresa de Cartagena (siglo XV)." In *Actas del VI Congreso Internacional de la Asociación Internacional de Hispánica de Literatura Medieval*, edited by José Manuel Lucía Megías, 1227–1239. Alcalá de Henares: Universidad de Alcalá de Henares.

Redondo Goicoechea, Alicia. 1992. "La retórica del yo-mujer en tres escritoras: Teresa de Cartagena, Teresa de Ávila y María de Zayas." *Compás de Letras* 1: 49–63.

Rivera-Cordero, Victoria. 2011. "Writing as Resistance: Self and Survival in Leonor López de Córdoba and Teresa de Cartagena." In *The Inner Life of Women in Medieval Romance Literature: Grief, Guilt, and Hypocrisy*, edited by Jeff Rider and Jamie Friedman, 179–201. New York: Palgrave Macmillan.

Sanmartín Bastida, Rebeca. 2007. "Una dama: pregunta a Diego Nuñez." In *Seis siglos de poesía española escrita por mujeres: pautas poéticas y revisiones críticas*, edited by Dolores Romero López et al., 39–50. Bern: Peter Lang.

Sanmartín Bastida, Rebeca and María Luengo Balbás. 2014. "Las Revelaciones de María de Santo Domingo (1480/86–1524)." *Papers of the Medieval Hispanic Research Seminar 74.* London: Queen Mary, University of London.

Seidenspinner-Núñez, Dayle. 1997. "'But I Suffer Not Woman to Teach': Two Late Medieval Women Writers in Late-Medieval Spain." In *Hers Ancient and Modern: Women's Writing in Spain and Brazil*, edited by Catherine Davies and Jane Whetnall, 1–14. Manchester: University of Manchester.

———, ed. 1998. *The Writings of Teresa de Cartagena*. Woodbridge: D. S. Brewer.

———. 2004. "Teresa de Cartagena." In *Castilian Writers 1400–1500*, edited by Frank A. Domínguez and George D. Greenia, Dictionary of Literary Biography, 286, 15–20. Detroit: Bruccoli Clark Layman.

Seidenspinner-Núñez, Dayle and Yonsoo Kim. 2004. "Historicizing Teresa: Reflections on New Documents Regarding Sor Teresa de Cartagena." *La corónica* 32 (2): 121–150.

Smith, Paul Julian. 1987. "Writing Women in Golden Age Spain: Saint Teresa and María de Zayas." *Modern Language Notes* 102 (2): 220–240.

Snow, Joseph. 1984. "The Spanish Love Poet: Florencia Pinar." In *Medieval Women Writers*, edited by Katharina M. Wilson, 320–332. Athens, GA: University of Georgia Press.

Surtz, Ronald E. 1995. *Writing Women in Late Medieval and Early Modern Spain: The Mothers of St Teresa of Ávila*. Philadelphia, PA: University of Pennsylvania Press.

———. 2010. "Iberian Holy Women: A Survey." In *Medieval Holy Women in the Christian Tradition c. 1100 – c. 1500*, edited by Alistair Minnis and Rosemary Voaden, 499–525. Turnhout: Brepols.

Thiébaux, Marcelle, trans. 1987. *The Writings of Medieval Women*. New York: Garland.

Trillia, Raquel. 2007. "Teresa de Cartagena: Agent of her own Salvation." *Revista Canadiense de Estudios Hispánicos* 32 (1): 51–70.

Twomey, Lesley K. 2013. *The Fabric of Marian Devotion in Isabel de Villena's Vita Christi*. Woodbridge: Boydell & Brewer.

Vicente García, L. M. 1989. "A Defense of Women as Intellectuals in Teresa de Cartagena and Juana Inés de la Cruz." *Mester* 18: 95–103.

Weissberger, Barbara F. 2001. "The Critics and Florencia Pinar: The Problem with Assigning Feminism to a Medieval Court Poet." In *Recovering Spain's Feminist Tradition*, edited by Lisa Vollendorf, 31–47. New York: The Modern Language Association of America.

7

AN INTERSTITIAL HISTORY OF MEDIEVAL IBERIAN POETRY

David A. Wacks

Whose history?

The Iberian Peninsula during the period ca. 1000–1500 was home to a poetic culture that was not defined by a national agenda. Poetry emanated from the monastery, the synagogue, the court, and the literary salon. Poets composed and performed in a variety of Ibero-Romance and classical languages, often more than one. The nationalism of the nineteenth and twentieth centuries has produced a literary historical legacy emphasizing the individual, national language – in some cases (Galician, Catalan) a language striving for political recognition. The works of medieval Iberian poets who wrote in more than one of these vernaculars – and there were many – were divided, edited, and studied as parts of separate traditions, the distinct patrimonies of Spain, Catalonia, Galicia, or Portugal. Hebrew and Arabic poets came to be identified with the national literary histories of other countries and linguistic groups who likewise divided their works according to national language and cast off those poems written in other tongues. Latin, the liturgical, administrative, and creative language of Christian Iberian kingdoms and to a lesser extent the Christian communities of al-Andalus, suffered tremendous marginalization in the modern era, and to this day there is a vast corpus of Iberian Latin belles lettres that has evaded the gaze of the modern literary critic. The resulting literary history is a series of silos, each containing a rich corpus and interpretive tradition of a single language, with little exception prior to the 1980s.

The most significant disruptor to this pattern of national literary history was Américo Castro, who during the second half of the twentieth century promoted the thesis of the Three Cultures, the idea that Spain's national culture was not a product of a Roman-Visigothic-Habsburgian cultural continuity, but rather was the hybrid product of the various religious and ethnic traditions who had always populated the Iberian Peninsula, including the Andalusi Muslim and Sephardic Jewish traditions (Castro 1948, 1954, 1961, 1962). While he did not go as far as displacing Castile from the center of Spanish studies, he opened the field to Hispano-Arabic and Hispano-Hebrew studies. One effect of this intervention was to privilege the literary voices of non-Christian residents of Christian Iberia. Castro's thesis was an important intervention and corrective to the excesses and particular distortions of the national literatures approach, but ultimately essentialist because his multicultural vision was still in service to a national

(Spanish) project. María Rosa Menocal later took Castro's work a step further, challenging the hegemony of Castilian and the idea of "Europeanness" that informed the approaches of her teachers' generation toward medieval Iberian culture (Menocal 1987, 1994, 2002).

The idea of examining these various textual traditions at their linguistic and religious interstices is not to ascribe a modern "national essence" to the medieval reality, but rather to demonstrate that the breadth, variety, and interaction of traditions that are now considered distinct was simply the regular state of affairs. That is, what to us appears to be interstitial was to audiences at the time not. The "hybrid," the "cross-cultural," the "mutual influence" are all anachronisms. Medieval Iberian audiences did not experience these forms in this way. To them it was poetry, plain and simple. They were not struggling against a national languages model of literary history – that's our problem today.

As a corrective to the national language approach that has dominated literary history for the past two centuries, John Dagenais suggests, in his contribution to the *Cambridge History of Spanish Literature*, that we "focus on the myriad points of intersection among traditions we might today recognize as separate literarily and linguistically" (Dagenais 2004, 47). In so doing, we can begin to develop a vision of the texture of the literary history of medieval Iberia that approximates how "they" lived it. This in itself presents at least two methodological and ideological problems. First, what does an "accurate" or "scientific" literary history mean? Can we actually aspire to a "better" representation of literary history? Any criteria we introduce to replace that of national language will have its own (flawed) ideological basis. Second, even in reacting to the national language model we are preserving its structures, observing it in the breach.

What is the problem, exactly? The national languages model of literary history serves a national linguistic policy that values uniformity and linguistic hegemony of a single language. A nationalist ideology is strengthened by common linguistic and cultural identity. This narrative, while perhaps productive from an early capitalist perspective (capitalism favors interchangeability, uniformity, reproduceability), is problematic from the point of view of a society (such as ours today) that at least officially values cultural and linguistic diversity. If we cannot avoid falling into the trap of shackling our literary history to a given ideology, at least we can try to be transparent about our motives.

I am going to begin with Arabic, not because it was the first language in which poets composed in the Iberian Peninsula, but because it is, in terms of Hispano-Romance literary history, the Elephant in the Peninsula. Despite the work of scholars such as Américo Castro and María Rosa Menocal who opened the literary history of Spain to the richness of its Semitic cultural legacy, the practice of Spanish literary history is still largely the history of Castilian. Only rarely in anything that bills itself as a literary history of Spain does Arabic appear. In the *Cambridge History of Spanish Literature*, John Dagenais (2004) and María Rosa Menocal (2004) discuss the plurilinguistic situation of "medieval Spain" (itself, as Dagenais points out, a back formation), but there is no chapter devoted to Arabic and/or Hebrew literature of the Peninsula, let alone Catalan, which in the medieval period is undeniably a richer, aesthetically superior corpus when compared with the Castilian. In fact, as Menocal herself points out, in all of the histories of Spanish literature produced in the nineteenth and twentieth centuries, only one dedicates a chapter to Hispano-Arabic literature (Millás Vallicrosa 1949). The other notable exception is the volume of the *Cambridge History of Arabic Literature* dedicated to al-Andalus, which spans the Arabic, Hebrew, and Romance literary production of what one might call "greater al-Andalus," for it includes authors such as Petrus Alfonsi and Ramon Llull, who lived in Christian Iberia (Menocal et al. 2000).

Arabic and Hebrew poetry in al-Andalus

Arabic was the official language of state in al-Andalus, first in the Umayyad Caliphate and then in the Party Kingdoms, the *muluk at-Tawa'if* that rose in the wake of the disintegration of the Caliphate. It was not the native language of all Andalusis, who spoke Arabic, Tamazigh, and Romance languages respectively, but rather was a lingua franca that united the various ethnic and religious groups living in al-Andalus. Classical Arabic was the language of Islam, of the court, the legal system, of scientific inquiry, of poetry (López-Morillas 1999; Wasserstein 1991). Arabic writers of al-Andalus participated in the vast literary culture of the Arab world, which stretched from al-Andalus in the West to Mughal India in the East. In some cases they introduced new styles that distinguished al-Andalus as a center of innovation at the far edge of the Arab world. Over time the Caliphal capital at Córdoba became known as a court that competed (or at least imagined itself competing) with Abbasid Baghdad in poetic, artistic, and intellectual refinement (Cachia 1992; Jayyusi 1992; Monroe 2004, 3–71).

As elsewhere in the Muslim world, religious minorities such as Christians and Jews were not barred access to public life and regularly served in highly placed positions at court. Jewish courtiers distinguished themselves, and by the reign of Abd ar-Rahman III in the tenth century a man such as Hasdai ibn Shaprut could rise to prominence at court, where he served the Caliph as physician, advisor, and diplomat. During this time Dunash ben Labrat developed a Hebrew poetics that mirrored the aesthetics of the Arabic poetry of his day, mapping Arabic meters, motifs, and genres onto Biblical Hebrew language (Brann 1991, 29–33; Cole 2007, 23–24; Schirmann 1956, 31–41). Over time, this Arabicizing Hebrew poetry became the dominant aesthetic in Hebrew poetry in al-Andalus and beyond. This embrace of Arabic poetics meant not only that Sephardic poets such as Dunash ben Labrat and those who came after him adopted the meters, motifs, and commonplaces of the Arab poets, but also that they began to use Hebrew poetry to express themes and give voice to ideas that were not in the service of liturgy (Schippers 1994). Arabic thus enabled Hebrew to move beyond the synagogue; for the first time since the Biblical era, Hebrew poets waxed lyrical over the generosity of great men, the beauty of young girls and boys, the delights of drinking wine in a fragrant garden, and the philosophical (but not always devout) musings of the poet. In turn, this secular poetics inspired new innovations in the poetry of the synagogue, which was now populated by the gazelles and beloveds of the Arab poets, who took their place beside the traditional Biblical motifs with which Hebrew poets had been praising God since the Biblical era (Cole 2007; Scheindlin 1986, 1991). In its mimicry of Arabic, Hebrew developed a secular poetics and a rich corpus of poetry both profane and devout that would go on to become the classical tradition of modern Hebrew literature. However, were one to open a modern history of Hebrew literature, the poems of Andalusi authors such as Solomon ibn Gabirol, and Moses ibn Ezra would not include their Arabic writings, which were just as "Jewish" as they were "Andalusi." Modern literary historiography obscures just as much as it edifies, and would have us think, as Menocal has written, that the work of medieval poets was "little more than the primitive stages of what will eventually become the real thing" (Menocal 2004, 61) whether that real thing be "Arabic," "Hebrew," or "Spanish" literature.

When literary critics write about cultural crossings, mutual influences, or exchange they inevitably turn to translation as one of the conduits of literary material between linguistic or national traditions. Poetry is notoriously resistant to translation, and in the medieval period we see almost no translation of poetry that is not scriptural. In the Andalusi period the closest we come to poetic translations are perhaps the Hebrew rhyming prose works translated from

Arabic, such as Judah al-Harizi's translation of the *Maqamat* of al-Hariri, the *Mahberet Itti'el* (al-Harizi 1952, 1965, 2001). However, even in these cases the poet replaces the Arabic verses of al-Hariri interspersed with the rhyming prose with new original verses in Hebrew.

At the court of Alfonso X "The Learned" of Castile-León, poets composed verse in several languages, including Latin, Galician-Portuguese, Provençal, and Hebrew (Alvar 1984; Cabo Aseguinolaza et al. 2010, 398; O'Callaghan 1993, 144–146; Procter 1951, 130–132; Salvador Martínez 2003, 2010; Snow 1977, 7; Targarona Borrás 1985). Only Castilian, the official language of Alfonso's court, was not used for poetry. So resistant was poetry to translation that even when the Castilian itself was not considered a fit vehicle for original poetic composition, there is still no evidence of poetic translation into Castilian (Burnett 1994; Gil 1985; Jacquart 1991; Sáenz-Badillos 1996a). Why might this have been? In a time and place where writers produced volumes of history, law, religious narrative poetry, scientific treatises, and all manner of secular prose in Castilian, not until the mid-fourteenth century do courtly poets begin to compose in the language of the court? Castile was ironically out of step with Galicia, Catalonia, Occitan, and Sicily, where poets had been composing profane courtly verse in the vernacular since the late eleventh century, when William X of Aquitaine famously penned the first lines of troubadour verse (Akehurst and Davis 1995; Bonner 1972; Gaunt and Kay 1999). Frederick II of Hohenstaufen's court at Sicily, in so many ways a cultural model for that of Alfonso X in Castile, was home to poets who wrote sonnets in the vernacular that would be the inspiration for the Tuscan *stil novisti* and in turn for Petrarch (Abulafia 1988, 272–279; Gensini 1986). But not in Castile. It was not for a lack of poets or appreciation of verse. Alfonso retained many poets who versified in Provençal, Galician-Portuguese, even Hebrew (C. Alvar 1978, 35–38, 54, 81, 123, 230; 1984, 181; Beltrán 2006, 165–166; Milá y Fontanals 1966, 179–199; O'Callaghan 1993, 144). Alfonso himself authored (or at least directed) a large collection of Marian verse in Galician-Portuguese, the *Cantigas de Santa Maria*, as well as a corpus of satirical and jocular verse in the same language, the *Cantigas d'escarnho e maldizer*. But although Castile thrived as a language of science, history, law, and even religious narrative poetry, it would make no inroads into courtly poetry until well after Alfonso's time (C. Alvar 1984, 7). Why?

We really cannot be certain. It is possible that Galician-Portuguese and Provençal, prestigious poetic languages in their own right, were sufficiently intelligible so as to be serviceable as poetic languages for educated Castilian speakers. Another is that courtly audiences did not feel it necessary to fully comprehend poetry presented at court – and to be honest, we have very little information about poetic performance at the court of Alfonso. What the poets themselves tell us mostly refers to Alfonso's patronage rather than to the actual conditions or practices of composition, performance, and circulation. It may well have been, and this could be the case for the whole of the Peninsula, that the material record that has arrived to us is only the tip of the iceberg of medieval poetic practice. We know very little about the performance practice of medieval poets (a bit more about the Arabic and Hebrew poets of the Peninsula who documented, or at least fantasized about poetic gatherings, readings, and the composition process, as did some of the Provençal troubadours). One Hebrew poet, Judah ibn Shabbetay, who lived during the reign of Alfonso VIII, reports having performed his rhyming prose narrative at court, where Alfonso rewarded his performance generously (Ibn Shabbetai 1991, 2: 33, ll. 779–793). This was probably a fictional, quite possibly parodic account meant to demonstrate the poet's influence, but gives us some idea as to the nature of poetic performance at courts where multiple poetic languages thrived (Cynthia Robinson 2001, 280; Nykl 1946, 381).

Interstitial poetics are the tip of the iceberg of poetic practice. National literary history tells us that the glorious present of your national language has a glorious past as well. Interstitial poetics appear as a blip on the screen of this narrative, a glitch, a fluke, or at best a quaint innovation. But these moments are indices of a broader poetic practice that has been lost to us by the literary scholarship of the nineteenth and twentieth centuries. This vision of medieval poetic practice was forged in a present that privileged monolingualism, and in which the role and function of poetry itself had changed and no longer looks very much like what is was in 1000 or 1400 CE. Today popular poetry is still very much a part of our lives, mostly in the form of popular recorded music, which we consume and enjoy, but we rarely sing for others, except perhaps in ritual settings (Christmas caroling, "Happy Birthday," etc.). The *romance*, or ballad, once a very living tradition, survives in Mexico as the *corrido* but even in Spain is in decline as a living tradition (Díaz Roig 1992; Catalán 1970; Menéndez Pidal 1968; Orta Velázquez 1981; Smith 1996). There is arguably little to no poetry at court or in the halls of power of our governments, and it is extremely rare that a high government official publish verse. Thus the practice of poetry itself has been transformed in such a way as to be unrecognizable to an aficionado of twelfth-century Santiago, León, Valencia, or Granada.

In al-Andalus itself this interstitiality was not always a question of Arabic/Romance bilingualism or diglossia. Andalusi vernacular Arabic differed a great deal from the Classical Arabic used in poetry; so much so that one had to learn the poetic register as a Classical language in school. The Arabic of the home and the market was not the Arabic of the mosque, the academy, and the court. Even so, there are poetic texts that tell us Andalusis sought to experiment with mixing the vernacular with the Classical, to bring the street and the court into contact in their verse. The earliest and most famous examples of these are two poetic genres that began life in al-Andalus and later spread through the Arab world.

The *muwashshah* was, according to legend, the innovation of a blind poet from Córdoba named Muqaddam of Cabra (10th century). In his day, Classical Arabic verse was declaimed or recited in monorrhyme verse, but was not sung to a melody. Muqaddam defied these conventions: he composed songs in Classical Arabic that were set to popular melodies from oral tradition that one might hear in the market. What's more, his verses were written in a variable rhyme scheme, like the popular melodies upon which he based his compositions. To make things worse, he ended his poems with a couplet from the popular tune itself. Critics would later call this couplet the *kharja*, or "exit" from the poem, which readers of Spanish will recognize as *jarcha* (Abu-Haidar 2001; Armistead 1987, 2005; Monroe 1992; Zwartjes 1998).

This inter-register interstitiality would become common practice with the learned *glosas* of popular couplets written by the courtly *cancionero* poets of fifteenth-century Castile, but in Córdoba in the tenth century it was highly unorthodox, even shocking to prevailing literary tastes. Muqaddam's experiment in linguistic and poetic interstitiality was a success, and soon poets throughout al-Andalus and the broader Arabic world began to compose *muwashshahat* based on popular melodies and incorporating a bit of a popular verse as the final couplet. The sudden shift in register and/or in language (in the case of a *kharja* in Andalusi Romance) shocked and delighted audiences, according to the twelfth-century literary historian Ibn Bassam (Zwartjes 1998, 59–60). Some poets took this example of early Arabic literary vernacularization and ran with it, composing *zajals* in Andalusi Arabic using a verse form (aaab cccb dddb, etc) which would come to be known in Italy as the *ballata* and in France as the *virelei* (Zwartjes 1998, 94–124). In the twelfth century, the Andalusi poet Ibn Quzman would achieve renown working in the zajal genre. He left an entire corpus of scandalous poetry in a quasi-colloquial register of Andalusi Arabic (Buturovic 2000; Ibn Quzman and Corriente 1984; Monroe 1985). However, because he operated in the interstices of what would become modern national literatures, he never achieved that status accorded to other Bacchic poets who wrote in Classical, rather than colloquial Arabic (Monroe 2013).

This literary appreciation of the Andalusi vernacular was a defining characteristic of Andalusi literary culture (López-Morillas 2000). Later, writers such as the Granadan Abu Yahya al-Zajjali would edit collections of popular sayings and proverbs that elevated Andalusi Arabic both as a poetic language and as a source of culturally authentic lore that passed muster at court (Al-Zajjali 1971).

The success of the muwashshah and zajal genres echoed through Arabic cultural history. Well into the age of recorded music, iconic Arab singers such as Fairouz (Lebanon) and most notably Umm Kulthum (Egypt) recorded dozens of hit muwashshahat. Singers throughout the Arab world continue to cultivate the muwashshah in both secular and devout settings (Reynolds 2000; Shannon 2006, 29–30, 32, 117–119, 132; 2007). Current-day practitioners of the zajal in Morocco or Lebanon use the form as a vehicle for parody, satire, and invective and do not necessarily consider it to be an Andalusi tradition (Beinin 1994; Hazran 2013).

The literary and linguistic porousness displayed by Arabic Andalusi poets inspired similar innovations in the Hebrew poetry of al-Andalus and later in Christian Iberia. Jewish Andalusi poets followed this fashion and composed scores of muwashshahat in Biblical Hebrew, with final couplets or kharjat written in either Andalusi Arabic or in the dialect of Romance spoken in al-Andalus. These Hebrew compositions added another voice to the interstitial poetics of their moment, blending the language of the Bible with the imagery, conceits, and habits of thought of the Arab poets of the dominant culture in which they lived.

Like their counterparts who wrote only in Arabic, Jewish courtiers in al-Andalus were well educated in Arabic letters, including the Qur'an and its commentaries (Decter 2006). Their Hebrew muwashshahat blended images from the Song of Songs with the gazelles and beautiful boys and girls of the Arab tradition, with the lovesick maid of popular Andalusi song (Roth 1982, 1991). Tradition tells us (though we would do well to question it) that the first poet to bring Arabic poetics over into Hebrew was the tenth-century courtier Dunash ibn Labrat, who studied in Baghdad under the sage Saadia Gaon and returned to al-Andalus to shock the Jewish literary establishment with his innovation which would forever transform Hebrew poetry. Labrat's innovation was to map the traditional meters of Classical Arabic poetry onto the Hebrew language, which some contemporary critics saw as hammering a square peg into a round hole. Despite these objections, Labrat's innovation transformed Hebrew poetry forever, and for centuries poets in the Iberian Peninsula and beyond wrote using the Arabic metrics he pioneered. Labrat's wife, whose name has been lost in the archive, is thought to be the author of the only surviving Hebrew poem composed by a woman from the Andalusi period.

Jewish writers would cultivate the zajal and muwashshah genres for centuries, in all the languages of the Peninsula. The great scholar Maimonides, who was born in Córdoba but later migrated to Fez and thence to Cairo, decried the composition of vernacular (Ar. *ajamiyya*, literally "non-Arabic" but in the Iberian context referring to either Andalusi Arabic or Andalusi Romance) as "improper," from which he can conclude that it must have been fairly commonplace among Andalusi and North African Jews (Monroe 1988). Andalusi Hebrew writers likewise cultivated narrative genres, such as the maqama (rhymed prose narrative interspersed with verse) in Hebrew, adapting the formal, thematic, and aesthetic conventions of the Arabic maqama in Hebrew (Drory 2000a, 2000b). As with poetic genres, they populated the structures of the Arab poets with Biblical Hebrew language, and in their lines the commonplaces and imagery of the Classical Arabic tradition mixed freely with Biblical toponymy; imagery drawn from the Psalms, the Prophets, and other poetic texts; the narratives of Genesis and Exodus; and even the technical priestly texts of Leviticus (Cole 2007, 253; Kozodoy 1977; Pagis 1976, 70–79; Schippers 1994; Yellin and Pagis 1972, 118–149).

La "thèse arabe" and national literary history

At the height of the Andalusi Arabic and Hebrew poetic ferment, a young nobleman in what is now Southern France began to compose courtly vernacular verse. At the end of the eleventh century this would have raised no eyebrows in Córdoba or Seville, where poets had been composing vernacular zajals for over a century, but across the Pyrenees this represented a revolutionary break in poetic practice. William IX of Aquitaine, the "first troubadour," is credited with writing the first verses of courtly poetry in the Romance vernaculars. This claim, made effortlessly by literary historians since the nineteenth century, is certainly disputable, given the pre-history of Romance kharjas and zajals in al-Andalus in the century before William IX's innovation. Without going into a round of "who got there first" brinksmanship, the question arises (and has generated volume after volume of scholarly speculation and no little controversy) as to whether and to what extent the two phenomena might be related. The so-called *thèse arabe* posits that Andalusi poetic practice crossed the Pyrenees with William VIII of Aquitaine in the form of a troop of Andalusi *qiyan* – technically singer-slaves but in practice closer to indentured professors of music. The father of the first troubadour had crossed the Pyrenees in the assistance of Sancho Ramírez of Aragon in the Siege of Barbastro (Huesca), then held by al-Muzaffar of Zaragoza. As part of the spoils of this successful campaign he brought back with him to Aquitaine a troop of Andalusi qiyan, who then introduced Aquitainian musicians, singers, and audiences to courtly strophic song in the form of muwashshahat and zajals (Boase 1977, 62–75; Menocal 1987, 28–33; Nykl 1946, 371–411; Robinson 2001, 295–299). As the story goes, young William IX, having been reared on such musical and poetic fare, simply followed the lessons of his father's qiyan in composing the first verses of troubadour verse, thus converting himself into the Muqaddam of Cabra or Dunash ibn Labrat of the north.

The poetic movement begun (according to tradition) by William IX soon spread southward into the Peninsula, where poets working in Provençal, Catalan, or Galician-Portuguese performed at the courts of Christian Iberian monarchs. Even by the thirteenth century, Alfonso X "The Learned" was patron to many poets who performed troubadouresque poetry in Provençal and Galician-Portuguese. These Romance languages, as we have noted, still held pride of place in poetic practice, while Castilian was as yet not used for profane courtly poetry (though by the time of Alfonso X it was already a well-established language of prosaic learning and religious narrative poetry). Modern literary history makes very little of this important poetic practice at the court of Alfonso X, and the courtly poetry performed in Provençal and Galician-Portuguese receives very little attention in literary histories of the period, particularly in those studies geared toward more general or student audiences (Alborg 1966; M. Alvar 1980; Deyermond 1980; Valbuena Prat 1937), with some exceptions (Deyermond 1971, 10–11; Filgueira Valverde 1949, 599–603).

This is to be expected, because the interstitial, the poetic practice that crosses the linguistic and national boundaries constructed in modernity, is often minimized or altogether omitted in the story of what poetry used to be. After all, if literary history is an "act of forgetting" (Gies 2001, 3), something must be forgotten. This can be true even in the case of a single author, such as the iconic King Alfonso X, who himself composed a great deal of verse. His canonical songs of devotion to the Virgin Mary, the *Cantigas de Santa Maria*, despite being written in Galician-Portuguese (due to their royal authorship) achieved canonical status. The same Alfonso is also author of a corpus of scurrilous invective poetry in Galician-Portuguese, the so-called *Cantigas d'escarnho e maldizer*, that have almost completely evaded the gaze of the literary historiographer (Snow 1990). This is most likely due to the off-color nature more than to the language in which they were written, but the fact that the *Cantigas de Santa Maria* pass muster while the *Cantigas d'escarnho* do not tells us much about how modern literary historiography distorts the data to produce neater, more linguistically and culturally homogeneous narratives that serve national and regional agendas.

This distortion is even more extreme in the case of non-Romance languages. Literary histories of the court of Alfonso X make almost no mention of the Hebrew poets working in the service of the Learned King, the most notable of which was Todros Abulafia, who wrote a number of poems in which he writes of Alfonso's literary patronage and of life at his court (O'Callaghan 1993, 144–146; Procter 1951, 130–132; Roth 1985, 440; Salvador Martínez 2003, 446 n 44). Seen from the angle of Hebrew literary history, Abulafia is an outlier for his experimentation with troubadouresque styles, and as a consequence has received less critical attention than other Hebrew poets of his era who hewed more closely to the Andalusi models favored by Sephardic poets. These models mixed freely in Abulafia's verse with Biblical, troubadouresque, and other themes, motifs, and techniques of his own innovation, in a massive corpus totaling more than 1,200 compositions (Brann 1991, 149; Cole 2007, 257; Doron 1989, 42; Schirmann 1956, 2: 416; Targarona Borrás 1985).

If one accepts this still debated *thèse arabe* or Andalusi genesis of troubadour verse, this mixture of Andalusi and troubadouresque verse performed at the court of a Castilian king is nothing less than a poetic family reunion. In Abualafia's verse, the Andalusi muwashshah that gave rise to the Provençal *cansó* are reunited in Hebrew back in the Iberian Peninsula, where interstitiality was the norm and was responsible for any number of important innovations. The role of the court of Alfonso X in the emergence of courtly lyric says otherwise: al-Andalus was home to unparalleled poetic traditions in both Arabic and Hebrew, celebrated to this day as important classical legacies in the histories of both languages. Provençal gave us the troubadours, Galician-Portuguese gave us Alfonso's great collection of Marian verse, but all that Castilian could manage in the thirteenth century, when the Sicilian poets were inventing the sonnet that would catapult Petrarch to immortality, was Marian and hagiographic verse for priests and the faithful, but nothing actually sung at court (Antonelli 1989; Pötters 1998; Weiss 2006). Castile-León during this period was home to a great deal of poetic innovation by poets working in the interstices of national linguistic traditions, who for purposes of the history of Spanish Literature were not Spanish, despite the fact that they might have lived their entire lives in Castile-León.

Similarly, poets writing in the interstices between Hispano-Romance language and Semitic languages or even simply Semitic alphabets have been glossed over in the history of the Peninsula's literature (and when we say this we often mean the history of Castile-León). A quick perusal of almost any literary history of Spain, Portugal, or Catalonia written in the twentieth century reveals little to no mention of the Hebrew, Arabic, or Hispano-Romance other than the national tradition in question. Even Hebrew poetry written in the full flower of Romance vernacularity does not make the cut, with very few exceptions (Barletta et al. 2013; Cabo Aseguinolaza et al. 2010; de Riquer 1997). Though the histories of Hebrew literature tend to minimize the contributions of poets who wrote after the flowering of Romance vernacularization in the thirteenth century, Hebrew poets in Castile and Aragon were active well into the fifteenth century. Their work (as demonstrated in the Andalusi period by the Hebrew muwashshahat with Romance kharjat) was in constant dialogue with the Romance literatures of the Peninsula, a dialogue likewise minimized by critics of medieval Hebrew literature, who have tended to focus on what they perceive as the hermetically "Jewish" aspects of the Hebrew literature of the period. Just as the Hebrew poet Todros Abulafia experimented with troubadouresque motifs and techniques, including the cansó (love song) and tensó (invective) forms, other poets working in Hebrew likewise participated in the poetic practice of the day, in ways that would not seem extraordinary among poets working in Romance languages (Sáenz-Badillos 1996b). Some, such as Shem Tov ben Isaac Ardutiel of Carrión (Castile, 14th c., known as Santob de Carrión in Spanish), wrote verse in both Hebrew and Castilian, and carried on an internal dialogue between both languages which, for the modern literary critic, is crucial to fully understanding Ardutiel's work (Alba Cecilia 2008; Ardutiel 1947, 1980; Shepard 1978; Wacks 2012; Zemke 1997). Others, such as Vidal Benvenist (Zaragoza, 14th–15th c.), adapted popular themes and motifs in learned Hebrew compositions. Benvenist's *Tale of Efer and Dinah* is a rhyming prose narrative gloss on the *canción de malmaridada*, in which a young girl laments her loveless marriage to an older man. Benvenist reworks this topos into a morality tale ostensibly sung – or perhaps produced on stage – for the Purim festival of the Jewish communities of Zaragoza (Benvenist 2003; Wacks 2013).

In other cases Hebrew poets borrowed the melodies themselves of popular lyrics for their compositions in Hebrew, as they did in the Andalusi period for the Hebrew and Arabic muwashshah. We have manuscripts of Hebrew poetry both devotional and secular from the fifteenth century that specify, at the end of each composition, the first line of the Castilian popular lyric that lends its melody to the poem (Seroussi and Havassy 2009). In Catalonia we have a collection of bilingual Catalan-Hebrew Jewish wedding songs in which the bulk of each verse is in Catalan, with rhyming words in Hebrew. These *Cants de noces* demonstrate a literary diglossia that (as the muwashshahat and other genres of lyric poetry practiced on the Peninsula) crossed both language and register, in this case colloquial Catalan with Biblical and Rabbinic Hebrew (Argenter 2001; Riera i Sans 1974).

It is not surprising that Jewish or Muslim Iberians sang the songs of their day in their native languages; nor is it surprising that they would produce poems in which elements of their colloquial and confessional languages intertwine. We should remember that at no point in their history did Iberian Jews speak Hebrew as a native language, and that by the fifteenth century there were significant populations of Iberian Muslims whose primary language was Castilian or Aragonese (Boswell 1977, 382; Harvey 1990, 7; López-Morillas 2000, 54–57). However, literary histories that focus on the poetic production of a single dialect of Hispano-Romance or a single Semitic language of the Peninsula tend to obviate these interstitial voices.

Just as the Jewish Iberian who wrote in Hebrew, and the Muslim poets who wrote in Arabic, have been marginalized in national literary histories, the poetry of the Iberian Muslims who wrote in Castilian or Aragonese, but in the Arabic alphabet, have likewise suffered poorly in literary history. The *aljamiado* poetry of the Morisco authors of the fifteenth through early seventeenth centuries gives us an example of Islamic Spanish literature that, like the poetry by Iberia's Jews, demonstrates a familiarity and facility with the poetics of the dominant culture while putting these in the service of Islamic religion in a specific ethno-cultural milieu (Harvey 1974; López Baralt 2009, 24–25; Vázquez 2007). While the majority of aljamiado texts are in prose, there is a corpus of aljamiado poetry that bears striking resemblance to the *mester de clerecía* genre of hagiographic and Marian verse that flourished in Castilian in the thirteenth century (Barletta 2005, 151–55). Later aljamiado poets, writing at or after the time of the Moriscos' expulsion from the Peninsula, write sonnets and other popular forms in imitation of the most renowned Christian authors of the day.

In similar fashion, the Jews expelled from the Peninsula in 1492 continued to practice poetic forms both popular and learned that they brought with them from Spain well into Modernity and throughout the Mediterranean and the New World. A tour of the "afterlife" of medieval Castilian poetic forms as practiced by Sephardic Jews would take you around the Mediterranean and across the centuries. In the seventeenth century you might attend a prayer service of the Muslim-Jewish donmeh sect of the false messiah Shabbetai Tzvi in Constantinople, where they would sing the ballad of "La linda Melosina" as a kabbalistic hymn for welcoming the Sabbath on Friday night (Perets 2006). One hundred years later we join a Purim celebration in Izmir where we hear the story of Queen Esther sung in *coplas de Purim* (Hassán 2010; Romero 2011). In another hundred years, while out walking in Salonika we hear a mother singing a medieval *romance* (ballad) to her child at bedtime (Díaz Mas 1992, 123). Finally in current-day Jerusalem we enjoy a drink in a café while a young singer fronting a jazz band performs a program including traditional songs such as *Los bilbilicos* and her own original compositions, likewise sung in a dialect of medieval Castilian mixed with loanwords from Hebrew, Arabic, Turkish, and French (Cohen 2011).

Other poetic forms forged in the interstices of medieval Iberian poetic practice continue to bear fruit in the present day. In the Arab world, popular singers perform muwashshahat and zajals. Classical Andalusi orchestras in North Africa, France, and Israel perform settings for compositions by Andalusi poets. Many of the popular Iberian poetic forms that were born at the interstices escaped literary history, and were free to live their own lives outside of books and without being linked to the modern national project.

Works cited

Abu-Haidar, Jareer A. 2001. *Hispano-Arabic Literature and the Early Provençal Lyrics*. Richmond: Curzon.

Abulafia, David. 1988. *Frederick II: A Medieval Emperor*. London: Allen Lane.

Akehurst, F.R.P. and Judith M. Davis. 1995. *A Handbook of the Troubadours*. Berkeley, CA: University of California Press.

Alba Cecilia, Amparo. 2008. "El *Debate del cálamo y la espada*, de Jacob ben Eleazar de Toledo." *Sefarad* 68 (2): 291–314.

Alborg, Juan Luis. 1966. *Historia de la literatura española*. Madrid: Editorial Gredos.

al-Harizi, Judah. 1952. *Tahkemoni* [Hebrew]. Edited by Yisrael Toporovsky and Yisrael Zamorah. Tel Aviv: Mehaberot Lesifrut.

———. 1965. *The Takhkemoni*. Translated by Victor Reichert. Jerusalem: Raphael Haim Cohen.

———. 2001. *The Book of Tahkemoni: Jewish Tales From Medieval Spain*. Translated by David Simha Segal. London: The Littman Library of Jewish Civilization.

Alvar, Carlos. 1978. *Textos trovadorescos sobre España y Portugal*. Madrid: Cupsa.

———. 1984. "Poesía y política en la corte alfonsí." *Cuadernos Hispanoamericanos* 410: 4–21.

Alvar, Manuel. 1980. "La poesía en la edad media." In *Historia de la literatura española*. Edited by José María Díez Borque, vol. 1, 211–388. Madrid: Taurus.

al-Zajjali, Abu Yahya Ubaid Allah. 1971. *Proverbes Andalous de Abu Yahya Ubaid Allah Az-Zaggali (1220–1294)*. Edited by Mohamed Bencherifa. Ministère d'Etat Charge des Affaires Culturelles et de L'Enseignement Originel. Fez: Ministère des Affaires Culturelles.

Antonelli, Roberto. 1989. "L'invenzione del sonetto." In *Miscellanea di studi in honore di Aurelio Roncaglia*, edited by Aurelio Roncaglia, vol. 1, 35–75. Modena: Mucchi.

Ardutiel, Shem Tov ben Isaac. 1947. *Proverbios morales*. Edited by Ignacio González Llubera. Cambridge: Cambridge University Press.

———. 1980. *Maase Ha-Rav*. Tel Aviv: Tel Aviv University.

Argenter, Joan A. 2001. "Code-Switching and Dialogism: Verbal Practices among Catalan Jews in the Middle Ages." *Language in Society* 30 (3): 377–402.

Armistead, Samuel G. 1987. "A Brief History of Kharja Studies." *Hispania* 70: 8–15.

———. 2005. "El Problema de Las Jarchas." In *Dejar Hablar a Los Textos: Homenaje a Francisco Márquez Villanueva*, edited by Pedro M. Piñero Ramírez, 57–64. Seville: Universidad de Sevilla.

Barletta, Vincent. 2005. *Covert Gestures: Crypto-Islamic Literature as Cultural Practice in Early Modern Spain*. Minneapolis, MN: University of Minnesota Press.

Barletta, Vincent, Mark L. Bajus and Cici Malik, eds. 2013. *Dreams of Waking: Late Medieval and Early Modern Iberian Lyric Poetry*. Chicago: University of Chicago Press.

Beinin, Joel. 1994. "Writing Class: Workers and Modern Egyptian Colloquial Poetry (Zajal)." *Poetics Today* 15 (2): 191–215.

Beltrán, Vicenç. 2006. "Trovadores en la corte de Alfonso X." *Alcanate. Revista de estudios Alfonsíes* 5: 163–190.

Benvenist, Vidal. 2003. *The Tale of Efer and Dinah* Hebrew. Edited by Matti Huss. Jerusalem: Magnes.

Boase, Roger. 1977. *The Origin and Meaning of Courtly Love*. Manchester: Manchester University Press.

Bonner, Anthony. 1972. *Songs of the Troubadours*. New York: Schocken Books.

Boswell, John. 1977. *The Royal Treasure: Muslim Communities under the Crown of Aragon in the Fourteenth Century*. New Haven, CT: Yale University Press.

Brann, Ross. 1991. *The Compunctious Poet: Cultural Ambiguity and Hebrew Poetry in Medieval Spain*. Baltimore, MD: Johns Hopkins University.

Burnett, Charles. 1994. "The Translating Activity in Medieval Spain." In *The Legacy of Muslim Spain*, edited by Salma Khadra Jayyusi, 1036–1058. Leiden: Brill.

Buturovic, Amila. 2000. "Ibn Quzman." In *The Literature of Al-Andalus. The Cambridge History of Arabic Literature*, edited by María Rosa Menocal, Raymond P. Scheindlin, and Michael Anthony Sells, 292–305. Cambridge: Cambridge University Press.

Cabo Aseguinolaza, Fernando, Anxo Abuín González, and César Domínguez, eds. 2010. *A Comparative History of Literatures in the Iberian Peninsula*. Amsterdam: John Benjamins.

Cachia, Pierre. 1992. "Andalusi Belles Lettres." In *The Legacy of Muslim Spain*, edited by Salma Khadra Jayyusi, 308–316. Leiden: Brill.

Castro, Américo. 1948. *España en su historia: cristianos, moros y judíos*. Buenos Aires: Editorial Losada.

———. 1954. *The Structure of Spanish History*. Princeton, NJ: Princeton University Press.

———. 1961. *De la edad conflictiva*. Madrid: Persiles.

———. 1962. *La realidad histórica de España*, vol. 2. México: Porrúa.

Catalán, Diego. 1970. *Por campos del romancero; estudios sobre la tradición oral moderna*. Madrid: Editorial Gredos.

Cohen, Judith R. 2011. "'No so komo las de agora' (I'm Not Like Those Modern Girls): Judeo-Spanish Songs Meet the Twenty-First Century." *European Judaism* 44 (1): 151–164.

Cole, Peter. 2007. *The Dream of the Poem: Hebrew Poetry from Muslim and Christian Spain, 950–1492*. Princeton, NJ: Princeton University Press.

Dagenais, John. 2004. "Medieval Spanish Literature in the Twenty-First Century." In *The Cambridge History of Spanish Literature*, edited by David T. Gies, 39–57. Cambridge: Cambridge University Press.Decter, J. P. 2006. "The Rendering of Qur'anic Quotations in Hebrew Translations of Islamic Texts." *The Jewish Quarterly Review* 96 (3): 336–358.

de Riquer, Martí. 1997. *Antologia de poetes catalans*. Barcelona: Galàxia Gutenberg.

Deyermond, Alan D. 1971. *The Middle Ages*. London: Benn.

———, ed. 1980. *Historia y crítica de la literatura española: 1/1 Edad media, primer suplemento*. Barcelona: Crítica.

Díaz Mas, Paloma. 1992. *Sephardim: The Jews from Spain*. Translated by George K. Zucker. Chicago: University of Chicago Press.

Díaz Roig, Mercedes, ed. 1992. *Romancero Viejo*. Madrid: Cátedra.

Doron, Aviva. 1989. *A Poet in the King's Court: Todros Halevi Abulafia, Hebrew Poetry in Christian Spain* [Hebrew]. Tel Aviv: Dvir.

Drory, Rina. 2000a. "The Maqama." In *The Literature of Al-Andalus*, edited by María Rosa Menocal, Michael Sells, and Raymond P. Scheindlin, 190–210. Cambridge: Cambridge University Press.

———. 2000b. *Models and Contacts: Arabic Literature and Its Impact on Medieval Jewish Culture*. Leiden: Brill.

Filgueira Valverde, José. 1949. "Lírica medieval gallega y portuguesa." In *Historia general de las literaturas hispánicas*, edited by Guillermo Díaz-Plaja, 545–644. Barcelona: Editorial Barna.

Gaunt, Simon and Sarah Kay, eds. 1999. *The Troubadours: An Introduction*. Cambridge: Cambridge University Press.

Gensini, Sergio. 1986. *Politica e cultura nell'Italia di Federico II*. Pisa: Pacini.

Gies, David T. 2001. "The Funes Effect: Making Literary History." In *The Cambridge History of Spanish Literature*, edited by David T. Gies, 1–12. Cambridge: Cambridge University Press.

Gil, José S. 1985. *La escuela de traductores de Toledo y los colaboradores judíos*. Toledo: Diputación Provincial de Toledo.

Harvey, L. P. 1974. "Oral Composition and the Performance of Novels of Chivalry in Spain." *Forum for Modern Language Studies* 10 (3): 270–286.

———. 1990. *Islamic Spain 1250–1500*. Chicago: University of Chicago Press.

Hassán, Iacob M. 2010. *Las coplas de Purim*. Madrid: Hebraica Ediciones.

Hazran, Yusri. 2013. "The Zajal: Popular Poetry and the Struggle over Lebanon's History." *Middle Eastern Literatures* 16 (2): 169–188.

Ibn, Quzman and F. Corriente. 1984. *El Cancionero Hispanoarabe*. Madrid: Editora Nacional.

Ibn Shabbetai, Judah ben Isaac. 1991. *The Offering of Judah, Succour of Women, and Wellspring of Justice* [Hebrew]. Edited by Matti Huss. Jerusalem: Hebrew University.

Jacquart, D. 1991. "L'école Des Traducteurs." In *Tolède, XII ᵉ–XIII ᵉ Siècles*, edited by Louis Cardaillac, 177–191. Paris: Editions Autrement.

Jayyusi, Salma K. 1992. "Andalusi Poetry: The Golden Period." In *The Legacy of Muslim Spain*, edited by Salma Khadra Jayyusi, 317–366. Leiden: Brill.

Kozodoy, Neal. 1977. "Reading Medieval Hebrew Love Poetry." *AJS Review* 2: 111–129.

López Baralt, Luce. 2009. *La literatura secreta de los últimos musulmanes de España*. Madrid: Trotta.

López-Morillas, Consuelo. 1999. "Lost and Found? Yça of Segovia and the Qur'ân among the Mudejars and Moriscos." *Journal of Islamic Studies* 10: 277–292.

———. 2000. "Language." In *The Literature of al-Andalus*, edited by María Rosa Menocal, Michael Sells, and Raymond P. Scheindlin, 33–59. Cambridge: Cambridge University Press.

Menéndez Pidal, Ramón, ed. 1968. *Romancero hispánico*. Madrid: Espasa-Calpe.

Menocal, María Rosa. 1987. *The Arabic Role in Medieval Literary History: A Forgotten Heritage*. Philadelphia, PA: University of Pennsylvania Press.

———. 1994. *Shards of Love: Exile and the Origins of the Lyric*. Durham, NC: Duke University Press.

———. 2002. *The Ornament of the World*. Boston, MA: Little Brown.

———. 2004. "Beginnings." In *The Cambridge History of Spanish Literature*, edited by David Gies, 58–74. Cambridge: Cambridge University Press.

Menocal, María Rosa, Raymond P. Scheindlin, and Michael Anthony Sells, eds. 2000. *The Literature of al-Andalus. The Cambridge History of Arabic Literature*. Cambridge: Cambridge University Press.

Milá y Fontanals, Manuel. 1966. *De los trovadores en España*. Barcelona: Consejo Superior de Investigaciones Científicas.

Millás Vallicrosa, José María. 1949. "Literatura Hebraicoespañola." In *Historia general de las literaturas hispánicas*, edited by Guillermo Díaz-Plaja, 145–193. Barcelona: Barna.

Monroe, James T. 2004. *Hispano-Arabic Poetry: A Student Anthology*. Piscataway, NJ: Gorgias Press.

———. 1985. "Prolegómenos al estudio de Ibn Quzman: El poeta como bufón." *Nueva Revista de Filología Hispánica* 34: 769–799.

———. 1988. "Maimonides on the Mozarabic Lyric." *La Corónica* 17 (2): 18–32.

———. 1992. "Zajal and Muwashshaha: Hispano-Arabic Poetry and the Romance Tradition." In *The Legacy of Muslim Spain*, edited by Salma Khadra Jayyusi, 398–419. Leiden: Brill.

———. 2013. "Why Was Ibn Quzman Not Awarded the Title of 'Abu Nuwas of the West?' ('Zajal 96', the Poet, and his Critics)." *Journal of Arabic Literature* 64 (3): 293–334.

Nykl, A. R. 1946. *Hispano-Arabic Poetry, and its Relations with the Old Provençal Troubadours*. Baltimore, MD: J. H. Furst.

O'Callaghan, Joseph F. 1993. *The Learned King: The Reign of Alfonso X of Castile*. Philadelphia, PA: University of Pennsylvania Press.

Orta Velázquez, Guillermo. 1981. *El corrido mexicano*. México: Porrúa.

Pagis, Dan. 1976. *Innovation and Tradition in Secular Hebrew Poetry: Spain and Italy* [Hebrew]. Jerusalem: Keter Israel.

Perets, Avner, ed. 2006. *Water, Fire, and Love: Love Songs and Other Mystical Poems of the Sabbateans* [Hebrew and Ladino]. Ma'aleh Adumim: Ben Gurion University.

Pötters, Wilhelm. 1998. *Nascita del sonetto: metrica e matematica al tempo di Federico II.* Memoria del tempo 13. Ravenna: Longo.

Procter, Evelyn. 1951. *Alfonso X of Castile: Patron of Literature and Learning.* Oxford: Oxford University Press.

Reynolds, Dwight. 2000. "Musical 'Membrances of Medieval Muslim Spain." In *Charting Memory: Recalling Medieval Spain*, edited by Stacy N. Beckwith, 229–262. New York: Garland.

Riera i Sans, Jaume, ed. 1974. *Cants de noces dels jueus catalans.* Barcelona: Curial.

Robinson, Cynthia. 2001. *In Praise of Song.* Leiden: Brill.

Romero, Elena. 2011. *Los yantares de Purim; coplas y poemas sefardíes de contenido folclórico: estudio y edición de textos.* Barcelona: Tirocinio.

Roth, Norman. 1982. "'Deal Gently With the Young Man': Love of Boys in Medieval Hebrew Poetry of Spain." *Speculum* 57 (1): 20–51.

———. 1985. "Jewish Translators at the Court of Alfonso X." *Thought* 60 (239): 439–455.

———. 1991. "'Fawn of My Delights': Boy-Love in Hebrew and Arabic Verse." In *Sex in the Middle Ages: A Book of Essays*, edited by Joyce Salisbury, 157–172. New York: Garland.

Sáenz-Badillos, Ángel. 1996a. "Participación de judíos en las traducciones de Toledo." In *La escuela de traductores de Toledo*, 65–70. Toledo: Diputación Provincial de Toledo.

———. 1996b. "Hebrew Invective Poetry: The Debate between Todros Abulafia and Phinehas Halevi." *Prooftexts* 16: 49–73.

Salvador Martínez, H. 2003. *Alfonso X, El Sabio: una biografía.* Madrid: Ediciones Polifemo.

———. 2010. *Alfonso X, the Learned: A Biography.* Leiden: Brill.

Scheindlin, Raymond P. 1986. *Wine, Women, & Death: Medieval Hebrew Poems on the Good Life.* Philadelphia, PA: Jewish Publication Society.

———. 1991. *The Gazelle: Medieval Hebrew Poems on God, Israel, and the Soul.* Philadelphia, PA: Jewish Publication Society.

Schippers, Arie. 1994. *Spanish Hebrew Poetry and the Arabic Literary Tradition: Arabic Themes in Hebrew Andalusian Poetry.* Leiden: Brill.

Schirmann, Jefim. 1956. *Hebrew Poetry in Spain and Provence* [Hebrew]. Jerusalem; Tev Aviv: Mossad Bialik; Dvir.

Seroussi, Edwin and Rivka Havassy. 2009. *Incipitario Sefardí: el cancionero judeoespañol en fuentes hebreas: siglos XV-XIX.* Madrid: Consejo Superior de Investigaciones Científicas.

Shannon, Jonathan H. 2006. *Among the Jasmine Trees: Music and Modernity in Contemporary Syria.* Middletown, CT: Wesleyan University Press.

———. 2007. "Performing Al-Andalus, Remembering Al-Andalus: Mediterranean Soundings from Mashriq to Maghrib." *The Journal of American Folklore* 120 (477): 308–334.

Shepard, Sanford. 1978. *Shem Tov: His World and his Words.* Miami: Ediciones Universal.

Smith, Colin. 1996. *Spanish Ballads.* 2nd ed. London: Bristol Classical Press.

Snow, Joseph Thomas. 1977. *The Poetry of Alfonso X, El Sabio: A Critical Bibliography.* London: Grant & Cutler.

———. 1990. "The Satirical Poetry of Alfonso X: A Look at its Relationship to the *Cantigas de Santa Maria*." In *Alfonso X of Castile: The Learned King (1221–1284)*, edited by Francisco Márquez Villanueva and Carlos Alberto Vega, 110–127. Cambridge, MA: Harvard University Press.

Targarona Borrás, Judit. 1985. "Todros Ben Yehuda ha-Leví Abulafia, un poeta hebreo en la corte de Alfonso X el Sabio." *Helmantica* 36 (110): 195–210.

Valbuena Prat, Ángel. 1937. *Historia de la literatura española.* Barcelona: Gustavo Gili.

Vázquez, Miguel Ángel. 2007. "Poesía morisca (o de cómo el español se convirtió en lengua literaria del islam)." *Hispanic Review* 75 (3): 219–242.

Wacks, David A. 2012. "Vernacular Anxiety and the Semitic Imaginary: Shem Tov Isaac Ibn Ardutiel de Carrión and His Critics." *Journal of Medieval Iberian Cultural Studies* 4 (2): 167–184.

————. 2013. "Vidal Benvenist's *Efer ve-Dinah* between Hebrew and Romance." In *A Sea of Languages: Literature and Culture in the Pre-Modern Mediterranean*, edited by Suzanne Akbari and Karla Mallette, 217–231. Toronto: University of Toronto Press.

Wasserstein, David. 1991. "The Language Situation in Al-Andalus." In *Studies on the Muwassah and the Kharja*, edited by Alan Jones and Richard Hitchcock, 1–15. Oxford: Oxford University Press.

Weiss, Julian. 2006. *The* Mester de Clerecía: *Intellectuals and Ideologies in Thirteenth-Century Castile*. Woodbridge: Tamesis.

Yellin, David and Dan Pagis. 1972. *A Theory of Sephardic Poetry* [Hebrew]. Jerusalem: Y.L Magnes.

Zemke, John. 1997. *Critical Approaches to the* Proverbios Morales *of Shem Tov of Carrión: An Annotated Bibliography*. Newark, DE: Juan de la Cuesta Hispanic Monographs.

Zwartjes, Otto. 1998. *Love Songs from Al-Andalus: History, Structure and Meaning of the Kharja*. Leiden: Brill.

8

REVISITING THE HISTORY OF MEDIEVAL TRANSLATION IN THE IBERIAN PENINSULA

Julio-César Santoyo

La part des traductions dans l'ensemble du corpus que nous a légué le Moyen Âge espagnol, si elle était établie quantitativement, étonnerait par son importance.
(Clare and Chevalier 1972, 159)

Tracing the history of medieval translation in the Iberian Peninsula is an extremely complex task, especially because a degree of periodization is rendered necessary by the very broad time span involved, and the existence of texts and documentation from different stages within it. Indeed, as far as the history of translation is concerned, the early and late centuries of the Middle Ages have virtually nothing in common, to such an extent that accounts of these two periods seem at times to be dealing with two separate countries; in fact, this formulation may not be so far from the truth, bearing in mind that for centuries there were two cultural and linguistic traditions inhabiting the Iberian space: the Christian and the Muslim. Only very tentatively, then, is the following schema suggested, by which the medieval millennium may be divided into three stages: 1) the fifth century to the eleventh, where both texts themselves and paratextual documentation are very rare; 2) the twelfth century, where texts are relatively abundant, but paratextual documentation is still very scarce; and 3) the thirteenth to the fifteenth centuries, a period where texts abound and paratextual documentation is more common, but which in turn must be subdivided into: a) the thirteenth century, when Arabic is the principal source language, and b) the fourteenth and fifteenth centuries, which feature a wide variety of source and target languages (Latin, Greek, Hebrew, Arabic, Castilian, Catalan, Galician-Portuguese, Aragonese, Provençal, French, Italian, English), and in which textual interaction within the Peninsula is common. Against these temporal co-ordinates three different religious and cultural traditions must be plotted (Jewish, Christian, and Muslim), as well as various nationalities which constantly influence one another and whose borders are unstable.

The picture is thus a complex one, but to see it clearly it is also necessary to correct several errors which have been perpetuated in previous studies, and some mistakes which have been the *communis opinio* for more than 100 years. The truth is that we are still far from having a panoramic view of what the translator's task was during the 1,000 years of the Peninsular Middle Ages, when a multi-faceted textual corpus was created, of which only one facet – the book – is now given the attention it deserves. In the meantime, other clearly distinct sub-corpuses have been ignored, not only for having a different textual status, but also, more importantly, because of the different translation strategies that each one of them requires. The frequent medieval testimonies of the everyday practice of translation, for example, tend to show that it was not uncommon, at least from the end of the tenth century; such evidence comes from innumerable town charters and legal codes translated into Castilian, along with documents detailing land divisions and royal, noble, and monastic privileges, private wills, diplomatic and other correspondence between Christian and Muslim kingdoms, papal bulls, and so on, all of which were translated with a strictly local purpose, and consistently show a clear desire for precision. In these works, the act of translation is the result of the immediate need for their content to be understood. *Est latine, non legitur*: since it is in Latin, it cannot be read, and therefore it is translated. The same may be said of Arabic: *est arabice, non legitur*. Everything indicates, in effect, that the practical importance of this type of everyday translation means that the search for a precise equivalence is the overriding objective. This is a long way from what Lemarchand (1995, 30) considers normal among medieval book translators, when she claims that "se sentían perfectamente autorizados para modificar el texto de un autor en función del público al que iba destinado." In fact, book translation and everyday translation are opposing practices, because they represent two opposing conceptualizations of translation carried out for clearly different purposes.

However, as well as stand-alone translations such as books and documents, a third sub-corpus of "inserted" translations is already very common by the thirteenth century; this has also been virtually, if not completely, ignored. These consist of the inclusion in an original text of isolated translations from other (Arabic or Latin) texts, which are at first grafted onto the framework of the original composition, usually as quotations of various kinds. These are fairly literal translations made by the author of the composition into which they are inserted, who provides a vernacular version of a textual fragment written in a language which the reader will not know. Such inserted translations are very frequent, for example, in the vast historio-graphical work of the collaborators of Alfonso X. And together with this kind of translated text, which is usually reasonably lengthy, comes a second, microtextual variant: very short translations inserted in vernacular texts such as sermons and homilies, which are very literal, are almost always produced by the author of the work. The texts in this group therefore feature very different translation strategies from those of the previous two sub-corpuses.

The gloss is another extraordinarily widespread phenomenon, in its twin form of translation glosses and explanation glosses. The first of these may be located in various parts of the page (they may be marginal, intratextual, interlineal, and so on), and were very common in the Iberian Peninsula from the days of the first texts, whether those texts were written in Latin or in Arabic, Hebrew, or the various Romance languages. Many of these glosses, especially the lexical glosses, are simply translations, and even though they do not constitute what we might call a "text," they form a very wide, diverse sub-corpus which differs from the characteristics of earlier texts, in terms of both typology and purpose. Meanwhile, it should not be forgotten that in the south and east of the Peninsula in particular, the daily need for this kind of interlinguistic mediation was the result of the extensive use of Arabic, which had to be rendered for the new Romance arrivals, whether Castilian, Aragonese, or Catalan. The constant presence of Arabic translators in day-to-day work should therefore come as no surprise. Oral translation was just as common as written translation, if not more so, and though it has obviously left no written texts, we do have a very wide sub-corpus of testimonies from across the whole medieval period, especially after 711, which often give us insight into the circumstances of the task of translation; these pieces of sociological-historical data are often just as important as linguistic data, if not more so. On the basis of these twin foundations of periodization and variety of corpus a story is built that will span 1,000 years, but the brief scope of this study means that, as so often, it will focus on book production.

* * *

It is eminently possible that the first translations to be known in the Iberian Peninsula from the mid-third century were variants of Old and New Testament texts from the *vetus latina*, which had earlier circulated among the Christian communities in northern Africa. Little is known of these, save for some speculation, until the late fourth century, when a married couple from Hispanic Andalucía, Lucinius and Theodora, received word of a new Latin version of the Bible and other texts, which Saint Jerome was working on in his Bethlehem retreat; they took what was then an unusual step, and sent six scribes there in the year 397, to make copies of Jerome's versions and bring them back to the Peninsula. Saint Jerome's letters make it quite clear that even during his own lifetime, a large part of the Vulgate Bible was known in Hispania, perhaps along with other original or translated works of his. Less than twenty years after the date of these letters, the Iberian Peninsula had its first translator, Avitus de Bracara (present-day Braga, in Portugal), who was in Jerusalem in 415. There he translated the story of the recent discovery of the tomb of the proto-martyr Saint Stephen from Greek into Latin. According to Gennadius of Massilia in his *De viris illustribus* (ca. 475), Avitus, "homo hispanus genere ante relatam Luciani presbyteri scripturam transtulit in Latinum sermonem et adiecta epistola sua per Orosium presbyterum Occidentalibus dedit" [(Avitus,) a Spaniard by race, translated the above mentioned work of the presbyter Lucianus into Latin, and sent it with his letter, by the hand of Orosius the presbyter, to the Western churches] (see Martínez Cavero and Beltrán Corvalán 2006, 593).

More than a century was to pass before the north-west of the Iberian Peninsula produced its first translators: in ca. 550 two clerics, Martinus and Paschasius, in a small monastery in Dume, once again near Braga, produced very literal Latin versions of several Greek originals – two collections of *exempla* and *sententiae*, and a run of 84 council canons. This was followed by almost four centuries of silence. The Muslim conquest of the Peninsula in 711 brought the collapse of the Visigothic kingdom, and with it the disappearance of all cultural activity in the small bastions of Christianity that survived in the mountainous north. In the rest of the country, the conquerors' Arabic was imposed over Latin, and what was left of the Christian population still living there – the Mozarabs – either lost their own language or became bilingual. If there was any kind of translation activity (as there must have been), hardly any evidence survives to attest to this fact. The texts that do survive are all very late, such as those from the second half of the tenth century: the four gospels translated into Arabic by Ishaq ibn Balasq al-Qurtubi in 946; the so-called *Calendar of Cordova*, a parallel text in Arabic with a Latin translation, which Bishop Recemundus presented to al-Hakam II in ca. 961; or the psalter translated by Hafs ibn Albar al-Quti in 989. There is little more. Perhaps the most notable translation was the Arabic version of Dioscorides' Greek pharmacopoeia *Περὶ ὕλης ἰατρικῆς* [On Medical Matters], which an embassy of the Byzantine emperor gave as a gift to Abd al-Rahman III, and which was then translated into Arabic by a small group of Jewish and Christian intellectuals in ca. 951. The Byzantine delegation also gave the caliph another codex containing Paulus Orosius's work *Adversus paganos historiarum libri septem*, which was also translated into Arabic. Around the same time, in 967, the young Gerbert d'Aurillac (the future Pope Sylvester II) came to study at the cathedral school in Vic, close to Barcelona and to the monastery at Ripoll, whose library contained a small selection of scientific treatises on topics such as the astrolabe, geometry, astronomy, and the manufacture of timepieces, all translated from Arabic into Latin.

Nor were these the only translations produced in Catalonia during the late tenth century: there is also a record of a treaty entitled *De multiplicatione et divisione numerum*, translated by a certain Joseph; a *liber de astrologia* translated by Sunifred Llobet; and a *Mathematica Alhandrei*, whose translator is anonymous. After these few examples, silence once again descends, scarcely to be interrupted throughout the whole of the eleventh century, save for very brief accounts of a very few Arabic to Hebrew and Latin to Arabic translations, the second of these groups including a significant collection of canons and papal decrees translated in 1049–50 by the Mozarabic priest Vincentius. Otherwise, the eleventh century is bereft of translations. In Europe as a whole, this was not a propitious time for the cultivation of the arts; still less for that of letters. In the Iberian Peninsula, this was a time of Christian and Muslim attack and counter-attack, including the reconquest of Coimbra (1064), Toledo (1085), and Valencia (1094), while the caliphate of Cordova was split into more than thirty local *taifas*; this, then, was a *siglo de hierro* in which, as Lemay notes, "on n'a pratiquement aucun vestige d'échange scientifique ou philosophique entre Latins et Arabes ou Mozarabes" (1963, 643–644).

* * *

Moses Sefardí, a Jew baptized as Petrus Alphonsus, physician to the King of Aragon and Henry I of England, opens our survey of the twelfth century with a classic of the Middle Ages, *Disciplina clericalis*: a miscellany of anecdotes and aphorisms taken from Arabic and even some Hebrew sources, translated from those languages and adapted to fit the work's moralizing tenor. His contemporary, Abraham ibn Ezra, traversed much of Europe while he made Hebrew translations of Arabic commentaries on al-Khwarizmi's astronomical tables, as well as texts on astronomy, astrology, and geomancy. Nonetheless, this century has been defined as the "first generation" of what has erroneously been termed the "School of Translators" in Toledo: there never was such a school in Toledo, either in the twelfth century with Archbishop Raimundus, or in the thirteenth with Alfonso X. All modern criticism without exception denies the existence of this "school," which is now unanimously seen as myth, fiction, or legend. It also denies that Archbishop Raimundus was the founder or patron of any such "school:" of all the twelfth-century translations written in Toledo, which number over 100, only one is dedicated to that prelate, and only one is dedicated to his successor in the seat of Toledo, Archbishop Juan. More than 200 years ago, Amable Jourdain deduced a whole "school of translators" from these two dedications and the presence of three translators in Toledo, but that "school" never existed. What is true – and this is all that is documented – is that only three of the twelfth-century translators who were traditionally ascribed to this non-existent "school" worked in Toledo; the rest worked in Tarazona, Barcelona, León, Limia (in Galicia), Tudela, or Segovia. These men worked individually or in one-off collaborations; some were itinerant, while others were based in one place; some were Christian, others Jewish; some from the Peninsula, others from lands beyond the Pyrenees, including Italy, England, Normandy, Belgium, Scotland, Istria, and Germany. In the early years of that century, for instance, Barcelona saw the frequent collaboration of Plato Tiburtinus (from Tivoli, near Rome) and Abraham bar Hiyya: the former produced around ten texts translated from Arabic into Latin, including Ptolemy's *Tetrabiblos*; the second wrote Hebrew translations of Arabic texts. For five years between 1138 and 1142, two friends and translators, Hermann of Carinthia and Robert of Ketton (or Chester), lived *circa fluvium Hiberum*, perhaps in Tudela (Navarre), where there was a significant Muslim, Mozarabic, and Jewish population; both men were engaged in the study and translation of Arabic texts on astronomy and geometry, such as al-Khwarizmi's *Algebra*, Euclid's *Elements*, or the

Liber de compositione alchymiae – the first such work known in Western Europe. In 1142, Peter the Venerable (Petrus Venerabilis), Abbot of Cluny, who was interested in Islamic texts and especially the *Koran*, paid a good sum of money to commission its translation from Robert of Ketton and Hermann of Carinthia, who spent months collaborating on the project; also involved were a Mozarab, Petrus Toletanus; a Muslim, Mohamed; and the Abbot's own secretary, Pierre de Poitiers. The translations commissioned by the Abbot – the *Koran* along with four minor texts – were completed in July 1143. However, all the indications are that the translation of the *Koran* in particular was the work of Robert of Ketton, with the contributions of the other members of the team limited to collaboration in isolated sections. Robert remained in the Peninsula until his death (post 1160), and his biography as arch-deacon of the diocese of Pamplona and Tudela, and a man trusted by the kings of Navarre, is familiar enough (see Santoyo 1999, 82–85).

Hermann, however, crossed the Pyrenees to Béziers and Toulouse before 1143 was out; thereafter, his name disappears from the record. At around the same time, the Norman cleric Hugo de Cintheaux (Hugo Sanctilliensis) was also working alone in Tarazona under the patronage of Bishop Michael (the fictitious name "Hugo de Santalla" has been attributed to this translator without foundation, along with the erroneous claim that he came from the north-west of the Peninsula). He was interested above all in texts relating to astrology, alchemy, geomancy, and the arts of divination, and penned a dozen Latin translations of Arabic originals which seem to have come from the library of the Banu Hud, petty kings of Rueda de Jalón between 1110 and 1131, which stands one or two days distant from Tarazona. Iohannes Hispalensis (*nom de plume* of Johannes ibn David [Avendauth], who was perhaps a *converso* or the son of one) began to work on translations in ca. 1118, in the Galician region of Limia, where he translated into Latin several texts of pseudo-Aristotle, Qusta ben Luqa, al-Tabari, al-Harrani, Masha'allah ibn Athari, Albumasar, and al-Farghani. From 1135, he worked on his translations in Toledo, until ca. 1150; irrespective of dates, he used variants of a certain formula in the majority of his translations, which identify them as his: *cum/sub/in laude Dei et eius auxilio*, *cum/sub laude Dei et eius adiutorio*, and so on. He was a translator of remarkable range, as his many works deal with topics including medicine, philosophy, mathematics, astronomy and astrology, the use of the astrolabe, and more. He collaborated with Dominicus Gundisalvi, arch-deacon of the Cathedral of Toledo, on three translations of ibn Gabirol, al-Gazzali, and Avicenna; in the last of these, in a statement which perhaps holds true for all three, the *modus operandi* is described by ibn Dawud as "me singula verba vulgariter proferente et Dominico archidiacono singula in latinum convertente" (Santoyo 1999, 114): ibn Dawud gave an oral translation of a fragment of Arabic in the vernacular, proceeding word by word, and Dominicus retranslated from the vernacular into Latin. Dominicus Gundisalvi also put his name to at least ten translations done without collaborators, most of which were of Arabic philosophical texts. Very soon after, now in the second half of the century, Gerardo de Cremona (Gherardus Cremonensis) came to Toledo, "magnus linguae arabicae translator." His name enters the record in Toledo in 1157, as his *socii* claim that he came to the city because he could not find a copy of Ptolemy's *Almagest* in Italy. Either alone, or in an imprecise collaboration with some of his *socii*, of whom we know only the Mozarab Galib, he translated around eighty works from Arabic into Latin, many of which were originally in Greek, including works on medicine, philosophy, physics and mechanics, mathematics, astronomy and astrology, geometry, and alchemy: his output as a translator was remarkable, yet he never put his name to the works.

Scarcely seventy years passed, then, between 1118, the probable date of the first translation by Iohannes Hispalensis, and the year of Gerardo de Cremona's death in 1187; but these seventy years were to mark a paradigm shift in the Peninsula and in Europe as a whole. Nothing would ever be the same again in European culture: these 100 or so works translated from Arabic, which passed from the Peninsula into the rest of Europe and were spread throughout the continent in manuscript copies, took with them a new kind of medicine, a new astronomy and astrology, a new alchemy, a new kind of philosophical thought, a new mathematics and geometry, and an introduction to Islamic religious texts; in short, this was "an entirely new summa of scientific knowledge, based on sources which were almost completely unknown fifty years previously, but which were to remain standard textbooks for many centuries to come" (Burnett 1978, 133).

* * *

A new generation of Arabic-Latin translators, unrelated to the earlier translators noted previously and apparently unrelated to one another, emerged in the late twelfth century and early thirteenth: Marcos de Toledo (Marcus Toletanus), who became Canon in 1198, was a physician, translated several treatises by Galen and Hunayn ibn Ishaq, and in 1209–10 produced a new Latin version of the *Koran*. He was followed by several foreigners who lived for some time on the Iberian Peninsula, such as the Italian Salione Buzzacarini (Salio da Padova), or Alfred of Sareshel and Michael Scott, from Britain. Scott spent more than five years in Toledo, where, with the help of a certain Abuteus, he produced Latin translations of Arabic copies of al-Bitruji's *De sphaera*, and Aristotle's *De animalibus*. The last, and youngest, of this second generation of itinerant translators was Hermannus Alemannus (Herman the German), Canon of Palencia and then of Toledo, and finally Bishop of Astorga. Between 1240 and 1246 in Toledo, he made Latin translations of several of Averroes's and al-Farabi's commentaries on Aristotle's *Ethics*, *Poetics*, and *Rhetoric*. As all this implies, until the mid-thirteenth century, translations were usually from Arabic into Latin (and vice versa). There is only very slight evidence of texts being translated into the emerging Romance languages on the Peninsula, and these were always from Latin, such as the Catalan version of the Visigothic *Forum Iudicum*, or the six sermons known as the *Homilies d'Organyà*, which are really adaptations, rather than translations, of a collection of French sermons. As regards Castilian, the real turning point for the abandoning of Latin and the adoption of Castilian as the target language of translation must be said to come with the express wishes of Alfonso X, even before he came to the throne in 1252. Translators formed part of Alfonso's courtly surroundings, as his court included a group of twenty Christian, Muslim, and Jewish men, some Hispanic and others Italian, who were clerics, *alfaquines* or physicians, notaries, and royal scribes; these men included Bonaventura da Siena or Pietro da Reggio, Judah ben Moshe ha-Kohen or Samuel ha-Levi, Garci Pérez, Álvaro de Oviedo, and Ferrando de Toledo or Bernardo el Arábigo. For more than thirty years, these and other translators translated into Castilian – and sometimes subsequently into Latin or French from the Castilian – a wide array of Arabic texts which almost always corresponded to a personal interest of the King, to such an extent that the King himself would intervene in certain parts of the process: the choice of text and translator(s), revision of language and style, details of the final edition, and so on; the texts involved ranged from the sixteen treatises that comprise the *Libros del saber de astrología* to the *Libro de la escala de Mahoma*, in a parallel translation into Castilian, Latin, and French, or the *Libro del açedrex, dados e tablas*.

As I have said, Alfonso X's translators never constituted a "school." Nor, if there had been such a "school," would it have been located in Toledo, which the King visited only very rarely. As was the norm at the time, the court of Alfonso X was an itinerant court: it went where the King was, and the ruler's translators were also to be found where the King was, simply because for many of them, their principal employment was as part of the retinue that surrounded the

King. This explains why it was in Seville (and not in Toledo) that in 1264 Bonaventura da Siena translated the *Libro de la escala de Mahoma* for the King, from Castilian into French; or why it was Seville (and not Toledo) that in 1283 saw the Castilian version of the *Libro del açedrex, dados e tablas*. As well as the great catalogue of stand-alone translations, Alfonso X's collaborators also made frequent use of "inserted" translations: textual fragments, which could be very significant in length, translated from Arabic or Latin and included in the composition of other works, such as the *General Estoria*, which contains the prose translation-adaptation of the whole ten books of Lucan's *Pharsalia*, as well as long passages from Ovid's *Heroides*, and a litany of sections directly translated, adapted, or summarized from Paulus Orosius, Eusebius of Caesarea, Saint Jerome, Pliny the Elder, Isidore of Seville, and so on. To that sizeable corpus of translations – inserted and stand-alone, partial and complete – must be added a good number of anonymously translated works of wisdom literature, which stem from the same courtly environment of Fernando III, Prince Fadrique, Alfonso X, and his successor Sancho IV; these included such works as the *Sendebar*, *Poridat de poridades*, the *Libro de los buenos proverbios*, the *Libro de Apolonio*, *Barlaam & Josafat*, and so on. Also from this period are a few translations which subtly foreshadow the new cultural tendencies that began to arrive from the other side of the Pyrenees, such as the Castilian translation which Alonso de Paredes and Pascual Gómez made to Sancho IV's commission in ca. 1292 of Brunetto Latini's *Livres dou tresor*. Nonetheless, the Castilian court did not have a monopoly on translation during that period. Away from the court and the interests of each monarch, Arabic medicine was a topic of considerable interest, especially among the Christian and Jewish practitioners who used their knowledge of the subject to translate into Latin, Romance, or Hebrew a good number of texts by Avicenna, Maimonides, Hippocrates, Qusta ben Luqa, Averroes, Galen, al-Razi, al-Zahrawi, and more. Outstanding among the Christian physician-translators are Arnau de Vilanova, his nephew Armengaud de Blaise, and Berenguer Eimeric, who translated al-Zahrawi's *Tasrif*, first from Arabic into Catalan and then from Catalan into Latin.

Farther south, in the *studium arabicum et hebraicum* founded by the Dominicans in Murcia, Fray Domingo Marroquino translated the *Liber de egritudinibus oculorum*, and his student Rufino Alejandrino translated the *Isagoge in quaestiones medicae*, by Hunayn ibn Ishaq. Jewish physicians translating the same authors into Hebrew included Sem Tob de Tortosa, his son Abraham de Tortosa, Jacob ha-Qatan, and Solomon ben Josef ibn Ayyub ha-Sefardi; but they were not alone in this task. Also worthy of mention is the activity of many other Jewish translators across the whole of the Peninsula, many of them wandering globe-trotters and insatiable visitors of all parts of Europe; in the main, their translations were exclusively from Arabic into Hebrew, for the benefit of their own linguistic communities. Perhaps the most notable of all was the first of that century: the poet Judah ben Solomon al-Harizi, who produced Arabic-to-Hebrew versions of a dozen works by Maimonides, al-Hariri de Basora, Hunayn ibn Ishaq, Galen, and Aristotle. Many others followed in his footsteps throughout the century, leaving an enormous body of translated work that is now scarcely mentioned and even less studied: Judah ben Solomon ha-Kohen, who translated his own encyclopaedic treatise *Midrash ha-Hokmah* from Arabic into Hebrew; Zerahiah Gracián, a physician and philosopher who, while he was in Rome, translated a considerable number of texts by Aristotle, Averroes, Avicenna, al-Farabi, Maimonides, and Galen; Abraham ben Samuel ha-Levi ibn Hasdai; Sem Tob ben Josef ibn Falaquera; Isaac Albalag; and so on. The century closed with one of the most remarkable figures of the age, the indefatigable Ramon Llull, a trilingual author and self-translator writing in Arabic, Catalan, and Latin, whose extensive and varied work includes theology, philosophy, and Christian apologetics.

* * *

The fourteenth century has been forgotten in the Peninsular history of translation, a no-man's-land between the translation activity of Alfonso X *el Sabio* and the wave of translations brought by the fifteenth century. Yet it represents a crucial period of that history insofar as it marked a decisive move away from previous tradition. With Arabic and Hebrew now limited to religious contexts or very restricted cultural circles, Latin instead became the essential source language for the whole of the fourteenth century, as there was a great abundance of translations from Latin across the whole of the Peninsula, and with Catalan a much more common target language than Castilian. The first hints of proto-humanist tendencies that reached the Peninsula from across the Pyrenees found an immediate and warm welcome in the Catalan language. The large group of Catalan translators includes Metge, Antoni Canals, Jacme Conesa, Guillem Nicolau, Ferrer Saiol, Pere Saplana, Antoni Ginebreda, Pons Saclota, Romeu Sabruguera, Guillem Corretger, Berenguer de Sarriera, and many more; there were also numerous anonymous translators active especially during the second half of the century, whose Catalan versions included not only a vernacular Bible and a *Koran* translated from the Latin, but also works by Seneca, Valerius Maximus, Ovid, Sallust, Palladius Rutilius, Frontinus, Boethius, Petrarch, André le Chapelain, Guido delle Colonne, Aegidius Romanus, Richard de Fournival, William of Conches, Albertano da Brescia, Laurent du Bois, Jacobus de Cessolis, and more. Not to forget the many practical and scientific translations, especially pertaining to medicine and veterinary science. Both in number and in range this is far greater than what is found in Castilian translation, but there too, especially in the second half of the century, we may still find a number of titles translated from Latin texts or from intermediary French versions, for which, at the end of the century, Chancellor López de Ayala was often directly or indirectly responsible; these include three decades of Livy, the *Historia troyana* of Guido delle Colonne, Boccaccio's *De casibus virorum et foeminarum illustrium*, the *Sententiae* of pseudo-Isidore of Seville, the Book of Job, and so on. To this short account of translations bearing López de Ayala's signature must be added a brief list of Castilian texts which ultimately derive from Latin originals, such as the *De regimine principum* of Aegidius Romanus, translated by Juan García de Castrojeriz; or Gottfried von Franken's *Tractado de plantar o enxerir arboles o de conseruar el vino*. Aragonese is also a popular language to translate into or to compose in during this century, to a degree that has perhaps been unmatched since then, especially as a target language for translations.

The patron of this vogue in translations was Juan Fernández de Heredia, Grand Master of the Hospitaller Order of Saint John of Jerusalem. Unlike other patrons such as Alfonso X or the Marquis of Santillana, Heredia's interests lay above all in historiographical topics. The list of Aragonese translations which were made under his patronage is certainly wide in scope, and includes the first translations into Aragonese from Greek (Thucydides, Plutarch, John of Zonoras), and from Italian, French, Latin, and Catalan (Orosius, Paulus Diaconus, Marco Polo, the *Crónica de los Reyes de Aragón*, the *Crónica troyana*, and so on); this formed "un corpus de obras realmente ingente, que en esta lengua no resulta parangonable con nada anterior ni posterior" (Alvar and Lucía 2002, 696). It is no surprise, then, that Heredia has been compared to Alfonso X: both showed a clear desire to give precedence to a Romance language as a target language, privileging Castilian or Aragonese over Latin. Nonetheless, the differences between the two cases are significant: by the time of the fourteenth century, the *auctoritas* of Arabic texts was somewhat reduced from the status they had held in the thirteenth; and the two men hardly shared the same personal tastes, as a brief survey of the texts each chose for translation will show. Indeed, these two men may illustrate the decisive move away from previous tradition alluded to in the foregoing discussion: Alfonso X is an archetypal example of the medieval world; Heredia, to a greater degree even than Chancellor Ayala, is a herald of the first stages of vernacular humanism.

The fourth Romance language with relevant activity in the field of translation is Galician-Portuguese, which offers for the first time during this century a short run of translations largely derived from Latin and Castilian texts. Moreover, it is also during this century that intra-Peninsular translations become a general phenomenon, with translations between Castilian and Galician-Portuguese (in both directions), and from Catalan to Castilian (the reverse, while not unheard of, was much less common). Indeed, the number of works translated from Catalan to Castilian was remarkable: in Riera's words, this body of work was "realmente impresionante: son muchísimos más de los que nadie había sospechado" (1989, 700). Finally, to this intra-Peninsular picture of translations from Latin, Greek, and Romance texts must be added the importance of three extra-Peninsular source languages: Italian, Provençal, and especially French, which included the works of John Mandeville, Laurent du Bois, Pierre Bersuire, Benoit de Sainte-Maure, and a good number of anonymous works, notably the Breton cycle, whose tales were translated into Castilian, Catalan, and Galician-Portuguese. This century also sees the first tentative steps on the Peninsula towards reflecting on translation itself, with embryonic analyses of the process of translation, its instruments, or the conditions under which it is carried out: these reflections are almost always clearly set down in a translator's prologue. Nonetheless, what is notable is that for the first time a meta-language is beginning to be developed concerning the process of translation, in the languages of the Peninsula.

In conclusion, then, our account of translation in the fourteenth century may be summarized thus: the practice of translation was widespread, especially in Catalonia, which often acted as a cultural bridge to the rest of the Peninsula; the "centre" of translation thus moved from Castile to the Kingdom of Aragon, and the growing activity of translation was uncoupled from royal patronage and "decentralized," spreading widely across the whole Peninsula and even to places beyond its borders, as translations were not made at court, but in Gerona, Montpellier, Barcelona, Paris, Cordova, Avignon, Valencia, Murcia, Alcobaça, or Bayona (see Santoyo 1999, 297). This wide reach meant that translation was consolidated as an established vehicle for cultural diffusion in all the Romance languages. The Arabic source texts of earlier centuries were replaced mainly by texts in Latin, Greek, French, Italian, or Provençal – a shift which also meant that the figure of the Jewish or Mozarabic collaborator no longer appeared; and there was a great proliferation in the number of source languages, as works were translated from Latin, Arabic, Castilian, Catalan, Hebrew, Greek, French, Portuguese, Italian, and Provençal. There was also a similar proliferation in target languages, as this was the first time translations of contemporary texts were made into, and between, the various Romance languages of the Peninsula, with translations into Catalan being particularly common; intra-Peninsular translations thus became standard practice. Finally, the century ends with the appearance of the first reflections on and critiques of translation, which also sets in motion the development of a meta-language of translation. In the whole history of translation on the Iberian Peninsula, there has been no greater moment of change, no greater movement away from established tradition, than that which took place in the fourteenth century. This was a fertile time of transition between the strictly medieval translation activity of the twelfth and thirteenth centuries, and the new currents of Renaissance humanism, which were to establish themselves definitively in the Peninsula during the fifteenth century.

* * *

"La historia de las traducciones peninsulares del siglo XV resulta asaz compleja y variada" (Russell 1985, 42). And indeed this is no overstatement, especially because "la mayoría de los escritores originales de este tiempo son también traductores" (García Yebra 1985, 78). The long list of fifteenth-century translators is almost a duplicate of the names cited by histories of literature in the various Romance languages: in Castilian, we may note Juan de Mena, the Marquis of Villena, Juan Rodríguez del Padrón, Alonso de Madrigal "el Tostado," Juan del Enzina, Antonio de Nebrija, Prince Carlos of Viana, or Alfonso de Palencia, among others; in Catalan, the outstanding names are Antoni Canals, Andreu Febrer, Ferran Valentí, Francesc Alegre, or Joan Roís de Corella. Indeed, this convergence of the author and the translator may have been a problem, as most of the many modern studies of fifteenth-century translation have focused on "important" authors or translators (in a literary or historical sense), while the rest of what is a very wide corpus has attracted very little interest. However, literary versions are merely a drop in the ocean of non-literary translation work – much of which was anonymous – with which the fifteenth century was inundated, so much so that it is no exaggeration to say that non-literary translation was a much wider-reaching phenomenon than the original work of Peninsular authors: this was essentially a century that existed in translation, and has therefore been misinterpreted by many scholars, whose focus has too often been on translated literature, whether Classical, medieval, or contemporary. Such works included translations of Virgil, Boccaccio, Cicero, Boethius, Eusebius of Caesarea, Leonardo Bruni, Seneca, Quintus Curtius Rufus, Sallust, Vegetius, Dante, Honoré Bouvet, Giannozzo Manetti, Pier Candido Decembio, Livy, and Valerius Maximus, among others: certainly they were translations which left a definite mark on the cultural outlook of the century, which grew ever more distinct from that of previous centuries. But neither the "classical" status of these works, nor their authors' fame, nor that of the translators, and their patrons in turn – in particular the Marquis of Santillana and his great network of collaborators – should have been legitimate reason to ignore other, very different areas of the activity of translation.

Insofar as the lands of Aragon alone are concerned, Josep Pujol has recently written that "la historia de la traducción durante los reinados de los dos primeros Trastámara de Aragón, Fernando I (1412–1416) y Alfonso IV (1416–1458), está todavía por hacer, e incluso por hilvanar" (2004, 641). If this *status quaestionis* is similarly applied to the remaining Peninsular lands, we may begin more clearly to see the enormous volume of work which remains to be done. The result of all this, at least for the case of the fifteenth century, is that we still have a very fragmentary view of Peninsular activity in translation, which extended into practically every sphere of human life. Such is the case – and it is one case among many – of religious literature, because the spiritual treatises (including evangelical, catechistic, doctrinal, hagiographic, ascetic texts and so on) translated into *every* Romance language of the Peninsula were legion; they are now hardly mentioned, but were nonetheless accessible to the reading public of the age, especially after 1472 with the establishment of printing in various areas of the Peninsula. "Se explica de este modo que *casi la mitad* de los textos traducidos en el siglo XV puedan agruparse bajo el rótulo de obras religiosas o morales" (Alvar and Lucía 2003, 1), and the same applies to Portuguese lands, where there is once again a proliferation of "traduções, sobretudo do latim, de obras de carácter religioso e filosófico, textos hagiográficos, ascéticos, místicos e espirituais" (Sampaio Lemos 2003, 163). Nevertheless, as Charles B. Faulhaber has written, "nótese que a pesar de su popularidad, son textos que jamás se estudian hoy, salvo entre los pocos especialistas del latín medieval o de la espiritualidad" (1997, 591). However, there is no doubt that in their own contemporary context, all of these texts (catechisms, saints' lives, confession manuals, and so on), addressed to all kinds of readers (and listeners), engaged a large audience, and were much more widely read than the majority of the Classical and humanist texts cited previously, which were in general no more than "the exclusive intellectual preserve of an educated elite" (Wright 1997, 14).

What caused this great tide of religious translations? The answer was repeated throughout the century as a *locus communis*, with such frequency that we must believe the many translators who had recourse to it: the reason was simply the desire to translate texts on Christian spirituality into the prevailing language in daily use, where those texts were in Latin or in other Romance languages and therefore inaccessible to the majority of the faithful. Thus understood, translation in all areas of the Peninsula becomes an exercise in catechesis: one more form of religious instruction for those who did not know Latin. A second strand of such translations given very little attention comes with the vernacular versions – in Castilian, Catalan, and Galician-Portuguese – of medical, surgical, pharmacological, or veterinary material, usually translated from Latin. As was the case in previous centuries, these translations have been little studied, yet they form a rich store of works from the period, and many of them appear in printed editions dating from the later decades of the century: these include Castilian versions of medical treatises by John of Ketham, Lanfranco da Milano, Valesco de Taranta, Lundino dei Luzzi, or Bernard de Gordon; Portuguese versions of Rogerio di Palermo, Arnau de Vilanova, or Jacobus Kamintus; Catalan translations of Guy de Chauliac, Petro d'Argellata, Pero Cellerer, Girolamo Manfredi, or Antonio Richart; as well as a raft of short, anonymous translations from Latin into all of those three languages, including *Maçer erbolario*, *Tractat de flobotomia*, *Tractat de la conaxença dels polsos*, *Tractat de les viandes*, and so on. There were also intra-Peninsular translations dealing with these same topics, such as Manuel Dieç's *Libro de albeytería*, translated from Valencian into Castilian by Martín Martínez de Ampiés, or the *Llibre dels cavalls*, an anonymous Catalan version of the *Libro de los caballos*. There are even examples of authors translating their own works, such as the physician Julián Gutiérrez, who wrote his *De potu in lapidis preservatione* in Latin, and soon afterwards translated it into Castilian as the *Cura de la piedra y dolor de la yjada*. The voluminous work of this century's many anonymous translators has also been largely forgotten, though this has recently been mitigated in the case of Castile by the exemplary study of Elisa Borsari (2011): there were anonymous translations of Lucian of Samosata, Cato, Johannes de Sacrobosco, Flavius Josephus, Eneas Silvio Piccolomini, Petrarch, Seneca, Thomas of Aquinas, Julius Caesar, Aesop, Albertano da Brescia, and so many more. And all this is to say nothing of translation in Portugal, whose own history is still waiting to be written. Given how incomplete our view of Peninsular translation in the fifteenth century still is, then, we must wait for new research finally to flesh out the complex and varied overview alluded to by Russell.

Works cited

Alvar, Carlos and Lucía Megías, José Manuel. 2002. *Diccionario filológico de literatura medieval española*. Madrid: Castalia.

———. 2003. "Repertorio de traductores del siglo XV: tercera veintena." In *Traducción y práctica literaria en la Edad Media románica*, edited by Rosanna Cantavella et al., 1–40. València: Universitat de València.

Borsari, Elisa. 2011. *Catálogo de traducciones anónimas al castellano de los siglos XIV al XVI en bibliotecas de España, Italia y Portugal*. Madrid: Biblioteca Nacional.

Burnett, Charles. 1978. "Arabic into Latin in Twelfth Century Spain: The Works of Hermann of Carinthia." *Mittellateinisches Jahrbuch* 13: 100–134.

Clare, L. and J. C. Chevalier. 1972. *Le Moyen Âge espagnol*. Paris: Armand Colin.

Faulhaber, Charles B. 1997. "Sobre la cultura ibérica medieval: las lenguas vernáculas y la traducción." In *Actas del VI Congreso Internacional de la Asociación Hispánica de Literatura Medieval*, edited by José Manuel Lucía Megías, vol. 1, 587–597. Alcalá de Henares: Universidad de Alcalá de Henares.

García Yebra, Valentín. 1985. *Traducción y enriquecimiento de la lengua del traductor*. Madrid: Real Academia Española.

Lemarchand, Marie-José. 1995. "¿Qué es un texto original? Apuntes en torno a la historia del concepto." In *Cultura sin fronteras: encuentros a torno a la traducción*, edited by Carmen Valero, 23–30. Alcalá de Henares: Universidad de Alcalá de Henares.

Lemay, Richard. 1963. "Dans l'Espagne du XIIe siècle: Les traductions de l'arabe au latin." *Annales: Économies Sociétés Civilisations* 18 (4–6): 639–665.

Martínez Cavero, Pedro and Domingo Beltrán Corvalán. 2006. "La desaparición de Orosio en Menorca." In *Espacio y tiempo en la percepción de la Antigüedad tardía*, edited by Elena Conde Guerri et al., 591–600. Murcia: Universidad de Murcia.

Pujol, Josep. 2004. "Traducciones y cambio cultural entre los siglos XIII y XV." In *Historia de la traducción en España*, edited by Francisco Lafarga and Luis Pegenaute, 623–650. Salamanca: Ambos Mundos.

Riera, Jaume. 1989. "Catàleg d'obres en català traduides en castellà durant els segles XIV i XV." In *Historia de la Llengua*, edited by Antoni Ferrando, 699–709. València: Institut Universitari de Filologia Valenciana.

Russell, Peter. 1985. *Traducciones y traductores en la Península Ibérica (1400–1550)*. Bellaterra: Universitat Autònoma de Barcelona.

Sampaio Lemos, Aida. 2003. "Textos de prosa literária escritos em português do século XV: a edição do Tractado das Meditações do Pseudo-Bernardo." *Diacrítica* 17 (1): 163–188.

Santoyo, J. C. 1999. *La traducción medieval en la Península Ibérica*. León: Universidad de León.

Wright, Roger. 1997. "Translation between Latin and Romance in the Early Middle Ages." In *Translation Theory and Practice in the Middle Ages*, edited by Jeanette Beer, 7–32. Kalamazoo, MI: Western Michigan University.

9

SUBJECTIVITY AND HERMENEUTICS IN MEDIEVAL IBERIA

The example of the *Libro de buen amor*

Robert Folger

The *Libro de buen amor* is a challenge – and a provocative one – for literary critics and modern readers in general, although it exemplifies many of the features deemed typical of medieval literature.[1] The text is framed by the autodiegetic narrator Juan Ruiz, Archpriest of Hita, but we have no definite information on its historical author. Despite this pseudo-autobiographical plot, the book does not construct a clearly identifiable authorial subject, much less a reliable narrator. The archpriest metamorphoses on occasion into a certain Don Melón; at one point the book itself addresses the reader. Another typically medieval feature of the text is its *mouvance* (Cerquiglini 1989), that is, the instability of a text which has come down to us in three manuscripts which differ significantly from one another. This textual instability contributes to the problem of establishing a date of composition, which may have been 1330, as indicated by the Gayoso manuscript, or 1343, if we consider the colophon of the Salamanca manuscript as evidence for the completion of the work (Lawrance 2004). The text itself does not show the degree of internal cohesion that the modern reader expects. Although the roamings and erotic adventures of the Archpriest provide a feeble overarching plot, the text is, in typical medieval fashion, a patchwork of original passages and set pieces which the poet reworked and parodied, ranging from brief *exempla* to adaptations of well-known texts, such as the *Pamphilus de amore*.

At the same time, the *Libro de buen amor* seems to challenge many commonly held assumptions about a monolithic Dark Age, with an emphasis on religious orthodoxy, a repudiation of eroticism, obscenity, and subversive humor, and, perhaps most importantly, a penchant for straightforward didacticism and indoctrination (see Aers [1992], who discusses the misconceptions of early modernists regarding medieval subjectivity). The introductory passages of the *Libro de buen amor* present the book essentially as an inquiry into the nature of "good love," opposing the pious love of God to the mundane pleasures of worldly passion and sex. However, the text does not provide its reader with clear answers, but with a wealth of ambiguous "love affairs" equally capable of celebrating sexual exploits and condemning them. The *Libro* is characterized by an irreducible polysemy that is often seen as the hallmark of modern forms of literature. Juan Ruiz eschews flat didacticism, focusing instead on the very process of determining the nature of good love. In recent decades, scholarship has indicated that this particular poetics of the *Libro de buen amor* is a masterful *mise en scène* of medieval hermeneutics (Muñoz-Basols 2010), rather than a historical oddity or case of Renaissance pluralism and valorization of earthly matters *avant la lettre*. As E. Michael Gerli (2002) has shown, in an article which draws on his earlier work regarding the influence of Augustine on the work, the *Libro de buen amor* is a reflection of the Augustinian idea that, in the fallen world of men, all signs are essentially polysemous and can at best be transcended in an anamnesis of the divine truth. John Dagenais, in particular, has reconstructed a form of medieval hermeneutics based on an "ethics of reading" that requires the active engagement and "a series of ethical meditations and of personal ethical choices" (1994, xvii) of a reader who does not seek an overarching meaning inherent in a text, but extracts and assimilates exemplary material to his own value system.[2]

These reconstructions of medieval hermeneutics help us understand the rationale of the text, but they do not allow us to fully explore the historical pragmatics of the text, that is, the effect it had on its readership, or was supposed to have. In hermeneutics, a notion of subjectivity is always implicit. It manifests itself both in the composition of a text and in its effect on the recipient; the literary text, the cultural artifact, indeed every phenomenon in a world that is supposed to be "authored" and made meaningful by God, requires the interpretive act of a subject that reacts to these phenomena (see further Hans Blumenberg's comments on the "Lesbarkeit der Welt" [readability of the world] [1979]). Juan Ruiz's text is unique in the degree of hermeneutic effort or violence which it requires from its reader, who has to come to terms with ambiguity and avoid the pitfalls of immorality, but the hermeneutic principle and the underlying notion of subjectivity are by no means exceptional in themselves.

The *Libro de buen amor* is arguably the most quintessentially "medieval" text of Iberian letters, in the sense that it is a dazzling display of medieval hermeneutics. It has a close formal relationship to the *mester de clerecía*, learned poetry in *cuaderna vía* (stanzas of four rhymed alexandrine verses with fourteen syllables), examples of which include the works of Gonzalo de Berceo or the anonymous *Libro de Alexandre*. Like the texts of the *mester de clerecía*, and the substantial body of didactic and gnomic medieval literature (such as the thirteenth-century *Poridat de poridades* and *Bocados de oro*, or Juan Manuel's *El conde Lucanor*, which is contemporaneous with Juan Ruiz's work; see Fernando Gómez Redondo [1998–2002], 241–294 and 1148–1183), the *Libro de buen amor* presupposes a reader who does not simply accept a didactic message, or strive for a global interpretation of a literary work that is supposed to encapsulate a meaning encoded by an authorial subject. Instead, the reader of these texts will draw his own "ethical" conclusions from elements which he finds in the larger text, such as Berceo's *exempla* or the deeds of Alexander. The pertinence of the *Libro de buen amor* to the medieval Iberian hermeneutic tradition is, perhaps, best highlighted by another quest for spiritual perfection in a world full of temptations: *El llibre d'Evast e Blanquerna*, composed around 1283 by the Catalan missionary, philosopher, and theologian Ramon Llull. Llull uses Blanquerna's "biography" to give his work an underlying structure, onto which he then grafts a concatenation of *exempla* and ethical reflections that are supposed to guide the reader, together with the protagonist, to a godly life (Johnston 1996).

At the same time, the *Libro* marks a watershed in Iberian letters because it explicitly reflects upon the underlying principles of epistemology and hermeneutics, particularly in the Salamanca manuscript with the prose prologue. We can only speculate that this explicit reflection is an indication that the medieval code of reading is on the wane, and there is therefore a need to spell out to the reader what the "natural" mode of reading was before. It is apparent, however, that after the *Libro*, the *mester de clerecía* faded from prominence, along with Sem Tob's *Proverbios morales* and Pero López de Ayala's *Rimado de palacio*. In the latter's *Crónica del rey Don Pedro*, we find the first clearly discernible indications of the emergence of a new form of subjectivity that is grounded on introspection and an opaque self that is sealed off from the environment (Gumbrecht 1990, 110–119). Of course, the model of subjectivity and hermeneutics underlying the *Libro de buen amor* do not suddenly disappear in the second half of the fourteenth century. Works such as the misogynist diatribes *El Corbacho*, written by Alfonso Martínez de Toledo in the 1430s, and Jaume Roig's *Espill*, composed roughly three decades later, bear witness to their survival, and even in the Golden Age of Spanish literature they are still "residual" and help us understand important aspects of the literature of the time.[3] However, the fifteenth-century vogue of literature *de amore*, with its typical reflections on the nature and effects of passionate love (Cátedra 1989), and its literary supplement, sentimental romance (in particular the works of Diego de San Pedro), indicate that a new form of subjectivity emerged which was predicated on a self that was capable of identification with other subjects imagined as possessing depth (Folger 2009).

In the following pages, I will focus on the role of subjectivity in medieval literature and its implications for poetics and hermeneutics. I will first trace a model of premodern subjectivity based on Galenic-Aristotelian ideas of the workings of the mind – in the light of "postmodern" theories of subjectivity. I will test this model against the *Libro de buen amor*. My objective is, on one hand, to contribute to our understanding of this enigmatic text. On the other, I propose that the *Libro de buen amor* highlights several essential characteristics of medieval literature in general. The following reflections on medieval subjectivity in the *Libro de buen amor* are thus offered so as to illuminate a range of medieval texts, notwithstanding the fact that emerging and residual epistemologies must be taken into account to understand the whole of medieval Iberian literature.

Premodern subjectivity

When scholarship addresses the issue of subjectivity in relation to medieval literature, it routinely does so to expose a deficiency. Subjectivity as the internal and autonomous reality of human beings is associated with modernity, to the point where it becomes a defining characteristic of modern man. From this perspective, "medieval subjectivity" is an oxymoron of sorts. An antithetical and, at the same time, complementary position to this view considers subjectivity as an anthropological characteristic that has determined the psychic reality of human beings in all periods of human history; the argument runs that as human societies evolved, subjectivity gradually prevailed over other modes of self-consciousness that are essentially determined by social groups.[4] However, subjectivity can also be seen as a configuration of the self which changed fundamentally over the course of history, requiring a form of historical explanation and contextualization that rejects teleological reductionism.[5]

In a study of subjectivity in medieval French literature, Peter Haidu has succinctly defined subjectivity as "potentiality for action" (2004, 114). Thus subjectivity is a mental structure that allows the 'I' to interact with an environment and other subjects. Since René Descartes postulated the split between *res cogitans* and *res extensa*, this potentiality for action is understood to give the individual a "unique or privileged access to his or her own inner discourse – an access that could not legitimately be contradicted by any collective process or external authority" (Heller and Wellbery 1986, 5). The autonomy of the modern Cartesian self is the decisive difference that sets it apart from premodern ideas of subjectivity, because the latter does not imagine subjectivity as interiority. Premodern subjectivity sees the self as embedded in and permeated by an environment that is not radically exterior.[6]

Following the lead of Jörg Dünne, this form of subjectivity may be described as "weak."[7] Unlike the autonomous, disembodied Cartesian subject that opposes an exterior world of objects, the "weak subject" is the result of a practice or "technology of the self" (Foucault 1993, 203) based on repetition. It works the phenomenal world into the self. The weak subject is not pitted against the exterior, nor does it mirror the exterior in an individual act of inte-riorization. In his interpretation of Michel Foucault's notion of subjectivity, Gilles Deleuze (1986b) speaks of a folding (*Le pli*), in which the subjective interior must be understood as the interior *of the* exterior, "le dedans *du* dehors" (Deleuze 1986a, 134).

The epistemic grounding of the self-practices of folding in is provided by Jacques Lacan's "scopic field." James F. Burke (2000) holds that the premodern subject can be understood in analogy with Lacanian subject constitution (Lacan 1966; see also Madeline Caviness [2001] on "scopic economy"). According to Burke, this subject is embedded into:

> [a] generalized, choric visual field that encodes within it the precepts of the symbolic order. This gaze involves a vast number, an enormous array, of projecting, interwo-ven ocular planes that can be understood to proceed not only from the eyes of those who look but also from inanimate objects that in the ancient and medieval under-standing were thought to emit *species* that in some fashion conveyed the imprint of their essence.
>
> (Burke 2000, 25)

Burke correlates this notion with medieval faculty psychology (a detailed description of fac-ulty psychology and reviews of pertinent scholarship is provided by Folger [2002, 33–56, 2009, 42–103]), which, in turn, is the expression and foundation of contemporary epistemol-ogy. Since Greco-Roman antiquity, two models of cognition and perception have co-existed. The older model, based on Platonic ideas, presupposes that an interior "fire" emits seeing rays through the eyes. These rays scan external objects, absorb the objects' light or "fire," and transmit it to the observer's mind.[8] With the enthusiastic reception of Aristotelian writing in the twelfth century, the so-called intromission model gained prominence and became the dom-inant view, particularly among learned natural philosophers. Intromission means that objects emit *species* (*formae, phantasmata*), which travel in the surrounding medium, normally the air, and are therefore also known as *species in medio* (Tachau 1982). The external senses convey the *species* to the brain and the internal senses, which are located in the ventricles of the brain.[9] The exteriorized *species* are no less than a protuberance of the observer's *anima sensitiva* (also known as "animal soul") beyond the limits of the body.

In the brain, *facultates*, mental faculties, process the *species*. The complex and varied architecture of the mind in individual treatises can be reduced to a model with three basic faculties, located in the three ventricles of the human brain.[10] The first ventricle is the seat of the *imaginatio*, the second is the location of the *vis aestimativa* [judgment], and in the third we find the *memoria*. Imagination receives *species*, disassembles them, and associates them with related *imagines* stored in the chambers of memory. Therefore, "thinking" is always an activity of composition and remembering. The *aestimativa* extracts so-called *intentiones*, which can be understood, according to Mary Carruthers (2000, 124–126), as "attitudes" or emotional inclinations and intensities. The activity of the *aestimativa* produces orectic impulses, *appe-titus*, which stimulate the heart to emit *pneuma* or spirit, the extremely rarified matter that is instrumental for all mental operations. Positive judgments of a *species* result in the desire to "obtain" an object and to "use" it (*appetitus concupiscibilis*); negative judgments have the opposite effect, that is, they cause flight response or aggression (*appetitus irascibilis*). This psychosomatic complex is called "passion" (*passio*). The resulting mental *imago*, which con-sists of species and "judgment," is finally permanently stored in the chambers of memory.

It must be emphasized that perception and cognition are essentially pneumofantasmatic (I adopt this notion from Giorgio Agamben [1977]). From an Aristotelian-naturalist perspective, all mental operations depend on *phantasmata*, including the operations of the rational soul. This soul is unique to human beings, consisting, according to St. Augustine, of intelligence, will, and memory. The faculties of the rational soul mirror the faculties of the sensitive soul: intellect allows more complex, abstract operations than imagination; will is the superior orectic faculty that checks the instinctual reactions of judgment; and rational memory is also a repertory of "memories" of the eternal divine truths. However, the higher faculties cannot operate without sensitive *species* and *imagines*. Thus, in *De memoria et reminiscentia*, Aristotle states that thinking is impossible without images – a view confirmed by the authority of Thomas Aquinas (Folger 2009, 48–50). This means that texts evoke images that are ontologically equivalent to images perceived by the external senses.[11]

The mental operations I have sketched belong to the realm of the *anima sensitiva*, the animal soul. Although the theological perspective privileges the rational soul as the defining feature of humanity, it is obvious that the *anima sensitiva* is an interface of sorts between man and world, which allows the individual to interact with the world. The sensitive soul is the location and instrument of the folding of world into self. The parallels Burke postulates between the medieval scopic field and the Lacanian theory of subject constitution are obvious. Lacan conceives of this scopic field as an aggregate of individual imagined gazes: "Things look at me, and yet I see them" (1998, 109). The subject is a function of impersonal, disembodied *regards* (gazes). They produce self-consciousness, founding man as a "*speculum mundi*" (Lacan 1998, 75). By analogy, the premodern subject can be understood as a *speculum mundi*, with the difference that the *regards* of "things" are not seen as imagined, but imagined as "real" *species*.

This subject is constituted by a scopic field produced through extromission (by objects) and intromission (by a subject). The individual is embedded into and, at the same time, permeated by this field. Theo Kobusch (1998, 747) emphasizes that *existimatio*, honor, reputations, and appreciation, granted by the others, determine a concrete individual as *ens morale* (moral being) in a social context. In the words of Petrus Aureoli: "esse morale non constitit in re extra, sed in aestimatione hominum" [being moral is not in an external thing, but in the esteem of the people] (quoted in Kobusch [1998, 747]). Guillaume de Conches, a twelfth-century author, explains that the onlookers' gazes imprint upon the viewed "qualities" through their appreciation or rejection (Hahn 2004, 175). Therefore, the cogito of the premodern subject is, in the words of Burke, "I see and am seen" (2000, 26–27). The subject is what it sees (and reads) and how it is seen.

The effects of seeing and being seen are, of course, not temporary but constitute what Stephen Greenblatt calls a "sense of personal order" (1980, 1). The ever-shifting constellations of *regards* and *species* are checked against the contents of memory and integrated into the psychic apparatus. Similar to Foucault's (1984) *cura sui* (self-care), the self is the result of a lifelong working-in of others'"opinions" (*existimatio*), which are always imagistically conceived; experiences; and, not least, readings. This practice establishes and fortifies *habitus* or *hexis* in memory (Burke 2000, 30). *Hexis* is a term originating in Aristotelian ethics. It provides, by means of repeated "mental actions," a stable, active disposition which encodes social norms and mental patterns of behavior and thought.[12]

This is the meaning of "potentiality for action." It implies that habitualization is not only and not primarily a somatic mechanization of actions, but also a mental regime, which was necessarily, in the context of medieval epistemology, a negotiation of sensorial *imagines*. In premodern understanding, the constitution of stable mental structures (*hexis, habitus*) implies the processing and fending off of "influences" in the form of *imagines* and *species*. *Habitus* are structures that establish an order among the semi-autonomous faculties of the sensitive soul. They provide the individual with "a sense of personal order, a characteristic mode of address to the world, a structure of bounded desires," as Stephen Greenblatt (1980, 1) characterizes the self.

It should be emphasized that *habitus* and *hexis* do not refer to innate structures or biological characteristics of a subject. They are the result of continuous mental exercise in which the sensorial input is transformed into the building blocks of socially accepted mental dispositions. This mental exercise is primarily related to the faculty of judgment: it is essential to extract the correct *intentiones* and evaluate them, which requires an already existing honed judgment, and fosters, if successful, the *habitus*. The notion of *hexis* and *habitus* and the need to build them up and foster them is essential for the understanding of the rationale of Juan Ruiz's *Libro de buen amor*.

Before I proceed to read the text against the backdrop of this notion, I would like to point out two important aspects of the corollary of premodern subjectivity for medieval literature. The notion of thinking as a process of judging that provides the building block for *hexis* implies that the text is broken up into "digestible" units that can be folded in. Texts preferably do not take the shape of longer, complex narrations with gradually unfolding plots as we know them from the modern novel. Modern forms of literature require from the reader an immersion and bracketing of experiential reality. This form of attention and suspension of judgment is alien to medieval literature. Premodern literature requires a punctual reading; that means stepping out of the fictional world and folding the reading matter back into the individual *hexis*.

Secondly, the medieval meaning of "intention" marks more than a semantic difference to our own understanding. Although an author has an intention, that is, a purpose for his writing activity, *intentio* is not essentially associated with the subject of enunciation: the text or textual units, as the basis for the formation of *imagines*, have intentions that must be properly judged by the reading subject. The author's intention is not the primary object of hermeneutic activity, because the literary artifact has its own intention, and this intention is not something to be merely discovered and accepted. On the contrary, the intention must be altered in the folding process, relating it to an already built-up *hexis*. The modern reader's habit of deciphering a coherent authorial intention in a text is therefore a futile and anachronistic exercise; the medieval author or narrator usually provides only a weak and unstable organizing thread, rather than the principle of textual coherence.

Both piecemeal poetics and hermeneutics, as well as the secondary importance of authorial intention and the emphasis on the intentionality of textual blocks, are characteristic features of the *Libro de buen amor* and medieval didactic literature in the broadest sense.

The *Libro de buen amor*: an instrument of *hexis*

The Salamanca manuscript of the *Libro de buen amor* begins with an "oración" (1989, 1) in which the poet expresses existential spiritual anguish and pleads for divine help.[13] This prayer is followed by a prose prologue that has puzzled modern readers because its apparently serious religious didacticism seems to clash with the following "erotic autobiography" of the Arcipreste.[14] In a 1967 article, Pierre L. Ullman debunked the widespread view of the prose piece as a parody of a sermon (*sermon joyeux*), analyzing it in terms of paraenetic rhetoric as a serious homily about the human inclination to sin. Ullman claims that the prologue is informed by Augustinian voluntarism, rejecting Thomist intellectualism as an important influence. He comes to the conclusion that the author marshalled "a justification using Augustinian voluntarism to argue that evil is in the eye of the beholder and not in the book" (1967, 161).

Ullman's otherwise incisive analysis is dissatisfying in two respects. Firstly, the exclusion of Aristotelian-Thomist thought is not admissible. Medieval treatises on the workings on the human mind are predominantly eclectic, privileging Aristotelian natural philosophy to explain the actual phenomenology of the subject, and drawing on Augustinian thought on the faculties of the rational soul to remedy the difficult theological problems implied by naturalism. Secondly, Ullman's interpretation of the prologue not only denies it the status of an introduction ("It is not initiatory; on the contrary, it was probably added in the second redaction" [1967, 154]), but also fails to indicate the purpose of the *Libro* and, more importantly, its *utilitas*, which was a crucial item in the *schema* of the *accessus* (Quain 1945, 215). In medieval eyes, a text merely claiming not to be harmful was by no means justified. It is advisable, then, to read the prose prologue not as a theological text, but as an actual paratext, or *accessus*, which provides the readers with clues on how to read difficult texts (Dagenais [1986] has related the prose prologue to the *accessus Ovidiani* tradition; see also Dagenais [1994, 37]).

The prologue is based on an exegesis of the psalm "Intellectum tibi dabo et instruam te in via hac gradieris firmabo super te oculos meos" (2) [I will give you judgment and teach you in the way you should go; I will counsel you with my loving eye on you].[15] The author recognizes in this psalm:

> tres cosas, las cuales dizen algunos doctores philósofos que son en el alma e propiamente suyas. Son éstas: entendimiento voluntad e memoria. Las quales, digo, si buenos son, que traen al alma consolaçión, e aluengan la vida del cuerpo, e danle onra con pro e buena fama. Ca, por el entendimiento, entiende onbre el bien e sabe dello el mal.
>
> (1989, 2)

In this passage, he is referring to the faculties of the rational soul, reflecting the Holy Trinity: intellect, will, and memory. Divinely infused intellect or understanding enables man to distinguish between good and evil. This is the basis for desiring the good:

> E desque está informada e instruida el alma, que se ha de salvar en el cuerpo, e pienssa e ama e dessea omne el buen amor de Dios es sus mandamientos. [. . .]. E otrosí desecha e aborresçe el alma el pecado del amor loco deste mundo.
>
> (1989, 2)

Understanding is supplemented by will, which naturally desires the good love of God. Will and intellect enable man to make the right judgments and act accordingly, choosing the love of God that will save him, and rejecting the temptations of the *loco amor* and earthly pleasures. Memory assures that the right actions are executed at all times:

> [D]evemos tener sin dubda que obras sienpre están en la buena memoria, que con buen entendimiento e buena voluntad escoge el alma e ama el amor de Dios por se salvar por ellas.
>
> (1989, 3)

Although God has given human beings an immortal soul with all the powers necessary to live a virtuous and holy life, they are always in danger of succumbing to evil: "E viene otrosí esto por razón que la natura umana, que más aparejada e inclinada es al mal que al bien, e a pecado que a bien" (1989, 3). Although there seems to be a contradiction between this pessimistic view of human nature and the harmonious picture of the human soul sketched in the initial sermon, the argument is consistent with premodern subjectivity. The "natura umana" refers to man's postlapsarian earthly existence, and hence the workings of the sensitive soul. The noxious *intentiones* of objects and people (particularly as potential sexual partners) generate "appetites" that lead the individual to commit sinful acts, if they are not properly checked. The onslaught of *imagines* weakens the faculties of the unprepared mind. The "mengua del buen entendimiento" and the "pobredad de la memoria" (1989, 4) are the reason and, at the same time, the result of this fatal attraction to carnal delights. In addition to devotional and meditative practices, reflected in the *Libro* in serious prayers (e.g., the Marianic *gozos* and meditation of the *passio Christi*), understanding must be trained, and memory must be stacked with appropriately processed materials. This is the rationale of the *Libro de buen amor*:

> E conpuse este nuevo libro en que son escriptas algunas maneras, e maestrías, e sotilezas engañosas del loco amor del mundo, que usan algunos para pecar.
> Las quales leyéndolas e oyéndolas ome o mujer de buen entendimiento, que se quiera salvar, descogerá e obrarlo ha.
>
> (1989, 4)

A person with a properly acquired and structured *hexis* will condemn *loco amor*. Judging the related examples of ungodly passion correctly, the examples of the *Libro* will be stored in the treasure house of memory with the appropriate "tag" ("good love" or "mad love"), further fortifying the *hexis* located in memory.

The author claims, however, that individuals who have not acquired a beneficial *habitus* will also benefit from his work:

> Otrosí los de poco entendimiento non se perderán; ca leyendo e coidando el mal que fazen o tienen en la voluntad de fazer, e los porfiosos de sus malas maestrías.e [sic] descobrimiento publicado de sus muchas engañosas maneras, que usan para pecar e engañar las mujeres, acordarán la memoria e non despreçiarán su fama: ca muchos es cruel quien su fama menospreçia.
>
> (1989, 4)

In the *Libro*, the archpriest makes public his deceitful ways and suffers humiliation after humiliation in his erotic quest. The reader who shares his delight in carnal pleasures will recognize that this behavior is detrimental to his *existimatio* and even though he does not have enough *entendimiento* to understand the superior values of spiritual salvation, he will refrain from sinning because it would harm his standing (*fama*) in the world of men.

The argument is weak, to say the least, as the author acknowledges in a disclaimer: "Enpero, porque es umanal cosa el pecar,si [sic] algunos, lo que non los consejo, quisieren usar del loco amor, aquí fallarán algunas maneras para ello" (1989, 4). This is the price the author is willing to pay to reach his goal of fortifying the faculties of the soul. Explicitly and unambiguously negative or positive examples are harmless, but they will not hone the mental skills necessary to live a virtuous life in a fallen world, where all signs are potentially or actually polysemous and require the right judgment. This is the reason why the other great theme of the *Libro de buen amor*, besides the nature of good love, is the reflection on and the practice of hermeneutics:

> Non tengades que es libro de neçio de devaneo,
> nin creades que es chufa algo que en él leo;

ca según buen dinero yaze en vil correo
ansí en feo libro está saber non feo.

> (1989, 5, stanza 16)

This "saber" is not simply a prefabricated truth, but knowledge of how to determine, or judge, whether the *amor* presented in the book is good, godly love, or harmful appetite. The presentation of the carnal desire and adventures of the Archpriest is perfectly suited to elicit the *appetitus* that the higher faculties of will and intellect are supposed to check, resulting in a beneficial *hexis*. This is also the reason why the book does not present *exempla* with obvious didactic messages, but lessons *in utroque*, requiring a violent act of interpretation or determination according to the pre-established mental habits of the reader, rather than a fixed meaning in the text.

This violent act of interpretation is foregrounded in the "disputaçión que los griegos e los romanos en uno ovieron" (1989, 9). The Romans and Greeks communicate in sign language, and the picaresque champion of the Romans, disguised as a learned man, misunderstands the Greek's theological arguments as insults. The Greek philosopher in turn misinterprets the recriminations of the Roman oaf as signs of the Romans' cultural maturity and decides that they are worthy of receiving Greek wisdom. This humorous story of *translatio studii* is, on the one hand, an exercise in the intricacies of interpretation and the treacherous nature of signs (Gerli 2002). On the other, the kernel of the story is also that an interpretation which exerts hermeneutic violence rather than doing justice to the intention of the producer of signs (the Roman *ribaldo*) may achieve beneficial effects (the revelation of the *dotrina*). The introductory matter of the *Libro* ends with the highly appropriate metaphor of the book as a musical instrument:

De todos instrumentos yo libro só pariente;
bien o mal, qual puntares, tal te dirá çiertamente.
Qual tú dezir quisieres y faz punto y tente;
si me puntar sopieres sienpre me avrás en miente.

> (1989, 11, stanza 70)

The *Libro* is an instrument for the honing of the mental faculties. The actual content is primarily matter for mental exercise, and thus secondary to the pragmatics of the text. Only if the book is "played," interpreted, and processed correctly will it "always be in the mind," as part of a mental habit in memory. The remaining text of the Archpriest's book is a corollary to this principle: from the Aristotelian argument that justifies the archpriest's appetite for "mantenençia" and "juntamiento con fenbra plazentera" (1989, 11, stanza 71), which requires the reader's acumen to recognize the logical flaw in confusing animal soul and rational soul (Rico 1985), to the final perplexing praise of the advantages of the book:[16]

Buena propriedat ha do quier que sea,
que si lo oye alguno que tenga muger fea,
o si muger lo oye que su marido vil sea,
fazer a Dios serviçio en punto lo desea.

> (1989, 170, stanza 1627)

Juan Ruiz is certainly right in affirming that "sobre cada fabla se entiende otra cosa" (1989, 170, stanza 1631), because this is the principle of the didacticism of the book:

The *Libro de buen amor* is a superb example of this perilous didacticism, because it will benefit the few already properly instructed ("ome o mujer de buen entendimiento;" 1989, 4), and possibly shame sinners into virtuous behavior, but it may also be misused as a text book for those addicted to the "amor loco deste mundo" (1989, 2). This was most certainly not the author's intention:

> E Dios sabe que la mi intençión non fue de lo [sc. el libro] fazer por dar manera de pecar, ni por mal dezir, mas fue por reduçir a toda persona a memoria buena de bien obrar, e dar ensienpro de buenas costumbres e castigos de salvación.

(1989, 4)

It was no unfamiliar concept during the Middle Ages that authorial intention was relevant to the interpretation of a literary text: the *intentio scribentis* was one of the subdivisions of the *accessus ad auctores* tradition that provided readers with clues to the understanding of a text.[17] It would, however, be misleading to suggest that this authorial intention was the hermeneutic guarantor of the meaning of the whole text. Instead, textual fragments have their own *intentiones*, and it is the reader's task to judge these intentions and fold the textual fragments into his or her own mental structures. In this *mise en scène* of medieval hermeneutics on the Iberian Peninsula, the *Libro de buen amor* is unique in its virtuosity, and an exemplary illustration of premodern subjectivity.

Notes

1 For an overview of *Libro de buen amor* studies, see Deyermond (1987) and Haywood and Vasvari (2004).
2 Manuscript S and its autobiographical rendition of the *Libro del Arcipreste* suggest that some readers in the fourteenth century already had different reading habits, indicating emerging forms of modern subjectivity; see Folger (2003).
3 I use the concepts of "residual," "dominant," and "emerging" following Raymond Williams (1977, 121–128) as indications for contemporaneity and the imbrication of discourses and power formations to explain the "overlapping" of stages of history.
4 Anthony Low holds that subjectivity gradually replaced the "emphasis on community," in a historical process of alienation through "psychological pressures that thwart personal desires" (2003, x and xviii).
5 For a more detailed discussion of scholarship on subjectivity, and the reasons for using the concept in relation to medieval texts, see my *Escape from the Prison of Love* (27–42).
6 In the sixteenth century, according to Natalie Zemon Davis, "the line drawn around the self was [still] not firmly closed. One could get inside other people and receive other people within oneself, and not just during sexual intercourse or when a child was in the womb" (1986, 56). On the "embodiment" of the premodern subject, see Biernoff (2002).
7 Dünne's study (2003) focuses on the literature of the late eighteenth and nineteenth centuries. Weak subjectivity is based on Deleuzian "naked" repetition, which is situated between the interior repetition of the "strong" subject and Nietzsche's eternal return, which actually negates subjectivity.
8 See Michael Camille (2000, 205). Boccaccio's Fiammetta, for instance, falls victim to lovesickness because she is caught by the pneumatic rays Pamphilo emits through his eyes; see also Ioan P. Couliano (1987, 29–30). Phenomena like the evil eye are also based on the assumption that a human being emits seeing rays; see Burke (2000, 63–77).
9 See Biernoff (2002, 63–107). Roger Bacon argues in his *Opus majus* (5.1.7.4) that *species* which are emitted by objects are "*aided* and *excited* by the species of the eye" (quoted in Biernoff [2002, 87]; Biernoff's emphasis).
10 The most common model is based on five internal senses; all premodern descriptions of the human mind show considerable variations in terminology; see Folger (2003, 27–33) and Wolfson (1935).

11 *Imagines* are not merely visual in our modern understanding, but synesthetic. "Common sense," situated in the front of the brain, is the first receptor of the sense impression; it has the function of fusing the visual stimuli with the sensorial data conveyed by the other external senses.

12 According to Thomas Aquinas, synderesis is the expression of a successful habitualization of virtuous thinking. Synderesis is the conscience of practical reason and *habitus*: "synderesis dicitur instigare ad bonum et murmurare de malo, inquantum per prima principia procedimus ad inveniendum et judicamus inventa" (1970, 188–190; *Summa* 1a. 79,12): see Philippe Delhaye (1968, 112–14). Bourdieu's notion of *habitus* as "structured structures predisposed to function as structuring structures" (2002, 72) of social practices and representations is indebted to this tradition, naturally reflecting a radical change in epistemology.

13 I use Anthony Zahareas' synoptic edition (Ruiz 1989) because it more faithfully reflects the text that the medieval reading subject encountered.

14 The prologue has attracted considerable critical attention and produced widely diverging interpretations. Alastair J. Minnis sums up the discussion (2001, 64–70). In his own view, the *Libro* is connected to the "Medieval Ovid:" "the art of love and its remedy are interrelated; the one presupposes the other" (2001, 69).

15 I have modified the standard English version of Psalm 32:8, which translates "Intellectum tibi dabo" as "I will instruct you," in order to emphasize the hermeneutic imperative that would be obvious to medieval readers.

16 In the Salamanca manuscript, after the colophon (stanza 1634) there are further materials that suggest a change in reading habits during the fourteenth century; see Folger (2003).

17 See Quain (1945). The *accessus* was reserved for actual *auctores*, but Juan Ruiz claims for his book, possibly tongue-in-cheek, the status of a "libro de testo" that deserves a "glosa" in the form of a "grand prosa" (1989, 170, stanza 1631).

Works cited

Aers, David. 1992. "A Whisper in the Ear of Early Modernists; or, Reflections on Literary Critics Writing the 'History of the Subject'." In *Culture and History, 1350–1600: Essays on English Communities, Identities, and Writing*, edited by David Aers, 177–202. Detroit, MI: Wayne State University Press.

Agamben, Giorgio. 1977. *Stanze: La parola e il fantasma nella cultura occidentale*. Torino: Einaudi.

Biernoff, Suzannah. 2002. *Sight and Embodiment in the Middle Ages*. New York: Palgrave Macmillan.

Blumenberg, Hans. 1979. *Die Lesbarkeit der Welt*. Frankfurt am Main: Suhrkamp.

Bourdieu, Pierre. 2002. *Outline of a Theory of Practice*. Translated by Richard Nice. Cambridge: Cambridge University Press.

Burke, James F. 2000. *Vision, the Gaze, and the Function of the Senses in* Celestina. University Park, PA: Pennsylvania State University Press.

Camille, Michael. 2000. "Before the Gaze: The Internal Senses and Late Medieval Practices of Seeing." In *Visuality before and beyond the Renaissance: Seeing as Others Saw*, edited by Robert S. Nelson, 197–223. Cambridge: Cambridge University Press.

Carruthers, Mary. 2000. *The Craft of Thought: Meditation, Rhetoric, and the Making of Images, 400–1200*. Cambridge Studies in Medieval Literature 34. Cambridge: Cambridge University Press.

Cátedra, Pedro M. 1989. *Amor y Pedagogía en la edad media: estudio de doctrina amorosa y práctica literaria*. Salamanca: Universidad de Salamanca.

Caviness, Madeline H. 2001. *Visualizing Women in the Middle Ages: Sight, Spectacle, and Scopic Economy*. Philadelphia, PA: University of Pennsylvania Press.

Cerquiglini, Bernard. 1989. *Éloge de la variante: histoire critique de la philologie*. Paris: Seuil.

Couliano, Ioan P. 1987. *Eros and Magic in the Renaissance*. Translated by Margaret Cook. Chicago: University of Chicago Press.

Dagenais, John. 1986. "A Further Source for the Literary Ideas in Juan Ruiz's Prologue." *Journal of Hispanic Philology* 11: 23–52.

———. 1994. *The Ethics of Reading in Manuscript Culture: Glossing the Libro de buen amor*. Princeton, NJ: Princeton University Press.

Davis, Natalie Zemon. 1986. "Boundaries and the Sense of Self in Sixteenth-Century France." In *Reconstructing Individualism: Autonomy, Individuality, and the Self in Western Thought*, edited by Thomas C. Heller, Morton Sosna, and David E. Wellbery, 53–63. Stanford, CA: Stanford University Press.

Deleuze, Gilles. 1986a. *Foucault*. Paris: Les Éditions de Minuit.

———. 1986b. *Le pli: Leibniz et le baroque*. Paris: Les Éditions de Minuit.

Delhaye, Philippe. 1968. *The Christian Conscience*. Translated by Charles Underhill Quinn. New York: Desclee.

Deyermond, Alan. 1987. "El *Libro de Buen Amor* a la luz de las recientes tendencias críticas." *Ínsula* 488–489: 39–40.

Dünne, Jörg. 2003. *Asketisches Schreiben: Rousseau und Flaubert als Paradigmen literarischer Selbstpraxis in der Moderne*. Romanica Monacensia 65. Tübingen: Gunter Narr.

Folger, Robert. 2002. *Images in Mind: Lovesickness, Spanish Sentimental Fiction and Don Quijote*. Chapel Hill, NC: University of North Carolina Press.

———. 2003. "Alfonso de Paradinas, ¿carcelero del Arcipreste de Hita?: *El libro de buen amor*, MS. S, como narrativa (anti) boeciana." *Revista de Estudios Hispánicos* 30 (2): 61–73.

———. 2009. *Escape from the Prison of Love: Caloric Identities and Writing Subjects in Fifteenth-Century Spain*. Chapel Hill, NC: University of North Carolina Press.

Foucault, Michel. 1984. *Histoire de la sexualité*. vol. 3: *Le souci de soi*. Paris: Gallimard.

———. 1993. "About the Beginning of the Hermeneutics of the Self: Two Lectures at Dartmouth." *Political Theory* 21: 198–227.

Gómez Redondo, Fernando. 1998–2002. *Historia de la prosa medieval castellana*. Madrid: Cátedra.

Gerli, E. Michael. 2002. "The Greeks, the Romans, and the Ambiguity of Signs: *De doctrina christiana*, the Fall, and the Hermeneutics of the *Libro de buen Amor*." *Bulletin of Spanish Studies* 79 (4): 411–428.

Greenblatt, Stephen. 1980. *Renaissance Self-Fashioning from More to Shakespeare*. Chicago: University of Chicago Press.

Gumbrecht, Hans Ulrich. 1990. *'Eine' Geschichte der spanischen Literatur*. Frankfurt am Main: Suhrkamp.

Hahn, Alois. 2004. "Wohl dem, der eine Narbe hat: Identifikation und ihre soziale Konstruktion." In *Unverwechselbarkeit: Persönliche Identität und Identifikation in der vormodernen Gesellschaft*, edited by Peter von Moos, 43–62. Norm und Struktur: Studien zum sozialen Wandel in Mittelalter und Früher Neuzeit 23. Köln: Böhlau.

Haidu, Peter. 2004. *The Subject Medieval/Modern: Text and Governance in the Middle Ages*. Stanford, CA: Stanford University Press.

Haywood, Louise and Louise O. Vasvári, eds. 2004. *A Companion to the Libro de buen amor*. Woodbridge: Tamesis.

Heller, Thomas C. and David E. Wellbery. 1986. "Introduction." In *Reconstructing Individualism: Autonomy, Individuality, and the Self in Western Thought*, edited by Thomas C. Heller, Morton Sosna, and David E. Wellbery, 1–15. Stanford, CA: Stanford University Press.

Johnston, Mark D. 1996. "The 'Good Upbringing' of Ramón Llull's *Blanquerna*: Appropriation and Misrecognition as Social Reproduction." *Essays in Medieval Studies* 12: 119–134.

Kobusch, Theo. 1998. "Person und Subjektivität: Die Metaphysik der Freiheit und der moderne Subjektivitätsgedanke." In *Geschichte und Vorgeschichte der Subjektivität*, edited by Reto Luzius Fetz, Roland Hagenbüchle, and Peter Schulz, 743–761. vol. 2. Berlin: De Gruyter.

Lacan, Jacques. 1966. "Le stade du miroir comme formateur de la fonction du Je telle qu'elle nous et révélée dans l'expérience psychanalytique." *Écrits*, 93–100. Paris: Seuil.

———. 1998. *The Four Fundamental Principles of Psychoanalysis*. Translated by Alan Sheridan. *The Seminar of Jacques Lacan*, edited by Jacques-Alain Miller, vol. 11. New York: W. W. Norton & Company.

Lawrance, Jeremy. 2004. "*Libro de buen amor*: From Script to Print." In *A Companion to the Libro de buen amor*, edited by Louise Haywood and Louise O. Vasvári, 39–68. Woodbridge: Tamesis.

Low, Anthony. 2003. *Aspects of Subjectivity: Society and Individuality from the Middle Ages to Shakespeare and Milton*. Pittsburgh, PA: Duquesne University Press.

Minnis, Alastair J. 2001. *Magister Amoris: The Roman de la Rose and Vernacular Hermeneutics*. Oxford: Oxford University Press.

Muñoz-Basols, Javier. 2010. "Más allá de la dicotomía del *sic et non*: *inventio, dispositio* y *elocutio* en el *Libro de buen amor*." *Bulletin of Hispanic Studies* 87 (2): 397–413.

Quain, Edwin A. 1945. "The Medieval *accessus ad auctores*." *Traditio* 3: 215–264.

Rico, Francisco. 1985. "'Por aver mantenencia': el aristotelismo heterodoxo en el *Libro de buen amor*." *El Crotalón* 2: 169–198.

Ruiz, Juan. 1989. *Libro del Arcipreste: también llamado Libro de Buen Amor*, synoptic edition by Anthony N. Zahareas (together with Thomas McCallum). Madison, WI: Hispanic Seminary of Medieval Studies.

Tachau, Katherine. 1982. "The Problem of the *Species in Medio* at Oxford in the Generation after Ockham." *Mediaeval Studies* 44: 349–443.

Thomas Aquinas. 1970. *Summa theologiæ*. vol. 11: *Man (1a. 75–83)*. Edited and translated by Timothy Suttor. New York: Blackfriars; McGraw-Hill.

Ullman, Pierre L. 1967. "Juan Ruiz's Prologue." *Modern Language Notes* 82: 149–170.

Williams, Raymond. 1977. *Marxism and Literature*. New York: Oxford University Press.

Wolfson, Harry Austryn. 1935. "The Internal Senses in Latin, Arabic and Hebrew Philosophic Texts." *Harvard Theological Review* 28: 69–133.

10

PATRONS, ARTISTS AND AUDIENCES IN THE MAKING OF VISUAL CULTURE IN MEDIEVAL IBERIA (ELEVENTH– THIRTEENTH CENTURIES)[1]

Manuel Castiñeiras

It is well known that between the eleventh and the thirteenth centuries, Medieval Iberia was a cluster of different cultures and artistic traditions (Vanoli 2006). Several political powers, religious beliefs and intellectual backgrounds were to be found in the multifaceted land which lay between the Mediterranean and the Atlantic, from colourful and multicultural al-Andalus to the emerging and creative Catalan Counties. From the end of the eleventh century onwards a number of artistic enterprises promoted by Christian rulers seem to herald a new era in the visual arts, placing them in the vanguard of Romanesque Europe.

Scholars of Spanish artistic historiography have so far focused on topics such as the itinerant artist, the circulation of models and dissemination of styles, often disregarding the ideological framework of the creation, the use of art as a means of communication, and the assessment of patrons and audiences as agents in the artistic process. Nonetheless, these issues must all be taken into account if we are to have a complete overview of the agents involved in the making of Spanish Medieval art.

There is thus a need for a series of case studies that allow us to develop a true microanalysis of all the agents involved. Art is predominantly an action, an attempt to transform reality, an expression of agency (Gell 2010). Hence the significance of the processes of reification, or objectification, in which a myth turns into a concrete feature of the Iberian geography, Christian symbols grow to be seen as an expression of the ideals of Gregorian Reform, and martyrdom as the ideal end for one who preaches against heresy, while St. James becomes a live saint in the eyes of his pilgrims. In each of these processes, artworks and images perform a specific role, like actors in a play, whose author was often the patron or the institution involved.

Hercules in the garden of the Hesperides:
a geographical myth in the Creation Tapestry?

The Creation Tapestry was made in the Catalan Counties at the end of the eleventh century, and it is intimately linked to the conditions of the relationship between the Papacy and the emerging power of the Catalan counts. As pointed out by Adeline Rucquoi (2010), it is clear that in the context of these turbulent years the episcopal sees as well as the main Catalan monasteries were firmly under the influence of the papal legates. Synods presided over by Hugues Candidus (1068), Amat d'Oloron (1077–1078), Bernard de Sedirac (1097) or Richard de Saint-Victor de Marseille (1101) took place in Girona to avoid simony and Nicolaism, reinforce Christian dogma, and ensure the submission of the Catalan counts' policy to the interests of the Holy See. To this extent, both the conquest of lands – mainly Tortosa and Tarragona – and the political status of the counts as vassals of St. Peter seemed to be the most important goals of this era.

It goes without saying that the institutions involved in this process – Church and nobility – acted as patrons of some of the most important works of art of the period, to ensure that many of these ideas were reflected in them. It is worth noting that some of these works were intended for a particularly wide audience, and their iconographical programme aimed to reinforce the dogma of the Roman Catholic Church as well as the submission of lay power to ecclesiastical power. The originality of the imagery of the Girona's Creation Tapestry, which was made around 1097, is therefore of interest here.[2]

It is highly likely that this tapestry was used as a ceremonial carpet for the 1097 council presided over by the Papal legate and archbishop of Toledo, Bernard of Sedirac; the meeting was intended to resolve the internal conflicts of the Catalan church, to affirm the power of the young count Ramon Berenguer III, under the protection of the Holy See, and to encourage the definitive restoration of the metropolitan see of Tarragona. The iconographical programme of the embroidery reflects a number of these concerns. Furthermore, as I have outlined in previous publications, the embroidery may well have been done in a convent under the guidance of an important lady of the nobility. The most likely candidates in this respect are the Benedictine nuns of Sant Daniel de Girona, who continue silently to produce liturgical ornaments by needlework to this day. This coenobitic monastery was founded in 1018 by the Countess of Barcelona, Ermessenda (also known as a patroness of the new Romanesque Cathedral of Girona), and by the end of the eleventh century this monastery was under the protection of Countess Matilde of Apulia (1060–1112?), widow of Ramon Berenguer II and mother of the young prince Ramon Berenguer III. Matilde is likely to have played an important role in the genesis of the Creation Tapestry (Castiñeiras 2011a).

Following the recent restoration carried out by the *Centre de Restauració de Béns Mobles de Catalunya* (CRBMC), the figure depicted in the top border on the right hand side, previously identified as Abel, is now thought to be Hercules, as some scholars had previously suggested (see Figure 10.1) (Castiñeiras 2011a, 67–68, figs. XLVIII–XLIX; Palol 1986, 27–28). Hercules is depicted in the Garden of the Hesperides carrying the skin of the Nemean lion on his shoulders. This discovery would not have been possible without analysis of the reverse of the work, which has recently been done for the first time. Indeed, the embroidered remains of the *titulus* HERCVLES were still visible on the reverse. Unfortunately, those remains were covered on the front of the work with a patch from an earlier restoration.

This discovery confirms an old suspicion about the model and sources of this classical image. In my opinion, this figure was made based on the illustrations of the *Aratea*, and in particular the Northern Hemisphere constellation *Engonasin* (Hercules), since there were similar representations in the eleventh- and twelfth-century Astronomy and Computus miscellanies held by the library of the Benedictine Abbey of Ripoll. These works are Vat. Reg. Lat. 123, f. 186v, a manuscript produced in Ripoll in 1055 under the direction of the monk Oliva, and Madrid, Ms. 19, f. 46r, a controversial codex also produced in Ripoll *circa* 1134 from a manuscript which arrived from Montecassino in the time of Abbot Oliba (1008–1046). Furthermore, it is no coincidence that this recent restoration has made it possible to prove the close

Figure 10.1 Hercules. The Creation Tapestry, upper border, c. 1097. Museum of the Treasury of the Cathedral of Girona.

© Catedral de Girona

connections between the embroidered programme and the Ripoll Abbey manuscripts. The use of the Medieval Latin term "HIEMPS" to refer to Winter can thus be seen both in the Creation Tapestry (Personification of Winter) and in the diagrams of the *Computus* miscellany made by the monk Oliva in 1055. They belong to the same monastic culture. However, producing a work of embroidery on such a scale requires a process with two distinct stages: the actual design or tracing of the iconographical programme (the work of the *auctor intellectualis*), and its reproduction on the cloth by the *auctor materialis*. Hence my proposal to take into serious consideration the possibility that Ripoll Abbey might have been both the source of most of the drawings, and responsible for the creation of the cosmological programme. The nuns in Sant Daniel at Girona then made this programme a reality by the silent practice of their craft of needlework.

On the other hand, the position of Hercules on the right hand side of the upper border aims to foster symmetry with that of Samson on the left. Both depictions must be connected with the caption REX FORTIS (Courageous King) that accompanies the central image of Christ Logos or Cosmocrator in the Creation Wheel. In fact, St. Augustine, in his *De Civitate Dei* (XVII, 19), compared the biblical Samson to the mythical hero Hercules, on the basis of his strength:

"Hebraeorum iudex Samson; qui cum mirabiliter fortis esset, putatus est Hercules" [Samson, judge of the Hebrews, was thought of as Hercules, because of his marvellous strength]. Both were considered prefigurations of Christ in the Middle Ages because of their strength, temperance and virtue (Frugoni 1976–1977, 138–140).

It is worth noting that Samson and Hercules were also role models for proper governance, implying a possible political interpretation of the embroidery. In fact, the Creation Tapestry might be conceived as a *speculum principis* for the new ruler: the young Count of Barcelona, Ramon Berenguer III, who came of age in 1097. Its design has precedents in its inclusion of objects conceived as attributes of imperial power, including the Chair of St. Peter, which was used as the throne of the emperor Charles the Bald for his Christmas coronation in 875. This luxurious seat was decorated with the Labours of Hercules on the front and with the depictions of the Constellations of Orion and Hercules on the backrest. The Greek hero also figured prominently in the coronation mantle of Henry II (ca. 1014). Hercules and cosmography have thus often been related to the tradition of princely programmes.

Furthermore, in our embroidery, the depiction of Hercules could be read as a mythical and geographical reference to the Count of Barcelona. As A. Rucquoi (2010) has pointed out, in the Spanish Middle Ages the Greek hero was named as the founder of cities such as Barcelona and Urgell, according to Rodrigo Jiménez de Rada (1989, 68), in *De Rebus Hispaniae* I, 5, and Alfonso X el Sabio (2011, 56–57), in his *Estoria de España*, 8. These thirteenth-century sources draw on Virgil's *Aeneid*, Lucan's *Pharsalia*, and Ovid's *Metamorphoses*. Most of these works were preserved in the library of Ripoll Abbey, whose possible role in the intellectual creation of the Tapestry's iconographical programme has been noted previously. In addition, from the fifteenth century onwards, other local legends cited by writers such as Joan Margarit i Pau (fifteenth century), Juan Roig i Galpí (1678) and Enrique Flórez (eighteenth century) attempted to explain the etymology of Girona as a derivation from the giant Geryon, a mythical founder of the city familiar from the tenth labour of Hercules (for all these sources, see Vivó 1989).

In addition, contemporary sources such as the *Geste de Robert Guiscard*, written by William of Apulia at the end of the eleventh century, mention that Ramon Berenguer II, Count of Barcelona and father of Ramon Berenguer III, was on his way from the Hesperides ("partibus Esperiae") when he travelled to Southern Italy in 1078, to request a blessing for his marriage to Mafalda of Apulia in 1078 (Aurell 1977, 363). It is thus very likely that the depiction of Hercules in the Creation Tapestry was designed to dignify the new Count of Barcelona in two ways: as a prince of the mythical western land of the Hesperides and as a courageous warrior. Similarly, Ralph of Caen, in his *Gesta Tancredi* 52 (2010, 78), compared the strength of the Norman Tancred (nephew of Bohemond, who was step-brother of Matilde of Apulia) to Hercules' club. Furthermore, it should not be forgotten that in the *Carmen Campidoctoris*, which was copied in a codex from Ripoll Abbey, the Cid, whose daughter was married to Ramon Berenguer III, was compared to other classical heroes such as Paris, Hector, Pyrrhus and Aeneas.[3]

The embroidery also contains other elements of the tradition of princely programmes, including the use of a luxurious purple tint in the base fabric, or the depiction of the emperor Constantine, the governor *par excellence*, which is still partially visible in the lower section of the work. Moreover, if Hercules and Samson were depicted as models of strength and virtue for the new ruler, then the bizarre scene of Adam naming the animals in the central wheel of the embroidery may be interpreted as a metaphor for the wide but limited power of princes descending from Adam, as Xenia Muratova (2007) has pointed out in discussion of the Golden Doors of the Cathedral of Suzdal (Russia). Ultimately, this theocratic view of power is based on the idea that the Almighty Cosmocrator manages the destiny of the created world and its rulers, as suggested by the *Donation of Constantine*. It means that the likely objective of the Creation Tapestry is to serve as a manifesto reflecting the ideals of the Papacy derived from the Church of the Gregorian Reform, in which lands and governors may be subject to the rule of the Pope. To this extent, the depiction of the pious and brave governor, Constantine, should be seen as Ramon Berenguer III's *alter ego*, whom the Almighty Cosmocrator allows to ensure the destiny of Christian society, thanks to the support and protection of the Church (Castiñeiras 2015).

Finally, we may also find further support for the idea that this large embroidery was intended to serve as a ceremonial carpet at the synod of 1097. This event was presided over by Bernard of Sedirac, archbishop of Toledo, who proclaimed Ramon Berenguer III as the new Count of Barcelona, while also promoting a Catalan alliance for the conquest of Tarragona and Tortosa. It is very likely that the Creation Tapestry was then placed on the choir or sanctuary together with the episcopal chair, which was also made for the occasion. This would be typical of the practice of Gregorian Reform: for instance, in the Council of Bari of 1098, together with the *mirifica sedes* or Abbot Elia's chair, the English historian William of Malmesbury (*De gestis*, 1c) tells us that the church floor was decorated with carpets.[4]

To this extent, the Norman lineage of Mafalda, daughter of Robert Guiscard, would explain some similarities between the Girona marble throne and the art of Apulia. I refer here to the episcopal throne of Canosa, which Ursone, Archbishop of Bari-Canosa (1078–1089), had made reusing the remains of a previous one (Belli d'Elia 1975, 86–91). According to the chronicles, the archbishop accompanied the Norman princess to Catalonia for her marriage to Ramon Berenguer II. The Cartulary of Charlemagne from the Cathedral of Girona confirms these fluid relations with Apulia: for example, it documents the reading of the will of Gaufret Guillem on 4 November 1080, after he died while returning from Apulia with the bishop of Girona, Berenguer (*Cartoral dit de Carlemany* I, doc. n 148; see Marquès, Josep Maria 1993, 277).

Dynastic relations, artistic exchanges and political interests thus all attest to an important relationship between Catalonia and the Papacy as well as the Norman domains in Southern Italy. This is the context which ought to inform our interpretation of the Creation Tapestry: in this exceptional work, Greek myth (Hercules), biblical archetypes (Samson) and Christian history (Constantine) are woven together in order to present the work of the Almighty Creator as an allegory for the political interests of the Church at the time of Gregorian Reform.

In the name of God: Moors and Christians on the Aragonese border

Few figures of twelfth-century Spain have been as intriguing as Alfonso I of Aragon (1104–1134), known as the Battler (*El Batallador*). On the one hand, his policy of military expansion against the Muslims allowed him to conquer Zaragoza in 1118. On the other, his invasion of territories belonging to his ex-wife Urraca, Queen of León, allowed him to take control of much of the Castilian plateau, including the region of Soria. During the 1130s, artistic styles and formulae that were alien to Castile were thus introduced or promoted by this new Aragonese milieu. This resulted in the production of great pictorial cycles such as those in San Baudelio in Berlanga (Soria), San Miguel at Gormaz (Soria) and Santa Cruz at Maderuelo (Segovia), which owed much to the rich experience of the distant church of Santa Maria de Taüll in the Pyrenees (Cook and Gudiol 1980, 105).[5]

The latter church, which was consecrated on 11 December 1123 by Ramon, Bishop of Roda, offers tremendous evidence of the didactic function of images at the time of the Gregorian Reform. The diocese of Roda d'Isàvena then ruled a territory that extended from the north of Aragon to Catalonia. From the end of the eleventh century, its bishops and canons were committed to a policy of parish reorganisation and endorsement of liturgical reform, in which mural and panel painting seem to play an important role. It is unclear whether the entire cycle of wall paintings in the apses, aisles and counter-façade of Santa Maria was completed in advance of its consecration. However, the unity of the iconographical programme implies that the work was shared among three masters or workshops from the start, in order that the church be ready as soon as possible. One master worked on the central apse, which features the *Maiestas Mariae*; a second decorated the right lateral apse, which is of excellent quality and closely resembles the paintings of Santa Cruz at Maderuelo (Soria) (Museo del Prado); and finally, a third master or workshop, known as the Master of the Last Judgement, was responsible for the cruder decoration of the nave and aisles, columns and counter-façade. This third team also produced the paintings of the left apse in Sant Climent at Taüll, which was dedicated to Saint Michel.

Furthermore, two minor sets of mural paintings dating from the same period are reminiscent of the style of the Master of the Last Judgement: namely, those of Santa Eulalia de Mérida (Susín, Huesca) (Museo Diocesano de Jaca) and San Esteban at Almazorre (Sobrarbe, Huesca). Although some Aragonese scholars have disputed the relationship between Susín and the Master (Borrás Gualis and García Guatas 1977, 145–155), it is difficult to deny this direct connexion, as Josep Gudiol has noted (1971, 78). In fact, the recent publication of the paintings of Almazorre by María del Carmen Lacarra (2010) seems to confirm that the style of the Master of the Last Judgement was visible throughout Aragon by a very early date, around 1131 – just a few years after the consecration of Santa Maria de Taüll – while Lacarra Ducay also confirms the leading role of the See of Roda in that process. The act of consecration of San Esteban at Almazorre also informs us that Arnaldo Dodon, bishop of Huesca-Jaca (1130–1134), performed the dedication on 6 January 1131 (Lacarra Ducay 2010, 23–25); this text can also be read on the captions accompanying the paintings on the central apse. It must be underlined that Arnaldo was a former canon of Roda d'Isàvena, and may therefore have had links with the workshop of the Master of the Last Judgement, whom he would later have called to Almazorre (Castiñeiras 2011b).

However, what really distinguishes these paintings is the battle scene depicted on the centre of the apse, just behind the altar, which shows two warriors fighting on horseback (see Figure 10.2). Unfortunately, the knight on the left, who was identified as a Christian, is now in poor condition. Nevertheless, the combatant on the right is quite well preserved and appears to be a Muslim warrior. The painting would then be the depiction of a battle between a Christian and a Moor. This subject will be common in late twelfth-century Soria, as we can see in the carved capitals of the churches of Santa Maria at Tiermes and San Pedro at Caracena (Monteira Arias 2005, 51–53, figs. 37, 38). However, because of its early date the Almazorre image has a very particular context: namely, the Almoravid attacks in southeast Aragon in 1131 and the subsequent campaigns of Alfonso the Battler against Mequinenza (1133) and Fraga (1134). This second battle, where the king was mortally wounded, also saw the deaths of the bishops Dodon of Huesca and Pedro Guillermo of Roda-Barbastro (Huesca 1797, IV, 179–181).

To an extent, one should thus consider the Almazorre paintings, which probably date from 1131, as a visual manifesto of the knightly ideals of Alfonso I and his entourage, in which Bishop Arnaldo played an important role as both warrior and churchman. This would explain the uncommon display of a battle scene on an apse, in which a Muslim warrior wearing a turban directs his spear against a medallion featuring a Chrismon. From the time of King Sancho I Ramírez (1063–1094), father of Alfonso I, this had been the symbol of the compromise of Aragon – as tributary to St. Peter – with the Holy See, and the Crusade against the Muslims. As

Figure 10.2 Detail of the warriors fighting. San Esteban de Almazorre (Huesca), mural paintings, apse, central register, c. 1131.

© Antonio García Omedes

the seal of God, the Chrismon was used in documents issued by the royal chancellery as well as in the tympana of the kingdom's main churches, such as the Cathedral of Jaca, Santa Cruz de la Serós or San Pedro el Viejo in Huesca (Ocón 2003). Ultimately, the double display of the sign in Almazorre, on both sides of the apse, accompanying both warriors, would be interpreted as the direct compromise between Church and King in the current war against the Almoravids.

Longing for Jerusalem

As part of Western Europe, the Peninsula was not isolated from the phenomenon of the Crusades, as is often suggested. Throughout the twelfth century there were close ties between Iberia and the Holy Land, both in institutional and private domains. To this extent, it is worth mentioning that a brotherhood joined the chapters of the Holy Sepulchre in Jerusalem and Santiago de Compostela from 1129. It is very likely that Patriarch Stephen then sent Gelmírez, Archbishop of Compostela, with the letter of *confraternitas*, the so-called *Lignum Crucis "of Carboeiro"* that is conserved in the Chapel of the Relics. It deals with a patriarchal cross-shaped reliquary belonging to a group produced by the *aurifabri* at the Holy

Sepulchre in Jerusalem between 1120 and 1170. Examples of these crosses are spread across Europe, and most were gifts given directly by the Patriarch of Jerusalem – as in the cases of Denkendorf, Angers and Grandmont.

Furthermore, some members of the Galician nobility, and in particular the family of Traba, made journeys to the Holy Land and gave numerous donations to the Holy Sepulchre. The name of Rodrigo Pérez de Traba stands out prominently among these. In 1138, apart from the hamlet of Pasarelos, located near the city of Santiago in Oroso (La Coruña), he endowed the Holy Sepulchre with an annual income of two silver marks: "duasque argenti marcas ad conservandam hujus doni mei stabilitatem et memoriam Sepulcri Domini canonicis annis singulis mittam" [I shall send two silver marks each year to the canons of the Lord's Sepulchre for the preservation of the stability and memory of this gift of mine] (Bresc-Bautier 1984, doc. 72, 170–171). Moreover, his name appears in the dedication of a description of the Holy Land written by Rorgo Fretellus of Nazareth in 1148 (Castiñeiras 2012b, 349–350). To this extent, the old comparison drawn between the new façade of the Holy Sepulchre, which was consecrated on 15 July 1149 (Boas 1999, 125–127), and the north and south façades of the Cathedral of Santiago, which were constructed between 1101 and 1111, requires further attention. Jerusalem seems to evoke Compostela, as a result of the web of cultural exchanges suggested here, to which I will return in future publications.

In Catalonia, meanwhile, the nobility shows very similar sentiments towards the Holy Land throughout the twelfth century. However, in this case, the phenomenon seems to have had its precedents in a long tradition of travelling to Jerusalem, particularly common during the eleventh century (Gudiol 1927). The rapid conquest of lands undertaken by Christians between 1117 (Tarragona) and 1148 (Lleida), and the settlement of the Knights Templar at the Castle of Miravet from 1153, ensured a wide and prosperous territory for this expanding society. This is the background against which we should read the Patriarchal Cross of Anglesola (Lleida), known as Vera Creu d'Anglesola (see Figure 10.3), which, as in the case of Compostela, belongs to the same group of crosses produced in twelfth-century Jerusalem. Scholars have determined that the family of Anglesola played a leading role in the acquisition of this reliquary. For Jaspert (1999, 463–465), its acquisition should be related to the 1154 donation of some houses in the village of Anglesola to the Order of the Canons of the Holy Sepulchre by Berenguer Arnau d'Anglesola and his sons Berenguer and Bernat, as well as by his brother Arnau Berenguer d'Anglesola and his sons. However, according to Jaspert, the reliquary should not have arrived until the end of the twelfth century when the canons of Santa Anna of Barcelona were well established and probably dedicated a chapel to the Cross there. On the other hand, Miquel Torres Benet (2012, 50–51) suggests that Berenger Arnau, Lord of Anglesola, was responsible for bringing this prestigious object on his return from the Holy Land in 1176.

This latter hypothesis seems to fit the date of the piece much better, and confers a special significance on the object as a "speaking" witness of the pilgrimage to Jerusalem. Thanks to a recent restoration by the CRBMC, the original aspect of the cross has been rediscovered. The reliquary currently has an ornate seventeenth-century base crowned by a Gothic case in the shape of a cross, which hides a very good twelfth-century *stauroteca* (Español 2015, 80–86). Although there is no doubt about the production of the latter in the workshop of the Holy Sepulchre or its attribution to the same group of the *Lignum Crucis* of Compostela because of the double cross-shaped openings or the depiction of the Tomb of Christ under the dome of the Anastasis, some details of the iconographical programme imply a later date around 1150–1170. This can be deduced by the prominence of Adam and the Deesis, who are both absent in the Cross of Compostela. Their presence in the Anglesola cross may well be related to the

Figure 10.3   Patriarchal Cross of Anglesola (Lleida), anvers. Jerusalem, c. 1150–70.

© Ajuntament d'Anglesola

decoration of the chapel of Adam in Calvary after the consecration of the Crusader's Anastasis in 1149. In any case, the special continuity of the devotion of the Anglesola family to the Holy Sepulchre is recorded in 1379, in which Berenguer d'Anglesola was summoned by Prince Joan of Aragon to recount his recent journey to Jerusalem and Cyprus (Vieillard 1936, 269).

Cathars and friars: the origins of the Inquisition

The turn of the century was a time of much tension within this expanding society. In this particular context, it is especially important to consider art as a means of communication. The great old diocese of La Seu d'Urgell, in northwest Catalonia, is a case in point. From the late twelfth century onwards, this see was the setting of a straight fight between the feudatory power represented by the viscounts of Castellbò and the Counts of Foix, and the power of the ecclesiastical see of Urgell. The first found their greatest ally in the emerging communities of Cathars or Albigensi on both sides of the Pyrenees, who were responsible for the systematic destruction of the liturgical furnishing of the diocese during 1195 and 1196. This wave of devastation attempted to destroy these sacred objects as symbols of the ecclesiastical hierarchy and the sacrament of the Eucharist (Gros 1996). Hence the reaction of the see of Urgell, which from the early thirteenth century onwards promoted the activity of a panel-painting workshop probably based in the cathedral which aimed to proclaim – in colourful and impressive images – the values of the dogmas which issued from the Fourth Lateran Council (1215).

After a second wave of devastations in the late 1230s, a powerful bishop of Urgell, Ponç de Vilamur (1230–1257), commissioned a written account of all the misdeeds carried out by the Cathars in this long and difficult period: *Memorials dels danys causats* (Marquès 2006–2008, 44–53). It is very likely that its composition between 1241 and 1251 was almost contemporary with another important event: the painting of the murals of the chapel of Saint Catherine (ca. 1242–1255), at the far south-west end of the transept of the cathedral of La Seu d'Urgell (Castiñeiras 2009). This set of mural paintings, which combined a hagiographical cycle (including the Dispute, Arrest and Martyrdom of Saint Catherine) with the scene of the Last Supper, was removed between 1927 and 1933 and divided into three fragments.[6] Its peculiar style is proof of the final transformation of Catalan Romanesque painting, which was then influenced by the French Linear Gothic style.

As far as Ponç de Vilamur is concerned, he was a noted persecutor of the Cathars in his bishopric. He undertook this task with the support of Dominican friars, such as the inquisitor Pons de Planès, who in 1237–1238 was poisoned by the inhabitants of Castellbò and later buried as a saint in the Cathedral of La Seu d'Urgell. In this context of a statement of Catholic orthodoxy, the patronage of this original cycle gave Pons de Vilamur the opportunity to express his ideas about the importance of the dialectics against the heretics, whether Cathars or Jews, as well as to highlight the importance of the sacrament of the Eucharist. At the time, the cult of the Alexandrian martyr – Saint Catherine – was particularly relevant to the emerging Dominican Order as a champion of orthodoxy and model of scholastic debates. Hence her particular depiction as a contemporary preacher in the scene of disputation (see Figure 10.4), where Catherine shows great dialectical skills, bearing a book and arguing with a group of pagan philosophers. Just below this, a large scene of the Last Supper proclaims the institution of the Eucharist, which was proof of the sacrifice and humanity of Christ, the most controversial issues where Catharism was concerned. Furthermore, it is very likely that this chapel of Saint Catherine was a place devoted to the reconciliation of heretics and the cult of Dominican martyrs.

Figure 10.4 Dispute and Arrest of Saint Catherine. Mural Paintings of Santa Caterina de la Seu d'Urgell, c. 1241–52.

© MNAC-Museu Nacional d'Art de Catalunya. Barcelona. Calveras/Mérida/Sagristá.

Two anachronisms in the Dispute of Saint Catherine can tell us much about the ideological background of the image: firstly, the saint is followed by a group of preachers – three canons and one Dominican friar wearing a white habit, who may have been members of the emerging tribunals of the Inquisition; secondly, the wise men (SAP/IEN/TES) are depicted as contemporary Jews, sitting on the floor, wearing pointed gowns and with ethnic features such as long beards and crooked noses. For a contemporary audience, this latter depiction evoked debates between Christians and Rabbis as well as the rising communities protected by King Jaume I of Aragon in Puigcerdà and Perpignan but regarded suspiciously by the ecclesiastical authorities. Unfortunately, a century later this weak balance would degenerate into a series of violent pogroms, and pitiless anti-Semitic programmes became a typical feature of Aragonese and Catalan Gothic painting (Mann 2010).

The apostle is present! From Compostela to Turégano

To return to Santiago de Compostela, it should be noted that at the turn of the thirteenth century Maestro Mateo established a new longitudinal axis (W–E) in the sacred topography of the Cathedral. This was made in three successive steps: the carving of an impressive sculpted porch in the western wall, known as the Pórtico de la Gloria (1168–1188); the building of a large stone choir in the central aisle; and finally the placing of the statue of St. James on the main altar for the solemn consecration of 1211. This dramatically altered the previous transversal axis (N–S) and itinerary created by Gelmírez around 1100, offering pilgrims a new longitudinal perception of the building. For these pilgrims the cathedral was primarily a sanctuary, the end point of a popular and crowded pilgrimage, whose location close to Finisterre helped at least some to see it as the legendary entrance to the afterlife.

That is precisely how the monument is described in the *Vision of Thurkill*, a text composed in England around 1206 which tells the story of an English peasant from Stisted (near Colchester, Essex), whose soul journeyed to Compostela. This is the first *ekphrasis* of the Pórtico de la Gloria, where St. James, wearing episcopal robes, received the soul of this pilgrim:

> intrantibus illis basilicam occurrit eis sanctus Iacobus quasi infulatus, qui videns per-
> egrinum suum, pro quo miserat, ait sancto Iuliano et sancto Dompnino, qui custos
> eiusdem erat loci, quantinus ostenderent peregrino suo loca penalia reorum necnon
> et mansiones iustorum (*Visio Thvrkilli* 1978, 10–11) [when they entered the basilica,
> it happened that Saint James appeared, as if wearing episcopal robes, and seeing his
> pilgrim and who had sent him, he told Saint Julian and Saint Domninus, who were
> the guardians of him in this place, to show his pilgrim the places of the punishments
> for the wicked as well as the houses of the righteous].

This clearly refers to the seated statue on the *trumeau* of the Pórtico, where, as in the text, St. James seems to be inviting us to look upon the punishment of the damned and the peace of the righteous, which are depicted on the right arch of the porch. These just souls are crowned and later rise up to Heaven, from where they can hear – as in the central arch of the Pórtico – all kinds of musical instruments (*Visio Thvrkilli* 1978, 32–33). A shocking experience awaited those who looked upon the new painted Pórtico, who would have perceived it as a true performance. The realism of these sculptures, with their painted lips, eyebrows and beards, would have fascinated a contemporary audience.

Nevertheless, the author of the *Vision of Thurkill* gives no sign of being aware of the very last works undertaken in the basilica. His account makes no mention of the statue of St. James the Great that presides over the high altar from 1211 onwards. That position was ideal for the Apostle to play his role as a true psychopomp and intercessor on behalf of his pilgrims. This original image was therefore soon to be echoed elsewhere in the Peninsula. Thus, in the Church of St. James in Turégano (Segovia), a series of carvings in the apse wall (see Figure 10.5), which have recently been restored by María Suárez-Inclán, provide the earliest evidence for the reception of the colourful sculptures of the Pórtico as well as the lifelike statue set behind the high altar (Castiñeiras 2012a). This series consists of a set of reliefs depicting a group of pilgrims standing or kneeling before the figure of the Apostle St. James bearing a book with the caption: "IA(C)/OBVS/APOSTO/LVS." It is very likely that this remarkable composition echoed the new scenery consecrated in 1211 in the main altar at the Cathedral of Santiago as well as the new pilgrim rites related to it.

In my opinion, these intriguing carvings were made around 1232 and they are directly related to a particular historical event. On 10 July 1232, the powerful archbishop of Toledo, Rodrigo Jiménez de Rada, and the bishop of Segovia, Bernardo, met in Turégano to issue an indulgence for those who visited the Cathedral of Saint Mary in Segovia on the anniversary of its consecration or during the feast of Magdalene (Villar García 1990, 185–186, docs. 129–130). It is very likely that the unusual presence of both prelates in Turégano is due to their probable participation in the consecration of two new parish temples in the village:

Figure 10.5   Saint James and his pilgrims. Santiago de Turégano (Segovia), apse, painted reliefs, c. 1232. © Manuel Castiñeiras.

those of St. Michael and St. James. It is worth noting that just a few years before, in 1228, Bernardo had consecrated the new Romanesque cathedral of Segovia, where there was an important altar, on the right lateral apse, dedicated to St. James the Great.

Furthermore, the construction of the church of Santiago de Turégano between 1220 and 1232 coincided with a change in the political situation of the Kingdom of Castile. From 1217, the realm was ruled by Fernando III – son of the King of Galicia and Leon, Alfonso IX (1188– 1230) – who was responsible for the permanent union of both monarchies (Castile and Leon) in 1230. It is very likely that this building was related to the renewed success of the cult of St. James in these lands, especially given his role as patron of the Reconquest. It must not be forgotten that from 1228 Fernando III embarked on a series of campaigns against the Muslims that culminated in the conquest of the symbolic city of Córdoba in 1236. There, according to Rodrigo Jiménez de Rada, *De Rebus Hispaniae* IX, XVII (1989, 351), the King recovered the bells of the Basilica of Santiago, which had served as oil lamps in the mosque from the time of Almanzor, and sent them back to Compostela.

In light of this, I would like to draw attention to the group of three aristocratic figures kneeling before the statue of St. James, in the lower register of the carving with pilgrims. From their lavish garments, the first two may be a royal couple, a king and a queen, while the third figure, who is wearing a mitre and leaning on a peculiar tau-shaped crosier, is undoubtedly a bishop. In my opinion, these figures represent Bernardo, bishop of Segovia, Queen Beatriz and King Fernando III, who, on 29 February 1232, were in Compostela (*apud Sanctum Iacobum*) to issue generous donations to the Basilica of St. James (Lucas Álvarez 1998, 306–310, docs. 158–160). Just a few months later, on 10 July 1232, came the consecration of the new building dedicated to St. James in Turégano, at which Bishop Bernardo was also present. Bishop

Bernardo would have commissioned these carvings as a record of his pilgrimage and devotion to St. James, as well as a statement of his episcopal power and his closeness to the King.

Furthermore, this innovative stone *retablo* is the earliest witness of the impact of a work placed on the high altar of the Cathedral of Santiago in 1211. According to the *Libro de Constituciones* I, f. 73r (ca. 1240) (Archivo de la Catedral de Santiago), the door to the railing that enclosed the sanctuary was opened at least once a day to allow pilgrims to enter and perform certain rites, in particular, to place almonds and light candles before the statue of St. James: "ponant candelas ante figuram beati Iacobi" (Plötz 2004). As the carvings in Turégano show, that is how the figure of St. James became alive in the eyes of his pilgrims (Castiñeiras 2016). He was finally a patron who presided over his home, pointing his finger at his tomb and expecting that in the afterlife he would develop his role as intercessor and leader of the souls of his pilgrims.

Notes

1 This chapter is the product of research undertaken as part of the project *Artistas, Patronos y Público. Cataluña y el Mediterráneo (siglos XI–XV)-MAGISTRI CATALONIAE* (MICINN-HAR 2011-23015).
2 Although from a technical point of view the Creation Tapestry is not actually a "tapestry" but an "embroidery," the term "tapestry" is used here following what was standard practice in the Middle Ages, by which "tapestry" was understood to refer to any type of embroidered fabric.
3 Paris, BN, Ms. Lat. 5132, ff. 79v–80v.
4 William of Malmesbury (1855), col. 1492.
5 For further refinement of this view, see Árnaiz Alonso (2008) and Guardia (2011, 211–213).
6 The fragment depicting the Dispute and Arrest is kept in the MNAC (Barcelona); the Martyrdom is in Abbeg Stiftung (Riggisberg, Switzerland); and the Last Supper is in the Museu Episcopal de Vic.

Works cited

Alfonso X el Sabio. 2011. *Alfonso X el Sabio. Prosa histórica*. Edited by Benito Brancaforte. Madrid: Cátedra.

Árnaiz Alonso, Benito. 2008. "En clave románica: las pinturas murales de San Miguel de Gormaz (Soria)." *Arevacon. Revista Cultural. Asociación de Amigos del Museo Numantino* 29: 28–48.

Aurell, Martin. 1977. "Du nouveau sur les comtesses catalanes (IXè–XIIè siècles)." *Annales du Midi* 109: 219–220, 357–379.

Belli D'Elia, Pina. 1975. *Alle sorgenti del Romanico. Puglia XI secoli*. Bari: Pinacoteca Provinciale.

Boas, Adrian J. 1999. *Crusader Archeology. The Material Culture of the Latin East*. London and New York: Routledge.

Borrás Gualis, Gonzalo and Manuel García Guatas. 1977. *La pintura románica en Aragón*. Zaragoza: Caja de Ahorros de la Inmaculada-Fundación General Mediterránea.

Bresc-Bautier, Geneviève. 1984. *Le Cartulaire du Chapitre du Saint-Sépulchre de Jérusalem*. Paris: L'Académie des Inscriptions et Belles-Lettres.

Castiñeiras, Manuel. 2009. "Santa Caterina retrobada: el programa de la Catedral de La Seu d'Urgell i el seu context." In *La princesa sàvia. Les pintures de Santa Caterina de La Seu d'Urgell*, edited by Manuel Castiñeiras and Judit Verdaguer, 23–37. Barcelona: Museu-Nacional d'Art de Catalunya-Museu Episcopal de Vic.

———. 2011a. *The Creation Tapestry*. Girona: Catedral de Girona.

———. 2011b. "El románico catalán en el contexto hispánico de la Edad Media. Aportaciones, encuentro y divergencias." In *El esplendor del románico. Obras maestras del Museo Nacional d'Art de Catalunya*, edited by Jordi Camps, 47–69. Madrid: Funadación Mapfre-Museu Nacional d'Art de Catalunya.

———. 2012a. "Un nuevo testimonio de la iconografía jacobea: Los relieves pintados de Santiago de Turégano (Segovia) y su relación con el altar mayor de la Catedral de Santiago." *Ad Limina* 3: 73–117.

————. 2012b. "Puertas y metas de la peregrinación: Roma, Jerusalén y Santiago hasta el siglo XIII." In *Peregrino, ruta y meta en las peregrinations maiores, VIII Congreso Internacional de Estudios Jacobeos, Santiago de Compostela, 13–15 Octubre 2010*, edited by Paolo Caucci von Saucken, 327–378. Santiago de Compostela: Xunta de Galicia.

————. 2015. "Le *Tapis de la Création* de Gérone: une œuvre liée à la réforme grégorienne en Catalogne?" In *Art et réforme grégorienne en France et dans la Péninsule Ibérique*, edited by Barbara Franze, 147–175. Paris: Picard.

————. 2016. "El Apóstol y sus adorantes peregrinos. El porqué de la imagen coral de Santiago de Turégano (Segovia)." In *De peregrinatione. Studi in onore di Paolo Caucci von Saucken*, edited by Giuseppe Arlotta, 749–790. Napoli: Edizioni Compostellane.

Cook, Water S. and Josep Gudiol i Ricart. 1980. *Pintura e imaginería románicas.* vol. VI of *Ars Hispaniae.* Madrid: Plus Ultra.

Español, Francesca. 2015. *La Vera Creu d'Anglesola i els Pelegrinatges de Catalunya a Terra Santa.* Solsona: Museu Diocesà i Comarcal de Solsona.

Frugoni, Chiara. 1976–1977. "L'ideologia del potere imperiale nella *Cattedra di San Pietro.*" *Bullettino dell'Istituto Storico Italiano per il Medio Evo e Archivio Muratoriano* 86: 67–180.

Gell, Alfred. 2010. *Art and Agency: An Anthropological Theory.* Oxford: Clarendon Press.

Gesta Tancredi. 2010. *The Gesta Tancredi of Ralph of Caen. A History of the Normans on the First Crusade.* Translated and edited by Bernard S. Bachrach and David S. Bachrach. Farnham: Ashgate.

Gros, Miquel dels Sants. 1996. "Devastació d'esglésies del bisbat d'Urgell entorn del 1200." In *Homenatge a mossèn Jesús Tarragona*, edited by Esther Balasch, Carme Berlabé and María Burrell, 167–177. Lleida: Ajuntament de Lleida.

Guardia, Milagros. 2011. *San Baudelio de Berlanga, una encrucijada.* Bellaterra: U.A.B. Servei de Publicacions.

Gudiol i Cunill, Josep. 1927. "De peregrins i peregrinatges religiosos catalans." *Analecta Sacra Tarraconensia* 3: 93–119.

Gudiol i Ricart, Josep. 1971. *Pintura medieval en Aragón.* Zaragoza: Institución Fernando el Católico.

Huesca, Ramon de. 1797. *Teatro histórico de las Iglesias del Reino de Aragón*, IV. Pamplona: La Imprenta de la Viuda de Longás e hijo.

Jaspert, Nikolas. 1999. "Un vestigio desconocido de Tierra Santa: la Vera Creu d'Anglesola." *Anuario de Estudios Medievales* 29: 447–475.

Jiménez de Rada, Rodrigo. 1989. *Historia de los hechos de España.* Edited by Juan Fernández Valverde. Madrid: Alianza Editorial.

Lacarra Ducay, María del Carmen. 2010. *Estudio histórico de la decoración mural interior de la iglesia de San Esteban de Almazorre.* Zaragoza: Gobierno de Aragón.

Mann, Vivian B. 2010. "Jews and Altarpieces in Medieval Spain." In *Uneasy Communion: Jews, Christians, and the Altarpieces of Medieval Spain*, edited by Vivian B. Mann, 76–129. New York and London: Museum of Biblical Art-D Giles Limited.

Marquès, Benigne. 2006–2008. "Els documents del Fons Caboet-Castellbò de l'Arxiu Capitular d'Urgell (1095–1251)." *Quaderns d'Estudis Andorrans* 8: 11–76.

Marquès, Josep Maria. 1993. *Cartoral dit de Carlemany, del bisbe de Girona s. IX–XIV.* Barcelona: Fundació Nogera.

Monteira Arias, Inés. 2005. *La influencia islámica en la escultura románica de Soria. Una nueva vía para el estudio de la iconografía en el Románico.* Madrid: Fundación Universitaria Española.

Muratova, Xenia. 2007. "Chiesa e Palazzo nella Russia medievale: la decorazione delle porte meridionali della cattedrale di Suzdal." In *Medioevo: la Chiesa e il Palazzo, Convegno Internazionale di Studi, Parma, 2005*, edited by Arturo Carlo Quintavalle, 543–556. Milan: Electa.

Ocón Alonso, Dulce. 2003. "El sello de Dios sobre la iglesia: tímpanos con crismón en Navarra y Aragón." In *El Tímpano románico. Imágenes, estructuras y audiencias*, edited by Rocío Sánchez and José Luis Senra, 77–101. Santiago di Compostella, Xunta de Galicia.

Palol, Pere de. 1986. *El Tapís de la Creació de la Catedral de Girona.* Artstudi: Barcelona.

Plötz, Robert. 2004. "Volviendo al tema: la *coronatio.*" In *Padrón, Iria y las tradiciones jacobeas*, edited by Vicente Almazán, 107–108. Santiago de Compostela: Xacobeo.

Rucquoi, Adeline. 2010. "Cluny, el Camino francés y la Reforma Gregoriana." *Medievalismo* 20: 97–122.

Torres Benet, Miquel. 2012. "Assaig contextual i religiós de la Santa Creu d'Anglesola, un reliquiari del segle XII, reformat al segle XVII." In *Ordes menors: Els trinitaris d'Anglesola, Avinganya i Lleida*, edited by Grup de Recerques de les Terres de Ponent, 33–70. Sant Martí de Maldà: Grup de Recerques de les Terres de Ponent.

Tumbo, A. 1998. *Tumbo A de la Catedral de Santiago.* Edited by Manuel Lucas Álvarez. Santiago: Cabildo de la Catedral de Santiago-Seminario de Estudos Galegos.

Vanoli, Alessandro. 2006. *La Spagna delle tre culture. Ebrei, cristiani e musulmani tra storia e mito.* Roma: Viella.

Vielliard, Jeanne. 1936. "Pèlerins d'Espagne à la fin du Moyen Âge." *Analecta Sacra Tarraconensia* 12: 265–300.

Villar García, Luis-Miguel. 1990. *Documentación medieval de la Catedral de Segovia (1115–1300).* Salamanca: Ediciones Universidad de Salamanca y Ediciones Universidad de Deusto.

Visio Thvrkilli. 1978. *Visio Thvrkilli.* Edited by Paul Gerhard Schmidt. Leipzig: Bibliotheca Scriptorvm Graecorvm et Romanorvm Tevbneriana.

Vivó, Carles. 1989. *Llegendes i misteris de Girona.* Girona: Diputación de Girona.

William of Malmesbury. 1855. *Gesta pontificum anglorum. Patrologia Latina*, CLXXIX. Edited by Jacques-Paul Migne. Paris.

PART II

The Iberian Peninsula in the Golden Age (sixteenth–seventeenth centuries)

History, politics and cultural studies

11

THE EARLY MODERN IBERIAN EMPIRES

Emulation, alliance, competition

Alexander Ponsen and Antonio Feros

[T]his union brings to the church and to all of Christianity in general one of the greatest benefits and comforts that could ever be offered [. . .] that joining the forces of my states with those of the Portuguese nation, so valiant and highly esteemed in the world for its military capabilities and conquests by sea and land, and for its industriousness in navigation, will raise Spain's reputation to such a point that all other nations will recognize and respect it as the most thriving and prosperous province of Christendom.

(Philip II [1579] 1845, 652–653)

Philip II's enthusiasm in 1579 at the imminent prospect of incorporating Portugal and its empire within his already vast dominions could hardly have been more palpable. The union was meant to cement Spain's reputation by achieving the long-sought reunification of the entire Iberian Peninsula under one Christian sovereign and by crowning Philip king of the largest composite monarchy the world had ever known. But six decades on, in the wake of Portugal's "Restoration" of independence in 1640, many Portuguese observers scorned the unification process in retrospect as an unjust conquest by a larger, aggressive neighbor, and later historians portrayed the sixty-year union as a "long night" of "submission" and "captivity," a regrettable blemish on Portugal's otherwise proud, distinctive history (Cueto 1992, 50). As a result of independence, Portugal recovered its pride as one of the largest monarchies in history, thanks to the exploits of Portuguese conquerors in Africa, Asia and the Americas. By that time, however, the Iberian monarchies were no longer the only great powers in an ever more expansionist Europe. The Portuguese and Spanish kingdoms were therefore the earliest examples of what Thomas Dandelet calls the "revival of imperial ambition [. . .] the master narrative that drove European political life for the entire early modern period" (2014, 3).

Here we analyze the Iberian cases within this imperial renaissance, attempting to understand why they expanded, how they integrated overseas territories into the pre-existing peninsular realms, but also the debates that this expansionism provoked in each political community. In this parallel history of the Portuguese and Spanish empires, the fundamental objective is to highlight the many connections between the two, the alliances and convergences as well as the competition between them (Martínez Torres 2014; Subrahmanyam 2007). The essay will also aim to explain the characteristics of the political communities which, though never officially self-declared empires, undoubtedly behaved as such, as heirs to the Roman Empire. In Castilian and Portuguese dictionaries of the sixteenth and seventeenth centuries, "empire" referred to the Roman Empire, or to its successor, the Holy Roman Empire. The Iberian monarchs never possessed the title of Emperor. *Imperio* as a concept meant simply, "power" and "dominion," "to reign" and "to command." This concept of "empire" as "government and command," explains titles like that of the mid-seventeenth-century manuscript by Alonso Martínez Calderón, *Imperio de la Monarquía de España* (Pagden 1995).

But despite not labeling themselves as empires the two realms did nonetheless have designs to dominate non-European peoples and territories, and sought to extend their power and *imperio* to all possible regions of the globe. The results of Iberian expansionism were without doubt "imperial," which is to say that they produced the creation of communities which integrated numerous territories on various continents. This complex mixture of concepts appears with clarity in the work of the Valencian Tomás Cerdán de Tallada who determined that the way to create a "state" was to subject diverse territories and peoples to the command, *imperio*, of a prince, "as has happened in this Spanish realm, that with time through marriages, and extrinsic juridical and natural successions, through laws, actions and conquests, conceded to the Kings of Spain by the Holy See, by just causes, had united in the Royal person of our King and lord, so many Kingdoms, Provinces, Lordships, and Republics" (1604, 2). It was the vastness of the territories under the monarch's *imperio* which convinced many that the king of Spain was more than just an ordinary king: he was the king of kings and of princes and lords. In this way, the Spanish monarch was head of the "most powerful kingdom," had subjected other "kingdoms and provinces," and had no "superior in the temporal" sphere (López Madera 1597, 7r-v).

This essay analyzes the imperial constitution of the Iberian realms from the beginning of their expansion in the fifteenth century, and the debates that accompanied their expansion. It also assesses what the integration of Portugal brought to the Spanish monarchy, how the non-European possessions of both realms were governed in this period, and the relationship of those possessions to the metropolis. The histories of Portuguese and Spanish imperial expansion are strongly connected, not only from 1580 but also earlier. Both kingdoms shared a common history, one without doubt characterized by conflicts, but also by imitations, emulations and convergences. Their mutual expansion produced exchanges and mimicry, both in the process of expansion itself and in the attempts to give an institutional political structure to the expanding realms. In addition, although the results of expansion were in many ways distinct – due fundamentally to different conditions in the territories where the Spanish and Portuguese ended up settling – the reality was that in conceptualizing their empires, they drew from a common juridical-political culture, which was shared throughout Europe and was not just Iberian.

Emulation

While historians have long recognized the joint religious and commercial motives behind Castile's early expansion under Ferdinand and Isabel, Portugal's initial forays into the Atlantic and Indian oceans have been portrayed until recently as overwhelmingly commercial in orientation, with their religious missionary element as secondary to what was first and foremost a profit-driven enterprise. But in addition to the search for profit, propagation of the faith played as central a role in the early expansion of Portugal as it did for Castile. This was true from the beginning, and the rulers of both kingdoms shared a worldview steeped in the juridical-theological culture of fifteenth century Christian Europe.

Iberian expansion was violently competitive at the outset. Well before the Iberians' arrival in the New World, Portugal and Castile clashed over possessions in the Canaries, Morocco, the Azores and Cape Verde. This expansion was not the result of an imperialist policy, but of attempts by the Portuguese initially, followed by the Spanish, to find new opportunities and commercial routes to replace those monopolized or closed by the Ottomans in the Mediterranean, North Africa and overland across parts of western and central Asia. The Portuguese took the first initiative. By the early fifteenth century they had already expressed their conviction that the best alternative route was that which, beginning in the Atlantic, rounded Africa and entered into the vast world of spices in the Indian Ocean and East Asia. As they went, they established an array of strategic strongholds to secure their commercial monopoly over the spice trade. Portugal's primacy in the fifteenth century is evident when we recall the papal bulls, *Dum Diversas* and *Romanus Pontifex* of 1452 and 1455, which granted Portugal full secular and ecclesiastical jurisdiction over the lands and seas from northwest Africa all the way to India. The main conditions of those bulls were ratified when the two kingdoms signed the Treaty of Alcaçovas in 1479, which established the first Portuguese *mare clausum* in African and Asian waters.

Within a matter of decades the expansion of each kingdom achieved results viewed by many as nothing short of miraculous. After extending its trade in gold and slaves along the west African coast in the late fifteenth century, Portugal established trade links with India in 1498 and laid claim to Brazil with Cabral's landing there in 1500. Over the next half century the Portuguese attacked and occupied Goa, Colombo in Sri Lanka, and several southeast Asian islands. As they secured their foothold in Brazil, they also established an informal trading presence in both East Africa and Macao. Already by 1501, King Manuel I had adopted the title, "Lord of the Conquest, Navigation, and Commerce of Ethiopia, Arabia, Persia and India," indicating his global ambitions.

The expansion of the Spanish realm was no less impressive. Although not without setbacks along the way, since 1493 the Spanish monarchy had sponsored, organized or facilitated numerous voyages of exploration, as well as the occupation and exploitation of several Caribbean islands. The pace of expansion picked up following the victory over the Mexica in 1521, secured by Hernán Cortés with the aid of a large native army, and the conquest of the powerful Inca empire in the 1530s by Pizarro and his companions. As a result of these conquests, by 1560 the most populous regions and cities in the Americas had been occupied and claimed for the Spanish realm, and virtually all of the future colonial centers or capitals had been founded, or re-founded. Not until the 1620s would other European powers begin to threaten Spanish hegemony in the Indies, and even then only in the Caribbean and the regions that would later form part of the United States and Canada.

Spaniards also tried their luck on other continents. The Spanish monarchy sponsored the first successful circumnavigation of the globe, claimed sovereignty over the Moluccas, over the Philippines from the 1560s, attempted the conquest of the isle of Formosa (Taiwan), considered plans for the exploration and conquest of Australia and even for the invasion of China itself. Alongside these possessions were the Canary Islands and various territories in North Africa: Ceuta (after 1640, having previously belonged to the crown of Portugal), Melilla in what is today Morocco, and Oran, a city under Spanish sovereignty from 1509 until the end of the eighteenth century, in modern Algeria.

In the wake of Columbus' voyage to the Americas, the comparative power of the two Iberian kingdoms began to level off as demonstrated by the 1493 *Inter caetera* Bull of Donation, which legitimized conquest in the name of Christianization and granted jurisdiction on the condition that the "barbarous nations" discovered "be overthrown and brought to the faith."

The bull, *Inter caetera*, recognized the rights of Isabel and Ferdinand and their descendants over all the lands and peoples discovered as a result of these voyages of exploration. The bull conceded not only territorial, political and commercial rights to the Spanish kings, but also imposed on them an unambiguous ideological purpose: the obligation to convert all of the pagan peoples they encountered, to provide sufficient education for them to become good Christians, and, ironically, to care for and protect them against the aggression of rapacious colonizers. The legitimation of Spanish expansionism, and in a way its success, would be forever linked to Spain's ability to integrate the natives into the Christian "civilized" world.

Before the moment of dynastic union in 1580 there were relatively few conflicts between the Portuguese and Spanish. The primary reason was that from the beginning of Spanish expansion both kingdoms agreed to a pact creating two separate spheres of jurisdiction and navigation, which were confirmed in the 1494 Treaty of Tordesillas and the 1527 Treaty of Zaragoza. The Segovian jurist and governor Alonso de Zuazo referred to this in 1518 as a pact between the Portuguese and Spanish to divide "the world as an orange, in two equal parts" (1864, 296–297). Despite some conflicts and misunderstandings the treaties between Spain and Portugal largely succeeded in eliminating violence between them until the rise of border skirmishes in South America in the seventeenth and especially the eighteenth centuries. Importantly, as Portugal and Spain competed to consolidate imperial rule within their respective spheres, the two empires became increasingly interlinked. Many Portuguese, including Magellan, were essential to the early phase of Spanish discoveries and conquests. And while many Spaniards were at the forefront of the expansion of the Portuguese empire in Brazil, Portuguese settlers usually constituted by far the largest group of foreigners in the cities and towns of early Spanish America.

Celebrating and debating empire

From the second decade of the sixteenth century, the Spanish and Portuguese both expressed a clearly triumphalist view of their accomplishments (Curto 1998; Hespanha 1996). One example of such imperialist celebration comes from a Castilian chronicler, and another from a Portuguese poet. "[T]he greatest event since the creation of the world, apart from the incarnation and death of the creator himself, is the discovery of the Indies," proclaimed Francisco López de Gómara in the epistle dedicating his history of the Indies to Emperor Charles V (1553). A few years later, the great Portuguese poet, Luiz Vaz de Camões, echoed these sentiments by celebrating the explorations, voyages, and conquests of his compatriots in one of the most influential texts of the early modern period, *The Lusiads*. It was an ode to the history of his Portuguese homeland, the discoveries, the expansion of Christianity, and the deeds of Vasco de Gama and Magellan, all of which made Portugal "predestined to accomplish great deeds" and "impose its law in the concert of nations" (Camões 1639). The eulogizing of Spanish exploits was taken up again by Spain's most influential historian of the early modern period, Juan de Mariana. For Mariana, the year 1492 was without parallel in the history of Spain, with the conquest of Granada and the expulsion of the Jews, as well as the "most memorable enterprise, the source of the greatest honor and profit to have taken place in Spain [. . .] the discovery of the Western Indies, which as a result of their greatness are called the New World. [. . .] No nation in the world," he wrote, "has in such a brief period of time advanced so far, or stretched the limits of its empire so much" (1854, 2: 241, 243).

Yet despite the unmistakably patriotic literary trends in Portugal and Spain, already in the first years of expansion this triumphalism was accompanied by strong debates about the justness of the expansion, about the legality of their dominion over non-European peoples and territories, and about the integration of these territories into pre-existing institutional structures. The main issues under scrutiny also reflected the general models that the two respective empires came to adopt. While Spanish debates revolved around the legality of their territorial claim to the Americas and the abuse of subjected indigenous populations, debates over Portuguese *imperium* centered primarily on the African slave trade and exclusive control over navigation and the distribution of Asian spices. Nevertheless, Portuguese and Spanish jurists, humanists and theologians all drew on a common juridical-theological discourse in justifying the expansion of their empires.

The controversy was perhaps most intense when its focus was the abuse of the natives (Pagden 1982; Todorov 1984). In 1511 Antonio de Montesinos, a Dominican priest in Hispaniola, had been the first to publicly denounce their enslavement and harsh treatment. We have innumerable testimonies of the horrors of the conquest, from a wide variety of sources, but it was the Dominican friar Bartolomé de las Casas who provided the first systematic account in his famous *Brief Relation of the Destruction of the Indies* (1552), which catalogued the crimes committed by Spaniards in each of the regions conquered until that time. "Among these gentle sheep," he wrote, "the Spaniards appeared [. . .] like famished wolves, and tigers, and lions," killing everybody and destroying everything. Tensions escalated to such a point that, in 1550, Charles V convened a *junta* of theologians to rule on a debate on the issue.

If early Portuguese expansion elicited less controversy, part of the reason was that, unlike in Spanish America, many Portuguese conquests in Africa and Asia were directed against local peoples that were either Muslim or were considered so barbarous that, as Gomes Eanes de Zurara first argued, their conquest and enslavement was easily justified in the name of conversion and civilization. The 1510 conquest of Goa from its Muslim rulers was justified on this basis, and in 1548 Damião de Góis and Diogo de Teive spoke of the military campaign at the island of Diu as "a pious and just war" for precisely the same reasons. Yet by the second quarter of the sixteenth century Portuguese and Spanish authors were criticizing Portuguese *imperium* as well, particularly on the issue of African slavery. Bartolomé de las Casas marveled at "the manner in which Portuguese historians [Zurara, João de Barros, and others] glorify as illustrious such heinous deeds, representing these exploits as great sacrifices made in the service of God," while the Portuguese Fernando Oliveira leveled an even more scathing critique, arguing that his Portuguese compatriots were responsible for the very invention of the African slave trade by providing a demand for it on an unprecedented scale. A decade and a half later, in 1569, Andalucian Dominican Tomás de Mercado criticized the unjust violence through which the Portuguese crown obtained its *imperium* on the West African coast and protested uniquely that the Iberians' slaving activities contributed gravely to the social and political instability in the African regions where the slaves were procured (Marcocci 2012, 417–424).

In the case of the Spanish monarchy, as a result of these critiques, from the 1530s onward ecclesiastical and secular authorities implemented measures and formed institutions aimed at changing the colonists' treatment of the natives. In the first place, they acknowledged the need to attenuate the effects of conquest on the indigenous populations by eliminating slavery, forced labor and wars of conquest. In 1536 Pope Paul III declared that the Indians were fully human, and in 1542 the Spanish ruler officially rescinded all previous decrees that allowed the enslavement of Indians. Henceforth only specific Indian populations could be legitimately enslaved – those designated as savages or barbarians, but in reality all those who resisted Spanish domination – and in later decades even these distinctions were abolished in favor of full freedom for all natives. This process of juridical and political stabilization culminated with the publication of the 'Ordinances for the discovery, settlement, and pacification of the Indies,' issued by Philip II in July 1573. These prohibited new campaigns of exploration not approved by the royal authorities, and enjoined officials and colonists to "forego the word conquest, using instead pacification and settlement," to ensure that the Indians were never "assaulted, or aggrieved" (*Recopilación Leyes de Indias*, 1681, bk. 4). Although the debates among the Portuguese over expansion were not as intense and in general did not elicit an institutional response as profound as in the Spanish case, they did elicit the creation in 1532 of the *Mesa da Consciência*, its aim being "to resolve and settle any possible conflict between secular power and moral theology" (Marcocci 2014, 477).

The most prominent of these debates, however, was the so-called "Controversy of the Indies," centered on Spain's lawful title to the Americas. In 1534 Francisco de Vitoria, a leading theologian of the School of Salamanca, forcefully denied the validity of the Papal Bulls of Donation, citing what he viewed as the Pope's lack of authority in secular affairs, and decried Castile's seizure of American territory as unlawful because the natives, as rational beings by nature, had held it as legitimate owners. Controversy over both kingdoms' titles to their overseas possessions slowly faded from view, however, if only because, as the Spanish Jesuit ethnographer José de Acosta contended, despite valid questions over the conquest's initial legitimacy, Castile's right to the Indies had nonetheless become legally enacted through its long and continuous occupation of the land (Gil Pujol 2007, 33–34). More important is that both the Spanish and Portuguese kingdoms justified their rights to empire over their non-European territories using a multitude of titles – from the papal bulls, to the right of conquest, their right to occupy unclaimed lands, and even theories about voluntary vassalage offered by native peoples (Pérez-Amador Adam 2011; Saldanha 2004; Solórzano Pereira 1647, book 1, chaps. 9–12).

Ruling the empires

Beyond justifying the occupation of the overseas territories, the Iberian kingdoms were even more concerned with resolving their juridical status and delineating with clarity how they would be legally integrated within kingdoms that had been exclusively European until almost the end of the fifteenth century. Both the Spanish and Portuguese kingdoms had long traditions in the dynamics of territorial aggregation and cohesion. Both were "composite kingdoms" during the early modern period, the result of the aggregation of diverse territories, first in Europe, and from the mid-sixteenth century with extended dominions in Africa, Asia and America (Gil Pujol 2012). As the historians Pedro Cardim and Susana Münch Miranda (2012) have reminded us, these territories were united or annexed by various means – dynastic marriage, conquest, the voluntary cession of sovereignty – and their juridical status was determined by their means of incorporation, the geographical location of the territory, and the ethnic composition of the population. In other words, the separation between the metropole and the overseas territories was reinforced by perceived racial differences, and in general this implied that a great majority of the populations of these territories were treated as dependent and subaltern.

This explains why in both realms the overseas territories received a juridical status inferior to that of the European kingdoms and territories. All of the former were considered to have been annexed by "conquest" or cession of sovereignty, and all were considered to be inhabited by populations in a state of civilization inferior to that of Europeans. The most important result was that, with a few exceptions in the Portuguese case, they respected none of the overseas territories' institutions and laws, prohibited natives from holding imperial offices, and abolished institutions of representation that had existed before the union or annexation.

The Spanish case was in many ways simpler. From the beginning, all of the non-European territories over which the Spanish monarch came to exercise sovereignty were incorporated within the kingdom of Castile – as Granada and the Canaries had been – and therefore governed according to Castilian law. The non-recognition of pre-existing indigenous institutions made it such that the crown directly governed these territories. Founded in 1524, the Council of the Indies advised the monarch on everything related to the administration of his American possessions. To govern the colonies, the crown created two viceroyalties, one with its seat in Mexico City, the other in Lima. The viceroys, named by the Spanish kings as their lieutenants in the Indies, held executive power. Their most important functions were to defend royal interests, and indigenous peoples from predatory colonists. In addition to the viceroyalties, the crown also created several high courts of justice, *Audiencias*, to hear cases presented by both Spaniards and natives. Alongside these secular bodies and offices, the monarchy encouraged the creation of bishoprics and the establishment of numerous religious orders throughout the Indies, whose most important function, apart from taking care of the spiritual needs of the Spaniards in the New World, was to convert the natives, and the hundreds of thousands of Africans transported to those lands (Solórzano Pereira 1647).

In Spanish realms the so-called *indios* were considered vassals of the king, but formed part of the *República de Indios*, a separate political body which supposedly conserved some indigenous laws and institutions of government. But *indios* also had access to Castilian law. The Spanish monarchs conceded special statutes to certain indigenous nations, such as the Tlaxcalas, for their collaboration in the defeat of the Mexicas, or to members of the original indigenous elite. To these, although they were prohibited from performing traditional religious functions, they granted status, property, power in the native community, and the hereditary nature of their titles, offices and wealth. The growing presence of "Spaniards" in these territories provoked discussions about their role in governance. The crown permitted the creation of new cities, which functioned more or less as the peninsular ones did, but the inhabitants of the Indies never had parliamentary representation of any sort. And yet, as "Spaniards," these populations were subject to Castilian law.

The situation of the overseas territories of the Portuguese kingdom was much more complex. First, the Portuguese kingdom's capacity of centralization seems to have been much less than that of the Spanish. As a result, there was a general lack of central institutions of imperial government throughout the sixteenth century, and many of the territories remained relatively autonomous, especially the African and Asian ones, as well as Brazil until the seventeenth century. But rather than simply ascribing this to the weakness of the Portuguese monarchy, it is important to recall the complexity of the juridical status of its diverse territories. As Luis Filipe Thomaz stated, "When confronted with the current notion of empire, the Portuguese State of India [*Estado da Índia*] presents us with something original and, at times, baffling. More than its spatial discontinuity it is the heterogeneity of its institutions and the imprecision of their limits, both geographical and juridical, which make it unusual" (Thomaz 1994, 230). According to Susana Münch Miranda, what characterized the Portuguese empire was "decentralization, physical distance, and the jurisdictional autonomy" of each and every one of its officials and institutions (2010, 276).

Distinct from the Spanish practice of treating its overseas territories as part of the whole, the Portuguese maintained, or were forced to maintain, the differences and idiosyncrasies of each one. In various African possessions, in Angola for example, the Portuguese were a minority in relation to the natives, which were not under Portuguese jurisdiction, and the same occurred with the so-called "indios bravos" of Brazil. In some territories the Portuguese permitted varying degrees of religious liberty, especially in African and Asian territories, made voluntary pacts of vassalage with the indigenous populations, permitted the persistence of native political institutions and in many cases the coexistence of various rights within the same territory (Hespanha 2001). The Portuguese inhabitants of these overseas territories had

Alexander Ponsen and Antonio Feros

a similar relationship with the metropole to that which the Spaniards had with their kingdom, the difference being that the Portuguese in these territories gained the right of representation in the meetings of Portugal's *Cortes* (Cardim and Münch Miranda 2012).

Union

By the 1570s the devout monarchs of Spain and Portugal remained convinced of the divine mission of their respective empires. This decade saw Spain's dramatic naval victory against the Ottomans at Lepanto in 1571, considerable Portuguese territorial expansion into Angola and East Africa, and the consolidation of the plantation economy in Brazil (Subrahmanyam 2007). In 1578, inspired by these recent developments and thirsty for military glory, Sebastian I of Portugal led an ill-conceived attempt to establish an "Algarve beyond the sea" in Morocco by overthrowing its Ottoman-backed sultan. Sebastian disappeared in battle, presumably killed, and when his successor, the childless Henry I, fell ill just two years later, Philip began advancing his legal claim as rightful heir to the Portuguese throne.

As the son of Portuguese Princess Isabella and grandson of Portuguese King Manuel I, Philip's claim was strong and he viewed it as his divine destiny to unite the entire peninsula under one Christian sovereign. An anonymous letter from late 1578 advised Philip that union with Portugal would enable him to "wage war against the Turk across the Red Sea and to enter the provinces of Egypt and Jerusalem" (Bouza 1997, 34). The death of Henry in 1580 and the attempts of Dom António to declare himself king of Portugal compelled Philip to order an invasion, but only after having placated most of the Portuguese nobility with bribes as well as informal promises of autonomy and patronage in return for their political support. Despite having ultimately used force to secure his succession, Philip rejected the advice of his trusted adviser, Cardinal Granvelle, to treat Portugal as a conquest, abolish its autonomous laws, and subsume it as a province within the jurisdiction of Castile. Instead, under the terms agreed upon at the *Cortes* of Tomar in 1581, Philip was proclaimed King of Portugal while promising to respect the kingdom's existing customs, laws and privileges. Portuguese officials would continue to administer the kingdom and its overseas possessions, Portuguese would remain the official language in all matters of state, and a permanent *Consejo de Portugal* would be established, composed solely of Portuguese councilors, to advise the king on all matters relating to Portugal and its empire (Bouza 1987; Cardim 2014a, 2014b; Schaub 2001).

Philip's succession to the Portuguese throne initiated a profusion of verbal and visual discourse celebrating the event. The famous 1583 coin emblazoned with the phrase, "The World is not Enough," was one of many examples. Several prominent Portuguese voices also celebrated the union for its potential in expanding the territorial reach of the Iberian empires in East Asia. In 1584, the Portuguese Bishop of Malacca, Dom João Ribeiro Gaio, presented a detailed plan stressing the ease with which a joint Iberian force could conquer and become lord of all the lands from India to Japan. The following year, another Portuguese India official, Jorge de Lemos, echoed the militant discourse of Gaio in claiming "that the conquest of Atjeh [in present-day Indonesia] would give the dual Iberian crown the economic resources for a war [. . .] to recover all Christian territory lost to the Muslims (including Jerusalem), and to overthrow the Ottoman empire" (Boxer 1969, 122–124). Portuguese and Spanish authors lauded the extension and power of the new kingdom, which extended its power right across the New World and, in the words of Gregorio López Madera, thanks to Portugal, to territories in Africa and Asia where "Roman power never reached, and which not even Alexander attempted to subject" (Curto 1998, 461).

The Portuguese benefited greatly during the first four decades of union. Lusophone slave traders in West Africa gained access to both the enormous Spanish American market as well as to Biscayan iron, one of the chief items of exchange for slaves in their African ports of origin. Access to Spanish American silver was perhaps the major draw, both through legal trade conducted on the peninsula, as well as through the largely illicit trade in East Asia and the Río de la Plata (Schwartz 1968, 44). Beyond that, a military alliance with Spain was a tantalizing prospect in the effort to stamp out the rise of northern European privateering everywhere from the South Atlantic to the Malacca Straits. Finally, the series of steps taken by Spain to facilitate inter-peninsular commerce by abolishing customs duties on the Spanish-Portuguese border and improving navigation on the Tagus River also proved beneficial to both sides (Bustos 1983, 172).

Throughout the period of union, Portuguese writers also continued to pen celebratory tracts in the tradition of Zurara, Barros and Camões. In his 1627 *Memorial de la preferencia, que haze el Reyno de Portugal, y su Consejo, al de Aragon, y de las dos Sicilias*, Pedro Barbosa de Luna argued that, given the breadth of its overseas jurisdiction and conquests in the name of Christ, Portugal deserved a more dignified status than Aragon or Sicily within the composite Spanish kingdom. Four years later, by which time Spanish-Portuguese relations were already under significant strain, António de Sousa de Macedo intensified the patriotic rhetoric further still, describing Portugal as an "independent sovereign kingdom," which within its borders recognized neither the authority of the Emperor nor the superiority of the kingdom of Castile (Cardim 2010; Curto 1998).

These defenses of Portugal and its empire, especially during the first decades of the seventeenth century, came largely in response to Castilian attempts to consolidate control over the kingdom and its possessions. There were decades of constant debate about the possibility of abolishing the agreements of Tomar. There were also attempts to introduce Castilian officials into the governance of the Portuguese empire and centralize it according to the Spanish model with the creation of a Council of India (*Conselho da Índia*), which existed from 1604 to 1614 (Hespanha 1989; Münch Miranda 2010). Some of the most significant reforms were undertaken under the Count-Duke of Olivares, who served Philip IV as royal favorite from 1622 to 1643. In his 1624 *Gran Memorial*, Olivares suggested: "Looking at the way they are nowadays governed, many people would rightly say that Your Majesty's power would be greater if there were fewer nobles" (Elliott and de la Peña 1978, 95). With respect to the relationship between the Spanish and Portuguese overseas empires, he had in mind both an economic integration of the two empires and a Union of Arms (Subrahmanyam 2007, 1381). As a consequence of these reforms, besides bringing prestige to the Spanish monarchy by vastly expanding its imperial holdings, the incorporation of Portugal and its overseas possessions also brought a number of material benefits. Spain gained a number of Portuguese Atlantic ports, including Lisbon, direct access to spices from Portuguese India and slaves from Portuguese possessions in Africa (Schwartz 1993, 167). In addition, its colonists at the distant edges of the empire in Buenos Aires and Manila benefitted enormously through intense yet illicit trade in silver, slaves and spices with their Portuguese counterparts in Brazil and Macao.

The period of union was also characterized by the increase of international conflict, or to put it in other words, by the growing expansion of other European competitors, a process which questioned and challenged Portuguese and Spanish dominion in Asia, Africa and the Americas. The Dutch seizure of a Portuguese carrack off Singapore in 1603 provoked the first major international juridical debate over Portugal's right to maritime monopoly in Asia. In the famous 1609 treatise, *Mare Liberum*, Dutch jurist Hugo Grotius argued that the sea was an international space, that all nations were free to trade across it and that no nation could claim it exclusively or restrict the passage of foreign ships. Grotius drew heavily on the ideas of Spanish jurists who argued against the right to exclusive dominion over the high sea, but his basic innovation was to claim that Dutch war against Portugal was fully justified since the latter had violated the common rights of "the freedom of the seas" by attempting to impose its exclusive dominion. By the mid-1620s, the Dutch and English had long since broken Portugal's maritime monopoly. Beyond the rapid rise of Dutch and English power across maritime Asia, the Dutch also occupied northeast Brazil from 1630 to 1654 and Angola from 1641 to 1648.

As frustrations mounted in both the Spanish and Portuguese empires, resulting in large part from the incursions of the Dutch, English and French, many Spaniards and Portuguese alike came to view each other, and the union in general, as a major cause of their respective woes. The *consulado* merchants of Seville and their partners in Peru brought rising anti-Portuguese sentiment to a head by protesting the impressive economic power of the Portuguese. The xeno-phobic frenzy reached its height in the 1630s, resulting in a purge of unprecedented proportion in the Spanish Americas. During Lima's so-called *Complicidad Grande* of 1635, the Peruvian Inquisition executed more than thirty suspected New Christians, the vast majority of them Portuguese. This had an impact on virtually the entire Portuguese population, and many had their assets seized in the process (Cross 1978, 162).

At the same time, anti-Spanish feeling had gathered force among the Portuguese, because of their sense of being undervalued within the broader body politic of the Spanish kingdom, and of the many injuries Portugal had suffered in recent years. Philip IV's 1631 plan to popu-late Brazil with Italians to protect against Dutch incursions further aggravated the Portuguese (Schwartz 1968, 47). And after Olivares expressed the idea of an Iberian Union of Arms, Por-tuguese jurist, João Pinto Ribeiro, published his 1632, *Discurso sobre os fidalgos e soldados Portugueses nao militarem em conquistas alheas desta Coroa*, which protested that, in accord-ance with the terms agreed upon at Tomar, Portuguese soldiers and mariners should never be forced to serve outside their own empire (Boxer 1967, 249).

Two empires

Tensions finally came to a head on 1 December 1640 when a group of Portuguese nobles seized a well-chosen moment to assassinate the Portuguese Secretary of State Miguel de Vasconcelos and imprison Margaret of Savoy, Portugal's vicereine under Philip IV. Faced simultaneously with another revolt in Catalonia and a war with France and the Protestant powers, Castilian forces were unable to respond adequately after the Duke of Braganza was proclaimed King John IV of Portugal the following day. Despite the persistence of anti-Castilian sentiment among the people throughout much of the period of union, the formal rebellion itself was only made possible once the King had threatened the collective power of the Portuguese nobility, thereby violating the terms of their informal pact (Bouza 1994, 344). The spew of patriotic pamphlets published in the wake of the Portugal's "Restoration" of independence justified the revolt as a legitimate reaction to tyrannical kingship and the steady degradation of Portugal's autonomous jurisdiction (Gil Pujol 2007, 72–73).

Responses to Portuguese Restoration in the overseas territories were less straighforward. Although in Portugal and its colonial capitals of Goa and Salvador, both the lower and ruling classes alike were quick to support the Restoration, colonists in Macao and southern Brazil, at the distant edges of the empire on the border with Spanish territories, were remarkably ambiv-alent. Macao's commercial life, if not also its naval protection, had grown far more linked to

Manila than to the Portuguese *Estado da Índia*. In 1642, Macao's municipal council entered into negotiations with Philip IV to rejoin the Spanish realm on condition that Castile send a permanent garrison to defend the port and that the Macanese be permitted to travel freely to Manila. Likewise, the notoriously autonomous colonists of São Paulo, many of whom were of Spanish descent, also offered their allegiance to Philip IV in return for two concessions: first, that they be permitted to continue capturing and trading indigenous slaves, which they viewed as their legal right through immemorial custom; and second, that he approve their 1640 expulsion of the Jesuits, who had vigorously opposed their indigenous slaving activities. Philip ultimately declined the proposals of both São Paulo and Macao, wary of the lack of guarantees and hopeful that he would soon quell the ongoing Portuguese "rebellion" and thereby return the entire Portuguese empire to his dominion without undermining the process through sub-agreements with individual colonies (Valladares 2001, 77–80). The conflict between Portugal and Castile lingered on through the mid 1660s, with intermittent fighting along the border. But because of the Spanish monarchy's weakened financial position and its various military entanglements elsewhere, its hope of reconquering Portugal never came to pass, and it eventually recognized formal Portuguese independence in 1668.

Portugal's patriotic identity and pride, fashioned through the history of expansion and the writings of its great poets and chroniclers, remained latent but never faded during the union, and re-emerged with the writings of António Vieira and others who hailed Portugal as a resurrected "Quinto Imperio" (Cardim 2010, 25–29). However, although both empires survived, after their separation they eventually lost their combined pre-eminence on the world stage. The new global political landscape had shifted with the increasing preeminence of the Dutch but especially the French and English empires. There is no doubt that after the 1660s Spain and Portugal continued defining imperial realities in southern and central America, but on the broader global scale, imperial supremacy and its dominant discourses were shifting from Iberia to Northern Europe.

Works cited

Bouza, Fernando. 1987. *Portugal en la Monarquía Hispánica, 1580–1640*. Madrid: Universidad Complutense.

———. 1994. "La relación de la nobleza portuguesa con la Monarquía española." In *Las relaciones entre Portugal y Castilla en la época de los descubrimientos y la expansión colonial*, edited by Ana María Carabias Torres, 337–344. Salamanca: Universidad de Salamanca.

———. 1997. "Portugal en la política internacional de Felipe II." In *A União Ibérica e o Mundo Atlântico*, edited by Maria de Graça Ventura, 29–46. Lisbon: Colibri.

Boxer, Charles. 1967. "Spaniards and Portuguese in the Iberian Colonial World: Aspects of an Ambivalent Relationship, 1580–1640." In *Salvador de Madariaga: Liber Amicorum*, 239–251. Bruges: De Tempel, Tempelhof.

———. 1969. "Portuguese and Spanish Projects for the Conquest of Southeast Asia, 1580–1600." *Journal of Asian History* 3 (2): 118–136.

Bustos, Manuel. 1983. "Los historiadores españoles y portugueses ante de la unidad peninsular de 1580 a 1640." *Gades* 9 (11): 161–181.

Camões, Luis de. [1572] 1639. *Lusiadas*. Madrid: Juan Sánchez.

Cardim, Pedro. 2010. "La aspiración imperial de la monarquía portuguesa (siglos XVI y XVII)." In *Comprendere le Monarchie Iberiche: Risorse materiali e rappresentazioni del potere*, edited by Gaetano Sabatini, 37–72. Rome: Viella.

———. 2014a. "The Representatives of Asian and American Cities at the Cortes of Portugal." In *Polycentric Monarchies: How did Early Modern Spain and Portugal Achieve and Maintain a Global Hegemony?* edited by Pedro Cardim et al., 43–53. Sussex: Sussex Academic Press.

———. 2014b. *Portugal unido y separado: Felipe II, la unión de territorios y el debate sobre la condición política del Reino de Portugal*. Valladolid: Universidad de Valladolid.

Cardim, Pedro and Susana Münch Miranda. 2012. "La expansión de la Corona Portuguesa y el estatuto político de los territorios." In *Las Indias Occidentales: Procesos de incorporación a las Monarquías Ibéricas, siglos XVI a XVIII*, edited by O. Mazín and J. J. Ruiz Ibáñez, 181–240. México, DF: El Colegio de México.

Casas, Bartolomé de las. 1552. *Brevísima relación de la destrucción de las Indias*. N.p.

Cerdán de Tallada, Tomás. 1604. *Veriloquium en reglas de estado*. Valencia: Juan Crisóstomo Garriz.

Cross, Harry. 1978. "Commerce and Orthodoxy: A Spanish Response to Portuguese Commercial Penetration in the Viceroyalty of Peru, 1580–1640." *Americas* 35 (2): 151–167.

Cueto, Ronald. 1992. "1580 and All That: Philip II and the Politics of the Portuguese Succession." *Portuguese Studies* 8: 150–169.

Curto, Diogo Ramada. 1998. "A literatura e o imperio." In *História da expansão portuguesa*, edited by Francisco Bethencourt and Kirti Chaudhuri, vol. 1, 434–454. Lisbon: Círculo de Leitores.

Dandelet, Thomas. 2014. *The Renaissance of Empire in Early Modern Europe*. Cambridge: Cambridge University Press.

Elliott, J. H. and José F. de la Peña, eds. 1978–1980. *Memoriales y cartas del Conde Duque de Olivares*, vol. 1, 95. Madrid: Ediciones Alfaguara.

Gil Pujol, Xavier. 2007. "Spain and Portugal." In *European Political Thought, 1450–1700: Religion, Law and Philosophy*, edited by H. A. Lloyd, G. Burgess and S. Hodson, 416–457. New Haven, CT: Yale University Press.

———. 2012. "Integrar un mundo. Dinámicas de agregación y de cohesión en la Monarquía de España." In *Las Indias Occidentales: Procesos de incorporación a las Monarquías Ibéricas, siglos XVI a XVIII*, edited by O. Mazín and J. J. Ruiz Ibáñez, 69–108. México, DF: El Colegio de México.

Hespanha, António Manuel. 1989. "O governo dos Áustrias e a modernização da constituição política portuguesa." *Penélope* 2: 50–73.

———. 1996. *Las Indias en la Monarquía Católica*. Valladolid: Universidad de Valladolid.

———. 2001. "A constituição do império português: Revisão da alguns enviesamentos correntes." In *O Antigo Regime nos Trópicos*, edited by J. Fragoso et al., 163–188. Rio de Janeiro: Civilização Brasileira.

López de Gómara, Francisco. 1553. *Historia general de las Indias*. Medina del Campo: Guillermo de Millis.

López Madera, Gregorio. 1597. *Excelencias de la Monarquía y reino de España*. Valladolid: Diego Fernández de Córdoba.

Marcocci, Giuseppe. 2012. *A consciência de um império*. Coimbra: Imprensa da Universidade de Coimbra.

———. 2014. "Conscience and Empire: Politics and Moral Theology in the Early Modern Portuguese World." *Journal of Early Modern History* 18: 473–494.

Mariana, Juan de. [1601] 1854. *Historia de España*. In *Obras de Juan de Mariana*, edited by P. Pi y Margall. 2 vols. Madrid: Rivadeneira.

Martínez Torres, José Antonio. 2014. "'There Is but One World': Globalisation and Connections in the Overseas Territories of the Spanish Habsburgs, 1581–1640." *Culture and History Digital Journal* 3 (1): 1–15.

Münch Miranda, Susana. 2010. "Organización financiera y práctica política en el Estado de la India durante la Unión Ibérica." In *Comprendere le Monarchie Iberiche: Risorse materiali e rappresentazioni del potere*, edited by Gaetano Sabatini, 261–292. Rome: Viella.

Pagden, Anthony. 1982. *The Fall of Natural Man: The American Indian and the Origins of Comparative Ethnology*. Cambridge: Cambridge University Press.

———. 1995. *Lords of All the Worlds: Ideologies of Empire in Spain, Britain and France, c. 1500–c. 1800*. New Haven, CT: Yale University Press.

Pérez-Amador Adam, Alberto. 2011. *De legitimatione imperii Indiae Occidentalis: La vindicación de la empresa Americana*. Madrid: Iberoamericana.

Philip II. 1845. "Carta de Felipe II al Duque de Osuna, 24 Agosto 1579." In *Colección de Documentos Inéditos para la Historia de España*, edited by Miguel Salvá and Pedro Sainz, vol. 6, 649–661. Madrid: Viuda de Calero.

Recopilación *de Leyes de los reinos de Indias.* 1681. Tomo 2, Libro Quarto. Madrid: Julián de Paredes.

Saldanha, António Vasconcelos de. 2004. *Iustum imperium: Dos Tratados como Fundamento do Império dos Portugueses no Oriente.* Lisbon: Instituto Superior de Ciências Sociais e Políticas.

Schaub, Jean-Frédéric. 2001. *Portugal na monarquia Hispânica, 1580–1640.* Lisbon: Livros Horizonte.

Schwartz, Stuart. 1968. "Luso-Spanish Relations in Habsburg Brazil, 1580–1640." *Americas* 25 (1): 33–48.

———. 1993. "Panic in the Indies: The Portuguese Threat to the Spanish Empire." *Colonial Latin American Review* 2 (1–2): 165–187.

Solórzano Pereira, Juan de. 1647. *Política Indiana.* Madrid: Diego Díaz de la Carrera.

Subrahmanyam, Sanjay. 2007. "Holding the World in Balance: The Connected Histories of the Iberian Overseas Empires, 1500–1640." *The American Historical Review* 112 (5): 1359–1385.

Todorov, Tzvetan. 1984. *The Conquest of America.* Translated by Richard Howard. New York: Harper and Row.

Thomaz, Luis Felipe Reis, 1994. "A estrutura política e administrative do Estado da Índia no século XVI." Chap. 6 in *De Ceuta a Timor.* Lisbon: Difel.

Valladares, Rafael. 2001. *Castilla y Portugal en Asia, 1580–1680.* Leuven: Leuven University Press.

Zuazo, Alonso de. 1864. "Capítulos de carta del licenciado Alonso de Zuazo." In *Colección de documentos inéditos relativos al descubrimiento, conquista y colonización de las posesiones españolas*, vol. 1, 292–298. Madrid: Manuel B. de Quirós.

12

THE IBERIAN INQUISITIONS IN THE SIXTEENTH AND SEVENTEENTH CENTURIES

Between coercion and accommodation

Helen Rawlings

The Iberian Inquisitions, first established in the kingdom of Castile (1478), then in the Crown of Aragon (1484), and half a century later in neighbouring Portugal (1531) as a deterrent against the threat of heresy, soon gained a collective reputation as a metaphor for religious and racial intolerance that has left its indelible mark on Iberian identity in particular and the history of western civilization in general for more than 500 years. But the infamy of the Inquisition as an historical phenomenon has very often distorted the actual historiographical record, giving rise to an enormous volume of 'black versus white' polemical discourse, coloured by the ideological and political bias of writers, as opposed to measured analysis. It was not until the beginning of the twentieth century that a major turning point was reached in inquisitorial studies when the American scholar Henry Charles Lea became the first historian to make extensive use of the archives of the Spanish Inquisition to conduct his research. His application of critical, objective methodology to the evidence transformed the discourse. In his four-volume *History of the Inquisition of Spain* (1906–07), Lea challenged liberal and conservative interpretations that had characterised inquisitorial historiography since the sixteenth century. While he criticised the severity of its practices, he also acknowledged that the Spanish Inquisition had been established for reasons that were seen as legitimate in their time and advised modern historians to be cautious in their judgement of it. He thus set the agenda for revisionist scholarship that would follow in the second half of the twentieth century.

Since the transition from dictatorship to democracy in both Spain and Portugal, a new generation of historians, building upon Lea's work, have set inquisitorial research on a variety of innovative pathways and overturned certain long-held preconceptions regarding its practices. Major work was undertaken in the closing decades of the twentieth century on the trial records of regional branches of the Spanish Inquisition (their working methods, spectrum of activity and purview) by pioneering historians such as Beinart (1981), Bennassar (1979), Contreras (1982), Dedieu (1989), García Arenal (1978), García Cárcel (1976, 1980), Haliczer (1994); Henningsen (1980), Monter (1990), Nalle (1992) and Poska (1998). Revisionist overviews of the history of the Spanish Inquisition have been published by Kamen (1997), Peters (1988) and Rawlings (2006), while Bethencourt (1997), as an extension of his work on the Portuguese branch of the Inquisition, has invited scholars to consider the global impact of the institution within a transnational context, including its pursuit of heresy in the overseas territories of the Iberian empire. As a result of the broadening of the panorama of inquisitorial research and its subjection to new techniques of interrogation, we can now perceive of the Iberian Inquisitions as being far more complex and less monolithic than has hitherto been understood, rather as multi-faceted bodies that skilfully adapted to time and circumstances, enabling the major Spanish branch to survive for more than 350 years.

Modern research also suggests that the Castilian, Aragonese and Portuguese inquisitions encountered distinct challenges in the exercise of their jurisdiction in the sixteenth and seventeenth centuries and, contrary to common understanding, were far more restrained than repressive in the practice of their authority. This was the period that witnessed the height of inquisitorial activity throughout the peninsula, but in the pursuit of their primary role – the elimination of heresy – Iberian tribunals found themselves increasingly conditioned by prevailing social, political and economic factors that determined the nature of their mediation. They responded by moderating, accommodating and realigning their practices, sometimes adopting corrective and conciliatory policies and at other times coercive measures in their dealings with different offenders of the faith, in accordance with the agenda set by the Church, Monarchy and State. This chapter focuses on the intervention of the Iberian Inquisitions in relation to three principal target groups, each addressed within a different time frame and regional context – the Old Christian, the *Morisco* and the Portuguese *converso* – that will allow us to evaluate the relative as opposed to absolute nature of the institution's power base in the early modern period.

The correction of old Christian ignorance and deviance

During the first half of the sixteenth century the Holy Office only had jurisdiction over formal heresy (Judaic, Islamic and Protestant), but from the 1560s onwards the Spanish branch of the Inquisition extended its sphere of activity to lesser infringements of the code of orthodoxy. In response to the Council of Trent's recommendations on doctrine and discipline, approved in its final session of 1562–63, Castilian and Aragonese tribunals intervened to correct the speech, beliefs and behavioural practices of the Old Christian (principally the rural masses), that veered from the accepted norm. Tens of thousands of Spaniards came before inquisitorial courts for the first time in the second half of the sixteenth century accused of acts of "minor heresy." Among the most common offences that figured under this category was the making of irreverent statements, known as "propositions," frequently based on a misunderstanding of true doctrine. Others were charged with the associated and potentially more serious crime of blasphemy. Blasphemous statements might include a denial of the power of the sacraments, disrespect of Mary and the Saints, opposition to tithe payments, the rejection of papal and/or inquisitorial authority and a refusal to observe official feast days. These same objections to aspects of the faith overlapped with those expressed by *conversos* and *Moriscos*, as well as alleged Protestants who were brought to trial by the Spanish Inquisition in the mid-sixteenth century, and the campaign against propositions within the Old Christian community may have been a precautionary warning about the possibility of contagion. In the case of Protestant offenders, such transgressions invariably led to their prosecution according to the degree of heresy deemed to be involved (Dedieu 1979, 269–271; Schwartz 2008, 24). However, where Old Christians were concerned, despite the obvious anti-religious and anti-authoritarian overtones of these statements, they were frequently judged by the inquisitors to have been uttered in anger, frustration, jest or simply out of habit, demonstrative of the naïve mentality or ignorance of the individual and hence devoid of any real heretical intent. As a result, minor penalties were generally applied, such as a fine or public penance rather than imprisonment. Nevertheless, culprits had to be singled out to serve as a lesson to others and to demonstrate Spain's leadership in restoring the Church's teaching mission. While the Church instructed, the Inquisition corrected, supporting and reinforcing the pedagogical role of bishops and priests. According to Contreras and Henningsen's data bank of inquisitorial trials (1986), in the second half of the sixteenth century (1560–1614), hearings for blasphemy and for the associated crime of propositions accounted for 45% of cases brought before Castilian tribunals and 27% of those in neighbouring Aragon (heavily preoccupied with its *Morisco* subjects), while in Portugal such offences were dealt with by ecclesiastical courts. The tribunal of Toledo took a leading role in the campaign to silence the verbal outbursts of its Old Christian clients. Its 'success' as an instrument of social disciplining can be measured by the 85% decline in such anti-doctrinal statements being brought before the local tribunal between 1551 and 1560 (486) and 1591 and 1600 (74) (Dedieu 1986, 181–182).

Two examples of trial records serve to underline the nature of religious deviance to be found at the local level in Castile, which the propositions campaign sought to eliminate. Bartolomé Sánchez was a struggling Castilian wool-comber from the village of Cardenete in the diocese of Cuenca, brought before the local tribunal of the Inquisition on a charge of heresy in 1553 (Nalle 2001). Following a visionary experience which led first to penance then rebellion, Sánchez began to expound his own radical ideas about doctrine. He attacked priests, the worship of idols, the celebration of the Eucharist, the payment of tithes and the authority of the Pope. He believed he spoke for God and that his mission, which he equated to that of the second Messiah, was to correct the injustices delivered on Spanish society by the Inquisition and the Catholic Church. While his neighbours tolerated his outbursts as symptomatic of his eccentricity, local inquisitors arrested him on a charge of heresy. The inquisitor assigned to his case, Pedro Cortés, took sympathy with Sánchez and sought via his hearings with the prisoner to rehabilitate him, attempting to correct his erroneous beliefs. Sánchez's obstructive behaviour, extending to his rewording of Christian prayers to reflect his prophetic relationship with God, did not deter Cortés in trying to prove that the defendant was insane rather than deviant. But the compassionate strategy failed. Sánchez refused to be tamed and he was sentenced to death for his views. However, en route to the execution ground in April 1554, he repented, only to break the conditions of his penance within two years and relapse into heretical behaviour again. Following a third trial in 1560, Sánchez was declared insane and sent to a mental hospital where inquisitors hoped he would be cured of his illness. This compelling tale, as well as redefining the image of the merciless inquisitor, invites us to look afresh at the dividing line between madness, heresy and ignorance and the relatively restrained role of the Inquisition in such cases.

Gabriel López from Galindos, near Ávila, was brought before the Toledan tribunal of the Inquisition in 1570 (aged 31) on a charge of heresy. His interrogation revealed that he was a man of Old Christian stock, baptised and confirmed, who regularly attended confession. He was able to recite the four prayers of the Church in both Latin and Castilian. He earned a living as a farm hand, beggar and prayer monger, frequently reciting a paraphrased version of the *Ave María* in exchange for money, in which he erroneously referred to Christ as "Three in One." Upon further questioning, it was discovered that, while he was able to correctly identify the three persons of the Trinity, he failed to understand the meaning of the word Trinity itself. Thus he could not distinguish between God the Father, God the Son and God the Holy Spirit. For Gabriel López (and presumably for all of those for whom he had recited the prayer), Christ *was* God. This confusion had a feminine counterpart: it was common for women, in their excessive veneration of the Virgin, to identify her as the fourth member of the Trinity. Here was evidence of how unsatisfactorily certain aspects of Catholic doctrine were accommodated in the minds of the populace. Following a period of imprisonment, the unbeknown "heretic," López, was forced to abjure his errors in an *auto de fe* held in the Plaza de Zocodover before returning to the community (Dedieu 1979, 258–261).

These examples of anti-orthodox behaviour reveal a considerable level of religious scepticism in Spanish society that prevailed despite official attempts at instruction and reform. The Counter-Reformation's educative programme, conducted by the Catholic Church, clearly did not wholly satisfy the needs of the faithful, especially at the rural level, who struggled to understand and therefore adhere to Catholic teachings, preferring instead their popular forms of devotion centred on local saints, shrines and holy brotherhoods. The exposure of this fundamental weakness in the Church's teaching mission prompted the measures adopted by the Spanish Inquisition to strengthen adherence to the faith via preventative rather than punitive means. By the beginning of the seventeenth century, the corrective strategy adopted by the Inquisition meant that individuals themselves frequently became censors of their own behaviour (and that of others) for fear of the consequences, hence the number of cases of so-called 'minor heresy' coming before inquisitorial courts declined substantially.

The acceptance and rejection of the *Morisco*

The plight of the *Morisco* in sixteenth and seventeenth century Iberia – a problem particular to Spain and not Portugal where the Moors never settled – is one coloured by alternating policies of acceptance and rejection. Following the end of the Christian Reconquest of the peninsula, the Moslem community had been given the same ultimatum as the Jews in 1492: either convert to Christianity or leave Spain. Mass conversions took place, first in Castile from 1502 and a quarter of a century later in Aragon. In southern and eastern regions of the peninsula, most densely populated with *Moriscos*, the majority converted under duress. For much of the first half of the century, Granadine *Moriscos* retained intact their Moorish cultural identity, including their practice of Islamic rituals, in exchange for the payment of subsidies to the Crown and taxes to the local aristocracy, while their co-religionists in Valencia, continued to live as Moors and enjoyed similar immunity from inquisitorial prosecution. Little or no initiative was taken by the Church in these areas to instruct and integrate them into the Catholic faith, to which they remained superficially attached only. That situation changed dramatically from the 1560s, following the implementation of Tridentine reform on raising standards of adherence to Catholicism (Coleman 2003, 177–180). The Granadine *Moriscos* rose up in revolt against the enforced eradication of their cultural traditions and religious customs (1568–1570), while those in neighbouring Aragon were subject to increasing prosecution by the tribunals of Valencia and Zaragoza for their obstinate refusal to abandon their old faith. The age of cooperation between the two cultures in these regions now appeared to be over. However, modern evidence suggests that the picture was actually more balanced and that attempts at conciliation continued alongside demands for the outright expulsion of the *Moriscos* from Spain.

At the beginning of the seventeenth century, there was no unanimous call to expel the *Moriscos*, either from within government, the *Cortés* or the Church. The Council of Inquisition was not formally consulted in the adoption of the final resolution. Divisions of opinion and of conscience continued to obstruct the decision-making process, just as they had done the attempted programme of integration. Those who favoured expulsion – men motivated by the political threat rather than the religious one – were actually in the minority. Ecclesiastical opinion in general did not support the harsh stand made by Archbishop Ribera of Valencia, who in 1602 had called for the *Moriscos'* exclusion as "heretics and traitors." The bishop of Segorbe, Feliciano de Figueroa, reported in 1604, as he had done three years previously, of his success in bringing the faith to his *Morisco* flock via teaching and missionary work. Cardinal Fernando Niño de Guevara as Inquisitor General (1599–1602) refused to allow a global condemnation of the *Moriscos*. The same stance was taken by Philip III's favourite, the duke of Lerma. In his treatise of 1606, the chronicler Pedro de Valencia, as well as acknowledging the failings of the *Moriscos*, also put forward a series of rational solutions to solving the problem of their lack of integration. He strongly advised against the use of religion for political purposes. Instead he proposed that measures should be taken to incorporate the *Morisco* into Christian society on equal terms and to provide for their proper conversion and assimilation into the Catholic Church. Valencia's paper bore witness to the endurance of a tolerant, dispassionate current of thought in Spanish society, humanist in spirit, free from the prejudice and fanaticism that prevailed in certain circles on the eve of the expulsion:

> In order to aid their conversion, the *Moriscos* must be compelled to abandon their Moorish dress and customs. But this must be done in a gentle rather than forceful way, without any intervention from the Holy Inquisition, for when they are subject to harsh tactics, they become rebellious and corrective measures, such as beatings and confiscations of goods, are interpreted as acts of vengeance by the enemy. As a result, they dig their heels in further [. . .] Not only should *Moriscos* be equal in status and honour to Old Christians, but everyone should now be called Old Christians without distinction.
>
> (Jones 1997, 168–169)

When the formal decision to expel the *Moriscos* was taken by the Council of State on 4 April 1609 (and approved by Philip III five days later), it came as a shock to those working on the ground to find conciliatory solutions. The date was chosen to coincide with the signing of a twelve-year truce with Dutch rebels. A major propaganda exercise was mounted to divert public attention away from the humiliating withdrawal of troops from the Netherlands and focus instead on eradicating the enemy from within. The first expulsion order was published in Valencia on 22 September 1609. Five days later, Archbishop Ribera delivered a sermon in which he justified the banishment of the *Moriscos* on religious grounds. He referred to the dishonour suffered by true Christians by their forced coexistence with infidels and the need to placate God for having tolerated non-believers for so long. The old crusading militancy of the Spanish Church, rooted in the Reconquest, was thus dramatically rekindled in order to win over public support (Domínguez Ortiz and Vincent 1978, 177–180). According to government figures, within four months of the order, an estimated total of 135,000 *Moriscos* were deported from the kingdom of Valencia, suspected of being in collusion with their Ottoman allies. They were followed by their co-religionists from Castile, Extremadura, La Mancha, Andalusia, Murcia, Catalonia and Aragon. By the end of March 1611, the main part of the operation was complete, with pockets of resistance having been successfully crushed. The official calculation was that a total of nearly 300,000 *Moriscos* had been forced to leave Spain for France and North Africa, while some 10,000 to 12,000 others are thought to have lost their lives in rebellions en route to their places of departure (Lapeyre 1986, 252). By presenting the event as a great moral victory for Catholicism, the political calculations inherent in the dispersal were disguised, as were the conflict of attitudes within both lay and ecclesiastical circles that lay behind it. But modern scholars have found evidence to question the definitive nature of expulsion and the failure of attempts at integration. How far did the *Morisco* survive?

Some continually evaded prosecution such as Diego Díaz, a *Morisco* from Daimiel in New Castile, whose personal testimony delivered to inquisitors reveals important insights into his faith and endurance. In 1609 he was forced into exile along with other converts from Islam, but within two weeks he had returned to resume life in his homeland. It was eight to ten years before the civil authorities caught up with him and promptly deported him via the port of Cartagena. He arrived in Algiers where he was taken captive, forced to convert to Islam and circumcised against his will, but sought confession and continued to practice Christianity in secret. He managed to escape on a fishing boat and find his way back to Spain to begin a new life as a meat-cutter in Cuenca. Thirteen years later in 1632, he and his wife were arrested by the local tribunal of the Inquisition, accused of the secret practice of Moorish rituals. Díaz skilfully deployed various defensive strategies in his trial. He successfully guessed the identity of those who had denounced him, therefore eliminating their charges. He also maintained that it was possible to be a *Morisco* and a faithful Christian at the same time, thus counteracting the accusation of heresy. He was eventually let off with a reprimand (Kagan and Dyer 2004, 119–151).

The *Morisco* community that inhabited the village of Villarubia de los Ojos in the region of Campo de Calatrava in La Mancha may be considered another exception to the rule, as illustrated by Dadson's research (2007). They had voluntarily been baptised as Catholics prior to the implementation of forced conversions in 1502 and, significantly, in this same year were granted equal status to their Old Christian neighbours by Ferdinand and Isabella. During the first half of the sixteenth century they gradually became assimilated into Christian society with little or no need for inquisitorial intervention, constituting a growing and economically significant minority of farmers, workers and labourers. From 1550 they had risen to assume middle-class positions in society such as town councillor and magistrate and were playing an active role in civic life. Fellow Old Christian villagers, together with their overlord the Count of Salinas, supported them in their struggle against the edict of expulsion, served upon them in the summer of 1611. They returned from forced exile to France and then resisted two further attempts to banish them in 1612 and 1613, insisting on their right to remain in their homeland. They resumed their role in the local community and in 1627 the ancient status of the *Moriscos* of Campo del Calatrava, granted 125 years earlier, was reconfirmed by royal decree.

In October 1611 Philip III signed an expulsion order on all the 2,500 inhabitants of the community of the Valle del Ricote in Murcia. Many appealed against this decision, including Fray Juan de Pereda (emissary of the royal confessor), who wrote an account in April 1612 of the different sorts of *Moriscos* who lived in the kingdom, insisting on the Christianity of those of the Valle del Ricote:

> And it is rare to find a witness that does not confirm that none dresses in Moorish fashion, that they usually drink wine and the majority eats bacon. In this they differ greatly from the *moriscos* of Granada and Valencia. [. . .] The difference is also manifest in their language, for those who are above 40 do not speak Arabic nor do they understand it. Lastly, all witnesses confirm that in all things pertaining to Christianity the *moriscos* [of the Valle del Ricote] are like saints compared to their compatriots in Granada, Valencia and Aragón. [. . .] Those people who speak most earnestly about the sincerity of their faith are confessors and those who have had individual contact with them.
>
> (Lapeyre, Appendix xvi)

But hardliners on the Council of State refused to be convinced by Pereda's appeal, alleging the inhabitants of the Valle del Ricote to be nothing but superficial Christians. Some, they claimed, had joined religious orders and feigned conversion to avoid enforced exile. The expulsion went ahead in October 1613 and a total of 6,000 to 7,000 *Moriscos* were forced out of their Murcian homeland. However, such was their devotion to their roots that many returned illegally from exile. Although subjected to punishment they continued to defy the secular authorities who gave up their chase in 1626 and allowed them to settle once again in *their* kingdom. Via the character of Ricote – drawn from historical reality – who appears in Part II of *Don Quijote* (1615), Cervantes expressed his own underlying sympathy (and possibly that of a wider public) for the banished *Morisco* by making him the mouthpiece of the sadness and bitterness of a condemned community and race. "To us," claimed Ricote, "it [exile] was the most terrible [punishment] that could be inflicted. Wherever we are we weep for Spain; for, after all, we were born here and this is our native country. Nowhere do we find the reception our misery requires," he lamented (*Don Quijote*, Part II, Chapter 53).

These stories of *Morisco* survival against the odds reveal an endurance of their influence and that of the old spirit of *convivencia* beyond expulsion that may have been much more widespread than the official propaganda would suggest. Along with sections of the religious community, the Spanish Inquisition, despite its outward alignment with the political agenda, remained open to conciliation with its *Morisco* neighbours.

The inclusion and exclusion of the Portuguese *converso*

The brutal persecution of crypto-Judaism has long remained synonymous with the activity of the Iberian Inquisitions. This generalisation needs qualifying in terms of time, geography and prevailing attitudes. Most historians agree that the primary religious motivation for the establishment of the Holy Office – to purify the peninsula of deceitful Christians who might threaten the stability of the Catholic state – was underscored by racial prejudice against the Jewish community and resentment at their socio-economic success. There is certainly widely documented evidence to support the severity with which the Castilian branch of the Inquisition dealt with its backsliding Jews, as well as those who practised two faiths simultaneously over the period 1480–1525, when it burned approximately 2,000 victims. Thereafter the incidence of crypto-Judaism declined substantially in Castile, while it had only a negligible impact in neighbouring Aragon where the Jewish community had never settled in large numbers. Meanwhile, a much more lenient policy towards converted Jews operated in Portugal. The *cristãos-novos* community included a considerable number of Spanish exiles who had left their homeland after the 1492 expulsion order. Although forced to convert within five years of their arrival, they enjoyed almost half a century of freedom from persecution in their adopted country, allowing them to maintain sophisticated links with Judaism. They became known as 'Men of the [Jewish] Nation' on account of their adherence to their Jewish faith and identity (Bodian 1994, 58–60). The Portuguese Inquisition was not fully operational until 1547, but during the first 33 years of its existence only around 2,000 New Christians were brought to trial by its tribunals – a relatively small number compared with the size of the problem they posed. Although rooted out for their Judaic practices and stigmatised for their race, they were also highly valued as bankers, merchants and traders. Their strategy of part-conformity and part-dissimulation in matters of the faith allowed Portuguese *conversos* to maintain sophisticated links with Judaism, as well as the opportunity for their commercial activities to prosper. But their long period of relative exemption from inquisitorial scrutiny was soon to come to an end.

The Portuguese Inquisition suddenly became a much more repressive instrument of racial and religious control following the annexation of Portugal to Spain in 1580. Fifty autos were held in Lisbon, Evora and Coimbra between 1581 and 1600 at which 3,000 were penanced and 212 were condemned to death. This forced the Portuguese New Christian community to seek alternative ways of preserving their ethnic identity and deploying their professional skills. Several thousand opted for migration to Castile, settling in commercial cities such as Madrid, Seville and Málaga, hoping for greater clemency from the Spanish Inquisition as opposed to that in their homeland. In practice, they found themselves subject to fluctuating strategies of inclusion and exclusion. In August 1605 a papal brief was issued which allowed more than 400 Portuguese New Christians, referred to as *portugueses de la nación judía*, to be released from inquisitorial custody in Portugal and enjoy immunity from prosecution for a limited period in return for a 1.86 million-ducat payment to Philip III. From 1607 through 1611 no *conversos* came before the courts of the Spanish Inquisition, but once the terms of the pardon had expired, those crypto-Jews who had enjoyed a temporary safe haven in Spain soon found the pressure stepped up against them.

Against this backdrop, a fierce debate was taking place within lay and ecclesiastical circles over the continued justification for the purity of blood laws that had prevented *conversos* from holding public office since 1449. The *limpieza* statutes were regarded by many as unfairly discriminating against *conversos* whose family connections with Judaism in Spain were so remote as to be indiscernible, yet who continued to be treated as suspect Jews and barred from advancement in the professions (Kamen 1997, 248–254; Rawlings 2002, 139–142). Where Portuguese New Christians were concerned, however, their Jewish ancestry was more recent and therefore the test of *limpieza* could be applied with greater certainty. In 1619, Martín González de Cellorigo, an employee of the Inquisition of Toledo, wrote a *Plea for justice from your Majesty on behalf of certain individuals from the kingdom of Portugal*. He argued for toleration to be shown towards Portuguese New Christians, less on religious than on financial grounds: the harnessing of their commercial expertise which was vital to the interests of the Spanish economy (Alpert 2001, 42–45). The first minister of Philip IV, the Count-Duke Olivares, spearheaded the modification of the *limpieza de sangre* laws, in which he had a particular interest through his own line of *converso* descent. He made his views known on the victimisation of the converted Jew in a discussion at the Council of State in 1625 at which he described the statutes as being 'unjust and impious, against divine law, natural law, and the law of nations. [. . .] In no other government or state in the world do such laws exist' (Lynch 1992, 148).

The financial crisis faced by Philip IV at the beginning of his reign forced him to give serious consideration to making use, as his father had done, of the entrepreneurial skills and capital of Portuguese New Christians, many of whom had fled from Spain under the renewed round of persecutions. Between 1626 and 1627, on the instruction of the Crown, the Spanish Inquisition issued Portuguese financiers suspected of Judaic practices with another temporary pardon for past offences and allowed them to compete for financial contracts (*asientos*) with Italian bankers. The following year they were granted free access to trade anywhere within the Spanish Empire. By the middle of the reign of Philip IV they were negotiating more than half of the loans required by the treasury to finance its debt payments and support Spain's vast military effort overseas. In return for bribes and payments, the Crown was able to make use of their highly valued financial and entrepreneurial expertise to rescue its ailing economy. In the case of Portuguese New Christians, therefore, it can be argued that political and economic considerations frequently took precedence over those of maintaining orthodoxy, but this situation only endured while it suited the expediency of the monarch. The protection offered to the Portuguese New Christians, now acting as royal bankers, was a major source of scandal. In particular it raised the concerns of traditionalists within the Church who saw religious ideals being discarded to meet the financial needs of a bankrupt government and exposed the underlying racial sympathies of Olivares, who drew up a radical proposal in 1634 to allow exiled

Jews to be able to return to Spain. The Spanish Inquisition never reconciled itself to the new deal for Portuguese *conversos* and maintained its vigilance over them despite government restraint and Philip IV's intervention to protect them (Lynch, 148–149).

In 1640 Portugal re-asserted its independence from the Spanish Monarchy. The Inquisition seized the opportunity to renew its zealous purge of the minority of Portuguese New Christians left in Spain – now its political adversaries – while also impressing its indispensability on the Crown as the 200-year-old protector of the nation's orthodoxy. Leading Portuguese financiers who had previously served the Crown became the target of attack. Whole families were reportedly arrested in Madrid (often on the basis of false testimony) and many took flight. Just over 60% of all trials conducted by the tribunal of Cuenca between 1650 and 1670 – where many of the cases denounced in Madrid were processed – were for the secret practice of Judaism. In Toledo the peak decade for the trial of crypto-Jews was 1651 to 1660 when they accounted for 76.5% of all cases (Alpert 2001, 91–92). By 1680, the rigorous pursuit of Portuguese New Christians had reached its climax. On 30 June of that year a grandiose *auto de fe* (depicted by the artist Francisco Rizi) was held in Madrid at which 56 judaisers were 'reconciled' or severely punished and 22 sentenced to death by burning, the majority of Portuguese origin. By the end of the seventeenth century, the Portuguese New Christian community in Spain had effectively been wiped out, although *conversos* continued to make up the majority who came before the courts of the Spanish Inquisition up to 1730. The alternating policy of persecution and accommodation adopted by Iberian governments towards Portuguese New Christians, based on economic imperatives, emphasises the way in which the Inquisition was forced to yield to secular priorities at the expense of the eradication of Jewish heresy.

Conclusion

The different case studies examined here lead us to reconsider the theory and practice of Iberian inquisitorial authority in matters of orthodoxy. The historical evidence suggests that the need to strengthen Spain's leadership of the Counter-Reformation lay behind the Spanish Inquisition's corrective policy towards Old Christian deviance from the faith. A re-examination of the decision to expel the *Moriscos* from Spain reveals a fundamental political motivation that did not necessarily converge with the will of the religious or inquisitorial authorities who favoured a more conciliatory approach. The plight of the Portuguese *conversos* can be seen as intrinsically linked to the value of their commercial and financial expertise to the economic survival of the state. As a result of this policy, crypto-Judaism was allowed to survive much longer than the Inquisition in either Spain or Portugal might have wished, hence the heavy-handed approach of Spanish tribunals when the *converso* finally fell from royal favour. We can conclude by proposing that the Iberian Inquisitions were not always the arbiters of their own actions in the sixteenth and seventeenth centuries, but rather responsive to different circumstances and policy decisions – at times coercive, at other times more measured – allowing us to redraw the balance between the institution's authoritarian reputation and its often acquiescent disposition.

Works cited

Alpert, Michael. 2001. *Crypto-Judaism and the Spanish Inquisition*. Basingstoke: Palgrave.
Beinart, Haim. 1981. *Conversos on Trial. The Inquisition in Ciudad Real*. Jerusalem: The Magnes Press.
Bennassar, Bartolomé, ed. 1979. *L'Inquisition Espagnole, XVᵉ-XIXᵉ siècle*. Paris: Hachette.
Bethencourt, Francisco. 1997. *La Inquisición en la época moderna*. Madrid: Akal.
Bodian, Miriam. 1994. "'Men of the Nation': The Shaping of *Converso* Identity in Early Modern Europe." *Past and Present* 143: 48–76.

Coleman, David. 2003. *Creating Christian Granada. Society and Religious Culture in an Old World City, 1492–1600.* Ithaca and London: Cornell University Press.

Contreras, Jaime. 1982. *El Santo Oficio de la Inquisición de Galicia, 1560–1700: poder, sociedad y cultura.* Madrid: Akal.

Contreras, Jaime and Henningsen, Gustav. 1986. "Forty-Four Thousand Cases of the Spanish Inquisition (1540–1700): Analysis of a Historical Data Bank." In *The Inquisition in Early Modern Europe: Studies on Sources and Methods*, edited by Gustav Henningsen and John Tedeschi in association with Charles Amiel, 100–129. Dekalb, IL: Northern Illinois University Press.

Dadson, Trevor J. 2007. *Los moriscos de Villarubia de los Ojos (siglos XV-XVIII): crónica de una minoría asimilada, expulsada y reintegrada.* Madrid and Frankfurt: Iberoamericana/Vervuert.

Dedieu, Jean-Pierre. 1979. "'Le modèle religieux: les disciplines du langage et de l'action' and 'Le modèle religieux: le refus de la Réforme et le contrôle de la pensée." In *L'Inquisition Espagnole*, edited by Bartolomé Bennassar, 241–267, 269–311.

———. 1986. "The Archives of the Holy Office of Toledo as a Source for Historical Anthropology." In *The Inquisition in Early Modern Europe*, edited by Gustav Henningsen and John Tedeschi, 158–189. DeKalb, IL: Northern Illinois University Press.

———. 1989. *L'Administration de la Foi. L'Inquisition de Tolède (XVIᵉ-XVIIIᵉ siècle).* Madrid: Casa de Velázquez.

Domínguez Ortiz, Antonio and Vincent, Bernard. 1978. *Historia de los moriscos. Vida y tragedia de una minoría.* Madrid: Alianza.

García-Arenal, Mercedes. 1978. *Inquisición y moriscos. Los procesos del tribunal de Cuenca.* Madrid: Siglo Veinituno.

García-Cárcel, Ricardo. 1976. *Orígenes de la Inquisición española. El tribunal de Valencia, 1478–1530.* Barcelona: Ediciones Península.

———. 1980. *Herejía y sociedad en el siglo XVI. La Inquisición en Valencia, 1530–1609.* Barcelona: Ediciones Península.

Haliczer, Stephen. 1994. *Inquisition and Society in the Kingdom of Valencia (1478–1834).* Berkeley, Los Angeles and Oxford: University of California Press.

Henningsen, Gustav. 1980. *The Witches' Advocate. Basque Witchcraft and the Spanish Inquisition (1609–1614).* Reno: University of Nevada Press.

Jones, John A. 1997. "*Fervor sin fanatismo*: Pedro de Valencia's treatise on the *Moriscos*." In *Faith and Fanaticism in Early Modern Spain*, edited by Lesley K. Twomey, 159–164. Aldershot: Ashgate.

Kagan, Richard L. and Abigail Dyer, eds. 2004. *Inquisitorial Inquiries: Brief Lives of Secret Jews and Other Heretics.* Baltimore, MD: Johns Hopkins University Press.

Kamen, Henry. 1997. *The Spanish Inquisition. An Historical Revision.* New Haven and London: Yale University Press.

Lapeyre, Henri. 1986. *Geografía de la España Morisca.* València: Diputació Provincial de València.

Lynch, John. 1992. "Spain after the Expulsion." In *Spain and the Jews. The Sephardie Experience. 1492 and after*, edited by Elie Kedourie, 140–161. London: Thames and Hudson.

Monter, William. 1990. *Frontiers of Heresy: The Spanish Inquisition from the Basque Lands to Sicily.* Cambridge: Cambridge University Press.

Nalle, Sara T. 1992. *God in La Mancha. Religious Reform and the People of Cuenca, 1500–1650.* Baltimore, MD: Johns Hopkins University Press.

———. 2001. *Mad for God: Bartolomé Sánchez, the Secret Messiah of Cardenete.* Charlottesville and London: University Press of Virginia.

Peters, Edward. 1988. *Inquisition.* New York: Free Press.

Poska, Allyson M. 1998. *Regulating the People: The Catholic Reformation in Seventeenth-Century Spain.* Leiden: Brill.

Rawlings, Helen. 2002. *Church, Religion and Society in Early Modern Spain.* Basingstoke: Palgrave.

———. 2006. *The Spanish Inquisition.* Oxford: Blackwell.

Schwartz, Stewart B. 2008. *All Can Be Saved. Religious Tolerance and Salvation in the Iberian Atlantic World.* New York and London: Yale University Press.

13

THE WAY BEHIND AND THE WAY AHEAD

Cartography and the state of Spain in Cabeza De Vaca's *Relación*

Kathryn M. Mayers

Early in Volume II of *Don Quijote*, as the now-recuperated hidalgo shows signs of giving his niece and housekeeper a third slip, his housekeeper attempts to divert him from his ill-errant chivalry by suggesting that he be one of those who "a pie quedo sirviesen a su rey y señor, estándose en la corte" (Cervantes 1978, 80). Don Quijote refuses her advice with a reference to cartography:

> [N]o todos los caballeros pueden ser cortesanos, ni todos los cortesanos pueden ni deben ser caballeros andantes . . . porque los cortesanos, sin salir de sus aposentos ni de los umbrales de la corte, se pasean por todo el mundo, mirando un mapa . . . pero nosotros, los caballeros andantes verdaderos, al sol, al frío, al aire, a las inclemencias del cielo, de noche y de día, a pie y a caballo, medimos toda la tierra con nuestros mismos pies; y no solamente conocemos los enemigos pintados, sino en su mismo ser . . . y . . . esta segunda, o, por mejor decir, primera especie de caballeros andantes . . . ha sido la salud no sólo de un reino, sino de muchos.
>
> (80–81)

What is interesting about this passage is not just the bleeding of cartography into literature, which had become commonplace by the early seventeenth century, nor Cervantes' anticipation of Alfred Korzybski's notion to the effect that a map is not the territory it represents, but rather the way Don Quijote's speech here contrasts two different methods of cartography as a device to express dissatisfaction with the current political shape of Spain. In emphasizing that true knights save kingdoms with knowledge drawn not from (illusionistic, two-dimensional) paintings but from (first-person, directly experienced) measurements, Cervantes uses the contrast between knowledge derived from abstract projection on paper and knowledge derived from first-hand empirical investigation as a figure for Don Quijote's dissatisfaction with the increasing bureaucratization of the court that had occurred in the transition from a medieval to a Baroque state.

Studies of early modern Spanish cartography have often overlooked this reflexive, national-constitutive dimension of their discourse.[1] This is particularly the case with scholarship on cartographic writing on Spanish territories *overseas*,[2] the exploration of which played a central role in re-shaping sixteenth-century Spain. Owing, perhaps, to the influence of postcolonial theory, studies of scientific writings on the Americas have largely focused on the way these early modern writings "map" the Amerindian Other. Studies of Alvar Núñez Cabeza de Vaca's 1542 *Relación*, for example – a text whose author could serve as the gold standard for "suffering heat or cold, hunger or thirst" and "measuring the whole earth with his own feet" – have focused on conflicts between European and Amerindian ways of knowing, and the way the text's ethnography of Amerindian peoples subalternized America and Amerindian orders of knowledge.

I would like to suggest in this essay, however, that the *Relación*, much like *Don Quijote*, uses a discourse of mapping to talk also about Spain. The author states in the early pages of the text that since he has been unable to conquer new lands, he will instead serve his King by "escrivi[endo] este camino" (24), enabling the king to "saber y ver . . . tod[o] lo que en nueve años . . . pude alcançar y conoscer" (18).[3] Linking his *Relación* directly to contemporary projects of the Spanish monarchs to achieve a totalizing view of the nation, he then draws together a number of the cartographic genres most favored by the Crown and enhances them with non-European forms of knowledge and points of reference. Studying this interplay between diverse rhetorics of mapping, I suggest that, in this particular text, the author uses a discourse of cartography to distinguish Spain from European nations following other paths to modernity. Complicating a "monarch of all I survey" matrix that underlay both feudal and early modern rationalized views of the nation, I argue, Alvar Núñez redefines Spain less as some form of rationally delimited territory or juridically controlled people than as an evolving approach to actively negotiating competing epistemological frameworks and reordering cross-cultural contact.

At the time Alvar Núñez wrote, Spain was already suffering the shift from a feudal to a mercantilist state to which Cervantes would allude nearly a century later. The consolidation of Spain as a nation-state was troubling traditional ways of positioning oneself in national space. However, other changes beyond the political were also contributing to a more general sense of disorientation. Discoveries in geography, astronomy, and mathematics were invalidating previous concepts of space and necessitating changes in notions of man's relation to totality. The rise of market capitalism was up-ending traditional ways of measuring the value of goods and services and of positioning oneself socially (Conley 1996, 1–2). And secularization of older forms of the sacred was producing a crisis in the narratives by which people understood the place of humans in history (Jameson 1988, 349). These broader developments across the political, economic, scientific and religious realms were producing an unprecedented sense of epistemological uncertainty across Europe and a need to cognitively map the new cultural space in which people found themselves caught as individual subjects.

In response to this sense of disorientation, the sixteenth century saw an explosion of mapping. The decades surrounding Alvar Núñez's expedition saw a tremendous increase not only in the number of maps but also in the number of *types* of maps printed. Whereas during the Middle Ages, the field of graphic mapping had been dominated largely by portolan charts and sacred *mappaemundi*, the late fifteenth century saw a widespread return to map forms with classical and Medieval roots and their development into multiple, complex new genres. Local topographical maps originating in simple Medieval administrative diagrams developed into elaborately colored, realistically detailed, Albertian views of cities, districts, estates, and battle scenes. *Isolarii* with roots in first-century Greek geographical poetry developed into thematically or alphabetically ordered depictions of the islands of the world combining pictorial regional topographical views with prose or verse descriptions of islands' history, mythology, ethnography, and archeology. And geographical maps with roots in Ptolemy's second-century use of Euclidean space developed into coherently measured, proportionately correct representations of the entire spherical earth, referencing space to a net of parallels and meridians.[4]

The purpose of these maps was to (re)orient the viewer in some coherent way to a changing reality. Their sum effect, ironically, was quite the opposite. For each of the genres that arose during this era constructed a different type of viewer, the particular "interests" of which led to conflicting conceptualizations of space. Topographical bird's-eye-view maps, for example, situated an implicitly land-owning or militarily victorious viewer in an elevated position before a vivid but non-rationalized scene. Encouraging him to read the arbitrary proportions and contiguities of the region as a symbol of the natural shape of his dominion, they encouraged a feudal view of the nation as a group of independent realms or federation of *comunidades* or city states (Mundy 1996, 7). Geographical maps, on the other hand, fixed a detached, abstract viewer before a mathematically calculated, Euclidean rendering of three-dimensional space. Encouraging the viewer to read the measured regularity of each geographical region as a reflection of the homogeneous belonging of every part to a finite greater whole, this genre fostered an imperial view of the nation as a single, homogeneous whole under a remote and impartial God or king (Mundy 1996, 5, 7; Woodward 1991, 83–84). By implying distinct viewers or notions of what it is that counts as knowledge – contiguity versus congruity; adjacency versus algebraic calculation – different types of maps led to conflicting notions of the shape of space and thus conflicting ideologies of the individuals' place within it.

In sixteenth-century Spain, this problem was particularly acute. In an effort to exert some form of control over how their realms would be understood, Spanish monarchs began sponsoring an array of large-scale, carefully detailed, mapping projects (see, e.g., Parker [1992] on these projects). The very diversity of their endeavors, however – maps that ranged from the *Padrón real* compilation of portolans begun in 1508 to the *Descripción y cosmografía de España* detailings of the particularities of some 7,000 villages of Castile begun in 1517 to the cross- and idol-adorned map of Tenochtitlán published with Cortés's letter to the Crown in 1524 to the *plus ultra*-bordered tapestry map created to celebrate Carlos V's 1535 conquest of Tunis – merely exacerbated a troubling opposition between Medieval and Renaissance notions of the state. Implicit in some of these maps is a notion of the nation as a form of juridical sovereignty over a particular people – "people" defined in some maps by religion and others by culture or history. Implicit in others is a competing notion of Spain as a form of territorial sovereignty over a particular place – "place" defined in some maps as a series of *comunidades* and in others as regions forming a larger whole.[5]

It is with an acute awareness of both the crown's interest in mapping its realms and the tension between conceptions of Spain within those realms that Alvar Núñez reframes the account of his disastrous expedition as a map in service to the Emperor. In the opening paragraph of his 1542 edition – an edition, which, Ralph Bauer has pointed out, would eventually be printed not with the author's family crest on the frontispiece but Charles V's personal coat of arms (2003, 35–36) – Alvar Núñez sets forth the cartographic nature of his *Relación*:

> Mas como ni mi consejo, ni diligencia aprovecharon para que aquello a que éramos idos fuesse ganado . . . no me quedó lugar para hazer más servicio de éste, que es traer a Vuestra Magestad relación de lo que en nueve años por muchas y muy estrañas tierras que anduve perdido y en cueros, pudiesse saber y ver, ansí en el sitio de las tierras y provincias y distancias dellas, como en los mantenimientos y animales que en ellas se crían, y las diversas costumbres de muchas y muy bárbaras naçiones con

quien conversé y viví, y todas las otras particularidades que pude alcançar y conoscer que dello en alguna manera Vuestra Magestad será servido.

(18)

To compensate for the failure of his expedition, the author explains, he will serve the King by providing an account that will allow the king to "see" what he himself saw as he wandered through foreign lands for ten years. This account will include his "route" (the province of sixteenth-century itinerary maps and portolano charts), the "disposition" of the lands he traversed (the province of geographical maps), the "forms of sustenance" and "diverse customs" of different lands and peoples (the province, today, of ethnography but, in the 1600s, of the widely popular *isolario*), and numerous "other particularities" (the province of *isolarii* and local topographical maps). Charting the space he traversed over the course of his journey, Alvar Núñez will contribute both to the knowledge of these peripheral regions of the empire so desired by the emperor and to the debate over different conceptualizations of the Spanish empire implicit in these very different forms of cartography.

Scholarship on the *Relación* has largely overlooked this spatial-discursive aspect of the text,[6] instead focusing primarily on the way Alvar Núñez relates (to) the *people* in the text. Two features of this ethnographic map have been especially influential. The first is the degree of detail of Amerindian beliefs and practices. Unlike the majority of accounts at the time, Alvar Núñez conveys not just an understanding of native practices and points of view, but also, in some cases, a blending of these practices with his own. His intimacy and identification with Amerindian peoples has led a number of critics (e.g., Molloy [1993]; Spitta [1995]) to identify in him a process of transculturation, and to argue that, for the first time in what would become a long history of Latin American cultural fusion, a Spanish noble entered a "third space" and recognized the fallacy of essentialist notions of identity and hegemonic claims to universalism that underwrote the discourse of conquest. The second feature, on the other hand, is the text's rhetorical objectivity. Alvar Núñez's sympathy for native peoples notwithstanding, his process of "writing" them and their customs employs, at certain times, narrative techniques that lead him, intentionally or not, to control the Other and to imply its backwardness. The distance between Alvar Núñez's first-person, transculturated observer and his third-person "objective" narrator has led other critics (e.g., Rabasa [2000]; Rojinsky [2006]) to identify a persistent coloniality, and to argue that, similar to Bartolomé de Las Casas, Alvar Núñez remained subject to a hubris of zero degrees[7] from which he was incapable of recognizing his own subalternization of Amerindian orders of knowledge.

However, readings that see in the *Relación* only an anti-hegemonic transcultural or hubristic colonialist view on the world over-simplify the complexity of its contribution to Early Modern Spanish history. A transculturation interpretation overlooks the ways Alvar Núñez's rendering of native codes mobilized asymmetrical power relations, while a hubristic reading leaves unexplored the manner in which his orchestration of native- and hybrid-self material into a coherent whole departs from other European traditions of organizing the reader's and spectator's gaze. Neither Alvar Núñez's sympathetic elevation of native orders of knowledge nor his rhetorical-objective subalternization of natives and their beliefs fully explains the complexity of his point of view on the surrounding world – an orientation which, Ralph Bauer has recently argued, involves "not so much a conflict between European and (Native) American cultures and ways of knowing – between a European self and an American other – as a conflict between two different [*European*] ideas of empire and . . . orders of knowledge as they arose in the geo-political dialectic between European expansionism and centralizing monarchy" (2003, 33–34).

In the *Relación*, the way the text maps Alvar Núñez with reference to space can help us better understand the text's intervention in this debate over knowledge and empire. In this study, I examine two different stages in the *Relación*'s mapping of Alvar Núñez's trek, looking not just at the protagonist's orientation to land but also at the author's orientation to rhetorical orders related to the process of diagramming land. Identifying the way in which the *Relación* elaborates, first, an empirical, conquering eye/I that grows frustrated with certain scientific-rational developments in European cartography, and later, an embodied communal eye/I that becomes attentive to certain nomadic reference points suppressed in modern Spanish cartography, I show how, while the text absorbs certain indigenous ways of seeing and knowing, it neither inverts nor does away with colonial hierarchies, but rather alters them to take in and re-purpose foreign knowledge. By combining different map forms in a way that fashions a particular kind of cross-cultural knowledge, I argue, Alvar Núñez carries Spain ahead, past the conflict between juridical and territorial notions of the nation, toward a Spain defined by its "knowledge of its enemies [not] merely in painting, but in their very being" (Cervantes 1978, 80, my translation).

In the early chapters of the *Relación*, which relate the series of calamities that reduce the original expedition to only four survivors, Alvar Núñez charts the physical space between the port of Sanlúcar de Barrameda, Spain, and Galvestan Bay in today's Texas. In part, this chart replicates the conventions of a narrative portolan. Describing the size, shape, and depth of rivers, coves, shallows, ports, and estuaries, it outlines the hydrographic reality of their route. Giving depths, distances, and orientation in the four cardinal directions, it estimates nautical distances covered and directions travelled. And noting types of winds and sounds of waves in different places, it suggests additional aids and hazards to future navigation. At times, this chart also replicates the generic conventions of the local topographical map. Describing certain views from an aerial perspective (e.g., a perch in a tree), it replicates the bird's-eye viewpoint typical of sixteenth-century regional maps. Detailing buildings' construction and design and noting varieties of animals, plants, and soil, it replicates local maps' focus on points of military significance and agricultural potential. And describing unusual types of trees and woods (e.g., the lightning-struck, fallen trees of the Everglades), it replicates local maps' attention to topographical singularity.

Portolans and topographical maps differed, of course, in the type of space they diagrammed, but they converged in some very basic ways in the forms of seeing they encouraged. Though the one charted hydrography and the other topography, they both included, as an essential part of their structure, combinations of landscape and the built environment (Mundy 1996, 4). Portolans used the names of cities and harbors where sailors might replenish their stores to anchor their representation of space as a series of connected points reducible by geometric means, while terrestrial topographical maps used views of buildings and other manmade constructions to define their representation of space as an area of land socially appropriated for use or exchange (Cosgrove 1998, xvi). Additionally, though portolans diagrammed progress along a route and topographical maps sketched stationary views, they both, by this point in the sixteenth century, also bore marks of increasing Euclidean rationalization. Portolans had begun to bear latitude scales derived from the idea of Potolemaic coordinates to indicate the proportions of land and water masses with relation to a larger whole, and terrestrial topographical maps had begun to display scaled segmentation of the entire map into a grid of uniform spaces to represent cities in measured proportion (Woodward 1991, 84). Though different in content, therefore, these genres both implied an anthropocentric, scientific-rational gaze on a separate, measureable earth – in the case of the portolan, an earth available for trade and access and in the case of the Albertian topographical map, an earth available for conquest or seigniorial dominion.

However, while this early part of the *Relación* very clearly borrows from a stock of portolan and topographical commonplaces, it changes this model of seeing. For the geographical and cardinal referents with respect to which Alvar Núñez would designate "where he is" are, he finds, largely missing or unrecognizable. To begin with, in contrast to other recent portolans and topographical maps, the *Relación* finds scant and problematical instances of built environment in sixteenth-century North America. While Alvar Núñez does mention a few landmark Indian villages and routes, most of his points of reference take the form of relative clauses that refer to the actions or beliefs of his own men: "el río que primero avíamos atravessado que entrava por aquel mismo ancon" (48); "la vía donde avíamos visto la canoa la noche que por allí veníamos" (78); "un río muy grande . . . , a quien avíamos puesto por nombre el Río de la Magdalena" (64); or "la vaía que pusimos nombre de la Cruz" (72). On account of the Spaniards' inability to identify humanly elaborated Indian fields, transportation routes, groves, villages, and burial grounds *as such*, the text omits reference, for example, to the many fire-controlled forests and mound-stippled maize fields that blanketed the Southeast (Mann 2005, 320). Furthermore, in those instances in which Alvar Núñez *does* incorporate views of villages and manmade structures, he sometimes openly suggests the Europeans' inability to read these landmarks correctly. Describing the bird's-eye view of Apalache gained by Lope de Oviedo from a tree, for example, Alvar Núñez reports that Lope "vio que la tierra estaba cavada a la manera que suele estar tierra donde anda ganado, y paresçióle por esto que devía ser tierra de christianos, y ansí nos lo dixo" (94). This village, Alvar Núñez knew at the time he wrote the text, was not a Christian one, but an Indian one. But by including Lope's obviously inaccurate reading of the (probably Indian-mounded) village as inhabited by Christians, Alvar Núñez relays that even where they were able to identify points of Amerindian built environment, these places did not orient them as they should. Where recent European maps constructed a viewer able to see space as an array of comprehensible, ethnically identifiable (and thus juridically governable) peoples, the *Relación* suggests, rather, a viewer blinded to crucial reference points and unable to read the nature of the nation(s) around him.

Additionally, in contrast to the Euclidean bent of recent portolans and local maps, the *Relación* includes imprecise and problematically self-referential measures of distance and direction. While the text does now and then mention cardinal directions of North, South, East, and West, it does not give precise compass readings, and as the expedition progresses, indications of direction increasingly take the form of verbs of motion modified by adverbs of direction ("entrar en la tierra *adentro*;" "ir . . . *adelante*") or deictics ("allá," "allí," "aquellos;" "estos") that indicate direction not in relation to an external referent but in relation only to the speaker himself. On account of the pilots' inability to relate their progress to a larger whole, the text omits description of the proportionate size and orientation of the lands traversed by the expedition. Furthermore, where Alvar Núñez does include specific instrumental, mathematical measurements of distance, he frequently implies their inaccurate nature and their role in misleading them. Bemoaning the expedition's disoriented "progress" along the Gulf Coast, for example, Alvar Núñez writes that, "a dicho y juramento de nuestros pilotos, desde la vaía que pusimos nombre de la Cruz hasta aquí anduvimos dozientas y ochenta leguas poco más o menos" (72). Opening this statement with the suspicious fact that the expeditions' *multiple* pilots felt compelled to swear to their instrument reading, and closing it with a qualifying "more or less," Alvar Núñez places an implicit question mark around ciphers of distance in the text, pointing out their inadequacy for locating them on a graticule and thus their inability to situate these lands within a picture of totality. Where recent European maps constructed a viewer who saw space from afar as an array of proportionate (and thus interconnectable and delimitable) territories, the *Relación* suggests, rather, a viewer trapped at close range, unable to "oversee" the territory around him.

Recognizing the ways these early chapters of the *Relación* depart from the conventions of ordinary sixteenth-century portolan and topographical maps complicates interpretations of Alvar Núñez as a transcultural hybrid or as a viewer from the hubris of zero degrees. While Alvar Núñez does question, repeatedly, the science of the expedition's pilots, he himself does not see key elements of the Amerindian-built environment and he certainly does not see as actual Amerindians do. The way he tries to situate himself in space – noticing, from a rational-scientific, bird's-eye view military resources and paths of access – is in no way Amerindian and is, in fact, frustrated by his inability to see as anything other than a European. At the same time, while Alvar Núñez does attempt to see as a European, his experiences with faulty instrumental measurements and readings of Amerindian built structures leads him, early on, to grow skeptical of the truth of an instrumentally calculated Euclidean view from afar or an empirically determined Albertian view from above. The way he abandons these methods of trying to situate himself in space – the way he increasingly identifies their position explicitly in relation to themselves – in no way situates the viewer "outside" or "before" the scene, in empirical inductive or non-empirical zero space.

In fact, if anything, the point of view on the world implicit in these initial chapters of the text suggests the limitedness of European modes of viewing and the need – both for the expedition's success and for the King's more accurate view of his whole nation – for an alternative model of viewing that could account for an entirely different (non-juridical, non-territorial) relationship between the individual and his/her surroundings. This view would "see" built environment, but the shapes it would recognize might not be stationary or urban; this view would "measure" the land, but distances might be more than physical-spatial; and this view would "situate" different areas in relation to a larger totality, but this totality might be something other than a grid of longitude and latitude. Beginning with the mix of genres it does, then, the *Relación* suggests the need for a type of science or knowledge that would make visible a nation for which there is no place in current European cartography.

The latter half of the *Relación* suggests one such type of knowledge. Following his stay on the Island of Malhado, Alvar Núñez relates the series of miracles by which he and his fellow survivors were able to locate a Spanish military outpost on the West Coast and eventually return to Spain. In the process, he charts the space between Galvestan Bay and the city of what is today, Culiacán, Sonora. As the terrain changes and he begins to travel with different Amerindian groups, the text gradually begins to take the form of two different but still European cartographic genres of the time. The underlying structure becomes that of a narrative itinerary. Adverbs of movement, measurements of distance between points, and markings of place names begin to trace the protagonist's progress along a terrestrial route. At the same time, chorographic detail that includes the ecological and epidemiological character of different areas and the alimentary and linguistic customs of different tribes overlays this itinerary structure with the encyclopedic, atlas-like qualities of later *isolarii*.

Like portolans and topographical maps, itinerary maps and *isolarii* differed with respect to their referents but converged in some of the basic ways they organized the spectator's gaze. Though itineraries focused primarily on distances between landmarks and *isolarii* focused more on the chorographic qualities of particular regions, they both structured the representation of space around the observations of an individual gazing on an object that was implicitly separate from that viewer: itinerary maps used a visual narrative of episodic places traversed by the mapmaker (Conley 2007, 406), while *isolarii* used an insistence (explicit in their prefaces, implicit in their style) on systematic personal experience of each area's singularities (Conley 2007, 401; Tolias 2007, 280). Additionally, though itineraries focused on the sequence of places between one point and another and *isolarii* focused on the particulars of randomly or alphabetically ordered places, they both presented the mapmaker's observations as those of a timeless viewer: itinerary maps conflated multiple measurements taken sequentially over time into a single, synchronous view, while *isolarii* combined perspective views on cities and multiple views taken of islands into a single composite view. Thus while different in content both from each other and from portolans and topographical maps, these genres likewise promoted a monadic, eternalized gaze on a separate, knowable earth – in the case of the itinerary, on a collection of points reducible to a series of individually measured routes, and in the case of the *isolario*, on a collection of singularities made meaningful by an individual scheme of comprehension.

However, while in this central part of the *Relación* Alvar Núñez continues to adhere closely to the commonplaces of these popular European genres, he once again departs from some of their customary reference points. And here, rather than signaling the *lack* of readable reference points, he increasingly incorporates points of reference used by his Amerindian companions to organize their own migratory image of space. As he grows more sensitive to these non-European reference points, he does not find a space that he considers civilized. However, he does grow far more able to navigate and to identify peoples and territories that went unaccounted for in European current methods of mapping. This ability to map his surroundings seems to spring from three basic changes in seeing that this Amerindian migratory cardinalization implies.

To begin with, as Alvar Núñez increasingly marks his route by the gathering points at which he and his companions stopped, instead of reducing the representation of space to the viewpoint of an imaginary individual, he suggests the viewpoint of multiple observers. Commenting on some of the fruits that marked certain points along his route, for example, he writes: "Ay muchas maneras de tunas, y entre ellas ay algunas muy buenas, aunque a mí todas me paresçían ansí, y nunca la hambre me dio espacio para escogerlas . . ." (149); and, "allegamos a un río donde assentamos nuestras casas. Y después de assentadas, fuimos a buscar una fruta de unos árboles que es como hierros" (154). In the first example, the contrast between his own imperception of different kinds of prickly pear ("all very good") and the perception of his companions ("*some* very good") reveals the way the groups with which he traveled taught him to see differences between diverse landmarks which he alone was unable to perceive. In the second, use of a simile ("like [the fruit of] a vetch") rather than a name to designate the fruit reveals that, because he himself was unfamiliar with this landmark before this experience, his ability to see it at all depended on the viewpoint of an Indian community that used it to structure their own migratory image of their lands. While this pluralized viewer does not imply an individually controlling, sedentary, feudal-monarchic, urban-agricultural, "civilized" relation to the earth, it does more effectively locate Alvar Núñez with relation to the land's botanical and social resources.

Secondly, instead of structuring his representation of space around the fiction of an eternal, temporal viewer, Alvar Núñez also begins to locate his observations in a specific time. In those same references to botany that mark his movement through space, for example, Alvar Núñez marks not only the plurality of his viewpoint but also its seasonal-cyclical temporality: "por [gran hambre] los indios que a mí me tenían se salieron de la isla, y . . . passaron a tierra firme, a una vahías adonde tenían muchos ostiones. Y tres meses del año no comen otra cosa, . . . Y assí estuvimos hasta el fin de abril que fuimos a la costa de la mar adó comimos moras de çarças todo el mes" (110–112). Inclusion of these markers of time and duration ("three months of the year;" "the whole month") reveals that Alvar Núñez's own particular view of things – the fact that he saw these coves and coasts *as* he did – owed to being in those places *when* he was. The oblique reference to his captivity ("que a mi me tenían") reveals, in addition, that as Alvar Núñez himself did not seek out those areas, his observation of them likewise owed to the gaze of his companions, who used knowledge not just of spatial distance but also temporal distance between food-gathering seasons to structure their cyclical-migratory understanding of space. This temporally located viewer does not imply an outside-of-time, permanently vigilant, accumulative relation to the earth, but it does situate the viewer within the rhythms of the land for non-sedentary, cyclical gathering and exchange.

And finally, as Alvar Núñez also increasingly marks his route by the dietary customs of the peoples he encountered, instead of basing his representation of space on the observations of a detached eye witness, he begins to incorporate a broad range of sensorial data. Commenting on the eating practices of the Mariame Indians that marked a stopping point in his passage across the Texas coastline, for example, he writes:

> Su mantenimiento principalmente es raízes de dos o tres maneras . . . ; son muy malas y hinchan los hombres que las comen. Tardan dos días en assarse, y muchas dellas son muy amargas, . . . Es tanta la hambre que aquellas gentes tienen que . . . comen tierra y madera y todo lo que pueden aver y estiercol de venados y otras cosas que dexo de contar; . . . Muchas veces estando con éstos, nos acontesçió tres o quatro días estar sin comer porque no lo avía.
>
> (138–142)

The emphasis here on the desperate hunger Alvar Núñez suffered while with this tribe ("many times . . . three or four days without eating because there was no food") suggests that his "observation" of this diet – the fact that he knew the bitter taste and bloating effects of roots, dirt, and deer excrement – owed to his own (non-ocular) experience of these foods. Furthermore, the tropes of inexpressibility that mark the passage ("all that they can find;" "and other things that I refrain from mentioning") suggest that, as Alvar Núñez himself found these foods too abhorrent for words, his ability to see them as sustenance at all likewise owed to the gaze of his companions, who used non-ocular, embodied knowledge to gain a more total image of their environment. While this sensorially informed "viewer" does not imply the rational objectivity and physical separation prized in societies organized around hierarchical dominion over land and people (the separation, furthermore, that would become the foundation of Northern European Enlightened modernity), it does equip the viewer to more completely know the land that was actually there – to better map the total world available for human sustenance.

Recognizing these ways that Alvar Núñez incorporates non-European knowledge in this central part of the text further complicates interpretations of him as a "neither Spanish nor Native American" hybrid (Spitta 1995, 51) or a viewer from the hubris of zero degrees. On the one hand, while Alvar Núñez does learn to see referents to which he was originally blind – "built" environment that consists not just of buildings but also of sites constructed from layers of social memory; "measures" of the land that include not just spatial but also temporal distances; a "totality" to which lands relate not only in proportion and disposition but also in range of available sustenance – he still does not "see" as Native Americans do. Whatever his ability to identify these coordinates, he does not embrace the "unspoken, unanalyzed relationship to the order of creation" (Mundy 1996, xii) implicit in the use of these coordinates to structure spatial understanding. "Civilization," for him, continues to be defined by a European ideology of man's (singular and eternal) dominion over the earth and all that is in it. On the other hand, while Alvar Núñez does continue to prefer a colonial ownership and sedentary accumulative relationship to the environment, his experience of the utility of Amerindian modes of understanding space – and his utter disgust, when, upon finally reaching a Spanish encampment, a simple two-day journey guided by four Spaniards results in the death of seven men from thirst – does lead him to view European modes of knowing space more skeptically. Whatever his gut-sense of European superiority, his closing condemnation of European scientific-rationalism demonstrates clearly that the hubris of zero degrees leads nowhere and is, for him and others, the way behind.

The way "ahead," the *Relación* implies, must necessarily involve the re-purposing of non-European knowledge. Only the recognition of non-European (communal, seasonal-cyclical, embodied) knowledges *as such* will allow European travelers to correctly read the appearances of peoples and territories and successfully move between one route and another. And for Carlos V, only a cartography that incorporates this material will enable him to see the true totality of his realms. At this time when elite cartographers grappled with regional versus national views of the Spanish realm and religious versus cultural definitions of the Spanish people, Alvar Núñez points out that the "totality" of Spain exceeds any of these definitions. Whether regional or geographical, territorial renderings of the nation only "saw" sedentary, accumulative relations with the earth and not the transitory attachment and cyclical frequentation of land of certain nomadic populations in the Americas and on the Peninsula. And whether religious or cultural, juridical demarcations of the nation both "saw" only Judeo-Christian "peoples" and not Amerindian (or gypsy or Arab, for that matter) tribes. A cross-cultural mapping of the nation could account for the fact that the real and actual "shape of Spain," increasingly, was not (just) a federation or nation-state made up of sedentary provinces or peoples with a common history or social structure, but rather an enormous, diverse interaction sphere with a constantly evolving exchange of symbols, ideas, and inventions. Like other royal mapmakers, Alvar Núñez does more than simply outline existing realms. He endeavors "to chart a state's designs for future expansion and to enunciate, in cartographic form, hopeful programs of state building" (Kagan and Schmidt 2007, 662). In the *Relación*'s case, this design is principally scientific-epistemological. It involves a type of authority based on intimate and mobile knowledge of particularities, or as Don Quijote would put it, "knowing the enemies [not] merely in painting, but in their very being." Situating himself (*avant la lettre*) as a "true knight" – "the salvation, not merely of one kingdom, but of many" – Alvar Núñez charts a scientific way ahead for the "heartland" of the nation as it transitions from the Medieval into the modern, global era.

Notes

1 Kagan and Schmidt: "the lack of comment goes in both directions: early modernists have not adequately made the case that nationalism and cartographic state building took place in the [Renaissance], while modernists have discounted the possibility that the mapping of the state might have taken place prior to the mid-eighteenth century" (2007, 662).

2 Notable exceptions are Ricardo Padrón's (2004) *The Spacious Word* and Arias and Meléndez's (2002) *Mapping Colonial Spanish America*, which complement recent work on graphic maps by scholars such as Dana Leibsohn, Walter Mignolo, and Barbara Mundy.

3 All quotations from the text are taken from the 1542 Zamora edition as transcribed by Adorno and Pautz (1999) and will be indicated by the page numbers as they appear in the Spanish version.

4 On the origins and evolution of these different genres in the Renaissance, see Woodward (1991) and chapters 8, 9, 19, and 20 of Woodward 2007.

5 On the historical transition from Classical to Medieval to Early Modern notions of sovereignty, see Kagan and Schmidt 2007, 662–664.

6 Studies have largely been limited to reconstructing Cabeza de Vaca's route (e.g., Adorno and Pautz 1999), "mapping" the text's cognitive spaces (e.g., Domínguez Castellanos 2004), and analyzing the way the journey motif structures the narrative (e.g., Nanfito 1994).

7 The hubris of zero degrees, as explained by Santiago Castro-Gómez, is the belief in a point of view (and capacity to know, measure, and determine universal values) independent of one's ethnic and cultural center of observation (2008, 278–279).

Works cited

Adorno, Rolena and Charles Patrick Pautz. 1999. *Alvar Núñez Cabeza de Vaca: His Account, His Life, and the Expedition of Pánfilo de Narváez.* 3 vols. Lincoln, NE: University of Nebraska Press.

Arias, Santa and Mariselle Meléndez, eds. 2002. *Mapping Colonial Spanish America. Places and Commonplaces of Identity, Culture, and Experience.* London: Bucknell University Press.

Bauer, Ralph. 2003. *The Cultural Geography of Colonial American Literatures: Empire, Travel, Modernity.* Cambridge: Cambridge University Press.

Castro-Gómez, Santiago. 2008. "(Post)Coloniality for Dummies: Latin American Perspectives on Modernity, Coloniality, and the Geopolitics of Knowledge." In *Coloniality at Large: Latin America and the Postcolonial Debate*, edited by Mabel Moraña, Enrique Dussel, and Carlos A. Jáuregui, 259–285. Durham, NC: Duke University Press.

Cervantes Saavedra, Miguel de. 1978. *El ingenioso hidalgo Don Quijote de la Mancha.* Edited by Luis Andrés Murillo. Madrid: Clásicos Castalia.

Conley, Tom. 1996. *The Self-Made Map: Cartographic Writing in Early Modern France.* Minneapolis, MN: University of Minnesota Press.

———. 2007. "Early Modern Literature and Cartography: An Overview." In *The History of Cartography*, edited by David Woodward, vol. 3, 401–411. Chicago: University of Chicago Press.

Cosgrove, Denis E. 1998. *Social Formation and Symbolic Landscape.* Madison, WI: University of Wisconsin Press.

Domínguez Castellano, Julia. 2004. "Cartografías imaginarias: La creación de espacios utópicos en el 'Lazarillo de Tormes,' el 'Quijote' y la 'Relación' de Cabeza de Vaca." PhD diss., University of Arizona.

Jameson, Frederic. 1988. "Cognitive Mapping." In *Marxism and the Interpretation of Culture*, edited by Cary Nelson and Lawrence Grossberg, 347–360. Urbana, IL: University of Illinois Press.

Kagan, Richard L. and Benjamin Schmidt. 2007. "Maps and the Early Modern State: Official Cartography." In *The History of Cartography*, edited by David Woodward, vol. 3, 661–679. Chicago: University of Chicago Press.

Mann, Charles C. 2005. *1491: New Revelations of the Americas before Columbus.* New York: Knopf.

Molloy, Silvia. 1993. "Alteridad y reconocimiento en los *Naufragios* de Álvar Núñez Cabeza de Vaca." In *Notas y comentarios sobre Álvar Núñez Cabeza de Vaca*, edited by Margo Glantz, 219–242. Mexico: Grijalbo.

Mundy, Barbara. 1996. *The Mapping of New Spain: Indigenous Cartography and the Maps of the Relaciones Geográficas.* Chicago: University of Chicago Press.

Nanfito, Jacqueline. 1994. "Cabeza de Vaca's *Naufragios y comentarios*: The Journey Motif in the Chronicle of the Indies." *Revista de Estudios Hispánicos* 21: 179–187.

Padrón, Ricardo. 2004. *The Spacious Word: Cartography, Literature, and Empire in Early Modern Spain.* Chicago: University of Chicago Press.

Parker, Geoffrey. 1992. "Maps and Ministers: The Spanish Habsburgs." In *Monarchs, Ministers, and Maps: The Emergence of Cartography as a Tool of Government in Early Modern Europe*, edited by David Buisseret, 124–152. Chicago: University of Chicago Press.

Rabasa, José. 2000. "Reading Cabeza de Vaca or How We Perpetuate the Culture of Conquest." In *Writing Violence on the Northern Frontier: The Historiography of Sixteenth-Century New Mexico and Florida and the Legacy of Conquest*, 31–83. Durham, NC: Duke University Press.

Rojinsky, David. 2006. "Found in Translation: Writing beyond Hybridity in Alvar Núñez Cabeza de Vaca's *Naufragios*." *Hofstra Hispanic Review: Revista de Literaturas y Culturas Hispánicas* 3 (1): 11–25.

Spitta, Silvia. 1995. *Between Two Waters: Narratives of Transculturation in Latin America.* College Station: Texas A&M University Press.

Tolias, George. 2007. "*Isolarii*, Fifteenth to Seventeenth Century." In *The History of Cartography*, edited by David Woodward, vol. 3, 263–284. Chicago: University of Chicago Press.

Woodward, David. 1991. "Maps and the Rationalization of Geographic Space." In *Circa 1492: Art in the Age of Exploration*, edited by J. A. Levenson, 83–87. New Haven, CT: Yale University Press.

———, ed. 2007. *Cartography in the European Renaissance. The History of Cartography*, vol. 3. Chicago: University of Chicago Press.

14

PURITY AND IMPURITY OF BLOOD IN EARLY MODERN IBERIA

Rachel L. Burk

The Spanish term *limpieza de sangre* and its Portuguese equivalent *limpeza de sangue* began as a legal designation of religious identity attributed to the supposed purity or impurity of one's blood. Instituted via local statutes beginning in the mid-1400s in Spain and a century later in Portugal, the *pureza* laws were propagated widely by the end of the sixteenth century in the whole of the Peninsula.[1] Local regulations on *limpieza-limpeza* prohibited recent converts to Christianity and eventually their descendants from holding select offices in government, the Church, guilds, schools, and universities. To qualify for these positions, proof of lineage free from Muslim and Jewish relatives even in generations past was required. With these entrance demands developed an inquisitional process for accessing and certifying a supposedly physical verity that ended in a set of documents called blood purity proofs, as well as a generalized social preoccupation with lineage.

Although the real discriminatory impact may have been small, the ideological shift blood purity instituted had far-reaching effects. From this point forward, identity – national, religious, ethnic – was associated with an internal differential, a difference in bodies regardless of creed. To be Old Christian (a *cristiano viejo* in Castilian, or *cristão-velho* in Portuguese) rather than a *converso* (converted Jew) or Christianized Moor (*Morisco* or *Mouresco*) bespoke an innate ancestral inheritance of superiority, registered physically in one's blood.[2]

The first blood purity law, the *Sentencia-Estatuto* for the Cathedral of Toledo issued in 1449, made explicit the association between genealogy and the physical body of Castilian subjects. The rules for excluding New Christians from Church employment emphasized that all *conversos* by their nature were *manchados* [stained] and thus *infames* [infamous], suggesting a religious category of lasting dishonor, a stain not removed by baptism akin to the curse of Ham. Envisioning this difference between peoples as explicitly corporal and located in the blood obviated practice, will, and belief in the creation of social identity. While medieval anti-Semitism had attributed to Jews a constellation of dishonorable qualities in addition to mistaken belief, blood purity located the source of infamy in a genealogical trace that could not be easily erased.

It can be said that blood law remained limited in scope, that in many places statutes went unenforced well into the sixteenth century, and that, in practice, the dispersed system of requirements was easy to sidestep. Nonetheless, the importance of blood purity is not that it did what it purported to do: that is, keep Iberian New Christians from participating in civic and economic life on equal footing with Old Christians. Rather, its significance is as a new idea in the larger history of exclusion, as an early instance of the institutionalization of biopolitics, and an ideological inheritance left to the Spanish and Portuguese colonies, but once there transformed. Blood purity modeled a kind of body-based power relationship that, although in many cases more symbolic than real, marked a significant ideational step in the progression from medieval to modern imaginations of community.

Ex illis: origins, laws, and blood purity as social phenomenon

The close of the Christian Conquest in 1492 marked the end of the last Iberian Islamic polity and the ascent of Castile-Aragon as the most powerful kingdom on the Peninsula. The incipient consolidation of the Spanish nation-state, along with the founding of the Hapsburg empire and growth of both Iberian empires, led to the forced conversion of Jews, Moors, gypsies, Amerindians, and non-Arabized Africans to Christianity. Portugal, less powerful than in previous centuries, felt Castilian influence acutely during the Iberian Union (1580–1640), as Feros and Ponsen in this volume discuss. Throughout the period, Portuguese and Spanish kingdoms acted reciprocally, although many times distinctly, on matters of minority populations. At the same time, both societies confronted the creation of new social categories of Old and New Christian and the bringing of the whole of the Iberian populace under the jurisdiction of the Inquisition.

Late medieval Iberia was home not only to a significant Islamic presence, but also to a large, ancient, and robust Jewish population that formed an influential portion of society.[3] As of the 1300s, tensions between majority Christians and minority Jews and Muslims were on the rise because of economic instability, brought on in part by internecine war and bouts of plague; jostling between princes, nobility, and rising bourgeoisie; and the consolidation of Christian dominance among other factors.[4] By a century later under the Catholic Kings and with the conquest of Granada, the double movement of unification of Iberian kingdoms at home and expansion abroad brought an end to medieval *convivencia-convivência* between Muslims, Christians, and Jews, who had lived together as unequal partners throughout the eight centuries of the Islamic rule and Christian Conquest. In advance of the imposition of the blood purity statutes, the scapegoating of Jews led many to convert to Christianity in the late fourteenth century. This was most prominently the case after 1391 when a pogrom broke out in Seville, followed by violence against Jews in Toledo, Valencia, and Barcelona. Similar events followed in 1412. The first generations of Spanish *conversos* encountered a varied landscape for integration into Christian society. Before the hardening and proliferation of the blood purity doctrine, many found acknowledged routes to success via the Church or state or were incorporated easily into a growing urban bourgeoisie. This kind of public assimilation was made difficult by the Decree of Alhambra in 1492, which demanded conversion or expulsion for all Spanish Jews, as Rawlings in this volume elaborates.

Jews in Portugal received better protection from the Lusitanian monarchs well into the period of Union. The late medieval incidences of anti-Semitic violence in Portugal were markedly fewer, and the kingdom protected its Jewish and *converso* population for almost a century and a half after the pogroms, creating distinct circumstances for them once Catholic orthodoxy was finally enforced. João II (1481–1495) resisted Spanish pressure to expel his Jewish population, and his successor, Dom Manuel I (1495–1521), managed a détente with Spain that allowed *conversos* religious and social latitude. As a result of Alhambra, approximately 120,000 Spanish Jews took refuge in Portugal legally in the 1490s. While the reprieve from mandated conversion was short – the official order came in 1497 – Jews and nominal *conversos* had fifty years mostly free from persecution before the Portuguese Inquisition was founded in 1536 (Costigan 2010).

Moors under Christian rule were less often victims of mob violence because they tended to live in isolated rural communities and had a less visible role in the economy. Indeed in Portugal the last vestiges of Moorish presence were gone by 1496. With the conquest of Granada, however, Castilian monarchies turned their attention to the remaining concentrated Moorish population in Iberia. After short-lived assurances that Granadines could remain Muslim, they were Christianized by force in the first two decades of the sixteenth century. Repressive edicts, prohibiting the use of Arabic along with other practices as much cultural as religious, followed, fomenting dissent that erupted in the Alpujarras War (1568–1571). As a consequence, Granadine *Moriscos* were dispersed by royal order to smaller communities and, although Christian, eventually expelled (1608–1614). Different from *conversos*, *Moriscos* were regularly seen as a Fifth Column, as colluding with the powerful Turkish empire. As several recent historical studies have elaborated, this slowly realized eviction was less than absolute: the Expulsion often ordered *Morisco* children into the care of Christian families. As well, there were many Ricotes, Sancho Panza's *Morisco* friend who, once expelled, sneaks back into Spain, a not unsurprising outcome among a group of Christians with weak ties to the larger Islamic world.

While throughout the sixteenth century New and Old Christians alike sought a peaceful incorporation of former religious minorities into the majority, *pureza de sangre-sangue* grew up to counteract the movement towards sanctioned assimilation. The humanistic vision of a big-tent Christian nation gave way to a more complex reality of official intolerance – at times acute – and extra-official lenience.

Out of this complex political and social landscape arose the doctrine of blood purity. Often referred to in relation to official statutes, blood purity extended beyond its initial life as a legal mechanism and grew into a full-fledged culture-wide obsession by the turn of the seventeenth century. What are often considered the first blood purity statutes were instituted by the ambitious mayor of Toledo, Pedro Sarmiento, in 1449. They banned *conversos* from holding Church positions on the basis not of any misdeed but genealogy as manifested in their impure blood, in the terms of the statute. Sarmiento's decree was one act in a larger revolt against Castilian King Juan II and his proxy, Álvaro de Luna, who was sympathetic to Jews and a *converso* himself. It concerned the imposition of what many Toledans considered an unjust tax in support of the Castilian war against Aragon. In response to the levy, a crowd attacked Alonso Cota, a *converso* tax collector and landowner, along with other wealthy New Christians in the Magdelena neighborhood. The blood purity statute was in support of the mob. When Toledo came back under monarchal control in 1451, Juan II forgave the rebels but disputed blood purity. Early incidents of blood purity discrimination suggest the ways in which it began as a convenient excuse, a secondary "offense" that would become primary, and that it did not have a stable coalition that supported blood purity so much as it was used opportunistically as a mechanism in larger politics (Sicroff 1985, 51–56).

Blood purity never constituted pan-Iberian law although at its height requirements were in place at a broad swath of religious, political, and social institutions. Instead, the statutes appeared unsystematically and spread piecemeal, reflecting the diffuse character of authority in the period and the debate that *limpieza-limpeza* provoked. Religious brotherhoods, churches, cathedrals, individual trade unions, schools, universities, and city governments established their own policies on blood purity, demanding "pure bloodedness" of their members in fits and starts. In the course of progressive implementation, requirements for blood purity were sometimes rescinded, reinstated, vigorously challenged, and kept but not enforced. The end result, however, was the impression of a general saturation that encouraged intense concern for blood purity as part of the culture of honor.

Soria Mesa (2013) among others has showed the ways in which blood purity postulated the far-reaching exclusion of former religious minorities, creating an image of what we might now call ethnic cleansing so impactful that it remains to the present. The reality was distinct, however. "The spectacular façade" (11) of blood purity law masked the documented presence of *conversos* in all ranks of Spanish government and aristocracy, not only in the fifteenth century as F. Márquez Villanueva (1965) had detailed previously, but throughout the period in which blood purity was on the books. Soria Mesa identifies a number of avenues for eluding blood purity requirements, from the common practice of falsifying proofs to the equally common practice of paying for advancement, including noble titles.

Blood purity grew up as a social phenomenon with legal grounding from the fifteenth through the end of the sixteenth century, when it reached a stable form. It went into decline by the end of the seventeenth century. Official suppression of the distinction between Old and New Christian was enacted by law in Portugal in 1773 and in Spain in 1870.

Scholars have offered differing accounts of what blood purity did to early modern society on large scale and whom it benefited. One significant result was that the spread of blood distinctions potentially provided every Old Christian Spaniard with a claim to a kind of nobility, particularly in the North where the Islamic empire ruled for only a short period or not at all. Everyone who could assert Old Christian status gained honorable standing ("honra de los villanos" in the term of the *comedias* of the time), conveying moral-cultural capital to non-nobles although no explicit legal rights. The role of the lower castes in upholding the statutes was substantial in the process for proving or disproving purity. The Santo Oficio demanded testimonies to lineage and denunciations by neighbor and kin, institutionalizing a form of community self-monitoring that created fear, regardless of ancestry. Kamen (1986) has argued that blood purity at first served as a check on the rising bourgeoisie and later brought together the rural peasantry with the urban underclass, forming a national popular culture that could be directed from above.

"Raza en los linges se toma en mala parte:" blood purity and the history of race

Early modern forms of exclusion are not the same as "race" in the eighteenth and nineteenth centuries, notably in the later period's emphasis on visible, external physical traits to distinguish one race from another.[5] Nonetheless, the early modern discourse of *limpieza-limpeza* in Iberia represents a critical transition in European thought from conceiving of divisions between what had been "peoples" or "nations" as multivariable, based on geography, culture, common history, beliefs, and caste as well as bodies, to a taxonomical system based explicitly and essentially on physicality and thus reducing difference to a single, unchanging term. In Covarrubias's *Tesoro de la lengua castellana o española* (e.p. 1611; 2006), he lists meanings for *raza* in horse breeding and weaving before arriving at "race in lineage," which he defines as having "some Jewish or Muslim race." Although in later manifestations *raza-raça* will come to mean skin color, the religio-racial identities discussed here did not correspond in any meaningful way to darkness or lightness of complexion. Fuchs (2007) explains: "[B]lackness emphatically does not equal Moorishness within Spain. Instead Spanish racial hysteria focused on covert cultural and religious practices, and on the much more ambiguous register of blood" (95).

Balibar and Wallerstein (1991), Mariscal (1998), and Mignolo (2007) have offered a corrective to generalist histories of race that disregarded Portugal and Spain, insisting on their centrality and the idea that the conceptual framework for race is born of religious difference and the suppression of Judaism and Islam in early modern Iberia. It is this proto-racial foundation, they proffer, which in turn is translated, adapted, and expanded by post-Enlightenment science and philosophy.

In Hispanism, the relationship between early modern blood purity and race has been at issue since the 1940s. Maravall (1979), Roth (1940), and Sicroff (1985) postulated a clear link to post-Enlightenment racism, while Kisch (1943) and Márquez Villanueva (1965) objected strongly to the notion of blood purity as a conceptual or practical forerunner of contemporary race. More recent historians and cultural critics, particularly Hering Torres (2003, 2012), Martínez (2008), and Nirenberg (2009) have eschewed easy anachronism and begun rethinking the premises of modern race in ways which allow us to respect continuities with past forms of difference as well as their historical specificity. The first generations of race theorists insisted on a time frame that views the advent of race as a radical disjunction from the past and a unique hallmark of modernity unknown to the premodern era. In this, they err, these critics would say, in replicating a fallacy of racism by insisting on a single definition of race rather than viewing the phenomenon as a related "series of historical racisms" in Martínez's term or "imaginaries of racism" according to Hering Torres. Further, within Iberian Studies, race and racial identity have tended to remain either peninsular or colonial, a trend reversed by recent transatlantic studies (Costigan 2010; Herzog 2012, 2013; Martínez 2008), as well as those that consider other parts of the empires such as Barreto Xavier (2003, 2012).

While unprecedented, the Castilian blood purity statutes did not appear *ex nihilo*. They grew out of a specific political and social climate in late medieval Iberia and have a place in larger religious-theological and cultural developments at work throughout Europe. Anidjar (2005) insists that conditions that facilitated the emergence of blood purity in the Iberian Peninsula (concern over the Eucharist; growing blood piety such as the veneration of blood relics and miracles of the stigmata; the association of Jews with blood, most notably the so-called blood crimes; etc.) were common to all of western Christendom.

Thanks to their inherent "impurity," *conversos'* status was as heretics, disobeyers within the fold, rather than heathens, disbelievers outside the fold. It was this double proximity, both spiritual and physical, that supposedly threatened Old Christians. (Unlike Jews and Muslims, New Christians no longer lived in separate enclaves and were party to Church institutions.) The lexicon of contamination, suggesting that the presence of New Christians put the orthodoxy of Old Christians in jeopardy, confused religion and biology. Alarm at what *conversos* might say or do in the company of non-*conversos* became a fear of their mere physical presence. This line of thought may have begun in fears about judaizing, that is, *marranos*, cheek to jowl with Old Christians, sharing their beliefs and thus spreading heresy. By 1600, however, the material body was so conflated with religion that it usurped belief as the more important term. As Nirenberg explains, "Judaizers were to be identified by their behavior, but that behavior only gained meaning in light of their genealogy" (1996, 82).

Root (1988) places the *limpieza de sangre* statutes in a dynamic relationship with an ideological progression taking place over the course of the sixteenth century in which Catholic orthodoxy and *españolidad*, a kind of proto-national identity, became equivalent. Heresy came to function as a social and genealogical category, rather than one purely indicative of religious affiliation (118). In the mandated culture of Catholicism, customs of all kinds, even those less associated with religious belief per se like language, dress, and cuisine, came under scrutiny and were lauded as orthodox or suppressed as heterodox. That heterodoxy was then understood as evidence of innate difference. Edicts of Faith, issued regularly by the Inquisition, criminalized cultural practices such as the use of Arabic and Hebrew, marking the Sabbath on

Saturday with clean linen and special foods, and avoidance of pork and wine. Distinguishing between Catholic and Moorish or Jewish conventions was not simple. Given the long history of *convivencia-convivência*, practice was often as much a cultural and regional as a religious matter, as explored by Fuchs (2009).

Blood purity laws initially extended the period of transition from one religion to another; the instantaneous conversion of baptism became a period of assimilation and a generation of converts, which in turn extended to generations. Ultimately, as the laws grew in scope to affect four or more generations post-conversion, *limpieza-limpeza* undermined genuine conversion under most circumstances. Blood purity naturalized social and cultural diversity, thus making it absolute in a way previously inconceivable, given that the multi-fold cultural, religious, historical, and geographical difference of old – what we would now call ethnicity – was inexact, open to conversion, chance, and change. At the level of the individual, blood purity became fundamental to creating and reproducing a new norm: old Christian, male, and aristocratic. At a larger societal level, blood purity promoted a new model of community that affected understanding of related notions such as Christendom, nation, and empire. It is the reduction of variables, hardening of categories, and prioritizing of physicality that are critical to modern notions of race that suggest that sixteenth-century blood purity should be viewed as continuous with race in its post-Enlightenment form.

Sangre enemiga, alma israelita: debate and resistance

From its beginnings, the notion of blood purity provoked a vigorous debate within the Old Christian community, as well as among New Christians, during much of the sixteenth century and again in the 1620s. *Pureza* as concept and institution met with vocal resistance from many quarters: among outspoken *conversos* and *Moriscos* such as Miguel de Luna and Francisco Nuñez de Mulay; among a few aristocrats who stood to lose standing because of prevailing documented Jewish ancestry and agricultural workers who farmed their lands; among reformers, humanists, and *alumbrados* who saw it as a perversion of Christ's Millennialism. Even some in positions of power openly resisted the statutes: Ignatius of Loyola famously refused to demand proof of purity for entrance into the Jesuits.

The founding tract against blood purity was published within a year of the events of Toledo. Alfonso de Cartagena's *Defensorium Unitatis Christianae* [*A Defense of Christian Unity*] (1450), an apology for *conversos*, argues that blood purity contradicts long-held notions of Christian community and denies the efficacy of baptism to incorporate new followers into the fold.[6] Cartagena uses the Old Testament story of Ruth, who converted to Judaism, as exemplary of the primacy of faith over blood, posed in no uncertain terms as the substance of difference: while she was born of "foreign blood, or better said enemy blood," by accepting the true faith she made "her soul an Israelite" (Mariscal, 190).

Many critics of blood purity pointed to the well-known practice of intermarriage in noble families that threatened to jeopardize their standing if *limpieza-limpeza* was taken into consideration. In 1449, Fernán Díaz, relator of Juan II of Castile, pointed to the riskiness of a genealogical system for the aristocracy, contending that most noble families had *converso* ancestry (Nirenberg 2007, 82). Indeed, the most infamous text of the age, the *Libro verde de Aragón* (1507), elaborated the "tainted" lineage of noble families, exposing just this caste vulnerability.[7]

Once blood purity had a firm foothold, reformers penned critiques to the end of changing its applications. These included Fray Domingo de Baltanás's *Apología* (1557), Fray Luis de León's *De los nombres de Cristo* (1583), and Juan de Mariana's *De rege et rege institutione*

(1598). In this vein, Fray Augustín Salucio in his *Discurso* (1599) suggests any test of blood purity should include an evaluation of Christian knowledge and practice. Further, he argues, dividing the Christian community into lesser and greater goes against the Pauline ideal of unity expressed in his letter to Galatians. All professed believers should be incorporated into the *corpus mysticum*, the mystical body of the Church, which constitutes the spiritual community of Christians, defined by practicing the sacraments, not birthright.

Miguel de Cervantes takes up this anti-*limpieza* strain of Christian thought, influenced by Erasmian humanism, in *El retablo de las maravillas* (published 1615) and *Numancia* (1582–87), as explored in Burk (2012). As Cervantes suggests in his one-act *Retablo* with satirical incisiveness, the doctrine preys on our worst instincts and fears of exclusion. His two shyster play producers, Chanfalla and Chirinos, convince a small town's leaders that a stage show, in which nothing actually occurs, can only be seen by the pure-blooded. No one fesses up to the sham for fear of betraying that they cannot see the production and doubt their own "purity" for it. The comedy closes with the arrival of a soldier unaware of the terms of the fake production. He sees nothing on stage, says so, and is taunted by the frenzied participants who call him "Ex illis" ["one of them"]. Enraged, he slays the audience, leaving Chanfalla and Chirinos to put on their performance again the following night, suggesting that adhering to blood purity is fatal yet the premise lives on.

Empires of blood

Blood purity arose in the Peninsula during the incipient moments of Iberian colonialism, as Portugal rapidly expanded its worldwide medieval possessions and Castile founded the first modern European empire. Recent transatlantic scholars such as Costigan (2010), Herzog (2012, 2013), Martínez (2008), and Monteiro et al. (2011) have explored the relationship between blood purity and the hierarchical *sistema de castas* that grew up in many parts of Latin America under Portuguese and Spanish rule. Others such as Barreto Xavier (2003, 2012) have considered blood purity as influential in race/caste structures in colonies outside the Americas, such as that in Goa. Although resulting social orders were manifestly different from those in early modern Iberia, blood purity bequeathed to the Spanish and Portuguese empires two ideological tenants of social organization: genealogy and faith. It passed on to colonial subjects the notion that inheritable characteristics, originating in religion, left a bodily trace.

To begin with, assuring blood purity was a determining factor in whom the Spanish allowed to immigrate abroad during most of the colonization period. Despite stipulations against New Christian colonizers, which were easily got around according to Soria Mesa, there were early-established and well-documented crypto-Jewish communities in Mexico City among other Latin American communities, as studied by Gitlitz (1996) and others. Cook (2016) even offers evidence of American *Moriscos* in Spanish America, although numbers were surely smaller. Because of the late introduction and slow implementation of the Inquisition to the Lusitanian empire (only beginning in 1596), Portugal allowed the immigration of Jews and *conversos* to the Americas early in colonization, many of whom played pivotal roles in the founding of Portuguese Brazil as well as the expansion of trade (Bomfim 2008, Olival Rigor 2004). But even the most generous estimates suggest that Old World New Christians were but a small percentage of colonial populations. Nonetheless, the specter of Moorishness and the threat of judaizing had outsized influence in these societies, especially in the first centuries after conquest.

To wit, the impact of blood purity in the American and Indian colonies was as a classificatory framework that lingered in spirit even though the European historical reality it described was distant in time and space. Martínez asserts that Iberian "blood purity," along with "caste" and "race," were reformulated in the distinct and changing circumstances of sixteenth- to eighteenth-century Mexico that included native communities with pre-Hispanic nobilities, African slaves, *mestizos*, and poor Spaniards. By the late seventeenth century, a tiered system of social classification based on European, indigenous, and African ancestry had grown up that also figured in caste and belief. *Limpieza de sangre* in this context was often vexed: for example, an Aztec could be seen as both pure, of "unmixed" blood and belonging to the parallel Indian Republic, and impure, that is, non-Spanish and non-Christian. The secularization of the concept in the eighteenth century linked purity to whiteness, resulting in an elaborated race rubric based on miscegenation and exemplified in *casta* paintings. Even then, however, the remaining religious dimension to late colonial categories of identity suggest the roots of the *sociedad de castas* found in blood purity.

The early establishment and longevity of Portuguese Goa (1510–1961), on the Indian west coast, makes it an interesting case. The majority of Indians under Portuguese rule converted to Christianity from Hinduism quickly after conquest. Xavier (2012) points out the ways in which blood purity standards were a Portuguese imposition, but also in juxtaposition with similar Indian concepts, as part of elaborated notions of bodily purity. Genealogical purity was a term in power struggles between elites to establish dominance, notably in opposition between the Portuguese born in India (*casados*) and those from Portugal (*reinóis*); the *reinóis* regularly accused the *casados* of mixed blood. The Goan colonial race/caste system included a "race of Indian," that was roughly equivalent to Jew or Moor in the Iberian context. Equally the pre-colonial purity discourses meant that *limpeza de sangue* served not only as an "imperial tool for social differentiation," but also as a "vehicle for empowerment of the colonized," that led to the association of whiteness with purity in order to ensure Portuguese dominance (Xavier 2012, 143).

"Bloody" Spain and the Black Legend

The irony of the blood purity doctrine and its performative insistence on purity as prerequisite to national identity was its perception outside the Peninsula. Early modern anti-Spanish propaganda, particularly of the 1580s and '90s, characterized Iberia as oriental as part of efforts to challenge its imperial domination by England, the Netherlands, Italy, and France. "Blood" was a central term condemning Spain's growing reputation as violent ("bloody" and "blood-thirsty") and racially, as well as religiously, impure ("of mixed blood"). Born of imperial rivalry, the Black Legend was a tenacious discourse of Spanish difference that conflated violence, heretical – this often meant Catholic as well as Muslim and Jewish – practice, and "blackness," qualities associated with or even ascribed to blood. In this view the Spanish were characterized by a fundamental, suspect, and unique hybridity, Spain as Europe's mongrel nation. Significant, much Black Legend rhetoric read Spain's continued Moorishness as physical as well as moral "blackness," although such an association had no currency in Spain itself (Fuchs 2007, 116–9).

It is fair to point to a broader, although less marked, anti-Iberian sentiment in Europe: Portugal was often painted with the same brush as Spain, but without the vehemence that its neighbor elicited, given the larger country's political and imperial weight. While Portugal escaped some of the negative repute of African-ness, at least in early modernity, anti-Lusitanian sentiment pegged Portuguese culture as appreciably Jewish, and Iberians abroad were often labeled "Jews" contemptuously.

Conclusion

Viewed transhistorically, blood purity served as a transitional concept, located in between older discourses on purity and modern race, with elements of both. The symbolic function of blood purity, its propagandistic role in creating embodied social categories, was crucial, though it did not reliably fulfill its stated intent. Through blood purity, the body itself came to be seen as recalcitrant: it passed on group, rather than exclusively familial, identity, irrespective of an individual's actions or desires. For all the instances in which pure-bloodedness ended up being a porous category, the idea of a physical, transmittable inheritance of religio-racial identity and its institutionalization contributed to an epistemic change in the European notions of collective identity.

Notes

1 The initial comprehensive historical studies of *limpieza de sangre* come from Caro Baroja (1961), Domínguez Ortiz (1955), Márquez Villanueva (1965), and Sicroff (1985). More recent contributions in monographs and broader works include Böttcher et al (2011), Hering Torres (2003, 2012), Hernández Franco (1996, 2011), Kamen (1986, 1996, 1999), Maravall (1979), and Méchoulan (1981). Portuguese blood purity has received recent attention by Barreto Xavier (2003, 2012), Figuerôa-Rêgo (2008), and Olival (2004).
2 *Converso* refers to converts from Judaism and their descendants in Portuguese and Spanish, but the term could indicate either Jewish or Muslim converts, depending on the situation. *Morisco – mouresco* (little Moor) always pertains to those converted from Islam. *Cristianos nuevos – cristãos-novos* includes both and was a less precise term used to differentiate new converts from *cristianos viejos – cristãos-velhos*.
3 Other European kingdoms exiled, or attempted to exile, their smaller populations of Jews by the twelfth century while Jews often prospered under medieval Iberian rulers, both Muslims and Christians.
4 Mounting conflict between religious populations in late medieval Iberia was a complex phenomenon. See Netanyahu (1995) and Nirenberg (1996).
5 For a discussion of the early modern terminology of race in Spain, see Hering Torres (2003); for Spanish America, see Hill (2015). For a broader study of racial lexicon in early modernity, see Loomba (2002).
6 Kamen (1996) details the movement against blood purity, with Cartagena as point of departure. Amelang (2013) traces different trajectories for *morisco* and *converso* communities throughout Iberia, including the resistance of Granadan Old Christians to laws that would discriminate against the majority of their fellow *granadinos*.
7 *El libro verde* and *El tizón de la nobleza* were anonymous compilations of genealogical information on principal noble families that cast doubt on the purity of lineage of many; copies were eventually banned. See Beusterein (1998).

Works cited

Amelang, James S. 2013. *Parallel Histories: Muslims and Jews in Inquisitorial Spain*. Baton Rouge, LA: Louisiana State University Press.

Anidjar, Gil. 2005. "Lines of Blood: *Limpieza de sangre* as Political Theology." In *Blood in History and Blood Histories*, edited by Mariacarla Gadebusch Bondio, 119–136. Florence: Sismel – Edizioni del Galluzzo.

Balibar, Etienne and Immanuel Wallerstein. 1991. *Race, Nation, Class: Ambiguous Identities*. New York: Verso.

Beusterien, John. 1998. "The Libro verde: Blood Fictions from Early Modern Spain." Ph.D. Diss., University of Wisconsin.

Bomfin Souza, Grayce Mayre. 2008. "Uma trajectoria racista: o ideal de pureza de sangue na sociedade iberica e na America Portuguesa." *POLITEIA* 8 (1): 83–103.

Bottcher, Nikolaus, Bernd Hausberger, and Max Hering Torres, eds. 2011. *El peso de la sangre: Limpios, mestizos y nobles en el mundo hispánico*. Mexico, DF: El Colegio de Mexico.

Burk, Rachel. 2012. "'La patria consumida': Blood, Nation, and Eucharist in Cervantes's *La Numancia*." *Journal of Spanish Cultural Studies* 13 (4): 1–19.

Caro Baroja, Julio. 1961. *Los judíos en la edad moderna y contemporánea*. 3 vols. Madrid: Ediciones Arión.

Cartagena, Alfonso de. 1943. *Defensorium Unitatis Christianae*. Edited by Manuel Alonso. Madrid: n.p.

Cook, Karoline P. 2016. *Forbidden Passages: Muslims and Moriscos in Colonial Spanish America, 1492–1650*. Philadelphia, PA: University of Pennsylvania Press.

Costigan, Lúcia. 2010. *Cracks in the Wall: Modern Inquisitions and New Christian Letrados in the Iberian Atlantic World*. New York: Brill.

Covarrubias Orozco, Sebastián de. 2006. *Tesoro de la lengua castellana or española*. Pamplona: University of Navarra Press.

Domínguez Ortiz, Antonio. 1955. *La clase social de los conversos en Castilla en la edad moderna*. Granada: University of Granada.

Figueirôa-Rêgo, João. 2008. "Family Genealogical Records: Cleansing and Social Reception (Portugal– 16th to 18th Century)." *E-JPH* 6 (1): 1–11.

Fuchs, Barbara. 2009. *Exotic Nation: Maurophilia and the Construction of Early Modern Spain*. Philadelphia, PA: University of Pennsylvania Press.

———. 2007. "The Spanish Race." In *Re-reading the Black Legend*, edited by Margaret Greer, Walter Mignolo and Maureen Quilligan, 88–98. Durham, NC: Duke University Press.

Gerli, E. Michael. 2017. "The Expulsion of the Moriscos: Seven Monumental Paintings from the Kingdom of Valencia." In *The Routledge Companion to Iberian Studies*, edited by Javier Muñoz-Basols, Laura Lonsdale, and Manuel Delgado, 184–200. London and New York: Routledge.

Gitlitz, David. 1996. *Secrecy and Deceit: The Religion of the Crypto-Jews*. Philadelphia, PA: Jewish Publication Society.

Hering Torres, Max. 2003. "Limpieza de sangre: ¿Racismo en la Edad Moderna?" *Tiempos Modernos Revista Electrónica de Historia Moderna* 4.

———. 2012. "Purity of Blood: Problems of Interpretation." In *Race and Blood in the Iberian World*, edited by Max Hering Torres, María Elena Martínez, and David Nirenberg, 11–38. Zurich: Lit Verlang.

Hernández Franco, Juan. 1996. *Cultura y limpieza de sangre en la España moderna: puritate sanguinis*. Murcia: University of Murcia Press.

_____. 2011. *Sangre limpia, sangre española: el debate sobre los estatutos de limpieza (siglos XV-XVII)*. Madrid: Cátedra.

Herzog, Tamar. 2012. "Beyond Race: Exclusion in Early Modern Spain and Spanish America." In *Race and Blood in the Iberian World*, edited by Max Hering Torres, María Elena Martínez, and David Nirenberg, 151–168. Zurich: Lit Verlang.

_____. 2013. "Judíos, musulmanes, conversos, indígenas y gitanos: Sobre la ida y vuelta de categorías jurídico-sociales entre el Viejo y el Nuevo Mundo." In *Les processus d'américanisation. vol.2: Dynamiques spatiales et culturelles*, edited by Louise Bénat-Tachot, Serge Gruzinski and Boris Jeanne, 59–84. Paris: Éditions Les Manuscrit.

Hill, Ruth. 2015. "The Blood of Others: Breeding Plants, Animals, and White People in the Spanish Atlantic." In *The Cultural Politics of Blood*, edited by Ralph Bauer, Kim Coles, Zita Nunez, and Carla Peterson, 45–64. Basingstoke: Palgrave MacMillan.

Kamen, Henry. 1986. "Una crisis de conciencia de la Edad de Oro en Espana: Inquisición contra limpieza de sangre." *Bulletin Hispanique* 88: 321–56.

———. 1996. "Limpieza and the Ghost of Américo Castro: Racism as a Tool of Literary Analysis." *Hispanic Review* 64 (1): 19–29.

———. 1999. *The Spanish Inquisition: A Historical Revision*. New Haven, CT: Yale University Press.

Kisch, Guido. 1943. "Nationalism and Race in Medieval Law." *Seminar: An Annual Extraordinary Number of* The Jurist I: 48–73.

Loomba, Ania. 2002. *Shakespeare, Race, and Colonialism.* New York: Oxford University Press.

Maravall, José Antonio. 1979. *Poder, honor y élites en el siglo XVII.* Madrid: Siglo Veintiuno de España.

Mariscal, George. 1998. "The Role of Spain in Contemporary Race Theory." *Arizona Journal of Hispanic Cultural Studies* 2: 7–22.

Márquez Villanueva, Francisco. 1965. "The *Converso* Problem: An Assessment. " In *Collected Studies in Honour of Américo Castro's 80th Year*, edited by M. Hornik, 317–333. Oxford: Oxford University Press.

Martínez, María Elena. 2008. *Genealogical Fictions: Limpieza de sangre, Religion, and Gender in Colonial Mexico.* Palo Alto, CA: Stanford University Press.

Méchoulan, Henri. 1981. *El honor de Dios: Indios, judíos y moriscos en el Siglo de Oro.* Translated by Enrique Sordo. Barcelona: Argos Vergara.

Mignolo, Walter. 2007. "What Does the Black Legend Have to do with Race?" In *Re-Reading the Black Legend*, edited by Margaret Greer, Walter Mignolo, and Maureen Quilligan, 312–324. Durham, NC: Duke University Press.

Monteiro, Rodrigo Bentes, Daniela Buono Calainho, Bruno Feitler, and Jorge Flores, eds. 2011. *Raízes do Privilégio. Mobilidade social no mundo ibérico do Antigo Regime.* Rio de Janeiro: Civilização Brasileira.

Netanyahu, Benzoin. 1995. *The Origins of the Inquisition in Fifteenth-Century Spain.* New York: Random House.

Nirenburg, David. 1996. *Communities of Violence: Persecution of Minorities in the Middle Ages.* Princeton, NJ: Princeton University Press.

———. 2007. "Race and the Middle Ages: The Case of Spain and its Jews." In *Re-Reading the Black Legend*, edited by Margaret Greer, Walter Mignolo, and Maureen Quilligan, 71–87. Durham, NC: Duke University Press.

———. 2009. "Was There Race before Modernity?: The Example of Jewish Blood in Late Medieval Spain." In *The Origins of Racism in the West*, edited by Miriam Eliav-Feldon, Benjamin Isaac, and Joseph Ziegler, 232–264. Cambridge: Cambridge University Press.

Olival, Fernanda. 2004. "Rigor e interesses: Os estatutos de limpeza de sangue em Portugal." *Cadernos de Estudos Sefarditas* 4: 151–82.

Ponsen, Alexander and Antonio Feros. 2017. "The Early Modern Iberian Empires: Emulation, Alliance, Competition." In *The Routledge Companion to Iberian Studies*, edited by Javier Muñoz-Basols, Laura Lonsdale, and Manuel Delgado, 139–151. London and New York: Routledge.

Rawlings, Helen. 2017. "The Iberian Inquisitions in the Sixteenth and Seventeenth Centuries: Between Coercion and Accommodation." In *The Routledge Companion to Iberian Studies*, edited by Javier Muñoz-Basols, Laura Lonsdale, and Manuel Delgado, 152–161. London and New York: Routledge.

Root, Deborah. 1988. "Speaking Christian: Difference in Sixteenth-Century Spain." *Representations* 23 (Summer 1988): 118–134.

Roth, Cecil. 1940. "*Marranos* and Racial Anti-Semitism: A Study in Parallels." *Jewish Social Studies* 2: 239–48.

Sicroff, Albert. 1985. *Los estatutos de limpieza de sangre: controversias entre los siglos XV y XVII.* Madrid: Taurus.

Soria Mesa, Enrique. 2013. "Los estatutos municipales de limpieza de sangre en la Castilla moderna. Una revision crítica." *Mediterránea* Ricerche Storiche 27: 9–36.

Xavier, Angela Barreto. 2003. *A invenção de Goa: poder imperial e conversões culturais nos séculos XVI e XVII.* Italy: European University Institute.

———. 2012. "Purity of Blood and Caste: Identity Narratives among Early Modern Goan Elites." In *Race and Blood in the Iberian World*, edited by Max Hering Torres, María Elena Martínez, and David Nirenberg, 125–150. Zurich: Lit Verlag.

15

THE EXPULSION OF THE MORISCOS

Seven monumental paintings from the kingdom of Valencia

E. Michael Gerli

The making of Spanish identity during the early modern period can be told from various perspectives. The most common one is triumphal and nationalistic: it tells a story of empire and of the Spanish Golden Age, *El Siglo de Oro*. It deals with territorial expansion, transoceanic adventure, social and political hegemony on a universal scale, and the flourishing of a literary and artistic culture of equal universal reach and transcendence. Yet below the surface of all this there is another tarnished tale, one with tragic human consequences that traces a story of powerful international and domestic conflict, of ethnic warfare and civil strife, as it sounds a somber counterpoint to the epic tenor of the golden plot. It is the saga of those Spaniards who were expelled from their nation in 1492, the Jews, and then much later the Moriscos (Muslims converted to Catholicism and their descendants) in 1609–1614, whose account is less well-known (see Boase 1990; Cardaillac 1977; Carr 2009; Chejne 1983; Domínguez Ortiz and Vicent 1978; Harvey 2005).

With the conquest of Granada in 1492, the Muslims of that kingdom were extended the status of *mudéjares* (Islamic subjects living under Christian rule) who, as had been the practice for centuries, were free to practice their religion and in most ways continue to govern themselves under their own laws. By 1502, however, Christian-Muslim relations in the kingdom had deteriorated significantly and conversion was imposed upon the Muslims of Granada as well as the rest of the Muslims of Castile. The same thing occurred in Valencia, Catalonia, and Aragon between 1521 and 1526, where Muslims were compelled to choose between baptism and exile. For the majority, baptism was the only real alternative. After 1526 all Spanish Muslims had become New Christians and were known collectively as *Moriscos*. Because they were nominally converts to Catholicism, they were, of course, subject to the Holy Office of the Inquisition. At the same time, although they were now ostensibly Christian, their commitment to Islam and to Islamic culture remained strong. Even those who had sincerely converted to Christianity persisted in following Muslim cultural practices, especially dietary habits and the use of Arabic in conducting daily affairs. Still others did not convert at all and continued to follow the Quran and practice Islamic rites clandestinely. The nature of conversion was thus for the most part problematic, a varied and difficult social, political, and religious puzzle, especially since numerous Muslims followed the practice of *taqiyya*, or cautious dissimulation, which in the face of repression made religious duplicity canonically acceptable (based on Quran 3:28). The situation led to persecution and wrenching social and political conflict.

To make matters worse, although officially Muslims were to have abandoned Islam upon voluntary or forced conversion, local authorities often deliberately overlooked the continued practice of Islam by many. In some cases, it was possible to pay a tax, or *servicio*, which guaranteed exemption from inquisitorial scrutiny. And, in unspoken complicity with the nobility of Aragon whose lands the Moriscos tended, the Church frequently ignored the continued practice of Islam so as to vouchsafe economic prosperity and the well-being of agriculture in the region. The Moriscos and their role in Spanish life would become the single most vexing and polemical domestic civic issue of the sixteenth century and, after much debate about their place in society and their allegiance to the Crown, especially during the last quarter of the century, the Moriscos were finally expelled from Spain between 1609 and 1614. A summary of the major events and key arguments leading up to their expulsion follows.

Tensions between Christians and Muslims grew after the surrender of the kingdom of Granada in 1492, culminating at the end of the century in several Muslim insurrections both in the city and the surrounding mountain communities. On January 2, 1500, reacting to Christian repressions in Granada against their coreligionists, the Muslims of the nearby villages in the Alpujarras Mountains rebelled. Their uprising was brutally suppressed and resulted in the enslavement of many of the insurgents. Although the revolt was limited to Granada and was soon contained, it was not forgotten. Subsequent widespread resistance and uprisings later in the sixteenth century provided the monarchy with a justification to embark upon the systematic extirpation of the presence of Islam in Spain. Although by the time of their expulsion in 1609 the descendants of Muslims had become citizens of Spain and, although some were sincere converts to Christianity, others still continued to practice Islam clandestinely. At the same time, regardless of their beliefs, both Christian converts from Islam and Muslims became victims of policies repeatedly based on baffling theological arguments and xenophobic racial claims that sought to exclude them from society.

After the forced conversions of 1521 to 1526, there was an interval in which the Moriscos were allowed to retain their language, customs, and traditional clothing. By the 1520s, however, it was clear that Islam and these signs of cultural identity were largely one of a piece, and that to suppress the religion it would be necessary to stamp out the cultural practices and the language that went with it. By 1567 every aspect of the Moriscos' existence would be proscribed, labeled as pagan and alien by both Church and State. To make matters worse, in the last years of the sixteenth century Spain was at war with England, France, the Dutch, and the Ottoman Empire. Amidst this climate of uncertainty, the conflict with the Turks in the Mediterranean and the proximity of Islam in North Africa heightened awareness of the Moriscos, who were seen as a fifth column threatening the internal stability of the nation. Numerous measures were proposed to confront the perceived menace of the Moriscos since it was generally assumed that they were both political and religious enemies of the state, potential collaborators who were living in the very midst of Spanish society. To deal with this state of affairs, and to stamp out all signs of religious and cultural difference throughout the realm, by 1567 Philip II forbade the use of all Muslim customs and religious practices, in addition to the use of the Arabic language. As a result, dietary preferences became suspect vis-à-vis religious orthodoxy: those who refused wine, pork, or shellfish ran the risk of being indicted by the Inquisition. In the eyes of both the Inquisition and the popular imagination, the consumption of certain foods, even listening or dancing to Arabic music, were un-Christian practices for which one could be obliged to perform public penance. In the 30 years before their expulsion from Spain, it is estimated that some 12,000 Moriscos were accused of apostasy by the Inquisition. Even those Moriscos who were sincere Christians (and there were many) were deemed second-class citizens and were often exposed to censure from Christians and clandestine Muslims alike.

Exasperated by the Monarchy's and the Inquisition's attempts to suppress their faith and way of life, the Moriscos launched the Second Rebellion of the Alpujarras (1568–1570). The result was a brutal war of attrition between the Moriscos and Philip II's professional army, led by the king's merciless half-brother, Don Juan de Austria, brought in specifically to crush the rebellion. In the end, the uprising was cruelly suppressed by Don Juan, whose worst atrocity was the destruction of the town of Galera on February 10, 1570, in the mountains east of Granada. After slaughtering 2,500 people, including 400 women and children, Galera was razed and sown with salt (Boase 1990). Immediately after the defeat of the revolt, the authorities dispersed some 80,000 Moriscos from Granada to other parts of Castile, just as they brought Christians from the north to settle on the Moriscos' lands, leaving the only large concentration of Muslims in the Peninsula in the kingdom of Valencia and the lower Aragon.

Philip II acceded to the throne of Portugal in 1580, putting within his grasp the ancient ambition of achieving complete Christian hegemony in Iberia. During the winter of 1581–1582 the Royal Council met in Lisbon and proposed the expulsion of the Moriscos as the best means for dealing definitively with their seditious presence. Although the economic and political problems caused by expulsion were fully understood by the Council, and the canonical impediment to sending baptized Christians to non-Christian lands noted, the argument favoring the unity and the internal peace of Spain won the day. There would be no more insurrections like the ones of the Alpujarras. The mass expulsion of the Moriscos had thus been decided upon nearly three decades before the monarchy actually dared carry it out. During the 1580s, several plans were presented to the Crown for the Moriscos' exodus that would end in their conclusive annihilation. One was to put them on ships that would be sunk on the open sea; another called for the castration of all Morisco males and the sterilization of the women, who would then be transported across the Atlantic to the Isla de los Bacalaos (Newfoundland), and be left there destined for extinction. The methods to be used to purge Spain of the Moriscos became matters of regular discussion in court and clerical circles; only the proposed procedures varied depending on the religious or political nature of the conversation. The debate concerning their fate eventually became intensely polemical, moved largely by zealots like Fray Jaime de Bleda, an inquisitor from Valencia; the *arbitrista* (government lobbyist) Martín González de Cellorigo; the historian Fray Marcos de Guadalajara; and, above all, the theologian Pedro Aznar de Cardona, for whom the expulsion marked the long-awaited closure of the teleological parenthesis in Spanish history set in place by the Muslim conquest of the Peninsula in 711 (Aznar Cardona 1612, II, 5,16–19).

Despite rampant xenophobia, a range of significant opposition also was voiced right up to the final expulsion of the Moriscos. The opponents of expulsion typically favored evangelization, tolerance, and mixed marriages between Old Christians and Moriscos, all of which would lead to assimilation. The single most eloquent voice in favor of moderation was that of the Royal Chronicler Pedro de Valencia, whose reputation for learning and moral probity were amply recognized. In 1608, Valencia wrote the *Tratado acerca de los Moriscos de España*, directed at Luis de Aliaga, Philip II's confessor and pawn of the influential Duke of Lerma. Aliaga is believed to have persuaded Philip III (1598–1621) to revive and implement the 1581 Lisbon recommendation for the expulsion. The *Tratado* remains the most important and succinct contribution to the dispute, the single most notable defense of the Moriscos in more than a century of heated polemic. The argument against the eradication of the Moriscos that Valencia develops is both clear and simple: the real question, he argues, is not the destiny of a menacing minority, but whether Spain, if it were to expel the Moriscos, could legitimately continue to be seen as the leader of Christendom and claim to be a Christian nation. Not surprisingly, the major opponents to expulsion were, like Valencia, largely *conversos*, or "New"

Christians of Jewish ancestry whose advocacy of the assimilation of the Moriscos, besides its profound ethical and religious foundations, flew in the face of Old Christian prejudices and blood purity statutes.

Strenuous opposition to the expulsion aside, whether the justifications for it were secular or religious, expulsion ultimately triumphed. The higher councils of the realm agreed to rid the land of the Moriscos' threatening presence. The issue thus became not whether they should be ejected but the method that was to be used to rid Spain of them. After settling on expulsion as the only viable solution, regardless of the harmful economic and social effects repeatedly predicted by the nobles of Aragon, caution prevailed and no final action was taken until 1609–10, when Philip III would finally issue the edict of expulsion first recommended at Lisbon in 1581. (For the text of the edict, see García Arenal 1975, 252). The action was approved unanimously by Phillip III's Council of State on January 30, 1608, at the urging of the Duke of Lerma, the king's favorite, whose father had been the Marquis of Denia in the Kingdom of Valencia, and who had recently undergone a change of heart when it was agreed that the lords of Valencia would receive the lands of the Moriscos in compensation for the deportation of their vassals. The Duke, however, failed in his attempt to gain inquisitorial and papal support for the edict. The Valencian parliament also resisted the expulsion, certain that it would destroy the economy of the kingdom and divide the social fabric of the realm. The warnings were to no avail: Philip signed the Edict of Expulsion on April 4, 1609. From the official perspective, the expulsion was an act against the enemy infidel despite the fact that some sincere Christians of Muslim descent would be swept up, contrary to earlier assurances that those who willingly accepted baptism would be permitted to remain.

To avoid insurrection, ships from the royal fleet were secretly prepared, just as they would later be joined by merchant vessels from Genoa, Sicily, and England surreptitiously brought in for the operation. The order of expulsion was promulgated across the Kingdom of Valencia on September 11, 1609. On October 2, the first 4,000 Moriscos sailed to Oran from Denia, arriving three days later. Another 14,500 were loaded onto vessels at Valencia in view of the Christians of the city, who went to the water's edge to buy precious laces, silks, and broadcloth for paltry sums from the departing Moriscos, who were obliged to leave their fineries behind.

Although the King's decree called for the immediate expulsion of all the Moriscos from Spain, the logistics of implementing the measure proved challenging and efforts continued on until 1614. The Moriscos of Aragon, Castile, Andalusia, and Extremadura did not begin to receive their orders for expulsion until 1610. While the majority of the Moriscos would go on to settle in Morocco or Tunis, their North African coreligionists were less than welcoming when they arrived: they took them to be aliens, Spanish in most every way: in language, dress, and customs. After decades of efforts to suppress their language and culture, the Moriscos were deemed foreign by North Africans. Most of the Moriscos that went to Tunisia, for example, bore Spanish surnames and spoke only Castilian or Valencian, identifying and associating more closely with exiled Sephardic Jews – who also preferred to remain apart from native North African Jews. In addition to North Africa, many Moriscos traveled to France but, after the assassination of Henry of Navarre in May 1610, they were compelled to move on to Italy and Sicily, many driven as far as Constantinople. In the midst of the upheaval, some actually relished the opportunity to flee the repression, even arranging for their own safe passage out of Spain. For the latter, flight seemed like an act of liberation that offered a chance to live freely as Muslims, rather than repressed citizens of the Spanish Crown.

Yet still, other Moriscos violently resisted expulsion, defying the large contingents of the King's army sent to force them from their homes and drive them to the sea for their journey into exile. While there is some disagreement about the number of Moriscos who died in the armed struggles, as well as the actual number of those who perished on the journey into banishment, a treatise by Pedro Aznar Cardona (1612) notes that between October 1609 and July 1611 more than 50,000 Moriscos died in the resistance, and some 60,000 others perished on land and sea during their expatriation, or finally at the hands of their fellow Muslims who beat, robbed, and murdered them as they disembarked on the beaches of North Africa. If these figures are accurate, nearly 20% of the original Morisco population of Spain died during the first two years of the expulsion. Estimates regarding the size of the Morisco population at the time of the expulsion vary significantly. Henri Lapeyre (1959) estimated from census reports and embarkation lists that, of a population of approximately 300,000, approximately 275,000 Moriscos were expelled between the years 1609–1614. This is an approximation inconsistent with many of the contemporary accounts, some of which put the figure upwards of 600,000. By all accounts, it is not unreasonable to assume that by 1620 the Kingdom of Valencia had lost almost a third of its population and that half of its villages had been deserted. One thing is sure, the events of 1609–1614 mark a chilling precedent in systematic, government-sponsored ethnic cleansing in European history.

Graphic evidence of the last chapter of this tarnished tale of the Spanish Golden Age lives on in striking visual images that can still be seen in a series of seven monumental paintings commissioned by Philip III in 1612, which few scholars have heard about and even fewer have actually examined closely for the events which they depict. Through the agency of the King's cousin, the Marquis of Caracena, Viceroy and Capitan General of the Kingdom of Valencia, himself a protagonist in the events of the expulsion, the canvases were ordered and completed between 1612 and 1613. They were painted by renowned local artists: Pere Oromig, Francisco Peralata, Vicent Mestre, and Jerónimo de Espinosa. These paintings have rarely been exhibited publicly, the last time in 1996. Although today six of them hang prominently in one of the centers of financial power in Spain – in Valencia in the conference room of the President of Bancaja, a large Spanish savings bank – access to them remains extremely limited and by special permission only. A seventh more inaccessible painting remains in private hands.

The history of the paintings of the Expulsion of the Moriscos from Valencia is known, chronicled in a catalogue edited by Jesús Villalmanzano Cameno (1997). The paintings were commissioned by Philip III and hung first in the Royal Palace at Madrid, moving then to the Royal Palace of Valencia where they remained until the latter's demolition in 1813; they subsequently passed through several hands until 1917, when they became the property of Elías Tormo Bisbal, and in 1982 they were purchased by the Caja de Ahorros de Valencia (subsequently Bancaja), where they now form part of Bancaja's permanent collection. We know, too, that the paintings were composed by the four artists shortly after the events that they portray, and that they were created using eyewitness accounts and detailed notarial documents, including ship manifestos, from the Crown archives that provided logistical and legal minutiae about the procedures and personages involved in the deportation of the Moriscos. Yet while all this is so, except for a perceptive study by Dopico Black (2003), virtually no interpretive work or close visual readings of the canvases has been undertaken. From the existing studies, we know the paintings largely as mute objects, silent panoramas that have come down to us from the past, rather than as striking graphic testimonials full of human drama that constitute visual witnesses to a critical event in the chronicles of the early modern Mediterranean: "to one of the boldest and most barbarous [acts] recorded in human annals," as Cardinal Richelieu, with just a soupçon of Schadenfreude, would refer to the expulsion (1908, I:124). The history of the gripping events that the paintings portray, and the powerful way in which they portray them, emerge from a close inspection of what they visually convey. In the fullness of their detail, the canvases are replete with multifaceted images of contradiction and heartbreak, populated by complex visual metaphors that display the artists' anxieties regarding the community to which they belonged and the scenes of civil strife they were commissioned to commemorate.

Two paintings in particular record the Moriscos' fierce resistance to the expulsion, one of the Muela of Cortes, and the other of the Sierra of Laguar. In the one depicting the Spanish infantry's assault on the Muela the artist portrays the multitude of the well-ordered, well-armed, well-protected troops of the Crown doing fierce battle with the tenacious Moriscos, who resist and defend the heights of their mountain redoubt only with farm implements, literally turning their plowshares into swords (see Figure 15.1). In its detail, strikingly reminiscent of the events of the ferocious resistance and the suicides of the Jews at the Roman siege of Masada as narrated by Flavius Josephus (1737, Chps. 8–9), the canvas also bears more than a casual resemblance to Botticelli's rendering of Hell in Dante's *Commedia*, a winding, but inverted, heap of torture, struggle, and suffering (see Figures 15.2, 15.3).

On October 25, 1609, resistance broke out amongst the Moriscos across the Valley of Laguar. By the end of the month, upwards of 20,000 Moriscos had gathered there on the Llano de Gargas on the heights of the surrounding mountains, taking final refuge in the higher elevations above the valley. After fierce fighting in the crags on the flanks of the surrounding mountains, what was left of them desperately sought sanctuary in the now vanished Castillo de Pop on the summit of Mont Cavall Verd, above Murla. There, like the Moriscos of Cortes, they battled with arms made mostly from farm implements against the assault of the King's armored *tercios* (infantry arrangements made up of pikemen, swordsmen, and arquebusiers in mutually supportive formations), who battered them with methodical discipline and ferocity. In the painting that records the assault of the Muela of Cortes, we see desperate Morisco women hurling themselves off cliffs with small children in arms to avoid a certain fate at the

Figure 15.1   Rebelión de los moriscos en la Muela de Cortes. Vicent Mestre, 1613. Valencia, Fundación Bancaja, Permanent Collection.

Figure 15.2 Sandro Botticelli, *The Abyss of Hell*, c. 1485. Biblioteca Apostolica, Vatican. Wikimedia Commons.

Figure 15.3 Detail, Sandro Botticelli, *The Abyss of Hell*, c. 1485. Biblioteca Apostolica, Vatican. Wikimedia Commons.

hands of the King's army. As one does so, however, she unexpectedly seems to take flight, limbs stretched, her distinctive robes gracefully opening almost like the wings of the angels seen decorating the firmament of the pious paintings of the high renaissance (see Figure 15.4).

The heights of the Sierra are defended by Moriscos with slings, mattocks, knives, pick-axes, and cudgels. The insurgents respond to the volleys of the King's cannon by hurling boulders and mill stones down the mountainside in the hope of crushing some of the on-rushing troops. Finally, the painting records the firing-squad execution of the "King" of the rebellious Moriscos. He was a miller from Confrides named Gerónimo Mellini, who also went under the name of Ahmed Sequien Al-Mellini. An outspoken critic of the expulsion and defender of the Moriscos' rights, the rebels had elected him as their sovereign. The upper left quadrant of the painting depicts the place and exact moment of Al-Mellini's summary execution, marked by a fiery volley from a disciplined squadron of infantrymen (see Figure 15.5).

In their totality, the paintings trace an arch that ranges from the celebration of the promise of deliverance from more than a century of captivity to dark irony and murder. They record the history of the vain hope the Moriscos were initially led to have of a new home in North Africa, a hope that suddenly turns to violence against those who chose not to leave, and then precipitously sinks into death and despair on the shores of Oran and Tunis, where both the willing and unwilling who were expelled from their homeland were received as strangers by their coreligionists, beaten, robbed, and left to die on the shores of the false promised land (see Figure 15.6).

In the canvas devoted to the expulsion at Denia, a dozen moriscas in traditional garb dance to the sound of a quartet of Morisco musicians. They are joined by a group of six richly dressed Christian women accompanied by their elegantly attired consorts (see Figure 15.7). To the right of them, we see four pairs of men engaged in contests of *lucha a la morisca* (Greco-Roman wrestling, similar to Turkish *Yağlı güreş*) which recall the traditional games organized by Aben Humeya, leader of the Second Rebellion of the Alpujarras, in Pucherna

Figure 15.4 Detail, *Rebelión de los moriscos en la Sierra de Laguar.* Jerónimo Espinosa, 1612–13. Valencia, Fundación Bancaja, Permanent Collection.

Figure 15.5   Detail, *Rebelión de los moriscos en la Sierra de Laguar*. Jerónimo Espinosa, 1612–13. Valencia, Fundación Bancaja, Permanent Collection.

Figure 15.6   Detail, *Desembarco de los moriscos en el Puerto de Orán*. Vicent Mestre, 1613. Valencia, Fundación Bancaja, Permanent Collection.

during September 1569. Aben Humeya had arranged for them as a measure of Morisco cultural assertion, and as a gesture of open defiance against the Crown's prohibition of Morisco cultural practices. Ginés Pérez de Hita describes the games in Chapter 14 of the second part of his *Guerras Civiles de Granada*.

In his narrative of events of the expulsion at Alicante, Jaime Bleda, a scrupulous chronicler and zealous defender of the expulsion, depicts the general air of exuberance and delight conveyed by many of the Moriscos when faced with the prospect of cultural freedom and the right to express themselves openly once safe in North Africa:

> A Alicante fueron a embarcarse los Moriscos . . . llegaban con tanta alegría y alboroço como si fueran a las más alegres fiestas y bodas que huvo entre ellos. Yvan cantando y tañendo con flautas, tamborines y dulçaynas y otros instrumentos que solían tener,

Figure 15.7 Detail, *Embarque de los moriscos en el Puerto de Denia.* Vicent Mestre, 1612–13. Valencia, Fundación Bancaja, Permanent Collection.

relinchando, y diziendo: viva el Turco que nos ha de recibir en su tierra, y nos ha de dexar vivir libremente en nuestra ley. Y viva Mahoma, que nos ha dexado ver estos tiempos tan felices, en los cuales vamos a vivir a tierra, de donde vinieron nuestros passados. . . . Muchos que por el camino se casaron contra las leyes de la Iglesia, llegados a Alicante celebraron las bodas con mucho regozijo de bayles y danças y música de laudes, y dulçaynas, las moriscas yvan vestidas lo mejor que podían. . . . Dezían que yvan con gusto adonde el Rey los echava; mas que presto bolverían, y nos echarían a nosotros.

(Bleda 2001, 1002–03)

This doubtless explains the gallows and ladder prominently displayed near the gate of the city just below the heavily armed turret, close to the ships set to carry the banished to North Africa. The gibbet stands as somber warning to Moriscos of the order forbidding them to display signs of the Muslim religion or their ancestral cultural practices (see Figure 15.8). Any celebratory atmosphere is foreclosed by the specter of summary execution. The King's men were given broad discretion to put to death Moriscos who refused to obey orders on their way into exile. In the bottom right of the scene, we see Don Baltazar Mercader, cross of the Order of Santiago boldly displayed on his chest who, according to the cartouche on the canvas, presided over the deportation of 45,800 Moriscos from Alicante.

Since their dances, marriage rites, games, music, and language had been banned, the Moriscos at Denia, like those described by Bleda on their way to Alicante, doubtless also sought to flaunt their culture in the face of the very authorities that had forbidden them to do so and had earlier sought systematically to extirpate them. The *lucha morisca*, dance, the playing

Figure 15.8   Embarque de los moriscos en el Puerto de Alicante. Pere Oromig and Francisco Peralta, 1612–13. Valencia, Private Collection.

of music, and the singing of songs are, thus, more than untroubled signs of joy at the prospect of newly found freedom. They are certain acts of civil disobedience, gestures of defiance and cultural affirmation from the Moriscos who, thinking they were at the threshold of liberty, under the very eyes of the Spanish authorities, abruptly broke out in public performances of the cultural identity that Spain had denied them.

The canvas recording the expulsion at Valencia broadly depicts the loading of the Moriscos onto the ships, just as on the distant horizon it records a plethora of the sails of the vessels that had already departed carrying the exiled to North Africa. The many small ships on the horizon emphasize graphically the size and scope of the exodus, while suggesting that the pained scenes of departure in the foreground of the painting are nothing but a recurrence of what had already taken place just minutes or hours before (see Figure 15.9). There we see the patron of the operation, the Marquis of Caracena, wearing the habit of the Order of Santiago, leading his entourage toward the seaside astride a prancing stallion. He is preceded by a court functionary bearing a document inscribed with the number 15615, corresponding to the number of Moriscos who, according to the cartouche in the upper left, "voluntarily" came to Valencia and paid for their passage into exile. As the Marquis arrives near the water's edge, he is received on horseback by General Agustín Mejía, the commanding officer of the operation who leads a contingent of cavalry with shields at the ready and helmeted soldiers with their arquebuses set to protect the official carriage behind them. The cartouche in the upper right of the painting records 3,490 Moriscos who came to Valencia from the Sierra de Cortes to be deported, along with an additional 1,903 rebellious Moriscos who were forcibly brought there from other parts of the kingdom by Don García Bravo (see Figure 15.10). But beyond the grand procession of officials, just ahead at the water's edge, we see a family of well-to-do Moriscos ready to be deported. They are dressed in all their finery, swathed in gold chains – the sum of all their wealth – as they are urged to move forward to the shore by two less prosperous Morisco women to their left ("Vestíanse las mugeres lo mejor que tenían para embarcarse," notes Bleda [2001, 1001]). Just at this moment the family's sumptuously dressed daughter is being turned over to a man to be lifted into a waiting boat. Behind them, to their right, there is another woman in the habit of the Poor Clares who prays fervently with clenched hands, conceivably a grieving compatriot pained by the sight of the banishment of her fellow citizens. The cruel, dehumanizing events of the expulsion, affecting both rich and poor, produced separations, deaths, and recurring assaults to human dignity that we know were met with great compassion by a minority of pious Christians and intellectuals (see Figure 15.11).

Figure 15.9   Embarque de los moriscos del Grau de Valencia. Pere Oromig, 1612–13. Valencia, Fundación Bancaja, Permanent Collection.

Figure 15.10   Detail, *Embarque de los moriscos del Grau de Valencia*. Pere Oromig, 1612–13. Valencia, Fundación Bancaja, Permanent Collection.

Figure 15.11   Detail, *Embarque de los moriscos del Grau de Valencia*. Pere Oromig, 1612–13. Valencia, Fundación Bancaja, Permanent Collection.

Just beyond this scene, to the upper left, we see an old man carried across the water by two stevedores (see Figure 15.12). The scene captures the moment narrated by Jaime Bleda in his *Corónica*, where he writes that:

> En las taraçanas del Grao estava un Viejo boqueando, y una palabra que habló a los otros quando se despedían dél para embarcarse fue dezirles que lo llevassen a embarcar, aunque se muriese luego, y cumpliose su desseo: porque apenas llegó a la saetía cuando murió, invocando a Mahoma, y le echaron en la mar.
>
> (Bleda 2001, 1002)

Figure 15.12 Detail, *Embarque de los moriscos del Grau de Valencia*. Pere Oromig, 1612–13. Valencia, Fundación Bancaja, Permanent Collection.

Immediately behind the old man three Christians seem to barter with a Morisco, while a woman who appears to be lamenting raises her eyes heavenward and places her hand on her young son's head, possibly at the moment of their separation, when the boy was being turned over to the Christian couple behind him.

The human complexity and heart-wrenching nature of the expulsion is displayed throughout the paintings, compounded by striking visual metaphors and contradictions that permeate them. There is an urgent need to explore these further to comprehend more fully the paintings' larger meaning, which is likely not entirely accessible or understood by today's viewers. To appreciate the conflict portrayed between the King's policy and its implementation in these canvases requires "competent viewers," or observers who can view deeply, as it were, and connect the events in the background as the necessary precursors of what is portrayed in the foreground. Yet, even before the actual sequence of events dawns upon us, we are implicated from the very outset in the enormity of the experience and cannot assume a detached position. The responsive viewer is compelled to look deeper into the many scenes that are being simultaneously portrayed. The result is a forced confrontation between two planes: the immediate official proceedings and their brutal background. The temporal simultaneity of the actions portrayed defies the constraints of the painting's outward illusionistic world. On the surface the paintings present themselves as chorographs (detailed pictorial representations of particular areas), when they are really full chronicles of events, wherein chorography is a genre devoted to the rendering of places, and chronicle the means for narrating about events in places and time. Attentive to the conventions of chorography, to panoramically depicting Denia, Valencia, Vinarós, Alicante, and the surrounding countryside in the Sierra de Cortes and the Valley of Laguar, and rubricated according to the place they are meant to evoke, this is, in fact, the way viewers are first meant to approach these paintings.

The canvases are far more than panoramic, static representations of the events of the expulsion, however. They are charged with poignant narrative and tell multiple stories that often foreclose any ideologically consistent message in them. There is clearly a foreground, meant to capture our immediate attention, and a background, that is much more difficult to discern both visually and semantically. Although encompassed by a unitary frame, the foreground and background seem often to oppose each other, as they narrate different versions of the events. We must look closely at the even more difficult to descry backdrop to grasp the complete meaning of the images, which forces us to search the entire setting for clues to the action unfolding in the foreground. The foreground/background relation, as a result of the miniscule nature of the background, seems willfully to minimize detailed scrutiny, at least for the casual observer.

The first things the casual viewer notices are the size of the paintings, their frames (on average 110 × 175 cm), and the images' panoramic sweep. Without the containing frame, each painting is fragmented, so detailed and diffuse that it seems chaotic. The frame implies a beholder and reinforces the notion of the integrity of the gaze, since the paintings have two dramatic and psychological focal points – the foreground and the background – each of which diffuses what the whole image actually displays. The complete focus of the painting is displaced, often diverted by the cartouches that provide only the most superficial information. Until foreground and background are joined by the observer the full narrative of the events remains inaccessible. In fact, the painting's full account comes from outside of it, from contemporary events, and implies the necessity of an informed viewer for more complete understanding. They are essentially ironical since they require careful contemplation to call the viewer's attention to the contradiction between what is ostensibly being narrated in the foreground and what is happening in the background. There is a clear tension between order and disorder in the portrayal of the events. At first, cued by the foreground images and the narrative medallions, viewers think they understand what is happening; but on second inspection they see that the overall scene is fraught with contradiction. Not just sight then but discernment is crucial to the paintings' full appreciation. The character of the conflict, its repressive and broad civil nature, is only revealed when we turn to the margins or the depths and see depictions such as Morisco women hurling themselves from cliffs, preferring suicide to prolonged extinction in an alien land. These figures have no apparent reason for existing other than to address a more complete version of the historical events; to be seen and portray the conflict and resistance of the community to the Crown's policies. Our complacency as spectators of panoramic canvases is disrupted by the tiny arresting images we can barely make out. On careful inspection of the multitude of minuscule figures, we discover what actually transpires there and begin to experience a discomfort as our scrutiny progresses. Suddenly, the lofty acts expected of the King's army are cast against a backdrop of self-destruction, cruelty, repression, armed advantage, steely discipline, technological superiority, and the criminal acts of war. Despite their obligation to portray the official version of the expulsion as per their commission, the artists repeatedly display sensitivity, empathy, and even partisanship in their rendering of the Moriscos' struggle against their exile and the suppression of their freedoms. They were, after all, also citizens of Spain, but especially of the Kingdom of Valencia, compatriots of the painters who like many in the kingdom expressed opposition to the Moriscos' surrender of their identities and citizenship. In this way, the scrutiny of the images discloses a difference between what is revealed in a mere glance – a panorama of multitude of actions – and looking at the minute details, features that belie surface appearances and force larger recognition and understanding. Amidst a plethora of specificity, the pictures challenge us to look more closely and understand the brutal nature of the conflict. The primary subject of the expulsion – the forced removal of the Moriscos by the King's military and administrative apparatus – is set into relief, then, by a series of contrasting small images, which remain pictorially secondary but denotatively primary because of the irony and clear contradiction they pose to the main action. In this way, though minor in size, and often skewed away from the centers and vanishing points of the paintings, the miniature figures remain central to the full understanding of the painted scenes.

The paintings were intended to portray the military victory and administrative efficiency of Imperial Spain. With the benefit of historical hindsight, however, it is clear that the canvases concede the moral victory to the Moriscos. In their contradictions, these compositions are frankly transgressive as the events portrayed in the backgrounds usurp the space usually reserved in chorography for the affirmation of the passage of time and daily life. We see in them the dramatization of the problem of what was claimed to be a just war against a perceived domestic enemy, and the awkward way war and aggression against one's own people play into the unity of the nation and its aspirations of empire. Two distinct facets of Spain battle against each other in them – a multicultural, multiconfessional Spain waging its own righteous resistance in defense of the last bastions of its existence next to the onslaught of an imperial Spain that fights a less easily justifiable combat against its own citizens, while failing to recall the need to combine strength and moral probity with clemency and tolerance in dealing with all people. In this way, the images pose the question whether any state, however upright its motivations or able its generals, can endure if its actions are not honorable and fair, and serve as an admonition to more observant Spaniards of this reality. When closely examined, it is evident that in the paintings of the expulsion the artists joined their vision of events to a prominent minority of resisters, including Pedro de Valencia, who from the latter half of the sixteenth century had condemned the repressive policies of the state not just beyond its immediate borders – that is, in Flanders and America – as tragic errors leading not to the preservation of empire but to its inevitable ruin. Seen in the context of this larger debate the canvases acquire shadings that are not immediately visible today in the offices of a savings bank: the Duke of Lerma, as a capable general who thought it far better to preserve by ethnic war for God and king a nation that was impoverished and even ruined, than, without the war save it, in his mind, for the benefit of Muslims and heretics. The ironic juxtaposition of the images no doubt provided much bitter reflection for Philip III's loyal dissidents. Cervantes, for one, would write about the conflict in painfully anguished and ambivalent terms, appreciating how both sides were devastatingly entangled in a clash of religious and political motives (Márquez Villanueva 2010). The strife between Moriscos and the King's regiments provides a classic, emblematic narrative which serves as a vehicle for meditation about the trajectory, legitimacy, power, burden, and mistakes of empire. If the painters' purpose had been solely to capture visually and chronicle the glory of the expulsion, a testament to a fading Imperial Spain, the detailed narrative of the Moriscos' example of resistance to aggression would not have been appropriate to include in the depictions. These are no simple exaltations of the righteous actions of the state. Rather they represent a Spain that had finally reached the depths of a troubled domestic religious and cultural conflict, one that had arrived at the final collapse of its ancient social institutions and ways of life. The canvases thus comprise a complex interweaving of multiple themes and preoccupations, many of them contradictory: prudence versus daring, sophistication versus simplicity, human enterprise versus fortune, a people's rights versus the demands of the state. It is to that complexity and tension that the paintings, when closely viewed, owe their compelling power. They capture a double perspective on Spanish history at a single moment in time: one that refuses to paint events in simple terms of black and white, and another that views them as a process laden with unending suffering and contradiction.

Works cited

Aznar Cardona, Pedro. 1612. *Expulsión justificada de los moriscos españoles*. Huesca: Pedro Cabarte.

Bleda, Jaime. 2001. *Corónica de los moros de España, dividida en ocho libros*. Facsimile, Edition and Preliminary Study by Bernard Vincent and R. Benítez Sánchez-Blanco. Valencia: Ajuntament, Universitat de València. (Originally published València: Imprenta de Felipe Mey, 1618.)

Boase, Roger. 1990. "The Morisco Expulsion and Diaspora." In *Cultures in Contact in Medieval Spain: Historical and Literary Studies Presented to L.P. Harvey*, edited by David Hook and Barry Taylor, 9–28. London: King's College.

Cardaillac, Louis. 1977. *Morisques et Chrétiens: Un Affrontement Polémique (1492–1640)*. Paris: Klincksieck.

Carr, Matthew. 2009. *Blood and Faith: the Purging of Muslim Spain*. New York: New Press.

Chejne, Anwar G. 1983. *Islam and the West: The Moriscos*. Albany: SUNY Press.

Domínguez Ortiz, Antonio and Bernard Vincent. 1978. *Historia de los moriscos: vida y tragedia de una minoría*. Madrid: Editorial Revista de Occidente.

Dopico Black, Georgina. 2003. "Espectros de la nación: la serie pictórica de la expulsión de los moriscos del reino de Valencia" In *Américo Castro y la revision de la memoria: el Islam en España*, coordinado por Eduardo Subirats, 179–99; 235–46. Madrid: Ediciones Libertarias, Prodhufi.

du Plessis, Armand Jean, Cardinal de Richelieu. 1908–31. *Mémoires*. 10 vols. Paris: Société de l'Histoire de la France.

Flavius Josephus. 1737. "De bello Judaico: The Jewish War." In *The Works of Flavius Josephus*. Translated by William Whiston. Sacred Texts: Judaism. http://sacred-texts.com/jud/josephus/war-7.htm.

García Arenal, Mercedes. 1975. *Los moriscos*. Madrid: Editora Nacional.

Harvey, L. P. 2005. *Muslims in Spain, 1500 to 1614*. Chicago: University of Chicago Press.

Lapeyre, Henri. 1959. *Géographie de l'Espagne morisque*. Paris: S.E.V.P.E.N.

Márquez Villanueva, Francisco. 2010. *Moros, moriscos, y turcos de Cervantes*. Barcelona: Ediciones Bellaterra.

Villalmanzano Cameno, Jesús, ed. 1997. *La expulsión de los moriscos del reino de Valencia*. València: Fundación Bancaja.

Literature and visual culture

16

THE INFLUENCE OF *TIRANT LO BLANCH* ON GOLDEN AGE IBERIAN AUTHORS

Rosa Navarro Durán

Literature has no frontiers but those of language, and these may be eliminated with the assistance of a good translator. In the sixteenth century, as a result of the wide diffusion of literary creations made possible by the revolutionary invention of printing, already firmly established by that time, the great fifteenth-century Catalan writers had a deep influence on the texts of Castilian authors, in what was to become a pivotal moment for the creation of new literary forms. In narrative, the crucial case is that of the greatest chivalric novel written on the Iberian Peninsula, *Tirant lo Blanch* by Valencian writer Joanot Martorell:[1] despite only being in print very briefly during the sixteenth century, its influence on Iberian literature was profound, as an examination of its many great readers will show.[2]

Firstly, I propose a hypothesis to account for its limited editorial success. I then proceed to an analysis of the presence of *Tirante el Blanco* in Alfonso de Valdés's two *Diálogos* and his *Lazarillo de Tormes*. Moving to the second half of the sixteenth century, I show traces of this great chivalric novel in *Don Clarisel de las Flores*, by Jerónimo de Urrea, the Spanish translator of *Orlando furioso*. Finally, I focus on the work of one of its most enthusiastic readers, Miguel de Cervantes, to show echoes of *Tirante* in *La Galatea* and *Persiles*, and I point out just a few of the many elements of it which may be seen in the *Quijote*.

Tirante el Blanco: a fleeting existence in print during the sixteenth century

The scrutiny of Don Quijote's library offers a true image of the hero: the different books he had read inform us about the models which Cervantes's creature, born of the act of reading, strived to imitate. The first book which Maese Nicolás hands over to Pedro Pérez is *Amadís de Gaula*, which the priest is determined to burn as the initiator "de una secta tan mala;" but the barber intercedes on its behalf and it is eventually salvaged for its artistic quality. After succinctly praising *Palmerín de Inglaterra*, the census of chivalric books seems complete, but at that moment a large volume falls at the barber's feet: the *Historia del famoso caballero Tirante el Blanco*.

Upon hearing the title, the priest exclaims: "¡Válame Dios, que aquí esté *Tirante el Blanco*! Dádmele acá, compadre, que hago cuenta que he hallado en él un tesoro de contento y una mina de pasatiempos." Upon remembering some of its characters, he continues: "Dígoos verdad, señor compadre, que por su estilo es este el mejor libro del mundo: aquí comen los caballeros, y duermen y mueren en sus camas, y hacen testamento antes de su muerte" (Cervantes 1998, 83). The priest, Quijote's friend, reveals himself as an enthusiastic reader of the translation of Joanot Martorell's *Tirant lo Blanch*, which Diego de Gumiel, the printer of the work's second edition (Barcelona, 1497), published as an anonymous work, without acknowledging the Catalan original, in Valladolid in 1511.[3]

Pedro Pérez's amazement at finding the book in Don Quijote's library is well justified: by that time, it might have been a rare book, because it was not reprinted after the first 1511 edition; indeed, only two copies of this unique edition now survive (Riquer 1975), both incomplete and lacking various pages (Mérida 2002). The original did not fare much better, as only two editions of *Tirant lo Blanch* were published, the first in Valencia in 1490 by Nicolás Spindeler, and the second in Barcelona by Diego de Gumiel in 1497. Very few copies of any of the three editions have survived. As López Estrada reminds us (1993, 448), Ferdinand Columbus bought a copy for his library "por 260 maravedises, y es uno de los más caros de la lista; el *Floriseo* le costó 128 maravedises."

Menéndez Pelayo notes that "el original catalán del *Tirante* había penetrado en Italia antes que estuviese traducido en ninguna lengua. Ya en 1500 lo leía Isabel de Este, marquesa de Mantua, y un año después comenzaba a traducirlo, a instancia suya, Niccolo da Correggio." He also cites imitations by Boyardo, Ariosto, Bandello, and Shakespeare, in his comedy *Much Ado About Nothing*, before noting the book's rapid fall into oblivion. He posits the possibility that this might be due to "su realismo demasiado prematuro para un libro de caballerías," or perhaps, to "su desenfrenada licencia en las pinturas eróticas;" he also reminds us that "la Inquisición no le puso nunca en sus índices" (Menéndez Pelayo 1943, vol. 1, 402–403).

Anyone who reads the book may suppose that there must have been a very specific reason, beyond the implausible distaste of readers, for such a wonderful work to fall into oblivion, as exceptional works usually manage to endure despite changes in literary taste. Moreover, this fall from grace occurred in the kingdoms of Aragon and Valencia, as well as in Castilla y León, as if both Catalan and Castilian readers shared this "mezquino" literary taste, while Italians continued to appreciate the book (the 1538 translation was twice reprinted, in 1566 and 1611).

Alfonso de Valdés, Charles V's secretary of Latin correspondence, read the book, and we can find traces of his reading in his two *Diálogos* and his *Lazarillo*. Another to read the work was Antonio de Guevara, Charles V's preacher, who placed the knight Tirant among historical heroes in a letter he wrote to Juan de Padilla, "capitán que fue de los comuneros contra el Rey, en la cual le persuade el autor que deje aquella infame empresa," on 8 March 1521 (though we should always be suspicious of any supposed fact from the mouth of the inventive Franciscan):

> Si vos, señor, tomáredes mis consejos, asentara os yo en mis crónicas entre los varones ilustres de España, es a saber: con el famoso Viriato, con el venturoso Cid, con el buen conde de Fernán González, *con el caballero Tirán* y con el Gran Capitán y otros infinitos caballeros dignos de loar y no menos de imitar.
>
> (Guevara 1950, vol. 1, 308)

Why did such a splendid work, whose hero was ranked among history's greatest by the Emperor's preacher, not have a successful life in print?

In attempting to explain why so few editions of *Tirant* and *Tirante* survived, it may be useful to recall an event contemporaneous to Gumiel's edition that has nearly disappeared from the historical record. In 1517, six years after *Tirant* was translated and published in Spanish, the young King Charles arrived in Spain. He was greeted by his grandfather's young widow, Germana de Foix, and they embarked on a passionate romance, the outcome of which was their daughter Isabel of Castile. Regina Pinilla Pérez de Tudela has unearthed documents that prove this daughter's existence. In her will, Queen Germana bequeathed a necklace of 133 pearls "a la serenísima doña Isabel, infanta de Castilla, hija de su Majestad el Emperador, mi señor e hijo;" moreover, the Duke of Calabria wrote to the Empress in this regard: "Vea V. M. el legado de perlas que dexa a la serenísima infanta doña Isabel, su hija" (Fernández Álvarez 2000, 98–99). As the priest of *El Quijote* notes, *Tirante* narrates the romance of "la señora Emperatriz, enamorada de Hipólito, su escudero." When the young man, with discreet clarity and "voz algo ronca y baja" finally seeks the love of the Empress, the old lady at first sensibly argues that her age is not "conforme" with his, adding: "que si tal cosa fuese sabida, ¿qué dirían de mí?: que me he enamorado de mi nieto" (*Tirante* 1974, vol. 3, 243). The book does not punish this unequal and adulterous love with a moralizing denouement; quite the contrary, the novelist rewards it with a happy ending: Tirante, the Emperor, and Carmesina all die, while the Empress, heiress of the Empire, rushes to marry Hipólito. The Spanish translation of *Tirant* was published in 1511. As these events occurred just a few years later, any courtier would easily associate the fictional love story with the real romance between the widowed Queen and the young Emperor. It is reasonable to assume that no printer, even though the book was not explicitly banned, would venture to republish it in the kingdoms of Castilla y León or Valencia, the latter being a territory directly linked to Queen Germana.

However, the literary success of *Tirant/Tirante* was far greater than its few editions and limited circulation may suggest, because the book had two great readers: the novelists Alfonso de Valdés and Miguel de Cervantes. This is clear from the indisputable echoes of *Tirante* in their work, which provide an elegant example of how the influence of *Tirant lo Blanch*, the first European novel, was to spread through the work of other writers. This therefore gives us another measure for the success of a book: the quality of its readers (in their alternative mode of literary creators), and the traces it leaves in those readers and their subsequent works.

Tirante in the works of Alfonso de Valdés

As Alfonso de Valdés's two *Diálogos* are primarily historical rather than fictional texts – albeit with a satirical bent – *Tirante el Blanco* provided him with words and worldviews, rather than specifically narrative resources. For example, in Valdés's *Mercurio y Carón* we find the hapax "artizar," by which he labels the French as tricksters who send peace envoys to the Emperor while getting ready for war: "como siempre suelen los franceses *artizar*, que estonces se muestran más deseosos de la paz cuando más se aperciben para la guerra, por tomar desproveídos a sus contrarios" (Valdés 1999, 158). This unusual word is also found in *Tirante*: as a true strategist, the young captain fortifies the city while, to escape, he simultaneously digs mines under the sites considered most "flacos:" "Como el Caudillo vio hacer a Tirante tan sotiles y *artizadas* obras, estaba el más maravillado hombre del mundo" (*Tirante* 1974, vol. 4, 43); according to Martín de Riquer, "artizar" is a translation of the Catalan word *artizades* ("artificiosas, hechas con ingenio").

The word "contramina" appears in its straightforward sense in *Tirante*: "Tirante dudaba que no minasen el castillo; y el Rey y los otros se tenían por perdidos; e ordenó que se hiciese una contramina" (*Tirante* 1974, vol. 4, 131). But in Valdés's *Diálogo de Mercurio y Carón* and in his third work, *La vida de Lazarillo de Tormes*, it is used in a figurative sense. In the former, the soul of the married woman refers to the condition of her husband thus: "Y dime tan buena maña, contraminando sus vicios con virtudes . . ." (Valdés 1999, 275). In the latter, Alfonso de

Valdés combines two words ("maña" and "contraminar") when Lázaro narrates the greed of the old blind man and how he managed to neutralize him: "Digo verdad: si con mi sotileza y buenas mañas no me supiera remediar, muchas veces me finara de hambre. Mas, con todo su saber u aviso, le contraminaba de tal suerte, que siempre, o las más veces, me cabía lo más y mejor" (Valdés 2011, 9).

Valdés's ideas also seem to have been influenced by *Tirante*. In the *Diálogo de las cosas acaecidas en Roma*, we find the same endorsement of peace as in *Tirante*. While on the Berber Coast discussing peace, Placer de mi Vida tells Tirante: "Bien sabes que dijo Jesucristo que bienaventurados serán los pacíficos porque ellos serán llamados hijos de Dios. E la noche de Navidad, cuando Jesucristo nació, los ángeles cantaban: 'Gloria sea dada a Dios en los cielos, y paz en la tierra a los hombres de buena voluntad'. Y pues tú eres cristiano, ¿por qué vienes contra sus mandamientos?" (*Tirante* 1974, vol. 4, 174–175). The same reference appears in Lactancio's wonderful speech against the Pope's war: "¿Dónde halláis vos que mandó Jesucristo a los suyos que hiciesen guerra? [. . .] Cuando Jesucristo nació, no tañeron al arma, mas cantaron los ángeles: *Gloria in excelsis Deo, et in terra pax hominibus bonae voluntatis!* [. . .] Pues el que esta [la caridad] no tiene, ¿cómo será cristiano?" (Valdés 1992, 101). The Emperor in the *Diálogo de Mercurio y Carón* has the same attitude towards happiness and sorrows as Tirante, who, in answer to the Queen of England's advice not to grieve in order better to display his virtue, states: "Jamás fue ninguno, serenísima señora, que me viese triste – dijo Tirante – por gran pérdida que me viniese; ni mucho menos alegrarme por más bien que se me siguiese" (*Tirante* 1974, vol. 1, 205). Furthermore, in Valdés's dialogue, the loyal secretary to the Emperor tells us: "El Emperador, aunque en todas sus cosas se conformó tan de verdad con la voluntad de Dios, que ni las prosperidades le dan demasiada alegría ni las adversidades tampoco tristeza . . ." (Valdés 1999, 136).

Tirant's influence can also be found in *Lazarillo de Tormes*. When Carmesina despises Tirant after hearing lies about him from the wicked Viuda Reposada, the brave captain, alone in his room, refuses to eat. Estefanía laments this situation and tells Diafebus: "¡Qué remedio podremos dar a su gran dolor, que tanto como yo adobo de día desbarata la Viuda de noche!" (*Tirante* 1974, vol. 3, 135). It is easy to see the similarities this excerpt shares with Lázaro's account of how his boss fixes the holes he has carved during the day in an old chest: "Torna a buscar clavos por la casa y por las paredes, y tablillas a atapárselos. Venida la noche y su reposo, luego era yo puesto en pie con mi aparejo, y cuantos él tapaba de día, destapaba yo de noche" (Valdés 2011, 23). It is also *Tirante* that gives us the clue to the concealed reference to the author's name in *La vida de Lazarillo de Tormes, y de sus fortunas y adversidades*. Its first three letters (read in reverse, as in Hebrew), added to the last three (read in Latin order) render LA V / DES (Valdés). This explains the strange article ("La") that opens the title, as such titular "lives" would usually dispense with the article, and begin "*Vida de . . .*" Tirante orders that his flag should bear the following message: "La letra que está primera / en el nombre de esta pintura / la llave es con que ventura / cerrada tiene la postrera" (*Tirante* 1974, vol. 2, 159). This motto is accompanied by golden "calnados," because the Catalan form for "padlock" is "cadenat," a word opening with the 'c' of Carmesina, and ending with the 't' of Tirant. Thus, Alfonso de Valdés might have obtained the idea of ciphering his last name in the title of his work from his careful reading of *Tirante*.

Another reader of *Tirante el Blanco*: Jerónimo de Urrea

Captain Jerónimo Jiménez de Urrea translated a key work of Renaissance literature from Italian, Ariosto's *Orlando Furioso* (1549). Even though the priest, going over Don Quijote's library, claims that the "señor capitán [. . .] le quitó mucho de su natural valor" (Cervantes 1998, 81), Cervantes had read this translation carefully. He had also read de Urrea's *Diálogo de la verdadera honra militar* (Navarro Durán 2013), as well as the manuscript of his chivalric novel *Don Clarisel de las flores* (unpublished until 1879), as evinced by the similarities between *Don Quijote* and that other delirious novel, similarly full of wizards. Within this chain of readers, it is also worth noting that Jerónimo de Urrea had also read *Tirante el Blanco*, as his *Clarisel* makes clear. The Aragonese writer was born circa 1510 (Geneste 1975, vol. 1, 72), and fought with Garcilaso in the skirmish at Muy, where Garcilaso died, as well as in the disastrous battle of Algiers. Always loyal to the Emperor, he was also part of his army in the successful battles of Dura and Mülhberg. It is not surprising, then, that he had read *Tirante el Blanco*. For proof of this it should suffice to note that when Urrea's Belamir *el fermoso*, accompanied by Gelander from Hungary, lies to the King of Macedonia's daughter, Leoniselda, and tells her that, even though they carry weapons, they are ladies, he comes up with the following invented names: "Buena señora, a esta mi hermana llaman Reposada y a mí Traviesa" (Urrea 1879, 291), *Tirante*'s Viuda Reposada being the obvious inspiration.

We can detect imitation of other minor details, for example in the death of a character as a result of a burst gallbladder. In *Tirante*, this is the fate which befalls the giant Quirieleisón as he rages in front of his master's tomb, after his defeat by Tirante: "[. . .] vio a su señor de la manera que estaba, tomole tanto dolor, mezclado con extrema ira, que le reventó la hiel en el cuerpo y luego arrebatademente murió" (*Tirante* 1974, vol. 1, 256); the same occurs to the disgraceful duke of Andria (vol. 2, 285). In *Don Clarisel*, a maiden knocked down by a palfrey dies in the same way: "[. . .] y a la doncella derribó con tal caída que la cuitada no movió más pie ni mano porque se le quebrantó la hiel en el cuerpo" (Urrea 1879, 200). There are also echoes of another scene. After a day of hunting, the unknown Nobleman (as Clarisel is often styled) "quiso reposar cerca de una fuente en lo bajo de la selva," and thus rested under "grandes y fojosos plátanos; sacando un pequeño libro, que siempre consigo traía, que de fechos de caballeros antiguos trataba, a lo que él muy aficionado era [. . .]" (Urrea 1879, 178). The same scene, including a wood and a fountain (though changing the plane-tree for a pine tree) appears in *Tirante*, in a "sitio muy deleitoso, con gran espesura de árboles," where the young knight finds the hermit who tells him about chivalric orders reading from Ramon Llull's *Llibre de l'orde de cavalleria*: "Hijo mío – dijo el ermitaño – , toda la orden es escrita en este libro, el cual yo leo algunas veces por traer a la memoria la merced que Dios me ha hecho en este mundo, porque yo honraba y mantenía a todo mi poder la orden de caballería" (*Tirante* 1974, vol. 1, 101–102).

Other details may be added, but the foregoing should suffice to prove that Captain Urrea had read *Tirante el Blanco*, and that the impressions which that book left on him were to emerge in the fanciful chivalric romance he wrote during the second half of the century. It is evident, then, that Joanot Martorell's novel continued to influence Castilian literature during the sixteenth century, by means of Gumiel's anonymously published 1511 edition. Moreover, this influence even extended beyond the sixteenth century, as one of its most enthusiastic readers was Miguel de Cervantes.

From *La Galatea* to *Persiles*: *Tirante* as background

Traces of *Tirante* in Cervantes's work are not limited to *El Quijote*. They are also evident in some of the *Novelas ejemplares* and, to a greater extent, in *Los trabajos de Persiles y Sigismunda*. *La Galatea* also displays some traces that might be attributed to Cervantes's reading of *Tirante*, in which case Cervantes might have read the book at an early date, before 1585, when his pastoral novel was published. For example, in the first book of *La Galatea*, Teolinda is narrating her romances when the shepherdesses hear a great clamour of herdsmen's cries and barking dogs. Hiding among the branches, they see a pack of hounds chasing a hare. The narrator says: "Y no tardó mucho que por el mesmo lugar donde las pastoras estaban, la vieron entrar y irse derecha al lado de Galatea" (Cervantes 1994, 75). The hounds follow the hare to the side of the shepherdess, who protects the animal. Arriving there, the herdsmen "quedaron admirados de la hermosura de Teolinda."

At the beginning of the fourth book "del venturoso y esforzado caballero Tirante el Blanco" we encounter him, shipwrecked and hopeless, in a Tunisian cave, along with a sailor who has also survived the disaster. The ambassador of the king of Tremicén is hunting in the area, and the narrator relates how they "hallaron una liebre, y por haber sido muy corrida con los perros y con los halcones, no podiendo haber otro reparo, se entró en la cueva donde estaba Tirante." When one of the hunters, chasing the hare, discovers Tirante, who is resting, he tells his master: "Yo no creo que natura pudo formar un cuerpo mortal con más perfición y hermosura que el que yo he visto" (*Tirante* 1974, vol. 5, 9–10).

The scenes presented in the two books are strikingly similar: chased by hounds, a hare takes refuge next to the main character, and when the hunters find the hare, they discover a beautiful unknown person, Teolinda or Tirante. We might add the image of scimitars glittering under the fire of a nocturnal Turkish attack on a coastal Catalan village: "A la luz de las furiosas llamas se vieron relucir los bárbaros alfanjes y parecerse las blancas tocas de la turca gente" (Cervantes 1994, 120). In *Tirante el Blanco*, Placer de mi Vida, alone on the Barbary Coast, naked, and deathly cold, witnesses a fight between Moors and Christians, and "con los relámpagos vía relucir las espadas a la ribera de la mar" (*Tirante* 1974, vol. 3, 363). Might this second similarity confirm Cervantes's early reading of Tirante? If so, he would have kept the book to hand for a long time, as it is a constant presence in all his later works.

Cervantes also wonderfully recreates a great scene from Martorell's novel in *El celoso extremeño*. One of the most charming – and sauciest – episodes of *Tirante* occurs in Carmesina's bedchamber. Placer de mi Vida has hidden the brave captain in a large chest, with holes through which he can breathe. Unaware of his presence, Carmesina undresses for her bath, while a cheeky Placer de mi Vida illuminates her body for the enjoyment of the voyeur:

> La Princesa se comenzó de desnudar, e Placer de mi Vida le puso el asiento que venía de cara de donde Tirante estaba, de manera que él la podía muy bien ver a su placer. E como del todo fue desnuda, Placer de mi Vida tomó una candela encendida, y por hacer placer a Tirante mirábala toda la persona, que allí no había nada encubierto.
>
> (*Tirante* 1974, vol. 3, 180)

In *El celoso extremeño*, we find a wealthy old man who lives with his young and beautiful wife in a Sevillian house that he keeps locked, as if it were a convent. The rogue Loaysa, after seducing with his music an old black eunuch slave who guards the house, manages to enter into the hallway. Having learned of the presence of the handsome musician, the lady of the house and her maids carve a hole in a turntable and take turns to spy through it; meanwhile, the slave passes a candle across the handsome young singer's body so they can admire the attractive boy: "Poníase una al agujero para verle, y luego otra; y por que le pudiesen ver mejor, andaba el negro paseándole el cuerpo de arriba abajo con el torzal de cera encendido" (Cervantes 1995, vol. 2, 42). When we compare the two scenes, we can appreciate the greatness of both writers and how much Cervantes enjoyed reading *Tirante*. He reversed the sexes of observer and observed, turning women into admirers of male beauty in *El celoso extremeño*: desire belongs to both sexes.

We move now to a very different scenario and a more melancholy tone in *Persiles*. When Tirante, who has undertaken to help the Emperor, reaches Constantinople, the Emperor appoints him as commander of his troops. Immediately, the knight goes to the palace to pay homage to the Empress and Princess Carmesina. "La cámara era muy escura, que no había en ella lumbre ni claridad ninguna," as the ladies are in mourning following the death of their son and brother. The knight asks for a torch to bring some light into the room. "Después que la lumbre entró en la cámara, vio un pabellón todo negro. Allegose a él e abriole y vio una señora toda cubierta de paño grosero con un gran velo negro sobre la cabeza que la cubría toda hasta los pies" (*Tirante* 1974, vol. 2, 118). In *Los trabajos de Persiles y Sigismunda*, a group of pilgrims is made to witness a bizarre scene at an inn: Claudino Rubicón has killed Count Lamberto of Scotland, and the widow, Mrs. Ruperta, "agraviada y airada" and seeking revenge, carries a bloody sword and her dead husband's head. The episode is very different save for the mourning; what brings both scenes together is the widow's chamber. When the pilgrims find this room, it is described as "un aposento todo cubierto de luto, cuya lóbrega oscuridad no les dejó ver particularmente lo que en él había, y estándole así mirando, llegó un hombre anciano, todo asimismo cubierto de luto." This old man, the widow's squire, tells them the story of the widow, and how she had vowed "que mi vestido será negro, mis aposentos lóbregos, mis manteles tristes y mi compañía la misma soledad" (Cervantes 2002, 589) until she fulfills her oath and takes revenge on her husband's death.

These are far from the only traces of Cervantes's reading of *Tirante* evident in his last novel, but I turn now to the pages of *Don Quijote de la Mancha* to underscore some of the debts this great work bears to *Tirante el Blanco*, starting from the very name of its main character.

From the title of *Don Quijote* to Cervantes's will: debts to *Tirante*

The *hidalgo* from La Mancha needed eight days to come up with "Don Quijote," a name befitting his new occupation as a knight-errant; he then remembered that Amadís had added to his own name "el de su reino y patria, por hacerla famosa, y se llamó Amadís de Gaula," and accordingly, he styled himself "don Quijote de la Mancha, con que a su parecer declaraba muy al vivo su linaje y patria, y la honraba con tomar el sobrenombre de ella" (Cervantes 1998, 42–43). As for the ideal birthplace for Cervantes's parodic knight-errant, this "de la Mancha" is strange in the name of a knight who is supposed to be unblemished, and should be understood in opposition to the "blanco" of "Tirante el Blanco."

Immediately after Don Quijote begins his adventurous life on a hot July day, he realizes he lacks something essential: he needs to be dubbed a knight. Overcoming an enormous grief that almost brings an end to his adventure, he finally decides to ask the first person he meets to knight him; and his habit of transforming reality is to help him turn a castle into an inn. After Quijote assaults two other guests, the innkeeper, himself a reader of chivalric novels, decides to "abreviar y darle la negra orden de caballería" right away to avoid further harm. As the "castle" has no chapel, he convinces Don Quijote that the setting is of no importance. He begins the ritual with the assistance of the two prostitutes who are accompanying a group of mule drivers to Seville. The innkeeper pretends to read prayers from his account book (where in reality he keeps a tally of the hay and barley he has given to the mule drivers), and touches Don Quijote's shoulders with the sword to confer his knighthood. One of the girls, Tolosa, fits his sword for him, and the other, Molinera, fastens on his spurs.

The parodical nature of the ceremony is intensified if we compare it to a parallel event in the life of Tirante el Blanco, who was knighted by the King and the archbishop of England in a vast room. He is first seated in "una silla grande de plata que estaba cubierta de un rico paño de seda verde," and the archbishop, dressed as a deacon and holding an open missal, takes his oath – the wording of which reminds us of what Don Quijote tells the shepherds about the Golden Age: "se instituyó la orden de los caballeros andantes, para defender las doncellas, amparar las viudas y socorrer a los huérfanos y a los menesterosos" (Cervantes 1998, 123). In *Tirante*, the King of England, placing the sword over the knight's head, declares: "Dios te haga buen caballero y señor San Jorge."

There is thus a clear contrast between the inn, in *Don Quijote*, and the luxurious platform that the King erects for Tirante's ceremony, as well as between the innkeeper and the archbishop and the King of England. In addition, a further parallel adds to the scene's humour. The account of the retinue in *Tirante el Blanco* is as follows: "Luego venieron siete doncellas vestidas de blanco, a significación de los siete gozos de Nuestra Señora, e ciñéronle la espada. Después vinieron cuatro caballeros, los mayores en dignidad que allí se hallaron, y calzáronle las espuelas, a significación de los cuatro evangelistas" (*Tirante* 1974, vol. 1, 167–168); in Don Quijote's case, we have the barley account book, the innkeeper, and the two prostitutes. In *Tirante*, there are seven maidens clad in white to symbolize the seven joys of the Virgin Mary; for Don Quijote, Tolosa and Molinera.

Don Quijote's adventures come to an end when the despair resulting from his defeat in Barcelona, and a strong fever, take him to the grave. In Tirante's case, he is struck by a sudden and severe pain in his side while taking a walk on the riverbank, only a day away from Constantinople and the happiness he would have found there. He is taken to the city, "e como fue echado en la cama," the "físicos" find no remedy for him. He then asks for his Franscican confessor, with whom he will also take communion and write his will. Don Quijote also asks for a confessor and a scribe. In his will, he includes Sancho, his housekeeper, and his niece, to whom he bequeaths all his possessions. The narrator adds: "Andaba la casa alborotada, pero, con todo, comía la sobrina, brindaba el ama y se regocijaba Sancho Panza, que esto del heredar algo borra o templa en el heredero la memoria de la pena que es razón que deje el muerto" (Cervantes 1998, 1221). Tirante's bequest remembers his servants, and declares "mi sobrino y criado Hipólito de Roca Salada" heir of his possessions and titles (*Tirante* 1974, vol. 5, 187). Carmesina dies from sorrow, as does the Emperor upon seeing his daughter's grief. In contrast, the narrator tells us of Hipólito: "Y no penséis que Hipólito toviese mucho dolor, que luego que Tirante fue muerto, hizo su cuenta que él sería emperador, e mucho más después de la muerte del Emperador y su hija, teniendo confianza del mucho amor que la Emperatriz le tenié" (*Tirante* 1974, vol. 5, 214). Inheritance thus assuages the pain of loss, and in both *Tirante* and *Don Quijote* the narrator underscores how these material gains can cause the inheritor to forget.

In addition to the heroes' wills, we find another legal document in both tales. In the first book of *Tirante el Blanco*, the King of Friesland, the King of Apollonia, the Duke of Burgundy, and the Duke of Bavaria appear before the King of England, though they remain anonymous. They hand the King a document in which the Mantuan notary Ambrosino certifies that they are "caballeros de cuatro cuartos," and bears witness that they have appeared before three cardinals, the patriarch of Jerusalem, and two great knights (*Tirante* 1974, vol. 1, 216). Something similar happens in Chapter LXXII of the second part of *Don Quijote*, during the knight's encounter with Álvaro Tarfe, a character from *Quijote*'s apocryphal second part by Alonso Fernández de Avellaneda. The character from the spurious book sees with his own eyes the differences between the Don Quijote he knows and the one in front of him, between this witty Sancho Panza he is now talking to and the greedy, dumb character of Avellaneda's book. After declaring that he is Don Quijote de la Mancha, "el mismo que dice la fama, y no ese desventurado que ha querido usurpar mi nombre y honrarse con mis pensamientos," and telling

Tarfe that he has never been to Zaragoza, as he avoided the city on learning that the usurper had gone to a jousting tournament there, he appeals to Tarfe's status as a knight, asking that he "sea servido de hacer una declaración ante el alcalde de este lugar de que vuestra merced no me ha visto en todos los días de su vida hasta agora, y de que yo no soy el don Quijote impreso en la segunda parte, ni este Sancho Panza mi escudero es aquel que vuestra merced conoció." By chance, the mayor and a scribe then happen to walk into the inn, and the declaration is thus effected (Cervantes 1998, 1208). The legal documents are different, as are their settings, but their functions are the same. The scribe from the village in La Mancha has a similar role to the notary in Rome who signs the text recognizing the knighthood of those who now present a letter to the King of England.

A thoroughgoing analysis of the presence of *Tirante el Blanco* in *Don Quijote* would require much more space than is available here. Nonetheless, the examples given herein should suffice to underscore, once again, the contention made at the outset of this study, that good literature has no linguistic borders. Joanot Martorell had a profound influence on literature written in Spanish because some of its greatest innovators had read their works. This paper is but a brief incursion into a fascinating topic: the way great authors of the Golden Age read contemporary works, and how these, in turn, influenced their own books, underscoring in addition the importance of the work of translators in the process of transmission that so often occurs among significant works of literature. While the influence of Greek and Latin models in the literature of the Golden Age is universally acknowledged, similar influence exerted by contemporary writers often goes unnnoticed. By carefully examining a text, we can detect the readings of particular writers, for good literature feeds on literature, more than it does on life.

Notes

1 I leave aside the issue of the possible intervention of Martí Joan de Galba in Martorell's work and direct interested readers to Villalmazo and Chiner (1992). I would nonetheless note here that if Martorell pawned his copy of *Tirant*, it was very likely a completed work; had it not been finished, the sum he was given by the pawnbroker – "cent reals" – would have been excessive.

2 Literary histories bear testimony to another great fifteenth-century Catalan novel, *Curial e Güelfa*, the manuscript of which, kept at the Biblioteca Nacional de España (BNE), was only discovered by Manuel Milà i Fontanals in 1876. There was no trace of its influence on any previous work, nor was any mention of it recorded anywhere. The reason for the late discovery of this otherwise unobserved work was that it was actually a "Gothic novel" created by Milà, as is clear from the traces of Romanesque works visible in it, from Muntaner's *Crònica* to the Italian *Novellino*; *Paris e Viana* and *Petit Jehan de Saintré*; the trobadours Rigaut de Berbezilh and Raimbaut de Vaqueiras; Alfonso de la Torre's *Visión deleitable* and the *Coplas* of Jorge Manrique; even *La Celestina*, Luis Milán's *El cortesano*, *Lazarillo*, and the *Quijote* (Navarro Durán 2014). This erudite and clever forgery (similar to the case of Macpherson's Ossian) serves to emphasize the central point of this essay: that great authors assimilate their reading of other literary works and exhibit it in writing their own.

3 In this paper I use the 1511 Spanish translation of *Tirant*, since that was the version read by the various writers analyzed here.

Works cited

Cervantes, Miguel de. 1994. *La Galatea*. Edited by Florencio Sevilla Arroyo and Antonio Rey Hazas. Alcalá de Henares: Centro de Estudios Cervantinos.

———. 1995. *Novelas ejemplares*. Edited by Rosa Navarro Durán. 2 vols. Madrid: Alianza Editorial.

———. 1998. *Don Quijote de la Mancha*. Edited by Francisco Rico. Barcelona: Crítica.

———. 2002. *Los trabajos de Persiles y Sigismunda*. Edited by Carlos Romero. Madrid: Cátedra.

Fernández Álvarez, Manuel. 2000. *Carlos V, el césar y el hombre*. Madrid: Espasa and Fundación Academia Europea de Yuste.

Garcilaso de la Vega. 1995. *Obra poética y textos en prosa*. Edited by Bienvenido Morros. Barcelona: Crítica.

Geneste, Pierre. 1975. *Essai sur la vie et l'oeuvre de Jeronimo de Urrea*. 2 vols. Lille: Université de Lille.

Guevara, Fray Antonio de. 1950. *Epístolas familiares*. Edited by J. M. Cossío. 2 vols. Madrid: Aldus and RAE.

López Estrada, Francisco. 1993. "El *Tirante* castellano de 1511 y los libros de viajes." In *Actes del Symposium Tirant lo Blanc*, 441–470. Barcelona: Quaderns Crema.

Martorell, Joanot and Martí Joan de Galba. 2005. *Tirant lo Blanch*. Edited by Albert Hauf. Valencia: Tirant lo Blanch.

Menéndez Pelayo, Marcelino. 1943. *Orígenes de la novela*. Edited by Enrique Sánchez Reyes. 4 vols. Santander: Aldus and CSIC.

Mérida, Rafael M. 2002. *Tirante el Blanco. Guía de lectura*. Alcalá de Henares: Centro de Estudios Cervantinos.

Milá y Fontanals, Manuel. 1876. "Notes sur trois manuscrits." *Revue de Langues Romanes*, 10: 225–240.

Navarro Durán, Rosa. 2013. "Cervantes leyó al capitán Urrea, de Épila." *Clarín* 106: 13–16.

———. 2014. "*Curial e Güelfa*, mélange de gothique et de renaissance." *El texto infinito. Actas del Congreso de la SEMYR*, September, 2012: 191–225.

Riquer, Martín de. 1975. "Un nuevo ejemplar del *Tirante el Blanco* de Valladolid, de 1511." *Miscellanea Barcinonensia* 47: 7–15.

Tirante el Blanco. 1974. *Versión castellana impresa en Valladolid en 1511 de la obra de Joanot Martorell and Martí Joan de Galba*. Edited by Martín de Riquer. 5 vols. Madrid: Espasa-Calpe.

Urrea, Jerónimo de. 1879. *Primera parte del libro del invencible caballero don Clarisel de las Flores y de Austrasia*. Sevilla: Francisco Álvarez impr., Sociedad de Bibliófilos Andaluces.

Valdés, Alfonso de. 1992. *Diálogo de las cosas acaecidas en Roma*. Edited by Rosa Navarro Durán. Madrid: Cátedra.

———. 1999. *Diálogo de Mercurio y Carón*. Edited by Rosa Navarro Durán. Madrid: Cátedra.

———. 2011. *La vida de Lazarillo de Tormes, y de sus fortunas y adversidades*. In *La novela picaresca I*, edited by Rosa Navarro Durán. Madrid: Biblioteca Castro.

Villalmazo, Jesús and Jaime J. Chiner. 1992. *La pluma y la espada. Estudio documental sobre Joanot Martorell y su familia (1373–1483)*. Valencia: Ayuntamiento de Valencia.

17

WOMEN FROM THE PERIPHERY IN *DON QUIXOTE*

Ekphrasis versus counter-narrative

Frederick A. de Armas

While the adventures of Don Quixote and his conversations with his more down-to-earth squire have enchanted audiences for centuries, and while the amorous adventures in the interpolated narratives have also caught the attention of many, the intrepid women that make an appearance during Don Quixote's adventures are sometimes forgotten, given the scope of his imaginings. This essay seeks to highlight two women from Iberia's periphery who in some ways counter the knight's imperial quest. In each of these adventures, the knight seems to dominate his surroundings by the use of his imagination. As dramatist and artist he transforms or paints over a quotidian space into a place for chivalric adventures. There is no question that the knight urges us to use our sight over and over again: "Ves allí, amigo Sancho Panza, donde se descubren treinta, o poco más desaforados gigantes" (1978, 129); "Dime, ¿no ves aquel caballero que hacia nosotros viene, sobre un caballo rucio rodado, que trae puesto en la cabeza un yelmo de oro? (1978, 253). Indeed, not only does he paint over the landscape, but also he shapes new characters derived from his chivalric imaginings. When asked about Dulcinea, he replies: "píntola en mi imaginación" (1978, 314). Don Quixote believes in the capaciousness of his words to create something new. In ancient rhetoric this capaciousness is tied to a kind of *descriptio* sometimes called *ekphrasis*. It is not my intention here to enter into the debates over this term.[1] While Leo Spitzer (1962) once described the technique as "the poetic description of a pictorial or sculptural work of art . . . the reproduction through the medium of words of sensuously perceptible *objects d'art*" (1955, 207), Murray Krieger claims as one aspect of ekphrasis the exhilaration felt when the word is able "to freeze itself into a spatial form . . . [to] recover the immediacy of a sightless vision" (1992, 10). The dazzling images that emerge from Don Quixote's mind are thus transformed into capacious writing and this grants him the exhilaration felt by the poet. Don Quixote as creator does not feel the opposite reaction that may emerge from ekphrasis: the "exasperation" created because "words cannot have that capacity, cannot be capacios because they have literally, no space" (Krieger 1992, 10). For the knight, the landscape and the characters are truly changed. If his vision is challenged, then it has to do with malefic enchanters who are intent on changing his reality.

In this essay I argue that the exhilarating ekphrasis of the knight is countered by a counter-narrative, the quasi-untold or unnarrated stories about valorous, willful and adventuresome women who stand in contrast to the illusory Dulcinea: a Basque lady viewed as a kidnapped princess and a servant/prostitute from Asturias also imagined as a princess. A brief interlude

213

with some Galician mares also comes to our attention. Thus this study reflects the tensions between painting with the imagination versus hiding a so-called ordinary tale, and the opposition between a knight who wishes to make Castile the center of the world versus women from the edges of the peninsula who try to stand their ground.

The case of the kidnapped princess: a Basque story

Steve Hutchinson has spoken of the "liberating and salubrious effects of feminine journeys" (1992, 106) in Cervantes fiction.[2] He argues that, since women "are possessed as objects, transferred, kept, robbed, bought, and constantly referred to as things of value . . . the journey . . . removes them from where they are controlled" (1992, 107). This section begins with the story of a forgotten traveler – forgotten because she is a woman from the periphery who seems to fade away against the brilliant but imagined visual images that are at the basis of the knight's adventures. Perhaps her invisibility is because she appears in one of the most narratable episodes in the 1605 novel, the adventure of the Basque. Indeed it is considered so narratable, so "worthy of being told" (Prince 1987, 56), that it is told four times. The four versions have been analyzed with great care and insight by Michael Gerli. But even he neglects our princess. Our purpose is to figure out why she is hidden and what it is that she is hiding.

As the knight watches the approach of two friars on mules, a carriage filled with damsels, four or five horsemen and two muleteers coming on foot, he works his magic by transforming the scene and making it into an adventure: "porque aquellos bultos negros que allí parecen deben de ser, y son, sin duda, algunos encantadores que llevan hurtada alguna princesa en aquel coche" (1978, 1.133).[3] Don Quixote aided by the narrators paint a canvas with consummate skill, creating an ekphrasis filled with marvel, thus erasing the mundane. As Juan Bautista Avalle-Arce reminds us, the figure of Don Quixote can be conceived as an artist who paints over reality, creating marvelous designs of the imagination. Avalle-Arce asserts: "El caballero sale al mundo para vivir la vida como una obra de arte" (1973, 51). He then cites Vasari's *Lives of the Artists* to explain the knight's and the novel's theory of imitation. Thus, the knight, aided by the narrators, paints with words a scene that he has viewed in the canvas of his mind. This is an ur-ekphrasis "existing as a concept of ekphrasis in the character's mind . . . thus foregrounding the process of artistic creation" (De Armas 2006, 10).

When these amazing and imagined ekphraseis are coupled with remarks by a doubting Sancho, the reader is asked to enjoy scenes that arouse laughter, curiosity, amazement and wonder. These images remain in our memory for further contemplation and they do so, in part, because the adventures are carefully fashioned to follow the dictates of the art of memory which was so prevalent in the Renaissance. Theorists of the time have argued that the images that best remain in the mind are those of heroic deeds. More generally, "rare and unusual things stay in the mind because they bring about wonder [*maraviglia*]" (Della Porta 2012, 103). And Don Quixote is forever inciting wonder. The Arts of Memory also claim that "horrible and frightful things," as well as "things that easily move us to enjoyment or laughter" are memorable (Della Porta 2012, 103). As Giovan Battista Della Porta shows, when opposites are combined, they are even more striking. And it is precisely the opposition between the quotidian and the marvelous, the lofty chivalric ideals with its humorous and mundane realities that create what is particularly memorable. Thus, the double narrative, the quotidian presented by a rather hostile narrator (Cide Hamete) and the exalted one imagined by the knight create a truly mnemonic space. As Soledad Fox has argued, "It takes exceptional genius to create magic, beauty, or heroism on the infertile soil of La Mancha" (2010, 53).

Although it could be indeed marvelous to find a kidnapped princess in La Mancha, her possible abduction would not be particularly surprising since the lady in the carriage is a woman of importance who is traveling on roads that were often dangerous. Banditry on Spanish roads was often a problem. And, the motif of the kidnapped princess is in itself a commonplace in the romances of chivalry. To cite but a few examples, in *Felixmarte de Hircania* the princess Martedina is kidnapped by savages and later freed by a savage woman named Belsagina; and in *Cristalián de España* the enchanter Algamaz kidnaps the wife and son of Lindedel (Ortiz-Hernán Pupareli 2009/10, 324–5). In *Duardos de Bretaña* by Pero Dacacova Carneiro, Carmelia de Tracia is kidnapped together with several other princesses, while the work concludes happily with her marriage to the protagonist, Don Duardos. A gender inversion occurs in *Clarisel de las Flores* written towards the end of the sixteenth century by Jerónimo de Urrea. Here, the female magician Filesa kidnaps the Doncel. Indeed, in her typology of women in the chivalric romances, Elami Ortiz-Hernán Pupareli lists more than twenty figures under the rubric: "doncella secuestrada o encantada" (2003, np).

Much more memorable than the frequently kidnapped princesses of the romances or the women metamorphosed by the knight into princesses in Cervantes's novel, are the friars that become enchanters and ride dromedaries. Even the Basque using a pillow for a shield while fighting a crazed knight of old with surprising valor stands out much more than the lady in the carriage. Thus, from the start, the "princess" is at a disadvantage, somewhat hidden in the canvas of memory. But her story is not untold, it does not seem part of the unnarrated;[4] it is just hinted at, fragmented and kept in the background. These bits and pieces may arouse the reader's curiosity. Once the friar/enchanters are defeated by the "valiant" knight, he approaches the carriage and seeks to communicate with the "princess" ("vuestra fermosura" 1978, 1.135), telling her and her companions that they are now free of the kidnappers. He also requests that the princess and her retinue go to see Dulcinea and tell her of his exploits. Thus their freedom is contingent since they have to tell Dulcinea "lo que por vuestra libertad he fecho" (1978, 1.135). Rather than freeing them, his imperious command imprisons them. Because there is no response from the "princess" she remains as part of the imaginary canvas, caught in the knight's imagination rather than enjoying the freedom of the journey.

But, a Basque squire who accompanies the carriage, realizing that they must turn away from their destination, takes up the fight. He considers himself as noble as Don Quixote. In garbled speech he asserts: "Vizcaino por tierra, hidalgo por mar, hidalgo por el diablo, y mientes que mira si otra dices cosa" (1978, 136). As this battle is about to start, the reader finally gets a glimpse at the lady's emotions and actions: "admirada y temerosa de lo que veía, hizo al cochero se desviase de allí algún poco y desde lejos se puso a mirar la rigurosa contienda" (1978, 136). The lady shows some agency, simply asking the coachman to move the vehicle so she can watch the battle from a safe distance. The adjectives, "admirada and temerosa," recall emotions that need to be aroused for the art of memory to work best. What she experiences can be termed *ekplexis*, a heightened sense of astonishment or marvel derived from striking visual images. Leonard Barkan (2013) equates it with *admiratio*. This may come from such extremes as bloody battles (Refini 2012, 46) or the extraordinary beauty of a woman such as Helen of Troy (Worman 2002, 132). Knowing the two extremes of the emotion, and being presented with the battle, a reader may hazard a guess that the narrative is hiding the extraordinary beauty of the princess, a point upon which the knight would agree.

She serves to increase the astonishment of the reader through her own emotions. As she watches, the reader may wish to see through her eyes. This seems to create a kind of metatheater where readers as spectators watch her and her retinue as they watch the action.[5] Diane Chaffee Sorace argues: "The lady's withdrawal from the center of the action to its periphery changes her role in the dramatic episode from participant to spectator and converts the battle into a well-defined theatrical event" (1989, 210). Her role is subservient to the events about to take place. Furthermore, she appears as ornamental as numerous ladies in the romances of chivalry, thus legitimizing Don Quixote's imaginative vision of her as a princess in distress. And to further diminish the importance of her very human emotions the narrator later asserts that all who watched the adventure were "temerosos y colgados" (1978, 1.137). Thus far the princess is forgettable as she is relegated to the backdrop by both knight and narrator. If this were all, her story would not just be untold but uninteresting and close to unnarratable.

Don Quixote, after being slashed by the Basque, invokes Dulcinea to succor him in his peril. A parallel movement occurs in the carriage. The lady and her attendants pray to countless Christian images of devotion and promise to make votive offerings if their squire is spared: "estaban haciendo mil votos y ofrecimientos a todas las imagines y casas de devoción de España, porque Dios librase a su escudero y a ellas de aquel tan grande peligro en que se hallaban" (1978, 1.137). This particular move raises their status, as the ladies compete with the knight in obtaining favors from above. We could almost be reading a (mock) classical epic where different gods and goddesses intervene in favor of opposing camps. But the results of such prayers have to wait, given that the manuscript ends.

This "frozen" moment (with the two opponents ready to do battle) recalls two epic instances: Ariosto's and Ercilla's "cantus interruptus" (Javitch 1980, 66–80). In *La Araucana*, there is an initial frozen duel between the "barbarous" Rengo and the Italian Andrea, a battle which is suspended between cantos fourteen and fifteen (De Armas Wilson 2000, 161–182; Lerner 1998, 207–220). Then: "The same brain bashing *bárbaro*, Rengo, returns to battle, not with a European opponent this round but with an Araucanian rival called Tucapel (29.53), whose sword remains in mid-air for over a decade between the publications of Part 2 (1578) and Part 3 (1589)" (2000, 176). Turning to Ariosto's *Orlando furioso*, David Javich points to a different kind of interruption, discussing how Angelica is about to be sacrificed by the Orc in Canto Eight but the reader must wait until Canto Ten for the resolution of this dire moment, thus arousing curiosity and suspense (1980, 66, 69). Such moments are less powerful when they occur in the midst of a Canto and are not resolved until much later since the reader loses curiosity because of the long deferral. In such a case, it is more a question of variety. However: "A recurring tactic of Ariosto's is to defy the expectation of closure at the end of the canto by terminating it at the start or at the height of a dramatic episode or action" (1980, 69). Grifone's revenge, begun in Canto Seventeen and continued in Canto Eighteen, may have some bearing on Cervantes' episode; however, Grifone's revenge is not completed here either (1980, 73). Thus the Cervantine text colludes with the knight to make this a truly epic moment recalling Ariosto and Ercilla. There is no thought here for the princess, for the lady in her carriage. She does not seem to exist in these maneuvers; she fades into the unnarrated since at the point of the sword, her story does not seem worth telling.

After the suspenseful break in the narrative, the "author" seeks a new manuscript while he praises the violence of the episode, recalling some of its key moments in what Gerli calls a "parody of unrestrained epic expression" (1995, 68). Indeed the author imagines that when the Basque and the knight's swords come down "se dividirían y fenderían de arriba abajo y abrirían como una granada" (1999, 1.8.139). The simile of the body as a fruit which exposes its red interior (the blood of the fighters) leads to an explanation of the savory flavors of violence. For Eric Graf, the *granada* or pomegranate has a number of meanings, among them, its many seeds recall the many lands that coexist in the Iberian Peninsula, the Basque abiding in its periphery.[6]

If we follow Eric Graf's lead in terms of the lady, we find that in paintings of the period the pomegranate is often held by the Virgin Mary. Such is the case of the *Madonna con bambino* by Botticelli or the *Madonna with Pomegranate* attributed to Leonardo.[7] Perhaps the violence aroused by the image of splitting the pomegranate is assuaged by religious images in the background as we recall the lady and her attendant praying to the Virgin Mary. Will the Virgin act through her? Diana de Armas Wilson, speaking of the dark aspects of liberation in Cervantes' novel, claims that there are two episodes that frame false liberation – the kidnapped princess in Chapters 8–9 and the statue of the Virgin in Chapter 52: "The matron's liberation costs don Quijote half an ear (1, 9) and the Blessed Virgin's, a shoulder smashed to pieces (1,52)" (2007, 250). I would add that the Virgin is not transformed into a princess, but becomes exactly what the earlier character was: "alguna principal señora" (1978, 1.598). Is this yet another clue that we are to view the princess's future actions in terms of Mary? Although never explicit, the pomegranate evoked by Graf and the second frame indicated by Wilson may point to the lady's intercession in the fourth version of the episode.[8]

The third telling of the story is an ekphrastic description of an illustration in the newly found manuscript. The illustration, like the narrative, point to the moment when the action is frozen: "pintada muy al natural la batalla de don Quijote con el Vizcaíno, puestos en la mesma postura que la historia cuenta, levantadas las espadas, el uno cubierto de su rodela, el otro de la almohada" (1978, 144). The illustration shows, to some extent, what would be the *punto crítico*, the climactic point of the whole adventure.[9] Much is made of the animals here, both the Basque's mule and Don Quixote's Rocinante – even Sancho and his beast are exhibited. But the women are erased from the illumination. As with the second version, any hint of the princess must be unearthed in ways that are truly tenuous. The ekphrasis seems to relegate her to the unimportant: "Otras algunas menudencias había que advertir, pero todas son de poca importancia y que no hacen al caso a la verdadera narración de la historia que ninguna es mala como sea verdadera" (1078, 144).

On the other hand, we have tangential details that can help in reconstructing the counter-narrative. We are given the Basque's name: Sancho de Azpeitia. Although a fairly common Basque name, it could point to the birth of Ignatius of Loyola in a town thus named. He fought with Castile, receiving the famous wound that led to his religious conversion.[10] Many paintings and illustrations show how he prayed to the Virgin, how she appeared to him, and how she even inspired him to write the *Ejercicios espirituales* in later years. Thus, it is easy to see how the princess's intervention might be seen in terms of the Virgin's interceding for Ignatius. Indeed, the name Sancho de Azpeitia may not only evoke a miraculous intervention in Cervantes' text, but may also have to do with the composition of place, a technique from Loyola's exercises, which derives in part from the Art of Memory. As Frederic Conrod (2008), Philip Davidson (2012) and others explain, Loyola's book influenced Cervantes' novel. Davidson traces the many writers that have seen a connection between Cervantes and Loyola throughout the centuries. Conrod, discussing the director/exercitant relation in Cervantes' novel argues that: "Don Quixote is not a director for Sancho nor vice versa; Sancho is simply doing a parallel mental pilgrimage and benefits from Don Quixote's greater capacity to establish a structure within his own mind" (2012, 111). The different mental images in Loyola are evoked by the succession of very different episodes in Cervantes. "Don Quixote takes Sancho along so that he can teach him the values of imagination and free will. At several stages he reveals the fundamental truth of the novel: every human perception is different. Of all Catholic orders, the Society of Jesus is the one that places most importance on casuistry and the relativity of perception . . ." (2012, 111). Thus, Loyola's *Exercises* bring together the visual, the imaginative and the emotional, three key elements in our adventure; and they even involve Sancho in this pursuit. In Cervantes' episode, the Basque's wounds, it can be argued, will bring about, if not his conversion, then an intercession from above. And the Exercises were said to have come about with the aid of the Virgin, and the saint is depicted in art writing under her tutelage.[11]

The fourth and final version, which begins in medias res, recounts that even though the Basque was able to wound the knight, taking half of his left ear, he in turn gave such a blow to his adversary that the squire fell from his mule bleeding from the nose, the mouth and the ears. Don Quixote, in the fury of battle, does not wait, and climbing down from his horse: "poniéndole la punta de la espada en los ojos, le dijo que se rindiese; si no, le cortaría la cabeza" (1978, 1.146). As Judith Whitenack has pointed out, this is a typical of the "conversion or death" threat in the romances of chivalry (1993, 67). The conversion in this case may well consist in the belief in Dulcinea's beauty and powers. Thus, while Don Quixote believes in an earthly goddess, the women prefer to pray to Christian images. Not able to respond, the Basque is about to meet his end when the ladies from the coach come forth and beg for mercy. The ladies' squire had previously spoken in jumbled Castilian, a typical strategy of humor in the literature of the period and used by Cervantes in *El Vizcaino fingido*.[12] But now the would-be princess and her attendants seem to address the knight in clear and respectful Castilian: "si las señoras del coche . . . le pidieran con mucho encarecimiento les hiciese tan gran merced y favor de perdonar la vida a aquel su escudero" (1999, 1.9.146). Although still in great fear, the women are able to save their squire through correct and persuasive speech.

This may not seem as much of a feat after the great battle, but I would argue that it is a major accomplishment which the bellicose gentleman seeks to minimize. The women, whatever they may think of Don Quixote, stand up to the knight and prevent a murder. Sancho Panza knows quite well that the whole adventure was not lawful. He realizes what almost happened and what did happen. He asks his master whether they should seek asylum in a church: "sería acertado irnos a retraer a alguna iglesia" (1999, 1.9.147). For surely the *Santa Hermandad* or Holy Brotherhood, which protects the countryside, would be after them after such an event. After all, their role is "to keep roads safe" (González Echevarría 2005, 64). Don Quixote rejects the idea, but his words are significant: "¿Dónde has visto o leído jamás que caballero andante haya sido puesto ante la justicia, por más homicidios que hubiese cometido?" (1999, 1.9.148). He knows quite well that if the ladies had not intervened, his choleric disposition may have led him to kill the Basque, and that this *homicidio* would be hard to explain.

The episode is now ended and knight and squire move on, curiously "sin despedirse ni hablar más con las del coche" (1978, 1.147). This lack of courtesy portrays the knight as a self-absorbed figure whose only goal is to win, no matter how much violence is unleashed. De Armas Wilson explains that: "Our fondness for Don Quixote should not allow us to overlook certain imperial (and imperious) strains of his mania" (2007, 251).

While the story tells how the friars left the battle, it is silent as to when or how the coach was able to resume its journey to Seville. And even though the text follows knight and squire into the forest, it turns away from the women of the coach and the voyage of the would-be princess who travels to meet her husband. Indeed, a longer journey awaits her on arriving in Seville, since her husband had received a "cargo honroso" in the Indies.

Although the tale of Don Quixote's adventure continues without a thought for the wounded squire, we know of his valor and of his lady's ability to match the knight in prayer and to stop a homicide that could well have landed the knight in jail or worse. While a man from Biscay can challenge Don Quixote and give him a very good fight, it is this woman from the periphery who succeeds in allowing the narrative to proceed unimpeded. She has saved the life and reputation of Don Quixote and she has saved the novel and its imaginative adventures for the time being. Only after the episode of the galley slaves, as Roberto González Echevarría states, do "both Don Quijote and Sancho become fugitives of the law" (2005, 63). It is then that the interpolated tales replace the knight's adventures as he hides out in Sierra Morena.

After crossing the peninsula from the northeast to the southwest, the lady from the Basque country will disappear from the narrative space as she and her husband travel to the Indies. Such a long voyage seems beyond Don Quixote, who is content to journey a short distance from his home. While she may witness real adventures at sea and in America, he will imagine all of his. The irony is that his episodes are recorded while hers would not make it to print. Such a digression would establish a counter-narrative that would challenge the knight. Its geographical amplitude would compromise a knight who seldom thinks of the lands north of Castile or beyond the sea, being content with evoking tenuous chivalric sites. Thus, Don Quixote and his narrators will conceal the narrowness of his journey and his lack of true exploits through powerful images, imaginative twists, mnemonic scenes and clever contrasts. And the knight has to have some worthy opponents: the illustration seeks to highlight the battle by making the Basque into a figure who can fight like his countryman, Ignatius of Loyola, and can be wounded just like him. Are these wounds a prelude to conversion and does the lady echo celestial interventions? We will leave such questions for the imaginative knights.

The fact is that we know nothing of the lady's background, as opposed to that of her squire. The gaps in the narrative allow the reader to create her own counter-narrative.[13] For all we know, Don Quixote was right. She could descend from royalty. According to legend, the Señorío de Vizcaya was formed when the daughter of a Scottish king traveled by sea to Biscay. There, she had a son who was chosen to command the troops of the area against the son of the King of Leon. Victorious in battle, and of royal blood, he became the Señor de Vizcaya. Such a genealogy for the lady from Biscay might be even worthy of the knight's imaginings.

In this first adventure, the lady from Biscay is a figure of power. She points to a story that is just beginning to be told, as her meeting with Don Quixote may be the first of her adventures. The geographical capaciousness of her travels seeks to rival the imaginative capaciousness of the knight's quests. Her prayers, countering those of the knight, might have leveled the playing field in battle. But most importantly, we rest assured that her keen intellect and her soothing and regal words, an intercession that echoes those of a celestial being or a woman of power, have prevented a dangerous strike by the knight and thus have allowed her to continue her journey and him to continue his quest unimpeded. Thus, the curious case of the kidnapped princess both hides and reveals her narrative, political and personal triumphs as she revels in the freedom of the road.

The Galician mares: an interlude

Chapter Ten, which immediately follows the episode of the Basque, is titled: "De lo que avino a don Quijote con el vizcaíno y del peligro en que se vio con una turba de yangüeses" (1978, 1.146). This is incorrect since the episode of the Basque concluded in Chapter Nine and that of the muleteers from Yanguas would not be told until Chapter Fifteen. It can be argued, then, that in the original plan for the novel, Cervantes intended to place the episode of the muleteers immediately after that of the Basque, but he later decided to insert a pastoral episode in between so as to ridicule some of the shepherd's lofty sentiment and the presence of Marcela as a *mujer esquiva*. Marcela's self-sufficiency mirror the behavior of the muleteers' mares.[14] There is a second apparent mistake in that these muleteers from Yanguas are also said to be from Galicia. To make matters even more confusing, there are two towns called Yanguas, one in the area of Soria and the second in Segovia. Most agree that the text points to the village in Soria since their muleteers were famous throughout Castile and even La Mancha in Cervantes' time. It has also been argued that the suppression of Galicia in favor of Yanguas was due to the editor or printer, and not the author. Thus, Juan de la Cuesta and his team may have been responsible. Indeed, his family had lands in the Yanguas area (Barroso Cabrera and Morín de Pablos 2009, 227–29). For our purposes, it is the author's initial intent to have these muleteers come from Galicia that is most important because the narrative would then move from an adventure with the Basque to a melee with these muleteers who are transporting Galician mares ("hacas galicianas [1978, 1.194]") and then on to a "princess" from Asturias in Chapter Sixteen. Thus, in three succeeding episodes, the novel would have dealt with three regions in Iberia's periphery: the Basque Country, Galicia and Asturias.

It may be useful, then, to take a brief look at Chapter Fifteen before turning to the second princess. Here, Sancho decides to let loose Rocinante so that he can graze at will, knowing that the horse is very tame. However, Fortuna or the devil brings the muleteers with their mares to this same valley. Rocinante suddenly becomes very feisty and excitedly pursues the mares, deciding to "refocilarse" with these female creatures. They in turn reject him quite violently. When the muleteers intervene to stop this melee, Don Quixote and Sancho go to defend Rocinante from what are now called Galician muleteers ("los gallegos" [1978, 1. 191]). Needless to say, the knight is badly beaten by this crowd. While Don Quixote had defeated the Basque and released the "kidnapped" princess, here he is unable to triumph over other figures from the periphery. Both the Galician mares and the muleteers are perfectly peaceful until attacked by the chivalric pair. It is as if they are the cause of conflict.

While the princess in the previous episode was able to triumph using correct and lofty Castilian to obtain the release of her squire, here the female animals are far from polite, using their heels and their teeth to beat away Rocinante. Chad Leahy, who has studied pamphlets and other writings critical of Galicians during this period in order to shed light on this episode, asserts: "El comportamiento de las yeguas en este sentido se muestra representativo de una naturaleza inherente al pueblo gallego, desde la imagen tipificada del gallego como criado vasallo rebelde y traidor, hasta la idea de la gallega como moza poco constante en el servicio y en el amor" (2008, 13).[15] Thus, Cervantes subjects inhabitants of the periphery to careful scrutiny and so far, they seem to have the upper hand. The Princess can speak perfect Castilian, is in control of her rhetoric and can win the release of her squire, while the Galician mares are not fickle but seem to defend their right to choose their mate. Indeed, just as in the previous episode a Basque squire shows honor and valor, here, in John Cull's words: "The *arrieros* beat Rocinante to the ground with their stakes to punish his boldness, then turn their wrath on Don Quixote and Sancho" (1990, 47).

While in the previous episode, the visual, narrative and epic-chivalric elements overwhelm the reader so that the princess's tale is almost untold, here, the knight fails to paint over the scene, to create a chivalric medium to excuse his attack. He ends up admitting that the god of war (Mars) has punished him for battling with those who are not knights. While Don Quixote is weakened and fails at ekphrasis, the men and female beasts from the periphery succeed. In addition, the action preserves a mnemonic quality since Della Porta asserts that comic and lewd images are easily remembered (2012, 103). I believe that this lowering of style and subject in this comic interlude prepares the reader to engage with the so-called princess from Asturias.[16]

The case of the trapped princess: a tale from Asturias

Knight and squire reach the inn in a sorry state. Don Quixote, although lying flat on Sancho's beast, is not to be deterred from his imaginings by one relapse into the quotidian. As Sancho takes up the mantle of chivalry assuring those present that Don Quixote's wounds are the result of falling down a cliff, the knight, being taken to a rustic bed, begins to imagine that the inn is a castle. Indeed, several beds are placed in succession away from the door: first Don Quixote's, then Sancho's, then a muleteer's. Indeed, the presence of an *arriero* connects this adventure with the previous interlude. What has been called a "bedroom farce" (Mendeloff 1975) and a bawdy tale that borrows from Boccaccio and Bandello (McGrady 1987) ensues as the servant from Asturias enters the room in darkness and in search of the *arriero* with whom she has a tryst, but runs into an eroticized knight, with his eyes "abiertos como liebre" (1978, 1.202), the hare symbolizing sexuality and a creature of Venus.[17] Indeed, for Carolyn Nadeau, Maritornes resembles Circe, a figure who keeps the hero from continuing his duties in the Homeric epic (2002, 19). Judith Whitenack adds that the *magas* of the romances of chivalry act very much like Circe, keeping "the hero enchanted for a long time," and attempt to make him forget not only the quest but also the lady (1993, 75). Analyzing Don Quixote's reaction to Maritornes, she sees here a glimmer of the *magas* of old, and adds: "Of course, part of the humor of the scene derives from the contrast between Don Quixote's self-designation as a faithful knight and his evident enjoyment of the rejection scene" (1993, 79).

Although we might think that these allusions to myth and chivalry may elevate the scene, this is not the case. Each attempt to turn to a higher style of narration ends in humor. Contrary to the story of the first princess, this tale is fully told although it seems to belong to the unnarrated, that which flaunts the conventions of writing. Indeed, in an aside, the narrator intervenes to criticize the author: "Benengeli fue historiador muy curioso y muy puntual en todas las cosas, y échase de ver, pues las que quedan referidas, con ser tan mínimas y rateras, no las quiso pasar en silencio" (1978, 1.201). In fact, the chapter delights in telling of the grotesque physique of Maritornes: "ancha de cara, llana de cogote, de nariz roma, del ojo tuerta y del otro no muy sana . . . no tenía siete palmos de pies a la cabeza, y las espaldas, que algún tanto le cargaban, la hacían mirar al suelo más de lo que ella quisiera" (1978, 1.198). This contrasts with Don Quixote's imaginings of a delicate and beautiful princess who abides in this castle/inn and must obviously desire him. This clash between beauty and ugliness, expectations and reality, the mythical/chivalric and the quotidian strengthen the mnemonic aspects of the scene through extreme contrasts. Don Quixote, on coming across Maritornes, not only enlivens his memory of chivalric books, but acts in a manner that seems to replicate a painting by Titian, *Tarquin and Lucretia*.[18] In this case the description is both an ekphrasis deriving from the mental image in the knight's imagination and a dramatic ekphrasis, one where both the knight and the narrators strive to paint the scene in terms of the Titian's canvas, while fully exposing the lurid reality.

On entering the room, Maritornes "topó con los brazos de don Quijote, el cual la asió fuertemente de una muñeca, y tirándola hacia sí, la hizo sentar en la cama" (1978, 1.203). In the Italian canvas, Sextus holds on to Lucretia's arm while she reclines on the bed. The similarities are thus striking. Furthermore, the knight decides to paint over this rather grotesque-looking servant into a princess from the romances utilizing instead Titian's painting of the Roman matron. Maritornes' hair becomes as golden as that pictured by Titian: "hebras de lucidísimo oro de Arabia 1978, 1.203); while the glass beads she wears on her wrists become Lucretia's bracelets "de preciosas perlas orientales (1978, 1.203). Moving back from the ur-ekphrasis to the dramatic ekphrasis, the narrator explains how "la moza forcejaba por desasirse y don Quijote trabajaba por tenella" (1978, 1.204). In the same manner, In Titian's canvas, Lucretia attempts to disengage herself from the threatening Sextus, pushing him away with one arm, while he holds on to her other arm. The approach of the *arriero*, who wishes to know what is transpiring, completes the ekphrasis of Titian's painting since the canvas shows a slave or servant as voyeur.

There is no need to recount here the many battles that ensue, where the knight is beaten over and over again and decides that the castle is haunted. What is of interest is the contrast between the two imagined princesses. While the first is in reality a lady of quality, the second is a servant and a prostitute; while the Basque lady is known for her voice, the Asturian servant is silent; and while the first is conceivably very beautiful, this second one has to be fully painted over by the knight. And yet, the two episodes have some things in common: the use of mnemonic techniques and contrasts; the importance of the ekphrastic to elevate the knight's adventures from the quotidian; and the presence of women from the periphery. While the Basque princess prays to religious images for the deliverance of her squire, Maritornes also shows her devotion. At the end of the events at the inn in Chapter Seventeen, Maritornes, seeing that Sancho has been tossed in a blanket over and over, decides to act: "La compasiva de Maritornes, viéndole tan fatigado, le pareció ser bien socorrelle con un jarro de agua, y así se lo trujo del pozo" (1978, 1.214). When Sancho asks for wine, she buys it for him from her own money. This charitable moment contrasts with Don Quixote, who either does not want or cannot intervene to save his squire as he is being tossed on a blanket for failing to pay for his and the knight's lodging at the inn.[19] While Sancho is often portrayed bouncing up into the air, to my knowledge there are no illustrations of Maritornes' charitable act. Although this event seems to have been forgotten, we can assert that the two princesses from the periphery show agency, goodness and devotion.

Although Maritornes will appear much later in the novel to extract her revenge for being forcibly kept on the knight's bed, it is time to end this essay, which has reviewed the importance of two women from the edges of Iberia, made into princesses by the knight's imaginings. In both instances as well as in the interlude with the Galician mares, it is the imperious and imperial knight who wishes to control the action, showing a combative nature. But the women from the periphery, each in their own way, counter the knight's aggression and ability to use a capacious and ekphrastic language, through counter-narratives that subtly or overtly point to his failures and their own triumphs. The Basque princess saves her squire and saves the novel with her prayers, her rhetoric and her fine Castilian; and the princess from Asturias, even though she is a prostitute, knows how to fight Don Quixote's advances, and knows the goodness of Sancho, showing him a kindness that no one else at the inn even considers. Both the Basque and the Asturian are women of power in their own realm. They challenge the knight's imperial and ekphrastic impetus through the fragmented, the untold and the unnarratable. Their tales are worthy of being told, as they begin a counter-narrative that can challenge our most beloved knight.

Notes

1 There is a controversy as to whether *ekphrasis* refers to a stop in a narrative to describe an art object or if it is a wider concept taken from ancient Greece: "a conception of the word as a force acting on the listener . . . words . . . to the ancient reader were alive with rich visual and emotional effects" (Webb 2009, 5).

2 He speaks of Preciosa in *La gitanilla*; Cornelia in *La señora Cornelia*; Auristela and Feliciana de la Voz in *Persiles y Sigismunda*; Dorotea, Luscinda, and Zoraida in *Don Quixote* I (1992, 105–106).

3 Although I am quoting from Murillo's 1978 edition, I have also consulted Francisco Rico's text and notes.

4 Her partially untold story does not fit into the unnarrated: it is neither too boring nor conventional, that is, "not worth narrating" (Prince 1988, 1–8); nor does it flaunt manners or literary convention and thus cannot be narrated (Prince 1987, 1–8).

5 Jill Syverson-Stork asserts: "The author has blocked his characters' movements as if they were performing on stage" (1986, 124).

6 On the *granada* see Eric Graf, who points to its many referents. For example: "The *granada* [pomegranate] at the beginning of Chapter 9 has two principal meanings, one geopolitical and the other moral. In the first case the *granada* refers to the kingdom of Granada . . . . [It] can still be seen today at the base of the Spanish coat-of-arms found in the center of the national flag" (2004, 44). In his

book, he argues that Botticelli's Madonna of the Pomegranate can be an "organizational device for Don Quijote" (2007, 115).

7 This small panel has also been attributed to Andrea del Verrocchio but today many think it is by Lorenzo di Credi. It is also called the *Dreyfus Madonna* because it was owned by Gustave Dreyfus from 1872 to 1930. It now hangs at the National Gallery.

8 Graf relates the pomegranate to a transcultural message: "The way to be free of the endless cycles of ethnic-religious violence is to affirm the Other (Zoraida) as the bearer of religious meaning (Mary), to learn to apply the antidote of a new and more ethnically diverse and tolerant Christian philosophy at the cites of cultural conflict"(54). But it is also a symbol of death and resurrection, the passion of Christ, Persephone's stay in the underworld because she ate seeds from the fruit.

9 Greg Baum (2013), pointing to the 1738 Carteret edition of the novel, shows how every illustration here appears at the *punto critico*. It is used here to supplement language in its inability to express certain things such as the movements of the soul. These illustrations also supplement the imagination and often foreground psychological complexity (Baum 2013).

10 Born in Azpeitia in 1491, Ignatius died in Rome in 1556. He was raised by the Castilian Juan Velázquez de Cuéllar, and often traveled with him to the Court at Valladolid. In 1521 he fights with the Castilian army in Pamplona against the French and Navarre forces who want to liberate the area.

11 The inspiration of the Virgin in composing the "Exercises" at Manresa is not based on any written testimony but upon a revelation made in 1600 to Marina de Escobar as told in the Life of *Father Balthazar Alvarez.*

12 Gerli compares his speech to that of Don Quixote: "Don Quijote's bombast is, as well parried by the near-unintelligible gibberish of the Biscayan . . . a veritable babble of knight-speak and nonsense" (1995, 65). On the Basque who speaks garbled Castilian in the literature of the Golden Age see Carmoná Tierno and the joint essay by Castillo Martínez and Ramírez Luengo (2008). Carmoná describes the break in the syntactic order as: "caos morfosintáctico del español . . . . Se quebrantan casi todas las normas de dicción castellanas, hasta el punto de que se hace necesario un intérprete para comprender lo que ha dicho el personaje" (2013, 344). This kind of speech appears for the first time in the *Tinelaria* (1517) by Torres Naharro.

13 Ross Chambers in *Loiterature* calls digressions a counter-narrative. Indeed, the partially missing tale may have to do with questions of identity, as Samuel Frederick (2012) states: "If plot is that which affirms its identity by appropriating difference [i.e., digression] then digression is that which affirms difference by repudiating that identity" (4). The gaps in the princess's tale allows for the creation of a counter-narrative and for the creation of a new identity in character and plot that has the potential of rivaling the main story.

14 Joaquín Casalduero was one of the first critics to point to this contrast and to also relate it to the ensuing episode with Maritornes: "el episodio de *Rocinante* y las jacas es una deformación burlesca de la pastoril y prepara la parodia del amor caballeresco," (1970, 97).

15 He even cites the *Búho Gallego* attributed to Cervantes' patrón, the Conde de Lemos. On Cervantes' Galician patron see also Casás Fernández 1949; and on Don Quixote and Galicia see Presado Garazo (2006) and Saavedra Pegerto (2005).

16 Curiously, this interlude may have as its model a passage in Apuleius's *Golden Ass*, which thus adds a sense of authority to the comic scene. See Prjevalisnky Ferrer (1948).

17 "it is also the case that rabbits and hares are standard symbols of lechery" (McGrady 1987, 7).

18 I will be brief in recounting the parallels between painting and action since I have already referred to this on two occasions (De Armas 2004, 2006, 186–187).

19 Carolyn Nadeau has stressed Maritornes' inner beauty and virtue, pointing out that outer beauty does not always accompany virtue (2007, 205–213). Although she recognizes Maritornes' double nature, she points to Casalduero: "De la misma manera que la cultura Antigua concibió de una raíz única dos Venus, la cultura cristiana le ha dado a la caridad también dos fases: la iluminada con la luz de la gracia y la que florece en medio de las ruinas humanas. Maritornes, que marcha en la oscuridad como ciega para satisfacer al arriero, al aire libre siente piedad por Sancho" (1971, 98).

Works cited

Avalle-Arce, Juan Bautista. 1973. "*Don Quijote.*" In *Suma cervantina*, edited by J. B. Avalle-Arce, Juan Bautista, and E. C. Riley, 47–80. London: Tamesis.

Barkan, Leonard. 2013. *Mute Poetry, Speaking Pictures*. Princeton, NJ: Princeton University Press.

Barroso Cabrera, Rafael and Jorge Morín de Pablos. 2009. "A propósito de un descuido cervantino: la alternancia yangüeses/Gallegos en el *Quijote*." *Cervantes* 29 (1): 221–229.

Baum, Greg. 2013. "'Mine though Abortive': Reading and Writing *Don Quixote* in Seventeenth-Century England." PhD diss., University of Chicago.

Carmona Tierno, Juan Manuel. 2013. "Las hablas de minorías en el teatro del Siglo de Oro: Recursos de comicidad." *Teatro de Palabras: Revista sobre Teatro Áureo* 7: 335–355.

Casalduero, Joaquín. 1970. *Sentido y forma del "Quijote."* Madrid: Ínsula.

Casás Fernández, Manuel. 1949. *Cervantes y Galicia: El Conde de Lemos, ilustre gallego, mecenas del inmortal autor del Quijote*. Madrid: Talleres Tipográficos AF.

Castillo Martínez, Cristina and José L. Ramírez Luengo, 2008. "La caracterización lingüística de los vascos en la literatura: habla vizcaína frente a habla aldeana." *Oihenart. Cuadernos de lengua y literatura* 23: 35–44.

Cervantes, Miguel de. 1978. *El ingenioso hidalgo don Quijote de la Mancha*. Edited by Luis Andrés Murillo. 2 vols. Madrid: Castalia.

———. 1999. *Don Quijote de la Mancha*. Edited by Francisco Rico. 3rd ed. 2 vols. Barcelona: Crítica.

Chaffee-Sorace, Diane. 1989. "Ekphrastic and Theatrical Interior Duplication: Irony and Verisimilitude in Don Quijote's Adventure with the Basque." *Romanische Forschungen* 101 (2): 208–220.

Chambers, Ross. 1999. *Loiterature*. Lincoln, NE: University of Nebraska Press.

Conrod, Frédéric. 2008. *Loyola's Greater Narrative: The Architecture of the Spiritual Exercises in Golden Age and Enlightenment Literature*. New York: Peter Lang.

Cull, John T. 1990. "The 'Knight of the Broken Lance' and His 'Trusty Steed': On Don Quixote and Rocinante." *Cervantes* 10 (2): 37–53.

Davidson, Philip. 2012. "Don Quijote de Loyola: sus asociaciones por lectores a lo largo del tiempo." *Cuadernos de Aleph* 4: 47–74.

de Armas, Frederick A. 2004. "Pinturas de Lucrecia en el *Quijote*: Ticiano, Rafael y Lope de Vega." *Anuario de Estudios Cervantinos* 1: 109–120.

———. 2006. *Quixotic Frescoes: Cervantes and Italian Renaissance Art*. Toronto: University of Toronto Press.

de Armas Wilson, Diana. 2000. *Cervantes, the Novel and the New World*. Oxford: Oxford University Press.

———. 2007. "Chivalry to the Rescue: The Dynamics of Liberation in *Don Quijote*." *Cervantes* 27 (1): 249–265.

Della Porta, Giovan Battista. 2012. *The Art of Remembering / L'arte del ricordare*, edited by Armando Maggi. Ravenna: Longo Editore.

Fox, Soledad. 2010. *Flaubert and Don Quijote: The Influence of Cervantes on Madame Bovary*. Sussex: Sussex Academic Press.

Frederick, Samuel. 2012. *Narrative Unsettled. Digression in Robert Walser, Thomas Bernhard and Adalbert Stifter*. Evanston, IL: Northwestern University Press.

Gerli, Michael. 1995. *Refiguring Authority. Reading, Writing and Rewriting in Cervantes*. Lexington, KY: University of Kentucky Press.

González Echevarría, Roberto. 2005. *Love and the Law in Cervantes*. New Haven, CT: Yale University Press.

Graf, Eric C. 2004. "The Pommegranate in Don Quixote 1.9." In *Writing for the Eyes in the Spanish Golden Age*, edited by Frederick A. de Armas, 42–62. Lewisburg, PA: Bucknell University Press.

———. 2007. *Cervantes and Modernity: Four Essays on Don Quijote*. Lewisburg, PA: Bucknell University Press.

Hutchinson, Steven. 1992. *Cervantine Journeys*. Madison, WI: The University of Wisconsin Press.

Javitch, Daniel. 1980. "Cantus Interruptus in the *Orlando Furioso*." *Modern Language Notes* 95: 66–80.

Krieger, Murray. 1992. *Ekphrasis. The Illusion of the Natural Sign*. Baltimore, MD: Johns Hopkins University Press.

Leahy, Chad. 2008. "Lascivas o esquivas? La identidad geográfica y sexual de las yeguas gallegas en Don Quijote (I.15)." *Cervantes* 28 (2): 89–118.

Lerner, Isaías. 1998. "Entre Cervantes y Ercilla: *Quijote* I, 8–9." In *El comentario de textos*, edited by Inés Carrasco and Guadalupe Fernández Arriza, 207–220. Málaga: Analecta Malacitana.

McGrady, Donald. 1987. "The Italian Origins of the Episode of Don Quijote and Maritornes." *Cervantes: Bulletin of the Cervantes Society of America* 7 (1): 3–12.

Mendeloff, Henry. 1975. "The Maritornes Episode: A Cervantine Bedroom Farce." *Romance Notes* 16: 753–759.

Nadeau, Carolyn. 2002. *Women of the Prologue: Imitation, Myth and Magic in Don Quixote I.* Lewisburg, PA: Bucknell University Press.

———. 2007. "Maritornes: algo más que la prostituta de la venta." In *Actas I Congeso Internacional El Quijote en clave de Mujer/es*, Valdepeñas, Spain, 2005, edited by Fanny Rubio, 205–213. Toledo: Empresa Pública Don Quijote de la Mancha.

Ortiz-Hernán Pupareli, Elami. 2009/10. "Los mil rostros del amor en *Cristalián de España* frente a otros libros de caballerías hispánicos." In *Caballerías*, edited by Lilian von der Walde Moheno and Mariel Reinoso. *Destiempos* 4.1 (23): 298–328.

———. 2003. "Hacia una tipología de los personajes femeninos en los libros de caballerías hispánicos." *Tirant*. Accessed November 21, 2015. http://parnaseo.uv.es/tirant/butlleti.6/art.resena.elami.htm.

Presado Garazo, Antonio. 2006. "Los ingeniosos hidalgos gallegos en la época de Alonso Quijano." In *El tapiz humanista. Actas del I curso de primavera IV centenario del Quijote*, edited by Ana Goy Diz and Cristina Patiño Eirín, 229–250. Santiago de Compostela: Universidade de Santiago de Compostela.

Prince, Gerald. 1987. *A Dictionary of Narratology*. Lincoln, NE: University of Nebraska Press.

———. 1988. "The Disnarrated." *Style* 22: 1–8.

Prjevalisnky Ferrer, Olga. 1948. "Del *Asno de Oro* a 'Rocinante': Contribución al estudio del Quijote." *Cuadernos de literatura* 3: 247–257.

Refini, Eugenio. 2012. "Longinus and the Poetic Imagination in Late Renaissance Literary Theory." In *Translations of the Sublime: The Early Modern Reception and Dissemination of Longinus Peri Hupsous in Rhetoric, the Visual Arts, Architecture and the Theatre*, edited by Caroline van Eck, Stijn Bussels, Maarten Delbeke, and Jurgen Pieters, 33–54. Leiden: Brill.

Saavedra, Pegerto. 2005. "Galicia nos tempos de *El Quijote*." In *IV Memorial Filgueiro Valverde no IV centenario de El Quijote*, 27–86. Pontevedra: Publicacións da Cátedra Filgueira Valverde.

Spitzer, Leo. 1962. "The 'Ode on a Grecian Urn,' or Content vs. Metagrammar." In *Essays on English and American Literature*, edited by Anna Hatcher, 67–97. Princeton, NJ: Princeton University Press.

Syverson-Stork, Jill. 1986. *Theatrical Aspects of the Novel: A Study of Don Quixote*. Madrid: Albatross.

Webb, Ruth. 2009. *Ekphrasis, Imagination and Persuasion in Ancient Rhetorical Theory and Practice*. Burlington, VT: Ashgate.

Whitenack, Judith. 1993. "Don Quixote and the Romances of Chivalry once Again: Converted *Paganos* and Enamoured *Magas*." *Cervantes: Bulletin of the Cervantes Society of America* 13: 61–91.

Worman, Nancy. 2002. *The Cast of Character: Style in Greek Literature*. Austin, TX: The University of Texas Press.

18

"PARA TIEMPOS DE VERAS / SE EJERCITAN EN LAS BURLAS"

Some uses of rehearsal on the Golden Age stage

Jonathan Thacker

Studying a part and rehearsing it within the *compañía* was an established element of the actor's daily life from the late sixteenth century in Spain. The practices of rehearsal must have developed as the troupes became more professional in a period which saw the establishment and rapid growth in popularity of the permanent theatres in Madrid and other towns and cities. The nature of play rehearsals – what went on in the *autor de comedias*'s house every morning from nine o'clock – may be difficult to establish with confidence and would not have accorded at all closely with today's rehearsal-room norms, but the importance of practice to enhance performance was recognised generally.[1] Thus, the *labrador* in Calderón's *auto sacramental*, *El gran teatro del mundo* (mid-1630s), plaintively echoes his fellow characters in objecting to the *autor*'s denial of rehearsal time to them as they take to the stage of life:

> Aun una comedia vieja
> harta de representar
> si no se vuelve a ensayar
> se yerra cuando se prueba.
> Si no se ensaya esta nueva,
> ¿cómo se podrá acertar?
> (Calderón de la Barca 1985, lines 453–58)

If even an old play from the repertoire requires practice, a new one will certainly fall flat without study and rehearsal time.[2] However, the *autor* (or God) who "directs" the play of life within this Corpus Christi play, advises His creations that the prompt-book, or *apunto* (line 478), will be His law which is to provide guidance in the extempore role-playing of life. Though the central allegory is somewhat strained by the lack of a chance to practise before performance, the *autor*'s point is overtly didactic and within Catholic theological norms: one's audience is God, the title of the play is unchanging and one's role is simple and uniform.

Beyond the conservatism of the seasonal *auto sacramental*, in a period when social roles were changing more rapidly than they had done before and individuals could countenance re-fashioning – to borrow Stephen Greenblatt's seductive term – and bettering themselves, the idea of rehearsing a role, a notion taken from the world of the popular theatre, was a serious one with far-reaching implications.[3] In their secular works for the Golden Age stage, dramatists are seen to concentrate metatheatrically on the *practising* of theatre, rather than making use of the fully-fledged play-within-the-play, the final rehearsed performance. This probably explains the hitherto unremarked fact that cases of on-stage rehearsal of plays and roles in the drama of the period are more common than examples of the play-within-the-play, a metatheatrical phenomenon which has more limited possibilities and functions.[4] Indeed, these rehearsals frequently constitute pivotal moments in the plays in which they occur, jolting and challenging the audience members through the momentary breaking of the dramatic illusion, and demanding that they reflect on their use and the scene's implications. They provide or open up possibilities for the interpretation of the works in question and reflect, I shall argue, the broader concerns of the period as a whole.

The plays to be considered here display the variety of uses of rehearsal which emerged in the *comedia nueva* as it matured during the opening decades of the seventeenth century. In Antonio Mira de Amescua's *El ejemplo mayor de la desdicha* (c. 1625), the text of a play being rehearsed principally by the court ladies, allows for characters to express themselves freely – to escape social niceties – using the dramatist's words as a code. In Agustín Moreto and Jerónimo Cáncer's *Nuestra señora de la Aurora* (c. 1650), the lines of a play being rehearsed in a rural setting permit a peasant woman to escape an undeserved slur on her honour. In Tirso de Molina's *El vergonzoso en palacio* (c. 1621), in a much-admired scene, rehearsal allows for the freedom of self-expression normally denied to the noblewoman, and something similar occurs in the same playwright's *El Aquiles* (c. 1626). In Felipe Godínez's *La cautela en la amistad* (c. 1635), the rehearsal of a ceremony creates a space in which real feelings can be made known.[5] In Lope de Vega's *El castigo sin venganza* (1631), the overhearing of a rehearsal introduces a central theme of the tragedy, the anxiety surrounding performance in elevated social roles. And the importance of rehearsal is fundamental, in complementary ways, to the whole conception of life in Lope's *Lo fingido verdadero* (c. 1608) and Cervantes's *Pedro de Urdemalas* (c. 1615). The definition of *ensayo* is stretched in two of these plays (Godínez's *La cautela en la amistad* and Tirso's *El Aquiles*, in which the rehearsals are of a wedding and a courtship respectively) but this elasticity is justified by the emphasis characters in them place on their status as rehearsals, not least in their repeated recourse to the term "ensayar" and its cognates.

Given what I intend to suggest in my analysis of rehearsal scenes in the *comedia*, it is important to bear in mind that this term "ensayar" possesses in Spanish a breadth of association that the English "rehearse" (whose origins relate it to repetition and whose meaning is now more restricted to its theatrical sense) does not.[6] Covarrubias, in his 1611 dictionary, explains that "vale hacer prueba" (2006, 789) and the third volume of the *Diccionario de Autoridades*, published in 1732, defines the verb as "examinar, reconocer, hacer prueba y experiencia de alguna cosa" (2014). Testing and trying out is often implicit in its meaning and modern Spanish dictionaries do not prioritise the theatrical sense of "ensayar" either. The rehearsals in the plays mentioned provide testing-grounds of distinct sorts for characters: they are not in general simple, potentially dull exercises in learning lines (*estudiar*) or merely repeating what is written on the *papel de actor*, but are privileged scenes in which characters evolve, plot develops and discoveries are made in a heightened atmosphere.

The rehearsal scene in Mira de Amescua's *El ejemplo mayor de la desdicha* constitutes a good example of how a play practice can be integrated into the main plot allowing the playwright to create a chance for self-expression which would normally be denied the characters in the performance of their social roles. Teodora, the empress of Constantinople, has decided to entertain the emperor on his birthday with a "comedia" performed by the palace "damas" (Mira de Amescua 2001, line 1000). The performance is partly to take his mind off the absence of his favoured general, Belisario, for whom he feels an excessive affection. Teodora, as it happens, has been trying to have Belisario killed, though the latter, who foils the attempts on his life, is unaware of who exactly his enemy is at court before the rehearsal scene starts. The play to be practised is "Píramo y Tisbe" (line 1035), and Belisario's unexpected return from war means that he can be asked to help out by playing the part of Pyramus, a fortuitous turn of events as he is secretly in love with Antonia, who is playing Thisbe.

Belisario is delighted at the chance to hear Antonia speaking loving words to him even if perhaps "fingidos" (line 1338). The rehearsal allows their love affair to develop as they realise that their feelings are mutual and that they can, paradoxically, speak openly to each other through another's words (line 1374). Belisario is able to establish that Antonia is not his enemy and, although he slips in and out of the part (calling Tisbe "Antonia" on one occasion), their role-play, part extempore in fact, but part scripted, is enough to cement their relationship. Antonia, using the code of the rehearsal lines and the well-known elements of the story, is even able to warn Belisario that Teodora is the "lion" trying to ruin their relationship but that she will die happy if she knows that they are in love. A lady-in-waiting, in on the act, warns Antonia that "tu madre está escuchando" (line 1478). The "madre" is of course the suspicious empress, who is reassured that this loving conversation is all part of the Pyramus and Thisbe play rehearsal. However, Teodora eventually senses that reality and fiction are becoming dangerously blurred and loses her temper, ripping up the play-text and promising that she will indeed be a lion to be feared. Floro, the *gracioso*, is moved to intone: "La comedia se acabó. / Perdón, ilustre senado" (lines 1493–94), comically breaking the tension that has built up during the rehearsal.[7]

The rehearsal scene, in this first case, provides some comic relief and vicarious pleasure at the evil empress being outwitted, and also develops the plot of the play. The lines written for another play by an anonymous playwright can be abused and added to cleverly to match the characters' needs. Suspicion is in part averted because characters can deny that what they are saying is an expression of their own feelings. This *modus operandi* can be seen as an example of Lope de Vega's "hablar equívoco" (Vega 2006, line 323), a recourse for the successful playwright and a way for a character to express him- or herself in a potentially hostile social environment.[8] At the same time, Belisario's naivety, which will cost him his life, is evident in the scene and the choice of play forewarns the audience of the tragic outcome. The rehearsal here is much better suited to the playwright's intentions than a play-within-the-play would have been. It allows for more nuance and subtlety in plot and characterisation.

In Moreto and Cáncer's co-written work, *Nuestra señora de la aurora*, rehearsal functions slightly differently, though its use might still be said to follow Lope's recommendation. A group of villagers rehearse a work intended to celebrate the creation of a new image of the Virgin by the village's *cofradía*. The play being prepared is a version of *El robo de Elena*, another classical story, whose title is chosen to shed ironic light on the plot of the frame play. A local nobleman, Don Diego, smitten by the peasant girl, Madalena, who has repeatedly rejected him, bribes another villager with a ring to allow him to see the rehearsal they are about to begin. Madalena's beloved, Manuel, is the peasant director and lead actor who takes the part of Menelaus to Madalena's Helen.

On this occasion it is not the lovers who use the play's lines, as one might have expected, to communicate secretly or even enjoy an illicit intimacy (as the *autor* Ginés does with his *primera dama* in Lope's *Lo fingido verdadero*). The "robo" in question is actually attempted by Don Diego during the rehearsal and a frightened Madalena, shouts out from off-stage as he tries to abduct her. Rather than reacting as a jealous lover, Manuel is frustrated that she is speaking her lines too early in the piece. However, when Madalena's father, Juan, suspecting that something is afoot, goes after her, she is able to hide Don Diego away to save everyone's blushes (and her own honour of course), claiming that she was just acting. Her quick-wittedness helps avoid a real crisis in the lovers' relationship and the amateur nature of the production is even adduced by her father to explain the way events have unfolded:

Manuel: ¿Pues quién aquí dentro estaba?
Juan: ¿No veis que representaba?
Madalena: Este es un paso que tiene
              mi papel.
Juan: Pues ¿de qué indicio
              se asustan, quiero saber?
              Miren lo que hace el no ser
              representantes de oficio.
                         (Moreto and Cáncer 2014)

As is the case with Mira's tragedy, the lines of the rehearsed play can possess a double meaning: they are fictional yet real. The rehearsal has allowed breathing space in a situation that was approaching a crisis, averting the sort of destructive conflict that society's strict codes might necessitate. In this case it is the freedom to err which rehearsal permits that provides the possibility of escape. Again, this would be harder to carry off if the scene involved a polished performance of the play.

One of the better-known rehearsal scenes in Golden Age drama occurs in act 2 of Tirso de Molina's *El vergonzoso en palacio*, and here too the practice allows a temporary freedom which normal social role-play would not permit. In this play the scene is prepared for when noblewoman Juana explains to her cousin, Antonio, that her mistress, Serafina, is not interested in love but in:

estudiar con sus doncellas
una comedia, que por ser mañana
Carnestolendas, a su hermana intenta
representar, sin que lo sepa el duque
[. . .] y esta tarde
conmigo sola en el jardín pretende
ensayar el papel, vestida de hombre.
            (Tirso de Molina 1989b, lines 473–76 and 478–80)

It is Carnival time then, when the world can be turned upside-down: the play is illicit, performed by an all-female cast and organised without parental permission, and Serafina will be dressed in male attire. In terms of its dramatic function the rehearsal gives Antonio the chance to have Serafina's portrait painted from a secluded position.

Serafina begins by convincing Juana of the merits of the theatre (lines 749–84). Her oft-anthologised speech, like that of the duke of Ferrara in *El castigo sin venganza*, encourages the audience to begin to consider the effect of theatre on real life in terms of its straight didactic function – being a mirror – but also in terms of the proximity of conscious play-acting and normally unconscious social acting. She defends her playing by saying that the audience will be only her sister, Magdalena, and her ladies. Nevertheless, Serafina wants to look right – she does not want her hair to fall down, like a lady's will, when she removes her hat – and she is dressed as a man even for the run-through: "Ensayemos el papel, / pues ya estoy vestida de hombre" (lines 843–44).

Serafina's play is a "farsa" called *La portuguesa cruel* and, rather than playing the lead, she chooses to play a "príncipe" who goes out into the country to fight a "conde" over the eponymous woman. Never having been in love, she does not know what jealousy is, but performs her speech so vividly that Juana fears for her life (lines 896–97); then she plays a tender scene with her lover, and Juana asks her, "¿es posible que quien siente / y hace así un enamorado / no tenga amor?" (lines 947–49). Finally she plays the same man, "loco," a complicated part in which she has to master several voices, strike herself, and attack a congregation.[9] Again her performance is a bravura one in which, crucially, she loses or forgets herself.

In terms of its structural function, the scene needs to provide a chance for a portrait of Serafina to be sketched by a painter: later she will find the portrait and fall in love with the mystery man in it. Yet the artist admits to having finished his work before the real rehearsal has even begun (lines 835–36). This is not mere comic relief either and so the scene is, strictly speaking, excessive, and might thus be seen to constitute a metatheatrical riff by a self-indulgent playwright and a chance for an actress to display her talents. However, the concentration on the rehearsal is more than that: within Serafina's praise of the theatre's ability to entertain and instruct, she asks "el ignorante, ¿no sabe?" (line 763), implying that the theatre can open one's eyes to things that one does not know, that one can learn from performance. In Serafina's case this awakening is to another side of her character, a part of her that she has been unable to express in her closeted life as a duke's daughter, as Jeremy Robbins has argued: "However categorized, it is clear that her [Serafina's] sense of self is markedly at odds with all social and sexual expectations of what was deemed normal for a woman" (1998, 129). Instinctively she expresses passion, freed from the confines of her sex's usual comportment, to the extent, as we have noted, that she loses herself and seems to *become* the passionate prince. This sudden alteration is permitted by the excuse of the *ensayo* but it will live on beyond the rehearsal, the (unseen) play-within-a-play and even the conventional end to the main play, as Galoppe suggests (2001, 202). Serafina's manliness does not put off Antonio who, from the bushes, admires her "donaire y gracia" (line 1045) even more than he did before, and it is no doubt a mistake, as Robbins also argues (129), to over-read the scene as demonstrating that she has latent masculine or lesbian desires. Serafina's wish to maintain her new dress, "quiero / vestirme sobre este traje / el mío, hasta que sea tiempo / de representar" (lines 1050–53), is a sign that she is keen to maintain something of this new sense of self, the freedom of expression she has discovered and that came with the role played, not that she actually wants to be a man. The scene contributes directly to the theme of a play that charts the "vergonzoso," Mireno's realisation of his proper place in the world and which contains Tirso's fine sonnet, sparked by the hero's change in clothes (lines 660–73).

For Robbins too, Serafina's 'performance' (128) is one example of Tirso's overall purpose in his work: "The exploration and adoption of other identities, and the possibilities this offers of allowing the expression of personal desires and aspirations otherwise forbidden by gender or class, is the driving force behind the entire play" (129). I would add, focusing on the scene's status as a rehearsal-within-a-play, rather than a play-within-a-play, that Tirso demonstrates that *rehearsal* is important for life because it allows an individual to discover something about herself without immediate consequences in the "real world." The audience members do not see the planned play performed but that is because the rehearsal, the trying out, is more important for their grasp of the character of Serafina, and perhaps all of us. Tirso's understanding of the possibilities of the individual is a characteristically sensitive and modern one. He is often sympathetic to those who have not found their part in life and frequently allows his characters to thrive and express themselves in disguise or through pretence. Of course, the rehearsal is to the play – as Serafina's paean to theatre indicates – , what the play, *El vergonzoso en palacio* or the *comedia nueva* in general, is to life beyond the theatre. The "sabios" (line 782) and the "discretos" (line 785), mentioned by Serafina and Juana, enjoy seeing plays for what they can learn from them about themselves and others. It might be said then that rehearsals are important in the *comedia* because the *comedia* itself functions, in part at least – and as good theatre should – as a sort of vicarious rehearsal, a testing ground, for the spectator's life, a safe space for practice.

This idea recurs but more overtly in another work by Tirso, *El Aquiles*. The rehearsal scene in act 2 of this play is not of a pre-existing dramatic work in fact, since Aquiles (dressed as a woman) asks Deidamia to practise an unscripted courtship scene with him: "Finge que mi dama eres / y yo tu galán" (Tirso de Molina 1989a, 983a), he urges her, metatheatrically. Even without a script individuals know the outlines of their roles in certain common situations, having heard, read or experienced them before. Aquiles sketches the reasons behind his desire:

> De esta manera
> se entretienen las mujeres
> cuando apetecen casarse,
> engañando el gusto así
> unas con otras; yo vi
> muchas damas ensayarse
> cuando niñas, que amor ciego
> travesea a todas horas.
> "Los señores y señoras"
> llaman los niños a un juego
> en que contentos imitan
> lo que a sus padres oyeron
> y en materia de amor vieron,
> con que después facilitan
> dificultades mayores
> que trae consigo el recato.
> (983a)

Interesting here is the protagonist's emphasis on rehearsal as a natural (here, female) practice beneficial in that it prepares the individual to overcome a potential problem, to ensure that future difficulties are avoided. As the leader-in-waiting, Ciro, explains while training his make shift peasant army, in Lope de Vega's *Contra valor no hay desdicha* (c. 1625–35), "Para tiempos de veras / se ejercitan en las burlas" (Vega 1857, lines 759–60).

The Aquiles-Deidamia scene, presented as a rehearsal/practice for real courtship (she is betrothed to another man, Lisandro), lasts until the end of the act. Aquiles asks whether he is being a good "galán." When Deidamia replies that "she" does in fact look like a *man* she recently fell in love with, he replies:

> Pues siendo así,
> saldrá la fiesta más propia.
> Veamos cómo se ensaya
> nuestro amor y mi ventura.
> (Tirso de Molina 1989a, 983a)

Aquiles "hace que sale del vestuario" in the stage direction (983b) and has to repeat his extemporised lines as she asks him to give himself a name before the practice proper begins. When Aquiles gets over-excited, and kisses her hand, she calms him, "Paso, prima, que parece / que va esto de veras" (984b). He has become the role he is playing, rather like Amón in a similar scene, though without the heavy stress on the idea of rehearsal, in Tirso's *La venganza de Tamar* (1621–24). Deidamia calls an end to the game and he asks her to watch him play the jealous lover: "hace que vuelve a salir" (985a). Aquiles, after delivering the jealous speech, this time in his female disguise of Nereida, goes off and appears in the *vestuario* as a man (987a). They declare their eternal love for one another. Thus Aquiles has used the "act" to jog Deidamia's memory and rekindle her love for him, first experienced when out hunting in act 1, and then surprise her with his real identity. This rehearsal is a means of expressing pent-up or repressed emotions and unblocking their flow, where a simple declaration by Aquiles/Nereida to Deidamia would certainly fail. It proves the value of an equivocal approach.

Godínez's *La cautela en la amistad* also contains an intriguing rehearsal of a ceremony, with a similar purpose. In act 2, the duquesa de Milán invites the relatively lowly Carlos Colonna to pretend to be her husband ostensibly so that she can play her role adequately on the day of her wedding to the royal Enrique. What seems to be a suggestive request becomes more highly-charged still when she encourages him to act so that it seems to be real, "no tan fingido, / que no parezca de veras" (Godínez 2014). The main interest of this play is the stress put on the likelihood of something practised, rehearsed, fictional in nature, becoming the truth. In act 3, as she tries to persuade Carlos to marry her for real, and faced with his hesitancy, the duchess makes clear to him what her earlier strategy was:

> Ea, que ya no te ensayas
> para ser el desposado,
> y si esto acaso es venganza
> de aquellas burlas, advierte
> que eran veras ensayadas.

It is the scene prior to this in act 2, however, which allows a more leisurely reflection on the status of the rehearsal. In a speech reminiscent of Aquiles's in Tirso's play, the *duquesa* suggests the idea of rehearsing to Carlos to assuage his melancholy thus:

> vos estáis triste y yo quiero
> divertiros por si acaso,
> como imagino, me caso.
> ¿Sabéis lo que considero,
> que en aquel lance primero
> de la esposa y del esposo,
> suele el menos vergonzoso
> turbarse, recién venido,
> y faltarle lo entendido
> o, por lo menos, lo airoso?
> Pues yo quisiera excusar
> aquel desaire en mis bodas
> en que al fin todos y todas
> suelen comúnmente errar,
> y quizá debe de estar
> en no pensarlo el error.
> ¡Qué invencionero es amor!
> El cuerdo que se previene
> en lo que hace y dice tiene
> más destreza y más primor.

El ensayo facilita
toda acción: decirle espero,
si quiera así, que le quiero.
Vaya la primer visita:
vos sois quien el novio imita
y yo vuestra esposa bella.
Fingid, pues, que entráis a verla.

Typically, the *gracioso*, Gandalín, understands the duchess's subtext and, faced with an uncertain master, astutely advises him:

Calla, y déjate engañar
que, pues lo quiere ensayar
agora con tal cuidado,
cuando lo tenga ensayado,
lo querrá representar.

The rehearsal itself is a characteristically ambivalent scene in which the duchess at times admits that she is not taking on her character – "pero vamos al ensayo, / que esto ha sido fuera dél" – , and advises Carlos to inhabit his own, "hablad sin miedo, ensayad / de modo que transforméis / en ese papel que hacéis." He does so to the extent of kissing her hand. His excuse is at the ready: "Agravio en besarla os hice; / pues perdonad, que lo dice /de esa manera el papel." (Unlike in Mira's *El ejemplo mayor de la desdicha* there is in fact no written role to be followed in this scene.) Towards the end of the encounter, and in forgiving him his indiscretion, the duchess is moved to introduce explicitly the *theatrum mundi* commonplace:

Corrido sin duda estáis,
aunque veis que todo ha sido
disimulado y fingido;
pero ya no os ensayáis
y aunque en la comedia hagáis,
como es lo más ordinario,
cada día un papel vario,
sabed que vuelve después
cada uno a ser quien es,
volviéndose al vestuario.

It is a metaphor that will simultaneously keep Carlos at arm's length *and* give him hope. He has demonstrated to her satisfaction that he can play the part of a "gran señor" – she has tested him through the rehearsal – and yet he must return to his usual social role ("quien es") once the scene is over. The rehearsal creates a safe space in which to try out words one would like to employ and actions one would like to perform. It is no surprise really that characters compare rehearsals to children's games or to education and it has a sound pedigree in Aristotle's assertion that man is the most imitative of creatures and learns by imitation.

The rehearsal that the duke, Ricardo and Febo come across during an evening on the streets of Ferrara in Lope's *El castigo sin venganza* has some parallels with the scene we have analysed in Tirso's *El vergonzoso en palacio*, though it is much briefer in duration (at just nine lines of rehearsal text). Here the duke is out at night looking for amorous adventure and entertainment when he and his men hear singing and arrive at the house of an "autor / de comedias" (Vega

2009, lines 178–79). The duke establishes that they are rehearsing (line 194) and listens in to Andrelina (thought to be the Italian actress and poet, Isabel Andreini) whose acting he admires.

The point of this scene is to show that the duke is affected by the theatre: the actual words, heard off-stage in this case, refer to a glorious past turning into a tragic present, "mi pasada gloria / conviertes en tormento" (lines 199–200). They are indeed "discursos tristes para alegres horas" (line 205) as the actress complains from within her apparently tragic role (about which we learn nothing more). This snatch of monologue apparently reminds the duke of his own situation – the imminent life-changing marriage to Casandra and the end to his immoral life of pleasure that should entail. He is suddenly "sin gusto" (line 208). We know that the acting in the rehearsal affects him because, as we see also with the Roman emperor in the same playwright's *Lo fingido verdadero*, it sparks a rumination on the relationship of acting to life and in particular the role of theatre as a teacher: the duke goes on to say that he has had one lesson from a "primera dama" that evening (Cintia, who has shut her window on him earlier in the act) and does not want to listen to more drama that will prick his conscience. The scene helps characterise the duke: he knows what he is doing wrong but does not have the strength of character to change, and becomes immediately melancholic. The fact that the intelligent duke sees parallels between life and theatre and finds a lesson to learn (line 173) in the rehearsal, but does not then profit from it, helps the audience to make up its mind about the moral lessons of the play. For Lope then, the rehearsal text, so convincingly performed, constitutes a clear warning for the future reality of not just a man but a man responsible for a realm. The fact that we overhear a *rehearsal* rather than a play in this case is verisimilar but probably not so important, although, with the next day's ceremonies so close, there could be an implied negative comment on the duke's own lack of preparation for his new role. Is this how he rehearses for the next day's formal entry?

Acting and the *theatrum mundi* topos are central concerns of Lope's *Lo fingido verdadero* as well. The histrionic themes of this saints play have been well documented, though in fact it does not contain such clear-cut rehearsal scenes as *El vergonzoso en palacio* or *El castigo sin venganza*. In act 1, the emperor Carino stalks the Roman streets looking for adventure, much like the duke of Ferrara. Unlike the duke, Carino is a simple character, a fool who rejects the comparison of life to a play until he is able to comfort himself that he is all but immortal, whilst an actor, such as Ginés, can only be a king for an hour and a half (Vega 1964, 63a). His sudden and dramatic death is a clear comment on his over-confidence and immoral ways.

In act 3, a rehearsal of sorts is set up by the new emperor, Diocleciano. The future patron-saint of actors, Ginés, alone, rehearses playing a Christian in a soliloquy as his troupe, off-stage, attempts to re-kindle the old play at the emperor's command. In his practice he uses his knowledge of what Christians do when praying and sits down as if "en un gran tormento" (95b), and then he mimics abusing the emperor as if he were there (commenting, at the same time, on how he's performing the role). He next turns his attention to the heavens, begging the saints to intercede and Christ to baptise him. The heavens do open and he hears a voice which he thinks, momentarily, must have come from one of the cast. Once the play starts and Ginés again goes off the page, the "soldado" (in character) complains: "El fin de este paso dudo; / que no se ensayaba así" (100a) and the other actors continue to be confused calling for prompts and eventually angering the emperor for not knowing their lines.

These scenes in Lope's *Lo fingido verdadero* emphasise the notion that underpins the rehearsal-within-the-play occurring elsewhere in Golden Age drama, that the words spoken in practice – privileged as they seem to be – contain a not immediately evident truth which has implications for the lives of the characters that speak or hear them. There are at least two interesting features in this particular case. First, there is the specifically religious aspect to Ginés's experience. By allowing himself to be subsumed into the role, Ginés is able to be heard in heaven and a divine voice replies to him. Like Serafina in *El vergonzoso en palacio*,

Ginés becomes in rehearsal the part that he is trying to play and to his own ultimate advantage. Whereas for the former, there is something to learn about her own self or identity from her instinctive desire to play, for Ginés the performance leads to conversion to Christianity, a higher truth still which takes the idea of rehearsing a performance into fresh territory. Rehearsal here unblocks a new route towards a sort of personal liberation which (in the only saints play discussed here) chimes with contemporary theology. The second aspect is that in this work, uniquely amongst the play-texts studied here, we see the rehearsal, its effect on the play-within-the-play (in which Ginés errs from the text but plays the Christian part correctly), and the subsequent effect on life itself (within the frame play of course), which is martyrdom, a great prize indeed in the eyes of the contemporary audience. The drama as a whole can be, if we follow the idea of the play itself as a vicarious rehearsal for the audience, a recognition of the power of practising in the search to discover a truth or to get something right. Genesius's uncertain rehearsal within the frame play is equivalent to the play in the *corral* seen by the audience in the seventeenth-century world.

Cervantes's *Pedro de Urdemalas*, while it is a secular play and while it undermines the Lopean model of the *comedia nueva*, is in fact quite similar to *Lo fingido verdadero* in an important sense, related to the theme of acting and rehearsing. The thematic unity of this picaresque play is also provided precisely by Cervantes's aperçus concerning the theatricality of life, in particular the importance of trying out roles. In act 3, as Pedro re-appears on stage in yet another garb – this time as a student – he produces a hymn of praise to mutability (Cervantes 1986, lines 2660–89). He is reaching a personal maturity, having spent years effectively rehearsing different parts, and celebrates his new understanding of life:

> Bien logrado iré del mundo
> cuando Dios me lleve dél
> pues podré decir que en él
> un Proteo fui segundo.
> (lines 2672–75)

Right on cue (line 2711), two actors arrive on the scene to help him fleece the *labrador* carrying his chickens, and Pedro accepts that his role in life is to be an actor: Malgesí's seemingly outlandish predictions about him can thus all come true:

> Ya podré ser patriarca,
> pontífice y estudiante,
> emperador y monarca;
> que el oficio de farsante
> todos estados abarca.
> (lines 2862–66)

Pedro's famous speech on the ideal actor is delivered to the *autor* who arrives to begin rehearsing and his fate is sealed. Of course Pedro's literal transformation into an actor is the result of a life of rehearsing different roles. The implication – and in this Cervantes goes further than his contemporary playwrights – is that life makes most sense when seen and experienced as a succession of roles played, and success can be had by those who have an ability to play.[10]

Pedro de Urdemalas ends inconclusively with the suggestion that this particular play, with its resistance to dramatic norms – "que no acaba en casamiento" (line 3169) – and its chaotic, insecure role-playing, is somehow truer to life than other dramatic fare. A play about a character seeking a role, about a man constantly rehearsing until discovering his vocation as an actor, about one play ending and another beginning (lines 3160–63), is further strong evidence of the contemporary concern with appearances and reality, with mutability and social mobility.

The rehearsal scenes in these *comedias*, all written most likely during the reigns of Philip III and Philip IV, are deftly employed by dramatists often in key moments in their works (usually major *salidas* of act 2), to allow them to develop plot and characters and address their principal themes. The rehearsal text can act as a code which enables characters to communicate secretly; it can hide or excuse an error, allowing an individual a second chance to correct behaviour; it can enable a journey of self-discovery; it can unblock a repressed or suppressed emotion; it can open up a "safe space" in which to explore a possibility; responses to a rehearsal can shed light on characters and their contribution to the theme or moral message of the play; and in our last two examples, one secular, one religious, we enter a more philosophical arena, hinted at in all of the earlier examples. In *Lo fingido verdadero* and *Pedro de Urdemalas* a staged rehearsal and the realisation that a life-time has been spent in rehearsal respectively, allow characters to discover a kind of freedom or self-confidence for which any audience-member might yearn.

What is more, the rehearsal seems to make a case both overtly and implicitly for the usefulness of drama not just by sparking the occasional paean to the theatre (which might of course alert the audience to the theme), but by demonstrating how theatre can work practically in life. If the play in the Golden Age, indeed in any period, can act for the audience as a vicarious rehearsal for life, a sort of preparation at one remove or exploration of modes of acting, then the rehearsal within the play is a particularly privileged scene. Rehearsals within plays are more frequent than plays-within-plays in the Golden Age because they actually enable a wider variety of possibilities than a play itself. *Pace* Calderón's *autor* of *El gran teatro del mundo* it is the theatre itself that becomes the period's prompt book.

Notes

1 I have summarised briefly the state of knowledge about play rehearsals in Golden Age Spain in my recent article (Thacker 2014). Oehrlein's (1993) is the best brief consideration of the topic in print. There are a number of parallels with the situation in Shakespeare's London, as can be seen by consulting Stern (2000).

2 Lope de Vega's *Lo fingido verdadero* provides a good sense of what it took to prepare a play already in the troupe's repertoire for a fresh performance. See Thacker (2014, 129–131).

3 See for example, though their approaches to this state of flux in the early modern period differ: Stephen Greenblatt, who (with English writers principally in mind) believes that "there appears to be an increased self-consciousness about the fashioning of human identity as a manipulable, artful process" (1980, 2); José Antonio Maravall, who argues that the Spanish individual "en virtud del amplio desarrollo de su vida durante casi dos siglos anteriores, se salía de los cuadros tradicionales del orden social" which had held him in check (1990, 18); Jeremy Robbins, who notes the "omnipresence of the notion of performance" in the seventeenth century (1998, 39); George Mariscal, for whom "an interplay of subject positions" (1991, 33) is a feature of the period; and the historian J. H. Elliott, who argues that, "As an age captivated by the art of the theatre, the seventeenth century displayed an almost obsessive concern with appearance" (1989, 163). I do not wish to labour this point about the histrionic tendencies of early modern individuals, which is generally accepted as self-evident, if not a defining feature of the early-modern period. The necessity for theatre-style *rehearsal* in a society in which role-play is essential has not, however, yet been explored in any detail by scholars.

4 A good example of the use of the play-within-the-play, to "catch the conscience of the king," as in Shakespeare's *Hamlet*, occurs in the third act of Lope de Vega's 1602 play, *El cuerdo loco*.

5 On the date and authorship of this play, sometimes attributed to Moreto, see Vega García-Luengos (1986, 91–98).

6 See Stern (2000, 22–25) on "rehearse" in English.

7 The play contains a fascinating "papel de actor" within the text of the rehearsal scene, which Floro, unaware of how he is meant to deliver his lines, reads out in full, cues and all. See Thacker (2014, 132–133).

8 Lope allows his characters to develop a coded speech in other plays too. See, for example, Thacker's (2000) exploration of the use characters in *Los locos de Valencia* make of well-known figures from Ariosto and the ballad.

9 This has been called "teatro dentro del teatro dentro del teatro" by Margrit Frenk (as quoted in Galoppe 2001, 199).

10 In act 3 of *La entretenida* (c. 1615), Cervantes becomes bolder still in pursuit of a similar idea, not allowing the audience to distinguish clearly between the rehearsed *entremés* and the "real world" of the play.

Works cited

Calderón de la Barca, Pedro. 1985. *El gran teatro del mundo*. Edited by Eugenio Frutos Cortés. Madrid: Cátedra.

Cervantes, Miguel de. 1986. *El rufián dichoso / Pedro de Urdemalas*. Edited by Jenaro Talens and Nicholas Spadaccini. Madrid: Cátedra.

———. 2013. *La entretenida*. Edited by John O'Neill. Accessed July 17, 2014. http://entretenida.out ofthewings.org/text/entretenida/performance/title.html.

Covarrubias Horozco, Sebastián de. 2006. *Tesoro de la lengua castellana o Española*. Edited by Ignacio Arellano and Rafael Zafra. Madrid and Frankfurt: Iberoamericana/Vervuert.

Diccionario *de Autoridades*. 2014. Accessed July 2, 2014. http://web.frl.es/DA.html.

Elliott, J. H. 1989. *Spain and Its World, 1500–1700*. New Haven, CT: Yale University Press.

Galoppe, Raúl A. 2001. *Género y confusión en el teatro de Tirso de Molina*. Madrid: Pliegos.

Godínez, Felipe. 2014. *La cautela en la amistad*. In *Teatro español del Siglo de Oro*. Accessed July 2, 2014. http://teso.chadwyck.co.uk. [Play attributed there to Agustín Moreto].

Greenblatt, Stephen. 1980. *Renaissance Self-Fashioning: From More to Shakespeare*. Chicago: University of Chicago Press.

Maravall, José Antonio. 1990. *Teatro y literatura en la sociedad barroca*. Barcelona: Crítica.

Mariscal, George. 1991. *Contradictory Subjects: Quevedo, Cervantes, and Seventeenth-Century Spanish Culture*. New York: Cornell University Press.

Mira de Amescua, Antonio. 2001. *El ejemplo mayor de la desdicha*. Edited by Maria Grazia Profeti. In *Teatro completo*, vol. 1, 221–302. Edited by Agustín de la Granja. Granada: Universidad de Granada.

Moreto, Agustín y Cáncer, Jerónimo de. 2014. *Nuestra señora del Aurora*. In *Teatro español del Siglo de Oro*. Accessed July 2, 2014. http://teso.chadwyck.co.uk

Oehrlein, Josef. 1993. *El actor en el teatro español del Siglo de Oro*. Madrid: Castalia.

Robbins, Jeremy. 1998. *The Challenges of Uncertainty: an Introduction to Seventeenth-Century Spanish Literature*. London: Duckworth.

Stern, Tiffany. 2000. *Rehearsal from Shakespeare to Sheridan*. Oxford: Oxford University Press.

Thacker, Jonathan. 2000. "Lope de Vega's Exemplary Early Comedy: *Los locos de Valencia*." *Bulletin of the Comediantes* 52: 9–29.

———. 2014. "Play Rehearsals on the Golden Age Stage." In *Artifice and Invention in the Spanish Golden Age*, edited by Stephen Boyd and Terence O'Reilly. Oxford: Legenda. 126–135.

Tirso de Molina. 1969. *La venganza de Tamar*. Edited by A. K. G. Paterson. Cambridge: Cambridge University Press.

———. 1989a. "El Aquiles." In *Obras dramáticas completas*, edited by Blanca de los Ríos, vol. 2, 961–1001. Madrid: Aguilar.

———. 1989b. *El vergonzoso en palacio*. Edited by Francisco Ayala. Madrid: Castalia.

Vega, Lope de. 1857. *Contra valor no hay desdicha*. In *Comedias escogidas de Frey Lope Félix de Vega Carpio*, edited by Juan Eugenio Hartzenbusch, vol. 3, 1–16. Madrid: Rivadeneyra.

———. 1922. *El cuerdo loco*. Edited by José F. Montesinos. Madrid: Centro de Estudios Históricos.

———. 1964. *Lo fingido verdadero*. In *Obras de Lope de Vega*, edited by Marcelino Menéndez y Pelayo, vol. 9, 51–107. Madrid: Atlas.

———. 2006. *Arte nuevo de hacer comedias*. Edited by Enrique García Santo-Tomás. Madrid: Cátedra.

———. 2009. *El castigo sin venganza*. Edited by Alejandro García-Reidy. Barcelona: Crítica.

Vega García-Luengos, Germán. 1986. *Problemas de un dramaturgo del Sigo de Oro: Estudios sobre Felipe Godínez*. Valladolid: Universidad de Valladolid.

19

IBERIAN MYTHS AND AMERICAN HISTORY IN BALBUENA'S *EL BERNARDO*

Rodrigo Cacho Casal

Early modern authors born in Spain who spent part or most of their life in America seem to inhabit a critical limbo. The adscription of their literary works is often contested between cognate areas of study, particularly peninsular and colonial studies. First developed in nineteenth-century Latin America, colonial studies fostered the rediscovery of texts that allegedly embodied the spirit of the newly constituted countries. Nowadays identitarian readings are still at the core of the discipline, buttressed by the development of postcolonialism, ethnic and subaltern studies (Adorno 2011, 3–6). On the other hand, more traditional European methodologies, such as those fostered by Hispanic Philology, have tended to appropriate texts written in the colonies, ignoring the American substrate of their political discourse. Taken to the extreme, such dichotomies can lead to rather narrow intellectual debates. For instance, Alonso de Ercilla's epic poem *La Araucana* (1569–89), which describes the clash between Spaniards and Mapuches, has often been regarded as mere continuation of European poetic codes or, conversely, as the embodiment of an early national identity upon which Chilean independentist claims would later rest.

The critical reception of Bernardo de Balbuena is an eloquent illustration of such binaries. Though born in Spain (ca. 1561–1562), the author spent most of his adult life in America, where he held several ecclesiastical appointments: first in Mexico, then promoted abbot of Jamaica (1608), and finally, in 1619, bishop of Puerto Rico (Rojas Garcidueñas 1982; Van Horne 1940). Balbuena's three most significant works were conceived in Mexico, between the end of the sixteenth century and the beginning of the seventeenth century. Here he obtained his first university degree, took orders and started making a name for himself as a poet. His ambitious artistic project was to replicate Virgil's tripartite literary career (*Eclogues, Georgics, Aeneid*), writing a pastoral book, *El Siglo de Oro en las selvas de Erífile* (1608); a modern georgic, *Grandeza mexicana* (1604); and the heroic poem *El Bernardo o victoria de Roncesvalles* (1624) (Cacho Casal 2015). Despite the presence of American themes in these works, the consideration of Balbuena within the canon of colonial studies rests on shaky foundations. Some critics find him to be representing echoes of an early Creole identity in Mexico, whereas others dismiss his writing as the product of a Spaniard who never really felt truly connected with the New World, and was only able to produce a narrow imperialistic and Eurocentric discourse (Balbuena 2011, 23–59).

Such controversies seem to have been fuelled also by the topic chosen for *El Bernardo*, the work which Balbuena regarded as his masterpiece. Rather than narrating the events of the conquest, such as Ercilla and other epic poets of the colonial period, the author focused his attention on the deeds of the legendary medieval Iberian hero Bernardo del Carpio. Balbuena's poem seems thus to lean more towards the construction of Spanish nationalistic myths rather than looking at American identity. The New World, however, has a central role in various books of *El Bernardo*, especially 18 and 19. Balbuena drew from American history and geography to describe Columbus's discovery, the arrival of Cortés to Mexico and the subsequent fall of Tenochtitlan. Despite its relative brevity, this is a key episode in *El Bernardo*, which allows the author to establish links between the past greatness of the Spanish crown and the colonization of the New World. Balbuena puts forward a teleological reading of the American conquest presented as the ultimate achievement within Spanish history; all previous glories and efforts were only meant to lead to this outcome: Spain would not be Spain without America. History is turned into myth, and vice versa.

The manipulation of myth and history in *El Bernardo* has its roots in the sixteenth-century heated debate on the nature of heroic poetry, revolving around neo-Aristotelian principles, the role of history and fiction in heroic poems, and the controversial relationship between epics and romance as embodied by Tasso and Ariosto. Ultimately, it is perhaps not so crucial to establish whether Balbuena belongs to the peninsular or the colonial tradition; whether he was Spanish, Iberian, Mexican or American. He was all of these at the same time since such categories did not possess the same political value that they hold nowadays (Brading 1998). What is likely to prove more fruitful is to analyze the ways in which Balbuena manipulated the literary tools to which he had access at the time, and how these were affected by their implantation in the New World; what was the meaning of concepts such as history and myth with regards to heroic poetry, and how this genre was used to voice contemporary political ideas. This essay considers dualisms and ambiguities as a defining feature of early colonial writing, looking at *El Bernardo* from two complementary angles: firstly, accounting for its literary tradition, paying close attention to the poem's prologue, where Balbuena summed up his theory of epic poetry; and secondly, considering its ideological discourse, analyzing the role of the conquest and Amerindians in the poem.

A double-faced discourse: history and myth in the heroic poem

The date of composition of *El Bernardo* is uncertain. Although it first appeared in 1624, the work underwent a long process of revision. Following the information provided in the preliminaries of the text, Van Horne (1927, 25–27) has argued the author completed the first draft of the poem around 1595, followed by an unsuccessful attempt to publish it in 1609. If Van Horne is right in assuming that Balbuena began to write *El Bernardo* in the 1580s, this would mean that it was composed during the critical years of the literary debate concerned with the heroic poem. This quarrel arose mainly in response to the *Orlando furioso* (1532). The initial success of Ariosto's *romanzo* was later met with strong criticism from the most rigid neo-Aristotelian scholars, who regretted its lack of unity and verisimilitude, and its inappropriate mixture of serious and burlesque themes. The controversy reached its climax after the publication of Tasso's *Gerusalemme liberata* (1581), which offered a more orthodox interpretation of heroic poetry in line with classical principles and poetics (Weinberg 1961, 954–1073).

Before the triumph of Tasso's model, Ariosto had offered the first important epic vernacular example to the Spanish authors of the sixteenth century. Despite its grotesque and marvellous elements, the *Furioso* was canonized as a veritable imitation of classical sources, especially the *Aeneid*, the ultimate model within the epic genre. Allegorical and political readings proliferated in commentaries and annotated editions, making Ariosto the modern Virgil (Chevalier

1966, 7–106; Javitch 1991). The first Spanish heroic poems followed on *Furioso*'s steps, shifting the protagonism of the French paladins to a more suitable national hero, Bernardo del Carpio. Born from the secret marriage of King Alfonso III's sister and the Count of Saldaña, he will play a crucial role in the battle of Roncesvalles, defeating the French army and killing Roland (C. Alvar and M. Alvar 1991, 381–408; Burton 1988, 14–23; Franklin 1937). This medieval legend was appropriated by Spanish epic poems of the sixteenth century, with an emphasis on its nationalistic message, which fed on contemporary military and political conflicts between Spain and France; Alfonso III and Charlemagne were masks for Charles V and Francis I, whilst the French defeat at Roncesvalles was read as a prefiguration of the 1525 battle of Pavia (Vilà 2012). This is the case for Nicolás Espinosa's *La segunda parte de Orlando* (1555), Francisco Garrido de Villena's *El verdadero suceso de la famosa batalla de Roncesvalles* (1555), Agustín Alonso's *Historia de las hazañas y hechos del invencible caballero Bernardo del Carpio* (1585) and, to a lesser extent, Luis Barahona de Soto's *Primera parte de la Angélica* (1586).

Undoubtedly, Balbuena had in mind these Spanish texts and, most importantly, the legacy of Boiardo and Ariosto when he began composing his poem. Balbuena broadly follows the intricate narrative style of the *Innamorato* and the *Furioso*, choosing a literary path that could be regarded as outdated at the time when he was writing (Vilà 2012, 59). In the first book of the poem we find two fairies, Alcina and Morgana, conspiring against the French and foreseeing the great deeds of Bernardo, who will avenge them. Here *El Bernardo* is clearly indebted with canto 1 of Barahona de Soto's *Angélica* (Chevalier 1966, 376), which reproduces the gathering of several fairies – comprising also Alcina and Morgana – organised by Demogorgone at the beginning of Ariosto's posthumous *I cinque canti* (1548). Balbuena, however, does not include this assembly and focuses only on the private meeting of the two fairies, a choice which can be regarded as a declaration of artistic intentions. Morgana has a leading role in the *Innamorato*, whereas Alcina in the *Furioso*. By linking them from the onset the poet seems to be implying that his goal does not only lie in the continuation of Ariosto's work, as it is the case for the other Spanish authors mentioned previously, but rather to combine the content and style of both texts in a final effort to culminate the quest of the Italian *romanzo* as a whole, as he declares in the prologue of *El Bernardo*: "Este poema se puede llamar el cumplimiento, la última línea y la clave que de lleno en lleno cierra el artificio y máquina de sus fábulas" (Balbuena 1624, ¶6ᵛ).

Key terms here are "artificio" and "máquina de sus fábulas," which define some of the main features of the Boiardo/Ariosto model as reworked by Balbuena; that is, the presence of a complicated narrative plot, magic and marvel. According to Aristotle's *Poetics* (1460a), the marvellous is a fundamental tool for the epic poet. In Homer and Virgil this is usually produced by the actions of pagan "deidades y semideos," whilst in *romanzi* wonderment is generated by "las hadas y encantamentos de los magos" (Balbuena 1624, ¶6ᵛ). Such predicaments appear to be a response to Tasso's *Discorsi dell'arte poetica* (1587), later reworked and expanded in the *Discorsi del poema eroico* (1594), which dominated epic theory in the later part of the sixteenth and in the first half of the seventeenth century. Although Tasso agrees that the marvellous is crucial, he prefers to present it as the symbolic clash between the Christian God and the Devil, angels and demons, and employing wizards and fairies only in the second instance (Tasso [1594] 1973, 38), as it is made abundantly clear in his *Liberata*. The kind of magic and supernatural actions found in *El Bernardo* are more in line with Boiardo and Ariosto, although the prologue accounts for ideas that seem to be in direct correlation with the *Discorsi*.

Balbuena has conceived his heroic poem as an ideal continuation of Homer and Boiardo (Balbuena 1624, ¶6ᵛ), founders of the genre in classical and modern times, as well as Virgil,

Ariosto and even Tasso, whose *Liberata* appears to be rather different from *El Bernardo*. In its prologue several instances seem to echo the *Discorsi*, and the second part of the poem – especially the last books – acquires a more austere tone combined with truly grandiose descriptions of epic battles. Balbuena's ambitious project was to produce the ultimate and all-inclusive heroic poem of his time, accounting also for the most prestigious text of the Spanish tradition, Ercilla's *La Araucana*. As it is well-known, Ercilla's first stanza (1.1) is a *recusatio* which rejects the *Orlando furioso*: "damas," "amor" and "gentilezas / de caballeros" are replaced with "hechos" and "proezas" of the Spanish soldiers deployed in Chile (Ercilla [1569–89] 2002, 77); this is what in the prologue the author calls "la historia verdadera" and "cosas de guerra" (Ercilla [1569–89] 2002, 69). Balbuena's opinion regarding the presence of history in heroic poems is radically different from Ercilla, following on Aristotle's idea (*Poetics*, 1451a–1451b) that poetry ought to be a creative imitation of life, and not an account of true events: "donde en la palabra *imitación* se excluye la historia verdadera, que no es sujeto de poesía" (Balbuena 1624, ¶6). It follows a strong criticism directed against Ercilla (who is never mentioned in *El Bernardo*) and his imitators:

> Donde de paso se verá cuán inadvertidamente hablan los que la principal calidad de sus obras en verso hallan que es el no haberse desviado un punto de la verdad, como quiera que cuanto más desta tuvieren, tanto ellos tendrán menos de poetas, [. . .] que es la razón porque tampoco Lucano es contado entre los poetas, con haber escrito en verso: porque la poesía ha de ser imitación de verdad, pero no la misma verdad, escribiendo las cosas no como sucedieron, que esa ya no sería imitación, sino como pudieran suceder, dándoles toda la perfección que puede alcanzar la imaginación del que las finge; que es lo que hace unos poetas mejores que otros.
>
> (Balbuena 1624, ¶6)

With these words, not only is Balbuena opposing *La Araucana* and other heroic colonial poems that dealt with the conquest of America, but also the whole Spanish epic tradition based on the deeds of Charles V and the Hapsburgs, beginning in the 1560s, especially after the publication of Luis Zapata's *Carlo famoso* (1566). The idealised medieval world of Boiardo and Ariosto, which "se funda sobre cimiento dudoso y aún por ventura de todo punto falso" (Balbuena 1624, ¶6), offered the poet more freedom to let his imagination fly than if he had to depend on real facts. Balbuena's defence of the fictional nature of poetry also challenges Tasso's theory that "truth provides a more suitable basis for the heroic poem" (Tasso [1594] 1973, 26), though such truth could – and indeed should – be embellished by invented episodes. The problem with Boiardo and Ariosto, Tasso believes, is that they go too far in their *romanzi*, lacking any real historical basis. The dubious veracity of their plots produces flaws with regards to verisimilitude: "what we are not sure has been done is thought less possible" (Tasso [1594] 1973, 28). Balbuena inverts such argument, turning an alleged flaw into a virtue, holding onto a very literal reading of Aristotelian poetics through which the writer expresses his aesthetic and political ideas.

Looking at the aesthetic motivations, it should be noted that Ercilla complains at the end of part 1 of *La Araucana* (15.4) about the lack of variety and "gusto" produced "por ir a la verdad tan arrimado / y haber de tratar siempre de una cosa" (Ercilla [1569–89] 2002, 430). To overcome such limitations, love stories and magic will make more frequent appearances in the remaining two parts of *La Araucana*. Balbuena, on the other hand, offers from the onset a "obra tejida de una admirable variedad de cosas," as we read in the title page of the book. In *El Bernardo* there are endless sentimental interludes and fantastic adventures, guided by the hedonistic principle according to which "de la imitación poética la porción mayor de su fin es el deleite" (Balbuena 1624, ¶7ᵛ); a closer look at the poem, though, shows that there are several episodes that rely on Spanish and colonial historiography. It is often through such digressions that Balbuena's political message becomes more apparent, emphasising its nationalistic and imperialistic content. We could perhaps claim that there is an inverted relationship between the use of fiction and history in *La Araucana* and *El Bernardo*. What appear as digressions from the central plot in Ercilla instead constitute the main core of Balbuena's poetic work.

Such dialectic between history and fiction rests on classical poetic and rhetorical principles that had a major role in the interpretation of heroic poetry throughout the Middle Ages and the Renaissance. This happened particularly thanks to Virgil's commentary attributed to Servius, which had a lasting effect on early modern epic theory (Dietz 1995; Lazzarini 1984). *Historia* was the kind of narration that described real past events (*res gesta*), whilst *fabula*, or *mythos*, dealt with fictional and inverisimilar episodes, such as those of pagan mythology. The juxtaposition of both kinds of narration was recognized by Servius as a fundamental semiotic tool in the construction of meaning in the *Aeneid*. According to him, Virgil refers to the events of a mythical foundational past that announces the birth and expansion of the Roman empire, and the greatness of Augustus, his patron. This is obvious from the beginning of the poem (1.5–7), where clear reference is made to Rome and the birth of the Latin lineage (*genus Latinum*). Both narrative planes merge in book 8, where the shield of Aeneas is described, including a foretelling of the great deeds of the emperor, culminating in the battle of Actium. This *mise en abyme* was the key section of the text that fostered a political and imperialistic interpretation of the epic genre for posterity (Quint 1993, 21–49). Political Virgilianism, also present in Ariosto and Tasso, permeates most heroic poems written in early modern Spain, as pointed out by Vilà (2001, 2010, 2011), highlighting their allegiance to the Hapsburg cause.

Servius's hermeneutical approach granted a twofold interpretation of the *Aeneid*; the poem consists of *historia* (especially book 8) and *fabula*: myths enclose natural, philosophical and religious truths. *Fabula* deals with universals, whilst *historia* with particulars; Aeneas is a representation of the good king, and he also foreshadows Augustus.[1] The *Aeneid* and subsequent imitations are – to use Lipsius's terminology – *mythistoria*.[2] Balbuena welcomes both *historia* and *fabula* in his work, though for him there is no doubt that the latter is the defining trait of poetry, linking both concepts, also thanks to Aristotle's distinction between history and poetry discussed previously. For the author of *El Bernardo*, poetry is essentially *fabula*, that is, *myth*, as the term was then understood: "un razonamiento de cosas fingidas" which contains "escondida moralidad y provechosa doctrina" (Pérez de Moya [1585] 1995, 65). It is the *fabula* that makes a poem, since this provides the ultimate source of entertainment (*delectare*) and moral instruction (*docere*). The "encubierta moralidad y alegoría" is in no way alienable from "el deleite de la fábula y sus colores retóricos" (Balbuena 1624, ¶7ᵛ). This explains the central role played by allegories in *El Bernardo* (Pierce 1949–50). This also explains Balbuena's rejection of the pseudo-historicist model put forward by Ercilla, where particulars predominate. Both writers authored *mythistoriae*, although the degree of these two components (history/myth) varies radically from one poem to the other.

Balbuena uses Aristotelian principles to claim that history is less entertaining and philosophical than poetry, and that its moral message is weaker since it rests on the actions of real human beings who are, by definition, imperfect. This is very apparent in Lucan's *Pharsalia*, populated by betrayal and anti-heroes. The role of poetry is to employ myths to overcome such limitations by presenting fictional characters who embody greater moral ideals. This is why, for both Servius and Balbuena, Lucan (Ercilla) was not a real poet, because in his text history is not veiled by allegory (Lazzarini 1984, 131), leaving no room for beauty, aesthetic pleasure and intellectual elevation. Ultimately, this is also a disservice to the nationalistic and imperialistic cause. As argued by Quint (1993, 8), the Virgilian model gave rise to the "epics of the imperial victors," and Lucan to the "epics of the defeated." The former aestheticize and universalize colonialism and warfare, whereas the latter does not hide the horrors and contradictions that ensue from armed conflicts and from the violent subjugation of a civilization by another. This is why *El Bernardo* can, at least in part, be regarded as an extensive response to Ercilla: an anti-*Araucana* where its ideals and poetic choices have been reversed, as it is apparent by the role that America and the conquest play in both poems.

From Iberia to America: Tlascalán and political allegory

Balbuena's contested presence in the colonial literary canon is also due to the superficial treatment of Amerindians in his works. According to Adorno (2007, 4–5), "the native – colonized or indomitable – stands always at the heart of colonial writings." But this does not seem to apply to Balbuena, who appears to be lacking any depth or real interest when dealing with pre-Columbian civilizations. Absent from *Siglo de Oro*, they are quickly dismissed as barbarians in the prologue of *Grandeza mexicana*. Here, the "indio salvaje" (Balbuena [1604] 2011, 161) responds to stereotypes associated with the rebellious Chichimecas, an image that appears drastically reversed at the end of the poem, where Balbuena describes the "indio feo" (Balbuena [1604] 2011, 249) as the tamed and dominated version of the savage encountered in the first pages of the book. The author fails to account for the *grandeza* of Mexico before the arrival of the Spaniards. In the second chapter he states that he has made the conscious decision to leave out Tenochtitlan and its history, focusing only on the present of "de lo que soy testigo" (Balbuena [1604] 2011, 177). A similar silence can be found in *El Bernardo*, where the poet openly rejects Ercilla's model. In *Grandeza*'s preliminary poem addressed to the Count of Lemos, he turns *La Araucana*'s opening *recusatio* on its own head:

> Otros canten de Arauco las bravezas
> y aquellos capitanes
> que llegaron a ver tras mil afanes
> un nuevo cielo y polo en sus cabezas.
> (Balbuena [1604] 2011, 87)

Balbuena prefers to recount instead the "antiguas victorias y hazañas" of "tu español Bernardo," whilst the fights against the Araucanians are degraded to "guerras bárbaras" (Balbuena [1604] 2011, 87). As I have argued elsewhere (Cacho Casal 2015), Balbuena's decision to obliterate the conquest from its discourse could also be read as an attempt to limit the literary projection of the Mexican *encomenderos* and their descendants, who produced several epic texts revolving around the figure of Cortés to support their claims (Mazzotti 2000). Moreover, it should be borne in mind that Balbuena made these statements in a poem dedicated to the Count of Lemos, Pedro Fernández de Castro, who was also the principal addressee of *El Bernardo*. Here the hero is presented as one of the legendary originators of the Castro lineage, similar to Aeneas and Augustus in Virgil, and Ruggero and Ippolito d'Este in Ariosto. This is made abundantly clear in the dedication of *El Bernardo* written for the Count's brother, Francisco, after Pedro had died; the main goal of the text is describing "la esclarecida decendencia de la excelentísima casa de Castro" (Balbuena 1624, ¶4). It is easier to recreate a legendary fictional lineage in a remote fantasy world. Also, locating the origin of the Castros in a distant past grants them more prestige.[3]

Unlike Ercilla, Balbuena compresses the conquest of America in a few books of *El Bernardo*, mainly 18 and 19. Here he offers a geographical vision of the New World, and describes the quarters of the wizard Tlascalán who foretells the arrival of Cortés to Mexico and his alliance with Tlaxcala in order to defeat the violent Mexicas. It could be argued that Balbuena had in mind Zapata, who in his *Carlo famoso* offered the first account of the discovery and conquest of America in a Spanish epic poem. Following mainly López de Gómara, Zapata recounts Columbus and Cortés's deeds in cantos 11 through 14. The principal dissimilarity between Balbuena and Zapata, however, is that in *Carlo famoso* the New World appears only as a series of interpolated episodes, which do not particularly stand out in relation to other events described in the text. *El Bernardo*'s case is rather different. Tlascalán's prophecy is a crucial episode in which various dichotomies converge: myth and history, Iberia and America, the Middle Ages and modern times. This is also the section in which some of the most relevant political ideas of the text are revealed.

As discussed earlier, the central political *mise en abyme* within heroic poems was usually located in ekphrastic scenes revolving around the description of the hero's shield or armour. Such a device was first used in the *Iliad* (book 18), and later imitated in the *Aeneid* (book 8) with a specific propagandistic content; a convention followed by early modern authors such as Zapata in his *Carlo famoso* (cantos 34–35). In *El Bernardo* the protagonist inherits Achilles's armour, but, despite the fact that these are mentioned on several occasions (books 2, 9 and 19), and that they are said to have engravings representing "una oculta decendencia / de héroes ilustres" (2.96), they never generate political panegyrics of great national leaders. It seems, however, not a coincidence that when the armour is mentioned there is often a foretelling related to Spanish distinguished figures. In book 2, Alcina enumerates the peninsular Gothic kings, and Iberia – personified as a nymph – gives account of the deeds of "nueve capitanes celebrados" (2.188), amongst who are Nuño Belchides (related to the Castro lineage), El Cid and Hernán Cortés. In book 19, Tlascalán refers to the conquest of Tenochtitlan, and Iberia appears once again, this time describing her tapestries where the names of great Spanish families are found. This catalogue ends with seven stanzas devoted to praise of Balbuena's own family, his father and himself (19.220–226).

Symbolically, Iberia and Tlascalán join forces in book 19. This section of the poem represents what Balbuena conceived as the unbreakable bond between Spain and the New World, looking at the past (the Goths, El Cid) and at the present (noble families, such as the Castros) in connection with the conquest (Columbus and Cortés). Spatial and chronological coordinates shift and merge in the name of Spanish imperialism. According to Balbuena, this is also achieved thanks to his poetic skills, which have enabled him to compress history and myth in a vast and imaginative text. The "nuevo mundo" is mentioned both at the start and at the end of *El Bernardo* (1.3, 24.186), as a recurring theme that gives meaning to Spanish history as a whole. Iberia's greatest achievement was the discovery of America, which stands as the foremost embodiment of Hispanic providential vision of world domination: "que el cielo ha dado a España el mundo todo: / suyo ha de ser en esta edad postrera" (2.79). If *El Bernardo* is an ideal sequel of Homer, Virgil, and particularly Boiardo and Ariosto's poems, it can also be said that for Balbuena the New World is the ultimate continuation (or *gionta*, to use a term dear to ariostesque tradition) of Iberia: Spain can only be complete and achieve its true destiny once reunited with its missing piece. The West Indies are the ultimate marker of Hispanic identity; *El Bernardo* transpires all of Balbuena's pride for being Spanish precisely because he feels also American; particularly his literary works are fashioned as an American product, which "a vueltas de su nuevo mundo fueron naciendo" (Balbuena [1608] 1989, 65), as he confesses to the Count of Lemos in the dedication to the *Siglo de Oro*.

The providential conception of the conquest in *El Bernardo* is never visualized as explicitly as in Tlascalán's episode. His prophecy regards the fall of Tenochtitlan as an inevitable event; a semi-divine act that joined together what was always meant to be united. The prophetic view of the American wizard projects a sense of predetermination onto Spanish colonialism. This is also made possible thanks to a native group met by Cortés in the New World, the Tlaxcalans, who are portrayed in a very different light than the Indian savages encountered in *Grandeza*. Tlaxcala stands in the poem as the missing link, the civilized force of the continent waiting to be reunited with Spain in their common effort against the unruly barbarians, here embodied by the Mexicas. The Tlaxcalans are described as "hidalga nación," the legitimate inhabitants of the land that has been appropriated by the Mexica, represented as foreign and violent invaders: "feroces estranjeras gentes" (19.10). Tlascalán is a symbol of the sophisticated culture of his nation, "mi constante pueblo altivo" (19.13), which joined forces with Cortés. Here Balbuena is reworking popular accounts of the conquest of Tenochtitlan, such as those written by Gómara and Cortés, where the Tlaxcalans, after their initial resistance against the Spaniards, became their most powerful allies. Their support was rewarded with tax exemptions and with the title of "Insigne, muy noble y muy leal ciudad de Tlaxcala" (Gibson 1952; Martínez Baracs 2008; Oudijk and Restall 2007).

The fictional role of 'liberator' from the evil Mexica invaders, attributed by Balbuena to Cortés, allows him to draw parallels with previous events of Iberian history: the *reconquista* against the Moors, initiated by the Gothic kings and culminated by the Catholic Monarchs, Isabella and Ferdinand, who will also be the promoters of the discovery of the New World, as recalled by Tlascalán: "su luz abrirá el alba a nuestra gente / y el sol dará en los mundos del poniente" (19.70). True events, mystifications, anachronisms, legends: they all seem to fit, to find their cohesive place in *El Bernardo*. Hidden amongst fairies and giants, history reaches the surface of *El Bernardo*, giving a whole new meaning to medieval Iberian myths and highlighting the political message of the poem, which is tightly connected with the representation of America. As pointed out by Nicolopulos (1998), the encounter with Tlascalán is an imitation and an outdoing of Fitón's episode in canto 23 of *La Araucana*. Ercilla's wizard is an old and feeble man, "anciano consumido" (Ercilla [1569–89] 2002, 644), whereas Balbuena's character appears as a "corpulento jayán, doblado en ciencia" (18.115); he is taller, stronger and more knowledgeable; he is also more threatening and imposing. He epitomizes the dualisms embedded in colonial discourse. He stands for the pre-Columbian sophisticated civilizations, and he also incarnates the dangers and violence of the New World.

Such dichotomies pertain also to the literary and symbolic registers. The dark side of America has been here represented with the stereotypical evil character found in European chivalric books and *romanzi*: the giant. Tlascalán is both a friend and a foe; both familiar and exotic: he is the ultimate allegory of the New World.[4] The very measure of his size matches the greatness of the continent's geography, described by Balbuena in book 18 (101–110) as a set of contradictions, where beauty and hostility meet: the *antípodas* are a combination of *riquezas* and *guerra*. *El Bernardo*'s verbal cartography is as well an adaptation and an extension of *La Araucana*'s account of Chile in its first canto (1.6–10). Ercilla's American world has been tamed and compressed in a few books of *El Bernardo*; as if Tlascalán had swallowed up Fitón and, with him, the whole ambiguous vision of the conquest that appeared in *La Araucana*, where the vanquished often seemed more worthy of praise than the vanquishers.

Balbuena's metaphorical discourse sheds a moralising and religious interpretation on the discovery, as it is made clear in the *alegoría* at the end of book 18. Malgesí's flight above America is compared to the wonders of contemplative life, which leads the mind to reach higher truths hidden underneath appearances: "con la cual llega a la felicidad del Nuevo

Mundo, que es la bienaventuranza prometida al hombre, como a la monarquía española las Indias Occidentales" (Balbuena 1624, 223ᵛ). *El Bernardo* combines political (particulars) and spiritual (universals) interpretations of the conquest, entertaining readers with its variety – or its "confuso amontonar de cosas" (12.130), distracting them from the darker realities of war and colonialism. Here lies the crucial substrate of Balbuena's use of myths in his poem. As pointed out by Barthes (1957, 216–230), mythology is a semiotic system which fosters stasis above change, de-historicising and de-politicizing language. Myths conceal the political contingency of imperialism, presenting it as a natural and inevitable outcome: *anti-physis* is disguised as *pseudo-physis*. This is why they have always been a powerful tool in the hands of conservative regimes.

Balbuena's *mythistoria* was conceived as a celebration of Spain, America and the Catholic Church, fulfilling thus some of the main goals that Tasso ascribed to heroic poetry: "establish the faith or exalt the Church and Empire" (Tasso [1594] 1973, 50). But greatness was also meant to be reached in the literary field. The all-encompassing need for variety and accumulation of episodes in *El Bernardo* reflects also the author's wish to set himself as the foremost epic poet, following on the inventor of the genre, Homer: "fuera Homero el segundo, yo el primero" (3.174). Balbuena's opening with a Homeric invocation to the Muse – "Cuéntame, oh Musa" (1.1) – and the organization of his poem in 24 books, as the *Iliad* and the *Odyssey*, are all clear indicators of this imitation. The same can be said for the assortment of themes discussed, which, as stated by the title page of the book, include history, geography, ethnography, architecture and moral philosophy. According to ancient interpretations, still very much alive in the sixteenth century despite its competition with Virgil, Homer was the greatest author, the originator of all literary genres, knowledgeable in all subjects and sciences (Ford 2007). Balbuena's ambitious project takes him back to the roots of literature and philosophy, writing his masterpiece, a heroic poem, which was regarded at the time as the most prestigious genre of the literary canon, as pointed out by Dryden ([1697] 1900, 154): "A heroic poem, truly such, is undoubtedly the greatest work which the soul of man is capable to perform."

Balbuena sets this Homeric background on the shoulders of the *romanzo*, conceiving it as a modern variation on heroic poetry. Also Tasso ([1594] 1973, 69) shared this view, though he found the structure of the works of Boiardo and Ariosto to be too loose, and their content often obscene and inadequate. Balbuena had similar concerns, since *El Bernardo* lacks the traits of humour and grotesque that characterized his Italian predecessors. Such purged interpretation of the *romanzo* is epitomized by the invention of a new character, Arcangélica. As her name suggests, she is a morally improved version of her mother, Angelica, and her relationship with Bernardo is always kept on a spiritual level. *El Bernardo* is both an exuberant heroic poem and an orthodox *romanzo*. The last scene of the poem, when the Spanish hero kills Orlando, seals Balbuena's imitation and outdoing of his literary models. This is achieved thanks to the symbiosis between author and character, which reaches its peak in book 17. Here the protagonist climbs to the top of mount Parnassus, where Apollo proclaims that his military victories will be sung by a modern poet. Bernardo the warrior is also Bernardo the writer on his way to fame: "ambos de un mismo nombre y un cuidado: / tú en hacer con tu espada maravillas, / y él con su humilde pluma en escrebillas" (17.89).

El Bernardo cannot be understood without taking into account Balbuena's literary ambition. His ultimate goal was to write a memorable poem, which would make him rise above the greatest models of the epic canon. To do so, he fashioned himself as a pan-Hispanic author, shared between two worlds, the Old and the New – "juntando de ambos, para el grave acento, / lo de mayor sustancia y fundamento" (16.149). Balbuena conceives *El Bernardo* as one of the best products resulting from the Spanish presence in America. Turning his back on the realities of colonialism, resting on the principle that all great literature is conceived in the first place by the imagination of the poet, Balbuena crafted a fictional world that, he hoped, was to culminate the long epic tradition. Set against the backdrop of Homer and Virgil, he put forward a personal reworking of *romanzi*, which would retain the entertainment produced by its typical accumulation of episodes without disregarding the high stylistic register conventionally attributed to heroic poetry, as well as its political and moral content. It has often been said that *El Bernardo* is a baroque poem (Pierce 1945). If this rings true, though, it is not because of its intricate style or complex metaphors, but rather down to the autonomy granted to the work of art. In *El Bernardo, fabulae* supersede reality; imperialism and national propaganda, Spain and America are components of a larger semiotic network, a poetic "mundo entero" (1.66) whose end is to teach readers what they already know, or should know, and, most importantly, to stimulate their imagination. Nothing, perhaps, can better express the aesthetic principles and ideological limitations of Balbuena's text than to say that the ultimate protagonist of *El Bernardo* is the poem itself.

Notes

1 Homer was the object of allegorical readings since antiquity, though, unlike the *Aeneid*, Homeric discourse could not be related to a particular dynasty and specific political leaders. Ideological approaches to Homer in the Renaissance (Ford 2007) tend to dwell on abstract themes (justice, the good king, etc.) rather than on finding equivalences between the characters in the poem and a real national referent outside the text.
2 In his 1600 letter to Nicolas de Hacqueville, Lipsius (1602, 62) distinguished between *historia* and *mythistoria*, defining the latter as a combination of history and myth ("fabulas vero mixtas").
3 Barahona de Soto, following on Ariosto, anticipated Balbuena, including a genealogical panegyric in his *Angélica*, linking Bernardo del Carpio with the Osuna family.
4 Also Cabello de Balboa's *Miscelánea antártica* (1586) compares the map of South America with "un corpulento y robusto gigante" (Firbas 2004, 272).

Works cited

Adorno, Rolena. 2007. *The Polemics of Possession in Spanish American Narrative*. New Haven, CT: Yale University Press.
———. 2011. *Colonial Latin American Literature: A Very Short Introduction*. Oxford–New York: Oxford University Press.
Alvar, Carlos, and Manuel Alvar, eds. 1991. *Épica medieval española*. Madrid: Cátedra.
Balbuena, Bernardo de. [1604] 2011. *Grandeza mexicana*. Edited by Asima F. X. Saad Maura. Cátedra: Madrid.
———. [1608] 1989. *El Siglo de Oro en las selvas de Erífile*. Edited by José Carlos González Boixo. Xalapa: Universidad Veracruzana.
———. 1624. *El Bernardo o victoria de Roncesvalles, poema heroico*. Madrid: Diego Flamenco.
Barthes, Roland. 1957. *Mythologies*. Paris: Seuil.
Brading, David A. 1998. "Patriotism and the Nation in Colonial Spanish America." In *Constructing Collective Identities and Shaping Public Spheres: Latin American Paths*, edited by Luis Roniger and Mario Sznajder, 13–45. Brighton: Sussex Academic Press.
Burton, David G. 1988. *The Legend of Bernardo del Carpio from Chronicle to Drama*. Potomac, MD: Scripta Humanistica.
Cacho Casal, Rodrigo. 2015. "Balbuena's *Grandeza mexicana* and the American Georgic." *Colonial Latin American Review* 24 (2): 190–214.
Chevalier, Maxime. 1966. *L'Arioste en Espagne (1530–1650). Recherches sur l'influence du "Roland furieux."* Bordeaux: Institut d'Études Ibériques et Ibéro-Américaines de l'Université de Bordeaux.

Dietz, David B. 1995. "*Historia* in the Commentary of Servius." *Transactions of the American Philological Association* 125: 61–97.

Dryden, John. [1697] 1900. "Dedication of the *Æneis*." In *Essays*, edited by W. P. Ker, 2: 154–240. Oxford: Clarendon Press.

Ercilla, Alonso de. [1569–89] 2002. *La Araucana*. Edited by Isaías Lerner. Madrid: Cátedra.

Firbas, Paul. 2004. "La geografía antártica y el nombre del Perú." In *La formación de la cultura virreinal, II. El siglo XVII*, edited by Karl Kohut and Sonia V. Rose, 265–285. Madrid and Frankfurt: Iberoamericana / Vervuert.

Ford, Philip. 2007. *De Troie à Ithaque: Réception des épopées homériques à la Renaissance*. Geneva: Droz.

Franklin, III, Albert B. 1937. "A Study of the Origins of the Legend of Bernardo del Carpio." *Hispanic Review* 5 (4): 286–303.

Gibson, Charles. 1952. *Tlaxcala in the Sixteenth Century*. New Haven, CT: Yale University Press.

Javitch, Daniel. 1991. *Proclaiming a Classic: The Canonization of "Orlando furioso."* Princeton, NJ: Princeton University Press.

Lazzarini, Caterina. 1984. "*Historia/fabula*: forme della costruzione poetica virgiliana nel commento di Servio all'*Eneide*." *Materiali e Discussioni per l'Analisi dei Testi Classici* 12: 117–144.

Lipsius, Justus. 1602. *Epistolarum selectarum centuria miscellanea*. Antwerp: Ex Officina Plantiniana, apud Ioannem Moretum.

Martínez Baracs, Andrea. 2008. *Un gobierno de indios: Tlaxcala, 1519–1750*. Mexico City: FCE.

Mazzotti, José Antonio. 2000. "Resentimiento criollo y nación étnica: el papel de la épica novohispana." In *Agencias criollas: La ambigüedad 'colonial' en las letras hispanoamericanas*, edited by José Antonio Mazzotti, 143–160. Pittsburgh, PA: Instituto Internacional de Literatura Iberoamericana.

Nicolopulos, Jaime. 1998. "Pedro de Oña and Bernardo de Balbuena Read Ercilla's Fitón." *Latin American Literary Review* 26 (52): 100–119.

Oudijk, Michael R. and Matthew Restall. 2007. "Mesoamerican Conquistadors in the Sixteenth Century." In *Indian Conquistadors: Indigenous Allies in the Conquest of Mesoamerica*, edited by Laura E. Matthew and Michael R. Oudijk, 28–64. Norman, OK: University of Oklahoma Press.

Pérez de Moya, Juan. [1585] 1995. *Philosofía secreta*. Edited by Carlos Clavería. Madrid: Cátedra.

Pierce, Frank. 1945. "*El Bernardo* of Balbuena: A Baroque Fantasy." *Hispanic Review* 13 (1): 1–23.

———. 1949–50 "L'allégorie poétique au XVIᵉ siècle. Son évolution et son traitement par Bernardo de Balbuena." *Bulletin Hispanique* 51 (4): 381–406, 52 (3): 191–228.

Quint, David. 1993. *Epic and Empire: Politics and Generic Form from Virgil to Milton*. Princeton, NJ: Princeton University Press.

Rojas Garcidueñas, José. 1982. *Bernardo de Balbuena. La vida y la obra*. Mexico City: UNAM.

Tasso, Torquato. [1594] 1973. *Discourses on the Heroic Poem*. Translated by Mariella Cavalchini and Irene Samuel. Oxford: Clarendon Press.

Van Horne, John. 1927. *"El Bernardo" of Bernardo de Balbuena*. Urbana, IL: University of Illinois.

———. 1940. *Bernardo de Balbuena. Biografía y crítica*. Guadalajara: Imprenta Font.

Vilà, Lara. 2001. "Épica e imperio. Imitación virgiliana y propaganda política en la épica española del siglo XVI." PhD diss., Universitat Autònoma de Barcelona.

———. 2010. "Épica y poder en el Renacimiento. Virgilio, la alegoría histórica y la alegoría política." In *La teoría de la épica en el siglo XVI (España, Francia, Italia y Portugal)*, edited by María José Vega and Lara Vilà, 23–59. Vigo: Editorial Academia del Hispanismo.

———. 2011. "*Compuesto de materia que es la verdad histórica*. Virgilianismo político y escritura épica." In *Estudios sobre la tradición épica occidental (Edad Media y Renacimiento)*, edited by Lara Vilà, 123–139. Madrid/Bellaterra: Editorial Caronte.

———. 2012. "De Roncesvalles a Pavía. Ariosto, la épica española y los poemas sobre Bernardo del Carpio." *Criticón* 115: 45–65.

Weinberg, Bernard. 1961. *A History of Literary Criticism in the Italian Renaissance*. Chicago/London: University of Chicago Press.

20

FALLEN IDOLS? VICE AND VIRTUE IN THE ICONOGRAPHY OF ICARUS AND PHAETHON

Richard Rabone

Out of the night I will ride,
Burning bright through the eye of my father.
Watch me until I am gone,
Friend. Watch me forever, and after.

(Glyn Maxwell, "Phaeton and the Chariot of the Sun")

The stories of these impetuous boys who dared to ascend to the skies have had a long and varied afterlife. Moreover, though the tales are usually separately told, the obvious narrative parallels between them have often made them seem a natural pair, or seen them used as vehicles for similar sentiments: both tell of a daring attempt to traverse the heavens (with a special focus on the sun), which fails as similar advice from both boys' fathers is ignored; both then fall to their deaths, Phaethon in the river Po, Icarus in the sea that will henceforth bear his name. Accounting for the wide variety of interpretations that were commonly tied to these tales in early modern Europe, however, is much less straightforward. Two strands recur with particular frequency in Golden Age literature and art. The first focuses on the daring of the ascent, and on the immortality it brings, as Icarus's name lives on forever in that of the sea where he died, for example; comparison is then easily made with a poet's daring in his writing and the immortality hoped for on the basis of his poetry, or with the situation of the Petrarchan lover and the daring of the approach to the beloved. As an example of this last use may stand Herrera's "Dichoso fue'l ardor, dichoso el buelo," printed in his *Anotaciones* to Garcilaso's twelfth sonnet (2001, 364). He also briefly notes there the second meaning widely read into these tales: "Algunos sinifican esta fábula moralmente contra los que presumiendo subir con temeraria osadía más alto que lo que pueden sus fuerças, al fin caen en tierra" (2001, 363). This chapter focuses on this second line of interpretation, taking examples from emblematic and artistic tradition to draw out an important ambivalence in the moralizing use of these fables, which were capable of being employed either to refer to a single, specific vice, or to refer to a more general moral principle that may be taken to underpin all virtuous action.

It is now well established that artists found an invaluable iconographical source in the emblem books that flooded Renaissance Europe (see especially Sebastián 1995). The most significant was that of Andreas Alciatus, *pater et princeps* of the genre, the first version of which was published in Latin in 1531. Daza Pinciano's 1549 translation undoubtedly did much to popularize the work in Spain, but there is clear evidence that Alciatus's book of emblems was already familiar in some Spanish circles: Infantes notes the earlier translation of four individual emblems (without illustrations) appended to Villa Real's *Emblema o scriptura de la Justicia* (1546), the emblems apparently selected to fill the blank leaves at the end of the book because of their relevance to its theme of justice (2000, 238–239); Egido draws attention to discussions of Alciatus's emblems by members of the epistolary circle of the Aragonese Antonio Agustín from the late 1530s (2004, 21–22); and Heiple also suggests the possible influence on Garcilaso's twelfth sonnet of Alciatus's two emblems whose illustrations depict Icarus and Phaethon (1994, 203–206). Moreover, the influence of the Latin versions was not confined to the early years of Alciatus's reception, as commentaries written by Spaniards on his Latin verses bear testimony that the idea of Alciatus's emblem book as a modern classic was by no means alien to Spain; these include at least the published Latin commentary of El Brocense (Sanctius Brocensis 1573), the Spanish explanation by Diego López (1615), and the manuscript commentary by Juan de Valencia covering seventy of Alciatus's Latin emblems (see Talavera Esteso 2001). The continued relevance of these Latin-based editions is significant: it suggests that Spanish intellectuals were aware of participating in a phenomenon that reached easily across European national boundaries, and implies that in questions of interpretation, we should be wary of a risk of over-privileging the account offered by the Spanish versions of these texts (see Egido 2004, 25); this is a particular risk in contexts where Mal Lara's doubts over the usefulness and fidelity of the vernacular versions may well have been shared.[1] We must therefore approach these emblems keeping their Latin originals in mind.

One example of this risk is afforded by Alciatus's Phaethon emblem (see Figure 20.1). Titled "In temerarios," this emblem is illustrated by an image of Phaethon's fall from the 1534 Paris edition onwards; Daza Pinciano titles his version "Contra los vanos príncipes." The difference is essentially one of emphasis, but it may be instructive. The Spanish title accentuates the association of the moral with rulers, leading many critics to insist on the political context of the emblem (see, e.g., Sebastián 1985, 93). However, there is no specific reference to princes in the title of the Latin original, and the gloss tells a similar story:

Aſpicis aurigam currus Phaëtonta paterni
Igniuomos auſum flectere solis equos.
Maxima qui poſtquam terris incendia ſparſit:
Eſt temerè inſeſſo lapſus ab axe miſer.
Sic plerique rotis Fortunae ad ſydera Reges
Euecti: ambitio quos iuuenilis agit:
Poſt magnam humani generis clademque ſuamque,
Cunctorum poenas denique dant ſcelerum.

(Alciatus 1550, 65)

[Here you see Phaeton; driver of the paternal chariot; he dared to guide the fire-vomiting horses of the Sun. After scattering enormous conflagrations all over the Earth, he fell disgraced from the vehicle which he had so recklessly mounted. Much the same happens to many kings who, driven by adolescent ambition, are carried toward the stars upon the wheels of Fortune. After having provoked much misfortune among the human race, they bring ruin upon themselves and, finally, they pay the penalties due for their crimes.]

(tr. Moffitt 2004, 75)

STVLTITIA. 65

In temerarios.

A∫picis aurigam currus Phaëtonta paterni
Igniuomos aursum flectere solis equos.
Maxima qui po∫t quam terris incendia ∫par∫it:
E∫t temere infe∫∫o lap∫us ab axe mi∫er.
Sic pleriqu: rotis Fortunæ ad ∫ydera Reges
Euecti: ambitio quos iuuenilis agit:
Po∫t magnam humani generis cladémque ∫uímque,
Cunctorum pœnas denique dant ∫celerum.

Figure 20.1   Andreas Alciatus, "In temerarios." In *Emblemata* (Lugduni: apud Mathiam Bonhomme, 1550).

Of this eight-line gloss, only lines 5–8 refer to royalty; 1–4 simply introduce the character of Phaethon and the moment of his fall, hinting at the meaning of the episode, before that meaning is then applied to the royal context in lines 5–8. The original, then, is not focused on the exclusive association of Phaethon with princes; rather, he and his fall have a specific ethical significance, which is then applied to the rulers who would do well to follow it. The focus on Phaethon's moral significance is clear enough from Golden Age commentators: López, for example, noting Horace's allusion to Phaethon and Bellerophon at *C* 4.11 in a context far removed from royalty, explains that "Amone∫tanos esta Emblema, que ninguno prete[n]da lo q[ue] no puede, ni procure co∫as mayores que las que pueda hazer, y acabar" (1615, 173v).

This is the essence of the moral advice embodied by Phaethon: the daring which was praised by Herrera remains an important feature of the tale, but the focus is now on whether what is being undertaken is commensurate with someone's abilities; if not, then the action

251

is no longer praised, but condemned, as an example of excessive daring. Moreover, there is no need to rely on the commentaries to make this meaning clear. In condemning Phaethon's daring as excessive, Alciatus's emblem is clearly echoing Aristotelian morality, which saw proper courage as a mean between cowardice (involving greater fear than a situation should warrant) and recklessness (where insufficient fear is felt in situations that ought to provoke it); that proper sense of fear should then prevent projects like Phaethon's being undertaken (see especially *Nicomachean Ethics* 1115b28–1116a9). Nor would this context have seemed terribly recondite to a contemporary audience: in the Spanish context alone, it is familiar enough for Sancho Panza to pick it up in passing in the *Quijote*:

> Y más, que yo he oído decir, y creo que a mi señor mismo, si mal no me acuerdo, que entre los estremos de cobarde y de temerario está el medio de la valentía: y si esto es así, no quiero que huya sin tener para qué, ni que acometa cuando la demasía pide otra cosa.
>
> (Cervantes 2004, 719–720)

Significantly, Sancho's term for this excessive daring is *temeridad*, the standard term used to denote this excess in Spanish as its cognate *temeritas* is in Latin. This specific vice, then, is already alluded to in the Latin title of Alciatus's emblem, which is echoed by the use of the adverb "temerè" [recklessly] in the gloss. The emblem thus reveals Phaethon as an example of the vice of temerity, while the illustration, which depicts his mortal fall, focuses the reader's attention on the negative consequences of that vice, revealing the disaster which it brought in Phaethon's case. These important lexical allusions are both obscured in the Spanish translation, where the title's description of the princes as "vanos" suppresses the signpost to the Aristotelian vice, and "temerè" is rendered colourlessly as "de ciego." Alciatus's original emblem is not simply vague advice to princes about the dangers of youthful impetuousness or blind ambition; instead, it is underpinned by a precise allusion to Phaethon as an exemplar of the specific vice of temerity.

This is no innovation on Alciatus's part: rather, the association of Phaethon with temerity was already commonplace, as may be conveniently illustrated by Ravisius Textor's *Officina*, a remarkable compendium of literary erudition, including a wide range of classical figures and their standard associations. The *Officina* contains a list of eight "Audaces et temerarii" [bold and reckless characters], of which Phaethon is the first example given (Ravisius Textor 1520, 351r). Moreover, the association of Phaethon with Icarus on narrative grounds, noted previously, finds a different kind of support here, as Icarus also has a place on this list. The two young fliers are thus also linked by their shared status as a convenient shorthand for this specific Aristotelian vice of temerity: daring without compunction what ought not to be undertaken.

This background is important for Alciatus's emblem 103 ("In astrologos"): the emblem refers to astrologers, but its gloss focuses on Icarus, and it is illustrated with an image of Icarus's fall from the 1534 Paris edition onwards (see Figure 20.2).[2] Its gloss reads as follows:

> Icare per ſuperos qui raptus & aëra, donec
> In mare praecipitem caera liquata daret,
> Nunc te caera eadem, feruenſque exulcitat ignis,
> Exemplo ut doceas dogmata certa tuo.
> Aſtrologus caueat quicquam praedicere. praeceps
> Nam cadet impostor, dum ſuper astra uolat.
>
> (Alciatus 1550, 113)

Figure 20.2 Andreas Alciatus, "In astrologos." In *Emblemata* (Lugduni: apud Mathiam Bonhomme, 1550).

[Oh Icarus, you who ascended through air up into the heaven, until the melting wax pitched you into the sea, now this same wax and the same burning fire bring you back to life as an example by which you will teach us your resolved doctrine. The astrologer must be careful with what he predicts, since the impostor falls head down when he flies above the stars.]

(tr. Moffitt 2004, 124)

The emblem's title might initially imply that the most relevant interpretative strand here is the rationalization of Icarus and Phaethon as pioneers in the field of astrology, a tradition noted by Herrera (2001, 360–361) and which draws on works such as Lucian's *Astrology*. However, line 4 suggests that in fact the moralizing reading is again in play here, as the *exemplum* by which Icarus's message is to be conveyed would easily bear the sense of a moral example. This suspicion is again confirmed by the commentators, who make frequent reference to the vice of temerity, or label Icarus a "temerario mancebo" (López 1615, 264r). Perhaps the clearest example of this is recorded in the great Tozzi edition of Alciatus's emblems (Thuilius 1621, 434):

> Icari fabulam hic Alciatus noſter torquet in Aſtrologos quoſdam falſarios & impoſtores, qui ſupra humanum captu[m] conantur aliquid, quaeque longiſſimè abſunt ab ingenio humano, vi mentis, & artis experientia ſe hariolari poſſe putant.

> [Our Alciatus here turns the story of Icarus to certain astrologers acting as forgers and impostors, who attempt something beyond human capability, and believe themselves able to predict things which are far beyond the human intellect, the power of the mind, and the experience of science.]

Crucially, then, the problem with these astrologers is that they are going beyond human capability, and essaying something they ought to recognize as beyond them, thus exemplifying the familiar vice of temerity. It is this moral correspondence that really underpins the parallel with Icarus, aptly captured by Pico della Mirandola's description of astrologers as "pennis temerariae profeſſionis in cęlum ſe ſubtollentes" [raising themselves up to the sky on the wings of the reckless profession] (recorded in Thuilius 1621, 435).

This emblem, then, in fact seems to work very similarly to the Phaethon emblem. Both illustrations depict the youths falling from the heavens, thus focusing our attention on the moment when the temerity both exemplify is punished. As in "In temerarios," the gloss again begins by briefly evoking Icarus's story, before proceeding to the continued relevance of the moral doctrine which Icarus exemplifies. The final two lines then apply this moral to a specific context. There remains some controversy among Renaissance commentators as to whether the moral is applied to all astrologers (López 1615, 264r–v) or only to those who claim knowledge they do not have (Sanctius Brocensis 1573, 317), but in either case what is important is that the condemnation is underpinned by the astrologers' attempts to act beyond their capability. It is only the readiness of both figures' association with this vice of temerity that allows Alciatus to apply his Icarus and Phaethon emblems to specific contexts as rapidly as he does, and as we have seen, the reference to that vice formed an important part of how early modern readers reacted to the emblems, both in Spain and beyond.

However, this picture begins to be interestingly complicated by one of the most remarkable emblem books produced anywhere in Europe: Otto Vaenius's *Quinti Horatii Flacci Emblemata* (or *Emblemata Horatiana*). Two Latin editions were printed in 1607, the second including short verse additions in French and Dutch; the vernacular element is much expanded in the 1612 edition, which also includes Spanish and Italian poems, together with new French and Dutch lines. These vernacular texts provide important evidence of the breadth of the work's intended audience, which reaches across Europe, and may extend beyond the learned circles in which Latin was common. They may also be the fruits of early responses to the initial Latin emblems (Thøfner 2003, 39), or evidence of an instinct to explain the emblems' content (Bath 1997, 90). Such an instinct is already visible in the Latin, as some emblems include short prose passages to clarify the meaning, printed among the other texts on the verso of the two-page spread each emblem occupies, alongside the Latin quotations (which remain largely, but not entirely, consistent between these editions), and such vernacular compositions as may appear. The recto page is then entirely devoted to the image, which is often remarkably intricate, and seeks to give visual expression to the ideas suggested by the quotations, at times in rare detail. Lavish Spanish editions are published in 1669, 1672, 1682, 1701, and 1733, usually under the title *Theatro moral de la vida humana en cien emblemas*; they retain the original illustrations, but follow the much-altered format of the 1646 French edition by Marin Le Roy, Sieur de Gomberville.[3] The emblems are presented in a revised order, and now feature an introductory explanation in Spanish, followed by a reduced number of Latin quotations, the Spanish poems from the 1612 edition, and a further short set of Spanish verses that are printed below the illustration on the recto page. (On this book, see especially the articles in McKeown 2012; Gerards-Nelissen 1971; and on the Spanish version, Sebastián 1983.)

Icarus makes his appearance in Vaenius's sixth emblem, "In medio consistit virtus," where he and Daedalus appear flying, with Icarus's wings already falling from his shoulders (see Figure 20.3). They figure in the background of a scene which depicts the virtue of Liberality, who stands at the centre of a circle and is flanked by her corresponding vices of Avarice and Prodigality: exactly as she is described in the Latin passage attributed to Aristotle on the facing page.[4] Once again, then, we are squarely in the field of Aristotelian morality. However, while this might seem to imply that the emblem deals principally with Aristotle's trio of virtue and vices pertaining to liberality, the inclusion of Icarus and Daedalus would then be surprising, since the temerity alluded to in Alciatus's Icarus emblem was specifically the excess of courage, and thus pertains to a quite different Aristotelian virtue. We might therefore suspect that specific virtues and vices are in fact not of primary relevance here; more important is the general virtuous principle which underpins both these examples: the Aristotelian idea that virtue is always a middle path between two vicious extremes. Indeed, this is the obvious implication of the emblem's title, and is well supported by the Latin quotations, which include some of the most famous Horatian formulations of the idea of a virtuous mean.[5]

Moreover, the details of the picture also support this more general interpretation, as the falling Icarus has encroached on the shaded area depicting the sun's rays, a visual representation of Ovid's quoted assertion that he was seeking to fly too high, while Daedalus flies a clear middle path between the shaded areas above and below him.[6] It is worth noting too that where the Icarus myth carries this more general meaning, Daedalus is often included as well, as a positive example of prudence to counterbalance Icarus's excess; or indeed he may even be depicted on his own, as a positive example of the exhortation to take the middle course.[7] This is the sense in which the myth is used in the present emblem: not as a condemnation of temerity in particular, but as a general example of the need to follow the middle path, avoiding vicious extremes in all matters of virtue, as is reiterated by the reference to Icarus in the Spanish sonnet included in the 1612 edition:

Es la virtud del hombre vna armonia,
Que de contrarios haze confonancia,
Entre afectado, y tofco vna elegancia,
Que aborrefce la falta, y demafia;
Es entre mas, y menos norte, y guia
Para la eterna immaterial eftancia,
De dos extremos liga, y concordancia,
Rachel hermofa entre vna, y otra Lia:
Es medio vniuerfal, por donde puede,
De fus vicios huyendo los extremos,
Sin que cayga qual Icaro atreuido,
Llegar el ho[m]bre al te[m]plo, en quien co[n]cede
La prudencia, que ofrezca vela, y remos,
Que à tal medio tal fin fe efta deuido.

                    (see Vaenius 1612, 18)

Figure 20.3 Anonymous after Otto Vaenius, "In medio consistit virtus." In *Quinti Horatii Flacci Emblemata* (Antuerpiae: Philippus Liſaert, 1612).

Once again, we might have expected Icarus's epithet "atrevido" to guide us to the specific vice of bold recklessness, but the preceding lines make the sense clear: Icarus is here being used as a general example of one who fails to keep to this "medio universal" by fleeing all "extremos" – the fundamental principle behind all Aristotelian notions of virtue.

The emblematic tradition, then, reveals an important ambivalence in the moral significance these myths may be taken to imply: they may be markers of the specific vice of temerity, or more general negative *exempla* of a failure to keep to the mean, which defines all virtuous action. Their appearance in Spanish art is perhaps comparatively infrequent, as is the case with mythological tales in general (see, e.g., Brown 1978, 71–72); nonetheless, where mythological themes are treated, emblems such as those discussed here are frequently cited as an interpretative crux, and would doubtless have been an invaluable iconographical source for contemporary painters (see especially Sebastián 1995), and a proper understanding of their implications is therefore essential. Moreover, while Icarus and Phaethon may be relatively infrequent, they are certainly not absent from the artistic tradition. One especially important context in this regard is early seventeenth-century Seville, which saw the creation of ceiling paintings including at least one of our impetuous youths in the Casa de Arguijo (1601) and the Casa de Pilatos (1604), both of which served as meeting places for the academy originally founded by Mal Lara. I focus here on the second of these, which includes both Icarus and Phaethon, in a context where the moralizing tenor is clear. It is difficult, however, to consider the Icarus and Phaethon panels in isolation, as their relationship to the ceiling's other *lienzos* is an essential, if controversial, factor in their interpretation. Nonetheless, I suggest that we may be more easily guided through the ceiling's decorative programme if we keep in mind the interplay between general and specific interpretations which emerges from the emblematic tradition.[8]

The layout of the ceiling may be briefly rehearsed (see Figure 20.4). It contains seven principal panels, interspersed among which are decorative motifs and two heraldic shields. The central panel depicts Hercules, clearly identifiable by his club and the Nemean lionskin, in the moment of his apotheosis, making his ascent to dwell among the Olympian gods who surround him in this painting. A dedicatory inscription next to Jupiter makes the moralizing context explicit: Hercules, the mythical founder of Seville also claimed as an ancestor by the family who owned the house (Kunoth 1964, 336), is here presented as a model for his alleged descendant, his apotheosis a reward for his virtuous conduct, in which the present duke is supposed to follow Hercules's lead.[9] Hercules's apotheosis is then flanked by large images of Icarus and Phaethon: on one side, Phaethon falling from his chariot; on the other, the falling Icarus, while Daedalus again seems to fly between two layers of cloud. Moving further out from the centre, each of these is then followed by two slightly smaller panels: after Icarus come Astraea/Justice and Ganymede, borne aloft to Olympus by Jupiter in the form of a great eagle; after Phaethon are Bellerophon (sometimes identified as Perseus) astride Pegasus, and a final figure usually given as Envy.[10] As may be seen at a glance, the ceiling is thus deliberately arranged, with a very obvious symmetry; due account must be taken of this in any overall interpretation of the work.

The Icarus and Phaethon panels flank the central depiction of Hercules, and may be seen to provide the key to the ceiling's symmetrical layout. Both panels once again focus on the moment of the fall, and have often been taken as negative *exempla*, along the lines of the two Alciatus emblems just examined. As such, Icarus and Phaethon would be images of vice that act as a counterpoint to the virtuous Hercules (López Torrijos 1985, 132–133; Sebastián 1995, 78), with those two failed attempts then further contrasted with the successful ascents of Ganymede and Bellerophon, the difference between success and failure perhaps coming "a causa de la virtud o del vicio representado a su lado [i.e. Justice or Envy]" (López Torrijos 1985, 135). This is an attractive interpretation; however, it does not convincingly account for the presence of Daedalus in the panel supposedly devoted to Icarus's fall as an example of vice, particularly as the emblematic background outlined previously might lead us to expect Daedalus's appearance alongside Icarus to shift the panel's emphasis onto a more positive reference to prudence, that general moral principle that a middle course must be kept. Moreover, it is difficult to tie Justice and Envy sufficiently closely to Ganymede and Bellerophon for them to be the cause

Figure 20.4   Francisco Pacheco, *Apoteosis de Hércules*, 1604. Tempera on canvas. Casa de Pilatos, Seville.

of their neighbours' success or failure, but the reason for their inclusion over other virtues or vices then remains somewhat unclear.

Similar questions are raised by Brown's analysis (1978, 77–80): though he takes Daedalus as an example of prudence, that is as a counter to Icarus's imprudence, and so with Phaethon as a figure of vainglory, both panels are again interpreted as warnings against vice, with Daedalus offering the additional suggestion that the Duke should cultivate modesty and prudence. The panels showing Ganymede and what he takes to be Perseus astride Pegasus are then seen to imply other particular qualities recommended to the Duke: namely, prudence in learning, and physical strength; or, if the emphasis is on Pegasus rather than his rider, courage, or fame. Once again, though, the appearance of Justice and Envy is acknowledged to cause some problems; they may be seen as general representatives of vice and virtue, but "it is hard to know why justice and envy have been singled out" (Brown 1978, 80). The ceiling's apparent symmetry also risks being obscured on this interpretation, as virtuous and vicious figures seem interspersed with no clear overarching pattern.

One solution to these problems is offered by Lleó Cañal (see especially 1998, 64–65; 1999), who sees the emphasis in the Icarus-Daedalus panel as being on the father figure, who stands as a positive example of prudence.[11] On the other side of Hercules, Phaethon would then give a counter example of temerity, as the ceiling is divided into three virtues which the young duke should cultivate, facing three vices which he must avoid. Thus, the Deadalus-prudence panel is supported by Justice, whose selection is explained because she is considered the "suma de todas las virtudes," and Ganymede, understood as a "símbolo de la pureza del alma;" opposed to them are Envy, as the root of all evil, and Bellerophon, pictured here not in virtuous victory, but in his hubristic attempt to scale the heavens, and thus to be understood as a figure of arrogance or pride (see Lleó Cañal 1999, 178–179).

This interpretation takes very plausible account of the symmetry of the ceiling, and is not easily countered; some of the specifics, however, still resist easy integration. If Justice, for example, is invoked as the sum of all virtue, then it is odd to relegate her to a corner panel, and give pride of place on the virtuous side to Icarus and Daedalus. The choice of Ganymede's purity as the third of the virtues also remains something of a surprise, and though López (1615, 19r–20r) gives useful details on this association of Ganymede with the delight of the pure soul engaged in divine contemplation, the reason why Ganymede's purity should be directly opposed by arrogance, as on Lleó Cañal's reading of Bellerophon, is still difficult to explain. Bellerophon himself may also have more precise implications than this, as he is elsewhere ascribed a specific moral value very close to that of Phaethon (see, e.g., Ravisius Textor 1520, 351r; and the allusion noted previously at Horace, *C* 4.11.25–31, where Phaethon and Bellerophon's attempted ascents are given as examples of overreaching). However, it is no easier to see why Bellerophon's overreaching should directly oppose Ganymede's purity, as the precise purpose of these oppositions suggested by the ceiling's symmetrical layout remains difficult to pin down.

With all this in mind, a final clue to the ceiling's meaning is afforded by a brief inscription, now lost to a recent restoration, which formed a halo above Hercules's head: "petitur hac caelum via" [by this path is heaven sought]. Lleó Cañal gives the inspiration for this as Ovid, *Fasti* 1.307, in a passage on astronomers (see especially 1998, 64; 1999, 178; 2012, 65). However, Ovid's exact phrase is "sic petitur caelum" [thus is heaven sought], and the alteration is significant. In fact, the phrase on Pacheco's ceiling is lifted *verbatim* from [Seneca], *Octavia* 476, where it is used to describe another virtuous apotheosis: that of Augustus. The shift in context here to that of Hercules is striking, too, for Hercules's own situation allows the phrase to take on new meaning. In this context, "hac . . . via" [by this path] must surely recall the famous moment of Hercules at the crossroads, faced with the choice of the two *viae* of virtue and vice; in his apotheosis, we are being shown the consequence of his choice of path, while the moment of that choice is simultaneously alluded to in the inscription. Moreover, this extra facet renders Hercules an even more appropriate model for the third duke, since Hercules made his choice when emerging from boyhood into the age of his independence (see Xenophon, *Memorabilia* 2.1.21), a precise parallel with the Duke, who was about to come of age at the time of the ceiling's painting (see Lleó Cañal 1998, 60).

The ceiling thus exhorts the Duke to make the same choice as his ancestor Hercules, now that his time has come to face the same twin paths of Virtue and Vice; those paths are then illustrated by the virtuous and vicious figures grouped on either side of the ceiling's central panel. However, Hercules's two paths are not usually associated with specific virtues and vices, but are understood in a much more general way. This returns us to the ambivalence found in the emblematic tradition, the final important piece of evidence to bear in mind when assessing Pacheco's ceiling. Our natural first instinct on seeing Phaethon's spectacular fall is to assume him an example of the specific vice of temerity; however, the opposing panel's depiction of both Icarus and Daedalus makes us hesitate, given their earlier appearance together in the context of an allusion to the doctrine of the mean, the guiding principle of all virtuous action. There is thus an apparent tension between the general and the specific interpretations of these myths, which is one reason why the contrast between the ceiling's two halves has been difficult to work through in detail. The foregoing interpretation of the central panel, with its allusion to Hercules's choice, suggests the relevance of the more general mode of interpretation, and this also helps explain the ceiling's symmetrical layout. While the specific virtues and vices alluded to in these six panels may well have been felt particularly pertinent to this duke and his station, the contrasts between particular pairs of these which the symmetry might suggest are not always straightforward. Instead, the layout of these panels might be seen as simply reinforcing the general choice represented by Hercules's crossroads: three panels standing for the path of virtue, and three for that of vice, between which the Duke must choose. This reading also makes sense of the decision to give Daedalus and Icarus pride of place on the virtuous side, with Justice placed less prominently in a corner panel, which was seen to be problematic if she was to be taken as the supreme virtue. If we privilege what has here been termed the general interpretation of the myths, then it is natural to set Daedalus and Icarus at the head of the virtues, since they together represent the principle of keeping to the mean, which underpins all moral action. The warning which emerged from study of emblematic tradition, that moralizing references to Icarus and Phaethon may not always be associated with the specific vice of temerity, is thus salutary here, as the more general alternative reading of the Daedalus-Icarus scene ties in closely with the image and inscriptions of the ceiling's essential central panel, as well as offering an explanation for certain details of its overall interpretation and its layout which have otherwise proved elusive.

Pacheco's ceiling thus provides a useful case study to show how an awareness of the emblematic tradition can enrich our understanding of other artistic works, which are so often said to use emblems as a source of iconographical information. Importantly, however, there has been no need here to posit the direct influence of these particular emblems on Pacheco – and indeed, in the case of the later Vaenius emblem, such a relationship would be chronologically impossible. Instead, the emblems and their commentaries can offer us a glimpse of what the mythological figures and commonplaces which they often took as their subjects really meant to the Renaissance mind. The potential double-meaning that this background suggests for the moralizing myths of Icarus and Phaethon is thus not a problem to be solved by specifying the influence of a particular source; instead, the emblematic tradition as a whole bears witness here to an ambivalence in what these figures implied in the general cultural consciousness, sometimes standing as an analogue for the vice of temerity, while other references suggest the more general *mediocritas* on which all virtuous action is based. The findings of this study therefore have a potentially wide relevance, as the influence of this possible double-meaning is not only felt in early modern visual culture, but extends across the full range of Golden Age cultural production.[12]

Notes

1 See Mal Lara (2013, 463): "Los quales [sc. the *Emblemas* of Alciatus], aunque andan en romance castellano y en vulgar toscano, viendo que aún no están entendidos, quise yo, como hombre que los he leído muchas vezes y trabajado sobre ellos, poner mi declaración, que más allegue a la letra y al sentido d'ellos."

2 The three earlier editions contain simply an image of an astrologer contemplating the stars. Manning (2002, 43) makes the very useful suggestion that the 1534 Paris edition was the first to benefit from Alciatus's involvement, and saw the beginning of a process whereby some illustrations used for the earlier editions were corrected, as an inability to read the Latin glosses had led to some emblems being inappropriately illustrated. This context might well explain the printing history for the Icarus emblem, where references to Icarus come only in the gloss, and if taken on its own, the title might suggest something more general on astrologers, which the early illustrations would fit well.

3 This title was used for all editions except that published in 1669, whose title read: *Theatro moral de toda la philosophia de los antiguos y modernos.*

4 This passage reads: "In circuli centro, poſita hic Liberalitas, Auaritiam inter, ac Prodigalitatem. *Virtus enim eſt mediocritas duorum vitiorum, alterius ſecundùm exceßum, alterius ſecundùm defectum, ratione ad nos ſervatâ*: ſine qua mediocritate nihil boni nobis aduenire poteſt; eâ autem ſeruatâ, nihil ad bene beateque viuendum ſubtrahi" [Liberality is placed here in the centre of the circle, between Avarice and Prodigality. *For Virtue is a mean of two vices, one of excess, the other of deficiency, even if [working out] the precise proportion has been left to us*: without that mean, nothing good can happen to us; but if it is preserved, nothing pertaining to good and happy living can be withheld] (see Vaenius 1612, 18). It is attributed to the second book of Aristotle's *Nicomachean Ethics*, noting also Cicero, *De officiis*; part of the italicized text, as far as "*defectum*," is indeed a Latin version of *Nicomachean Ethics* 1107a2–3, but it is only that section which corresponds directly to Aristotle's text here. (I am grateful to Rhiannon Ash for her advice on this piece of Vaenius's Latin.)

5 "Virtus eſt medium uitiorum in utrimque reductum" [Virtue is a mean between vices set back from both sides] (see Vaenius 1612, 8; cf. *Epistles* 1.18.9); "Eſt modus in rebus, ſunt certi denique fines, | Quos ultra citraq[ue] nequit conſiſtere rectum" [There is a mean in things, and then there are fixed limits, and it is impossible for virtue to dwell beyond those limits on either side] (see Vaenius 1612, 8; cf. *Satires* 1.1.106–107).

6 The quoted Ovidian lines are: "Dum petit infirmis nimium ſublimia pennis | Icarus, Icariis nomina fecit aquis" [As Icarus seeks to go too high on his fragile wings, he has given a name to the Icarian waters] (see Vaenius 1612, 8; cf. *Tristia* 1.1.89–90, though some modern editors prefer the reading "aequoreis" for "Icariis").

7 See, for example, Griffin (2005, 153–154), who reproduces a printer's mark used by both Pierre Regnier and Denis de Harsy, which depicts a flying Daedalus emblazoned with the command to avoid both extremes, and instead follow the middle way. Griffin also notes the possible irony in Regnier's use of the image, as his own situation might rather have resembled the negative example of Icarus.

8 For interpretations of the Arguijo ceiling, see especially Brown (1978, 73–77); Lleó Cañal (2012, 70–74); López Torrijos (1999; 1985, 102–111).

9 The inscription reads: "D. FERD. HENRICIO. A. RIBERA. DVCI. ALCALAE. III. HEROICA. VIRTVTE. ARDVVM. AD. GLORIAM. ITER. PARANTI. EXEMPLAR. PROPOSITVM." [Proposed as an example to Don Fernando Enríquez de Ribera, III Duke of Alcalá, as he prepares the difficult journey to glory with heroic virtue].

10 This identification rests on an obscure object clasped in the figure's hands, taken to be a heart, and thus a reference to the widespread tradition of Envy eating her own heart, as recorded, for example, in Alciatus's emblem "Invidia," or in Ripa (1992), *Iconologia*, s.v. "Invidia."

11 Given the foregoing study of the emblematic background, I take this approach to be more promising than that which the same author advances elsewhere (Lleó Cañal 2012, 64), seeing Daedalus as a "mero apéndice iconográfico de Ícaro;" his presence in fact suggests the possibility of quite a dramatic shift in meaning, as illustrated previously.

12 I am grateful to Jonathan Thacker and Oliver Noble Wood for their comments on this chapter, and to Sofia Kaba-Ferreiro for her help in editing the images for publication.

Works cited

Alciatus, Andreas. 1550. *Emblemata*. Lugd[uni]: apud Mathiam Bonhomme. Accessed January 20, 2015. http://www.emblems.arts.gla.ac.uk/alciato/books.php?id=A50a.

Bath, Michael. 1997. "Vaenius Abroad: English and Scottish Reception of the *Emblemata Horatiana*." In *Anglo-Dutch Relations in the Field of the Emblem*, edited by Bart Westerweel, 87–106. Leiden: Brill.

Brown, Jonathan. 1978. *Images and Ideas in Seventeenth-Century Spanish Painting*. Princeton, NJ: Princeton University Press.

Cervantes, Miguel de. 2004. *Don Quijote de la Mancha. Edición del Instituto Cervantes*. Edited by Francisco Rico. 2 vols. Barcelona: Galaxia Gutenberg.

Egido, Aurora. 2004. *De la mano de Artemia: Literatura, Emblemática, Mnemotecnia y Arte en el Siglo de Oro*. Barcelona: José J. de Olañata and Edicions UIB.

Gerards-Nelissen, Inemie. 1971. "Otto van Veen's *Emblemata Horatiana*." *Simiolus* 5: 20–63.

Griffin, Clive. 2005. *Journeymen-Printers, Heresy, and the Inquisition in Sixteenth-Century Spain*. Oxford: Oxford University Press.

Heiple, Daniel L. 1994. *Garcilaso de la Vega and the Italian Renaissance*. University Park, PA: Pennsylvania State University Press.

Herrera, Fernando de. 2001. *Anotaciones a la poesía de Garcilaso*. Edited by Inoria Pepe and José María Reyes. Madrid: Cátedra.

Infantes, Víctor. 2000. "La primera traducción de Alciato en España: Hernando de Villa Real y su *Emblema o scriptura de la Justicia* (1546)." In *Emblemata aurea: La emblemática en el arte y la literatura del Siglo de Oro*, edited by Rafael Zafra and José Javier Azanza, 235–250. Madrid: Akal.

Kunoth, G. 1964. "Francisco Pacheco's *Apotheosis of Hercules*." *Journal of the Warburg and Courtauld Institutes* 27: 335–337.

Lleó Cañal, Vicente. 1998. *La Casa de Pilatos*. Madrid: Electa.

———. 1999. "Los techos pintados de la Casa de Pilatos." In *Velázquez y Sevilla: Estudios*, edited by Luis Méndez Rodríguez and José Luis Romero Torres, 172–181. Sevilla: Junta de Andalucía, Consejería de Cultura.

———. 2012. *Nueva Roma: Mitología y humanismo en el Renacimiento sevillano*. 2nd ed. Madrid: CEEH.

López, Diego, 1615. *Declaración magistral sobre las Emblemas de Andres Alciato con todas las Historias, Antiguedades, Moralidad, y Doctrina tocante a las buenas costumbres*. Nájera: Juan de Mongaston. Accessed January 20, 2015. http://www.emblems.arts.gla.ac.uk/alciato/books.php?id=A15a&o.

López Torrijos, Rosa. 1985. *La mitología en la pintura española del Siglo de Oro*. Madrid: Cátedra.

———. 1999. "El techo de la casa del poeta Juan de Arguijo." In *Velázquez y Sevilla: Estudios*, edited by Luis Méndez Rodríguez and José Luis Romero Torres, 182–196. Sevilla: Junta de Andalucía, Consejería de Cultura.

Mal Lara, Juan de. 2013. *La Philosophía vulgar*. Edited by Inoria Pepe Sarno and José-María Reyes Cano. Madrid: Cátedra.

Manning, John. 2002. *The Emblem*. London: Reaktion.

McKeown, Simon, ed. 2012. *Otto Vaenius and His Emblem Books*. Glasgow: Glasgow Emblem Studies.

Moffitt, John F., ed. and trans. 2004. *A Book of Emblems: The Emblematum Liber in Latin and English, by Andrea Alciati (1492–1550)*. Jefferson, NC: McFarland.

Ravisius Textor, Ioannes. 1520. *Officina, Partim Historiis Partim Poeticis Referta Disciplinis*. Paris: Reginaldus Chauldiere.

Ripa, Cesare. 1992. *Iconologia*. Edited by Piero Buscaroli. Milan: TEA.

Sanctius Brocensis, Franciscus (El Brocense). 1573. *Comment[aria] in And[reae] Alciati Emblemata*. Lugduni: apud Guliel[mum] Rouillium.

Sebastián, Santiago. 1983. "*Theatro moral de la vida humana*, de Otto Vaenius. Lectura y significado de los emblemas." *Boletín del Museo e Instituto "Camón Aznar"* 14: 7–92.

———, ed. 1985. *Alciato: Emblemas*. Madrid: Akal.

———. 1995. *Emblemática e historia del arte*. Madrid: Cátedra.

Talavera Esteso, Francisco J. 2001. *Juan de Valencia y sus* Scholia in Andreae Alciati Emblemata*: Introducción, edición crítica, traducción española, notas e índices*. Málaga: Universidad de Málaga.

Thøfner, Margit. 2003. "Making a Chimera: Invention, Collaboration and the Production of Otto Vaenius's *Emblemata Horatiana*." In *Emblems of the Low Countries: A Book Historical Perspective*, edited by Alison Adams and Marleen van der Weij, 17–44. Glasgow: Glasgow Emblem Studies.

Thuilius, Ioannes, ed. 1621. *Andreae Alciati Emblemata cum commentariis Claudii Minois I.C. Francisci Sanctii Brocensis, & Notis Laurentii Pignorii Patavini*. Patavii: Petrus Paulus Tozzius.

Vaenius, Otho. 1612. *Quinti Horatii Flacci Emblemata, Imaginibus in a[e]s incifis, Notifq[ue] illuſtrata*. Antuerpiae: Philippus Lifaert.

PART III

The Iberian Peninsula in the eighteenth and nineteenth centuries

History, politics and cultural studies

21

HISPANO-IRISH WOMEN WRITERS OF SPAIN'S LATE ENLIGHTENMENT PERIOD

Elizabeth Franklin Lewis

Spain's Enlightenment was, until the second half of the twentieth century, almost completely overlooked by scholars. Primarily understood as being a time of foreign imitation (an idea debunked by Russell Sebold 1967, 1970), many have considered the Spanish Enlightenment not to have produced anything original or good, with the great exception of Goya. However, some recent studies have emphasized this period as a time of major social, cultural, and political changes that propelled Spain towards modernity: Joaquín Álvarez Barrientos (2005) outlines features of the Spanish eighteenth century that connect it to the larger Enlightenment movement, and that propel Spain into a "mentalidad moderna" (12), while Michael Iarocci (2006), tracing Spanish Romanticism to José de Cadalso's *Noches lúgubres* (1775), also identifies the beginnings of modernity in the eighteenth century. This was especially the case for Spanish women (see Bolufer and Burguera 2010): for the first time Spanish women began to publish translations, treatises on education, and poems and plays in significant numbers. They led and participated in the culturally and politically influential *tertulias* of the day such as the *Academia del Buen Gusto* in Madrid. They were both contributors and subscribers to increasingly popular periodical publications such as the *Semanario de Salamanca* and the *Diario de Madrid* (see Jaffe 2010). Women also participated in important male groups such as the Royal Economic Society of Madrid, and formed their own all-female civic organizations that attempted to solve difficult social problems of poverty and the lack of education in groups such as the *Junta de Damas* and the *Asociación de Señoras* (see Bolufer 1998; Jaffe and Lewis 2009; Lewis 2004; Palacios Fernández 2002, Smith 2006, and García Hurtado 2016).

These Enlightened women were both commoners and aristocrats, living in Madrid and the provinces, and notably, a number of them came from wealthy immigrant families from Ireland. Four of the most influential of these Hispano-Irish Enlightenment women were Inés Joyes y Blake, Margarita Hickey y Pellizzoni, María Gertrudis Hore y Ley, and Frasquita Larrea y Aherán, all of whom made significant contributions to the advancement of women in Spanish culture, education, and politics of their day. They were women of economic and sometimes political privilege, yet commoners excluded from some aristocratic circles. Many resided in the provinces (especially Cádiz and Málaga), but with strong ties to Madrid. Their unique multicultural and multilingual perspectives allowed them to successfully negotiate conservative male expectations of Spanish women, while they also contributed to a changing notion of women's importance to the modernization of Spanish society through their writings and through their intellectual and social exchange.

Spain found itself at the end of the Hapsburg dynasty and the turn of the eighteenth century with a number of pressing problems – an economy that was underdeveloped and lagged behind the rest of Europe, waning political influence on the world stage, an education system that was outdated for men and practically non-existent for women, and a perceived decadence in literature and art that held tightly to the successes and excesses of its *Siglo de Oro* baroque style. The new Bourbon dynasty sought ways to address these problems and to consolidate and increase their own political power. Their new, more cosmopolitan court in Madrid brought French and Italian influences to government and culture (see Bergamini 1974), while they also encouraged the participation of reform-minded Spanish *ilustrados*, who looked to French models, but also to English ideas for possible solutions to Spanish problems. Enlightenment British authors including Sir Francis Bacon, Thomas Hobbes, John Locke, Alexander Pope, Edmund Burke, Samuel Johnson, Edward Young, and Mary Wollstonecraft have all been cited as important influences on Spanish *ilustrados* from Benito Feijoo, to Gaspar Melchor de Jovellanos, Juan Meléndez Valdés, and Josefa Amar y Borbón among others (for more on British influences in Spanish eighteenth-century authors, see Fuentes 2004; García Calderón 2007; Glendinning 1968; Polt 1964; and Sebold 1970).

The Irish diaspora in eighteenth-century Spain

Coinciding with this increased interest in adapting British Enlightenment ideas and reforms in Spain came a rise in English-speaking migration from Ireland. Irish immigrants began coming to Spain in large numbers at the end of the seventeenth century as a result of the defeat of the Jacobites by the supporters of William III. Irish Catholics who as a result of the conflicts with Britain lost their social positions, livelihoods, and even civil rights, continued to immigrate to Spain throughout the eighteenth century, concentrating in coastal cities such as Bilbao to the north and especially in Cádiz and Málaga to the south, as well as in the Spanish capital Madrid. Unlike later Irish migrations to the Americas, these eighteenth-century migrants were for the most part wealthy, educated, and urban (Bolufer 2009a, 172). Embraced for their shared Catholic faith and for the infusion of capital they offered Spain, Irish immigrants were welcomed first by the Hapsburg King Carlos II in the late seventeenth century, and later by the Bourbon Felipe V in the eighteenth, who gave Irish men who married Spanish women the right to own real property and to conduct their commerce freely (Bolufer 2009a, 172). They came as military officials, merchants, and exiled priests. Many went on to build prominent businesses and hold important military and government positions, and to raise their families in Spain (see Villar García 2000). After a few generations they were absorbed into Spanish society. However a few – both men and women – are remembered as having made lasting contributions to Enlightenment Spain: men such as economist Bernardo Ward, minister of finance for Felipe VI, who also published two books on economics and charity; General Enrique O'Donnell, who fought for Spain in the Peninsular War against Napoleon; and intellectual and journalist José María Blanco White, an important liberal thinker and cultural critic in the early nineteenth century (see Bolufer 2009a; Lewis 2012 ; and Villar García 2000). Included in this list of important Hispano-Irish figures in Spanish society were several women: translator and essayist Inés Joyes y Blake, poet and translator Margarita Hickey y Pelizzoni, poet María Gertudis Hore, and intellectual and author Frasquita Larrea y Aherán, all of whom wrote and published in the late eighteenth and early nineteenth centuries. These four women stand out among a handful of eighteenth-century women writers in Spain, and together with them made important contributions to the advancement of women in Spanish culture.

Enlightenment voices in defense of women: Feijoo to Amar

Fray Benito Feijoo, in his famous 1726 essay "Defensa de la mujer" from the *Teatro crítico español*, affirmed women's "aptitud para todo género de ciencias, y conocimientos sublimes" (1778, 325–326). His essay sparked a heated debate throughout the century over women's education and place in Spanish society (see Lewis 2004, chs 1 and 2), and by the end of the century, women were openly contributing to this discussion, as well as to Spanish culture overall with their publications, their participation in important *tertulias* and academies, and their social action through their own civic groups, forming what Theresa Smith has called an *emerging female citizen* (2006). Many recent studies on eighteenth-century women such as Inés Joyes y Blake, Josefa Amar y Borbón, María Rosa Gálvez, María Gertrudis Hore, and María Lorenza de los Ríos, Marquesa de Fuerte Híjar, have clearly shown the importance of this group of women intellectuals and artists to the period (Bolufer 2008; Establier 2012; Jaffe 2013; López Cordón 2005; and Morand 2007). They are united by themes of education, of the defense of women's rights and abilities, of the importance of love and friendship among women, a critique of heterosexual love and marriage, and an exploration of women's active role in society and the family. A comparison of an important Castilian female voice, Josefa Amar, to the Hispano-Irish women writers we study in this essay, reveals both points of contact in their shared concerns and the ways in which they addressed them, as well as distinct differences, stemming from their unique bicultural and bilingual perspective.

Born in Zaragoza, and later a member of the Economic Society of Zaragoza, Josefa Amar y Borbón (1749–1833?) is one of a handful of eighteenth-century Spanish women studied by late twentieth and early twenty-first century historians as an early feminist writer. Her two major original works – her 1786 "Discurso en defensa del talento de las mujeres" and her 1790 book on female education – the *Discurso sobre la educación física y moral de las mugeres* – have gone from complete oblivion to almost canonical status in the past twenty years, with frequent appearances of these two main works in course reading lists, encyclopedia articles, and essay collections. Amar also published two translations from original Italian texts, which not only legitimated her work as an intellectual gaining acceptance for her as part of the elite group of Spanish eighteenth-century *ilustrados*, but they also helped to set the trajectory of her brief but remarkable career as a thinker and writer, as scholars such as López-Cordón and Sullivan have noted (see López Cordón 2005, 77–98; Sullivan 1992).

The "Discurso en defensa del talento de las mujeres, y de su aptitud para el gobierno, y otros cargos en que se emplean los hombres" was published in the *Memorial literario* in response to the controversy over women's admission to the Economic Society of Madrid and in particular to two previously published essays in the *Memorial literario* for and against female admission by Gaspar Melchor de Jovellanos and Francisco Cabarrús. In the essay, Amar defends women's equal abilities and talents and calls for their acceptance into the Madrid Economic Society for the important public role they could play (see Lewis 2004 for a deeper analysis of Amar's essay, compared with essays by Feijoo, Jovellanos, and Cabarrús):

> Concluyamos, pues, de todo lo dicho que si las mugeres tienen la misma aptitud que los hombres para instruirse; si en todos tiempos han mostrado ser capaces de las ciencias, de la prudencia, y del sigilo, si han tenido y tienen las virtudes Sociales;

[. . .] con tales hipótesis, lejos de ser perjudicial la admisión de las mugeres, puede y debe ser conveniente.

(Amar 1786, 430)

Amar's strong defense of women has been compared to Mary Wollstonecraft's *Vindication of the Rights of Women*, although Amar's essay predates Wollstonecraft's publication by six years (see Bolufer 2009b; López-Cordón 2005; and Sullivan 1992). Amar's book on female education, the *Discurso sobre la educación física y moral de las mugeres*, was published by the prominent Madrid printer Benito Cano. It is both a book of medical advice on pregnancy, childbirth and child-rearing, as well as a guide for women and their daughters about women's education and their social role in Spain. One important topic in the book is marriage. Amar counsels careful consideration of the choice girls must make between marriage and convent, the only two available, she notes, since a single woman "es un cero" in the eyes of society (Amar 1790, 225). She warns that girls educated in the convent might either decide to stay "de haberse familiarizado" (226) or to get married because they think it will bring happiness "que acaso no existe" (227). Happiness came instead from the "recto uso de las facultades racionales para obrar con cordura y discreción" (135). Mónica Bolufer points out Amar's rejection of the popular sentimental model that was taking hold of Europe and Spain in the late eighteenth century, especially in the novel, in which women found happiness within their domestic confines. Instead, Amar's views on marriage are pragmatic, and happiness for women comes from "hallar por sí mismas otras fuentes de satisfacción, de las que el estudio y la escritura, como placer íntimo y como ocasión de reconocimiento público, fueron las más apreciadas" (Bolufer 1997, 212).

Inés Joyes y Blake

While her life and writings were extraordinary, Amar was not the only Spanish woman of her time translating important foreign works, defending women's abilities and rights, or giving advice to daughters. Inés Joyes y Blake (1731–1808) also published an important translation and wrote about women's education and women's role in society through a published letter addressed to her own daughters. Born in Madrid to a wealthy Irish family originally from Galway, she married her distant cousin Agustín Blake, a businessman in Málaga, raised nine children, was widowed at age 50, and published one book in 1798 at the age of 67, a translation of Samuel Johnson's 1759 *The History of Rasselas, Prince of Abisinnia*. She accompanied her translation with a small original treatise, "Apología de las mugeres en carta original de la traductora dirigida a sus hijas." Mónica Bolufer calls Joyes' essay "one of the most lucid and vehement texts on women's condition in eighteenth-century Spain" (Bolufer 2009b, 27), and points to similarities between Joyes' text and previous publications on women's education and women's rights by Benito Feijoo (1726), Josefa Amar y Borbón (1790) and Mary Wollstonecraft (1792). The "Apología" does not specifically reference the translation of Johnson (1798) that it follows, yet Bolufer finds that the two texts coincide in their praise of certain Enlightened values – the exultation of wisdom and virtue over riches and frivolity, and of reason over passion (Bolufer 2003, 145). Both also are critical of marriage, and yet both see it as an important element of order in the family and society. Lastly, in both there is a tension between the individual's pursuit of happiness, and the good of society. In her essay, Joyes urges women not to underestimate themselves, and she uses strong words to describe male oppression. She goes on to urge women to respect themselves and to support one another, which will win respect from men too: "respectaos a vosotras mismas y os respetarán: amaos unas a otras" (Joyes 1798, 204).

Joyes criticizes more forcefully than Amar the limited choices eighteenth-century Spanish women had between convent and marriage: "¡Máxima perniciosa, erradísimo concepto que es causa de infinitos casamientos disparatados e infelices, y de que se vean tantas arrepentidas!" (Joyes 1798, 195). While Amar's tone is calm and distant (she makes no personal references to her own experience as a woman), Joyes shows her indignance at male hypocrisy that subordinates women: "Los hombres en general las quieren ignorantes porque solo así mantienen la superioridad que se figuran tener" (203). Joyes passionantly wants to get through to women her message of empowerment: "Yo quisiera desde lo alto de algún monte donde fuera posible que me oyesen todas darles un consejo. Oíd mujeres, les diría, y no os apoquéis: vuestras almas son iguales a las del sexo que os quiere tiranizar" (203–4). She concludes her treatise connecting women's individual happiness to the positive effects their good education and virtue will have on society: "tendréis la Gloria de reformar las costumbres haciendo amable la virtud; irá decayendo el lujo: vuestro exemplo hará moderados a los hombres: vuestros maridos os amarán y apreciarán: vuestros hijos os venerarán: vuestros hermanos se tendrán por dichosos con vuestro trato: viviréis felices quanto cabe en el mundo, y moriréis con la gloria de dexar una posteridad virtuosa" (204). Despite Joyes' hope for a better future, her optimism was not shared by all eighteenth-century women writers.

Margarita Hickey y Pellizzoni

Margarita Hickey y Pellizzoni, the daughter of an Irish father and an Italian mother, was born in Palma de Mallorca in 1728 (Pierruci 2006, 13). Her father served in the military (Pierucci 2006, 13–14; Salgado 2009, 62). She grew up in Barcelona and married Juan Antonio Aguirre (from Navarre); the couple was living in Madrid by 1759, when Hickey appeared on the literary scene (Deacon 1988, 399–400; Pierucci 2006, 16–17). Philip Deacon has identified that Hickey attended Agustín Montiano's literary *tertulia*, where she met and befriended playwright and poet Vicente García de la Huerta, with whom she maintained correspondence during Huerta's self-imposed exile in France (1988, 403–405), and also exchanged poetry (1988, 406–408). Her only published collection *Poesías varias sagradas, morales y profanas o amorosas: con dos poemas épicos*, was published by the Royal Press in 1789. It included a translation from French to Spanish of Racine's *Andromaca*, two epic poems dedicated to military hero Pedro Ceballos, and 49 lyrical poems, many of which treat the injustices of heterosexual love for women. As with Amar and Joyes, Hickey also offered advice to young women about marriage and love. Hickey strongly criticized male oppression of women, portrayed marriage as an undesirable state for women, and defended women's intellectual abilities as writers in particular.

Throughout the poems, Hickey criticizes men's actions, and cautions women to beware. Women suffer the injustice of an inferior economic and social position, she complains:

> De bienes destituidas,
> Víctimas del pundonor,
> Censuradas con amor
> Y sin él desatendidas;
> Sin cariño pretendidas,
> Por apetito buscadas,
> Conseguidas, ultrajadas,
> Sin aplausos la virtud,
> Sin lauros la juventud,
> Y en la vejez despreciadas.
> (Pierucci 2006, 138)

Unlike Joyes' optimism over the power of women to change society through the example of their virtue, Hickey offers a pessimistic view of a male-dominated society that oppresses women at every turn. Likewise, while Amar saw a certain social utility in marriage, Hickey clearly rejects it. In "Décima aconcejando una dama a otra amiga suya que no se case," the poet urges a friend not to marry:

> Conserva libre tu mano
> Huye del lazo inhumano
> Que el amante más rendido
> Es, transformado en marido,
> Un insufrible tirano. (137)

Men are not just tyrannical in love; in their rejection of women's talents they also oppress. In a poem directed to a male friend, *Danteo* (identified as sainetista Tadeo Moreno González by Pierucci (2006, 285), following Serrano y Sanz), Hickey closes her collection explaining her purpose for writing and her frustrations. She begins with a typically feminine denial of her seriousness of purpose:

> Amigo Danteo
> Por fin te remito
> Estas producciones
> De los ocios míos. (285)

She elaborates on the topic of love found in so many of her poems:

> Hallarás en ellas
> Documentos finos
> De amar noblemente
> Con afectos dignos. (286)

But although writing is supposedly merely light entertainment for her, she is not afraid to criticize male poets, and begins with none less than Ovid:

> No de amar un arte
> Como la de Ovidio,
> Que más de amor
> Es arte de vicio. (286)

María Salgado (2009) points out how Hickey both borrows from and re-works canonical male poetry and poetic themes, highlighting the author's critique of Ovid, of Luís de Góngora and of Lope de Vega, forming a "strategy of validating her voice by placing her poems within a very canonical tradition. She was indeed conscious of the literary context within which she wrote and of the parameters her feminist discourse had to overcome" (Salgado 2009, 64–65). Later in this poem, Hickey addresses her critics:

> No dudo, Danteo,
> Persuadida vivo,
> Que los Aristarcos

y Momos del siglo
hincarán su diente
con audacia y brio,
diciendo, arrogantes
tanto como altivos,
que quién me ha inspirado
o quién me ha metido,
no habiendo las aulas
cursado ni visto . . . (287)

These men expect her to dedicate herself to activities proper for her sex – "la rueca, el huso, / la aguja, y el hilo" (287) – and that women should naturally prefer to speak of fashion, dresses, and hairstyles. To this Hickey declares "que el alma no es hombre / ni mujer, y es fijo / que en entrambos casos / su ser es el mismo" (290). The structure of this collection is significant. Both the Racine translation and the epic poem dedicated to Ceballos have a prologue (see Llosa Sanz 2008 for a discussion of the prologue to the Ceballos poem), but the lyrical poetry does not. Instead, Hickey ends with this poem, a sort of epilogue, defending her work, defending herself, and criticizing, again, the men who would reject or put limits on her.

María Gertrudis Hore y Ley

Another poet, María Gertrudis Hore y Ley (1742–1801), criticized women's inferior social role as did Hickey before her. Morand points out a possible acquaintance between Hickey and Hore, given their similar family backgrounds, some time that Hore spent in Madrid in 1774 or 1775, and a poem by Hickey addressed to a female friend "Fenisa," a poetic name Hore used for herself (Morand 2007, 111–112). Also known by her pen name *Hija del Sol*, Hore was born to a wealthy Irish merchant family in Cádiz. Much like Hickey, Hore was well known in her day in important literary and social circles. She participated in the *tertulia* of Antonio de Ulloa in Cádiz, corresponded with members of the Escuela de Salamanca, and published her poems in important contemporary journals in Madrid and Barcelona (Morand 2009, 37 and 44–45). Bolufer believes that, although from different Southern coastal cities (Cádiz and Málaga), Hore's family and Joyes' family had social and economic ties, and it is likely they knew each other (Bolufer 2006, 95). Yet despite being well regarded and published during her lifetime, Hore is remembered as much for a mysterious decision to leave her marriage to businessman Esteban Fleming and enter the convent of Santa María in Cádiz at the age of 35 as for her extraordinary poetry. Fernán Caballero romanticized this story in "La hija del sol," published in 1857 (see Lewis 2004, 62–63). Some of her writings are religious in nature, but many of them also deal with friendship and poetry, and some follow the popular anacreontic style of the day (a poetic form imitating the hedonistic odes by Classical Greek poet Anacreon), seemingly unsuitable topics for a cloistered nun.

While one might think, given that Hore left marriage for a religious vocation, that her poetry would contain a similar indictment of marriage and men as Hickey expressed in her poetry, rarely does Hore even mention marriage, although she does frequently address the subject of romantic love and some of her manuscript poems speak of, or even to, specific lovers by poetic names such as *Mirteo*, *Mirtilo*, and *Ergasto*. But many more of her poems exalt female friendship and contrast a frenetic social life outside the cloister that impedes creativity, to a pleasant and tranquil exchange among friends that encourages it. In one of these light-hearted poems, "La ensalada," published in May 1795 in the *Diario de Madrid*, Hore presents an idyllic scene among female friends enjoying a fresh salad together. The poem begins describing the chaos of the outside world: "De riñas y cuestiones / ardiendo está la Aldea, / todas hablan a un tiempo, / y no hay quien las comprenda" (197). She calls her friends to shut out the noise and gather together for a light meal together: "Niña, de la cabaña / Cierra pronto la puerta . . . y en tanto que ellas rabian / tráeme tú Filena, / con agua serenada / la talla portuguesa" (197). Hore takes the traditional hedonistic homosocial anacreontic ode, so popular during her day, especially among poets such as Meléndez Valdés, to an all-female setting, portraying a salad shared with girlfriends as being as sumptuous and enjoyable as any Bachanal gathering (see Irene Gómez-Castellano 2012 for a study of the anacreontic among the poets of the Escuela Salmantina). Her imagery appeals to the senses, with colors, flavors, and fragrance: "el rubí del tomate," "la Esmeralda bella del pimentillo dulce," "ambar del pepino" and "el orégano [. . .] fragante" (197).

In another anacreontic ode, published in 1795 in the *Diario de Madrid*, the poet encourages a female friend to leave society life behind: "¿Hasta cuándo Gerarda, / tu peregrino ingenio / en frívolos asuntos / malgastarás conceptos?" (201). Gerarda needs to stop wasting her talents on the "contrario sexo / que solo en nuestra ruina / fabrica sus trofeos" (202). Yet in this poem, it is not just heterosexual romantic love or men's treatment of women that the poet criticizes, but rather that her friend wastes her poetic talent writing about them. Instead, says the poet, if Gerarda looks to a woman (who is perhaps the Virgin Mary) as her poetic guide – "nuestra común amiga sea tu nuevo Febo" – she will be rewarded by climbing the heights of the "most sacred Parnassus" (203).

Morand (2009) has pointed to the many ways in which Hore, despite being a cloistered nun during the most active time of her poetic career, was very much a part of Enlightenment Spanish society – from the contents of her library to her important male and female contacts. She was well acquainted with many Enlightenment debates and topics of discussion, and did, like many other women writers, translate texts from Italian to Spanish. In one unpublished poem, the long hendecasyllabic "Meditación," Hore evokes a popular British text, Edward Young's *Night Thoughts*. Young's 1742 poem had inspired other Spanish writers, notably José de Cadalso, also from Cádiz, whose *Noches lúgubres* (composed in 1775 and published between 1789–1790) was influenced by Young and which is commonly cited as an example of an early Romantic sensibility in Spain. Hore's dramatic poem is also in this vein, forming part of an aesthetic shared by numerous *ilustrados* including Jovellanos, who found in English philosophy and sentimental literature an expression of their own frustrations with the failures of Enlightenment reforms (See Yvonne Fuentes 2004). In this poem, again addressed to a female friend, Hore speaks of her attraction to the morbid settings in Young's poem:

> Mas como aquel filósofo del Támesis,
> huyendo, sí, sus engañosas dichas
> y los vanos objetos que interpone
> para que la verdad se nos resista,
> se entra por los altísimos cipreses
> y con el mayor gusto ve y visita
> sepulcrales cavernas a quien solo
> de la muerte blandones iluminan. (337)

Well read, and very much a participant in the trends of her times, this cloistered nun found inspiration and delight in the imaginative macabre settings of Young's poem, which also spoke to her own melancholy:

¡Sí, sí, divino Young! contigo entro:
al ver tu ejemplo, mi valor se anima,
y de ti acompañado sin Recelo,
compararé la muerte con la vida. (337–8)

Frasquita Larrea y Aherán

The youngest of our group of Hispano-Irish women not only participated in the sensibility of her time as Hore did before her, but also is actually credited with influencing it. Francisca Javiera (Frasquita) Ruiz de Larrea y Aherán (1775–1838) was born in Cádiz in 1775, daughter of a Basque merchant father and Irish-born mother. She grew up near Cádiz, in Chiclana, but is thought to have spent time in her youth in England and France, where she met her husband, the German Johann Nikolas Böhl Von Faber. This couple is known for bringing the so-called conservative Romantic movement to Spain, and for being the parents to Spain's great Realist novelist Fernán Caballero, Cecilia Böhl de Faber (Carnero 1978, 1990). Juan Nicolás (as he was known in Spain) and Frasquita were intellectual peers who were intensely interested in literature, philosophy, and culture, which they debated in letters to each other, and undoubtedly in their homes in both Germany and Spain. Their sometimes rocky relationship led to a six-year separation from 1806 to 1812 (Orozco 1977, 73–89). Larrea was well traveled throughout her adult life, and spent time in England, as well as France, Switzerland and, of course, Germany and Spain. She had few publications but maintained correspondence with various important intellectuals of her day, including José María Blanco White, another son of Irish immigrants. Her papers are housed in the Osborne Archives, which Orozco Acuaviva was able to consult and present in his book (1977). We find in these texts evidence of Larrea's literary and political interests – from her frequent citations in English and French of authors as diverse as Shakespeare, Chateaubriand, and Rousseau, to her outspoken criticism of Napoleon and of the Cortes in Cádiz (see Cantos Casenave 2002, 2009). Although Larrea was the best traveled and most worldly of the Hispano-Irish women we have studied, she also was the most nostalgic defender of Spain as her homeland.

One of her early writings, *Ela* (1807), displays some of Larrea's important ideas about nature and love, rooted in contemporary sentimental literature and early Romanticism, and has been identified as somewhat autobiographical, representing her nostalgia for her own childhood in Chiclana (Orozco 1977, 104). The story of the young girl begins with an epilogue in French from Romantic writer Chateaubriand. Ela was close to nature – "Su infancia fue íntima con la naturaleza" (Orozco 1977, 251) – and "la vida campestre fortaleció su físico y purificó sus sentimientos." She was free, even in her thinking: "Examinaba libremente toda opinión antes de apropiársele" (251). She meets a young German man, Wilhelm, and their pure love for each other is almost other-worldly: "Tenía el antesabor de otra existencia aun quando gozaban de todas las delicias de ésta" (253). Wilhelm and Ela never marry. Instead, Ela is struck by lightning and killed as she admires the power of nature.

Politics was another frequent topic of Larrea's writings. In an 1808 manuscript text, "Una aldeana Española a sus patricias," the author forcefully urges women to do all that is in their power to oppose Napoleon and support the Spanish cause against the French: "Y nosotras españolas usémos también las armas que nos son propias. Recordemos a nuestros esposos e hijos sus obligaciones. Pintémosles las dulzuras de una muerte en defensa de su Religión y Patria" (260). She ends by exclaiming "¡Morir o vencer, Españoles! ¡Rogad y persuadid, Españolas!" (260).

Frasquita traveled extensively through Europe both alone and with her family, and in some of the archived manuscripts she describes her many trips north. In the essay "Chiclana," written from a cold and dreary Brighton, England, in December of 1811, Larrea expresses her nostalgia for her native Andalusia: "entre yelos de otro clima, en la tierra del extrangero, vuestra idea acompaña mi agitada carrera . . . . Al través de un velo de neblina miro los desnudos troncos y pienso en los mirtos, naranjos y laureles de la Andalucía, vanos en su días de diciembre" (272). The most cosmopolitan of the women we have studied, Frasquita Larrea was also the most nostalgic and patriotic, yearning for the Spain of her own idyllic and innocent past.

Conclusion

These four Hispano-Irish late-eighteenth-century women were united by the circumstances of their families' origins, and, as members of a tightly knit and small community, perhaps were even acquainted with one another, at least by reputation. When compared with other Spanish women writers of the period, like Josefa Amar, they were certainly among the most important, most active, and most outspoken women during the late Enlightenment period in Spain and they shared many of the same interests and concerns. Their cosmopolitan and multilingual upbringing – growing up in port cities in families that dealt in international trade – gave them special access to ideas coming to Spain from the outside, notably from England. Their exposure to texts in English also distinguished them from most Spanish women, and they seem to have all reflected in their own writings similar affinities to British philosophy and literature, as well as to ideas about the importance of friendship, of women's autonomy, and of women's role in society, even while they decried male oppression and injustice much more forcefully than did writers such as Amar y Borbón. But was there anything particularly Irish about them, or did they bring an Irish Enlightenment to Spain? Given that Ireland too was on the "periphery" of the Enlightenment (Butterick et al. 2008), probably not. But their unique perspectives certainly made an impact on Spanish culture, and through figures such as Fernán Caballero in the mid-nineteenth century, certainly we can say that they helped shape the direction of women's writing in Spain.

Works cited

Álvarez Barrientos, Joaquín. 2005. *Ilustración y neoclasicismo en las letras españolas.* Madrid: Síntesis.
Amar y Borbón, Josefa. 1786. "Discurso en defensa de las mugeres y de su aptitud para el gobierno, y otros cargos en que se emplean los hombres; Compuesto por Josefa Amar y Borbón, Socia de mérito de la Real Sociedad Aragonesa de los Amigos del País." *Memorial Literario* VIII (32): 400–430. Accessed December 15, 2014. http://www.ensayistas.org/antologia/XVIII/amar-bor/
———. [1790] 1994. *Discurso sobre la educación física y moral de las mugeres.* Madrid: Benito Cano. Edited by María Victoria López Cordón. Madrid: Cátedra.
Bergamini, John D. 1974. *The Spanish Bourbons: The History of a Tenacious Dynasty.* New York: Putnam.
Bolufer Peruga, Mónica. 1997. "Josefa Amar e Inés Joyes: dos perspectivas femeninas sobre el matrimonio en el siglo XVIII." *Historia de la mujer e historia del matrimonio*, edited by Montserrat Carbonell Esteller and María Victoria López-Cordón, 203–217. Murcia: Universidad de Murcia.
———. 1998. *Mujeres e Ilustración: la construcción de la feminidad en la España del siglo XVIII.* Valencia: Institució Alfons el Magnànim.
———. 2003."Traducción y creación en la actividad intelectual de las ilustradas españolas: el ejemplo de Inés Joyes y Blake." In *Frasquita Larrea y Aherán. Europeas y españolas entre la Ilustración y*

el Romanticismo, edited by Gloria Espigado Tocino and M. José de la Pascua, 137–155. Cádiz: Universidad de Cádiz.

———. 2006. "¿Escribir la experiencia? Familia, identidad y reflexión intelectual en Inés Joyes (s. XVIII)." *Arenal. Revista de Historia de las Mujeres* 13 (1): 83–105.

———. 2008. *La vida y la escritura en el siglo XVIII. Inés Joyes: apología de las mujeres*. Valencia: Universidad de Valencia.

———. 2009a."Irlandeses en España: los Trenor y otros más" In *Trenor. La Exposición de una gran familia burguesa*, edited by Anaclet Pons and Justo Serna, 165–198. València: PUV.

———. 2009b. "Women of Letters in Eighteenth-Century Spain: Between Tradition and Modernity." In *Eve's Enlightenment: Women's Experience in Spain and Spanish America, 1726–1839*, edited by Catherine Jaffe and Elizabeth Franklin Lewis, 17–32. Baton Rouge, LA: Louisiana State University Press.

Bolufer Peruga, Mónica and Mónica Burguera. 2010. "Presentación." *Género y modernidad en España: de la Ilustración al liberalismo. Ayer* 78 (2): 13–23.

Butterick, Richard, Simon Davies, and Gabriel Sánchez Espinosa, eds. 2008. *Peripheries of the Enlightenment*. Oxford: Voltaire Foundation.

Cantos Casenave, Marieta. 2002. "El discurso de Frasquita Larrea y la politización del romanticismo." *Cuadernos de Ilustración y Romanticismo* 10: 3–13.

———. 2009. "Entre la tertulia y la imprenta, la palabra encendida de una patriota andaluza, Frasquita Larrea (1775–1838)." In *Heroínas y patriotas: mujeres de 1808*, edited by Irene Castells, Gloria Espigado, and María Cruz Romeo, 269–294. Madrid: Cátedra.

Carnero, Guillermo. 1978. *Los orígenes del romanticismo reaccionario español: el matrimonio Böhl de Faber*. Valencia: Universidad de Valencia.

———. 1990. "Francisca Ruiz de Larrea (1775–1838) y el inicio gaditano del romanticismo español." In *Escritoras románticas*, edited by Marina Mayoral, 119–130. Madrid: Fundación Banco Exterior.

Deacon, Philip. 1988. "Vicente García de la Huerta y el círculo de Montiano: la amistad entre Huerta y Margarita Hickey." *Revista de Estudios Extremeños* 44 (2): 395–422.

Establier Pérez, Helena. 2012. *El teatro trágico de María Rosa Gálvez de Cabrera en el tránsito de la Ilustración al Romanticismo*. Alicante: Biblioteca Virtual Miguel de Cervantes. Accessed December 15, 2014. http://www.cervantesvirtual.com/obra/el-teatro-tragico-de-maria-rosa-galvez-de-cabre ra-en-el-transito-de-la-ilustracion-al-romanticismo.

Feijoo, Benito Jerónimo. 1726. "Defensa de las mujeres." In *Teatro crítico universal*, vol. 1, 325–398. Madrid: Ibarra. Accessed December 15, 2014. http://www.filosofia.org/bjf/bjft116.htm.

Fuentes, Yvonne. 2004. "British Aesthetics and the Picturesque in Spain: Jovellanos's Affinity with England." *Hispania* 87 (2): 210–219.

García Calderón, Ángeles. 2007. "La poesía inglesa de la naturaleza en el siglo XVIII y su influencia en Meléndez Valdés." *Revista de Literatura* LXIX.138: 519–541.

García Hurtado, Manuel-Reyes. 2016. *El siglo XVIII en femenino*. Madrid: Síntesis.

Glendinning, Nigel. 1968. "Influencia de la literatura inglesa en España en el siglo XVIII." *Cuadernos de la Cátedra de Feijoo* 20: 47–93.

Gómez-Castellano, Irene. 2012. *La cultura de las máscaras: disfraces y escapismo en la poesía española de la Ilustración*. Madrid and Frankfurt: Iberoamericana/Vervuert.

Hickey y Pellizoni, Margarita. [1789a] 2006. "Décima aconsejando a una dama a otra amiga suya que no se case." *Poesías varias sagradas, morales y profanas o amorosas: con dos poemas épicos*. Madrid: Imprenta Real. In *Margartia Hickey y Pellizoni Poesías*, edited by Daniela Pierucci, 137. Pisa: Edizioni ETS.

———. [1789b] 2006. "Otra defendiendo la infeliz constitución de las mujeres en general." *Poesías varias sagradas, morales y profanas o amorosas: con dos poemas épicos*. Madrid: Imprenta Real. In *Margarita Hickey y Pellizoni Poesías*, edited by Daniela Pierucci, 138. Pisa: Edizioni ETS.

———. [1789c] 2006. "Remitiendo a un conocido estas poesías." *Poesías varias sagradas, morales y profanas o amorosas: con dos poemas épicos*. Madrid: Imprenta Real. In *Margarita Hickey y Pellizoni Poesías*, edited by Daniela Pierucci, 285–296. Pisa: Edizioni ETS.

Hore, María Gerturdis. [1795a] 2007. "Anacreóntica. La ensalada." *Diario de Madrid* May 21: 577–578. In *Una poetisa en busca de libertad: María Gertrudis Hore y Ley (1742–1801)*, edited by Frédérique Morand, 197–198. Cádiz: Diputación de Cádiz.

———. [1795b] 2007. "Anacreóntica: ¿Hasta cuándo Gerarda?" *Diario de Madrid* August 9: 897–898. In *Una poetisa en busca de libertad: María Gertrudis Hore y Ley (1742–1801)*, edited by Frédérique Morand, 201–203. Cádiz: Diputación de Cádiz.

———. [N.D.] 2007. "Meditación." Manuscript held at Biblioteca Menéndez Pelayo Santander. 199, fol. 6d. In *Una poetisa en busca de libertad: María Gertrudis Hore y Ley (1742–1801)*, edited by Frédérique Morand, 201–203. Cádiz: Diputación de Cádiz.

Iarocci, Michael. 2006. *Properties of Modernity: Romantic Spain, Modern Europe and the Legacies of Empire*. Nashville, TN: Vanderbilt University Press.

Jaffe, Catherine. 2010. "Lectora y lectura femenina en la modernidad: El *Semanario de Salamanca* (1793–1798)." In *Género y modernidad en España: de la Ilustración al liberalismo*. Special issue of *Ayer* 78 (2): 69–91.

Jaffe, Catherine and Elizabeth Franklin Lewis. 2009. *Eve's Enlightenment: Women's Experience in Spain and Spanish America, 1726–1839*. Baton Rouge, LA: Louisiana State University Press.

Jaffe, Catherine and Elisa Martín Valdepeñas y Yague. 2013. "Sociabilidad, filantropía y escritura: María Lorenza de los Ríos y Loyo, marquesa de Fuerte-Híjar (1761–1821)." In *Mujeres y culturas políticas en España 1808–1845*, coord. Ana Yetano Laguna, 85–126. Barcelona: Universitat Autònoma de Barcelona.

Johnson, Samuel. 1798. *El Príncipe de Abisinia: novela traducida del inglés*, trans. Inés Joyes y Blake. Madrid: Sancha.

Joyes y Blake, Inés. 1798. "Apología de las mugeres en carta original de la traductora dirigida a sus hijas." In *El Príncipe de Abisinia, Novela traducida del inglés*, trans. Inés Joyes y Blake, 177–204. Madrid: Sancha.

Larrea, Frasquita. [1807] 1977. "Ela." In *La gaditana Frasquita Larrea, primera romántica española*, edited by Antonio Orozco Acuaviva, 250–255. Cádiz: Sexta.

———. [1808] 1977. "Una aldeana española a sus patricias." In *La gaditana Frasquita Larrea, primera romántica española*, edited by Antonio Orozco Acuaviva, 260–261. Cádiz: Sexta.

———. [1811] 1977. "Chiclana." In *La gaditana Frasquita Larrea, primera romántica española*, edited by Antonio Orozco Acuaviva, 271–273. Cádiz: Sexta.

Lewis, Elizabeth Franklin. 2004. *Women Writers in the Spanish Enlightenment: The Pursuit of Happiness*. Aldershot: Ashgate Publishers.

———. 2012. "Enlightenment Politics and Catholic Charity in Spain: Bernardo Ward's *Obra pía* (1750) and *Proyecto económico* (1762)." *1650–1850: Ideas, Aesthetics, and Inquiries in the Early Modern Era* 19: 295–312.

Llosa Sanz, Álvaro. 2008. "'Como si acaso el alma tuviera sexo.' Margarita Hickey: el sexo y la escritura." *Hispanófila* 152: 53–66.

López-Cordón, María Victoria. 2005. *Condición femenina y razón ilustrada: Josefa Amar y Borbón*. Zaragoza: Prensas Universitarias de Zaragoza.

Morand, Frédérique. 2007. *Una poetisa en busca de libertad: María Gertrudis Hore y Ley* (1742–1801). Cádiz: Diputación de Cádiz.

———. 2009. "Enlightenment Experience in the Life and Poetry of Sor María Gerturdis de la Cruz Hore. In *Eve's Enlightenment: Women's Experience in Spain and Spanish America, 1726–1839*, edited by Catherine Jaffe and Elizabeth Franklin Lewis, 33–50. Baton Rouge, LA: Louisiana State University Press.

Orozco Acuaviva, Antonio. 1977. *La gaditana Frasquita Larrea, primera romántica española*. Cádiz: Sexta.

Palacios Fernández, Emilio. 2002. *La mujer y las letras en la España del siglo XVIII*. Madrid: Ediciones Laberinto.

Pierucci, Daniela, ed. 2006. *Margarita Hickey y Pellizoni Poesías*. Pisa: Edizioni ETS.

Polt, John H.R. 1964. *Jovellanos and His English Sources: Economic, Philosophical and Political Writings*. Philadelphia, PA: American Philosophical Society.

Salgado, María. 2009. "Margarita Hickey's Guide to the Traps of Love." In *Eve's Enlightenment: Women's Experience in Spain and Spanish America, 1726–1839*, edited by Catherine Jaffe and Elizabeth Franklin Lewis, 62–83. Baton Rouge, LA: Louisiana State University Press.

Sebold, Russell. 1967. "A Statistical Analysis of the Origins and Nature of Luzán's Ideas on Poetry." *Hispanic Review* 35 (3): 227–251.

———. 1970. *El rapto de la mente*. Barcelona: Anthropos.Smith, Theresa Ann. 2006. *The Emerging Female Citizen: Gender and Enlightenment in Spain*. Berkeley, CA: University of California Press.

Sullivan, Constance. 1992. "Josefa Amar y Borbón and the Royal Aragonese Economic Society." *Dieciocho* 15 (1–2): 95–148.

Villar García, María Begoña. 2000. *La emigración irlandesa en el siglo XVIII*. Málaga: Universidad de Málaga.

22

THE END OF EMPIRE AND THE BIRTH OF THE MODERN NATION, 1808 TO 1868

Jesús Cruz

On the night of March 17, 1808, a mob took over the esplanade of the Aranjuez Palace near Madrid to stop the possible escape of the Spanish Royal family to the American colonies. Rumors spread that the first minister Manuel Godoy was behind this escape plan, fearing that the advance of the Napoleonic troops into Spanish territory could endanger the monarchs. While these rumors were the spark that ignited the riot known as the Revolt of Aranjuez, the causes of these discontents were deep and long-standing, the most immediate being the defeat and decimation of the Spanish navy in 1805 in the disastrous battle of Trafalgar, consequence of Manuel Godoy's unfortunate international policies. The defeat not only eroded the morale of the Spanish military and political elites, but also worsened the state of the national finances, spreading economic hardship to all levels of Spanish society. The prestige of King Charles IV was also jeopardized because of his political inhibition, weak spirits, and lack of charisma. He delegated all his political responsibilities to Manuel Godoy, a member of the royal bodyguards who was always perceived as an outsider by the aristocratic King's entourage and by the selective clique of the monarchy's high administration. Because of this exchange of responsibility, Godoy amassed too much power. This accumulation of power evolved in proportion to his political isolation and lack of support from all entities of Spanish society, from the upper classes to the common people. But beyond his eventual political mistakes and unfortunate international alliances, the causes of discontent were cumulative: they were the expression of a profound crisis of the Spanish political, social, and economic system – the Spanish *Ancien Regime* – that demanded radical transformations.

The events on the night of March 17, 1808, at the Royal Site of Aranjuez mark the end of the Ancien Regime in Spain and the beginning of the liberal era. Its most immediate impact was the abdication of Charles IV in favor of his son Ferdinand VII, and the resignation of Manuel Godoy, thus creating the worst crisis in the Spanish monarchy since the late seventeenth century. It may be true that the mob assembled in Aranjuez was carefully manipulated by the angry foes of Godoy, the members of what was known as the Fernandine party. This party was composed of a group of courtier notables that Godoy describes in his memoirs as the "faction." Despite the intervention of this network, whose main connection was their hatred of the first minister, the movement was much more than a palace coup. The event known as the Revolt of Aranjuez actually consisted of several riots that started in that city and extended to the capital. In Madrid, the rebellion was carried out by spontaneous popular groups who looted the residences of Godoy and his acolytes. The fact that palaces were pillaged and set on fire by an angry mob with no intervention to stop the plunder demonstrates the state of malaise that exceeded the limits of the high politics of the court. The riots reflected not only the rejection of the traditional dominant groups towards Godoy's attempted reforms, but also the commitment of politically advanced groups, who claimed the need for a profound intervention to cure the long-term illnesses of the Spanish imperial system. These groups, known as the *Ilustrados*, were composed of educated elites who began embracing the ideas of the Enlightenment in the mid-eighteenth century. The *Ilustrados*, well represented in the circles of the administration of the monarchy, backed reformist policies to remedy the deficiencies of the Spanish Imperial system. The French Revolution, and the failure of Godoy's despotic reformist policies, radicalized a segment of the *Ilustrado* elite that later adopted the banner of liberalism and proposed radical revolutionary solutions to modernize Spain. The Revolt of Aranjuez, and the uprising against the occupation of Madrid by the troops of Napoleon which occurred on May 2 of that same year, were popular actions in part inspired by the ideas of liberalism. Both occurrences anticipated a style of Spanish rebellion that would repeat itself throughout the nineteenth century, marking the beginning of the period known in Spanish history as the Liberal Revolution.

The Spanish Liberal Revolution (1808–1843)

Between 1808 and 1843 Spain underwent a profound transformation, from an absolutist imperial monarchy to a modern liberal nation-state. It was a period of change in a broad sense sparked by the two transnational impulses that affected the history of the West in the last third of the eighteenth century: the ideas of the Enlightenment, and the technological, scientific, and economic developments taking place in parts of the Western world. In Spain, as in other parts of Europe, both impulses ignited the process of political and social transformation that is known as the Liberal Revolution. However, as Juan Pablo Fusi has pointed out, that revolution was an intermittent, uneven, undefined, long process, and in a number of aspects incomplete (Fusi Aizpurúa 1997, 16). It did not occur during a time of substantial transformation of the Spanish economy and did not produce enough economic prosperity to soften endemic social inequality. It was above all a period of political and institutional change that in part occurred under the exceptional historical circumstances of the Napoleonic Wars. By means of constitutional forms of government, the traditional social structure of estates was replaced by a society integrated by citizens equal before the law. Nevertheless, this new society remained oligarchic in nature, with a small middle class, dominated by a combination of old established elites and new ascendant groups that exercised dominance by means of a social system based on patronage, loyalty, and personal dependence. The privileges of the nobility were abolished, especially those of taxation, criminal justice, inheritance, and old established seigniorial rights. Nonetheless, the aristocracy remained strong within circles of royal and local power and maintained an atavistic social and cultural ascendance. The power of the Church was substantially diminished. The tithe was suppressed, the assets from the *manos muertas* (a form of tenure in which property donated to the church was forever unalienable) were forbidden, the menacing Spanish Inquisition finally abolished. Still, the four different constitutions drafted during this period recognized Catholicism as the religion of the Spanish nation.

Revolutionary politics caused the disintegration of the Spanish empire. The management of the empire became more and more complex during the second half of the eighteenth century because of the lack of financial resources, international competition, and the rise of autochthonous colonial elites that felt alienated by the imposition of rules and rulers from far away. The monarchy tried hard to remedy the crisis by implementing a series of new policies known as the Bourbon Reforms, aimed at improving colonial administration. Reforms came too late and proved insufficient in stopping the rise of revolutionary movements for national emancipation that brought about the independence of the major colonies of the Spanish empire.

Liberalism was the political ideology behind the revolution. Liberal ideals were pro-democracy as they favored political representation, but were not fully democratic because the right to vote was limited by a variety of restrictive prerequisites. In Spain, as in the rest of the Western world, liberalism was not the patrimony of a single class or social group, though the ideology was more attractive to the educated middle and lower segments of society. Some historians and social thinkers have questioned the strength of Spanish liberalism as a political force and denied the existence of a Spanish contribution in what became the main political credo of the West during the nineteenth century. For these scholars, the Spanish liberal movement only captivated a social minority that borrowed the ideas of the French and English Enlightenment and its successive philosophical ramifications. The paradox of this approach is that the term "liberal" entered the English and French political vocabulary in reference to the Spaniards who were drafting the first Spanish Constitution in the city of Cádiz around 1812. The essence of the liberal program embraced by Spanish liberals was a set of ideals stemming from the Enlightenment with one central theme: the search for freedom and the rejection of despotism. But recent scholarship has shown that the embodiment of these principles in the early Spanish Constitution of 1812 established an original contribution that transcended the frontiers of Spain. From a political point of view, Spanish liberalism was not an ideology of minorities, or poorly organized, or a failure when compared with the liberal experiences of other European cases considered models of nineteenth-century liberal success. As María Cruz Romeo points out, considering the long periods of authoritarian government in France, and the institutional fragmentation of Germany and Italy, Spain can be credited with having the longest years of parliamentary government among the large continental European countries, beginning in the 1830s and ending in the early twentieth century (Romeo 2010, 106).

The first stage of the Liberal Revolution took place under the exceptional circumstances of the Napoleonic occupation of Spain between 1808 and 1814. The control of the Iberian Peninsula was an essential strategic component of Napoleon's imperial project. With the cooperation of the Spanish monarchy, the emperor signed a series of treatises of friendship with Spain between 1801 and 1807. The most transcendental, the Treaty of Fontainebleau (1807), allowed the entrance of French troops into Spanish territory to facilitate Napoleon's invasion of Portugal. Most Spaniards disliked the military incursions of the French that in Catalonia and the Basque Country began as early as 1794. The riots of 1808, and especially the uprising of May 2 in Madrid, demonstrated the depth of anti-French sentiment among Spaniards and brought Napoleon's tactic of cooperation to an end. The emperor then decided to substitute his previously friendly imposition for a de facto invasion that forced the abdication of Charles IV and his son, the future Ferdinand VII, in favor of his own brother Joseph. While a significant segment of the Ilustrado elite welcomed the French emperor as a beneficial modernizer and cooperated with the invaders, thus becoming committed "afrancesados," the majority of the Spanish people declared war on the French and the imposed king Joseph I. The War of Independence, the name given to the Peninsular War in Spain, was, according to Stanley Payne, the broadest and most intense popular and national reaction to Napoleonic domination in Europe (Payne 2011, 140). The fight comprised a combination of actions carried out by the regular army in conjunction with a popular guerrilla movement. The intervention of British troops was decisive in defeating the French army on the battlefield. At the same time, the continuous and unpredictable activity of the guerrillas in different parts of the territory eroded the morale of Napoleonic troops by creating a feeling that victory could never be fully accomplished.

The war transformed the abstract idea of the Spanish nation, used before by the Ilustrado reformers, into a material reality in which "el pueblo" (the people), now fighting against an invader, became the main protagonist. The large majority of Spanish people understood the fight against Napoleon as a patriotic act to defend a territory, a culture, and a monarchy. However, Spanish sentiment was split concerning the political, social, and cultural form the new national community should adopt (Álvarez Junco 2011, 99). One side favored maintaining the traditional order of the absolutist monarchy and the society of estates, and the other supported the transformation of Spain into a constitutional monarchy and a society of citizens equal before the law. The proponents of change were still a social minority, but had clear goals and were better prepared and organized for the political battles to come.

Opponents to Joseph I established Juntas Provinciales (Provincial Councils) and a Junta Central. These were alternative institutions that rejected the legitimacy of what they called the intruder king and assumed the sovereignty of the Spanish nation. The Junta Central took shelter in Cádiz, a city the French never managed to subdue, and called for the meeting of the Cortes Extraordinarias – a special meeting of the traditional Spanish parliament. Parliamentary sessions started in September 1810, after a wartime election that gave the liberals many seats. The social archetype of these liberals was a young, highly educated member of the middle and lower ranks of the provincial elites, with a background in public administration, higher education, or commerce. Good examples of this archetype were the three most celebrated deputies of this parliament: the lawyers Agustín de Argüelles and Evaristo Pérez de Castro, and the cleric and university professor Diego Muñoz-Torrero, all in their thirties and all belonging to families of the middle ranks of the provincial gentry. The influence of the liberal majority was noticed when the Cortes approved a bill to legalize freedom of speech despite the opposition of the conservatives, now known as the serviles. Additional legislation abolished seigneurial privileges, the corporate structures of artisan guilds, and the Inquisition. A commission was charged to draft the first Spanish liberal constitution.

The Cádiz Constitution was approved in March 1812 and was the most celebrated liberal charter across Europe and South America until the 1830s. It inspired liberals in Italy, Germany, Russia, and, against the intention of its drafters, the forces that brought about the dismantling of the Spanish empire. The ideas embodied in the text stemmed from the philosophical traditions of the French and Anglo-Scottish Enlightenment, and included elements inspired by the doctrines of natural law of the Spanish-Catholic-Scholastic school. The Constitution introduced the principles of equality before the law, national sovereignty, and the division of powers meant to limit the authority of the absolutist monarch. According to the Constitution, the nation was to be represented in the Cortes by elected deputies following a complicated electoral process of indirect male suffrage. The powers of the king were reduced substantially: his orders had to be validated by the first minister, he did not have the power to suspend the legislature, and his ministerial appointments had to be approved by the parliament. Some individual rights were recognized, including free speech, education, and property, but the Constitution did not include a bill of rights and did not acknowledge the right to choose a religion other than Catholicism.

The Constitution of 1812 attempted to create a centralized state that emphasized the sovereignty of the national community over that of the individual subject; it was assumed that the nation was the source of all individual rights. It did not mention what the future held for long-established fiscal and institutional arrangements in some parts of Spain, including the Basque Country and Navarre. The 1812 liberals intended to eliminate feudal privilege by creating a national community of universal taxpayers in an open socio-economic order that valued merit over inheritance. With an absolute and no doubt naive confidence, they called for a peaceful transition towards the new state and social order.

The defeat of Napoleon brought about the restoration of the Bourbon monarchy in Spain. The new king, Ferdinand VII, returned to Spain in March 1814 in an atmosphere of patriotic excitement and popular support. It was now the responsibility of the new monarch to accept, reject, or negotiate with the Cortes the Constitution of Cádiz. Soon the conservative opposition, the *serviles*, took action by drafting a manifesto (*Manifiesto de los Persas*) encouraging the king to restore absolutism. On May 4, Ferdinand VII, a ferocious anti-liberal, approved a decree that dictated the suspension of the Cortes, the abolition of the 1812 Constitution, and the restoration of the old political and social order.

In Spain, as in the rest of Europe, the "Restoration" of 1814 promised to be a transitory moment in the long conflict initiated by the Enlightenment in the eighteenth century between the forces of change and the defenders of tradition. The 1812 liberals lost their first battle because they were an advanced radical minority in a country still dominated by traditional Catholicism and old established social loyalties. But those who held liberal ideologies were on the right side of history, and little by little its social base became wider, more persistent, and better organized. The "spirit of 1812" survived in the minds of many members of the upper ranks of the army whose ascent had taking place during, and because of, the war. These liberal military men became a fundamental force in the ascent of liberalism in nineteenth-century Spain. After 1814 the most frequent iteration of the Spanish liberal uprising was a sort of coup known as a *pronunciamiento* that involved the combined action of the military and civilians. It was usually an urban rebellion comprised of two fundamental steps: a period of secret conspiracy to design intricate plans to take over the government, and a military coup backed by revolutionary civilians who barricaded the streets. The success or failure of these revolutionary upheavals mainly depended on the role played by the military. The first of many *pronunciamientos* took place in 1820 and was led by Rafael de Riego, a young military general with a social profile similar to the liberal deputies of the Cortes of Cádiz: he was of the provincial gentry, well educated, and a romantic patriot.

Riego restored the Constitution of 1812 and forced Ferdinand VII to pledge allegiance to it. Riego's imposing attitude toward a king that had sent explicit signs of displeasure caused the first split among the Cádiz liberals. A more moderate wing was in favor of amending the charter to give the monarch more power and to establish a bicameral legislature with one chamber for the upper classes of society. Regardless, the spirit of radical liberalism prevailed, the possibility of an amendment was rejected, and the liberal divide intensified. This fissure created an unstable political environment. Those in favor of a traditional political system took advantage of this instability and launched a geographically localized but substantially armed uprising in which all opponents to liberalism were united in a dynamic of violent action. The liberal government reacted to this uprising by speeding up its increasingly anti-clerical revolutionary policies, which now focused on dismantling the power of the Catholic Church.

It is in this tumultuous political climate that the Spanish American colonies achieved independence. The liberals of 1812 and 1820 failed to provide mechanisms of political representation to the colonial elites. The *criollo* deputies in the Cortes of Cádiz were coopted by the imperial administration, not elected by a democratic constituency. The Spanish liberals were not willing to cede any political autonomy to Spanish American elites. After 1820, independence became the only feasible option for the *criollo* groups. Under the leadership of Simón Bolivar and José de San Martín, by 1824 the bulk of the Spanish American empire was transformed into a series of independent republics.

By 1823 Riego's government was on the edge of collapse, plagued by anti-liberal forces, the division among liberals, and the uncontrolled activity of radicalized groups. In April of that same year the anti-liberal European coalition of the Austrian and Russian empires sent a French battalion to Spain that overthrew General Riego. Ferdinand VII's absolutism was restored and the general was jailed and publicly executed a few months later. The Spanish Liberal Revolution now had its first popular hero, but after three years of liberal rule the liberals were divided. The ten years leading up to the death of Ferdinand VII in 1833 were years of political persecution, though the liberal movement remained fairly active, in a constant state of conspiracy, and by all means unstoppable.

At the time of Ferdinand VII's death, his daughter and the inheritor of the Spanish crown, Queen Isabella II, was only three years old. Her mother, María Cristina of Naples, became the temporary Regent of Spain. María Cristina had two options from which to choose when forming her new government: continue with the absolutist style of her husband or negotiate with the liberals. While she did not sympathize with the liberal credo, she understood that liberalism could no longer be kept at bay. During the 1820s, the most influential sectors of the dominant social groups embraced liberalism, and its ideals captured a popular following also. Having said this, María Cristina could not stomach the spirit of the Cádiz Constitution and decided instead to govern using the support of the most moderate wing of the liberal spectrum. She gave the position of first minister to Francisco Martínez de la Rosa, a prestigious intellectual and former deputy of the Cortes of Cádiz who belonged to the moderate group. Martínez de la Rosa drafted an alternative charter (the Royal Statute of 1834) to replace the Constitution of 1812. However, his experiment did not generate enough support among the liberals and was drastically rejected by the absolutists. The division between temperate and radical liberals widened to the point of splitting into two separate political parties: the Moderate Party and the Progressive Party. Each party held differing views over how quickly Spain should be transformed into a modern liberal democracy, a division that characterized Spanish politics during the central years of the building of the modern nation. On the other side of the political spectrum, the absolutists declared war on the Regent María Cristina and her liberal government. They questioned the legitimacy of Isabella to inherit the Spanish crown, proclaiming instead that the ultra-conservative Carlos María Isidro, brother of Ferdinand VII, was the legitimate heir. This war, known as the Carlist War (1833–1839), was the first in a series of three violent civil confrontations between liberals and absolutists (Carlists) in the nineteenth century.

Martínez de la Rosa's reticent liberalism failed in its attempts to unify the liberals and fight the reactionary forces represented by Carlism; in short, his political vision could not definitively bring freedom to the Spanish nation. He left the government in 1835, creating a period of ascent for the progressives that lasted until 1844. The Spanish liberal revolution reached its peak in a context of exacerbated political confrontation between moderates and progressives, while both groups still fought a war against the forces of the *Ancien Regime*. The main difference between the moderate and progressive parties lay in the degree of political and social change brought on by revolution, as well as the means used to implement these transformations. Both parties were in favor of constitutional monarchy, but disagreed on the amount of power the monarch should keep. Both were in favor of a restricted form of suffrage, but they differed in the level of restriction. These differences were irreconcilable when drafting electoral law or when spreading democracy to municipal life. The progressives were in favor of making the municipal councils and the mayors elected officials, a measure the moderates drastically rejected. The moderates prioritized order and authority, where the progressives emphasized democratic participation. Both were in favor of the protection of private property and realized the need to disentail the properties of the Church, but the progressives wanted to create more measures than the moderates to constrain the economic power of the Catholic Church. Both relied on military *pronunciamientos* to seize power instead of elections. The difference lay in the amount of popular involvement each party relied on to make the coup successful. Progressive *pronunciamientos* were generally carried out by military garrisons in coordination with rioters in the streets building barricades, while the moderates preferred palace coups without the participation of the masses. The progressives created a body of National Militias (*Milicia Nacional*) integrated by civilians whose mission was to defend and promote revolution. The moderates opposed these militias drastically and called for their dissolution.

Until 1842 the two main figures in the Progressive Party were Juan Álvarez Mendizábal and General Baldomero Espartero. In 1835 Mendizábal, a financier with experience in international trade who was well connected in British economic circles, was offered a ministry in the cabinet. Progressive party leaders felt he would be able to fix the persistent Spanish deficit now aggravated by the war. Mendizábal's main contribution to the revolution was the implementation of the program of disentailment of the Church's property. Mendizábal's policies were drastically contested by the moderate opposition, and backed in the streets by radical liberals who desired the restoration of the Constitution of Cádiz. A *pronunciamiento* in August 1836 known as the coup of the "Sergeants of La Granja" reinforced the position of the progressives, who were now ready to restore constitutionalism. They now had two options: either reinstate the Constitution of 1812, so hated by the moderates, or draft a new constitution. They decided to follow the second track, because it was the only feasible alternative that could guarantee a long period of political stability. A new constitution was drafted and approved in 1837. The Constitution of 1837 struggled to find a balance between moderate and progressive liberal agendas. It established a bicameral system with a Senate whose members were proposed by the Cortes but elected by the monarch. All laws had to be approved by both chambers. Cabinet ministers were also nominated by the monarch but needed to be endorsed by the Cortes. Catholicism was again declared the official religion of Spain, but the practice of other religions was permitted. The state agreed to economically support the clergy, to repair the harm caused by the disentailment of Church property.

For María Cristina and a substantial portion of the Moderate Party, the Constitution of 1837 was still too radical. It generated political stability, but only for a short period that coincided with the defeat of the Carlists on the battlefield and the end of the First Carlist War. The leader of the moment was the progressive General Baldomero Espartero, who was victorious in 1839. Espartero was a product of the Spanish Liberal Revolution: the son of a craftsman from a small village in central Spain promoted to the rank of general thanks to the wars and the opportunities offered by the new liberal system. In 1840 the charismatic general, now highly popular, was endorsed by the progressives to become the new Regent of Spain, taking the place of María Cristina, who was sent into exile. The progressives hoped that his popularity and political commitments would guarantee the continuation of the Liberal Revolution. However, Espartero behaved more like Napoleon and less like the civilian politician most progressives had desired. By 1843 the consensus of support for the general's regime had been eroded, mainly because of the disillusionment of the politicians. An ad hoc alliance of moderates and progressives engineered a series of conspiracy plots that culminated in *pronunciamientos* and forced Espartero from his position.

At this point a significant segment of the dominant groups, including the monarchy, the moderate military, and the Catholic Church felt that the revolution had gone too far. The defeat of the Carlists served to reinforce the prestige of the monarchy, thus creating an atmosphere of stability that would foster the political rearrangement of the dominant Spanish groups. Under these new conditions the momentum of radical politics waned. As in France in 1795, so in Spain in 1843, the moment for the taming of the revolution had arrived. What happened during these years was certainly not unique to Spain. It was a process that occurred in all nineteenth-century European revolutions. After a period of radical enthusiasm marked by dramatic political alterations, the revolutions were either completely halted or else re-channeled by the insurgent forces of order. This same phenomenon occurred in the Spanish revolution after 1843, when the Moderate Party took control of the political process and Queen Isabella II, on her thirteenth birthday, was declared of age and became the new Queen.

Unlike the brief period of Progressive control, the Moderate period of hegemony, beginning in 1843, lasted for most of the rest of the century. In the long term the transformation of Spain into a liberal state was mainly the achievement of the moderate stream of liberalism (Esdaile 2000, 85–88). The progressives held power only during short intervals that were normally linked to revolutionary episodes. These were decisive moments in the process of the transformation of Spanish political and social structures, to be sure, but the long periods during which the liberal system matured were controlled by moderates. Thus, the years between 1843 and 1868 mark the beginning of this moderate hegemony that lasted until 1923. These were the years in which the Moderate Party forged the political and administrative foundations of the Spanish liberal state.

Taming the liberal revolution: the conservative turn (1843–1868)

The formal task of taming the revolution was undertaken by the three internal forces that balanced Isabella II's constitutional monarchy: the crown, the army, and the bulk of the dynastic parties. The crown was unequivocally conservative, if not anti-liberal. Publicly, both María Cristina during her regency, and the Queen herself during her rule, were committed to liberal reforms, but they feared the liberal revolution because it represented a threat that would limit the power of the throne (Burdiel 2010, 20–22). The monarch still had the right to designate and dismiss ministers and to grant a decree to end the legislature and call for new elections. Isabella II took advantage of this option whenever she felt threatened by liberal radicalism, a tendency that consistently favored the Moderate Party. Thus, the Progressives felt that they were being deliberately neglected by a partisan monarch who was constantly challenging the liberal revolution, and little by little started to endorse the idea of finding a possible successor who would be willing to accept the rules of constitutional parliamentarianism. In the beginning the idea appealed only to the radical wing of the Progressive Party and to the new left wing, which had situated itself in a separate group known as the Democratic Party. However, with the passage of time – especially after 1863 – the idea of replacing the monarch found support among all members of the Progressive Party and even among significant representatives of the Moderate center.

The military formed the second internal force that worked for the control of liberal radicalism. The propensity of the military to actively intervene in politics in nineteenth-century Spain is a phenomenon that cannot be explained in simple terms. Likewise, it is also a simplification to consider this interventionist propensity, which continued into the twentieth century in Spain as well as the greater Hispanic world, as the most evident manifestation of the existence of a "distinctive" Spanish authoritarian tradition. Militarism, understood as the active intervention of the military in the process of political decision making, was a common phenomenon in all of continental Europe in the nineteenth century. In a general sense, modern militarism has resulted mainly from the weaknesses of civil society in countries in which political democratization is guided by political elites, but it also has to do with the different role assigned to the military in the context of the new liberal state.

After 1843 the military's political intervention increasingly abetted the conservative shift in liberal politics (Vincent 2007, 32). The fall of the charismatic General Baldomero Espartero marked the beginning of a period of military realignment with the Moderate program. It is true that the generals adopted independent styles of governing not always in tune with the civilian programs they were supposed to represent. Nonetheless, what generally prevailed were arrangements along the lines of the two major civilian political forces active on the Spanish political scene: the Moderates and the Progressives. Espartero, despite his Napoleonic propensity, was considered the candidate of the rogressives. Ramón María Narváez, despite his exaggerated authoritarianism, along with the more conciliatory Leopoldo O'Donnell, the military leaders of the period between 1843 and 1868, became the sentinels of Moderate liberalism. In the last instance, the military hierarchy was more attracted by the moderate message of an ordered and controlled transition than by the progressive program of democratic insurgence.

Along with the crown and the military, the last and most important force in the process of political readjustment initiated after 1843 was the Moderate Party. In the 1840s the moderates believed the most critical steps for the implantation of a liberal order had already been taken in the previous decade. They argued that the years of progressive radical politics had been a threat to the political, social, and economic stability that Spain needed to prosper. It was their task, they believed, to return Spanish politics to the path that would lead to the completion of the still unfinished task of constructing an authentic liberal order.

After 1843 the moderates and the crown worked together to exclude the progressives from government, but that exclusion was also the result of the progressives' misguided political strategies. They had decided to adopt a position of *retraimiento* (systematic electoral abstention) to protest the impudent favoritism that the crown showed towards the moderates. The strategy was a complete failure because it served to entrench the power of the moderates. The progressives were divided between a radical and a more pragmatic wing. The problem they continually faced was finding a way to control the revolution and keep it from extreme radicalization. This tension was always a handicap for the rogressives and the reason for their tactical hesitancy. The Progressives' reluctant policies resulted in the split of the party. In 1849 an excision from the progressives formed the Democratic Party, determined to bring an authentic democracy to Spain. The political positions of the democrats were diverse. The leadership of the group still believed in the constitutional monarchy, but many were republicans, some of them federalists who called for a kind of multinational state. There was also a socialist component represented by followers of Fourier. The Democrats were active in all of the revolutionary attempts that challenged the moderate hegemony. They provided the popular element that sparked the upheaval of 1868, and in 1873 they were the main promoters of the first republican experiment in Spain.

The main instrument the moderates used to tame the revolution was the "reform" of the constitution that the progressives had adapted in 1837. In fact, the so-called reform ended in the formation of a new Constitution of 1845. Despite the repetition of many articles, this new body of laws differed substantially in spirit from the progressive constitution, to the point that it transformed the nature of the entire political system. Under the Progressive constitution, national sovereignty had rested with the parliament, but the Moderates established a new form of sovereignty in which part of the crown's traditional powers were restored. This restoration was made by limiting the responsibilities of parliament and, subsequently, reinforcing the power of the monarch, the cabinet, and the senate in the decision-making process. There was a new senate whose members, undetermined in number, would be exclusively appointed by royal designation from among the notables of the kingdom. Also, the constitution opened the door to limiting freedom of expression. Along with this, it suppressed the national militia that had been a key instrument used by the Progressives to implement their revolutionary program. Once the constitution had established the framework for the new order, the Moderates embarked upon a feverish legislative program to consolidate their rule. The main outcome of this process was the elaboration of new electoral laws and new norms for the regulation of freedom of speech. Both legal instruments were, of course, restrictive and designed to continue the consolidation of their power.

But the Moderates were not only cunning political manipulators, they were also good administrators. The moderate years bequeathed a set of institutions, laws, and practices that survived the turbulence of daily politics and helped to consolidate the Spanish liberal state. The Moderates reformed the old Spanish National Bank, converting it into the modern financial institution it is today. They also introduced the postal stamp to Spain and the use of the peseta as the national monetary unit, and took the first measures to create a state-supported education system. Regarding the administering of justice and public order the moderates succeeded in formulating a new criminal code in tune with the spirit of rationalization that characterized liberal law. They advanced the process of building a modern court system, and created in 1844 the controversial and historic Spanish Civil Guard, a government-controlled local police force in charge of maintaining public order. One of the moderates' more lasting projects was the reform of the national treasury that made the collection of taxes more balanced and efficient. They also initiated a series of reforms of the state's administration to make it more professional. Among the most important steps of this reformist task before 1848 was the creation of the new departments of Commerce, Education, and Public Works, the completion of the administrative division of Spanish territory in the provinces, and the approval of a bill to regulate municipal and regional powers that implied a tighter control of central government over provincial life.

The first serious revolutionary challenge to moderate rule occurred during the spring of 1848. The progressives tried to replicate in Spain the revolutionary movements that were taking place in other parts of Europe. However, conditions were not favorable and the effort was a complete failure. Narváez acted rapidly and resolutely to repress the revolution. The Progressives were unable to mobilize the masses to man the barricades for the revolution. They were divided regarding the goals of the revolution; there was a good deal of hesitation among those who feared that popular mobilization would end in a social revolution. The result was a split in the Progressive forces that gave birth in 1849 to the Democratic Party. So, despite the failure, 1848 demonstrated that the seeds of revolution were nestled in Spanish soil and could germinate under more advantageous conditions.

This moment arrived in 1854. The political situation had so deteriorated that it was finally possible to create a broad consensus favoring change. As usual, the military was the key to revolutionary success, by means of repeated armed pronunciamientos that ended in the neutralization of the government. The movement attained its goals in July 1854 when General Espartero was called to take the presidency of a new cabinet. Between 1854 and 1856, Espartero, with the Progressives' and O'Donnell's consent, tried to go back to the situation as it had been before 1843. The Progressive program included the promulgation of a new constitution that would make it possible to extend freedom of speech, decentralize the state, reform the tax system, expand suffrage, continue with disentailment, and restore the national militia. The program only partially succeeded in its economic goals. A new constitution was written and approved by parliament in 1856, but it was never promulgated and consequently had no lasting impact. Progressive rule did not substantially alter the functioning of the liberal state as it had been established by the Moderates. The 1854 revolution brought about more a change of government personnel than a change of vision and policy; consequently, it was contested from the very beginning by those who dreamed of the coming of a new order. Now the voice of revolution was represented by the new Democratic Party, whose rhetoric and program were even more radical. In fact, the more rebellious the Democrats seemed the more hesitant and ambivalent appeared the progressives. It was this combination of factors that brought to an end the progressive biennium. In 1856 Espartero, unable to stop the revolutionary pressure of the democrats and the criticisms of the moderates, decided to resign. General Leopoldo O'Donnell became the new prime minister.

The fourteen years that separate the 1854 revolutionary episode from the Gloriosa revolution of 1868 were marked by the attempt to build a liberal center with a new political experiment guided by Leopoldo O'Donnell, known as the Liberal Union. A coalition more than a party, the Liberal Union worked better as an experiment for the future than as a solution for the problems of the moment. The idea was promising, but in reality the experiment was sponsored by an alliance of notables with few popular links and strongly convinced that in politics order should prevail over liberty. The Liberal Union brought about the longest period of stable government since 1833, but it finally failed in what was supposed to be its main goal: the unification of the entire liberal family in a common endeavor. Like the moderates before 1854, the unionist government ended up practicing a policy of exclusion of the political opponent. The fear of a popular revolution was again the excuse to neglect and repress those who supported greater democracy and social reform. In this, politicians were backed by the crown, which was more and more identified as the main obstacle to democracy.

The coming of the 1868 upheaval shows the inability of Spanish liberals to achieve a stable political system for Spain. As we have seen, the years of the moderate hegemony were decisive for the consolidation of a liberal state, but overall liberalism failed to provide the liberty and prosperity that many Spaniards would have expected from the early liberal project. This political failure was in the last instance the consequence of the poor performance of the Spanish economy and the persistence of traditional social structures. Indeed, in a society marked by the existence of deep social divisions, traditional Spanish elites had little margin to both warrant political stability and at the same time maintain their domination. This explains the hesitations of the Progressives and the refusal of the Moderates and Liberal Unionists to open the political system to a higher degree of democratic participation. Under these circumstances, Spanish political life would continue to be marked by the menace of revolution, but now the social characteristics of that revolutionary potential threatened more than ever the traditional liberal elites. In the future the maintenance of a stable political system would depend on the capacity of the elites to remain united, a condition that proved to be impossible in Spain's turbulent political life.

Works cited

Álvarez Junco, José. 2011. *Spanish Identity in the Age of Nations*. Manchester: Manchester University Press.

Burdiel, Isabel. 2010. *Isabel II: una biografía (1830–1904)*. Madrid: Taurus.

Esdaile, Charles J. 2000. *Spain in the Liberal Age: From Constitution to Civil War, 1808–1939*. Oxford: Blackwell.

Fusi Aizpurúa, Juan Pablo, and Jordi Palafox Gámir. 1997. *España, 1808–1996: el desafío de la modernidad*. Madrid: Espasa.

Payne, Stanley G. 2011. *Spain: A Unique History*. Madison, WI: University of Wisconsin Press.

Romeo, María Cruz. 2010. "Las guerras civiles del siglo XIX: ¿una ruta excepcional hacia la modernización?" In *¿Es España diferente?: una mirada comparativa (siglos XIX y XX)*, edited by Nigel Townson, 65–110. Madrid: Taurus.

Vincent, Mary. 2007. *Spain 1833–2002: People and State*. Oxford: Oxford University Press.

23

CARLISTS AGAINST LIBERALISM

Counter-revolution in the Iberian Peninsula during the nineteenth century

Jordi Canal

Carlism belongs to a wider category of what have been termed "counter-revolutionary" movements visible in most Western European states over the course of the nineteenth century, including Miguelism in Portugal or the Legitimist movement in France. It was primarily opposed to liberalism and revolution. It was not the only expression of counter-revolutionary sentiment to be seen in Spain (consider, e.g., the popularity of royalism during the Liberal Triennium), but it was undoubtedly the most important, in every sense. This has often led "Carlism" to be understood as a synonym for "counter-revolution," especially in accounts of nineteenth-century Spain (see Canal 2000a, 2006; Rújula 1998). That century saw Carlists take a leading role in two major civil wars – the First Carlist War (1833–1840) and the Second Carlist War (1872–1876) – as well as various insurrections, cavalry raids, coups, and minor skirmishes. These conflicts involved thousands of people, and were an essential part of the process by which the contemporary nation-state took shape. As such, the Carlist movement is of fundamental importance for the contemporary history of Spain.

God, King, and Country

Carlism may be defined as a socio-political movement which is anti-liberal and anti-revolutionary in nature, formed soon before the fall of the *Ancien Régime* and still surviving to the present day, albeit in a clearly diminished form. The terms "Carlism" and "Carlist" were coined during the second absolutist restoration of Fernando VII, between 1823 and 1833; they were derived from the name of the prince, Carlos María Isidro de Borbón, who would later become the legitimists' King Carlos V; and they represented the culmination of several pre-existing trends, whose principal outlet had previously been royalism. The situation was similar in neighbouring Portugal: the terms "Miguelism" and "Miguelist" referred to a counter-revolutionary movement led by Dom Miguel, King Miguel I of Portugal from 1828 to 1834, who remained a pretender to the throne after being deposed at the end of a fratricidal war (see Lousada and Ferreira 2006). Although Carlism really took root in Spain and rose to prominence from 1833 onwards, its rise must be set alongside those of other royalist movements which have their origins in the conflicts of the early nineteenth century, and which begin to play a significant role in events during the 1820s (see Aróstegui 1975; Canal 2000a).

The widespread acceptance of the terms "Carlism" and "Carlist" resulted in other similar – but not completely equivalent – expressions falling into disuse, although they did not disappear entirely; these included "royalism" and "absolutism," or terms such as "ultra," "apostólico," "servil," or "royalist." In certain cases, words such as "absolutist" or "servil" acquired distinctly pejorative connotations over time, even within the counter-revolutionary movement itself. Others, such as "faccioso," "latrofaccioso," or "carca," were applied to Carlists by their enemies, the product of an intensely confrontational atmosphere. Likewise, referring to the Carlist rebels as a "facción" was common. In Catalan, as well as "facció" and "facciós," "fàccia" was also used as a synonym for the former. The origins of the term "carca" lay in Portugal, where liberals referred to counter-revolutionaries or Miguelists as "corcovas," "corcundas," or "carcundas." The Portuguese and Galician "corcunda" or "carcunda," which were variant forms of "corcova" (a hump, a hunchback, an egoist), were the root from which the Spanish "carcunda" and the abbreviated, jargonistic form "carca" ultimately derived, aided by phonetic similarity to the term "Carlist" ("carlista").

The term "traditionalism" is also worthy of note; in the nineteenth century it was often associated, and sometimes even synonymous, with "Carlism." In Jaime Lluís y Navas's words, Carlism "con el tiempo sería llamado tradicionalismo" (1967, 309). In reality, the situation is more complex. It is true that following the Democratic Sexennium, in the era of the Comunión Católico-Monárquica, and especially during the Restoration and subsequently during the Second Republic (Carlism's loss of vigour after the Carlist uprisings was not irrelevant to this process), the term "traditionalism" came to be used as a synonym for "Carlism." However, although all forms of Carlism were traditionalist (at least during the nineteenth century, since the late twentieth-century battle between traditionalist and socialist manifestations of Carlism is another question entirely), not all forms of traditionalism were Carlist. The case of Juan Donoso Cortés, Marquis of Valdegamas, may be instructive. "Traditionalism" essentially referred to a system of thought, to a doctrine and an attitude, as Francisco Canals has recognized (1977, 193–198). Carlism's identification as traditionalist thus reaffirmed a distinctive and essential part of its nature (as did its identification as Catholic), while also facilitating its underlying tendency to unite various related movements under a single banner.

Although this question has been of little interest to historians, it is worth adding here that colours were used as terms of reference for both Carlists and, of course, liberals. Thus, "blanco" was common currency in nineteenth-century Spain to designate the followers of Carlism, while "negro" – or "beltza" in Basque – indicated an adherent to liberalism. While the former had its roots in the association of that colour with the Bourbon dynasty (counter-revolutionaries were also known as "blancs" in France), the latter – which is openly contemptuous – appeared in Spain during the 1820s, and must be related to the processes of political purging or purification, and to the supposed purity or otherwise of the soul (see Canal 2008).

The dynastic question, which confronted advocates of Isabel II and those of her uncle Carlos María Isidro regarding the succession to Fernando VII, is not itself sufficient to explain the birth of Carlism and its prolonged existence. However, the influence of this controversy has often been overplayed. Queen Amalia, Fernando VII's third wife, died in May 1829, whereupon the King, now a widower without an heir, decided quickly to contract a new marriage. His bride was one of his nieces, the young María Cristina of Naples who was sister to Luisa Carlota, the wife of Prince Francisco de Paula. The marriage took place in December of that year, and a few months later it was announced that the Queen was expecting. In late March 1830, Fernando had the Pragmatic Sanction, passed in 1789 but never promulgated, formally enacted. The Pragmatic Sanction constituted the annulment of the Salic law which had been in force since the reign of Felipe V; it introduced substantial changes in the matter of succession, removing the masculine preference and the resulting near-exclusion of women. The child of Fernando and María Cristina would therefore inherit the throne, regardless of gender.

Much critical ink has been spilled over the promulgation of the Pragmatic Sanction, since it formed the legal basis for the conflict between Carlists and liberals. The points of contention were several: could Fernando VII take this decision? And if so, could he do so without the approval of the Cortes? Did enacting the Pragmatic Sanction affect Prince Carlos, who was born before 1789? Were the acts of 1713 and 1789 in fact valid? Many questions thus required clarification, and each side answered them according to its own interests, providing further evidence that the matter of succession was really secondary, and essentially designed to provide a legal justification for dispute and civil war. The Carlist uprisings were truly socio-political conflicts. The decree passed in 1713, which barred women from succession in the event of there being a direct or collateral male heir, was updated under Carlos IV. In 1789, the Cortes voted to restore the old customs of succession set down in the *Partidas*, according to which there should be no distinction on the basis of gender. However, this modification was not published, and was therefore not incorporated into the *Novísima Recopilación* of 1805. In March 1830, King Fernando VII simply took the next step following the approval of the Cortes, which was to promulgate the law. When Princess Isabel was born in October of that year, her uncle, Carlos María Isidro, and groups of "ultras" in particular began to see the accession to the throne which they had so longed for now in serious danger (see Burdiel 2010; Canal 2000a; Moral Roncal 1999). The suggestion advanced by Gloria Martínez Dorado and Juan Pan-Montojo (2000), that in studying the origins of Carlism the dynastic question should be interpreted as a form of political opportunism, is worthy of consideration.

The dynastic question was not an essential issue for Carlism, nor was the movement ever solely a defence of the rights of Carlist Bourbons to the throne. The elements of continuity with previous counter-revolutionary movements, as well as the scale of the Spanish civil wars, give the lie to any exclusively dynastic interpretation of Carlism. In any case, the Carlists were driven by an idea or a set of principles not only personified in the Carlist king, but also for which he became an emblem, as well as being a permanent point of reference for the movement's followers. They thus fought on the battlefield and in the political arena not for a king's own person, but for what the figure of that king represented: namely, a particular worldview and the possible projects that might bring it to fruition. The legitimist publicist Juan María Roma wrote in the *Álbum histórico del carlismo* that the Carlists "lucharon por una idea más que por un Trono y una Dinastía" (1935, 25). The dynasty and the various claimants to the throne were to become essential parts of the movement, in a symbolic and emblematic sense. Despite the attempts of some Spanish Marxist historians, however, it is not possible to explain Carlism without the real and symbolic figure of the king-pretender: Carlos V, Carlos VI, Juan III, or Carlos VII, in the twentieth century. Although not exclusively so, Carlism was a legitimist movement, as Miguelism and Chambordism were. The figure of the king-pretender always had a role to play in bringing together various different counter-revolutionary interests into a single body (see Canal 2011a; Torras 1976).

The Carlist cause supported the maintaining of tradition, and fought against liberalism and everything that it represented or implied, both in reality and on an abstract level. God, King, and Country were the essential pillars of an ideology that was in fact remarkably ill-defined (see Canal 2001, 297–299; Ugarte 1998, 420). The *Fueros* did not always come in under the Carlist banner, and often did not do so until the end of the nineteenth century; when they did it was always strictly in support of traditional liberties, and not an expression of nationalism or the desire for regional autonomy. The First Carlist War was not a war fought over regional charters, but these were a part of what was at stake in some areas. The so-called "abolición feral" ("Abolition of Municipal Charters") of 1876, together with the emergence of regionalisms and nationalisms subsidiary to the wider construct of the state, which had some overlap with Carlism, often led to a fourth element being added to that fundamental trilogy of God, King, and Country (see Mina 2011). In any case, the indistinct nature of their ideology made it easier for differing opinions and heterogeneous sectors of society to coexist within the Carlist movement, united in the face of other options to which they considered themselves opposed, and which they therefore saw as threatening.

Carlism's foundations were strongest in the north of Spain, especially in the Basque Country, Navarre, and Catalunya, with important centres elsewhere in Valencia and Aragon. The movement's geographical reach was apparently unaltered with the passing of the decades, varying only in the scale of its support. The Carlist territory par excellence was the Peninsular north, which was particularly strongly affected by several widespread and intensive transformative processes from the early years of the twentieth century; these included everything from industrialization and agricultural specialization to the arrival of new ideas and attempts at reform, along with changes to forms of ownership or the perceived socio-cultural value of certain activities or institutions. Any analysis of the roots of the Carlist movement should be wary of overlooking either the inheritance of previous counter-revolutionary mobilizations, from the War of Independence (1808–1814) to the so-called Ominous Decade (1823–1833); or the impoverishment of several areas, as has been demonstrated in the case of Catalunya; or the attitude of traditional élites, particularly in the north (see Agirreazkuenaga and Ortiz de Orruño 1990).

As time passed, the wellspring of Carlist support was to grow concentrated in specific areas – above all, in Navarre – which became self-perpetuating enclaves of deeply rooted Carlist political culture (see Caspistegui 2005, 2008; Millán 1998). These places provided an ideal environment for Carlism to build its own microcosm and to think of itself as a true counter-society, without the inaccessible possession of the State ever destroying what was really a victimizing myth. However, other areas were always able to join these heartlands, on a more or less provisional basis, always as a result of an intense proselytizing process. This was the case, for example, in several Andalusian provinces during the Second Republic (see Blinkhorn 1975). Nonetheless, there is a clear continuity to be observed which extends throughout Carlism's prolonged existence, taking into account both its ideology and its affiliations, structures, and legacy. This movement has been sustained by one single political culture, constantly in the process of being remade (see Pérez Ledesma 1996; Rújula 2014).

Social heterogeneity is one of the touchstones of Carlist identity. Peasants and craftsmen were the most common adherents to the movement and formed the heart of its popular base, along with landowners and the clergy, and not forgetting soldiers, administrative professionals, and merchants. Some studies of the first wave of Carlism in the centre of Navarre, for example, yield the following approximate results: 66.4% agricultural labourers – mostly peasants (54.5%), along with some day labourers (10.2%); 10.2% clergy; 7.7% craftsmen; 7.2% rentiers; 4.7% working in administration; and 3% soldiers. In Pamplona, however, the proportions vary somewhat: craftsmen are most common (34.3%), along with the clergy (22.6%), followed by those in administrative jobs (17.3%), agricultural trades (11%), those working in education (4.6%), rentiers (2.3%), and merchants (1.9%); the final 3.5% of the sample comprises those working in minor trades, or who are unemployed (see Pan-Montojo 1990).

According to the Carlists, liberalism and the revolution, in any of their varied manifestations, were the cause of the transformations – some of which had already taken place, with others still to come – which were calling into question, weakening, or shattering completely their political or social positions, their economic foundations, or their cultural universe (which was not limited to religion, although that was a fundamental component of it). Carlists were united by mutual support in their battle for a common goal, despite differences between them which were many and significant. Although the movement's overall direction was controlled by the most well-to-do sectors of society and the old élites, there is no substance to the Marxist interpretation of Carlism, namely, that the movement should be understood in terms of a manipulation or exploitation of a popular revolt by more powerful members of society, who would become, on this interpretation, the true counter-revolutionaries. Neither is the opposite view tenable, advanced by neo-Carlist historiography, which argues for the existence of a popular Carlism that was the movement's true form, and which was then manipulated by the powerful (see Canal 2007b). The truth is that Carlism was really a temporary and circumstantial confluence of people from different parts of society – which nonetheless endured on occasion – based on interests, aspirations, wrongs, dangers, enemies, languages, and ideologies which were partially or entirely held in common, even if they were not identical.

The Carlist wars

Carlism was at its height in Spain between 1833 and 1876, in terms of both its reach and its importance. This was the era of the Carlist uprisings (see Aróstegui et al. 2003; Moral Roncal 2006; Rújula 2014). Both the First Carlist War (or the "Seven-Year War") and the Second Carlist War took place at a critical juncture, and could be seen as potentially or actually revolutionary. The first, which took place during the regency of María Cristina of Naples (1833–1840), the wife of Fernando VII, occurred when the *Ancien Régime* was in the throes of crisis and the liberal revolution was unfolding. In this context, the links between the first Carlist uprising and the struggles of the royalists during the Liberal Triennium (1820–1823), or those of the "agraviados" in 1827, are clear. The second uprising occurred during the Democratic Sexennium (1868–1874), a turbulent period which began with Isabel II being deposed from the throne, and includes the reign of Amadeo I – who was fought fiercely by the Carlists as an enemy of the Pope, on account of the actions of the House of Savoy during the unification of Italy – and the brief period of the First Republic. Both conflicts essentially centred on northern Spain, and at some stages resulted in the formation of true Carlist states in the Basque Country and in Navarre (see Molina 2005; Montero 1992). Between the two wars of the 1830s and 1870s, as well as a wide variety of attempted insurrections – in 1855 and 1860, during the reign of Isabel II, and in 1869 and 1870, in the early stages of the Democratic Sexennium, to mention only the most significant – those years also included the "Guerra de los Matiners" (1846–1849), which only affected Catalunya (see Vallverdú 2002).

The First Carlist War was without doubt the most important, and broke out following the death of Fernando VII. The uprisings in favour of the pretender Carlos V, which seemed to be under control and close to being quashed in almost every part of Spain in early December 1833, then entered a new phase in which the incipient Carlist movement took on a markedly different form. Firstly, it showed a clear tendency to focus exclusively on certain areas, particularly the Basque Country and Navarre, but also Catalunya, Valencia, and Aragon. City revolts also gave way to an insurrectionism with a fundamentally rural basis. Finally, a combination of political, social, and cultural factors replaced the decidedly political motivation behind the uprisings of October and November 1833. The Carlist movement grew in followers and became more consistent as the months passed, through a dialectical process where revolution and counter-revolution each gave fuel to the other. Acts including the killing of monks and clergy in 1834 and 1835, the "desamortizaciones" (i.e., the ecclesiastical confiscations of Juan

Álvarez Mendizábal), or the progressive changes in government all spurred certain sectors of society to align themselves to the cause which Carlos represented. The battle would last seven long years.

Navarre and the Basque Country were the primary theatre of war during the period from December 1833 to mid 1835. Aside from the capitals, some coastal areas and part of Álava, in June 1835 the north of Spain was in Carlist hands. In those circumstances, the decision was taken to attack Bilbao. Tomás de Zumalacárregui was wounded during the failed siege of the city, and he died a few days later. Until mid 1837, the war in the north saw the armies of the Carlists and the government relatively evenly matched, the latter having been strenuously reinforced by the liberals in power. In the rest of Spain, after the weak Carlist mobilization of 1834 and 1835, a clear development in Catalan and Valencian-Aragonese lands is particularly noteworthy.

In May 1837, what was termed the "Royal Expedition" left Navarre, comprised of 12,000 cavalrymen and infantrymen, with Carlos himself at their head. The causes of this expedition were more political than military, and differed substantially from other expeditions, both previous and subsequent. The months leading up to the expedition saw ties begin to be established at the Neapolitan court between the pretender Carlos and the regent María Cristina, who was disquieted by the advance of the revolution, aggrieved by the liberals and the Calatrava government's treatment of her, and unhappy with the other powers who made up the "Quadruple Alliance." The Baron of Milanges played a prominent role in negotiations, in which he proposed that marriage be contracted between the young Isabel and the prince Carlos Luis, as a means of securing peace. The ruling queen even showed herself willing to cede power to the Carlist pretender in exchange for certain concessions for her and her family.

The presence of Carlos near the capital was considered an advantage. As a result, the Royal Expedition reached the outskirts of Madrid in mid September, having passed through Aragon, Catalunya, and Valencia. However, the Carlists made no attempt to enter the city, which was well defended with General Baldomero Espartero also making his approach at the time; nor did they have any news of María Cristina, who was closely watched by ministers and by her family, and who had won some support from the military. The Carlist troops began a long and difficult retreat towards Basque-Navarrese territory. The enterprise had turned out badly and the discontent among the Carlists was palpable. Although the effects of this military excursion were not to prove too serious, it may nonetheless be seen as a political fiasco. The balance which had so far been maintained between moderate and extremist forms of Carlism was to tip in favour of the latter.

The 31st of August 1839 saw the well-known meeting of the Carlist and liberal armies, along with the famous Embrace of Vergara. That pact contained the basis of an accord that was accepted by a significant portion of the Carlist combatants. It was not the first attempt to establish a dialogue, nor the first peace project to be essayed during the conflict. Early intentions to establish concord between the two parties were already in evidence before the outbreak of war in 1833, via the marriage of the young Isabel to a son of Carlos María Isidro, a proposal which was never completely discarded and which always remained available to be brought to the negotiating table. The first successful attempt led to Vergara and the subsequent breaking up of the Carlist army, which was sharply divided between those in favour of the treaty and those against it.

The war may be said to have ended in the Basque Country and Navarre by September 1839, but that was not true of the rest of Spain. In mid 1838, the Valencian-Aragonese region saw one of the crowning moments of the Carlist movement, driven on by Ramón Cabrera (see Sauch 2004). It had been a spectacular progression. Neither the Catalan Carlists, nor the followers of the Count of Morella, nor the majority of the few scattered rebels from other lands accepted the Vergara pact, and they therefore continued to fight. In any case, the conflict between liberals and Carlists had taken a dramatic turn that was soon to prove decisive. Only the arrival from France in late 1839 and early 1840 of Castilians, Basques, and Navarrese who had not accepted the treaty managed to prolong, for a few months more, a war which almost everybody was to some extent weary of, after six years of fighting. The First Carlist War ended in mid 1840.

It was not until the 1870s that Carlism again found itself capable of provoking another civil war on a large scale, on the basis of a new set of counter-revolutionary factors. Around 1868, as before 1833, the prevailing conditions were again favourable for the building of Carlist sentiment – even if the situation was not identical, as Spanish society had undergone significant changes in the intervening years. Carlism became the focal point of a protest with various interests and multiple causes, but which above all based its unity on the fight against a common enemy, even if that enemy was an abstract one: the revolution of 1868. This new counter-revolutionary amalgamation which was formed during the Democratic Sexennium was also to build on the experiences of the middle years of the century, the idealization of earlier battles, identification with certain particular emblems, and the political and ideological dimensions which the conflict took on. The revolutionary events of 1868 and the first measures enacted by the new rulers paved the way for united action from both Carlists and neo-Catholics – a group led by Cándido Nocedal who were more right wing than the moderates (see Romeo 2011; Urigüen 1986) – who were to merge from 1870 to form the Comunión Católico-Monárquica. After initial attempts to precipitate conflict by various means in 1869–1871 – including via politics, parliament (winning 23 seats in the Cortes in the 1869 legislative elections), propaganda, and journalism – in 1872 Carlism took up arms. There had already been rebellions in 1869 and 1870, but the order to go to war was given definitively in April 1872. It was to last four years, until February 1876 (see Garmendia 1976, 1985; Sesmero 1998).

Each of the various Carlist uprisings ended with a significant political exodus. The Carlists found themselves forced to leave Spain with each defeat that they suffered in their constant battle with the ruling liberals (see Canal 2014). Two significant emigrations, after each of the two major civil wars – the First and Second Carlist Wars – as well as others on a more reduced scale, provide the roll call of Carlist exiles during the nineteenth century. Pedro Rújula has correctly seen exile as "una presencia constante en el horizonte carlista" (2007, 167), and it was to become a central tenet of Carlist mythology and culture.

The archetypal model of Carlist mobilization between 1833 and 1876 involved different bands of soldiers being brought together to form a Royal Army. The exception was the "Ortegada" of 1860, a failed attempt to land on the Catalan coast which took the form of a coup led by Jaime Ortega, Captain General of the Balearic Islands, and which entailed, among other things, the capture of the pretender Carlos VI, Count of Montemolín, and his brother Fernando (see Ceamanos Llorens 2003). The step from forming smaller bands of fighters to building a Carlist army or state did, however, require certain specific conditions to be fulfilled. This was achieved during the wars of 1833–1840 and 1872–1876, especially in the north, and was attempted on several other occasions with varying degrees of success. These squads of soldiers, guerrilla warfare, and full-scale insurrections were thus the most typical forms of Carlist violence.

Taking to the hills, with its explicit reference to the rural nature of the struggle during that period, was a tactic employed over and over again. The independence and mobility of the Carlist squads were key to their success, but these strengths came at a cost, as they also meant that the soldiers were difficult to organize and control. For that reason, when the leadership of the

Carlist movement was weak, as was the case after each of the two great Carlist uprisings, these squads could descend into little more than fringe groups engaged in acts of banditry. In sum, violence was a constant presence during the long civil war between Carlism and liberalism, with varying levels of organization, brutality, and regulation – as Lord Eliot was to discover in 1835, a refusal to recognize the opponent's status as a war combatant was hardly conducive to a struggle which respected even basic norms of conduct, whether in relation to prisoners or to the population at large.

In any case, defeat in the Second Carlist War marked the end of the bellicose facet of Carlism, leaving aside, of course, the isolated incident of October 1900 – the so-called "Octubrada" – and the significant Carlist participation on the rebel side in July 1936 (see Canal 2000b). 1876 was the year when the last great amalgamation of counter-revolutionary forces brought together around Carlism was broken apart (see Canal 2000a). The new rulers of the Restoration (1875–1923) made a significant investment of both human and material resources in ending the succession of Carlist-dominated conflicts, which had been present throughout the process of building the liberal state in Spain. In the end, the fruits of that enterprise were positive. The Restoration offered an extraordinary period of stability in modern Spain. This was the end of an era in the history of Carlism, one defined by Carlist uprisings and the head-to-head struggle against liberalism.

Conclusion: counter-revolution and civil war

Whether it was open hostility or latent tension, civil war formed the backbone of the nineteenth century in Spain. The country spent the larger part of that century suffering the effects of a long civil war – conflict was not continuous but it did endure, as phases of open combat alternated with attempted insurrections, exiles, and periods of what was really only an illusory sense of tranquillity. Confrontation between revolution and counter-revolution was constant, as can easily be shown for the years 1808 to 1876. Further conflicts of varying intensity would follow thereafter. The War of Independence was really the lead-up to the feuds that would dominate the Peninsula during the nineteenth century (see Marías 1985; Rújula 2008, 2012). Nevertheless, it was during the Liberal Triennium that those feuds re-emerged in a more serious guise. Carlism was the primary outlet for contemporary Spanish counter-revolutionary movements, and the Carlist-liberal dialectic was to dominate the middle decades of the century. However, there has been a certain tendency to overlook or conceal the fratricidal nature of many of the armed confrontations which took place during those years. These conflicts have undoubtedly not received the attention they deserve, as the term "civil war" is reserved almost exclusively for the Spanish Civil War of 1936–1939. Something very similar could be said of the widespread political emigration during the nineteenth century and the great exile of 1939. In any case, civil war must be acknowledged as a defining feature of nineteenth-century Spanish history (see Canal 2004, 2007a; Ranzato 1994).

However, this is not an exclusively Spanish phenomenon. Civil war has played a role in the genesis or formation of various modern nations and states, both in Europe and elsewhere. The history of the nineteenth century simply cannot be understood without reference to the concept of civil war. This is clearly the case both in western and southern Europe, in France and in Spain, in Portugal and in Italy. These countries lived and suffered through a long and important civil war which lasted for most of the century. Of course, each nation-state's civil war inevitably took on its own distinctive hue, in terms of chronology and intensity as well as in their various implications, characteristics, and repercussions. There is no doubt that these considerations may equally be applied, *mutatis mutandis*, to other neighbouring countries and to some lands farther afield (see Guerra 1999; Pérez Vejo 2010).

The case of Portugal may be the most similar to Spain. There too the Triennium of 1820–1823 was marked by tensions between revolution and counter-revolution which ultimately led to a civil war several years later, pitching Miguelists and liberals against each other between 1828 and 1834 – and especially from 1832 to 1834. The triumph of the liberals over proponents of Miguelist absolutism, many of whom were exiled, did not mark the end of this counter-revolutionary movement which had "Deus, Patria, Rei" as its motto (see Cardoso 2007; Lousada 1987; Lousada and Ferreira 2006; Silva 1993). In Portugal, as in Spain, conflicts of lesser intensity then followed after the war – a mixture of guerrilla warfare and banditry – until the revolts of Maria da Fonte and Patuleia broke out in the second half of the 1840s (see Ferreira 2002; Mónica 1997). To this should be added the political instability which affected the liberal side, which has led the historian Maria de Fátima Bonifacio to define the period 1834–1851 as a "guerra de todos contra todos" (1999, 160–181). The *Regeneraçâo* of 1851 brought an end to this long era of confrontation, rebellion, and civil strife in Portugal (see Sardica 2001).

The links between various counter-revolutionary movements in European countries were permanent, providing at least an informal basis for a real "White International" during the middle decades of the nineteenth century (see Canal 2011b, 2011c). Men and women, money and arms, political practice and ideas were in permanent circulation in western Europe and America (see Albònico 1979; Cancio 2015; Dupont 2014, 2015; Sarlin 2009, 2013; Tronco 2010). The Carlists received ample financial support during the two civil wars of the nineteenth century, and many foreign legitimists fought on their side. Likewise, many counter-revolutionaries from France, Spain, Belgium, Germany, Portugal, and elsewhere gave their support to the King of Naples and the cause he represented, whether that was in person or through donations and propaganda. It is thus worth asking seriously whether the different civil wars between revolutionaries and counter-revolutionaries in various incipient nation-states throughout nineteenth-century western Europe might really be considered as parts of an overarching European civil war (see Canal 2011c).

Works cited

Agirreazkuenaga, Joseba and José María Ortiz de Orruño. 1990. "Algunes puntualitzacions sobre la insurrecció carlina al País Basc: l'actitud dels notables rurals." In *Carlisme i moviments absolutistes*, edited by Josep M. Fradera, Ramon Garrabou, and Jesús Millán, 169–186. Vic: Eumo Editorial.

Albònico, Aldo. 1979. *La mobilitazione legittimista contro il regno d'Italia: la Spagna e il brigantaggio meridionale postunitario*. Milan: Giuffrè.

Aróstegui, Julio. 1975. "El carlismo en la dinámica de los movimientos liberales españoles. Formulación de un modelo." In *Actas de las I Jornadas de metodología aplicada a las ciencias históricas. IV. Historia contemporánea*, 225–239. Santiago de Compostela: Universidad de Santiago/Fundación Juan March.

Aróstegui, Julio, Jordi Canal, and Eduardo González Calleja. 2003. *El carlismo y las guerras carlistas. Hechos, hombres e ideas*. Madrid: La Esfera de los Libros.

Blinkhorn, Martin. 1975. *Carlism and Crisis in Spain 1931–1939*. Cambridge: Cambridge University Press.

Bonifacio, Maria de Fátima. 1999. *Apología da história política. Estudos sobre o século XIX português*. Lisbon: Quetzal Editores.

Burdiel, Isabel. 2010. *Isabel II. Una biografía (1830–1904)*. Madrid: Taurus.

Canal, Jordi. 2000a. *El carlismo. Dos siglos de contrarrevolución en España*. Madrid: Alianza Editorial.

———. 2000b. "La violencia carlista tras el tiempo de las carlistadas: nuevas formas para un viejo movimiento." In *Violencia política en la España del siglo XX*, edited by Santos Juliá, 25–66. Madrid: Taurus.

———. 2001. "La longue survivance du Carlisme en Espagne: proposition pour une interprétation." In *La Contre-Révolution en Europe, XVIIIe–XIXe siècles. Réalités politiques et sociales, résonances culturelles et idéologiques*, edited by Juan-Clément Martin, 291–301. Rennes: Presses Universitaires de Rennes.

———. 2004. "Guerra civil y contrarrevolución en la Europa del sur en el siglo XIX: reflexiones a partir del caso español." *Ayer* 55: 37–60.

———. 2006. *Banderas blancas, boinas rojas. Una historia política del carlismo*. Madrid: Marcial Pons.

———. 2007a. "Los exilios en la historia de España." In *Exilios. Los éxodos políticos en España, siglos XV–XX*, edited by Jordi Canal, 11–35. Madrid: Sílex.

———. 2007b. "El carlismo en España: interpretaciones, problemas, propuestas." *Trienio* 49: 193–215.

———. 2008. "Matar negros, hacer blancos: los colores y los nombres del enemigo en las guerras civiles de la España contemporánea." *Espacio, tiempo, forma. V. Historia contemporánea* 20: 19–36.

———. 2011a. "El Rey de los carlistas. Reflexiones sobre las palabras, las personas y las cosas." In *IV Jornadas de estudio del carlismo. Actas. "Por Dios, por la Patria y el Rey": las ideas del carlismo*, 227–249. Pamplona: Gobierno de Navarra.

———. 2011b. "Internationale blanche." In *Dictionnaire de la Contre-révolution*, edited by Jean-Clément Martin, 307–311. Paris: Perrin.

———. 2011c. "Guerres civiles en Europe au XIXe siècle, guerre civile européenne et Internationale blanche." In *Pratiques du transnational. Terrains, preuves, limites*, edited by Jean-Paul Zuñiga, 57–77. Paris: Centre de Recherches Historiques (EHESS).

———. 2014. "Gli esili nella Spagna dell'Ottocento." In *Il Risorgimento. Mito e storiografia tra Italia e San Marino*, edited by Maurizio Ridolfi, 63–78. San Marino: Centro Sammarinese di Studi Storici.

Canals, Francisco. 1977. *Política española: pasado y futuro*. Barcelona: Acervo.

Cancio, Raúl C. 2015. *España y la Guerra Civil americana o la globalización del contrarrevolucionismo*. Alcalá de Henares: Instituto Franklin/Universidad de Alcalá de Henares.

Cardoso, António Manuel Monteiro. 2007. *A Revolução Liberal em Trás-os-Montes (1820–1834). O Povo e as Elites*. Porto: Ediçôes Afrontamento.

Caspistegui, Francisco Javier. 2005. "'Spain's Vendée': Carlist identity in Navarre as a mobilizing model." In *The Splintering of Spain. Cultural History and the Spanish Civil War, 1936–1939*, edited by Chris Ealham and Michael Richards, 177–195. Cambridge: Cambridge University Press.

———. 2008. "¿Carlismo en Navarra o Navarra carlista?: paradojas de una identidad conflictiva entre los siglos XIX y XX." In *El carlismo en su tiempo: geografías de la contrarrevolución (I Jornadas de estudio del carlismo)*, 205–243. Pamplona: Gobierno de Navarra.

Ceamanos Llorens, Roberto. 2003. *Del liberalismo al carlismo. Sociedad y política en la España del siglo XIX: General Jaime Ortega y Olleta*. Zaragoza: Ayuntamiento de Gallur/Diputación de Zaragoza.

Dupont, Alexandre. 2014. "¿Hacia una Internacional neocatólica? Trayectorias cruzadas de Louis Veuillot y Antonio Aparisi y Guijarro." *Ayer* 95 (3): 211–236.

———. 2015. "Une internationale blanche. Les légitimistes français au secours des carlistes (1868–1883)." PhD diss., Université de Paris I Panthéon-Sorbonne.

Ferreira, Maria de Fátima Sá e Melo. 2002. *Rebeldes e Insubmissos. Resistencias Populares ao Liberalismo (1834–1844)*. Porto: Afrontamento.

Garmendia, Vicente. 1976. *La Segunda Guerra Carlista (1872–1876)*. Madrid: Siglo XXI.

———. 1985. *La ideología carlista (1868–1876). En los orígenes del nacionalismo vasco*. Zarautz: Diputación Foral de Guipúzcoa.

Guerra, François-Xavier. 1999. "Editorial." *Bulletin Institut Pierre Renouvin* 7. Accessed May 20, 2015. http://ipr.univ-paris1.fr/spip.

Lluís y Navas, Jaime. 1967. "Las divisiones internas del carlismo a través de la historia. Ensayo sobre su razón de ser (1814–1936)." In *Homenaje a Jaime Vicens Vives*, edited by J. Maluquer de Motes, vol. 2, 307–345. Barcelona: Universidad de Barcelona.

Lousada, Maria Alexandre. 1987. "O Miguelismo (1828–1834). O discurso político e o apoio da nobreza titulada." PhD diss., Universidade de Lisboa.

Lousada, Maria Alexandre and Maria de Fátima Sá e Melo Ferreira. 2006. *D. Miguel.* Lisbon: Círculo de Leitores / Centro de Estudos dos Povos e Culturas da Expressâo Portuguesa.

Marías, Julián. 1985. *España inteligible. Razón histórica de las Españas.* Madrid: Alianza Editorial.

Martínez Dorado, Gloria and Juan Pan-Montojo. 2000. "El primer carlismo, 1833–1840." *Ayer* 38: 35–63.

Millán, Jesús. 1998. "Una reconsideración del carlismo." *Ayer* 29: 91–107.

Mina, María Cruz. 2011. "El carlismo y los fueros." In *"Por Dios, por la Patria y el Rey." Las ideas del carlismo. Actas de las IV jornadas del carlismo,* 251–292. Pamplona: Gobierno de Navarra.

Molina, Fernando. 2005. *La tierra del martirio español. El País Vasco y España en el siglo del nacionalismo.* Madrid: Centro de Estudios Políticos y Constitucionales.

Mónica, Maria Teresa. 1997. *Errâncias miguelistas (1834–1843).* Lisbon: Cosmos.

Montero, Julio. 1992. *El Estado Carlista. Principios teóricos y práctica política (1872–1876).* Madrid: Aportes XIX.

Moral Roncal, Antonio. 1999. *Carlos V de Borbón (1788–1855).* Madrid: Actas.

———. 2006. *Las guerras carlistas.* Madrid: Sílex.

Pan-Montojo, Juan. 1990. *Carlistas y liberales en Navarra (1833–1839).* Pamplona: Gobierno de Navarra.

Pérez Ledesma, Manuel. 1996. "Una lealtad de otros siglos (En torno a las interpretaciones del carlismo)." *Historia Social* 24: 133–149.

Pérez Vejo, Tomás. 2010. *Elegía criolla. Una reinterpretación de las guerras de independencia hispanoamericanas.* Mexico: Tusquets.

Ranzato, Gabriele, ed. 1994. *Guerre fratricide. Le guerre civili in età contemporanea.* Turin: Bollati Boringhieri.

Roma, Juan María. 1935. "Por una idea, no por un trono. Vindicando a los mártires de la tradición." In *Centenario del tradicionalismo español. Álbum histórico del carlismo 1833–1933–35.* Barcelona: Gràfiques Ribera.

Romeo, María Cruz. 2011. "'¿Qué es ser neocatólico?.' La crítica antiliberal de Antonio Aparisi y Guijarro." In *"Por Dios, por la Patria y el Rey." Las ideas del carlismo. Actas de las IV Jornadas del carlismo,* 129–164. Pamplona: Gobierno de Navarra.

Rújula, Pedro. 1998. *Contrarrevolución. Realismo y carlismo en Aragón y el Maestrazgo, 1820–1840.* Zaragoza: Prensas Universitarias.

———. 2007. "Carlistas." In *Exilios. Los éxodos políticos en España, siglos XV–XX,* edited by Jordi Canal, 167–190. Madrid: Sílex.

———. 2008. "La guerra como aprendizaje político. De la Guerra de la Independencia a las guerras carlistas." In *El carlismo en su tiempo: geografías de la contrarrevolución (I Jornadas de estudio del carlismo),* 41–63. Pamplona: Gobierno de Navarra.

———. 2012. "La guerra civil en la España del siglo XIX: usos políticos de una idea." In *Guerras civiles. Una clave para entender la Europa de los siglos XIX y XX,* edited by Jordi Canal and Eduardo González Calleja, 39–58. Madrid: Casa de Velázquez.

———. 2014. "El antiliberalismo reaccionario." In *Historia de las culturas políticas en España y América Latina. 2. La España liberal, 1833–1874,* edited by María Cruz Romeo and María Sierra, 377–409. Zaragoza: Prensas Universitarias/Marcial Pons.

Sardica, José Miguel. 2001. *A Regeneração sob o signo do Consenso: a política e os partidos entre 1851 e 1861.* Lisbon: Imprensa da Ciências Sociais.

Sarlin, Simon. 2009. "Los carlistas en Italia en el siglo XIX." In *Violencias fratricidas: carlistas y liberales en el siglo XIX (II Jornadas de estudio del carlismo),* 223–238. Pamplona: Gobierno de Navarra.

———. 2013. *Le légitimisme en armes. Histoire d'une mobilisation internationale contre l'unité italienne.* Rome: École Française de Rome.Sauch, Núria. 2004. *Guerrillers i bàndols civils entre l'Ebre i el Maestrat: la formació d'un país carlista (1808–1844).* Barcelona: Publicacions de l'Abadia de Montserrat.

Sesmero, Enriqueta. 1998. "¿En armas a su pesar? Ensayo sobre la evitabilidad de la Segunda Guerra Carlista en Bizkaia." *Vasconia* 26: 179–190.

Silva, Armando Barreiros Malheiro da. 1993. *Miguelismo. Ideologia e mito*. Coimbra: Livraria Minerva.

Torras, Jaume. 1976. *Liberalismo y rebeldía campesina, 1820–1823*. Barcelona: Ariel.

Tronco, Emmanuel. 2010. *Les Carlistes espagnols dans l'Ouest de la France (1833–1883)*. Rennes: Presses Universitaires de Rennes.

Ugarte, Javier. 1998. *La nueva Covadonga insurgente. Orígenes sociales y culturales de la sublevación de 1936 en Navarra y el País Vasco*. Madrid: Biblioteca Nueva.

Urigüen, Begoña. 1986. *Orígenes y evolución de la derecha española: el neocatolicismo*. Madrid: CSIC.

Vallverdú, Robert. 2002. *La guerra dels Matiners a Catalunya (1846–1849). Una crisi econòmica i una revolta popular*. Barcelona: Publicacions de l'Abadia de Montserrat.

24

FROM PATRIOTISM TO LIBERALISM

Political concepts in revolution

Javier Fernández Sebastián

This chapter offers an overview of certain decisive changes in Spanish political language over the course of the late eighteenth and early nineteenth centuries. I begin by treating the unease felt among various sections of the learned élite regarding the unstable meanings of certain key terms, and the semantic battles waged with ever-increasing intensity in that time of transition between the late Enlightenment and the early stages of liberalism. As I show, such controversies over meanings gave rise to interesting political-philological debates over whose remit it was to define the correct use of words. Finally, I show that with the crisis of the Spanish monarchy in 1808, and the following process of politicization, a set of interlinked concepts – including "patria," "revolución," "nación," "independencia," "libertad," "constitución," and several others – quickly gained prominence in contemporary discussions, and provided the foundations for political vocabulary to be comprehensively updated. My focus is essentially historical-conceptual, and seeks to integrate several different perspectives, including political-intellectual history, and certain developments in cultural history. Rather than eminent authors and political treatises, I rely on evidence from other types of sources, particularly ephemeral or circumstantial sources, such as parliamentary oratory, political pamphlets, or early examples of the newspaper press.

The turn of the century and upheaval in political vocabulary: the example of "patria"

Not coincidentally, at the very height of the Enlightenment and the Bourbon Reforms the whole Hispanic world began to echo to the sound of ever more frequent complaints about a supposed political-linguistic disorder, corrupting the language and distorting certain words' straightforward meanings. This concern over the abuse of words, which was not unique to Spain in the Western world, is clearly present in the work of various Peninsular authors with markedly differing sensibilities, from Cadalso, Forner, and Jovellanos to Arroyal, Capmany, and García del Cañuelo (Fernández Sebastián 2012a, 244–249). For some, of course, this unease over the flexibility of the language was not without more positive facets, too. Writers and members of the learned élite were well aware that linguistic and conceptual innovation largely depended on new cultural practices and social centres, which had caused certain words to be more frequently used, thus making them fashionable; some of these emerging terms were themselves capable of creating expectations and giving impetus to the reforms. Thus, at the end of the 1770s, one of the founders of the Real Sociedad Bascongada de Amigos del País notes the following with some satisfaction:

> *[e]l Patriotismo, la Economía política, la Industria, etc.*, son voces que hasta estos últimos tiempos sólo se oían en boca de un corto número de Políticos; pero a resultas del fermento Patriótico que de Provincia en Provincia se ha ido difundiendo por el Reino, se han introducido ya en las conversaciones familiares, y han llegado a ser los términos favoritos del lenguaje del día, despertando con su uso continuado las ideas análogas, aplicando éstas a los respectivos objetos determinados y realizando los tales objetos en establecimientos prácticos.
>
> (Munibe 2002, 183; italics in the original)

Despite the unbridled optimism of the Conde de Peñaflorida, the truth is that at the time of his writing, the words he mentions in his speech were still rather bookish terms, whose use in erudite circles was certainly on the increase, but which were still rare among the illiterate masses. Nonetheless, patriotic language had progressed sufficiently during the eighteenth century for the philologist Antonio de Capmany to propose to the Real Academia Española during the 1780s that the term "patriotismo" should be included in the Academia's official dictionary (Étienvre 2001, 207).

However, to whatever extent these words were standard by the turn of the century, the high watermark for the use of such vocabulary was to follow soon afterwards. From spring 1808, after the sudden politicization brought on by campaigning against the favourite of Charles IV, the hated Manuel Godoy, together with the mutiny of Aranjuez and the subsequent Napoleonic invasion of the Peninsula (see Fernández Sebastián 2000, 2013a), as well as the forced abdication of the newly installed King Ferdinand VII at the hands of the French emperor, the word "patria" could be heard in all quarters, both in Peninsular Spain and in Spanish America (see Entin 2014; Lomné 2014). Decades later, Alcalá Galiano would record that this was the point when "de término usado solamente en los libros, [la palabra patria] pasó a ser aclamación popular" (Alcalá Galiano 1955, II, 319).

The uprising of the Spanish people against their French occupiers was accompanied by a huge number of pamphlets, manifestos, and proclamations in which the rebels justified their actions and called on their compatriots to support them, systematically appealing to topics that were at the forefront of the public consciousness and had great potential to mobilize their audience, such as "religión," "rey," and "patria" (Vilar 1982, 236–237). In these documents, many of which were signed by the improvised insurrectional *juntas* formed against the Bonapartes, metaphors of fire and electricity are common: very frequent reference is made to the fire of patriotism that burns in good Spaniards' hearts, for example, or to the uprising having spread through the whole country with lightning speed, and so on.

For centuries, the term "patria" had predominantly been used to allude simply to a place of birth; yet despite this ambiguity, in the eighteenth century it had begun increasingly to refer at once to the monarchy and the Spanish nation (Fernández Albaladejo 2001; Fernández Sebastián 1994). However, the pragmatic and discursive context in which this word and its cognates appeared was usually economic and educational, rather than strictly political. It was a matter of improving education, agriculture, and trade, by searching for more efficient ways in which to increase the wealth of the country and the prosperity of its inhabitants. Indeed, the *sociedades económicas* which spread through the whole realm from the 1770s, under the influence of Minister Campomanes, were also known as "sociedades patrióticas."

Of course, in learned speeches, where the duties which the "ciudadano" owed to his "patria" were often mentioned, the writers' classical training is clearly on display, as a great number of references to "republican" texts are included, from Cicero to Montesquieu, not to mention Suárez, Mariana, and other treatise writers from the Salamancan school. In such contexts, talk of patriotism – the great civic virtue of loving one's *patria* – was primarily a means of emphasizing the traditional call to sacrifice any thoughts of personal gain for the public profit of the nation, always preferring the common good to private interest (Smith's idea of the invisible hand, which was to allow the two factors to be reconciled, was far from widely known at the time).

On the other hand, "patria," patriot, and patriotism bear a strong emotional charge which was easily associated with safeguarding native customs and institutions (including religion) against any threat that might come from outside. In the dramatic circumstances of Napoleonic aggression and the abdications of Bayonne (May 5, 1808), as popular resistance spontaneously broke out against what most Spaniards felt was a tyrannical power being illegitimately imposed, the emotional facet of this vocabulary became a tremendously important factor. Perhaps because of this, lexicometric evidence shows that written sources for this torrent of public opinion had a strong preference for using the term "patria" over "nación" (Vilar 1982, 236–237). Defending, loving, honouring, and serving the "patria:" these were the verbs that commonly took the "patria" as an object of veneration in the earliest calls to insurrection. Only at a later stage, when the *Cortes* were convened, did another more "technical," abstract set of concepts come into play, such as "nación," "constitución," and "soberanía." The ardent language of the "patria" thus emerged before the language of the "nación" (or, to put it another way, calls to arms to fight for independence preceded the demand for political liberty), which fits well with the historical sequence of events on a political, military, and institutional level.

That said, the patriotic fight against despotism was immediately linked, in certain areas of public opinion, with the need for sweeping reforms designed to safeguard the rights of citizens. The clamour for the *Cortes* to convene in order to provide the country with a new constitution was quickly heard all across the Peninsula. Significantly, when making its announcement to call the *Cortes* to convene, the *Junta Central* addressed the Spanish people, saying that "por una combinación de sucesos tan singular como feliz, la providencia ha querido que en esta crisis terrible no pudieseis dar un paso hacia la independencia sin darle también hacia la libertad" (Sevilla, October 28, 1809).

Otherwise, contemporary texts demonstrate that without losing one iota of its emotional force, "patria" was equally capable of more politicized and intellectualized meanings, in certain contexts. This versatility – which was shared by other concepts, such as "libertad" – allowed this crucial piece in the political chess game to be played on two boards simultaneously: both in the immediate response to the invasion and in the reclamation of civil and political liberties. In comparing the ancient and modern meanings of the word, the poet Manuel J. Quintana was pleased to see the "sagrado fuego" of patriotism being kindled again among Spaniards, bringing with it the longed-for rebirth of the traditional meaning of "patria" as that "estado o sociedad" whose laws assured its citizens of their liberty and well-being (*Semanario Patriótico*, September 15, 1808).

A few weeks later, Quintana himself wrote a *Manifiesto de la Junta Central a la Nación*, dated October 26, 1808, in Aranjuez, which included the following claim: "La Patria, Españoles, no debe ser ya un nombre vano y vago para vosotros: debe significar en vuestros oídos y en vuestro corazón el santuario de las leyes y de las costumbres, el campo de los talentos y la recompensa de las virtudes." The illocutionary force of the text is striking here, clear from the admonitory tone of "debe significar . . ." whose goal is to persuade the reader to modify the content generally attributed to that expression. Many newspaper articles, pamphlets, and parliamentary speeches of the time, especially those whose authors were liberals, showed a similar desire to redefine other key political terms ("ciudadano," "nación," "constitución," "soberanía," "representación," "opinión pública," and several others).

As far as the concept under discussion here is concerned, the focus of all this rhetoric was that the *Cortes* of the nation should convene as soon as possible for its representatives to set down a constitution for the country. "¡Dadnos una patria!" was the cry issued to the provisional authorities in the edition of *Semanario Patriótico* published on September 15, 1808. Since, according to Quintana, Flórez Estrada, and many others, the "verdadera patria" in a republican sense only existed under a constitutional regime, then only when "despotismo" was definitively in the past and liberty was guaranteed could it be confirmed, strictly speaking, that the Spanish people at last belonged to a "patria" – the claim emphatically made by one representative, Agustín de Argüelles, when he presented the text of the constitution in 1812 (see Fernández Sebastián and Fuentes 2002, 515–517).

However, it is no less true that, as noted by Alcalá Galiano, patriotism was already present before the constitutional regime gave it a republican hue: proof of this is the fact that Spaniards threw themselves into battle in 1808 "a la voz de patria unida con la de rey," four years before the constitution was promulgated (Alcalá Galiano 1984, 24).

Governing the language

Under pressure as events developed at a startling rate, many other concepts changed not only their meaning, but also their political and moral overtones during those years. One of the most remarkable examples of this transvaluation is the word "revolución." This term, whose abuses during the decade of the French Revolution had rendered it a hateful word, was rehabilitated on being applied to the Peninsular context. According to the manifesto published by the *Junta Central* on October 26, 1808, "la revolución española tendrá [. . .] un carácter totalmente diferente de la revolución francesa." While the French Revolution was usually seen as the sum of all political evils, the revolution in Spain was considered inevitable and beneficial, even in circles that were not necessarily constitutionalist. The Conde de Montijo, for example, reclaimed for himself the title "revolucionario" (which he considered honourable, as opposed to the deplorable epithet "faccioso"), and made a careful distinction between the concepts of "revolución" and "motín." While a "motín" could never be acceptable, Montijo's contention was that in the circumstances in which Spain found itself, "revolución" effectively denoted a patriotic obligation: "Es necesario revolver para ordenar lo que está fuera de orden, y aun es un deber de los pueblos el revolverse contra cualquiera fuerza extraña o doméstica que tiránicamente los intente oprimir. He aquí nuestra revolución; todos estamos obligados a sostenerla; todos somos revolucionarios" (García Godoy 1999, 47; 58; Montijo 1810).

This kind of political-linguistic polemic was not only the concern of those who wrote for an abundant newspaper press, making early use of the freedom of the press decreed by the *Cortes* in Cádiz in November 1810; rather, it also comprised a significant part of parliamentary debate (Fernández Sebastián 2008, 2012a). Strictly speaking, this was nothing new, since, as indicated previously, debates on language and its relationship to public life were already the order of the day in the intellectual media as early as the late eighteenth century.

In a short book published in 1806, the diplomat and philologist Santiago Jonama categorically affirms that "el lenguaje es una república libre, y no sufre más leyes que las que dicta la pluralidad" (Jonama 1836, 19). This metaphor of language as a democracy may surprise a reader unaware of just how far politics and philosophy of language overlapped each other in those early years of the nineteenth century. Indeed, many political, historical, and philosophical issues then appeared to be inextricably intertwined.

The political-semantic controversies referred to previously, and which will be the focus of the next section, were in turned linked to another theme that was no less contentious, which may be summarized by the following question: Who is the ultimate authority on the meanings of words? Is it the common people, or the educated few?

This is a thorny issue and has been the focus of debate between many authors since Antiquity, with arguments advanced on both sides.[1] The matter is further complicated by the fact that since the medieval period, there has also been a temporal aspect to this question. Where should the best guides for correct use of the language be sought? Should the normative model be the language of the best writers of a remote "golden age," or that of contemporary writers, or even the courtier's manner of speech Or should attention be paid instead to the common usage of the majority of current Spanish speakers, which implicitly tips the scales towards the masses and the contemporary lower classes?

Learned Spaniards of the late eighteenth century who discuss this issue (including, among others, Antonio de Capmany in his *Filosofía de la elocuencia* [1777], or José López de la Huerta in his *Examen de la posibilidad de fijar la significación de los sinónimos de la lengua castellana* [1789]) in general reject "la autoridad de nuestros clásicos" in matters concerning the meanings of words, since those meanings change every day and grow more precise, thanks to "los progresos de la literatura, de las artes, de la sociabilidad y el comercio o recíproca comunicación de las ideas" (López de la Huerta 1789, ix–x). Capmany, not unlike the later Wittgenstein, contrasts the authority of the academic dictionary with close observation of the use which speakers make of words in their everyday conversation: the "regla sabia del uso," he says, "nos dará la particular y propia definición" of every word (Étienvre 1983, 268).

The question of governing the language, and of controlling political language in particular, is an extremely delicate one during such a time of constitutional change, where new legislation is to be designed. In the eyes of many, the constitution was seen as the political "tablas de la ley," or even as a real "gramática de la libertad" (Fernández Sebastián 2012a, 270, 277). On the eve of the crisis in 1808, Santiago Jonama emphatically claimed that "el *uso común*," i.e. "[el] convenio de los hombres sobre el sentido de cada voz [. . .] debe ser la norma del lenguage" (Jonama 1836, 21; 25–26). And furthermore, in a display of radical 'linguistic contractualism,' so to speak, he added that "[l]a norma del lenguaje es el uso del día," since "es claro que si el convenio de la multitud pudo formar el lenguaje, el mismo convenio podrá reformarlo, desusando unas voces, inventando otras nuevas, limitando o extendiendo la acepción de las ya conocidas, y aun mudándola enteramente. Por eso mi norma no será precisamente el lenguaje que hablaron Herrera y Garcilaso, sino el que hoy hablan Meléndez y Moratín" (Jonama 1836, 27–28).

Such opinions, which bore a striking similarity to the political debates of the day, as those debates focused on the suitability of rewriting Spain's historical constitution or establishing a new constitutional code, were to be reinforced just two years later. It was not in vain, as many eyewitnesses corroborated and as general historiographical opinion would later agree, that the undoubted protagonist of the insurrection in 1808 was "la nación en masa:" the starring role in that drama, in such extreme circumstances, was undoubtedly played by the Spanish people (Costa 1992, 151). While the aristocracy, high-level functionaries, and cultured élites were amenable to collaboration – with varying degrees of enthusiasm – with the government of José I (who had taken up the throne at the wish of his brother, the Emperor, after he had overthrown the legitimate Bourbon dynasty), the lower classes instead chose rebellion against the French, thus bringing about politicization on an enormous scale, which, in the name of wounded patriotism, "trocó el Gobierno español en popular" (Alcalá Galiano 1955, II, 463). As Galiano saw, in those first days of the uprising, Spain effectively became a fully fledged democracy: the power vacuum caused by the *vacatio regis* was immediately filled by the people, and even at times by the lower classes, who took charge of the destiny of the country in the face of the desertion of a large section of their ruling classes, the *afrancescados*, who transferred their allegiance to Napoleon (Alcalá Galiano 1955, II, 46).

Against this background it is easier to see why not only the resulting constitution, but also the spheres of politics and culture gave a pre-eminent role to the Spanish people. At a time when, as Donoso wrote, "toda la nación era pueblo" (Donoso Cortés 1970, I, 246–251; Fuentes 1988), and every institution, from suffrage to the army, was throwing open its doors to the most populous levels of society, control over the language could not be an exception to this trend. Nor was it. The idea that it was "el convenio de la multitud," to use Jonama's formula, which was responsible for making and unmaking the meanings of words was the predominant feeling among the Spanish *literati* over the following years.

However, this "gobierno popular de la lengua" was open to two different interpretations. For conservatives and traditionalists, the principle implied that no one had the authority to twist received meanings, in current use by the majority of the population, in order to impose new meanings on words. The "diccionario de los demagogos" was not to take priority over the "diccionario del pueblo" (Donoso Cortés 1837; Fernández Sebastián 2012a, 256–257). On the other hand, particularly progressive liberals emphasized the contractual/voluntarist facet and had no hesitation in actively promoting reconceptualizations; they would go as far as subverting inherited meanings or the assessment of certain fundamental concepts to advance their political agenda of reform. In these cases, as has been shown previously in the example of "patria," half-forgotten layers of meaning in old Greek and Latin words were available to be reactivated in certain pragmatic situations. Thus newly sharpened, these terms could be wielded in debates with political adversaries, and proved to be incisive weapons in the cut-and-thrust of the early nineteenth century parliament and media.

A significant number of these same liberal authors, who followed the epistemological sensationalism espoused by Locke, Condillac, and the *idéologues*, even cherished the goal of establishing a perfect language, whose definitions were clear, stable, and precise. They believed that this would settle many political disputes. During the second constitutional period (1820–1823), Alberto Lista and the moderate journalists at his side continued to aspire towards fixing the "verdadero significado" of each political term once and for all, believing that errors caused by "la mala inteligencia de las palabras" were much to be lamented. "Si fuera posible," they continue, "que todos los hombres diesen el mismo valor a las voces, es decir, expresasen con cada una de ellas una misma idéntica idea, se acabarían para siempre las disputas, y no habría en el mundo más que una sola opinión" (*El Censor*, November 8, 1821).

Fighting for the dictionary

We have now come to terms with the fact that politics and rhetoric are inseparable, and so such disputes are impossible to resolve. However, this was not the prevailing view of early nineteenth-century Spain, among either reformists or conservatives.

The War of Independence (1808–1814) offered a good opportunity for pre-liberal groups, who were unsatisfied first with Godoy's government and then with that imposed by Napoleon, to put their planned reforms into action.

From the earliest days of the uprising, the notions of "independencia" and "libertad" went hand in hand in many texts produced by the rebel faction. For those early liberals, expelling the intruder king, Joseph Bonaparte, was not enough. Instead, they had to go one step further and put an end to "despotismo ministerial," by constructing a new regime which included a written constitution, with a division of power and a series of rights and freedoms. And many of them believed that this was the inevitable consequence of a profound reform of political language.

However, not all those who fought against the French shared the same opinion. More conservative groups among the rebels, who supported the traditional monarchical order, fought valiantly against the positions of those who argued for constitutionalism. It was this which, especially after the meeting of the *Cortes* in Cádiz, led to a kind of literary-political war being waged in addition to the war against the French invader (the latter in turn being a war which presented certain features of civil strife, given that a number of Spaniards, particularly civil servants and members of the élite, supported the invading French); and this literary-political war split the anti-French side. Although there are various shades of nuance among the different groups who fought these ideological battles (for which the major battlegrounds were the political press), there were two essential distinctions: firstly, the line which divided the so-called "afrancesados" from the "patriotas" (who saw the former as traitors); and secondly, among patriots, liberals were starkly distinguished from absolutists, whom liberals pejoratively labelled "serviles."

Given that this ideological battle between these three principal factions – "afrancesados," "patriotas," and "serviles" – was fought above all over semantics, and the leaders of those factions were usually men of letters, we may say that each party possessed not only its own related periodicals, but also its own lexicon (and its own anti-lexicon). Indeed, much ink was then expended on the publication of various *sui generis* dictionaries, whose authors – beneath the cloak of anonymity – maliciously included a series of pseudo-definitions of dozens of key words, and attributed them to their adversaries. While various conservative authors, including the politician Justo Pastor Pérez or the friar Luciano Román (who also translated the work of Lorenzo Thjulen), satirized the "nuevo vocabulario filosófico-democrático" of the "lengua revolucionaria" of the "nuevos filósofos," others, such as Bartolomé J. Gallardo, took the opposite view, fighting fiercely against the "diccionario del fanatismo" and exalting the "idioma de la libertad," the language which constituted the real "diccionario de los hombres libres" (see Álvarez de Miranda 1984; Fernández Sebastián 2012a, 260ff.; Gallardo 1811; Pastor Pérez 1811; Seoane 1968; Thjulen 1813).

Nor were *afrancesado* publicists slow to enter this ideological struggle. The pages of the official press of Joseph Bonaparte's regime, composed under the direction of José Marchena, contain several sardonic jokes directed against the "diccionario de la revolución," including a series of words with false and disparaging definitions which took as their target the "patriotic" guerrillas, reframing them as revolutionaries who deceive the people and "excitan a la rebelión" (see *Gazeta de Madrid*, September 28, 1811; *Gazeta de Oficio del Gobierno de Vizcaya*, October 11, 1811). At exactly this time, in the city of Cádiz and safe from French troops, the respective authors of the *Diccionario razonado-manual* and the *Diccionario crítico-burlesco* were embroiled in bitter disputes over the contradictory meanings which were variously assigned to the terms "patriota" and "patriotismo" (see Gallardo 1811, 27–29; 116; Pastor Pérez 1811, 52–55).

This three-sided conceptual struggle between liberals, absolutists, and Bonapartists, which extended to the definition of several dozen key words, bears eloquent testimony to the importance taken on by this lexical field in the Spain of the early nineteenth century.

One clear symptom of the profound transformations which Spanish society underwent during that era, beginning in the last third of the eighteenth century, is the drastic change in the use of the phrase "sociedades patrióticas." While in 1770 this label was used to designate the *sociedades económicas* stimulated by the government, by 1820, "sociedades patrióticas" instead meant active political clubs inspired by the most radical fringe of liberalism (see Gil Novales 1975). The intense politicization of the years 1808–1814, and especially of 1820–1823, explains such a dramatic shift in meaning, as the leap is made from forms of conviviality more typical of the Enlightenment and the pleasant gatherings of notable members of rural and provincial society, to the bustling new centres of a liberal kind of conviviality, whose political meetings took place in the foremost cafés of most cities. The half-hearted "patriotismo" of the eighteenth century, conceived in essentially economic and patrician terms, was expanded in 1808 to include a much more passionate, political, and plebeian patriotism – a new patriotism which in 1820 was to become markedly liberal. In this light, it is revealing that during the Liberal Triennium, the areas of Spain with the highest number of periodicals that included the term "patriota" in their title were Catalonia and the Basque Country, two areas with a budding bourgeois population. All the indications are that almost a century before the rise of sub-state "nacionalismos" in these parts of the country, liberal Spanish patriotism was a sentiment felt with particular fervour among the urban middle classes in Basque and Catalan cities (see Fernández Sebastián 1991, 272ff, especially 277–278 and map 2).

From the recovery of Spanish independence to the invention of liberalism

It seems clear, however, that the movement from a predominantly economic agenda to the proposal of constitutional reform was a gradual one. Indeed, in the work of such essayists as Cabarrús or Arroyal, it is no easy task to determine where economics end and political aspirations begin. Moreover, as the eighteenth century moved into the nineteenth, "política" "politics" was generally held to refer to a combination of political economics and public law (see Fernández Sebastián 2013b). Indeed, in some authors' work, the shift was almost imperceptible as they moved from the request for economic improvements to the demand for a constitution as the only guarantee of citizens' rights, liberty, and property (see Portillo Valdés 2007, 2010).

The enormous weight given to the emerging concept of independence in the wake of the crisis of the Spanish monarchy was linked almost from the outset to the demand for a constitution (see Fernández Sebastián 2013a). It is no coincidence that Article 2 of the Constitution of Cádiz (and that of several Spanish American constitutions, following the Cádiz model) proclaimed the nation's sovereignty and independence, not only from any foreign power, but also from its own legitimate kings: "la Nación española es libre e independiente, y no es ni puede ser patrimonio de ninguna familia ni persona." In this sense, the liberal revolution in Spain, and Hispanic revolutions in general, might be characterized as a series of movements which linked the fight for liberty to the affirmation of the sovereignty of the people – or rather, the sovereignties of the peoples, where each city or local community may constitute a separate *pueblo* (see the articles in Ferreira 2009; Goldman 2014; San Francisco 2014). In sum, then, all those revolutions in the Iberian Atlantic between 1810 and 1825 may be seen as one great "revolución de independencia," which led to the dissolution of the two imperial monarchies. And the term "independencia" was to remain a fundamental political watchword throughout the nineteenth century: at different junctures during the revolution, Spanish liberals would again repeatedly invoke the independence of Spain as one of their primary political goals.

* * *

To conclude, I would like to draw attention to two little-known aspects of the liberal revolution in Spain, which are of some interest from a linguistic and cultural point of view. The first of these is an internal, local feature; the second has a more external, global relevance.

Firstly, Hispanic reformers worked hard to make sure that the principles of constitutionalism were known both in the regional languages of Peninsular Spain and in Amerindian tongues. Secondly, those *liberales* were the first to be referred to as such, both in Europe and in the world as a whole.

The proselytizing zeal of the leaders of the Spanish Revolution explains their systematic recourse to all forms of political propaganda. As well as the polemical dictionaries mentioned previously, and all kinds of pamphlets, periodicals, songs, images, and symbols, those early liberals published several political catechisms, and had no hesitation in adapting any genre or format to help serve the purpose of legitimizing the new regime which they sought to implement. Once again it became clear that the transformations in the printed matter made available to the public, and the semantic alterations at the level of individual words, were processes that were far from independent of each other. This, then, is further testimony, if such were needed, that modern intellectual historians have much to learn from specialists in cultural history and the history of the book, and vice versa (see Fernández Sebastián 2012a, 269–274).

Various translations into languages other than Castilian, with a greater or lesser presence in the Hispanic world, likewise testify to this determination to see the constitutional message reach every corner of the realm, especially during the 1820s. There is no doubt that the translators of those texts were the same men that had given all they could in a cause which was ultimately to prove impossible: transforming the Spanish imperial monarchy into a multi-ethnic, constitutional nation. Moreover, since this objective implicitly required turning the overwhelming majority of adult males – including the American aboriginals – into citizens, by a process similar to the evangelizing efforts of three centuries earlier, the "missionaries" of this new "constitutional Gospel" made every effort to translate their fundamental precepts into the vernacular languages of the New World. A leaflet published in Mexico, for example, entitled *La Malinche de la Constitución*, summarized the contents of the 1812 constitutional text in Nahuatl and Spanish, and we know that several partial translations of that same constitution were made in Mesoamerica, "en lenguas como el quiché y otras mayas" (Clavero 2000, 87; 332–333). According to one observer, these attempts at indoctrination were not in vain: the 1812 constitution did indeed profoundly alter the political language of the natives (see Clavero 1995, 2000, 307; Sierra O'Reilly 1955–1957, vol. 2, 67).

In the metropolis, too, where languages other than Castilian were spoken, it was necessary to overcome linguistic barriers. Works such as *Jaquinbide Iritarautia Españiaco Neurquidaren*, an 1820 Basque translation of a widely known Spanish constitutional catechism, stand as evidence of their authors' desire to propagate modern ideologies – in this case liberalism – in a rural environment where orality was still the norm (see Amundarain 1820; Gallastegi Aranzabal 2009; Ibisate 1994).

* * *

As will have been noted, most of the vocabulary of that nascent political modernity is composed of familiar words with revised meanings. However, those crucial years also saw the birth of a set of neologisms. Perhaps the most significant of these is "liberalismo," especially if we keep in mind the brilliant future which the following two centuries held in store for this, the first of the political – *ismos*, and the true herald of the ideological era.[2]

Whatever term we apply to it, this emerging ideology, political system, or movement, which was still not yet fully formed, and whose ideological traits look somewhat confused and ill-defined from our modern perspective, was given precisely this name of "liberalismo" at the *Cortes* of Cádiz. That was where, in late 1810, a group of young European and American constitutionalist parliamentarians were christened "liberales," for having the word "libertad" constantly on their lips during their impassioned speeches.

From that Andalusian city on the Atlantic coast, the political epithet "liberal" – as well as other related, but less common, expressions, such as "partido liberal" and "liberalismo" – spread rapidly to other cities on the Peninsula, and soon afterwards to the rest of Europe and America. There is some evidence to show that texts published in England, France, Germany, and the United States initially used the Spanish spelling of the word, or in any case employed it to make reference to the Hispanic liberals (see Fernández Sebastián 2006, 2012b).

During the 1820s, when the words "liberales" and "liberalismo" – already recognizable from Cádiz to St. Petersburg, from Boston to Santiago de Chile – started to become common currency on the other side of the Atlantic, the countries and languages of Iberia again played a decisive role in this step-change from regional to global significance. The aftereffects of these constitutional experiences were felt far away from the Peninsula, far away from Europe and from America. If the news and new languages reached the Philippines via the usual colonial routes, a more complicated course also took them to the Indian subcontinent. In Calcutta, the founder of Indian liberalism, Rammohan Roy, held several public celebrations in honour of the Iberian revolutions of 1820–1823, enthusiastically acknowledged the restoration of the Constitution of Cádiz, and was the recipient of a copy of that same legal text, with a dedication written in Spanish which included the word "liberalismo" (see Bayly 2007, 26–28; Collet 1962, 161–163).

It is therefore no surprise that until the eve of the French Revolution of 1830, the word "liberalismo," little used at the time, remained much more common in Spanish than in any of the other principal languages of Western Europe (see Figure 24.1):

Liberalismo had originally been considered by its enemies to be a kind of ideology, a party or a political-religious sect that pertained strictly to Spain, if with foreign roots (see *El Sensato*, July 1, 1813); however, from the 1820s, Spanish sources began to view it as a European, or even Euro-American phenomenon, which seemed destined to spread across the entire world.

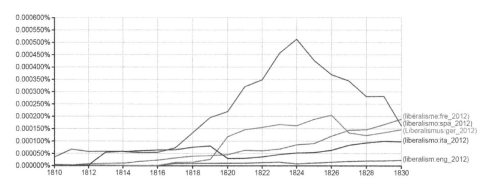

Figure 24.1   Relative frequency of the use of the term "liberalism" in five European languages, 1810–1830.

Source: Google Ngram Viewer, July 25, 2014.

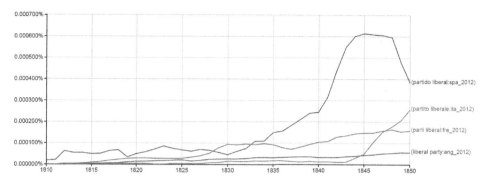

Figure 24.2   Relative frequency of the use of "liberal party" in four European languages, 1810–1850.
Source: Google Ngram Viewer, July 25, 2014.

Despite such universalizing designs, during the first half of the nineteenth century, and especially the decade of the 1840s, the likelihood of the phrase "partido liberal" appearing in a work composed in Spanish was considerably higher than that of finding an equivalent phrase in texts published in French, English, or Italian (see Figure 24.2):

In light of the data presented in the figures, it is surprising to note that nowadays Hispanic liberalism, historically the first liberalism to exist anywhere in the world, occupies an almost insignificant place not only in the classical manuals of Western liberalism used in British and North American universities, but also in much specialized historiography. How are we to explain this blind spot in intellectual history? As well as the familiar issue of Anglocentrism, part of the problem here is doubtless the strange silence resulting from the focus on a small canon of "great authors" in traditional histories of political theory – among which, of course, there is not a single figure who wrote in Spanish or Portuguese.

For my part, I am less interested in the works and authors of the classical canon than in the social transmission and circulation of concepts, and so my historical focus tends more towards languages than "theories," looking at how words are used rhetorically rather than at ideas in an abstract sense. From this perspective, Spanish liberalism – or, to be more precise, the liberalisms of Spain and Latin America – become once again a subject of great interest. In particular, they retain the interest which always pertains to the ways in which a society perceives itself in its own time; that is, to how a society's members seek solutions to their problems, debate them amongst themselves, and respond to the collective challenges with which they are presented.

As far as Spain is concerned, we have seen that during the later eighteenth century and the early nineteenth, the political language used by Spaniards underwent a period of profound renewal. Following the loss of almost all her American territories, Spain became a second-tier European power. The old monarchy which spanned two hemispheres was thus reduced to a nation-state of moderate size, which was fundamentally peninsular. At the same time as its lands were dramatically diminished, the country also began a period of intermittent political and constitutional revolution, which was only to reach a certain level of stability once the first third of the nineteenth century had passed, with the definitive triumph of representative government which would last for the remainder of the century. Paradoxically, significant changes to the array of concepts upon which the new institutions were built did not only affect Peninsular Spain: following a trajectory which ran parallel to that of the old mother-country, the young republics which had been separated from the monarchy (and here the same may be said of imperial possessions in Brazil, in reference to the Kingdom of Portugal) similarly renewed their political vocabularies during the first half of the nineteenth century, which quickly allowed the creation of a repertory of concepts that typified modern politics, and which were common to the rest of the Western world, although subject to differing interpretations. The *Iberconceptos* project attempts to chart the varying evolution of a set of twenty of these fundamental ideas which helped to open up Iberian paths by which modernity might be reached (see Fernández Sebastián 2009, 2014).

Notes

1 A different issue, though still associated with the fixing of meaning, is the question of who can provide models of writing and eloquence.
2 I leave aside *patriotismo*, a word already formed during the eighteenth century, and some other, minor –*ismos*, in particular those linked to the French Revolution, such as *jacobinismo*.

This article is part of the work of the Group IT615-13 and the Research Project HAR2013-42779-P (*Iberconceptos*), financed by the Basque Department of Education, Universities and Research, and by the Ministry of Economy, Government of Spain, respectively.

Works cited

Alcalá Galiano, Antonio. [1843–1844] 1984. *Lecciones de Derecho Político*. Madrid: CEC.

———. 1955. *Obras escogidas*. 2 vols. Madrid: Atlas.

Álvarez de Miranda, Pedro. 1984. "Algunos diccionarios burlescos de la primera mitad del siglo XIX (1811–1855)." In *Romanticismo, 2. Atti del III Congresso sul Romanticismo spagnolo e ispanoamericano. Il linguaggio romantico*, 155–167. Genoa: Facultà di Magistero dell'Univ. di Genova.

Amundarain, José Félix. 1820. *Jaquinbide Iritarautia Españiaco Neurquidaren edo Constitucio berriaren erara adrezatua Erritarren arguidoraraco, Gazteen icasbideraco, eta Escola-maisuen usoraco, Erderatik Eusquerara itzuli du Apez Vicario D. J. J. F. A. Guipuztarrac, 1820n urtean* (a manuscript version in Basque of: José Caro Sureda. 1812. *Catecismo político arreglado a la constitución de la monarquía española: para ilustración del pueblo, instrucción de la juventud, y uso de las escuelas de primeras letras*. Cádiz: Imprenta de Lema.)

"Apéndice al vocabulario de la lengua castellana, o explicación del diccionario de la revolución para la inteligencia de necios y discretos." *Gazeta de Madrid*, November 28, 1811: 1123–1124.

Bayly, C. A. 2007. "Rammohan Roy and the Advent of Constitutional Liberalism in India, 1800–1830." *Modern Intellectual History* 4: 25–41.

Clavero, Bartolomé. 1995. "Cádiz entre indígenas: Lecturas y lecciones sobre la Constitución y su cultura en tierra de los mayas." *Anuario de Historia del Derecho Español* 65: 931–992.

———. 2000. *Ama Llunku, Abya Yala: Constituyencia indígena y código ladino por América*. Madrid: CEPC.

Collet, Sophia D. 1962. *The Life and Letters of Raja Rammohun Roy*. Edited by D. K. Biswas and P. C. Ganguli. Calcutta: Sadharan Brahmo Samaj.

Costa, Joaquín. [1875] 1992. *Historia crítica de la Revolución española*. Edited by A. Gil Novales. Madrid: CEC.

Donoso Cortés, Juan. 1837. "Semejanza de voces; confusión de ideas." *El Porvenir*, Madrid, June 30.

Entin, Gabriel. 2014. "El patriotismo americano en el siglo XVIII: ambigüedades de un discurso político hispánico." In Véronique Hébrard y Geneviève Verdo, eds., *Las independencias hispanoamericanas. Un objeto de historia*, edited by Véronique Hébrard and Geneviève Verdo, 19–33. Madrid: Casa de Velázquez.

Étienvre, Françoise. 1983. "Filosofía de la sinonimia en la España de las Luces." *Anales de Literatura española* 2: 251–279.

———. 2001. *Rhétorique et patrie dans l'Espagne des Lumières. L'œuvre linguistique d'Antonio de Capmany (1742–1813)*. Paris: Honoré Champion.

Fernández Albaladejo, Pablo. 2001. "Dinastía y comunidad política: el momento de la patria." In *Los Borbones. Dinastía y memoria de nación en la España del siglo XVIII*, edited by P. Fernández Albaladejo, 485–532. Madrid: Marcial Pons and Casa de Velázquez.

Fernández Sebastián, Javier. 1991. *La génesis del fuerismo. Prensa e ideas políticas en la crisis del Antiguo Régimen (País Vasco, 1750–1840)*. Madrid: Siglo XXI de España.

———. 1994. "España, monarquía y nación. Cuatro concepciones de la comunidad política española entre el Antiguo Régimen y la Revolución liberal." *Studia Historica. Historia Contemporánea* 12: 45–74.

———. 2000. "The Awakening of Public Opinion in Spain. The Rise of a New Power and the Sociogenesis of a Concept." In *Opinion*, edited by Peter Eckhard-Knabe, 45–79. Berlin: Berlin Verlag Arno Spitz.

———. 2006. "*Liberales y liberalismo* en España, 1810–1850. La forja de un concepto y la creación de una identidad política." *Revista de Estudios Políticos* 134: 125–176.

———. 2008. "La crisis de 1808 y el advenimiento de un nuevo lenguaje político. ¿Una revolución conceptual?" In *Las experiencias de 1808 en Iberoamérica*, edited by Alfredo Ávila and Pedro Pérez Herrero, 105–133. Mexico, DF: UNAM/Universidad de Alcalá.

———, ed. 2009. *Diccionario político y social del mundo iberoamericano. La era de las revoluciones, 1750–1850*. vol. 1. Madrid: CEPC.

———. 2012a. "Guerra de palabras. Lengua y política en la Revolución de España." In *Guerra de ideas. Política y cultura en la España de la Guerra de la Independencia*, edited by Pedro Rújula and Jordi Canal, 237–280. Madrid: Marcial Pons Historia.

———. 2012b. "Liberalismo en España, 1810–1850. La construcción de un concepto y la forja de una identidad política." In *La aurora de la libertad. Los primeros liberalismos en el mundo iberoamericano*, edited by Javier Fernández Sebastián, 265–306. Madrid, Marcial Pons Historia.

———. 2013a. "La independencia de España y otras independencias. La transformación radical de un concepto en la crisis del mundo hispano." In *Las declaraciones de independencia. Los textos fundamentales de las independencias americanas*, edited by Alfredo Ávila, Érika Pani, and Jordana Dym, 41–79. Mexico: El Colegio de México/UNAM.

———. 2013b. "What did they Mean by *política*? Debating over the Concept, Value and Place of Politics in Modern Spain." In *Writing Political History Today*, edited by Willibald Steinmetz, Ingrid Holtey, and Heinz-Gerhard Haupt, 99–126. Frankfurt and New York: Campus Verlag.

———, ed. 2014. *Diccionario político y social del mundo iberoamericano. Conceptos políticos fundamentales, 1770–1870*. Part II. 10 vols. Madrid: CEPC.

Fernández Sebastián, Javier and Juan Francisco Fuentes. 2002. "Patria." In *Diccionario político y social del siglo XIX español*, edited by Javier Fernández Sebastián and Juan Francisco Fuentes, 512–523. Madrid: Alianza.

Ferreira, Fátima Sá e Melo, ed. 2009. "Pueblo." In *Diccionario político y social del mundo iberoamericano. La era de las revoluciones, 1750–1850*, edited by Javier Fernández Sebastián, vol. 1, 1115–1250. Madrid: CEPC.

Fuentes, Juan Francisco. 1988. "Concepto de pueblo en el primer liberalismo español." *Trienio* 12: 176–209.

Gallardo, Bartolomé J. 1811. *Diccionario crítico-burlesco del que se titula "Diccionario razonado manual para inteligencia de ciertos escritores que por equivocación han nacido en España*. Cádiz: Impr. del Estado Mayor General.

Gallastegi Aranzabal, César. 2009. "La primera traducción al euskera de un texto parlamentario español." In *Nomografía y corredacción legislativa*, edited by Andrés Urrutia, 145–184. Bilbao: Universidad de Deusto.

García Godoy, María Teresa. 1999. *El léxico del primer constitucionalismo español y mejicano, 1810–1815*. Granada: Universidad de Granada.

Gil Novales, Alberto. 1975. *Las sociedades patrióticas (1820–1823)*. 2 vols. Madrid: Tecnos.

Goldman, Noemí, ed. 2014. "Soberanía." In *Diccionario político y social del mundo iberoamericano. Conceptos políticos fundamentales, 1770–1870*, edited by Javier Fernández Sebastián, vol. 10, 15–234. Madrid: CEPC.

Ibisate, Ángel. 1994. "El doctor Don José Félix Amundarain (Cegama 1755–Mutiloa 1825) autor del *Jaquinbide Iritarautia* (1820)." *Boletín de la Real Sociedad Bascongada de Amigos del País* 50 (1): 159–169.

Jonama, Santiago. 1836. *Ensayo sobre la distinción de los sinónimos de la lengua castellana*. 2nd ed. Barcelona: Imprenta de Oliva (1st ed., Madrid: Imprenta Real, 1806).

La *Malinche de la Constitución. En los idiomas mejicano y castellano*. Mexico: Alejandro Valdés, 1820.

Lomné, Georges, ed. 2014. "Patria" In *Diccionario político y social del mundo iberoamericano. Conceptos políticos fundamentales, 1770–1870*, edited by Javier Fernández Sebastián, vol. 8, 15–228. Madrid: CEPC.

López de la Huerta, José. 1789. *Examen de la posibilidad de fijar la significación de los sinónimos de la lengua castellana*. Viena: Imprenta de Ignacio Alberti.

Montijo, Conde de. 1810. *Manifiesto de lo que no ha hecho el Conde de Montijo, escrito para desengaño o confusión de los que de buena o mala fe le dicen autor de sediciones que no ha hecho, ni podido hacer* [September 22, 1810]. Cádiz: Impr. de M. S. de Quintana.

Munibe, Javier María de, Conde de Peñaflorida. 2002. *Introducción a la Asamblea General de la R. S. B. en 1779*. Mss. In *Discursos inéditos de Javier María de Munibe, Conde de Peñaflorida*, ed. Jesús Astigarraga, 182–203. Vitoria: Ararteko.

Pastor Pérez, Justo. 1811. *Diccionario razonado, Manual para inteligencia de ciertos escritores que por equivocación han nacido en España*. 2nd ed. Cádiz: Impr. de la Junta Superior.

Portillo Valdés, José M. 2007. "Constitucionalismo antes de la Constitución. La Economía Política y los orígenes del constitucionalismo en España." *Nuevo Mundo Mundos Nuevos* [online]. Accessed December 20, 2014. http://nuevomundo.revues.org/4160.

———. 2010. "Entre la historia y la economía política: orígenes de la cultura del constitucionalismo." In *Historia y Constitución: trayectos del constitucionalismo hispánico*, edited by Carlos Garriga, 27–57. México, DF: CIDE.

San Francisco, Alejandro, ed. 2014. "Independencia." In *Diccionario político y social del mundo ibero americano. Conceptos políticos fundamentales, 1770–1870*, edited by Javier Fernández Sebastián, vol. 4, 15–221. Madrid: CEPC.

Seoane, María Cruz. 1968. *El primer lenguaje constitucional español (las Cortes de Cádiz)*. Madrid: Moneda y Crédito.

Sierra O'Reilly, Justo. 1955–1957. *Los indios del Yucatán*. 2 vols. vol. II. *Consideraciones históricas sobre la influencia del elemento indígena en la organización social del país (1848–1851)*. Edited by Carlos R. Menéndez. Mérida: Fondo Editorial del Yucatán.

Thjulen, Lorenzo. 1813. *Nuevo vocabulario filosófico-democrático, indispensable para todos los que deseen entender la nueva lengua revolucionaria*. 2 vols. Sevilla: Viuda de Vázquez.

Vilar, Pierre. 1982. *Hidalgos, amotinados y guerrilleros. Pueblo y poderes en la historia de España*. Barcelona: Crítica.

25

THE MODERN CITY, 1850 TO 1900

Urban planning and culture in Barcelona, Madrid and Bilbao

Benjamin Fraser

Urbanization in nineteenth-century Spain – particularly as it unfolded during the second half of the century – was a cultural process as much as it was a material one. This is true both in the general and in the particular senses.

First, that is, the plans for restructuring cities were themselves inevitably cultural from the outset. Here, it is necessary to adopt a broad and interdisciplinary perspective on culture, one that focuses not merely on artistic expression but also on its ties with historical, social, geographical, political and economic forces and circumstances. From this perspective, all human activity may be considered cultural in nature – to one degree or another, perhaps. To wit: Hispanic Studies – a traditionally literary field – has been rejuvenated in recent decades by cultural studies approaches pushing for just this sort of broad and interdisciplinary understanding of culture. The volume you are presently reading is, in fact, testament to the growing primacy of this approach.

Second, however – and more importantly – it is the task of this chapter to delve into the cultural dimensions of Spain's urbanization in a more specific way. There are two complementary parts to the understanding of the urban phenomenon charted out herein. One part concerns the "culture of urban planning" itself, while the other part concerns "urban culture." Each is related to the other, such that neither should be viewed in isolation. Rather than precise terminology, these terms are mere provisional instruments for making sense of a larger process. Grasping this larger process entails returning urbanization to the wider context of human history. Doing so reveals that in producing urban environments we humans have been refashioning ourselves. This is true at once at both the grand scale of urban design and also at the scale of the everyday. Even though this chapter emphasizes the cultures of urban planning over urban culture considered more generally, it does make the effort to link the two together.

The cultural processes of designing and building urban environments find their complement in the everyday cultural processes by which we inhabit and live in cities. To see this, we must not take the city as a static object. That is, the city is not a mere container for our activities. Instead we must recognize that, just as we shape the city, the city shapes us in return. In fact, this reciprocal influence between human beings and our urban environment has long been a central part of the discourse of urban culture – one that can be traced through the twentieth century to the present day (e.g., Harvey 2012; Park 1968; Simmel 2010). Nevertheless, late nineteenth-century urban planning and urban culture remain a privileged moment even in twenty-first century understandings of the city, as it was then that the urban became synonymous with the cultural project of modernity (Berman 1982; Choay 1969; T. Hall 1997; Harvey 2006; Larson and Woods 2005; Lefebvre 1995).

The culture of urban planning

The "culture of urban planning" as it developed in the second half of the nineteenth century was clearly tied to a nexus of historical, political and economic circumstances (Lefebvre 1996; Sennett 1992, 2008). Waves of industrialization had effected rapid technological change, increasing the density of urban areas as well as contributing to the uneven geographical development of the city (Mumford 1938, 1961). That is, variation in the contours of the urban form tended to produce both areas of lower density with upper-class residents and also areas of higher density where poor living conditions often went hand in hand with poverty and disease (Cerdà 1991; Engels 1935, 1987; P. Hall 2002; Riis 1996). Governments launched systematic urban improvement projects both to combat the poverty and disease that unevenly affected urban populations and also – as had been evidenced already by King Carlos III's late eighteenth-century beautification of Madrid, for example – at once to reimagine urban environments as emblematic triumphs of the modern age (Afinoguénova 2013; Fraser 2007a). The rise of the modern urban planner in the nineteenth century was thus linked organically to the technological changes wrought by industrialization and the renewed focus on the importance of cities as centers of economic trade and political power.

The role played by the planner in nineteenth-century society was also a direct result of the bourgeois specialization of knowledge that accompanied the increasing class division of capitalist labor (Lefebvre 2003). It may be noted that Hispanic Studies as a discipline has traditionally used the rhetoric of exceptionality to downplay both the spread of Enlightenment ideals in Spain and the presence there of bourgeois revolution (Carr 1970, 2000; Subirats 1981). Nevertheless, such a traditional approach has been critiqued by a strong recent tendency within the discipline (Afinoguénova and Martí-Olivella 2008; Ginger 2007; Lewis 1999). The strength of Spain's planning traditions provides ample evidence that the country was very much subject to the same social dynamics that affected Western Europe during the 1900s (Chueca Goitia 2011; Fraser 2011a). As a specialized class endowed with the social power to shape urban space, European planners appeared to embody the scientific rationality of the Enlightenment tradition. In this sense, at least, Spain was no exception.

As a cultural practice, European planning activities were carried out in a decidedly social, political and economic context. Readers may be familiar, for example, with Baron Georges-Eugène Haussmann's urban restructuring of central Paris in the second half of the nineteenth century (Choay 1969; Harvey 2006). That is, it is frequently said that the broad avenues produced by Haussmann's urban renewal scheme had been designed to facilitate the march of a modern metropolitan police force, thus aiding in the control of potentially unruly and politically motivated urban crowds (Miles 2007). Yet even if the planner's work was not driven directly by political power, it was necessarily a product of a certain class-inflected vision of the city.

Empowered by the metaphor of the city as an organism – following the seventeenth-century debates surrounding the circulation of blood through the body – nineteenth-century planners often envisioned the city as a vast circulatory system (Cerdà 1867; Fraser 2011b; Sennett 2008). Seen through this metaphorical thinking, streets became arteries, and part of the planner's job was to assure the free, unimpeded movement of traffic throughout the city. The insistence on maintaining this flow of traffic, of course, belied a commitment to intensified trading activities and capitalist commerce. Yet, the city was simultaneously a respiratory system, and the harmonious integration of green space into the urban fabric was also seen as paramount. The reasons for this had to do both with the realities of disease in dense city areas and also with the culture of urbanism (Cerdà 1867). That is, on one hand, trees and vegetation acted as the city's green lungs, keeping the air fresh and, it was believed, minimizing the potential for disease transmission. On the other, through planned green spaces, the city was turned into a garden of sorts. As was the case with public gardens already existing in Spain – modeled on the British and French traditions – the urbanite could visually consume the city's urban fabric and at once appreciate the domination of culture over nature (Fraser 2013; Frost 2008).

Emboldened both by these metaphors and by the social power they enjoyed, nineteenth-century planners cultivated a distanced, rational, even geometrical form of spatial thinking (Fraser 2011b; Resina 2003; Sennett 1992). Problematically, however, this thinking in essence reduced a living organism to a two-dimensional diagram (Lefebvre 1995). In this way, they dealt not with the city in time but with the city as a simple spatial object. The planned city manipulated in blueprints and representations was an abstracted, conceived space (Lefebvre 1995). Acting as surgeons, planners operated on the city as they might have a cadaver. They cut into the city's urban tissue and believed that in changing the built environment alone they might solve the greatest problems of humanity (Cerdà 1867; Fraser 2011a, 2011b; Soria 1996). In the end, the spatial and fragmenting approach to the city evident in urban plans from Spain's nineteenth century can be best understood as one particular way in which scientific bourgeois knowledge in general reduced a complex social totality into a number of presumably isolated parts (Lefebvre 2003).[1]

Building on the foregoing necessarily concise articulation, the following subsections – on Barcelona, Madrid and Bilbao – are intended to give neither a totalizing nor chronological account of the rise of city planning and urban culture in Spanish cities. Instead, these brief vignettes are to serve as privileged points of entry into key moments and aspects of urban transition in Spain. This account of the country's urban transitions illustrates the dynamics associated with European planning as a whole, but is related also to the astounding urban population growth affecting Spain's cities in particular during the second half of the nineteenth century. By the beginning of the twentieth century, that is, Barcelona's population had topped half a million inhabitants, and Madrid's population had almost doubled, increasing from under 300,000 in 1850 to more than 500,000 in 1900 (Fox 1989; Ugarte 1996). Spurred on by an industrial boom, even Bilbao's population almost tripled leading up to the turn of the century, surpassing 50,000 residents by 1900 (Basurto Ferro 1993; Zulaika 2003). Of course, the interested reader is advised to explore the readings listed in the works cited at the end of this chapter to acquire a more thorough background in the dynamics of urban change in nineteenth-century Spain.

Barcelona

Perhaps more than any other nineteenth-century planner in Spain, the extensive urban writings of Ildefons Cerdà (1815–1876) provide insight into the connections between culture and planning outlined previously. Renowned for reportedly having coined the word *urbanización*, the Catalan planner was the author of numerous theoretical works on the nature of the urban phenomenon such as *Teoría de la viabilidad urbana y reforma de la de Madrid* (1861) and the two-volume *Teoría general de la urbanización* (1867) (Choay 1969; Degen 2008; Fraser 2011a,

2011b; Hughes 1992; Resina 2008). Cerdà is most well known, however, for his nineteenth-century design masterpiece: an expansion of Barcelona's central core (or *casco medieval*) known as the Eixample. Outlined, in part, in the *Teoría de la construcción de las ciudades aplicada al proyecto de reforma y ensanche de Barcelona* (1859), for this project he drew on his own statistical study (from 1856) of the poor living conditions of the working class in Barcelona. Following up on Friedrich Engels' already completed study of *The Condition of the Working Class in England* (1987 [1844]) – and anticipating Danish-born photojournalist Jacob Riis' polemic titled *How the Other Half Lives* (1996 [1890]), which would document life in the tenements of New York at the century's close – Cerdà hoped to apply the bourgeois science of urban planning to effect real social change where it was needed.

Interestingly, Cerdà's theoretical musings knowingly harnessed the organic metaphor of the city's environment so popular in nineteenth-century urban discourse. In his *Teoría general*, he purposely cast himself in the role of urban surgeon, proclaiming that "Introduciendo el escalpelo hasta lo más íntimo y recóndito del organismo urbano y social, se consigue sorprender viva y en acción la causa originaria, el germen fecundo de la grave enfermedad que corroe las entrañas de la humanidad" (1867, I: 16–17). In line with what would become known as the Haussmannization of Paris, Cerdà's rational and rectilinear vision subjected the city to a geometrical grid, touted the benefits of broad avenues and incorporated green space into the urban fabric of the Eixample at regular intervals. In fact, one of the planner's dictums cited the need to "urbanizar lo rural, ruralizar lo urbano [urbanize the rural, ruralize the urban]." Additionally, his invention of the *xamfrà*, or truncated corner – also implemented in Bilbao's nineteenth-century urban reform – was conceived as a way of allowing traffic to flow more freely through intersections in the city. This innovation not only anticipated the importance of automobile traffic in the early twentieth-century city, but it was also motivated by his realization that the construction of urban-built environments had been driven historically by modes of transportation and patterns of circulation (Cerdà 1867; Epps 2002; Fraser 2011b; Resina 2008; Soria 1996).

And yet, the contradiction visible in the Cerdà plan was one common to nineteenth-century planning as a whole. That is – perhaps despite his utopian socialist-inspired conception of the city and sympathy for the working class – the famed Catalan planner separated the lived city from the conceived city. Despite its originator's emphasis on mobility and movement, the plan – which was clothed in the triumphant and triumphalist rhetoric of modernity (Lefebvre 1996) – nevertheless reduced the city to being a simple object or set of static structures. The result was an area soon inhabited by the middle class and progressively distanced from the working-class culture that had fueled industrialization and concomitantly the urbanization of the modern nineteenth-century city. Robert Goldston puts it well: "The entire district is removed from the sight, smell and sound of the factories from which its wealth was drawn. Businessmen living in the Ensanche had no need to be aware of the hideous slums growing up in other parts of the city; they lived a suburban life, abandoning the central city to commerce, industry and the makeshift life of the poor" (1969, 78). Manuel Vázquez Montalbán would later remark that the planner's legacy is "an Eixample which has turned out to be as far from Cerdà's dreams as it is from the malevolent schemes of the speculators" (1990, 76).

Madrid

In contrast to Barcelona (and Bilbao), Madrid boasted relatively little industry even by the mid-nineteenth century. Nonetheless, it, too, was soon subjected to the planner's blueprints for urban change. The political center of Castillian Spain ever since Felipe II had named it the Spanish capital in the sixteenth century, Madrid's built environment was similarly reimagined as part of the process of cultural modernization that affected other cities in Spain. As the authors of the book *El ensanche de Madrid: historia de una capital* explain:

> A mediados del siglo XIX, las principales ciudades europeas parecían decididas a traspasar el umbral de la Modernidad, afrontando una serie de profundas transformaciones que alteraría por completo las formas de vida del hombre urbano. [. . .] En la década anterior a la aprobación del Ensanche, los tejados madrileños vieron elevarse alguna columna de humo industrial (la fábrica de Gas); la plaza de Oriente pasaba de inhóspito descampado a regio espacio público; la sede de la soberanía se erigía sobre las recias columnas del Congreso; abría sus puertas, por fin, el Teatro Real, escaparate de lujo y envidias, escenario de anhelos de ascenso social; la Puerta del Sol dejaba de ser calle, se desperezaba y desenrollaba, a su vez, alguna de las arterias que venían a desembocar en ella; nuevos burgueses ricos plantaban sus palacetes, cual medallas a su triunfo social; las fuentes daban la bienvenida a las vivificadoras aguas del Lozoya; reverberaban los primeros silbidos del ferrocarril, y el gas, al tiempo que iluminaba cafés, lujosos salones y escaparates con la nueva moda venida de París, alumbraba míseras barriadas y sucias callejuelas, un panorama, en definitiva, lleno de luces y sombras.
>
> (Carballo *et al.* 2008, 59–60)

These historical and cultural shifts that accompanied urbanization during the second half of the nineteenth century in particular brought increased attention on the central areas of the city.

A new wave of urbanism sought to connect the centrally located (and then newly renovated) Puerta del Sol with the area that is today known as Callao and also with what is now the Plaza de España (Baker 2009; Haidt 2005). These urban changes, which were of course directly experienced by numerous Madrilenians, were captured on film by photographers intrigued by the city's refashioning as driven by the ideal of the modern city (Fontanella 1981). The Castro plan of 1860 had been an important attempt to formalize the city's expansion, and other, more ambitiously conceived plans were to follow (*Guía de la ciudad lineal* 2011; Fernández de los Ríos 1868). Importantly, the opening of the city's central areas occurred alongside the development of new transportation systems such as the tranvía – whose first line opened in 1871 and was dramatized in a prose work by Galdós (*Madrid en Galdós* 1988, 198–199) – which connected newly constructed peripheral areas to Madrid's urban core. Of course, in connecting bourgeois neighborhoods with the city center, this modern transportation also allowed the city's uneven geographical development to persist.

Another important outcome of this focus on rethinking Madrid's central neighborhoods was the idea to construct the Gran Vía beginning at Calle de Alcalá's intersection with the Palacio de las Comunicaciones (commonly referred to as Cibeles). Construction on the Gran Vía began on 4 April 1910 and, at a short 1362 m, the road would in time become synonymous with twentieth-century urban modernity in Spain (Baker 2009; Baker and Compitello 2003; Larson 2011; Ramos 2010). Importantly, however, although the 1907 plan used for the Gran Vía officially was the work of architects Francisco Andrés Octavio and José López Sallaberry, the idea for the road dates back to an 1886 plan by Carlos Velasco and, some say, can be traced back even as far as 1856 (Baker 2009; Fernández Cifuentes 2003).

Bilbao

Conceived during a population boom that began in the second half of the nineteenth century, the 1876 Expansion plan for Bilbao was designed by engineers Pablo Alzola and Ernesto Hoffmeyer and the architect Severino Achúcarro (Basurto Ferro 1993; Cruz 2011; Zulaika 1999, 2003). As it had been with Haussmann's Paris and Cerdà's Barcelona, the plan for Bilbao was very much guided by an abstract, geometrical visual logic which saw the city as a set of static structures that needed to be opened up to increase movement and flow. An additional issue in this case, however, was that the city was envisioned in quite reductive terms, making its further expansion problematic.

> Quizás lo más sorprendente del Plan de Bilbao era la ausencia de una visión metropolitana. Cierto que el Plan debía atender al territorio del ámbito municipal; igualmente cierto es el hecho de que no existía ningún ente de rango superior aglutinante de prioridades para los municipios de Bilbao Metropolitano. [. . .] Como consecuencia de esa falta de visión o vocación metropolitana de Bilbao, el plan estrangulaba el desarrollo de la ciudad con la proposición de un cinturón de ronda, un anillo, en una estructura, la del Bajo Nervión, de carácter lineal. La lectura del plano reflejaba cómo se había extraído la ciudad de Bilbao de su contexto metropolitano. Se había abordado el plan como si de una isla se tratara. Cuando la realidad era bien diferente.
> (Cenicacelaya 2009, 20–21)

As evident in this description, the fact that the Nervión River runs through the city on its way to the Cantabrian Sea did not sufficiently figure into the plan for Bilbao. But another problematic aspect of the plan – once again, one common to many urban plans of the nineteenth century – came from the way in which it dealt with the city's static structures alone and left the human city out of the equation. Of note here is the brief polemic, for example, evident in the pages of a Bilbao periodical appropriately named *El Nervión*, which involved Miguel de Unamuno (1864–1936). Therein, Unamuno – who has long been regarded as one of Spain's most noted authors, poets and philosophers – alleged that the urban reforms were motivated by the potential benefits they held for increased collective rents (Rivero Gómez 2008; Serrano 1986; Unamuno 1999). In the end, urban planning in Bilbao – just as in Madrid and Barcelona – was a much more complex process than the specialized scientific knowledge base of planning which was so widespread during the nineteenth century was able to admit.

If the work of contemporary critic Manuel Delgado Ruiz (1956–) is any indication, critics of urbanism in Spain today continue to draw attention to the distance between the city as conceived from above and as lived on the ground (Delgado Ruiz 1999, 2007a, 2007b; Fraser 2007b, 2011a). It may thus also be said that the main problem planners faced in the nineteenth century persists even today in the twenty-first century. That is, there is still a need to more fully recognize the social, political and economic context and implications of urban planning, just as there exists the need to define the city not merely as a set of structures, but also as a complex human organism.

Urban culture

Although this chapter has focused more on the culture of urban planning, it is important to keep in mind that the pressures that urban population growth put on Spain's urban environments were not merely a matter for planners to consider. Their effects were palpable and were felt by a cross-section of urbanites. That is, we must not overlook that at the same time that the specialist class of urban planners was dealing with the city as a conceived space, nineteenth-century urbanites were engaging with the city as a lived space. There were new forms of art, culture and social life – new ways of thinking and being in cities – that manifested themselves amongst urban populations. It is fair to say that the increased attention given to the urban form by specialized planners found its complement in the increased emphasis placed on city life by authors and artists.

In canonical examples of Spanish literature, authors turned increasingly toward representing the city (Baker and Compitello 2003; Frost 2008; Parsons 2003). In the first half of the nineteenth century, for example, public literary figures had emerged whose work privileged the urban environment (Baker 1991; Haidt 2005). Among these were Mariano José de Larra (1809–1837) and Ramón de Mesonero Romanos (1803–1882), who both resided in the Spanish capital and shared a similar interest in the city's streets. Mesonero was himself simultaneously a writer and also an active planner who helped to shape Madrid's urban fabric in no small way. While Mesonero saw the city as a triumphant and quintessentially human accomplishment, however, Larra tended to see in the everyday life of the city streets a darker side informed by the consequences of powerful institutions, which humans had created (Fraser 2011a, 2011c).

Building implicitly on such earlier costumbrist depictions of urban life in Spain, the second half of the century undoubtedly saw the cultivation of a modern sort of metropolitan aesthetic in prose works and the arts (Haidt 2009, 2011). Thus many writers either explored the textures of everyday life in the Spanish city directly (most significantly, author Benito Pérez Galdós in Madrid; as well as Narcís Oller, in Barcelona) or else interrogated this rapidly urbanizing society somewhat indirectly by focusing on the city-country opposition (e.g., the work of Emilia Pardo Bazán or Juan Valera) (Baker and Compitello 2003; Cruz 2011; Frost 2008; Mercer 2013; Resina 2008; Williams 1973). Importantly, too, literary products by these and other authors set an urban tone that was to be discernable, also, in early twentieth-century works (see Baker and Compitello 2003; Fraser 2011a; Larson 2011; Ramos 2010; Ugarte 1996).

It must be acknowledged, of course, that there is a difference between urban culture, on one hand, and the culture of urban planning, on the other. Above all else, this means accepting that studies of the monumental city alone are, in reality, a study of those same power structures and cultural assumptions (social, political and economic assumptions) which drove urban reform in the nineteenth century. In the prologue to his fundamental study *Materiales para escribir Madrid* (1991), Edward Baker regards narrow definitions of urban culture with suspicion for their potential complicity with non-democratic power: "Este punto de mira supone el rechazo de la concepción pseudomonumentalista y sacralizadora de la capitalidad, y parte del convencimiento de que Madrid es y debe ser cada día más villa que corte, movimiento necesario hacia el control colectivo, aún más lejano, de las condiciones en que se desenvuelve la existencia de cuatro millones de madrileños" (1991, xiii). Appropriately, this comment may be taken both as a specific critique of Francisco Franco's monumental urban nationalism and also as a more general call to democratize the notion of urban culture in the monumentalized forms that have endured from the nineteenth century until the present day (see also Baker 2012).

In truth, the connections between cultural texts (whether literary in the traditional sense or not) and their nineteenth-century urban contexts have not been sufficiently explored as of yet. It is significant that interdisciplinary work on urban culture in Hispanic contexts can claim a history dating back at least three decades. For example, two days in late October 1983 – at the ninth annual Hispanic Literature conference on "Los escritores y la experiencia de la ciudad moderna" – twenty-eight scholars presented a series of original and quite novel papers on the city, edited for publication by Dr. Juan Cruz Mendizábal. Hispanist scholars have increasingly turned to investigating the urban culture of the twentieth century in Spain, more often than not focusing on Madrid or Barcelona, and likewise the urban cultures of cities across Latin America. Still, there remains much work to be done in the exploration of the urban phenomenon as it relates to Spanish cultural studies in the nineteenth century in particular (Fraser 2012; Graham and Labanyi 2000).

As emphasized throughout this chapter, it is important to see the modern city as a construction stemming from two complementary cultural forces: on one hand, the culture of urban planning as it was conceived by a specialist class, and on the other, the urban culture experienced by inhabitants in that city. It is true that, because of the often divergent social, political and economic interests that shape each of them, these two forces may be seen as necessarily antagonistic to each other. Yet it is the concept of culture that links them both. Ultimately, a more capacious view of culture is necessary if we are to understand the complexity of Spain's nineteenth-century urban modernity.

Note

1 Françoise Choay builds on discussion of Ildefons Cerdà and Eugène Haussmann specifically to enumerate three relevant points that define the nineteenth-century planning process in general and which are supremely important for understanding urbanism as it unfolded in Spain. These are "1) the city is conceived as an object: both theoretically and in its reality, the modern city came out of the same type of reflective effort that produced the nineteenth-century concepts of art and labor. [. . .] As a consequence of this process and of the century's general awareness of history, the concepts of historical monument and preservation of the past were created;" "2) An analytical method is used, both in the study of the object and in the elaboration of projects. The key words are *classification* and *system*. Its use of classification, in which visual factors were extremely important, appears to have been borrowed from the natural sciences. Moreover, the concept of function evolved by the new biology becomes the basis of the systems created by the city planners who also apply to the city biological images such as circulation, nucleus and cell;" and "3) Two objectives are given exclusive priority: traffic and hygiene" (Choay 1969, 26–27).

Works cited

Afinoguénova, Eugenia. 2013. "Liberty at the Merry-Go-Round: Leisure, Politics, and Municipal Authority on the Paseo del Prado in Madrid, 1760–1939." *Journal of Urban Cultural Studies* 1 (1) 85–106.
Afinoguénova, Eugenia and Jaume Martí-Olivella, eds. 2008. *Spain Is (Still) Different.* Lanham, MD: Rowman & Littlefield.
Baker, Edward. 1991. *Materiales para escribir Madrid: Literatura y espacio urbano de Moratín a Galdós.* Madrid: Siglo XXI.
———. 2009. *Madrid cosmopolita: La Gran Vía, 1910–1936.* Madrid: Marcial Pons y Fernando Villaverde.
———. 2012. "Madrid de *caput regni* a capital nacional: toponimia y cultura conmemorativa de 1812 a 1840." In *Capital Inscriptions: Essays on Hispanic Literature, Film and Urban Space in Honor of Malcolm Alan Compitello*, edited by Benjamin Fraser, 105–22. Newark, DE: Juan de la Cuesta.
Baker, Edward and Malcolm Alan Compitello, eds. 2003. *Madrid. De Fortunata a la M- 40: un siglo de cultura urbana.* Madrid: Alianza.
Basurto Ferro, Nieves. 1993. "El primer ensanche de Bilbao: oportunismo y vacío legal." *Cuadernos de Sección Historia-Geografía* 21: 229–242.
Berman, Marshall. 1982. *All that Is Solid Melts into Air.* New York: Simon & Schuster.
Carballo, Borja, Rubén Pallol, and Fernando Vicente. 2008. *El ensanche de Madrid: historia de una capital.* Madrid: Editorial Complutense.

Carr, Raymond. 1970. *Spain 1808–1939*. Oxford: Oxford University Press.

———. 2000. *Spain: A History*. Oxford: Oxford University Press.

Cenicacelaya, Javier. 2009. "Bilbao y la urgencia de un urbanismo sostenible." In *Urbanismo en el siglo XXI*, edited by Jordi Borja and Zaida Muxí, 17–33. Barcelona: Escola Técnica Superior d'Arquitectura de Barcelona.

Cerdà, Ildefons. [1859] 1991. *Teoría de la construcción de las ciudades aplicada al proyecto de reforma y ensanche de Barcelona*. In *Cerdà y Barcelona*, 107–450. Madrid: INAP/Ajuntament de Barcelona.

———. [1860] 1991. *Pensamiento económico*. *Cerdà y Barcelona*, 457–71. Madrid: INAP/Ajuntament de Barcelona.

———. [1861] 1991. *Teoría de la viabilidad urbana y reforma de la de Madrid*. *Cerdà y Madrid*, 45–280. Madrid: MOPT/Ayuntamiento de Madrid.

———. 1867. *Teoría general de la urbanización*. 2 vols. Madrid: Imprenta Española.

Choay, Françoise. 1969. *The Modern City: Planning in the Nineteenth Century*. Trans. Marguerite Hugo and George R. Collins. New York: George Braziller.

Chueca Goitia, Fernando. 2011. *Breve historia del urbanismo*. Madrid: Alianza.

Cruz, Jesús. 2011. *The Rise of Middle-Class Culture in Nineteenth-Century Spain*. Baton Rouge, LA: Louisiana State University Press.

Degen, Mónica Monserrat. 2008. *Sensing Cities: Regenerating Public Life in Barcelona and Manchester*. London: Routledge.

Delgado Ruiz, Manuel. 1999. *El animal público*. Barcelona: Anagrama.

———. 2007a. *Sociedades movedizas: pasos hacia una antropología de las calles*. Barcelona: Anagrama.

———. 2007b. *La ciudad mentirosa. Fraude y miseria del "modelo Barcelona."* Madrid: Catarata.

Engels, Friedrich. 1935. *The Housing Question*. New York: International.

———. 1987. *The Condition of the Working Class in England*. Edited by Victor Kiernan. London and New York: Penguin.

Epps, Brad, ed. 2002. "Barcelona and the Projection of Catalonia." Special section of the *Arizona Journal of Hispanic Cultural Studies* 6: 191–287.

Fernández Cifuentes, Luis. 2003. "Fachadas del 98: la reconstrucción del escenario metropolitano a raíz de las guerras coloniales." In *Madrid de Fortunata a la M-40: un siglo de cultura urbana*, edited by E. Baker and M. A. Compitello, 87–113. Madrid: Alianza.

Fernández de los Ríos, Ángel. 1868. *El futuro Madrid*. Madrid: Imprenta de la Biblioteca Universal Económica.

Fontanella, Lee. 1981. *La historia de la fotografía en España desde sus orígenes hasta 1900*. Madrid: El Viso.

Fox, E. Inman. 1989. "Introducción." In *Aventuras, inventos y mixtificaciones de Silvestre Paradox*, edited by Pío Baroja, 9–44. Madrid: Espasa-Calpe.

Fraser, Benjamin. 2007a. "Madrid's Retiro Park as Publicly – Private Space and the Spatial Problems of Spatial Theory." *Social & Cultural Geography* 8 (5): 673–700.

———. 2007b. "Manuel Delgado's Urban Anthropology: From Multidimensional Space to Interdisciplinary Spatial Theory." *Arizona Journal of Hispanic Cultural Studies* 11: 57–75.

———. 2011a. *Henri Lefebvre and the Spanish Urban Experience*. Lewisburg, PA: Bucknell University Press.

———. 2011b. "Ildefons Cerdà's Scalpel: A Lefebvrian Perspective on Nineteenth-Century Urban Planning." *Catalan Review* 25: 181–200.

———. 2011c. *La urbanización decimonónica de Madrid: textos de Larra y Mesonero Romanos*. Doral, FL: Stockcero.

———. 2012. *Capital Inscriptions: Essays on Hispanic Literature, Film and Urban Space in Honor of Malcolm Alan Compitello*. Edited by Benjamin Fraser. Newark, DE: Juan de la Cuesta.

———. 2013. "Madrid, Histological City: The Scientific, Artistic and Urbanized Vision of Santiago Ramón y Cajal." *Symposium: A Quarterly Journal of Modern Literatures* 67 (3): 119–134.

Frost, Daniel. 2008. *Cultivating Madrid: Public Space and Middle-Class Culture in the Spanish Capital, 1833–1890*. Lewisburg, PA: Bucknell University Press.

Ginger, Andrew. 2007. "Spanish Modernity Revisited: Revisions of the Nineteenth Century." *Journal of Iberian and Latin American Studies* 13 (2): 121–132.

Goldston, Robert. 1969. *Barcelona: The Civic Stage*. London: Collier-Macmillan Ltd.

Graham, Helen and Jo Labanyi, eds. 2000. *Spanish Cultural Studies: An Introduction*. Oxford: Oxford University Press.

Guía de la Ciudad Lineal. [1928] 2011. Valladolid: MAXTOR.

Haidt, Rebecca. 2005. "Visibly Modern Madrid: Mesonero, Visual Culture and the Apparatus of Urban Reform." In *Visualizing Spanish Modernity*, edited by Susan Larson and Eva Woods, 24–45. New York: Berg.

———. 2009. "Flores en Babilonia: los 'Gritos' de Madrid y el imaginario urbano hacia 1850." *Journal of Spanish Cultural Studies* 10 (3): 299–318.

———. 2011. "Commodifying Place and Time: Photography, Memory, and Media Cultures around 1850." In *On Photography, History and Memory in Spain*, edited by Maria Nilsson. *Hispanic Isues On Line Debates* 3: 10–29.

Hall, Peter. 2002. *Cities of Tomorrow*. Oxford: Blackwell.

Hall, Thomas. 1997. *Planning Europe's Capital Cities: Aspects of Nineteenth – Century Urban Development*. London: E and FN SPON.

Harvey, David. 2006. *Paris: Capital of Modernity*. New York: Routledge.

———. 2012. *Rebel Cities*. London: Verso.

Hughes, Robert. 1992. *Barcelona*. New York: Knopf.

Larson, Susan. 2011. *Constructing and Resisting Modernity: Madrid 1900–1936*. Madrid and Frankfurt: Iberoamericana/Vervuert.

Larson, Susan and Eva Woods, eds. 2005. *Visualizing Spanish Modernity*. Oxford: Berg.

Lefebvre, Henri. 1995. *Introduction to Modernity*. Translated by John Moore. London and New York: Verso.

———. 1996. *Writings on Cities*. Edited and translated by E. Kofman and E. Lebas. Oxford, Blackwell.

———. 2003. *The Urban Revolution*. Translated by Robert Bononno. Minneapolis, MN: University of Minnesota Press.

Lewis, Tom. 1999. "Structures and Agents: The Concept of 'Bourgeois Revolution' in Spain." *Arizona Journal of Hispanic Cultural Studies* 3: 7–16.

Rodríguez Puértolas, Julio. 1988. *Madrid en Galdós, Galdós en Madrid*. Work by Galdós (*Madrid en Galdós* 1988: 198–199). Madrid: Comunidad de; Madrid: Consejería de Cultura.

Mercer, Leigh. 2013. *Urbanism and Urbanity: The Spanish Bourgeois Novel and Contemporary Customs (1845–1925)*. Lewisburg, PA: Bucknell University Press.

Miles, Malcolm. 2007. *Cities and Cultures*. New York: Routledge.

Mumford, Lewis. 1961. *The City in History: Its Origins, Its Transformations, and Its Prospects*. New York: Harcourt, Brace & World.

———. 1970. *The Culture of Cities*. 1938. New York: Harcourt, Brace Jovanovich.

Park, Robert. 1968. "The City: Suggestions for the Investigation of Human Behavior in the Urban Environment." In *The City*, edited by R. E. Park, E. W. Burgess and R. D. McKenzie, 1–46. Chicago: University of Chicago Press.

Parsons, Deborah L. 2003. *A Cultural History of Madrid: Modernism and the Urban Spectacle*. Oxford: Berg.

Ramos, Carlos. 2010. *Construyendo la modernidad: Escritura y arquitectura en el Madrid moderno (1918–1937)*. Lleida: Universitat de Lleida.

Resina, Joan Ramon. 2003. "From Rose of Fire to City of Ivory." In *After – Images of the City*, edited by Joan Ramon Resina and Dieter Ingenschay, 75–122. Cornell, NY: Cornell University Press.

———. 2008. *Barcelona's Vocation of Modernity. Rise and Decline of an Urban Image*. Stanford, CA: Stanford University Press.

Riis, Jacob. 1996. *How the Other Half Lives: Studies Among the Tenements of New York*. Edited by David Leviatin. Boston, MA: Bedford Books of St. Martin's Press.

Rivero Gómez, Miguel Ángel. 2008. "Desarrollo político en el joven Unamuno: Antecedentes de su etapa socialista." In *Miguel de Unamuno: estudios sobre su obra III*, edited by Ana Chaguaceda Toledano, 165–79. Salamanca: Ediciones Universidad Salamanca.

Sennett, Richard. 1992. *The Conscience of the Eye: The Design and Social Life of Cities.* New York: W. W. Norton.

———. 2008. *The Craftsman.* New Haven, CT: Yale University Press.

Serrano, Carlos. 1986. "Unamuno y El Nervión de Bilbao (1893–1895)." In *Volumen-Homenaje cincuentenario de Miguel de Unamuno,* edited by María Dolores Gómez Molleda, 303–322. Salamanca: Universidad de Salamanca.

Simmel, Georg. 2010. "The Metropolis and Mental Life." In *The Blackwell City Reader,* edited by Gary Bridge and Sophie Watson Malden, 103–110. Oxford: Wiley – Blackwell.

Soria y Puig, Arturo. 1996. *Cerdà: las cinco bases de la teoría general de la urbanización.* Barcelona; Madrid: Fundació Catalana per a la Recerca; Sociedad Editorial Electa España.

Subirats, Eduardo. 1981. *La ilustración insuficiente.* Madrid: Taurus.

Ugarte, Michael. 1996. *Madrid 1900: The Capital as Cradle of Literature and Culture.* University Park, PA: Pennsylvania State University Press.

Unamuno, Miguel de. 1999. *Escritos Bilbaínos (1879–1894).* Edited by José Antonio Ereño Altuna and Ana Isasi Saseta. Bilbao: Erando/A. G. Rontegui.

Vázquez Montalbán, Manuel. 1990. *Barcelonas.* Translated by Andy Robinson. London: Verso.

Williams, Raymond. 1973. *The Country and the City.* New York: Oxford University Press.

Zulaika, Joseba. 1999. "'Miracle in Bilbao': Basques in the Casino of Globalism." In *Basque Cultural Studies,* edited by William A. Douglass, Carmelo Urza, Linda White, and Joseba Zulaika, 263–274. Reno, NV: University of Nevada/Basque Studies Program.

———. 2003. *Guggenheim Bilbao Museoa: Museums, Architecture and City Renewal.* Reno, NV: University of Nevada/Center for Basque Studies.

Literature and visual culture

26

BUILDING NATIONS THROUGH WORDS

Iberian identities in nineteenth-century literary historiography[1]

Santiago Pérez Isasi

National identities, literary histories

The birth and expansion of nationalism between 1800 and 1918 is one of the most remarkable phenomena in the history of contemporary European history. In just a little more than 100 years, a relatively marginal ideology managed to become the fundamental principle guiding international relations, with extremely significant, and sometimes tragic, consequences. Of course, nationalism did not materialize out of thin air: it had its roots in eighteenth-century ideas, such as "Herder's belief in the individuality of nations, Rousseau's belief in the sovereignty of the nation, [and] a general discourse of national peculiarities and 'characters'" (Leersen 2006, 125–6). However, the core doctrine of nationalism, as A. Smith calls it, only developed and became prominent during the nineteenth century, and it consisted of a set of propositions which have been summarized as follows:

1 The world is divided into nations, each with its own individuality, history and destiny.
2 The nation is the source of all political and social power, and loyalty to the nation overrides all other allegiances.
3 Human beings must identify with a nation if they want to be free and realize themselves.
4 Nations must be free and secure if peace and justice are to prevail in the world. (1991, 74)

Fascinating as they may be, we will not have time or space to deal with the debates on the relevance, or even existence, of pre-national ethnic communities and traditions (which Anthony Smith defends and Ernest Gellner (1983), among others, denies or minimizes), nor with the conditions that triggered the appearance of national movements that sometimes coincided with preexisting dynastic states (such as Spain, Portugal, France or England), or promoted the creation of new entities by means of unification (Italy or Germany) or separation (Catalonia or Scotland).

When considering, as we intend to do, the construction of Iberian national identities during the nineteenth century, it is important to remember that even in those cases where there existed an established state with fixed boundaries (such as Portugal and Spain), there still was a need to "nationalize" the people, to (re)construct the past of the nation, a task which during the nineteenth century was carried out mostly by a liberal *intelligentsia* using all the resources of political, cultural and social power: a growing centralized bureaucracy, a national army, a new education system, national symbols and commemorations, and so on.

Of course, literature, literary studies and literary history were also affected by this shift in the paradigm of collective identities, which coincided with other significant modifications brought about by Romanticism, in areas such as History, Aesthetics or Poetics. The first wave of Romantic Literary Criticism (cfr. Behler 1993; Bowie 1997), systematized by August Wilhelm and Friedrich Schlegel, respectively, in *Über dramatische Kunst und Literatur* (1809–11) [*Lectures on Dramatic Art and Literature*, 1815] and *Geschichte Der Alten Und Neuen Literatur* (1812) [*Lectures on the History of Literature, Ancient and Modern*, 1842], applied the Herderian concept of *Volksgeist* (meaning "spirit of the people" or "national character") to the study of European and World literatures, firmly establishing the idea that each nation creates art – including literature – according to its national character; and that therefore not all national literatures can be judged by the same criteria (i.e., the classical pseudo-Aristotelian rules), but should be studied individually and historically.

Iberian literatures were no exception in the expansion of this new paradigm of literary history and literary criticism; in fact, Portuguese and, even more significantly, Spanish literature played an important role in the creation of a Romantic scheme of European literatures, by offering an outstanding example of a Southern, Latin, Catholic, Romantic literature which could be opposed to other Northern, Germanic and Classical literatures, and which demanded, in their view, a specific set of critical tools different from the ones provided by classical literary theory. These ideas contributed, or quite simply provoked, the recovery and reconsideration of Spanish and Portuguese medieval poetry, and particularly of seventeenth-century Spanish drama, with Calderón de la Barca as the champion of Catholic and Romantic literature.

It can be no surprise, then, that the first literary histories of both Spanish and Portuguese literatures were written by foreigners, and published outside the Iberian Peninsula: for instance, the *Geschichte der Poesie und Beredsamkeit seit dem Ende des dreizehnten Jahrhunderts* [*History of Poetry and Eloquence from the End of the Thirteenth Century*], published by Friedrich Bouterwek between 1801 and 1819, which was partially translated as *Historia de la literatura española* in 1829; Jean Charles Léonard Simonde de Sismondi's *De la Littérature du Midi de l'Europe* [*On the Literature of the South of Europe*] (1813–4), again partially translated as *Historia de la literatura española* (1841–2); Ferdinand Denis's *Résumé de l'histoire littéraire de Portugal* [*Summary of Portuguese Literary History*], published in Paris in 1826; and the *History of Spanish Literature* written by George Ticknor in 1849 and translated into Spanish in 1851–6. The image of Iberian literatures – and nations – was therefore first developed abroad, by foreigners, and only later (mainly after 1850) adopted and adapted by the inhabitants of the Iberian Peninsula themselves, who in some cases modified or rejected, but in many others simply perpetuated, the views and configurations of their history supplied by these foreign scholars.

In the following pages, I offer some considerations on the way in which the Iberian Peninsula as a whole, and the Spanish and Portuguese nations individually, were conceptualized in the literary histories written during the nineteenth century. I hope to show how the Romantic vision of Spain and Portugal conditioned both the formation of the literary canon in each of these countries, and the narrative literary history constructed with it.

The idea of "Iberia"

As we have seen, the first wave of European Romanticism constructed a critical, philosophical and historiographical system that incorporated a very specific view of the ethnic, cultural and geopolitical distribution of nations in Europe and worldwide. This new conception of the world established the existence of nations with recognizable characters and features, which were permanent through history and yet could be captured in the form of historical narrations. As we have also pointed out, this Romantic conceptualization divided nations into families or categories, such as Classical versus Romantic, Catholic versus Protestant, Germanic versus Latin, etc. These classifications do, in fact, overlap to some extent (e.g., they tend to appear integrated as Northern, Germanic, Protestant versus Southern, Latin, Catholic), but they are not mutually interchangeable, since they do not always respond well to these amalgamations and can vary from one literary critic to the other. For instance, Mme de Stäel establishes a triple division of European peoples, between Latin, Germanic and Slavic, as opposed to the twofold divisons that appear in the Schlegel brothers' works:

> On peut rapporter l'origine des principales nations de l'Europe à trois grandes races différentes: la race latine, la race germanique et la race esclavonne. Les Italiens, les Français, les Espagnols, ont reçu des Romains leur civilisation et leur langage; les Allemands, les Suisses, les Anglais, les Suédois, les Danois et les Hollandais sont des peuples teutoniques; enfin, parmi les Esclavons, les Polonais et les Russes occupent le premier rang. Les nations dont la culture intellectuelle est d'origine latine sont plus anciennement civilisées que les autres. [The origin of the main nations in Europe can be brought back to three different races: the Latin race, the Germanic race and the Slavic race. The Italians, Spanish and French people have received their civilization and their language from the Romans; the Germans, Swiss, English, Swedish, Danish and Dutch are Teutonic peoples; finally, among the Slavic peoples the Polish and the Russians occupy the first rank. The nations in which the intellectual culture has a Latin origin were civilized earlier than the others.]
>
> (de Stäel 1813: I, 45)

The Iberian Peninsula was consistently classified, as a whole, among the Southern, Latin, Catholic nations (the European *Midi* or *Meridione*), but with a strong Romantic component, as demonstrated by Simonde de Sismondi's history:

> Nous avons trouvé dans toute l'Europe méridionale, ce mélange d'amour, de chevalerie et de religion, qui a formé les moeurs romantiques, et qui a donné à la poésie un caractère particulier. [We have found in all of Southern Europe a mixture of love, chivalry and religion, which formed the romantic customs and gave their poetry a particular character.]
>
> (Sismondi 1813–4: IV, 557)

This concept of the South, of course, is not just a geographical indication, but a complex ideological operation (cfr. Vecchi 2013, Domínguez 2006) that idealizes Iberia and at the same time transforms it into a primitive, exotic and wild space, almost in association with the myth of the "noble savage." As Sismondi puts it, "ils vivent encore avec la nature" [they still live among nature] (Sismondi 1813–4: IV, 270).

This view of the Iberian Peninsula must then be analyzed in relation with the general classification of nations, according to ethno-linguistic, religious or aesthetic criteria, but also in relation to the opposition between centers and peripheries within Europe. And the center of the system, of course, is situated in the northern European countries (Germany, France and

England). In the southern part of Europe, only Italy is qualified as "central," for instance, by Friedrich Schlegel in his *Lectures on the History of Literature, Ancient and Modern*:

> It is quite evident that four countries alone in the centre of Europe, Italy, Germany, France, and England, as they have occupied the first place in the political history of modern Europe, so in the history of literature also have they distinguished themselves to such a degree, that from the time of the first awakening of the European intellect under Charlemagne, down to the present day, it is scarcely possible to point out a single great incident in the annals of philosophy, a single remarkable discovery, extension, retrogression, or error,–or, in short, to fix upon a single great name in the history of philosophy, which does not belong to one of them.
>
> (F. Schlegel 1841, 232)

Not only are Iberian literatures peripheral in the European context but also for some historians they are not even *strictly speaking* European, given their geographical position, their cultural isolation and their close relation with the East. This idea of Iberia's isolation from Europe appears in F. Schlegel ("Spain remained at all times cut off in some measure from the other districts of Europe, not more by geographical position, politics, constitution, and manners, than by her peculiarity both of language and of intellectual cultivation," 1841, 227–8) and Simonde de Sismondi ("D'ailleurs, [la littérature Portuguaise] c'est une littérature qui est hors de la portée du reste de l'Europe" [Furthermore, Portuguese literature is beyond the reach of the rest of Europe], 1813–4: IV, 262), and has a strong rhetorical and ideological tradition that prevails even to this day.

This peripherality of the Iberian nations is reflected in the ignorance – or fragmentary or imperfect knowledge – of their respective literatures, notable in the critics and historians themselves: A. W. Schlegel, Bouterwek or Sismondi are just a few examples of significant authors who, although they included Iberian literatures in their works, admitted that they knew little about them. This gap in the knowledge of Iberian literatures is particularly blatant in the case of Portuguese literature. For instance, F. Denis begins his *Résumé* with a chapter entitled, "Pourquoi la littérature portuguaise est peu connue" [Why Portuguese literature is little known].[2] Sismondi's case is also extreme: in his work he accepts that he knows close to nothing about Portuguese literature, and that he follows almost to the letter what Bouterwek had previously written on this subject – which, naturally, brought him fierce criticism from Portuguese scholars later in the century (Sismondi 1813–4: IV, 262). Of course, this lack of knowledge gives these early literary histories what we could call a "civilizing" purpose: by filling gaps in the knowledge of the European past, they are offering (or recovering) cultural and artistic models for those same countries that were "left behind" by the history of European nations. This combination of both retrospective and prospective intentions (narrating the past to modify the present and the future) is implicit in all literary histories, and even explicit in some of them, such as Schack's *Geschichte der dramatischen Literatur and Kunst in Spanien* [*History of Spanish Dramatic Literature and Art*] (1845–6), translated into Spanish as *Historia de la Literatura y del Arte Dramático en España* (1885):

> A los españoles podrá servir este ensayo de una historia de su literatura dramática . . . para recordarles vivamente el periodo de su grandeza y originalidad literaria, y a exhortarlos quizás, en medio del tumulto de sus luchas actuales de partido, a no olvidarse de aquellos grandes hombres que llenaron de orgullo a sus abuelos, y cuya memoria debe ser entre ellos sempiterna, si no quieren despreciarse a sí mismos.
>
> (1885: I, 47)

We have spoken, so far, without distinction, of Spanish and Portuguese literatures as "Iberian literatures." Do Romantic literary histories offer a unified image of both Iberian nations? The answer to this question must be dual, and somewhat paradoxical: Romantic literary histories insist on the similarity and the continuity between the two countries, but also on their mutual independence and individuality. This is the case with Bouterwek's *Geschichte* (the volumes devoted to Spanish and Portuguese literature were in fact translated together into English in 1847); Sismondi's *De la littérature* (1813–14) and, a bit later, the *Studien zur Geschichte der Spanischen und Portugiesischen Nationalliteratur* [*Studies on the History of Spanish and Portuguese National Literatures*] (1859) by Ferdinand Wolf (1840), translated into Spanish by Miguel de Unamuno, and annotated by Marcelino Menéndez y Pelayo, with the title *Historia de las literaturas castellana y portuguesa*. However, all of these works are structured on the principle of nationality and national literatures; this is to say that even if Iberian literatures are shown to be close neighbors and even members of a common family, they are also studied in different chapters, books or volumes, separated even in relation to those times when the two nations were part of a diverse cultural, linguistic and political continuum (such as before 1492, when the Iberian frontiers were stabilized almost definitively), or when they were united under a common dynasty (between 1580 and 1640). Continuity and unity are hinted at or pointed out in the text, but diversity and separation are much more strongly suggested by the configuration of the historiographical work itself. We cannot really speak of a history of Iberian literatures, but of the histories of Spanish and Portuguese literatures brought together by geographical proximity and certain historical and cultural connections.

This tension between unity and diversity, proximity and separation, continuity and difference, is present in several of the first nineteenth-century literary histories, such as F. Schlegel's, Bouterwek's or Sismondi's:

> Le royaume de Portugal fait proprement partie de l'Espagne; les Portugais eux-mêmes se considèrent comme Espagnols, et en prennent le nom, tandis qu'ils appellent toujours castillan le peuple leur voisin et leur rival, qui partage avec eux la souveraineté de l'Espagne. Cependant, le Portugal a une littérature à lui; sa langue, au lieu de demeurer un dialecte de l'espagnol, a été regardée, par un peuple independant, comme une marque de sa souveraineté, et a été cultivée avec amour. [Strictly speaking, the kingdom of Portugal is a part of Spain; the Portuguese themselves consider themselves to be Spaniards, and they adopt that name, although they still call "Castilian" the people of their neighbor and rival, which shares with them the sovereignty of Spain. Nevertheless, Portugal has a literature of its own; instead of remaining just a dialect of Spanish, the Portuguese language has been seen by this independent people as a sign of its own sovereignty, and they have cultivated it with love.][3]
>
> (Sismondi 1813–4: IV, 261)

To sum up, both Iberian nations form a historical and literary unity, when considered from the distant point of view of the European (literary, cultural and political) center; they are together and similar in their geographical, linguistic and historical isolation; they are both, then, peripheral and Southern – with all the consequences that this entails. However, when they are compared with one another, differences and discontinuities become apparent – at least from the point of view of the Romantic definition of national literatures: one nation, one *Volksgeist*, one literature. And when Spanish and Portuguese literary histories start to be written by Iberian historians themselves, any idea of Iberian proximity and continuity vanish quite quickly: these literary histories, written mainly from 1850 onwards, may mention occasionally the other

Iberian nation and literature (more frequently in the case of Portuguese literary histories than the other way round), but they always establish very clear boundaries and limits that coincide, as we might expect, with the political territories of the nineteenth-century states of Spain and Portugal.

The next part of this chapter is devoted, precisely, to understanding how the Spanish and the Portuguese *Volksgeist* differed from that of other European nations, and from each other, and the consequences these differences had in the formation of their literary canons and the construction of their literary histories.

The chivalrous Spaniards, the sweet Portuguese

As we have seen, historians such as F. Schlegel, Sismondi or Bouterwek considered the Iberian Peninsula as a historical and cultural unity that was severed from the rest of Europe and preserved its common peculiarities through time; however, this unity and continuity disappears, as we have also seen, when we consider Spain and Portugal separately. And this is what happens in nineteenth-century literary histories when they are devoted to each of the national literatures, from their birth to the present moment, as we see herein.

It is common in Spanish and Portuguese literary historiographies to identify the Middle Ages with the moment when both national characters are created.[4] The Middle Ages are the starting point for most literary histories too: the birth of the nation is equated with the birth of the romance languages, and therefore literatures. This medieval period also provides what became a key element in the conceptualization of Iberian literatures: the Islamic conquest of the Iberian Peninsula and the long years of struggle (or peaceful coexistence, depending on the historian) between Eastern and Western peoples.[5] This same idea is repeated in almost every history of the nineteenth century (see Pérez Isasi 2011). According to the Romantic vision, the Christian inhabitants of the Iberian Peninsula simultaneously rejected and were influenced by the long centuries of war and cohabitation with the Moors: they fought against them, but also lived with them; they adopted some of their key customs, and reaffirmed some of their own in opposition. This is why the Iberian Peninsula is often referred to as an "Eastern space," or as a bridge between Europe and Asia: an imaginary *locus* filled with often fantastic connotations (César Domínguez 2006). Iberian "orientalism" is easier to find, in fact, in the histories written by foreigners, and progressively disappears as the century progresses, and as Iberian scholars contribute more to literary historiography.[6]

Here I stress two more points regarding the "birth" of the Iberian nations and literatures: firstly, that the Moors (and, for that matter, any inhabitants of the Iberian Peninsula before the Visigoths) are not considered, as such, Spaniards or Portuguese, and therefore no effort is made by historians to include them or their literary productions in the narration of the history of Iberian literatures; secondly, that this mixture of gruesome war and friendly cultural exchange between peoples is crucial to the way in which Romanticism conceptualized both the Spanish and Portuguese *Volksgeist*: as fighters for freedom and religion (in the case of Spain), or as peaceful, bucolic poets (in the case of Portugal).

There are, in fact, three main characteristics of Spanishness which stand out in these first foreign attempts to write the history of Spanish literature (cfr. Pérez Isasi 2013): orientalism; chivalry (connected with an exacerbated sense of honour and with a sense of gallantry); and piety or religiosity. All of them appear with surprising regularity in the histories of Spanish literature written in the first half of the nineteenth century, for instance in Sismondi, Ticknor or Schack:

La nación española otro tiempo tan valerosa, tan caballeresca, y cuyo orgullo y dignidad son proverbiales en Europa, se ha retratado al vivo en su literatura.

(Sismondi 1841, I: 2)

Hay en la literatura española dos signos tan peculiares y exclusivos de ella, que es forzoso fijarlos desde el principio como puntos de partida, a saber la fe religiosa y la lealtad caballeresca.

(Ticknor 1851–1856, I: 109)

A semejante resultado contribuyeron los dos grandes factores de la civilización moderna, cuyas consecuencias han sido en todos uniformes, a saber: el espíritu caballeresco y la influencia del cristianismo.

(Schack 1885–1888, I: 87)

Spanish literary historians, reluctant as they were to accept the idea of Iberian orientalism, happily accepted, however, the other two characteristics: in Amador's *Historia crítica*, for example, we can read that "*Dios* y la *patria*: he aquí el doble dogma del arte castellano" (Amador de los Ríos 1861–1865, III: 4), and Gil de Zárate, too, explicitly defines Spanishness as "religion, honour and gallantry":

La religión, el honor y la galantería: estos son como hemos visto los tres ejes sobre los cuales ha girado la civilización de los tiempos medios, y las tres fuentes de todas las bellezas propias de su literatura. Estas tres causas han influido poderosamente en nuestra patria, y tal vez con más eficacia que en ninguna parte.

(Gil de Zárate 1844, I: 11)

Of course, this characterization of the Spanish national character has, as we have already pointed out, deep implications for the formation of the national canon. For instance, the supremacy given to "chivalry" and "piety" in the definition of the national character implied giving more importance to certain genres, such as epic or mystic poetry, and underestimating, on the contrary, others such as lyric poetry or the novel (with the obvious exception of Cervantes's *Don Quixote*). In the case of Spanish literature, this essentially meant gathering popular "romances" (short popular, epic-lyrical medieval poems which had already attracted the attention of Herder and F. Schlegel) as they were considered to constitute the "true national poetry:"

Ya hemos visto en el poema del Cid y aún volveremos a ver en los romances la poesía de los guerreros, la poesía verdaderamente nacional, la que guarda perfecta armonía con las costumbres, las esperanzas y los recuerdos de todo un pueblo, la que está inspirada por el entusiasmo y la que servía para conservarle en el corazón y en la mente de los españoles.

(Sismondi 1841–2: I, 55)

Medieval epic poetry (which included both long epic poems such as the *Mio Cid*, and the much shorter "romances") was not the only genre exalted as "national:" from the very origins of German Romanticism, Spanish Golden Age drama was singled out as the perfect representative of Spanishness (because of its identification with Catholicism, honour and gallantry), especially the work of Calderón de la Barca; in the first half of the nineteenth century Lope de Vega was considered his inferior or immediate predecessor (although the balance shifted towards Lope in the second half of the century).

The case of Portugal is different to the Spanish one in some key aspects. Firstly, Portuguese literature was deemed of secondary importance by European Romanticism, with the single exception of Luis de Camões, who was considered a true literary genius. Its reception was, in a way and up to a point, mediated by that of Spanish literature, with which it was supposed to share a geographical and, above all, ideological or symbolic space. As noted previously, in foreign literary histories both literatures tend to appear closely linked, as is the case, for instance, of Bouterwek's *Geschichte*, which not only often makes frequent references to Spanish literature in the chapters devoted to Portuguese literature, but also concludes with a very significant section entitled "Comparison of Portuguese and Spanish literatures." This does not mean that Portuguese literature lacks individuality or that it is in no way different from Spain; in fact, Romantic historians stress that, because of its long tradition of political independence, the Portuguese nation and its language and literature acquired very specific and unique features; quite different, in fact, from those of the Spaniards. Instead of the fierce brutality of the Spanish nation, the Portuguese are characterized as a sweet, soft, friendly nation, devoted to poetry and the arts, favoured by the climate and washed by the Atlantic Ocean. Nouns such as "sweetness," "tenderness" or "softness" often appear as *leitmotifs* when referring to the Portuguese language, literature or national character.

References to the climate are not fortuitous: in fact, Sismondi justifies the Portuguese *Volksgeist* with reference to its geographical and climatic conditions, opposing the roughness of mountains to the soft influence of the sea: "D'ailleurs la langue est adoucie, come le sont le plus souvent les dialectes des côtes, par opposition aux langues rudes et sonores des montagnes" [Furthermore, the language is sweetened, as often happens with coastal dialects, as opposed to the rude and sonorous languages of the mountains] (Sismondi 1813–4: IV, 262). Portuguese historians themselves, such as Borges de Figueiredo, for example, also mention these same elements, climate and language ("um clima encantador, uma lingua sonora e majestosa," 1844, 151), thus accepting the self-image proposed by center-European historians.

If chivalry and piety were the main features of Spanish national identity according to early Romantic historians, the Portuguese are characterized not only by "tenderness" but also by a certain "technical ability," which manifests itself in different ways: in their capacity to navigate the seas, but also in their literary dexterity and scientific interests:

> O amor ás Lettras, e a aptidao intellectual para as cultivar com dignidade e aproveitamento é um dos caracteres da gente Portugueza.
>
> (Carvalho 1845, 17)

> Na verdade a propensão para as Letras e sua cultura data entre nós de tão longe, que era opiniao corrente, dominando o Imperador Octaviano Augusto, que os Turdulos ou Turdetânos, isto é, os habitadores naquelle tempo de grande parte da Andaluzia e Algarve, ou, para melhor dizer, os seus antepassados, que moravam entre o Tejo e o Douro, eram os mais doutos dos Hespanhoes; pois usavam de *Grammatica* [. . .] e conservavam muitas poesias e leis, postas em verso, com varios monumentos de grande antiguidade, em que não só mostravam as gloriosas memorias dos seus progenitores, mas a elevada sciencia dos seus antepassados.
>
> (Carvalho 1845, 20)

Again, this definition of a national character is not a rhetorical preliminary merely packaged together with the rest of the literary history: it is, on the contrary, as we have already said, a theoretical and ideological framework that conditions the selection of literary works, genres and periods. In the case of Portuguese literature, the predominance of "tenderness" and technical ability (over, for instance, religiosity and chivalry), makes lyrical and bucolic poetry the preferred genre, at least until the appearance of Camões, the cornerstone of the Portuguese literary canon:

> A amenidade do clima de Portugal e ao gosto pelos prazeres campestres que sempre tiveram os seus habitantes cumpre attribuir a appariçao da poesia bucolica n'alvorada de sua civilizaçao, e o gráo d'aperfeiçoamento que reveláram os seus primeiros ensaios.
>
> (Pinheiro 1862, 26)

Conclusions

As we pointed out at the beginning of this article, it would not be possible to argue that nineteenth-century nationalist movements appeared without precedent: they were built upon a previous rhetorical, political and anthropological tradition, which was then used for national movements and parties to create a self-image, often in opposition to the *other*, the outsider, the "barbarian." However, as we have also pointed out, it was only in the nineteenth century that these ideas were systematized and applied to the (re)construction and diffusion (most frequently in a top-down manner) of specific national identities, which in some cases coincided with previously established dynastic states (as was the case of Spain and Portugal). Literary history, closely linked with the new state-based education system, was one of the tools used in this nationalization process, and it was dependent on the principles of early Romantic criticism: the idea that the world is divided into nations; that each nation has a *Volksgeist* or "national character," and that this character was clearly visible in the literary productions of each nation. Not only that but Romantic literary criticism also established that there was a difference between groups of nations and literatures: some were Classical, and could be judged according to the Classical principles of Poetics and Rhetoric, while others were Romantic and had developed a new literary or poetic model which was still waiting to be described and systematized.

This philosophical, critical and historiographical paradigm was put into practice in relation to European and World literatures, and also, of course, in relation to Iberian literatures: Center-European historians created a vision of the Iberian Peninsula as a peripheral, exotic, Southern unity, severed from the rest of Europe and conditioned by its long centuries of interaction with the Moors; an image that combined an idea of Iberian unity with the national duality that corresponded with the two dynastic states of Spain and Portugal. This means that nineteenth-century literary historians also created (or described, as they would put it) a series of features related with each of the national characters: chivalry, gallantry and piety in the case of Spanish literature; tenderness and technical ability in the case of the Portuguese. While Iberian historians in some cases rejected the vision that came from abroad (for example, in relation to the oriental character of Iberian peoples and literatures), they in any case conditioned greatly the way in which they wrote their own literary histories during the nineteenth century.

In the short pages of this article, we have not been able to analyze with any detail the historiographical consequences of these ideological constructions of the Iberian nations. It is obvious, however, that different works, authors, genres and periods are privileged accordingly and transformed into the center of each of the literary canons, for instance, medieval epic poetry and Golden Age theater, which are considered to best represent the Catholic and chivalrous Spain, and lyrical and bucolic poetry in the case of Portuguese literature. Of course, a much more detailed analysis of both the Spanish and the Portuguese literary canon would be needed to do justice to all the nuances and variations to these very general considerations: the subtle (or not so subtle) differences between historians and histories; the complexity of the Romantic aesthetic and historiographical project; or the evolution and modification of these very general concepts through the nineteenth and until at least the first half of the twentieth century.

Notes

1 This article is a result of my ongoing research project, "Nationalism and Literary Regenerations in the Iberian Peninsula (1868–1936)," funded by the Fundação para a Ciência e a Tecnologia of Portugal (Ref. IF/00838/2014).
2 He even risks a geographical and geopolitical explanation: "Cela tient sans doute à la position géographique du Portugal, et plus encore aux relations politiques des deux pays. Les Portugais, puissants en Asie, n'etaient rien en Europe; l'Espagne imposa ses lois et ses arts à une partie des peuples voisins" [This has to do, no doubt, with the geographical position of Portugal, and even more with the political relations of both countries. Portugal, powerful in Asia, was nothing in Europe; Spain imposed its laws and arts to some of its neighbors] (Deniz 1826, 2).
3 This same idea of diversity-in-unity lies at the heart of many of the texts that supported cultural Iberianism in the second half of the nineteenth century, such as Oliveira Martins' *História da Civilização Ibérica* (1879). In the worlds of Teófilo Braga, for example, "No problema da raça não ha hespanhões nem portugueses. A separaçao começa na formação da nacionalidade" (Braga 1872, 12).
4 The *Historia Crítica de la Literatura Española* by Amador de los Ríos, published between 1861 and 1865 in seven volumes, is an exception to this rule: de los Ríos starts his history from the very first texts written in the Iberian Peninsula, in Latin, Hebrew and Arabic. However, he did not get to complete this very ambitious work: the seventh volume ends at the beginning of the sixteenth century.
5 According to Amador de los Ríos, for instance: "Fórmase en esta lucha [la Reconquista] el pueblo español propiamente dicho . . . ella es el campo siempre abierto, donde se fortalecen sus creencias, donde nace y florece su patriotismo, donde se crea, finalmente, su carácter" (Amador de los Ríos 1861–5, I, XCIX); and in the case of Portugal: "No celebrado campo d'Ourique, onde cinco estandartes mouriscos cáem nas maos dos Portuguezes; proclamado rei, Affonso Henriques funda a monarchia, e dá as primeiras leis a um povo amante da independencia e da victoria" (Borges de Figueiredo 1844, 153).
6 It still appears, for instance, in Schack's work, written in 1849: "Este rasgo característico de su fisonomía, que proviene de la influencia de un pueblo no europeo, y es efecto de la unión de los dos elementos oriental y occidental, la distingue de manera singular" (Schack 1885–1888, I: 87). However, it is interesting to note that the Spanish translators of Simonde de Sismondi's *De la littérature* already rejected, in 1841, this idea of Spain as an Eastern, or at least mixed nation: "Tampoco es exacto lo que asienta el autor pocas líneas más arriba cuando dice que la literatura española difiere esencialmente de las demás de Europa, y que puede decirse que éstas son europeas mientras que aquella es oriental. Nuestra literatura ha tenido diversas épocas y no deben confundirse en un juicio común" (Simonde de Sismondi 1841, I: 29, note A).

Works cited

Amador de los Ríos, José. 1861–5. *Historia crítica de la literatura española*. 7 vols. Madrid: Imprenta de José Rodríguez.
Behler, Ernst. 1993. *German Romantic Literary Theory*. Cambridge: Cambridge University Press.
Borges de Figueiredo, Antonio Cardoso. 1844. *Bosquejo histórico da Litteratura Classica, Grega, Latina e Portugueza*. Coimbra: Imprensa da Universidade.

Bouterwek, Friedrich. 1847. *History of Spanish and Portuguese Literature*. London: David Vogue.

———. 1829 [2002]. *Historia de la literatura española*. Madrid: Verbum.

Bowie, Andrew. 1997. *From Romanticism to Critical Theory*. London: Routledge.

Braga, Teófilo. 1872. *Theoria da historia da litteratura portugueza*. Porto: Imprensa Portugueza.

Carvalho, Francisco Freire de. 1845. *Primeiro Ensaio sobre Historia Litteraria de Portugal*. Lisboa: Typographia Rollandiana.

Denis, Ferdinand. 1826. *Résumé de l'histoire litteraire de Portugal*. Paris: Leconte e Durey.

de Staël, Anne Louise Germaine. 1813 [1968]. *De l'Allemagne*. París: GF-Flammarion.

Domínguez, César. 2006. "The South European Orient: A Comparative Reflection on Space in Literary History." *Modern Language Quarterly* 67 (4): 419–449.

Gellner, Ernst. 1983. *Nations and Nationalism*. New York: Cornell University Press.

Gil de Zárate, Antonio. 1844. *Resumen histórico de la literatura española*. 3 vols. Madrid: Boix.

Leersen, Joep. 2006. *National Thought in Europe. A Cultural History*. Amsterdam: Amsterdam University Press.

Pérez Isasi, Santiago. 2011. "The Origins of the Portuguese and Spanish Nations in Romantic Literary History." Proceedings of conference *Europe of Nationalities*, Universidade de Aveiro, 9–11 May 2011. CD-ROM.

———. 2013. "The Limits of Spanishness in 19th-Century Literary History." *Bulletin of Hispanic Studies* 90 (2): 167–188.

Pinheiro, Joaquim Caetano Fernandes. 1862. *Curso elementar de litteratura nacional*. Rio de Janeiro: Livraria de B. L. Garnier.

Schack, Adolfo Federico de. 1885. *Historia de la Literatura y del Arte Dramático en España*. Madrid: Imprenta y Fundición de M. Tello.

Schlegel, August Wilhelm. 1815. *Lectures on Dramatic Art and Literature*. London: Baldwin, Cradock and Joy.

Schlegel, Friedrich. 1841. *Lectures on the History of Literature, Ancient and Modern*. New York: J. & H.G. Langley.

Simonde de Sismondi, Jean-Charles-Leonard. 1813–1814: *De la litterature du Midi de l'Europe*, 4 vols. Paris: Treuttel & Wurtz.

———. 1841–1842. *Historia de la literatura española*. Sevilla: Imprenta de Álvarez y Compañía.

Smith, Anthony. 1991. *National Identity*. Reno, NV: University of Nevada Press.

Ticknor, George. 1851–1856. *Historia de la Literatura Española*. 4 vols. Madrid: Imprenta de la Publicidad.

Vecchi, Roberto. 2013. "Thinking from Europe about an Iberian 'South': Portugal as a Case Study." In *Looking at Iberia*, edited by Santiago Pérez Isasi and Ângela Fernandes, 69–85. Oxford: Peter Lang.

Wolf, Ferdinand. 1840. *Historia de las literaturas castellana y portuguesa*. 2 vols. Madrid: La España Moderna.

27

THE POETIZED PEOPLING OF NINETEENTH-CENTURY SPAIN/S[1]

Ronald Puppo

The social and spiritual dislocation concomitant to the political and industrial jolts of nineteenth-century Spain ushered in a multilingual polyphony of poets' voices rising often from Spain's distinct peripheral cultures and language communities. Particularly striking in the poetic statement of peripheral stamp are the groundbreaking works of Galicia's Rosalía de Castro (1837–1885) and Catalonia's Jacint Verdaguer (1845–1902). Rosalía de Castro's landmark poetry volumes in Galician, *Cantares gallegos* (1863) and *Follas novas* (1880), stand as watershed achievements in Galician literature whose impact touches also on the historical, given their decisive role in the recovery of the Galician language, for centuries dormant as a vehicle of written culture. Furthermore, the fact that the foundational voice of Galicia's *Rexurdimento* was a woman's amounts to a quantum leap in gaining ground against a male-dominated discursive network, despite efforts for decades to package the woman and her poetry under a parochial label. In Catalonia, it was the rural-bred Jacint Verdaguer's prolific works of poetry in Catalan – above all, his *L'Atlàntida* (1878) and *Canigó* (1886), foundational epics of Spain and Catalonia, respectively – that would prove decisive in projecting the Catalan language both at home and abroad, laying the literary and, *pari passu*, linguistic groundwork for the recovery of Catalan far beyond the vernacular. Later, amid literary triumph and acclaim, the poet-priest's long, bitter and widely publicized clash with his own Church higher-ups in Barcelona would polarize public opinion, forcing onto discursive platforms of the day sharp debate not only about the man's character, but also about the meaning of Christian faith and practice as well. Verdaguer, for whom the transcendence sought by humankind was unquestionably divine (he was, after all, a Catholic priest), nevertheless turned his poetic attention, as did Castro, also to worldly injustice, producing a number of poems classifiable as *social* poetry.

A peripheral people womanly voiced: Rosalía de Castro

Although Rosalía de Castro stands, unquestionably, as the uncontested foundational figure of the *Rexurdimento*, Rosalian scholarship during the past half-century has argued repeatedly and convincingly that the image of the woman projected for several decades by critics – beginning with her own husband Manuel Murguía (1833–1923) – is one that was intentionally skewed. In her seminal article, Davies (1983) reviews salient mid-twentieth-century Rosalian criticism while stressing the need for a new approach to the woman and her work, punctuating the social clout of many of her poems and other writings, and pointing out how Rosalía de Castro "was in more than one sense a real danger to Restoration society:"

> El sistema se considera obligado a defenderse de una serie de peligros ofrecidos por Rosalía de Castro: novedades formales, imaginación y sensibilidad, la "filosofía" alemana, la mujer compitiendo con el hombre y, . . . el galleguismo frente al centralismo.
>
> (C. Blanco Aguinaga et al., *Historia social de la literatura española* [Madrid: Castalia, 1979], vol. 2, 136 [as quoted in Davies 1983, 218])

Elaborating further on the vital link between the writer and her social context, Bermúdez (2002, xx–xxvi), Davies (1990, 11–16) and Lama López (1995, 11–19) have outlined the turbulent social and political backdrop, which looms all the larger in Castro given her husband's high-profile role as political and cultural activist:

> Murguía asociábase non soamente á causa progresista radical, senón tamén ó provincialismo galego [. . .] Murguía sería eminente historiador e polígrafo e axiña se converteu en líder e primeiro teórico do movemento nacionalista galego en xermolo, responsable máis tarde da fundación da Real Academia Galega no 1906.
>
> (Davies 1990, 8–9)

By the same token, Murguía was to prove instrumental in the publication, dissemination and reception of Castro's works: "a débeda con Murguía é inmensa no que respecta ás relacións coas institucións e o mercado" (Lama López 2007, 178). On the other hand, Murguía projected an image of his wife's contribution to advancing Galician letters and culture within a progressive political framework that would nonetheless be tempered by prevailing mores concerning the accepted scope of women writers, thus staking out a critical trend that passed over a more accurate, more complete Castro in all her heterodoxy (I follow Geoffrion-Vinci in referring to the poet and novelist by her last name – despite the prevalence of "Rosalía" in Galician- and Spanish-language reception – since, as Geoffrion-Vinci [2002, 5] points out, calling her by her first name "fails to accurately valorize this important literary figure's status as a writer and an intellectual"). Thus, tailoring "Rosalía" to fit the gender roles of the day, Murguía "establece as principais liñas de interpretación da súa obra, condicionando a crítica posterior en grande medida" (Lama López 2007, 178). The frequently cited woman-violet comparison speaks eloquently of Murguía's notion of a woman's place:

> Siempre se dirá de la mujer que, como la violeta, tanto más escondida vive, tanto es mejor el perfume que exhala. La mujer debe ser sin hechos y sin biografía, pues siempre hay en ella algo a que no debe tocarse. Limitada su acción al círculo de la vida doméstica, todo sanctifica desde que entra en su hogar. Tiene en la tierra una misión de los cielos.
>
> (as quoted in Lama López 2007, 176)

Olga Castro (2012, 209), in her study of Rosalian works disseminated in English translation, finds additional examples of this "motherly" and "saintly" image being paid tribute, exported abroad as paratextual commentary accompanying translations well into the twentieth century:

Son obras que en cierta manera enfatizan el mito galaico construido alrededor del símbolo de la *naiciña*, la *santiña*, la mujer llorona y desasosegada y, en definitiva, la imagen rosaliana mitificada y canonizada que borra completamente su discurso transgresor de género.

This saintly and trivializing distortion of the poet and, by extension, also of Galicia itself as depicted by her, amounts to the disempowerment of both the woman and the land:

> converter unha e outra – Rosalía e a Galiza – nunha realidade defunta, inexistente a efeitos práticos e concretos, converté-las a ambas en símbolos inofensivos, en iconos moi grabados en determinados planos de retórica compensatoria, mais descargados de toda forza, de toda virtualidade real e ferinte.
>
> (Pilar García Negro, "A orixinalidade de Rosalía." In *Rosalía de Castro. Unha obra non asumida* [A Coruña: Xistral, 1985], 34 [as quoted in Lama López 2007, 173])

Paradoxically, this disempowerment stands in stark contrast to Castro's signal achievement. Alonso Montero (1972, 30, 59–60), for instance, has shown how the publication in 1863 of *Cantares gallegos* marks the end of the prehistory of the *Rexurdimento*, ushering in Galicia's modern literary history. Underscoring the magnitude of the event, the Real Academia Galega – on the occasion of the centennial of Castro's 1863 signing of a copy of *Cantares* dedicated to Fernán Caballero – instituted 17 May as the Día das Letras Galegas.

Despite the fact that, seventeen years later, the publication in 1880 of *Follas novas* would mark yet another historic year in Galician letters (Alonso Montero 1972, 62–87; Carballo Calero [1974] 2013, 20–21; Davies 1990, 18–19), the end of the Democratic Sexennial (1868–1874) spelled hardship for Murguía and Castro, with repercussions on the reception of her works – marginal in Spain, yet thriving in Galician communities across the Atlantic:

> por estar Rosalía implicada co rexionalismo de Murguía, co reformismo e o anti-clericalismo, por ser a súa unha voz inconformista, a súa poesía publicada despois de 1875 non recibiu en España o recoñecemento merecido. Só as comunidades gale-gas de La Habana e Buenos Aires aclamaron a Rosalía con entusiasmo e mesmo a axudaron a publicar os seus traballos.
>
> (Davies 1990, 20)

Particularly significant was the role of the Galician community in Havana, where the Real Academia Galega was founded the year before its official inauguration in A Coruña in 1906, with Murguía presiding over the institution from its inception until 1923. The first edition of *Cantares* had sold widely in Cuba, where Galician expatriates were culturally active and supportive of Murguía and Castro, and where the first edition of *Follas novas* was published:

> Resulta revelador de la cada vez mayor dependencia del galleguismo cultural de la metrópoli cubana que el segundo libro de Rosalía fuera directamente publicado allí [. . .] De La Habana llega el dinero que funda escuelas laicas en la abandonada Galicia, con-struye carreteras, ayuda a redimir los campos de los foros, crea monumentos cívicos, etc.
>
> (Pereira-Muro 2008, 121)

This enormous cultural and material support from a far-off Galician diaspora (see, e.g., Fol-kart [2008]) bespeaks the conditions of extreme poverty, corruption, caciquism, and Spanish political and administrative centralism to which Galicia was subjected repeatedly throughout the nineteenth century – all magnified by the mid-century famine: "La tremenda hambruna de 1853 es el pistoletazo de salida para una sangría humana, que lleva a la emigración a América, según datos recientes, a más de dos millones de gallegos" (Pereira-Muro 2008, 119). Castro was sixteen when she saw firsthand the horrible toll of famine in the streets of the capital during the harsh winter of 1853. Davies (1990, 14) notes, "As escenas de penuria producidas en Santiago por mor da fame de 1853–54 afectaron a Rosalía profundamente," and Alonso Montero (1972, 19–20) – quoting at length Castro's moving account of the famine – concludes: "probablemente el primer hecho colectivo que incide seriamente en su sensibilidad." In a good number of her poems Castro does not only bear witness to the suffering, indifference and injustice inflicted on Galicia's poor; in addition, she foregrounds quite clearly her own sense of outrage in a way that exposes and challenges the prevailing moral complacency.

Poetry with a subversive edge

Castro's experience of the famine is inscribed in her bold, disturbing and not-so-subtly subversive poem "*Tembra un neno no húmedo pórtico*" (*Follas novas* [henceforth, *FN*] III, 41). The first three stanzas describe a cold, hungry, orphaned boy who lies shivering in a damp stairwell, his face against the stonework; in the fourth, well-to-do passersby see the boy on their way to church, but remain impassive: *van e vén ¡a adoraren ó Altisimo! / fariseios, os grandes da terra, / sin que ó ver do inocente a orfandade / se calme dos ricos / a sede avarienta*. In the poem's penultimate fifth stanza, the poet's voice shifts to first person with a feeling of anguish before the sorry scene of suffering and indifference – *O meu peito ca angustia s'oprime* – then queries the Almighty about why such suffering and indifference should exist: *¡Señor! ¡Dios do ceo! / ¿Por que hai almas tan negras e duras? / ¿Por que hai orfos na terra, Dios boeno?* Finally, in the concluding sixth stanza there comes the one, inescapable form of worldly justice that lies beyond the reach of all human design:

> *Mais n'en vano sellado está o libro*
> *dos grandes misterios. . .*
> *Pasa a groria, o poder i a alegría. . .*
> *Todo pasa na terra. ¡Esperemos!*

The greatest of equalizers – death – will balance the scales in the end. María Xesús Lama López, in an email to me, 19 May 2014, articulates Castro's stance in the following way: "De acordo, gañádesnos esta batalla (da vida), estamos sen armas nin munición, non temos posibilidade ningunha de darlle a volta á situación, pero non esquezades que isto é transitorio. A nosa arma é a paciencia e só precisamos esperar, e verémosvos caer." What comes through so clearly here is that the humble solace of religious faith is ruled out – and strikingly so, given the religious imagery in the poem: the appearance not only of the churchgoing passersby but also the poet's own appeal to the Deity in the penultimate stanza. The only solace comes from the knowledge that the outrageous injustice here depicted will be set right by the eventual demise of the impassive *fariseios, os grandes da terra*.

Significantly, this poem stands in stark contrast to "*Ora, meu meniño, ora*" (*Cantares gallegos* [henceforth, *CG*] 20), where a poverty-stricken mother, while laboring in the fields, must leave her suckling infant alone in their tumbledown hovel pierced by the rain and cold: *e neve e chuvia en ti caen / por antr'as fendidas tellas*. The denouement, however, is a miraculous one, with care and comfort given by a divine hand: *i a Virxen santa, vestida, / con vestido de inocencia, / porque de fame non morra / e fartiño s'adormeça, / dálle maná do seu peito / con qu'os seus labios refresca.* As also pointed out by Professor Lama López in her correspondence with me (see previously), this wondrous outcome is entirely consistent with the traditional and popular imagination to which Castro had given voice in her *Cantares gallegos* nearly two decades before *Follas novas*. Furthermore, the additional character in the poem – Rosa, who witnesses the appearance of the Virgin – folds a layer of magical perspective into the account, with Rosa herself slipping away into the thick fog after revealing the identity of the infant's benefactor to the returning mother. By contrast, in *"Tembra un neno no húmedo pórtico. . ."* there will be no miracles or disappearing acts – only the direct voicing of the poet's feeling of outrage and her climactic indictment.

Narrowing in further on the question of worldly justice, the dilemma between Christian morality and rightful vengeance is brilliantly encapsulated in the poem *"Para uns, negro. . ."* (*FN* III, 22). Torn between opposing instructions, first those of his father on his deathbed (*Sé astuto s'é que sabes; / víngate das ofensas s'é que podes*), then those of his mother on hers (*perdoa a quen t'ofenda, / fai ben decote a amigos i enemigos*), the son strikes a compromise that seems to weigh in more on the side of his father's directive: *Ña nai, fareille ben a quen cho fixo. / Meu pai, vinganza piden os teus ósos.* Again, the notion of relying on justice to be done in the hereafter recedes in favor of action calibrated to the measure of circumstances. More forceful still is the hard-hitting statement of *"A xusticia pola man"* (*FN* II, 25), in which the poem's persona, a woman, tells of how she has been robbed, evicted, vilified and dishonored by those reputed to be *honrados*, and whose exploitation of her has resulted even in the death of her children: *meus fillos . . . ¡meus anxos! . . . que tanto eu quería, / ¡morreron, morreron ca fame que tiñan!* Mocked by the judges – *De min se mofaron* – in her appeal to legal justice, her appeal to the Almighty proves also fruitless: *Tan alto que estaba, bon Dios non m'oíra.* Then, taking the law into her own hands, like a rabid or injured wolf (*cal loba doente ou ferida*), she murders her tormentors swiftly while they sleep: *dun golpe ¡dun soio!, deixeinos sin vida*, and sitting serenely beside her victims (*contenta* and *tranquila*), the murderess awaits the light of day, whereat she concludes in the poem's final two-line stanza: *I estonces . . . estonces cumpreuse a xusticia: / eu, neles; i as leises, na man qu'os ferira* (in Castro's own translation of the poem into Spanish, the final lines read: *Y entonces . . ., sólo entonces se cumplió la justicia / Yo en ellos, y las leyes en mi mano homicida* [Alonso Montero 1972, 160]). In a word, the same laws to which she turned to no avail will be quick in delivering justice on behalf of her victims. The poem's bold step in exposing the failure of worldly justice to set wrong things right, especially where the impoverished and exploited are concerned, culminates in the inevitable; but it is by no means an invitation to, nor an apology for, violence. It is, however, as Alonso Montero (1972, 76) has noted, groundbreaking in that "hasta entonces nadie había escrito un poema tan implacable sobre la perversidad del mundo y menos un poema sobre la inevitabilidad de la violencia como respuesta."

The more somber tone and content of *Follas* with respect to *Cantares* stems largely, as underscored by Lama López (1995, 42), from the failure of the ideal of social reform during the Democratic Sexennial: "A protesta social faise agora máis elocuente e directa," and more broadly:

> En ocasións traspasa os límites da situación de Galicia para dirixirse a cuestións de carácter xeral. Nas composicións máis subxectivas mostra a confusión e o fondo pesimismo derivado da perda de confianza nunha posible orde universal.

This lack of universal order so poignantly felt by the poet is frequently expressed through the iconic Rosalian image of *sombra* – widely popularized by the poem *"Cando penso que te fuches*" (*FN* II, 20) set to music under the title "Negra sombra" by composer Xoán Montes (1840–1899). In his analysis of the poem, García Sabell (1952, 48) laments the conversion of the poem into song: "Es una pena que tan pura fuerza lírica se haya popularizado a través de una música, mejor o peor, pero, en todo caso, ajena al espíritu del poema." The lyrical strength of the poem lies in its representation of *sombra* as a vital force: "Esa Sombra no es algo negativo, una ausencia de la luz, sino una fuerza, una capacidad básica del Ser" (52). This *sombra*, this experience of the solitary nature of being, felt deep in the core of one's self, is ever-recurring, revisiting the poet again and again, in all things: *Cando maxino que es ida, / no mesmo sol te m'amostras / i eres a estrela que brila / i eres o vento que zoa.* [. . .] *En todo estás e ti es todo, / pra min i en min mesma moras, / nin m'abandonarás nunca, / sombra que sempre m'asombras.* Paradoxically, this essential subjective experience and its expression in intimist poems is the starting point for outward and commonly shared experience in the world, and ultimately, its expression through poems of social significance and even subversive impact on the status quo. Remarking on this fusion of the solitary with the solidary, Lama López writes: "nin sequera as composicións máis intimistas son alleas ó compromiso coa colectividade" (1995, 43).

Of course, separately but inextricably, no small part of Castro's subversive impact on the status quo lay in her voicing, with universal appeal and effectiveness, the particulars of her and her people's sufferings and joys in her native Galician language. As Carballo Calero (1952, 27) points out incisively:

> Porque n-iles Rosalía elevábase á temática lírica de máis pura intimidade e univer-
> salidade. E isto era insólito en galego. O galego era unha fala campesiña. E non debía
> sair do seu marco rural. Como o galego non fora empregado ate de aquela máis que
> no ámbito do realismo pintoresco, a inercia esixía que se non pasara de ahí.

Along with the recognition of one's peripheral language as a proper vehicle for complex and nuanced literary expression, and rooted in the common social life of that language-sharing community, there comes also a strengthening of the sense of a national identity distinct from that imposed by Spanish politico-economic and administrative centralism. Nowhere is the subversion of this imposition more forcefully stated than in Castro's renowned poem "A gaita gallega" (*CG*), penned by way of reply to the poem that Salamancan writer Ventura Ruiz Aguilera (1820–1881) dedicated to Murguía titled "La gaita gallega" (*El museo universal*, 26 Nov. 1860), in which he reiteratively posed the question of whether, when Galician bagpipes played, they were in fact singing or weeping: *Hoy si la gaita gallega / el pobre gaitero toca, / no acierto a deciros / si canta o si llora.* Castro's lyrical reply (taking Aguilera's original as a formal template, but twenty verses longer) concluded: *E cando a gaita gallega / aló nas Castillas oias, / ó teu corazón pergunta, / verás que che di en resposta / qu'a gaita gallega / non canta, que chora.* More striking still, however, is the Aguilera – Rosalian palimpsest in the opening verses of section IV. Where Aguilera had written:

> *¡Pobre Galicia! . . . Tus hijos*
> *huyen de ti, o te los roban,*
> *llenando de íntima pena*
> *tus entrañas amorosas.*
> *Y como a parias malditos,*
> *y como a tribus de ilotas*
> *que llevasen en el rostro*

sello de infamia o deshonra,
¡ay! la patria los olvida,
la patria los abandona [. . .]

Castro now writes:

Probe Galicia, non debes
chamarte nunca española,
qu'España de ti s'olvida
cando eres ¡ay! tan hermosa.
Cal si na infamia naceras,
torpe, de ti s'avergonza,
i a nai qu'un fillo despreça
nai sin coraçón se noma [. . .]
Galicia, ti no tes patria,
ti vives no mundo soia [. . .]

It was this spirit of reasoned rebellion and strong affirmation of distinct cultural identity on the Iberian periphery that caught the eye of Víctor Balaguer (1824–1901), historian, poet and cabinet minister during the First Spanish Republic (1873–1874), who published a Catalan translation of both Aguilera's query and Castro's reply in his own *Esperances i records* (1866), along with "*Castellanos de Castilla.*" (*CG* 28), Castro's portrayal of the degraded socioeconomic relations between Castile and Galicia, which as Julià (2013, 5) observes, bears a notable resemblance to Balaguer's "Los quatre pals de sang" (1862): "Tots dos amb una tornada que esdevé molt popular i símbol de la reivindicació de les respectives identitats." Enlarging the peripheral factor, the awards ceremony of Barcelona's 1868 Jocs Florals was to spotlight multiculturalism in literary production. Presided that year by Balaguer (just returned from political exile in Provence) – and attended by Occitan writer Frederic Mistral (1830–1914, Nobel laureate 1904), Teodor Llorente (1836–1911, leading figure in the Valencian Renaixença and one of four Valencian poets to officiate that year [see Roca Ricart 2012b, 205]), and Castilian poets Gaspar Núñez de Arce (1834–1903), José Zorrilla (1817–1893) and Ventura Ruiz Aguilera as well – the ceremony was to include Rosalía de Castro, also invited as an honored guest: "La presència de Rosalía hagués representat la tríade de literatures i identitats 'germanes' que reclamava Balaguer al seu discurs: Castella, Galícia i Catalunya–Provença" (Julià 2013, 11). The reasons why Castro did not attend are not known. Rosalía de Castro's womanly voicing of Galicia embraces an entire spectrum of exceptional contribution, ringing out against social injustice, laying the foundations of the *Rexurdimento* and spearheading innovation in poetic form (see, e.g., Davies [1990, 42, 44–46] and Lama López [1995, 81–83] on Castro's innovative meter), dignifying the use of Galician (shunned by detractors as unfit for all purposes), exploring the solitary self and its solidary potential in the common social life, and exposing Spain's centripetal disdain for her own peripheral peoples. This bold voice – a woman's – arising from both the people around her and from deep within herself, anticipates, as noted by Olga Castro (2012, 205–206), Virginia Woolf's *A Room of One's Own* (1929) by sixty-five years. Keenly aware of her uncanny role as gender intruder, Castro ironized about womanhood and writing in her Spanish-language essays *Lieders* (1858) and *Las literatas: Carta a Eduarda* (1866); and in her prologue to her first novel, *La hija del mar* (1859), concluded: "Porque todavía no les es permitido a las mujeres escribir lo que sienten y lo que saben." What women might feel and know, in effect, Castro novelized and poetized throughout her twenty-five-year writing career, perhaps most masterfully in the thirty-one poems comprising the concluding section of *Follas novas* – "As viúdas dos vivos e as viúdas dos mortos" – causing readers also to feel and to know what so many women in her troubled land, in singing or in weeping, felt and knew.

Voicing the Catalan periphery: Jacint Verdaguer

A tale of two epics

It was at this landmark 1868 edition of Barcelona's Jocs Florals that the nearly twenty-three-year-old Jacint Verdaguer was introduced to Mistral and Llorente (see Verdaguer Pajerols [2012] on Verdaguer and the Jocs Florals), and though the heartland-bred seminarian had been awarded a number of literary prizes at the 1865 and 1866 Jocs (see Torrents 1995, 138–139), he took none that year for his *L'Atlàntida enfonsada i l'Espanya naixent de ses ruïnes*: the embryo of *L'Atlàntida*, which – following his first bouts with tuberculosis in 1872; nine crossings to the Antilles (1874–1876) as chaplain aboard the ships of transatlantic magnate Antonio López, the poet-priest's patron (see Pinyol i Torrents [2007] for a brief English-language biography of Verdaguer); and after nearly a decade of expanding and revising the some 2,600-line foundational epic of Spain – would win the "Premi extraordinari" at Barcelona's Jocs Florals in 1877. Hailed as the cornerstone restoring Catalan literature's place among the literatures of Europe after a hiatus of three centuries, *L'Atlàntida* melded the destruction of Atlantis (inflicted on the Atlanteans for presuming to rival the gods) with the Judeo-Christian providentialism resulting in Columbus's first voyage: the continents united once more, the "pattern of cosmic retribution and renewal" (Terry 2003, 7) was now complete; and in the ideological synthesis of the ancient classical and Judeo-Christian worlds into one universe where the latter prevailed, the poem celebrated, as Farrés (2003, 70) points out, "el destí d'Espanya en la transmissió del cristianisme," or as Torrents (2004, 105) notes, Spain's role in spreading "la primera ideologia de la globalització," even as the heroism of classical antiquity cemented the foundational mix in which Hercules, by wedlock with Hesperis (the widowed queen of Atlantis), emerges as the progenitor of a new Iberian people.

By July 1877, two months after the Jocs, Mistral had penned a hearty congratulations to Verdaguer, likening *L'Atlàntida* to Milton's *Paradise Lost* and Lamartine's *La chute d'un ange*, and proclaiming, *Tu Marcellus eris!*—Mistral's letter in Occitan would close Verdaguer's own prologue to the first edition of *L'Atlàntida* published the following year, with facing prose translation into Spanish by poet and critic Melcior de Palau (1843–1910). By autumn of 1877, praise for *L'Atlàntida* appeared in literary magazines in Paris and New York, and with the circulation of the bilingual edition in 1878, the work found favorable reception by Spanish-language critics as well, notably Marcelino Menéndez y Pelayo (1856–1912), who described the poem as "inverosímil en estos tiempos, rico, vigoroso y espléndido, portento de audacia y de armonía," and to whom Verdaguer proved "superior en condiciones descriptivas a todos los poetas catalanes, castellanos y portugueses que yo conozco," and finally: "Gracias al autor de *L'Atlàntida*, nada tiene que envidiar España a los Tennyson, Longfellow, Carducci, Mistral y demás grandes poetas de otras tierras" (*El Fenix*, March 1879; quoted in Farrés [2003, 61]). By the mid 1880s there had appeared a verse translation into Spanish, verse and prose translations into French and Italian, and in the 1890s verse translations into Czech and German, a prose translation into Provençal, and by 1909 also a verse translation into Portuguese (see Farrés [2003, 67–72] for more details on the translations); of the English-language translation, undertaken by the Irish-born *félibre* William Bonaparte-Wyse (1826–1892), only the opening and concluding sections were completed before the translator's death (Wyse's splendid verses are reproduced with the Catalan text facing in Puppo [2007, 37–51]).

The new Iberian peopling whose epic origins are recounted in *L'Atlàntida* comprises in fact a plurality of peoples – distinct from each other in their respective historical and cultural self-representations, and several in their widespread use and longstanding transmission of vehicular languages other than Spanish: plain for all to see in the Rosetta-like first edition of the poet-priest's homage to Spain. Turning to the periphery, in his foundational epic of Catalonia, *Canigó: Llegenda pirenaica del temps de la Reconquista* (1886), Verdaguer celebrates the particular and distinct historical and legendary mix fueling the Catalan imaginary, drawing from Catalonia's early medieval origins, the reconquest of the Spanish March (Catalonia), and the symbolic conflict between, on the one hand, a powerful folk mythology rooted in the natural geography (in the storyline, the fate of the newly knighted Gentil's countrymen is interlaced with his encounter with Flordeneu, queen of the Pyrenean faeries) and, on the other, the widely institutionalized universalism of Christianity. As in *L'Atlàntida*, it is the Christian order that prevails in the fusion of the two. The poem, remarks Soldevila (2002, 19), is Verdaguer's response to the need for reaffirming Christian values and reflects the moderately pro-Catalan conservative thought later formulated in *La tradició catalana* (1892) by Bishop Josep Torras i Bages (1846–1916) – for whom "Catalunya serà cristiana o no serà" – in contrast to the growing secular progressivism and republicanism articulated in *Lo catalanisme* (1886) by statesman and writer Valentí Almirall (1841–1904). That said, Torrents (2003, 244) shows how Verdaguer's addition of the epilogue, "Los dos campanars," in the second edition (1901) of *Canigó* recasts the poem's ending, changing it from *hymnal* to *elegiac*: the climactic planting of the cross on Mount Canigó's summit and expulsion of the Pyrenean faeries now gives way to the lamentation personified in the dialogue between the bell towers of the crumbling abbeys of Sant Martí del Canigó and Sant Miquel de Cuixà, lying abandoned below the Canigó massif. Perhaps, as Torrents suggests, the poem's final lines convey a sobering realization that the ingredients of national identity may change with the centuries:

> *Lo que un segle bastí l'altre ho aterra,*
> *mes resta sempre el monument de Déu;*
> *i la tempesta, el torb, l'odi i la guerra*
> *al Canigó no el tiraran a terra,*
> *no esbrancaran l'altívol Pirineu.*

The natural monument – the mountain, Catalonia symbolized – endures, with or without the abbeys; transmuting the well-known phrase attributed to Torras i Bages, Torrents allows for a redrawing of parameters: "Catalunya serà, encara que no sigui cristiana" (2004, 132). Thus, concludes Torrents, the poem's final lines posit a "telluric" or geographic identity that is more fundamental than that rooted in Christendom (2003, 245). In any event, Verdaguer's conceptual framework – beyond any particular religious doctrine or denomination – is largely the legacy of Enlightenment deism: in a word, nature, and nature's God, have endowed land and life with vigorous diversity, and Verdaguer's depictions of the life-giving quality of the landscape resonate with a cultural multiplicity that thrives as an extension of nature's own diversity (see Puppo [2010, 276–278] for more on this important point).

Vilardell Domènech (2013) has rigorously catalogued, detailed and assessed the numerous translations (partial and complete) of *Canigó* into Spanish by no less than eleven writers/translators during the fifty-year period following its first edition in 1886 and its critical reception in Barcelona, València, Mallorca and Madrid; among the translations during Verdaguer's lifetime are, most notably, the 1886 prose version published serially in the conservative Catholic magazine *La Hormiga de Oro* (Barcelona) by writer Jaume Nogués i Taulet (1850–1902), the several cantos in verse translation by writer Constantí Llombart (1848–1893) in various Valencian magazines in 1886 and 1887, and the widely circulated part-verse, part-prose translation by the Castilian historian, author, academician and excursionist Jerónimo López de Ayala-Álvarez, Conde de Cedillo (1862–1934), published in Madrid in 1898; in a long, warm letter of approval and gratitude to López de Ayala dated October 1897, Verdaguer, having read the translation slated for publication, writes: "Me alegro de que mis humildes cantos al Canigó se difundan por los países donde se habla la lengua castellana, despojados de su rudeza nativa y adornados con las galas poéticas de la inspiración de usted y con las preciosas ilustraciones que los acompañan" (in Molas and Cònsul 2003, 1151). Farther abroad, a partial verse and prose translation into Italian appeared in 1888, and Josep Tolrà de Bordas (1824–1890), for his 1889 prose translation into French, obtained Verdaguer's permission to include the epilogue – preceding its appearance in the second Catalan edition by eleven years (see Camps Casals [2013] for a thoroughgoing treatment of translations of Verdaguer's works into French). *Canigó* drew praise once again from Llorente and Mistral, and Menéndez y Pelayo, who compared it with Victor Hugo's *La Légende des siècles*, judged *Canigó* to be superior to *L'Atlàntida*, although Vilardell Domènech has found that most critics asserted the superiority of *L'Atlàntida*, adding that "perhaps if the new poem had been originally published in a bilingual Catalan-Spanish edition, as was *L'Atlàntida*, its echo in both the Catalan and the Madrid-centred press might have been greater" (2013, 391–392).

Solidarity, rebellion, reconciliation

Verdaguer, at age thirty-nine, was at the height of his literary career – and his stature was about to soar with the triumph of his second major epic, *Canigó*, in a year's time – when a devastating earthquake struck, on Christmas Day 1884, the Andalusian provinces of Granada and Málaga. Campaigns for aid to victims and reconstruction were quickly organized throughout Spain and abroad by charitable societies, authorities, the Church, the press and other concerned groups (Vidal Sánchez 2012, 30–38), including initiatives by poets such as Llorente (see Roca [2012a] for details on action by writers in València) and, in particular, Verdaguer. In less than three weeks' time, Verdaguer's collection of thirty poems under the title *Caritat* (several of which had already appeared separately) was submitted to the censor for approval, and by 30 January the volume was available for sale; a second edition came out in May with four additional poems and some revisions, followed by a third edition in 1893 with two more poems. Proceeds from the first edition surpassed the amount collected by the entire diocese of Vic (Cònsul 2005, 289). Two of the poems, "Per què canten les mares?" and "La boira," depicting poverty-stricken mothers, recall analogous portrayals of social injustice in Castro's poetry. In the first, an ailing husband and father, too sick to work again, asks why his wife sings with such joy to their child: *Per què, esposa del meu cor, / per què tan alegre cantes?* to which she replies, *Perquè el nostre fill no plore.* Her song – and a crucifix – are all they have left, both of which represent acts of charity: the mother through her song follows the example of the Cross. In "La boira," a young widowed mother must labor in the fields while her infant lies nearby under a hot sun; miraculously, cool mists descend from Canigó's summits to shield them from the punishing heat – recalling the care and comfort given by the divine hand in the Rosalian poem *"Ora meu meniño, ora . . ."* (*CG* 20).

Still, for Verdaguer the Christian faith, if only observed in appearance and not put into practice, would not measure up. On returning from his pilgrimage to the Holy Land and Egypt in 1886, Verdaguer began putting his faith into practice more rigorously through more prayer, fasting, almsgiving – encouraging his patron's wife to contribute more of the family's money to Barcelona's poor – and associating himself with a group of radical Catholics who performed exorcisms. The Marqués de Comillas, now anxious to cut ties with his unorthodox family chaplain, enlisted the cooperation of the bishops of Barcelona and Vic to have Verdaguer sent away; confined to a provincial parish, Verdaguer flouted Church authorities by returning to Barcelona without permission, prompting the suspension in 1895 of his priestly duties and functions. The salvo of articles penned by Verdaguer in his own defense over the next two years – published, in Catalan, in Barcelona's left-leaning Spanish-language daily *La Publicidad* – dramatically polarized Catalan public opinion until the matter was finally resolved in 1897, thanks largely to the Augustinian friars at El Escorial, Madrid, who arranged an agreement that proved satisfactory to both parties (see Torrents 1995, 90–95).

Coda: *Escolta, Espanya*

Verdaguer, despite the perspicacity of his social gaze, proved adamant in his faith in a transcendent universal order. However, for Joan Maragall (1860–1911) – Verdaguer's turn-of-the-century successor in powerfully poetizing the joys and sufferings of his peripheral people – religious transcendence and solace would fall short of the mark, unable to placate the growing awareness of the need for resolving deep-rooted social ills. For Maragall, it was the men and women of Barcelona who must themselves win back conviviality in the wake of the social turmoil that culminated in the Setmana Tràgica of 1909, just as the men returning from the horror and defeat of the last of the Cuban wars of independence (see Puppo [2012a, 2012b] on Maragall's important poems and writings on these troubling events) must once again take heart; and these things they must do through a kind of public-spirited love and the celebration of Spain's diversity on the periphery – diversity to which Mother Spain, in Maragall's "Oda a Espanya" (1898), seems oblivious:

> *Escolta, Espanya,–la veu d'un fill*
> *que et parla en llengua–no castellana;*
> *parlo en la llengua–que m'ha donat*
> *la terra aspra:*
> *en 'questa llengua–pocs t'han parlat;*
> *en l'altra, massa [. . .]*

The question of how preferential and peripheral linguistic communities – Spain's peoples – are to negotiate, or refuse to negotiate, conviviality; divergent views on historical memory competing for discursive and symbolic space; ideological tensions arising from Spain's variegated cultural fabric; all these crucial issues confronting the Spain/s of more than a century ago remain, for the most part, unresolved to this day.

Note

1 Research for this chapter was funded by a grant from the Spanish Ministry of Education (FFI2011-26367), and conducted by the consolidated research group (2009 SGR 736) "Textos Literaris Contemporanis: estudi, edició i traducció," Universitat de Vic.

Works cited

Alonso Montero, Xesús. 1972. *Rosalía de Castro*. Madrid: Ediciones Júcar.

Bermúdez, Teresa, ed. 2002. "Contextualización da obra." In *Follas novas*, Rosalía de Castro, xxi–xxxi. Vigo: Editorial Galaxia.

Camps Casals, Núria. 2013. "La recepció de Verdaguer a França: traductors i traduccions." PhD diss., Universitat de Vic.

Carballo Calero, Ricardo. 1952. "Arredor de Rosalía." (See *Siete ensayos sobre Rosalía*, 19–39).

———, ed. (1974) 2013. "Introducción." In *Cantares gallegos*, Rosalía de Castro, 9–36. Madrid: Ediciones Cátedra.

Castro, Olga. 2012. "La traducción como mecanismo de (re)canonización: el discurso nacional y feminista de Rosalía de Castro en sus traducciones al inglés." *Quaderns: Revista de Traducció* 19: 199–217.

Cònsul, Isidor. 2005. "Introducció [a *Caritat*]." In *Jacint Verdaguer: Poesia, 1*, vol. 3 of *Totes les obres de Jacint Verdaguer*, edited by Joaquim Molas and Isidor Cònsul, 287–289. Barcelona: Proa.

Davies, Catherine. 1983. "Rosalía de Castro, Criticism 1950–1980: The Need for a New Approach." *Bulletin of Hispanic Studies* 60 (3): 211–220.

———. 1990. *Rosalía de Castro e Follas Novas*. Translated into Galician by Leandro García Bugarín. Vigo: Editorial Galaxia.

Farrés, Pere. 2003. "Introducció [a *L'Atlàntida*]." In *Jacint Verdaguer: Poemes llargs/Teatre*, vol. 2 of *Totes les obres de Jacint Verdaguer*, edited by Joaquim Molas and Isidor Cònsul, 67–70. Barcelona: Proa.

Folkart, Jessica A. 2008. "Itinerant Identities: Galician Diaspora and Genre Subversion in Manuel Rivas's *A man dos paíños*." *Anales de la literatura española contemporánea* 33 (1): 5–29.

García Sabell, Domingo. 1952. "Rosalía y su sombra." (See *Siete ensayos sobre Rosalía*, 43–56.)

Geoffrion-Vinci, Michelle. 2002. *Between the Maternal Aegis and the Abyss: Woman as Symbol in the Poetry of Rosalía de Castro*. Madison and Teaneck: Fairleigh Dickinson University Press.

Julià, Lluïsa. 2013. "Rosalía a Catalunya: recepció i debat identitari." Paper presented at the symposium titled "Catalunya i Rosalía de Castro: 150 anys de *Cantares gallegos*," Institut d'Estudis Catalans, Barcelona, November 14.

Lama López, María Xesús, ed. 1995. "Introducción." In *Cantares gallegos*, Rosalía de Castro, 9–119. Vigo: Editorial Galaxia.

———. 2007. "Apuntes arredor dunha biografía de Rosalía de Castro: 'tras dun olvido, outro olvido'." In *Actas do VII Congreso Internacional de Estudos Galegos. Mulleres en Galicia. Galicia e os outros pobos da Península. Barcelona 28 ó 31 de maio de 2003*, edited by Helena González and M. Xesús Lama López, 171–179. Sada: Ediciós de Castro/Asociación Internacional de Estudos Galegos (AIEG)/Filoloxía Galega (Universitat de Barcelona).

Molas, Joaquim and Isidor Cònsul, eds. 2003. *Jacint Verdaguer: Prosa*, vol. 1 of *Totes les obres de Jacint Verdaguer*. Barcelona: Proa.

Pereira-Muro, Carmen. 2008. "Emigración, nacionalismo y literatura: los gallegos de Cuba en la obra de Rosalía de Castro y Fernando Ortiz." *Revista Hispánica Moderna* 61 (2): 119–134.

Pinyol i Torrents, Ramon. 2007. Introduction to *Selected Poems of Jacint Verdaguer: A Bilingual Edition*. Edited and translated by Ronald Puppo, 1–19. Chicago: University of Chicago Press.

Puppo, Ronald, ed. 2007. *Selected Poems of Jacint Verdaguer: A Bilingual Edition*, with an introduction by Ramon Pinyol i Torrents. Chicago: University of Chicago Press.

———. 2010. "Making Room for Small-Language Imports: Jacint Verdaguer." *Babel* 56 (3): 259–281.

———. 2012a. "How Maragall's Notion of a Public-Spirited Love Resonates in English Translation." *Haidé: Estudis maragallians* 1: 93–107.

———. 2012b. "The Poetry of Troubles: Maragall's *Els tres cants de la guerra* (Three songs of war) and their translation." *Journal of Catalan Studies / Revista Internacional de Catalanística* 14 (2011): 217–236.

Roca Ricart, Rafael. 2012a. "L'aportació de la Renaixença valenciana als terratrèmols d'Andalusia (1885)." *Anuari Verdaguer* 19: 419–431.

———. 2012b. "Valencians als Jocs Florals de Barcelona (1862–1893)." In *Joc literari i estratègies de representació*, edited by Josep M. Domingo, 199–247. Barcelona: Institut d'Estudis Catalans.

Siete *ensayos sobre Rosalía*. 1952. Edited by Luis Pimentel, Teixeira de Pascoaes, Ricardo Carballo Calero, Domingo García Sabell, Jacinto de Prado Coelho, Celestino F. de la Vega, Ramón Piñeiro López, J. Rof Carballo and Salvador Lorenzana. Vigo: Editorial Galaxia.

Soldevila, Llorenç, ed. 2002. "Introducció." In *Canigó: Llegenda pirenaica del temps de la Reconquista*, Jacint Verdaguer, 7–28. Barcelona: Proa.

Terry, Arthur. 2003. *A companion to Catalan literature*. Woodbridge: Tamesis.

Torrents, Ricard. 1995. *Verdaguer: un poeta per a un poble*. Vic: Eumo Editorial.

———. 2003. "Introducció [a *Canigó*]." In *Poemes llargs/Teatre*, vol. 2 of *Totes les obres de Jacint Verdaguer*, edited by Joaquim Molas and Isidor Cònsul, 241–245. Barcelona: Proa.

———. 2004. *A la claror de Verdaguer*. Vic: Eumo Editorial.

Verdaguer Pajerols, M. Àngels. 2012. "Jacint Verdaguer i els Jocs Florals de Barcelona: De la plataforma a la mitificació." In *Joc literari i estratègies de representació*, edited by Josep M. Domingo, 289–325. Barcelona: Institut d'Estudis Catalans.

Vidal Sánchez, Francisco. 2012. "El Terremoto de Alhama de Granada de 1884 y su impacto." *Anuari Verdaguer* 19: 11–45.

Vilardell Domènech, Laura. 2013. "La recepció de *Canigó*, de Jacint Verdaguer, a Barcelona, València, Mallorca i Madrid (1886–1936)." PhD diss., Universitat de Vic.

28

DEATH AND THE CRISIS OF REPRESENTATION IN NARCÍS OLLER'S *LA FEBRE D'OR* AND PÉREZ GALDÓS'S *LA DE BRINGAS*

Elisa Martí-López

What comes to my mind when thinking about the nineteenth century is the critical and ideo-logical possibilities – and dangers – of *Iberian* Studies. What new avenues of reflection are being opened up, and under what new and old constraints? The critical contributions of studies that aim to "congregar, confrontar" the work by Narcís Oller with that of Benito Pérez Galdós, or to study "las interrelaciones literarias dadas entre dos de las tradiciones peninsulares – la castellana y la catalana – ante una propuesta literaria específica como es el Realismo" (Arroyo 1998–1999, 18) are indeed relevant to the understanding of these two authors and the function-ing of the Catalan and the Spanish literary systems. However, I find myself resisting the idea that the study of Iberia requires some sort of comparative approach, and uneasy discussing Oller and Galdós side by side within a critical paradigm whose practices and political implica-tions for the study of the literatures and cultures of the Iberian Peninsula are unclear. Moreover, I think that these two authors' interest in representing urban experience in the late nineteenth century claimed different allegiances, resorted to different narrative strategies, and resulted in highly different city imaginaries. I agree with Joan Gilabert and Joan Ramon Resina that these authors present diverging representations of the city: "la glorificación del presente" drives Oller's writing of Barcelona, while Pérez Galdós's concern was "el rechazo absoluto del pas-ado que es anacrónicamente presente" (Gilabert 1977, 157; see also Resina 1994–1995, 261).

The question to pose to comparative approaches and, more particularly, to all studies written under the rubric of *Iberia* is what Iberian imaginary, if any, they bring forth. Are we reproducing old forms of national imagination framed now by wider or looser – and not always explicit – notions of territorial coherence? Is *Iberia* a premise for new literary and cultural affinities? Moreover, is *Iberia* a new definition for a national inside (conceived now as multipolar and multilinguistic) and a foreign outside? Is it the continuation of the privileging of production over reception? What new exclusions do Iberian Studies effect? How should we read the Modern Language Association's recent decision to link Iberian Studies to Spanish (but not to Catalan or Galician) in its new forum format? As the Modern Language Association's deci-sion clearly brings forth – Iberian Studies' "natural" place is with Spanish – it is questionable how effectively *Iberia*, as critical object, supports an epistemology that undermines the deeply rooted hierarchical positionality of different Iberian languages and literary traditions. In more general terms, it is not evident to me why we should privilege – and, thus, institutionalize – *Iberia* as the frame for a set of multipolar and multilinguistic relations that can be inscribed more productively in other ways.

At the same time, I am intrigued by the critical possibilities *Iberia* as both object of representation and site of enunciation may open for the discussion of literature and culture. The deconstruction of the capital as metaphor for the nation and other deeply naturalized and hierarchical oppositions, such as that between capital and provinces, are exciting critical developments for the thinking of Iberia. In this sense, still pending is a radical revision of well-established readings of Galdós's Madrid that reproduce the Spanish State's discourse on the nation and, thus, are "a means of political legitimation" of the State (Resina 2001, 59; see also Martí-López 2005, 148–167). I find, however, that these critical insights are of little use when writing about Oller's *La febre d'or*. Barcelona has quite successfully resisted its political and literary reduction to a province (vis-à-vis Madrid as capital) and, thus, its subsumption into the imaginary of the Spanish nation. At the same time Barcelona, while functioning as *cap i casal* of Catalonia, has never been the capital of a nation-state. How, then, does one write about Oller for a collection on Iberian Studies? Here I try to contribute to this volume in a way that avoids any a priori notions that might confirm the existence of *Iberia* instead of contributing to its critical discussion.

Oller's novel, *La febre d'or*, is the focus of this essay, but not the only work I discuss. I have decided to try my hand at *Iberia*, discussing Oller alongside both a personal literary enjoyment – Galdós's *La de Bringas* – and a critical one – Hazel Gold's and Jo Labanyi's readings of the novel, in particular, their analyses of the cenotaph which opens *La de Bringas*. In another collection I would have privileged other enjoyments that would give Oller's work different and always provisional contexts of discussion. The recognition of such enjoyment is my critical compromise with the discussion intended by this collection of essays. Since I have nothing to add to these critics' analyses of Francisco de Bringas's cenotaph, I have chosen both Galdós's literary image of the hair cenotaph and Gold's and Labanyi's analyses of it to bring the discussion of death and the city in *La febre d'or* to the point where I would like to start.

A "close-up" of a hair cenotaph

The hair cenotaph at the beginning of *La de Bringas* (1884) is "the most arresting feature of Galdós's novel" (Franz 1996, 259). At the time of the novel, hair cenotaphs were already obsolete but, as has been pointed out, it is not its obsolescence that makes it "arresting," but rather the description of its aberrant shape. The description of the extravagant hair memorial Francisco de Bringas is putting together throughout most of the novel takes up the entire first chapter, thus effectively delaying the beginning of the story-as-plot. The meticulous and ironic description of this *memento mori* by the narrator focuses exclusively on the object itself, on its monstrous – chaotic – nature. No indication is given at this time of its intended recipient or function, and only at the very end of the chapter is its maker identified: it is Francisco de Bringas, husband of the protagonist. Later on we are told that the hair cenotaph is Francisco's cheap way – at no cost for him – of repaying Manuel Pez for the favor of securing employment for the Bringas's young son.

Literary descriptions are never simply a likeness of something else, but rather a way of building and conveying meaning and, as Hazel Gold comments, the cenotaph – the juxtaposition of disparate motifs that characterize its overall composition – "is no mere costumbrista digression but rather a principal device in the unification of the work" (1986, 54). As summarized by Gold, the cenotaph's "ineradicable heterogeneity" includes "virtually every icon of death known to Romantic painting and sculpture ("torches, urns, amphorae, owls, bats, winged water-clocks . . . floral crowns, etc.), . . . details from diverse sources (the pyramids of Egypt . . . the temples of classical antiquity . . . and – among many other things – gargoyles of the great cathedrals of the Middle Ages)," and a "disordered mix of architectural styles (Classical, Gothic, Plateresque, late Renaissance, and Tyrolean)" (55). Francisco de Bringas's execution of the hair memorial is "simultaneously reminiscent of every major form of printmaking, etching, engraving, woodcut drawing, pencil sketching and includes hair from different sources (the deceased girl, mother and siblings)" (55). All of this adds up to an "oppressively over-ornamented mausoleum" whose "heterogeneity means virtually nothing" (54). The meaning of cenotaph is an "empty tomb" (61).

The empty sign of the tomb and the ocular illnesses that result from the meticulous work it requires – Bringas suffers temporary blindness and blurred vision – have been discussed as a metaphor for Bringas's blindness to his wife's spendthrift and sexual exploits, as well as for the political decadence of the ruling classes just before the 1868 Revolution. In her reading, however, Gold analyses how the cenotaph and the ocular illnesses it produces articulate the novel's reflection on the problematics of perception and representation: "the blur of indifferentiation which clouds his existence is nowhere more evident than in the *cenotafio*" (1986, 56). In particular, the cenotaph represents a form of false knowledge, a misrepresentation of reality – a literal realism – Galdós is interested in denouncing: "Unable to perceive where reality lies in his own life, his [Francisco de Bringas's] attempts to picture reality in the *cenotafio* can never transcend the mechanics of technique. In perhaps no other Galdosian novel does the reader find such a mordant critique of a certain brand of realism that paradoxically bears no allegiance to the real" (66).

We find out later that the cenotaph at the beginning of Galdós's novel is meant to commemorate the death of Juanita Pez, the young daughter of Manuel Pez, a well-established and affluent civil servant. The cenotaph – a representational displacement of death – thus stands for an absence and for what is hidden: the corpse and its putrefaction. Following Gold's connection between the cenotaph and the novel's reflection on the production of meaning – "At the same time that Bringas is observed creating the *cenotafio*, the narrator is engaged in his own special brand of creation: the production of meaning within the text" (1986, 61) – I propose that we read the incongruent ornamental excess of the cenotaph not as a short-sighted literalism. Rather, it could be read as the positing at the beginning of the novel of the radical gap between representation and what Georges Bataille called the "irrevocably real," that is, what "is not susceptible to traditional representations . . . [what] is external and foreign to ideal human aspirations" (Schleifer 1993, 312). The cenotaph, thus, is a metaphor for the struggle for meaning, for the futility of all forms of representation. This approach opens up different possibilities of interpretation. What if the ironic tone the narrator adopts when describing the cenotaph replicated Bringas's self-assurance in representation? Could this irony be a foretelling of the narrator's complacent and corruptive ways, a mark of what critics have described as the narrator's lack of an authoritative voice? Moreover, what if the duplicity of language found in the narrator's irony would be the result not only of the ridiculous heterogeneity of the cenotaph and its literal realism, but also the appropriate verbal style for the articulation of the empty sign represented by the cenotaph? Death, as has been often pointed out, is outside of language. What, thus, if we read the "depersonalized clichés" (Gold 1986, 61) that describe the cenotaph as signs for the radical ineffectiveness – arbitrariness – of all meaning systems and representations? Jo Labanyi's reading of the cenotaph goes in this direction.

In Labanyi's analysis, "Francisco Bringas's hair picture provides a false start" (1990, 26). This "false start" – the pause brought on by the description – initiates the novel's self-conscious exploration of literary representation, our reliance on the beginnings and endings that frame stories, and the limits of narrative perspective. In *La de Bringas*, "references to blurred vision and distorted perspectives are part of a wider examination of what happens when framing devices fail to hold" (25). Moreover, Galdós's novel shows how "the same perspective that confers intelligibility to the story is an illusion" (27). In Labanyi's reading, like in Gold's, Bringas's hair memorial is also a "flawed work of art" (27), but it is so for a very different reason. If, in Gold's analysis, the cenotaph represents a short-sighted realism and its failure to capture reality – "it is a worthless object" (1986, 49) – for Labanyi, the cenotaph is a *mise-en-abyme* exploration of the limits and dangers of representation: "The cemetery represented in the hair picture is an attempt to contain heterogeneity in a deathly stasis, but by including so much that the artistic structure breaks down, it defeats its own purpose" (27). Thus, the cenotaph plays out the danger of bourgeois confidence and reliance on closed frames to represent reality. And it is precisely the failure of framing devices to hold representation and to produce meaning, and death "as object lesson in the importance of framing" (27), that I discuss in *La febre d'or* by Narcís Oller.

Panoramic views: from gold to carpentry by way of death

In *La febre d'or* (1890–1892), "the first attempt in Catalan literature to produce a bourgeois epic" (Resina 1994–1995, 259), death can be found at every step and at all levels. Death is often used by characters to talk about themselves and others, and about city experience; it organizes the novel's plot both structurally and symbolically; and it is key to the novel's narrative strategies. In my reading of *La febre d'or* the representation of death (or, rather, of death's metonymies), with its "structural dialectic of revealing and concealing" and its "inevitable configurations of power and powerlessness" (Goodwin and Bronfen 1993, 19), is directly related to the narrating of a city constituted by speculative exchange relations. Moreover, I contend that, in Oller's novel, the limits of realist writing as a means to represent – give form and meaning to – Barcelona's modernity are exposed precisely through death. Death both articulates and destabilizes the narrative strategies the novel puts forward to order and make sense of the chaos of Barcelona's particular processes of modernity.

La febre d'or focuses on a period of two years – from 1880 to 1882 – when the bullish stock market that started in 1876 and lasted until 1886 had the greatest impact on Barcelona. Oller wrote about the effects of speculation and of fraudulent financial companies investing in the extension of the railway through the quick rise and fall of a self-made man, Gil Foix. The rapid success and ruin of a self-made man – one of the great themes in the nineteenth-century novel – allows Oller to build "a historical canvas of fin-de-siècle Barcelona" (Resina 2008, 15). The titles of the two parts of the novel – "Pujada" (ascent, rise, climb) and "Estimbada" (falling down a "timba," or precipice), respectively – use spatial metaphors for movement to describe the "ups" and "downs" of the social fortune of the novel's protagonist. The fact that, in later editions, Oller preferred "Estimbada" instead of "Cayguda" (fall, downfall) – the title used for Part II in the 1892 edition of *La febre d'or* published by *La Ilustració Catalana* – would indicate that the titles of the two parts of the novel also point to the cause of Foix's social mobility: gambling or, in this case, playing the stock market, two activities often confused in nineteenth-century fiction ("timba" also means "gambling house").[1] "Pujada" (up) and "Estimbada" (down), the spatial metaphors that summarize Gil Foix's story, also can be read as Oller's preferred spatial viewpoints from which to depict Barcelona. The choice of visual perspective – that is, viewing the city from above, from street level, or from below – is not an inconsequential one: it determines the image of the city being described (Pike 1981,

33). In *La febre d'or* Oller combines the street-level view (down) and the perspective from above (up). The remarkable thing about this is that death always makes its appearance in all perspectives from above and in significant instances of street-level view. In all of these instances, death indicates the problematic reliability of what is being represented (Barcelona), as well as testing the limits of the realist representation of the city's modernity.

In *La febre d'or* panoramic views constitute moments of suspended action when Barcelona's visibility or lack of visibility is the central focus of the narrative, and they all have at their core particular figurations of death. These moments are but few in the novel. On these occasions, the city is laid out in front of numerous characters, but only two stop to observe it attentively: Gil Foix and his daughter, Delfina Foix. These instances are quite different in the visual scope they provide and in the amount of writing the novel invests in them – from a few paragraphs to a simple word – but in all of them, the novel plays out its dependence on death not only to make the city's modernity visible, but also to explore the limits of realism's reliance on visibility to represent Barcelona's modern image. In this essay, I focus my analysis on the panoramic views narrated when Gil Foix looks at the city from above.

The first panoramic view we encounter in the novel appears in Part One, Chapter XIII, during a party given by Giró – a speculator who has had a few lucky strikes playing the stock market – at his newly acquired *torre* (summer house) in Pedralbes, at the time a rural area outside Barcelona. When Gil Foix, his wife, and daughter Delfina approach by carriage the white walls surrounding the *torre* to attend the celebration, it is remarked that the entrance to the property – with its "reixat de ferro . . . llargues parets . . . emblanquinades i amb llurs cerreres eriçades de vidres" – is that of a burial ground: "Era ben bé l'entrada d'un fossar" (I, 168). This observation – the identification of the entrance to a fashionable summer house with that of a burial ground – is less unexpected if we realize that Delfina's state of mind when arriving at Giró's *torre* is highly perceptive to issues of wealth and representation. She has spent most of her ride musing over her young uncle Francesc, a painter, with whom she is falling in love. She is angry at her uncle's mockery of her elegant dress, and at his refusal to enter the art marketplace. Fashionably and expensively dressed in preparation for Giró's party, happy to be a valuable asset in the upscale market of marriage, she does not understand his refusal to circulate – "conèixer i tractar la gent rica" (I, 163). More importantly, she is angry at her own incapacity to know him, to see through his mockery and judgmental wit: "Era desesperador, per a ella, pensar que unes voltes el veia d'una manera, i tot d'un plegat d'una altra, sempre, sempre enigmàtic, mai prou clar" (I, 161).

Still infatuated with a deceiving baron interested only in her father's wealth, she nevertheless has not forgotten nor ceased to believe in the old pre-capitalist view – pragmatic but essentialist – on work and family inherent in her *menestral* origins. Thus, when one of her fashionable friends reminds her at the party that marriage in their social circle is about wealth and not love, she thinks the idea "repugnant:" "restà tota pansida, com vexada en el més íntim del cor" (I, 171). From the very beginning of the story, Delfina is able to articulate a suspicion of reality that later on in the story will take her to dissociate herself completely from the risks of desire and debauched spending her father has embraced, to become what Leo Bersani has described as a "heroine of stillness," a character "whose main function seems to be to smother desire, to stifle all movement" (1976, 77). Being a heroine of stillness, her suspicion of reality takes the form of a belief in fixed images, that is, in a world where signs and values have objective referents even when hidden under confusing appearances. Annoyed with her uncle's "mirar indesxifrable," frustrated with that "ésser estrany" whose eyes refract reality instead of reflecting it, she wishes she could read her uncle's "mind" and "heart" looking through and beyond his eyes: "alguna nit, se n'hauria anat de puntetes a obrir-los per veure què hi havia allí dins" (I, 161, 163). There, she believes, she would find her uncle's true value: "que aquell xicot era molt formal, molt bo, molt intel·ligent . . . tot un home" (I, 161).

Aware of the problematics of visibility and representation, Delfina recommends that her uncle visit the houses of the wealthy to "observar, veure, què es el que falta als artistes d'aquí quan volen pintar o descriure el món elegant" (I, 163). Moreover, when her uncle refuses to accept her mother's request to make a painting of a saint intended as a gift for her husband – "Que hi voleu combregar . . . o ballar, a la sala? . . . Jo, jo pintar sants? Per qui m'heu pres?" – she understands that Francesc's rebuff is an objection to both the object and the manner of representation proposed to him, and that, like his "gargots" – doodles – it responds to "un tractat de filosofia artística, o cosa així, que ella endevinava" (I, 162, 163). And when her uncle mockingly suggests that she choose an appropriate painting for her father from a well-known art gallery, Sala Parés, she responds defiantly: "ja ho veurà, si hi entenc; ja ho veurà, si sé escollir" (I, 162). It is not surprising that Delfina's concerns about the appearance of people and things, and how they are represented, precede the description of Giró's *torre* and the gathering of fashionable Barcelona as "un fossar:" "The representations of death often serve as metaphors for the process of representation itself: its necessity, its excesses, its failure, and its uses for the polis" (Goodwin and Bronfen 1993, 4). Giró's *torre* as *fossar* provides both the frame and the meaning for a mise-en-scene where the value of things as well as people is its representative value. Death mirrors the endless circulation of signs tied to no referent, the endless sliding of signifiers played out in the speculative wealth Giró's *torre* has come to represent: the *torre*, the old site of landed wealth – it used to belong to a marquise – has recently been auctioned twice: "¿No es més just, senyor Giró, – says Foix – aquest vaivé de la propietat actual?" (I, 169). "Villa Nabab" or "casino burgès" are the proper names for the *torre* according to Emilia Llopis, an opinionated and *cursi* bluestocking whose early experience in Paris may explain her talent to name the fashionable Barcelona (I, 181, 172). At the party, one of Giró's sons tells his friends that the family decided against naming the house after his dead mother because it would remind them of her: "Li volíem posar el nom de la mamà; però la mamà és morta, i cada cop que hi vindríem ens recordaríem d'ella" (I, 181). They were right. To maintain the illusion of representation – its deception and pretense – one needs to keep their spectral nature hidden, just like the Catalan bourgeoisie hid the body's putrefaction under ostentatious mausoleums in the *Cementiri de Montjuïc*. Thus, the same long line of elegant carriages entering the *torre*'s gate reappears later on in a funeral procession to the *Cementiri de Montjuïc* from where Barcelona's modernity again becomes visible to Gil Foix (I, 168, 297).

From Pedralbes's heights, Gil Foix views and admires with great exclamations the "boniques vistes que allí es descobrien" of Barcelona (I, 169) – "Vista Alegre" is another name the family is considering for the *torre*. He feels the bourgeoisie's pleasure for "the boundless city," its clamor "for space and visibility" after the demolition of the city walls (Resina 2008, 21). Through his eyes, the city as a whole seems to become visible: he "surveys the expanding city" in a detailed description "in which Foix's gaze traces the emerging topography" of Barcelona (2008, 21). The legibility of the city from Giró's *torre* is sustained by the apparent distance that transforms a character or narrator into a "solar eye" – a "god-like perspective" – and the panoramic view into an organized topography (de Certeau 1988, 92). Indeed, the view from Giró's *torre* encompasses a diversity of objects distinctly enumerated within clear coordinates: "A l'esquerra, un tros de Barcelona . . . estenent-se al peu de Montjuïc. . . . Sos barris de Llevant . . . la costa . . . Montjuïc, [la] platja . . . els blancs poblets de marina" (I, 169). This "solar eye" view that transforms "the bewitching world by which one was 'possessed' into a text that lies before one's eyes" (de Certeau 1988, 92), makes Barcelona both visible – it extends itself in front of the character and readers – and deceptive. The narrated view is a text that lies: "The same perspective that confers intelligibility is an illusion" (Labanyi 1990, 27). It is not only that the panoramic view of the city "hid[es] the unpleasant sources of value" (Resina 2008, 44) creating false knowledge. The view of Barcelona from Giró's *torre* also subverts the realist reliance on visibility to represent the city's modern image. Bernat Foix, brother of Gil – a failed inventor who sees social and economic upheavals as "lleis naturals" (I, 167) and the guarantors of human progress – is not deceived by the illusion of totality and meaning – the harmonious whole – sustained by the "detailed description" of Barcelona's topography: "no tanco els ulls davant de la veritat, per trista o esfereïdora que sigui" (II, 179).[2] He identifies speculative wealth as the origin – or point – from which the view of the city originates, and, consequently, its inevitable and also necessary distortion of reality: "Els diners del joc no duren gaire, i els que es fiquen a la Bolsa a mi em sembla que s'embarquen en un globo de paper. El globo els enlaira per ensenyar-los panorames encisadors; però tot plegat s'encén, i, barrabum! a baix!" (II, 179). It is thus not surprising that the other possible name mentioned for Giró's *torre* is "Villa Oro" (I, 181). Just as the fleeting ownership of the Pedralbes property marks its entrance in the capitalist economy and its transformation from index – the site of aristocratic, landed, money – into sign (a commodity), the impossibility of fixing a name that would properly represent Giró's *torre* – the constant sliding of signifiers used to name it: Villa Nabab, Buena Vista, Vista Alegre, Villa Oro; no definitive name is ever given – transfigures Giró's summer house into a *fossar*. Giró's *torre* as *fossar* metaphorizes the crisis of representation – the "fever" – that informs Oller's panoramic views of Barcelona's modernity. As we will see, the city's "panorames encisadors" turn out to be, like death, "a signifier with an incessantly receding, ungraspable signified, always pointing to other signifiers" (Goodwin and Bronfen 1993, 4). But before discussing Barcelona's problematic visibility from the paper balloon made out of money – or, in Gil Foix's words, out of "el barrim-barram actual de la riquesa" (I, 166) – and its effects on realist representation, we need to discuss why it is the narrator, not the character himself, who gives voice to Gil Foix's gaze and takes upon himself the task of describing Barcelona's modernity.

Barcelona's panoramic view leaves Foix – a character whose financial success has transformed him into "un discursaire" (II, 48) who often overwhelms family and business associates with "llargs parlaments" (I, 165) – speechless: the view in front of him, says the narrator, "li travava la llengua" (I, 169). As businessman and man of action, Foix himself proudly acknowledges to his wife and daughter his ineptitude for details on their way to Giró's *torre*: "M'he acostumat ja a veure les coses a l'engròs, en gran, a abarcar d'una mirada els grans horitzons del negoci . . . i a despreciar, per insignificants els detalls. És el secret dels grans homes" (I, 165). Foix's "grans horitzons" are not those of a contemplative observer or detached flâneur, but rather those of the city dweller who "allows time only for activity" (Moretti 2005, 126). For him, the city is not so much a space to be viewed but, rather, "the most gripping story possible" (126). In Foix's "gripping story," the making of his fortune and reputation in Barcelona by playing the stock market – "El carril seria un fet dintre de pocs dies . . . Si els Nords seguien pujant, seria ric, i ric de debò, ben aviat" (I, 164) – the city is simply a "background," not an "object of attention in and for itself" (Moretti 2005, 126). Because he does not yet have enough capital at the time of Giró's party to project upon the city his own ambitious business plans, the city appears out of focus. All Foix sees is the undifferentiated object of his desire, the great expectations arisen by the city – not the city itself. It is the excitement for, the anticipation of things to come, that fill him with an emotion that cannot be put into words – "li travava la llengua – but his eyes reflect – "feia espurnejar els ulls" (I, 169). Foix's view of the city from the *Cementiri de Montjuïc* after the funeral of his mother-in-law later on in the novel – after he has acquired enough financial power to think he can make his dreams come true – confirms both his incapacity to see the city and the ensuing loquacity triggered by his projects: his gripping story in the making is the city under the focus of his ambition. It also confirms Oller's reliance on death to look into questions of visibility and representation.

After depositing his mother-in-law's body in the cemetery, his mind again full of business ventures, Foix takes his associates to the top of the cemetery to explain his last project: an "arsenal marítim" (II, 34). "Els horitzons se m'eixamplen" are his words (I, 187). From the cemetery, Barcelona's visibility is determined by Foix's ambitious plans: "Sa vista, encesa d'ambició, s'esplaiava per aquella immensa plana" (I, 298). The "immensa plana" is the background for the narrow focus of Foix's ambition delineated here in the stretch of beach and land where he wants to invest. The narrator, aware that Foix does not see the city at his feet but, rather, his own success story – the city dweller's life is "always framed and defined by exigencies of a temporal order" (Moretti 2005, 126) – focuses instead on his eagerness and activity, on his constant movement: "I tot era moure's, anar i venir, i assenyalar amb aquell bastó inquiet els grans rodals de terra que ja veia seva, que adqueriria sens dubte" (I 298). The city that Foix does not see and the arsenal that is not there generate the long "discurs" that his friends – transformed into "oients" – listen to with deference and resignation, but that the narrator does not care to reproduce: "Sos acompanyants el seguien, l'escoltaven sense pestanyejar, com l'estat major d'un general que traça el pla de batalla" (I, 298).

The Foix "discursaire" swings here into high gear to put into a flow of words his incapacity to distinguish seeing from desiring and possessing. Gil Foix is not Eugène Rastignac, who – viewing Paris from the high ground of the Cemetery of Père Lachaise at the end of *Père Goriot* – understands that "Paris must be legible if one is to possess it" (Brooks 2005, 133). Foix's visionary perspective of Barcelona from the *Cementiri de Montjuïc* conceals "the space that catches human beings by their throat, and does not let go" (Moretti 1998, 90) in order to support his illusory representation of both himself and the city. The complexity and hostility of the city vanish in front of him and are replaced by a "panorama encisador" he does not recognize for what it is: the "lie" before or, rather, in one's eyes. This is his mistake. If Rastignac's introspection from Père Lachaise – that ends with his brief defiance: "A nous deux maintenant!" – initiates his conquest of Paris, Foix's lack of attention to details – his "grans horitzons" – and "rius de paraules" mark his false consciousness (I, 167).

At the top of the cemetery, death reappears in another of its displacements to correlate the cemetery as point of view – death as a trope about representation – and that of the paper balloon made out of money with Foix's false consciousness. Surrounded by business associates, a sudden thought stops Foix's verbosity to remind him that a wealthy man like him should have a pantheon. The pantheon – the radical gap between representation (the fashionable tomb) and what it hides (the body's putrefaction) – stands for the delusional nature of Foix's representation of both himself and the city based on debauched and libidinal spending. The "arsenal" Foix's desire sees is not in the "immensa plana" and it will never be. However, in the empty site of the cemetery where he focuses his false consciousness – "el punt on el faria fer [el panteó]" – he will build a (funerary) monument to the spectral representations of speculative wealth that make him temporally a very rich man and Barcelona a modern city.

The "barrim-barram" of wealth, the "zum-zum" made by people (I, 166, 169), and Foix's speechlessness at Giró's *torre*, all find their voice in the novel's narrator. An allegorical description by the narrator of "tot aquell trasbalsament de riquesa invisible" that constituted Barcelona's modernity (Oller 1962, 132) substitutes for the indistinct words uttered by Gil Foix, his difficulty in naming what he sees, and his inability to metaphorize the city.[3] Speaking from Foix's perspective, and identifying with his emotion (but not his pragmatic aims or prosaic style), the narrator gives form and meaning to the luminosity and glowing sparks found in Foix's teary eyes. In the narrator's view, modern Barcelona is a blast of light and color. The city is like a *luminista* painting by Roig i Soler (I, 170). Under the bright light that dazzles the eye, the distinctiveness of objects and the limits of spaces become an undifferentiatied "conjunt de tons finíssims" where one thing seems to melt – evaporate – into the next.

The only reference to Barcelona's industrial wealth or urban development are the chimneys in Poblenou that, in the narrator's description of the city, become "alteroses xemeneies." The rest of the city is a "gilded" landscape – everything is "daurat," "tot daurat" (I, 170, 181) – not so much by the "gold" of the novel's title, but rather, by the "fever" of speculation that substitutes for it. Barcelona's metaphorical "radiance" cancels out all pretense of bourgeois objectivity – and Realism's claim to transform reality into objective information – to voice instead the bourgeoisie's own subjectivity. As Emilia Llopis – the *cursi* bluestocking – comments, that afternoon, at Giró's *torre*, light was a "claror enlluernadora" (I, 172). The city's metaphorical "radiance" does not describe the city, but rather represents "the optimism of a class that mirrors itself in something that is alive and growing" (Resina 2008, 21). It is a figment of the bourgeoisie's imagination. The dazzling light in Foix's eyes – his excitement for things to come – corresponds to the confident self-image the narrator shares with the Catalan bourgeoisie and also with Narcís Oller. In fact, the narrator's luminous showing of Barcelona – its allegorical brightness – seems to take its cue from Oller's object of narration – "l'ardent febrada del 80 i 81" – and the author's own excitement: "desitjava deixar historiada la gesta més esplendorosa de l'estimada Barcelona dels meus dies" (1962, 105). Narcís Oller's "objectiu temàtic no era la ciutat sinó la riquesa i el progrés" (Castellanos 1997, 150).

The narrator's view of the city as a blast of light and color that dazzles the eye and blurs one's vision not only mirrors the Catalan bourgeoisie's optimism of those years, but also the origin of its speculative wealth. In the narrator's dazzled eyes and Barcelona's specular representation, the stock market is an "ardent" venture, and brokers, "haurat[s] Jason[s]." The allegorical subjectivity that metaphorizes Barcelona's modernity captures, at the expense of Realism and its claims to objectivity and thingness, capitalism's endless process of exchange tied to no referent or objective value, the specular nature of speculative wealth. Barcelona "blanca, nova, immensa, com una gran metròpolis" both appears and disappears under "la brillantor del sol" that lights up and dematerializes its different neighborhoods. Moreover, in the narrator's impressionistic "llapissades" (I, 169) we find the "metonymic confusion" that characterizes the bourgeois sign and threatens realist writing (Barthes 1999, 40): Barcelona recedes under its signifiers. Like Balzac's obsession with detail, the reverie and dreamy quality of Barcelona viewed from a paper balloon made out of money menace – "with collapse, mined from within by the thread of non-meaning" (Brooks 2005, 33) – Oller's Realist purpose to chronicle the transformation of Barcelona into a modern metropolis. Realism's frames of representation fail to hold the vision of the crazed new heroes – "L'espectacle que allò oferia era el d'un nosocomi de delirants excitants fins el més alt grau" – as well as that of their chronicler, Oller, whose admiration and fear transfigure them into "nous argonautes" en "perillosa expedició a Colquida, sens el favor d'una altra Medea ni saber qui d'ells seria l'haurat Jason" (1962, 132).

At the end of the novel, Gil Foix, ruined and psychologically unstable, has a last chance to view the city. Following the doctor's recommendation, his wife takes him for a walk to "la Bona Nova" from where the sea and "un bon tros del Pla de Barcelona" are fully visible (II, 174). There Gil Foix stops to contemplate the city one last time and, suddenly, starts sobbing: "començà a plorar, i plora que plora, no el podien arrencar d'allí" (II, 174). The city is finally in focus but, just like before, Foix has no words to express either what he sees or his emotion;

his failure, the frustration of his desire. Back at home he falls into a delirious hectic activity, again planning ways to regain his dream: locked in his room, "somiant amb l'arsenal, vinga fer càlculs i més càlculs, despacientant-se, enfurismant-se, rebatent la ploma a cada instant perquè les operacions no li sortien bé" (II, 174). For a while, every time they take him out into the city, he falls into the same feverish activity. Bernat, saddened by his brother's nervous breakdown – he is suffering from "neuràstenia" (II, 175) – points out that Gil's failure is not due to his "bona fe," as his daughter thinks, but rather to his lack of vision: "[anava] a ulls clucs" (II, 178). Gil Foix himself seems to have finally arrived at the same conclusion. His grandiose plans for Barcelona shattered for good, he locks himself in his room "a les fosques" (II, 175). The darkness that surrounds him represents both his inability to see and a new consciousness: knowing that he is unable to stop his desire from creating false views of himself and the city, he gives up his sight (vision). Locked in a metaphorical tomb, darkness substitutes for the dazzling light of false knowledge, but also threatens to stop the energies unleashed by a debauched libidinal economy and the illusion of totalizing views that sustain the bourgeoisie's and the novel's historical optimism: progress and modernity.

The "cure" for Gil Foix – and for *La febre d'or*'s precariousness of limits – seems to be found in carpentry. At the very end of the final chapter, Bernat and Francesc discover Foix in the painter's room engaged in making frames for his son-in-law's paintings. Foix, says his brother, has returned to his origins, since his old craft was carpentry: "Potser això el curi" (II, 182). They think he is working out of pride: "l'orgull," says Francesc, "se li rebel·la a deixar-lo viure a despeses meves. Somia amb renumerar-me!" (II, 182). Thus, Foix's activity is, for these characters, another sign of his delusion. But perhaps there is another reason for his activity, a reason that may shed light on why in Galdós's *La de Bringas*, Francisco de Bringas's ophthalmologist also recommends that he – a character so radically different from Gil Foix – spend time engaged in "trabajos mecánicos" like carpentry (2000, 158–159). For very different reasons – debauched libidinal spending and the hoarding of capital, respectively – both the stock market player and the miser have the same problem of vision: their incapacity to picture reality. Gil Foix's (and also the narrator's) excessively imaginative dazzled eyes, as well as Francisco de Bringas's "strabismic close-up" (Gold 1986, 57), threaten the bourgeois reliance on close frames for representation. "[U]n nuevo armario para la ropa" for Rosalía is Francisco de Bringas's new project, his old understanding of art as mirror of the hoarding of capital remains unchanged. In *La febre d'or* wooden frames seem to be the metaphorical solution to contain Realism's failing devices of representation. Carpentry, a *menestral* craft, refers us to an earlier pre-capitalist time when money "revealed" and was an index that "furnished a fact, a cause, it had a nature" (Barthes 1999, 39). Like the old "reliable" money, Gil's wooden frames stand for a conception of art in which the work reveals reality's ultimate truth, for the belief that the image has a referent other than the endless sliding of signifiers. These wooden frames would be Gil's – and maybe Oller's – guarantors of the truth of representation. Oller knows, however, that frames are no longer, in John Berger's (1972) words, a "safe let in a wall" where the "visible has been deposited" (as quoted in Labanyi 1990, 27). Gil's "bastiments" will support his son-in law's social and financial success – "'ja veuràs com s'enfila,' predicts Bernat" (I, 179) – and frame his modernist paintings: the doodles that put an end to Realism. Oller's retelling of one of the great themes of the nineteenth-century novel, the rapid success and ruin of a self-made man, "inaugurated Barcelona as a literary subject" (Resina 2008, 15), but it is the crisis of representation that threatens *La febre d'or* that marks the definitive entrance of Barcelona in modern literature.

Notes

1 On the confusion between gambling and playing the stock market in nineteenth-century fiction, see Moretti 2005, 122.
2 Bernat "formula ya desde un principio la dialéctica social por la cual se moverá toda la obra" (Gilabert 1977, 140–141).
3 The process of "reduc[ing] the city to words . . . is one of metaphorization" (Pike 1981, 12).

Works cited

Arroyo Almaraz, Antonio. 1998–1999. "Benito Pérez Galdós y Narcís Oller: formulación y percepción narrativas de la ciudad." *Revista de Lenguas y Literaturas Catalana, Gallega y Vasca* 6: 17–27.

Barthes, Roland. 1999. *S/Z*. New York: The Noonday Press.

Berger, John. 1972. *Ways of Seeing*. London: BBC and Penguin Books.

Bersani, Leo. 1976. *A Future for Astyanax: Character and Desire in Literature*. Boston, MA: Little Brown.

Brooks, Peter. 2005. *The Realist Vision*. New Haven, CT: Yale University Press.

Castellanos, Jordi. 1997. *Literatura, vides, ciutats*. Barcelona: Edicions 62.

de Certeau, Michel. 1988. *The Practice of Everyday Life*. Berkeley, CA: University of California Press.

Franz, Thomas R. 1996. "Don Francisco as Fate: The Construction of the Cenotaph in *La de Bringas*." *Neophilologus* 80: 259–267.

Gilabert, Joan. 1977. *Narciso Oller: estudio comparativo con la novela castellana del siglo XIX*. Barcelona: Marte.

Goodwin, Sarah Webster and Elisabeth Bronfen. 1993. "Introduction." In *Death and Representation*, edited by Sarah Webster Goodwin and Elisabeth Bronfen, 3–25. Baltimore, MD: Johns Hopkins University Press.

Gold, Hazel. 1986. "Francisco's Folly: Picturing Reality in Galdós's *La de Bringas*." *Hispanic Review* 54 (1): 47–66.

Labanyi, Jo. 1990. "The Problem of Framing in *La de Bringas*." *Anales Galdosianos* 25: 25–34.

Martí-López, Elisa. 2005. "Autochthonous Conflicts, Foreign Fictions: The Capital as Metaphor for the Nation." In *Spain beyond Spain*, edited by Brad Epps and Luis F. Cifuentes, 148–167. Lewisburg, PA: Bucknell University Press.

Moretti, Franco. 1998. *Atlas of the European Novel 1800–1900*. London: Verso.

———. 2005. *Signs Taken for Wonders: On the Sociology of Literary Form*. London: Verso.

Oller, Narcís. [1890–1892] 1993. *La febre d'or*. Barcelona: Edicions 62.

———. 1962. *Memòries literàries: Història dels meus llibres*. Barcelona: Aedos.

Pérez Galdós, Benito. [1884] 2000. *La de Bringas*. Alicante: Biblioteca Virtual Miguel de Cervantes. Accessed March 20, 2015. http://www.cervantesvirtual.com/nd/ark:/59851/bmcdn428.

Pike, Burton. 1981. *The Image of the City in Modern Literature*. Princeton, NJ: Princeton University Press.

Resina, Joan Ramon. 1994–1995. "The Sublimation of Wealth and the Consciousness of Modernism in Narcís Oller's *La febre d'or*." *JHR* 3: 259–275.

———. 2001. "Madrid's Palimpsest: Reading the Capital against the Grain." In *Iberian Cities*, edited by Joan Ramon Resina, 56–92. London and New York: Routledge.

———. 2008. *Barcelona's Vocation of Modernity*. Stanford, CA: Stanford University Press.

Schleifer, Ronald. 1993. "Walter Benjamin and the Crisis of Representation: Multiplicity, Meaning, and Athematic Death." In *Death and Representation*, edited by Sarah Webster Goodwin and Elisabeth Bronfen, 312–333. Baltimore, MD: Johns Hopkins University Press.

29

PERFORMING THE PENINSULA

Costumbrismo and the theatre of the eighteenth and nineteenth centuries

Alberto Romero Ferrer

The "rediscovery" of popular culture, from the Enlightenment to the Romantics

The popular classes burst onto the political and social scene with the coming of the French Revolution, a unique set of circumstances which mark the beginning of the modern era, and which were to bring about dramatic cultural change founded on the ideals of liberty and equality. The people were to play the central role in this process, which was also to lead to a new political regime. However, after the events of Napoleon's rule, that new system was to enter a period of decline, which demanded – for the sake of peace and order – that this revolutionary ideology be to some extent forgotten.

Yet it did not disappear entirely. Those popular classes who had been the driving force in the revolution did not vanish, for the cultural world quickly came to see them as a source of material which could be exploited to make connections between the new mentality and the emerging Romantic nationalist movement, which had the rediscovery of *lo popular* at its heart. Poets, playwrights, painters, musicians, illustrators, and journalists would thus treat this popular reality in their works, incorporating elements, characters, and situations which they found in its "rediscovery." A cultural pact was thus established between these artists and the people, on which much discussion of a newly established "modernity" was to focus. In *costumbrismo*, this pact found one of its most important forms of artistic expression, especially if we focus on the case of southern Europe and the Iberian Peninsula.

The rise of *costumbrismo* in the eighteenth century, as well as its development in the nineteenth as a new way of looking at and reflecting Peninsular life in literature and theatre, in painting and music, both entail the discovery of "popular reality." This requires accepting the existence of a range of customs, features, and character types that might conflict with more strictly uniform neo-classical dogmas, especially in the realm of theatre. These changes were also linked to the emergence of the bourgeois class as a new locus of power, particularly in the nineteenth century. Thus began the formal discovery of the popular classes, which the middle classes rapidly came to see as grist for their artistic mill, in the ceaseless search for essential national realities which could only be confirmed by these wide sectors of society still uncontaminated by modernity, and its grand plan for cultural uniformity. Burke sums this up as follows:

> Craftsmen and peasants were no doubt surprised to find their houses invaded by men and women with middle-class clothes and accents who insisted they sing traditional songs or tell traditional stories.

(1978, 3)

Songs, traditional customs, settings, and figures were soon given form in the theatre, as the platform of the stage thus codified an Hispanic-Peninsular imagination grounded in this recently discovered culture with ties to the realm of "craftsmen and peasants," and in what it had to say about those supposedly native qualities in the different regional identities of the Iberian Peninsula.

This process, which began as early as the first half of the eighteenth century, really came into focus during the transition from the Enlightenment to Romanticism (1750–1850), once the resistance of the enlightened élites, who rejected *lo popular* and saw it as something barbarous, had been overcome (Escobar 1984). This conflict was particularly visible in the theatre, both because of the medium's wide reach and because of the hope placed in it as a vehicle for the politics of the Enlightenment, as a means of education and a school of morality.

The *sainete* and the *tonadilla escénica*: Madrid versus Andalusia

The stage would soon bear witness to the restlessness that accompanied this "rediscovery" of the popular classes. This was partly due to the established tradition of short Baroque theatre which made use of characters and situations of popular heritage, but also because of the disappearance of the *entremeses de Trullo*, which were taken off the Court stage in 1780, to be replaced by the *tonadilla escénica* and the new eighteenth-century *sainete*. These changing tastes and dramatic practices would become one of the most intricate and hotly contested aspects of the battle fought over the theatre by the Enlightenment with its great programme of cultural modernization, which had no place whatsoever for the popular world which these theatrical forms endorsed.

Despite the process of refinement which the *sainete* and the *tonadilla escénica* had undergone with regard to their seventeenth- and early eighteenth-century predecessors, official Enlightenment culture was unrelenting in considering them both an anti-aesthetic kind of theatre, both inadequate and immoral, which had to be banished and which needed to be civilized, for they represented the lowest kind of cultural debasement. This conflict resulted in those forms of theatre taking on a markedly combative character, which led to a radicalization of their aesthetics, their characters, and their language, both at the level of the dramatic text and in terms of their staging.

The reflection of *lo popular*, and consequently of its defining regional, social, and linguistic variety was partly down to the influence of the theatrical antecedent of the old *entremés*, but it must also be linked to the more recent shifts in how reality was perceived, and the resulting impact on various artistic fields – a phenomenon known in literature as "mimesis costumbrista" (Escobar 1988). This approach is exemplified by Ramón de la Cruz, in his defence of his theatre as modern and civilized:

> Pintura exacta de la vida civil y de las costumbres españolas [. . .] No hay ni hubo más invención en la dramática que copiar lo que se ve, esto es, retratar los hombres,

sus palabras, sus acciones y sus costumbres. Y queda convencido que yo invento cuando retrato los payos y los hidalgos extravagantes de las provincias de mi Nación, y los majos baladrones, las petimetras caprichosas y los usías casquivanos de mi lugar [. . .] Los que han paseado el día de San Isidro su pradera, los que han visitado el Rastro por la mañana, la Plaza Mayor de Madrid la víspera de Navidad, el Prado antiguo por la noche.

(1786: liv–lvi)

This perspective renders the *sainete* and the *tonadilla* two of the most important buttresses supporting the creation of an imaginary relating to national reality; and while the *comedia* focused its attention on the interests of the bourgeoisie, this new cultural imaginary demonstrated a wide regional and linguistic diversity, taking in situations, spaces, and characters which had to be interpreted – as indeed they were – as a more or less faithful mirror of life in the country, or a "[p]intura exacta de la vida civil." Its references were therefore to real, everyday life on the street. Indeed, this is one of its most vital characteristics: its close relationship to contemporary popular reality.

In another light, we should not forget the possibilities opened up for *costumbrismo* by the revolution in stage design which essentially stemmed from the 1767 reforms of the Conde de Aranda, who ordered the *Junta de Teatros* "que se retiren los paños o cortinas de la escena y se sustituyan por decoraciones pintadas" (Arias de Cossío 1991, 30). Painters thus became indispensable in the creation of theatre sets, as the techniques and materials used to make them were rapidly updated, via the incorporation of scenery and backcloths which brought a greater realism to the stage. Nor were authors such as Ramón de la Cruz blind to these developments: he was thus able to bring the real world into his *sainetes* in a much more convincing way.

Of this real world comprised of "los hombres, sus palabras, sus acciones y sus costumbres" (Cruz 1786, liv), two aspects stand out. These are the *majismo* and *plebeyismo* of Andalusia and Madrid (Sala Valldaura 1988), to say nothing of other regional links – the gallery of characters from other stock, the Galicians, Biscayans, Cantabrians, and Murcians, all with their own idiosyncrasies of language, profession, and fashion, which may be seen in the *zarzuela Las labradoras de Murcia* (1769) or the grand finale *Las provincias españolas unidas por el placer* (1789). Nonetheless, it is the *majismo* of Andalusia and Madrid that demand most attention, as the theatrical correlates of a curious process of cultural vulgarisation visible among the most aristocratic strata of society (Martín Gaite 1972), who were to adopt as their own the fashions, behaviours, and linguistic patterns supposedly thought to belong to the common people, in a complex process of social transvestism and transculturalization which tends to give us an idealized picture of those sectors – peripheral *barrios*, craftsmen's guilds, rural society – which are seen through the lens of eighteenth-century *majismo*.

The causes of this phenomenon, and importantly of its location in Andalusia and Madrid, lie in the respective economic and social contexts of those two places, being very specifically associated with the cities of Madrid and Cádiz. These were the two cities most exposed to cosmopolitan contamination, and therefore most inclined to imitate outside influences: Madrid because it was the capital of the kingdom, Cádiz because it was so cosmopolitan and had the monopoly on overseas trade. Drama also played a significant role in both cities, whose theatres became mirrors on their respective social and urban surroundings, reflected in the scenery and in the characters on stage. It is therefore no surprise that the *sainete*'s influence was both more widely and more consistently felt in these cities, as it echoed in comedic form the social dialectic of the dandy *petimetre* and *majo*.

This may be seen in the works of Ramón de la Cruz, or the Cádiz playwright Juan Ignacio González del Castillo – the two most professionalized *saineteros* of the period – as well as in many of Madrid's *tonadillas*, by musicians such as Blas Laserna, or the Andalusian works of an important composer such as Manuel García.

Many *sainetes* by both Cruz and Castillo made use of contrasts between the dandyism of *petimetría* – the emblem of modernity – and *majismo* – the image of more old-fashioned ways – as part of a play on more straightforward oppositions as the more "civilized" world of the city was systematically set against that of the rustic *payo*. This opposition was accentuated by the contrast between *currutaco* dandies and peasants, and the superiority complex of the former against the simple rusticity of the latter: peasants and craftsmen, villagers and inn-keepers, *majos* and *majas* from the periphery. The perspective of drama, which always looked favourably upon these villagers and *majos*, would set about ridiculing all kinds of affectations, whether in behaviour, speech, clothing, or action, as well as the resulting supremacy of *brío* or *bizarría* as the equivalents of being honest or natural, which were seen as the particular characteristics of the people, who were now being given a place on stage.

Both playwrights went through a particularly intense period, as far as this confrontation between *petimetres* and *payos* or *majos* is concerned, towards the end of the eighteenth century, whether that came via a recreation of a rural scene (such as La Mancha, or a cattle fair), or directly from dramatizing the ways of the city. This may be seen in Cruz's *La civilización* and *Las usías y las payas*, or in Castillo's *Un lugareño en Cádiz* and *La feria del puerto*. In all of these, censure is focused on the frivolousness of the customs which are fashionable in the city, the excesses of its luxury, and the importance placed on appearances, as opposed to a basic identity whose roots may be traced to other sectors of society which have not let themselves be contaminated by the invasion of modernity, presented as something alien to native qualities.

The first *costumbrista* images of peninsular life thus began to arise in the theatre, part idealization of the rustic world and part moral censure of *petimetría*. These images were projected from the enlightened perspective of the city, in order to indicate the design shaping the supposed cultural diversity of the Peninsula. That is the reason for the claim recorded in *El Censor* that "Madrid daba implacablemente la pauta a las provincias, y muchos de los lugareños que visitaban la corte se sentían intrusos en ella y se quejaban de ser puestos continuamente en evidencia a causa de su *rusticidad*" (Martín Gaite 1972, 54).

The *sainete* sees Madrid transformed into a literary stage, especially in the case of Cruz, who recreated the city both in his prolific run of short theatre pieces and in his *zarzuelas* (*Las segadoras de Vallecas*, 1768), paying special attention to the busiest public spaces, which offered better scope for a panoramic view of daily life. Thus, in *La pradera de San Isidro*, "se descubre la vista de la ermita de San Isidro en el foro, sirviendo el tablado a la imitación propia de la pradera" (Cruz 1996, 66).

In the case of Andalusia, evidence comes from such works by González del Castillo as *La boda del Nuevo Mundo*, *El día de toros en Cádiz*, *La feria del Puerto*, *La casa de vecindad*, *Felipa la Chiclanera*, *El fin del pavo*, *La maja resuelta*, and *El triunfo de las mujeres*. These offer a vivid description of life on the city streets, as an example of which may stand *Un lugareño en Cádiz*:

La escena se representa en la plaza de San Juan de Dios con puestos, vendedores, etc. A izquierda, tienda de mercader, con TENDERO. El POBRE MENDIGO tendrá delante del pecho dos manos postizas. El SARGENTO y los SOLDADOS estarán paseándose. El CIEGO, a un lado, con su guitarra. El CALESERO se paseará con su látigo en la mano; el AGUADOR, con su cántaro y vasos.

(2008, 314)

It is also worth mentioning the work of the Sevillian Manuel García in this southern context, whose time spent in the theatres of Cádiz between 1791 and 1797 should not be forgotten for the construction of southern models of lyrical theatre which we find in his *tonadillas escénicas El majo y la maja* (1798) and *La declaración* (1779), the operettas *El seductor arrepentido* (1802) and *El criado fingido* (1804), or the monologue opera *El poeta calculista* (1805) (Subirá 1928–30).

This obsession with offering a portrait of city life also gave the *sainete* an added value as a fairly detailed record of various aspects of *intrahistoria*: dress, food and drink, decoration and furniture; when allied to the linguistic idiosyncrasies of its protagonists, this lent the *sainete* an extraordinary mimetic capacity. The purpose was precisely that of showing scenes of everyday life which were close to the spectators, and transmitting an illusion of reality, which was beginning to be constructed as the *costumbrista* imaginary of the Iberian Peninsula.

Romantic *costumbrismo* in the theatre

However, if the eighteenth century saw the beginning of this championing of *casticismo*, it was during the nineteenth century that the *costumbrista* outlook on Spanish reality really took hold in the theatres, as the bourgeoisie began to play a more central role in society. The development of this aesthetic took it from its incipient forms and its roots in the earlier tradition of the *sainete*, transforming it into one of the pillars of the theatrical and literary history of the period. In its more developed form, it had a wide variety of literary manifestations, and had significant implications for the moral, political, and administrative order of the country: in 1822, the state was divided into 52 provinces; these then were grouped into 15 regions in 1833.

The first step of this process is provided by Romantic *costumbrismo* and its designs on rediscovering Spanish reality, its attempts to preserve and bear witness to a world which the bourgeois mentality saw as being in danger of extinction. Spain had to be rediscovered. Literature and drama were thus full of "tipos populares, vistos en Madrid o en las diferentes provincias; gente que no vista a la europea, que habite en cuchitriles; alguna vez, tipos extrasociales o francamente fuera de ley" (Fernández Montesinos 1965, 120). This was a world essentially inhabited by:

> [. . .] el torero, el barbero, la criada, la nodriza, el aguador, la lavandera, el alguacil, la gitana, el mendigo, el cochero, el calesero, el cartero, la celestina, la comadre, el sereno, la posadera, la cigarrera, el celador de barrio, los buhoneros, el portero, el ciego; en cierto modo, la doncella de labor.

(120–121)

Nonetheless, not every kind of character, location, or situation was ripe to be used in the theatre. The literary stage of Andalusia thus saw the development of a very particular line of thought regarding what would come to be termed the "género andaluz" (Romero Ferrer 1998). This was an original dramatic form, short in length as González del Castillo bears witness, but which incorporated the new contributions relating to technique and meaning afforded by articulating customs; it is defined by Fernández Montesinos as "narración dramática" (1965, 14), and predominantly depicts scenes and character types which are linked to the south. It may therefore be established that Andalusian fashion gains a foothold in theatrical tradition through these works, whether comic or melodramatic in tone, which have a decidedly southern edge to them, marked by the areas discovered by Romantic travellers such as Mérimée, Dumas, Scribe, Lord Byron, Washington Irving, Gautier, Davillier and Doré, or Richard Ford; moreover, the particular historical, geographical, linguistic, and social forces that apply in the case of Andalusia see this southern take on the theatre become the cultural paradigm for the whole Iberian Peninsula in this period. Nor, in the theatrical context, should the relevance of the incorporation and development of southern dance be underplayed. The *género andaluz* was thus a syncretic hybrid of the *sainete*, dramatic dance, and the *tonadilla escénica*, which alternated with a show's main performance.

We are thus presented with a repertoire of material from the period 1839–1861, which ranges from the ethnic "cuadro de costumbres gitanas" to the "escena andaluza" or the picturesque "entremés lírico-taurino." As Caro Baroja (1969) has observed, the vitality of the "pasillo andaluz" came from its grounding in the neo-classical model and later adjustment to the techniques of *literatura de cordel*, anchored during the nineteenth century in stereotypes associated with the most "savage," and therefore more Romantic, part of the Peninsula. A non-theatrical equivalent to this process may be seen in Estébanez Calderón's *Escenas Andaluzas* (1847).

Examples are easily found in the plays of Tomás Rodríguez Rubí, who also published a collection of poetry, *Poesías Andaluzas* (1841), containing works which had already appeared in the *Seminario Pintoresco Español*, and his two collaborations on Andalusia in *Los españoles pintados por sí mismos*. Relevant works include: *Toros y cañas* (1840); *El contrabandista* (1841), which included music by Basilio Basili; *La simpatía o el cortijo de Cristo* (1842); *La venta de Cárdenas* (1842); or *La feria de Mairena* (1843).

The preference for the Andalusian stage may also be explained in terms of the potential this "Puerta de Oriente" offered for the aesthetic programme of Romanticism, where existing on the periphery was seen as one of a literary character's fundamental qualities. The character types of the gypsy, the outlaw, the bandit, and the *pícaro* all found in Andalusia a setting that was true to life, according to their literary needs, but it also provided them with a set of references and allusions closely tied to aspects of the social reality of the south. Andalusia was a highly visual theatrical space, as well as being a place of significant artistic prestige, outstanding in various areas of graphic design, engraving, and painting.

The stage was filled with crowds, festivals, and dances, which constituted a dramatic motif in themselves. The contexts and spaces chosen by a playwright allowed other fragments of reality to be suggested to the audience, whether visually or aurally. He would make use of situations that were clearly marked by native characteristics, but always focusing on expectation or surprise at what was put on stage. He had a choice of different motifs open to him, such as city or country; and within the city, he might use an inn, a street, or a tobacco factory as the most suitable setting in which to dramatize "everyday" action. Rodríguez Rubí's *La venta de Cárdena* (1842), José Sánchez Albarrán's *La fábrica de tabacos de Sevilla* (1850), or Gutiérrez de Alba's *Un jaleo en Triana* (1861) may stand as examples of this.

The initial *costumbrista* tendency of these works would solidify into a specifically Andalusian rural environment that was markedly agrarian and firmly set against the various changes whose influence on that century was now clearly felt. This may be seen, for example, in Rodríguez Rubí's *La feria de Mairena. Cuadro de costumbres andaluzas* (1857):

> Vista del campo de Mairena: varios puestos repartidos convenientemente de fruteros, aguaduchos, buñolerías, etc., etc. Concurrencia de gente de todas clases: algazara que

se confunde con las voces de los que venden y con el ruido de las guitarras, castañue-
las y panderos de una fiesta.

(3)

This description reveals to us an obsession for painting an image of the countryside of Andalusia that shows it as suspiciously inward-looking, totally unaffected by conflicts, and featuring
a vivid *casticismo*. This image was to be frequently reproduced as the defining contemporary
depiction of Andalusia, and at times even the definitive image of what was typically Spanish.

Costumbrismo, ruralism, and regionalism: from the *género chico* to rural drama

Up to the mid-nineteenth century, as far as the theatre is concerned, the Peninsular imagination
had focused almost exclusively on Madrid and Andalusia, with other regional realities firmly
relegated to a secondary role, including such types as the Galician night watchman, the rustic
Aragonese, or the Cantabrian of the *sainete*. However, this situation was to change considerably during the second half of the century. Following the lead of Romantic *costumbrista* publications such as *Los españoles pintados por sí mismos* or the *Seminario Pintoresco Español*, an
attempt was made to take the cultural diversity with which Peninsular reality had been drawn
(however artificially) and transfer it to the theatre, always bearing in mind the theatrical trends
and tastes of the day, although the results were not always successful.

After the initial fervour over Romantic drama had calmed, new directions were sought
for serious theatre in Spain. Realism and its aesthetic offshoots and successors, from *costumbrismo* to ruralism, which had already found success in the novel, were also incorporated into
the theatre, if with a certain reticence. As was noted by Yxart (1894–1896), realism will have
only a small role on stage in a theatrical environment such as the Spanish, which is far from
welcoming of this kind of perspective, especially in the declamatory genres.

These circumstances are most easily explained by the fact that these perspectives were
being introduced to the dramatic context by way of musical theatre, as part of a debate over
the creation of a national opera, as opposed to the Italian and French models. Dramatic realism seems to find its home in the *zarzuela*, thanks to the *casticista* revolutions introduced
to the genre by Ramón de la Cruz. This is essentially the case in *zarzuelas* such as Arrieta's
Marina (1855), later made into an opera in 1871, and Barbieri's *Pan y toros* (1864) (see
Cotarelo 1934).

However, the political background of the last third of the nineteenth century was one of
instability, as there had already been signs to indicate that the liberal regime would fail as a
national project, and nationalist cries were beginning to be heard again from the periphery,
giving voice to the Peninsula's other cultural realities, in the Catalan *renaixença*, Galician
federalism and *rexionalismo*, the Basque problem, and Aragonese regionalism. In such a context, it was felt necessary to air these anxieties in the public forum offered by the stage, and
these years saw the rebirth of the Catalan and Valencian *sainete*, as well as the appearance of
Galician *enxebrismo*, the Basque and regionalist *zarzuela*, *ruralismo escénico*, and, vitally,
the *género chico*. These theatrical forms contained an attempt to move away from a unified,
monolithic view of Spanish reality, painting it instead as the sum of the various different cultural and linguistic traditions that made up the Iberian Peninsula. In short, they offered a new
way of constructing and deconstructing the Peninsular imaginary.

During the last third of the nineteenth century, the Spanish theatre devoted itself to an
intensely regionalist mode of theatrical depiction, with a wide array of titles including

especially the abundant *zarzuelas* of this sort, which went hand in hand with the resurgence of poetry in dialect and the regionalist novel. There was a great proliferation of different types of *costumbrismo* – Aragonese, Valencian, Murcian, Galician, Manchego, Catalan, and Andalusian – which all coincided with an important moment of incipient success for regional economies, especially on the periphery, as well as with a vindication of the emerging provincial middle classes keen to identify with their regions' most distinguishing traditions (Mainer 1972).

This new context brings us two further theatrical phenomena of quite a different ilk, but which combine to produce an image of the Peninsula grounded in a sense of what makes it different. The first of these is the *género chico*, a type of play-writing that was born to support the *teatro por horas* (Romero Ferrer 1993, 2000; Versteeg 2000), which could be seen on the Madrid stage from 1870. It was comprised of short, one-act pieces, with or without music, which were performed continuously with separate admission to each play. The objective was to make the theatre a less expensive place to go, thus opening it up to other sections of society whose means were more restricted (Membrez 1987).

One of the most interesting aspects of this phenomenon is precisely its kinship with Romantic *costumbrismo*. Indeed, we may even talk of a clear line of literary progression, which is already evident from the account of contemporary theatre. Here we find dramatic works where the story is little more than a pretext linking a series of scenes where certain character types are placed with some precision against an easily recognizable backdrop, representing the place with which they are indelibly associated. This is therefore a kind of theatre that is based on a reasonably short series of portraits of customs, as may be explicitly seen in titles such as Tomás Luceño's *sainete* – without music – *Cuadros al fresco* (1870), where the action takes place "en Madrid: época, la actual" (Romero Ferrer 2005, 268), and which stages a procession of the characters of "la viuda, la cuca, la verdulera, la criada, el cesante, el jornalero, el cafetero, el barbero, el ciego, el inválido, el agente de policía, el sereno, el jugador: gente del pueblo" (268). The approach taken to scenes and character types in this articulation of customs thus coincides with the perspectives offered by the modern *sainete*.

Within this essential schema, *género chico* works then focus on the same sections of "popular Spain" – the peripheral districts of Madrid or the Peninsula's rural environments – which had seemed to be the site of what was typically and particularly Spanish, the home of its most essential qualities. Into this aesthetic framework were then incorporated different landscapes, modes of dress, songs, dances, customs, and languages; it included music and rhythms that were drawn from popular or folkloric material; and drew the collaboration of set designers such as Augusto Ferri, Giorgio Busato, Bernardo Bonardi, Luis Muriel, and Amalio Fernández.

As had been the case in the eighteenth century, one of the defining geographical locations was Madrid, following the *casticista* fashions which gripped Spanish society at the end of that century. This may be seen in lyrical *sainetes* such as Ricardo de la Vega's *La verbena de la Paloma* (1894), José López Silva and Carlos Fernández Shaw's *La Revoltosa* (1897), or Miguel Ramos Carrión's sketch *Agua, azucarillos y aguardiente*. All of these feature a succession of various "genuine" images and character types from popular life – scenes which in *La Revoltosa* are confined to a "patio de una casa de vecindad" (189), in *La verbena de la Paloma* to "una calle" (415), and in *Agua, azucarillos y aguardiente* to the "jardines de Recoletos" (370).

This dramatic realization of "los españoles pintados por sí mismos" thus brought into the world of the theatre the new realist-naturalist artistic model that implied considering "la sociedad como modelo de arte" (Yxart 1894, 82), which represented a tremendous innovation over the stagnant state of the rest of contemporary theatre. This was a new dramatic literature which allowed the interaction of Spanish theatrical tradition and the new realist model, which within the realm of literature was supposed simply to extract "[lo] más auténtico y lo más real de la vida misma" (82).

This preoccupation with an objective reflection of reality implied an obsession with the accumulation of facts, though this always had to be tempered in order that it complement the overall premise of society being an artistic model whose ultimate aim was to portray the popular way of life, a clear nod to the *sainete* tradition of the second half of the eighteenth century. When Luceño wrote *¿Cuántas, calentitas, cuántas?*, he would add the subtitle "continuación de *Las Castañeras picadas* de don Ramón de la Cruz," thus providing clear testimony of its artistic heritage. So from the *majo* of *Manolo* comes Julián in *La verbena de la Paloma*; from the *maja*, *La Revoltosa*'s Mari Pepa; from the *petimetra*, the affected *señorita* of *Agua, azucarillos y aguardiente*; from the old *currutaco*, Don Hilarión's *viejo verde* – though things were moving in the direction of the grotesque tragedy of Arniches, or even Valle-Inclán's *esperpento*.

Nonetheless, the *género chico* was also marked by the cultural influence of the periphery, and by a strong *casticismo*. The world of the Valencian orchard, the lands of Aragon, the saffron fields of La Mancha, the coastal setting of Cantabria, or a town in Guipúzcoa, together with the olive groves and farms of Andalusia, were all transformed into honoured stage settings full of literary prestige and dramatic force, both in the comic mode supported by previous tradition, and in its more melodramatic facet. The latter was grounded in the greater verisimilitude which the drama could exploit in the withdrawn, rustic world of the countryman, which was transferred to the painted sets in minute detail. Relevant here for the southern context are Burgos's *El mundo comedia es o El baile de Luis Alonso* (1896), a comic work set in the working-class Cádiz district of La Viña, or Julián Romea's *La Tempranica* (1900), a melodrama set in the plain of Granada. Miguel Echegaray's comic *zarzuela*, *Gigantes y cabezudos* (1898), is a useful example of Aragonese realism; the dramatic *zarzuela* by García Álvarez y Paso, *La alegría de la huerta* (1900), represents the orchards of Murcia, as Arniches's *María de los Ángeles* (1900) does the coast of Santander; Fernández Shaw's *El tirador de palomas* (1902) may stand as an example for Peninsular Levante, as Burgos and González del Castillo's *A fuerza de puños* (1912) does for Guipúzcoa.

The landscapes of these different Peninsular regions would then have to be given in great detail, as may be seen in *La alegría de la huerta*:

> La escena representa un pedazo de la huerta de Murcia. La vegetación llega hasta el pie de la sierra elevada y escabrosa que se verá al foro. Campos de maíz, grupos de higueras chumbas, moreras, cipreses, palmeras, etc., etc. A lo lejos vence también casetas blancas y barracas de los huertanos. Dividen el suelo varias sendas; por el centro de la escena y cerca del foro cruza una acequia, que se pasa por un puentecillo de tablas. A la izquierda del espectador y a todo foro, una cuesta o rampa que figura la que baja al puente de tablas.
>
> (Valencia 1962, 527)

Or again, in *La tempranica*:

> Una explanada en la sierra cercana a Granada. A la izquierda, en segundo término, fachada de un cortijo y casa de cazadores, en cuyo centro está la puerta de entrada. Continúa formando escuadra con la dicha fachada con otro cuerpo de edificio que llega hasta el proscenio. Este trasto tiene una ventana a una altura que no puede ser

dominada sino subiéndose en el banco de fábrica que hay debajo adosado al muro. Otros bancos del mismo género a los lados de la puerta. Foro derecha, camino estrecho, por el que llega a la casa. Rocas y maleza al fondo. Es de noche. Se percibe el resplandor de la luna, que se pone poco a poco, haciéndose noche oscura.

(557)

As a final example of this tendency may stand Manuel de Falla's *La vida breve* (1913), and his "gitanería en un acto" *El amor brujo* (1915), written for Pastora Imperio and drawing on texts by Fernández Shaw and Martínez Sierra, respectively, where many elements of flamenco were also included.

In sum, this all came together to form a dramatic frieze which revealed a hidden and distinctive Spain, grounded in a regionalist ruralism which acted as a contrast to the genre's excessive *madrileñismo*, although rooted in the same traditional, folkloric background. It therefore offered a picture of Spain as a multicultural puzzle, with a great artistic depth in the first third of the twentieth century.

The second theatrical phenomenon which reflects Peninsular regionalism is rural drama (Paco 1971–1972). Under the influence of naturalism, the last decade of the eighteenth century saw the rise of a type of drama which also bears the strong imprint of regionalist *costumbrismo*, as well as that of Golden Age peasant drama such as *Fuenteovejuna* and *El alcalde de Zalamea*, and the rustic plays of Bretón de los Herreros (*A Madrid me vuelvo*, or *El pelo de la dehesa*).

However, beyond the extreme presentation of human passions, and the conflicts over an outmoded conception of honour very much modelled on Baroque predecessors, rural drama was always to feature a regional setting, whether that belonged to peasants or simply to the popular classes.

This was a kind of theatre conceived by and for the bourgeoisie, as opposed to the *género chico*, whose wider audience also included the lower classes. As a result of this bourgeois perspective, the vision offered of the rural environment often plays on an idealized view of it as a pure world of archetypal models of conduct, with rudimentary ethics and unmodified emotions, in stark contrast to the artificiality and deceptive appearances that typified the environment of the city. This was a *topos* present in the literary image of rural society throughout the eighteenth and nineteenth centuries. It was, therefore, a bourgeois vision of Spanish peasantry, reflecting values the middle classes could themselves admire, but only through the lens of an artistic contemplation of their identity.

This new literary means of lending dignity to the people, who now acquired all the honour of a tragic hero rather than maintaining their more usual comic manifestations, considered it important to a work's artistic integrity that the stage be transformed into a depiction of real life. One of its defining characteristics was therefore the construction of characters with distinguishing dialectical marks, which included an abundance of common expressions and popular sayings, in a constant attempt to convey the linguistic reality of the people depicted, as if they were a direct echo of real life. The same intentions lay behind the veristic staging which aimed to put the Iberian Peninsula on stage, by means of its different regional realities.

This is what we find in the naturalist regionalism of Ángel Guimerá, which makes the jump from neo-Romantic drama to *costumbrista* theatre with titles clearly linked to the Catalan *renaixença*, such as *María Rosa* (1894), *La festa del blat* (1896), or *Terra baixa* (1897) – a work which met with great success, and quickly became a classic of the Catalan repertoire. It is a strongly realist drama, where the weight of the setting and the hotly passionate characters, whose emotions were grounded in the love-honour code, are counterbalanced by the work's psychological study of them, and its detailed analysis of their external appearance and their language. This all takes place in a rural context that forms a perfect background for conflicts to be played out, especially the protagonists' internal conflicts. In all these examples, Catalan regionalism also seems to see rural drama as a useful way of making itself heard, which must also be related to emerging ideologies that sought to reclaim the Catalan nation and its cultural and linguistic identity.

However, this Spain of the people and the countryside also made itself felt in other parts of the Peninsula, as may be seen in the plays of Feliú y Codina. His successful *La Dolores* (1892) was set in the Aragonese context of Catalayud, while *María del Carmen* shows us the Murcian orchard, and *Miel de la Alcarria* (1895) takes place in austere Castile, as will Benavente's plays *Señora ama* (1908), "en un pueblo de Castilla la Nueva" (1991, 52), and *La malquerida* (1913). Many other works were also to focus on the Peninsula's southern lands, as was the case in Codina's *La real moza* (1897). Indeed, the south was to find in rural drama yet another way to give expression to its own peculiar distinguishing characteristics.

It should therefore come as no surprise that Andalusia returns once again to the stage, although lacking its previous relaxed image, in different dramatic registers. This may be seen, for example, in *Malvaloca* (1912), by the Álvarez Quintano brothers, which features a suffocating Andalusian world full of prejudices relating to the protagonist's honour and the lover's untrammelled passion. Moreover, in this southern environment we will also find writers of other ideological persuasions, such as López Pinillos "Pármeno," as well as a considerable number of texts that focus on the social complexities of the world of the Andalusian labourer, and offer a harsh, coarsely realistic picture of that environment, for the sake of a certain kind of regenerationist discourse. We may see this in works such as *El Pantano* (1913), *Esclavitud* (1918), or the later works *La red* (1921) and *La tierra* (1921), to say nothing of the plays by Lorca in which this line of inquiry finds its culmination: *Bodas de sangre* (1935), and his "drama de las mujeres en los pueblos de España," *La casa de Bernarda Alba* (1936).

In one form, this great abundance of dramatic riches represented by the *género chico* and rural drama may be said to reach its peak in the early decades of the twentieth century with Sorolla's series of fourteen murals for the Hispanic Society of America, entitled *Las regiones de España* (1913–1919), which depicted the most characteristic scenes, landscapes, and customs of the different regions of Spain and Portugal. They represented two different ways of producing and understanding theatre which, whether consciously or not, were to make it their aim to project a multifaceted image of what was typical of the Peninsula, while also keeping in mind the tensions and conflicts between centre and periphery which mark the political and cultural rhythms of turn-of-the-century Spain, as well as incorporating the strong *costumbrista* tradition seen in earlier theatre. Along with other artistic and literary movements of the eighteenth and nineteenth centuries, this rich seam of theatrical production was mined in order to advance the construction of national, regional, and provincial imaginaries that teemed with contradictions and remained in a state of permanent revision.

Works cited

Arias de Cossío, Ana María. 1991. *Dos siglos de escenografía teatral en Madrid*. Madrid: Mondadori.

Benavente, Jacinto. 1991. *Señora ama. La malquerida*. Edited by Mariano de Paco. Madrid: Espasa-Calpe.

Burke, Peter. 1978. *Popular Culture in Early Modern Europe*. New York: Harper and Row.

Caro Baroja, Julio. 1969. *Ensayo sobre la literatura de cordel*. Madrid: Revista de Occidente.

Cotarelo y Mori, Emilio. 1934. *Historia de la zarzuela, o sea del drama lírico en España, desde su origen a finales del siglo XIX*. Madrid: Tipografía de Archivos.

Cruz, Ramón de la. 1786. *Teatro, o colección de los sainetes y demás obras dramáticas de D. Ramón de la Cruz y Cano, entre los Árcades Larisio Dianeo*. Madrid: Imprenta Real.

———. 1996. *Sainetes*. Edited by Josep Maria Sala Valldaura. Barcelona: Crítica.

Escobar, José. 1984. "Más sobre los orígenes de *civilizar* y *civilización* en la España del siglo XVIII." *Nueva Revista de Filología Hispánica* 33: 88–114.

———. 1988. "La mímesis costumbrista." *Romance Quarterly* 33: 261–270.

Fernández Montesinos, José. 1965. *Costumbrismo y novela. Ensayo sobre el redescubrimiento de la realidad española*. Madrid: Castalia.

González del Castillo, Juan Ignacio. 2008. *Sainetes escogidos*. Edited by Alberto Romero Ferrer and Josep Maria Sala Valldaura. Sevilla: Fundación José Manuel Lara.

Mainer, José-Carlos. 1972. "José López Pinillos en sus dramas rurales." In *Literatura y pequeña burguesía en España (Notas 1890–1950)*, 89–120. Madrid: Edicusa.

Martín Gaite, Carmen. 1972. *Usos amorosos del dieciocho en España*. Madrid: Siglo XXI de España.

Membrez, Nancy J. 1987. *The "Teatro por Horas": History, Dynamics and Comprenhensive Bibliography of a Madrid Industry (1867–1922)*. Santa Barbara, CA: University of California.

Paco, Mariano de. 1971–1972. "El drama rural en España." *Anales de la Universidad de Murcia* 30 (1): 150–155.

Rodríguez Rubí, Tomás. 1857. *La feria de Mairena. Cuadro de costumbres andaluzas*. Madrid: Imprenta de Don Cipriano López.

Romero Ferrer, Alberto. 1993. *El Género Chico. Introducción al estudio del teatro corto fin de siglo*. Cádiz: Servicio de Publicaciones de la Universidad de Cádiz.

———. 1998. "En torno al costumbrismo del género andaluz (1839–1861): cuadros de costumbres, tipos y escenas." In *Costumbrismo Andaluz*, edited by Joaquín Álvarez Barrientos and Alberto Romero Ferrer, 125–148. Sevilla: Secretariado de Publicaciones de la Universidad de Sevilla.

———. 2000. "Del género chico al sainete arnichesco." *Ínsula* 639–640: 23–26.

———, ed. 2005. *Antología del Género Chico*. Madrid: Cátedra.

Sala Valldaura, Josep Maria. 1988. "El majismo andaluz en los sainetes de González del Castillo." In *Al margen de la Ilustración. Cultura popular, arte y literatura en la España del siglo XVIII*, edited by Javier Huerta Calvo and Emilio Palacios Fernández, 145–168. Amsterdam: Rodopi.

Subirá, José. 1928–1930. *La tonadilla escénica*. Madrid: Tipografía de Archivos.

Valencia, Antonio, ed. 1962. *El Género Chico (Antología de textos completos)*. Madrid: Taurus.

Versteeg, Margot. 2000. *De fusiladores y morcilleros. El discurso cómico del género chico (1870–1910)*. Amsterdam: Rodopi.

Yxart, José. 1894–1896. *El arte escénico en España*. Barcelona: Imprenta La Vanguardia.

30

PAINTING IN THE SPANISH ENLIGHTENMENT

Artists at court and in the academy

Andrew Schulz

Two events in the early 1750s had an important impact on the course of painting in Spain during the second half of the eighteenth century. Although both occurred during the reign of Ferdinand VI (ruled 1746–1759), they were the culmination of lengthy preparation and the legacy of the centralized arts policy imported from France by Philip V (ruled 1700–1746). The first of these events was the execution of the initial ceiling frescos in the new royal palace in Madrid, undertaken by the Neapolitan painter Corrado Giaquinto (1703–1766). With the notable exception of Francisco Goya (1746–1828), the decoration of the new palace would occupy the most important foreign and native painters working in Spain during the second half of the eighteenth century. The other signal event was the founding of the Royal Academy of Fine Arts of San Fernando (hereafter "the academy") in 1752. Of the thirteen painters, sculptors, and architects who composed the academy's preparatory committee (created by royal decree in 1744), six had been called to Madrid from abroad to work at the Bourbon court. The institution they established provided a training ground for the Spanish-born artists who came to dominate painting in Spain by the late 1770s.

Focusing on the court and the academy as interrelated institutional actors that helped to shape artistic production, this essay offers a broad overview of painting from the mid-eighteenth century to the aftermath of the Peninsular War (1808–1814). While it might be tempting to characterize this period in terms of a transition from the theatrical and painterly late Baroque style of Giaquinto and his followers to the Neoclassical outlook promoted by the academy, closer examination reveals that a plurality of styles coexisted simultaneously. And although the late eighteenth and early nineteenth centuries correspond to the artistic maturity of Francisco Goya, this singular artist was but one of many painters vying for a position of prominence during these decades. I close with a brief consideration of Goya's artistic practice in the 1790s, which begins to challenge the conventions of artistic patronage by charting a course founded on the imagination of the artist and the whims of the market and, in those respects, gestures toward Romanticism.

The early death of the sickly and childless Charles II (r. 1665–1700) caused a dynastic crisis that was settled by the War of Spanish Succession (1701–1714). As a result, the Duke of Anjou, grandson of Louis IV of France, ascended to the throne as the first Spanish Bourbon monarch. Among the rather dismal royal residences that the new king inherited from his Hapsburg predecessors was the Alcázar, located on the western edge of Madrid, capital city of the Spanish empire since the 1560s. This ninth-century Islamic fortress had been rebuilt in the fourteenth century and modified time and again to keep pace with the shifting tastes of the Trastámara and Hapsburg monarchs who occupied it. A fire on Christmas Eve 1734 (thought to have begun in the apartments of court artist Jean Ranc) rendered the Alcázar uninhabitable. The Italian architect Filippo Juvarra (1676–1736) arrived in Madrid by April of the following year to design a new palace on the same site, only to die a matter of months later. His pupil Giovanni Battista Sacchetti (1690–1764) oversaw construction until 1760, when Charles III (ruled 1759–1788) appointed Francisco Sabatini (1721–1797) as chief architect.

The design, construction, and decoration of the new palace constituted the most important artistic undertaking in Spain during the final two-thirds of the eighteenth century. This imposing, classically inspired edifice allowed the successive kings of the new dynasty (through the agency of court administrators and artists) to forge out of mythology, allegory, religion, and, to lesser extent, history a visual iconography that legitimized the Bourbon monarchy as inheritor of Spain's classical tradition and protector of the Catholic faith. Martín Sarmiento (1695–1772), a member of the Benedictine order and an important intellectual at the court of Philip V, was charged in 1743 with creating the iconographical program for the palace (Sarmiento 2002). Over the next quarter century he created an erudite sculptural scheme that was then dismantled under Charles III (ruled 1759–1788). Unfortunately, any instructions for painters that Sarmiento may have written have yet to come to light.

By 1753 construction on the palace had progressed to the point where ceiling frescos could be executed. These paintings were a key site of Bourbon propaganda and are important monuments in the history of painting in Spain. The Venetian artist Jacopo Amigoni (c. 1685–1752) – who had arrived in 1747 as court painter to Ferdinand VI and became director of the academy – would have begun the frescos, were it not for his untimely death. In 1753 Corrado Giaquinto arrived from Italy to take Amigoni's place as first court painter, and he remained in Madrid until 1762 (Cioffi 1992; Pérez Sánchez 2006). Giaquinto first decorated the palace chapel, painting *The Coronation of the Virgin* in its dome. He then moved on to the vaults above the twin ceremonial staircases (later modified on two occasions under Charles III), on which he painted *Spain Rendering Homage to Religion and the Catholic Church* (c. 1757–58; above what is now the single palace staircase) and *The Birth of the Sun and the Triumph of Bacchus* (1761–62; in what is now the Hall of Columns). The late Baroque dynamism, vibrant palette, and lively handling of paint that characterize Giaquinto's art had an important influence on Spanish-born painters who reached maturity in the 1750s and early 1760s and came to dominate painting in Madrid during subsequent decades.

In the early 1760s, as part of sweeping changes that accompanied his ascension to the throne, Charles III summoned to Madrid two of the greatest court painters of the eighteenth century, Anton Raphael Mengs (1728–1779) and Giambattista Tiepolo (1696–1770), each of whom decorated the vaults of important spaces in the palace. A native of Bohemia, Mengs had spent the previous decade in Rome, making his reputation as a leading proponent of Neoclassicism in close alignment with the German historian and theorist Johann Joachim Winckelmann and a circle of international artists resident in the Eternal City. Early in his career, Mengs had served the Dresden court of Charles's father-in-law, Augustus III of Poland, and he visited Naples in 1759 toward the end of Charles's tenure as King of Naples and the Two Sicilies (ruled as Charles VII, 1734–1759). Mengs spent two extended periods in Madrid, from 1761 to 1769 and from 1774 to 1776, and following Giaquinto's death in 1766 he was named first court painter (Hollweg 2006; Roettgen 2003, 217–78, 344–61). In the Madrid palace, Mengs's principal contributions were *The Triumph of Aurora* (Queen's Apartments, 1762–64), *The Apotheosis of Hercules* (Antechamber of Charles III, 1762–69), and *Apotheosis of Trajan*

(Saleta of Charles III, 1774). The subjects of the latter two works are typical of the palace frescos in connecting Spain to the classical past. Trajan was one of the Roman Emperors born in Hispania, and, as we shall see in other frescos, Hercules was often deployed as a symbol of Spain and the Spanish monarchy. While in Spain, Mengs also executed religious paintings that were highly prized by Charles III and spent much of his time painting portraits of the royal family and other dignitaries. Elements of his decorous painting style, which emphasized the selective imitation of nature, careful study of the human form, and a highly finished manner of painting, can be discerned in the works of the young Spanish painters who entered his orbit in the 1760s.

While Mengs arrived in Madrid at the height of his powers and fame, Tiepolo came to the Spanish court toward the end of his long and distinguished career – and only after doing his best to resist the invitation to decorate the palace throne room ceiling, on which he painted *The Wealth and Benefits of the Spanish Monarchy under Charles III* (1762–64). (On Tiepolo in Spain, see Christiansen 1996, 242–53; Sánchez Cantón 1953; Whistler 1985, 1986). As it turned out, Tiepolo (assisted by his sons Lorenzo and Giandomenico) went on to fresco the adjacent Audience Hall (*The Apotheosis of the Spanish Monarchy*, c. 1764) and the Guard Room (*Venus Charging Vulcan to Forge the Arms of Aeneas*, 1764–66). Between 1767 and 1769, in what would turn out to be his final commission, Tiepolo and sons executed seven altarpieces for the new church of San Pascual Baylon at Aranjuez (Whistler 1985). Indicative of the shift toward Neoclassicism at the Bourbon court, Tiepolo's paintings were replaced in 1775 by depictions of the same subjects executed by Mengs and two of his Spanish acolytes, Francisco Bayeu y Subías (1734–1795) and Mariano Salvador Maella (1739–1819). At the time of his death in 1770, Tiepolo was planning frescos for the dome of the Church of the Colegiata at the royal palace of San Ildefonso de La Granja. Bayeu and Maella also carried out that project, which was largely destroyed by fire in 1918.

Although Tiepolo's artistic impact is difficult to discern, the divergent styles of Giaquinto and Mengs would exercise considerable influence on Spanish artists. Under the sponsorship of Ferdinand VI's first minister, José del Castillo (1737–1793) went to Rome to study with Giaquinto in 1751 and then accompanied him to Spain in 1753. For other young artists, Antonio González Velázquez (1723–1794) served as an important intermediary to Giaquinto's art. A student of the provisional academy that preceded the institution's official charter, González Velázquez also trained under Giaquinto during his sojourn to Rome, which began in 1747. He worked alongside the Neapolitan artist in Santa Trinità degli Spanguoli, in which Giaquinto painted the altarpiece and González Velázquez the ceiling frescos. Once back in Spain in 1752, González Velázquez frescoed the dome of the chapel in the Basilica of El Pilar in Saragossa, employing the young Francisco Bayeu as an assistant. In 1758, Bayeu received a scholarship to study at the Madrid academy under González Velázquez, but remained only a short time in the capital before returning to Saragossa. Maella also studied with González Velázquez before his departure for Rome in 1757. González Velázquez occupied important positions at court and in the academy, and he had a hand in many of the most significant religious projects, such as those at the Monastery of the Encarnación, Salesas Reales, and San Francisco el Grande, and he designed some seventy cartoons for the royal tapestry factory. Antonio's elder brothers, Luis (1715–1763) and Alejandro (1719–1772), were also important painters, and all three worked under Giaquinto's direction on the fresco decorations of the church of the Monastery of the Salesas Reales, completed in 1761. Looking forward into the nineteenth century, Antonio's son Zacharías (1763–1834) carried on the family tradition, training with Maella and becoming a leading artist at the court of Ferdinand VII.

In the 1760s and 1770s, talented young Spanish painters entered into the orbit of Mengs, who was in need of assistance in carrying out fresco decorations and designing tapestry cartoons. Mengs encountered Francisco Bayeu during his visit to Saragossa in 1762, and he called Bayeu to court the following year to work on the palace frescos. (On Bayeu, see Morales y Marín 1995). Bayeu's first assignment was *The Surrender of Granada* on a ceiling in the Queen's apartments. This courtly, elegant image shows Ferdinand V of Aragon accepting the keys to the Alhambra while Mohammed XII (the final Muslim ruler on the Peninsula) bows before Isabella of Castile as putti carrying symbols of victory descend from above. Bayeu's work apparently met with approval, and in 1764 he executed *The Fall of the Giants* on the ceiling of the *sala de conversación* in the apartments of the Prince and Princess of Asturias (the future King Charles IV and Queen María Luisa). In contrast to the historical character and rococo charm of *The Surrender of Granada*, *The Fall of the Giants* depicts the Greek myth in which a race of mortals attempts unsuccessfully to overthrow the gods of Olympus. Hercules, who played a pivotal role in this struggle, is represented prominently in Bayeu's image for reasons discussed previously.

Painted when Bayeu was thirty years old, *The Fall of the Giants* is the major achievement of his early career. In it, he demonstrates his skill in handling perspective and in depicting the body in a variety of poses. This work synthesizes the competing styles of Mengs – in the arrangement of the figures around the cornice, the accurate study of the body, and the use of classical models – and Giaquinto – in the dynamism of the composition and the vibrant palette, the latter particularly visible in the presentation sketch. Typical of Bayeu's art, the finished work was the result of careful study, as evidenced by the many preliminary drawings related to this composition (now in the collection of the Museo del Prado), which reveal the artist's skill as a draftsman. Bayeu's oil sketches (see Figure 30.1) exhibit a lively handling of paint – also the legacy of Giaquinto – that he found difficult to translate into fresco. A few years later, Bayeu painted *The Apotheosis of Hercules* (1768–69) on another ceiling in the same apartments, at which point he was given a supplement of 6,000 *reales* for his efforts.

Bayeu attained the salaried position of court painter in 1767, and following Mengs's departure for Rome a decade later he emerged as the most influential painter at court. Known for his incessant work (which may have contributed to his relatively early death), he executed frescos in other royal residences occupied by the monarchs during the course of the year, and undertook important commissions in the Basilica of El Pilar in Saragossa, some of which were carried out by other artists, including Goya, under his supervision. Bayeu also became an important figure in the academy, to which he gained membership shortly after his arrival in Madrid in 1763. In 1788, he succeeded Antonio González Velázquez as the academy's director of painting, and in 1795 (the year of his death) he was elected director general.

Bayeu's career was interwoven in various ways with that of his slightly younger contemporary, Mariano Maella (1739–1820), including the aforementioned projects in the church of San Pascual in Aranjuez and the Church of the Colegiata at the royal palace of La Granja. (On Maella, see de la Mano 2011). Born in Valencia, Maella studied at the Madrid academy in the 1750s, where he began his training under court sculptor Felipe de Castro before studying painting under the tutelage of Antonio González Velázquez. Maella went to Rome in 1757 and was elected to the academy upon his return in 1765, at which point he became closely aligned with Mengs. The following year, Maella executed a ceiling fresco in the Madrid palace depicting *Hercules Between Virtue and Vice* (Prince's dressing room), and in 1797 he painted *Apotheosis of Hadrian* (dressing room of Charles III). In 1776, Bayeu and Maella shared a commission to fresco the cloister of Toledo Cathedral, and Maella would go on to execute altarpieces for

Figure 30.1 Francisco Bayeu y Subías, *El Olimpo. Batalla de los gigantes*, 1764, oil on canvas, 68 × 123 cm.
© Museo Nacional del Prado, Madrid [P604].

the same church. Following Bayeu's death in 1795, Maella took over the role of general director of the academy, and in 1799 he and Goya were elevated to the rank of first court painter.
During the Peninsular War, Maella worked for the "intruder king," Joseph Bonaparte, and was
therefore forced to renounce his positions at court and in the academy after the defeat of the
French in 1814. But Maella's legacy did live on, as his most important pupil, Vicente López,
became the favored portraitist at the court of Ferdinand VII (ruled 1814–1832), employing in
a polished Neoclassical style that represents a return in some respects to the ideals of Mengs.

Among the duties at court given to Bayeu and Maella was the task of supervising painters
employed by the royal tapestry factory. Dedicated to Santa Barbara, the tapestry factory was
the first in a series of manufactories created by Spanish Bourbon monarchs along the French
model of centralized state sponsorship of the arts. Others produced glass, porcelain, illusionistic tabletops composed of hard stone, and other luxury goods to decorate and furnish the
various palaces occupied by the royal family during the course of the year. The tapestry factory
was founded in 1720 on the outskirts of Madrid to replace the supply of Flemish tapestries that
was lost along with the Spanish Netherlands in the War of Spanish Succession.

The tapestry factory flourished under the patronage of Charles III, who appointed Mengs
as its artistic supervisor. It provided an important source of employment for young Spanish artists, including Bayeu, Castillo, Maella, and Goya, as well as Andrés Ginés de Aguirre
(1727–1800) and Ramón Bayeu (1744–1793; younger brother of Francisco). Painters created
thematically coherent ensembles of works of varying sizes and shapes to decorate a given
room. They rendered compositions in full-sized, oil-on-canvas designs (referred to as "cartoons") that workers followed – with varying degrees of success – to produce woven tapestries. At the time of their creation, tapestry cartoons were not considered works of art in their
own right and were either discarded or stored for possible reuse. In addition to their decorative
purpose, the woven tapestries served the practical function of providing insulation against the
harsh Castilian winter, which explains why most were intended for the Escorial and Pardo
palaces, occupied by the royal family during the fall and winter, respectively. Other tapestries
were destined for the small pleasure houses constructed on the grounds of those palaces for
the future Charles IV.

As was the case for other artists of his generation, the tapestry factory provided Goya's
initial foothold at the Madrid court, although he eventually came to resent these assignments
as beneath his rising ambition. A native of Aragon, Goya received training in Saragossa, where
he came into contact with Francisco Bayeu, who is described as his teacher in a document
dating from the early 1770s. After twice failing to gain entry to the Madrid academy through
its student competitions, Goya travelled to Italy in 1769 at his own expense (as he reports in
a document soliciting the position of court artist in 1779). He returned to Saragossa in 1771,
took on various local religious commissions, and married Bayeu's sister Josefa in 1773. In late
1774 – and most likely at Bayeu's suggestion – Mengs summoned Goya to Madrid to design
cartoons for the tapestry factory. His first assignment was a series of hunting scenes (a favored
pastime of the Spanish monarchs) executed after drawings by Bayeu for the dining room of
the Prince and Princess of Asturias in the Escorial Palace. During the next fifteen years, Goya
would make a total of seven suites of cartoons, comprising sixty-three designs in all (Tomlinson 1989). The majority of these decorative ensembles was for the Prince and Princess of
Asturias, who would become Goya's most important patrons during their twenty-year reign,
which lasted from 1789 to 1808.

Goya's cartoons (and those of his contemporaries) are genre scenes that feature contemporary types, some engaged in labor and others in various popular pastimes. These works reflect

Figure 30.2   Francisco de Goya y Lucientes, *El quitasol*, 1777, oil on canvas, 104 × 152 cm.
© Museo Nacional del Prado, Madrid [P773].

such current fashions as francophilia and *majismo*, and rely on a variety of sources, including contemporary theatre and traditional iconography drawn from emblem books. Goya's tapestry cartoons also exhibit a diversity of emotional tenor, ranging from the "comic and rustic" (as one series was described in a contemporary document) to the elegance of works such as *The Parasol* (see Figure 30.2), which depicts a fashionably dressed young woman gazing flirtatiously at the viewer.

The Parasol forms part of Goya's second series of tapestry cartoons, which he famously described as "of my own invention." This group of ten images was painted between 1776 and 1778 for the dining room of the Prince and Princess of Asturias in the Pardo Palace. Intended as the design for a tapestry that would fit over a door, *The Parasol* exhibits a playful eroticism and rococo charm typical of this series, in which *majos* and *majas* engaged in popular entertainments make their initial appearance in Goya's art. Thematically, *The Parasol* brings to mind contemporary French painting by Jean-Honoré Fragonard (1732–1806) and others, as well as a genre of theatre known as the *sainete* popular at the time in Madrid. The technique is also noteworthy, as vibrant colors are applied with a virtuoso brushwork that would have presented challenges for the tapestry weavers. This sketch-like approach to creating finished works – termed *bocetismo* by Enrique Lafuente Ferrari – is a signature quality of Goya's oeuvre that would periodically cause problems for the artist (Enrique Ferrari 1947, 77–81). In 1778, the tapestry factory returned to Goya a cartoon entitled *The Blind Guitarist* (from his third series, for the antechamber of the Prince and Princess of Asturias in the Pardo Palace) for corrections and further elaboration so that the workers could follow it. Goya made the requested changes, but demonstrated his pride in the original conception by recording it in an etching, his largest work in that medium. He would run into similar problems in 1780–81 over his commission to paint *Mary, The Queen of Martyrs* in one of the domes of the Basilica of El Pilar in Saragossa, which led to a falling out with Francisco Bayeu.

In addition to the demand for decorative painting, portraiture was an important source of employment for artists working at court and for private patrons. Dissatisfied with the efforts of the painters he found in Madrid early in the century, Philip V imported French artists to create likenesses of the royal family. Michel Ange Houasse (1680–1730; in Madrid 1715–1730), Jean Ranc (1674–1735; in Madrid 1722–1735), and Louis Michel Van Loo (1707–1771; in Madrid 1736–1753) fulfilled the king's expectations for a grander and more opulent style of portraiture, which had been shaped by the paradigm of Hyacinthe Rigaud (1659–1743), who had himself declined an invitation to come to Madrid. As Philip's reign progressed, a preference for Italian painting and culture emerged under the influence of his second wife, Isabel Farnese. This trend continued under Philip's son and successor, Ferdinand VI, who in 1747 called Jacopo Amigoni to Madrid at the suggestion of his courtier Carlo Broschi, the great Italian castrato singer (1705–1782; better known as Farinelli).

Charles III's desire early in his reign to have Anton Raphael Mengs come to Madrid would have been motivated in large measure by his skill as a portraitist. The significant time that Mengs had to devote to creating royal likenesses led him to recruit Bayeu, Maella, and Antonio González Velázquez to paint frescos in the Madrid royal palace in the 1760s. Mengs's talents as a portraitist are on full display in a pair of paintings of the Prince and Princess of Asturias, the future King Charles IV and Queen Maria Luisa, painted around the time of the sitters' marriage in 1765. These three-quarter-length likenesses eschew the elaborate trappings favored by the earlier Spanish Bourbons. The restrained elegance of the painting of the fourteen-year-old María Luisa established a prototype for out-of-door aristocratic portraiture that younger painters would emulate, as did Goya (albeit in his own particular manner) in his *Portrait of the Marquesa de Pontejos* (c. 1786; Washington, D.C., National Gallery of Art).

Mengs's portrait of the future king in hunting costume (see Figure 30.3) recalls the Habsburg iconography of royal hunting portraits found most memorably in Velázquez's paintings of King Philip IV, Prince Baltasar Carlos, and the Infante Don Fernando as hunters (all Museo del Prado), created in the early 1630s for the royal hunting lodge known as the Torre de la Parada. In the eighteenth century, these works hung in the Madrid royal palace, where Mengs and other court painters and their patrons would have seen them. In 1776, Mengs wrote an appraisal of the Spanish royal collection in which he celebrated the naturalism of Velazquez's art. The less polished surfaces and slightly looser handling of paint in Mengs's pair of portraits may reveal Velázquez's influence on his style (Petzel 1968, 130).

Velázquez had an even more important impact on the art of Francisco Goya. In the late 1770s, Goya undertook a series of etchings after works by Velázquez in the royal palace, including the three hunting portraits already mentioned (Vega 1995). Twenty years later, in the fall of 1799 – at the time he was made first court painter together with Maella – Goya painted his magnificent portrait of Charles IV in hunting costume (see Figure 30.4; illustrated here in contemporary copy rather than the original, which still hangs in the Madrid palace). The unmistakable reference to Velázquez's royal hunters would have been intended to suggest that Goya's relation to Charles IV was similar to that between Philip IV and Velázquez, who was the only painter sanctioned to depict the Hapsburg king. Goya's dialogue with his great predecessor at court continued the following year when he depicted himself at work within his large-scale *Family of Charles IV* (1800; Madrid, Museo del Prado), in emulation of Velázquez's position in *Las Meninas* (1656; Madrid, Museo del Prado).

Figure 30.3 Anton Raphael Mengs, *Carlos IV, Príncipe de Asturias*, c. 1765, oil on canvas, 152.5 × 111 cm.
© Museo Nacional del Prado, Madrid [P2188].

Although Goya would paint some of his most accomplished portraits for private patrons in the first decade of the nineteenth century, his favored position at the court would prove to be short lived. In the aftermath of the Peninsular War (1808–1814), Goya painted several images of Ferdinand VII; however, these were commissioned by ministries and other institutions and not by the monarch himself. Ferdinand's love of medals and decorations, and of flattery, was better served by the portraiture of Vicente López, who was called to court in 1814. The highly polished and elegant style of López's portraits represents a return to the ideals of Mengs, which López had inherited as a student in the studio of Maella.

Turning now from the court to the academy, as was noted in the introduction the Royal Academy of Fine Arts of San Fernando played an important role in shaping artistic practice during the second half of the century (Bédat 1973; Úbeda de los Cobos 1988). Although not given its royal charter until 1752, during the reign of Ferdinand VI, the academy of fine arts was one of a series of state-sponsored cultural institutions launched during the long reign of

Figure 30.4 Francisco de Goya y Lucientes (copy), *Carlos IV*, 1799, oil on canvas, 207 × 127 cm.
© Museo Nacional del Prado, Madrid [P727].

Philip V. Others included the Spanish Academy, founded in 1713 with the aim of providing official oversight of the Spanish language, and the Royal Academy of History, chartered in 1738 and charged with writing a national history freed from myth and superstition.

The genesis of the academy of fine arts can be traced to sessions held beginning in 1741 in the studio of Giovanni Domenico Olivieri (1706–1762), who arrived from Genoa the previous year to serve as court sculptor to Philip V. In 1744, the king sanctioned the formation of a preparatory committee comprised of artists engaged in the building and decorating of the Madrid palace. Officially founded by royal decree in 1752, the academy received its definitive statutes in 1757, which put control not in the hands of artists, but rather of aristocrats who played important roles in affairs of state. The king's chief minister of state – essentially the prime minister – served as protector of the academy and bore ultimate responsibility for, and authority over, its affairs. Thus, although created in emulation of the academies in Paris and then Rome, the Madrid academy differed in this important respect from similar institutions that sprung up in European capitals during the course of the eighteenth century.

Nevertheless, the Madrid academy was linked to broader eighteenth-century academic culture in its privileging of the art and architecture of antiquity and the revival of classical ideals in fifteenth and sixteenth centuries. The members of the preparatory committee made clear the importance of classical precepts by agreeing at their first meeting to make a series of allegorical paintings. These erudite works, created in the late 1740s and intended to provide models for students to emulate, include *The Allegory of the Founding of the Royal Academy of Fine Arts* painted in 1746 by Antonio González Ruiz (1711–1788) and *The Education of Love by Mercury and Venus* created two years later by Louis-Michel Van Loo (1707–1771). (Both works remain in the academy's collection.) In addition, celebrations of the classical past pervade the orations given by important officials of the academy at the prize-giving ceremonies held annually until 1757 and triennially thereafter. Similar to the visual arguments presented in the Madrid palace frescos discussed previously, these orations posit the Spanish Bourbons, culminating with Charles III (who as King of Naples had sponsored excavations at Pompeii and Herculaneum), as inheritors and upholders of classical principles. And, as was the case elsewhere in Europe, the Madrid academy sent its most promising students in painting, sculpture, and architecture to Rome so they could study first-hand the monuments of classical antiquity.

The academy's primary function was to train students in the disciplines of painting, sculpture, architecture, and printmaking. With classes open to all – both native and foreign born, and regardless of social class – the academy was one element in the broad program of educational initiatives and reforms undertaken under royal sponsorship during the Spanish Enlightenment. The institution's success can be measured in quantitative terms by the dramatic growth in the number of students, from about 300 in the late 1750s to roughly 1,000 in 1800. This growth necessitated its relocation in the 1770s from the Casa de la Panadería to a nearby palace on the Calle de Alcalá, adorned with a new, classically inspired façade by Diego Villanueva (1715–1774) as declaration of academic principles.

The academy adopted a highly rationalized educational program rooted in the belief that artistic creation should be governed by fixed rules derived from the art of antiquity. Students progressed from studying geometry, to copying prints and drawings of canonical works, to working from casts of classical sculptures, and, finally, to studying the live male model. Although Mengs had a contentious relationship with the academy, the Neoclassical principles outlined in his writings – such as the selective imitation of nature as a means of creating ideal beauty – exerted a powerful influence over the academy. This was particularly true in the 1780s, following the publication in Spanish of his collected writings, edited by his friend, Joseph Nicolás de Azara, who served as Spanish Ambassador to Rome (Schröder and Maurer 2013). In an oration delivered in 1781, Gaspar Melchor de Jovellanos – an advisor to the academy and a leading figure of the Spanish Enlightenment – described Mengs's writings as "the catechism of good taste and the code of practitioners and lovers of the arts" (Jovellanos 1781). Charles III's predilection for Mengs's style is signaled by his directive that an unfinished *Annunciation* be installed in the council room of the academy in 1780. At the academy's prize-giving ceremony held the following year, Francisco Gregorio de Salas read a "poetic copy" of the painting that he had composed for the occasion (Tomlinson 1992, 29).

A cornerstone of the academy's activities was student competitions in the various disciplines taught by the institution (Azcárate Luxan 1994). The competitions took place every three years and were divided into three classes corresponding to different levels of student advancement. The competition in each class consisted of two components: a *prueba de pensado* for which entrants were given a fixed amount of time to create a finished work depicting the prescribed theme, and a *prueba de repente*, which entailed treating a theme in one sitting under the watchful eye of professors of the academy. For painting and sculpture, the subjects chosen were historical, religious, and mythological, and allegorical in nature, with approximately half of them relating to illustrious events in the history of Spain, usually drawn from the *Historia general de España* written by Juan de Mariana (1536–1624).

In contrast to the state patronage of history painting in France during the second half of the eighteenth century, artists in Spain had few opportunities to paint the kinds of subjects called for in the Madrid academy's student competitions. The demand for religious painting did, however, provide one important outlet for ambitious painting depicting significant human action – as well as an important source of income. The most important and interesting religious project during the final quarter of the century was the rebuilding and decoration of the convent church of San Francisco el Grande. Allegedly founded by Saint Francis himself while on a pilgrimage to Santiago de Compostela in 1217, San Francisco el Grande was one of the most important religious institutions in Spain. Shortly after arriving in the capital in 1759, Charles III decided to replace the old church with a new one to showcase the talents of contemporary architects and artists. Designed by court architect Francisco Sabatini – who was also in charge of work on the nearby royal palace – construction began in 1775 and was completed in the early 1780s.

A royal order issued on July 20, 1781, commissioned large-scale altarpieces for the main altar and chapels from the leading artists working in Madrid, including Bayeu (main altar), Castillo, González Velázquez, Goya, and Maella, as well as Andrés de la Calleja (1705–1785) and Gregorio Ferro (1742–1812). The project was overseen by José Moniño, Count of Floridablanca (1728–1808), first minister to Charles III from 1777 to 1792 and a proponent of the pragmatic reforms that characterized the Spanish Enlightenment. As the king's first minister, Floridablanca acted as protector of the academy, which explains why all but one of the artists selected were members of that body. (Castillo was the one exception; Goya had gained entry into the academy only in May of the previous year.) Moreover, all of these painters had been born in Spain, exemplifying the shift from foreign to native artists discussed in relation to the royal palace. As a point of comparison, consider the decoration of the Church of the Salesas Reales, undertaken in the late 1750s under the sponsorship of Barbara of Braganza, wife of Ferdinand VI. In that case, French and Italian artists created altarpieces under the supervision of first court painter Corrado Giaquinto.

The large-scale paintings created for San Francisco el Grande reveal the diverse artistic idioms that characterize Spanish painting in the early 1780s, which to some extent matched the variety of themes (many relating to Franciscan saints) given to the artists. Once unveiled to the public in 1784, the altarpieces appear to have been poorly received, at least in official circles. Reacting to requests for payment made in 1785 by Goya, Castillo, and Ferro (who were not salaried court artists), Floridablanca responded, "Pay each another 4,000 *reales*; although the paintings were no great masterpieces, at least those by these artists were not the worst" (Tomlinson 1992, 2). Eugenio Llaguno, a leading politician and intellectual, provided an even more damning assessment in a letter to the academy's secretary, Antonio Ponz: "I wish the paintings at San Francisco had never been done, because, without them, we would have no proof of our great ignorance of the Art of Painting" (Kasl and Stratton 1996, 201). For his part, Goya considered his depiction of *Saint Bernardine of Siena Preaching Before Alfonse V of Aragon* (in situ), in which he treats the theme in historical rather than visionary terms, to have been a triumph. Indeed, he goes so far as to claim in a letter to his childhood friend Martín Zapater that it had been judged the best of the lot.

Whatever the truth about the reception of Goya's painting, his participation in the decoration of San Francisco el Grande signals his rise to prominence during the 1780s. As noted previously, the decade had opened with his acceptance as an artist member (*académico de mérito*) in the academy, a position he probably sought as a result of the closure of the tapestry factory in the face of the economic conditions caused by the outbreak of war with England. Perhaps the most important development of these years was Goya's emergence as a leading portraitist at court and among the cultural elite, which begins with the full-length portrait of the Count of Floridablanca (1783; Madrid, Banco de España), probably painted shortly after completing the altarpiece for San Francisco el Grande. He also executed several portraits for the Infante Don Luis (1783–84), brother of Charles III, as well as for the Duke and Duchess of Osuna and the Count and Countess of Altamira. These relationships would result in further patronage, particularly in the case of the Osunas, who from the mid 1780s until the end of the century were Goya's most important private patrons, commissioning not only portraits, but also decorative and religious works, and purchasing four sets of his landmark print series *Los Caprichos* (1799). Goya also enjoyed success at court, attaining the salaried position of painter to the king in 1786 and first court painter in 1789, the year of Charles IV's ascension to the throne (ruled 1789–1808). As noted previously, many of Goya's tapestry cartoons had been painted to decorate rooms occupied by Charles and María Luisa, and now they turned to Goya for several sets of royal portraits.

Goya's ascendancy continued in the 1790s. He received important commissions for portraits, religious paintings, and decorative works, with some of his greatest paintings in each of these genres dating from these years. He continued to play a role in the affairs of the academy, delivering an address as part of the call for pedagogical reforms in 1792. And in 1799 he would rise to the highest rung of the artistic hierarchy at court and be named (along with Mariano Maella) to the post of first court painter, which had remained unfilled since Mengs's death in 1779.

But this decade was also an important watershed for Goya. Toward the end of 1792, in his mid forties, he suffered a mysterious illness that left him permanently deaf and fundamentally altered the course of his life and artistic career. As he recovered in 1793, Goya undertook a group of uncommissioned cabinet paintings, which he describes in a famous letter to Bernardo de Iriarte, vice-protector of the academy, dated January 4, 1794:

> In order to use my imagination, which has been painfully preoccupied with my illness and my misfortunes, and to offset the expenditure I have inevitably incurred, I set out to paint a group of small pictures, in which I have managed to include observations of subjects which would not normally fall within the scope of commissioned work, in which there is no room for the inventive powers and inspiration of the imagination [*capricho e invención*]
>
> (trans. Glendinning 1977, 46–47)

The paintings alluded to in this letter were shown to the members of the academy the following day, and in a second letter to Iriarte, dated January 7, Goya thanks the vice-protector for his intervention and alludes to the "generous reaction to my works." He then goes on to mention ". . . a final [painting], which I have already begun, which shows a yard with lunatics, and two naked figures fighting while the keeper beats them, and others in sacks (it is a scene I once saw in Saragossa). I will send it to Your Excellency in order to complete the series" (trans. Wilson-Bareau and Mena 1994, 200). This remarkable painting (see Figure 30.5), executed in oil on tin-plated iron, was identified in the late 1960s and – by virtue of its scale, unusual media, and

Figure 30.5 Francisco de Goya y Lucientes, *Corral de locos*, 1794, oil on tin-plated iron.

© Meadows Museum, Algur H. Meadows Collection, Dallas, Texas [67.01].

style – provided the point of departure for reconstructions of the series (Wilson-Bareau and Mena 1994, 189–209). There is now general scholarly consensus that half of the twelve paintings that comprise this series portray scenes of bulls and bullfighting. The other half depict a variety of themes including a fire, a shipwreck, an assault on a coach, and the interior of a prison, which together with the *Yard with Lunatics* focus on extremes of human emotion and experience, bringing to mind Romantic conceptions of the sublime.

The letter of January 4 to Iriarte states that by virtue of their uncommissioned nature these works opened up new expressive possibilities, which Goya memorably describes as encompassing *capricho e invención*. As I have discussed elsewhere, contemporary sources define *capricho* as describing something outside of the ordinary rules (Schulz 2005, 55, 100–101). Although Goya continued to undertake commissions for the remainder of his life, from this moment forward he developed a parallel body of work, comprised primarily of drawings, prints, and occasionally, paintings, in which he explored the creative freedom afforded by working outside of the constraints of patronage. Such an approach put Goya out of step with the mainstream of early nineteenth-century Spanish art, which came to be dominated during the reign of Ferdinand VII by a rather tepid Neoclassical style. Viewed in retrospect, Goya's interest in the expressive powers of the imagination positions him as perhaps the first of the moderns and an essential point of reference for artists working in a wide range of media down to the present day.

Works cited

Azcárate Luxan, Isabel et al. 1994. *Historia y alegoría: los concursos de pintura en la Real Academia de Bellas Artes de San Fernando (1753–1808)*. Madrid: Real Academia de Bellas Artes de San Fernando.

Bédat, Claude. 1973. *L'Académie des beaux-arts de Madrid: 1744–1808*. Toulouse: Associations des publications de l'Université de Toulouse-Le Mirail.

Christiansen, Keith, ed. 1996. *Giambattista Tiepolo, 1696–1770*. New York: Metropolitan Museum of Art.

Cioffi, Irene. 1992. "Corrado Giaquinto at the Spanish Court, 1753–1762. The Fresco Cycles at the New Royal Palace in Madrid." PhD diss., New York University.

de la Mano, José. 2011. *Mariano Salvador Maella. Poder e imagen en la España de la Ilustración*. Madrid: Fundación de Arte Hispánico.

Glendinning, Nigel. 1977. *Goya and His Critics*. New Haven, CT: Yale University Press.

Hollweg, Pia. 2006. *Anton Raphael Mengs' Wirken in Spanien*. Frankfurt: Peter Lang.

Jovellanos, Gaspar Melchor de. [1781] 1952–1963. "Elogio de las bellas artes." In *Obras publicadas e inéditas de D Gaspar Melchor de Jovellanos*. 5 vols. Edited by Candido Nocedal. Madrid: Atlas.

Kasl, Ronda and Suzanne L. Stratton. 1996. *Painting in Spain in the Age of Enlightenment: Goya and His Contemporaries*. Indianapolis, MN: Indianapolis Museum of Art.

Lafuente Ferrari, Enrique. 1947. *Antecedentes, coincidencias e influencias del arte de Goya*. Madrid: Sociedad Española de Amigos de Arte.

Morales y Marín, José Luis. 1995. *Francisco Bayeu. Vida y obra*. Zaragoza: Ediciones Moncayo.

Pérez Sánchez, Alfonso E. 2006. *Corrado Giaquinto y España*. Madrid: Patrimonio Nacional.

Petzel, Thomas O. 1968. "Anton Raphael Mengs and Neoclassicism: His Art, His Influence, and His Reputation." PhD diss., Princeton University.

Roettgen, Steffi. 2003. *Anton Raphael Mengs, 1728–1779. Leben und Wirken*. Munich: Hirmer.

Sánchez Cantón, F. J. 1953. *J. B. Tiepolo en España*. Madrid: Instituto Diego Velázquez, del C.I.S.C.

Sarmiento, Martín. 2002. *Sistema de adornos del Palacio Real de Madrid*. Edited by Joaquín Álvare Barrientos and Concha Herrero Carretero. Madrid: Sociedad de Conmemoraciones Culturales.

Schröder, Stephan F. and Gudrun Maurer. 2013. *Mengs y Azara. El retrato de una amistad*. Madrid: Museo Nacional del Prado.

Schulz, Andrew. 2005. *Goya's* Caprichos*: Aesthetics, Perception, and the Body*. Cambridge: Cambridge University Press.

Tomlinson, Janis. 1989. *Francisco Goya: The Tapestry Cartoons and Early Career at the Court of Madrid*. Cambridge: Cambridge University Press.

———. 1992. *Goya in the Twilight of Enlightenment*. New Haven, CT: Yale University Press.

Úbeda de los Cobos, Andrés. 1988. *Pintura, mentalidad e ideología en la Real Academia de Bellas Artes de San Fernando, 1741–1800*. Madrid: Editorial Universidad Complutense.

Vega, Jesusa. 1995. "Goya's Etchings After Velázquez." *Print Quarterly* 12: 145–63.

Whistler, Catherine. 1985. "G. B. Tiepolo and Charles III: The Church of S. Pascual Baylon at Aranjuez." *Apollo* 121: 321–327.

———. 1986. "G. B. Tiepolo at the Court of Charles III." *The Burlington Magazine* 128: 198–203.

Wilson-Bareau, Juliet and Manuela B. Mena Marqués. 1994. *Goya, Truth and Fantasy: The Small Paintings*. London: Royal Academy of Arts, and Chicago: Art Institute of Chicago.

PART IV

The Iberian Peninsula during the twentieth century

History, politics and cultural studies

31

THE IDEA OF EMPIRE IN PORTUGUESE AND SPANISH LIFE, 1890 TO 1975

Filipe Ribeiro de Meneses

Portuguese and Spanish life in the twentieth century was in great part dominated by the experience of dictatorship, which began to take hold in the 1920s and then lasted, with the interregnum of the Second Republic in Spain, until the mid 1970s. Much has been written about the origins, nature, and consequences of the Salazar and Franco regimes, which undeniably shared a number of characteristics, but which also differed in a number of key areas. Some of these differences were born out of the personality, background, and world view of the two dictators; others reflected the economic, social, and cultural realities of Portugal and Spain. One issue brought all these factors together: Empire.

From the British Ultimatum of 1890 until decolonization in 1974–1975, Portugal's colonial dimension played an ever greater role in the country's life and politics. In the same period, meanwhile, Spain lost the remainder of its American and Asian empire, became embroiled in North Africa through the Moroccan Protectorate, and then, without much fuss (except for the Southern Sahara) divested itself, in the final years of the Franco dictatorship, of almost all its African possessions. The political consensus in Portugal around Empire across most of this period was striking, but for all the commitment to Portugal's "civilizing mission," there was remarkably little pragmatic thought given, across three very different regimes, to its purpose, value, and consequences. Empire, ultimately, was a myth through which Portugal's political, economic, and cultural elites could find both common ground and a justification for their role and privileges. Given the importance and resources of Portugal's overseas possessions, this was a powerful and intoxicating myth. How the rest of the country, poor and, by Western European standards, underdeveloped, viewed the enterprise, seemed not to matter. Because of the smaller size of Spain's territorial holdings, losses in Morocco at the time of the Annual disaster (1921), and genuine popular participation in the country's affairs during the Second Republic (1931–1936), the situation in Spain was different. Popular indifference or even hostility to the creation by force of a new colonial empire was made manifest. Nevertheless, the idea of "Empire," however nebulous, was used by the Franco regime to point to a redeeming future, and to justify ongoing sacrifices.

The aim of this article is to compare the idea of Empire in Portugal and Spain during this period, which in both countries involved an evolution from liberal monarchy to republic to dictatorship. The article pays close attention to the mythic status of Empire and its manipulation by successive regimes, stressing, however, that the Portuguese Empire was a more significant entity than its Spanish counterpart, playing a greater role in national life. It should be kept in mind that dictatorships, by censoring public debate, made difficult any accurate evaluation of the real popularity of conceptions of Empire and corresponding ambitions.

Portugal before Salazar

The history of contemporary Portugal cannot be written in a strictly national fashion, focusing exclusively on events in the metropolis. As Fernando Tavares Pimenta put it recently, "O 'Século XX Português' foi radicalmente distinto do 'Século XX Europeu.' Essa distinção foi uma consequência direta do peso desproporcionado do fator colonial na história portuguesa" (Pimenta 2010, 8). From 1900 to 1933, Portugal moved from constitutional monarchy to the First Republic, and then to Salazar's New State. There were differences in the three regimes' colonial policies, but these were not as important as the continuities that bound them together: for all the hopes pinned on the colonies, and all the sacrifices made in their name, Portugal's hold over them was always relatively feeble, due not only to internal and external threats, but also to the enormous gulf that separated imperialist rhetoric from reality. While the latter was true of all colonial empires, with claims to a civilizing mission falling far short of the reality on the ground, Portugal's unique position as an economically weak colonizer meant that even hard-nosed arguments about bringing the indigenous populations into the world economy against their will, or making use of resources that such populations were too backward to tap into, fell flat.

It was the sight of other powers scrambling for parts of Africa which the Portuguese had long considered, in a vague way, theirs, that woke Portugal from its lethargy at the close of the nineteenth century. Not much thought was given to why, or with what purpose, Portugal laid formal claim to territory in the wake of the Berlin Conference of 1884–5, just a sentiment that others were trespassing on Portuguese lands. And so, without much consideration for available resources, material and human, by 1887 Portugal, in the now famous "mapa cor-de-rosa," was laying claim not only to Angola and Mozambique, whose borders had been more or less delineated, but also to all the territory in between. This dizzying vision of a second Brazil in Africa, stretching from the Atlantic to the Indian Ocean, was quickly felled by the British ultimatum of January 1890, which forced the Portuguese to withdraw from what is today Zimbabwe. What had begun as a venture into State-fomented nationalism by the Crown became a national humiliation which benefited the rising Portuguese Republican Party, but few paused to ask why Portugal needed such vast tracts of territory, how it proposed to develop them, and how it could impose its will on their inhabitants.

The inability to find Portuguese investors to operate in the colonies led to the creation of Crown companies, which were active in Mozambique, but with disappointing results. The colonies were also disdained by Portuguese emigrants, who continued to cross the Atlantic in their thousands every year, mostly to Brazil. Portugal had colonies (officially labelled "overseas provinces"), but its hold on them was slight. On the ground, it was a desire for enrichment that drove a handful of Portuguese settlers, and they displayed little concern for the well-being of the local populations, whatever their level of material advancement. There was little sense that the "white man's burden" weighed on the shoulders of the Portuguese.

The coming of the Republic in October 1910 deepened Portugal's attachment to the myth of Empire. All republicans believed that Empire, as a living link with a glorious past, would play a key role in reawakening the national genius, dulled by centuries of monarchist and clerical reaction. Maria Cândida Proença writes, "Conscientes da força do império na formação da unidade e identidade nacionais, os republicanos, desde cedo, incorporaram no seu discurso cultural e político a defesa da salvaguarda, manutenção e desenvolvimento dos territórios ultramarinos como um dos vetores da sua propaganda política" (2009, 205). And there remained, of course, the hope of extracting considerable wealth from the colonies. But such ideological readings of history and pious hopes for the future could not overcome the fact that Portuguese economic agents had not amassed sufficient capital to transform the colonies. Whatever investment occurred was carried out by the State, or was heavily guaranteed by it, to the detriment of the impoverished metropolis.

The difficulties proved insurmountable. The Republic's colonial programme, based on decentralization, amounted to little in the end. The regime, which relied on the income provided by import and export duties charged on trade with the colonies (Oliveira 2011, 303), had little to say on the ideal relationship with the indigenous population, or on tensions between that population, the (very few) white settlers, and metropolitan business interests, who for the most part simply re-exported colonial goods. Without financial investment in the Portuguese colonies, these remained, for the most part, in the doldrums, and subject to periodic rebellions against Portuguese rule. Portugal's colonies saw plenty of fighting during the First World War (Meneses 2014). These were sad campaigns, which consumed many lives and much gold for very little gain and which, more often than not, were still "pacification" efforts. But it might be said that enough was done – enough men died – to guarantee that Portuguese rule over the colonies continued throughout the interwar period, despite frequent allegations of labour abuses. Republicans attempted to portray this sacrifice as part of the national renewal they had initiated. It is worth recalling the words of the interventionist feminist Ana de Castro Osório, in her children's history of the conflict:

> Nunca em Portugal se deve ensinar nas escolas nem nas famílias que a nossa Pátria
> é pequena, pois essa não é a verdade. E pela vida fora, quando diante dum português
> tal falsidade se disser, têm a obrigação de defender-se como duma verdadeira injúria.
> (Osório 1918, 32)

A new impetus was given, after the war, to the material transformation of Angola and Mozambique. High Commissioners, backed by Legislative Councils, were empowered to take out international loans to fund the development of their respective province, while the mercantilist link with Portugal was broken, but the results attained still fell well short of the desired goal. The central problem continued to be the lack of investment capital, now allied to the distrust of the autonomy granted to the colonies on the part of economic groups tied to the re-export of colonial goods (Proença 2009, 218). These groups made the most of a series of scandals, notably the Alves dos Reis "Angola e Metrópole" bank forgeries, to warn that the Empire was in danger, weakening the regime. And as the ultimate guarantor of colonial loans, the Portuguese State became liable for debts whose contraction it could not control.

Spain before Franco

The consequences for Spain of defeat by the United States of America in 1898 are by now well understood. Defeat and the loss of American and Asian territories did not lead to a coup by a wounded army, jealous of its prerogatives, or to a social revolution. Neither did it lead to economic crisis and stagnation. But 1898 did result in heightened political tension, with which the Restoration monarchy did not cope well; a more politically active – and united – officer class; and much soul-searching by Spanish intellectuals about the country's place in the world, now that the last links with the great Empire of the past had been cut. The year 1898 also had a powerful effect on the young man who soon after rose to the throne. Alfonso XIII enjoyed close links with the army and wanted to consolidate his political position at home. African military adventures were a shortcut to this goal.

The army's desire for a leading role in national life, allied to a growing awareness of the "Scramble for Africa" among certain economic interest groups, pushed Spain into an unlikely and costly colonial venture in Morocco. Alfonso de la Serna writes, "La tentación colonial africana sería entonces la gran trampa que el destino iba a tender a España" (2001, 190), before asking, having laid out the diplomatic scenario, "Cómo podía nuestro país ser indiferente al gran juego político, económico y militar que se abría sobre el estratégico tablero extendido ante nuestras costas?" (2001, 191). The seeds were in place: military activity in the region throughout the nineteenth century; a powerful if anachronistic legate in the shape of Isabel la Católica's will, which urged her heirs to continue the conquest of Africa and the struggle against the "infidels;" and the creation of a number of learned societies such as the "Sociedad de Africanistas" (1864), the "Sociedad Geográfica de Madrid" (1876), and the "Asociación Española para la Exploración de África" (1876). Joaquín Costa was an early proponent of a greater commercial contact with Africa, sponsoring caravans from the Saharan coast to the Sudan, and then serving as the point of contact between this reputedly fabulous trade, Europe, and Spanish-speaking America. There was an enormous gulf, however, between the ambitions of these early *africanistas* and the possibilities of the Spanish state, which watched impotently as France laid claim to the territories it coveted.

Coincidentally, the creation of a Spanish sphere of influence was required by the other powers interested in the peaceful carve-up of North Africa. But the Protectorate over northern Morocco was a poisoned pill, given the ferocity with which its population resisted Spanish "pacification." This constant demand for military action proved unpopular at home – beginning with Barcelona's "Tragic Week" in 1909 – and led to the creation of a specialized officer corps, at odds with the broad mass of the population, civilian politicians, and even their Peninsula-based comrades (Balfour 2002). The blood-letting at Annual, twenty-three years after the 'disaster' of 1898 (with the significant milestone of the costly 1909 Melilla campaign halfway between the two) consolidated popular opposition to wars of expansion. General Primo de Rivera's initial popularity was due in no small part to his "abandonista" stance in relation to Morocco. It was hard to conceive of the Moroccan Protectorate, consolidated only in the mid 1920s after the final defeat of Riffi leader Abd-el Krim, as the worthy heir of the Spanish Empire of the past, but some commentators tried to do just that (Meneses 2005).

However, there was another dimension to Empire in Spanish minds, notably among nationalist thinkers. This was an entirely spiritual dimension, born of the nostalgic belief that Empire had been a mission in pursuit of which Spain, a grouping of different kingdoms, had been forged, and had attained greatness. While the formal links with the old colonies were gone, it was still believed – and vehemently preached – that Spain's role as a beacon for the rest of the Hispanic world remained valid and indeed necessary. Quite how this role was to be fulfilled was by no means evident, but the general view was that this kind of Empire would be more elevated, and less materialistic, than its Anglo-Saxon equivalent. Spain would be a guide to its successor states on the American continent, and it would be able to count on the support of Spanish emigrants now residing in those states. José Antonio Primo de Rivera, who rarely mentioned Spain's actual colonies (Nerín and Bosch 2001, 36), was one of the principal proponents of this strengthening of cultural links with Latin America. Others were Ramiro de Maeztu, author of *Defensa de la hispanidad*, and Antonio Tovar, the Falangist author of *El imperio de España*. This whole scheme was at the very least delusionary. As *The Times* put it on the eve of the Second World War, "In Argentina and Uruguay, where a mixed European immigrant population predominates, there was before the Civil War a tendency to despise Spain as being picturesque but materially backward. South Americans who visit Europe find hygiene less advanced than in the big cities of the New World" ("Spain across the sea" 1939). Manuel Chaves Nogales, a republican in exile writing for *The Washington Post*, explained that:

> As for the restoration of the Spanish empire of the sixteenth century, this is an idea which is discussed by many good Spanish patriots. For 40 years – that is, since the war with the United States and the loss of the Spanish colonies – it has been an idea shared by all honest and intelligent Spaniards that any attempt at national reconstruction should be based upon the admission of Spain's present inferiority. This intellectual discipline, imposed by a series of national catastrophes due to the disproportion that long had existed between Spain's real strength and the amplitude of her enterprises, is actually the cause of the division between the two Spanish parties. Against this principle of the true limits of Spain, Franco, obsessed with the dawning imperialism of the totalitarian countries, has resuscitated the idea of this empire – which is merely a will to power devoid of any real basis. The only resource left to Spanish imperialism is to exercise its influence in the Spanish-speaking world in the hope of some day assuming a kind of spiritual mandate over the 16 American republics of Spanish origin.
>
> (Nogales 1939)

Salazar's new state

The Portuguese Republic was replaced in 1926 by a military dictatorship, whose leaders quickly invited António de Oliveira Salazar to be the country's "financial dictator." In 1932 he was appointed Prime Minister, and unveiled a new regime, the "New State." Salazar did not, initially, view the colonies as his main preoccupation. This was reserved for resolving the country's financial situation, using the political capital accrued by this success to make himself indispensable. This in turn meant bringing the colonies to heel, financially and economically speaking. We should remember, too, that the Great Depression, which coincided with Salazar's rise to power, saw a collapse in the value of colonial exports, which lessened the importance of the colonies in his eyes. Securing Portugal's overseas possessions was, however, an important part of shoring up his power, and so Salazar unveiled a new legal framework for the relationship between the metropolis and the colonies – the Colonial Act, drafted with the help of an established ideologue, Quirino de Jesus, and a rising political star, Armindo Monteiro. This legislation, which formally constituted an Empire and introduced the word "colony" into Portuguese legal terminology, reasserted unequivocally the authority of the metropolis.

The Colonial Act was welcomed by existing economic interest groups in Lisbon, nationalist circles, and the armed forces, who generally administered the Empire. It set out to redefine the relationship between Lisbon and the colonies, but also to proclaim, more clearly than ever before, the reason for Portugal's overseas efforts:

> É da essência orgânica da Nação Portuguesa desempenhar a função histórica de possuir e colonizar domínios ultramarinos e de civilizar as populações indígenas que

neles se compreendam, exercendo também a influência moral que lhe é adstrita pelo Padroado do Oriente.

("Ministério das Colónias" 1930)

One of the missions Portugal set itself was ensuring the well-being of the native populations under its charge, preserving them from abuses and labour exploitation (these were merely pious expressions of intent, with little in the way of substance to back them up). What the Act failed to do, however, was to address Empire's future. Could the indigenous population ever be accepted as full citizens? What would happen when Angola or Mozambique could survive and thrive on their own – would they be set free? Could they become new Brazils?

Armindo Monteiro, who took over the Colonies portfolio (1931–1935), attempted to generate an imperialist sentiment in Portugal. It was his aim to make the Portuguese appreciative and worthy of the Empire they had supposedly inherited from their ancestors, proud of its size and power, and willing to engage productively with the colonies. With Armindo Monteiro began the age of colonial exhibitions (which culminated later, in 1940, with the *Exposição do Mundo Português* in Lisbon), in which the Empire was brought home to the Portuguese. Salazar allowed this propaganda to go ahead, as he allowed other ministers' pet projects, but his heart was not in it, and he eventually lost interest. He understood that there remained strict limits to what could be done even by those whose enthusiasm for the colonies had been awakened. Settlement was not encouraged; foreign investment was discouraged; and all around, thanks to poverty, underemployment, and illiteracy, was abundant evidence that Portugal's status as an imperial nation was questionable.

Portugal remained neutral in the Second World War, and the regime survived. But as other European countries began to wind up their colonial empires, willing or unwillingly, the New State woke up to the need to reform its own, especially in light of the United Nations Charter. True to form, the change envisaged was extremely restricted to a legal/constitutional setting, having little impact on settlers and Africans alike. No serious consideration was as yet given to inviting Africans to participate in decision-making at any level, while white settlers were distrusted, given their support for the democratic opposition movement in the 1945 elections. The Empire was rebadged *Ultramar Português*, while its individual units reverted to the more traditional designation, *Províncias Ultramarinas*. Legislative Councils were created in Angola and Mozambique, although their powers were extremely limited, they met infrequently, and most of their membership (white, "mestiço," and black) was appointed, not elected. Power remained in the hands of the Governor General and, through him, the Overseas Ministry in Lisbon. The economic subordination of the colonies to Lisbon also remained in place. There was one important change after the war: a sudden government enthusiasm for white settlement in Africa, notably Angola, which was now given official sanction and some support. From 44,083 in 1940 and 78,826 in 1950, the population rose to 172,529 in 1960 (from 1.2% to 3.6% of the total population). The numbers for Mozambique in the same period were 27,438, 48,910, and 97,245 (from 0.5% to 1.5%) (Pimenta 2010, 95). It was hoped that these arrivals would strengthen the Portuguese claim to the territory, and that they would dilute the spirit of opposition to Lisbon among the established white community, but this was not always the case (Pimenta 2010, 95).

More importantly, the Portuguese imperial myth reinvented itself in the face of the mounting challenge to colonialism. The brutal assertion of strength and domination typical of the Colonial Act was now replaced by "luso-tropicalism," an idea posited by Brazilian sociologist Gilberto Freyre. This was a uniquely Portuguese approach to life in the tropics that facilitated a cultural exchange unblemished by racism. Luso-tropicalism was manna from heaven for the Portuguese, who used it to differentiate their overseas action from the crude, materialistic colonialism of other Europeans. Portugal was building multi-racial societies in its overseas provinces; it did not have colonies, but was one nation, with one outlook and purpose, spread out over a variety of continents. That white Europeans occupied the most important positions was simply a measure of their head start in the modern world, but they had no innate right to those positions. This set of beliefs, which flew in the face of so much concrete evidence (in terms of established economic exploitation, such as compulsory cultivation of cotton, the labour abuses denounced by Henrique Galvão (1961, 57–71) and the kind of brutal repression evident in Pindjiguiti, Portuguese Guinea, in 1959 and in Mueda, Mozambique, in 1960), was to colour Portuguese thinking in relation to colonial matters until decolonization and, for great swathes of the population, ever since.

Spain under Franco

The hopes for both a larger and more permanent presence in North Africa and a spiritual/ intellectual leadership of the Hispanic world can be discerned in the rhetoric and actions of Francisco Franco. Nerín and Bosch write:

> el discurso africanista de los vencedores de la guerra civil no procedía ni de la vieja Falange ni del carlismo. Para crear una nueva ideología colonial se hubo de fundir la ideología militar africanista con algunos elementos de la retórica imperial falangista, con retazos del pensamiento regeneracionista y con los fundamentos ideológicos del africanismo decimonónico de las sociedades geográficas.
>
> (2001, 38)

Franco, whose career prospects and world view had been transformed by fighting in Morocco, easily adopted the Falangist discourse of Empire, born of a preoccupation with the seemingly relentless loosening of the bonds that held Spain together. This was an imperialism of the mind, impossible to realize in the face of Spanish weakness and the indifference, if not outright hostility, of other Spanish-speaking countries (Kennedy 1946); but instilling this will to Empire was seen by the Nationalist authorities as an essential task. As early as November 1940, a *Consejo de Hispanidad* was created in Madrid. An American observer wrote in the 1940s:

> What Franco and his imperialist intellectuals dreamed of was a league of totalitarian governments stretching all the way from Cape Horn to the Rio Grande. Whether they would be out-and-out Fascist government or would merely lean to Fascism would depend on local conditions. These governments, from the very nature of things, would be cooperative with Franco, as indeed some of them are already. Fascist Spain, therefore, would be in a position to act as their spokesman and tutelary genius in the same way that England, as a democracy, acts in many things for Canada, Australia and New Zealand.
>
> (Hamilton 1944, 467)

The Second World War presented for a brief moment the possibility of turning imperial aspirations into concrete reality. Might Spain be able to profit from others' (notably France's) misfortune? Might a victorious Germany reward Spain with a larger slice of North Africa, leading to the establishment of a viable Empire (Goda 1998)? The territories lusted after included all or part of the French Protectorate (based on all kinds of argumentation that "demonstrated" the strong affinities, if not actual unity, of Spain and Morocco, their land and their people) and the area around Oran, where there was a substantial Spanish settler population. Good diplomatic fortune might even lead to the acquisition not just of Gibraltar, but, some extremists thought, possibly of Portugal as well – and with it Portuguese colonies across Africa and Asia (Hamilton 1944, 465). Even the Philippines were occasionally mentioned as a possible avenue for expansion. Those same powers that had helped the Nationalist camp in the Civil War were now at war – and defeating – the countries that had traditionally stood in the way of Spanish colonial expansion, France and Great Britain. Newspapers such as *El Alcázar* speculated feverishly about the possibilities opened up before Spain: "Before the prospect of a readjustment of colonial dominions in Europe, we are forced to put on record that Spain has been repeatedly frustrated as far as her rights in Africa are concerned, and that one way or the other it will be necessary to end an unjust situation which does not conform to her geographical position or history, nor allow for her excess population" (English 1940b). Writing some years later, Thomas J. Hamilton noted how:

> Times have changed since the summer of 1940, when gangs of Fascists roamed the streets of Madrid shouting their claims to Gibraltar, and the Franco government put up official posters laying claim not only to Cuba and the Philippines but to California, Arizona, Texas and Florida. In those exuberant days Fascist toughs stoned both the British and American embassies, Fascist newspapers made daily attacks upon the "decadent pluto-democracies" in the best Goebbels style, and either Franco or his brother-in-law Serrano Suñer delivered a weekly speech attacking the Allies and threatening that Spain would enter the war at any moment.
>
> (1944, 466)

Falangist ambitions were eventually codified into the *Reivindicaciones de España*, published in the summer of 1941 by José María de Areilza and Fernando María Castilla, on behalf of the party's Institute of Political Studies. It demanded Gibraltar, Tangier, French Morocco, and most of Algeria, "plus a broad strip of desert from the southern reaches of Algeria to the Atlantic below Rio di [*sic*] Oro" (Hamilton 1944, 466).

Falangist groups and their press might have dreamed of an expanding empire, but how far did Spanish society share these ambitions? Given their lack of popularity before 1936, and the moral and material state of the country after 1939, it is almost impossible to conceive that anyone saw Spain's resurgence as a great power as a realistic goal, whatever the outcome of the war. The generalized distrust and dislike of the Falange must also be borne in mind. As one observer put it, "The country is in such a state that, if the Germans were not on the frontier, the Falange, and with it both Franco and Serrano Suñer, would almost certainly disappear overnight" (Situation in Spain 1940). But the Falange was not the only organization that craved expansion. The Army was equally ambitious and ready to intervene should the Pétain government collapse, or de Gaulle stage a coup in the French Protectorate. In any case, in the summer of 1940 the regime launched a major campaign to turn territorial aggrandizement into a true national goal – insofar as this was possible in post Civil War Spain. Newspaper articles and columns became progressively more annexationist as France's woes deepened. Robert Gale Woolbert wrote, shortly after the Second World War's end:

> This enthusiasm is not shared by the average Spaniard, for whom African adventures have in the past almost invariably spelled unwanted military service, higher taxes and

national humiliation. Since the end of the Civil War the Spanish imperialists have tried valiantly to counteract this popular hostility and to arouse a pride in Spain's imperial past, an interest in her present modest colonial empire and a faith in its glorious future.

(1946, 724)

Spain carried out one act of international aggression – the seizure of the city of Tangier, an internationally run enclave within the Spanish protectorate (English 1940a; Preston 1993, 361–362) – but refrained from taking matters further, despite, for example, assuming an aggressive posture on the borders of French Morocco (and fomenting unrest among that territory's indigenous population), and massing troops outside Gibraltar. The difficulties involved in either of these operations dwarfed the limited means available to the Spanish armed forces. Spain's dependence on Great Britain for the supply of essential goods also undercut any aggressive action. Ultimately, an African empire could only have been built on the back of a German military victory, but there was even no guarantee that in the aftermath of such a victory Spain would emerge as Germany's favourite, deserving of such rich prizes. In the wake of France's armistice with Germany, Pétain, with Berlin's blessing, moved troops into North Africa to preserve the status quo. No change was possible. Following this brief dalliance with North Africa, Spanish imperialist dreams focused once again on *Hispanidad*: "Not even the wildest *Falangista* really ever believed that the Spanish flag would again fly over any of the twenty nations of Latin America. But there is ample evidence of the Franco regime's determination to assert itself in that area to the maximum" (Hamilton 1944, 467).

As a result, the pacified Protectorate continued to be Spain's principal African possession, of little bearing in Spanish life, alongside other territories such as the Spanish Sahara and the neighbouring enclave of Ifni. Awarded to Spain at the Berlin Conference in 1884 (at a time when Madrid's eyes were still firmly set on the Caribbean and the Philippines), Ifni was sparsely inhabited by Berbers and, interestingly, was occupied only in 1934, during the Republic's "Bienio Negro"). Farther south, Spanish Guinea was a classic example of colonial inactivity. Taken together, these territories were of little economic value. Spanish Guinea's offshore oil deposits had not yet been identified, and the colony was a backwater, eventually gaining its independence in 1968. By then the Protectorate had long been absorbed by the rest of Morocco as it recovered its full independence. Spanish authorities had been reduced to using the Protectorate as a way of ingratiating themselves with the Arab world, posing as friends of Moroccan nationalism – in contrast with the French, whose policies they were sabotaging. This did not prevent a last bout of repression in the Spanish zone before Franco "showed a sense of realism" and accepted the Protectorate's immediate demise (Preston 1993, 644). Less realism was shown towards Spanish Sahara and Ifni. A decree of 10 January 1958 would declare Ifni and the Sahara to be Spanish provinces, an integral part of Spain. This was as absurd for Spain as it was for Portugal and, as in Portugal, the move was a response to the anti-colonial threat posed by the United Nations. Unlike Salazar, however, Franco would eventually recognize that this was an untenable situation, and military action against Moroccan forces alternated with negotiations and the return of territory. In the Spanish Sahara, a Berber resistance group, the Polisario Front, fought a guerrilla war against Spanish forces, but it was eventually pressure from Morocco, at a time when Spain was focused on Franco's impending death, that forced Madrid's withdrawal. These conflicts were always low-level, and did not affect Spanish life – wrapped up in economic growth – greatly. By the 1960s, moreover, there was no thought of these remaining African territories fitting into some kind of imperial scheme, or a wider narrative of Spanish imperial mission.

Portugal's colonial wars

In 1961 the wave of African nationalism finally crashed down on Angola. Under fire in Africa and at the UN, Portuguese colonialism, while resorting to arms, once again attempted to reinvent itself. This happened in many stages. Adriano Moreira, appointed Overseas Minister in 1961, was perhaps the most fervent believer in official Portugal in the luso-tropical model, and wanted to formulate policy anchored in this reading of the Portuguese overseas action. He was trapped, however, between the deep conservatism of the man he served – Salazar – and the white Angolan elites' desire for a radical overhaul of their province, allowing for much greater economic freedom and rapid development. These elites found in Governor-General Venâncio Deslandes a champion. Moreira was also searching for a political solution to the conflict begun in March, based on a gradualist approach to autonomy and, eventually, self-determination of the overseas provinces, to be arrived at in partnership by the metropolis and the local elites, whatever their colour. To bring this about he needed immediate changes on the ground, as well as a review of the legal framework for Portuguese practices overseas. Numerous early measures introduced by Moreira included the abolition of the *Código do Indigenato*, the end of compulsory cultivation of cotton, the reinforcement of the Governors' powers and each province's representation in the National Assembly, greater public investment in Overseas Portugal and the opening up of the colonial economies to international investors (Moreira 1962). But his thunder was stolen in Angola by the "Deslandes Plan," approved on 7 October by the Legislative Council of Angola. It contained reforms in all sectors: the economy, education, public works, transport and communications, health, etc. It also promised to reinforce the power of the Council, leading to greater popular involvement in decision-making. Deslandes took the search for collaborators as far as establishing a line of communication with Agostinho Neto's MPLA, not yet engaged in a violent campaign against Portugal. In a letter to Salazar, Deslandes defended a federal approach for Angola and Mozambique. The tipping point came on an issue close to Salazar's heart: university education. The ensuing political crisis was eventually resolved by the twin removal of Deslandes, who at one stage described himself as the head of government of the largest portion of national territory, as well as the leader of the strongest military force Portugal had ever assembled, and Moreira, seen as having stirred up a hornet's nest. In the meantime, the rapid loss of the Portuguese State of India in December 1961 came as a shock to the country and to Salazar himself.

A second period of reform was unveiled under the overall control of Salazar's energetic successor, Marcelo Caetano. Caetano had long been associated with an evolution of Overseas Portugal along federal lines. Appointing him Prime Minister, Admiral Américo Tomás, the President of the Republic, was taking a gamble – one he thought was worth taking, given the fact that he himself had now considerably more power than under Salazar. Caetano understood this, and defended a policy of "progressive and participatory autonomy," by which legislative and executive power would be devolved slowly, as each province revealed itself able to cope with it. The main beneficiaries of this gradual approach, Caetano hoped, would be the white settlers, who would eventually – in a distant future – inherit power, as had occurred in British Dominions (although this was a view that Caetano could not exactly espouse in public), keeping their respective territory, once independent, within a wider Portuguese community. In their diplomatic contacts with friendly governments, Caetano and his Foreign Minister, Rui Patrício, stressed the unique nature of Portugal's mission to create independent, multi-racial societies (Patrício 2012; Pimenta 2008, 316).

To his credit, Marcelo Caetano, as Prime Minister, did something Salazar had never done in all his years of power – he toured the "Overseas Provinces," selling his idea of gradual devolution of authority. He came back impressed by the growing strength of the Portuguese presence in Africa, and more determined than ever to preserve it. Settlers' economic associations welcomed this development, and were extremely active in this period. There was a trade-off: immediate political support at national level for an embattled Caetano, in return for the promise of future control over Angola and Mozambique. Many of the deputies elected by Angola in the 1969 legislative elections represented these interests. But still, against the hopes and aspirations of the settlers, stood the conservative faction of the New State, headed now by Thomaz (Pimenta 2008, 314–343). And so the changes made were essentially cosmetic, beginning with the promotion of Angola and Mozambique to "States." The governor-general continued to be appointed by Lisbon, but was now seen as a cabinet member in the metropolitan government, while presiding over his respective State's government. Legislative Assemblies were unveiled, more powerful than their predecessors, the Councils. There was a rise in the number of deputies sent to Lisbon (from seven to twelve) and in the number of overseas electors, from 183,000 to 628,000. It was hoped that recently enfranchised *mestizo* and black electors would act as a bulwark to the nationalist movements, and help the whites to build an – eventually – independent Angola. What Caetano could not do, however, was end both the financial subordination to Lisbon and the war. Ultimately, Caetano was deluding himself and the country. The continuation of the war saw Portugal increasingly reliant on some very unsavoury friends whose stated racial policies were the opposite of the Portuguese multi-racial mission: Rhodesia and South Africa. Their intelligence services met regularly and exchanged information; South African investment made a number of emblematic projects possible, notably the Cahora Bassa Dam in Mozambique; and their armies, grouped in what was called Exercise ALCORA, collaborated in the destruction of what was now deemed a common enemy (Meneses and McNamara 2012).

Conclusion

For Portugal, Empire ended in tragedy. The idea of Empire, which was meant to unite the nation, ended up dividing much of it: on one side, the ever larger number of settlers attracted by the late blossoming of the colonial economy, at a time when the entire enterprise was doomed. On the other, those called upon to sacrifice their lives for Overseas Portugal, but who could discern no end to wars that counter-insurgency doctrine taught them could only be resolved by a political solution. The result was not only the 25 April 1974 revolution, but also the confused and often chaotic decolonization process that ensued, which in the case of Angola led directly to civil war, and in the case of East Timor to Indonesian occupation. The great wave of *retornados* should have brought home to Portugal the cost of its imperial folly, but their surprisingly easy integration into Portuguese life, at a time of great political and social agitation, ensured the survival of certain benign interpretations of Portuguese colonialism. In Spain, the real cost of Empire had been learned much earlier, and there was no chance of any late blossoming of popular enthusiasm for colonial ventures. Both discourse and reality were an idiosyncratic characteristic of a regime which at times seemed completely divorced from the reality of Spain's place in the world. While decolonization was a footnote in the history of Spain's transition to democracy, it provided the immediate cause of Portugal's transition, as well as playing a major role in its course, if nothing else because it placed Portugal at the very centre of an international conflict between the superpowers that it could not hope to control.

Works cited

Balfour, Sebastian. 2002. *Deadly Embrace: Morocco and the Road to the Spanish Civil War*. Oxford: Oxford University Press.

English, Maurice. 1940a. "Spanish Occupy Tangier; Call It Start of Empire." *Chicago Daily Tribune*, June 15.

———. 1940b. "North Africa Is Our Rightful Sphere, Says Spanish Press." *Chicago Daily Tribune*, June 23.

Galvão, Henrique. 1961. *Santa Maria: My Crusade for Portugal*. Cleveland: World Publishing Company.

Goda, Norman J. W. 1998. "Franco's Bid for Empire: Spain, Germany and the Western Mediterranean in World War II." *Mediterranean Historical Review* 13 (1–2): 168–194.

Hamilton, Thomas H. 1944. "Spanish Dreams of Empire." *Foreign Affairs* 22 (3): 458–468.

Kennedy, Paul K. 1946. "Franco Espouses Cultural Empire." *New York Times*, October 13.

Meneses, Filipe Ribeiro de. 2005. "Popularizing Africanism: The Career of Víctor Ruiz Albéniz, *El Tebib Arrumi*." *Journal of Iberian and Latin American Studies* 11 (1): 39–63.

———. 2014. "The Portuguese Empire." In *Empires at War, 1911–1923*, edited by Robert Gerwarth and Erez Manela, 179–196. Oxford: Oxford University Press.

Meneses, Filipe Ribeiro de and Robert McNamara. 2012. "The Last Throw of the Dice: Portugal, Rhodesia and South Africa, 1970–1974." *Portuguese Studies* 28 (2): 201–215.

"Ministério das Colónias. Secretaria Geral. Decreto 18:570." 1930. *Diário do Governo*, July 8.

Moreira, Adriano. 1962. *Portugal's Stand in Africa*. New York: University Publishers.

Nerín, Gustau and Alfred Bosch. 2001. *El imperio que nunca existió: la aventura colonial discutida en Hendaya*. Barcelona: Plaza & Janés.

Nogales, Manuel Chaves. 1939. "America Held Franco's Best Imperial Hope." *Washington Post*, May 24.

Oliveira, Pedro Aires. 2011. "O factor colonial na política externa da Primeira República." In *A Primeira República Portuguesa: Diplomacia, guerra e império*, edited by Filipe Ribeiro de Meneses and Pedro Aires Oliveira, 299–332. Lisbon: Tinta da China.

Osório, Ana de Castro. 1918. *De como Portugal foi chamado à guerra: História para crianças*. Lisbon: Casa Editora "Para as Crianças."

Patrício, Rui. 2012. "Política externa portuguesa, 1970–1974." In *Marcelo Caetano: Tempos de transição*, edited by Manuel Braga da Cruz and Rui Ramos. Oporto: Porto Editora.

Pimenta, Fernando Tavares. 2008. *Angola, os brancos e a independência*. Lisbon: Edições Afrontamento.

———. 2010. *Portugal e o Século XX: Estado-Império e descolonização (1890–1975)*. Lisbon: Edições Afrontamento.

Preston, Paul. 1993. *Franco: A Biography*. London: Harper Collins.

Proença, Maria Cândida. 2009. "A questão colonial." In *História da Primeira República Portuguesa*, edited by Fernando Rosas and Maria Fernanda Rollo, 205–228. Lisbon: Tinta da China.

Serna, Alfonso de la. 2001. *Al sur de Tarifa. Marruecos-España: Un malentendido histórico*. Madrid: Marcial Pons.

"Situation in Spain." Note by the Prime Minister. National Archive, London, Cabinet Papers, CAB 66/12/12 Secret W.P. (40): 382, 21 September, 1940, War Cabinet.

"Spain across the Sea. Echoes of the Civil War. From our Buenos Aires Correspondent." 1939. *The Times*, June 19.

Woolbert, Robert Gale. 1946. "Spain as an African Power." *Foreign Affairs* 24 (4): 723–735.

32

THE FATE OF SPAIN'S "NATIONALISMS" DURING THE SPANISH CIVIL WAR, 1936 TO 1939

George Esenwein

Today it is widely accepted that Spain is composed of multiple nationalities and regions, which, despite their autonomous status, form an integral part of the nation. Yet, from the nineteenth century on, the Castilian-centred Spanish state struggled to come to terms with the regional populations who felt themselves to be both historically and culturally distinct. This was particularly evident in the last quarter of the nineteenth century, when both regionalist and secessionist aspirations of the Basque and Catalonian provinces crystallized into full-blown nationalist movements. Despite the reforming efforts and centralizing tendencies of Restoration (1876–1923) politicians of the late nineteenth and early twentieth centuries, the political and national unity of Spain was never fully achieved. Rather than seeking ways of accommodating regionalism within a national framework, the Primo de Rivera dictatorship (1923–1930) sought more directly to subdue Spain's ethno-nationalisms by imposing a top-down approach. Yet, after nearly six years of subjugation, regionalism not only survived the dictatorship but it experienced a robust revival under the short-lived Second Republic (1931–1936). The outbreak of civil war in July 1936 marked a new and unique phase in the development of Iberian nationalisms. During this exceedingly turbulent period, both the Basque and Catalan autonomous movements briefly achieved an unprecedented degree of independence from the central government. After the Spanish Nationalists under Francisco Franco emerged triumphant in 1939, regionalists were forced to operate in the shadows of an oppressive state system which actively sought to erase all traces of Spain's deeply rooted ethno-nationalist identities. It was not until democracy returned to Spain in the late 1970s that the autonomous movements would reestablish themselves as fundamental features of the nation's political and cultural landscape.

To understand why Spain's Civil War and its outcome represented a watershed event in the evolution of Iberian nationalisms in the twentieth century, this chapter highlights the achievements of the Basque and Catalan movements between 1936 and 1939. In the first part of the essay we are concerned with identifying the distinguishing characteristics of the Basque and Catalan varieties of nationalism. We then turn to an examination of these movements during the Spanish Civil War period, 1936–1939. In this section, special attention is paid to the conflicts which arose between Basque and Catalan groups striving for greater self-rule and the left-wing forces who sought to centralize all operations of the Republic.

Background: a tale of two nationalisms

By the time civil war erupted on the Iberian Peninsula in July 1936, both Basque and Catalan nationalisms had become dominant forces in their respective regions. But even though the two movements rallied in defense of the Republic against the military-led insurgency, the fact is that they had done so for substantially different reasons. This is because, despite sharing the overarching goal of achieving greater autonomy for their own distinctive communities, the Catalan and Basque nationalists were representative of different varieties of Spain's ethno-nationalisms. In the case of Catalonia, for example, the nationalist agenda was being largely shaped and directed by liberal, progressive forces on the left as represented by the republican party, *Esquerra*. On the other hand, the dominant *Partido Nacionalista Vasco* (PNV) and other Basque nationalist parties comprised mostly conservatives who believed that separatism was the best way of preserving the traditional lifestyle and values of the Basque peoples against the intrusions of both liberal (republican) and reactionary (Carlist) influences. To gain a greater sense of how the differences between these two anti-Spanish nationalisms conditioned their respective experiences of civil war and revolution, it is necessary to review briefly some of the distinguishing features of both movements.

With the advent of fully fledged regionalist political parties at the turn of the twentieth century, the contrasting aspects of the nationalist visions of both the Basques and Catalans became increasingly apparent. Catalan political nationalism, which was first given expression by the *Lliga Regionalista* (Regionalist League), was largely the creation of the industrial bourgeoisie. Though clearly wanting to assert their region's autonomy in social and cultural affairs, this group was above all concerned with advancing Catalan economic interests within the framework of Spain's national power structures. As a result, this variety of Catalan nationalism appealed not to the increasingly populous and left-leaning working classes, but to the more moderate and pragmatic elements of middle-class society.

In contrast, Basque political nationalism was cast in an entirely different mold. Its ideological foundations were laid by the *bilbaíno* Sabino Arana during the closing years of the nineteenth century. Deeply moved by his visceral dislike of the disruptive forces of capitalist industrialization as well as for all things Spanish, Arana envisioned the creation of a bucolic Basque nation, Euzkadi, which would embody the racial and cultural peculiarities of the Basque-speaking peoples (*euskaldun*). Apart from stressing the centrality of cultural identity, Arana's romantic brand of nationalism differed from *catalanismo* in every important respect. Instead of embracing modernization, it extolled age-old Basque customs and traditions, and instead of being disposed to diversity it insisted upon exclusivity, particularly in matters relating to race and religion. A propos the role of race in defining the Basque citizens, it is essential to bear in mind that Arana followed J. G. Fichte and the Romantic nineteenth-century nationalists in seeing race (better understood as ethnicity) as the *sine qua non* of all nations. He therefore believed that the Basque nation could only be achieved by excluding all non-Basques from their community. As far as religion was concerned, Arana's nationalist ideology assigned Catholicism a special and indispensable status. Above all he believed that, because liberal Spain had eroded Basque religious sentiment and had undermined the purity and unity of Catholicism, it was necessary to establish an independent Basque Catholic Church. In this way, Catholicism was conceived as a national religion which would form an essential part of the Basque homeland.

It has already been mentioned that *catalanismo* owed its existence to the middle classes, whereas Basque nationalism drew its inspiration from the peasantry and groups displaced by industrialization. This sociological fact imbued the two movements with distinct economic orientations. Rather than being pro-capitalist like their Catalan counterparts, Arana and his followers associated capitalist development with Spain and therefore they strongly opposed what they saw as the two main protagonists of Basque industrialization: the Spanish immigrant proletariat and the Basque industrial oligarchy. In the former case, the influx at the turn of the century of non-Basque workers to the mining districts and shipbuilding industries centered in Vizcaya had been accompanied by the spread of socialism to the region. The nationalists' early efforts to reduce socialist influence by creating a Catholic-inspired all-Basque trade union in 1911, Solidarity of Basque Workers, SOV – later called the *Solidaridad de Trabajadores Vascos* (STV) – were largely unsuccessful. It was only during the period of the Second Republic (1931–1936) that the STV began seriously eroding the socialists' hegemony among the workers.

Though the major tenets of Basque nationalism formulated by Arana established an ideological framework for the movement right up to the Civil War, they did not serve as a practical guide for the PNV, the party Arana had founded in 1895. In fact, Arana himself and his successors were increasingly obliged to modify the party's agenda over time, granting it a greater flexibility so that the PNV could adapt to the ever-changing social, political, and economic landscape. During the Second Republic, for example, the rise of the anti-nationalist right after 1933 compelled the PNV to downplay its anti-Republican rhetoric and support the left at the polls (Conversi 1997, 76; see also Balcells 1974, 1996). The party's pro-republicanism owed a great deal to the pragmatic thinking of a younger and less dogmatic generation of Basque nationalists led by the lawyer and former football player, José Antonio de Aguirre. Though they vehemently objected to the anti-clerical policies of the left, Aguirre and other moderate elements in the PNV nonetheless showed a willingness to make common cause with republicans if that meant obtaining some form of self-government for the Basque provinces (Fusi 1984, 2002; see also Aguirre et. al 1979; Arenillas 1970; Heiberg 1989).

The coming of the Second Republic had an even greater impact on the development of Catalan nationalism. During the municipal elections which swept the Monarchists from power in April 1931, the recently created *Esquerra* and its republican allies were catapulted into the forefront of regional politics. Their determined efforts to obtain self-rule for Catalonia came to fruition in September 1932, when the Madrid government approved a statute granting Catalan autonomy. Despite the strong resistance they later faced from the anti-regionalist and right-wing forces which rose to prominence during the 1933–1935 period, the Catalans managed to conserve their autonomous status before civil war broke out in July 1936. As we shall see in this chapter, conditions for expanding regional self-government during that conflict were much more favorable in Catalonia than they were in the Basque Country. At least during the first half of the war, the Catalans managed to greatly expand upon the dimensions of their previously won autonomy by effectively creating the basis for an independent Catalan state within the Republican zone.

War and revolution in Catalonia: 1936

Not long after it was launched in Northern Africa on July 17, it became apparent that the military rebellion had had the unintended effect of unleashing a sweeping popular revolution in the towns and countryside where the coup had failed. This was particularly true in Barcelona and other regions which had a long tradition of left-wing radicalism. The CNT-FAI, Spain's classic revolutionaries, were among the first non-governmental organizations to spring into action. In Barcelona the insurgents planned to seize the local garrisons and take over the *Generalitat* (Catalonia's regional government) and other key institutions. But when they began their assault in the wee hours of of July 19, improvised anarcho-syndicalist militias along with a mix of pro-Republican police and civilian groups immediately began cutting off the rebel advances. Following some thirty-six hours of fierce and bloody street fighting, which included a brazen anarchist-led attack on the Atarazanas fortress (one of the city's main military fortresses), the insurgents surrendered, thus depriving them of control of a key Republican region. Of the various groups resisting the uprising, the CNT-FAI emerged as the most powerful force in Catalonia. The then President of the *Generalitat*, Lluis Companys, later recalled the dramatic moment when the fighting had ended and, for a fleeting moment, the reins of power were in the hands of the revolutionaries. Upon entering the halls of the *Generalitat* Palace, anarchist leaders were met by Companys, who indicated to them that he was ready to surrender his government to the victorious workers. According to one eyewitness, the commissioner of public order, Major Federico Escofet, Companys reputedly told the anarchist chiefs: "Today you are the masters of the city and of Catalonia . . . . You have conquered and everything is in your power . . ." (Fraser 1979, 111). Companys went on to assure the CNT-FAI representatives that he would resign his post and support their anti-fascist struggle if they so desired. To his surprise, the anarchists refused to take power, accepting instead Companys' offer to join a power-sharing scheme. Under this proposal, the Catalan government would exist alongside a newly created governing body, the *Comitè Central de Milícies Antifeixistes* (Central Antifascist Militias Committee), or CCMA, comprised of both leftist revolutionary and middle-class parties. This unprecedented development would have a profound impact on the future course of events in Catalonia (Bolloten & Esenwein 1990; see also *Catalunya i la Guerra Civil* 1988, and Termes and Porredon 2008). Above all, the revolutionaries' unwillingness to impose their own revolutionary regime meant that the moderate republican parties, including the *Esquerra*, would be able to salvage the basic machinery of the Catalan state system and begin rebuilding its power base in the region.

Meanwhile, the anarcho-syndicalists dominated local affairs by assuming control of the key portfolios in the CCMA: public order, war, and transportation. Through their militias, neighborhood defense committees, and police squads (*patrullas de control*), for example, the anarcho-syndicalists replaced the civil and republican Assault Guards as the symbols of authority. On the economic front, the CNT-FAI channeled their energies into a thoroughgoing collectivization programme. Under their direction, countless small businesses, industries, and agricultural enterprises were taken over and reorganized along libertarian lines.

The stridently anti-Stalinist *Partido Obrero de Unificación Marxista* (POUM), which had been formed only a few months before the uprising, also used the opening phase of the Civil War to undertake its own revolutionary projects and gain greater traction in Catalonia's crowded political arena (Alba and Schwartz 1988).

But from the outset it was apparent that the POUM was saddled with a number of debilitating handicaps, not least being its political isolation. Rejected for its Marxist politics by the anarcho-syndicalists, the POUM was no more popular with the moderate republican parties. Perhaps its greatest political setback came during the first week of the war and revolution when its future nemesis, the *Partit Socialista Unificat de Catalunya* (PSUC) came into being.

Among the numerous political parties then operating in republican Spain, the formation of the PSUC held greatest significance for the *Partido Comunista de España* or PCE (Spanish Communist Party), which had never attracted more than a few hundred followers in Catalonia. At the beginning of the Civil War, the PCE was adhering to the anti-revolutionary "Popular Front" policy which the Communist International had adopted in 1935. Among other things, this reformist political strategy called for forming broad alliances between all anti-fascist working-class and middle-class parties. Amidst the climate of political dissolution and heady revolutionary transformations which prevailed in Catalonia during the first weeks of the war, the communists were especially fearful that their minuscule forces might be absorbed by their left-wing rivals. To avoid this, they stepped up their efforts to have the handful of unaffiliated Catalan socialist factions merge with their movement. Though initially concerned that such a union would result in communist domination, Joan Comorera of the *Unió Socialista de Catalunya* (USC) and other moderate *catalanista* elements swallowed their misgivings once the revolutionary organizations in Catalonia were in the ascendant. They therefore withdrew their objections to unification even though this meant adhering to the Communist International and, to all intents and purposes, subordinating the new party to the dictates of Moscow. As events would later prove, the concerns Comorera and others had earlier voiced were not misplaced, for the PSUC served primarily as a vehicle for extending communist power and influence in Catalonia throughout the war.

Given its reformist stance on most social and economic issues and in view of its allegiance to the anti-revolutionary Comintern, it is hardly surprising that the PSUC found itself on the same side of the Catalan political spectrum as the *Esquerra*. Yet this did not mean that the overall aims of the two parties were compatible. For while the *Esquerra* saw as its main objective the establishment of an independent Catalan state, the PSUC was obliged to subordinate its regionalist aspirations to the broader national and international goals defined by the communists. In the event, for the first half of the war the two parties entered into a marriage of convenience when it came to curbing the revolutionary movement in the region.

Meanwhile, after having successfully withstood the revolutionaries' initial efforts to dismantle the pillars of liberal political rule in Catalonia, the *Esquerra* wasted little time in mounting a counter-offensive aimed at putting an end to the region's dual power-sharing system. Taking advantage of the fact that rank-and-file anarcho-syndicalists proved incapable of successfully pursuing their revolutionary projects while their politically ineffectual leaders collaborated with the government, President Companys and the *Esquerra* took the first decisive steps towards restoring the *Generalitat's* ruling powers. On September 26 Companys scored a major political victory when he formed a new government comprised of both working-class and middle-class parties – commonly referred to as the "anti-fascist government of unity" – which he used as a stepping-stone to abolish the anarchist-dominated CCMA. On October 1 the CCMA dissolved itself, and its former functions were absorbed by the new *Generalitat* Council. This latest turn of events strengthened the hand of the moderate forces in various ways, but not least because it significantly enhanced the authority of the *Generalitat* and thereby gave the *Esquerra* and other pro-nationalist parties greater political leverage in their efforts to exercise social and economic influence over Catalan affairs.

In the coming months, the broadening of Catalonia's self-governing powers was well underway. With the CCMA no longer acting as a brake on its actions, the *Generalitat* set itself the task of reorganizing Catalonia's war industries and military affairs along non-revolutionary lines. For example, in late October the government's Department of Defense issued a Decree for the Militarization of the Militias, which was meant to end revolutionary control of the improvised militias or columns which had sprung up throughout the region in the early days of the Civil War.

On another level, the council of the Catalan government sought to rationalize the region's ill-coordinated economic activity by establishing legal uniformity for the commercial and industrial enterprises which had been previously caught up in the whirlwind of revolutionary takeovers. Of particular significance in this regard was a sweeping measure passed on October 24, 1936. Among other things, this decree legalized the collectivization of large-scale enterprises which employed more than 100 employees, but placed limits on the practice in smaller commercial operations. In this way, it was possible to appease the revolutionary members of the *Generalitat's* ruling council – who had earlier agreed to dissolve their anti-fascist militias committees throughout Catalonia – while at the same time afford some relief to small property owners and shopkeepers whose firms were no longer obliged to undergo a process of revolutionary reorganization. The Catalan government was also active in other spheres of regional affairs. On the social front, for example, efforts were made not only to safeguard churches, buildings, and monuments which had been damaged or threatened by overzealous revolutionaries, but also to extend the *Generalitat's* oversight of schools, museums, and other cultural institutions which had formerly been under the administration of the Madrid government. By the end of 1936, the Catalan government was functioning on many levels as a sovereign state. In addition to raising its own army (*Exèrcit Popular Regular de Catalunya/* Regular People's Army of Catalonia), it was issuing its own currency, establishing diplomatic ties with foreign countries, and negotiating its financial and political relations with the Popular Front government on an equal footing.

Nevertheless, it was not long before the Catalan nationalists were forced to confront the fact that the impressive gains they had made during the first year of the war at the expense of the revolutionaries could not be taken for granted. Political pressures between pro- and anti-revolutionary forces in Catalonia continued to build throughout the last months of 1936 and into the following year, finally coming to a head during the notorious May Events of 1937. At this time, the *Esquerra's* decision to ally itself with the PSUC and other pro-Popular Front parties of the central government would change the course of Catalan politics for the last year and a half of the Civil War.

Basques at war, 1936 to 1937

In the Basque region, the events which followed in the wake of the July military revolt followed a different trajectory than they did elsewhere in Spain. Unlike in Catalonia, where the uprising was met with a wide-ranging revolutionary movement which quickly overwhelmed the regional and national governments, no revolution occurred in the Basque areas which supported the Republic. Thus, while ad hoc defense juntas composed of leftist and nationalist parties sprang up in Vizcaya and Guipúzcoa in the first few weeks of fighting, their appearance did not signal the beginning of a revolutionary state of affairs. The few signs of social disruption which did occur – such as a rash of anticlerical assaults carried out by revolutionaries who helped to put down the military insurrection – were quickly contained by the dominant PNV and moderate parties. More problematic for the Basque nationalists was the fact that only a fraction of the Basque Country – the provinces of Vizcaya and Guipúzcoa – remained loyal to the Republic. Not surprisingly, the profoundly conservative and anti-separatist provinces of Navarre and Alava immediately sided with the insurgents. Enthusiasm for the rising was particularly evident in Navarra, the stronghold of the reactionary monarchists who belonged to the Carlist movement (Blinkhorn 1975). In the provincial capital of Pamplona, the *pronunciamiento* issued by General Mola – a pivotal figure in the conspiracy – was treated by the town's citizenry as an occasion for celebration. Wearing paramilitary uniforms and their distinctive red berets (*boinas*), Carlist *Requetés* (militias) marched through the city's central streets singing their signature battle cry, ¡*Viva Cristo Rey!* (Long live Christ the King), while throngs of onlookers cheered them on. In the following weeks, thousands of well-trained *Requetés* (later fully militarized as the Navarrese Brigades) helped the Nationalists conquer more Basque territories, most notably in Guipúzcoa and its strategically important border town of Irún (Gamboa and Larronde 2005).

The PNV reacted to the rapidly evolving circumstances in the region with predictable caution. While they held no brief for the left's pronounced secularism and radical agenda, they were no less repelled by the Carlists and their anti-regionalist allies on the right. Their initial ambivalence towards both sides was finally dispelled when pro-nationalist villages came under attack by Mola's advancing forces and *Requeté* shock troops. From that point on, the PNV decided that it was in the Basques' best interests to support the Republic.

From the beginning, the Basque nationalists made it clear that their commitment to the republican war effort would be conducted on their terms. Foremost on the PNV's agenda was securing formal approval of the Basque statute of autonomy, which had been held in abeyance since the outbreak of civil war. Their opportunity to do so came after a broad-based Popular Front coalition government was formed in September. At the insistence of the socialist premier Francisco Largo Caballero, the new administration offered to ratify the statute if the PNV-dominated Basque junta based in Bilbao was willing to appoint a representative to serve in his cabinet. Negotiations between the two sides were completed after the PNV deputy, Manuel de Irujo, entered the Largo Caballero government towards the end of the month as a minister without portfolio. On October 1, 1936, a rump session of the Republican Cortes voted in favor of granting the Basques their long-standing desire for self-government (Payne 1971). At this historic assembly, the soon-to-be president of Euzkadi, José Antonio de Aguirre, demonstrated his political acumen by publicly identifying the Basque cause as part of the greater struggle in Spain between democracy and fascism while at the same time reaffirming the Catholic underpinnings of the new state. On October 7, in a ceremony conducted under the ancient oak tree of "Gernika" (Sp. Guernica), the autonomous state of Euzkadi was proclaimed and Aguirre was inaugurated as its new president (*Lehendakari*). From then until its physical dissolution in the summer of 1937 he would preside over a government based in Bilbao which included four members of the PNV and five representatives from the left-wing parties – two socialists, one communist, and one left republican – all of whom showed a willingness to cooperate with Aguirre and the nationalists. The harmony which existed among the disparate ruling factions produced a degree of political and economic stability in the region that was unmatched in the rest of republican Spain.

The most urgent problem facing the Basques at this point in the war, however, was how to stop the relentless advances of the Nationalist and *Requeté* detachments. Since the outset of hostilities, the boundaries of the anti-nationalist zones in the Basque region had been seriously eroded, leaving only Vizcaya and a small portion of Guipúzcoa free of Franco's forces. Partly because it was physically isolated from the main republican zone and partly because the Basque regime refused either to place its armed forces under the command structure of the Republic's Popular Army or to coordinate its own army's actions with those of neighboring republican provinces (Asturias and Santander), the Basque region became a backwater of military engagements. Though resolved to defend themselves at all costs, the Basques themselves seemed ill prepared for undertaking such an ambitious logistical project. Not only did their nationalist militia units (*Euzko Gudarostea*, popularly called *gudaris*) lack any formal military training, but they also suffered from a shortage of essential material. The deficiencies of the Basque army became acutely apparent following the failure of its first major offensive mounted in late 1936. In the meantime, the Basques concentrated most of their energies into building a series of defensive fortifications (*cinturón de hierro*, or iron belt) around Bilbao (Preston 2006). By doing so, it was hoped that they could deter any military efforts aimed at taking the capital.

It was not until the Nationalists launched a major offensive against the isolated northern republican sectors in the spring of 1937 that fighting in the Basque region took center stage

(Cardona 1986; Martínez Bande 1969, 1971). At the end of March, General Mola and his Army of the North attacked the Biscayan front with a force of some 26,000 troops. Though they did not vastly outnumber the Basque defenders, Nationalist soldiers (including Carlist and Moorish shock units) were better trained and more battle hardened than their opponents. More importantly, they could count on the airpower provided by Italian bombers and the German Condor Legion, which had at its disposal some sixty bombers and cutting-edge fighter aircraft such as the Messerschmitt Bf-109. The force of this invasion had a devastating impact on a population that had not as yet become accustomed to intense fighting. Most of all, the relentless aerial bombardments to which Basque towns and villages were now subjected produced horrifying results for them and the rest of the world. After conducting a series of terror-bombing raids against civilian populations in Elgeta, Ochandiano, and Durango, the Nationalists turned their attention to the remote market town of Guernica, the historic and spiritual capital of the Basque region. On April 26, 1937, an event occurred there which was destined to become the most widely publicized atrocity of the Spanish Civil War. Using heavy high-explosive and incendiary bombs, a fleet of Italian and German bombers nearly leveled Guernica in the space of a few hours. According to one seasoned reporter who arrived on the scene the following day, an untold number of civilians had been killed or wounded, and only the lucky few who had found refuge in dugouts during the attacks could be seen rummaging amidst the still-burning ruins of the town's centre. Tellingly, the bombing mission had not destroyed what were presumably the main strategic targets of the assault, the local arms plant and the Rentería bridge.

Given that Guernica was an open city, news of its destruction by aerial bombing immediately sparked a scandal of international proportions. Perhaps the most reverberating of all the responses to the incident came from the renowned Spanish artist, Pablo Picasso, who was so struck by the enormity of the tragedy that he composed a massive painting simply entitled, "Guernica." Through his use of somber colors and startling imagery, Picasso managed to convey on canvas a moving parable, not only of the tragic fate of Guernica but also of the anonymous victims of modern warfare. Closer to home, the publicity surrounding the bombing served to underscore the high price ordinary Basque citizens were paying for their participation in the Civil War. President Aguirre summed up the stark reality facing all Basques in a press release the day after the bombardment of Guernica: "Before this outrage all we Basques must react with violence, swearing from the bottom of our hearts to defend the principles of our people with unheard stubbornness and heroism if the case requires it" (Quoted in Steer, April 28, 1937, p. 17+).

In the weeks following Guernica, the Nationalists resumed their campaign to conquer the Basque region. Though delayed by bad weather for most of May, the offensive reached the outskirts of Bilbao by mid June. The defending forces of the capital, already cut off from the outside world by a Nationalist-imposed blockade of the city's harbor, were short on supplies and therefore unprepared for a long siege. To make matters worse, morale among the Basque troops had ebbed in recent weeks because of their growing disillusionment with the republican regime. In light of the fact that Aguirre's repeated requests for military assistance from the Valencian government had gone answered, Basque nationalists in particular were at the point of breaking all ties with the Republic. In the event, what were widely assumed to be impenetrable fortifications surrounding Bilbao did not hold, and the city fell to the Nationalists on June 19. Aguirre and his administration had fled on the 16th, transferring their "government in exile" to France before returning to the republican zone in October and taking up residence in Barcelona. Meanwhile, the retreating Basque units did all they could to make life difficult for Franco's forces entering Bilbao. Besides destroying key bridges linking traffic to both sides of the city's main river, they disrupted the water supply, telephone system, and the electrical power services.

The collapse of Bilbao signaled the impending end of Basque resistance in their homeland. Surviving units of the Basque army made their way to Santander only to face defeat there several weeks later. Attempts by the Basque nationalists to sue for a separate peace with the occupying Italian forces was blocked by Franco, who refused to accept surrender without reprisals. By October the few remaining republican holdouts in the northern zone were over-run by the Nationalists (Payne 1975).

After they had conquered the north, Franco's occupying forces immediately imposed a strict and – as far as the Basque nationalists were concerned – unforgiving code of justice and social order. Because they were seen as traitors, pro-republican elements of the Basque population were summarily court martialed. Thousands were either imprisoned or sentenced to die. This included some sixteen so-called "red" Basque priests, who were executed for hav-ing sided with the "enemies of God" (Raguer 2007). No less ignored during the repression were the outward expressions of Basque identity. Nationalist symbols, such as the Basque flag, or *ikurrina*, were outlawed as was the use of *Euskera* and other distinctively Basque cultural practices.

Above all, the Nationalist victory meant that, if Basque nationalism were to survive, it would have to do so outside of Euzkadi, which, in the eyes of the Francoists, no longer existed. For many Basques the decision whether to live under Nationalist rule or retain their independ-ence had been made before the fighting in the north had ended. In advance of the invading Nationalist troops, thousands of Basques had already begun a long and arduous trek to foreign destinations. For some, like the 4,000 Basque children who were safely evacuated to Great Britain before the fall of Bilbao, this would mean living most, if not all, of their lives in exile (Bell 2007; Legarreta 1984; *Spain at War*, July 1938). Others, like the Euzkadi government officials who relocated to Barcelona, stayed in Spain for the time being, making their way to safe havens in the unconquered areas of the republican zone.

May events and Catalonia, 1937 to 1939

As noted earlier, during this same period the Basques were fighting to retain control over their homeland, political tensions in Catalonia were coming to a head. Despite their commanding position in the *Generalitat*, the Catalan nationalists were nevertheless obliged to share power with their rivals on the far left. In addition to holding portfolios in the government, the revo-lutionaries wielded considerable authority through their neighborhood defense committees, police squads, and unions operating in the collectivized sectors of the economy. Finding it impolitic to confront the massive CNT-FAI head-on, the *Esquerra* was nevertheless amenable to the PSUC's plan to undermine the strength and influence of the relatively weak anti-Stalinist POUM. Since its formation in July 1936, the PSUC had rapidly developed into a mass party. Given its strong opposition to the popular revolution, it is hardly surprising that the vast major-ity of its supporters came from the middle classes, who flocked to PSUC economic organ-izations such as the Catalan Federation of Small Businessmen and Manufacturers, GEPCI (*Gremis I Entitats de Petits Comerciants i Industrials*). In addition, after having absorbed the POUM's syndicalist-wing the FOUS (*Federación Obrera de Unidad Sindical*), the party now possessed a foothold in the unions. Emboldened by these gains and by the important backing it received from the Comintern and Spanish communists, the PSUC began waging a vocifer-ous campaign of denunciation aimed at wholly discrediting the POUM's political standing in the republican camp. The pressures the PSUC brought to bear against the Tarradellas cabinet in December resulted in the expulsion of Andreu Nin, who had since September served as the Councillor of Justice and who was the only POUM representative in government. The next few months saw an escalation not only of the PSUC/POUM struggle, but also of the rivalry for power between the anti-revolutionary parties on the one side and the revolutionaries on the other.

On May 3, 1937, the police, on orders from the PSUC and ERC officials, attempted to eject the anarcho-syndicalists from their dominant positions in the main telephone exchange in Barcelona. The bold actions of the government authorities triggered a violent response from the revolutionaries, who immediately reacted by deploying their own forces against their aggressors. Behind the barricades stood the rank-and-file members of the CNT-FAI, who were supported by their counterparts in the POUM. Opposing them were the PSUC, the ERC, and their allies. Fighting between the two sides – the war within a civil war which George Orwell later vividly captured in his eyewitness account, *Homage to Catalonia* – went on for several days before central government reinforcements arrived on the scene. By May 7, the fighting was over and the barricades which had been erected in the working-class districts throughout the city were taken down.

The occupation of Barcelona marked a turning point both for the revolutionary movement in the region and for Catalan nationalism. From this point on, the real power of the anarcho-syndicalists began to dwindle as instanced by the fact that they never again gained the leverage they had once enjoyed through their participation in the *Generalitat* and central government. Because they had proved incapable of subduing the May uprisings on their own, the Catalan government and the nationalist parties also experienced a steep and steady decline in their strength and influence. The intervention of the central government had broadened its control in the region, not least because, in the wake of the May events, it took over all of the rearguard police (*Mossos d'Esquadra*) and military authorities (*Somatent*) formerly under the control of the *Generalitat*. When, in October 1937, the seat of the republican government was transferred to Barcelona, the decline of the *Generalitat's* autonomous powers was accelerated. This became especially evident during the witch hunt and repression that was unleashed against the POUM in the weeks following the May disturbances. Though it played only a minor role in the fighting, the POUM was accused by the PSUC and communists of being a "nest of Francoist spies" which was responsible for the uprising. Despite his misgivings about the shrill and violent conduct of this communist-led campaign of persecution – which was underscored by the arrest and unexplained disappearance of Andreu Nin – the newly appointed premier of the republic, Juan Negrín, took advantage of this development by extending central government control over the Catalan judiciary (Bolloten 1991, 514). At the same time, he stepped up his administration's efforts to nationalize the war industries in the region, eventually placing them, like the courts, under the republican government's military authority. And, finally, Negrín's persistent refusal to bow to the pressures of the Catalan politicians who sought in vain greater representation in his cabinets revealed the extent to which the tide had turned against their efforts to defend the autonomy of Catalonia against the intrusions of the republican government.

During the last year of the war the Catalan and Basque parties worked in tandem to resist the centralizing policies of Negrín and his pro-communist Popular Front government. When a crisis over the government's plans to militarize the war industries, the ports, and courts of law prompted the resignation of the ERC minister of labour Jaume Aiguadé in August 1938, Manuel Irujo, the minister of justice and only Basque representative in the cabinet, resigned in solidarity. Apart from the PNV, however, the ERC had no other firm political allies. Its formerly transactional partnership with the communist-directed PSUC completely crumbled when Negrín replaced Aiguadé with Josep Moix, a Catalan trade-unionist leader and member of the PSUC. No longer allowed a voice in government affairs, the *Esquerra* was relegated to a position of minor importance for the duration of the Civil War.

Though the struggle between Republicans and Nationalists would drag on for another several months, the war for Catalonia (and the Basque nation) effectively came to an end in January 1939. Bereft of any meaningful self-governing powers, the *Generalitat* found itself at the beginning of the year helpless to mount a last-ditch defense against Franco's rapidly advancing army. In any case, by this point in the conflict the civilian population was so weary from war-induced deprivations that they no longer had the will to continue fighting. By January 15, Tarragona was occupied, and on the 23rd Negrín ordered his government to leave Barcelona for safer quarters in Figueres (Girona) near the French border. Surviving members of the Basque and Catalan governments followed suit, later joining the never-ending stream of republican refugees who were then crossing the Pyrenees into exile. On January 25 Nationalist troops under the command of General Yagüe reached the outskirts of Barcelona. They met no resistance as they entered the vanquished city the next day.

End of Spanish nationalisms?

The war's end brought to a close a significant chapter in the development of the Basque and Catalan nationalisms. Having had their expectations for nationhood rise and then fade during the Second Republic and Civil War period, both the Basque and Catalan nationalists would see their respective autonomous movements languish during Francisco Franco's dictatorship. As the undisputed leader of *el nuevo estado* ("the New State") he would rule for the next thirty-six years, Franco made a point of rewarding those groups which had supported his *movimiento* during the war and punishing those which had not. For example, in the post-war years the pro-Nationalist Basque provinces of Alava and Navarre were accorded rights of (corporatist) self-government and special tax privileges. By contrast, pro-republican Catalans and Basques – particularly those coming from a working-class or peasant background – fell victim to a regime bent on exacting a harsh post-war revenge on its former enemies (Juliá Díaz 1999; also Casanova et al. 2004; Ruíz 2005). Those who were not condemned to death by military tribunals or sentenced to long prison terms were subject to economic, social, and political hardships. Franco's post-war repression was equally concerned with eradicating the cultural practices and institutions associated with Basque and Catalan ethnicities. In the Basque Country, this took many forms, including the burning of Basque-language publications and the forcible closures of "separatist" schools and cultural associations. *Euskera* was banned from public use and even Basque names recorded in civil registries and official documents had to be translated into Spanish. A similar repression was imposed on Catalonia, where overt manifestations of Catalan identity were equated with political subversion. The assaults on Catalan identity mirrored those being carried out against the Basques: besides burning books written in Catalan, the government abolished or suppressed educational and cultural institutions. Even Catalan street names were translated into Castilian or changed to reflect the new Spanish order. With their own widely based language proscribed, Catalans were told in no uncertain terms to "Talk like a Christian. . . . speak [Spanish] the language of the Empire." Reprisals against the Catalans were not limited to the political and cultural spheres. Nationalist extremists, who tended to treat Catalonia as an occupied foreign country, also called for subordinating the region's industries to the demands of Franco's neo-fascist economic institutions (Harrison 2009).

While the dictatorship's offensive against Spain's ethno-nationalisms dealt a crushing blow to the infrastructure of their movements, Franco was not able to extinguish completely the autonomous aspirations of both the Basques and Catalans. Resistance to the regime came from various sources. In the immediate aftermath of the Civil War, nationalist politicians living in exile – such as Aguirre and Companys – attempted against overwhelming odds to salvage the remnants of their autonomous governments. Their hopes in this regarded faded after the outbreak of the Second World War and again at the end of the war when the prospects of overthrowing Franco's quasi-fascist regime never materialized. Back in Spain, pro-regionalist sentiments in the Basque Country and in Catalonia found concrete expression in the recurring protests of illegal trade unions and in the grass-root activities of clandestine organizations which were willing to pay a high price to preserve their respective ethnic moral and cultural communities. But it was not until the 1960s that both the Catalan and Basque movements began resurfacing into the public arena.

The resurgence of Catalan regionalism during the 1960s was conveyed in a variety of ways, but most notably through their music, literature, and popular culture. An example can be found in the performances of the noted balladeer Raimón, who helped to launch the *Nova Cançó* musical movement that sought to resist Francoism through the Catalan language. Along with other cultural dissidents, he was able to promote *catalanismo* in both domestic and foreign venues. Even institutions which had supported Franco's anti-republican crusade, such as the Catalan Catholic Church, eventually came round to opposing the dictator's inflexible attitude towards the national question. Over time, more and more Church representatives and institutions began defending the Catalans' right to self-expression.

In the Basque provinces, the PNV played a dominant role in shaping the cultural contest the nationalists waged against the Castilian-centric regime. By adopting a non-violent approach to conserving Basque ways – such as celebrating Basque festivals and reviving their folkloric customs – the party hoped to avoid head-on confrontations with the dictatorship. However, their pacifism as well as their understanding of the overall aims of the Basque movement were challenged from the late 1950s on by a younger and more ideologically driven generation of militants. The emergence of the ETA (*Euzkadi ta Askatasuna*, Basque Land and Freedom) in 1959 marked the opening of a new chapter in the Basque nationalist movement. Rather than being reformist and staunchly Catholic like the PNV, the new organization embraced a revolutionary brand of Marxism – *tercermundismo* ("third-worldism") – and direct action tactics. Above all, they were dedicated to the idea of waging war on any Spanish government which opposed the creation of an independent Euzkadi. For the next several decades, the ETA's violent deeds – including the spectacular assassination of Franco's designated successor in 1973 – would cast a long shadow over the entire Basque nationalist movement. And while the forces of moderation in the region eventually prevailed after democracy returned to Spain in the late 1970s, the bloody record of the ETA was a palpable reminder of the impact the Civil War had had on the development of Basque nationalism.

The Catalans' road to autonomy, though not problem-free, was not nearly as dramatic as that of their Basque counterparts. In the wake of Franco's death in November 1975, the nationalist movement rapidly gained momentum. Popular pressures demanding the restoration of Catalan rights – which were highlighted in the autumn of 1977 by the return of Josep Tarradellas, the President of the *Generalitat* in exile – were so immense that it became apparent that Spain's transition to democracy would have to address this pressing issue. While framing the country's first democratic constitution in more than forty-seven years, Spanish politicians bore this in mind by inserting a clause into the document which recognized and guaranteed "the right to self-government of the nationalities and regions of which it is composed and the solidarity among them all." This act was followed by the passage of a Statue of Self-Government for Catalonia, which the Catalans ratified by a popular referendum in 1979. Building upon these and other pro-regionalist measures passed since the return of democracy, Catalonia has today evolved into one of the most stable and self-contained regions within the Spanish state system.

Works cited

Aguirre, José María, et al. 1979. *Historia General de la Guerra Civil en Euskadi*. Bilbao: Haramburu-Naroki.

Alba, Victor and Stephen Schwartz. 1988. *Spanish Marxism and Soviet Communism: A History of the P.O.U.M*. New Brunswick, NJ: Transaction Press.

Arenillas, José María. 1970. *The Basque Country, Euzkadi: The National Question and the Socialist Revolution*. Leeds: ILP Square One Publications.

Balcells, Albert. 1974. *Cataluña contemporánea*, vol. 2 (1900–1939). Madrid: Siglo Veintiuno.

———. 1996. *Catalan Nationalism: Past and Present*. Ed. and intro. by Geoffrey J. Walker. New York and London: St. Martin's Press.

Bell, Adrian. 2007. *Only for Three Months: The Basque Children in Exile*. Norwich: Mousehold Press.

Blinkhorn, Martin. 1975. *Carlism and Crisis in Spain, 1931–1939*. Cambridge: Cambridge University Press.

Bolloten, Burnett. 1991. *The Spanish Civil War: Revolution and Counter-Revolution*. Chapel Hill, NC: University of North Carolina Press.

Bolloten, Burnett and George Esenwein. 1990. "Anarchists in Government: A Paradox of the Spanish Civil War." In *Elites and Power in Twentieth-Century Spain: Essays in Honour of Sir Raymond Carr*, edited by Frances Lannon and Paul Preston, 153–177. Oxford: Clarendon Press.

Cardona, Gabriel. 1986. "De Madrid a la caída del Norte." *El País Semanal. La Guerra de España 1936–1939* 12: 177–192.

Casanova, Julián, et al. 2004. *Morir, matar, sobrevivir. La violencia en la dictadura de Franco*. Barcelona: Crítica.

Catalunya i La Guerra Civil (1936–1939). 1988. Montserrat: Publicacions de L'Abadia.

Conversi, Daniele.1997. *The Basques, the Catalans and Spain*. London: Hurst.

Fraser, Ronald. 1979. *The Blood of Spain*. New York: Pantheon Books.

Fusi, Juan Pablo. 1984. "The Basque Question, 1931–1937." In *Revolution and War in Spain, 1931–1939*, edited by Paul Preston, 182–201. London: Methuen.

———. 2002. *El País Vasco 1931–37. Autonomía. Revolución. Guerra Civil*. Madrid: Biblioteca Nueva.

Gamboa, José María de and Jean-Claude Larronde, eds. 2005. *La Guerra Civil en Euskadi. 136 testimoniois inéditos*. Lapurdi: Editions Bidasoa.

Harrison, Joseph. 2009. "Early Francoism and Economic Paralysis in Catalonia, 1939–1951." *European History Quarterly* 9: 197–216.

Heiberg, Marianne. 1989. *The Making of the Basque Nation*. Cambridge: Cambridge University Press.

Juliá Díaz, Santos, ed. 1999. *Víctimas de la Guerra civil*. Madrid: Temas de Hoy.

La Guerra Civil a Catalunya (1936–1939). 2004–5. 4 vols. Barcelona: Edicions 62.

Legarreta, Dorothy. 1984. *The Guernica Generation: Basque Refugee Children of the Spanish Civil War*. Reno, NV: University of Nevada Press.

Martínez Bande, J. 1969. *La Guerra en el Norte*. Madrid: Editorial San Martin.

———. 1971. *Vizcaya*. Madrid: Editorial San Martin.

Payne, Stanley G. 1971. "Catalan and Basque Nationalism." *The Journal of Contemporary History* 6 (1): 15–51.

———. 1975. *Basque Nationalism*. Reno, NV: University of Nevada Press.

Preston, Paul. 2006. *The Spanish Civil War: Reaction, Revolution, and Revenge*. New York: W. W. Norton.

Raguer, Hilari. 2007. *Gunpowder and Incense: The Catholic Church and the Spanish Civil War*. Abingdon: Routledge.

Ruíz, Julius. 2005. "A Spanish Genocide? Reflections on the Francoist Repression after the Spanish Civil War." *Contemporary European History* 14 (2): 171–191.

Spain at War. A Monthly Journal of Facts and Pictures. 1938. 1–9, April–December. London: United Editorial Limited.

Steer, George. 1937. "The Tragedy of Guernica." *The Times*, April 27.

Termes, Josep and Arnau Cònsul Porredon, eds. 2008. *La guerra civil a Catalunya (1936–1939)*. Barcelona: Editorial Pòrtic.

33

BEYOND THE NATION

Spanish Civil War exile and the problem of Iberian cultural history

Sebastiaan Faber

The outbreak of the Spanish Civil War in the summer of 1936 and the defeat of the Republic three years later forced a half million citizens of the Spanish state to leave their country. An estimated 160,000 of them would end up in a form of long-term exile (Alted 2005, 52; Rubio 1977, 206–207). Although this amounted to less than 1% of the country's population at the time, the displaced included a significant portion of Spain's cultural elites: writers, artists, academics, politicians, and professionals. Among them were many of the individuals who had shaped two decades' worth of extraordinary intellectual flourishing since the 1910s and helped devise and implement the wide-ranging reforms of the failed Second Republic (1931–1936), which envisioned the Spanish state as a modern, secular, and multinational democracy.

The largest groups of Spanish Republican exiles took up residence in France and Mexico; other host countries that were significant in terms of numbers or status of the exiles they received included the United Kingdom, Argentina, the United States, the Soviet Union, Venezuela, and Chile (Pla Brugat 2007, 19–22). The Franco regime depicted the exiles as traitors, representatives of the anti-Spain, responsible for the outbreak of the Civil War, and agents of dangerous, un-Spanish ideologies. Through strict censorship and other means, the regime succeeded in all but excluding the exiles and their work from public life in the Spanish state, particularly during the 1940s and '50s. If any exile texts circulated in Franco's Spain, it was clandestinely or in very limited forms. The host societies, meanwhile, often benefited significantly from the exiles' presence. Despite the tensions and difficulties that accompany long-term political exile, Spanish Republicans left lasting cultural, academic, political, and economic legacies throughout the world. These legacies – schools of thought, cultural institutions, universities, publishing houses, whole academic fields – are generally acknowledged in the host countries but have remained largely underappreciated in post-Franco Spain.

What has become known in Spanish as *el exilio republicano de 1939* is one of several large-scale displacements from Western and Central Europe throughout the 1930s and '40s, fueled by the rise of Nazi- and Fascist-inspired oppression in Italy, Germany, Portugal, Spain, and the territories under their control. Yet in contrast to most other antifascist exiles, for the Spaniards the defeat of the Axis powers and the end of World War II in 1945 did not herald the possibility of a return home. While Hitler and Mussolini went down with their regimes, the Allied forces permitted Franco to stay in power, forcing the exiles who were still banking on an imminent and triumphant homecoming to adjust their plans and outlook. In fact, the intensification of the Cold War in the late 1940s allowed Franco to further strengthen his hold on his country's reins. Spain's Republican government in exile formally remained in operation until 1977, 38 years after being established and two years after Franco's death. By then, many of the exiles had died as well.

One single essay cannot do justice to the sheer size and diversity of almost four decades' worth of work by thousands of cultural producers in dozens of different host countries. In what follows, I focus on a core set of problems conjured up by a massive, politically motivated displacement like the one the Spanish Republicans suffered – problems that affect not just the exiles and their hosts, but also the home nation and the scholars tasked with writing a coherent narrative of the history of the exiles' fate and cultural output. In addition to giving an overview of the main trends in Spanish Civil War exile and scholarly approaches to it, particularly in literary and cultural studies, I focus on the *nation* as a category that has been central and problematic in both. After all, while the physical reality of long-term exile undermines the bond between individual and nation, the loss of nationhood tends to endow it with new meaning and weight. By way of example I take a brief closer look at the case of Catalan- and Castilian-speaking intellectuals in Mexico.

The challenges of cultural history

The magnitude, quality, and length of the Spanish Republican exile experience pose difficult challenges for historians of culture whose primary categories of organization are national language and identity. Since their rise in the nineteenth century, histories of national art, literature, or thought are chronological narratives that assume a level of organic unity in their corpus of study: an internal coherence woven by genealogical lines of influence and inspiration, a shared language, and a shared physical space, public sphere, and collective destiny. In the case of twentieth-century Spain – multinational, multilingual, deeply divided, and geographically dispersed – the existence of such an organic unity is not by any means self-evident (Epps and Fernández Cifuentes 2005, 11–45). Does a novel written in Castilian by a Spanish exile who has lived in Buenos Aires for thirty years still qualify as a Spanish novel, even if it was never published, reviewed, or read in Spain? Should it, and its author, be considered part of Spanish literary history, Argentine literary history, or no literary history in particular? And what if the novel was written in Catalan and published in Mexico City? In what national tradition should we include the work of Jorge Semprún, an exile from Spain who wrote most of his extensive prose production in French, and whose recurring themes place him closer to Primo Levi and Arthur Koestler than to most of his Spanish contemporaries? Is it proper to consider Eugenio Granell – a novelist and well-known late Surrealist painter whose trajectory of displacement included the Dominican Republic, Guatemala, Puerto Rico, and New York – as a Spanish artist? There are two obvious arguments against that claim. First, he did not pick up a paintbrush until finding himself exiled to the Caribbean; he most likely would not have considered a painting career had he not been uprooted by the Civil War. Second, he saw himself as much a Galician as a Spaniard – even though he wrote in Castilian.

Two additional elements further complicate the relation between notions of national identity and overarching narratives of cultural history. The first of these is the fact that the Franco regime insisted on constructing official histories of Spanish culture that consistently marginalized the exiled Spanish Republicans, along with culture produced in Catalan, Basque, and Galician, while allowing very little margin for any alternative views. As Fernando Larraz has shown in relation to Spanish literary history, regime-sanctioned or regime-tolerated narratives were fatally skewed but nevertheless became deeply ingrained in the institutional DNA of Franco's Spain – Royal Academies, encyclopedias, anthologies, cultural canons, and awards and, most importantly, school and university curricula and doctoral dissertation topics. Rather than "un bloqueo total" of the exiles' cultural production, Larraz writes, "lo que se produjo fue una manipulación mucho más dañina para los intereses de los exiliados;" "los prejuicios de toda índole impidieron casi siempre lecturas limpias y adecuadas" (Larraz 2009, 15). Curiously, these histories were not fundamentally revised after the country's transition to democracy, which left many basic institutional structures intact. In this way, post-Franco histories of culture continued to be marred by the "inercias y tópicos" produced under Francoism (Larraz 2009, 15). The exiles, to be sure, produced alternative histories of culture based on different conceptions of Iberian history and its relationship to modernity. But, as Mari Paz Balibrea has argued, those, too, have been largely ignored in post-Franco Spain (Balibrea 2007, 29–30).

The second complicating element is the fact that among a significant portion of the republican exiles the experience of displacement spurred a newly intensified focus on their own national identity. In some, this fueled a resurgence of different forms of cultural nationalism and pan-nationalism whose tenets harkened back to the eighteenth and nineteenth centuries. In some way this rise of cultural nationalism was surprising, given the profoundly cosmopolitan, internationalist outlook of Spanish cultural elites in the 1920s and '30s (Blanco Aguinaga 2005, 85–97). On the other hand, celebrations of national history and identity had been expressly encouraged among the global Left during the four years of the Popular Front period (1935–1939), in an attempt to counter the mobilizing power of the rabid nationalism embraced by the fascist and conservative Right (Faber 2002, 28–51). Finally, and more generally, Yossi Shain (1989) and Judith Shklar (1998, 38–55) have shown that exile often exacerbates nationalistic tendencies. The struggle for cultural and political hegemony that political exiles are forced to wage in their confrontation with the hostile home regime almost inevitably takes the nation as its main reference point (Shain 1989, 20–21).

Reactions to displacement

If the size, quality, and length of Spanish Republican exile pose certain difficulties for historians of Spanish national culture, historians of Spanish Republican exile as such face challenges of their own. How does one construct a coherent, evolutionary narrative from an infinitely wide range of experiences that occurred in dozens of countries spread over several continents? Not only were there many kinds of exile, but also the very term "exile" is not always the most fitting one to describe the experience of displacement lived by citizens of the Spanish state in the wake of the Civil War: groups and individuals left for different reasons, under different circumstances, enjoyed different kinds of legal status, and faced different options when it came to the possibility or desirability of return. (As we see in a moment, for example, the notion of return took on a different meaning for Catalan exiles than for Spanish ones.) The term "Republican," for its part, may be accepted as a generally accurate indication of the exiles' disagreement with the Franco regime, even if that disagreement manifested a wide range of gradations. Yet "Republican" does little justice to the exiles' ambivalent views about the five years of Republican government in Spain, and fails to acknowledge the dynamic variety of their political identities and affiliations in an ever-changing international context. The adjective "Spanish," finally, blurs the extent to which the very definition of Spanishness – if there was such a thing to begin with – was one of the major political and cultural stakes in the Civil War and its aftermath. An exile who, from abroad, refers to "*el país*" or "*la patria*" may be invoking Spain, but she may also well be invoking Catalonia, Galicia, or the Basque Country.

The exiles' reactions to their forced displacement varied enormously as well. This variation was in part a function of age, background, and temperament, but also of the exiles' widely different circumstances: exile environments and trajectories ranged from fairly luxurious to highly precarious or outright life-threatening. The handful of Spanish intellectuals housed from 1938 on in the Mexican "Casa de España," for example, enjoyed a warm welcome, including a good salary and plenty of opportunities for teaching and publishing without the handicap of a language barrier. A core group found long-term employment in El Colegio de México, the prestigious graduate institution into which La Casa de España soon evolved (Lida and Matesanz 1988). Those academics – relatively few in number but high in prestige – who were lucky enough to land jobs in the rapidly expanding world of United States higher education, too, tended to be well off materially. Yet they often found themselves isolated in cultural, geographical, and linguistic terms, an isolation that in the 1960s evolved into a decidedly conservative profile (Faber 2008, 65–72; Resina 2005). On the other end of the spectrum, thousands of Spanish Republicans ended up in French concentration camps; more than 10,000 Spanish refugees were taken prisoner by the Germans after the French capitulation (Pike 2000, 3); and thousands ended up in Nazi extermination camps, including, prominently, the Mauthausen-Gusen complex. Others risked or lost their lives fighting in the European resistance against the Nazis or working as liaisons with the anti-Francoist struggle in Spain itself (Pike 1993).

Exile politics

The exiles' relationships with their host governments were often complicated. Problems started with conditions for admission and behavioral expectations once admitted. In the wake of the Great Depression many states around the world had adopted stringent immigration policies that affected not only Jewish refugees from Central Europe but other anti-fascists looking for asylum as well (Wyman 1984). As Hannah Arendt has argued, the rise of the modern nation-state and the concomitant definition of individuals' rights as a function of their legal status within nation-states have allowed governments to punish unwanted individuals and groups with denationalization or expulsion, leaving them practically without rights (Arendt 1973, 276–80). The fate of the thousands of stateless Spanish refugees in French concentration camps before and during the German occupation illustrates this well. Not surprisingly, Spanish exiles were all too aware of the fact that their survival depended on the willingness of foreign governments to take them in. Feelings of gratitude and dependency often conditioned exiles' place and role in their host societies, as did legal restrictions on the activities and rights of refugees, permanent residents, or naturalized citizens.

The Republicans' clearly pronounced political profile did not help matters. The United States, for example, applied a very restrictive immigration policy and party militants on the Left had a difficult time getting into the country (Alted 2005, 302; Namias 1992, 93–94). Those that did manage to get an entry visa often lived for years under the watchful eye of US intelligence services and became targets of suspicion or even persecution, as occurred with the filmmaker Luis Buñuel and his friend José Rubia Barcia, who in the late 1940s became a target of the House Un-American Activities Committee, was arrested and threatened with deportation (Fox 2008, 175–85; Martín 2010, 421–521; Namias 1992, 92–102; Rips 1981, 120–21). The group of Spanish exiles that ended up in the Soviet Union included the almost 3,000 children who were sent there between 1937 and 1939 and who were not able to return to Spain after the Republic's defeat and the outbreak of World War II (Alted 2002, 131). Some among the adult exiles in the USSR, between 1,000 and 2,000 in number, attracted the suspicions of the Stalin regime (Alted 2002). A particularly curious case was that of the Dominican Republic, whose right-wing dictator Rafael Leónidas Trujillo accepted a contingent of some 3,000 Republican exiles, whom he saw in part as a means to "whiten" his country's population, assigning them to agricultural colonies. The Spanish Republicans faced enormous difficulties dealing with their host country's climate in both meteorological and political terms, and many left for friendlier environments as soon as they had the chance (Lloréns 1975; Naranjo Orovio and Puig-Samper 2009). Still, the Republicans' legacy on the island is significant; among other things, they helped organize the opposition against the dictatorship (Vega 1984).

The government of Mexico, led until 1940 by President Lázaro Cárdenas, was by far the most generous and welcoming of all the host countries. Between 1939 and 1942 it would end up giving shelter to more than 20,000 Spanish Republican refugees. Yet even in Mexico the exiles faced strict regulations – participation in Mexican politics was strictly forbidden, for example – and a never-absent undercurrent of distrust. While the exiles in the Spanish-speaking Americas did not have to deal with the language barrier that their companions in the United States, France, or the United Kingdom faced, there was plenty of cultural and political friction between the representatives of the former empire and those of their former colonies (Faber 2002, 242). Still, in no other country have exiles from the Spanish state – Spaniards, Catalans, Basques, Galicians, Valencians – left a more indelible mark in the spheres of publishing, philosophy, science, industry, education, art, anthropology, literature, and film (Faber 2013).

In addition to the complex relationships with different types of host regimes, Spanish Republican exile communities were plagued by deep internal divisions of a political and personal nature. For some, the defeat of the Republic and the failure of the Allied Forces to liberate Spain after vanquishing fascism led to political disenchantment. For others, it meant a sharpening of their political commitment and resolve. Tensions that had been mounting during the Civil War – between anarchists and communists, for instance – grew stronger in defeat and spurred decades' worth of exclusions, accusations, recriminations, and even physical violence (Glondys 2013, 37–38). To complicate things further, political affiliations were cross-cut by personal and regional feuds and alliances. As had been the case during the war, these conflicts were in part a function of larger geopolitical developments. From the late 1940s on, the Cold War in particular shaped the Spanish Republican exile experience. As Franco positioned himself as the anti-communist "Sentinel of the West" the international isolation that had marked Spain in the immediate post-Civil War years turned into gradual acceptance: a treaty with the United States (1953) and admission into the United Nations (1955). And while many members of the Spanish Communist Party (PCE) in exile remained beholden to the Soviet Union (Morán 1986; Pike 1993), those exiles most radically opposed to the USSR – anarchists, liberals, and anti-Stalinist communists – were recruited into the so-called Cultural Cold War, in particular through the CIA-sponsored Congress for Cultural Freedom (Glondys 2013). For someone like Max Aub, a socialist who was critical of the Soviet Union and Communist Party policy but who nevertheless refused to join the anti-communist camp, the Cold War became "un falso dilema" that impeded the adoption of a third way between capitalism and communism (Aub 1967, 49; Aznar Soler 1996).

Exile and national identity: the case of Mexico

Regardless of geography, displacement came with numerous challenges. Leaving Spain compelled the exiles to reconsider their national identity, the role and function of their work, their relation to what they considered to be their homeland (be it Spain, Catalonia, Basque Country, or Galicia) and, especially in the case of the writers, the identity and location of their audience and their own relationship to that audience. Did it make sense for exiled poets, novelists, and essayists to continue to direct themselves to readers in Franco Spain, for instance, even though in practice those were all but unreachable? Should they write for their fellow exiles? Or was it more advisable, or effective, to try to reach out to the reading public in their host countries? Francisco Ayala, who took on this question in a seminal 1947 essay, urged his fellow exiles to wrestle themselves free from their obsession with Spain and concluded that the exiles wrote "para todos y para nadie" (Ayala 1990, 213).

Exile, as a concept and as a phenomenon, derives its meaning – its attraction and its pain, its charm and its echoes of tragedy – from a simple notion: the connection between culture and place. The curse that plagues writers and other cultural producers who choose exile, or who are forced into it, is the romantic idea that the only culture that is authentic to and relevant for a particular space is the culture produced within that space by people who can, moreover, claim an organic relation to that space. By this logic, only someone born in France, writing in France and in French, or born in Italy and writing in Italy and in Italian, is worthy of inclusion in the master narrative of French or Italian literature. An added problem is that exiles often lose the institutional power to define the limits of relevant spaces, and the power to consecrate cultural products as being authentic and relevant. This is why they themselves often end up excluded from cultural histories, or relegated to their margins. Much of exiles' lives and work is dedicated to resisting this dynamic: to proving that it is they who most authentically represent the nation they left behind. The irony is that, even if that is true at the beginning, it becomes necessarily less true with each passing year.

These are, in essence, the ingredients of what I have called a struggle for cultural hegemony. Among the exiles from Republican Spain, the tactics followed in this battle were diverse, and their results uneven. Some prominent intellectuals in the exile community doubled down on cultural nationalism, aggressively and obsessively identifying their work and language with some kind of national essence. Others worked in the opposite direction, seeking to subvert the connection between organicity and cultural value, claiming that the experience of uprootedness is itself as a source of superiority or privilege: a road toward emancipation and enlightenment. This idea lives on in the connection that Roger Bartra – son of Catalan Republican exiles in Mexico – establishes between melancholia and lucidity (Balibrea 2005, 127). The need to defend the exiles' definition of Spanish culture, past and present, also spurred productive and innovative institutional work. José Bergamín's publishing venture in Mexico, Séneca, managed to publish a range of outstanding books, including the complete works of Antonio Machado and the first edition of Federico García Lorca's *Poeta en Nueva York* (Faber 2002, 138–41). Philosophers such as José Gaos, Eduard Nicol, and María Zambrano dedicated their professional work to a critique of modernity from a position of Hispanic cultural specificity, thus partly paving the way for later innovations in Latin American thought (Balibrea 2007).

While some exiles built on the internationalist legacy of the avant-garde 1920s and embraced a new form of cosmopolitanism, others gave in to an exalted cultural nationalism that, among those in the Spanish-speaking Americas, could manifest itself in forms of Pan-Hispanism with a curious undertone of imperial nostalgia. The poet Juan Larrea, for example, who served as the driving force behind the Junta de Cultura Española and its journal *España Peregrina* (a precursor of *Cuadernos Americanos*), defended the curious argument that the defeat of the Spanish Republic in 1939 inaugurated a new era in which the spirit of Spain, embodied in the Republican exiles, would turn the Western hemisphere into the savior of civilization. In practice, Larrea's millenarian rhetoric only serves to underscore the exiles' actual marginalization. A certain fascination with Spain's imperial past, seen as a source of glory and pride and as the positive foundation of modern Spanish-American culture, is also present in

Luis Cernuda's exile poetry written in the United Kingdom (1938–1947), the United States (1947–1952, 1961–1963), and Mexico (1952–1963) (Blanco Aguinaga 1998; Faber 2000). There are clear rhetorical and conceptual points of connection between the pan-Hispanist ideas embraced by some of the Republican exiles and the discourse on Hispanidad as it was articulated around the same time by the Franco regime – points of connection that signal a common nineteenth-century genealogy. Both stipulate a basic linguistic and cultural unity of the entire Spanish-speaking world, minimizing the specificity of Spain's former colonies; and in both, the assumption of Spain's central place within that unity serves as a source of hope or pride. Yet while some of the Republican exiles fell prey to a form of imperial nostalgia, it is important to point out that Franco's Hispanidad, with its emphasis on Catholicism and hierarchy, tapped into a much more reactionary vein than the exiles' versions of Pan-Hispanism, which often emphasized shared progressive, liberal, or radical traditions (Rehrmann 1996) and rejected imperialism on principle.

The resurgence of pan-Hispanist ideas among Spanish-speaking exiles in Latin America serves to underscore the extent to which their experience differed from that of Republicans who identified with a different linguistic and national tradition. The community of Catalan exiles in Mexico, for example, which included anthropologist Joan Comas, philosopher Eduard Nicol, and the writers Josep Carner, Vicenç Riera Llorca, Agustí Bartra, Lluís Ferran de Pol, Avel·lí Artís-Gener, and Pere Calders, undertook a wide range of professional initiatives while also founding Catalan-language publishing houses and journals whose relative isolation in the host country was much more evident than those undertaken in Castilian. Still, some 170 books and dozens of journals in Catalan appeared in Mexico between 1939 and 1975 (Férriz 1998; Noguer Ferrer & Guzmán Moncada 2004, 12).

Joan Ramon Resina has convincingly argued for the specificity of Catalan exile after the Civil War. "El exilio catalán de 1939," Resina writes, "ni puede subsumirse sin más en el español, ni en la vaguedad de una abstracción que acaba siempre invocando otras expatriaciones, otras ausencias" (2012). Three principal factors determine this specificity: the political and cultural situation of Catalonia during the years of the Republic, marked by a measure of political recognition after four decades of energetic cultural development; the political and cultural situation of Catalonia during the Franco regime, shaped by ruthless repression of Catalan language, culture, and activism; and the fact that, given these realities, Catalan-speaking exiles related very differently not only to their homeland but also to the continuing legacies of Hispanic and Hispanist imperialism in Spain's former colonies. If the Spanish-speaking exiles tended to identify unwittingly with the colonizers, the Catalans identified with the colonized: their language and culture, too, had suffered under Spanish dominance. Given the blanket repression of Catalan culture by the Franco regime, moreover, the Catalan exiles felt the burden of responsibility for cultural survival even more heavily.

Exile and Iberian cultural history

From a scholarly perspective, the study of Spanish Civil War exile opens up central questions that affect the field of twentieth-century Iberian studies as a whole. Most of these questions can be framed as a problem of relations. How should historians of culture understand the relation between the culture produced in Spain and that produced by (former) citizens of the Spanish state abroad over a period of almost forty years? Are the culture of *la España del interior* and *el exilio* to be seen most fruitfully as two separate entities, or as part of an organic whole? Is one the core or rump and the other a peripheral appendix? Are those relations between exile and home front different for culture produced in Catalan, Castilian, Basque, or Galician? More in general, how should we understand the relation between culture produced in Castilian and culture produced in other Spanish languages? What is the relation between history and politics, on the one hand, and art and literature, on the other? How do we assess culture produced by citizens of the Spanish state – whether in Spain or in exile – in relation to modernity, however defined? Were the exiles stubbornly or tragically "stuck" in the past, whereas their countrymen in Spain remained contemporaneous with the rest of the (Western) world? Or was it precisely the other way around – that is, was the widening gap between the exiles and the cultural producers in Franco Spain due to the latter's isolation from twentieth-century normality, whereas the exiles could read and write much more freely?

Scholars and intellectuals have adopted widely divergent positions on these questions. Within the field of literary history, it was Francisco Ayala – an exile himself – who in 1981 argued against the notion of "exile literature" as an organizing principle. For Ayala, displacement was a non-literary factor that had no decisive, let alone consistent, influence on the content or form of narrative fiction produced by exiled writers (Ayala 1981, 63). If any group of authors was affected by the aftermath of the Civil War, it was those who remained in Spain, not those who left. The exiles' work could evolve more freely and naturally, more in touch with their times, than that of the writers living under the Franco regime (1981, 65). That said, Ayala's minimizing of the experience of displacement also assumes that the Spanish exiles never cease to be Spanish. His inversion of the hierarchy between the culture produced within the boundaries of the Spanish state and that produced outside of it by individuals born within it, returns in a different guise in Henry Kamen's *The Disinherited: The Exiles Who Created Spanish Culture* (2007). Kamen, a British historian of Spain, argues that the authors of many of the canonically central works of Spanish cultural history were in fact expelled from their home country or forced to leave. While representing Spain as cursed with a chronically intolerant state, he also, at the same time, relativizes the importance that Spanish exiles granted themselves and their work.

Literary histories published in Spain during and after the dictatorship, on the other hand, tend to place the center of gravity and normality within the Iberian Peninsula. In the first couple of decades, mentions of the exiles and the work were unlikely to pass the censor's muster; later, they were awkwardly relegated to appendices (Balibrea 2007, 42–50; Larraz 2009, 81–100). Since the late 1990s, research groups have formed – most prominently the Grupo de Estudios del Exilio Literario (GEXEL) at the Universitat Autònoma de Barcelona – whose main purpose has been to recover the intellectual legacy of Spanish Civil War exile for democratic Spain, starting from the premise that that legacy was unjustly ignored or trivialized both during the dictatorship and in the first decades of post-Franco democracy. In addition to scholarly studies and conferences, GEXEL has also spearheaded a biographical dictionary and editions of exiles' works that had never appeared in Spain.

Mari Paz Balibrea has provided a convincing and combative rationale for the need of recovery while pointing out that such a recovery can never be total. If the Transition of the 1970s largely ignored the significant cultural and political legacy of the exiles, she argues, it did so at the nation's peril. Spain today is far from a perfect democracy; it continues to suffer from the unaddressed legacies of Francoism. One major source of *alternative models* for a Spanish democracy – and therefore a major source of inspiration for reform – is precisely the largely untapped and forgotten legacy of the Republican exiles. In *Tiempo de exilio* (2007), Balibrea makes this argument specifically in relation to the work of Max Aub, María Zambrano, and Eduard Nicol. The value of their contribution lies precisely in its exilic difference, in the fact that it cannot be completely assimilated into post-Franco Spain.

At the opposite side of a polemical divide stands the work of Barcelona critic Jordi Gracia. In *A la intemperie. Exilio y cultura en España* (2010), Gracia makes three central arguments.

First, that Spain's democracy today has largely freed itself from the Francoist legacy. Second, that this democracy was born out of the efforts – initially tentative but increasingly courageous – of formerly Francoist writers within Franco Spain to carve out a space for liberalism and democracy. And third, that those who had left Spain – that is, the exiles – only contributed to this process to the extent that they abandoned their stubborn loyalty to the republican cause and their corresponding illusions of cultural superiority, and recognized instead that their role was a subservient, supportive one in relation to *la cultura del interior.* Gracia insists, however, on the notion that *la cultural del exilio* and *la cultura del interior* should be seen as part of "un solo cauce" (Gracia 2010, 19).

If Gracia, Balibrea, and others largely continue to read, interpret, and assess the cultural production of Spanish Civil War exiles in relation to the Spanish state, other critics – particularly those working outside of Spain – have attempted to turn the difficult relationship between exile and home culture into a lever for rethinking the overall structure of the scholarly fields tasked with studying the culture and history of the Iberian Peninsula and its diasporas. Such attempts have been made most prominently and productively under the umbrellas of Trans-Atlantic Studies, Iberian Studies, and Trans-Area Studies. What all three have in common is a desire to move beyond accounts of cultural history that privilege the nation-state, and instead to pay attention to individuals, currents, and genealogies that cross cultural and linguistic borders.

In reference to understanding Spanish Civil War exile, all three have valuable contributions to make. Trans-Atlantic Studies rejects the division of the Spanish-speaking world as an object of analysis into "Peninsular" and "Latin American" studies, while also recognizing the multicultural and multilinguistic nature of the geographical space that once made up the Spanish and Portuguese empires (Gabilondo 2001; Gerassi-Navarro & Merediz 2009). Iberian Studies, for its part, rejects the hegemony of Castilian in the fields that study the cultural production in the Spanish state – and the chronic repression, by that state, of non-Castilian cultures – emphasizing the multicultural and multinational nature of Spain and Portugal (Resina 2009, 2012). Within exile studies, Iberian Studies has served to underscore that the multicultural and multilingual are also defining features of Spanish Civil War exile communities, and to highlight the double marginalization of Basque, Galician, Catalan, and Valencian exile production. At a more general and polemical level, Iberian Studies has functioned as a basis from which to articulate a critical analysis of the ways in which Castilian-speaking exiles in U.S. universities and elsewhere laid the basis for a Hispanism that sidelined non-Castilian Hispanic cultures and attempted to re-assert the cultural hegemony of Spain over Latin America (Faber 2008, 55–72; Resina 2005). Trans-Area Studies, finally, seeks to abandon scholarly approaches to culture that assume a static relationship between place and production – such as the traditional philologies – in favor of models and fields that privilege movement. More dynamic models, the argument goes, are simply more fitting to understand the cultural production of a century such as the twentieth, which not for nothing has been dubbed "the century of displacement" (Ette 2012, 30).

If these three new approaches provide a deeper, more complete, and more rigorous understanding of the cultural production of Spanish Civil War exile – and therefore of twentieth-century Iberian culture as a whole – the narrow disciplinary framework, inherited from the philological school and reinforced by Francoism, that defines Spanish culture as culture produced in Spain, by Spanish-born individuals in the Castilian language has, by contrast, proven quite unproductive for that purpose. And yet somehow its tenets remain in force. This is clear from recent literary histories such as José Carlos Mainer's nine-volume *Historia de la literatura española*, which fails to acknowledge, let alone take to heart, any of the critiques leveled at the field from Iberian or Trans-Atlantic Studies. Tellingly, Mainer cavalierly announces in the editor's prologue that his monumental history will only occupy itself with works written in "nuestra lengua" (2011, vii), pointing to a chronic problem in the field of *Filología Española* (Santana 2006, 115). Similarly, the volumes dedicated to the nineteenth century and the first half of the twentieth minimize the extent to which the evolution of literature in Spain was shaped by developments originating in Latin America (Mejías-López 2009).

Conclusion

Many of the displaced intellectuals from Republican Spain, in particular writers and artists, continued to identify with the home nation throughout their long years of exile. They lived and worked for Spain, Catalonia, the Basque Country, or Galicia. But that does not necessarily mean that they can be unproblematically incorporated into Iberian cultural history alongside those who stayed behind. Two stubborn facts militate against that procedure. First, it is beyond dispute that the displacement itself – leaving the geographical space of home for a long-term existence in another country, culture, and sometimes language – transformed the exiles' work and worldview. It did not change it in uniform ways, as Ayala is right to point out – but change it certainly did. Second, in countless cases the exiles' work has had a greater influence on their host environments – students, readers, critics, colleagues, and peers; institutional landscapes and cultural histories – than in Spain, whether during or after the dictatorship. Gracia is right to argue that the exiles and their legacy played a relatively minor role in the transition to democracy. He is wrong, however, to invoke that fact in order to minimize the exiles' cultural or political influence: their influence was simply felt elsewhere.

Central in the debates over the relation between the exiles' work and *la cultura del interior* have been notions of relative quality, relevance, normality, and contemporaneity. Can the exiles' work be generally described, as it is by Gracia and others, as anachronistic, nostalgic, out-of-touch, and weighed down by dogmatically held political commitments? Or does the immense corpus of art, literature, thought, film, and science produced by Civil War exiles distinguish itself from the culture produced in Franco Spain – stunted by censorship, repression, and isolation – by the fact that it was of higher quality and more in touch with its times? If these debates have been less than productive, it is because they have been taking place largely within the confines of a single academic field, *Filología Española*. Here, again, a widening of the scholarly scope is helpful.

Any approach to cultural history that takes the nation-state as its principal organizing unit is bound to misunderstand or underestimate exiles' life, work, and genealogy. Given the massive impact of displacement on twentieth-century culture, particularly culture produced by individuals born in the Iberian Peninsula, it can be argued that the nation-based framework is insufficient to understand Iberian cultural production generally. In that sense, Spanish Civil War exile studies have proven to be a productive locus of innovation for the field as a whole.

Works cited

Alted, Alicia. 2002. "El exilio español en la Unión Soviética." *Ayer* 47: 129–153.
———. 2005. *La voz de los vencidos: el exilio republicano de 1939*. Madrid: Aguilar.
Arendt, Hannah. 1973. *The Origins of Totalitarianism*. New York: Harcourt Brace Jovanovich.
Aub, Max. 1967. *Hablo como hombre*. México: Joaquín Mortiz.
Ayala, Francisco. 1981. "La cuestionable literatura del exilio." *Los cuadernos del norte* 2 (8): 62–67.

————. 1990. *El escritor en su siglo*. Madrid: Alianza Editorial.

Aznar Soler, Manuel. 1996. "Política y literatura en los ensayos de Max Aub." In *Actas del congreso internacional "Max Aub y el laberinto español,"* edited by Cecilio Alonso, 568–615. Valencia: Diputación de Valencia.

Balibrea, Mari Paz. 2005. "Interview with Roger Bartra." *Journal of Spanish Cultural Studies* 6 (1): 123–131.

————. 2007. *Tiempo de exilio: una mirada crítica a la modernidad española desde el pensamiento republicano en el exilio*. Barcelona: Montesinos.

Blanco Aguinaga, Carlos. 1998. "Ecos del discurso de la Hispanidad en poetas del exilio. El caso de Cernuda." In *El exilio literario español de 1939. Actas del Primer Congreso Internacional*, vol. 2, edited by Manuel Aznar Soler, 273–294. Sant Cugat del Vallès: Cop d'Idees; GEXEL.

————. 2005. "Max Aub y la cultura internacional del exilio republicano." In *Homenaje a Max Aub*, edited by James Valender and Gabriel Rojo, 85–97. México, DF: Colegio de México.

Epps, Brad and Luis Fernández Cifuentes. 2005. "Spain beyond Spain: Modernity, Literary History, and National Identity." In *Spain beyond Spain: Modernity, Literary History, and National Identity*, edited by Brad Epps and Fernández Cifuentes, 11–45. Lewisburg, PA: Bucknell University Press.

"España Peregrina." 1940. *España Peregrina* 1: 3–6.

Ette, Ottmar. 2012. *Transarea: Eine literarische Globalisierungsgeschichte.* Berlin: De Gruyter.

Faber, Sebastiaan. 2000. " 'El norte nos devora.' La construcción de un espacio hispánico en el exilio anglosajón de Luis Cernuda." *Hispania* 83 (4): 733–744.

————. 2002. *Exile and Cultural Hegemony: Spanish Intellectuals in Mexico, 1939–1975*. Nashville, TN: Vanderbilt University Press.

————. 2008. "Economies of Prestige: The Place of Iberian Studies in the American University." *Hispanic Research Journal* 9 (1): 7–32.

————. 2013. "Los exiliados españoles y las instituciones mexicanas: Entre la autonomía y la cooptación." *Historia del Presente* 22: 75–84.

Férriz Roure, Teresa. 1998. *La edición catalana en México*. Zapopan: Colegio de Jalisco.

Fox, Soledad. 2008. "Clamando en el desierto. El exilio de José Rubia Barcia." In *Contra el olvido: el exilio español en Estados Unidos*, edited by Sebastiaan Faber and Cristina Martínez-Carazo, 175–186. Alcalá de Henares: Universidad de Alcalá, Instituto Universitario de Investigación en Estudios Norteamericanos Benjamín Franklin.

Gabilondo, Joseba. 2001. "Introduction." *The Hispanic Atlantic. Arizona Journal of Hispanic Cultural Studies* 5: 91–193.

Gerassi-Navarro, Nina and Eyda Merediz. 2009. "Introducción: Confluencias de los transatlántico y lo latinoamericano." *Revista Iberoamericana* 75 (228): 605–636.

Glondys, Olga. 2013. *La guerra fría cultural y el exilio republicano español: "Cuadernos del Congreso por la Libertad de la Cultura (1953–1965)*. Madrid: CSIC.

Gracia, Jordi. 2010. *A la intemperie: exilio y cultura en España*. Barcelona: Anagrama.

Kamen, Henry. 2007. *The Disinherited: The Exiles who Created Spanish Culture*. London: Allen Lane.

Larraz, Fernando. 2009. *El monopolio de la palabra: el exilio intelectual en la España franquista*. Madrid: Biblioteca Nueva.

Lida, Clara E. and José Antonio Matesanz. 1988. *La Casa de España en México*. México, DF: El Colegio de México.

Lloréns, Vicente. 1975. *Memorias de una emigración: Santo Domingo, 1939–1945*. Barcelona: Editorial Ariel.

Mainer, José-Carlos. 2011. *Historia de la literatura española. Modernidad y nacionalismo, 1900–1939*, vol. 6, coord. José-Carlos Mainer. Barcelona: Crítica.

Martín, Fernando Gabriel. 2010. *El ermitaño errante: Buñuel en Estados Unidos*. Murcia: Tres Fronteras.

Mejías-López, Alejandro. 2009. *The Inverted Conquest: The Myth of Modernity and the Transatlantic Onset of Modernism*. Nashville, TN: Vanderbilt University Press.

Morán, Gregorio. 1986. *Miseria y grandeza del Partido Comunista de España, 1939–1985*. Barcelona: Planeta.

Namias, June. 1992. *First Generation: In The Words of Twentieth-Century American Immigrants*. Urbana, IL: University of Illinois Press.

Naranjo Orovio, Consuelo and Miguel Ángel Puig-Samper. 2009. "De isla en isla. Los españoles exiliados en República Dominicana, Puerto Rico y Cuba." *Arbor* 735: 87–112.

Noguer Ferrer, Marta and Carlos Guzmán Moncada. 2004. *Una voz entre las otras: México y la literatura catalana del exilio.* México, DF: Fondo de Cultura Económica.

Pike, David Wingeate. 1993. *In the Service of Stalin: The Spanish Communists in Exile, 1939–1945.* Oxford: Clarendon Press.

———. 2000. *Spaniards in the Holocaust: Mauthausen, The Horror on the Danube.* London: Routledge.

Pla Brugat, Dolores. 2007. "Introducción." In *Pan, trabajo y hogar: el exilio republicano español en América Latina,* edited by Pla Brugat, 19–34. México, DF: SEGOB, Instituto Nacional de Migración, Centro de Estudios Migratorios.

Rehrmann, Norbert. 1996. *Lateinamerika aus spanischer Sicht: Exilliteratur und Panhispanismus zwischen Realität und Fiktion (1936–1975).* Frankfurt: Vervuert.

Resina, Joan Ramon. 2005. "Cold War Hispanism and the New Deal of Cultural Studies." In *Spain beyond Spain: Modernity, Literary History, and National Identity,* edited by Brad Epps and Luis Fernández Cifuentes, 70–108. Lewisburg, PA: Bucknell University Press.

———. 2009. *Del hispanismo a los estudios ibéricos: una propuesta federativa para el ámbito cultural.* Madrid: Biblioteca Nueva.

———. 2012. "Presentación." *Fractal* 66–67. Accessed July 2, 2014. http://www.mxfractal.org/Revista Fractal6667Presentacion.htm.

Rips, Gladys Nadler. 1981. *Coming to America: Immigrants from Southern Europe.* New York: Delacorte Press.

Rubio, Javier. 1977. *La emigración de la guerra civil de 1936–1939: historia del éxodo que se produce con el fin de la II República española.* Madrid: Librería Editorial San Martín.

Santana, Mario. 2006. "Mapping National Literatures: Some Observations on Contemporary Hispanism." In *Spain beyond Spain: Modernity, Literary History, and National Identity,* edited by Brad Epps and Luis Fernández Cifuentes, 109–124. Lewisburg, PA: Bucknell University Press.

Shain, Yossi. 1989. *The Frontier of Loyalty: Political Exiles in the Age of the Nation-State.* Middletown, CT: Wesleyan University Press.

Shklar, Judith N. 1998. *Political Thought and Political Thinkers.* Chicago: University of Chicago Press.

Vega, Bernardo. 1984. *La migración española de 1939 y los inicios del marxismo-leninismo en la República Dominicana.* Santo Domingo: Fundación Cultural Dominicana.

Wyman, David S. 1984. *The Abandonment of the Jews: America and the Holocaust, 1941–1945.* New York: Pantheon Books.

34

TRANSLATION AND CENSORSHIP UNDER FRANCO AND SALAZAR

Irish theatre on Iberian stages[1]

Raquel Merino-Álvarez

For most of the twentieth century the totalitarian regimes of Franco in Spain (1939–1975) and Salazar in Portugal (1933–1974) influenced Spanish and Portuguese cultural production, and theatre life in particular. Both dictatorships are the backdrop against which the study of theatrical culture on Iberian stages are tackled in this contribution by gauging the role of censorship in favouring or opposing the importation of foreign (Irish) drama.

Apart from the obvious chronological parallelism – Salazar's Estado Novo was founded three years before the beginning of the Spanish Civil War and came to an end barely a year before the demise of Francoism – the two Iberian dictatorships share obvious traits, but at the same time differ visibly when subjected to scrutiny. The foremost difference can be found in the way both regimes were born: the Portuguese out of a referendum and a "political" Constitution (Pena 2013), the Spanish counterpart as a result of a cruel civil war in which foreign forces took active part.

When comparing "two mutually inimical authoritarian regimes," the Portuguese and the Czechoslovak, Spirk affirms that they "actually had more in common than meets the eye" (2014, 23). The reverse may be said of the two seemingly friendly Iberian regimes. From the outset the political and economic circumstances in both countries were radically different. Spain, devastated after the Civil War, was perceived as a crucial front and a silent battleground where Axis forces fought to gain influence and challenge the position of the Allies, whereas neutral Portugal profited from trade with both Germany and Britain, and its territory was not considered crucial for the unfolding of WWII.

The effects of censorship under Salazar in relation to translation have been at the centre of recent research projects (Seruya 2009) focused mainly on printed literature. In Spain, under the auspices of the TRACE project, the history of translated literature, theatre and cinema in the Franco era has been mapped out. However, very little comparative research of the two Iberian contexts has been published to date: Fiuza's (2009) study of censored popular music being an exception.

Foreign ("English") theatre on Iberian stages

Published histories of (Spanish) theatre have traditionally overlooked the role played by translations, placing their focus on the "national" rather than the "foreign." The sporadic references found in such histories do not usually serve as a starting point to reconstruct the history of theatre in (Spanish) translation (Delgado and Gies 2012; Huerta 2003).[2] Research based on references in the daily press (Mahanta 1994) or compilations of publications linked to stage productions (Puebla 2012) usually adopt a more inclusive view, not excluding translated drama. In this respect, the Spanish censorship archives (AGA) have been paramount in attempting to reconstruct the history of translated theatre on Spanish stages. Translations of foreign theatre played a central role in the very existence of Spanish theatrical life; they helped renew topics and contributed both quantitatively and qualitatively to the development of stage productions; hence the need for an account of the plays, authors and topics that found their way onto Spanish stages via translation. The compilation of catalogues of translations and the study of textual corpora has been at the centre of TRACE (Spanish censorship) studies (Merino 2009, 2012). Since all productions had to seek official permission from the Francoist bureaucratic censorship offices, the traces left in the form of millions of documents are an exceptional documentary resource to mine. The Portuguese archives at the *Torre do Tombo* have also been instrumental in compiling databases of theatre translations (TETRA) or bibliographies of printed translations (Seruya 2009).

We have consulted TETRA and CETbase for information on theatre productions in Portugal, and the AGA (Spanish censorship archives, theatre section) and TRACE-theatre databases for the Spanish situation. A comparative overview of these sources shows that Anglophone cultures (British and US) seem to have prevailed in both Iberian contexts. In Portugal, plays originally written in English were often imported through the more influential French language and culture (Seruya 2009, 82). The events leading up to WWII made the leanings of Portugal and Spain gravitate from pro-German to Anglophile positions, with the pro-English stance remaining established from the mid 1940s onwards.

So far the TRACE (Translation and Censorship) project has identified a substantial corpus of translated drama texts and provided a comprehensive catalogue of productions of foreign theatre in Spain. These catalogues show the pre-eminence of Anglophone (British) drama since the 1940s and the quantitative and qualitative presence of plays by US authors since the 1950s, with plays by Irish authors to be found across the twentieth century in Spanish productions. In terms of numbers, the situation of Anglophone Irish theatre may be compared with that found in Portugal (Carvalho 2009a) or even in a non-totalitarian European country such as Finland (Aaltonen 1996).

The CETbase, established in 1992 by the *Centro do Estudos de Teatro*, is a general database of stage productions in Portugal, whereas the TETRA (Theatre Translation) project database has specifically addressed the issue of censorship. Carvalho has dealt with translations of Irish theatre in Portugal, drawing data from CETbase (2009a, 599). The data available for Portugal has been contrasted with the information compiled for a specific catalogue of translations (productions) of plays by Irish authors and drawn from AGA-censorship archives (TRACEtirl, www.ehu.es/trace). These sources, when compared, allow us to establish similarities and differences between the Portuguese and Spanish theatrical systems, in relation to the importation of plays originally written in English by Irish authors, under similar censorship restrictions (see Appendix).

Carvalho (2009a, 85) cites a compilation by theatre historian Jose Luiz Rebello of foreign theatre plays staged in Portugal between January 1940 and December 1949 which shows that Spain and France (48 and 46 entries, respectively) were the main sources of foreign imports, followed by Britain (17), Hungary (11) and the US (8). Carvalho's corpus, for the period 1956–2005, includes a total of 40 productions of Irish playtexts (2009a, 22).

In the case of Spain, (British and Irish) English playtexts were imported via translation right after the Civil War, with American melodrama of the pre-war period still present on

Spanish stages (Pérez 2005). In 1942, a pioneering production of Priestley's *Time and the Conways*, in the María Guerrero Theatre, directed by Luis Escobar-Kirpatrick, and possibly instigated by the director and founder of the British Institute in Madrid, the Irishman Walter Starkie (London 1997, 64), is reviewed and praised in the press alongside a film directed by Kimmich (Goebbels's brother-in-law) and the military fund-raising show of the Italian *Fascio* (*ABC*, November 18, 1942, 12).

Although Escobar sided ideologically with the Franco government after the war, and was even deemed pro-German (Quirós 2010), as head of the María Guerrero Theatre he tried to continue the theatrical tradition first established by *La Barraca* group with whom he had cooperated, albeit without the group's ideological agenda. Escobar's Anglo-Spanish origin favoured his role as influential mediator and successful translator. As director of one of the national theatres, he was persuaded to import most British plays from London's West End, as a means to counteract German influence on Madrid's stages at critical moments for the allies in WWII (García 2007, 96; London 1997, 41), and he also spent some time in London with funding from the British Council in the mid 1940s.

Irish theatre on Iberian stages: Shaw, Wilde, Beckett

The Spanish AGA censorship archives database for theatre performances record slightly more than 100 entries of plays by Irish authors. A direct search in the AGA files has led to a compilation of a larger catalogue of 200 translations of plays by Irish authors. From a quantitative point of view, entries for productions of Beckett's plays, along with those by Wilde and Shaw, make up two thirds of the total, while translations of plays by O'Casey and Synge represent barely 15% of the catalogue. Lastly, entries for Behan, Joyce or Yeats are restricted to sporadic productions.

In Portugal Irish authors were staged from the mid 1950s onwards (Carvalho 2009a, 599–607), starting with the 1956 premiere of Synge's *Riders to the Sea* or the 1959 production of Beckett's *Waiting for Godot*, establishing a trend in favour of Irish theatre as vehicle for the renovation of Portuguese theatrical repertoires (Carvalho 2005).

Among the first theatre productions to be staged after the Spanish Civil War are Oscar Wilde's *Lady Windermere's Fan* (1940), *A Woman of no Importance* and *Salomé* (1941). Wilde's plays were staged at a rate of about one per year in the 1940s, a tendency that slowed down in the 1950s and 1960s, only to return in the 1970s (Constán 2009) and continue well into the twenty-first century (Mateo 2010).

Spanish productions of Shaw's plays began with *Candida* (1941) and *Pygmalion* (1942) and continued at a steady pace through to the end of the 1970s (Isabel-Estrada 2001). Most of the translations of Wilde and Shaw produced in the period had been published before the Civil War, and new productions as well as translations of the more popular plays were put on stage. Both authors were considered (and labelled) "English" rather than "Irish," and given their well-established status in Europe, they were not deemed dangerous by censors on the whole. Wilde's *Salomé* was staged eight times during the Franco years, but was also the most polemical and so was occasionally banned or given the same restrictive classifications applied in the US (Sova 2004, 238). Wilde's *The Importance of Being Earnest* was staged six times, as was Shaw's *Pygmalion*, without much resistance from the censorship offices. *Major Barbara* and *Mrs. Warren's Profession* found more opposition and were banned in the first instance (Isabel-Estrada 2001).

In Portugal, Wilde and Shaw seem to have been perceived as established "English" classics (Marques dos Santos 2012; Ramos 2010, 2012), and are thus not included in studies on the reception of Irish theatre in Portugal, their plays not dealing with themes "specifically Irish or representing Ireland" (Carvalho 2009a, 16).[3] An exception is made for Beckett in Carvalho's study in considering him an extra-territorial author (Carvalho 2009a, 263–310). Beckett's plays were frequently staged in Portugal from 1959 onwards: all of his plays have been translated into Portuguese (Fernández 2009), and most have been produced by experimental groups.

Samuel Beckett is not specifically identified as Irish in Spain either. The premiere of *Waiting for Godot* in 1955 marked the beginning of a constant presence of his plays in productions for club sessions by independent groups. Beckett is labelled "English," "French" or "Irish" in the censorship records consulted, and it is not unusual to find references to the Paris or London productions of his plays in the reports by censors or in documentation submitted by the theatre groups. Martínez-Trives, translator and champion of Beckett's plays in Spain, impressed by the 1953 production of *Waiting for Godot* in Paris, decided to have it staged in Spanish (Fernández 2009). In the AGA censorship records consulted, Beckett seems to be perceived as an experimental playwright, whose plays are quite incomprehensible for the common censor, and therefore not considered especially dangerous.

Irish theatre on Iberian stages: O'Casey, Synge, Yeats

If some authors such as Shaw and Wilde are not specifically perceived as "Irish," but rather as "English" classics, or culturally hybrid (Beckett), then John Millington Synge and Sean O'Casey, along with W. B. Yeats, are playwrights committed to an Irish identity that has been highlighted in both Iberian contexts.

Reconstructing the introduction and development of Spanish productions of O'Casey's plays is an interesting exercise that provides an overview of the evolution of Spanish theatre under Franco's dictatorship. The first play to be granted permission for the stage is *Juno and the Paycock* in 1955, first staged in Finnish in 1952 (Aaltonen 1996, 221) and in French in 1953. The application was submitted to the censor by Enrique Llovet, at the time Spanish consul in Paris, and filed under Llovet's name as translator and Walter Starkie's as O'Casey's *representante* in Spain (AGA record no. 109/55). Starkie had been director of the British Institute in Madrid (1940–1954) but before that he occupied the chair of Spanish at Trinity College Dublin, where Llovet had been a student. Starkie favoured the presence of authors from the British Isles on Spanish stages, and his influence in theatre circles is made clear by this early successful introduction of O'Casey to Spanish audiences.

In 1955, the official register for *Teatros de Cámara* (experimental studio, theatres) was established, which allowed small theatre groups to present avant-garde productions imported from Paris, London or New York, while permitting Spanish authorities to demonstrate abroad that Spain was already in tune with Europe and willing to be included in international affairs.

The 1964 approval for a production of *End of the beginning / Pin y pon hacen sus labores* (AGA record no. 217/64), followed by *Bedtime Story / Cuento para la hora de acostarse* in 1966 (AGA record no. 274/66) directed by Enzo Casali, and *Red Roses for Me / Rosas rojas para mí* directed by José María Morera in 1967 (AGA record no. 226/67) consolidated O'Casey in Spain, coinciding with the short period of "apertura," or opening up, from within the Ministry for Information and Tourism (Theatre and Cinema Division) under Manuel Fraga (Muñoz-Cáliz 2006). The 1969 translation by Spanish playwright Alfonso Sastre of *Red Roses for Me* (AGA record no. 258/69) proved more polemical, as did *Cock-a-Doodle Dandy / Canta gallo perseguido* (AGA record no. 446/73) in 1973. With a change of ministerial team in 1969, a harsher censorship policy was applied: many applications were delayed or rejected. The clash between a modern progressive society and a regressive government resulted in a theatrical upheaval by 1975. Just before the death of Franco (1975), productions of controversial plays were not only granted permission for commercial productions but also became hugely successful: Peter Shaffer's *Equus* (with male and female nudity on stage), the musical *Jesus Christ Superstar* (with its irreverent perspective of the Christian religion) or Crowley's depiction of a party of homosexuals in *The Boys in the Band* (Merino 2007, 243–286).

Opposition and resistance from within the censorship offices were counteracted by applications for plays by foreign authors, usually manipulated to fit specific political agendas. In this context, the socialist O'Casey, whose plays circulated in East Germany and the Soviet Union, but also in the network of French state-subsidized theatres (Moran 2013, 157), was chosen by playwright Alfonso Sastre, a member of the Communist Party, to help boost the presence of socialist ideas on Spanish stages.

The censorship process leading up to the 1973 production of *Cock-a-Doodle-Dandy* was fraught with interventions from all possible fronts. The first application, submitted by director Adolfo Marsillach, was presented with the translation by Ana Antón Pacheco, published (along with *Oak Leaves and Lavender*) by Cuadernos para el Diálogo in 1972. The text, a copy of the published book, was accompanied by a note from the director stating that the "harsh" language of the Spanish translation "needs to be softened," and one of the censors (Zubiaurre) affirmed in his report that the play "has been feebly translated." Problematical sections were discussed by censors and negotiated with the director, specifically those felt to be attacks on Catholics and Catholicism. The successive versions of the Spanish text submitted to the censor are signed by the Spanish playwright Antonio Gala. Additional documentation in the record shows that the original translator (Ana Antón-Pacheco) filed a complaint and a request to have the censorship office check whether the so-called version by Gala was in fact her own translation slightly modified. Upon consultation with the legal department, a letter is sent to the translator stating that the censorship offices were not in charge of copyright matters. In a newspaper interview on the occasion of the premiere, Gala explains how he had been asked to write a version of *Cock-a-Doodle-Dandy* and explains that, as author of the version, he had "re-created" O'Casey's text, that "the essence" of the original text had not been modified but made more "perceptible" and "acceptable" to Spanish ears by making lines "lighter and faster." Gala remarks that by being "unfaithful" to O'Casey, by modifying and substituting the author's expressions, he managed to better serve O'Casey (*ABC*, November 30, 1973, 89).

O'Casey was often staged in Spain in the 1960s, a time of *apertura* from within the regime, and his plays seemed to be well-established in Spanish theatre, but in the troubled early 1970s the *Esperpento* theatre group's production of *A Bedtime Story*, after a successful tour in Europe and around Spain (*ABC*, May 10, 1973, 46), ended with an abrupt cancellation by the military authorities for alleged insults against the army, and the five members of *Esperpento* were nearly taken before a military tribunal (AGA record no. 274/66; *El Faro de Vigo*, June 1, 1973). The same year, 1973, Alfonso Sastre published his Spanish version of *Shadow of a Gunman / Irlanda, Irlanda* with an introduction on the struggle of the Irish to gain independence. In an interview (http://www.jornada.unam.mx/2005/01/02/102e1cul.php) he confirmed that he wanted to prompt the setting up of a Basque independent theatre following the Irish example.

Sean O'Casey's works were translated and published in Portugal from the 1960s (Carvalho 2009b), but while Portuguese editions were readily available, productions of his plays were performed only after Salazar's regime was over. The premiere of *Hall of Healing* by a professional group took place in 1976. But the first application to stage the play, filed in the early 1960s, resulted in a ban and the ensuing "non-production." Follow-up of the Portuguese censorship records for O'Casey's *Hall of Healing* (Fundo de Teatro, 11A-7763 6395 and 7763) (Carvalho 2009a, 233) could be an excellent starting point for further research, very much in line with the study of non-translation of Czech literature under Salazar (Spirk 2014).

A global appraisal of the position of O'Casey's plays on Portuguese stages may be that of a vacuum but the simple statement that O'Casey was not staged in Portugal until the advent of democracy begs for further research: How many times were his plays submitted to the censor in the 1960s, what reasons were adduced for banning them and who were the various agents involved in the process that resulted in the lack of productions? It is telling that the translation of *Hall of Healing*, which marks the debut of O'Casey among Portuguese readers back in 1957 and of his belated stage debut (in 1971 by an amateur group and in 1982 by a professional company), corresponds to a play widely popular in Eastern Germany and the Soviet Union (Moran 2013, 157).

While O'Casey's presence in Iberian theatre after 1955 (the year Portugal and Spain became members of the United Nations) is fairly clear, the reception of Synge and Yeats is to be traced in two distinct periods: a few translations of both playwrights appeared before the Civil War, but it was not until the late 1950s onwards that they started to form part of the Spanish and Portuguese repertoires. In Spain there are references to a translation of Synge's *Riders to the Sea / Jinetes hacia el mar* by Spanish writer Juan Ramón Jiménez and his wife, Zenobia Camprubí, published in 1920 and staged at Madrid's Ateneo in 1921 in a production attended by Spanish dramatist Lorca (Alonso 2009; Andrews 1991, 70; de Toro 2007; London 1997, 233, 127). Also in the 1920s, a Portuguese literary figure, Fernando Pessoa, had plans for a translation of *Riders to the Sea* (Carvalho 2009a, 167). The Spanish production of *Riders to the Sea* supposedly influenced the writing of Lorca's *Blood Wedding* and even inspired him to put on a Spanish production of *Playboy of the Western World* with the La Barraca theatre group (de Toro 2007, 10).

There were translations of Yeats' works published from 1918 in Spanish, Catalan, Galician and Basque until just before the Spanish Civil War (Hurtley 2006). A symbol of the Irish Literary Revival, Yeats was an inspiration for the Galician *Rexurdimento* (1920–1936) and was often quoted along with Synge as a successful example of the "Celtic race" (de Toro 2007).

None of the Celtic nationalist connotations found in relation to Yeats and Synge in Galicia seem to have a parallel in Portugal. As Carvalho (2009a, 232) aptly points out, it is the writings of actor-critic Mário Vilaça in the journal *Vértice* and Luiz Francisco Rebello's 1957/1965 volume *Teatro Moderno: Caminhos e Figuras* that effectively introduced Irish plays through translation to readers and theatregoers.

Synge arrived on Portuguese stages with a half-century delay (Carvalho 2009a, 159–231). In 1956 the TUP (Porto University Theatre) presented *Riders to the Sea*, and a year later RTP (Portuguese public television) broadcast the play and *Playboy of the Western World* was first produced by the TEP (Teatro Estudio Porto). In 1959 Yeat's *Cathleen ní Houlihan* was staged and Synge's *The Tinker's Wedding* was refused permission for performance on account of its "bad quality" and "ill-treatment" of the characters of the priest and the father (censorship record 5812 [Carvalho 2009a, 164]).

In the case of Spain, six plays by Synge were staged between 1956, when the National Chamber Theatre (*Teatro Nacional de Cámara y Ensayo*), under the direction of Modesto Higueras, presented *Playboy of the Western World*; and 1978, when two so-called *ordenación* (regulatory) records authorised productions of *Playboy of the Western World* in Catalan and *Well of the Saints* in Galician. This was, of course, the year that new freedoms were granted to theatres and the Spanish Constitution was passed in Spain.

Two distinct productions of *Playboy of the Western World* were authorised in 1961 (*El farsante más grande del mundo*, AGA record no. 147–61) and 1971 (*El botarate del mundo ocidental*, AGA record no. 345–71), respectively. The play was also broadcast by TVE (Spanish public television) in 1969.[4] *Deirdre of the Sorrows*, translated into Spanish by theatre critic Alfredo Marqueríe for the Malaga-based group ARA, was granted an extremely lenient approval in 1964 that included a rare permission for radio broadcast (AGA record no. 125–64). Spanish versions of *The Tinker's Wedding* and *Shadow of the Glen* were approved in 1969 (AGA records no. 363–69 and 463–69). In 1972, permission was granted for the Galician stage version of *Riders to the Sea/Cabalgada cara ó mar* by DITEA. DITEA theatre group, under Agustín Magán's direction, staged plays by Osborne, O'Neill and Albee in the 1960s, and produced Synge, O'Casey and Yeats in the 1970s (Rodríguez-Villar 2005). This is the first and only production of the play recorded in the AGA censorship database; the last record for Synge was in 1975 for *Well of the Saints* (AGA records no. 161–72 and 184–75). One year after the death of Franco, in 1976, DITEA was given permission to stage O'Casey's *Red Roses for Me* in Galician, coinciding with the Catalan production of the play.[5]

Translation as transculturation and resistance

In attempting to give an account of Irish theatre productions in Spain and Portugal under totalitarian regimes, we have tried to find similarities and establish parallelisms. It seems apt to affirm that both Iberian regimes share a historical period and a geographical space in the (southern) periphery of Europe. Although Salazar made use of Portuguese propaganda in favour of Franco, he did so more to reaffirm his own position than that of his neighbour. There is little doubt that the Portuguese press controlled by Salazar made sure that Franco was portrayed as a victorious hero in the battle against communism in the Iberian Peninsula, while presenting the Estado Novo as a model to follow in post-war Spain (Pena 2013, 2014). Luso-Spanish relations were not as close as might be expected; in fact, there was a much closer affinity between Portugal and Ireland, at least in the 1940s in relation to the defence of Catholicism and the need to maintain order and traditional values (Szmigiero 2006). Even the form and structure adopted by the censorship apparatus in both Iberian countries was, at best, dissimilar (Merino 2007; Seruya 2009).

The influence of foreign theatre on both theatrical cultures shows a pre-eminence of English as a source language, and Britain (and, with the victory of the Allies in WWII, the US) as source countries. In the case of Spain, the deliberate introduction of British plays served, through the intervention of the British Council, to counteract the influence of German trends (Corse 2013). However, it remains to be established whether a parallel situation occurred in Portugal.

The 1920 translation into Spanish of Synge's *Riders to the Sea* remains a rare reference, ingrained in a pre-Civil War literary tradition, related to the generations of writers of the period. So are the translations into Spanish, Galician and Catalan of Yeats' works (Hurtley 2006), texts anchored in the pre-war period, often used as examples of the influence of the Irish literary revival authors on their Spanish counterparts. The 1933 translation into Galician of Yeats' *Land of Heart's Desire*, by the Villar Ponte brothers, first published in the Galician Literary Revival Journal *Nos*, was used to mark the Day of Galician Literature in 1977. Yeats' text was thus implanted on a Spanish (Galician) stage in an attempt to make Galician nationalism rise from the ashes of the *Rexurdimento*.

Although Anglophone-Irish theatre was imported into both Spain and Portugal from the 1950s, the process in each setting was slightly different. In Spain, Irish authors were chosen for reasons of both ideology (O'Casey) and identity (Synge, Yeats), and were instrumental in establishing a struggle in favour of nationalism (and political change) in Galicia, Catalonia and the Basque Country. Ireland's political independence from Britain and Irish linguistic identity were taken as models from the periphery of Europe in the periphery of Spain, so that translation was a fundamental part of a transculturation process (de Toro 2007, 54) that led to the assimilation of Irish drama in Spain. In Portugal the wish to accommodate to European stage trends seems to have formed part of a process of renewal of Portuguese repertoires that was intended to counteract the official ideology, but it had no connotations of nationalist identity. In this case, the use of translation to introduce new "foreign" ideas and aesthetics was a form of resistance against the status quo.

Unlike "English" Shaw and Wilde (Coletes 1985; Constán 2009), whose plays had been translated and staged before Franco and Salazar's times, and continued to be staged and published throughout the twentieth century, other "Irish" playwrights, such as O'Casey or Synge, were introduced as belated novelties in both Iberian contexts. In the late 1960s and 1970s, productions in Galician and Catalan were staged because of their inherent "Irishness" or the accompanying political connotations. Productions of plays by Behan in the 1960s, or by Joyce (Uribe-Echevarría and Merino 1994; Merino and Uribe-Echevarría 1996) and Yeats in the 1970s (Alonso 2009; Andrews 1991; de Toro 2007), complete a global perception of Irish theatre produced in Spain. In Portugal, Synge's position on the stage was reinforced with O'Casey's influence in published form.

Beckett was staged in Spain and Portugal without much delay in relation to the Paris-London premieres, and was soon integrated into the repertoire of experimental companies following European avant-garde trends. Audience protests at the Paris premiere of *Waiting for Godot* "turned an exclusively Parisian phenomenon into an event reported worldwide" and Beckett "had acquired one of the ingredients of commercial success: the patina of fame" (Morash 2004, 200), making him one of the most popular playwrights to date (Rodríguez Gago 2006).

The study of Irish theatre on Iberian stages has naturally led us to European and international links both for the 1940s and the second half of the twentieth century. The fact that Irish authors were imported for a non-totalitarian context in the (northern) periphery of Europe (Aaltonen 1996), staged in the British Isles and the cultural centres of the European continent (both east and west), confirms Morash's claim that "as much as Irish theatre imagined itself as national, it has always been at its most vibrant when it has been most international" (2004, 275).

Notes

1. University of the Basque Country, UPV/EHU. Consolidated Research Group GIC12/197, Basque Government IT728/13. Project FFI2012–39012-C04–01T and G15/75, MINECO, Spanish Ministry of Economy, Industry and Competitiveness.
2. In the volume edited by Huerta (2003) a short section is devoted to "Foreign Theatre in Spain" between 1900 and 1939 (2575–2600), with just three pages on "English" theatre (2595–2597). The chapter on German theatre does mention the reception and influence of Brecht in Spanish dramatists Buero and Sastre (Huerta 2003, 2997–3019), but there is no mention of the influence of North American drama. The chronological tables (3012–3051) list titles for "Spanish" and "International" theatre without any reference to translations of foreign theatre in Spain. In Delgado and Gies (2012) a few references to translations are found in Chapter 17 ("Theatre under Franco," 341–370).
3. Aaltonen (1996, 221–223) includes both authors in her study of Irish drama in Finland.
4. Along with Synge's *Playboy of the Western World*, O'Casey's *Juno and the Paycock* (1964), Beckett's *Waiting for Godot* (1978) and Joyce's *Exiles* (1979), various pieces by Shaw and Wilde were broadcast on Spanish television in the 1960s and 1970s (http://www.imdb.com).
5. The AGA database records 428 entries for theatre manuscripts submitted in Catalan, 48 in Galician and 35 in Basque.

Works cited

Aaltonen, Sirkku. 1996. *Acculturation of the Other: Irish Milieux in Finnish Drama Translation*. Joensuu: Joensuu University Press.

AGA. "Archivo General de la Administración." Accessed April 30, 2014. http://www.mecd.gob.es/cultura-mecd/areas-cultura/archivos/mc/aga/fondos-documentales.html.

Alonso Giráldez, José Miguel. 2009. "*Jinetes hacia el mar*, una traducción afortunada: sobre la recepción en España de John Millington Synge." *AEDEAN Nexus*. Accessed April 30, 2014. http://aedean.org/?page_id=309.

Andrews, Jean. 1991. *Spanish Reactions to the Anglo-Irish Literary Revival in the Early Twentieth-Century: The Stone by the Elixir*. Lewiston, NY: The Edwin Mellen Press.

Carvalho, Paulo Eduardo. 2005. "Dramaturgia irlandesa e teatro português: Alguns elementos para uma cartografia de representações." *Cadernos de Literatura Comparada. (Teatro em Tradução)* 12–13: 163–176.

———. 2009a. *Identidades reescritas: figurações da Irlanda no teatro portugués*. Porto: Afrontamento.

———. 2009b. "Um encontro adiado: Sean O'Casey no Portugal do Estado Novo." In *Traduzir em Portugal durante o Estado Novo*, edited by Teresa Seruya, Maria Lin Moniz, and Alexandra Assis Roca, 229–249. Lisboa: Universidade Católica Editora.

CETbase Database. "Teatro em Portugal." Accessed April 30, 2014. http://ww3.fl.ul.pt/CETbase/.

Coletes, Agustín. 1985. "Oscar Wilde en España, 1902–1928." *Cuadernos de Filología Inglesa* 1: 17–32.

Constán, Sergio. 2009. *Wilde en España. La presencia de Óscar Wilde en la literatura española (1882–1936)*. León: Akrón.

Corse, Edward. 2013. *A Battle for Neutral Europe: British Council Propaganda during the Second World War*. London: Bloomsbury.

Delgado, Maria M. and David T. Gies, eds. 2012. *A History of Theatre in Spain*. Cambridge: Cambridge University Press.

de Toro, Antonio. 2007. *La literatura irlandesa en España*. La Coruña: Netbiblo.

Fernández, José-Francisco. 2009. "Beckett a Long Time Coming: The Critical Response to Samuel Beckett in Spain and Portugal." In *The International Reception of Samuel Beckett*, edited by Mark Nixon and Matthew Feldman, 272–290. London: Continuum.

Fiuza, Alexandre Filipe. 2009. "Censura y represión a los músicos españoles y portugueses en las décadas de 1960 y 1970." In *Crisis, dictaduras, democracia. I congreso internacional de Historia de Nuestro Tiempo*, edited by Carlos Navajas and Diego Iturriaga, 237–247. Logroño: Universidad de La Rioja.

García Ruíz, Víctor. 2007. "*El baile* de Edgar Neville: un tiempo dormido." In *Universo Neville*, edited by J. A. Ríos Carratalá, 87–115. Málaga: Instituto Municipal del Libro.

Huerta Calvo, Javier, ed. 2003. *Historia del teatro español*. Madrid: Gredos.

Hurtley, Jacqueline. 2006. "Lands of Desire: Yeats in Catalonia, Galicia and the Basque Country, 1920–1936." In *The Reception of W. B. Yeats in Europe*, edited by Klaus Peter Jochum, 76–94. London: Continuum.

Isabel-Estrada, M. Antonia. 2001. "George Bernard Shaw y John Osborne: recepción y recreación de su teatro en España durante el franquismo." PhD diss., Universidad Complutense.

London, John. 1997. *Reception and Renewal in Modern Spanish Theatre: 1939–1963*. London: Modern Humanities Research Association.

Mahanta Kébé, Serigne. 1994. "Crítica teatral de posguerra en el periódico madrileño Arriba." PhD diss., Universidad Complutense.

Marques dos Santos, Ana. 2012. "Teatro de Oscar Wilde no palco da Emissora Nacional – os textos." In *Depois do Labirinto. Teatro e Traduçao*, edited by Manuela Carvalho and Daniela Dipasquale, 273–292. Lisboa: Nova Vega.

Mateo, Marta. 2010. "The Reception of Wilde's Works in Spain Through Theatre Performances at the Turn of the Twentieth Century and Twenty-first Centuries." In *The Reception of Oscar Wilde in Europe*, edited by Stefano Evangelista, 156–172. London: Continuum.

Merino Álvarez, Raquel, ed. 2007. *Traducción y censura en España (1939–1985). Estudios sobre corpus TRACE: cine, narrativa, teatro*. Bilbao: Universidad del País Vasco.

———. 2009. "Building TRACE (Translations Censored) Theatre Corpus: Some Methodological Questions on Text Selection." In *Translation and Cultural Identity: Selected Essays on Translation and Cross-Cultural Communication*, edited by Micaela Muñoz-Calvo and Carmen Buesa-Gómez, 129–153. Newcastle: Cambridge Scholars Publishing.

———. 2012. "A Historical Approach to Spanish Theatre Translations from Censorship Archives." In *Iberian Studies on Translation and Interpreting*, edited by Isabel García-Izquierdo and Esther Monzó, 123–140. Oxford: Peter Lang.

Merino Álvarez, Raquel and Inés Uribe-Echeverría. 1996. "Spanish Translations of Joyce's Exiles." In *The Knowledges of the Translator: From Literary Interpretation to Machine Classification*, edited by Malcolm Coulthard and Patricia Anne Odber de Baubeta, 291–298. Lewiston, NY: Edwin Mellen.

Moran, James. 2013. *The Theatre of Sean O'Casey*. London: Bloomsbury.

Morash, Chris. 2004. *A History of Irish Theatre 1601–2000*. Cambridge: Cambridge University Press.

Muñoz-Cáliz, Berta. 2006. *El teatro crítico español durante el Franquismo visto por sus censores*. Madrid: Fundación Universitaria Española.

Pena Rodríguez, Alberto. 2013. "Los grandes héroes ibéricos. Salazar, Franco y la Guerra Civil española: prensa y propaganda." *Journal of Spanish Cultural Studies* 14 (1): 36–51.

———. 2014. "Mensaje del verdadero Portugal. Los intelectuales portugueses, la IIª República española y el fascismo ibérico: prensa y propaganda." *Arbor* 190 (766).

Pérez López de Heredia, María. 2005. "Inventario de las traducciones censuradas de teatro norteamericano en la España de Franco (1939–1963)." In *Transvases culturales: literatura, cine y traducción* 4, edited by Raquel Merino Álvarez, José Miguel Santamaría and Eterio Pajares, 97–112. Vitoria: Universidad del País Vasco.

Puebla, Lola. 2012. *Colección Teatro de Editorial Escelicer*. Madrid: Centro Documentación Teatral.

Quirós Alpera, Gabriel. 2010. "Historia de la dirección escénica en España: José Luis Alonso." PhD diss., Universidad Complutense.

Ramos Pinto, Sara. 2010. "Traduçao do vazio: a variaçao linguística nas traducçoes portuguesas de *Pygmalion* de Bernard Shaw, e *My Fair Lady* de Alan Jay Lerner." PhD diss., Universidade de Lisboa.

———. 2012. "Quando o palco e a página se encontram na traduçao." In *Depois do Labirinto. Teatro e Traduçao*, edited by Manuela Carvalho and Daniela Dipasquale, 213–249. Lisboa: Nova Vega.

Rodríguez Gago, Antonia. 2006. "Beckett después de Beckett." *Nexus* 2 (11): 72–77.

Rodríguez Villar, Alejandra Juno. 2005. "La cultura teatral en Galicia. El caso de DITEA, 1960–1986." PhD diss., Universidad de Santiago de Compostela.

Seruya, Teresa. 2009. "Introdução a uma bibliografia crítica da tradução de literatura em Portugal durante o Estado Novo." In *Traduzir em Portugal durante o Estado Novo*, edited by Teresa Seruya, Maria Lin Moniz, and Alexandra Assis Roca, 69–86. Lisboa: Universidade Católica Editora.

Sova, Dawn S. 2004. *Banned Plays. Censorship Histories of 125 Stage Dramas*. New York: Facts on File.

Spirk, Jaroslav. 2014. *Censorship, Indirect Translations and Non-translation: The (Fateful) Adventures of Czech Literature in 20th–Century Portugal*. Newcastle: Cambridge Scholars Publishing.

Szmigiero, Katarzyna. 2006. "Fabulism and Irish Censorship." *Estudios Irlandeses* 1: 112–118.

TETRA Database. "Teatro e Tradução." Accessed April 30, 2014. http://tetra.letras.ulisboa.pt/base/.

TRACE Database. "Translation and Censorship." Accessed April 30, 2014. http://www.ehu.es/trace/cata logos_eng.php.

Uribe-Echevarría, Inés and Raquel Merino-Álvarez. 1994. "Tradición y traducción: *Exiliados* de J. Joyce." In *Transvases culturales: literatura, cine, traducción* 1, edited by Federico Eguíluz et al., 433–444. Vitoria: Universidad del País Vasco.

APPENDIX

Table 34.1 Number of entries for plays by Irish authors.

	CETbase	TETRAbase	AGA teat	TRACEti
Behan	0	0	4	1
Beckett	112 [1959[1]]	47	33	22
Joyce	5 [1982[1]]	2	2	3
O'Casey	10 [1976[1]]	2	12	4
Shaw	7 [1945[1]]	25	24	14
Synge	11 [1956[1]]	7	8	1
Wilde	44 [1909[1]]	41	28	18
Yeats	3 [1964[1]]	2	1	1

35

UNSETTLING THE IBERIAN TRANSITIONS TO DEMOCRACY OF THE 1970S[1]

Pamela Radcliff

There is no question that one of the most dramatic turning points in twentieth-century Iberian history was the transition from authoritarian to democratic regimes in Spain and in Portugal in the mid 1970s. Almost from the beginning, the two processes were linked together, and, along with Greece, celebrated as the Southern European vanguard of Samuel Huntington's famous "third wave" of democratic transitions. The "transitology" sub-field that emerged in the 1980s to explain this unexpected "third wave" identified the Southern European transitions as model exemplars and yardsticks that could potentially be exported to other locations, especially Latin America or Eastern Europe. But by the mid 1990s, the hegemonic view of the model Spanish and Portuguese transitions began to unravel, as competing interpretations, both scholarly and popular, pulled out foundational threads from the seamlessly celebratory narrative. While these debates have been multi-faceted, they are clustered around two different sets of questions. The first generally accepts the success of the transitions, but debates which factors were most important in the democratization process. The second reconsiders the unqualified success of the transitions, especially in Spain, where critics unhappy with the perceived deficits of democratic practice today have claimed to locate at least part of their origins in the inadequacies of the transition process. This article maps out these debates and suggests ways in which the disaggregation of the Spanish and Portuguese cases from the singular Iberian model might enrich these debates and shed new comparative light on both democratic transitions.

The aggregation of the Spanish and Portuguese cases within a Southern European model was consolidated in a series of books on the transition to, and consolidation of, democracy. Building on Emmanuel Wallerstein's categorization of Southern Europe as a "semi-peripheral" region, the authors of the first volume sought to draw the neglected region into comparative political science models (O'Donnell et al. 1986). More importantly, they argued that the recent transitions had, at long last, brought Southern Europe into the range of "normal" Western European patterns, a conclusion confirmed by a later volume that identified these new democracies as unique models of consolidation within dozens of "third-wave" democratic transitions (Stepan and Linz 1996). The new "transitology" interpretation emerged from the apparent conundrum of these unexpected transitions, which did not seem to fit what had been the dominant theory of democratization: namely, that before a country could transition successfully to democracy, according to the argument in Seymour Martin Lipset's seminal 1959 article, it had to pass through certain stages of economic and social "modernization." Instead of a gradual long-term transition over generations, Spain and Portugal underwent political transitions from long-standing authoritarian regimes to western-style democracies within a few short years. Their new explanatory model emphasized the role of actors over structural changes and of contingency over determinism, of transitions as an uncertain space in which human agency, particularly that of elite political actors, was decisive. By the end of the 1980s, when another series of transitions from authoritarian rule took place in Eastern Europe, it was the Southern European "elite actor" model that was held up as the preferred road map.

At the same time that the model was consolidated, there was always an underlying tension between the Spanish and Portuguese cases. Coming from the post-hoc perspective of consolidated democracies, Philippe Schmitter (1998) used the term "equifinity" to conceptualize how countries can take radically different paths to the same general destination. Their considerable differences had to be minimized in order to shoehorn them into the same interpretation; thus, at the outset, Portugal's revolutionary rupture, set off by a colonial crisis that provoked a left-wing military coup in April 1974 that in turn unleashed a grass-roots popular revolution, could not have looked more different from Spain's "pacted" transition between old regime and opposition elites. In fact, Spanish elites in 1975–76 viewed Portugal as a negative model to avoid, and the fear of "portugalization" was itself a stimulus for the famous Spanish "consensus." The unitary Iberian model only functioned when the revolutionary period in Portugal was viewed as a temporary deviation on the road to the "normal" Western European democracy that it eventually became. From the November 1975 counter-coup, moderate elites began to take control of the process and the revolutionary forces were largely defeated. Even so, it was clear that, in reality, it was the Spanish transition that was the "ideal type" for the Southern European model that transitologists were eager to export (for a more extended analysis of the scholarship on the "Spanish model," see Radcliff 2015).

The optimism that this model could be exported anywhere reflected the confidence that structural obstacles need not be an impediment to democratization if political actors made good decisions. However, it was precisely the fact that so few other democracies outside Southern Europe managed to consolidate that eventually undermined the conviction that elite agency had been the only key factor in their success. Thus, the faltering of democratic legitimacy in Latin America, the uneven consolidation in the ex-Soviet bloc and the virtual halt of the third wave of new democratizations after the early 1990s began to chip away at what had been the dominant theoretical approach in the 1980s. While few scholars would discount the importance of short-term elite decisions and "crafting" in precipitating regime change and constructing solid democratic institutions, most would now qualify that they are necessary but not sufficient to a successful transition and, even more so, to consolidation.

Instead, the trend since the 1990s has been to turn the spotlight on other factors – and other actors – in explaining the Southern European "success" model. In particular, much of the scholarship over the past couple of decades has emphasized that transitions cannot be made only by a handful of farsighted men, and sought to demonstrate that the broader population – of men and women – were also active agents in determining the outcome. In general terms, there has been a widespread critique of the "top down" view of the pacted transition, both as an ideal model but also as a description of reality. In this latter category are a plethora of works that approach the transitions "from below," arguing that the "elite agency" narrative offered only a partial view of the transition process.[2]

From a culturalist perspective, scholars have argued that elites operated within symbolic frameworks and cultural norms that both shaped their actions and operated as mobilizing myths (Edles 1995; 1998). In her path-breaking book on the Spanish transition, Paloma Aguilar (1996) argued for the role of collective memory in structuring the options of political actors as well as the attitudes of the broader population. In particular, she made the case that the widespread desire to avoid re-opening the cleavages that had produced the Civil War helped frame the context in which an unlikely consensus between regime reformers and anti-Francoist opponents was imaginable. During the transition, the myth of national reconciliation, supported by all major political players from the Communists (PCE) to the new center-right party (UCD), provided the foundation for negotiations and eventual pacts, including the agreement to "forget" the traumatic past, which was epitomized by the 1977 Amnesty Law that freed anti-Francoist political prisoners but also foreclosed prosecution of Francoist officials or any sort of "truth and reconciliation" discovery process.

In Portugal, the very different context of an unwinnable colonial war in Africa had discredited the Salazar dictatorship so badly that there were few defenders of this past in 1974. Also different from Spain was the lack of a polarizing civil war at the dictatorship's origins. As a result of this distinct context of simultaneous decolonization and democratization, the coup and revolution opened a process of rupture or "radical discontinuity" that unleashed an extensive process of purging and transitional justice, not amnesty and reconciliation (Costa Pinto 2006). It was only after the revolutionary forces were defeated that the moderate elites constructed their myth of national reconciliation, based on the rejection of both the "authoritarianism of the right" (the dictatorship) and the "authoritarianism of the left," as the revolutionary period was framed. Thus, the eventual transition to a Western-style liberal democracy after 1976 was constructed upon its own culture of "forgetting," in this case of the revolutionary origins of the new regime (Maxwell 1995).

As part of the broader trend to explore the transitions "from below," scholars have been bringing the Portuguese revolution back into the center of the story. The revolutionary period used to be the exclusive property of Marxist historiography, which celebrated this period as a heroic but failed socialist revolution, but this interpretation paradoxically reinforced the notion that it was a dead-end process with no impact on the subsequent democratization process. More recently, social movement scholars have explored the diverse and widespread grass-roots movements as popular actors in a much more complex transition process that integrates the revolutionary period instead of suppressing or bracketing it (see Palacios Cerezales 2003 for an overview). Instead of being reduced to either "authoritarianism of the left" or failed socialism, popular mobilization during the revolutionary period has been re-framed as part of a wide-ranging debate over empowerment, forms of democracy and citizenship, and competing visions of the future society that left a lasting imprint on Portuguese society (Fishman 2011). From this perspective, rather than a simple alternative between authoritarianism and democracy, the transition played out different versions of a democratic future (for a re-framing of the constitutional debates along these lines, see Monica Brito Vieira and Filipe Carreira de Silva (2010).

Despite important differences in the nature and scope of popular participation in the Spanish case, the social movement scholarship has followed similar lines of inquiry, resurrecting alternative democratic visions in the popular mobilization of the transition. In both countries, scholars have explored the more familiar trade unions and working-class organizations, which they identified as key popular and often "early riser" players in the transitions (Domènech 2008). But they have also turned increasing attention to the less studied phenomenon of urban social movements, often rooted in neighborhood-based groupings and associations, which created alternate visions of modern urban life that would empower ordinary citizens against developers, landlords and an indifferent state (Molinero and Ysás 2010; Pérez Quintana and Sanchez León 2008; Radcliff 2012; Ramos Pinto 2013). Even under the dictatorships, urban residents began to petition the government for adequate housing and services, from education to running water, and in the process created new conceptions of citizenship and identity that became increasingly politicized over time. While popular mobilization around these issues was limited during the dictatorship, the networks and identities constructed formed the basis for the urban movements that exploded during the transition period. In a classic work on the urban movement in Madrid, scholar-participant Manuel Castells (1983) celebrated the unique scope of the Spanish phenomenon in a post-1968 European context, but more comparative analysis might confirm a broader Iberian phenomenon rooted in the specific urbanization problems of authoritarian capitalist regimes, in which unregulated private development and an unresponsive state leave ordinary urban residents without effective legal channels to pursue their claims to a liveable city.

Exploration of the transition "from below," especially from the perspective of urban social movements, also opened the door for the inclusion of female actors in the story, although the Iberian cases have received less attention than in scholarship on transitions in Latin America and Eastern Europe. Because women rarely held high government positions in the authoritarian regimes, or were prominent among opposition leaders, the elite agency narrative was essentially a masculine one. Feminist scholars have made the general argument that women are more likely to participate in politics at an informal level, especially in community-based organizations linked to quality-of-life issues. In transitions from authoritarian regimes, women's groups usually focus on prisoners, cost of living and women's rights. Research on the Spanish case has demonstrated that women indeed formed prisoners' support groups and housewife associations that lobbied for lower consumer prices, joined neighborhood improvement associations, and held the first feminist conference at the end of 1975, just after Franco's death (for an overview, see Threlfall 2005; see also Radcliff 2008, 2012, chs. 3 & 5). During the Constitutional debates, feminist leaders framed such issues as adultery, divorce, abortion, childcare and birth control as gendered democratic rights. In Portugal, most of these rights except for abortion were granted up front by the revolutionary state, which may explain the lack of a visible feminist movement there (Ferreira 2011). In any case, aside from specific gender studies, women's participation is still largely sidelined in the master narratives, especially in the Portuguese case, and even in the social movement scholarship on the transitions "from below."

Beyond revealing similarities in popular participation and social movements in the two transitions, social movement studies have also illustrated significant differences which deserve further exploration and comparison. Most dramatically, in Portugal the popular movements, whether of urban dwellers, industrial workers or landless laborers, engaged in revolutionary forms of activism that directly challenged not only the political power of the old regime but also the economic and social structures and hierarchies of a capitalist society. These included massive land expropriation and collectivization in the south, worker management experiments in industries and systematic home occupations in the major cities. An earlier generation of scholars tended to interpret this activity through the narrow ideological lens of communist revolution, but recent studies have suggested a more heterogeneous and even contradictory set of motives that emerged from a largely uncoordinated grass-roots process. From any angle, this was precisely the "portugalization" scenario that Spanish elites sought to avoid through a combination of negotiations with anti-Francoist parties and unrelenting police repression against strikes and demonstrations. Initial comparative analysis suggests that the state's capacity and willingness to repress and contain popular mobilization was the decisive factor in distinguishing the scope and form that mobilization took in each national case (Durán Muñoz 2009). Whereas in Portugal, the left-wing military coup and the precipitating colonial quagmire divided the political and military elites and unleashed a crisis of state authority, in Spain the military and policing apparatus, as well as the state administration, remained intact. Thus, it was the crisis of the state, rather than a distinctively radical ideological starting point that provided much greater scope for popular mobilization to transgress political and economic boundaries in Portugal and develop ever more radical forms.

The significance and impact of all these popular movements on the course of the two transitions and the shape of the future democracy is still a subject of lively debate. Although there are plenty who still defend the more familiar story that downplays the significance of popular participation in shaping the outcome of the transitions, social movement scholars have produced a growing number of studies that suggest plausible alternate narratives. In the Portuguese case, the question revolves around what legacies the revolutionary mobilization left in the legal, political, social and economic structure of the democratic regime established in 1976. Was the Constitution more participatory as a result of popular pressure, was the state more responsive to popular demands, or did the eventual "de-socialization" of the Constitution that occurred over the course of the 1980s wipe out all traces of the initial radical projects? In contrast to Portugal, where scholars are only beginning to examine the role that popular mobilization had in precipitating the crisis of the regime (Accornero 2012), in Spain the focus has been on demonstrating the causal link between popular mobilization and the origins of the transition. Thus, they have made the case that popular mobilization, growing in intensity from the early 1970s, was a significant factor in forcing regime change. On the one hand, increasingly vociferous protests torpedoed the Francoist elites' initial plans for minimal reforms, and on the other they strengthened the hand of the opposition parties in eventual negotiations. Instead of a pre-designed peaceful transition to democracy "bestowed" by Francoist reformers, as implied in some of their memoirs, democracy was "conquered" by pressure from below (see Pere Ysàs (2010) for a concise presentation of this argument).

All of this scholarship on the transition "from below" has aimed to unsettle the apparently idyllic story of peaceful, negotiated and somehow seamless transitions that still lingered in popular culture. In the alternate narrative, the Western-style democracies that emerged from this process were constructed at least in part on the suppression and/or demobilization of popular struggle and distinct visions of a democratic future. In recognition of this element of struggle, recent scholarship has also sought to re-inscribe the role of violence and conflict, as well as the uncertainty that accompanied it, into the transition process (Baby et al. 2009; Bermeo 1997; Costa Pinto 2006). In the Portuguese case, the reintegration of the revolution into the transition story both opens up other possible futures and shines a light on how they were disarticulated in the process of consolidating a liberal democracy. While there was no armed revolutionary "storming of the winter palace," there was significant coercion, intimidation and threats in the grass-roots attacks on property owners and "savage purges" (Costa Pinto 2001, 79) of police and other officials, few of which were actually controlled by the Communist Party (PCP), despite claims to the contrary on both sides of the political spectrum. At the same time, counter-revolutionary groups, particularly in the north, carried out violent attacks on communist offices and symbols, and, of course, the state and the army finally recovered its repressive capacity in violently containing the revolutionary movements after November 1975.

In the Spanish case, popular contestation and violence were more contained by the coherent resolve of the state, but a combination of left- and right-wing terrorism and repressive policing created an ongoing current of violence that belies any simple picture of peaceful consensus. Scholars debate the scope of this violence and its consequences on the quality of the subsequent democracy, but many would agree that it must be better taken into account in calculating the real costs of the transition. Moreover, there is broad agreement that, in the case of the Basque Country, the high level of violence there during and after the transition created its own regional dynamic. Violence took the form of massive unruly protests, police repression and, of course, escalating Euskadi Ta Askatasuna (ETA) terrorist attacks, all of which seriously undermined the legitimacy of the new democratic regime among the population. If the greater acknowledgment of violence throughout Spanish territory reduces the black and white contrast between "peaceful" Spanish and "violent" Basque transitions, few would question that the Basque case was in a category of its own, a virtual failed transition, which included low levels of support for the new Constitution, a polarized party system and strong anti-systemic movements (Muro 2011). With the recent rise in separatist sentiment in Catalonia, reflected in the pro-independence electoral victories, the larger question of how well the Spanish transition dealt with the regional nationalist question, or the territorial structure of the state, has become part of a broader re-evaluation of the achievements of the transition in public and scholarly debate.

In fact, over the past decade, there has been a rising trend towards more critical perspectives on the Spanish transition as a whole, arising from dissatisfaction or concerns with the current practice of democracy, which has been tainted by corruption scandals, political polarization and deep economic crisis, in addition to the separatist challenge. On the one hand, critical voices have always existed: the official ETA and Herri Batasuna positions on the new regime in 1977 were that it was a "continuation, reform or mere change of image of the dictatorship" (cited in Aguilar 2001, 101); whereas on the other, defenders of the successful pacted transition remain (Encarnación 2011; Gunther 2011); but there is no question that, in recent years, attacks on the "myth" of the "model" transition have gained momentum. Although few would argue that the democratic regime was not an improvement on what preceded it, and most Spaniards still probably view it as an achievement (in a 2001 poll 86% of Spaniards reported being proud of the transition [Moral 2001]), critics blame the "democratic deficits" of the present on either the "incomplete," "limited" or "flawed" transition, or even the "non" transition or "post-dictatorship."

At the core of these critiques is the accusation that the pacted and controlled transition, so extolled by the transitologists, failed to make a complete rupture with the authoritarian regime, leaving the ghosts of that past literally haunting the new democracy. One focus is the exploration of the "authoritarian legacies" that resulted from the continuity in personnel at all levels of state, military and judicial administration. Another is to draw links between the secretive "top-down" transition and the perceived "low-quality" democracy with limited popular participation and lack of transparency at the top. Partly drawing on both of these claims is the contention that one of the key "original sins" of the transition was the political decision to view the traumatic past as a "shared tragedy" perpetrated by "two demons" instead of assigning responsibility to the dictatorship. This latter issue has generated a virtual "memory war" in the public sphere, waged by both defenders and critics of the 1977 Amnesty Law and the broader agreement to "bury the hatchet" in the name of national reconciliation (Graham 2012, ch 7).

The memory wars in Spain were unleashed by two precipitating events: the 1998 extradition order against Pinochet that exposed Spain's own lack of transitional justice and the first exhumation of a Francoist mass grave in the year 2000. Civil society groups such as the Association for the Recuperation of Historical Memory began to advocate for digging up and identifying more "*desaparecidos*," but also for more public recognition of the victims of the dictatorship. In response, conservatives rejected the charged label of "disappeared" victims and argued against opening what they viewed as a Pandora's box, citing fear of unleashing past hatreds. During the Socialist government of 2004–8, the PSOE (*Partido Socialista Obrero Español*) responded to grass-roots pressure with the so-called "Law of Historical Memory," a "post-transitional justice" measure passed after much amendment and discussion in 2007 (see

Alves Raimundo 2012 for a comparative analysis of post-transitional justice in Spain). For the first time, it officially condemned the Franco regime as illegitimate and committed the State to rehabilitate its victims. Not surprisingly, the law did not satisfy everyone, with those on the left upset that Francoist judicial sentences were not to be overturned and the conservative Partido Popular (PP) party refusing to vote for it, on the grounds that it provocatively poked open old wounds. While the PP had presented a law in 2002 condemning "totalitarian" regimes and expressing moral support for their victims, the party has yet to directly condemn the Franco regime itself.

What this current debate in Spain has revealed is the continuing lack of consensus, not only about memory politics during the transition, but also about the longer trajectory of twentieth-century Spanish history leading up to that moment (Boyd 2008). Taking shape in both popular and academic historical scholarship are conflicting master narratives (including various inter-mediary positions) that assign distinct political meanings to the transition and what it pro-duced. For conservatives, the "pacted" reformist transition was the result of a gradual process of democratization that began during the Restoration liberal regime (1875–1923), was derailed by the radical and intolerant Second Republic (1931–1936), and was facilitated once again by the stability and economic growth provided by the Franco regime in its later phases, by which time it had left its fascist and violent past behind. This narrative culminates in the peaceful transition led by reformist Francoist elites, who planned the final step of political transition, which they implemented after Franco's death. Feeding into this version of twentieth-century history is a revisionist neo-Francoist strain of popular history that justifies the military coup of 1936 as a patriotic response to a chaotic republic.

The contrasting left-wing narrative argues that the only source of Spain's democratic tradi-tion lies, not in the elitist Restoration regime but in the popular democratic Second Republic, which was brutally crushed by a fascist dictatorship that derailed the country's modernization and contributed nothing to the democratic transition, whether directly or indirectly. In this nar-rative, Spain's democratic tradition was preserved and carried forward by the anti-Francoist opposition, culminating in the popular mobilization that forced regime elites towards real rupture. The left narrative diverges at this point as to whether the anti-Francoist democratic culture ended up completely crushed, or even betrayed by the official left parties, culminating in the "non" transition outcome, or whether the complex balance of forces produced an admit-tedly imperfect transition with both "lights and shadows."

The debates on the memory politics of the transition reflect this divergence. From the lat-ter perspective, the Amnesty Law and the politics of national reconciliation were pragmatic and functional solutions embraced by a left that viewed them as the best hope for democratic consolidation, as the then PSOE leader Felipe Gonzalez has reiterated in recent years. Far from being a "self-amnesty" imposed by the Francoist elites, the Amnesty Law was pushed by the left on reluctant conservatives. Amnesty, in contrast to amnesia, was a conscious decision not to let the past count in the future, a decision which did nothing to stem the outpouring of pub-lications on the traumatic past in the decades to come (Juliá 2010). Further, in an international context that preceded the current transitional justice conceptual and institutional framework, it would be anachronistic to expect that opposition groups should have demanded trials for Francoist officials. Without significant pressure groups advocating for transitional justice, and in a context in which military authority was still intact, a viable alternative path is difficult to envision (Aguilar 2001). At the same time, this path left various "shadows" of authoritarian legacy, including the continued influence of Francoist police, judges, bureaucrats and military officials, as well as public symbols such as street names and the massive memorial to the Francoist war dead, the "Valley of the Fallen." Although there is disagreement as to the level of damage this legacy inflicted on the democracy moving forward, most in this camp agree that the current democracy would be strengthened by acknowledging the costs of decisions made during the transition.

From the other, more uncompromising perspective, the "pact of oblivion" was mistakenly agreed to by opposition parties primarily out of fear, in a transition defined not by hope but by military supervision. The pact institutionalized the "impunity" of torturers and murderers and abandoned the victims to an imposed official amnesia that suppressed their voices and denied their very existence. In this view, the pact was not simply a political agreement but an enforced culture of silence that permeated not only official institutions and discourse but also most of the mainstream press (Resina 2000). While these critics acknowledge that academic scholars published works that uncovered the perspective of the victims of the Civil War, these did not permeate public or popular culture until the literal "unearthing" of the mass graves brought the violence into full view (Jerez Farrán and Amago 2010). The silence encompassed not just the victims of the past but the radical left of the popular transition, whose alternative democratic projects were actively demobilized and then marginalized under the neo-liberal hegemony of the center right and left parties that took control of the post-Francoist regime. This culture of "repressed memories" left a wounded society whose transition to a truly democratic society was blocked by its inability to work through its difficult past (Martín Cabrera 2011). Some have called for a new "second transition" which would move beyond the limits of the first incomplete, or inauthentic transition (Fontana 2005).

In this debate about the transition's contribution to the current "democratic deficits" in Spain, there is surprisingly little in-depth comparative analysis of the "deficits" of other European democracies with distinct origins. Without such comparison it is not always clear which deficits are rooted in Spain's "peculiar" experience and which are shared by other "postmodern" democracies. Before reviving what sometimes sounds like the 3.0 version of the classic "failure" narrative of Spanish history, it is important to place Spain within broader discussions about the crisis of democratic modernity in a post-'68 and post-'89 Europe.

But the most intriguing and under-explored comparative touchstone should be Portugal. Given that the first phase of the Portuguese transition contained many of the elements that critics of the Spanish case wish had occurred in their own country, comparing the impact of this different path on the quality of the two democracies seems like a fruitful research agenda. Under the transitology model, the revolutionary phase in Portugal was bracketed as ephemeral to the real story of the establishment of a liberal democracy by center left and right moderate parties. But if the revolution left real legacies in the shape of Portugal's democracy, as recent studies suggest, then disaggregating the homogenizing "Iberian model" would open space for exploring possible distinct outcomes from Portugal's "dual transition."

Thus, in regards to historical memory and authoritarian legacies, the Portuguese revolution took a very different path from Spain that, despite later reversals, was never completely obliterated. With the rupture of the coup and the crisis of the state, the Portuguese transition opened precisely the radical break with the past that anti-Francoists desired. With a dominant antifascist discourse, the revolutionary government unequivocally condemned the Salazar regime as fascist and undertook the most extensive process of transitional justice and symbolic delegitimation of all three Southern European countries (Costa Pinto 2001, 2006). Between the banning of existing conservative political parties and the purging of individuals, it was difficult for the Salazar elite, in contrast to the Francoist elite, to re-constitute itself in the new democracy. Thus, even though many purged military and political elites were reincorporated in the late 1970s, most did not come back to play leading roles and there was no important political party that carried the legacy of the authoritarian regime. In contrast, some 30,000 Francoist officials transferred seamlessly to the democratic civil service, in addition to continuity in the upper echelons of military and political elites, including a major political party led by an ex-Francoist Minister, Manuel Fraga. On the symbolic level, the Portuguese state undertook a coherent and immediate campaign to remove statues, change national holidays and institute secularization measures. The government even funded a Commission, not dissolved until 1991, which was granted access to state archives, and whose job was to publicize and disseminate documentation on repression and censorship as well as create a museum of the resistance. At the same time, grass-roots revolutionary groups carried out their own unauthorized "savage" purges, targeting the political police, capitalists, media elites and local political figures. The anti-capitalist or anti-monopolist purging of private sector economic elites made Portugal the only example of socio-economic "re-distributive" transitional justice in Southern Europe, resulting in massive land seizures in the south and worker-controlled industries around Lisbon. This multi-faceted effort to break with the dictatorial past and create an egalitarian democracy embodied the aspirations of many anti-Francoist militants in the 1970s as well as their defenders today.

Of course, many of these revolutionary measures were reversed over the course of the following decade, which was why it has been plausible to minimize the impact of the period on the later democracy. In particular, the re-distributive transitional justice projects were disarticulated, with most purges, worker self-management and expropriations reversed by the end of the decade, leaving Western-style capitalism in more or less the same dominant position as in Spain. Formal procedures of transitional justice were also halted, under a new rhetoric of national reconciliation and re-integration. The Constitution that established a mandate to "build socialism" through the "democratic power of the working class," and which declared nationalizations and expropriations to be irreversible was gradually "de-socialized" over the 1980s. But at the same time, it appears that many of the symbolic measures linked to the uncontested rejection of the dictatorship were never dropped (such as the commitment to the "ideals of April 25"), and that continuity of personnel was significantly disrupted by the purges. While there was a certain "culture of forgetting," it was aimed more at the revolutionary period than at the dictatorship itself. Thus, at least some of the legacies identified by critics of Spain's democracy seem to be weaker in the Portuguese case.

The question of whether these differences have left a measurable impact on the quality of the two democracies has generated some comparative research, but it is neither extensive nor conclusive. It does seem clear that the "memory wars" that have exploded in the past decade in Spain are not as powerful in Portugal,[3] with less interest in Portugal in challenging the dominant narrative of the past or the perspective on the transitional justice process (Alves Raimundo 2012). However, the different level of public debate does not speak directly to the quality of democracy in each country. More research needs to be done on the impact of continuity versus rupture on the subsequent functioning of their democratic regimes. One recent comparative study argues that, paradoxically, the police forces in Spain were subject to structural overhaul much more quickly than in Portugal because of the greater need to establish democratic legitimacy among a force that had played such a repressive role during and immediately after the transition (Palacios Cerezales 2010). On the other hand, another study argues that the revolutionary origins of Portugal's democracy left a stronger civil society with more capacity for self-organization and greater recognition by the state than in Spain (Fernandes 2015), while another argues that democracies born in social revolution like the Portuguese one are more likely to have a higher quality of democracy (Fishman 2011). However, another tempers these claims, arguing that demobilization in the Portuguese case led to greater marginalization of social movement voices than in Spain, because of the greater transfer of social movement activists to government positions in the latter case (Ramos Pinto 2013).

These suggestive studies offer a tantalizing window into the insights about the legacies of transition paths that could emerge out of a more developed comparative "Iberian Studies" framework. Ironically, this research agenda both confirms and unsettles the transitology model that first brought Spanish and Portuguese transition studies together. On the one hand, it confirms that the transitions away from authoritarian regimes, occurring in the same corner of Europe only a few years apart, offer an obvious point of comparison. But on the other hand, it unsettles the homogenizing process that paradoxically reduced ongoing comparison between two cases that were seen as exemplars of the same model. Instead, it encourages scholars involved in reassessing the transitions in each country to bring the Iberian counterpart back into the analysis, drawing not only on the obvious similarities but also on the striking differences, offering a fresh perspective on both cases for the next generation wrestling to come to terms with the past.

Notes

1 I thank Antonio Costa Pinto and Pedro Ramos Pinto for their suggestions based on an earlier draft of this article.
2 See, for example, the special issue of *Ayer* 79/2010 (3) dedicated to the transition, which lays out this agenda. A widely cited early theoretical source was Tarrow (1995).
3 See Perdigao Ribeiro (2011), for an interesting discussion of the albeit limited public debate over the government's framing of April 25, 1974, as "evolution" versus "revolution" during the 2004 celebration.

Works cited

Accornero, Guya. 2012. "Contentious Politics and Student Dissent in the Twilight of the Portuguese Dictatorship: Analysis of a Protest Cycle." *Democratization* 20 (6): 1036–1055.

Aguilar, Paloma. 2001. "Justice, Politics and Memory in the Spanish Transition." In *The Politics of Memory: Transitional Justice in Democratizing Societies*, edited by Alexandra Barahona de Brito, Carmen González Enríquez, and Paloma Aguilar, 92–118. Oxford: Oxford University Press.

Alves Raimundo, Filipa. 2012. "Post-Transitional Justice? Spain, Poland and Portugal Compared." PhD diss., European University Institute.

Baby, Sophie, Olivier Compagnon, and Eduardo González Calleja, eds. 2009. *Violencia y transiciones políticas a finales del siglo XX.* Madrid: Casa de Velázquez.

Bermeo, Nancy. 1997. "Myths of Moderation: Confrontation and Conflict during Democratic Transitions." *Comparative Politics* 29 (3): 305–322.

Boyd, Carolyn. 2008. "The Politics of History and Memory in Democratic Spain." *Annals of the American Academy of Political and Social Science* 617: 133–148.

Brito Vieira, Monica and Filipe Carreira de Silva. 2010. *O Momento Constituinte: os Direitos Sociais na Constituição.* Coimbra: Almedina.

Castells, Manuel. 1983. *The City and the Grassroots: A Cross-Cultural Theory of Urban Social Movements.* Berkeley, CA: University of California Press.

Costa Pinto, Antonio. 2001. "Settling Accounts with the Past in a Troubled Transition to Democracy: The Portuguese Case." In *The Politics of Memory: Transitional Justice in Democratizing Societies*, edited by Alexandra Barahona de Brito, Carmen González Enríquez, and Paloma Aguilar, 65–91. Oxford: Oxford University Press.

———. 2006. "Authoritarian Legacies, Transitional Justice and State Crisis in Portugal's Democratization." *Democratization* 13 (2): 173–204.

Domènech, Xavier. 2008. *Clase obrera, antifranquismo y cambio político: pequeños grandes cambios, 1956–1969.* Madrid: La Catarata.

Durán Muñoz, Rafael. 2009. "Fortaleza del estado y acción colectiva en el cambio de régimen: España y Portugal en perspectiva comparativa." In *Violencia y transiciones políticas a finales del siglo XX,* edited by Sophie Baby, Olivier Compagnon, and Eduardo González Calleja. 157–177. Madrid: Casa de Velázquez.

Edles, Laura Desfor. 1995. "Re-thinking Democratic Transition: A Culturalist Critique and the Spanish Case." *Theory and Society* 24 (3): 355–384.

———. 1998. *Symbol and Ritual in the New Spain: The Transition to Democracy after Franco*. Cambridge: Cambridge University Press.

Encarnación, Omar. 2011. "Democratizing Spain: Lessons for American Democratic Promotion." In *The Politics and Memory of Democratic Transition: The Spanish Model*, edited by Gregorio Alonso and Diego Muro, 236–256. New York: Routledge.

Fernandes, Tiago. 2015. "Rethinking Pathways to Democracy: Civil Society in Portugal and Spain, 1960s–2000s." *Democratization* 22 (6): 1074–1104.

Ferreira, Virginia. 2011. "Engendering Portugal: Social Change, State Politics and Women's Social Mobilization." In *Contemporary Portugal: Politics, Society and Culture*, edited by Antonio Costa Pinto, 153–192. Boulder, CO: Social Science Monographs.

Fishman, Robert. 2011. "Democratic Practice after the Revolution: The Case of Portugal and Beyond." *Politics and Society* 39 (2): 233–267.

Fontana, Josep. 2005. "Bases cap u una segona transició." In *La transició democràtica als Països Catalans: Historia i memòria*, edited by Pelai Pagès i Blanch, 411–423. València: Universitat de València.

Graham, Helen. 2012. "The Afterlife of Violence: Spain's Memory Wars in Domestic and International Context." In *The War and its Shadow: Spain's Civil War in Europe's Long 20th Century*, 125–142. Portland, OR: Sussex Academic Press.

Gunther, Richard. 2011. "The Spanish Model Revisited." In *The Politics and Memory of Democratic Transition: The Spanish Model*, edited by Gregorio Alonso and Diego Muro, 17–40. New York: Routledge.

Jerez Farrán, Carlos and Samuel Amago, eds. 2010. *Unearthing Franco's Legacy: Mass Graves and the Recovery of Historical Memory in Spain*. South Bend, IN: University of Notre Dame Press.

Juliá, Santos. 2010. "Echar al olvido: memoria y amnistía en la transición." In *Hoy no es ayer: ensayos sobre la España del siglo XX*, 303–333. Madrid: RBA.

Lipset, Seymour Martin. 1959. "Some Requisites of Democracy: Economic Development and Political Legitimacy." *American Political Science Review* 53 (1): 69–105.

Martín Cabrera, Luis. 2011. *Radical Justice: Spain and the Southern Cone beyond Market and State*. Lewisburg, PA: Bucknell University Press.

Maxwell, Kenneth. 1995. *The Making of Portuguese Democracy*. Cambridge: Cambridge University Press.

Molinero, Carme and Pere Ysàs, eds. 2010. *Construint la ciutat democràtica. El moviment veïnal durant el tardofranquisme i al transició*. Barcelona: Icaria Editorial.

Moral, Félix. 2001. *Veinticinco años después: la memoria del franquismo y de la transición a la democracia en los españoles*. Madrid: CIS.

Muro, Diego. 2011. "The Basque Experience of the Transition to Democracy." In *Politics and Memory of Democratic Transition: The Spanish Model*, edited by Gregorio Alonso and Diego Muro, 159–180. New York: Routledge.

O'Donnell, Guillermo, Philippe Schmitter, and Laurence Whitehead, eds. 1986. *Transitions from Authoritarian Rule: Southern Europe*. Baltimore, MD: Johns Hopkins University.

Palacios Cerezales, Diego. 2003. *O Poder Caiu na Rua: Crise de Estado e Ações Colectivas na Revolução Portuguesa, 1974–75*. Lisbon: Imprensa de Ciencias Sociais.

———. 2010. "Repressive Legacies and the Democratization of Iberian Police Systems." *South European Politics and Society* 15 (3): 429–448.

Perdigão Ribeiro, Filipa. 2011. "Uma revolução democrática é sempre uma revolução inacabada – or – A Democratic Revolution Must Always Remain Unfinished:" Commemorating the Portuguese 1974 revolution in newspaper opinion texts." *Journal of Language and Politics* 10 (3): 372–395.

Pérez Quintana, Vicente and Sánchez León, Pablo. 2008. *Memoria ciudadana y movimiento vecinal*. Madrid: Catarata.

Radcliff, Pamela. 2008. "Ciudadanas: las mujeres de las asociaciones de vecinos y la identidad de género en los años setenta." In *Memoria ciudadana y movimiento vecinal*, edited by Vicente Pérez Quintana and Pablo Sánchez León, 54–78. Madrid: Catarata.

———. 2012. *Making Democratic Citizens in Spain: Civil Society and the Popular Origins of the Transition, 1960–1978*. Basingstoke: Palgrave Macmillan.

———. 2015. "The Spanish Transition in Comparative Perspective." In *Is Spain Different? A Comparative Look at the 19th and 20th Centuries*, edited by Nigel Townson, 159–182. Portland, OR: Sussex University Press.

Ramos Pinto, Pedro. 2013. *Lisbon Rising: Urban Social Movements in the Portuguese Revolution, 1974–75*. Manchester: Manchester University Press.

Resina, Joan Ramón. 2000. "Introduction." In *Disremembering the Dictatorship: Politics of Memory in the Spanish Transition*, edited by Joan Ramón Resina, 1–16. Atlanta, GA: Rodopi.

Schmitter, Philippe. 1998. "The Democratization of Portugal in Its Comparative Perspective." In *Portugal e a Transição para a Democracia, 1974–76*, edited by Fernando Rosas, 337–363. Lisbon: Edições Colibri.

Stepan, Alfred and Juan Linz, eds. 1996. *Problems of Democratic Transition and Consolidation: Southern Europe, South America and Post-Communist Europe*. Baltimore, MD: Johns Hopkins University Press.

Tarrow, Sidney. 1995. "Mass Mobilization and Regime Change: Pacts, Reform and Popular Power in Italy and Spain, 1975–76." In *The Politics of Democratic Consolidation*, edited by Richard Gunther, et.al., 205–230. Baltimore, MD: Johns Hopkins University Press.

Threlfall, Monica. 2005. "Gendering the Transition to Democracy: Re-Assessing the Impact of Women's Activism." In *Gendering Spanish Democracy*, edited by Christine Cousins, Monica Threlfall and Celia Valiente, 11–54. London: Routledge.

Ysàs, Pere. 2010. "La Transición española: luces y sombras." *Ayer* 79 (3): 31–57.

Literature and visual culture

Literature and visual culture

36

BUÑUEL, LORCA, AND DALÍ

A new tradition

Agustín Sánchez Vidal

In 1559, by order of a decree issued on November 22 in Aranjuez, Philip II prohibited Spaniards from studying in any foreign universities except Bologna, Rome, Naples, and Coimbra, under pain of heavy sanctions. The effect was to significantly undermine Hispanic humanism, as the Iberian Peninsula was cut off from Protestant Europe.

It was not until almost three centuries later that this historical cycle was finally reversed. The real turning point came in 1843, when Gómez de la Serna, Minster of the Interior, gave financial support to Julián Sanz del Río that allowed him to further his education at the University of Heidelberg. That same year, of course, also saw the birth of the outstanding author of Spanish Realism, Benito Pérez Galdós.

On his return from Germany, Sanz del Río would bring Krausist doctrine back to Spain: a line of thought rooted in the work of Karl Christian Friedrich Krause (1781–1832), and which sought to harmonize the legacy of Kant and Fichte with that of Schelling and Hegel. Above all, this was a doctrine which defended a liberalism founded on the individual, against the budding totalitarianism implicit in certain interpretations of Hegelian philosophy. It also suggested a move away from the French cultural hegemony still very much in force, while its secular, pro-European tendencies stood in opposition to conservative, clerical traditionalism.

This is not to suggest that Spanish Krausists were necessarily or primarily anti-Catholic. However, a raft of university professors who subscribed to the doctrine were removed from their posts precisely because they refused to swear an oath of allegiance to the Church and the throne. Among them was Francisco Giner de los Ríos, who led them in founding the *Institución Libre de Enseñanza* (ILE) in 1876, soon after the restoration of the Bourbon monarchy with Alfonso XII. This gave them a platform to promote a private, secular education, initially at university level, but later with a wider scope which included primary and secondary education.

If Julián Sanz del Río emphasised German philosophy and learning, Francisco Giner built on this with the inclusion of pedagogical systems modelled on those used in England. This was the beginning of one of the most ambitious attempts to see Spain integrated into Europe, from both an intellectual and a moral standpoint, by re-establishing those links which had been severed by the *cordon sanitaire* against Lutheranism enacted in the mid-sixteenth century.

Such initiatives meant that Krausism gradually made its mark at all levels of intellectual development, resulting in an educative movement of a rather puritan nature. This would give rise to organizations ranging from the *Junta de Ampliación de Estudios* (whose president,

Santiago Ramón y Cajal, attempted to maintain intellectual links abroad) to *Misiones Pedagógicas* (whose role focused on cultural dissemination in rural areas during the 1930s). Its effects were also felt in the *Residencia de Estudiantes*, an idea conceived and realized by teachers who were very aware of their objectives and their place in history. Only the ILE could have carried out an undertaking of this sort, as the only sustained and coherent educative project which existed outside the Church in Spain.

Nothing in the *Residencia* was the product of improvisation; rather, this was a place designed to facilitate interdisciplinary dialogue, following the lead of the colleges in England. Everything had been calculated in minute detail by its director, Alberto Jiménez Fraud, with the aim of producing a ruling élite composed of a refined blend of the Spanish *caballero* and the English gentleman. The model to be avoided at all costs was the Spanish *señorito*, product of the "España de charanga y pandereta."[1]

The *Residencia* had 150 places, and was attended by 900 students in total, but its influence on Spanish culture was remarkable. In its most famous period (1915–1936) it was located in Madrid's Altos del Hipódromo, near the "Paseo de la Castellana," where it still stands today. At that time, it was almost completely surrounded by open fields, and had its own sports facilities. It also put on a wide range of cultural events, with programmes rarely bettered, in terms of their contemporary relevance and quality, in all Spanish history.

The young students who stayed there could learn at first hand about such recent events as the discovery of the tomb of Tutankhamun or the ascent of Everest, from hearing the testimony of those involved, Harold S. Carter and General Bruce. They could attend talks given by such luminaries as Einstein, Marie Curie, H. G. Wells, Paul Válery, Chesterton, Marinetti, Max Jacob, Duhamel, Cendrars, Claudel, R. Tagore, Mauriac, Bernard Shaw, Keyserling, Keynes, Le Corbusier, Walter Gropius – and Louis Aragon, who was to lecture on surrealism in 1925.

Encounters

It was in this setting that the friendship between the young Federico García Lorca, Luis Buñuel, and Salvador Dalí was born – a friendship which was to prove decisive for all three. Moreover, were it not for the *Residencia*, it is unlikely that they would ever have met, as Lorca came from Granada as a student of law and Buñuel from Aragon to study agronomy, while Dalí was a Catalan painter.

Buñuel arrived at the *Residencia* in autumn 1917, at 17 years of age; Lorca arrived at the age of 21, in spring 1919; Dalí was 18 on his arrival in September 1922. The future film director was to stay for seven years, until 1925, when he moved to Paris; Lorca also stayed until 1925, although he would continue to make frequent visits after he left; Dalí remained until 1926, when he was permanently expelled from Madrid's *Escuela Superior de Bellas Artes de San Fernando*. The crucial period for their friendship therefore runs from 1922 to 1925, a significant length of time during one's formative years.

Their affection for the old imperial capital of Toledo, city on the Tagus, may stand as an example. The significance of Toledo was outlined by Fernando de los Ríos, former Chair of the University of Granada where Lorca undertook his studies of law, and the man who set Lorca on his way to the *Residencia* and his later stay in New York. In his lecture entitled *Sentido y significación de España*, given in Mexico in 1945 and considered by its author to be a "[m]anifiesto sobre la tolerancia," Fernando de los Ríos admitted that his work as Minister of Public Instruction during the Second Spanish Republic had been guided by a particular model: the three cultures of Toledo. Moreover, he did not think Toledo an isolated example, but part of the current of free-thinking heterodoxy that began with Priscilian and continued with the Erasmians of the sixteenth century and the Enlightenment Encyclopedists of the eighteenth.

Similarly, the director of the *Residencia* and close friend of Fernando de los Ríos, Alberto Jiménez Fraud, began his *Historia de la Universidad Española* with a chapter titled "Peregrinación a Toledo," where he framed the School of Translators as a crucial moment in the history of the West – a moment when journeys were made to Toledo from all over Europe in search of the Greek learning preserved there in Arabic translation, the high water mark of a cultural unity in the Mediterranean that was one of history's greatest achievements.

Also relevant here is Manuel Bartolomé Cossío, founder of the *Misiones Pedagógicas*, who had revived the great artistic spokesman for the city on the Tagus, El Greco; a visit to Toledo thus became obligatory for any student staying at the *Residencia*. Nor was this the only proposal seeking to revive Toledo which had currency in the *Residencia*: others may be found in the symbolic weight given to the old imperial capital in novels such as Pérez Galdós's *Angel Guerra*, Azorín's *La voluntad*, or Pío Baroja's *Camino de perfección*, the high point of the search for the innermost depths of the national soul and the causes of the country's fall.

Of course, this fascination with the city did not mean that the young residents had to be reverent in their attitudes towards it; as testament to this stands Buñuel and his *Orden de Toledo*, founded in 1923. Among the places they visited was the tomb of Cardinal Tavera, located in the hospital which bears his name; the tomb was the work of the renowned sculptor Berruguete and showed the cardinal's body already in a state of decomposition. This tomb thus became the emblem of what were known in the *Residencia*'s own idiolect as "putrefactos."

This term was used to refer to anything old-fashioned and aesthetically outdated, contrasting it with the emotional detachment of the modern. One of the greatest expressions of this last tendency was to be the "Oda didáctica a Salvador Dalí," published by Lorca in 1926 in the *Revista de Occidente*.[2] The ode sets the painter against a Cubist Mediterranean background, drawing on the intellectual classicism advocated by Cocteau's *rappel à l'ordre* or Ortega y Gasset's *La deshumanización del arte*. The poet's lines mention "la amistad o la esgrima," undoubtedly a reference to the exchange of suggestions and stimuli in the work of the two friends, a process which culminated in 1927. That year saw them spend part of the spring and summer together at Cadaqués, while Dalí painted the backdrops for Lorca's play *Mariana Pineda*.

Nonetheless, it is impossible to ignore the ruptures that quickly followed, and the reticence visible on the part of the painter in the dense prose of his "San Sebastián," published in July 1927 in the Sitges journal *L'Amic de les Arts*. It contains an appeal to "Holy Objectivity," and to the impassivity of the eponymous martyr as he was shot with arrows, without showing any signs of pain. This thus stood as a translation, in homoerotic key, for an attitude of distance which acted as a barrier to the ode which Lorca had dedicated to Dalí, and the caution with which the painter responded to his affection.

This was to be the beginning of a dialectic between Putrefaction and Holy Objectivity, between sentimentalism and impassivity, manifest in the confrontation between biologism, with its excesses of blood and other bodily fluids, and the objectualism of what Dalí termed the *aparatos* – those mechanical devices that emerged from detailed reflection on those of Giorgio de Chirico. This conflict is at the heart of an enormously complex oil painting originally entitled *El nacimiento de Venus*, later altered to *Los esfuerzos estériles*, and finally *Cenicitas*. It took a long gestation period of nine months for Dalí to paint it, during the course of his military service in Figueras. He completed it in early 1928.

Following a process typical of much of his work, Dalí here began from a classic theme, the *Birth of Venus*, and turned it into the origin of the sexual impulse during adolescence. He then applied this to his relationship with Lorca, attempting to translate into visual images the rich world of Lorca's poetic imagery. These were the common reference points which both were using to construct their own personal worlds, when they began to grow apart, leaving behind the remains, the embers or ashes (*cenicitas*) of what could have been.

For 1928 was to be another story. In late July that year, Lorca published his *Romancero gitano*, a quite brilliant meeting of the discoveries of modernity and an apparently folkloric neo-popularism which extends to every possible aspect of the work. Lorca was at the centre of this non-rupturist avant-garde, which had celebrated the centenary of the Baroque poet Luis de Góngora the year before, and which would become known as the *Generación de 1927*.

The book met with spectacular success. Everyone heaped praise upon it – except for Dalí and Buñuel, who found it too "traditional." Both by this point had begun to incline towards surrealism: Buñuel, because he was in Paris, with first-hand knowledge of the deeds and writings of the circle of André Breton; Dalí, because he already showed signs of the influence of Joan Miró, Max Ernst, and Yves Tanguy.

After an intense effort to undermine Lorca, Buñuel succeeded in winning Dalí to his cause. The bait he offered was his collaboration in *Un chien andalou*, a short film that marked his first steps as a director in 1929. Such is the fame of this episode, there is no need to go into further detail here; it is enough to note that this film was to become a reference point for the avant-garde across the full breadth of Spanish culture. It marks several changes of direction at that crucial turn of the decade, as the fall of Primo de Rivera's dictatorship would quickly lead to the proclamation of the Second Republic on April 14, 1931.

Distancing

We cannot be sure that Federico García Lorca saw *Un chien andalou* in 1929, since he had left for New York on June 19, and would not return to Spain for more than a year. Nonetheless, during his time in New York he did write a brief screenplay, *Viaje a la luna*, intended to be brought to the screen by the Mexican director and painter Emilio Amero, who included Buñuel and Dalí's short film among his influences.

There are certain passages in Lorca's screenplay which bear a remarkable similarity to *Un chien andalou*, for example, the close-up of an eye being cut through by fish; a large head emerging dead from a mass of silkworms, in front of a sky with a severed moon; or a girl defending herself from a boy threatening to gouge out her eyes with his thumbs. His two friends' adventure in film had a profound effect on Lorca, who saw an allusion to himself and took offence at its title, its themes, and its imagery. It was this that prompted his first and only foray into writing screenplays and his adoption of surrealism, visible in *Poeta en Nueva York* and other works conceived in that city.

For Buñuel and Dalí, the success of their first collaboration was justification enough to think about shooting a longer film with sound: *L'Âge d'or*. They met during the summer of 1929 in Cadaqués, to plan the venture; however, their harmonious relationship was broken by the appearance of Gala, wife of the French surrealist poet Paul Éluard, who soon provoked as much dislike in the director as she did fascination in the painter. Accounts differ as to what happened thereafter. According to Buñuel, his former collaborator did no more than send him a few ideas for the film by letter, of which Buñuel used only one: the man going for a stroll with a stone on his head. Dalí maintained that his participation had been much greater, but that his role had been distorted by the director, who had brought a mere caricature of his ideas to the screen.

These testimonies, which are not contemporary and which bear the traces of their later quarrels, may now be usefully supplemented, and in some cases rejected, by documentary evidence which has become available. Particularly useful are letters from Dalí to Buñuel, and the correspondence between Buñuel and the patron of *L'Âge d'or*, Viscount Charles de Noailles.

It may be seen from this correspondence that the painter suggested various ideas to him which related to some of the film's most important sequences, and these were indeed incorporated by the Aragonese director. Dalí would therefore expect proper compensation for this, given his precarious situation, as his father had thrown him out of the family home and Camille Goemans, who exhibited his work, was recently bankrupt. Gala was also seriously ill, and required an operation. This was the first time Dalí had been without economic means, and he had great hopes of *L'Âge d'or*, which had tremendous financial backing, eventually totalling more than 750,000 francs. Buñuel received 6,000 per month while the technical screenplay was prepared, and 12,000 while the film was shot.

Dalí felt marginalized by his friend, and felt he was betraying him in the moment of his and Gala's greatest need. From that moment on, their paths would diverge. When surrealism was divided in 1932 by the great schism that set André Breton and Louis Aragon against each other, Dalí remained on Breton's side, while Buñuel left the group to join the Communist Party. This brought him to his 1933 documentary project *Tierra sin pan / Las Hurdes*.

Nonetheless, while their friendship had cooled since Gala became a part of Dalí's life, it did not visibly deteriorate until May 1934. This was the moment when hostilities really commenced, as a result of a dispute over the credits for *Un chien andalou* and *L'Âge d'or*. After seeing a re-run of *Un chien andalou* in Paris and being dumbfounded to see that Buñuel had removed his name, Dalí wrote an outraged letter to him, threatening legal action.

Before he recovered from this shock, Dalí had the same thing happen to him again when *L'Âge d'or* was shown in Barcelona: his name had once again been pulled from the credit sequence. Buñuel's answer must have been unsatisfactory, leading Dalí to take the matter up again in a long, hostile letter reproaching him for his lack of honesty and friendship.

If this were not enough to widen the breach between the two men, subsequent events would ensure they had little to do with each other. Dalí would continue to find success as a painter, and travelled to New York for the first time in November 1934, while Buñuel, who married on June 23 that year and was awaiting the arrival of his first child, worked on dubbed films for Warner Brothers; in 1935 he came together with Ricardo Urgoiti at the Filmófono production company to undertake populist projects involving *zarzuelas* and *sainetes*.

The Spanish Civil War marked a significant turning point in many respects. Lorca was shot by the Francoists in August 1936. The two survivors were both in the United States in 1939, by which time the painter had become famous, and was, according to the press, a multi-millionaire, while the film director's situation was very precarious. It was at the beginning of that year that he wrote to Dalí to test the waters regarding a possible collaboration in Hollywood. Dalí, however, rejected the idea. He was deeply affected by the harm done to his family by anarchists and republicans, and firmly committed to reconciling with them: he wanted to re-establish ties with his father and his family, and to turn back towards Spain. He concludes: "En el pasado nuestra colaboración ha sido mala para mí: acuérdate que me fue necesario un *esfuerzo* para que mi nombre fuera *reproducido* en el *chien andalou*" (see Figure 36.1).

The reference to the credits of their first filmic collaboration undoubtedly has the air of revenge. Buñuel must have been very hurt by these rejections, and was forced to content himself with a much more bureaucratic job at the Film Library of the Museum of Modern Art (MOMA) in New York, which he joined in early 1941. In October 1942, Dalí's *Vida Secreta*

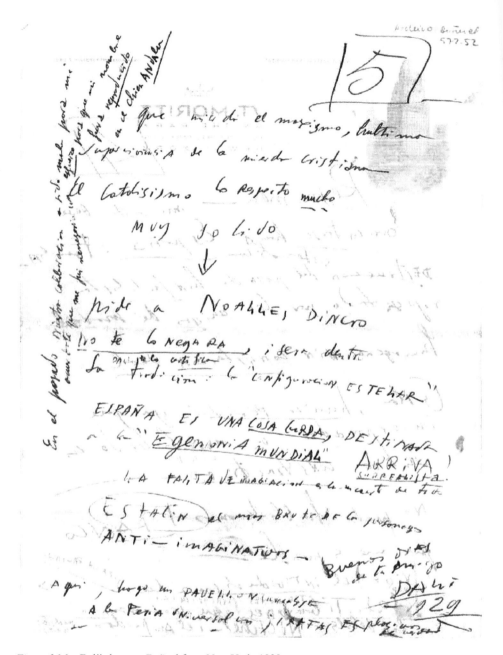

Figure 36.1 Dalí's letter to Buñuel from New York, 1939.

appeared in New York, and on June 30, 1943, Buñuel was obliged to hand in his resignation at MOMA. He has always maintained that the two events were linked, though so far nobody has found conclusive proof.

It seems rather that Buñuel was a victim of the early stages of what would become known as the "witch hunt" of Senator Joseph McCarthy. It is possible that Dalí's idiosyncratic autobiography was a cog in this larger machine, but it seems unlikely, if proper analysis is made of the forces in play. Whatever we might think of the *Vida secreta* today, its immediate reception was hostile, considered fatuous, megalomaniac, and untrustworthy. To suggest that such a work really had the effect on Buñuel's employment at MOMA that has been attributed to it is hardly plausible without evidence to that effect, particularly given that there is no lack of evidence for the left-leaning tendencies of both the director himself and his supporters.

Many years later, Dalí would attempt to call off hostilities with Buñuel, but the director appears to have been utterly unyielding. And in his 1955 film *Cela s'appelle l'aurore*, he included Dalí's *Cristo* as the background to a conversation in which a police commissioner tries to convince the film's protagonist to denounce a workman he has hidden in his house. Buñuel is thus accusing his old friend of being a "pintor de comisaría," or even, more clearly, a grass.[3]

From time to time, Dalí sent Buñuel messages of reconciliation, but the latter was unrelenting and unresponsive, save perhaps to say that they were past the point of no return. Dalí had still not admitted defeat by November 6, 1982, when he sent Buñuel the following telegram: "Querido Buñuel: cada diez años te envío una carta con la cual no estás de acuerdo, pero yo insisto. Esta noche he concebido un film que podemos hacer en diez días, a propósito no del Demon filosófico, sino de nuestro querido diabloncillo. Si te da la gana, pasa a verme al castillo de Púbol. Un abrazo. Dalí" (see Figure 36.2).

Buñuel wrote in reply to decline the offer of collaboration: "Recibí tus dos cables estup. idea sobre diabloncillo, pero me retiré del cine hace cinco años y ya no salgo de casa. Lástima.

Figure 36.2   Dalí's telegram to Buñuel, November 6, 1982.

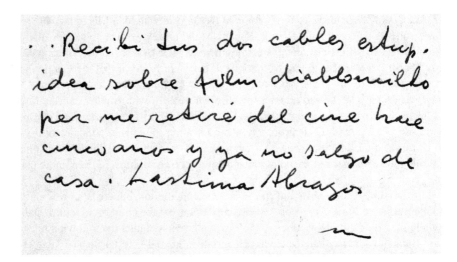

Figure 36.3 Buñuel's reply to Dalí's telegram.

Abrazos" (see Figure 36.3). This retirement from cinema was final, as he was to die eight months later.

A new tradition

Of the three friends, it was undoubtedly Lorca who made the most sustained defence of cultural tradition, even during the period when he was most in the grip of the modern, and produced works such as *Poeta en Nueva York*. This may be seen, for example, in his "Danza de la muerte," in which Wall Street is the background for his evocation of an African mask which looms above the crowd of people condemned, day and night, to keep the great machine running. Or, as he writes in the poem: "Y el director del banco observaba el manómetro / que mide el cruel silencio de la moneda."

What stands out here is the seamless integration of the old medieval or tribal dances with Goya's *El entierro de la sardina*, his own time spent in New York, and the Moloch-Machine sequence from Fritz Lang's *Metropolis* (1927), a sequence which in turn combined a vision of New York and modern technology with the ancient practice of human sacrifice, drawing for the latter on *Cabiria* (Giovanni Pastrone 1914).

It is therefore no surprise that the great, primitive mask should pass judgement over Wall Street's cement cliffs, just as in *Metropolis*, where skyscrapers are judged by the Tower of Babel; aerial motorways by the underground passageways of catacombs; the Promethean power of turbines by the crucifixion of the worker looking after them; the robot by the alchemist; the pleasure district by the allegory of the dance of death and the seven deadly sins which adorn the cathedral.

Returning to these questions after his time in New York, in his lecture *Teoría y juego del duende* Lorca considers the poetic hierarchy that brings art into the realm of the ineffable. But how to give form to the *duende*'s ethereal ideal? To this end, Lorca gives a survey whose breadth is illuminating. For, following Lorca's own order in his lecture, *duende* may appear unexpectedly in the spirit of Nietzschean tragedy, being nourished by "Pena" (great sorrow) [mourning], since "el duende no llega si no ve posibilidad de muerte." But it may also appear in the dark sounds of the *cante jondo*, or in Falla's *Nocturno del Generalife*. It appears in the ecstasy of the mystics Santa Teresa de Ávila or San Juan de la Cruz; in Goya's dark paintings, or in Jorge Manrique's *coplas*; in Quevedo's *El sueño de las calaveras*, or in Valdés Leal's *Obispo podrido* (the name given in the *Residencia* to his *Finis gloriae mundi*, painted in 1672 at the Hospital de la Caridad in Seville); in Berruguete, who created the statue of Cardinal Tavera in the Hospital de Tavera in Toledo, and in Velázquez; in Juan de Mena and Martínez Montañés; in Rimbaud and Lautréamont; in the Cervantes of the "Cueva de Montesinos" episode; in the flamenco singer Niña de los Peines; in the bullfighters Rafael el Gallo, Lagartijo, Joselito, Belmonte, and Cagancho. Or else in the poet Pedro Soto de Rojas, or the actress Eleonora Duse; in the image of Paganini we are given by Goethe; in the tower of Sahagún, or the Mudéjar style of the master builders in Catalayud or Teruel; in El Greco's yellow lightning, or in the apse of El Escorial, or in the song and dance of the sibyls in the cathedrals of Mallorca and Toledo . . .

What leads Lorca to make a catalogue on this scale? It is no coincidence that music features so often in these comparisons, as their trigger, guiding thread, and conclusion: Lorca always gave it a central role in any attempt to formalize his aesthetic. Of his important theoretical works, only *La imagen poética de Don Luis de Góngora* moves away from music into another field, as the Baroque poet is considered a visual creator, one who produces images rather than sounds.

The debt of Lorca's neo-popularist outlook to the example of Falla is well known, from *La vida breve* to the Cante Jondo competition they organized together in Granada in 1922. Falla inherited from his master Felipe Pedrell – himself often cited by Lorca – an idea which is vital for understanding the poet's attitude to these matters: that *lo popular* is visible not only in oral sources, but also in the most literary texts. This was founded on the understanding that the *Cantigas* of Alfonso X or *vihuela* players, for example, had themselves echoed the popular music of their own day, which had only managed to achieve written form following the intervention of the higher echelons of society.

This search for the popular requires, of course, an excellent ear. And here we begin to perceive a crux of Lorca's thought: the segregation of the spurious populism that was the product of picturesqueness or the *españolada*. This led to his radical opposition of *cante jondo* and flamenco: while the former represents spiritual colour, as a manifestation of something eternal whose creation predates all recorded time, flamenco is burdened by local colour and the lingering influence of the eighteenth-century outlook under which it was codified.

This had already been seen by Ortega y Gasset when he evoked the Esquilache riots of 1766, one of the pretexts for which was the rejection of the three-cornered hats set to replace the broad-brimmed *chambergo*. The word *chambergo* had been incorporated into Spanish as an adaptation of *Schomberg*, the surname of the commander of the Flemish guard brought to Spain a century earlier, during the reign of Charles II: In its own day, therefore, it had been just as unpopular and foreign as the French-style three-cornered hats were now. When the Spanish descendants of those subjects of Charles II fought to defend "their" *chambergo*, believing that a foreigner was attempting to deprive them of one of the defining markers of their identity, they were therefore fighting the descendants of those same Walloon guards from whom they had taken that hat. Moreover, by the time of the *Romancero gitano*, the *sombrero de tres picos* – internationalized by Falla, Picasso, and Diáguilev, in the ballet named after it – had become one of the distinguishing symbols of eternal Spain, in the form of the *tricornio* of the *Guardia Civil*.

To get to the root of such heritage, it is therefore necessary to dispense with period elements, replacing them with later artistic practices which update them – such as the various avant-gardes. For *lo popular*, on Lorca's various definitions, does not necessarily discriminate between aristocratic and common, high and low, rural and urban, oral and written, clear and inscrutable, rational and irrational, minority-based and commercial, sacred and profane, living folklore and the museum of ethnography, classical and baroque, or other standard dichotomies. It does not even distinguish between the different arts, but melds them together, along with their different techniques and discoveries.

Lorca's conception of *lo popular* is not only based on what is typical, excluding everything not considered authentic; rather, it includes what is external and foreign, but assimilated and treated as if it really belongs, provided that its origins remain visible. Such is the case with Japanese haikus, or the Afro-American culture of New York and Cuba.

To put it another way: given that one of the surest guarantors of this open concept of *lo popular* lies in its links with the great myths, with fundamental metaphors and essential rituals, these elements should not necessarily be assigned to the past, but should rather be associated with the new web of mythology being spun in the present day. This opens the way for associating – without the need of continuity – Greek tragedy, *autos sacramentales*, *esperpento*, jazz, Buster Keaton, and the raft of mythogenic material derived from the silver screen.

Dalí has suffered much greater misunderstanding, in large part as a result of his own attitude, as he was an inveterate trickster. Nonetheless, we must be unequivocal on the classicist background to his work, so clear in his early periods. Above all, we cannot doubt that his evolution through almost every trend in modern painting is precisely that of a member of the avant-garde, *malgré lui*. This is the only explanation for his idiosyncrasies within surrealism, and the profound alteration in his character and his work which took place during the 1930s. This change was in process throughout the Spanish Civil War, but really took hold at the outbreak of the Second World War, emerging particularly virulently in 1941: that was the year Dalí finished his *Vida secreta*, which can only really be understood in the light of his novel *Rostros ocultos*, the most enigmatic of his written works.

For the present investigation into the establishment of a new tradition, 1941 is also relevant as the year which saw a musical comedy based on Aristophanes's *Clouds*, the butt of whose satire was the surrealists. Dalí also released his ballet *Laberinto*, while extending the run of *Bacanal*, which he had shown on the New York stage in 1939. His intention was to complete the trilogy by adding a third ballet entitled *Sacrificio*, which was to take place in Toledo and El Escorial. If *Bacanal* represented the annihilation of a Wagnerian romanticism which was on its last legs, *Laberinto* showed the way out of this chaos by means of the Ariadne's thread of Tradition. *Sacrificio* was to be the triumph of religion and spiritual values, given form by the painting of El Greco and the music of Bach.

Sacrificio, then, represented his recovery of those childhood visits to Toledo, alongside his friends from the *Residencia*. During those same years, between 1940 and 1945, he painted the *Resurrección de la carne*, which he considered a "seismograph" of his reactions to the Second World War. It features a whole series of rotting corpses attempting to reconstruct their bodies as they emerge from the crypt of the Capuchin church in Toledo.

This would be followed by his *Manifiesto místico* in April 1951, with its vindication of Santa Teresa de Jesús, San Juan de la Cruz, and El Escorial; or his collaboration in making the sets for Luis Escobar's version of *Don Juan Tenorio*, and a very interesting "neo-mystic" film project entitled *El alma*. After his *Cristo de Port Lligat*, which bore the hallmarks of San Juan, the example of Velázquez would also be crucial, crystallising all these tendencies towards a return to Spanish tradition in the face of the frequent changes of direction in contemporary painting, which, he maintained, revealed its lack of style, intelligence, and conviction.

Unlike Dalí or Lorca, however, Buñuel was forced to confront much more specific problems when embarking on his most experimental period. Both *Un chien andalou* and *L'Âge d'or* had been independently financed, away from the commercial machine: the first was paid for by the director himself, while the second relied on the patronage of the Viscounts of Noailles. Moreover, *Tierra sin pan / Las Hurdes* was largely financed by Ramón Acín, a friend who owed his wealth to a lottery win. However, the ascent to power of a right-wing government resulted in a ban on showing the film. By 1934, Buñuel was therefore a director renowned for being radical, but whose films remained underground and made no impact on the box office.

As noted previously, the need to provide for his family led Buñuel to venture into commercial cinema in 1935 and 1936, with the production company Filmófono – a foray that would be ended by the Spanish Civil War. However, it was this commercial experience, together with the time he spent in 1940s Hollywood working on dubbing, which allowed him to advance so rapidly and successfully in the Mexican field, as he came to shoot certain films in as little as four, three, or even two weeks.

Buñuel was 46 on arrival in Mexico, by which time his personality was definitively fixed; his cultural background thus remained entirely Spanish, even though his themes, plots, and characters all took on features of his adopted country. Carlos Arniches is still behind *La hija del engaño* (1951), a new version of *Don Quintín el amargao*, already adapted for Filmófono. Similarly, Galdós is in the background of *Nazarín* (1959), and *Los olvidados* evokes the Spanish picaresque, or Pío Baroja's *La busca*.

All of which is to say nothing of the telling example of *Viridiana* (1960), which in principle was to be shot in Mexico, but was eventually made in Spain. Along with *Nazarín* and *Tristana* (1970), *Viridiana* forms a triptych of films inspired by Galdós, since it draws on two of his novels, *Halma* and *Angel Guerra*, the latter being set partially in Toledo, where the entirety of *Tristana* takes place, despite the novel's action being predominantly located in Madrid. The whole film is an homage to Toledo, and includes, of course, the tomb of Cardinal Tavera and other sites which Buñuel often visited on those *Residencia* visits, together with Lorca and Dalí.

In a letter to Ricardo Muñoz Suay of October 8, 1960, Buñuel admitted that in filming *Viridiana*, he was making his return to "ese famoso realismo español." In other words, more than three decades later, he is here picking up more or less where he left off in 1933 with *Las Hurdes*, and his explicit appeal to the painters Ribera and Zurbarán. However, other films from his second French period are no less replete with elements of Spanish tradition: *La vía láctea* (1969) owes much to Menéndez Pelayo's *Historia de los heterodoxos españoles*, among whose number was the Priscilian invoked by Fernando de los Ríos. Moreover, the central idea of the abortive dinner in *Le charme discret de la bourgeoisie* (1972) comes from *Don Juan Tenorio*, some lines of which are quoted on a theatre stage in the dinner sequence.

Nonetheless, Buñuel's most productive phase, when it comes to evaluating a tradition and founding a new one, is perhaps his Mexican period. The films that he shot there put forward a concrete proposal which has not always received the attention it demands. This is doubtless the result of the pull of the "surrealist" label so often attached to him, despite the fact that he spent the bulk of his career in Mexico, often in a context very different from his own beginnings, or his final French period. If pushed to assign this Mexican period a contextualizing label, we might perhaps opt for "Third Cinema," as it was coined and used by filmmakers such as Glauber Rocha, Fernando Solanas, and Octavio Getino, contrasting it with a domineering, commercial Hollywood, and with the European tradition of the *auteur*.

In this field, Buñuel's influence has been decisive. On the one hand, he helped to bring an end to the false dichotomy of slogans dividing filmic practices between American commercial aspirations and Soviet doctrinal aims ("neither Hollywood nor Mosfilm"). On the other hand, he updated the melodrama in ways that prove interesting in the light of subsequent developments in the Latin American audiovisual industry. Central to the question of his influence, above all, was his intuiting and avoidance of some of the dangers of Italian neo-realism, fortified by the presence, patronage, and prestige of Cesare Zavattini in certain Hispanic circles, including Cuba. The Aragonese director never hid his instinctive dislike of the overblown sentimentality so common to that kind of cinema, or of the obvious way it conveyed its messages, as it brushed aside the irrational moments that come with real human behaviour. Without that lesson from Buñuel, neither Brazilian *Cinema Novo* nor Cuban *Nuevo Cine* would have advanced towards originality and pluralism as quickly as they did.

It is no coincidence that these matters were raised by someone who had worked with Buñuel in Mexico: Alfredo Guevara, founder and director of the *Instituto Cubano de Arte e Industria Cinematográficos* (ICAIC). When he took charge of that institution and had to define the area with which the new, revolutionary cinema would concern itself, he insisted that the "Cine de la Libertad" took as its framework two classic Buñuel films, *Tierra sin pan* and *Los olvidados*, which demonstrated an engagement with an impoverished reality.

In some of his later polemics, Guevara would insist that Buñuel did not only constitute an ideal when producing this "realist" cinema with a social message. Rather, he was still an ideal to be aspired to when he returned to his old ways – which bore closer resemblance to surrealism – in films such as *El ángel exterminador*, which the party line in Cuba was to criticize as "bourgeois," and which Guevara himself knew well, having been part of the team which shot the film.

In this respect, a good part of Buñuel's legacy to the *Tercer Cine* was not a matter of content, but of form, suggesting non-reductionist ways of putting across his criticisms or reflecting social reality. Moreover, he did this while not falling prey to avant-garde traps, as well as avoiding stumbling into formalism, with a *mise-en-scène* that incorporated, and even concealed, his complexity of purpose beneath visual formulations that were obviously classicizing in appearance. This gave even more power to the irrational images that flashed through those neutral filmic mechanisms.

Properly considered, this approach is really not far from that of Lorca or Dalí. In their own ways, each of the three men returned to the great store of Spanish tradition that had nourished them in the *Residencia de Estudiantes*. Yet they made this return not to endorse that tradition, but to renew it, bringing to it some of the most advanced avant-garde features of their era. In doing so, they created new foundations for the cinema, literature, and painting of the twentieth century.

Notes

1 This famous phrase was coined by the poet Antonio Machado (himself associated with the ILE) in his poem "El mañana efímero" (1910), and refers to the vulgar, uncreative, dormant Spain that has yet to be reborn.

2 The poem was titled "Oda didáctica a Salvador Dalí" when Lorca, introduced by Jorge Guillén, read it in Valladolid on April 8, 1926, and was published with its definitive title as "Oda a Salvador Dalí" in the April edition of the *Revista de Occidente* (Laura Arias Serrano, *Las fuentes de la historia del arte en la época contemporánea*. Barcelona: Ediciones del Serbal, 2012, 474).

3 In the Spanish text of this chapter the author is making a pun on the word "comisaría," meaning both police station and commission.

Works cited

For a more detailed analysis of the relationship between Buñuel, Lorca, and Dalí, see:

Sánchez Vidal, Agustín. 1988. *Buñuel, Lorca, Dalí: el enigma sin fin*. Barcelona: Planeta.

——. 2007. "Dalí-Buñuel: encuentros y desencuentros." In *Ola Pepín! Dalí, Lorca y Buñuel en la Residencia de Estudiantes*, 23–79. Madrid: Residencia de Estudiantes.

For the Institución Libre de Enseñanza and the Residencia de Estudiantes, see:

Jiménez Fraud, Alberto. 1971. *Historia de la universidad española*. Madrid: Alianza.

——. 1972. *La Residencia de Estudiantes y Visita a Maquiavelo*. Barcelona: Ariel.

La *Institución Libre de Enseñanza y Francisco Giner de los Ríos: nuevas perspectivas*. 2013. Madrid: Fundación Giner de los Ríos [Institución Libre de Enseñanza] and Acción Cultural Española. 3 vols:

Vol. 1. Moreno Luzón, J., and F. Martínez López, eds. *Reformismo Liberal. La Institución Libre de Enseñanza y la política española*.

Vol. 2. García-Velasco, J., and A. Morales Moya, eds. *La Institución Libre de Enseñanza y la cultura española*.

Vol. 3. Capellán de Miguel, G., and E. Otero Urtaza, eds. *Antología de textos*.

Ríos, Fernando de los. 1997. *Obras completas*. Edited by Teresa Rodríguez de Lecea. Madrid: Fundación Caja de Madrid and Anthropos.

37

RECLAIMING THE GOODS

Rendering Spanish-language writing in Catalan and Galician

María Liñeira

In recent years the culture of translation in Spain has witnessed notable changes. Best-selling novels written in Spanish by Catalan writers, such as Carlos Ruiz Zafón's *La sombra del viento* (2001; trans. 2002), are routinely translated into Catalan; and canonical works written in Spanish by Galician writers, such as Rosalía de Castro's *La hija del mar* (1859; trans. 2001), are periodically translated into Galician. Notwithstanding their differences, both examples illustrate how the translation into Catalan and Galician of literary works written in Spanish by Catalan and Galician authors has carved out a place for itself in their respective literary fields.

Drawing on the work of Rainier Grutman (2011, 70), this type of translation might be identified as an endogenous vertical infra-translation: a translation between languages spoken asymmetrically by the community, and in which the direction of translation is from the hegemonic into the minorized language.[1] Despite its growing significance in contemporary Spain, this is an ill-studied phenomenon. Not only does it share in the general invisibility suffered by minorized languages in Translation Studies (Cronin 2003), but it also raises uncomfortable questions about the fraught relationship between language and ethnicity in modern Spain. The endogenous vertical infra-translation of literary works written in Spanish by Catalan and Galician authors affords a vantage point from which to study translation in Spain and can, more broadly, shed light on the dynamics of translation in minorized cultures.

Following Michael Cronin's clarion call for "historical research into the past experiences of minority languages" (2003, 153), this chapter reflects upon the literary translation into Catalan and Galician of works written in Spanish by Catalan and Galician authors during the twentieth century, a period vital to the evolution of both national literatures. This phenomenon has produced a limited corpus, but one which can nevertheless help us to situate the Catalan and Galician national literatures within two broader contexts: the development of a Spanish inter-literary community and the discussion of how translation facilitates the formation of cultural identities.

The near impossibility of receiving an education in Catalan or Galician until the late 1970s ensured that most people could read better in Spanish. Yet the catalogue of works translated into Catalan and Galician included not only works already available in Spanish, such as the plays of William Shakespeare, but also those originally penned in Spanish. The Catalan *Renaixença* has been described as a time of a "mania cervàntica:" *Don Quijote*, the most canonized Spanish-language text, has accumulated more Catalan translations than any other literary text (Bacardí 2010).

While pervasive, translation from Spanish into Catalan and Galician remains a contested topic. To commentators such as the Galician-language writer Xosé Fernández Ferreiro, writing in his 1963 review apropos the Galician translation of Camilo José Cela's *La familia de Pascual Duarte* (quoted in Dasilva 2013, 90), translation is a necessary evil, stemming from our inability to understand foreign languages; to translate a text from Spanish into Galician is therefore unnecessary, if not absurd. The Spanish-language writer Juan Marsé, born in Barcelona, used similarly strong language when he refused permission to translate his celebrated novel *Últimas tardes con Teresa* (1966) into Catalan: "me pareció un hecho inútil y estúpido" (Ibáñez 2013). To others, for whom it represents an opportunity to generate writing in the target language, this practice forms part of a crucial strategy to revitalize a minorized language and ultimately "posar-la al nivell literari" of neighbouring hegemonic languages, as the translator Antoni Bulbena i Tusell has claimed (quoted in Bacardí 2010). The findings of Xosé Manuel Dasilva (2008) and Maria Josepa Gallofré i Virgili (1991) show that, aware of the power of translation, Franco's zealous censors were vigilant of translation into Catalan and Galician.

However, the cases of Catalonia and Galicia are by no means exceptional. "[T]ranslation takes place in settings where it is *not* necessary to ensure communication," note Albert Branchadell and Lovell Margaret West (2005, 10; italics in the original). As Itamar Even-Zohar writes, in minorized language settings "translated literature simply fulfills the need of a younger literature to put into use its newly founded (or renovated) tongue for as many literary types as possible in order to make it serviceable as a literary language and useful for its emerging public" (1990a, 48). Furthermore, as Judith Woodsworth notes, the "[e]mergence of one literature always occurs in relation to another literature: it is a matter of differentiation, hence of relations of dominant and minor, or periphery and centre" (1994, 58). Endogenous vertical infra-translation is key to the development of the minorized national languages and literatures precisely because it encourages cultural and linguistic differentiation.

In this light, translation from Spanish into Catalan and Galician must be seen as empowering for nation building. In 1937, Bulbena i Tusell described the project to "catalanitzar lo castellà" as a natural successor to his first undertaking: to "descastellanitzar lo català" (quoted in Bacardí 2010). The act of translating from Spanish into Catalan was, for Bulbena i Tussell, a strategy by which to promote a more symmetrical relationship between the two languages. Cronin does, however, caution that "translation itself may in fact endanger the very specificity of those languages that practice it, particularly in situations of diglossia" (1995, 89). In contemporary Catalonia and Galicia, Spanish, the hegemonic language, remains the main source language, mediating between these cultures and the world. Cronin speaks of the paradoxical relationship between minorized languages and translation, rendered even more complex in cases in which a minorized language competes against a hegemonic language. In her examination of Spanish-Catalan translation, Montserrat Bacardí summarizes the potential impact of this type of translation with a rhetorical question: "[s]i, d'una banda, podia veure-s'hi encara el pes de la tradició castellana, no significava de l'altra, una separació de cultures i, al capdavall, un esforç de sistematització de la llengua d'arribada?" (1999, 59). As Lawrence Venuti concludes, "Translation is a cultural practice that is deeply implicated in relations of domination and dependence, equally capable of maintaining or disrupting them" (1998, 158).

In situations of literary emergence, as Even-Zohar (1990b, 79) notes, "A literature can be dependent upon another literature to a relatively large extent, and may use it as if it were part of itself." If the literature is fragile, it does so by becoming part of a bi- or multi-lingual polysystem and, if it is more robust, it does so by translating (81–82). As the comparatist Dasilva (2013) notes, Dyonýz Ďurišin (1984) explained this relationship with a visual model: national literatures belong to clusters of national literatures called interliterary communities, which are hierarchically organized. Spanish literature is at the centre of the Spanish interliterary community, and Basque, Catalan and Galician literatures are at the periphery; or, to be more precise, and proceeding from Pascale Casanova's model, they are inserted in "a continuum of different situations in which the degree of dependence varies greatly" (2005, 80). For historical and economic reasons, Catalan literature is less dependent upon Spanish than Galician literature. The communities within an interliterary community interact primarily with one another, and their literary agents (from authors to publishers, readers and reviewers) are often binational, as in the case of Catalans and Galicians, who are also Spanish.

Binationality encourages biliterariness, a state of affiliation to two national literatures. Where national literatures are governed by the language criterion, authors must write in the national language to be considered national writers. "Language is not an instrument of exclusion," challenges Benedict Anderson, "in principle anyone can learn any language" (2006, 134). In practice, however, many people cannot or at least they cannot necessarily learn to use it as a literary language. The Catalan Spanish-language writer Luis Goytisolo insists that not everyone can freely choose his or her literary language: "No elegí la lengua sino que fui elegido por ella" (quoted in King 2005, 53). In either case, the dynamics of language maintenance and shift in diglossic societies are more complex than these two statements suggest. To be biliterary, writers must be ideally bilingual and if not, must be translated into the national language; however, where two languages are spoken asymmetrically by the community, biliterariness comes at a cost. To write in the hegemonic language is often tantamount to betrayal in the eyes of a minorized culture; take, for instance, the controversy that dogged the Mallorcan Maria de la Pau Janer and the Galician Alfredo Conde's decision to write in Spanish to broaden their readership (Parcerisas 2009, 119–120; Vilavedra 2010, 86–95).

The act of translation – which, according to Cronin, allows people to "change identities or claim different identities through translation" (Kapsaskis 2012, 172), but, as Venuti points out, often provokes "fear of inauthenticity, distortion, contamination" (Venuti 1998, 32) – can help authors to achieve biliterariness. This chapter describes endogenous vertical infra-translation as a controversial strategy by which to provide writers with biliterariness and thereby expand the repertoire of writers active within the minorized language. Although translation, or self-translation, from Spanish into Catalan and Galician is rarely riddled with the same tensions as translation in the opposite direction, such as the risk of making the minorized language invisible, it has encountered resistance. In my own analysis, I am guided by the preliminary questions advanced by Bacardí: "What gets translated when the need for translation has disappeared? Who does the translation and why? On what criteria? Who reads the translated work?" (2005, 258).

Source texts are chosen by the target literature for many reasons, but all of them are governed by the main function of translating: assimilation, or "the inscription of a foreign text with domestic intelligibilities and interests" (Venuti 1998, 11). Texts about the Catalan or Galician communities are of special interest to the target literature. From this perspective, the Catalan translations of *Don Quijote* are an homage to a writer who, in the words of one of its modern translators, Joaquim Civera Sormaní, "va dir coses belles de Catalunya i va lloar la llengua catalana" (quoted in Bacardí 2010); that is, they offer a validation of Catalan culture and language.

Venuti's useful definition of assimilation does, however, have one shortcoming: he seems to be thinking exclusively of exogenous translation, that is, translation between two languages which are not in a direct hierarchical relationship. This assumption seems to be predicated upon a concept of "foreignness" which does not account for shades of difference. Translated texts may not be, however, foreign from an ethnic or cultural point of view; take, as a case in point, the linguistic assimilation of native texts examined here. In the pages to follow, I explore the reasons why only certain texts written in Spanish by Catalans and Galicians have been translated into Catalan and Galician. Adhering to a distinction more practical than epistemological, I examine these from the perspective not only of the writer, but also of the literary institutions of the emergent literature.

What is in it for the writer?

Authors self-translate or have their works translated to gain access to other literary fields where they can acquire monetary, cultural and symbolic capital. In a diglossic context, binational authors are translated more often from language B (Catalan and Galician) into language A (Spanish) because more capital is available to language A writing. Occasionally and significantly, authors, nevertheless, choose to translate texts written in language A into language B. Let us now examine several examples from both communities.

Self-translation: embracing biliterariness

As second best to original writing in the language, self-translation is key to positioning the writer as part of the national literature, that is, to becoming biliterary. It is easier to do so, particularly in national literatures that rely heavily upon language specificity, if the self-translation is opaque instead of transparent. According to Dasilva's (2013) terminology, opaque self-translations are unmarked translations passed off as originals, becoming pseudo-originals. They function indistinguishably from an original work within the national literature and can, accordingly, be canonized. An instance of the controversy generated by contested originals – that is, texts which might or might not be originals – is Lorenzo/Llorenç Villalonga's novel *Bearn, o, La sala de las muñecas* (1956) / *Bearn* (1961). There is a long-standing and heated debate, fuelled by the writer's conflicting statements, about which version was written first (Grimalt 2012). Regardless of its original language, thanks to the author's binationality and the native subject matter of the novel (the decadence of the Mallorcan nobility), the novel has been successfully assimilated by Catalan literature – it is considered one of the most influential twentieth-century novels written in Catalan. Like Villalonga, the Catalan Jordi Sierra i Fabra, a prolific and successful author of young adult fiction, writes in or self-translates into both Spanish and Catalan. By participating as original authors in both literary fields, these authors have successfully achieved biliterariness.

Seeking the status of translated writers

On occasion, however, the difficulties inherent to self-translation are insurmountable, and writers who cannot satisfy their own desire to be translated into the minorized language – because of a real or imagined inability to write in that language – have turned to others. One such author was the Galician-born Camilo José Cela. Throughout his life, Cela encouraged and promoted translations of his work both to the centre and to the periphery. As he said in letters to friends, among all the possible translations of *La familia de Pascual Duarte* (1942), the Galician translation was closest to his heart (Dasilva 2013). Thanks to it, Cela sought to participate in Galician literature and, in so doing, render his literary capital available to its national literature.

Cela began the process of publishing *A familia de Pascual Duarte* in 1952. He started the translation himself but, after working on the text for several months, confessed to a friend an inability to overcome perceived linguistic inadequacies; his Galician – in which Cela spoke and read, but rarely wrote – felt regional and uncouth. He found a suitable translator in the canonical writer Vicente Risco, who gave Cela symbolic capital.

Between 1952 and 1962 Cela tried to get the book published, but none of the main Galician publishers were interested (Dasilva 2013); only a subscription system set up among bibliophiles could finally get it into print. If, as George Steiner has argued, "[t]o class a source-text as worth translating is to dignify it immediately and to involve it in a dynamic of magnification" (2000, 196), to class one as unworthy of translation is to correspondingly belittle it. That this was an endogenous translation played an important part in the publishers' lack of interest: they viewed it as unnecessary (Dasilva 2013); but Cela's political allegiances with Franco's dictatorship and his textual aesthetics, alien to the contemporary hegemonic branch of *galeguismo*, were also decisive. Some publishers were unwilling to publish an endogenous infra-translation of Cela's work but not of other writers', such as the poet Luis Pimentel, as we see later.

The publishers' attitude contrasts with that of Ramón Otero Pedrayo who, in his prologue to the translation claims that, thanks to the translation, the novel was "hoxe devolta con amore e respeito á nosa lingoa galega" (1962, xx). That is, as he clarified in a letter to Cela: "quise decir como la novela volvía a la lengua verdadera de su autor" (quoted in Vázquez-Monxardín Fernández 2003, 201). Otero Pedrayo's claim that Cela's true language is Galician is not based on the author's biography but on the conflation of Galician ethnicity and the Galician language.

The idea of translation as restitution recalls George Steiner's conception of translation as a hermeneutic of trust, penetration, embodiment, and restitution (2000, 197). Restitution, also called compensation, is achieved because translation "can provide the original with a persistence and geographical-cultural range of survival which it would otherwise lack" (Steiner 1998, 416). The translated text is given new life in a new culture. Only *A familia de Pascual Duarte* did not find a place in Galician literature. Based on André Lefevere's argument that "[t]he degree to which the foreign writer is accepted into the native system will [. . .] be determined by the need that the native system has of him in a certain phase of its evolution" (2000, 243), it can be inferred that the most important Galician literary institutions were not interested in either Cela's political allegiances or his work's aesthetics.

The refusal of *galeguismo* did not prevent Cela from trying again. Although not a commercial success, *A familia de Pascual Duarte* has been reissued twice (1982, 1996), maybe as a result of Cela's Spanish and international canonization which culminated in him winning the Nobel Prize in 1989. Cela would also go on to encourage a Galician translation of *Mazurca para dos muertos* (1983), a novel set in Galicia, in 1999. Yet, thus far, Cela's position vis-à-vis Galician literature has remained problematic.

What is in it for the emergent literature?

For Lawrence Venuti, translation "has inevitably been enlisted in ambitious cultural projects, notably the development of a domestic language and literature" (1998, 77); translation contributes to the expansion of non-existent or little-developed linguistic functions and the creation of new literary repertoires (Even-Zohar 1990b, 80). Translation is, moreover, a useful strategy by which to acquire cultural and economic capital for the national literature. A word must, however, be said about cultural and linguistic differentiation before we examine how this search for capital determines which native texts are translated from Spanish into Catalan and Galician.

"Hay que traducir clásicos y actuales" because it is a strategy to "buscarle las cosquillas a nuestro idioma," asserted Álvaro Cunqueiro (quoted in Nicolás 1994, 182). For instance, in

1983 Conde embarked upon the Galician translation of Gonzalo Torrente Ballester's *La isla de los jacintos cortados: carta de amor con interpolaciones mágicas* (1980) not on the basis of its intelligibility, but for the linguistic challenge it offered: "Necesitabamos que o galego se prestase a todas as torsións da linguaxe" (quoted in Dasilva 2013, 90). Endogenous translation provides a unique opportunity to explore the boundaries of the target language; the first Catalan translations of *Don Quijote* were, for example, an "exercici de comparació" (Bacardí 1999, 51–52) between Catalan and Spanish.

It also plays a role in fixing those boundaries. In addition to widening the literary repertoire, for the *noucentistes* translation was instrumental in creating a model of literary language rooted in Pompeu Fabra's codification of Modern Catalan. Robert Neal Baxter (2002) contends that the various linguistic choices made in Portuguese-Galician translations increase the linguistic distance between Portuguese and Galician, with the aim of creating two different *Abstand* languages. Baxter's conclusions can also be applied to translations from Spanish. For instance, differentiation seems to be at the heart of the self-translated title that the Galician Luz Pozo Garza chose for one of her bilingual poetry collections in 1976: the original Spanish, *Últimas palabras*, was self-translated into Galician as *Verbas derradeiras*. The poet could have chosen *Últimas palabras*, since it is perfectly meaningful in Galician, but she decided instead on a title different from the Spanish one. Instead of the more neutral *palabras* and *últimas*, she opted for the more literary *verbas* and the slightly different in meaning *derradeiras* (as in *final*).[2] Apart from the practical reason of advertising a bilingual edition by means of the title, these choices were mainly aimed at promoting cultural difference. Yet there is another translation decision which gives us a glimpse into a differentiation that also speaks to stylistic choice. Pozo Garza also inverted the adjective order: the resulting title, *Últimas palabras/ Verbas derradeiras*, becomes a verse shaped by anadiplosis. The title, which is characteristic of the rest of the self-translated book, suggests that the Galician version is a stylistic revision of the original, as is often the case during self-translation. In sum, this is an act of translation motivated by both differentialism and aesthetics. Helena Buffery's *Shakespeare in Catalan: Translating Imperialism* (2007, 145) suggests a fruitful line of inquiry: to examine the linguistic attributes given to authors in the translation, to determine how each translation differentiated the literary language of the minorized from that of the hegemonic speech community. To achieve this, we might usefully consult the body of historical and canonical works selected for their cultural capital.

Filling the gaps in literary history: translating the diglossic past

Even-Zohar argues that (re)emerging literatures may also lack "a repertoire which is felt to be badly needed vis-à-vis, and in terms of the presence of, that adjacent literature" (1990a, 48). As cultural mediators, translators can help to develop the missing repertoire. Endogenous vertical infra-translation, for instance, affords the opportunity not only to fill the gaps in literary history, but also to correct the community's diglossic past.

In her 2007 article, "Restituir la història, les traduccions del castellà al català d'Alfons Maseras per a la Col·lecció Popular Barcino," Barcardí offers an insightful account of a translation project that sought to restore Catalan writing in Spanish to the national literature. Until 1939, the publishing company Barcino, founded in Barcelona in 1924 and still active today, published more than forty translations in its Col·lecció Popular Barcino; this corpus included ten endogenous infra-translations, one of them of a book of poetry. As Bacardí (2007) points out, "es tractava de restituir la veu *pròpria* als precursors de la Reinaxença, víctime d'una situació de diglòssia col·lectiva tal vegada irrepetible" (147; italics in the original). Some books appeared under the telling subtitle, "Versions d'obres no catalanes d'escriptores nacionals." These texts emerged from a project outlined by their translator, Alfons Maseras, in the prologue to each edition. For sociolinguistic reasons every work had been written in Spanish but, because its author was ethnically Catalan, his "intrínsec i natural" (153) language was also Catalan. They were "una flor exòtica o parasitària" (151) in Spanish literature and should be reinstated to the national Catalan literature through translation into Catalan. A relatively easy task, claimed Maseras: they had been "pensades catalanescament" (152). How, then, does this project attempt to rewrite the national story? It maintains that the Spanish-language writing of binational authors is a mistake to be corrected according to a monolingual ideal.

This linguistic correction could also happen in real time. The Spanish-language poetry of Luis Pimentel was translated into Galician by his *galeguista* friends because his biography and aesthetics were of interest to the *galeguista* movement. Pimentel is widely regarded as a canonical Galician-language poet, although scholars have long showed that almost all his Galician-language poetry is a pseudo-original (Herrero 2009). It can be argued therefore that it was a successful act of restitution in Steiner's sense because, although "there is a dimension of loss, of breakage" inherent to translation, "[t]he work translated is enhanced" (Steiner 2000, 196). It is restituted to a linguistic tradition and to a national literature.

Canonicity: translating Ramón del Valle-Inclán

For Pascale Casanova, "[p]restige is the quintessential form power takes in the literary universe" (2005, 83). Minorized literatures, starved of autochthonous prestige, turn to translating canonical authors in their own search for power. Buffery has shown that "[t]he great burst of translation which takes place at the end of the first decade of the twentieth century in Catalonia, and continues up to the Civil War, was presented as a way of enriching Catalan culture by importing universal values" (2007, 150). Few Galician translations were published as books during this period, but the theoretical culture of translation was similar. Álvaro Cunqueiro, a prolific poetry translator for periodical publications, claimed that "[u]na lengua culta tiene que tener a Homero y a Shakespeare, a Cervantes y a Goethe en ella. Y, por otros motivos bien más profundos, los Santos Evangelios" (quoted in Nicolás 1994, 182).

A minorized literature can be enriched when a member of its community achieves critical acclaim for texts written in the hegemonic language; critics have argued that translations of this corpus will more effectively re-assign its literary prestige to the minorized literature than lauded works by other, alien writers. Yet, as pointed out earlier, these authors, especially those who started writing in the minorized language and then shifted to the hegemonic language, are often also seen as traitors. Hence, they embody the tensions of the binational and biliterary community. The anxieties which stir when canonical authors refuse to write in a minorized language and the ensuing struggle to assimilate them through translation are no more clearly exemplified than in the failed and successful Galician translations of Ramón del Valle-Inclán.

As Antón Villar Ponte, one of the leaders of the incipient Galician nationalist movement and his fervent admirer, eloquently put it, Valle-Inclán was "gallego, y no de partida de bautismo solamente, como muchos otros, sino gallego de alma, con alma de gallego y galaica sensibilidad" (Ínsua 2012). However, apart from some verses written in the beginning of the twentieth century, Valle-Inclán withheld his considerable cultural capital from Galician literature. Although closely connected to many *galeguista* intellectuals, he was vocal against the rehabilitation of the Galician language (Ínsua 2012). And yet between 1918 and 1919, the nationalist newspaper, *A Nosa Terra*, published six authorized translations of his work (González-Millán 1992, 37), likely undertaken by Villar Ponte, the periodical's director. As Carmen E. Vílchez

Ruiz (2008, 178) has shown, some of the textual variants in one of the translations, "Os tres romances" – in which "La mengua de nuestra raza" becomes "A mengua da España" and "Castellano de sojuzgadores" is converted to "Castelán de domeadores e sojuzgadores" – represent an attempt to position Valle-Inclán's text and, ultimately, his persona within the coordinates of *galeguismo*. The agents of Galician literature have persevered in the struggle to assimilate an author who has been embraced as one of the community's canonical writers but did not write in Galician. Of the many possible examples, one stands out.

In 1998, the Centro Dramático Galego, the Galician national theatre company, produced *Valle-Inclán 98*, an ambitious programme of four plays in the original Spanish. This decision polarized Galician society and sparked a serious debate about whether public funds should be used to promote theatre in Spanish and how to negotiate the legacy of a canonical author who wrote in Spanish. That Valle-Inclán should be embraced as an ethnically Galician author was a consensus among the *galeguista* ranks, according to Dolores Vilavedra (2002). They were, however, divided as to whether it was necessary to translate Valle-Inclán's works.

For some, translation was unnecessary because his texts could already be assimilated as Galician in Spanish; to others, Valle-Inclán used an untranslatable idiolect, as the company's director put it, "Valle non escribiu en galego nin en castelán, senón en Valle-Inclán" (quoted in Vilavedra 2002, 718). The argument in favour of translation is neatly summarized by the playwright Manuel Lourenzo, one of Valle-Inclán's high-profile supporters, in the defense of his own 1981 Galician translation of *La doncella guerrera*, a play written in Spanish in 1934 by Rafael Dieste: "deixar de verter *A doncela guerreira* ao noso idioma sería sobre [todo] cobardia, estupidez, e desde logo unha inxustiza" (1981, 16). To translate the Spanish-language works of Galician authors was, for Lourenzo, to bravely and justly reinstate each text to the original language of the community and, by extension, its author. Valle-Inclán could not – and cannot – be legally translated because his estate refuses to grant permission for it, but activists mobilized against this refusal by translating the four plays and organizing readings in many Galician towns and cities on the day of the premiere. Translation was used as a political weapon in the struggle to improve the status of Galicia and try to assimilate Valle-Inclán's legacy into the national literature.

Popularity: translating popular novels

If a minorized literature is to survive, it must first broaden its readership beyond activist readers. One solution is to offer a wide range of books, particularly popular genre novels, but the minorized literature often lacks the cultural prestige and resources of the hegemonic literature. Translation might, in such circumstances, be used to jump on the bandwagon of a Spanish or internationally best-selling publication.

A similar trend in Spain encouraged the agents of both minorized literatures to publish affordable popular novels in Catalan and Galician throughout the 1920s and the 1930s. Endogenous infra-translations were listed in the catalogue of the popular novel series issued by two Galician publishing houses: Céltiga (1921–1923) and Lar (1924–1927). The former published *A santa compaña* (1923), a fictionalized account of the Galician superstition of the same name, written by the medical doctor Roberto Nóvoa Santos and transparently translated by Céltiga's editor, Jaime/Xaime Quintanilla. The latter published *O ilustre Cardona* (1927) by Wenceslao Fernández Flórez, an opaque translation, probably done by Lar's editor Leandro Carré Alvarellos, of a text originally published in Madrid in 1923. Lar also published two novels widely considered pseudo-originals: *A miña muller* (1924) also by Fernández Flórez and *O anarquista* (1924) by Leandro Pita Romero. However, given the lack of evidence, at present I prefer to consider them contested originals.

These translations were done with the aim of contributing to broadening not only readership but also authorship in Galician. As the editorial note to *O ilustre Cardona* puts it, "desexamos que o interés [de Wenceslao Fernández Flórez] atope noutros estimados literatos galegos estímulo para arrequentar tamén, con algunha sua producción, as letras rexionaes" (quoted in Mato 2007, 78). In Catalonia, the novels *Flor de maig* and *La Barraca*, written in Spanish by the widely successful Valencian author, Vicente Blasco Ibáñez, were published in 1926 and 1927, respectively. The latter, a prime example of a regionalist novel, was tellingly published as part of a Col·lecció Grans Èxits under the subtitle "novel·la valenciana." Its author's origin and the subject matter were of interest to readers in Catalan but, like Cela and Valle-Inclán, Blanco Ibáñez was too well-known as a writer in Spanish to have been assimilated into the minorized literature.

In the late 1960s, the Catalan José/Josep M. Gironella, a commercially successful novelist in Spanish, was also translated into Catalan. The book cover justifies the translation of his famous trilogy – *Els xiprers creuen en Déu* (1967), *Ha esclat la pau* (1968a) and *Un millió de morts* (1968b) – with the arguments already seen in this chapter: the author and the story are Catalan; therefore Catalan is their natural vehicle (Gironella 1967). Or, in the words of the book band of the first volume: "L'obra d'un català, pensada en català i redactada finalment en català." The aim of the translation was also to provide Catalan readers with a better experience: "la seva lectura serà, per al lector català, molt més suggestiva i apassionant" (Gironella 1967). This is a rare example of publishers' direct interpellation to the readers persuading them to choose a translation over an original.

In the 1980s, in a bid to attract new readers, Galician publishers set out to nurture an indigenous tradition of popular narrative genres. One of the titles published in the Edicións Xerais de Galicia crime series, Negra, is a translation of the type studied here. Translated by María Dolores Cabrera, *O fracaso de Clayton* (1994) by Darío Álvarez Blázquez was originally published as *El fracaso de Klayton* (1939), under the pseudonym – and name of the novel's amateur detective protagonist – Dr Lázaro Evia. First published at a time when no novels were published in Galician, this translation provided the 'missing link' of Galician crime novels. One year earlier, in 1993, Blázquez's son, Darío Álvarez Gándara, published *Sireno*, a crime novel featuring Evia, and, in 1996, added yet another title to the series, *O fracaso de Lázaro Evia*. It is noteworthy that, unlike *El fracaso de Clayton*, set in Great Britain, Álvarez Gándara's Evia is active within the coastal Galician city of Vigo, so the series is assimilated through space and language. To translate *El fracaso de Clayton* represented an opportunity to assimilate a text by a native author, who belonged to an important *galeguista* family, to Galician literature. For his son, it was also an opportunity to appropriate his familial and literary genealogy. After all, translation can become a public acknowledgment of a personal or social debt.

Álvarez Gándara's cousin, Alfonso Álvarez Cáccamo, embarked upon a similar process of appropriation when he translated two of his father's Spanish-language novels into Galician: *Na vila hai caras novas* (1993) and *Enchen as augas* (1995). José/Xosé María Álvarez Blázquez was a prolific writer in both Spanish and Galician who had some success in Spanish in the first decades of the postwar: *En el pueblo hay caras nuevas* (1945) was the runner-up in the Premio Nadal of 1944, famously won by Carmen Laforet's *Nada*, and *Crecen las aguas* (1956) was awarded the Premio Galdós de Novela 1955. Álvarez Cáccamo's translations were more meaningful than that of his uncle's novel because, unlike Darío, José/Xosé María Álvarez Blázquez was a prolific writer in both Spanish and Galician; he already occupied a secure position within Galician literature.

Conclusion: holding on to the national language

This chapter has explored Cronin's claim that "both the concept and reality of a minority language in translation raises fundamental questions about the activity [of translation]" (1995, 99). Instances of translation from a neighbouring and hegemonic language into a minorized language demonstrate that intelligibility is only one of many possible criteria that determine why and which texts are translated; in cases such as this, it is often the least important. Spanish remains the main source language for translations into Catalan and Spanish. This endogenous translation constitutes a social intervention: it not only seeks to gather cultural, economic and symbolic capital for emergent literatures, the end-game of all translation, but also to reinstate the Spanish-language texts of native authors within the minorized language and its literature. It should thus be considered a language-planning strategy to broaden the number of authors and works in the language and thereby develop the national literature. Endogenous infra-translation also admits authors to the national literature, even if the author and text will only be incorporated into a literary repertoire or canon to the extent that the translation is opaque and presented as an original. Authors and texts are selected for translation according to manifold criteria, but canonicity and popularity are among the most prominent. However, as a vicarious strategy by which to join the national literature, endogenous infra-translation should be approached with caution. How might it affect the minorized language? Is it a symptom of the autonomization of the national literature in the Bourdiean sense, or would its increase and acceptance discourage writers from writing directly in the minorized language?

Notes

1 To draw attention to the fact that "minority is a relation [and] not an essence" (Cronin 1995, 86), I have chosen to use the term *minorization* instead of *minority*. See Donna Patrick (2010, 176) for a definition of *minorization*.
2 As a matter of fact, *verba* is also a Spanish word, albeit an archaic one which was mostly used with the meaning of *loquacity*. In the twentieth century *verba* was popularised as a more Galician synonym or a more literary alternative to *palabra*. Although it is still widely used thus, the present edition of the dictionary of the Real Academia Galega only includes the meaning of *loquacity*.

Works cited

Álvarez Blázquez, Darío. 1994. *O fracaso de Clayton*. Translated by María Dolores Cabrera. Vigo: Edicións Xerais.

Álvarez Blázquez, José María. 1945. *En el pueblo hay caras nuevas*. Barcelona: Destino.

———. 1956. *Crecen las aguas*. n.p.: Sígueme.

———. 1993. *Na vila hai caras novas*. Translated by Alfonso Álvarez Cáccamo. Vigo: Ir Indo.

———. 1995. *Enchen as augas*. Translated by Alfonso Álvarez Cáccamo. Vigo: Ir Indo.

Álvarez Gándara, Darío. 1993. *Sireno*. Vigo: Cumio.

———. 1996. *O fracaso de Lázaro Evia*. Vigo: Cumio.

Anderson, Benedict. 2006. *Imagined Communities: Reflections on the Origin and Spread of Nationalism*. London: Verso.

Bacardí, Montserrat. 1999. "La mania cervàntica. Les traduccions del *Quixot* al català (1836–50?–1906)." *Quaderns: Revista de traducció* 3: 49–59.

———. 2005. "Translation from Spanish into Catalan during the 20th Century. Sketch of a Chequered History." In *Less Translated Languages*, edited by Albert Branchadell and Lovell Margaret West, 257–268. Philadelphia, PA: John Benjamins.

———. 2007. "Restituir la història, Les traduccions del castellà al català d'Alfons Maseras per la Col·lecció Popular Barcino." In *Literatura comparada catalana i espanyola al segle XX: gèneres, lectures i traduccions (1898–1951)*, edited by Miquel M. Gibert, Amparo Hurtado Díaz and José Francisco Ruiz Casanova, 145–156. Lleida: Punctum & Trilcat.

———. 2010. "*El Quijote* reescrito en catalán." In *IV conferencia científica internacional de hispanistas (Moscú, 2010)*. http://confhisp2010.wordpress.com/2010/04/21/bacardi-m-uab-espana.

Baxter, Robert Neal. 2002. "El paper de la traducció en la consolidació de la percepció social del gallec com a *Abstandsprache*." *Quaderns: Revista de traducció* 7: 167–181.

Blasco Ibáñez, Vicente. 1926. *Flor de maig*. Translated by Miquel Duran de València. Barcelona: Mentora.

———. 1927. *La barraca: novel·la valenciana*. Translated by Miquel Duran de València. Barcelona: Mentora.

Branchadell, Albert and Lovell Margaret West. 2005. *Less Translated Languages*. Philadelphia, PA: John Benjamins.

Buffery, Helena. 2007. *Shakespeare in Catalan: Translating Imperialism*. Cardiff: University of Wales Press.

Casanova, Pascale. 2005. "Literature as a World." *New Left Review* 31: 71–90.

Cela, Camilo Xosé. 1962. *A familia de Pascual Duarte*. Translated by Vicente Risco. Vigo: Talleres Faro de Vigo.

———. 1982. *A familia de Pascual Duarte*. Translated by Vicente Risco. 2nd ed. Vigo: Edicións Xerais.

———. 1983. *Mazurca para dos muertos*. Barcelona: Seix Barral.

———. 1996. *A familia de Pascual Duarte*. Translated by Vicente Risco. 3rd ed. Santiago de Compostela: Xunta de Galicia.

———. 1999. *Mazurca para dous mortos*. Translated by Xesús Rábade Paredes. Santiago de Compostela, Xunta de Galicia.

Cronin, Michael. 1995. "Altered States: Translation and Minority Languages." *TTR: Traduction, Terminologie, Rédaction* 8 (1): 85–103.

———. 2003. *Translation and Globalization*. London: Routledge.

Dasilva, Xosé Manuel. 2008. *O alleo é noso. Contribucións para a historia da tradución en Galicia*. Noia: Toxosoutos.

———. 2013. *Estudios sobre la autotraducción en el espacio ibérico*. Bern: Peter Lang.

de Castro, Rosalía. 1859. *La hija del mar*. Vigo: Compañel.

———. 2001. *A filla do mar*. Translated by Olga Patiño. Noia: Toxosoutos.

Ďurišin, Dyonýz. 1984. "Specific Interliterary Communities." *Neohelicon* 11 (1): 211–241.

Even-Zohar, Itamar. 1990a. "The Position of Translated Literature within the Literary Polysystem." *Poetics Today* 11 (1): 45–51.

———. 1990b. "Interference in Dependent Literary Polysystems." *Poetics Today* 11 (1): 79–83.

Evia, Dr. Lázaro [Álvarez Blázquez, Darío]. 1939. "El fracaso de Klayton: (Novela policiaca)." *Letras: Revista literaria popular* 28.

Fernández Flórez, Wenceslao. 1923. *El ilustre Cardona*. Madrid: La Novela de Hoy.

———. 1924. *A miña muller*. A Coruña: Lar.

———. 1927. *O ilustre Cardona*. A Coruña: Lar.

Gallofré i Virgili, Maria Josepa. 1991. *L'edició catalana i la censura franquista (1936–1951)*. Barcelona: Publicaciones de L'Abadía de Montserrat.

Gironella, Josep Maria. 1967. *Els xiprers creuen en Déu*. Translated by Bartomeu Bardagí i Moras. Barcelona: Argos.

———. 1968a. *Ha esclat la pau*. Translated by Bartomeu Bardagí i Moras. Barcelona: Argos.

———. 1968b. *Un millió de morts*. Translated by Bartomeu Bardagí i Moras. Barcelona: Argos.

González-Millán, Xoán. 1992. "Valle-Inclán y la revista *Nós*." *Revista Hispánica Moderna* 1: 35–44.

Grimalt, Josep A. 2012. "Llorenç Villalonga i la llengua catalana." *Estudis Romànics* 34: 209–229.

Grutman, Rainier. 2011. "Diglosia y autotraducción 'vertical' (en y fuera de España)." In *Aproximaciones a la autotraducción*, edited by Xosé Manuel Dasilva and Helena Tanqueiro, 69–91. Vigo: Academia del Hispanismo.

Herrero Figueroa, Araceli, ed. 2009. *Obra completa (Luis Pimentel)*. Vigo: Editorial Galaxia.

Ibáñez, M. Eugenia. 2013. "Juan Marsé, desde los 80." *La Lamentable*, February 1. Accessed 20 March, 2015. http://www.lamentable.org.

Ínsua, Emilio X. 2012. "Valle Inclán e Antón Villar Ponte, entre a polémica e a admiración." *Galicia Confidencial*. Accessed February 9, 2014. http://www.galiciaconfidencial.com.

Kapsaskis, Dionysios. 2012. "Translation, Necessity, Vulnerability: An Interview with Michael Cronin." *Synthesis* 4: 168–181.

King, Stewart. 2005. *Escribir la catalanidad: lengua e identidades culturales en la narrativa contemporánea de Cataluña*. Woodbridge: Tamesis.

Lefevere, André. 2000. "Mother Courage's Cucumbers: Text, System and Refraction in a Theory of Literature." In *The Translation Studies Reader*, edited by Lawrence Venuti, 239–255. London: Routledge.

Lourenzo, Manuel. 1981. "Introduction." In *A doncela guerreira* by Rafael Dieste. Translated by Manuel Lourenzo. A Coruña: Cadernos da Escola Dramática Galega.

Mato, Alfonso, ed. 2007. *Ánxel Casal, un editor para un país: catálogos de Lar e Nós*. Santiago de Compostela: Consello da Cultura Galega; Seminario de Estudos Galegos.

Marsé, Juan. 1966. *Últimas tardes con Teresa*. Barcelona: Seix Barral.

Nicolás, Ramón. 1994. *Entrevistas a Cunqueiro*. Vigo: Nigra.

Nóvoa Santos, Roberto. 1923. *A santa compaña.* Translated by Jaime/Xaime Quintanilla. Ferrol: Céltiga.

Otero Pedrayo, Ramón. 1962. "Prólogo." In *A familia de Pascual Duarte* by Camilo Xosé Cela. Translated by Vicente Risco, ix–xx. Vigo: Talleres Faro de Vigo.

Parcerisas, Francesc. 2009. "De l'asymétrie au degré zéro de l'autotraduction." *Quaderns: Revista de traducció* 16: 117–122.

Patrick, Donna. 2010. "Language Dominance and Minorization." In *Society and Language Use*, edited by Jan-Ola Ösma and Jef Verschueren, 166–191. Amsterdam: John Benjamins.

Pita Romero, Leandro. 1924. *O anarquista*. A Coruña: Lar.

Pozo Garza, Luz. 1976. *Últimas palabras/Verbas derradeiras*. A Coruña: Moret.

Ruiz Zafón, Carlos. 2001. *La sombra del viento*. Barcelona: Planeta.

———. 2002. *L'ombra del vent.* Translated by Josep Pelfort. Barcelona: Planeta.

Steiner, George. 1998. *After Babel: Aspects of Language and Translation*. Oxford: Oxford University Press.

———. 2000. "The Hermeneutic Motion." In *The Translation Studies Reader*, edited by Lawrence Venuti, 193–198. London: Routledge.

Torrente Ballester, Gonzalo. 1980. *La isla de los jacintos cortados: carta de amor con interpolaciones mágicas*. Barcelona: Destino.

———. 1983. *A illa dos xacintos cortados: carta de amor con interpolacións máxicas*. Translated by Alfredo Conde. Sada: Castro.

Vázquez-Monxardín Fernández, Alfonso. 2003. "A traducción galega de *A familia de Pascual Duarte*." *Boletín Galego de Literatura* 29: 167–220.

Venuti, Lawrence, 1998. *The Scandals of Translation*. London: Routledge.

Vilavedra, Dolores. 2002. "*Valle-Inclán 98*: achegas para un modelo de análise da recepción teatral." In *Homenaxe a Fernando R. Tato Plaza*, edited by Ramón Lorenzo, 715–725. Santiago de Compostela: Universidade de Santiago de Compostela.

———. 2010. *A narrativa galega na fin de século: unha ollada crítica dende 2010*. Vigo: Editorial Galaxia.

Vílchez Ruiz, Carmen E. 2008. "La estrategia de la escritura de *La lámpara maravillosa*, el papel de la prensa gallega." *Anales de la literatura española contemporánea* 33 (3): 163/503–182/522.

Villalonga, Lorenzo/Llorenç. 1956. *Bearn, o, La sala de las muñecas*. Palma: Atlante.

———. 1961. *Bearn*. Barcelona: Club Editor.

Woodsworth, Judith. 1994. "Translators and the Emergence of National Literatures." In *Translation Studies: An Interdiscipline*, edited by Mary Snell-Hornby, Franz Pöchhacker, and Klaus Kaindl, 55–64. Amsterdam: John Benjamins.

38

POSTWAR SPANISH FICTION AND THE PURSUIT OF SPANISH REALITY

David K. Herzberger

During the first two decades following the Spanish Civil War (1936–39), and well into the 1960s, most Spanish novelists stood primarily as literary and political outliers. This is so for a number of reasons. Above all, nearly all of the writers whose work garnered critical recognition in Spain during this period sharply opposed the very existence of the Franco regime: a dictatorship that had used raw military might to defeat the opposition during the War set out over the next two decades to consolidate its power and sustain its authority over government institutions, all forms of media and communication, and the diverse strains of cultural production. To a large extent during these years, Spain stood isolated from European and other Western democracies. This led in many ways to prolonged economic scarcity and rampant poverty in large segments of the Spanish population, yet it also coincided with an on-going celebration by the Nationalist (Francoist) victors of what they viewed as a return to the values and ideals of the authentic Spain. The trauma caused by the Civil War itself remained broadly suppressed for several decades, but in fact it was hidden in plain sight. The Regime sought to create (without consent of the people) laws and normative values for Spain whose purpose was to forge a mythic and unified national identity summarized in the lapidary assertion of "one language, once race, one religion."

The repeated insistence by the Regime on a canonical and permanent set of national values circumscribed nearly the entire cultural context of postwar Spain. As writer and Franco supporter Manuel Fraga Iribarne proclaimed, these values were constituted "ante Dios y ante la Historia" (1958, 516). While God was evoked naturally and easily by the Regime with the support of the Church, History was less easily managed, though the government persistently sought to do so. Indeed, the recurrent claims of conformity and consonance for Spain as a nation held sway over the writing of history, the purpose of which was to create a usable past to support the aims of the Regime. Such a posture, of course, inflicted sharp intellectual violence on the possibility of fully understanding history and precluded the construction of a meaningfully open culture in the present. More specifically, it engendered a past that became radicalized as essentially and rigidly authentic, while confining to the periphery all that stood outside the narrowly conceived core. As José Antonio Biescas put it, "Los vencedores del 39 quisieron hacer tabla rasa de toda aquella tradición que no fuese la suya, dogmática, institucionalizada, identificada como la nacional; el resto era marginado, expulsado de la convivencia intelectual" (1980, 516). This marginalization, of course, applied to Spanish novelists, whose work, as we see in this chapter, became important venues for representing elements of Spanish culture that defied the "convivencia intelectual" desire by the Franco regime.

In this context, the role of language itself in the composition of the novel and in the general composition of the cultural milieu in Spain bears mention. To a large degree the Franco regime repressed, and frequently disallowed, the use of regional languages – Basque, Catalan, and Galician – in various forms of cultural production. While it is not my aim here to offer a history of the novel in these languages in the postwar period, a few observations might summarize the challenging context of writing fiction (and representing the reality of Spain) in languages other than Spanish. First of all, the Regime's main cultural enterprise to impose unity on the nation was based less on the idea of conversion of the many into one (the idea of *e pluribus unum*) than to deny or suppress the very concept of the many in its history – the essential and authentic Spain was to be rooted in the erasure of differences to begin with. Thus, following the Civil War the Regime set out to diminish and in many instances prohibit the use of other languages in the education system, in administrative functions, and in various forms of oral and written culture. As Chris Perriam and his collaborators have noted in the history of postwar writing in Spain, names of people, streets, towns, and commercial products could be recorded only in their Castilian versions; even inscriptions on gravestones had to be in Spanish. Books in Catalan, Basque, and Galician were destroyed, and publishing in these languages (regarded as inferior 'dialects') was made virtually impossible throughout the 1940s (2000, 5).

The novel of social realism

Given the firmly drawn parameters of the cultural context in Francoist Spain that were either created or sanctioned by the Regime, Spanish novelists writing in the 1940s and 1950s (and with strong carryover even into the 1960s and early 1970s) faced both esthetic and ethical dilemmas. To a large extent, they resolved the esthetic challenge by evoking both the tradition and methods of realism, which provided them at the same time with a vehicle for their ethical response to the Regime. For example, in 1959, at a gathering of authors from Europe and the United States in Formentor (Spain) to discuss the current state of novel-writing, nearly all of the non-Spanish writers proclaimed the death of the grand narratives of realism from the nineteenth century. Not only had that kind of writing been superseded in their view by the more stylized, experimental, and formal paradigms of the best writers of the twentieth century (Faulkner, Joyce, Proust, and Kafka, to name only a few) but also the very idea of a hyper-realism bound to the faded principles of representation and referentiality were cast aside as both naïve and ineffective. Spanish novelists, however, dissented from the mainstream, proclaiming not only the power of the novel to re-present the real but also the ethical obligation to do so in a society that had scant access to information about the social ills and unequal justice that plagued the nation beyond individual circumstance.

Censorship and government control had indeed succeeded in excluding from public discourse most forms of cultural production that might undermine the felicitous view of Spain that had been promulgated by the Regime through its support of writers and publishers sympathetic to its ideas. Camilo José Cela, writing in the prologue of his 1951 novel *La colmena*, perhaps most poignantly describes (and prescribes) what may be seen as the foundational ethos of novel-writing for an entire generation of authors during the 1950s and 1960s: "Mi novela *La colmena* no es otra cosa que un pálido reflejo, que una humilde sombra de la cotidiana, áspera, entrañable y dolorosa realidad [de España]' (1967, 9). In 1962, when realism in the novel had flourished for more than a decade as an important literary tool for social criticism among a group of young writers known as the Generation of 1950, many Spanish novelists echoed the intentionality of Cela's earlier observations in a series of interviews. Armando López Salinas seemed to best sum up the prevailing attitude among novelists of this generation: "El servicio que puedo prestar a los otros hombres de mi país es el de desvelar las relaciones sociales y mostrar el mundo tal y como creo que es. La obra literaria, en un amplio sentido, puede ayudar a la creación de nuevas condiciones [sociales]" (Corrales Egea 1971, 61–62).

In the early 1940s, before the emergent novelists of the Generation of 1950 brought realism to prominence, Carmen Laforet had portrayed postwar Barcelona in her novel *Nada* (1944) as an impoverished and decayed city in which few were able to flourish. Although family life was set forth as one of the cornerstones of Francoist propaganda, it is portrayed in *Nada* as a gloomy, nightmarish, and violent institution for the young narrator, Andrea, who begins her university studies after arriving in the city from a town in rural Spain. Andrea meets sons and daughters of the wealthy at the university, but her own life is marked by scarcity (of food, clothing, and opportunity) as her once middle-class family in Barcelona is barely able to survive its own disintegration. Laforet represents both existential emptiness and social vulnerability as the foundational elements of postwar Spanish reality, but she does so without directly attributing these to the War itself, and certainly not to the policies of the Regime. To do so, of course, would have invited official disapproval and perhaps the silencing of her work. Nonetheless, the inferences to be drawn about Spanish society are clearly marked in the novel – deprivation and decay permeate the infrastructure of postwar Spain, a nation that is barely able to sustain itself.

Representing the Civil War directly remained a privilege of the victors in postwar Spain, but the implicit link between the War and the Franco regime on the one hand, and the general inability to explore the destructive consequences (political, social, economic) of the conflict on the other, shaped much fiction until the dictator's death in 1975. This can be seen in two principal ways: first, in the overt representation of contemporary Spanish reality viewed from the margins in the works of the Generation of 1950, who set out to frame their works as instruments for social change. The novels of this period, therefore, grow largely from the desire to represent all that is observable in contemporary Spanish society but frequently absent from reporting by the media. Although Spain as a whole, and thus many individuals as well, carried the burden of the lived trauma of the War (especially those who had opposed the Franco forces), the novelists of the Generation of 1950 showed scant interest in probing the lives of individual characters or exploring postwar anxiety with psychological depth. Instead, they tend to create a collective protagonist in their works (e.g., the impoverished people of Madrid in Cela's *La colmena*; the bored youth of the bourgeoisie in Rafael Sánchez Ferlosio's *El Jarama*, 1955) with a focus on the quotidian and external events of their lives. In *La colmena*, for example, the narrative evokes various aspects of the daily living of more than 300 characters, with a vivid representation of the lower classes struggling to survive amid the postwar poverty of Madrid. As Cela himself wrote about the novel, it is "un estrato determinado de la ciudad, que es un poco la suma de todas las vidas que bullen en sus páginas, unas vidas grises, vulgares y cotidianas" (1958, 14). In contrast to the story that the Regime wished to tell, Francoist Spain emerges in *La colmena* not as a tranquil and prosperous country but as a cauldron of misery with no prospects for change.

Second, rural Spain was presented no less harshly by writers of this period, who voice a purposeful dissonance from the rhetoric emanating from the Regime. The image of a bountiful and prosperous country (one chosen and blessed by God, according to the rhetoric of the time) is perhaps most persistently portrayed in the schools and textbooks during the Franco years. As Andrés Sopeña Monsalve notes in his humorous memoir of Spanish education during the 1950s and 1960s, everything about Spain taught in the schools – its history, its imperial influence, its cultural standing – elevated the nation to the level of myth, with Franco and his followers portrayed as heroic warriors who had saved the nation from the infidels (the Republicans during the Civil War) just as El Cid and his followers had rescued Spain from the Moors eight centuries earlier. Beyond the heroic nature of Francoist soldiers during the War, however, Spain itself was proclaimed to be physically and geographically blessed, and thus able to flourish more vigorously than other nations. As Sopeña Monsalve notes, his textbooks offered more propaganda than intellectual scrutiny of Spain. For example: "El Señor quiere mucho a España. Por eso la puso en el mejor sitio del mundo, donde no hace ni mucho frío ni mucho calor. (Pues en otros sitios o está siempre todo helado o hace tanto calor que no se puede vivir.) . . . . Y le dio un cielo muy azul, y unos montes muy altos, y unos campos muy grandes y muy ricos" (1994, 164). As a result of its favorable geographical position, Spain was destined to prosper without the aid of others: "Rodeada por el mar en su mayor extensión y embellecida con los mejores regalos de la Providencia, España lo contiene todo y es una de las naciones más completas del mundo" (165). In brief, as the textbook explains, "todos los hombres querían vivir en España" (165).

But, of course, many Spanish novelists of the time proposed an alternative reality in their works. Jesús Fernández Santos's *Los bravos* (1954) serves as a prime example. The novel is set in an unnamed rural village in northern Spain. There is a kind of geographical determinism at work in the town, whose inhabitants are submerged in a desolate landscape from which they cannot hope to escape – a sharp contrast with the sanctified Spain proclaimed by the Regime: "El pueblo estaba vacío. Las casas, el río, los puentes y la carretera parecían desiertos de siempre, como si su único fin consistiera en existir por sí mismos, sin servir de morada o tránsito" (1954, 12). Further, the infertile land fails to provide the villagers any hope of earning enough money to leave the area, and each year the meager harvest continues to diminish. This sense of isolation amid the hostility of the natural environment defies representations of Spain offered by the Regime of the wealth and abundance provided by the Spanish earth and, of course, by God himself. To be sure, rural Spain in the novels of this period is seen as a trap – a space of unforgiving harshness that impinges upon daily survival rather than nourishes it.

The novel and the nation

The isolation and paralysis of the small town portrayed in *Los bravos* is also sharpened by the suspension of time, which is pointedly conveyed by the image of the clock on the church tower: "El reloj aparecía inmóvil, falta de sus saetas, en una hora inverosímil . . . " (1954, 12). For the Franco regime, time became a critical component for the legitimization of their victory in the discursive practices of writing history. As the Regime saw it, past time and present time must be understood as bound up with the victory by the Nationalist forces in the Civil War. But it was a tricky intellectual maneuver to demonstrate that the past of Spain inevitably progressed toward the outcome of the War while proclaiming that progression beyond the current state of affairs was no longer required. On the one hand, a happy ending had been reached with the establishment of the Franco regime, while on the other the Regime asserted that a debilitating stagnation would not set upon the country even as history had come to a close. Franco himself viewed the Civil War as a culminating moment of liberation from the forces of the anti-Spain and labeled the Nationalist victory as "la coronación de un proceso histórico" (1940, 20). In this way he was able to assert the inherent value of the present linked to the past at the same time that he envisioned the arresting of temporal progression because Spain had now reached the legitimate apex of its destiny. The principal task of the Regime for defining the future thus became the preservation of the actual.

While obstacles to publishing in languages other than Spanish were slowly removed during the Franco years, novelistic production was clearly affected. Nonetheless, it is possible to affirm in broad terms that the development of the novel in Galician, Basque, and Catalan for the first two decades after the War followed the tendencies of the postwar novel written in Spain in general. The Galician novel of the 1950s, for example (often associated with the Galaxia publishing group), tended to provide a realistic portrayal of the harsh conditions of the Galician countryside linked to temporal stagnation, but with an overarching "local" nationalism that stood in sharp contrast to the Spanish nationalism promoted by the Regime. In other words, while the content of the Galician novel of this period drew from the regional reality of northwestern Spain, the foundational elements of this novel reflected a shared perspective on the nature and purpose of the novel written in Spanish at the time. This can be seen, for example, in works such as Xosé Neira Vilas's *Memorias dun neon labrego* (1959), which portrays merciless poverty among the young people of Galicia. As linguistic restrictions eased in the 1960s, the Galician novel gained moderate prominence as it turned from the realistic esthetic of the 1950s (similar to the novel written in Spanish) to works that use memory and fantasy to portray a complex Galician social structure and at times a contentiousness related to conservative versus liberal political positions and the shaping of Galician nationalism: the works of Xosé Luis Méndez Ferrin, for example, convey many of these issues, as well as the feminist and nationalistic fiction of María Xosé Queizán. It should also be pointed out that a major outlier from the dominant fiction of the 1950s and 1960s is Alvaro Cunqueiro, who produced works of fantasy in Spanish that were well received at the time, but who also wrote important novels in Galician such as *Merlin e familia* (1955) and *As crónicas do sochantre* (1956).

The Basque novel of the postwar period also generally evolved following the course of fiction in Spain in general, from a realistic, even "costumbrista" portrayal of local conditions during the 1950s to an existential focus in the 1960s with a heightened sense of universal dilemmas and experimentation with novelistic technique. However, translations of American and European novelists began to appear during this time (e.g., Twain, Hemingway, Kafka, and Camus), and a more modern approach to fiction can be seen in novels such as Ramón Saizarbitoria's *Egunero hasten delako* (1969) – highly sophisticated technically, it also draws to the fore the political realities of ETA (the pseudo-military organization in Spain and France fighting for Basque independence). The first edition of the novel was suppressed by the Spanish government and, as Mari Jose Olaziregi has noted, "readers chose to see it as a nationalist [Basque] manifesto" (2008, 252).

The Catalan novel by far has been the most produced and consumed in Spain outside of fiction written in Spanish during the postwar period and transition to democracy. But it too suffered from the rigorous restrictions imposed by the Franco government. This is seen not only in literature, of course, but in Cataluña as a whole – its desire for greater autonomy (and self-rule, for many), its widely supported tilt toward Europeanization, and with it, the embrace of modernity all clashed with the normative values promulgated by the Regime. These values, of course, mirror those that the government sought to overlay on resistant cultures throughout Spain: "Catholicism, Castilian monolinguism, and conservative social and political structures," as Josep Miquel Sobrer has shown (2008, 227). As occurred with a large number of writers and intellectuals throughout Spain, many Catalan novelists left the country after the War and during the early years of the Regime, and little that was written in the Catalan language during the 1940s and 1950s has made its way into the mainstream today. In 1962, however, Mercè Rodoreda published *La plaça del Diamant* (written from exile in Switzerland), the first novel of the postwar period in Catalan. The work gained significant recognition (especially when it was translated into Spanish), with its focus on life in postwar Barcelona. In general, Catalan fiction followed the broad social and existential trends of the novel in Spain during the first two decades of the Franco regime (with Manuel de Pedrolo's *Una salva com la teva*, 1960, serving as a prime example).

Social and cultural transformations

By the middle of the 1960s Spain was experiencing inevitable social and economic changes (though political transformation remained more than a decade away), which served as a catalyst for cultural change as well. In 1959, for example, the American president Dwight Eisenhower traveled to Madrid to sign an agreement that called for military bases in the country, a move that not only signaled international political support for the Regime as Spain increasingly moved to open its doors to foreign capital, but also brought to the nation the coincident influx of outside ideas. This new openness was further enhanced by a dramatic increase in tourism, which Franco himself lauded as part of a prosperous Spain. While such an increase was generally welcomed by the Regime, it also made what drew tourists to the country – the sun and the beaches, of course, but also the perception of Spain as an exotic other to the mainstream cultures of central and northern Europe – even more entrenched. The tourist slogan "Spain is different" thus became double edged: the nation embraced and marketed its distinctive essence (gypsies, bulls, horses, flamenco, and Moorish culture, among other things) while becoming vulnerable to the influx as well as the demand for more liberal ideas and permissive behaviors.

In the Spanish novel, social realism began to fade in the early 1960s, and writers slowly embraced the new literary techniques associated with the Latin American "boom" and the high modern novels of twentieth-century Europe and the United States. Yet for the most part the social focus of the novel on the reality of Spain remained strong. The portrayal of the Civil War (still somewhat tentative, given the political climate of the time), the relatively underdeveloped Spanish economy, with its coincident poverty, and the undemocratic conditions of Spanish society remained the referential base of much Spanish fiction, while many of the novelists who had embraced the techniques of realism in the novel during the 1950s created their work anew. In brief, as Spain drifted toward a more open social and political climate in the final years of the dictatorship, and then moved to create a democratic state in the early years that followed Franco's death in 1975, the social reality of Spain remained the primary focus of many Spanish novelists: trauma, violence, the Civil War, and memory sustained much of Spanish narrative even as no single movement or generational esthetic coalesced in the same way that social realism had shaped the writing of young authors following the War.

History and the novel of memory

Perhaps the most significant turn in narrative fiction of the 1970s and early 1980s coincides with a more purposeful attempt to explore the past, at the same time that both the Franco regime and the new democracy in Spain continued to resist opening the past to scrutiny. That is to say, while the official stance of the political institutions (and to a large extent, the judiciary as well) was to seek reconciliation for the nation by avoiding or willfully "forgetting" much of the suffering of the previous four decades, many novels of memory set out to explore the lived past of the Civil War and the strains of dissent that anticipated the conflict and persisted in its aftermath. Though by no means single-voiced in its propositions or tied to a precise set of literary principles, the novel of memory commingles past and present to seek definition of the self located within the flow of history and the social and political elements that constitute it. Importantly, however, while the earlier novels of social realism transferred life to literature through the principles of logical causality and narrative followability (i.e., past events accumulate to present consequences) the novels of memory unravel the plots of the past that had been denied or appropriated by the Franco regime and thus offer a more intimate rendering of the historical realities of Spain that for four decades had often been repressed and censored.

One of the most important aspects of the novel of memory has to do with how it engages writing about the past – the writing of history – that had been overtly restricted and manipulated by the Regime. Although an engineer by profession, Juan Benet (1927–1993) stands as one of the most prominent writers of the second half of the twentieth century to explore an alternative history to that promoted by the Regime, and he does so both in his fiction and his essays. From the beginning of his career in the early 1960s, Benet had staunchly opposed both the intention and the practices of social realism when it came to representing Spain and its past, yet by no means did he disengage from historical reality. For example, he wrote forcefully to protest the obstacles faced by historians attempting to understand much of the military strategy of the Civil War. As he pointed out, the "facts" of the war contained in the files of what the government called the "Archives of the War of Liberation" had remained closed to scholars who did not parrot the official posture of the Regime (1983, 60–61). His own brief history of the war, *¿Qué fue la guerra civil?* (1976b), draws out the violence perpetrated by both the Republican and Nationalist forces in the conflict, and he sees complete annihilation (not only victory) as the end game of both sides. Published a year after Franco's death, Benet's book sparked considerable controversy – one might say a healthy debate that most likely would have been disallowed a few years earlier.

But it is in his novel, *Volverás a Región* (1967) where Benet draws fully on history and memory to portray the destructive past of Spain as a determinant precursor to its ruinous present. The novel consists of a complex framework of third-person narration and first-person memories evoked by the two principal characters (Marré Gamallo and Dr. Daniel Sebastián), who recreate the past from the pre-Civil War period to the present in the isolated town of Región in northern Spain. Through the memories of the two characters (and with the historical backdrop of the twentieth century filled in by the third-person narrator) we are able to reconstruct the ruination of Región and its inhabitants throughout its history. Of primary importance, however, Benet uses the novel as a kind of metonymic remembrance of Spain as a whole over four decades. As Ricardo Gullón notes in the title of his well-known essay on Benet, Región indeed is "una región laberíntica que bien pudiera llamarse España."

Benet portrays the war and its aftermath as a lingering trauma, both for Spain as a nation and for the survivors of the conflict in Región. In effect, the people of the town (and in particular the two main characters) are so completely overwhelmed by the past that the present ceases to exist and the future is merely a continuation of all that has come before. To the dismay of these people, as Dr. Sebastián fully understands, "El presente ya pasó y todo lo que nos queda es lo que un día no pasó; el pasado tampoco es lo que fue, sino lo que no fue; sólo el futuro, lo que nos queda, es lo que ya ha sido" (1967, 245). In contrast to writers of social realism, whose testimonial perspective focuses on the pure present that is observed and recorded, and whose representation of trauma seems unhinged from specific events that may have caused it, Benet locates trauma along a temporal path that implies it is both aftermath and consequence. The Civil War stands prominently at the center of the historical trauma of Spain, and the memories of the two principal characters remain shaped by the conflict two decades after the Nationalist victory.

Another crucial aspect of *Volverás a Región* turns upon its implied renunciation of Francoist historiography. Francoist historians repeatedly characterized Spanish history as a movement from chaos to stability, with the rigid truth of myths asserted as the essential and eternal Spain. As we have seen, the Regime envisioned itself located at the end of history, which was signaled by the present time of peace and prosperity – the destiny of Spain fulfilled as the nation returned to its unifying core in language, race, and religion. In *Volverás a Región*, as well as in many of his essays on history, Benet purposefully undermines both the Francoist writing of history and the mythic structures that underpin it. For Benet the past is always closely bound up with how we express our desire to understand it. In other words, it is dependent always upon the telling of stories, upon the nature of narration and upon the belief that narration configures the past rather than simply reflecting it as if it could be told in a single story with a single truth.

Above all for Benet, narrative combines with time to eliminate from our understanding of the past what he calls "el demonio de la exactitud" (1976c, 48), while he asserts the contrary idea that "sólo la ambigüedad tiene capacidad de hacer historia" (1976a, 56). Thus in *Volverás a Región*, for example, when Benet writes at length about the political, historical, and even military aspects of the War, ambiguity, enigma, and contradiction move to the fore. His historical representation bears scant resemblance to the coherent structures of historiography as outlined by historians of the Regime – he construes the truths of narrative as well as of history as wholly contingent and deathly pale. This view permeates every aspect of his representation of Región. In this sense, Benet's Región echoes Cela's Madrid of *La colmena*, but with a critical difference: while both present the tragedy of the present, Benet's Spain is deeply rooted in history, which the characters seem helpless to overcome. In contrast to Francoist historiography, Benet proposes an end to myth rather than to history, and thus at least opens the past to re-presentation, if not to redemption. Not only does this subvert the Francoist approach to creating a usable past that serves the oppressive actions of the Regime, but also it suggests a diverse Spanish reality whose meaning is open to scrutiny and transformation. This, of course, represents a crucial turn in how Spanish fiction depicted Spain at the time.

One of the best-known memory novels of this period, Carmen Martín Gaite's *El cuarto de atrás* (1978), also challenges the Francoist view of history that the Regime utilized to frame the present. Published three years after Franco's death during the early transition to democracy, the novel rejects the testimonial representation of contemporary Spanish reality but by no means eschews the task of using Spanish society as its principal reference. It does so, however, with a commingling of memory and fantasy and explores both the present and past of Spain. The narrator (who is referred to as C, and clearly the voice of the author) shuttles between the present and past during the course of the novel, and the reflections that she offers on her life are intimately bound up with the past of Spain. The historical myths propagated by the Regime about Isabel la Católica serve as a highly pertinent example of how Martín Gaite challenges the single-voiced narrative of Francoist historians, and relates as well to the way in which the lives of women were shaped during the Franco years. Indeed, just as historians of the Regime exalt Isabel as the visionary matriarch who gave birth to Spain and its imperial glory and who cast pureness for women as the coequal of Spanishness, Martín Gaite locates Isabel at the center of the Francoist myths that are used to understand the past. Above all, the narrator of the novel recalls the imposition of values in her childhood by the state education system that come directly from the myth of Isabel: "Se nos ponía bajo su advocación, se nos hablaba de su voluntad férrea y de su espíritu de sacrificio, había reprimido la ambición y el despotismo de los nobles, había creado la Santa Hermandad, expulsado a los judíos traicioneros, se había desprendido de sus joyas para financiar la empresa más gloriosa de nuestra historia" (1978, 95).

It is clear, however, that the narrator evokes the myth of Isabel not to embrace it but to expose it as a paradigm for control instigated by the government – indeed, C is too astute a student of history not to penetrate the truth of the historiographic deceit that has shaped the myth.

As she reflects on how the past has impinged on her own life, this deceit moves to the fore: "Le escucho pensando en Isabel la Católica, en la falaz versión que, de su conducta, nos ofrecían aquellos libros y discursos, donde no se daba cabida al azar, donde cada paso, viaje o decisión de la reina parecían marcados por un destino superior e inquebrantable" (1978, 103–104). What is critical here, of course, is the way in which the narrator now sees the past always as contingent. The influence of that past on her own life, though still profound, is now open to question and doubt that was always discouraged and often disallowed for nearly four decades.

There are, of course, many other novels of memory written near the end of the Franco dictatorship and the early years of the transition to democracy – from Juan Goytisolo's *Señas de identidad* (1966), in which the protagonist evokes his life from the Civil War to the present (his rebellion not only against the Franco regime but also his rejection of the traditions and history of Spain as a whole), to Luis Goytisolo's 1973 masterpiece, *Recuento*, in which he criticizes overtly the barren lives of the young bourgeoisie and political Left in postwar Spain. These and other novels to a large degree seek to evoke past time in the context of the present, with Spain as primary referent near the end of Franco's rule and during the early years of its fledgling democracy. Also during this period the historical novel gains a prominent position in representations of the past, often linked to memory. Antonio Muñoz Molina's *El jinete polaco* (1991), for example, begins with a compulsion by the main character Manuel to disremember the past and to live outside of history, but the novel in fact shows that this is impossible to achieve. When Manuel returns to his hometown of Mágina after a long absence, he is forced to explore the lived history of the Civil War, the Franco regime, and what he has always thought of as a vacuous period of transition to democracy.

Lourdes Ortiz's *Urraca* (1982) explores the more distant past – the life of Urraca (1080–1126), first queen of the Christian kingdoms of León and Castile – but with clear relevance to democratic Spain during the transition. Narrated in the first person by Urraca, the historical perspective of the novel depends primarily on defining herself and medieval Spain against the grain of perceived orthodoxy. Above all, the world that she portrays is deeply rooted in a perspective that was largely rejected by mainstream Spanish historians for many centuries: the essential hybridity of Spain as a nation born of different cultures. Not only does her narrative speak to an Iberian community enriched by the mingling of Jews, Christians, and Moors, but also lays out a key historiographic concept – the essence of Spanish history, as well as its identity, grows not from the unifying imposition of Christianity on diversity but rather from a fusion of cultures that allowed diversity to engender a richness unique to Spain and central to its national identity.

Novels in regional languages create diverse paths during this period, but frequently share an interest in history and memory. For example, during the late Franco years, and as Spain moved deeper into the transition to democracy, the Basque novel (like other literature) developed in a variety of directions that lacked a unified center. It is clear, however, that the novel of memory became an important way for writers to evoke the cultural past that had been largely suppressed and ignored for many decades during the Franco years, as well as the recent past associated with the violence of resistance and terrorism associated with ETA. Ramón Saizarbitoria's *Hamaika pauso* (1995) represents the reality of ETA for many of those involved in violence, while Bernardo Atxaga's *Gizona bere bakardadean* (1993) explores the devastation brought on by such violence.

In the Catalan novel during this period, there is a visible attempt to treat a more diverse range of topics, especially toward the latter years under Franco as Cataluña gained a greater sense of independence from Madrid and was increasingly seen as a vital center for literature and the arts with close ties to Western Europe. At the same time, however, there appears a more intensely critical view of the middle- and upper-class society of Barcelona not unlike that found in the novels of Luis Goytisolo (e.g., *Recuento*) or Juan Goytisolo (*Señas de identidad*) written in Spanish. Beyond these well-known works in Spanish, however, Terenci Moix's *El dia que va morir Marilyn* (1966), and a novel such as Montserrat Roig's *El temps de les cireres* (1977), which portrays the angst of a young woman who had sought an abortion in England, both aim their criticism at the Catalan middle class even as the region emerges from decades of repression by the central government of Madrid.

Conclusion

The desire by Spanish novelists to represent the reality of Spain in the postwar period grew from the perceived distortion of its representation in nearly all forms of writing sanctioned by the State. It is important to point out, however, that the novels written during the first decades of the Franco regime were not born from a utopian quest to change the course of Spanish history but, somewhat more modestly, to dissent from claims about the felicitous state of affairs made by the Regime now that the authentic Spain had been restored and the anti-Spain had been kept at bay with the Nationalist victory in the Civil War. When the Franco dictatorship ended in 1975, the lingering desire to explore the present and to uncover the past remained a powerful concern among novelists, but democratization opened Spanish society and culture in ways that were at once embraced and resisted – the desire to know the past and work through its still present trauma was countered by a coincident desire to forget the past for the sake of reconciliation.

During the 1980s, what Robert Spires (1996) has termed "post-totalitarian fiction" began to take shape with new works by familiar authors, as well as by younger writers less concerned with Franco and the Spain of the recent past than with more universal concerns related to gender, identity, and the wielding of social authority. Furthermore, as Spain entered into a more mature phase of democratization, no compelling set of esthetic norms or a common perspective on political dissidence guided the novel, as had occurred during the four decades of dictatorship. It is hardly the case, of course, that Spanish novelists ceased to write about various aspects of life in contemporary Spain. However, the novel in general during this time might be best understood as shaped not in opposition to an overriding state of oppression in which writers sought social redemption for their work, but as an affirmation of openness to new ideas and techniques. Indeed, urgency to dissent, to use fiction as an instrument for social transformation or historical enlightenment, yielded to a more diffuse type of fiction that no longer set out to explore, as Teresa Vilarós has aptly noted (citing Rob Wilson and Wisural Dissanayake), "an 'imagined community' of coherent modernity [shaped] through warfare, religion, blood, patriotic symbology, and language (2003, 254). In other words, Spain as a nation, and large parts of its cultural production, began to lurch toward internationalism in ways previously eschewed under Franco, when Spain had persistently (and officially) imagined itself as different from the rest of Europe. The ethos of difference, of course, changed dramatically when Spain was admitted to the European Community in 1986 and was able to proclaim, "We are finally European."

The novel of memory of the 1970s and 1980s, with its interest both in history as well as the writing of history, managed to lay bare the truths and deceptions of those who sought to remember the past and those who preferred to forget. No longer circumscribed by the authentic Spain envisioned by the Franco regime, Spanish novelists used their freedom, in fact, to be free of many of the encumbrances that had plagued their writing for nearly forty years. Trauma and injustice, inequality and national identity are topics still woven into the basic fabric of the

Spanish novel during the 1980s and beyond, but they are not framed by a single point of view or even by a single language. Hence the role of novelists is no longer to incite readers to action, as during the 1940s and 1950s, but as is the case with literature in general, to stir the public to contemplate anew the complex world that surrounds them.

Works cited

Benet, Juan. 1967. *Volverás a Región*. Barcelona: Destino.

———. 1976a. *El ángel del Señor abandona a Tobías*. Barcelona: La Gaya Ciencia.

———. 1976b. *¿Qué fue la guerra civil?* Barcelona: La Gaya Ciencia.

———. 1976c. *En ciernes*. Madrid: Taurus.

———. 1983. "'La marcha sobre Madrid': Archivo histórico militar." *Artículos*, vol. 1. Madrid: Ediciones Libertarias.

Biescas, José Antonio and Manuel Tuñon de Lara. 1980. *España bajo la dictadura franquista*. Barcelona: Labor.

Cela, Camilo José. 1958. "Prólogo." *Mrs. Caldwell habla con su hijo*. Barcelona: Destino.

———. 1967. *La colmena*. 9th ed. Barcelona: Noguer.

Corrales Egea, José. 1971. *La novela española actual*. Madrid: Cuadernos para el Diálogo.

Fernández Santos, Jesús. 1954. *Los bravos*. Barcelona: Destino.

Fraga Iribarne, Manuel. 1958. "El articulado de la ley fundamental de 17 de mayo de 1958." *Arbor* 40 (151–151): 515–522.

Franco, Francisco. 1940. *Franco ha dicho*. Madrid: Ediciones Voz.

Gullón, Ricardo. 1973. "Una región laberíntica que bien pudiera llamarse España." *Ínsula* 29 (319): 3–10.

Martín Gaite, Carmen. 1978. *El cuarto de atrás*. Barcelona: Destino.

Olaziregi, Mari Jose. 2008. "Basque Fiction." In *A Companion to the Twentieth-Century Spanish Novel*, edited by Marta E. Altisent, 247–257. Woodbridge: Tamesis.

Perriam, Chris, Michael Thompson, Susan Frenk, and Vanessa Knights. 2000. *A New History of Spanish Writing: 1939 to the 1990s*. Oxford: Oxford University Press.

Sobrer, Josep Miquel. 2008. "The Catalan Novel." In *A Companion to the Twentieth-Century Spanish Novel*, edited by Marta E. Altisent, 225–234. Woodbridge: Tamesis.

Sopeña Monsalve, Andrés. 1994. *El florido pensil: memoria de la escuela nacionalcatólica*. Barcelona: Grijalbo Mondadori.

Spires, Robert. 1996. *Post-Totalitarian Spanish Fiction*. Columbia, MI: University of Missouri Press.

Vilarós, Teresa. 2003. "The Novel Beyond Modernity." In *The Cambridge Companion to the Spanish Novel: From 1600 to the Present*, edited by Harriet Turner and A. López de Martínez, 251–263. Cambridge: Cambridge University Press.

39

CELLULOID CONSENSUS

A comparative approach to film in Portugal during World War II

Isabel Capeloa Gil

The visual construction of national consensus: a comparative approach

Portuguese dictator António de Oliveira Salazar suffered from an acknowledged iconophobia. On several occasions he was reported to be suspicious of the power of images both for their superficiality and for their astounding ability to move. The fear of the visible is transported to political action and the dictator and the State *mutatis mutandis* embody a rhetoric of invisibility, as philosopher José Gil (1995) claims, that informs the body politic with the dictator's self-effacement and promotes a repressive logic of the hidden and obscure in political action. The contentious relation of the "invisible" dictator with film is contrasted with Francisco Franco's desire to be visible and to the power imparted to film by the Nationalists in the wake of the Spanish Civil War. And yet, despite the distinctive personalities of the dictators and the different conditions under which films were produced in the two Iberian countries in the 1930s, it is clear that the moving image, in films, documentaries and newsreels, was pivotal in setting up the totalitarian imaginary of the dictatorships.

Despite Salazar's avowed aversion to it, film was key in strengthening the cultural and political hold of the Portuguese New State [*Estado Novo*]. This was mostly due to the work of António Ferro (1933), the director of the National Propaganda Secretariat (SPN), later renamed National Information Secretariat (SNI), from 1933 to 1949. Inspired by Paul Valéry's politics of the spirit, Ferro set out to create his own brand of Portuguese spirit. He set up a string of policies ranging from awards to funding programs aimed at giving visibility and aiding those artists, writers and filmmakers whose work supported the imagination of the regime. As far as film is concerned, Ferro is credited for setting up the Cinema Fund in 1942, aimed at boosting the production of quality films and steering it away from the commercial film genres, amongst them the widely popular "Portuguese comedies," which he considered the cancer of national film (1950, 25). As a member of the intellectual modernist artistic elite, António Ferro was particularly influenced by his visit to the Hollywood factory of dreams in 1927, the same year he published *Viagem à volta das ditaduras* [*A Journey Around the Dictatorships*], a book in which he profiled the dictator type, modeled after Mussolini or Primo de Rivera, as the leadership model of an organic state. In fact, the construction of the dictator type and the passion for moving images went together, because what Ferro sought in the features of European dictatorships was deeply dependent on the possibility of visual implementation.

In *Hollywood, capital das imagens* [*Hollywood, Capital of Images*] (1931), film is described as the art of the century. Not only was it capable of producing arresting images but also it had an ability to literally *trans-figure* and anticipate, by producing a reservoir of a reality to be that would sustain the decoding of events to come. In other words, film provided the visual conviction for an idea of the state as a paradigm of order and of the nation as community of brethren united by tradition, history and religion (see Gil 2003, 312–313; Pita 2000, 43–47).

As Luís de Pina (1978) comments, the beginning of the New State and the emergence of a national Portuguese cinema went hand in hand, which is not to say that the relation was unproblematic. Overall the New State viewed film with sympathy, but with caution and even slight mistrust. In one of his interviews with António Ferro, Salazar lamented the lack of ideological orientation in cinematic artistic expression (Ferro 2003), while Ferro himself felt that the major errors of national cinema were a "lack of resources and a true absence of higher guidance" (1950, 46). He presented the creation of the Cinematic Fund and the refining of the censorship mechanisms as measures to steer misguided cinephiles onto the right path.

For the Propaganda Secretariat, film had a twofold mission: one internal – the moral and aesthetic education of the masses – the other external, as a means of propagating the Portuguese way of life as a model. The venture, however, had a third target: it aimed to create a national cinematography that not only served the purposes of the New State, but also made it simultaneously the epitome of the Portuguese national character. Deep down, for Ferro it is life that imitates art and the New State actually drew on the celluloid visuality of an invented country to steer its 48 years of existence.

This, however, was not done by the direct means of propaganda films as these were relatively scarce. Notable exceptions are *A Revolução de Maio* [*The May Revolution*] (1935), a proper "conversion" film with a screenplay by António Ferro and directed by António Lopes Ribeiro fictionalizing the transformation of a member of the Communist Party into an enthusiast of the New State, or *Camões* (1946), directed by Leitão de Barros and selected for the Venice Film Festival. King Sebastian's speech at the end of the film, as he is about to leave for the ill-fated 1578 battle of Alcácer Quibir in Morocco, after the national poet Luiz Vaz de Camões finishes reading the final lines of the *Lusiads*, is representative of SPN's drive to implement the visual construction of the regime through nationalist film. "This book is worthy of Portugal. I shall bring it with me to Africa and my captains shall read it. It has come at the time of my journey against the enemies of Our Lord Jesus Christ. [. . .] The spirit of the *Lusiads* will travel with me" (1:42'47). Like the epic poem, the film would create a community of affect with viewers. In the filmic economy, however, the close-up of the King's youthful face uttering these grand words works ambiguously. Clearly, the film reflects what Luís Reis Torgal (2000, 71) has named indirect or contextual ideology. It conveys the notion of the nation as a community that needs to be continuously reinforced by means of collective struggle against its enemies, which are also the enemies of Christendom, while suggesting its universal vocation and substantiating Portugal's colonial design. The year 1578 is read in the context of the mid 1940s with the film acting as a spectral surrogate to Camões' epic poem. Ultimately, just as *The Lusiads* invented the nation, so too does *Camões* enact the visual construction of the New State. The film promotes a staging of the memory of Portugal (see Sapega 2008) for which the creation of a specific brand of national cinematography was critical.

But this is not the whole picture, and the foregoing sequence also suggests a reverse appropriation. Álcácer Quibir represents in Portuguese cultural memory a tragic debacle and the viewer knows that the King's uplifting words are indeed ominous. Not only will the expansionist dream of an inexperienced ruler bring about the loss of sovereignty, but also the event depicted on film suggests a dire warning about the dangers of the imagination. This ambivalence suggests a visual discourse out of control. Particularly in the framing of Alcácer Quibir, which is a site of contention, a moment of struggle in the national narrative, this crack in the system becomes quite evident.

The film ends with the blending of the battle footage with four important dates for the nationalist narrative: 1640 (the Restoration of sovereignty), 1810 (the French campaign in Portugal), 1895 (the battle of Chaimite in the Occupation Wars in Mozambique) and 1940 (the date chosen by the New State regime to mark the double anniversary of the nation's foundation in 1143 and the Restoration in 1640). The film overlaps national sacrifice with a narrative of renewal and strength. Finally, the poet's dead body is identified with the death of the national body as it becomes the seed for rebirth in the present.

This chapter addresses, from a comparative perspective, the ways in which film became a tool in the imaginary construction of the Portuguese New State during World War II in view of the systemic movie flows between the European fascist regimes before and during the conflict and the way in which certain genres, such as the Portuguese comedies, or the Spanish Nationalist propaganda films about the Spanish Civil War, instilled a visual consensus with a dire social impact. Visuality, that is, the semiotic and cultural system that structures the way visual artifacts are produced, interpreted and disseminated, is arguably deeply transvisual. It works across dialogue and hybridity, through citation, borrowing and adaptation. As Nick Mirzoeff argues: "[. . .] modalities of visuality do not exist by themselves. They are necessarily imbricated with others to a greater or lesser extent. Visual culture is therefore a comparative mode of visual practice" (2009, 9). Despite the rhetoric of cultural singularity hailed by the authoritarian regimes, the system of images that made up the fascist optical regime in Portugal and Spain was profoundly transvisual.

Firstly, through a comparative discussion of Portuguese film productions of the World War II period with other cinema produced by fascist states seen in Portugal, the article engages in a comparative visual criticism, suggesting that despite their differences, there is a negotiation of tropes, techniques and ideology amongst these products that is evocative of a pervasive transfilmic fascism. But secondly, it is my contention that the visual containment aimed at with these products can never be quite accomplished. As in the final scene from *Camões*, representation, even of a totalitarian kind, can never be fully contained. In fact, as Mary Elizabeth O'Brien argues regarding the limited power of Nazi illusion aesthetics, "[o]nce the dream comes into being, it cannot be controlled" (2004, 13). Cornered by the claustrophobic image system, the spectator seems to be trapped within its closed economy and yet s/he is never fully absorbed into the filmic economy. Although the optical regime that framed the particular visuality of the Portuguese New State sought to create a rhetoric of social consensus, naive bliss, patriotic self-consciousness, religious piety, familial harmony and patriarchal submission, the fact of the matter is that no visual regime can aim at totality. As Laura Mulvey (2000, 75) contends, the system must provide an outlet for its own inconsistencies. Despite the fact that New State film seemed to have been crammed with propagandist ideology, even the comedies, consensual as they were, both in their appeal to all audiences as well as in the treatment of social issues, also worked to exceed this regime.

Clearly, one of the ways in which these films exceed the self-contained representational system of the New State is their somewhat contentious and perhaps schizophrenic relation to World War II. A representative discussion of two comedies, Jorge Brum do Canto's *João Ratão* (1940) and *Pátio das Cantigas* (1942) by Francisco Lopes Ribeiro, will seek to render a reverse or resistant appropriation of the rhetoric of peace and modernity hailed by the official discourse of the regime, and step out of the consensual way of seeing that has framed historical, filmic and cultural criticism of these visual products.

Film culture in Portugal, 1933–45

Until the 1930s, film viewing in Lisbon, particularly, was quite eclectic and cosmopolitan. Major European cinema, including Danish, Swedish, Austrian, German, Italian, Spanish, French and Soviet films, as well as the much beloved Hollywood pictures, were available not long after premiering in their home countries. This visual cosmopolitanism changed gradually during the 1930s, and Hollywood film guaranteed a substantial hegemony in the market share. Given that Hollywood film made up, on average, roughly 85% of films viewed in Portugal from 1930 to 1948, the remaining share was disputed between the German and the British. Spanish films, however, particularly those featuring the actress Imperio Argentina, were greatly admired.

Florián Rey's 1938 *Carmen la de Triana* opened to great applause in Lisbon in April 1942, at the Condes film theater. *Carmen* represented a folkloric image of Spain for the Portuguese viewer, a beloved *españolada*, and provided a visual outlet for the seductive exoticism the flamenco dancer connoted for Portuguese audiences. Still, the invented Spain conveyed by this popular musical film was also a transvisual exploit. The film is a keen instance of the transfilmic fascism addressed earlier: a German-Spanish production with two language versions by the Hispano-Film-Produktion company, founded in Berlin in 1936 and intent on becoming a key instrument in the expansion of German film productions to Spanish-speaking countries, it produced a folkloric image of Spain that affected the structuring of nationalist communities of viewers in European authoritarian regimes. The German-Spanish cooperation produced mainly typecast renditions and escapist fantasies of a Spain of bullfighters and seductive, exotic *femmes fatales*. Of the five films that came out of the joint venture, three were broadcasted in Portugal and distributed by Lisboa Filme. Apart from *Carmen*, Benito Perojo's *Mariquilla Terremoto* (1939) opened in August 1943 at Condes Cinema and *El barbero de sevilla* (1938) was screened later, in May 1946. Strikingly, this typecast image and even the hair-do of the protagonist in *Carmen* (see Figure 39.1) were resoundingly evocative of a contemporary UFA (Universum Film) blockbuster, Detlev Sierck's (a.k.a. Douglas Sirk) 1937 production *La Habanera*, an exotic warning against the lure of the South set in the tropics. *La Habanera* was produced a year earlier than *Carmen* and the latter film's aesthetics reflect a similar style of invented exoticism. In Lisbon, Sierck's film opened a year before Florián Rey's, in 1941, and drew the Zarah Leander fan base to the movie theatre Cinearte. In the play of mutual citation, Zarah Leander's invented *habanera* in Sierck's film haunts Argentina's *Carmen*, indeed suggesting a mutual interference in the construction of a German-based Hispanidad (see Figure 39.2).

UFA's interest in exploiting non-English-speaking markets followed the intent to combat Hollywood's hegemony in film production and distribution, viewed as Jewish and degenerate. A new international film body under Nazi control, the International Film Chamber (IFK), was lavishly launched in Berlin in April 1935 by the *Reichsministerium für Volksaufklärung und Propaganda (*RMVP*)*, gathering representatives from 18 different countries, including Portugal and Spain. Apart from creating a specific European film style under German guidance, the IFK also wished to foster its own star-system to respond to the flight of film industry workers and actors to Hollywood, and both Zarah Leander as well as Imperio Argentina fitted ideally into this new celebrity system.

Figure 39.1   Poster for *Carmen la de Triana*, Hispano-Film-Produktion, 1938.

Figure 39.2   Zarah Leander in Detlev Sierck's *La Habanera*, UFA, 1937.

Arguably for the Iberian film industry, the importance and allure of German UFA film lay precisely in its more commercial mode, represented by the melodramas and comedies that were a regular presence on Portuguese screens. Although critics such as Carsten Strathausen (1999) claim that UFA cinema was systematically a warring cinema, an attack on the senses, that stressed the unreliability of rational knowledge and the productive power of irrational aesthetics, it is probably fairer to argue that UFA's effect was less one of attack than of seduction into war, and in this it shared a common strategy with Hollywood's cinema of illusion.

In Portugal, most of these films, the first Zarah Leander exploits for UFA, or Detlev Sierck's melodramas, had a significant fan base, as shown by the many film reviews in *Cinéfilo*, *Kino* or *Animatógrafo* and *Boletim Cinematográfico*.

In Spain after the Civil War, the National Department of Press and Propaganda intended to reconstruct the film sector in the fields of production and distribution and was thus concerned with a major inflow of foreign film (Paz and Montero 2007, 260–1). A controversial agreement was struck in 1939 with the Reich's Film Camera to set up a quota of films exempt from the payment of rights, but the interests of the two sides never really met. As in Portugal, it was mostly the musicals and melodramas that struck a chord with local audiences. These escapist fantasies nonetheless lasted solely until the end of the war, as after signing the Bretton Wood Agreements, Spain no longer showed German films. In Portugal, the situation was different, for despite the fear of Allied exclusion, the distribution of films made under Nazi-UFA continued well into the 1950s. As far as distribution was concerned, between 1934 and 1944, Portugal Filme, later renamed Mundial Film, a company that owned the Ginásio movie theatre, stood out as the major player in German film import (Ribeiro 1983). Together with Sonoro Filme they kept a steady stream of reels coming despite the difficulties of communication with the Reich after 1944. In fact, both Sonoro Filmes and Mundial secured the royalties for distribution after 1945, when the UFA was closed down by the Allies, and German film banned from Allied-controlled areas and put under the control of the occupation forces.

Despite the overwhelmingly pro-Allied public sentiment, the sympathy for the Nazi regime, evident in intellectual, artistic, political and certainly military circles, as well as Salazar's policy of "neutralidade geométrica," kept away the more radically anti-Nazi American pictures from the screens. Charlie Chaplin's *The Great Dictator*, Raoul Walsh's *Objective Burma*, Edward Dmytryk's *Hitler's Children*, Howard Hawks' *Air Force*, Alfred Hitchcock's *Lifeboat* and even Michael Curtiz' *Casablanca* were not released until 1945, either after the German capitulation or close to the Axis' demise. Yet, as Lauro António reports (1978), defeat did not hinder a general brawl in the room between pro-German and pro-Allied supporters when *Casablanca* finally opened on May 17, 1945, at the Politeama movie theatre.

Comedies and melodramas made up the core of German film screened in Portugal from 1933 to 1945. The radically anti-Semitic propaganda films, such as Veit Harlan's notorious *Jüd Süss* or Fritz Hippler's *Der ewige Jude*, were never shown on Portuguese screens, and only a few of those considered by the Nazi Film Censorship Office as "politically valuable" or as "politically and artistically specially valuable" passed Portuguese censorship. No doubt, the prudence of the censors played a role in containing the more overtly Nazi racist products though, as Lauro António remarks (1978), they were clearly relying on the commercial as well as ideological judgment of the distributors. Free choice was nevertheless limited by the moral code of the regime. Hence a viewing ban was imposed on movies considered "[. . .] bad for the people's education, which were prone to crime incitement, and subversive vis-à-vis morality and the regime's social and political guidelines" (195). Scenes depicting the torture of humans or animals, naked characters, raunchy dances, surgery, executions, brothels, murder and rape were considered unfit for public viewing. UFA films had similar moral concerns. In Portugal, as in Spain, for the optical unconscious of fascism, the southerners' Catholicism and the northerners' atheism was no more a hurdle in matters of social morality than in political affairs.

A somewhat distinct stance was taken in relation to two Francoist films about the Civil War which effectively provided visual endorsement of the Nationalist narrative about the war. They portrayed a violent tale with graphic theatrical shots that would otherwise be cut by the censor's blue pencil. Augusto Genina's *Sin Novedad en el Alcázar* (1940) opened at the São Luiz Theatre in Lisbon on April 14, 1942, and told an epic tale of heroic resistance in the Alcazar in

Toledo against the treacherous forces of the "communist" Republic. The film opens with the shot of a Greek field of statues, evoking the epic frame of Leni Riefenstahl's 1935 *Triumph of the Will*, and inscribing the events that are about to be shown in the grand Homeric tradition. The critique of party-based democracy, particularly of parliament as the root of chaos, anti-religious sentiment, immorality and atrocity, is contrasted with images of order, hierarchy and the fear of God, embodied in the military forces and the Alcazar. But furthermore, the film works on the basis of a dichotomy between civilization and culture, between the heathen modern values of civilization and the grounded familial and pious culture of the nation, values which the IFK strongly backed as fitting with its strategy of creating a European counter-style to Hollywood's civilized materialism.

Then again, the violence on screen was somewhat hallowed as a defense of the three values that both Salazar and Franco adapted as guiding lights of their regimes: God, Fatherland and Family. The Portuguese regime's military aid to the Francoist forces was unquestionable during the years of the war, despite the defensive nationalism of Salazar's policies (Loff 1996, 200) and the fact that there was never absolute trust between the two dictators, as Salazar was suspicious of Franco's colonial appetites, while Portugal did not really fit into the latter's picture of a unified Iberia. *Sin novedad en el Alcázar* ends with an iconic inflow of shots of the fascist salute, suggesting the return to collective consensus and the final destruction of democratic dissent.

In a similar vein, José Luis Sáenz de Heredia's *Raza* (1942) was shown for the first time in Lisbon at the São Luiz Theatre, on November 10, 1942. With a screenplay written by the *Caudillo* himself, under the pseudonym Jaime de Andrade, *Raza* inscribes the Civil War in the 1898 debacle of the Spanish-American War. The Civil War becomes in this narrative the hallmark of national renewal, starting with the symbolic insurrection of the colonial Moroccan troops under Franco. Sponsored by the *Consejo de la Hispanidad*, *Raza* resorts to a central trope in nationalist rhetoric, the construction of the family as metonym of the nation. In the feuding brothers, one Nationalist, the other a Republican politician, the film projects the tensions of the body politic. The most infamous scene is arguably the execution of the Saint John of the Cross Friars, an extremely rare event in filmmaking of the time due to its graphic nature. As with the *Alcázar*, the movie repeats in visual form the official narrative of the victors and effectively promotes a repressive visual message. This is a film decidedly aimed at manufacturing consent that is ultimately conveyed in the shot of the children's fascist salute (see Figure 39.3).

But in fact, apart from these two more programmatic movies, consensus was fostered through entertainment. UFA's illusion films constituted a mode that worked in the creation of the shared political and moral imaginary of the Iberian regimes on account of what Peter Brooks has called the emotional cognitive moment (1976, 18), that is, the instant of knowing prompted by affective sentimental identification. The illusion of home, peace, sentimental resolution through marriage, and even the excitement of war, triggered a kind of fictional paradox, defined by Noël Carroll as "[t]he mystery of how one can be emotionally moved [. . .] by something you know does not exist" (2008, 153). It is precisely because the viewer knows that the optical regime is a hoax, that what she is looking at is fictional and can never take place outside the limited economy of the darkened theatre, that the spectator learns more convincingly, because emotionally, from the pathos of fiction. Film provides a fictional model of enjoyment that fosters a community of *jouissance* through consumption while enforcing the political dictates of the *Nação, Nación* or the *Volksgemeinschaft*. Although the cognitive-emotional argument might be convincing, for this as for other cases of film viewing it is by no means the whole picture.

Figure 39.3   Still from José Luis Sáenz de Heredia's *Raza*. Consejo de la Hispanidad, 1942.

In light of the transnational nexus of film cultures, I suggest the larger framing of the visuality of Portuguese comedies with other filmic traditions is not only useful, but also necessary to understand the structure of repressive social consensus that lasted until 1974. This discussion may be pursued on the macro level of comparative film analysis, or rather trimmed out in the energies that flow from the particular to the general through a micro comparative transvisual analysis. As Carlo Ginzburg argues in his reading of Siegfried Kracauer, this microanalysis, or close-up, explores a new way of seeing, narrating, and thinking, moving from minutiae to the general (2007, 182).

Microanalysis: *João ratão* and *the Courtyard of Ballads*

Although it has been argued (Granja 2000) that comedy is a contained genre in fascist aesthetics, that its appeal rests on a transgression in the end negotiated within the limits of the ideological context, I suggest that, as Stanley Cavell pointedly remarks, despite the mode of recognition and thus creative constraint it imposes, membership in a genre is "radically open-ended" (1996, 5), as it is prone to change and accommodates differing, even resistant discursive practices. Clearly, comedy rests on the radically subversive possibility of laughter despite outer coercion, which as argued by Mikhail Bakhtin in *Rabelais and His World*, "overcomes fear, for it knows no inhibitions, no limitations. Its idiom is never used by violence and authority" (1984, 35). The Portuguese comedies of the 1940s, far from being simplistic products, negotiate the dire reality of everyday fascism and disclose a subversive visuality that renders (in)visible a pervasive identity crisis, a sense of lack and castration, as well as a belatedness and displacement from modernity. In this I borrow from Stephen Greenblatt's theory of negotiation, to define the negotiation process in culture not as a means of surrendering and waving resistance, but rather as a way of using the hegemonic culture to also refract dissonance and discontent (1991, 3). Then again, this is not unique to the Portuguese brand of entertainment films in totalitarian times. Even in the most fiercely controlled visual regimes, such as in Nazi Germany, filmic visuality created its own mode of reverse appropriation, and became a place to vent dissatisfaction with the entrapment of daily life.

What I want to suggest is less a direct propagandist indoctrination of the Portuguese film company Tobis by the Nazified German conglomerate, but rather an oblique inspiration in the imaginary of illusion that was in fact to mark Portuguese filmmaking well into the 1950s. Then again the healed world presented by UFA musicals and melodramas resounded with the regime's ideologues and was negotiated on the provincial Portuguese level with the special national brand of petty bourgeois folklore and morals.

How did film contribute to foster this provincial consensus and what was specific to Nazi film production that was enlightening in this regard? Quite aware that cinematic technological concerns are not located in a hallowed ground beyond social and political usage, especially during the war, German nationalist authors sought to develop a particular kind of German, in this case read aryanized, filmmaking, that would contrast with the overtly "degenerate" modernism of Weimar film, the visual politics of Soviet film and its fast cutting, creative montage and revolutionary close-ups, and the commercial and Jewish star system of the Hollywood image factory. All of these efforts/theories were a hard sell, because filmmakers, even those close to the Nazi elite, such as Veit Harlan or Leni Riefensthal, did make use of fast cutting, the subjective camera or even empowering close-up shots. One of the most interesting theoretical references in this concern was Ernst Iros' *Wesen und Dramaturgie des Films* [*Nature and Dramaturgy of Film*] (1938), which sought to promote the Reich's specific brand of technical framing and narrative development. This approach looked at film as a means of "educating the masses and forming public taste," an expression that is quite close to António Ferro's famous defense of education through film.

Iros cautioned against modernist montage and fast tracking, a device particularly used in Hollywood adventure movies and westerns. Back projection was also hailed as unbecoming to the struggle for authenticity that should guide German film. For this purpose directors and cinematographers should use an emphatic static camera and work towards pictorial framing, collecting on frame every detail needed for the resolution of the sequence. This effort at hyper-containment was the filmic counterpart to the political *Gleichschaltung*. After all, the effort was simply a consequential resolution of the modern totalitarian obsession with the regulation of visibility.

If identity in the German context was being negotiated in the ambivalent UFA visuality as a preparation for war, in the hybrid Portuguese comedies, a mix of slapstick, melodrama and musical, the war was a totally absent reality. This derealisation and lack of any kind of interpellation of real historical conditions has been widely discussed by film scholars. After all, claims João Bénard da Costa (1991), this was a cinema that inevitably repeated the values of the New State: God, Fatherland and Family. There was no place "for an imaginary that opposed the regime's imagination" (1991, 71). One effective discursive practice used by the state to control the disruptive message of the European war whilst at the same time humouring both Axis and Allied powers alike was that of neutrality and peace. The regime sought by every means possible to control information about the war (Ribeiro 2011).

The rhetoric of peace is precisely where the war was hiding, for this rhetoric is in itself *guerroyant*, as Foucault indicates (1997, 40–41). The repressive discourse of peace became a practice of attack upon those who were at odds with the state. The comedies produced in the war period in Portugal, contained as they were, negotiated invisibility by comic relief, fostering an imaginary space where large-scale conflict escaped the fine threads of the regime's imaginary net. Film viewing provided an outlet for anxiety and fear over social and political repression, whilst at the same time depicting the narrative of the nation, of collective identity and submission to the fatherly pedagogical character of the dictator as a hollow signifier struggling to erase a pervasive sense of lack and displacement.

The tension between visibility and invisibility is indeed dealt with on the micro level of character interaction on screen. Visibility is here understood as a concept that does not necessarily pertain to the domain of visuality, but rather exceeds it, addressing instead the power discourses that render a character or event socially and politically visible. The Second World War, raging beyond Portugal's borders and a cinematic taboo, erupted subversively in minor brawls. These were usually brawls over a love affair, as shown by the war sketch in *O Pátio das Cantigas* [*The Courtyard of Ballads*] (1942) or by the row between the protagonist and the pharmacist in Jorge Brum do Canto's *João Ratão* (see Figure 39.4). Albeit petty, these minor scuffles anticipated the reinstating of consensus in the end, and were indeed comedy's way of using the law of minor causes that frames the genre to address larger issues. In fact, as Vasco Diogo has argued, there is a clear tension in narrative and character development, particularly between the conservative values of home and the longings and demands of the modern world, a tension best enacted in the representation of women, but which the plot's economy reduces and contains. This becomes apparent in the domestic petit-bourgeois idyll, made visible in order to render the real social tension and dissatisfaction invisible (2001, 322). This tension between inside and outside, between domestic values and what lies beyond, hovers as a phantasmagorical antagonist on screen. And between 1939 and 1945 this phantasmagorical outside is the ravaging war in Europe that seems completely absent from Portuguese screens. A remarkable instance of the spectrality of this outside is seen in the opening shot of the comedy *A Menina da Rádio* [*The Radio Girl*, 1944]. As Lisbon appears on frame, a caption indicates the time of the events about to take place: "At the time when there were still pastries for sale in the bakeries," that is, before the war and before Lisbon was swarmed by a wave of exiles fleeing the German advance in Europe.

The claustrophobic atmosphere of the small neighbourhood, the small urban house or the *patio*, were favourite images of the "fortress Portugal" the regime sought to convey. Within this micro-world, however, peace was always threatened. Whilst it is true that, in the end, the films return to the "imaginary wholeness" of the community or neighbourhood, a.k.a. the nation, yet the filmic economy provides a space for the ventilation of conflict that had no other place within the social arena. António Ferro's image of the comedies as the "cancer of national cinema" is revealing because it is the image of an illness that spreads, contaminates until it takes over the land with "what is most backward and gross in our street lives" (1950, 69). Laughter, after all, is democratic . . . and contagious. And if official rhetoric emphasises consensual peace as the hallmark of progress, it views these lapses into brutish conflict as a sign of pre-modern displacement. Yet, it is precisely by means of representing and addressing hostility and war that the films engage in a dialogue with modernity and allow a glimpse of the world outside the walled world on frame.

One example of how war is hiding in these comedies and destabilising the rhetoric of peace is Jorge Brum do Canto's *João Ratão* (1940), the story of a Portuguese soldier in World War I who fights valiantly, but returns home to his village and fiancée only to be enmeshed in a web of petty intrigue. The film ends with the reestablishment of order. Based on a popular vaudeville show of 1918, *João Ratão* provides a glimpse into a world without peace, but

Figure 39.4 Jorge Brum do Canto, *João Ratão*. Tobis Portuguesa, 1940.

which allows the petty farmer to experience modernity. Dire as it may be, the experience of the trenches is necessary for the inhabitant of the modern world. By contrast, the small village in Vouga seems to be truly displaced from time, and it is João Ratão who gives its inhabitants the fleeting experience of what goes on in a tiny fraction of the world beyond the walled community. Film critic João Bénard da Costa pointedly remarks that the director made a "total sacrifice to war and nothing to peace" (1991, 73).

A musical scene at the trenches in France presents war as happy endeavour, that only the soldier's melancholy brings to a halt. The music accompanies the shifting mood, from a foxtrot to the *fado das trincheiras* ("fado at the trenches"). The happy life of battle, women and wine which the foxtrot evokes is contrasted with the longing for rural life and happy bliss in the second. The scene plays in a trench, contrasting light providing the distinction between back darkness and forefront action, whilst hanging on to ensemble lighting to provide equality and cohesion. If entertainment and song are outlets for the soldier, then they at times reduce the duress of combat to spectacle. In this semiotic blend, shelling is trivialised as "music" ("temos música!"). For the rural soldiers in *João Ratão*, war is the only opportunity to experience the modern world. It is war that provides an opportunity for social mobility and prestige, and is the catalyst for the love story between the officer in charge of the regiment and the *fidalga* (noble woman). Before the dawning spectacle of World War II, World War I provides a blueprint of war as an entertaining and positive force, not uncommon in either fascist or in American and British productions of the period. Far from providing a peaceful message, the film lets audiences know that Portugal is not after all that far off from the modern conflict. The footage of real combat is a rarity for Portuguese film at the time and, whilst rendering the ravishing destruction of war visible, does not convey a pacifist message. After all, the rhetoric of peace covers up the regime's warring disposition that would come to the fore a decade later with the dictator's brutal demand to all combatants in the former Portuguese colony of Goa to never surrender. As Salazar claimed, there could be only one kind of soldier, either victorious or dead.

The last instance of this hidden discourse of war is the much debated brawl scene of Francisco Lopes Ribeiro's *Pátio das Cantigas* [*The Courtyard of Ballads*] (1942), a true parodic *mise-en-abyme* of the war, filled with everything from the German Flak guns, to air bombing, shelling, capture of the enemy and care for the wounded. The scene is best known for the final punch line when the character of Narciso Fino, the former drunkard healed by love, played by the imposing Vasco Santana, takes the children to safety in a cellar and places them in a wagon named Salazar. This rhetorical pun on Portugal as peaceful haven for refugees also mimics the dictator's fatherly role: "Rest assured, you will be safe here!" Albeit a parody of the war, the scene discloses the latent anxiety over the unfolding events and provides an outlet for the State's oppressive discourse. At the same time, as comedy convention suggests, it is a war in reverse, one that mimics heroism through cowardice, military virility through cross-dressing. As such, one of the lead characters Narciso Fino Filho, played by the frail actor Ribeirinho, also the film's director, functions as a parody of the virile romantic leading man acting as female nurse in the brawl scene, and another hero the fat Narciso Fino, the children's saviour, is depicted as a drunken slob. In this small sequence, petty morality and the rationale of the state are the object of a reverse appropriation that provides a glimpse of visual resistance to the hegemonic codes. This is clearly a mode of resistance that ultimately submits, but one that nonetheless sought to address the latent anxieties of the society of viewers through the aesthetic means available.

Coda

Fascist film systems in the 1930s and '40s are enmeshed in a web of invisible connections that share on the social and political level a similar appeal to social mediocrity and petty bourgeois values, presenting the abstraction of the nation, *Volksgemeinschaft* or home as self-referential signifiers of a common discourse seeking to quell the anxiety over identity. The comedies produced in Portugal share with the Spanish nationalist Civil War films and UFA's entertainment films a common sense appeal, and refract the dictatorial regime's drive to consensus through a visuality that wages war on the senses, be it through seduction (in the celebrity films of Zarah Leander or Imperio Argentina), shock and awe (as in the Francoist Civil War films), or even laughter. Yet, as artistic products these films also vent a visuality that can never be fully controlled and allows the viewer to be seduced into resistance. It is precisely because the audience knows that the fiction on screen does not exist that s/he is emotionally moved, and thus cognitively learns through an ambivalent, perhaps even resistant submission to an (in)visible totalitarian visuality.

Works cited

António, Lauro. 1978. *Cinema e Censura em Portugal.* Lisboa: Arcádia.

Bakhtin, Mikhail. 1984. *Rabelais and His World.* Bloomington, IN: Indiana University Press.

Brooks, Peter. 1976. *The Melodramatic Imagination. Balzac, Henry James, Melodrama and the Mode of Excess.* New Haven, CT: Yale University Press.

Carroll, Noël. 2008. *The Philosophy of Motion Pictures.* Oxford: Blackwell.

Cavell, Stanley. 1996. *Contesting Tears. The Hollywood Melodrama of the Unknown Woman.* Chicago: Chicago University Press.

Costa, João Bénard da. 1991. *Histórias do Cinema Português.* Lisboa: Bertrand.

Diogo, Vasco. 2001. "Comédias Cinematográficas dos anos 30–40." *Análise Social,* 36 (158–159): 301–327.

Ferro, António. 1933. *Salazar: O Homem e a sua Obra.* Prefaced by A. O. Salazar. Lisboa: Empresa Nacional de Publicidade.

———. 1950. *Teatro e Cinema 1936–1949. Política do Espírito.* Lisboa: SNI.

———. 2003. *Entrevistas de António Ferro a Salazar.* Lisboa, Parceria A.M. Pereira.

Foucault, Michel. 1997. *Il faut défendre la société: cours au Collège de France 1975–1976.* Paris: Gallimard/Seuil.

Gil, Isabel Capeloa. 2003. "A sedução dos fascismos e a avant-garde." In *Homenagem a Manuel de Costa Freitas,* 301–325. Lisboa: UCE.

Gil, José. 1995. *Salazar, a Retórica da Invisibilidade.* Lisboa: Relógio d'Água.

Ginzburg, Carlo. 2007. "Minutiae, close-up, micro-analysis." *Critical Inquiry* 34 (1): 174–189.

Granja, Paulo Jorge. 2000. "A comédia à portuguesa, ou a máquina de sonhos a preto e branco do Estado Novo." In *O Cinema Sob o Olhar de Salazar,* edited by Luís Reis Torgal, 194–233. Lisboa: Círculo de Leitores.

Greenblatt, Stephen. 1991. *Marvellous Possessions. The Wonders of the New World.* Chicago: Chicago University Press.

Loff, Manuel. 1996. *Salazarismo e Franquismo na época de Hitler (1936–1942).* Porto: Campo das Letras.

Mirzoeff, Nicholas. 2009. *An Introduction to Visual Culture.* London: Routledge.

Mulvey, Laura. 2000. "Visual Pleasure and Narrative Cinema." In *Film and Theory: An Anthology,* edited by Robert Stam and Toby Miller, 483–494. Oxford: Blackwell.

O'Brien, Mary-Elizabeth. 2004. *Nazi Cinema as Enchantment: The Politics of Entertainment in the Third Reich.* Suffolk: Camden House.

Paz, Maria A. and Julio Montero. 2007. " German Films on the Spanish Market before, During and after the Civil War 1933–45." In *Cinema and the Swastika: The International Expansion of Third Reich Cinema,* edited by Roel Van de Winkel and David Welch, 253–264. London: Palgrave Macmillan.

Pina, Luís de. 1978. *Panorama do Cinema Português. Das Origens à Actualidade.* Lisboa: Terra Livre.

Pita, António Pedro. 2000. "Temas e Figuras do Ensaísmo Cinematográfico." In *O Cinema Sob o Olhar de Salazar,* edited by Luís Reis Torgal, 42–61. Lisboa: Círculo de Leitores.

Ribeiro, M. Félix. 1983. *Filmes, Figuras e Factos da História do Cinema Português 1896–1949*. Lisboa: Cinemateca Portuguesa.

Ribeiro, Nelson Costa. 2011. *The BBC Broadcasts to Portugal in World War II*. London: Edwin Mellen Press.

Sapega, Ellen. 2008. *Consensus and Debate in Salazar's Portugal: Visual and Literary Negotiations of the National Text 1933–1948*. University Park, PA: Pennsylvania State University Press.

Strathausen, Carsten. 1999. "Nazi Aesthetics." *Renaissance and Modern Studies* 42: 5–19.

Torgal, Luís Reis, ed. 2000. *O Cinema Sob o Olhar de Salazar*. Lisboa: Círculo de Leitores.

Archives:

Arquivo Nacional da Torre do Tombo (ANTT)–Film Registry 1941–1953 (SNI–DGE, IGAC).

La *Habanera*, SNI, DGE, IGAC, Proc. 732, 748. ANTT.

40

(INTER)NATIONAL SPECTRES

Cinema in mid-twentieth-century Iberia

Brad Epps

The spectre of death marks the opening of two of the most celebrated films associated with the *Nuevo Cine Español* and the *Escola de Barcelona*, two cinematic currents from the 1960s and early 1970s whose oppositional pairing has both stimulated and exasperated critics and whose enduring, if contested, relevance raises questions about the contours of Spanish, let alone Iberian, cinema. Miguel Picazo's *La tía Tula* (1964), based on a short novel by Miguel de Unamuno, begins with a tracking shot of a little boy carrying a bulky funeral wreath along a deserted pavement as a bell tolls; Vicente Aranda's *Fata Morgana* (1965), based on a screenplay by Aranda and Gonzalo Suárez, begins with alternating static shots of a graphic crime novel and photographs of two young women depicted as murder victims, one preterit and the other predicted, the face of the first woman progressively lighted, or darkened, in a way that makes it resemble a skull. Linked by images of death, the two films are separated by form, structure, style and tone. In *La tía Tula*, filmed in black and white, death appears in the familiar Catholic guise of a wake with weeping mourners, dour nuns, shiny black casket, white shrouded corpse, candles, flowers and the aforementioned wreath. In *Fata Morgana*, filmed in Eastmancolor, death appears in the familiar pop cultural guise of a series of comic book vignettes and photographic stills that seem to quiver between forensics and fashion and that suggest a sexually charged violence tagged by commodity fetishism. In both films, ritual is at work, albeit in significantly different ways. In *La tía Tula*, we find the well-established rituals of provincial Catholicism and of the national literary canon, with a peculiarly Unamunian sense of sexual sublimation updated (the film is set in the 1960s) in a manner that conveys the *refusal to update* of "eternal" Spain; in *Fata Morgana*, we find the newly established rituals of urban consumerism and of the international counter-canon, with a diffusely psychoanalytic sense of sexual trauma recycled (the film is set in the near future) in a manner that conveys the *rush to outdate* of "modern" Europe. Both films insinuate ironic critiques of their respective rituals, whose symbolic sweep extends to the currents to which the two films are said to pertain: in the case of *La tía Tula*, a muted, for politically restrained, critical realism, and in the case of *Fata Morgana*, a resolute, but also politically restrained, experimentalism. Between the two currents, a national if not plurinational cinema is configured whose troubled status, signalled by a plethora of mortal metaphors, is only heightened when brought into play with the *Novo Cinema Português* "next door"—yet still so far away – in the Iberian Peninsula.

Deadly semblances and ritualised practices suffuse, of course, cultural products quite generally, but the almost ritualistic insistence with which metaphors of mortality, fragility and failure inflect critical discourse on the *Nuevo Cine Español*, the *Escola de Barcelona* and the *Novo Cinema Português* is nonetheless notable and bears on the temporal and spatial sweep, perhaps indeed the very viability, of the Iberian moniker showcased in the present volume. For strictly speaking, it may well be that Iberian cinema does not exist – or has existed only sporadically and haphazardly in the form of academic trends, disciplinary reformulations, cultural aspirations, personal relations and more insistent geopolitical markers. With respect to cinematic production, arguably at no time is such a deliberately provocative statement – which might be amplified to query the stability of "Spanish," "Portuguese," "Catalan," "Basque" and other component parts of "Iberian" – more resonant than during the 1960s and early 1970s, when cinema in the Iberian Peninsula undergoes a series of refurbishments in which novelty is enshrined as a badge of distinction and in which the maintenance of decrepit dictatorial regimes bent on a unified vision of nationality at once compels and constrains the films produced. The refurbishments, augured and accompanied by others in other countries across the world, are haunted, practically from the beginning, by senses of precariousness, inadequacy, failure and impending demise that pertain not only to the dictatorial regimes but also, and quite importantly, to the possibility of effective cinematic resistance to the regimes. These mortally inflected refurbishments take the form, as noted, of the *Nuevo Cine Español*, centred in Madrid in the 1960s, but linked to the "Primeras Conversaciones sobre Cine Español" held in Salamanca in 1955; the *Escola de Barcelona*, centred in Barcelona, but linked to the "Primeras Jornadas Internacionales de Escuelas de Cinematografía" held in Sitges in 1967, and the *Novo Cinema Português,* centred in Lisbon, but linked to the "Semana de Estudos sobre o Novo Cinema Português" held in Porto, also in 1967.[1]

The three rubrics, each with its primary and secondary sites, are as insistent as they are inadequate, at once summoning up a semblance of homogeneity and undercutting it with heterogeneous works in which the imprint of the director as *auteur* imposes itself only to end up becoming, as Sally Faulkner persuasively notes with respect to the production context of *La tía Tula* (2006, 101–102), likewise as insistent as it is inadequate. Recognizing, then, the inadequacy of rubrics both collective and individual, it nonetheless bears noting that, along with *La tía Tula*, the films most insistently associated with the *Nuevo Cine Español* include *Los golfos* (Carlos Saura, 1960, usually presented as a "pioneering" work), *Young Sánchez* (Mario Camus, 1963), *La niña del luto* (Manuel Summers, 1964), *Nueve cartas a Berta* (Basilio Martín Patino, 1965), *De cuerpo presente* (Antonio Eceiza, 1965), *La busca* (Angelino Fons, 1966), *La piel quemada* (Josep María Forn, 1965, notable for its engagement of immigration to Catalonia and its inclusion of spoken Catalan) and, most famously, *La caza* (Carlos Saura, 1965), films in which, to varying degrees, social problems are staged. Along with *Fata Morgana*, whose relation to the Escola as "precursor" is itself the subject of debate, the films most insistently associated with the *Escola de Barcelona* include *Noche de vino tinto* (José María Nunes, 1966), *Circles* (Ricardo Bofill, 1966), *Dante no es únicamente severo* (Jacinto Esteva y Joaquim Jordà, 1967, often considered the "manifesto" of the *Escola*), *Cada vez que . . .* (Carlos Durán, 1968), *Biotaxia and Sexperiencias* (José María Nunes, 1968), *Después del diluvio* (Jacinto Esteva, 1968), *Ditirambo* (Gonzalo Suárez, 1969) and *Liberxina 90* (Carlos Durán, 1970) as well as, if only as outliers, early works by Pere Portabella such as *No compteu amb els dits* (1967), *Nocturn 29* (1968) and *Vampir-Cuadecuc* (1970), films in which, to varying degrees, formal experiments are highlighted. With respect to the *Novo Cinema Português*, the films most insistently associated with it include *Dom Roberto* (Ernesto de Sousa, 1962), *Os verdes anos* (Paulo Rocha, 1963), *Belarmino* (Fernando Lopes, 1964), *Domingo à tarde* (Antônio de Macedo, 1965), *Mudar de vida* (Paulo Rocha, 1966), *Nojo aos cães* (Antônio de Macedo, 1970), *O cerco* (António da Cunha Telles, 1970) and *Uma abelha na chuva* (Fernando Lopes, 1972), films in which both social problems and formal experiments figure prominently, perhaps because the "new" is not so visibly and tendentiously divided as it is in the neighbouring country.

In all three cinematic ventures, and more tensely in the two that take place within the Spanish State, national questions are, to employ a phrase from Zunzunegui (2002, 106), critically and cryptically at play. The interplay of the critical and the cryptic in and around the national is conditioned by an often arbitrarily enacted censorship and by an ultimately unconvincing semblance of "normalcy" and "modernity" that accompanied participation in international festivals. The right-wing dictatorships in place in both Spain and Portugal, in which traditional values of family, country and church were presumably condensed in the persons of Francisco Franco and António de Oliveira Salazar, recognised the potential for cinema, as a mass medium, both to shore up and to subvert the regimes' dogmatic origins and aims. "In the Estado Novo dictatorship," as Paulo Granja notes, "films were financially supported by the regime in the hope that something like a popular cinema marked by its nationalist ideology would be produced" (2010, 62). In the Francoist dictatorship, as Casimiro Torreiro remarks, "un intento de rentabilizar políticamente la defensa de una determinada concepción de la cultura nacional a través del cine" (2009, 308) led to the implementation of a series of measures aimed at fortifying a positive image of the regime at home and abroad. Along with the production of a popular cinema of positive images, the production and maintenance of a cohesive, compliant national public was, in both countries and under both regimes, as important as it was impracticable. For if the ideology of Lusotropicalism and the contested status of the African territories meant that the concept of a national public had a violent intercontinental dimension for Portugal, the long-standing claims to alternative nationalities and the presence of languages other than that of the State meant that the concept of a national public had a tense intranational dimension for Spain.

The status of a national public and a popular cinema was further complicated, of course, by such factors as socioeconomic class, education and even taste, which perturbed even a relatively monolingual country like Portugal, where Mirandese was recognised as a regional language in 1999, long after the end of the Estado Novo. According to Paulo Cunha, "a geração que promoveu o designado *novo cinema português* tentou, numa primeira fase, conquistar o grande público sem prescindir da qualidade estética das suas propostas" (2011, 83). That the "public at large" remained largely indifferent to the *Novo Cinema* contributed to what Cunha calls "a falência deste primeiro período do novo cinema" (83). A similar situation obtained in a Spain whose multilingual reality, though disavowed and impugned by the Francoist regime, was undeniable. José Enrique Monterde, for instance, considers "la incapacidad – o imposibilidad – de generar un nuevo público, ése que podríamos definir como de 'arte y ensayo,' dispuesto a sostener intelectualmente al movimiento de renovación" to be one of "los grandes lastres del NCE y la EB" (2003, 12). What both Monterde and Cunha indicate, in other words, is that none of the "new cinemas" captured the nation in its fractured, vital entirety. The point is important, for one of the primary "accusations" that the detractors of the *Escola de Barcelona* have leveled against it is, as Rosalind Galt has noted (2010, 503), its elitist irrelevance, its inability, if not indeed its hypocritical refusal as the "*gauche divine*," to engage a wider national audience, be it Spanish or Catalan. In some respects, experimentalism would appear to be neither here nor there, for even in those films that attempted to depict contemporary problems in a fairly accessible manner, such as Rocha's *Os verdes anos* or Camus's *Young Sánchez*, the very pretense to intellectual and aesthetic quality was, it seems, a deterrent to a public accustomed to the patriotic fare of the regime and, no less importantly, the largely diversionary fare of Hollywood, typically dubbed and censored, when not outright banned, in Spain.

The inability of the "new cinemas" to generate "new publics" in their respective national settings is a recurrent topic in critical and historical studies on them and dovetails, and at times even motivates, the previously noted rhetoric of dissolution and demise that implicates, to differing degrees, both the films and the contexts in which they arise. For all three currents purchase their novelty, their edge, their *raison d'être* by implicitly or explicitly positing existing cinematic practice in Spain and in Portugal – and hence, it would seem, in Iberia – as being in a state of stagnation, even decrepitude, a state, that is, of dissolution and demise that merits dissolution and demise. It is within this depleted, beleaguered context that, in Portugal, César Moreira Baptista, who was named director of the Secretariado Nacional de Informação, Cultura Popular e Turismo in 1958, declares the need for new cinematic talents (Monteiro 2001, 5–6), and that, in Spain, José María García Escudero, who was named Director General de Cinematografía y Teatro in 1962, sets in motion the institutional reforms that undergird a relative loosening of prior strictures encapsulated in the buzzwords "aperturismo" and "posibilismo." Critics and historians of Spanish cinema generally take the appointment of García Escudero – a *comparatively* open-minded conservative jurist, journalist, military man and film critic whom dissident director Juan Antonio Bardem called "un hombre de bien" (1995, 28) – as the point of departure of a new cinematic environment in which paternalist protectionism and international projection ambivalently spurred innovation. Many filmmakers and critics alike promptly cast such institutionalized innovation into suspicion if not worse, seeing it as a ruse and an illusion, a cynical exercise in cultural cosmetics, what Torreiro has called a "lavado de cara del régimen" (2009, 300) and Monterde a mode of "travestismo" (2003, 13). With respect to Portugal, a group of filmmakers and technicians working more or less in concert with the Fundação Calouste Gulbenkian in the late 1960s sought, and to some extent achieved, similar modes of protection and promotion, including the creation of the Centro Português de Cinema, but, as Jacques Lemière notes, there too the "legitimidade interna" that accompanied these developments "se revelou sempre precária" (2006, 738).

Institutionalized innovation, in which a certain risk is promoted and protected, constitutes, of course, a paradox, but the paradox is all the more striking when the legitimacy of the regime is itself in question. For if "artistic freedom" is always already compromised by the now converging, now clashing forces of global capitalism and national sponsorship, it is even more compromised under dictatorship. The precarious, contested legitimacy of filmmaking in Spain and Portugal under Franco and Salazar in which totalizing concepts of the nation held ascendancy, spilt into the international domain. For both regimes, their *image abroad* was critical to their material and symbolic maintenance at home, especially as they became further entangled in multinational, technocratic networks. The image or images so produced did not, however, proceed in a unidirectional manner, inside out, but were often as not reprocessed or recycled, outside in, complicating in the process the very contours of the national and the pan-national. In the words of Anthony De Melo: "[a]lthough an ostensibly national movement, the Cinema Novo Português was, at the same time, profoundly conditioned by a world cinema culture" (2009, 8) and "drew inspiration from various world cinema figures, most notably Visconti, Rossellini, Renoir, Cassavetes, Mizoguchi, Bergman and Antonioni" (6). And in the words of Monterde: "los 'nuevos cines' españoles tuvieron mucho de mimetismo, de adopción de alternativas foráneas, todo lo más cruzadas con ciertas tradiciones propias, por supuesto venidas de más allá del campo estrictamente cinematográfico" (2003, 12). What comes to the fore is a national-international dialectic that, according to De Melo, "was evident in the history of Portuguese cinema as early as 1930" (2009, 8), but that was, in fact, at work in Portugal, Spain and elsewhere from the very origins of the cinematograph. Questions of *portugalidade*, *catalanitat* and *españolidad*, variously broached by Maria do Rosário Lupi Bello, Galt and others, are thus inevitably entangled in questions far beyond them.

It bears noting that Monterde refers to new Spanish *cinemas* in the plural, effectively linking the Madrid-based *Nuevo Cine Español* and the *Escola de Barcelona* and referring to a "double expression" in which the nation-state of Spain is at once reaffirmed and bisected. He is by no means alone. In a roundtable discussion on the "Barcelona School" held in Murcia in 1991, Florentino Soria, screenwriter, actor and former director of the Filmoteca Española, declares that the *Nuevo Cine Español* and the *Escola de Barcelona* were two faces of a new cinema and, moreover, that *both* were supported by the Administration, by which he means García Escudero (Paco 1991, 35–36). José María Nunes, the Portuguese-born director who was one of the central players and most persistent proponents of the *Escola de Barcelona*, concurs, claiming that at least two of his films, the glorious *Noches de vino tinto* (1966), with its inebriated, amorous nocturnal ramblings through the old city of Barcelona, and the stilted *Biotaxia* (1968), with its anxious, adulterous diurnal wanderings through the Eixample and the Parc Güell, were at least partly financed by the State (Paco 1991, 38); so too, if indirectly, was Aranda's *Fata Morgana* (Torriero 2000, 91). Although filmmaker Joaquim Jordà, another of the principal figures of the *Escola de Barcelona*, scoffs at Nunes' portrayal of García Escudero as a lover of cinema—"Sí, y Hitler también, y Franco también" (Paco 1991, 38)—he does not dispute that members of the *Escola* received support from the Administration. He recounts, for example, how Ricardo Muñoz Suay, a Valencian who had collaborated with Bardem and Luis García Berlanga (arguably the two most accomplished Spanish filmmakers of the fifties and early sixties) and who is generally considered to be the principal verbal architect, publicist or manager of the *Escola*, arranged a meeting between García Escudero, Jordà, Jacinto Esteva and Carlos Durán at which the Director General de Cinematografía reportedly said that he would continue to subsidize their films as long as they did not feature members of the working class (Paco 1991, 37–38).

Anecdotes aside, there is little doubt that State censorship and State sponsorship intertwined and implicated *both* the *Nuevo Cine Español* and the *Escola de Barcelona*. Moreover, as José María Caparrós Lera notes, "el 'padre' del NCE," José María García Escudero, "habló de dos tendencias, la de Madrid – 'social y celtibérica, en torno a la Escuela Oficial de Cinematografía' – y la de Barcelona, la célebre 'escola'" (1983, 43). The two tendencies, faces or sides, linked as they are to two cities whose modern history – the Civil War notwithstanding – has been marked more by competition than by collaboration, at once rive and reinforce the notion of Spanish cinema. Esteve Riambau, along with Casimiro Torreiro and Jean-Paul Aubert, one of the undisputed experts in the cultural history of the *Escola*, admirably encapsulates how such competition – or, as he puts it, confrontation – functions as a distinguishing feature of "Spanish cinema" in its would-be "unified" state *before* the creation of the autonomous communities and the asymmetrical devolution of power that mark the democratic return:

> Dicha confrontación es aparentemente insólita en otros Nuevos Cines, pero, en realidad, no cumplía otra función que la de enmascarar la oposición entre la influencia neorrealista fuertemente arraigada en Madrid, a partir de los precedentes constituidos por Juan Antonio Bardem, Luis G. Berlanga y Marco Ferreri, y las características de la Escuela de Barcelona, nacida, en cambio, a veinte años vista del neorrealismo y en el seno de unos Nuevos Cines mucho más desarrollados que cuando apareció el movimiento de renovación en Madrid.
>
> (2002, 5)

The apparently unwonted confrontation that differentiates the new Spanish cinema(s) from other new cinemas, including that of Portugal, remits, in Riambau's reading, to matters of cinematic influence and development that elide long-standing cultural, linguistic and political differences between the centre and the periphery, the meseta and the coast.

And yet, in dictatorial Spain, where a principle of national unity was authoritatively enforced in a manner that strove to enmesh language and culture in a univocal Spanish grasp centred in Madrid, it was the *Escola de Barcelona* that found itself not just in a geographically peripheral but also a politically ectopic position – a position that the Barcelona-based filmmakers were quick to style to their advantage. According to Juan Amorós, director of photography of Esteva's and Jordà's *Dante no es únicamente severo*, Durán's *Cada vez que . . .* and Esteva's *Lejos de los árboles* (1963, 1972): "Había una pugna entre lo que era la costa y la meseta, y de esa pugna nació la Escuela de Barcelona" (Paco 1991, 32). The "pugna," or tug-of-war, was ideologically charged, with the landlocked "meseta" evoking close-minded traditionalism and the "costa" evoking open-minded innovation in tune with Europe or – in a pregnant precision – the "rest" of Europe, Barcelona's much-touted cosmopolitanism having long functioned as a sign of its difference from a presumably parochial Spain. It is not insignificant that Amorós, along with countless others, refers to the proximity of "la frontera" (Paco 1991, 32), nor that the border, even without the precision of 150 km, was understood to be French, not Portuguese, for it was to the provincial city of Perpignan, not to the capital city of Lisbon, itself under dictatorial rule, that cinephiles from Spain made secular pilgrimages to see films prohibited or otherwise unavailable in Spain, just as it was to Jean-Luc Godard – Saint Godard, as celebrated critic and historian Román Gubern quipped in Jordi Cadena's documentary *La passió possible* – and not to, say, Manoel de Oliveira, that Jordà, Esteva and other Barcelona-based filmmakers turned for inspiration. Then again, it was not just the Portuguese capital but also the Spanish capital that remained at what often seemed an insurmountable distance from Barcelona; in the words of Riambau: "Para la Escuela de Barcelona, París quedaba mucho más cerca que Madrid y, por tanto, es en la capital cultural europea donde deben buscarse las principales influencias del grupo" (2002, 6).

In Lisbon it would also seem that Paris, or Rome, was closer than Madrid. Studies of the *Novo Cinema Português*, no less than those of the *Escola de Barcelona*, are rife with references to the *Nouvelle Vague* as well as to the English Free Cinema, Fluxus, the New York School, and the Polish and Czech New Waves (Galt 2006, 3; Ledesma 2013, 256; Riambau and Torreiro 1999, 199), but unlike their Barcelona counterparts, the Portuguese studies contain, on the whole, virtually no substantive reference to cinema in Spain. The situation appears to be mutual, because cinema in Portugal figures scarcely if at all in accounts of the *Nuevo Cine Español* or the *Escola de Barcelona*. While contention, competition and confrontation characterise cinematic relations between the "meseta" and the "costa" in the Spanish State, unfamiliarity and indifference appear to characterise cinematic relations between the two nation-states of the Iberian Peninsula. This is not to say that contention is absent from Portuguese cinema, for as in Spain the so-called "new" cinemas are founded, in no small part, on the denigration and rejection of "older" national cinemas, on a temporal break that, in the case of the Spanish State, fuels a spatial break as well. But along with relatively general categories of time and space the specificities of personhood are also here at issue – and to such a degree that what de Melo writes about the proponents and practitioners of the *Novo Cinema Português* holds, *toutes proportions gardées*, for those of the new cinemas of the Spanish State: "The explosion of 'young' cinemas worldwide inspired them to make *personal* films as distinct from those of their Portuguese forbears, as they were similar to the various national new cinemas" (2009, 6, emphasis added). The reference to the personal is by no means incidental and buckles back to the figure of the *auteur*. As one of the salient traits of the *Nouvelle Vague* and its theorization and promotion in *Cahiers du Cinéma*, the *auteur*, as polemically posited by François Truffaut in 1954, stands in tension with both the literary adaptor and the cinematic industry and, as reformulated by Andrew Sarris in 1962, signals a mixture of technique, personal style and, most importantly if ineffably, "interior meaning" (51). As such, the *auteur*, though implicated in the national, shimmers internationally, but in a manner that is at once infranational (too specific to represent the nation in its generality) and supranational (too general to represent the nation in its specificity).

The person and persona of the *auteur* complicates the aforementioned national-international dialectic in a manner that, going beyond the constraints and contradictions that critics rightly link to the dictatorships, impinges on the critical viability of the Iberian moniker before, during or indeed after Franco, Salazar and Marcello Caetano, Salazar's successor from 1968 to 1974, under whose government, as Ana Bela Morais notes, "a atuação dos censores não divergiu muito da que estava vigente durante o regime salazarista" (2014, 148). For in one study after another, whatever its historical coordinates, the emphasis almost invariably falls on the national (Spanish, Portuguese, Catalan, Basque, Galician), the international (European, Western, global), and/or the personal (Picazo, Aranda, Rocha), as well as on questions of genre, technology, industry, financing and reception. References to something Iberian – which is effectively a restricted mode of the international – are, as already intimated, as rare as any sustained dialogue on the cinematic production of the nation-states of Spain and Portugal. With regard to Portugal, Lupi Bello signals two principal and counterpoised tendencies: one that maintains that the search for something "Portuguese" is vacuous and vain, and another that proceeds "como se a busca dessa eventual 'portugalidade' fosse condição *sine qua non* para a adequada compreensão e contextualização de cada objecto cinematográfico de nosso País" (2010, 19). Similar concerns animate works on cinema in Spain, with some, like film-maker José Luis Borau, advocating a film's independence from "non-cinematic constraints" (1999, xxii), including nationality, as the paradoxical sign of Spanish cinema's "coming into its own," and others, like critic Santos Zunzunegui, insisting on a film's immersion in national tradition (see Vernon 2002, 99). The Madrid-based *Nuevo Cine Español*, with its engagement of the "problem of Spain," might appear to correspond more closely to what Kathleen Vernon has called Zunzunegui's "claustrophobic closing of the hermeneutic circle that restricts the focus to an exclusively Spanish cultural patrimony" (99) than to the *Escola de Barcelona*, which largely eschews both Spanish and Catalan traditions, at least in any direct or explicit manner. Perhaps not surprisingly, however, the traditional topic of traditions is more complex.

For all their purported Spanish "centralism," the filmmakers of the *Nuevo Cine Español* took many of their cues – or so the story goes – from Italian neorealists such as Roberto Rossellini or Vittorio de Sica and demonstrated, on the whole, an eagerness to participate in wider, inter-national circuits. Despite its derisive designation by some as "cine mesetario," the *Nuevo Cine Español*, with its "hambre de realidad" (Gubern 1966, 6), was by no means "landlocked," any more than it was unfettered because it occupied an ostensibly privileged position in the central-ised State. Subject to censorship and co-option, the Nuevo Cine did not issue in straightforward critiques of an oppressive system; far from it. This is not to suggest that the *Nuevo Cine Español* issued in reticular and opaque works such as the *Escola's Dante no es únicamente severo* or *Fata Morgana*, for Saura's *La caza*, one of the most celebrated films associated with the *Nuevo Cine*, is quite clearly an allegory of the Civil War. Nor, for that matter, is it to suggest that the *Escola de Barcelona* would perforce have eschewed the elliptical, fragmentary aesthetic that distinguishes it even if those associated with it could have worked in conditions that would have allowed them to be – to loop Jordà's much-cited witticism – Victor Hugo instead of Mallarmé

(Paco 1991, 25). Rather, it is to note, simply yet significantly, that despite the aforementioned ethos of contestation and competition, evident in subsidies, prizes, and other promotional and protectionist measures, and despite a lengthy history of intranational tension, the works variously associated with Madrid and Barcelona are more mutually entangled than the rhetoric of opposition that informs both the conception and reception of the films indicates. Indeed, contestation, competition and even opposition are all critical signs of entanglement. The entanglement does not extend, however, to the entirety of the Iberian Peninsula, or at least not nearly so intensely, for as already noted, the two nation-states, however marked by belatedness, insufficiency or embattled grandeur, enjoy an internationally recognised sovereignty that does not extend to, for instance, Catalonia, the Basque Country or Galicia.

Entangled or not, endowed with a state apparatus or not, there is no national rubric, including that of Portugal, that is not internally fractured and fissured. Such fractures and fissures, though often gainsaid by appeals to some sort of framing unit (Catalonia, Spain, Portugal, Iberia, Europe, etc.), are not merely adventitious, for as Andrew Higson rightly remarks: "Communities are rarely self-sufficient, stable or unified. They are much more likely to be contingent, complex, in part fragmented, in part overlapping with other senses of identity and belonging that have more to do with generation, gender, sexuality, class, ethnicity, politics or style than with nationality" (2000, 66). Fissured, hybrid and impure, the "modern cultural formations" that Higson signals as "always re-fashioning themselves" (67) – and whose more radical formulation might be Gilles Deleuze's "swarm of differences" (1994, 50) – seem particularly germane to the *Escola de Barcelona*, which Eduardo Ledesma links to practices of intertextuality and, more compellingly, of intermediality, in which various media careen and collide, intersect and overlap. In the words of Ledesma, the *Escola de Barcelona* "mobilized political critique by engaging in 'impure' and 'contaminated' media practices, especially in regard to relations between the verbal, the visual and the aural" (2013, 254). That the political critique that resulted was often deemed to be unintelligible or accessible to only a small number of "discerning" viewers fuelled previously noted tensions between the meseta and the coast as well as tensions among leftist artists and intellectuals, with their attendant vocabulary and accusations of populism and privilege or, as Faulkner puts it, naïveté and elitism (2006, 126). The politics of nationality and form almost invariably implicate questions of totality, singularity and purity, all of which are at play, often in the negative, in cinematic production. For if cinema has been international since its beginnings (technological exchanges, co-productions, subtitles and dubbings, distribution circuits, immigrant, exilic personnel), it has also been intermedial (drawing on and bringing together a variety of techniques, modes and media), even before the term gained currency in the 1990s (Ledesma 2013, 256).

Ledesma's reading of the *Escola de Barcelona*, in which he persuasively defends the anachronistic deployment of the term "intermedial," might be productively extended, at least in part, to the *Novo Cinema Português*, which, as Paulo Filipe Monteiro remarks, is paradoxical inasmuch as it is the *Estado Novo* that creates the conditions of possibility – principal among which, for Monteiro, the assault on "cineclubismo" – and supports some of its most avant-garde and experimental endeavours. Citing Paulo Rocha's declaration that "'[n]o começo do anos 60 a juventude europeia estava na moda. Ser novo, ter ideias novas era de repente um valor,'" Monteiro extends the cult of the new to the State itself: "[m]esmo no Portugal salazarista, como se poderá ver pela rápida ascensão dos novos valores" (2001, 312). Just as some of the experimental works of the *Escola de Barcelona* were implicated in, and even conditioned by, the regime's policies (as Jordà sardonically remarked, since it was easier to say the truth about a billiard ball than the Civil War or the working class, he would stick to speaking about billiard balls [Paco 1991, 37–38; Riambau and Torreiro

1993, 141; 1999, 178]), so too were some of the works of the *Novo Cinema Português*. It is important to remember, of course, that the *Novo Cinema Português* does not "divide" itself so doggedly into neo-realist and anti-realist modalities as occurs with the *Nuevo Cine Español* and the *Escola de Barcelona* and that both the relatively straightforward narrative of *Os verdes anos*, with its "green" protagonist, and the decidedly more tortuous narrative of *Uma abelha na chuva*, with its jaded married couple, are associated with it. It is also important to remember that the divisions that have characterized "new cinema" – or "new cinemas" – in the Spanish State have long been marked and marred by stereotype and, moreover, that the intermediality that Ledesma understandably associates with the more experimentalist works of the *Escola de Barcelona* is in fact so widespread that many so-called mainstream works employ it as well, although almost always less conspicuously.

The mixing of writing, sound and image that constitutes, at a minimum, the "promiscuous" and "impure" core of intermediality is operant, for instance, in adaptations of literary works whose status as films has also long been disputed, even impugned. True, it is a mixing that often as not dissembles itself, just as camera, photogram and material base also often as not dissemble themselves, dissemblance being the price not just of the mainstream feature but also, ironically, of many modes of realism (social, poetic, psychological), and exposure, in the guise of self-referentiality and meta-critique, being a mainstay of the arthouse feature and, more pointedly still, avant-garde experimentation. The dissemblance or exposure of a promiscuous plurality of forms, media and materials, in many respects parallels, moreover, the dissemblance or exposure of a promiscuous plurality of people, places and practices. In *Fata Morgana*, which lays bare a variety of media (photography, comic books, advertisements) and foregrounds a cosmopolitanism whose background remains enigmatic and apocalyptic, the city of Barcelona is defamiliarised and signs of national identity largely made to go "missing" (Galt 2007, 209). For Torreiro, *Fata Morgana* is a collage that bears little if any identifiable relation to "la exigua, por no decir raquítica, herencia cinematográfica" of Spain (2000, 94); for Aubert, it constitutes "une sorte de mosaïque de mots, solgans publicitaires, entretiens journalistiques, badinages incohérents" (2006, 22), a film in which "la ville est devenue un vaste terrain vague que parcourent sans raison des êtres privés d'identité" (2009, 160). For Gubern, in one of the first essays published on Aranda's film, however, *Fata Morgana* is "una obra que se define precisamente . . . por sus características de desarraigo y de rechazo" (1966, 6), a work produced "en el seno de una cultura cuya negación no hace sino afirmarla" (6). In other words, Gubern persuasively contends that it is amidst loss that something Barcelonan, indeed something Catalan, is to be found, and that it is in "un cosmopolitismo generalizado" (9), a diffuse internationalism, that the specificity of an uprooted, stateless culture is to be identified.

And yet, even in such "identifiably" Spanish works as *La tía Tula*, of which a contemporary reviewer said that it would be pointless to search for "los descubrimientos formales de las últimas tendencias del cine moderno" (Gortari 1964, 692), it would be "naïve," as Faulkner notes, "to state that Picazo's frame of filmic reference is . . . Spanish, as any notion a pure national cinema is a fallacy that overlooks the transnational hybridity of film" (2006, 106). True as it is, the invocation of the transnational hybridity of film is also so general as to risk sapping its critical force, something that Faulkner seems to recognise when she goes on to note both that "Picazo is less concerned with his place among European New Cinemas than other NCE directors" (106) and that *La tía Tula* is "indebted to earlier practices in Spanish film photography, rather than the technical developments in vogue in contemporary European New Cinemas" (108). As Picazo himself has declared: "Me he movido en un cine muy concreto, que es el español" (Gregori 2009, 383). Still, as Faulkner remarks, moments such as the "static camera and trick long take" of the credit sequence (110) contribute to the sense of imprisonment and stagnation that is at the thematic core of *La tía Tula* and that is, tellingly enough, repeatedly adduced as the environment of cinematic production in Spain more generally. Meek as *La tía Tula* may be in formalist terms, Patino's *Nueve cartas a Berta*, which is often considered to be even more emblematic of the *Nuevo Cine Español* than *La tía Tula* (just as *Dante no es únicamente severo* is considered to be more emblematic of the *Escola de Barcelona* than *Fata Morgana*), is decidedly more robust in its deployment of a number of formal devices that include stillness, accelerated montage and disjunctures between sound and image that give the lie to the notion that formal experimentation was the exclusive province of the *Escola de Barcelona*.

The problems involved in taking *La tía Tula* or *Nueve cartas a Berta*, *Fata Morgana* or *Dante no es únicamente severo*, *Os verdes anos* or *Uma abelha na chuva*, as "emblematic" or even "representative" of particular movements, groups or schools is related, of course, to the problems involved in taking any selection of works, attitudes or styles as representative of a particular nation or assemblage of nations, Iberia undoubtedly included. The exhaustion, frustration and even exasperation with which many critics have lately come to address questions of national identity is in some ways anticipated by José María Nunes's insistence that his is a cinema of Barcelona, not of Catalonia (Paco 1991, 24). Nunes's assertion is bolstered by the fact that, unlike either the *Nuevo Cine Español* or the *Novo Cinema Português*, the "Escola de Barcelona" – or, rather, the "Escuela de Barcelona," for the Catalan language, though defended by Jordà and others, was massively censored under Franco – spotlights the Catalan capital and not some nationally modified "new," overshadowing, in the process, a presumptive *Nuevo Cine Catalán*, let alone a *Nou Cinema Català*. And yet, even when it is dismissed or demonized, the national continues to lurk, often *sous rature*, in such designations as "European," "cosmopolitan" and "Iberian," and, more noticeably, in such prefixed variations as "international," "pan-national," "transnational," "supranational" and "postnational." It lurks, however, not necessarily as some master signifier, essentialist anchor or determinative force, but rather as a problem, a question, a remainder and a reminder of both the insistence and the insufficiency of identity categories more generally. In the case of recognised *nation-states*, the national, in its very insufficiency, obviously insists, and so much so that, as Higson notes, "[i]t would be impossible – and certainly unwise – to ignore the concept altogether" (2000, 73), just as it would be unwise not to query "what sort of cultural developments it can embrace and what it makes difficult" (70).

It is in the light of both the insistence and the insufficiency of national designations that the relatively discrete entities that go by the name of *Novo Cinema Português*, *Nuevo Cine Español* and *Escola de Barcelona* find themselves hounded, in their critical treatment but also in their very themes and conditions of production, by the rhetoric of dissolution and demise noted at the outset of this essay. Whether it be in Zunzunegui's mobilisation of the phrase "de cuerpo presente" – which refers to a cadaver that is prepared and displayed before burial but which is also the title of a 1967 film directed by Antonio Eceiza – to lament what he sees as the inability or unwillingness of the filmmakers associated with the *Nuevo Cine Español* to draw nourishment from an extensive Spanish literary and artistic tradition (2002, 106); or in Riambau and Torreiro's reference to "la simultánea frustración provocada por la prematura defunción del NCE y el abortado intento de gestación de un Nuevo Cine Catalán" (1999, 184); or in Riambau's presentation of "una Escuela [de Barcelona] ya agonizante" as a "Crónica de un suicidio anunciado" (2002, 3; 10); or in Ricardo Muñoz Suay's "Nacimiento de una escuela que no nació" (1967); or in João Bénard da Costa's *O cinema português nunca existiu* (1996), the spectre of death, failure and non-existence looms large. Stated more broadly, in all three cinematic movements, spanning the fractured and fissured Iberian Peninsula at a time of dictatorially constrained, (inter)nationally inflected innovation, something at once momentous and momentary, dynamic and depleted, is adumbrated. Torn between social realism and avant-garde experimentation, constrained denunciation and ironic consumerism, the "new" cinemas of the 1960s and early 1970s are also torn between modes of protracted localism and surging globalism in which questions of statehood and statelessness become involute.

A comparative reading of filmic production that moves beyond the overdetermined oppositional pairing of the *Nuevo Cine Español* and the *Escola de Barcelona* to encompass the *Novo Cinema Português* conjures up the prospect of an Iberian cinema whose innovative success and promise are shadowed, like those of its would-be component parts, by inadequacy, expiration and failure. There can be little doubt that, as the editors of the present collection contend, the fading of the Franco and Salazar regimes ushered in new social and cultural realities in which the multicultural richness and linguistic diversity of the region came increasingly to the fore. And yet, it remains to be seen to what degree such richness and diversity are "Iberian" – circumscribed, that is, to a geopolitically naturalized "peninsula" – and to what degree they remain marked by signs both larger (European, Western, international, trans-Atlantic, global, etc.) and smaller (Spanish, Portuguese, Catalan, Basque, Galician, etc., but also individual, personal, *auteurial*), signs that endure, at times ghost-like, and that return, at times zombie-like, in an age of corporate capitalism, neoliberal reason and splintered democratic devolution.

Note

1 The *Novo Cinema Português* is also linked to the document *O Ofício do Cinema em Portugal* that followed in 1968. Its prehistory is, however, considerably longer. As de Melo notes: "The desire for a new cinema to emerge in Portugal was articulated as early as 1957, when cine-club enthusiast and eventual film director, José Fonseca e Costa, argued for a fundamental change in the national film practice in an article titled, 'Cinema novo' ('New Cinema'), and published in the first issue of the magazine, *Celuloide*" (9). Not surprisingly, precursors to the *Nuevo Cine Español* and the *Escola de Barcelona* also exist.

Works cited

Aubert, Jean-Paul. 2006. "Une poésie du coq à l'âne: l'École de Barcelone et la subversion du récit." In *Transitions, transgressions dans l'iconographie hispanique moderne et contemporaine*, edited by Sylvie Mégevand and Jean-Michel Mendiboure, 19–30. Carnières-Morlanwelz: Éditeur Lansman.

———. 2009. *L'École de Barcelona: Le cinéma d'avant-garde en Espagne sous le franquisme*. París: L'Harmattan.

Bardem Muñoz, Juan Antonio. 1995. "El cine y la sociedad española." In *El cine español, desde Salamanca (1955–1995)*, 25–30. Salamanca: Consejería de Educación y Cultura.

Borau, José Luis. 1999. "Prologue: The Long March of Spanish Cinema towards Itself." In *Spanish Cinema: The Auteurist Tradition*, edited by Peter William Evans, xvii–xxii. Oxford: Oxford University Press.

Cadena, Jordi. 2000. *La passió possible: l'Escola de Barcelona*. Film.

Caparrós Lera, José María. 1983. *El cine español bajo el régimen de Franco (1936–1975)*. Barcelona: Publicacions i Edicions de la Universitat de Barcelona.

Costa, João Bénard da. 1996. *O Cinema português nunca existiu*. Lisboa: CTT, Correios de Portugal.

Cunha, Paulo. 2011. "Radicalismo e experimentalismo no novo cinema português (1967–74)." In *Cinema em Português: Actas das II Jornadas*, edited by Frederico Lopes, 83–92. Covilhã: Livros LabCom.

Deleuze, Gilles. 1994. *Difference and Repetition*. Translated by Paul Patton. New York: Columbia University Press.

De Melo, Anthony. 2009. " 'Finally, we have our own nouvelle vague.' António da Cunha Telles Productions and the Cinema Novo Português (1963–1967)." *eSharp*. Special Issue: New Waves and New Cinemas. Accessed 10 June, 2014. http://www.gla.ac.uk/esharp

Faulkner, Sally. 2006. *A Cinema of Contradiction: Spanish Film in the 1960s*. Edinburgh: Edinburgh University Press.

Galt, Rosalind. 2006. "Mapping Catalonia in 1967: The Barcelona School in Global Context." *Senses of Cinema* 41. Accessed 12 January, 2015. http://sensesofcinema.com/2006/feature-articles/barcelona-school.

———. 2007. "Missed Encounters: Reading, *Catalanitat*, the Barcelona School." *Screen* 48 (2): 193–210.

———. 2010. "Impossible Narratives: The Barcelona School and the European Avant-Gardes." *Hispanic Review* 78 (4): 491–511.

Gortari, Carlos. 1964. "*La tía Tula* por Miguel Picazo." *Film Ideal* 154: 691–692.

Granja, Paulo. 2010. "Paulo Rocha *Os verdes anos* (1962) and the New Portuguese Cinema." *Portuguese Cultural Studies* 3: 61–68.

Gregori, Antonio. 2009. *El cine español según sus directores*. Madrid: Ediciones Cátedra.

Gubern, Román. 1966. "Fata Morgana, epifenómeno de una cultura en crisis." *Nuestro Cine* 54: 6–9.

Higson, Andrew. 2000. "The Limiting Imagination of National Cinema." In *Cinema and Nation*, edited by Mette Hjort and Scott MacKenzie, 63–74. London: Routledge.

Jordá, Joaquín. 1967. "La escuela de Barcelona a través de Carlos Durán." *Nuestro Cine* 61: 36–41.

Ledesma, Eduardo. 2013. "Intermediality and Spanish Experimental Cinema: Text and Image in the Lyrical Films of the Barcelona School." *Journal of Spanish Cultural Studies* 14 (3): 254–274.

Lemière, Jacques. 2006. "'Um centro na margem': O caso do cinema português." *Análise Social* 41 (180): 731–765.

Lupi Bello, Maria do Rosário. 2010. "A implosão do cinema português: Duas faces de uma mesma moeda." *Portuguese Cultural Studies* 3: 19–32.

Monteiro, Paulo Filipe. 2001. "Uma margem no centro: a arte e o poder do 'novo cinema'." In *O cinema sob o olhar de Salazar*, edited by Luís Reis Torgal, 306–338. Lisbon: Temas e Debates.

Monterde, José Enrique. 2003. "Introducción. En los límites de los posible." In *Los 'nuevos cines' en España: Ilusiones y desencantos de los años sesenta*, edited by Carlos F. Heredero and José Enrique Monterde, 11–14. València: Institut Valencià de Cinematografia Ricardo Muñoz Suay.

Morais, Ana Bela. 2014. "A censura aos filmes ibero-americanos na governação de Marcello Caetano." In *Literaturas e culturas em Portugal e na América Hispânica: Novas perspectivas em diálogo*, edited by Magdalena López, Ângela Fernandes et al. Ribeirão: Edições Húmus.

Muñoz Suay, Ricardo. 1967. "Nacimiento de una escuela que no nació." *Fotogramas* 22: 964.

Paco, José de. 1991. *La Escuela de Barcelona*. Murcia: Semana de Cine Español/Filmoteca Regional.

Riambau, Esteve. 2002. "De Víctor Hugo a Mallarmé (con permiso de Godard): influencias de la *Nouvelle Vague* en la Escuela de Barcelona." Alicante: Biblioteca Virtual Miguel de Cervantes. Accessed 10 June, 2014. http://www.cervantesvirtual.com/obra-visor/de-victor-hugo-a-mallarme-con-permiso-de-godard-influencias-de-la-nouvelle-vague-en-la-escuela-de-barcelona--0/html.

Riambau, Esteve and Torreiro, Casimiro. 1993. *Temps era temps: El cinema de l'Escola de Barcelona i el seu entorn*. Barcelona: Generalitat de Catalunya-Departament de Cultura.

———. 1999. *La Escuela de Barcelona: el cine de la 'gauche divine.'* Barcelona: Editorial Anagrama.

Sarris, Andrew. 1973. *The Primal Screen: Essays on Films and Related Subjects*. New York: Simon and Schuster.

Torreiro, Casimiro. 2000. "Todo encuentro es una historia de amor: *Fata Morgana* y el origen de la Escuela de Barcelona." In *Miradas sobre el cine de Vicente Aranda*, edited by Joaquín Cánovas, 83–98. Murcia: Primavera Cinematográfica de Lorca/Universidad de Murcia.

———. 2009. "¿Una dictadura liberal? (1962–1969)." In *Historia del cine español*, edited by Román Gubern, José Enrique Monterde, Julio Pérez Perucha, Esteve Riambau, and Casimiro Torreiro, 295–340. Madrid: Cátedra.

Vernon, Kathleen. 2002. "Recent Books on Spanish Cinema in the 1990s: A Global Perspective." *Post Script* 21 (2): 90–99.

Zunzunegui, Santos. 2002. "De cuerpo presente: En torno a las raíces literarias del 'Nuevo Cine Español.'" *Cuadernos de la Academia* 11/12: 103–116.

PART V

Iberian studies in the twenty-first century

History, politics and cultural studies

41

PRO-SOVEREIGNTY POLITICS IN CATALONIA AND THE BASQUE COUNTRY

Are the two cases comparable?

Richard Gillespie

At a time when several stateless nations of Europe are making claims to sovereignty, Spain has become a key point of international reference, not least for the European Union. This is largely as a result of the rise of *soberanismo* (pro-sovereignty feeling and assertiveness) in Catalonia although there is also the emerging issue of how Basque politics will evolve following decades of political violence. While the rise of pro-sovereignty politics may be attributable partly to aspects of globalization including the repercussions of the international financial crisis of 2008, the different paths followed by nationalist movements in Catalonia and the Basque Country demonstrate the need for analysis to take full account of the endogenous features of each case. Among these, in what follows, particular attention is paid to different structures of political competition, contrasts in political and economic status between the Basque and Catalan autonomous communities and dissimilarity in the relationship between political elites and civil society.

This contribution aims to account for the marked contrast between the two territories in respect of the *soberanista* challenge faced by Spain today.[1] Is there really such a stark contrast between a Catalan national movement pushing to redefine Catalonia's relations with the Spanish state and a Basque nationalism that has become more circumspect in this regard? If so, this would represent a dramatic departure from historical patterns and necessitate a rethinking of traditional stereotypes associated with Basque and Catalan nationalism, whereby the former was "radical" and the latter "moderate" (Conversi 1997).

The chapter focuses primarily on the political orientations of the traditional mainstream Catalan and Basque nationalist forces, namely *Convergència i Unió* (CiU), a two-party federation in office in Catalonia between 1980 and 2003 and again between 2010 and 2015, *Convergència Democràtica de Catalunya* (CDC, or simply *Convergència*), the main component of CiU which continued to head the Catalan government after CiU's dissolution in 2015, and *Euzko Alderdi Jeltzalea-Partido Nacionalista Vasco* (EAJ-PNV, from now on PNV), the party of government in the autonomous community of Euskadi from 1980 to 2009 and since 2012.

For the most part, these mainstream Catalan and Basque nationalist political forces have viewed each other as nearest equivalents and have cooperated in elections to the European Parliament. In recent decades, both CiU and PNV managed to appeal to a range of nationalist opinion, from Basques and Catalans seeking incremental increases in autonomy to those advocating more decisive steps towards independence. Traditionally, both have been the senior nationalist forces in their respective territories, overshadowing the (since 1989) pro-independence *Esquerra Republicana de Catalunya* (ERC) until 2015 and successive parties of the so-called *Izquierda Abertzale* ("Patriotic Left"), including Batasuna in the past and Sortu today.

However, they are not similar in every respect. CiU, until its breakup in 2015, was a more recent, post-Franco federation involving the nationalist CDC led successively by Jordi Pujol and Artur Mas and the Christian Democrat *Unió Democràtica de Catalunya* (UDC), led from 1987 until 2016 by Josep Antoni Duran i Lleida (Barberà Aresté 2011; Barberà and Barrio 2006; Guibernau 2004, 120–151). The PNV is a much older, single party, although for a while it had a regular nationalist coalition partner in *Eusko Alkartasuna* (EA) (de Pablo and Mees 2005; Pérez-Nievas 2006).

Beginning with an overview of the distinctive nationalist paths undertaken by CiU and the PNV since the 1990s, the study goes on to highlight and discuss the three major variables behind the contrasting orientations mentioned previously. The concluding section adds some final thoughts on the value of comparing the two cases.

Changing places and defying the stereotypes? An overview of the PNV and CiU sovereignty strategies

At an impressionistic level (at least), the past twenty years have seen the mainstream Catalan and Basque nationalist parties – and essentially CDC and the PNV – engage in a dramatic process of "role reversal," after appearing to external observers to be quite embedded in their respective traditions for a substantial part of the last century. Indeed, until only a decade ago the relatively few academic studies that made comparative reference to the two cases were fairly uniform in seeing Basque nationalism as more radical and sovereignty-oriented and Catalan nationalism as distinctively moderate and "accommodationist" in the sense of looking to pursue objectives within the framework of the Spanish state (Conversi 1997; Díez Medrano 1995; Payne 1971). In a short space of time, successive developments then conspired to challenge these stereotypes and place the two nationalisms at different ends of the analytical spectrum, although this depiction must be qualified by the greater degree of autonomy sought and achieved by the Basques during the late 1970s, when Spain's model of devolved government was designed on the basis of individual statutes negotiated with each of the new "autonomous communities" established as regional units of the state.

The Basque evolution has involved a shift from assertive *soberanista* politics under former president of the Basque government Juan José Ibarretxe (*lehendakari* 1999–2009) to a more cautious, less urgent approach to the national question under Íñigo Urkullu (from 2012); while beyond the PNV there has been ETA's decision to abandon armed attacks and facilitate a turn to institutional political participation by radical pro-independence forces in 2011. CiU nationalism meanwhile was seen to radicalize more recently than in the case of the PNV, especially from 2012, after Catalans had mobilized to express their growing discontent over successive decisions taken in "Madrid" – notably, by Spain's Constitutional Court in 2010, with its unfavourable ruling on key aspects of the new Catalan Statute of 2006, which had promised enhanced autonomy and recognition of Catalonia as a nation; and by Prime Minister Mariano Rajoy in rejecting CiU demands for a better financial deal, specific to Catalonia, in 2011–12. Adding to the sense of radicalization in Catalonia, there have been several huge feats of popular mobilization, emanating from a powerful civil society movement that has its own dynamics and tended to push CiU towards the road to independence (Dowling 2014).

PNV radicalization took the form of a proposal to make Euskadi semi-independent through establishing a relationship of co-sovereignty, to be achieved by negotiation with Madrid (Keating and Bray 2006; Mees 2009). There were two main drivers behind Ibarretxe's initiative in the early 2000s, which progressed through adoption by his party, government and the Basque Parliament. One was a sense that the Statute of Gernika which had granted autonomy to Euskadi in 1979 had gone as far as it would in terms of actual transfers of powers to the Basque government: after 20 years a number of *competencias* had still not been transferred by Madrid, others had been transferred but then undermined by new Spanish laws and there were now moves to recentralize by the People's Party (PP) government of José María Aznar, once it had achieved an absolute majority in the Spanish Parliament in 2000. The other was an attempt on the part of the PNV to convince ETA to renounce violence by showing that the governing party and its coalition partners in Euskadi were prepared to push for a greater degree of home rule and thus there was now a stronger possibility of changing the status quo through political action.

The term "radicalization" is questioned by some in the PNV since the party historically had entirely *soberanista* roots and had never renounced its tradition despite becoming more ambiguous on the question of autonomy versus independence (de Pablo and Mees 2005). Ibarretxe himself had been a technocrat in the previous nationalist-led government headed by the pragmatic José Antonio Ardanza (1985–99) and as *lehendakari* continued to act within the Spanish constitutional framework when presenting his proposal for co-sovereignty and a "free association" between Euskadi and Spain. He made no demands about neighbouring Navarre, still a focus of Basque irredentist ambition. However, he did give priority to the PNV claim that ultimately the Basque people had a "right to decide" on the future political status of the Basque Country, through a referendum, and his government concentrated on pro-sovereignty politics far more than did the Ardanza governments, noted for achieving economic improvement. Thus "radicalization," in the sense of a *shift* from more "accommodationist" patterns of behaviour towards an emphasis on pro-sovereignty territorial demands (Gillespie 2015), is an apt term to apply to the evolution of Basque Nationalist priorities and policy emphases at this time.

Yet this development did not signal a revolution in the PNV. A party 'general assembly' (congress) in January 2004 saw a narrow victory for Josu Jon Imaz in the election of party president and his support for the Ibarretxe plan became somewhat conditional: Imaz defended the need to find a constitutional formula that would meet with sufficient public acceptance to cross the nationalist/unionist divide in the Basque Country and insisted that this would not be feasible until ETA had finally decided to abandon violence. Sectors of the party showed little enthusiasm for the plan, waiting for it to be frustrated by the Spanish authorities rather than opposing it openly. When it encountered rejection in Madrid, Ibarretxe and the PNV were devoid of a "plan B" and the emphasis on sovereignty politics began to be questioned more openly within the party amid electoral setbacks in 2005 and 2007. Imaz himself tried to set "red lines" to constrain *soberanismo* by publishing a newspaper article in July 2007,[2] but he never had a strong enough institutional base within the PNV to return to the approach of the Ardanza plan of 1998 which had sought a transversal basis for a new autonomy statute.

Only after Urkullu had been elected president as a supposed "unity candidate" in the fifth assembly of the PNV in December 2007 did the party begin to offer more authoritative reassurances regarding its ideas on a "consultation" of the Basque people, but Ibarretxe's final push for authorization to hold a referendum continued to be blocked by Prime Minister José Luis Rodríguez Zapatero in Madrid. The more moderate, conciliatory approach of Urkullu gradually triumphed in the course of a reassessment of the party's orientation, made inevitable by its displacement from power, temporarily, following elections in March 2009, after thirty years permanently in office. When it returned three years later, after a period of PP-backed Socialist minority government under Patxi López, both the PNV and a minority Urkullu government were united around the priorities, being recovery from economic recession and post-conflict pacification, ahead of any fresh effort to change the constitutional status of the Basque Country. Urkullu's government did eventually start a dialogue and parliamentary process aimed at achieving a "new political status" for the Basque Country, but it took a more cautious and gradual approach than Ibarretxe had, insisting that a consensus across the nationalist/unionist divide was imperative and would not come through seeking support for a preconceived party plan; rather, the PNV would explore the positions of the other Basque parties before defining its own proposal.[3]

While replacement of the Statute of Gernika was an ambition largely confined to Basque Nationalists and smaller allied parties, moves for statute reform in Catalonia came initially from a tripartite coalition that straddled the nationalist/non-nationalist divide while being united by Catalanism[4] and centre-left ideas. It was formed by the *Partit dels Socialistes de Catalunya* (PSC, a component of the *Partido Socialista Obrero Español*, PSOE), the nationalist *Esquerra Republicana de Catalunya* (ERC) and *Iniciativa per Catalunya Verds-Esquerra Unida i Alternativa* (ICV-EUiA, a postcommunist/ecosocialist alliance embracing a range of preferences regarding the future political status of Catalonia). While CiU, towards the end of its 23-year initial period in office, showed little sign of radicalization and had been collaborating politically with the PP from 1996, it was the federalist PSC leader, Pasqual Maragall, who took the initiative on statute reform after being able to form a governing coalition in 2003.

Reform of the statute was to face a more positive reaction from Rodríguez Zapatero than from the preceding Aznar government in Madrid. The PSOE leader looked to collaboration with a range of left-wing, nationalist and regional parties to overcome the parliamentary ascendancy of the PP in 2000–04. He was open to statute reform in all the autonomous communities (except Euskadi, while ETA violence persisted) as part of a "second transition" to renew and deepen democracy (Muro 2009). Besides, the PSOE relied on Catalonia for a large part of its vote: hence, Rodríguez Zapatero's pledge ahead of the 2004 general election that he would accept any new statute that was approved by the Catalan Parliament, a process achieved by September 2005 with eventual support from CiU which left the Catalan PP isolated in opposition. Frustration ensued, however, from a watering down of the statute at the insistence of the PSOE as the approved text was modified in negotiations with the government and in the Spanish Parliament before the resulting document was approved in a referendum in Catalonia in June 2006 (with turnout only 48.48%).[5]

Rodríguez Zapatero had expected a more moderating role to be played by PSC deputies in the Catalan Parliament but had underestimated the Catalanism of Maragall and his colleagues. He thus used parallel negotiations with CiU (despite it being an opposition party in Catalonia) to ensure that unacceptable aspects of the text (e.g., concerning the national status of Catalonia) were diluted (Orte and Wilson 2009, 424–30). Later it was to be the actions of the PP under Rajoy (street demonstrations and a mass petition against the statute, followed by an appeal to the Constitutional Court) that were to become dominant in narratives of Catalan grievance against Madrid, yet there was always an important sector of the PSOE too that remained opposed to any special status being granted to Catalonia, arguing that this would be at the expense of other regions.

Pro-sovereignty politics had begun to emerge within CiU in the late 1990s and it also underwent leadership changes with the retirement from front-line politics of its historical founder-leader Jordi Pujol in 2003. While this turnover brought some new programmatic emphases,

Pujol's choice of Artur Mas as his successor at the head of *Convergència* was initially seen as a setback for an incipient *soberanista* current (Barberà and Barrio 2006, 114). During CiU's years in opposition (2003–2010) Mas did call for a "refounding" of Catalanism but resisted *soberanista* pressures at CDC's fifteenth congress in July 2008, believing that talk of independence would alienate an electorally important sector of Catalanist opinion and jeopardize CiU prospects of returning to dominate the centre ground of Catalan politics electorally.[6] Yet many party members, anticipating an adverse ruling by the Constitutional Court, did become sceptical about the feasibility of further autonomist gains and they were responsible for the adoption of a euphemistic reference to independence ("a state of our own") at the following CDC congress, in March 2012, at which Oriol Pujol, *soberanista* son of the former president, became general secretary.[7]

The years in opposition saw "sovereignty" being used often in an instrumental, rhetorical way by CiU in a competition with ERC to establish pre-eminent "national" credentials and to embarrass it for the compromises involved in governing alongside non-nationalist coalition partners at a time of deepening economic crisis. *Esquerra* leaders were coming under huge pressure from their own militants.

Soberanismo became more evident within *Convergència* than in *Unió*, but even in CDC radicalization was a gradual, somewhat tortuous process at first. When the Constitutional Court finally ruled against controversial aspects of the 2006 statute in June 2010, the initial reaction of many CiU leaders was to defiantly resurrect the proposals approved by the Catalan Parliament in 2005, while insisting on a Catalan "right to decide." While the ruling had some radicalizing effect, the main CiU emphasis over the next two years was on economic grievance. On political sovereignty, there was an initial pragmatic retreat rather than a surge forward when CiU returned to power, under Mas, in late 2010.

Like the PNV when elected two years later, but facing a much worse financial situation than the Basques, CiU initially prioritized the economic challenges of debt and deficit. Forced to make dramatic spending cuts, the new government relied on collaboration with the centralist PP for its governing majority. Only when Mas got nowhere with demands for an improved financial deal for Catalonia (both before and after Rajoy's triumph in the general election of 2011) did CiU, and particularly CDC, begin to call for a referendum specifically on independence.

Even then, traditional moderates such as Mas only took up the sovereignty banner decisively when faced with huge pressure from civil society. The massive demonstration in Barcelona on the Catalan national day (*Diada Nacional de Catalunya*) of 11 September, in 2012, convinced pro-independence politicians within CiU that a window of opportunity had opened, while other senior figures played catch-up, concerned at the prospect of being by-passed as popular support gravitated towards the pro-independence ERC, itself no longer constrained by alignment with the PSC and ICV-EUiA. Catalonia saw a shift in the whole nationalist/Catalanist mainstream towards *soberanismo*, confirmed by the rise of *Esquerra* in the Catalan election of November 2012, in further displays of mass mobilization by pro-independence associations and in the results of elections to the European Parliament in May 2014, which for the first time saw ERC outpoll CiU, a pattern confirmed by the Spanish general election of December 2015 although qualified by changes in the Catalan party system and by enhanced political collaboration between *Convergència* and ERC from 2015, eventually leading to an agreed roadmap aimed at the creation of a Catalan state.

For the traditionally hegemonic party federation, this pattern of evolution was not without contradictions. Part of CiU, especially UDC leader Duran i Lleida, was far from happy with the eventual agreement reached by pro-*soberanista* Catalan forces to proceed with plans for a referendum or (if that were prevented) a plebiscitary election. However, the problem facing advocates of a "third way" (to enhance autonomy but avoid the uncertain road towards separation) was that the Rajoy government remained inflexible and had nothing substantial to offer to the many Catalans who sought better treatment but did not ideally wish to break with Spain completely.

CiU's eventual breakup in mid 2015 did not mean an end to the bid for independence, for CDC was able to form an alliance with ERC and Catalan civil society organizations and thereby retain pre-eminence through a common *Junts pel Sí* ("Together for Yes") platform in the next regional election in September, hoping – with the road to a referendum blocked – to use this event instead to demonstrate the existence of a popular mandate for moves to bring Catalan independence. The alliance won the election, but fell just short of an overall majority of the votes, and also of the seats in the Catalan Parliament. It thus relied now on conditional support from the radically anti-capitalist *Candidatura d'Unitat Popular* (CUP) in order to govern and one dramatic consequence for *Convergència* was that Artur Mas was prevented from forming another government. Instead, the new Catalan administration formed in January 2016 would be presided over by a more long-standing advocate of independence, the former CDC mayor of Girona, Carles Puigdemont.

Variables along the nationalist path

In discussing variation in the trajectories of mainstream Basque and Catalan nationalist parties, one must go beyond a focus on the parties themselves and highlight key contextual variables that influence elite decisions on whether to emphasize autonomist or *soberanista* demands in practice, the former seeking to reconcile Basque or Catalan home rule with a Spanish and European context, the latter seeking direct representation within the EU. Since it is necessary here to be selective rather than exhaustive in order to discuss such variables, only those deemed of greatest importance are the subject of this section.

Political competition

Electoral competition in both autonomous communities has involved the traditionally larger nationalist forces in competition mainly with more radical nationalist parties and with socialist parties. The PP has been weak in both communities, although a major force to contend with in Araba, the smallest of the three provinces of Euskadi.

In relation to their "electoral frontier" with other nationalist forces, CiU for a long time tended to dwarf ERC, a party noted for pervasive factionalism and instability arising from direct forms of internal decision making and ideological debates about the balance between nationalism and socialism (Culla 2013; Lucas 2004). The electoral gap between nationalist parties left CiU with considerable scope to cooperate with the major Spanish parties, mostly the PP within Catalonia and the PP or PSOE in Madrid, especially at times of minority government. This situation favoured the politics of accommodation, so long as it was seen as bringing incremental increases in Catalan autonomy and/or financial benefits for the community. However, a different balance of forces emerged from 2011 as CiU bore the costs of governing during financial crisis and recession while ERC grew for several reasons: it finally united after a string of electoral setbacks between 2006 and 2010; brought in non-sectarian candidates with no baggage from old internecine battles to head its electoral lists; reflected the rise of pro-independence public sentiment more quickly and unitedly than CiU; and initially managed to gain political influence without actually accepting the responsibility of office, by negotiating a pro-referendum (and wider programmatic) pact with CiU at the start of the latter's second term of office under Mas, in December 2012. A CiU setback in the Catalan election of that year had left it in need of allies and there was strong *soberanista* support for alignment with ERC within CDC. While some leaders may have been manoeuvring just to match ERC's programmatic "offer," others held that Catalonia now had a historic opportunity to press for independence and thus *soberanista* unity was crucial, even if it brought a *sorpasso* of CiU by *Esquerra*.

In contrast, in the Basque Country, electoral and other pressures from radical nationalists to make the PNV commit to independence politics have been weaker. Owing to the historical association of a large part of the *Izquierda Abertzale* with ETA, nationalist unity was never in prospect so long as political violence lasted. The PNV viewed ETA as a fundamental impediment to pushing for further autonomy or independence, since if it did so, rivals would claim it was legitimizing terrorism. Moreover, the party became convinced that no Spanish government would agree to transfer all the powers envisaged in the Statute of Gernika, since Madrid would want to keep back something to "concede" in the event of any of the peace negotiations undertaken by PSOE or PP administrations finally prospering. When the PNV under Ardanza and Ibarretxe tried to develop plans designed to bring an end to violence by securing an eventual referendum on a cross-party Basque agreement on future status (and thus, it was hoped, leave ETA without a justification to carry on), it was at times when the *Izquierda Abertzale* itself was concerned about a growing civil society repudiation of ETA attacks, not least among Basques. The early failure of these efforts, signalled by the collapse of an ETA ceasefire in late 1999, prevented any "normalization" of political contestation in the Basque Country, especially after changes to Spain's law on political parties were used from 2002 to ban parties such as Batasuna, on the grounds of involvement with ETA.

Only following ETA's announcement of a "definitive" and permanent end to violence was the *Izquierda Abertzale* (having itself made sustained efforts to achieve this outcome in recent years) allowed to participate again in elections, initially through the alliances Bildu and Amaiur. It proceeded to present a challenge to PNV pre-eminence within the nationalist community by taking a quarter of the vote in the Basque election of 2012, largely at the expense of the PNV. However, the dynamics of inter-nationalist rivalry remain very different to those in Catalonia, given an absence of nationalist mobilization on the Catalan scale, pressure on the radicals to convince Basque sceptics that their commitment to democratic praxis is sincere and irreversible, and significant differences in how the radical and moderate nationalist parties envisage territorial politics.

The Socialist presence in Basque and Catalan political life has been greater in the past, and PSOE affiliates have tended to do better in general and local elections than in regional ones. The *Partido Socialista de Euskadi-Euskadiko Ezkerra* (PSE-EE) has functioned as a loyal branch of its mother party whereas the PSC is the result of a merger and has experienced strong Catalanist influence in competition with an ultimately prevailing PSOE orientation. Although the PSE seemed almost a "natural" partner of the PNV under the pragmatic governments of Ardanza, it was always critical of the Ibarretxe plan and sceptical of PNV efforts to reach agreements with the *Izquierda Abertzale* aimed at conflict resolution. Referring strategic questions to Madrid, the Basque Socialists gravitated towards alignments with the PP, seen in the existence of competition between nationalist and unionist blocs in elections in 2001 and 2009. Despite periodic attempts to give the PSE a greater "Basque" identity, this never went so far as to create tension with the mother party. The nature and evolution of the PSE were thus something of an impediment to any pro-sovereignty shift by the PNV. Certainly, nationalist parties together have often taken 50% to 55% of the vote in Basque elections, but have not been able to unite or claim the level of endorsement claimed by CiU for *soberanismo*, whose adherents won 87 of 135 seats in the Catalan election of 2012 and 83 (including the *Catalunya Sí que es Pot* left-wing alliance and the CUP) in 2015.

Despite the Catalanist influence, the PSC did not in the end subscribe to the *soberanista* pact of 2012, but it had supported the broad notion of a Catalan "right to decide," so long as it was approached through reform of the Spanish Constitution. Those who argue that the rise of sovereignty politics has been more from above than below, as a result of CiU language and education policies introduced by the Generalitat, may regard the Socialists as having facilitated nationalist radicalization by embracing the idea of mainstreaming Catalan culture in public life. However, support for the policy of making Catalan the basic language of delivery in education had enjoyed much broader cross-party support within Catalonia, including from the PP. More certainly, the PSC facilitated the trend towards *soberanismo* simply by falling victim to its own internal disagreements over the national issue and PSOE-PSC relationship.

Regional financing arrangements

Attracting increased attention during the economic recession, the financial context of the autonomous communities in which the Basque and Catalan nationalists operate is an important key to the contrasting political itineraries of the PNV and CiU. The fact that Euskadi (together with neighbouring Navarre) has near fiscal autonomy under an agreement known as the *Concierto Económico* (*Convenio* in Navarre) whereas Catalonia comes under the common financing regime that applies in all other regions of Spain has given the Basque government greater control over its finances and greater resources during the financial crisis and its aftermath. Since the Basques collect their own taxes and the law governing the quota (*cupo*) that they pay to the state is subject to bilateral agreement, they are in a stronger negotiating position when this comes up for review than Catalonia (which negotiates its financing alongside fourteen other regions with conflicting priorities). PNV leaders claim to have had a better overall record of economic management and probity than CiU has had and maintain that their funding arrangements in themselves place them further along the road to independence than Catalonia, though they are envious of the scale of active support for *soberanista* goals in Catalan society.[8]

The generalized system of funding undoubtedly worked to Catalonia's disadvantage during the recession, since inter-regional redistribution had quite extreme effects in pushing Catalonia down the ranking of regional per capita fiscal resources (Gray 2014, 25). It is this, together with complaints about public investment in the region and political frustration that has led to support for independence outgrowing its traditional identity-based core and extending to non-nationalist Spanish-speaking sectors. Catalans are well aware that the region of Madrid has become economically dominant since the 1980s as Catalonia has slipped (Dowling 2014, 228–29), and they know that Euskadi's *Concierto* helps account for better-quality health care and lower unemployment levels than in Spain overall. A dominant theme behind the demands for a "fiscal pact" was for Catalonia to be granted its own unique funding model, although not a replica of the Basque *Concierto* since Catalan politicians have generally been adverse to the unilateral risk that this entails. If hypothetically applied to Catalonia, the *Concierto* arrangement would imply a much higher contribution to the Spanish exchequer than Catalan advocates of fiscal sovereignty would find palatable because of Catalonia's far greater weight in the Spanish economy (c. 18–20% of Spanish GDP versus c. 6–7% in the Basque case).

A related factor complicating the assertion of *soberanista* claims in the Basque Country is that fiscal and political authority is subjected to a more decentralized institutional structure reflecting greater territorial complexity compared with Catalonia (Goikoetxea 2013; Ibarra Güell 2011). Under the *Concierto* and the Basque Law of Historical Territories, it is Euskadi's three provinces of Bizkaia, Gipuzkoa and Araba that collect taxes and in turn provide a proportion of the funding to the Basque regional government (a proportion of which is contributed to the Spanish treasury). Thus the provincial level of government is uniquely important in Euskadi and elections linked to municipal elections can, as in May 2011, lead to different parties and coalitions controlling this tier of government in each province and potentially constraining the options open to the regional government in Vitoria. Thus, even without considering debates about the wider Basque Country (including the *Pays basque* in France and at least parts of Navarre), Basque nationalists – including the *Izquierda Abertzale* – have difficult issues to consider about how and where a Basque "right to decide" might be operationalized even if a sufficient consensus were to exist or emerge within Euskadi itself in support of a referendum. In contrast, Catalan politics are dominated by the city and province of Barcelona and although ERC retains a residual attachment to the notion of the *Països Catalans* (including the Valencian Community, French Catalonia and the Balearic islands, where it is organized as *Esquerra Republicana*), the campaign for a Catalan state has focused entirely on the autonomous community of Catalonia. Thus territorial parameters have not been a source of divergence within the *soberanista* camp.

Party-society relationship

A third area where mainstream Basque and Catalan nationalist parties have found themselves in different circumstances has been in the relationship between political forces and society. Following Spain's transition to democracy, Basque society continued to be deeply marked by political conflict, whereas Catalonia has enjoyed peace and a relatively soft, fuzzy community division around language and identity that has allowed for an unconstrained evolution of civil society. The Basque Country remains more internally divided, owing to a combination of factors: the marked historical impact of immigration from other parts of Spain (which bears comparison with Catalonia), the ethnic basis of early Basque nationalism and the impact of political violence. Although at times since the 1980s the nationalist-unionist divide has been bridgeable through PNV-PSE coalitions, there have also been periods of polarization or at least political tension between two "fronts." As a result, associational life in the Basque Country has tended to be segmented and colonized by political forces divided over the national question. Nationalist trade unions, for example, account for some two-thirds of union members in Euskadi, in contrast to Catalonia where the leading trade unions have been those that prevail throughout Spain, but are *soberanista*.[9] Even today, notwithstanding recent initiatives by pro-independence platforms in the Basque Country to borrow from Catalonia's mobilization repertoire, Basque associational life remains dominated by political acronyms.[10]

Modern Catalonia meanwhile has been free of organized political violence and in Catalanism has had a powerful ideological, cultural and political current that has offset the potential clash of nationalisms by embracing both nationalists and forces for which attachment to the national community has been combined with explicit loyalties to class or left-wing ideas. This helps explain why the anti-Franco movement in Catalonia was broad and unitary notwithstanding organizational fragmentation. Despite salient electoral rivalry between CiU and the PSC from 1980, there was a widespread consensus within Catalonia over political autonomy and the privileged status of Catalan in education.

Comparing the two episodes of radicalization in leading nationalist parties, the different politics-society configurations help account for the contrast between a Basque initiative under Ibarretxe that was an initiative "from above" and the rise of *soberanismo* in Catalonia which received considerable impetus "from below." In the Basque case, the initiative came purely from the party and government and was carried forward by the Parliament despite ETA's resumption of hostilities in early 2000. No attempt was made by the PNV to mobilize mass support, which would have been impossible at this time given the impact of conflict on associations and on individuals. Public responses were mixed and partisan (Keating and Bray 2006, 358–361). Public involvement was limited to a consultative process involving some 65 hearings by the Basque Parliament and appeals for electoral endorsement by Ibarretxe.[11] Little surprise then that there was no public protest when Ibarretxe met with rejection in Madrid or when the initiative finally died with the end of PNV-led government in 2009.

In contrast, the process of statute reform in Catalonia, a "prequel" to the rise of *soberanismo*, was made possible by transversal developments such as PSC efforts under Pasqual Maragall to appeal beyond the party's traditional base and ERC interest in collaboration with other Catalanist forces on the left. Public identification with the notion of a "right to decide" (pioneered by Ibarretxe) was evident by 2006, as some 200,000 Catalans protested over the dilution of the statute approved by their Parliament to a version acceptable to the government in Madrid. Opinion polls registered a gradual rise in independence preferences from 13.6% to 25.2% between 2005 and 2010,[12] while Catalanist mobilization grew in volume; pro-independence sentiment then became truly massive and more sustained from 2012.

Developments relating to identity and to Catalan and Spanish attitudes towards one another played a part in the rise of *soberanismo*, but what took independence politics into the mainstream was a wider *combination* of diverse drivers and the fact that (in contrast to the Basque case) a catalyst (the fate of statute reform)[13] or arguably a series of catalysts (anti-crisis measures, statute verdict, rejection of fiscal pact) existed to spark mobilization (Crameri 2014). An important role has been played by the Catalan National Assembly (ANC) as a horizontal umbrella structure for pro-independence groups working together on an inclusive basis, capable of appealing transversally across Catalan society to such an extent that CiU felt tempted and indeed obliged to harden its position, play catch-up in relation to pro-independence sentiment and participate in *Diada* mobilizations from 2012. The experience of *Òmnium Cultural*, which organized the demonstration against the court ruling in July 2010, is also instructive. Dedicated to the promotion of Catalan language and culture, it recovered from earlier symptoms of stagnation to reach a membership of 38,000 by early 2014, becoming sociologically and demographically more transversal and more geographically widespread in the process. Nationalist cultural associations in the Basque Country have been much smaller and more closely identified with nationalist parties.[14]

The interplay between top-down and bottom-up dynamics in the interpretation of how the nation-building project and (eventually) *soberanista* politics have become mainstream in Catalonia has been the subject of academic controversy which has tended to emphasize one perspective or the other,[15] yet it would seem plausible and necessary to include both in analysis. It is beyond the remit of this contribution to do so, but in any case one should be wary of framing the debate as purely one about nationalism. *Soberanismo* in Catalonia cannot be understood simply as a manifestation of nationalism – indeed it owes its potency to the movement's transversal nature which has allowed it to capture multiple sources of dissatisfaction with the current political and economic order and incorporate a significant part of the Spanish-speaking population.

Adding value through comparison?

While this study shows important differentiating factors that affect nationalist party behaviour in the Basque Country and Catalonia, the very fact that both Basque and Catalan parties have been involved in assertions of sovereignty relative to the Spanish state make them comparable, even if the leaderships of these parties do not always identify with the terminology of accommodation and radicalization used by analysts. Moreover, nationalist political movements, while tending to emphasize singularity, do gaze across at one another, often only to draw lessons about what *not* to do in their own communities, but sometimes to borrow ideas and concepts from the other. This is certainly true of the Catalan and Basque cases.[16]

What this particular comparison shows about the dynamics of mainstream nationalist parties is that shifts along the sovereignty-accommodation axis are far from unidirectional and should not be assumed to be permanent. Processes of radicalization may lose impetus; reversion to more accommodating or cautious strategies can occur, as in the Basque Country. A key factor facilitating reversion there was the fact that the *soberanista* initiative was elite-led and -controlled. Equally the PNV was under relatively little pressure from radical nationalist electoral competition, there was some risk of it losing centrality to statewide parties if their competition was ignored, and the party upon returning to office in 2012 faced far less advantageous economic conditions than it had known under Ibarretxe and thus had to focus on managing crisis, in view of its responsibilities under the *Concierto*.

The strength of *soberanismo* as a transversal movement and not merely a political force must mean that complete reversion is less likely in Catalonia, although even many *independentistas* acknowledge that windows of opportunity are of limited duration and mass mobilization cannot be sustained indefinitely. In 2012–14 the option of changing tack was simply not open to CiU once it had committed to a referendum: accommodationism lacked a suitable disposition on the part of central government, the PP and at least sections of the PSOE; the economic situation was a fundamental constraint; CiU had no potential partnership alternative to ERC, as the PSC broke with the "right to decide" alliance and was hit by crisis; and pressures from the ANC found a ready response from a majority within *Convergència* and among many *Unió* members. While reconsideration was being urged by some of the (big) business interests close to CiU, no alternative other than the discredited one of a "fiscal pact" was being posed from within. Certainly, *soberanismo* in Catalonia still faced an up-hill struggle by the start of 2015. There were tensions between *Convergència* and *Esquerra*, not to mention the wider range of pro-sovereignty forces, partly as a result of the decision of Artur Mas to accept a Spanish ban on the referendum on independence which these forces had been organizing for November 9, 2014.[17] Instead a more informal, unofficial consultation was held, in which it was largely the supporters of independence who took part.[18] There was also evidence of the pro-independence viewpoint losing ground in Catalonia by 2015–16.[19] And there were also indications that the new Spanish anti-establishment party, *Podemos*, which supported a Catalan "right to decide" but opposed separatism, would provide a formidable challenge to pro-independence parties in the future, both here and in the Basque Country.[20] Nevertheless, the *soberanista* challenge continued to be maintained, bolstered by the pact between *Convergència* and *Esquerra* ahead of the Catalan elections of September 2015 and encouraged by the loss of the PP's absolute majority and the difficulties surrounding the establishment of a stable Spanish government following the general elections of December 2015 and June 2016. Yet party responses to these developments affecting Spain's own governance showed *Convergencia*, as it contemplated its own "refoundation" in July 2016, and even more clearly the PNV, to be still keen to have an option on negotiation with the Spanish parties, even as rank and file pressures in the Catalan party were forcing the leadership around Mas to retain the *independentista* definition for the refounded party in preference to the more ambiguous term *soberanista*.[21]

Notes

1 This chapter is based on research undertaken as part of a project on "The Dynamics of Nationalist Evolution in Contemporary Spain," funded by the Economic and Social Research Council, UK (ES/J007854/1). It draws upon scores of personal interviews with Basque and Catalan political representatives in 2012–14. The author gratefully acknowledges feedback on an earlier draft from Andrew Dowling (2013) and Caroline Gray.

2 Jon Josu Imaz, "No imponer, no impedir," *El Correo*, July 15, 2007.

3 Interviews with Andoni Ortuzar and Iñaki Goikoetxeta, PNV, April 2014.

4 Catalanism is noted for diverse ideological currents but invariably involves demands for political and cultural recognition of Catalonia's distinctiveness and regards the territory as a fundamental framework for political action.

5 *El País*, 24 June, 2006.

6 "La ola nacionalista agita Cataluña," *El País*, September 16, 2007; "Mas defiende el derecho a decidir como base para refundar el catalanismo," *El* País, November 21, 2007; "Convergència quiere que Cataluña sea una nación libre y soberana," *El País*, July 13, 2008; "Otra vuelta de la tuerca," *El País*, editorial, July 14, 2008.

7 Oriol Pujol abandoned this post in March 2013 after being charged with political corruption offences. This was one of several cases involving members of the Pujol family, the biggest political fallout coming after the former President of the Generalitat, Jordi Pujol, announced in July 2014 that he himself was under investigation for tax offences.

8 Interviews with Andoni Ortuzar, Iñaki Goikoetxeta, Emilio Olabarria, PNV, April 2014.

9 Interviews with Ander Gurrutxaga, University of the Basque Country, April 2013, and Txema Montero, political analyst, April 2014.

10 Conversation with Iñaki Zabaleta, University of the Basque Country, April 2014.

11 Interviews with Joseba Egibar and Juan José Ibarretxe, PNV, April 2014.

12 *Centre d'Estudis d'Opinió* data, reported in *El País*, September 13, 2009, and November 6, 2010.

13 Interview with Laura Mintegi, Bildu, April 2014.

14 Interviews with Muriel Casals and Jordi Gabaró, ANC, February 2014.

15 Miley (2007, 2013) is critical of the work of Conversi (1997) and Guibernau (1999) for understating the role played by nationalist elites. Crameri (2014) and Dowling (2014) take the debate beyond the confines of nationalism. The former sees the process as pre-eminently "bottom-up" whereas the latter depicts a complex interaction, noting the important role played by cultural elites in the Catalan pro-independence movement.

16 One recent example is the emulation of the ANC's *Via Catalana* human chain in support of independence by the Basque *soberanista* platform *Guru Esku Dago* (It is in our hands) in June 2014: an attempt to go beyond the politically exclusive initiatives of the past. At the institutional level, the Basque and Catalan premiers Íñigo Urkullu and Artur Mas announced an intention to work together against what they viewed as a "growing recentralization" of the Spanish state under Mariano Rajoy ("Urkullu y Mas harán frente juntos al proceso recentralizador de Rajoy," *El País*, December 28, 2014).

17 "El frente soberanista exhibe su división en el Parlamento catalán." *El País*, October 15, 2014.

18 Of the 2.3 million Catalans who took part, 81% voted for independence (*El País*, December 1, 2014).

19 According to surveys by the *Centre d'Estudis d'Opinió* (CEO), funded by the Catalan government, public support for an independent state in Catalonia was highest in 2013–14, reaching a peak of 48.5% in November 2013. By March 2016 it stood at 38.5%. See "Baròmetro d'Opinió Política. 1ª onada 2016," at http://www.ceo.gencat.cat, accessed 9 June 2016. Support for independence in Euskadi, which had reached 37% in 2013, was also falling by this time: a Euskobarómetro survey published in April 2016 found 24% of Basques wanting independence while larger cohorts preferred either federalism or the existing system of autonomy. See "Euskobarómetro. Enero 2016," at http://www.ehu.eus/euskobarometro, accessed June 9, 2016, and *El País*, April 8, 2016.

20 In fact, the platform identified with Podemos, *Catalunya Sí que es Pot*, came a disappointing fourth in the Catalan election of September 2015, winning 11 of the 135 seats, but an equivalent alliance, *En Comú Podem*, won in Catalonia in the Spanish general elections of 2015–16. In the Basque Country, a Podemos-led alliance came third in its first regional election, in September 2016, behind the PNV and Bildu.

21 The decision to refound *Convergència* was strongly influenced by a desire to dissociate the party from a succession of corruption scandals associated with CDC funding and the Pujol family. The party presided over by Mas adopted the name *Partit Demòcrata Català* on 10 July 2016, after delegates rejected other names proposed by the leadership. Subsequent judicial challenges led this to be changed to *Partit Demòcrata Europeu Català* (PDeCat). For reports on the congress, see *La Vanguardia*, *El País* and *El Periódico*, 7–11 July 2016. For analysis of competing internal party currents within CDC and the PNV, which were again in evidence at this refoundation congress, see Gillespie 2016.

Works cited

Barberà Aresté, Oscar. 2011. *Alianzas políticas, relaciones de poder y cambio organizativo: el caso de Unió Democràtica de Catalunya (1978–2003)*. Madrid: Centro de Investigaciones Sociológicas.

Barberà, Òscar and Astrid Barrio. 2006. "Convergència i Unió from Stability to Decline." In *Autonomist Parties in Europe: Identity Politics and the Revival of the Territorial Cleavage*, edited by Lieven De Winter, Margarita Gómez-Reino and Peter Lynch, vol. 1, 101–141. Barcelona: Institut de Ciències Polítiques i Socials.

Casals, Muriel. 2014. Interview with the author, February 12.

Conversi, Daniele. 1997. *The Basques, the Catalans, and Spain: Alternative Routes to Nationalist Mobilisation*. London: Hurst.

Crameri, Kathryn. 2014. *"Goodbye, Spain?" The Question of Independence for Catalonia*. Eastbourne: Sussex Academic Press.

Culla, Joan B. 2013. *Esquerra Republicana de Catalunya 1931–2012: Una història política*. Barcelona: La Campana.

de Pablo, Santiago and Ludger Mees. 2005. *El péndulo patriótico: Historia del Partido Nacionalista Vasco (1895–2005)*. Barcelona: Crítica.

Díez Medrano, Juan. 1995. *Divided Nations: Class, Politics and Nationalism in the Basque Country and Catalonia*. New York: Cornell University Press.

Dowling, Andrew. 2013. *Catalonia since the Spanish Civil War: Reconstructing the Nation*. Eastbourne: Sussex Academic Press.

———. 2014. "Accounting for the Turn towards Secession in Catalonia." *International Journal of Iberian Studies* 27 (2–3): 219–234.

Egibar, Joseba. 2014. Interview with the author, April 8.

Gabaró, Jordi. 2014. Interview with the author, February 12.

Gillespie, Richard. 2015. "Between Accommodation and Contestation: The Political Evolution of Basque and Catalan Nationalism." *Nationalism and Ethnic Politics* 21 (1): 3–23.

———. 2016. "The Contrasting Fortunes of Pro-Sovereignty Currents in Basque and Catalan Nationalist Parties: PNV and CDC Compared." *Territory, Politics, Governance*. First published online 14 September, at: www.tandfonline.com/doi/full/10.1080/21622671.2016.1212732

Goikoetxeta, Iñaki. 2014. Interview with the author, April 10.

Goikoetxea, Jule. 2013. "Nationalism and Democracy in the Basque Country (1979–2012)." *Ethnopolitics* 12 (3): 268–289.

Gray, Caroline M. 2014. "Smoke and Mirrors: How Regional Finances Complicate Spanish Catalan Relations." *International Journal of Iberian Studies* 27 (1): 21–42.

Guibernau, Montserrat. 1999. *Nations without States: Political Communities in a Global Age*. Oxford: Polity Press.

———. 2004. *Catalan Nationalism: Francoism, Transition and Democracy*. London: Routledge.

Gurrutxaga, Ander. 2013. Interview with the author, April 11.

Ibarra Güell, Pedro. 2011. "Political Institutions in Hegoalde." In *Basque Political Systems*, edited by Pedro Ibarra Güell and Xabier Irujo Ametzaga, 33–51. Reno, NV: Centre for Basque Studies/ University of Nevada.

Ibarretxe, Juan José. 2014. Interview with the author, April 8.

Imaz, Jon Josu. 2007. "No imponer, no impedir." *El Correo* (Bilbao), July 15.

Keating, Michael and Zoe Bray. 2006. "Renegotiating Sovereignty: Basque Nationalism and the Rise and Fall of the Ibarretxe Plan." *Ethnopolitics* 5 (4): 347–364.

Lucas, Manel. 2004. *ERC. La llarga marxa: 1977–2004. De la il·legalitat al govern.* Barcelona: Columna.

Mees, Ludger. 2009. "Visión y gestión: el nacionalismo vasco democrático 1998–2009." In *¿Crisis? ¿Qué crisis? España en busca de su camino*, edited by Walther L. Bernecker, Diego Iñiguez Hernández, and Günther Maidhold, 161–205. Madrid and Frankfurt: Iberoamericana/Vervuert.

Miley, Thomas Jeffrey. 2007. "Against the Thesis of the 'Civic Nation': The Case of Catalonia in Contemporary Spain." *Nationalism and Ethnic Politics* 13 (1): 1–37.

———. 2013. "Blocked Articulation and Nationalist Hegemony in Catalonia." *Regional and Federal Studies* 23 (1): 7–26.

Mintegi, Laura. 2014. Interview with the author, April 7.

Montero, Txema. 2014. Interview with the author, April 9.

Muro, Diego. 2009. "Territorial Accommodation, Party Politics, and Statute Reform in Spain." *South European Society and Politics* 14 (4): 453–468.

Olabarria, Emilio, 2014. Interview with the author, April 10.

Orte, Andreu and Alex Wilson. 2009. "Multi-level Coalitions and Statute Reform in Spain." *Regional and Federal Studies* 19 (3): 415–436.

Ortuzar, Andoni. 2014. Interview with the author, April 10.

Payne, Stanley. 1971. "Catalan and Basque Nationalism." *Journal of Contemporary History* 6: 15–51.

Pérez-Nievas, Santiago. 2006. "The Partido Nacionalista Vasco: Redefining Political Goals at the Turn of the Century." In *Autonomist Parties in Europe: Identity Politics and the Revival of the Territorial Cleavage*, edited by Lieven De Winter, Margarita Gómez-Reino, and Peter Lynch, vol. 1, 31–63. Barcelona: Institut de Ciències Polítiques i Socials.

42

GOING GLOBAL

The international journey of Basque culture and literature[1]

Mari Jose Olaziregi

"A Basque map of the world"

One of the international bestsellers about Basques, *The Basque History of the World* (1999) by the American journalist and writer Mark Kurlansky, recalls a well-known joke about *bilbainos* and their excessive pride. "According to a popular Bilbao joke, a *bilbaino* walks into a store and asks for a 'World map of Bilbao.' The shop owner unflinchingly answers, 'Left bank or right?'" (Kurlansky 1999, 4). I do not know whether Basques have ever thought of themselves as being at the center of the world or believed the world to revolve around them, but among the ways in which Basque culture has projected itself onto the world stage, few initiatives have had such international (or profitable?) repercussions as the inauguration of the Guggenheim Museum Bilbao on October 18, 1997. The Bilbao Guggenheim Museum is the best example of the fact that the cultural policies favored by Basque nationalist governments have also been influenced by the dominant market logic in the new world scenario. A desire to regenerate the great Basque metropolis, Bilbao, and transform it into a city geared toward services that would make it attractive to tourists led Basque politicians to "fall for" the seductive charm of Thomas Krens (Zulaika 1997, 11). Yet this desire was also based on locating Bilbao "within the global culture of travel and consumerism, bridging transatlantic distances, linking New York with Bilbao, and thereby facilitating traffic in modern art, museum franchises, tourism, and reformulated urban images" (Douglass and Zulaika 2007, 344). It was precisely this visibility and profitability that justified the major local investment underpinning the project: the creation of an architectural landmark, a masterpiece, whose artistic attraction was unquestionable and that helped to put the Basque Country on the world map for a reason other than its so-called "troubles" (the terrorism of ETA). Kurlansky (1999, 299) mentions the fact that 85% of published news items about Basques in the last decades of the twentieth century in the United States referred to the terrorism problem. The data concerning the appeal and profitability of what has been termed the first global museum are beyond any doubt: it had a million visitors in 2012, and the museum is now one of the world's top-ranked culture infrastructures for self-financing.

In fact, the lure of this world-famous museum has guided the Basque government's international publicity campaigns in recent years (see www.euskadi.net/turismo). The successful refrain "Zatoz eta konta ezazu / Ven y cuéntalo" in the late 1990s gave way to the slogan "Euskadi, atsegin handiz / Euskadi, con mucho gusto" in the early 2000s, in which an image of the museum was combined with that of a dolmen, representing both modernity and tradition. Later there were slogans such as "Euskadi, sekulako hiria / Euskadi, un país increíble," with a clearly dreamlike quality, and the sensual "Euskadi, goza ezazu / Euskadi, saboréala," with an obvious allusion to the Basque Country's renowned cuisine. Meanwhile, the "Euskadi, Basque Country" brand, unveiled by the Basque government in June 2013, seeks to showcase the positive values associated with the Basque Country, with the eventual aim of reactivating the economy and creating employment. The advertisement that heads the campaign shows a Basque rowing boat with a mixed male and female crew and, with each stroke of the oars, an off-screen voice mentions economic data about the Basque Autonomous Community, including its per capita income, the third highest in the EU behind Luxembourg and Holland. The brand is associated with a country whose economic and social indicators (with a high level of university graduates in the sciences and technology and a leading position in human development rankings) distance it from the serious crisis in the Spanish economy. The strength and coordination of the rowing crew in the advertisement, together with the typography used for the logo of the Basque Country brand considered typical of Basque writing, symbolize values traditionally associated with the Basque collectivity such as *indarra* [strength, force] and *sendotasuna* [physical prowess, strength of character]. These were also key elements in the successful image and positive reputation of Basque emigrants in the Americas as hard workers (Douglass and Bilbao 1975, 407–409). The advertisement states that, "we are there to help you, in seventy countries, to achieve your goals" and displays a crew that is rowing along with us, a crew that moves forward, looking toward the future, as rowers do in traditional Basque regattas. This is a team, a Basque collectivity, which is presented as traditionally accustomed to collaborating in communal projects, a form of *auzolan*, or the system that is supposedly at the root of Basque cooperativism (Douglass and Zulaika 2007, 335), a term that is still fully applicable today as one can see in the strategic agenda of the current Basque government's Department of Education, Language Policy, and Culture, which termed its cultural plan for 2014–15 "Kultura Auzolanean" (see kulturauzolanean.net/eu).

We can thus see that the internationalization strategy of the Basque government, with its "Euskadi, Basque Country" brand, clearly differs from that used by the Spanish government for decades, in which, following Elena Delgado's diagnosis, culture has been the main exportable asset and the principal element of national cohesion (Delgado 2014, 150). This official Spanish culture has not been understood as an expression of diverse, complex, and contradictory social realities (Delgado 2014, 102), but has instead functioned as a kind of "glue" (Delgado 2014), and has been based "on the 'myth of the universal language' and the resulting assumption that, through Spanish, the culture transmitted in that language enjoys a worldwide projection" (Delgado 2014, 85). The dissolving of cultural specificity into the universal has made the heterogeneity of the diverse cultures in the Spanish state invisible. This is the case of Basque-speaking culture, whose language, Euskara, is currently spoken by almost a million people on both sides of the Pyrenees. The newly granted co-official status of Euskara in the Peninsular Basque Country, granted in 1982 in the Basque Autonomous Community and in 1986 in the Basque-speaking areas of the Foral Community of Navarre, as well as its compulsory introduction into the school curriculum in these same communities, has meant that, thanks to language policies in the Basque Country as a whole, there are at present 318,000 more Basque speakers than there were thirty years ago, some 200,000 of whom are the product of this educational system. The highest levels of bilingualism – 73% to be precise – are to be found among those aged under twenty-five. Even allowing for the fact that the use of Euskara has grown, above all, in formal settings and that it is supported by the population of the BAC (in which 82.3% of people choose it as the main language for the schooling of their children), its use in less formal and family settings is one of the most important challenges the language must face in the future (see *V. Inkesta Soziologikoa*, 2011). Nonetheless, these figures make for an optimistic reading of the situation and dispel the myth that the language is disappearing. In fact, if we follow the logic of David Crystal in his well-known book, *The Language Revolution*, Basque meets the criteria he considers necessary to ensure survival or, at the very least, to avoid joining the list of endangered languages: the Basque language has a number of speakers that is considerable and clearly well over 100,000; it has a political infrastructure that, at least in the Spanish Basque Country, defends, subsidizes and legislates measures for its promotion and standardization; it has a significant television and media presence; and, above all, it is clear that, for many Basque speakers, or *euskaldunak*, the Basque language is their most essential mark of identity (Crystal 2004). The positive figures about the recovery of the Basque language in the Spanish Basque Country and the worrying decrease of Basque speakers in the French Basque Country, where the Basque language has no official status, serve as a basis for demanding, as the current Basque government has just done through its *Euskararen Agenda Estrategikoa, 2013–2016*[2] [Strategic Agenda for Euskara], active policies in favor of the language. As regards its international projection, there are objectives that seek to encourage collaboration with institutions located not just in the Basque Country but in the wider Iberian framework, as well as collaboration with the *Agencia Vasca de Cooperación para el Desarrollo*. The creation of the Unesco Chair of World Language Heritage at the UPV/EHU (University of the Basque Country) in 2010, and the agreements between the UPV/EHU and Latin American universities to offer graduate studies on language planning and policy (University of the Basque Country 2013), among other things, are similarly important steps in a process of linguistic cooperation intended to preserve minoritized and threatened languages. As we can see, then, the cultural and political logic that governs the international projection of the Basque language inevitably differs from that regarding the Spanish language. Words and phrases such as "linguistic rights," "preservation," "aid," and "cooperation," as noted in the aforementioned strategic agenda, call for a place in the world for minoritized languages such as Basque.

Basque language and literature: facts and figures

The book of poems, *Linguae Vasconum Primitiae* (1545), by Bernard Etxepare, marks the beginning of Basque Literature. As Arcocha-Scarcia and Oyharçabal (2012) point out, it is a collection of poems whose paratext already makes clear the international ambition of the poet: the use of Latin for the title and the declaration that it is a work of *primitiae*, first fruits, support this evaluation. Encouraged by the benefits that he saw in the invention of the printing press for the diffusion of a small literature like ours, Etxepare exhorted, "Euskara, jalgi hadi mundura!" [Basque language, set out into the world!], declaring his strong desire that the Basque language should hold a place in the Republic of Letters. Thus, poetry not only became the founding genre of Basque literature, but also the genre that would lead to the establishment of Basque literature, around 1950, as an autonomous activity within Basque society (Olaziregi 2012, 152).

Bernard Etxepare's verses have inspired public institutions such as the Instituto Vasco Etxepare/Etxepare Euskal Institutua/Etxepare Basque Institute (see www.etxepare.eus), which was created by the Basque government in 2007 and has been active since 2010, with the goal of promoting and disseminating Basque language and culture internationally. When it comes to the task of promoting the Basque language, the Etxepare Basque Institute encourages spaces of interaction with other languages and communities, and sets up international programs to better understand and research the Basque language and culture. This work involves a network of university lecturers, provides grants for students on these courses, offers chairs of Basque

Studies to visiting professors, and trains instructors in the Basque language. Furthermore, the Institute participates in top-level international language fairs, such as Expolangues in Paris or the Language Show in London, and organizes numerous events related to the language, approaching and informing foreign institutions and individuals about the Basque language.

The Etxepare Basque Institute now has agreements with forty international universities in seventeen countries (including twelve in the Americas, twenty-three in Europe, and one in Asia) and there are twenty-eight Basque language and culture lecturers at universities all over the world. Approximately 2,800 students were enrolled in Basque language and culture courses in the 2013–2014 academic year. Furthermore, the Etxepare Basque Institute has to date created eight international university chairs, all of which undertake annual academic programs in Basque Studies, mainly at postgraduate level. Research fields such as Basque Literature and Linguistics (the Bernardo Atxaga Chair at the Graduate Center of the City University of New York; the Jean Haritschelhar Chair at the Université Bordeaux-Montaigne), Basque Studies (the Koldo Mitxelena Chair at the University of Chicago), Basque Arts (the Eduardo Chillida Chair at the Goethe University of Frankfurt), Basque Politics (the Manuel de Irujo Chair at the University of Liverpool, UK), and the Basque Diaspora (the Jon Bilbao Chair at the Center for Basque Studies, University of Nevada, Reno, and the Eloise Garmendia Chair at Boise State University) and Basque Cultural Studies (the William Douglass Chair at the University of Massachusetts, Amherst) are those that have, to date, been covered by these agreements.

Literary translation is another essential dimension of the Institute's work and as such it has multilingual (Basque, Spanish, French, and English) publications on cultural topics both in book form and available online. On average, between 2011 and 2014, twenty-two literary works a year were awarded grants for translation from Basque into other languages by the Etxepare Institute (with an average expenditure of 40,000 euros per year). As stated previously, literature written in the Basque language began to establish itself from the mid-twentieth century onward (Olaziregi 2012, Preface), a process that involved, among its aims, gaining cultural prestige by means of translation into majority languages. Pascale Casanova argues that translation, beyond being a form of naturalization (in the sense that it implies a change of nationality), entails *littérarisation* or becoming literary – building up one's literary capital – before legitimating institutions. And in a market in which intellectual and publishing logics have grown apart, as the commercial model takes over, it is clear from the outset than an author who already writes in a "majority" language can avoid having to be culturally "validated" by translation when competing for a place in the world rankings (Casanova 2004, 63–163). For this reason, translations are much less common in literary production in the United States or the United Kingdom, where they account for approximately 3% of literary production. Indeed, this low figure compares starkly with the 25% of publishing output in the Basque language, which equates to 1,500 new titles annually. Indeed, the central place of translations in the Basque literary system is proof of its weakness and relatively short life to date.

The Basque literary scene, which is occupied by artists who write not only in the autochthonous language but also in others such as Spanish in the Peninsular zone and French in the continental zone, has led experts such as Jesús María Lasagabaster to speak of "Basque literatures" (Lasagabaster 2002). Moreover, this plurilingual and plurisystemic reality has become an interesting focus of current Basque literary historiographical debate (Manterola 2014, 40–43; Olaziregi 2012); this debate has also dominated current Spanish literary historiography in its attempts to overcome its monolithic vision (Cabo Aseguinolaza 2012, 532–545). Publications by the research group led by Fernando Cabo Aseguinolaza (see Abuín and Tarrío 2004) have underlined the need to apply concepts such as Dionýz Ďurišin's "interliterary communities" to the analysis of the relationships between the various literary systems which coexist in the Iberian context. As Arturo Casas maintains, "The geocultural Iberian space could be stud-ied as an example of a (macro)polysystem, understood [. . .] as a group of national literatures that are historically linked and maintain among themselves a series of hierarchical relations and repertory-related fluxes or interferences" (quoted by Resina 2013, 12). Indeed, recent theses such as those of Domínguez (2010) and Manterola (2014) have analyzed, on the basis of Ďurišin's specific interliterary concept, translation trends in Peninsular children's literature and Basque literature, respectively. There is, moreover, an interesting reflection on the need to apply Ďurišin's concept to the analysis of relationships between the different literary systems that exist in Catalonia (Martí 2013, 68).

The data reported by Hooft Comajuncosas (2004) are quite remarkable and encourage reflection on the hierarchical relationships and interferences among the various literatures of the Iberian sphere. Hooft Comajuncosas describes the Spanish intercultural space from 1990 to 1998 as very unbalanced as a result of the dominance of the Spanish language over other Iberian languages as a vehicle for translating novels, stories, and poetry written originally in Catalan, Galician, and Basque; in sum, Spanish served as the *lingua franca* during this time. The statistics do not change significantly for the period from 1999 to 2003: the Catalan, Gali-cian, and Basque systems continued translating a large percentage of their works into Spanish. However, the extremely low number of works that are translated from Spanish into the other languages of the Spanish state is particularly striking. While 317 works written in Basque, Catalan, and Galician were translated into Spanish from 1999 to 2003, only 20 were translated from Spanish into the minority languages.

When it comes to translation trends in Basque literature, the abovementioned thesis by Eli Manterola (2014) offers interesting new data. With a total of 480 titles translated into thirty-eight languages up to 2010, Basque literature written in the Basque language offers a highly uneven reality with regard to the target languages and the global impact of the 161 Basque-language authors translated. In effect, Manterola confirms the leading role played by transla-tions into Spanish, as these translations make up almost half of the entire production (2014, 241), which is a clear example of the dependency of the Basque literary system on its Spanish counterpart. Catalan and English are the next most popular target languages, followed by Galician. It is, though, debatable whether in the case of translation into Spanish we can speak in terms of "exportation," given that the target readership is largely located within the origi-nal territory and culture. Only 44.66% of the books analyzed were translated directly from Euskara, and both self-translation (into Spanish) and allographic translation are similar in percentage terms (Manterola 2014, 242). As regards translated works by author, there is a sig-nificant distance between Bernardo Atxaga and other Basque authors. Thirty-five of Atxaga's works have been translated into thirty-one languages, and *Obabakoak* (1988) undoubtedly marked the beginning of a new era inasmuch as it encouraged a notable quantitative leap in the number of Basque literary works that were translated (245 in the 1990s; see Manterola 2014, 199). I am referring here to the most translated Basque-language work ever (Olaziregi 2005), a work that gave its author global visibility and an assured place in both the Basque and Spanish literary systems, mostly as a result of his winning Spain's National Prize for Narra-tive in 1989. Atxaga's central position in the current Basque literary system has paralleled his canonization in the potential Iberian interliterary system. One only need recall, following the argument of Mario Santana (2009), that of the 121 narrative books awarded the Critics' Prize since 1976 in Spain, Atxaga's *The Accordionist's Son* was the first to be translated into all the languages of the Spanish state. This is an interesting state of affairs, given that the prize itself was established to encourage relations among the literatures of the four languages of the Span-ish state. For my part, I would contend that, even though six Basque authors have won this award (Unai Elorriaga, Mariasun Landa, Anjel Lertxundi, Kirmen Uribe, and Josu Zabaleta), only Kirmen Uribe's international career has benefited from winning the prize in a comparable way to that of Atxaga, in that his *Bilbao-NY-Bilbao* (2008) has been translated, at present, into fourteen languages, while his more recent *Mussche* (2012) has already been translated into six languages, including Japanese and Chinese.

Basque studies beyond the Iberian Peninsula: present and future

The tendencies noted previously in areas such as language policy, cultural promotion, and literary translation are again visible in the field of teaching and research in the international university framework, where the political and legal structure of the administrations that make up the Basque Country as a whole condition its expansion. Except for the William Douglass Center for Basque Studies at the University of Nevada, Reno, in the United States, founded (as the Basque Studies Program) in 1967 (www.basque.unr.edu), the remaining Basque Studies centers are located in Basque-speaking territories, such as IKER (Centre de recherche sur la langue et les textes basques; UMR 5478), which is based in Baiona (Bayonne) in the Department of the Atlantic Pyrenees, Aquitaine, France. Moreover, a glance at the cartography of the international teaching of Basque Studies outside Basque-speaking territory reveals that, to date, only five universities in Spain (Salamanca, Complutense, UNED, the Universitat Autònoma de Barcelona, and the Universitat de Barcelona) and two in France (the Université de Bordeaux-Montaigne and Université de Pau et des Pays de l'Adour) have had tenured professors in Basque Studies. To these one should add the University of Liverpool, which has decided to create the first permanent Basque Studies position in the United Kingdom. Thereafter, while we possess some data on more than forty professors who teach subjects that incorporate some element of Basque Studies, in truth there is at present no up-to-date information on the presence of tenured professors in foreign universities. This outlook unquestionably places Basque Studies at the tail end of the international expansion in foreign university teaching of and research into all the official languages within the Iberian framework. The question of how Catalan Studies came to be implemented at an international level, in this regard, is truly noteworthy. According to the data of the Ramon Llull Institute's Academic Office, 157 universities all over the world offer courses in Catalan Studies, 88 of which receive financial aid from the Ramon Llull Institute and 69 of which do not.

The Spanish university system, even following its progressive revamp of curricula after fully implementing the Bologna Plan in 2010, continues to be chained to a philological tradition that centers some of its procedural focus on comparative (Spanish) philology, textual criticism, and publication of edited texts. In short, it is a tradition that has not disappeared from the nomenclature of university departments, whose curricula are still being only very slowly or gradually updated, and this thanks in part to the influence of a renovating breath of fresh air that cultural studies, gender studies, and postcolonial studies, among others, have brought to Hispanism.

The extremely limited space afforded to the study of various Iberian languages and literatures in undergraduate and graduate programs in Spanish universities clearly contrasts with the enthusiastic reception these studies have enjoyed outside Spain's borders. The numbers speak for themselves. If, for example, we take the case of Basque Studies, in the Iberian sphere this can only be studied, as noted previously, in five universities outside the Peninsular Basque Country, and in four of them (Complutense, UNED, Universitat de Barcelona, and the Universitat Autònoma de Barcelona) the Etxepare Basque Institute has lectureships to reinforce or complement those positions. The conclusions are obvious: As regards the situation of teaching Basque language and culture at a university level within the Spanish system, interest is not very high and is mainly driven by the Basque autonomous government; that is, it is not widely considered an area of "state" study. But the same could also be said of Galician or Catalan studies within the Spanish university system.

For its part, Galician Studies, sponsored by the Xunta of Galicia, exists in seven universities outside Galicia, and Catalan Studies are offered in ten universities outside the Catalan-speaking territories, two of them subsidized by the Institut Ramon Llull. One should clarify, moreover, that currently there is no undergraduate or graduate degree that covers Iberian Studies as a whole within the Spanish sphere; and that any undergraduate or graduate degree related to any of the cultures or official languages of the Spanish state are mainly studied in their respective autonomous communities. Master's programs such as the "Máster Universitario en Literaturas Hispánicas (Catalana, Gallega, y Vasca) en el Contexto Europeo," which has been offered by the UNED since the 2007–2008 academic year, are very rare.

This outlook clashes with the renovation that traditional Hispanism has been experiencing in recent years at the international level thanks to the gradual introduction of what is called for by the new discipline of Iberian Studies, a discipline whose novelty centers on "its intrinsic relationality and its reorganization of monolingual fields based on nation-states and their postcolonial extensions into a Peninsular plurality of cultures and languages pre-existing and coexisting with the official cultures of the state" (Resina 2013, vii), a "subfield of comparative studies" (Resina 2013, 11) that, in contrast to national philologies or national literatures, does "not serve a political entity or legitimize a state" (Resina 2013, 14). Although its epicenter is to be found in American universities such as those pointed out by Santana (2013, 55), and the work in particular of Joan Ramon Resina (2008, 2013) has been fundamental in the creation of a theoretical framework for this new direction, it is also true to say that the criticism at the root of this new discipline – specifically, that of the obsolete nature of Hispanism in general and, more particularly, of a mode of Spanish literary historiography that was dominant until quite recently – has been embraced in important recent publications such as those by Epps and Fernández Cifuentes (2005), Faber (2008), and Moraña (2005), to mention just a few. All of these welcome a new approach that would overcome the monolingual concept of the Spanish state "by delving into either the place of the so-called peripheral languages and literatures (Catalan, Galician, and Basque) or the place of emigrants and exiles in Spanish literary history" (Epps and Fernández Cifuentes 2005, 20). Moreover, current projects such as the cultural history of Spanish literatures headed by Jo Labanyi and Elena Delgado for Polity Press, with the collaboration of Kirsty Hooper, Helena Buffery, and Mari José Olaziregi, are moving in the same direction by incorporating, in a general reflection on the transformation of Peninsular literatures, the contributions of these literatures not just as a mere appendix to the study of literature written in Spanish, but as a dialogue with the latter, analyzing the interactions among them. In fact, it is interesting to note that some scholars have recently underlined this objective in their reflections on interactions among the Iberian literatures by mentioning it right at the beginning of their publications, in the paratexts (see Lafarga et al. 2009).

The aforementioned studies and methodological proposals are creating the basis for Iberian Studies to be constructed as a clear epistemic paradigm, as a field of study that rigorously examines the relationships, convergences, tensions, exchanges, dependencies, translation flows, and so on of the various literatures in this context. Reviewing and encouraging creative or research anthologies that incorporate the contributions of each Peninsular literature, fostering the teaching of and research into all the literatures involved in the Iberian sphere, and so on, are important steps in making people more aware of the multicultural reality that traditional Hispanism has overlooked. Yet such initiatives should also be followed by plans of action that encourage academic dialogue among experts in the different Peninsular literatures.

Here we find some recently formed groups in the Peninsula such as the LIJMI (Red Temática "Las Literaturas Infantiles y Juveniles en el Marco Ibérico e Iberoamericano"), founded at the University of Santiago de Compostela in 2004; and the "Historical Memory and Iberian Literature" researchers network, which since 2011 has organized three international seminars on the topic.

Yet how should one approach the study of the interferences and interactions among the different languages in the Iberian sphere? What is the methodology to do so, and how can we proceed in our analysis of these languages? Does the adjective "Iberian" imply comparing all the different literatures at the same time? How might we implement these studies within the current set-up of university departments of Hispanic Studies? Mario Santana has lucidly outlined the challenges posed by this new paradigm of Iberian Studies when it comes to being incorporated into university curricula (Santana 2013). The three areas that, in his opinion, need developing and updating are, in order of importance: 1) reconfiguring what have come to be understood as "national literatures," with a concomitant questioning of the monolingualism with which such literatures have been addressed, and "rethink[ing] the nature of the interactions among producers and consumers of literature across linguistic and political boundaries" (Santana 2013, 55); 2) educating professors of Iberian literature in more than one Peninsular language, an education that demands a questioning of the ideology of monolingualism, or "the notion that everything can be reinscribed and eventually done exclusively in one dominant language" (Santana 2013, 58); and 3) a critical review of the discipline.

The difficulty, obviously, surrounds the real options that a minoritized language such as Euskara has, not just in making itself heard in the World Republic of Letters, but also in establishing itself as one of the literatures that are part of a truly comparative framework that overcomes the ideological-theoretical Hispano-centrism that has reigned among Spanish scholars. One should recall, when considering all the possibilities, that a minoritized literature has to adopt a comparatist approach. Gayatri Chakravarti Spivak's well-known advice about "resuscitating" comparative literature when she defends the need to embrace the language of the Other, and not just as a "field study" language (quoted in Domínguez 2013, 25), is crucial, even though she herself points out that such advice goes against the fact that there are few hegemonic European languages and countless languages in the Southern Hemisphere. The renovation that, for example, comparative European literature has experienced in recent years parallels the Europeanization that Europe itself experienced through the creation of political bodies such as the EU. And this same renovation is implying, in turn, the transformation of national cultures through their integration into this new body as a whole. For Domínguez, this is the root cause of the growing strategic importance of culture in the EU when he affirms that, "[l]a Comunidad contribuirá al florecimiento de las culturas de los Estados miembros, dentro del respeto de su diversidad nacional y regional, poniendo de relieve al mismo tiempo el patrimonio cultural común" (Domínguez 2013, 27). The importance of culture and creativity as guarantors of European social cohesion and economic growth has placed EU member states' intercultural promotion policies at the center of current European cultural policy. As far as European literature is concerned, in 2008 the Parliamentary Assembly of the Council of Europe approved the Document 11.527, titled "Promoting the Teaching of European Literature," which contends that knowledge of European literature contributes to the strengthening of a "European citizenry," and it therefore urges EU member states both to promote the learning of European languages in order to access works in their original languages and to foster the production of translations (Domínguez 2013, 28). This demonstrates the growing importance of translation grants in recent calls for proposals published under the Creative Europe Programme (European Commission 2013).

Moving forward: cultural networking and the internationalization of Iberian cultures

Just as the focus on those other languages and cultures should be at the center of the debate in the sphere of comparative European literature, where the linguistic and cultural diversity of Europe needs to be taken into account, so it should also be given a central role in the debate surrounding Iberian Studies at university level, as noted previously. Any promotion of this dynamic will necessarily have to include a parallel promotion of studying the different Iberian languages themselves. This is an issue that both Santana (2013, 59) and Dominic Keown, in his interesting analysis of the reality of Hispanism and Iberian Studies in Great Britain and Ireland (2013, 33–34), have pointed out, underscoring the efforts that public institutions such as the Institut Ramon Llull and the Etxepare Basque Institute have undertaken in this regard through their subsidizing of lectureships to teach the Iberian languages in the international academic context.

Yet, as mentioned already, there is no comparison when it comes to examining how the different Iberian languages are being promoted at the international level. Data on the two state languages, Spanish and Portuguese, and the ways in which those languages have been promoted for centuries, are revealing in this regard. In the Spanish case, for example, one only need consult the records of the Instituto Cervantes; tools such as the Portal del Hispanismo; calls for Spanish-language lecturers published by the Agencia Española para la Cooperación Internacional (AECID) which, in its most recent call for the 2014–2015 academic year, had 108 places for lecturers; or the many activities associated with cultural promotion on the part of cultural agencies such as Acción Cultural Española, to cite just a few. For its part, the responsibilities of the Instituto Camões differ from those of the Instituto Cervantes in that, apart from the subsidies it offers to create Centers for Portuguese Language and Culture and many other activities, there is already a network of lectureships and professorships that has, for example, 177 lecturers in universities all over the world, 14 of which are in Spain. Meanwhile, the Institut Ramon Llull manages an international global network of 88 lecturers in Catalan language and culture but, as noted previously, the discipline of Catalan studies has been implemented to an even greater extent in universities beyond Iberian borders, with 157 universities offering Catalan Studies. As regards Galician, the Secretaría Xeral de Política Lingüística of the Xunta de Galicia (regional government of Galicia's General Commission for Language Policy) is charged with the task of promoting the language internationally. It has agreements with 40 universities, resulting in a total of 29 lecturers in the Galician language worldwide. Finally, data on lectureships in Basque language and culture administered by the Etxepare Basque Institute reveal 34 agreements with universities all over the world and 28 currently active lecturers. The clear numerical differences between the levels of implementing lectureships, as well as university programs, curricular itineraries, and departments at universities all over the world, bear witness to how much the situation can vary between the different languages and cultures concerned, which is obviously reflected in the abysmal gulf in financial resources available to the institutions involved. Behind the efforts undertaken for centuries to promote and develop "universal" languages such as Spanish there has been an economic logic, as in the case of the first chair of Spanish in the United States at Harvard University, which was established, as Resina contends (2009, 47), as a result of the nineteenth-century commercial interests of New England in Latin America. To return to the themes mentioned at the outset of the article, the issues involved are thus linked to what José Luis Marzo terms a "strategic object of visualization" (cited in Delgado 2014, 101). The use or not of culture, as well as of the language that underpins it, as an internationalization strategy marks out clear differences, as noted at the beginning of this article, between the cultural policies pursued by governments such as that of the Basque

Autonomous Community and the Spanish state. One could say that the scale of authority of a given government (the number of speakers it represents, its transnational language, and so on), economic interests, and linguistic-cultural marketing coincide with one another.

Conclusions

The desire of the author of the first book published in Euskara, Bernard Etxepare, expressed in his well-known poems, "euskara, jalgi hadi mundura" [Euskara, set out into the world!], has served as a guide in this brief reflection on the logic that the internationalization of Basque language and culture has had in recent times. Although the adjective "universal" or global, in the Basque context, has been most prominently exemplified by the Guggenheim Museum in Bilbao, it is also true that the striking development and consolidation that the Basque language has experienced in recent decades has resulted, among other things, in the fact that both artistic creation and academic research undertaken in that language are at present flourishing in different contexts, including academia. The internationalization of the Basque language, whether by means of active policies encouraging translation in order to correct the asymmetries in the Basque literary system today, or of fostering Basque Studies at university level internationally, is a demand that has only been met in recent years on the part of public institutions in the Basque context. In this sense, and as regards literary research, here I have underscored the contribution currently being made by comparative specialists in the Peninsular sphere in their analysis of the interactions among the different Iberian literatures, as well as the growing importance of the new discipline of Iberian Studies in international universities. Thanks to theoretical developments such as these, and to the implementation of academic programs and positions that specialize in the diverse literatures in the Iberian context, Iberian literatures may gain, among other things, a more visible and active status than they have had to date in traditional Spanish literary historiography, in which they have been largely relegated to an anecdotal sideshow. I should perhaps end by returning to Bernard Etxepare and hoping that, in the case of the Basque language and culture, *debile principium melior fortuna sequatur* [may better fortune follow a humble beginning]. As it should.

Notes

1 Translated by Cameron J. Watson. This chapter belongs to the project IT 1047-16. A shorter version was published in *BOGA: Basque Studies Consortium Journal* 3 (1) (Olaziregi 2015).
2 http://www.erabili.com/zer_berri/berriak/dokumentuak/2014/Euskararen_Ajenda_Estrate gikoa_2014–06–24.pdf. Accessed August 15, 2014.

Works cited

Abuín González, Anxo and Anxo Tarrío Varela,, eds. 2004. *Bases metodolóxicas para una historia comparada das literaturas da península Ibérica*. Santiago de Compostela: Servicio de Publicaciones de la Universidad de Santiago de Compostela.
Arcocha-Scarcia, Aurèlie and Bernard Oyharçabal. 2012. "The Sixteenth Century: the First Fruits of Basque Literature." In *Basque Literary History*, edited by Mari Jose Olaziregi, 69–88. Reno, NV: Center for Basque Studies/University of Nevada.
Basque Government. 2013. "Basque Country Spot." *Basque Government*. Accessed September 15, 2014. https://www.youtube.com/watch?v=gcN4K5WqO3o.
Cabo Aseguinolaza, Fernando. 2012. *Historia de la literatura española. 9. El lugar de la literatura española*. Barcelona: Crítica.

Casanova, Pascale. 2004. *The World Republic of Letters*. Translated by M. B. DeBevoise. Harvard, MA: Harvard University Press.

Crystal, David. 2004. *Language Revolution*. Cambridge: Polity Press.

Delgado, Luisa Elena. 2014. *La nación singular. Fantasías de la normalidad democrática española (1996–2011)*. Madrid: Siglo XXI.

Domínguez, César, ed. 2013. *Literatura europea comparada*. Madrid: Arco/Libros.

Douglass, William A. and Jon Bilbao. 1975. *Amerikanuak. Basques in the New World*. Reno, NV: University of Nevada Press.

Douglass, William A. and Joseba Zulaika. 2007. *Basque Culture. Anthropological Perspectives*. Reno, NV: Center for Basque Studies/University of Nevada.

European Commission. 2013. "Creative Europe." Accessed September 15, 2014. http://ec.europa.eu/culture/calls/index_en.htm.

Epps, Brad and Luis Fernández Cifuentes. 2005. *Spain beyond Spain: Modernity, Literary History, and National Identity*. Lewisburg, PA: Bucknell University Press.

Faber, Sebastiaan. 2008. "Economies of Prestige: The Place of Iberian Studies in the American University." *Hispanic Research Journal* 9 (1): 7–32.

Hooft Comajuncosas, Andreu van. 2004. "¿Un espacio literario intercultural en España? El polisistema interliterario en el estado español a partir de las traducciones de las obras pertenecientes a los sistemas literarios vasco, gallego, catalán y español (1999–2003)." In *Bases metodolóxicas para una historia comparada das literaturas da península Ibérica*, edited by Abuín González and Anxo Tarrío Varela, 313–333. Santiago de Compostela: Servicio Editorial de la Universidad de Santiago de Compostela.

Keown, Dominic. 2013. "Dine with the Opposition? ¡No, gracias! Hispanism versus Iberian Studies in Great Britain and Ireland." In *Iberian Modalities*, edited by Joan Ramon Resina, 23–36. Liverpool: Liverpool University Press.

Kurlansky, Mark. 1999. *The Basque History of the World*. London: Jonathan Cape.

Lafarga, Francisco, Luis Pegenaute, and Eric Gallén, eds. 2009. *Interacciones entre las literaturas ibéricas*. Berlin: Peter Lang.

Lasagabaster, Jesús María. 2002. *Las literaturas de los vascos*. Bilbao: Universidad de Deusto.

Manterola Agirrezabalaga, Elizabete. 2014. *La literatura vasca traducida*. Berna: Peter Lang.

Martí Monterde, Antoni. 2013. "Interliterariness and the Literary Field: Catalan Literature and Literatures in Catalonia." In *Iberian Modalities*, edited by Joan Ramon Resina, 62–80. Liverpool: Liverpool University Press.

Moraña, Mabel, ed. 2005. *Ideologies of Hispanism*. Nashville, TN: Vanderbilt University Press.

Olaziregi, Mari Jose. 2005. *Waking the Hedgehog. The Literary Universe of Bernardo Atxaga*. Reno, NV: Center for Basque Studies/University of Nevada.

———. ed. 2012. *Basque Literary History*. Reno, NV: Center for Basque Studies/University of Nevada.

———. 2015. "The International Location of Basque Studies." BOGA: *Basque Studies Consortium Journal* 3 (1). http://scholarworks.boisestate.edu/boga/vol3/iss1/3.

Resina, Joan Ramon. 2009. *Del hispanismo a los estudios ibéricos. Una propuesta federativa para el ámbito cultural*. Madrid: Biblioteca Nueva.

———, ed. 2013. *Iberian Modalities*. Liverpool: Liverpool University Press.

Santana, Mario. 2009. "On Visible and Invisible Languages: Bernardo Atxaga's *Soinujolearen semea* in Translation." In *Writers in Between Languages: Minority Literatures in the Global Scene*, edited by Mari Jose Olaziregi, 213–230. Reno, NV: Center for Basque Studies/University of Nevada.

———. 2013. "Implementing Iberian Studies: Some Paradigmatic and Curricular Challenges." In *Iberian Modalities*, edited by Joan Ramon Resina, 54–61. Liverpool: Liverpool University Press.

Unesco Chair of World Language Heritage. 2010. Accessed September 15, 2013. http://www.mho-unesco-katedra.org/w/about.html

University of the Basque Country. 2013. "Master in Language Policy and Planning." Accessed September 15, 2014. http://www.ehu.es/en/web/masterpoliticaslinguisticas/aurkezpena

Zulaika, Joseba. 1997. *Crónica de una seducción. El museo Guggenheim Bilbao*. Madrid: Nerea.

43

DEMOCRACY, *INDIGNADOS*, AND THE REPUBLICAN TRADITION IN SPAIN[1]

José Luis Martí

Over the course of the current economic crisis, Spain has been the focus of much world-wide concern. The crisis is particularly acute in that country, some of the worst fallout being extremely high unemployment rates, reaching 25% in 2014. As the thirteenth-largest economy in the world and the fifth largest in Europe, Spain's turbulence has seriously affected the rest of the globe. In 2011, however, the country caught the eye of the world in a different, more positive way.

In May 2011, hundreds of thousands of citizens took to the streets of major Spanish cities to protest against cutbacks in the welfare state imposed by the Troika (International Monetary Fund, European Commission, European Central Bank) and approved by the government of President Rodríguez Zapatero. As part of the protest, thousands camped in the central city squares for several months. Some of the protesters had read *Indignez-vous*, a small pamphlet by Stéphane Hessel calling citizens to take action to resist the injustices of capitalism and defend democracy (Hessel 2011). Some began to call themselves *indignados* ("the indignant"), and the label was quickly popularized in the media. The movement also became known as *15M* in reference to the start date of the protests (May 15).

What the *indignados* were demanding was much more than a review of austerity policies: they were seeking a true democratic revolution (Serrano et al. 2014; Taibo 2011b; Viejo 2011). Dissatisfied and disappointed with Spanish democracy in general, they were outraged with politicians, political parties, and the representative institutions in particular. *No nos representan* ("they do not represent us") was their main slogan. Spain's representative institutions had, they felt, deceived and betrayed the people (Taibo 2011b; Velasco 2011). Their aim was to bring about a profound change to the democratic system, fuelled alike by outrage and hope alike (Castells 2012; Perugorria and Tejerina 2013).

The *indignados* movement had, and continues to have, an enormous impact on Spanish politics. It mobilized hundreds of thousands of citizens, significantly influenced public deliberation, created successful new parties, and is now forcing the traditional political parties to adapt their discourse to these new circumstances. Its most valuable contribution to Spanish democracy, however, was the result of what happened in the squares: protesters began to experiment with democratic revolution by themselves, spontaneously and with no support from public institutions. They organized open and innovative face-to-face deliberations, creating a grand forum for public participation and deliberation, and an excellent school of democracy and civic culture was created. Their actions constituted one of the most interesting spontaneous initiatives in participatory and deliberative democracy ever seen.

In this chapter, I interpret the *indignados'* concerns, values, and proposals, as well as their innovative actions and methods, as distinctly republican. I argue that this movement is in fact a continuation of a long tradition of republican thought that has remained very influential among scholars and intellectuals in Spain. The next section briefly summarizes the main facts of the *indignados'* protests and the evolution of the movement. In the following section, I offer a reflection on the crisis of democracy in Spain and elsewhere, necessary to understanding the scope and aims of the *indignados* movement, as well as its potential impact. This is followed by a brief survey of the long republican tradition in Spain. Finally, in the last section I return to the *indignados* movement to highlight its republican elements.

Toma la plaza: how the *indignados* occupied the city squares and the public sphere

It all started on May 15, 2011. Thousands of citizens marched through the streets of major cities in Spain. A myriad of very small social organizations including Democracia Real Ya, NoLesVotes, and Anonymous had called for the protest. The number of participants in these demonstrations was significant (50,000 in Madrid, 20,000 in Barcelona, and 10,000 in Valencia; see Castells 2012), but still a long way below some earlier protests in Spain, such as the march against the Iraq war on February 15, 2003 (1.5 million in Madrid and 700,000 in Barcelona).

The participants were moved by outrage and indignation over the effects of a crushing economic crisis that had been created by the economic and political élite (Castells 2012; see also Perugorria and Tejerina 2013). They protested against the austerity packages imposed by the Troika and approved by the Spanish government the previous year. They were deeply disappointed with politicians and political parties. They no longer trusted their representative institutions. They felt politically orphaned and unrepresented (della Porta 2012; Hughes 2011; Maeckelbergh 2012; Martí i Puig 2011; Ovejero 2013; Romanos 2016; Taibo 2011a, 2011b; Viejo 2011), and they felt they had to do something to change the system. After the demonstration, about 40 protesters decided to camp that night in front of the city hall of Madrid in Puerta del Sol, one of its central squares. The police pulled them out, and 19 were arrested.

The following evening, May 16, dozens of people returned to Puerta del Sol; others did likewise in Plaza de Catalunya in Barcelona. The idea was to occupy the square, worded in Spanish as *tomar la plaza*. Two days later the number of protesters gathered in Madrid rose to 10,000, and those in Plaza de Catalunya numbered in the hundreds. They decided to stay at least five days more, until May 22, when local elections were to take place in the country. The initiative spread to other large cities very quickly. *#tomalaplaza* and *#spanishrevolution* became popular slogans and Twitter hashtags. The idea was not only to protest, but also to take control of part of the public sphere in the form of public squares. When on the following day the National Electoral Commission in Spain declared the sit-ins illegal by electoral law, the government did not dare to order police to pull all the protesters out by force; the numbers were unexpectedly high, and the world's media were already covering the events. Pictures of big tents sheltering the crowds of young protesters in the main squares of Spain resembled recent images of the Arab Spring, especially those of Tahrir Square in Cairo just five months before. In fact, there is a connection between the two movements despite their many differences, and they link up also with later events in Portugal and Greece and the Occupy movement in the US, the UK, Canada, and other countries (Byrne 2011; Gould-Wartofsky 2015;

Meyer 2015; Milkman et al 2015; Romanos 2016). More recently, we have witnessed similar civil demonstrations in other countries, including Turkey, Brazil, and Hong Kong. In every case we find the same combination of outrage over a lack of democracy and transparency in the country's government together with the hope for change (Castells 2012; Perugorria and Tejerina 2013; Romanos 2016).

The precise demands of each movement were, of course, very different. While the Arab Spring protesters demanded more transparency, the granting of a small number of rights, and free elections, the *indignados*, and later Occupy, expressed their dissatisfaction with these same minimal conditions of democracy. Yet they all pursued the goal of a democratic revolution that would improve the democratic conditions of their respective countries.

In addition, these movements all had another significant element in common: the generalized, frequent, and highly efficient use of information and communication technologies (ICTs) and social media. ICTs were used to coordinate action, call for general support and participation, keep the public informed, and connect with other similar movements or supporters around the world. Technology became more than a tool for coordination and communication, however; it helped participants to create new networks of power, and for *indignados* and Occupy protesters it was also an essential part of their ideology and culture. Many of them shared the values and principles of free culture and the culture of the commons (Byrne 2011; Castells 2012; Fuster 2012; Gould-Wartofsky 2015; Milkman et al 2015; Monterde et al. 2015; Peña López 2013; Peña López et al. 2014; Romanos 2012, 2016; Serrano et al. 2014).

The *indignados* occupied the city squares of Spain for several months in 2011. In less than one month they had gained the respect of the public and received substantial popular support. In response to their call for a massive demonstration, on June 19 a million citizens marched through the streets of Madrid, Barcelona, and other Spanish cities. Eighty-one percent of Spanish citizens believed that the *indignados* were generally right in their claims, and 66% felt sympathetic towards the movement's methods (Castells 2012, 121).

By the end of that month, however, the *indignados* in Barcelona and other cities had been moved out by the authorities. The movement held out somewhat longer in Madrid. Several marches began in July in a number of cities and continued for hundreds of miles, with the goal of converging on Madrid. On July 23, 250,000 protesters gathered in and around the Puerta del Sol to keep the flame of the movement alive. Throughout August, Sol was cleared and reoccupied several times. Finally, on October 15, the *indignados* and Occupy coordinated their efforts and millions of people marched in approximately 900 cities around the world. Once again, hundreds of thousands of Spanish citizens took over the streets to express a wish for a profound change in Spanish democracy (for a full and detailed chronology of the movement, see Castells 2012, 248–252; see also Milkman et al. 2015).

After that day, the *indignados* movement underwent a transformation. Leaving the city squares, it spread throughout major cities to work directly in the neighborhoods on a more local and focused basis. Several other demonstrations and assemblies, some of them virtual, took place in 2012. Several campaigns and initiatives were organized, such as 15MpaRato and Democracia 4.0. Organizations that had emerged from the movement, such as Democracia Real Ya, were consolidated, and new political parties, including Podemos and Partido X, were created.

The effects of these events remain visible in Spanish politics. In the European election of June 2014, despite having been dismissed or largely ignored by the mainstream media, Podemos was the fourth most popular political party, with 8% of the vote. In the legislative elections in December 2015, Podemos was again the fourth most voted party, gathering more than 12% of the vote. And in June 2016, in the following legislative elections, they consolidated as the third most popular party, with more than 13% of the vote. We still do not know where all this will end. But the powerful impact on Spanish democracy sought by the *indignados* has already been achieved.

The crisis of (Spanish) democracy

What made the *indignados* seek such a transformation of Spanish democracy? Why did they demand a "Spanish revolution"? After the long authoritarian regime of Francisco Franco, democratic elections in Spain were held in June 1977; since then twelve other general elections have taken place. Three different political parties, one with a centrist ideology, one leftist, and the other right wing, have been in power. Six different prime ministers, two from each party, have held office. The Spanish constitution of 1978 has the honor of being by far the longest to have endured in the history of the country. Two kings have exercised symbolic powers, and despite the coup d'état attempt of February 1981, the transition to democracy in Spain has been successful and admirable in many respects. There is no doubt that democracy is fully consolidated in the country.

However, one of the two main concerns for the *indignados* in 2011 was the state of democracy in Spain, the other being the economic crisis. While deeply dissatisfied with the austerity policies of the Zapatero government the previous year, the protesters' complaint was much more general: "They do not represent us." Disappointed with politicians in general, and political parties in particular, they claimed that the Spanish parliament did not truly and effectively represent the judgments and preferences of the people. Politicians were corrupt and subordinated to the interests of the financial system and the economic élite. They had contributed to the political alienation of the Spanish people by fooling them into believing they were living in a real democracy. They claimed that political parties in Spain were simply hierarchical, opaque organizations disconnected from the real needs of the people. It is telling that the main social organization associated with the *indignados* was named Democracia Real Ya ("Real Democracy Now"). Much of the content of the manifesto promoted by this organization in 2011 was intended to incite a profound revolution within Spain's democratic institutions (DRY 2011).

If we look carefully at the concrete proposals, however, we see that the "democratic revolution" advocated by the *indignados* was in fact more reformist than revolutionary. It was a call for, among other things, a more proportionally representative electoral system; compulsory referendums on the main issues on the parliamentary agenda; initiatives to make the internal activity of political parties more open, transparent, and democratic; tougher rules against corruption, including more institutional transparency and accountability; and less control over the Internet (DRY 2014; Velasco 2011). These proposals, and many others related to the economy, formed an ambitious reformist agenda with the explicit aim of regenerating and deepening democracy, but they did not represent a revolution.

Is it plausible to say that Spanish democracy was in crisis in 2011? First, it is important to note that in some ways democracy has been in permanent crisis throughout its entire history. The institutions associated with democracy have been undergoing constant change and evolution from the very outset. Intellectuals and scholars have often singled out the deficits and flaws of their respective democratic systems. Thinkers as dissimilar as John Dewey, Carl Schmitt, and Harold Laski all proclaimed the crisis of democracy in the first half of the twentieth century. Since the 1960s, many political scientists – including Campbell, Almond, Verba, Crozier, and Huntington – observed very poor turnout rates in elections and raised the alarm about the political disinterest and disaffection of citizens in consolidated democracies. It is telling, however, that at this exact time several social movements in the US and Europe rose up to call for more direct participation, and a new model of participatory democracy emerged, defended by theorists such as Pateman, Barber, Macpherson, and Mansbridge.

In any case, it is true that political distrust and disaffection has grown in most consolidated democracies, including Spain. Electoral turnout and political interest were understandably very high during the first two decades of Spanish democracy after almost forty years of authoritarian regime and oppression. The Spanish people were very enthusiastic about their new democratic institutions. However, in the last decade they began to experience the same kind of political disaffection as their counterparts in other consolidated democracies (Montero et al. 1998; Torcal 2006; Torcal and Montero 2006).

By 2011, the distrust among Spanish voters towards government and its representative institutions skyrocketed to a higher degree than in any other Western democracy. According to results from the national polling center in Spain, the *Centro de Investigaciones Sociológicas* in June 2011, 84% of citizens believed that corruption was very widespread or quite widespread in Spain. Sixty percent considered it to be a problem of maximum importance in Spanish democracy – scoring between 8/10 and 10/10 in terms of concern. Seventy percent of Spaniards considered Spain's political situation to be bad or very bad, and only 2% felt it was good or very good. Although only 14% of Spaniards were completely dissatisfied with Spanish democracy, politicians and political parties were cited as the third most serious problem in the country, after unemployment and the economic situation in general. In line with these results, 70% of polled citizens reported that they had a positive or very positive opinion of the *indignados* protests (CIS 2011a).

The situation had not improved by October that year, when 38% of citizens polled said they had zero trust in political parties, and political parties were seen as the least trustworthy institutions in Spain. In addition, very low levels of confidence were expressed in the government and in parliament. When asked what they felt about politics, 40% of respondents said "distrust," 16% "indifference," 15% "boredom," and 13% "outrage." The most widespread positive feeling was "interest," expressed by only 9% of participants (CIS 2011b).

The *indignados* believed democracy was in crisis in Spain, and most citizens agreed. What they wanted was a more authentic form of democracy. They did not reject the idea of representative institutions, but such institutions were expected to truly represent the people and work for the common good, not for the interests of the powerful. They were required to engage in dialogue and close contact with their constituents. They had to be under the effective control of the people. The *indignados* also wanted more emphasis to be placed on public deliberation, and they intended to play a central role on it.

All these beliefs, claims, and proposals are essential to the republican view of politics and democracy, which has a long-standing tradition in the political history of Spain.

A historical overview of the republican tradition in Spain

Republicanism is a venerable strand of political thought that has its origins in the works of Aristotle and Cicero. These two thinkers had already outlined most of the distinctly republican ideas that have characterized this tradition for the past 25 centuries. First and foremost, the republican form of government – the government of the many, as opposed to monarchy or oligarchy, the government of one or the few – is characterized by the idea of mixed government, which includes some kind of proper separation and balance of powers. Another central idea is the importance of the common good as the supreme political value. The main ingredient of this common good is the central value of freedom, which is mostly understood as the absence of domination and can only be realized within the framework of the rule of law.

The idea of *vivere libero*, living free from the domination of others, articulates a holistic political vision in terms of the role of government – the establishment of laws and institutions necessary to make such freedom possible – and the role of citizens, who are required to be virtuous, active members of the community, committed to the common good and participants in the common affairs that protect their freedom through processes such as public deliberation. Citizens may only be free in a republic in which these freedoms are protected by law and the citizens themselves have ultimate control over all public decisions made by the government and democratic institutions (for a complete definition see Martí and Pettit 2010; Pettit 1997, 2014).

In modern times, republicanism is usually identified by way of the Italian Renaissance (with Machiavelli as its leading figure), the commonwealth tradition of seventeenth-century Britain (Locke and Harrington), pre-revolutionary France (Rousseau and Montesquieu), and eighteenth-century America (Madison and Jefferson). Historians, however, have largely neglected the significant role that republicanism played in Spain, especially from 1300 to 1700 (some exceptions include Alonso Baelo 2007, Gil Pujol 2005, and Villacañas 2005). Spanish republicanism in that period was exceptional, distinctive, and nearly as important for Spain as it was for Italy.

Machiavelli was certainly a central figure in rehabilitating and adapting the ideas of Aristotle and Cicero for modern times. However, Cicero's ideas had never completely disappeared from the Spanish Christian tradition: they were in fact preserved and disseminated through the work of early medieval thinkers such as Isidore of Seville (560–636). The first clear precedent of Hispanic republicanism was the fourteenth-century Franciscan friar Francesc Eiximenis (1330–1409), educated in Oxford, Paris, and Toulouse; yet his contribution to Spanish republicanism has been largely ignored (for an exception see Giner 2010). However, his book *Lo Regiment de la Cosa Publica* (*The Rule of the Commonwealth*, the twelfth book of his magnum opus *Lo crestià*), addressed to princes and higher officials and, remarkably, written in Catalan, provides us with an entire treatise on good government containing many republican ideas. He defended, for instance, the modern idea that the government and the prince should receive their power exclusively from the people, who would transfer it only through a type of covenant or agreement which was designed for their mutual advantage, and which made it clear that the essential condition of this transfer of power was that government should be concerned with promoting the common good and preserving the freedom of the people.

As in northern Italy, the explosion of republican ideology in Spain came with the Renaissance in the sixteenth century, associated with Christian Scholasticism and the School of Salamanca in particular. Its greatest representative was the Dominican friar Francisco de Vitoria (1485–1546), one of the fathers of international law (Miras Albarrán 2009; Villacañas 2005). Vitoria was deeply influenced by Aristotle and Cicero, but also by Isidore and Thomas Aquinas. Like Eiximenis, he believed that the people were directly sovereign, that their authority had been granted by God and that they could in turn delegate it to the king. Furthermore, the king's powers were also conditional on the preservation of the common good and the liberty of the people.

Before Vitoria's main works were in print, Alonso Castrillo published in Castile his *Tractado de republica* (1521), a treaty on the ideal organization of the community and its cities, which once again cited Aristotle, Cicero, and Isidore, and argued for the active role of citizens in the management of public affairs. Castrillo wrote his treatise in reaction to the commoners' revolt in Castile from 1520 to 1522 (Alonso Baelo 2007; see also Gil Pujol 2005), which started as a protest against excessive taxation by Charles I but evolved into a general movement advocating the freedom of Castilian cities, with the explicit aim of becoming free republics.

It is important to mention, on a more practical level, some remarkable and enduring republican institutions which were created in certain Castilian towns in that period, including the *Concejo Abierto*, an open council through which Castilian citizens (i.e., male property owners) were able to directly participate in the governing of their towns by gathering and deliberating in the town's main square. These *concejos* were genuine bodies of deliberation and direct participation, and were exported by the Castilians to the South American colonies, where they have endured for centuries. Some historians in fact see them as a precedent for the *indignados'* deliberations in city squares (see Botella-Ordinas, Centenero and Terrasa 2011).

In addition to Vitoria and Castrillo, many other important theologians and humanists advocated republican ideas during the sixteenth and seventeenth centuries: Bartolomé de las Casas, Domingo de Soto, Juan Ginés de Sepúlveda, Fernando Pérez de Oliva (who notably offered an early defense of liberty as the basis of human dignity in his *Diálogo por la dignidad del hombre* of 1585), Juan de Mariana, and Diego Saavedra Fajardo, among others. Three names from those centuries, however, merit closer attention: Juan Luis Vives, considered the father of modern psychology and one of the greatest European humanists of his time; the great jurist Francisco Suárez, with his outstanding and highly influential *De legibus* (1612); and Baltasar Gracián, whose three remarkable political works *El político* (1640), *El discreto* (1646), and the earlier *El héroe* (1637), in which he describes the ideal of the good citizen and good government in moral terms, act as a counterpoint to Machiavelli's *The Prince*.

Spanish republicanism, however, dramatically declined during the eighteenth, nineteenth, and part of the twentieth centuries. In the eighteenth century, it is worth noting the enlightened ideas of intellectuals such as Gaspar Melchor de Jovellanos. In the nineteenth, three outstanding politicians again maintained and advanced republican ideologies, and in fact became presidents during the *Sexenio Democrático* (1868–1874): Francesc Pi i Margall, Nicolás Salmerón, and Emilio Castelar. In the first forty years of the twentieth century, important intellectuals and politicians such as Francisco Giner de los Ríos, Julián Besteiro, Adolfo Posada, Pablo Iglesias, Indalecio Prieto, and Manuel Azaña took credit for maintaining republican ideas which ran counter to the dominant ideologies in the rest of Europe, namely liberalism, communism, and fascism. Spanish republicanism, however, was not as strongly articulated during this period as it had been during the sixteenth and seventeenth centuries though, paradoxically, this is the period that has been studied most, at least by Spanish historians (see Gil Novales 1996; Martínez López and Ruíz García 2012; Suárez Cortina 2011, 2013).

It was not until the restoration of democracy in 1978, and particularly during the past thirty years, that Spain really saw a remarkable revival of republican thought. Important Spanish intellectuals such as Salvador Giner, Félix Ovejero, Antoni Doménech, Victoria Camps, Fernando Vallespín, Andrés de Francisco, Adela Cortina, Aurelio Arteta, Ramon Vargas-Machuca, and José Rubio Carracedo, among many others, have produced an endless list of books, journal articles, and newspaper editorials in defense of republican political ideas. In fact, there is probably no other country in which republicanism is currently as strong and widespread among intellectuals and scholars as Spain.

It should not have been surprising, then, when in 2000 José Luis Rodríguez Zapatero, newly elected the leader of the Socialist Party, then in opposition, introduced himself ideologically as a republican and heir to Pablo Iglesias and Indalecio Prieto, and a particular disciple of Philip Pettit. Rodríguez Zapatero won the next legislative elections in 2004 and became president of Spain. According to some analysts, his first term in office served to advance a truly republican agenda (see Martí and Pettit 2010). Reelected in 2008, he remained in power until December 2011. His second term, however, was marked by the economic crisis. His policies and strategies to address it, especially after 2010, when he adopted the austerity measures imposed by the Troika, became a prominent target of the *indignados* in 2011.

Some have interpreted the *indignados*' opposition to Rodríguez Zapatero's economic policy as a clash between two forms of republicanism: one more vertical and favorable to the representative governments associated with President Rodríguez Zapatero and the ideas of Philip Pettit, the other more horizontal and inclined towards direct participation and popular assemblies as embodied by the *indignados* (Botella-Ordinas 2011). But exactly how republican are the ideas and values defended by the *indignados*?

The republican character of the *indignados*: deliberation, popular control, and the common good

As stated in previous sections, the *indignados* movement has had an enormous impact on Spanish democratic politics. Besides the direct effect it may still have on elections and the institutional system, its most important aim was to change the way in which ordinary citizens engage in politics by improving their capacity for political judgment and increasing their control over institutions and political parties. They wanted to transform and strengthen public deliberation within the informal public sphere, and in this respect they had remarkable success.

The *indignados* were able to organize themselves in the squares in an innovative, deliberative, and complex way. They immediately formed open, horizontal popular assemblies, which were the only empowered bodies in the movement that could decide on what initiatives to undertake (Maeckelberg 2012; Serrano et al. 2014; Taibo 2011b). Despite their permanent, mutual communication and coordination, these assemblies (one in each occupied square) were totally autonomous. The assembly of Puerta del Sol was independent from the assembly of Plaza de Catalunya, or any other assembly in Spain. The most interesting aspect of this, however, was that each general assembly was divided into different, autonomous subgroups to discuss the main topics of concern (Benski et al. 2013; Hughes 2011; Ovejero 2013; Romanos 2011, 2016; Tejerina et al. 2013). Such deliberative groups were numerous, highly diverse, decentralized, independent, and open to any citizen who wanted to participate.

The *indignados* constituted a very heterogeneous and diverse movement. The core protesters, the most active members who took part in demonstrations and sit-ins from the beginning, were more homogeneous as they were essentially both young and educated. Some had considerable experience participating in anti-capitalist and anti-globalization movements, while others were participating for the first time (Taibo 2013). All the other participants – people who came to the squares and took part in deliberations, as well as those who only attended large demonstrations – were much more diverse: they came from all age groups and had varying levels of education and a wide range of different life experiences (Ferrer et al. 2014).

Each deliberative group was meant to specialize in one issue or a range of issues, but deliberations flowed freely, and a group could decide to discuss topics that in theory were not relevant. No topic or issue was excluded, and ideologies were neither prohibited nor presupposed, nor were they taken for granted. Moreover, each group was able to make its own decisions, even if they were contradictory to the decisions made by other groups. This sometimes presented a problem in terms of developing a single collaborative strategy. However, the goal was not always to propose joint actions, but rather to improve their own understanding of the situation and achieve some degree of consensus.

Social consensus about the main issues under debate was in fact the central aim for all these deliberative groups. Despite the initial diversity of views, the *indignados* aspired to find widespread general agreement that could represent society as a whole. For that reason, they tended to avoid divisive issues that might bring about a clash of interests among citizens, as did Occupy, who claimed to represent 99% of the people (Byrne 2011; Gould-Wartofsky 2015; Meyer 2015; Milkman et al. 2015; Romanos 2016). Their focus was on the common good, the underlying assumption being that when something is part of the common good, everyone can recognize it as being in their own interest, at least after a fair process of deliberation. This ideal of the people acting together in defense of the common good was exactly what, according to the *indignados*, political parties and partisan politics had forgotten, ignored, or neglected, and it constituted one of the most distinctively republican features of the movement. Decisions were thus not being taken by majority rule. This aspect was in stark contrast to previous, otherwise similar movements such as Alter-globalization, which viewed the pursuit of consensus as conducive to impasse or blocking actions (Maeckelberg 2012). Total unanimity was not required by the *indignados* either, but it was necessary to find at least some degree of general agreement. Given the diversity of the participants, this made it naturally impossible for groups to make decisions on many issues and, again, there was an opportunity lost in terms of joint action. Their main focus, however, was not on action, but deliberation.

The *indignados'* deliberations were very well organized. They aimed to generate direct political participation in qualitative public deliberation among ordinary citizens by using all available technology while relying at the same time on face-to-face conversations and personal contact. They normally involved a chairperson or facilitator who structured the conversation and maintained order, but leadership was avoided as a rule. From the very beginning, the *indignados* who camped in the squares refused to choose their own leaders, representatives, or speakers. This was a problem, especially for the political authorities who wanted to negotiate and the media who wanted information; as a horizontal movement of ordinary citizens, no bosses or leaders were allowed. They shared an almost visceral rejection of the emergence of leaders, who were seen as potential power-seekers and dominators. The intervention of participants who tended to assume a main role or exert some leadership were discouraged or minimized. Their desire to avoid leaders was so strong that even the position of chairperson or moderator had to rotate permanently from one volunteer to another to avoid certain faces becoming too prominent. This avoidance of leadership stalled the efficient organization of action, but action was, of course, not the main objective, and was only pursued when full consensus had been reached, as a sign of having achieved a truly common good. This interest in avoiding potential domination by such leaders connects very clearly with republican ideas.

The discussions held in city squares were substantial despite the objective difficulties of the meetings (Ovejero 2013): the groups were too large and they had no proper space in which to deliberate; they made do with sitting directly on the paving stones. Many participants were very poorly informed about the issues at stake, and the range of knowledge and experience varied greatly. As ordinary citizens, not experts or technocrats, some did not even read the newspaper. However, the *indignados* displayed a high level of civic virtue in most of their actions, as republicanism demands. They were not violent and showed great respect for the rule of law. While they opposed the existing democratic system, their aim was to reform it through legal procedures. They were also very respectful of the diversity of their own views (Ferrer et al. 2014). In addition, they proved to be strongly engaged in political issues in a disinterested way, without looking for immediate rewards or compensation. They wanted to learn together.

Discussions were held together, generally as a cooperative educative process, and most people were happy to learn and felt that they were all in the same boat. Their constant search for consensus as a means to identifying the common good, and their avoidance of divisive issues that could only be decided on the basis of simple majority, helped them to sustain this feeling. It was for this reason that there was very little of the hindrance or resistance normally seen in partisan political conversations. Deliberations were more likely to involve genuine exchanges of arguments and reasons, allowing participants to learn from others' points of view and sometimes producing a change in opinion (Martí 2006; Ferrer, Martí, and Fernández et al. 2014). Once again, this way of characterizing public deliberation as a cooperative, communal process is recognizable as a distinctively republican claim.

The *indignados* did not intend that this model should replace parliament in the manner of a popular Athenian assembly. They were aware that they had no authority to make binding political decisions on their own. They were simply trying to improve and take part in public deliberation within the informal public sphere. However, they also aimed to exert some effective control over their government and representatives. The central idea of the movement was that this type of ultimate control by the people is not possible unless citizens are empowered, sufficiently knowledgeable, and possess reasonable judgment. On this basis, *indignados* can accurately be described as a participatory, deliberative social movement, and in this respect it can be linked to republican concerns.

In short, the *indignados*' republican affinity is clearly visible in various features of the movement. These include: its commitment to deliberative democracy, with special emphasis on spontaneous public deliberation occurring in the informal public sphere; the vindication of citizens' political participation and ultimate control over the representative institutions; the insistence on the common good as the only legitimate political goal; the rejection of all divisive issues and decisions; the reticence displayed towards any kind of political leadership as a potential form of domination; and the idea that citizens should be empowered but also display adequate civic virtues in order to participate politically (see Botella-Ordinas 2011; Martí and Ovejero 2011; Pettit 2011).

Ultimately, what occurred in the public squares of Spain in 2011 was one of the most remarkable experiments in popular deliberative democracy in history, and an extraordinary school of civic culture for those who took part in it. The *indignados*' ultimate aim was to carry out a democratic revolution, and take significant steps towards genuine participatory and deliberative democracy. Only time will tell if they succeeded.

Note

1 I thank Sabrina Voss for editing the final version of this chapter.

Works cited

Alonso Baelo, Pablo Luis. 2007. "El Tratado de República de Alonso de Castrillo. Una reflexión sobre la legitimidad de la acción política." *Res Publica* 18: 457–490.

Benski, Tova, Lauren Langman, Ignacia Perugorría, and Benjamín Tejerina. 2013. "From the Streets and Squares to Social Movements Studies: What Have We Learned?" *Current Sociology* 61 (4): 541–561.

Botella-Ordinas, Eva. 2011. "La democracia directa en la Puerta del Sol." *Books and Ideas / La Vie des Idées*. Accessed January 7, 2015. http://www.booksandideas.net/La-democracia-directa-de-la-Puerta.html

Botella-Ordinas, Eva, Domingo Centenero de Arce, and Antonio Terrasa Lozano. 2011. "Una tradición hispana de democracia local: los cabildos abiertos desde el siglo XVI hasta nuestros días." *Books and Ideas / La Vie des Idées*. Accessed November 24, 2014. http://www.booksandideas.net/Una-tradicion-hispana-de.html

Byrne, Jabet, ed. 2011. *The Occupy Handbook*. New York: Back Bay Books.

Castells, Manuel. 2012. *Networks of Outrage and Hope: Social Movements in the Internet Age.* Cambridge: Polity Press.

CIS. 2011a: *Barómetro de junio*, Centro de Investigaciones Sociológicas. Accessed January 7, 2015. http://www.cis.es/cis/export/sites/default/-Archivos/Marginales/2900_2919/2905/Es2905.pdf

———. 2011b: *Barómetro de octubre*, Centro de Investigaciones Sociológicas. Accessed January 7, 2015. http://www.cis.es/cis/opencms/-Archivos/Marginales/2900_2919/2914/Es2914.pdf

della Porta, Donatella. 2012. "Mobilizing against the Crisis, Mobilizing for 'Another Democracy': Comparing Two Global Waves of Protest (Event Analysis)." *Interface: A Journal for and About Social Movements* 4 (1): 274–277.

DRY. 2011. "Manifesto." Accessed November 24, 2014. http://www.democraciarealya.es/manifiesto-comun/manifesto-english/

———. 2014. "Proposals." Accessed November 24, 2014. http://www.democraciarealya.es/documento-transversal/

Ferrer, Mariona, José Luis Martí, and Charlotte Fernández. 2014. "The Democratic Culture of the 15M in Spain." Unpublished manuscript.

Fuster, Mayo. 2012. "The Free Culture and 15M Movements in Spain: Composition, Social Networks, and Synergies." *Social Movement Studies: Journal of Social, Cultural and Political Protest* 11 (3–4): 386–392.

Gil Novales, Alberto. 1996. "Del liberalismo al republicanismo." In *Republicanos y repúblicas en España*, edited by Manuel Chust and José Antonio Piqueras, 81–95. Madrid: Siglo XXI.

Gil Pujol, Xavier. 2005. "Republican Politics in Early Modern Spain: The Castilian and Catalan-Aragonese Traditions." In *A Shared European Heritage. Volume 1: Republicanism and Constitutionalism in Early Modern Europe*, edited by Quentin Skinner and Martin van Gelderen, 263–288. Cambridge: Cambridge University Press.

Giner, Salvador. 2010. "Orígenes del pactismo republicano." *El País*, January 13.

Gould-Wartofsky, Michael. 2015. *The Occupiers*. Oxford: Oxford University Press.

Hessel, Stéphane. 2011. *Indignez-vous*. Paris: Indigène Editions.

Hughes, Neil. 2011. "Young People Took to the Streets and All of a Sudden All of the Political Parties Got Old: The 15M Movement in Spain." *Social Movement Studies: Journal of Social, Cultural and Political Protest* 10 (4): 407–413.

Maeckelbergh, Marianne. 2012. "Horizontal Democracy Now: From Alterglobalization to Occupation." *Interface: A Journal for and About Social Movements* 4 (1): 207–234.

Martí i Puig, Salvador. 2011. "15M: The *Indignados*." In *The Occupy Handbook*, edited by Jabet Byrne, 209–217. New York: Back Bay Books.

Martí, José Luis. 2006. *La república deliberativa: Una teoría de la democracia*. Madrid: Marcial Pons.

Martí, José Luis and Félix Ovejero. 2011. "Republicanismo y participación ciudadana." *Books and Ideas/La Vie des Idées*. Accessed November 24, 2014. http://www.booksandideas.net/Republicanismo-y-participacion.html

Martí, José Luis and Philip Pettit. 2010. *A Political Philosophy in Public Life: Civic Republicanism in Zapatero's Spain*. Princeton, NJ: Princeton University Press.Martínez López, Fernando and Maribel Ruíz García, eds. 2012. *El republicanismo de ayer a hoy*. Madrid: Biblioteca Nueva.

Meyer, David. 2015. *The Politics of Protest. Social Movements in America*. Oxford: Oxford University Press.

Milkman, Ruth, Stephanie Luce, and Penny Lewis. 2015. "Occupy Wall Street." In *The Social Movements Reader. Cases and Concepts*, edited by Jeff Goodwin and James M. Jasper, 30–44. Oxford: Wiley-Blackwell.

Miras Albarrán, Joaquín. 2009. "La Res Publica, la pensé politique de Francisco de Vitoria." In *Républicanismes et droit natural*, edited by Marc Belissa, Yannick Bosc, and Florence Gauthier, 31–40. France: Kimé.

Monterde, Arnau, Antonio Calleja-López, Miguel Aguilera, Xabier E. Barandiaran, and John Postill. 2015. "Multitudinous Identities: A Qualitative and Network Analysis of the 15M Collective Identity." *Information, Communication & Society* 18 (8): 930–950.

Montero, J. R., R. Gunther, and M. Torcal. 1998. "Actitudes hacia la democracia en España: legitimidad, descontento y desafección." *Revista de Investigaciones Sociológicas* 83: 9–49.

Ovejero, Félix, 2013. *¿Idiotas o ciudadanos? El 15M y la teoría de la democracia.* Madrid: Montesinos.

Peña López, Ismael. 2013. "Casual Politics: From Slacktivism to Emergent Movements and Pattern Recognition." Unpublished manuscript.

Peña López, Ismael, Mariluz Congosto, and Pablo Aragón. 2014. "Spanish *Indignados* and the Evolution of 15M: Towards Networked Para-Institutions." *Journal of Spanish Cultural Studies* 15 (1–2): 189–216.

Perugorría, Ignacia and Benjamín Tejerina. 2013. "Politics of the Encounter: Cognition, Emotions and Networks in the Spanish 15-M." *Current Sociology* 61 (4): 424–442.

———. 2014. "Synchronizing Identities. Crafting the Space of Mobilization in the Spanish 15M." In *The Debt Crisis in the Eurozone*, edited by Nicholas Peotropoulos and George Tsobanoglou, 282–304. Cambridge: Cambridge University Press.

Pettit, Philip. 1997. *Republicanism.* Oxford: Oxford University Press.

———. 2011. "Republican Reflections on the 15M movement." *Books and Ideas/La Vie des Idées.* Accessed November 24, 2014. http://www.booksandideas.net/Republican-Reflections-on-the-15-M.html

———. 2014. *Just Freedom. A Moral Compass for a Complex World.* New York: W.W. Norton & Co.

Romanos, Eduardo. 2011. "El 15M y la democracia de los movimientos sociales." *Books and Ideas/La Vie des Idées.* Accessed November 24, 2014. http://www.booksandideas.net/El-15M-y-la-democracia-de-los.html

———. 2012. "Esta revolución es muy *copyleft.*" *Interface: A Journal for and about Social Movements* 4 (1): 183–206.

———. 2016. "From Tahrir to Puerta del Sol to Wall Street: The Transnational Diffusion of Social Movements in Comparative Perspective." *Revista de Investigaciones Sociológicas* 154: 103–118.

Serrano, Eunaté, Antonio Calleja-López, Arnau Monterde, and Javier Toret, eds. 2014. *15MP2P. Una mirada transdisciplinar del 15M.* Accessed November 24, 2014. http://civilsc.net/sites/default/files/15MP2P_Mayo2014.pdf.

Suárez Cortina, Manuel. 2011. "El republicanismo en la España liberal (1820–1931): una aproximación historiográfica." *Bulletin d'Histoire Contemporaine de l'Espagne* 46: 11–42.

———. 2013. "El siglo XIX y la República: de historia e historiografía republicana." In *El republicanismo de ayer y hoy*, edited by Fernando Martínez López and Maribel Ruiz García, 27–46. Madrid: Biblioteca Nueva.

Taibo, Carlos. 2011a. *El 15-M en sesenta preguntas.* Madrid: Los libros de la catarata.

———. 2011b. *Nada será como antes: sobre el movimiento 15-M.* Madrid: Los libros de la catarata.

———. 2013. "The Spanish *Indignados*: A Movement with Two Souls." *European Urban and Regional Studies* 20: 155–158.

Tejerina, Benjamín, Ignacia Perugorría, Tova Benski, and Lauren Langman. 2013. "From Indignation to Occupation: A New Wave of Global Mobilization." *Current Sociology* 61 (4): 377–392.

Torcal, Mariano. 2006. "Desafección institucional e historia democrática en las nuevas democracias." *Revista SAAP* 2 (3): 591–634.

Torcal, Mariano and José Ramon Montero. 2006. *Political Disaffection in Contemporary Democracies.* London: Routledge.

Velasco, Pilar. 2011. *No nos representan. El manifiesto de los indignados en 15 propuestas.* Madrid: Temas de Hoy.

Viejo, Raimundo, ed. 2011. *Les raons dels indignats.* Barcelona: Pórtico.

Villacañas, José Luis. 2005. "Republicanismo clásico en España: Razones de una ausencia." *Journal of Spanish Cultural Studies* 6 (2): 163–183.

44

MEDIATIZING A PAST OF CONFLICT

The Spanish Civil War through TV documentaries in the twenty-first century[1]

Enric Castelló

During his time as a war correspondent in Spain, Ernest Hemingway (2007 [1938]) wrote a story, as short as it was devastating, entitled "Old Man at the Bridge." With a dialogue and two descriptive brushstrokes, he masterfully captures the desolation of an inhabitant of Sant Carles de la Ràpita before the advance of the Nationalist troops to the Ebro. From the bridge, Hemingway uneasily surveys the African-like landscape of the delta, and wonders how long it will take the enemy to arrive. When he asks the old man which side he is on, the reply is neither, that he is seventy-six years old, has walked twelve miles, and can go no further. This character is now anchored to the bridge, despondent, and worried about the cat, four pairs of pigeons, and two goats left behind in his yard. The old man can be read as a metaphor for memory: he is too exhausted to continue, too terrified to turn back, teetering between the two banks of the present, which is advancing as relentlessly as the river.

The journalistic reports of the Spanish Civil War published by newspapers around the world have been widely used in its historical reconstruction. These chronicles of troop movements, descriptions of bombing and destruction, and statements by politicians represented the first narratives to mediatize the war. The story of the battle of the Ebro was especially widely disseminated, on account of the number of casualties and the spectacular nature of its military operations. Hemingway may already have suspected that the story of the war would remain alive in the memory of the Spanish people several generations later. The grandchildren and great-grandchildren of characters like the old man at the bridge would continue to question their elders about the tragedy: about where they were, what they saw, and what they felt.

The Spanish Civil War, like all the wars of the twentieth century, was mediatized from the beginning, and many of its chroniclers offered biased accounts, putting their expertise at the service of propaganda. Examples include documentary films such as *Reportaje del movimiento revolucionario en Barcelona* (Santos 1936) or *Heroic Spain* (Reig et al. 1938), which have been studied by various authors (e.g., Gubern 1986; Pingree 2007). For example, one of the first documentaries about the battle of the Ebro includes footage shot by Manuel Aznar *(La batalla del Ebro*, 1938) for one of those propaganda films.

The issue of using journalism and documentary film as an ideological tool was debated among these first narrators of the war. Paul Preston explains how the *New York Times* correspondent, Herbert L. Matthews, was concerned about the impartiality of his writing. Reporting from the Republican side, which he openly supported, Matthews always maintained that taking part in the war was not incompatible with explaining the truth in his chronicles. However, the reporter showed a somehow naïve confidence in history, if only journalists would stick to the following criterion: "History will never fail so long as the newspaperman writes the truth" (Matthew quoted in Preston 2008, 23).

The truth is that the victory of fascism in Spain led to the exile of leftist intellectuals, and the media became a tool of indoctrination at the service of the National Catholic ideology of Francisco Franco's totalitarian regime. After nearly forty years of dictatorship without freedom of expression (1939–1975), the *Transición* (1975–1979) would bring Spain democracy, but, as many authors have pointed out, at the cost of accepting a sort of *pact of silence*. This is a controversial issue whose detailed analysis is beyond the scope of this chapter. However, Carme Molinero (2010, 35) summarizes this unwritten pact by arguing that: "Defenders of the Franco regime had agreed to accept democracy and the anti-Franco sectors 'forgot' forty years of dictatorship." The pact was sealed with the Amnesty Act (1977), which served to prevent the investigation and trial of crimes committed during the Civil War and the dictatorship, even when petitioned by the UN (Junquera 2013a, 2013b). Thirty years later, the *Ley de Memoria Histórica* (2007), passed by the Socialist government of José Luis Rodríguez Zapatero and criticized by the right-wing Popular Party, was a step forward in the recognition of the victims of Francoism, but it was unable to resolve problematic issues such as the exhumation of mass graves. The Francoist regime spent forty years honouring its fallen, but, aside from this gesture, Spanish democracy has failed to make equivalent reparations to the opposite side.

The present article deals with the television documentaries on the Spanish Civil War produced in the twenty-first century, particularly in the context of the seventy-fifth anniversary of the military uprising against the Republic in 1936. These documentaries have developed a function of visually resurrecting discourses and narratives, bringing into the public sphere the memories of many Spaniards who had chosen to remain silent, had had no previous opportunity to speak, or had never been asked to do so. Although it is inappropriate, in ontological terms, to speak of a "recovery" of memory – a concept that has been problematized elsewhere and implies a "reification" of memory (see, e.g., Castelló and O'Donnell 2006; Labanyi 2008) – it should be noted that some of these documentaries have been instrumental in stirring consciences and raising awareness of a troubled past that contemporary Spain is yet to come to terms with, however much institutional discourses insist on the story of "reconciliation."

The collective past and the media

The relationship between the media and collective memory has been discussed by various authors within the framework of a multidisciplinary field of research that has adopted the label of "memory studies." The concept of mediatization essentially refers to the idea that the media act as "agents of social change" (Hjarvard 2008) or as "moulding forces" (Hepp 2009) of society and culture. The mediatization of memory, according to Andrew Hoskins (2009, 31), evolves in two stages: firstly, the mass media establish dominant narratives, before archives, testimonies, and personal memories are revisited and interconnected. This second phase, following the author, is an inherent feature of the "post-broadcast" era. A social network of collective memory is formed, producing unlimited clusters of meaning. In addition, this second mediatization phase that Hoskins refers to does not take place only in the network; today the availability of recording devices, widespread access to archives, and easy editing of images in multiple formats has turned this second phase into a genuinely experimental field in which the hegemony of large media operators in establishing a collective memory is strongly contested.

Mediatization affects collective memory and to a degree transforms it. There is no doubt that Maurice Halbwachs's (1992 [1952]) long-established definition of collective memory now needs to be revisited, since today the public and private spheres are far less clearly demarcated than they were sixty years ago. In this regard, José van Dijck has drawn attention to the concept of "cultural memory" as a means of identifying the problematic relationship between the public and private spheres when it comes to defining memory, and the willingness of individuals to share their personal memories with a group. For this author, the mediation of memory (she does not use the term "mediatization") implies that the media highlights, corrupts, extends, and even replaces memory (van Dijck 2007, 16).

In an effort to understand the process of mediatization of collective memory, we can refer to the three factors outlined by Joanne Garde-Hansen: the first involves the media as an institutional means of registering the past, central to which are institutions such as museums or public television stations and their archives; secondly, the media serve as technological means of recording the past through devices such as cameras, smartphones, and computers; and thirdly, the media can act as memorials that bestow recognition on an individual, a group or a particular episode in history. In this last sense, the media can be understood as spaces of memory and remembrance of wars, their victims, and historical figures. These dynamics function simultaneously, but I would emphasize the prominent participation of citizens in the third of these. Memory organized "top-down" (promoted by institutions, public policy, etc.) is mutating into citizen-driven memory, with a central role being played by associations, NGOs, etc. On the third dynamic, Garde-Hansen (2011, 65) writes:

> This increased media practice coming from bottom up has impact for understanding how social and cultural heritage and history is changing. Ordinary people are engaged not just in genealogical research but also in civic and community entrepreneurship activities.

Such an empowerment of individuals and groups, who only a decade ago had far less access to the means of production and mass distribution of messages, is building a new collective memory. Memory is arguably something of a civil right, a matter of justice linked to public policy (Lee and Thomas 2012, 15). If we look at this question from the point of view of media ecology, deficits or gaps not covered by public policy would today be filled by collectives who organize events, produce material, and share their experiences in networks.

In the case of the Spanish Civil War, Joan Ramon Resina (2010) undertakes a psychoanalytical foray into the issue by referring to a "collective unconscious," as opposed to the concept of "collective memory," specifically implying an archive of shared memory that has disappeared from public view for political or social reasons. In twenty-first-century Spain and Catalonia, this unconscious, which stems from an unresolved traumatic experience, is reflected in the documentaries about the war, both those perpetuating the hegemonic discourse established by post-Francoism and the *Transición*, and those who oppose this hegemonic discourse that dominates the mainstream media. Moreover, this collective unconscious also turns into memory when what has been silenced is brought out and released into the vast narrative repository of the network.

The memory conflict

Reams of pages have been written about the Spanish Civil War by historians, but there has been little analysis of the television documentaries dealing with this event. Hernández Corchete (2012a, 12) suggests that this deficit is due to the difficulty of keeping up with the sheer volume of production, and this is surely correct; a systematic analysis of all television documentaries made only in the last ten years would provide material for a very extensive case study. Television began to narrate the conflict in documentary form during the 1980s – most prominently with the thirty-episode series *España en guerra* (Cervera 1987) – and more productions of this type followed in the 1990s. However, the television war documentary flourished after the turn of the century, particularly in the context of the seventy-fifth anniversary.

On the other hand, television is still discredited as a medium worthy of academic study. To give only one example, Sánchez-Biosca (2006, 16) considers that it is not particularly concerned with upholding "methodological rigour." This stance is supported by the low quality of some productions and initiatives, as well as the tendency of television in the "post-broadcast" era to prioritize entertainment in historical and scientific programming, often sacrificing quality and accuracy of content in the process. For Sánchez-Biosca (2006, 18):

> Hace ya tiempo que los medios de comunicación han abandonado la modestia de ilustrar discursos a los que reconocen un rango superior, como sería el caso de la Historia, y se comportan con una soberbia sólo parangonable a su ignorancia.

Sánchez-Biosca has pointed out two parallel trends in the public narration of the Spanish Civil War: on the one hand, the huge output; and on the other, the way many of these documentaries and reports constitute "an extremely belligerent and accusatory narrative," an opportunity for "neo-propaganda," characterized by simplification and the power of emotional narrative (Sánchez-Biosca 2006, 17). To an extent, the mediatized account of the war has become a jumble of perspectives that mixes documents and facts with fictionalization, historical reconstruction, re-enactments, and dramatization. The hybrid nature of these programmes has meant that historians tend to keep their distance, but it has also drawn interest from other disciplines of the humanities. Nevertheless, these discrediting features do not apply to every case, and mediatization has also produced some unprecedented and original narratives which would have been unthinkable only a few years ago.

Media narratives of the Civil War also include revisionist accounts by conservatives and the political right, who Balfour (2008, 179) suggests have learnt to mimic academic protocols, inverting discourses, and decontextualizing and reinterpreting readings in a presentist mode. Their views are reflected today across all media platforms, including reports broadcast on television, accessed online, or sold on DVD. This fragmentation of the narratives on the war has become universal, and in addressing particular audience profiles the ideological premise is converted into just another target-defining element.

Catalan and Basque national channels have also contested the hegemonic discourse of the Civil War, which until the 1990s operated at state level. Both have developed an approach that aims to problematize the so-called *pact of silence*. In Catalonia, journalistic reporting has shed light on highly controversial topics not dealt with previously (including the abducted or indoctrinated children of Republican parents, the mass graves of people murdered after the war, deportations to concentration camps, etc.; Castelló 2012), while in the Basque Country, the narratives have emphasized aspects related to the national conflict (see de Pablo 2012).

Finally, in the context of the aforementioned second phase of mediatization, a third trend is worth noting which involves contributions to the narrative that are shared on online social networks or distributed directly. I am referring to low-cost or local productions circulated by citizens with minimal resources, such as students of journalism or film preparing their first audiovisual projects, cultural associations of all types, ideological organizations, political party foundations, audiovisual amateurs, or history buffs. This amalgamation of stories, which is extremely difficult to keep track of, can range from worthy local or family-based productions (the testimony of relatives, politicians and local characters; anecdotes, local history, etc.), to others that enter the realm of propaganda.

In sum, the mediatization of the Spanish Civil War in the twenty-first century may be described as converting its narration into a case of memory-conflict. Its narrative production operates in a field of ideological dispute over the past, with a variety of purposes and objectives grounded in the present, and with the expectation of a particular outcome in the near future, examples of which may include public recognition, blaming or pointing out responsibilities, legitimizing or discrediting particular groups, or just remembering trauma or personal accounts on the war.

Viewpoints on the war

This section offers a brief examination of some recent war documentaries that contribute to the mediatization of Spanish collective memory from very different, even confrontational, perspectives. I focus particularly on several broadcasts on Spanish public television (TVE), one documentary from the San Pablo CEU Foundation broadcast on Telemadrid (TM), some productions by Television de Catalunya (TVC), and an independent film with support from Memorial Democràtic.

TVE (Televisión Española) and the Civil War

Since its inception in 1956, and at different stages of its life, TVE has taken a variety of approaches to the Civil War (Hernández Corchete 2012b; Montero and Paz 2011). According to Hernández Corchete (2012b, 50), after the transition to democracy, documentaries on Spanish television reinforced the idea of apportioning blame and moving on, placing particular emphasis on the human tragedy. In the first decade of the new century, this trend would continue, but the period of the right-wing government of José María Aznar (1996–2004) culminated in two controversial episodes of the historical series *Memoria de España* (Andrés 2004) about the Second Republic and the Francoist regime. Julián Casanova (2005) labelled them "historical revisionism" and an example of "the neo-Francoist syndrome," while advising against "whitewashing the past." In the first term of the socialist government of José Luis Rodríguez Zapatero (2004–2008), TVE launched the series *La memoria recobrada* (Domingo 2006) which, according to Ibáñez (2012, 75), "takes the side of the defeated," while being an "outstanding document of a time when it was still conceivable that a Law of Historical Memory would bring justice to all victims of Francoism."

In this context, TVE screened *El laberinto español* (Reverte 2006a), consisting of thirteen documentaries, each followed by a historical debate. Ibáñez's remarks (2012) about *La memoria recobrada* are also applicable to this series, which was made at a time when Zapatero's government was on the verge of passing the *Ley de Memoria Histórica*. Two of its episodes were concerned with showing and discussing *La batalla del Ebro* (Reverte 2006b), adapted by the director from his own book (Reverte 2006c), which combined history and journalism. It was a two-part documentary that was not a mere adaptation but an innovative audiovisual work that has been already noted as one of the most interesting TVE productions in recent years (Palacio and Ciller 2010).

The first part of this documentary offers comprehensive contextualization and assembles many archive images, interviews with historians, and testimony of all kinds. Highlights include survivors of the "Quinta del biberón," elderly men who recall how they forded the river and the battles where thousands of their youthful companions died.[2] Ex-soldiers on the Francoist side also provide eyewitness accounts of military operations: a colour code (a red or blue filter) is used to introduce testimony from both sides, which helps the viewer interpret what is being related.

Elements of dramatization are kept to a minimum, limited to glimpses of soldiers in a dark forest, or another carrying a water canteen. These resources often consist of subjective camera work from the perspective of a moving soldier and are interspersed with archive footage, testimonials, and photographs. Shots of the river try to recreate the tension of the moment for the viewer without actually resorting to a reconstruction, which risks ridicule if attempted with insufficient resources. It includes animated maps, a huge amount of data, numbers, locations, and facts, all interspersed with the memories of the surviving soldiers. It therefore has an informative value and a carefully honed aesthetic, replete with spectacular aerial images of the area. The viewer's interest is held by illustrative anecdotes, which are reasonably justified within the context of what the documentary seeks to convey. Overall, *La batalla del Ebro* helps the viewer understand how the battle evolved, step by step.

This documentary does not touch on the viewpoint of the population or the impact of the war on the villages, but that is not its declared aim. Focused almost exclusively on military activity and the historical context, it takes a journalistic rather than ethnographic approach. It is certainly a piece of work that Herbert L. Matthews would have liked to see, because in some ways it fits into what the American reporter aspired to provide for future generations of journalists and historians. Like *La memoria recobrada*, *La batalla del Ebro* fits in with the new socialist period of TVE, at a time when the government was working towards passing the *Ley de Memoria Histórica*, but it aspired to achieve documentary rigour, harmoniously combining action with a series of audiovisual resources.

Right-wing "myths"

The right-wing vision, or revision, trains its focus on the violence committed by the Republicans during the Civil War. On the occasion of the seventy-fifth anniversary of its outbreak, the clash of viewpoints even affected the obituary sections of the main Spanish newspapers. In the words of Rodrigo (2009, 213–214), for a few days a real "war of obituaries" broke out in *El País*, *El Mundo*, and *ABC*, in which each side remembered their dead. Many initiatives focused on the war marked this anniversary. Television producers and channels of all types launched numerous reports and discussions focused on different topics, often taking opposing ideological views.

Molinero (2010, 48) states that with the arrival of democracy in Spain, the generation of the grandchildren of those who suffered reprisals under Franco wanted to know what had happened, why their grandparents were shot, and where they were buried. There was a forceful emergence of a "memory of the vanquished," as opposed to the "memory of the victors." The latter still dominates today, and is present in the streets named or monuments such as El Valle de los Caídos (the Valley of the Fallen). For the Right, this new discourse of "the vanquished" violated the silence-based pact of the *Transición*. Therefore, it broke with what Resina (2003,

88) has labelled a "programmed amnesia" and triggered a reaction in the form of audiovisuals and television programs (debates, interviews, etc.) aimed at strengthening the testimony of the victors, which had monopolized the public space in Franco's time but now had to deal with a counterpoint.

An example of this trend is the documentary series from the San Pablo-CEU Foundation, *La Guerra Civil Española. Mitos al descubierto* (Bullón and Togores 2012).[3] With the occasion of the screening of the first episode of the series on Telemadrid (*El asesinato de Calvo Sotelo*) in the programme *Madrid opina* (Sáenz de Buruaga and Arribas 2006), some scholars expressed their objections and disapproval.[4] For example, the historian Santos Juliá (2011), described the production as a "regrettable manipulation," while Socialist Party advisers denounced the work on Madrid's public television network as "tendentious" and "biased" (Galló and Gómez 2011).

In this symbolic struggle, the term "myth" is often used to counter that of "history." Sánchez-Biosca (2006, 23) refers to myth in terms of the original Aristotelian meaning, which is the opposite of *logos*, or reason. In *La Guerra Civil Española: Mitos al descubierto*, the narrative tries to counteract accounts of the war that show Francoists as unjust or villainous. The use of the word "myth" in the title of the series aims to discredit the discourses generated by the stories of the defeated. It thereby problematizes the categories that have come to define the Nationalist/Republican conflict in much of the historiography and democratic memory of the war: respectively, perpetrators/victims; rebels/legalists; fascists/democrats, etc. The aim of the revision is to try and unseat the terms of this antagonistic discourse in relation to the "truth."

The series contains some two hundred minutes of historical re-enactment and draws on a range of experts, local historians, and personal accounts. Much of the narrative is geared towards spotlighting the victims of Republican aggression, with an emphasis on the murder of religious believers and the destruction of church property. Other atrocities committed by the Republican side are featured, including the Paracuellos murders, presented as "the largest organized genocide in the history of Spain" ("El Partido Comunista y la defensa de Madrid: La masacre de Paracuellos"); the uncontrolled violence of anarchist groups towards Nationalist supporters and religious orders ("Violencia en la retaguardia"); assaults on the church and the murder of priests ("La persecución religiosa"); and conflict and strife in the Republic ("Divisiones internas en el bando republicano"). The recreations in the series are largely dramatizations of executions or arrests, with an overwhelming emphasis on those committed by anarchists. Expert voices, reenactments, and memories are interwoven with archival footage, including material from the Fundación Nacional Francisco Franco, an organization that works to disseminate the memory and work of the dictator.[5]

Paul Preston (2014, 24) argues that the revisionists' accounts underplay the suffering of the victims on the Republican side, attributing this to a kind of historians' conspiracy. In the episode "La toma de Badajoz: entre la verdad y la leyenda" the "truth" is said to lie in the repressive actions of Republican militias, and in the assaults and chaotic situation which preceded the Nationalist military conquest. The alternative view or "legend" is countered with comparative data that apparently tries to balance out the excesses on both sides, but which effectively consigns the disproportionate Francoist repression in Badajoz to "myth" or "legend," (thereby problematizing the nature of "truth").

A story of proximity

Mediatization also provides many opportunities to narrate stories of proximity, as occurs in *La batalla de la memoria* (Pons Múria 2009), a documentary co-produced by TVC and Mario Pons Produccions Audiovisuals, with the collaboration of Memorial Democràtic and the

Institut Català d'Indústries Audiovisuals,[6] as well as the support of various municipal councils near the Ebro.[7] The documentary explores how the battle of the Ebro was experienced by the population through a series of mechanisms that portray the complexity of the conflict. The documentary uses footage from No-Do and the Spanish National Film Archive, but the real value of the production lies in the use of witness accounts.

Pons Múria was advised by the historian Josep Sánchez Cervelló, a specialist in local history and specifically in the wars this territory has endured throughout its history (e.g., Sánchez Cervelló 2001). The professor features in the documentary as a narrative guide, along with one of his students, who is investigating the death of his grandfather in a prison after the war. The documentary contrasts opposing versions of the conflict, but the prevailing theory is that Francoist repression in the area was disproportionate, ruthlessly cruel, and directed against many people who were not significantly involved or were innocent of any crime.

La batalla de la memoria recalls the crimes committed by anarchist brigades in villages of the Ebro, and includes accounts from relatives of religious and right-wing victims. These memories are offset by stories from the other side, such as those of the student's grandfather or the execution of Republicans after the entry of Franco's troops. The aim is to highlight the deep wounds the war left in the population, creating a social breakdown that lasted for generations, and the injustice committed on both sides, with a special focus on post-war Nationalist repression. As Sánchez Cervelló puts it, "the Left committed crimes first. But they [the Francoists] spent forty years avenging them." Moments of particular tension include the discovery of human bones in the hills where fighting took place, or the meeting at the end, which brings together people from both sides.

Though it relied on the support of regional television, Pons Múria's documentary is an example of a second phase in the mediatization of memory, since it is based on testimonial contributions and is austerely produced. A recognition and visualization of memory is achieved by a modest deployment of unspectacular techniques. This documentary shows that the Spanish Civil War has entered a dynamic in which local history, the memory of citizens, and the interest of new generations – embodied by the student investigating the death of his grandfather – is generating new discourses from perspectives which have hitherto been ignored. This phase of mediatization has access to limited or scarce technical resources (as is the case here), a good network of contacts, and the collaboration of various actors in the field.

The achievement of *La batalla de la memoria* is enhanced by its aesthetics: the everyday scenes of village life and of people working in the vineyards and cellars, and frequent landscape shots of the river and the buttressed sierras of Cavalls and Pàndols, accompanied by the rhythmic compositions of Quico el Célio, El Noi, and El Mut de Ferreries, popular music which distils a whole philosophy of life and culture emanating from the people who live along the last stretch of the Ebro. Ultimately, the uniqueness of this production lies in its point of view, which focuses on the villages of the area and the complexity of the conflict, with the participation of people who suffered on both sides, and who sometimes lived only a few metres away from each other in the same street.

New formats and initiatives

The Spanish Civil War is a narrative repository that forms the basis of new productions, both documentary and fictional. Some even navigate between these two genres. Another standout production in this crossover between documentary and fiction is *Mirant al cel/ Looking at the Sky* (Garay 2008), which deals with the 1938 bombing of Barcelona. The mediatization of the Civil War involves experimentation and breaking away from the classical canons of genre aesthetics. *Mirant al cel* presents two parallel stories, one fictional, with parts played by actors, and the other comprising the testimony of older people who remember the suffering and fear produced by the bombing. An old man in the fictional part plays one of the Italian pilots who took part in the bombing. The programme was the result of a collaboration between the writer Juan Goytisolo, historians, journalists, and the doctor Moises Broggi, who attended many of the victims during the attacks. Overall, this production is clearly in line with the "restoration" of the collective memory of the city of Barcelona.

The widespread and indiscriminate bombing of civilians in Barcelona is also dealt with in the TVC documentary, *Ramon Perera, l'home que va salvar Barcelona / Ramon Perera, the Man who Saved Barcelona* (Armengou and Belis 2006), which explores the construction of shelters by this Catalan architect. His work would subsequently be studied in London during the Blitz. Montse Armengou and Ricard Belis, journalists for Catalan public television, deserve special mention for their work on silenced aspects of the Civil War and the Franco regime, as several authors have pointed out (Castelló 2014; Herrmann 2008).

Mediatization implies that citizens and novice creators have access to the media to create new stories, and create visual memories of their family, neighbourhood, and local area. Documentary initiatives are emerging from young creators such as the three directors of *Han bombardejat una escola* (Corbera et al. 2010), recovering the little-known story of *Escola del Mar* in the Barceloneta neighbourhood. This school, which was a model of modernity in the Republican education system, was bombed and destroyed in 1938. Participating in this production are elderly women who as girls endured both the war and the loss of their school. This documentary also explores the end of the Republican educational system, which was much more advanced in its modern values and respect for women than what would be imposed by the dictatorship.

Han bombardejat una escola is another example of how mediatizing collective memory can have very different outcomes, resulting in a product that is intimate, original, and of documentary interest, and one which is close to the people. Its work is that of a municipal archive, making contact with neighbours and family archives, to create a story that combines emotion and documentary value.

Relativism and pigeonholing

The human tragedy lives on in the people who suffered it, and their families. The mediatization of the memory of the Spanish Civil War has many facets, but the hegemony exercised by the mass media in the late twentieth century has found a counterpoint in all manner of productions in the second decade of the twenty-first century. These recent narratives contribute to what some authors have identified as a true postmemory of the Spanish Civil War that encompasses not only cinema (Coronado 2016; Quílez 2016), but all types of platforms, including graphic literature (Galán and Rueda 2016) or even board games (Gonzalo 2016). In the field of the television documentary, we find series and one-off productions driven by organizations, small producers, educational institutions, local or regional television, and even individual citizens concerned with capturing memory, writing about their past or problematizing what others have written about their people.

The existence of multiple visions of the war should not lead to the radical relativism which is beginning to be voiced in some quarters, a relativism that considers all views on the past as equally legitimate, and therefore all historiography as valid (or even invalid). This is not the place to deal with this scepticism in the depth that the issue requires, but it would be unfair to view serious documentary work in the same light as productions which attempt to contort the past to their own ideological ends. Victims of all kinds have a right to memory, but using it to legitimize or delegitimize stories based on historical fact is a very different exercise. In the mediatization of the Civil War, not all accounts are on the same level: the right to construct or even "rescue" memory does not mean that every engagement with this subject is of the same kind. Moreover, one cannot equate the memory of the defeated with that of the victors, whose discourse dominated the collective narrative of the war in the decades of repression, censorship, and lack of freedom.

Today the mediatization of the Spanish Civil War is also yielding innovative work, which breaks new ground when compared with the first audiovisual productions and documentaries on the subject. Their interpretation and evaluation should not be limited to ideological pigeonholing on a left-right axis. Both pigeonholing and relativizing discourses would perhaps serve to undermine them and strip them of some of their merits. but some of these productions can constitute valuable pieces of research, drawn from the memories of survivors and their families, which can contribute to the recognition of the suffering experienced by war victims and make future generations aware of the barbarism endured by their predecessors in a graphic and engaging way. A major problem for a diverse audience is to distinguish such material from its counterpart.

In Spain today the construction of a memory of the Civil War and Franco's dictatorship requires overcoming various obstacles. The courts do not allow for the review of cases such as the execution of Salvador Puig Antich in 1974, and historians have had difficulty accessing certain public records for their research. Meanwhile, monuments exalting Francoism, such as the Valley of the Fallen, are still standing and the United Nations' experts urge Spain to investigate the atrocities during the Civil War and under Franco's dictatorship without a response from the state (UN 2014). This institutional framework may offer no help, but nothing seems to stop citizens in their determination to engage with the memory of the victims and to capture their memories on screen.

Notes

1 This article is part of the research projects entitled "The media construction of political and territorial conflicts in Spain. Study of discourses and narratives" (CSO-2010–20047) and "Second-Degree Memories: Postmemory of the Civil War, Francoism and democratic Transition in contemporary Spain " (CSO2013–41594-P), supported by the Spanish Ministry of Economy and Competitiveness.
2 The "Quinta del biberón" (Baby-bottle Call-up) was mobilized by Republican authorities in 1938–1939 and recruited young people born in 1920 and 1921.
3 The San Pablo CEU Foundation is an organization of the Asociación Católica de Propagandistas (Catholic Association of Propagandists), whose educational aims fall within the framework of the Catholic Church. Accessed April 7, 2014. http://www.ceu.es/fundacion/quienes-somos.html.
4 Mitos al descubierto. Accessed April 7, 2014. http://www.telemadrid.es/mitosaldescubierto.
5 This organization was funded by the government of the Partido Popular, which was strongly criticised by the leftist parties of the Spanish parliament (see Cué 2002).
6 Memorial Democràtic is an institution of the Generalitat de Catalunya aimed at "recovery, remembrance, and fostering democratic memory during the period 1931–1980." Accessed April 7, 2014. http://www20.gen cat.cat/portal/site/memorialdemocratic.
7 See the project "La batalla de la memòria." Accessed 7, 2014. http://labatalladelamemoria.blogspot.com.es/.

Works cited

Andrés, Elías. 2004. *Memoria de España*. Spain: Radio Televisión Española.
Armengou, Montse and Ricard Belis. 2006. *Ramon Perera, L'home que va salvar Barcelona*. Spain: Televisió de Catalunya.
Aznar, Manuel. 1938. *La batalla del Ebro*. Spain: Departamento Nacional de Cinematrografía.

Balfour, Sebastian. 2008. "The Concept of Historical Revisionism: Spain since the 1930s." *International Journal of Iberian Studies* 3 (1): 179–186.

Bullón, Alfonso and Luis Eugenio Togores. 2012. *La Guerra Civil Española. Mitos al descubierto.* Spain: Fundación San Pablo-CEU.

Casanova, Julián. 2005. "La Historia que nos cuenta TVE." *El País*, April 3. Accessed April 7, 2014. http://elpais.com/diario/2005/04/03/opinion/1112479208_850215.html

Castelló, Enric. 2012. "Memoria en conflicto. Guerra civil y posguerra en los documentales de la televisión catalana." In *La guerra civil televisada. La representación de la contienda en la ficción y el documental españoles*, edited by Sira Hernández-Corchete, 79–100. Salamanca: Comunicación Social.

———. 2014. "Disrupting 'Wills to Truth.' How Catalan TV Documentary Contributed to the Democratization of Spanish Civil War Narratives." *Memory Studies* 7 (2): 223–238.

Castelló, Enric and Hugh O'Donnell. 2006. "Historias de Cataluña: Ficción y memoria histórica en la televisión pública catalana." In *Historias de la pequeña pantalla. Representaciones históricas en la televisión de la España democrática*, edited by Francisca López, Elena Cueto, and David R. George Jr., 175–196. Madrid and Frankfurt: Iberoamericana/Vervuert.

Cervera, Pascual. 1987. *España en guerra*. Spain: RTVE.

Corbera, Mireia, Sandra Olsina, and Anna Moregón. 2010. *Han bombardejat una escola*. Spain. Accessed April 7, 2014. http://vimeo.com/77693848.

Coronado, Carlota. 2016. "Postmemory of the Spanish Civil War: Cinematographic Construction of the Conflict in the Twenty-first Century." *Catalan Journal of Communication and Cultural Studies* 8 (1): 31–43.

Cué, Carlos E. 2002. "El PP rechaza retirar las subvenciones de la Fundación Francisco Franco." *El País*, 16 October. Accessed April 7, 2014. http://elpais.com/diario/2002/10/16/cultura/1034719204_850215.html.

de Pablo, Santiago. 2012. "¿Invasión o conflicto fraticida? El País Vasco y la guerra civil en Euskal Telebista." In *La guerra civil televisada. La representación de la contienda en la ficción y el documental españoles*, edited by Sira Hernández Corchete, 101–118. Salamanca: Comunicación Social.

Domingo, Alfonso. 2006. *La memoria recobrada*. Spain: Radio Televisión Española.

Galán, Elena and José C. Rueda Laffond. 2016. "Those Wars Are also My Wars: An Approach to practices of Postmemory in the Contemporary Spanish Comic." *Catalan Journal of Communication and Cultural Studies* 8 (1): 63–77.

Galló, Isabel and Rosario G. Gómez. 2011. "La guerra civil, según Telemadrid." *El País*, July 5. http://elpais.com/diario/2011/07/15/radiotv/1310680802_850215.html.

Garay, Jesús. 2008. "Mirant al el." Spain: Massa d'Or Produccions, Silverspace Animation Studies, TVC, ETB, Istituto Luce S.p.A. Accessed April 7, 2014. http://www.tv3.cat/videos/323359.

Garde-Hansen, Joanne. 2011. *Media and Memory*. Edinburgh: Edinburgh University Press.

Gonzalo, Juan Luis. 2016. "Simulating history in Contemporary Board Games: The Case of the Spanish Civil War." *Catalan Journal of Communication and Cultural Studies* 8 (1): 143–158.

Gubern, Roman. 1986. *1936–1939: La Guerra de España en la pantalla, de la propaganda a la historia.* Madrid: Filmoteca Española.

Halbwachs, Maurice. 1992. *On Collective Memory*. Chicago: University of Chicago Press.

Hemingway, Ernest. 2007 (1938). "El viejo en el puente." In *Cuentos*, 106–108. Translated by Damián Alou. Barcelona: Lumen.

Hepp, Andreas. 2009. "Differentiation: Mediatization and Cultural Change." In *Mediatization: Concept, Changes, Consequences*, edited by Knut Lunby, 139–158. New York: Peter Lang.

Hernández Corchete, Sira. 2012a. "Introducción. La televisión española como instancia productora de la memoria colectiva e histórica sobre la guerra civil." In *La guerra civil televisada. La representación de la contienda en la ficción y el documental españoles*, edited by Sira Hernández Corchete, 9–20. Salamanca: Comunicación Social.

———. 2012b. "La mirada documental de la guerra civil en el tardofranquismo y la Transición. De la celebración de la paz a la búsqueda de la reconciliación nacional." In *La guerra civil televisada. La representación de la contienda en la ficción y el documental españoles*, edited by Sira Hernández Corchete, 23–52. Salamanca: Comunicación Social.

Herrmann, Gina. 2008. "Documentary's Labours of Law. The Television Journalism of Montse Armengou and Ricard Belis." *Journal of Spanish Cultural Studies* 9 (2): 193–212.

Hjarvard, Stig. 2008. "The Mediatization of Society. A Theory of the Media as Agents of Social and Cultural Change." *Nordicom Review* 29 (2): 105–134.

Hoskins, Andrew. 2009. "The Mediatization of Memory." In *Save As . . . Digital Memories*, edited by Joanne Garde-Hansen, Andrew Hoskins, and Anna Reading, 27–43. Edinburgh: Edinburgh University Press.

Ibáñez, Juan Carlos. 2012. "Historia y relectura del consenso transicional en los documentales televisivos: El caso de La memoria recobrada." In *La guerra civil televisada. La representación de la contienda en la ficción y el documental españoles*, edited by Sira Hernández Corchete, 53–78. Salamanca: Comunicación Social.

Jefatura del Estado. 1977. *Ley 46/1977, de 15 de Octubre, de Amnistía*. Madrid: *Boletín Oficial del Estado*. Accessed April 10, 2014. http://www.boe.es/boe/dias/1977/10/17/pdfs/A22765–22766.pdf.

———. 2007. *Ley 52/2007, de 26 de Diciembre, por la que se reconocen y amplían derechos y se establecen medidas en favor de quienes padecieron persecución o violencia durante la guerra civil y la dictadura*. Madrid: *Boletín Oficial del Estado*. Accessed April 10, 2014. http://www.boe.es/boe/dias/2007/12/27/pdfs/A53410–53416.pdf.

Juliá, Santos. 2011. "Una lamentable manipulación." *El País*, July 13. Accessed April 15, 2014. http://elpais.com/diario/2011/07/13/radiotv/1310508006_850215.html

Junquera, Natalia. 2013a. "La memoria histórica vuelve a los tribunales españoles." *El País*, December 30. Accessed April 15, 2014. http://politica.elpais.com/politica/2013/12/30/actualidad/1388437601_806015.html

———. 2013b. "La ONU insta a España a cumplir 'su obligación' y buscar a los desaparecidos." *El País*, November 15. Accessed April 15, 2014. http://politica.elpais.com/politica/2013/11/15/actualidad/1384521012_539699.html

Labanyi, Jo. 2008. "The Politics of Memory in Contemporary Spain." *Journal of Spanish Cultural Studies* 9 (2): 119–125.

Lee, Philip and Thomas, Pradip N. 2012. "Introduction. Public Media and the Right to Memory: Towards an Encounter with Justice." In *Public Memory, Public Media, and the Politics of Justice*, edited by Philip Lee and Pradip N. Thomas, 1–22. New York: Palgrave Macmillan.

Molinero, Carme. 2010. "La Transición y la 'renuncia' a la recuperación de la 'memoria democrática'." *Journal of Spanish Cultural Studies* 11 (1): 33–52.

Montero, Julio and María Antonia Paz. 2011. "The Spanish Civil War on Televisión Española during the Franco Era (1956–1975)." *Comunicación y sociedad* 24 (2): 149–197.

Palacio, Manuel and Carmen Ciller. 2010. "La mirada televisiva del pasado. El caso español (2005–2010)." In *Memoria histórica e identidad en cine y televisión*, edited by Juan Carlos Ibáñez and Francesca Anania, 38–55. Comunicación Social: Zamora.

Pingree, Geoffrey B. 2007. "The Documentary Dilemma and the Spanish Civil War." In *Teaching Representations of the Spanish Civil War*, edited by Noël Valis, 305–316. New York: The Modern Language Association of America.

Pons Múria, Mario. 2009. "La batalla de la memòria." Spain: Televisió de Catalunya; Mario Pons Productions; Institut Català d'Indústries Culturals and Memorial Democràtic. Accessed April 7, 2014. http://www.tv3.cat/videos/1046719.

Preston, Paul. 2008. *We Saw Spain Die. Foreign Correspondents in the Spanish Civil War*. London: Constable & Robinson.

———. 2014. "La Guerra Civil al cap de setanta anys." In *La Guerra Civil Espanyola*, 11–26. Barcelona: Base.

Quílez, Laia. 2016. "Feminine Resistances: The Figure of the Republican Woman in Carolina Astudillo's Documentary Cinema." *Catalan Journal of Communication and Cultural Studies* 8 (1): 79–93.

Reig, Joaquin, Paul Laven, and Fritz C. Mauch. 1938. *España heroica*. Spain: Falange Española Tradicionalista y de las Jons/Hispano Filmproduktion.

Resina, Joan Ramon. 2003. "Introduction." In *Disremembering the Dictatorship. The Politics of Memory in the Spanish Transition to Democracy*, edited by Joan Ramon Resina, 1–16. Amsterdam: Rodopi.

———. 2010. "Window of Opportunity. The Television Documentary as 'After-Image' of the War." In *Teaching Representations of the Spanish Civil War*, edited by Noël Valis, 406–424. New York: The Modern Language Association of America.

Reverte, Jorge M. 2006a. *El laberinto español*. Spain: Televisión Española.

———. 2006b. *La batalla del Ebro*. Spain: Televisión Española. Accessed April 7, 2014. http://www.rtve.es/alacarta/videos/la-batalla-del-ebro.

———. 2006c. *La batalla del Ebro*. Madrid: Crítica.

Rodrigo, Javier. 2009. "España era una patria enferma. La violencia de la guerra civil y su legitimación en la extrema derecha española: Entre historia, representación y revisionismo." *Revista de Historia Jerónimo Zurita* 84: 189–230.

Sáenz de Buruaga, Ernesto and Víctor Arribas. 2006. *Madrid opina*. Spain: Telemadrid.

Sánchez-Biosca, Vicente. 2006. *Cine y guerra civil española. Del mito a la memoria*. Madrid: Alianza Editorial.

Sánchez Cervelló, Josep. 2001. *Conflicte i violència a l'Ebre: De Napoleó a Franco*. Barcelona: Flor del viento.

Santos, Mateo. 1936. *Reportaje del movimiento revolucionario en Barcelona*. Spain: CNT-FAI. Oficina de Información y propaganda. Accessed April 7, 2014. http://www.youtube.com/watch?v=UDUZ30XndYg.

United Nations. 2014. "UN Expert Urges Spain to Probe Alleged Atrocities during the 1930's Civil War." *UN News Centre*. Accessed July 4, 2016. http://www.un.org/apps/news/story.asp?NewsID=47082#.V3o7X5OLTJw

van Dijck, José. 2007. *Mediated Memories in the Digital Age*. Stanford, CA: Stanford University Press.

45

A TRANSMODERN APPROACH TO AFRO-IBERIAN LITERATURE

Cristián H. Ricci

The literature of migration (re)presents radical renegotiations of personal identities and nationalities through "archeological excavations" and "transversal communications" that put in motion the "impure" and hybrid quality of identity. At a more formal level, migration literature emanates from linguistic impurities and heteroglossia, errant perspectives, foreign voices, and foundling, multidimensional and rhizomatic narrative and poetic forms. Sten Pultz Moslund associates the rhizomatic nature of migration texts with "linguistic homelessness," producing a cacophony of voices and languages (6). Gilles Deleuze's poetics accumulate an entire vocabulary of geographical and migratory terms, such as root-networks, nomads, movement, speed and lines of flight, territories and borders, in-betweenness and multiplicities. Minor literature is rhizomatic: it involves a linguistic deviance, an impoverished vocabulary, and improper use of grammar; an unadorned, minimalistic style, which turns it into a sign machine that avoids closure, that keeps pushing language to its limits, breaking down signification and multiplying meaning potentials. Minor literature is thus supposed to radically disrupt the purity and homogenising unity of major cultures (2010, 7–8).

I have analyzed elsewhere the paradigms of Moroccan and Equatorial Guinean literatures dealing with the Maghrebi and sub-Saharan diaspora in Spain, which began in the 1960s and continues to the present.[1] Building on this previous work, I pose the following series of questions: What is the potential readership of this literature of diaspora? Why does it not have a place in Spain's book market? What is its future? In this essay, I frame Moroccan and Equatorial Guinean literature written in Castilian and Catalan within the broader context of border studies and approach it from the theoretical perspective of intercultural and postcolonial studies. There is a group of Moroccan authors who show in their writings what Enrique Dussel (2005) calls "alteridad cultural de la poscolonización," incorporating the best of Spanish and European modernity to develop, not a cultural style that tends to a globalized unit, undifferentiated or empty, but a *trans-modern pluriverse* that draws on a number of cultural contexts: European, Asian, African, Islamic, Christian, and Latin American. Before I begin my analysis of Moroccan and Equatorial Guinean literature, I want to acknowledge that there is also a very prolific and active group of Saharawi authors who write poetry, narrative, and theater in Castilian. Because of the limited space of this article, and because most (if not all) Saharawi literature in Castilian does not reflect hybridizing processes, I do not analyze it in this article.[2]

An overview of Afro-Iberian literature

The first literary works addressing the modern migration of African citizens to Europe during the seventies were written in Arabic: Abdallah Laroui (*al-Gurba*, 1971, translated in English as *The Exile* or *The Loneliness*) and Mohamed Zafzaf (*al-Mar'a wa-l-warda*, 1970, in English *The Woman and the Rose*). Since the second largest arrival of Maghrebis to Spain on February 7, 1992, new Moroccan authors have opted to use Castilian to address the migration outburst in Moroccan and Spanish newspapers and literary journals. Moroccan literature in Castilian remained somewhat dormant between 1956 and 1992, except for literary publications in *L'Opinion*'s weekly section called "La página en español," and *La mañana*, Rabat's first and only Spanish-language newspaper produced by Moroccan nationals. As the result of the awakening of this literature, Mohamed Azirar and Mohamed Sibari published the first two Moroccan novels written entirely in Spanish, *Kaddour "el fantasioso"* (Azirar, 1988, as a feuilleton in *L'Opinion*), and *El caballo* (Sibari, 1990 as a feuilleton in *L'Opinion*, and as a book in 1993). The latter is the story of a migrant from Larache, whose trip to Spain is frustrated by Tangier's mafia. After *El Caballo*, there have been a number of other short stories published in Spanish, principally by Sibari, Mohamed Bouissef Rekab (today, Morocco's second most prolific writer, with nine novels and one book of short stories), and León Cohen Mesonero, a Sephardic writer from Larache. Ahmed Daoudi's *El diablo de Yudis* (1994), addressing the subject of migration, is the first novel by a Moroccan author in Spanish to have been published in Spain. In all these texts, the desire to migrate, the moral degradation of the characters, and a moralizing rhetoric are recurrent features.

Some of the Castilian-language texts about the customs and people of Morocco help to demystify a series of ethnocentric clichés that many travelers, historians, and European literati had made about Morocco and the rest of the non-Western world. However, if we take into account that most of these authors do not manage to sell their books in Spain (nor in the rest of the Spanish-speaking world), we cannot measure the impact these texts have in reducing the prejudices that exist about Morocco and its customs, nor do we know if these texts will be taken seriously by researchers. In this vein, Alicia Gaspar de Alba says that a book gives a writer a green card to venture into the world of letters. However, as in all such worlds, there are different levels of cultural citizenship (2000, 14). To avoid being a "literary wetback," these writers would have to fulfill at least two guidelines: to begin writing what the Western market is consuming at the moment, or to be exotic, magical, and sensual enough to captivate the Western reader, "always eager and restless for romanticism" (Said 1978, 10). Therefore, Moroccan borderland writers have reconstructed their alternative position within European modernity from an outsider's perspective; that is to say, from a worldwide standpoint, as opposed to the provincial perspective of the European. Consequently, as Homi Bhabha (1995, 12) proposes, transnational histories of migrants, of colonized (or neo-colonized), or of political refugees are the fertile lands where a worldwide literature could settle.

Regrettably, Spanish publishers are not interested in the Moroccan literature written in Castilian that narrates the crossing of the Gibraltar Strait. At this point, it is necessary to clarify that the realist aesthetic and the didactic-moralizing nature of these writings (chronicles, diaries, memoirs) are common to the sprouting of other borderland literatures that try to show the socioeconomic and cultural problems of migrants. Simultaneously, this kind of literature essentially responds to the Arabic tradition in Moroccan literature. More particularly, the short narratives of the seventies respond to a concept of social intention. In this sense, it seems that these texts on the crossing of the Gibraltar Strait have not managed to overcome the immediacy of a testimonial urgency, without greater historical depth. It is also true that with time, this type of literature begins a process of maturity towards purer forms of fiction that incorporate myths, the fantastic or supernatural effects, and the use of non-linear time. As Jean Cazemajou states (quoted in Martín-Rodríguez 2000, 255), mythical structures contribute to organize the narrative in order to be presented to distant readers. This rhetoric contributes to the enjoyment of the work by a non-Moroccan reader.

The opening towards Western literature can result in the loss of the Oriental flavor of Moroccan literature. As pointed out by Said, those same "Orientals," using Western methods of *Orientalization*, might weaken their raw material. In other words, there is a plea for a multi-cultural and multi-dimensional literature, but not one that is committed to assimilation, because assimilation implies an acceptance of superiority of the target culture (Said 1978, 278). I do not believe there is any risk of the latter, because while Western travelers to the East defined their identity in contrast to the image of the Other, Moroccan writers such as Ahmed Ararou, Ahmed El Gamoun, Larbi El Harti, and Mohamed Lahchiri are very conscious of the ontological and epistemological differences between both cultures, and can cross from one side to the other (from Occident to Orient) and criticize both cultures, with no need to request a "visa" from any academic guard, neither from the East nor from the West. Without apostatizing their Arab-African-Muslim culture, in many cases they have a better knowledge of "la hermosa casa del vecino [España], más que la propia" (El Harti 2004, 40).

In the narratives of Ararou, El Gamoun, El Harti, and Lahchiri, there is a "selective rejection" of Westernization, which is typical of postcolonial literature. These narratives are consistent with the concept of the philosophy of liberation. In this regard, they are not revolutionaries who fight for a completely new beginning; they do not represent the typical liberal discourse that mystifies national emancipation from Spain, nor are they Indigenists who deny history after the French and Spanish invasions. They propose, instead, to reconstruct their integrity within an Eastern and Western historical framework. In this sense, they recapture the historical identity of Morocco, a history that shares some characteristics with other post-colonialist literatures – a history that is conscious of the neocolonial relations that the new world order imposes.

Ahmed Ararou's fiction is a part of this literary paradigm, which is still marginal and trying to find its way. When I interviewed him in 2005, he described himself as a "writer without a portfolio." He talks, for example, about comparative linguistics, applied psychology, and literary criticism, uses stylistic resources taken from both Western and Eastern canonical writers, and incorporates stories or anecdotes from Moroccan folklore. From this amalgam of literary resources, Ararou constructs a marginal work that is immune to being reduced by categorization. Nonetheless, as a writer who affirms the modern Western literary canon, his narratives also contrast with those who pride themselves in being transgressors semantically and structurally. Ararou manages to surpass the artistic flexibility of postmodernism through the recognition of cultural differences and their coexistence with tradition. In this sense, his literary project exceeds, in form and content, the mere tracking of roots and the romanticizing of the Arab presence in al-Andalus. Whereas in the case of Moroccan writers of the eighties, such as Miloudi Chaghmoum and Mustafa Al-Misnawi, the stories of exploitation, submission, and the evolution of resistance strategies are authenticated from the periphery, Ararou situates the reader on what Homi Bhabha (1995) and García Canclini (2001) refer to as the cultural hybridization of the borderland condition. The hybridization allows Ararou to translate – and therefore to make a record of – the social imaginary of the metropolis as well as the cultural and technological modernity imposed upon or consented to in Morocco.

Writers such as Ararou, El Gamoun, and El Harti are aware that the pact of civilizations is based upon an implicit recognition of a multicultural space, with an enormous variety of traditions from which to choose the elements for a new model of literary development. The writer is not confined to espouse a single literary technique. At the same time, this type of literature is inseparable from the modernization of Morocco. Yet it observes analytically the Western imposition of products and beliefs, especially those that arrive through the signals of satellite television. Leafing through the annals of mythology is fundamental to the narratives of El Gamoun and Ararou, so that the Spanish reader, regardless of their familiarity with Moroccan and Arab myths such as Gilgamesh, can relate the narration to other utopian territories in literary history. In this regard, I see that a peripheral dialogue "South-South" exists between these Moroccan writers and others who face imperialistic cultures. I am referring here to thinkers from Asia and Latin America, as well as indigenous North Americans and Chicanos. The literary projects of El Gamoun and Ararou manifest what Enrique Dussel and the Moroccan philosopher Mohamed Mesbahi (2006) call "popular post-capitalist culture," that is, they surpass the reductive limits of a fallacious monolithic culture, reconstructing the cultural history of Morocco within the frame of global history: from Asia, through the Asian-Afro-European proto-history all the way to Hispanic Christianity; through the Spanish protectorate and onto postcolonial and neocolonized Moroccan culture.

Imazighen (Berber)-Catalan and Afro-Iberian identity

Castilian is no longer the only language of the Peninsula used by Moroccans; nor is it any longer the case that men dominate the literary field. In the past ten years, Catalan presses have been publishing female Moroccan-Amazigh voices, who write in Catalan and who have lived in Catalonia since childhood.[3] The significance of these narratives adds controversy to the ongoing political and language rivalry between Castilians and the different nationalisms of the Iberian Peninsula (particularly Catalan). Laila Karrouch published her autobiography in 2004, *De Nador a Vic* ("Premi Columna Jove," published by Planeta/Oxford in Castilian in 2005 under the title *Laila*). During the same year (2004) the Catalan press Columna, published Najat El Hachmi's autobiography, *Jo també sóc catalana*. Moreover, in 2008, El Hachmi was awarded the "Premi de les Lletres Catalanes Ramon Llull" for her first novel *L'últim patriarca* (in Castilian, *El último patriarca*, 2008), a novel that could be defined as autobiographical fiction. El Hachmi published a second novel, *La caçadora de cossos* (in Castilian, *La cazadora de cuerpos*) in 2011. Saïd El Kadaoui, the only male among these writers, published a novel in Castilian, *Límites y fronteras*, in 2008, and an autobiographical essay, *Cartes al meu fill. Un català de soca-rel, gairebé*, in 2011. Finally, Jamila Al Hassani published *La lluita de la dona bereber* in 2013. These narratives of cultural and economic survival bind together the immigration experiences of Karrouch, El Hachmi, El Kadaoui, and Al Hassani with the founding texts on exile by the already mentioned Muhammad Zafzaf, Abdellah Laroui, and Rachid Nini, a sociological narrative in Castilian by Pasqual Moreno Torregrossa and Mohamed El Gheryb, *Dormir al raso* (1994), and the essays of Sami Naïr and Juan Goytisolo, *El peaje de la vida* (2000) and *España y sus ejidos* (2003).

The four Imazighen-Moroccan authors refer to their writing as a therapeutic process that assists the characters towards the closure of their life-learning cycles. In this respect, Morocco (the Rif) lies in the past and Catalonia in the future. Linguistically, these authors confirm that their "Catalanness" does not define itself through antithesis with their "Moroccanness" or "Amazighness," but rather, their identities multiply themselves according to their class status, the male or female version of their testimony, and their place in the generational lines. Thus, my goal is to analyze how the subaltern voices of immigrants may disrupt (or antagonize) the modern canon of the literatures of the Peninsula, as well as, following Anjali Prabhu's reminder, how hybridity discourses are able "to dismantle power structures" (2007, xiv). In the same vein, Marianne David and Javier Muñoz-Basols indicate that diaspora narratives generate "a multitude of sub-narratives, each one unstable and specific to place and moment, each a distinct and idiosyncratic language system of pain and hardship with its own history and tradition, its own socioeconomic and political underpinnings" (2011, xvi).

Given the implicit pedagogical and moral intention of the author to promote tolerance and *convivencia*, Karrouch's autobiography tends to lessen the identity crisis she suffers upon arrival in Catalonia. However, it does bring forth the economic hardships that her family must overcome to live in Spain, and the contradictory role of Muslim women living in the West that must submit to the will of their husbands and fathers. Al Hassani in *La lluita de la dona bereber* is emphatic on this point when she claims that:

> mai he sabut què és l'amor d'un pare i què és realment tenir un pare, suposo que si hagués estat un nen hauria tingut més sort [. . .]. No volia seguir el pas de la mare, que es va casar amb un desconegut, sense amor, sense respecte, només per procrear i cuinar [. . .]. [S]empre he vist un dictador a casa i no un pare. D'ara endavant treballaré fort per oblidar la teva cara, aquella cara d'horror, d'odi, d'indiferència cap a nosaltres.
>
> (11, 27, 109–110)

At the same time, Al Hassani does not hesitate to blame Amazigh women for contributing to their "esclavisme" (86), for accepting that women should not go to college and must wear the hijab and djellaba (61–62); "la lluita pels drets d'un mateix comença a casa" (84). However, Al Hassani, following El Hachmi in *Jo també sóc catalana*, concludes that Western women are also victims of male abuse: "la dona occidental no anava tapada però també perdia la seva identitat quan havia de patir maltractament físic y psicològic" (90). Learning Catalan is the key to success in Al Hassani's character's "fight" to overcome prejudices and become a lawyer on behalf of oppressed women: "El fet de dominar la llengua li va obrir moltes portes [. . .] [E]star més preparada per ajudar-se i ajudar els seus fills [. . .] tot allò que era prohibit per les famílies tradicionals dels pobles berebers" (62, 79).

El Hachmi combines the contradictory feelings arising from the contact between languages with a certain degree of alienation that will "regnar en [her] vida " (2004b, 47). Such an assertion suggests a parallel to the mental state of *nepantlismo* ("being or feeling in between") that Chicana writer Gloria Anzaldúa asserts in *Borderlands/La Frontera*, and that refers to the "transference" of cultural and spiritual values from one group to another (1985, 78); *nepantlismo* that, in the specific case of Muslim women "located between god and man," Abdelkebir Khatibi translates as "the *mise en abyme* of theological order" (1985, 80). In *L'últim patriarca*, the narrator's (and main character's) intention is to "negotiate" her beliefs with God as well as the ritual practices of Islam, and, above all, mark her situation as a "retournée" to emphasize her condition of *mestiza*, of foreigner both in her North African culture as well as in Europe.

Thus, it is not coincidental that Najat El Hachmi assumes a traumatic-anomalous-deviated discourse in writing *L'últim patriarca*. That is, with this novel, El Hachmi accounts for the complex, controversial and contradictory literary and hybridizing processes of marginal and borderland literatures, aware that the colonial difference of the "borderland enunciating subject" (Mignolo 2000, 28) is not only uttered through a resisting and dissenting discourse, but is also materialized in the literary representation of the pain and anger of her "fractured" stories, of her memories, of her subjectivities. Overall, the novel highlights the *misovire* (neologism coined by Cameroon writer Warewere Liking) nature of the narrator; that is, of a woman who does not seem to find a man worthy of admiration, as well as the clear intention to apply what Abdelkebir Khatibi defines as "the double criticism of the paradigm-Other" (2001, 72); the narrator questions and "disengages" (2001, 73) the values imposed by Muslim-Amazigh society, "so theological, so charismatic, so patriarchal" (2001, 72), and the hegemonic structure of Western society, be it Catalan/Spanish/European. The coexistence with the Catalans/Spanish, her Muslim-Amazigh origins, and the voluntary adoption of Catalan as a means of artistic expression results in four perfectly defined cultures, with their sum acting as the basic foundation for a fifth: hybrid, interstitial, and interpellating in equal amounts Amazigh and Catalan culture.

In the writings of Karrouch, El Hachmi, and Al Hassani there is evidence of a continuous conflict between exoticism and the universal scope of North African literature, reinforced in this case when dealing with female writers. For her part, Najat El Hachmi writes a "Carta d'un immigrant" in 2004, a message to an anonymous immigrant whose ending I consider very appropriate for the development of the borderland concept: "Aprendràs a viure, finalment, a la frontera d'aquests dos mons, un lloc que pot ser divisió, però que també és encontre, punt de trobada. Un bon dia et creuràs *afortunat de gaudir d'aquesta frontera*, et descobriràs a tu mateix *més complet*, *més híbrid*, més immens que qualsevol altra persona" (2004a; my emphasis). In this mutation process, we must acknowledge, as Walter Mignolo points out, that language is not merely a neutral tool that represents the honest wish to tell the truth, but also – as borne out by the narratives of Ararou, El Gamoun, El Harti, Lahchiri and, of course, El Hachmi – a tool for the construction of a history and the invention of realities (Mignolo 1993, 122).

I concur with Prabhu in making a distinction between diasporic and creolization narratives, as while the first is premised on a past trauma that constitutes and links the members of a group in a discourse of victimhood, the second can be seen to display an overweening pride in hybrid agency, being forward-looking and concerned with interaction (2007, 13–14). According to David and Muñoz-Basols, host nations and migrant writers should be engaged in "the exploration of legitimate demands and aspirations together with adaptive modes and strategies with the goal of community building" (2011, xviii). Altogether, host countries must adapt "to a changing world, balancing competing interests, and revising traditional concepts of nationhood to make them more capacious and tolerant of difference" (David and Muñoz-Basols 2011, xviii). Najat El Hachmi combines both impulses, crucial to the forging of a discourse adequate to the multiple tactics required for a successful postcolonial praxis. This is why I consider El Hachmi's literary project to be significant, because it goes beyond a merely feminist view of the social situation, to render what could be the origin of an Afro-Iberian identity, critically engaged in feelings of *unhomeliness* and exclusion.

Judging by the marketing strategy of Editorial Planeta (including the book cover design and the spending of more than euros 300,000 in "Orientalist" advertisements in *El País*), some people might argue that El Hachmi is a doubly colonized subject (by gender and race). Planeta is certainly more interested in selling postcolonial women's writing – and, at the same time, fulfilling the European's desire for exoticism – than giving voice to those traditionally kept in the shadows. The fact that Spanish publishing houses care about publishing subaltern voices of immigration is surely a good sign (and, in fact, there are positive examples as the above-mentioned presses in the Castilian section); however, we should investigate what exactly the authors are willing to "negotiate" for their books to appear in display windows of bookstores.[4]

I end this section with a note from El Hachmi with regard to what kind of reader *Jo també sóc catalana* was aiming for: "A los que se llenan la boca con la inmigración y sólo han visto al inmigrante de lejos. Pero también a los que están preocupados por el tema de la identidad catalana" (Nuria Navarro 2007). Regardless of the Orientalist marketing strategies of Planeta, *L'ultim patriarca*, by showing critical perspectives in relation to the double postcolonial oppression of women, and not leaving up the task of unmasking the differences in race, class, and gender in the immigration communities, finally achieves the objective El Hachmi has previously delineated in her autobiography: "desferme del meu propi enclaustrament, un enclaustrament fet de denominacions d'origen, de pors, d'esperances sovint estroncades, de dubtes continus, d'abismes de *pioners* que exploren *nous mons*" (2004b 14; my emphasis).

Colonial and postcolonial literature of Equatorial Guinea

The progressive transformation of a collective patrimony into a more personal imprint culminates in 1953 with the appearance of the first African novel in Castilian, *Cuando los combes luchaban (Novela de costumbres de la Guinea Española)* by Leoncio Evita.[5] The novel is about the life of a white Protestant missionary in pre-colonial continental Guinea who acts as an asymmetrical literary symbol of contrast with the native characters. There is an ethnographic approach to the autochthonous culture in the plot, but in turn, there is a departure from a traditional lifestyle, which is measured up against the superior civilization. The phenomenon is obviously striking, particularly because the other relevant novel of the colonial period, *Una lanza por el boabí* (1962),[6] written by Daniel Jones Mathama – even when its main character is not white – still admits that the *boabí* becomes a better man through contact with the superior civilization, and considers it "an inescapable duty to proclaim all the way the great work Spain is doing on the island" (1962, 309; my translation). Although this narrative of "un-resistance," which defends and even justifies the colonial enterprise, is regarded by Ndongo-Bidyogo "as a positive sign of serenity and respect for the folklore and tradition of Guineans" (1984, 30; my translation), there is a clear point of divergence from other African literatures such as those written in French and English, which master the discourse of anticolonialism and a quest for black identity. This uniquely Guinean trait of "tolerance" towards domination shows a clear alienation as well as the impossibility of self-recognition, the *aliénation intellectuelle* described by Frantz Fanon (1961, 16).

After Equatorial Guinea's independence in 1968, and its later coup d'etat (1969), all cultural production came to a sudden halt. Francisco Macías Nguema's dictatorship not only suspended the previous constitution (Decree n° 115, May 7, 1971), but also jailed or murdered nearly half of the population, expelled all foreigners (Lipski 2002, 70), and "silenced" the voices of dissidents and any sort of intellectual expression, a prohibition that resulted in a massive Guinean exile during the mid seventies. These years of silence, 1969–1979, meant that all creative work was produced in exile (N'gom 1993, 414). The literature of writers in exile was fragmented from within as there was little or no contact between exiles, given their presence in Spain was not only clandestine, but also geographically scattered. Had these writers found one another and gathered in literary/intellectual circles in cities such as Madrid or Barcelona, I believe that the creative production and collective artistic and literary testimonies of Guineans could have followed a similar pattern as that of the Latin American *boom* in Barcelona or the earlier *négritude* movement in Paris.

Guinean exiles include writers such as Juan Balboa Boneke. Their diasporic discourse is clearly against the dictatorial regime and makes a point of exploring the historical and cultural trauma experienced by Guinea. The poetic genre of the time introduces the configuration of an alternative form of fixated nostalgia that embodied itself in the rhetoric of orphanhood. This diasporic poetry coexists with the emergence of the narrative of writers such as Donato

Ndongo-Bidyogo and Francisco Zamora Loboch. These authors again evoke the loss of their Motherland in opposition to the un-homely European city. However, according to N'gom, after the end of the Macías' regime and with Teodoro Obiang's coup d'etat, a renaissance of these dislocated writers was possible, both through the now democratic Madrid of the late seventies and the Centro Hispano-Guineano of Malabo's Press under the direction of Donato Ndongo-Bidyogo (1993, 416). The latter publishes *Las Tinieblas de tu memoria negra* (1987) [trans. in English by Michael Ugarte, *Shadows of Your Black Memory*], a point of inflection for the modern *postcolonial* Afro-Hispanic novel, and the first volume of his diachronic trilogy *Los hijos de la tribu*, completed by *Los poderes de la tempestad*, 1997, and *El metro*, 2007. The title of Ndongo's first novel, *Las tinieblas*, is a reflection (and translation) of a poem by Léopold Sédar Senghor, and "a homage to the cultural *négritude* movement" (Fra Molinero 2002, 163). The child protagonist of Ndongo's novel is torn between two excluding paradigms. On the one side, his uncle (Tío Abeso) appears as the symbol of a traditional culture that resists colonial ideological oppression while reassessing the indisputable value of the native culture, and on the other, his own father impersonates "the white mask," the mimicry of the agent of civilization. The boy acts as a dislocated translational link between his uncle and Padre Ortiz, the Catholic priest of the colonial *mission civilisatrice*. As Baltasar Fra Molinero points out, "[a]s a linguistic interpreter, this boy has to alternatively adopt the voice of the two adults without being able to speak out his own opinions" (2002, 167). Also, during this highly productive period for Guinean literature and the subsequent Spanish discovery of these outlying emerging signs, another relevant and versatile author, Francisco Zamora Loboch, publishes an ironic essay of black resistance against racism in Spain, *Cómo ser negro y no morir en Aravaca* (1994) and, five years later, a poetry book entitled *Memoria de Laberinto* (1999).

The women writers of this period, though, had left Equatorial Guinea when they were young. The first Guinean female writer is Raquel Ilonbé, who in 1978 published a book of poems titled *Ceiba*, and in 1987, a book of children's literature entitled *Leyendas guineanas*. Her poetry does not reflect the diasporic experience present in the poetic corpus of her contemporaries, but rather she delves into a fascinating search for a traditional culture and its influence in the Western world (N'Gom 1996, 60). On the other hand, María Nsué Angüe, author of *Ekomo* (1985), introduces a novel that explores cultural attitudes towards African women through the voice of a male character, and more interestingly, addresses new questions that arise from the growing conflict between the patriarchal Fang tradition on the verge of extinction and the realization of a changing modern present. According to Adam Lifshey, this is the first post-independence novel of Equatorial Guinea, whose "[. . .] collective cultural memory at hand is being lost at a tribal and continental level, not being gained within a new national context" (2003, 173). Among the few female voices present in the literature of Equatorial Guinea, there is also a playwright, Trinidad Morgades Besari, and a writer of short fiction, María Caridad Riloha. In 2005, Guillermina Mekuy made her debut with a novel entitled *El llanto de la perra* (Plaza y Janés 2005). Mekuy's first novel was a success and soon she became a mass media phenomenon. In 2008, Mekuy published *Las tres vírgenes de Santo Tomás*, which narrates the story of three mulatto sisters under the strong influence of a black African father who believes he is the reincarnation of St. Thomas Aquinas, and a white Spanish mother, an animist sorcerer initiated in Africa. This parental crossing-over of cultures ("[. . .]tenían las almas cambiadas" 2008, 39), enables an extreme metaphysical dialogue between African traditional beliefs and a mystic, radical version of Christianity.

Moreover, the first group of authors to have been writing since the nineties and into the twenty-first century are identified with the "Nuevo costumbrismo nacional" or "Nueva narrativa nacional." José Fernando Siale Djangany's *Autorretrato con un infiel* (2007) presents the reality of Equatorial Guinea through an African "mythical realism," which not only offers a new symbolic cartography of historical trauma (*Poór Donanfer*, Fernando Poo; *Franck Nkó* for Franco; *Isco de Coor*, Isla de Corisco), but also where the author builds a plot of underlying criticism aimed at both the old colonizing empires (*Puerto Galo* for Portugal and *Cabo Norte* for Spain) and the new African state. This novel depicts a polyphonic representation of the transition from the colonial to the postcolonial era as a much needed mechanism to avoid the loss of history; the literary figures of historians, anthropologists, sociologists, and missionaries all act to adulterate and conspire to destroy material records of African history. The painting by Father Delatorre, "Autorretrato con un infiel," that gives the novel its title is an ironic statement asserting that the subaltern cannot yet "sketch himself." In other words, the African character is still being drawn by the dominating powers in their own aesthetic terms. The other revealing element is the figure of the traditional storyteller who is asked about the underlying meaning of the folk tales, and is not able to answer at all; and while in the novel, reading is also censored, the native characters are trapped in a space where they are not able to speak out their own culture (the traditional rites and customs have lost their original content and act as empty containers, pure forms) nor have access to the typographical culture. In Siale's novel there is an absolute nullification of the postcolonial subject dispossessed both of the oral and the written. "Do you exist?" asks Roberto Fernández Retamar (1995, 23), evoking the colonized as a distant echo, a cultural and historical void.

In the same way, references to the past in Siale's novel (as well as in other African authors such as Ben Okri and Nuruddin Farah) is construed through common mechanisms of interpreting the chaotic present. Such a narrative strategy is not only designed to represent a re-visiting of the past, but also attempts to determine whether the old colonial framework has really collapsed or whether it is maintained under different signs through neo-colonial practices. *Nambula* (2006), a short novel by Maximiliano Nkogo Esono, also follows the narration of the process of formation of a new African republic:

> El vendaval de la democracia y su irresistible corriente multipartidista procedente del Norte levanta auténticos torbellinos de ambiciones fratricidas y sacude con portentosa fuerza los sagrados pilares sobre los que hasta ahora se había asentado cómodamente el tradicional modo de ser del Sur.
>
> (2006, 5)

This making and unmaking of African reality through corruption, incompetence, unemployment, mercenarism, bureaucracy, and paramilitary violence brings forth the depiction of an "Afro-Occidental" political parody, in which there is a clear questioning of the authenticity of the African transition process towards the creation of modern nation-states shaped after "democratic-civilized" Western models.

In the novels of the authors mentioned previously, the characters see themselves as involuntary protagonists of a situation they disapprove of and, therefore, mock through an absurd exaggeration of charismatic power demonstrations, and humorous misinterpretations of Western political formulae. There is still a manifest depiction of traditional African elements that find themselves unnaturally placed in a fossilization process that clashes deeply with what seems to be a rehearsal of modern, foreign ways. In this "Nueva narrativa nacional," we find issues such as the coexistence of tradition (amulets, fetishes, witchcraft, initiation rites, griots), Western political methods, and theatrical diplomatic equations that are narrated as clumsily embedded in African society. Such deeply hypercritical, yet comical passages, are absorbed into the text in a satirical manner, ridiculing not only the new African politics, but also its original Western forms, expressing the disillusionment of the postcolonial era and overcoming simultaneously the "rhetoric of blame" against the West (Said 1978, 19). This group of writers shares two major themes with other African authors: the clash between a modern way of life and tradition, and the need to reconcile past and present, using literature as an agent of social transformation; and they agree that even if the idea of European modernity cannot be validated, neither can the newly installed African republic, which is as deceitful as the previous one.

The twenty-first century marks a period of dynamic coexistence between this last generation, that produced the Guinean literature of the past two decades of the twentieth century, and what I consider the breakthrough work of César Mba Abogo, who in 2007 opened up a new path for Guinean literature with his eclectic *El porteador de Marlow. Canción negra sin color*, and continued in 2010 with the publication of *Malabo blues. La ciudad remordida*. The structure of *El porteador de Marlow* and *Malabo blues* combines short stories, vignettes, poetic prose, poetry, and short descriptive catalogues of European, African, and Latin American cities. In *El porteador de Marlow* there is an explicit intertextual relationship with Italo Calvino's *Invisible Cities*, a literary game that also interconnects the gazes of Marco Polo's West and Genghis Khan's Far East. At the same time, both Mba's books introduce a new literary object that cannot be properly defined except on its own terms. The configuration of the books is polyhedral, subverting the rigid form of European narrative by introducing a flexible and pragmatic aesthetic sense, more akin to African oral traditions. Mba's texts do not share the coordinates in content and style of his contemporaries, but rather occupy a contingent in-between space that innovates and interrupts the discourse of the past: "Estoy condenado a vivir en una frontera / En la desidia ambigua y en la tormenta del exilio / No hay paredes en este mundo para mis rótulos" (2007, 100), a "[l]iminal space, in-between designations of identity" (Bhabha 1995, 5). In this way, the narrator is a "transeúnte" that portrays himself as a sort of alien that, indeed, recognizes his borderland path, but at the same time attempts to legitimize his ontological search for belonging:

> Había vivido aventuras insólitas en las capitales modernas; en Malabo yo era como todos ellos, mi piel no desentonaba con el latido de la calle, conocía las especias y licores locales, y sin embargo me sentía tan extranjero en Malabo como en todas partes. Recuerdo que viajo por el mundo pero en realidad viajo a mí mismo.
>
> (243–44, 248)

The *retournée*'s mission of *Malabo blues* is to alert Africans "de las patologías coloniales "[. . .], de la mentira de la razón cínica de Occidente" (2010, 77). However, the narrator of *Malabo blues* soon realizes the opposite, that *retournées* are "caballos de Troya que ocultan un tumulto de ideas importadas en sus entrañas. S[ueltan el] vómito occidental y envenen[an] la percepción de hermanos y hermanas" (2010, 78). The narrator blames his parents for the irreparable damage: "Deberían haber tenido huevos y criarnos aquí en lugar de mandarnos a España o a donde quiera que soplaran los vientos" (2010, 87). The interstitial location, caught in between monolithic and directly opposing identities, offers the chance of a hybridizing outlook that not only negotiates difference without the presence of identitary hierarchies, but also searches for a new definition, a definition that targets the colonized subject as well as the old colonizing Metropolis. Europe is no longer taken as the absolute symbolic ego of postcolonial rejection, as an ontological trap for the Other's creative expression, but becomes an ambivalent scenario of "newness:"

> Así, pues, no paro de avergonzarme de mi cotidianidad en esa Europa en la que soy a la vez hijo y forastero. Pero, por mi parte, cuanto más intento vaciarme de las nomenclaturas de la historia para ser tan transparente como la conjunción de varios neo-mundos que forman un todo-mundo inédito que ignora las nociones de centro y periferia y del que ninguna sociedad es la metrópolis de otra, el lamento de Wallcot en su *A Far Cry from Africa*, ya sea en forma de mosquitos o libélulas, siempre acaba llegando hasta mí y aplastándome bajo su peso.
>
> (2007, 123)

The subversive dialogism that attempts to level an outdated North-South discourse through literature, endures simultaneously a social and ideological fragmentation within a single estranged language of Europe-as-Self and Europe-as-Other: "He vivido en Europa / He vivido en el paraíso / He vivido en el infierno / Cuando me reúna con mi gente / Hablaré de los hombres y las mujeres de Europa / hombres y mujeres como nosotros" (2007, 97–98). This challenging division in the locus of enunciation is perfectly defined in a dreamlike episode of one of the characters: "Mantuvo una conversación indescifrable con un hombre muy extraño. Tenía dos bocas, una estaba donde están las bocas habituales y la otra en la nuca "[. . .]. Hablaron como si fueran miembros de una familia desunida y extensa" (2007, 51). As I suggested already, following Bhabha (1995) and García Canclini (2001), the borderline engagements of cultural difference may as often be consensual as conflictual and indeed, as Mba points out (2007, 2010), the postcolonial subject has now two mouths from which he can speak, one mouth "where it should be," the other hidden yet not silent.

To end this article, I quote César Mba Abogo: "[E]s preciso sembrar algo en este continente que arrastra tantos monólogos y diálogos inconclusos" (2007, 120). In this regard, the reader is not sure exactly which continent he is referring to, or whether the message is aimed at both Europe and Africa in a timid statement of a transmodern project of Afro-Europeanization, present in what I believe to be an inaugural work for Afrohispanic literatures in the twenty-first century. To close the circle I proposed at the beginning of this essay, a question remains: Where is Iberian literature produced? As Rebecca L. Walkowitz states, texts belong to the places where they are classified and given cultural and social purposes ([2006] 2013, 919, 921). Iberian literature is no longer imagined to exist in a single literary system but in several, through various and uneven practices of world circulation. The multilingual circulation of immigrant fiction destabilizes nation-based conceptions of literary culture. As I have described herein, African authors who write in Spanish or Catalan rely on multiple literary traditions, trends, and techniques in others to fulfil two immediate needs: to speak about their fractured, hybridized condition, and to insert themselves in the Iberian literary market, a market that has not always welcomed African writers. The case of Imazighen-Catalan writers is quite different because of linguistic and political circumstances, equating culture with community and literary inclusion with national inclusion, presenting this as an alternative social model that distinguishes Catalonia from other parts of Spain. In short, African literature is written, printed, and read in multiple places, and the authors mentioned in this essay force us, as philologists and literary critics, to rehearse different strategies of theoretical analysis, to consider the relationship between the production and circulation of non-canonical and marginal literature because – apart from being read within several literary systems – African literature makes the Iberian system less inclusive.

Notes

1 Ricci (2010, 2014).
2 Adolfo Campoy-Cubillo (2012) wrote a chapter of his book, *Memories of the Maghreb: Transnational Identities in Spanish Cultural Production*, on Saharawi literature.
3 Mohamed Toufali published in 2007 an anthology of Contemporary Imazighen authors (*Escritores rifeños contemporáneos. Una antología de Narraciones y Relatos del Rif*). Some of the writers in the anthology, like himself, Karima Toufali, Karima Aomar, Driss Deiback, Rachid Raja, and Mohamed Lemrini write in Castilian.
4 For this article, let's say that addictions and (supposed) perversions depicted by the characters of both *L'últim patriarca* and *La caçadora de cossos*, Muslim as well as "Christian" (alcohol, drugs, lesbian episodes, prostitution) are recurrent topics in other "rebellious writers" from Africa: authors such as Ken Bugul, Calixte Beyala, or Halima Ben Haddou, first Moroccan woman to write a novel (*Aïcha la rebelle*, 1982), who express in critical ways the degradation of the moral values of the West as a starting point for a search of another Africa. A clear case of self-orientalization is mentioned in my book, *¡Hay moros en la costa!* (2014).
5 The Combé or Ndôwé tribe is an ethnic group of Equatorial Guinea.
6 A *boabí* is a minor monarch in African political systems.

Works cited

Al Hassani, Jamila. 2013. *La lluita de la dona bereber*. Sitges: Ediciones Oblicuas.
Anzaldúa, Gloria. [1985] 1999. *Borderland/ La Frontera*. San Francisco, CA: Aunt Lute Books.
Ararou, Ahmed. 2006. Interview by Cristián H. Ricci. Unpublished interview. Rabat. June 1.
Bhabha, Homi K. 1995. *The Location of Culture*. New York: Routledge.
Campoy-Cubillo, Adolfo. 2012. *Memories of the Maghreb: Transnational Identities in Spanish Cultural Production*. New York: Palgrave Macmillan.
David, Marianne and Javier Muñoz-Basols. 2011. "Defining and Re-Defining Diaspora: An Unstable Concept." In *Defining and Re-Defining Diaspora: From Theory to Reality*, edited by Marianne David and Javier Muñoz-Basols, xi–xxiv Oxford: Inter-Disciplinary Press.
Dussel, Enrique. 2005. "Transmodernidad e interculturalidad. Interpretación desde la filosofía de la liberación." Web de la Asociación de Filosofía y Liberación. Accessed April 22, 2006. http://www.afyl.org.
El Hachmi, Najat. 2004a. "Carta d'un immigrant." *Inauguració del Congrés Mundial dels Moviments Humans i Immigració, organitzat per l'Institut Europeu de la Mediterrània.*
———. 2004b. *Jo també sóc catalana*. Barcelona: Columna.
El Harti, Larbi. 2003. *Después de Tánger*. Madrid: Sial.
———. 2004. "La alienada." In *La puerta de los vientos. Narradores marroquíes contemporáneos*, edited by Marta Cerezales, Miguel A. Moreta and Lorenzo Silva, 11–18. Barcelona: Destino.
Fanon, Frantz. [1961] 2002. *Les damnés de la terre*. Preface Alice Cherki and postface of Mohammed Harbi. Paris: Éditions La Découverte/Poche.
Fernández Retamar, Roberto. 1995. *Calibán. Contra la leyenda negra*. Lleida: Universitat de Lleida.
Fra Molinero, Baltasar. 2002. "La educación sentimental de un exiliado africano: *Las tinieblas de tu memoria negra* de Donato Ndongo-Bidyogo." *Afro-Hispanic Review* 21 (1–2): 161–170.
García Canclini, Néstor. 2001. *Culturas híbridas. Estrategias para entrar y salir de la modernidad*. Buenos Aires: Paidós.
Gaspar de Alba, Alicia. 2000. "Literary Wetback." In *Literatura chicana: reflexiones y ensayos críticos*, edited by Rosa Morillas Sánchez and Manuel Villar Raso, 9–18. Granada: Comares.
Goytisolo, Juan, prologue. [1978] 2003. *Orientalismo* by Edward Said. Barcelona: Debolsillo.
Jones Mahatma, Daniel. 1962. *Una lanza por el boabí*. Barcelona: Casals.
Khatibi, Abdelkebir. 1985. "Double criticism." In *Contemporary North Africa: Issues of Development and Integration*, edited by Halim Barakat, 9–19. London: Groom Helm.

————. 2001. "Maghreb plural." In *Capitalismo y geopolítica del conocimiento: el eurocentrismo y la filosofía de la liberación en el debate intelectual contemporáneo*. Comp. and Introduction by Walter Mignolo, 71–92. Buenos Aires: Ediciones del Signo.

Lifshey, Adam. 2003. "Ideations of Collective Memory in Hispanophone Africa: The Case of María Nsué Angüe's *Ekomo*" *Hispanic Journal* 24 (1–2): 173–185.

Lipski, John. 2002. "The Spanish of Equatorial Guinea: Research on 'La Hispanidad's Best-Kept Secret." *Afro-Hispaic Review* 21 (1–2): 70–97.

Martín-Rodríguez, Manuel. 2000. "¿Quién es el público y dónde se lo encuentra?" In *Literatura chicana: reflexiones y ensayos críticos*, edited by Rosa Morillas Sánchez and Manuel Villar Raso, 253–261. Granada: Comares.

Mba Abogo, César. 2007. *El porteador de Marlow. Canción negra sin color*. Madrid: Sial.

————. 2010. *Malabo blues. La ciudad remordida*. Barcelona: El Aleph Editores.

Mekuy, Guillermina. 2005. *El llanto de la perra*. Barcelona: Plaza y Janés.

————. 2008. *Las tres vírgenes de Santo Tomás*. Madrid: Suma.

Mesbahi, Mohamed. 2006. "La otra cara de la modernidad de Averroes." *Hesperia Culturas del Mediterráneo* 3: 183–197.

Mignolo, Walter. 1993. "Colonial and Postcolonial Discourse: Cultural Critique or Academic Colonialism?" *Latin American Research Review* 28 (3): 120–134.

————. 2000. *Local Histories/Global Designs: Coloniality, Subaltern Knowledges, and Border Thinking*. Princeton. NJ: Princeton University Press.

Navarro, Nuria. 2007. "Entrevista. Najat El Hachmi. La 'pornografía étnica' también nos hace daño." Accessed August 8, 2007. http://www.gencat.net/salut/portal/cat/_notes/trans/nachat.pdf.

Ndongo-Bidyogo, Donato. 1984. *Antología de la literatura guineana*. Madrid: Editora Nacional.

N'gom, M'bare. 1993. "La literatura africana de expresión castellana: La creación literaria de Guinea Ecuatorial." *Hispania* 76: 410–418.

————. 1996. *Diálogos con Guinea. Panorama de la literatura guineoecuatoriana de expresión castellana a través de sus protagonistas*. Madrid: AECI.

Nkogo Esono, Maximiliano. 2006. *Nambula*. Malabo: Morandi.

Prabhu, Anjali. 2007. *Hibridity: Limits, Transformations, Prospects*. Albany, NY: State University of New York Press.

Pultz Moslund, Sten. 2010. *Migration Literature and Hybridity: The Different Speeds of Transcultural Change*. London: Palgrave.

Ricci, Cristián H. 2010. "African Voices in Contemporary Spain." *Hispanic Issues* 37: 203–231.

————. 2014. *¡Hay moros en la costa! Literatura marroquí fronteriza en castellano y catalán*. Madrid and Frankfurt: Iberoamericana/Vervuert.

Said, Edward. [1978] 2003. *Orientalismo*. Prologue by Juan Goytisolo. Barcelona: Debolsillo.

Toufali, Mo. 2007. *Escritores rifeños contemporáneos. Una antología de narraciones y relatos del Rif*. E-Book: Lulu.

Walkowitz, Rebecca L. [2006] 2013. "The Location of Literature. The Transnational Book and the Migrant Writer." In *Global Literary Theory. An Anthology*, edited by Richard J. Lane, 818–929. New York: Routledge.

Literature and visual culture

46

FERMENTED MEMORY

The intemperance of history in the narrative of Ramón Saizarbitoria

Joan Ramon Resina

When José Saramago received the Nobel Prize, there was no unanimity among the critics. Some considered Antonio Lobo Antunes a superior writer, and his name had in fact circulated in connection with the Nobel. Portugal is too small and too lightweight politically to reasonably expect two Nobel awards in one generation. This geopolitical limitation, wherever it exists, engenders similar dichotomies. Fortunately, the canon's ongoing readjustment makes the omission from an award, even the Nobel, of no consequence for an author's posterity. The history of contemporary literature is stock-full of authors who were never distinguished by the Swedish Academy, while the annals of the Nobel teem with names that no longer command the esteem they once did.

If I mention this dichotomy in Portuguese literature rather than the classic one between Tolstoy and Dostoevsky, it is because such dualisms arise more frequently in literatures considered "minor." The alternative "Tolstoy or Dostoevsky," the title of a renowned work by George Steiner, concerns a choice between generic modalities of writing (epic versus drama) rather than a dispute about literary eminence. Had the Nobel Prize existed in the nineteenth century, a fair number of Russian authors could have been candidates. A restrictive list would have included Chekhov, Pushkin, Gogol, Turgenev, and Herzen. On the contrary, the dichotomy I have in mind tends to polarize the options to the exclusion of others and is often the mark of subaltern literatures, where international success confers inordinate symbolic capital on a single author. If the Swedish Academy had been inclined to award the Nobel Prize to one Czech novelist of the last century (Jaroslav Seifert received it for poetry in 1948), would it have favored Milan Kundera or Bohumil Hrabal? It is, of course, a moot question. For decades there has been speculation on who the long overdue Catalan Nobel laureate for literature will be. Some years ago the names in circulation were Baltasar Porcel and Miquel Martí i Pol, but both died without the Swedish Academy recognizing their work; Salvador Espriu and Josep Vicenç Foix received only unsuccessful nominations before their own deaths. In Catalonia everyone knows that if the Nobel committee does one day recognize Catalan literature, there will be room for one prize only. This awareness automatically changes the question of relative merit to one of absolute preeminence. This is not the case in "normalized" literatures. In the French case, the awarding of the Nobel Prize to Albert Camus in 1957 did not imply a judgment on the superiority of Camus over the author that dominated the literary scene at the time. Jean-Paul Sartre would also receive the award seven years later. And priority does not entail precedence.

Temporal anticipation could not, in this instance, be construed as meritorious advantage. Let us recall that Sartre's major literary work, *Nausea*, was published in 1938.

I have begun with this reflection because it seems to me that, even without intervention from the Nobel committee appearing imminent, the representational dilemma typical of a small-size literature such as the Basque weighs on the estimation of Bernardo Atxaga and Ramón Saizarbitoria. Given that literary values are subject to fluctuations and often respond to extrinsic factors, one might ask what lies behind the tendency to consider Atxaga the most exportable of Basque writers, as is clearly reflected in the number of translations, reviews, awards, and invitations that he and his works have received, and even in the endowment of university chairs with his name. Might this swift differentiation of one single voice be the effect of a circular logic? It surely does seem that, in the haste to produce one visible "national author," Atxaga has been invested with the role played by Camões, Cervantes, and Llull in other Iberian literatures. But unlike these authors, whose names are seamlessly embedded in a centuries-old tradition, the future status of a modern classic is unpredictable and remains reversible for quite some time. For the time being, though, it can be affirmed that, while those earlier classics could not foresee their posthumous sovereignty in their respective languages, Atxaga enjoys in life his anticipated posterity through his official crowning as the writer of reference in Euskera. I would hazard that, more than market factors traceable to the relative scarcity of competition in a literature with a small demographic base, what best reveals the willful nature of this investiture is the synchrony between the institution of Basque literature as a national literature and the consecration of an author to represent it. Although undeniably flattering to Atxaga and stimulating for the younger authors who aspire to emulate his success, the fact is that boosting one single voice over the polyphony needed to build a literature throws as much shadow as light over the field of Basque letters. At the very least it presents the drawback of subduing Saizarbitoria's work and literary personality.

Saizarbitoria himself has talked about the advantages that a small-footprint literature like the Basque can obtain in drawing from its own resources rather than measuring itself by inapplicable standards. "We often put aside our resources because they are not in themselves those of a normal people or culture, and it seems that this happens to us because we want to be as normalized as the others. One does not become big by walking on tiptoe" (Etxeberria 2002, 157). These are wise words, and despite the discretion with which Saizarbitoria refers to Atxaga at all times during the interview, they apply to this writer. There was a moment when Atxaga started tiptoeing, mistaking globalization with stature. I do not criticize the ambition. There is nothing wrong with aspiring to become the García Márquez of Basque literature. Yet one must be clear that while the Colombian Nobel Prize recipient was able to launch Macondo onto the global scene by relying on an imaginative transcription of Colombia, Atxaga appears to believe that one becomes a global writer by writing for the world.

When Hasier Etxeberria, underscoring the difference between the two writers – "two ways of looking at literature: yours, more social, and Atxaga's, more literary"– suggests that Saizarbitoria's joining the journal *Ustela* prompted Atxaga to leave (2002, 127), Saizarbitoria does not dispute that distribution of roles, but shuns the implication of a clash between personalities. The interviewer insists: "There were also different writing styles and different literary interests." Saizarbitoria agrees: "Yes, that is also true. I had nothing to do in that other style. Borges, whom they so much appreciated, never interested me, and the reason is not that he sent us, Basques, to tend the cows" (Etxeberria 2002, 127). Etxeberria drives the point home: "Perhaps you preferred a literature with a social foundation to mere literary play." The reply: "It is possible. I lived in a different world. It seems that in the third issue of *Ustela* we departed from Atxaga's objectives; and something similar happened with the later *Oh! Euzkadi"* (Etxeberria 2002, 128).

Although the distinction between social literature and literary literature is perplexing, especially in relation to an author who had absorbed the lessons of the *nouveau roman*, it seems possible to draw a distinction between the fictional world of *Obabakoak*, which borders on magical realism, and Saizarbitoria's narrative, which is quite explicitly centered on memory. "The writer – he asserts – works with memory and with feelings. Those are his raw materials" (Etxeberria 2002, 166). I suggest that by "memory" Saizarbitoria understands a core of objectivity that resists the writer and which, as a result, allows him to build a solid work. Thus understood, memory is for him what the marble blocks were for Michelangelo: an exterior resistance in which he excavated his idea. Similarly, Saizarbitoria anchors imagination in memory, forcing experience to gravitate toward those anchor points: "The novel is imagination, and imagination is memory. As someone said, imagination is fermented memory" (Etxeberria 2002, 150).

I would like to dwell on this phrase and explore its implications for the narrative technique employed in three of his works. But first a common misconception requires attention. Although the author embeds terrorism in his plots as a reality that has been present in Basque society, this aspect does not justify reducing his work to political commentary. There could be no objection if those who perform such extrapolations acknowledged the arbitrariness of allowing a contextual element to overshadow the aesthetic object and rise up to the level of narrative truth. Such critics take to heart Hasier Etxeberría's categorical distinction between "social literature" and "literary literature," expelling Saizarbitoria from the latter. The error stems from the confusion between the verbal nature of theoretical constructs and the deductive mechanism employed to set up a misleading correspondence between the verbal play and the complexity of reality. On the level of self-awareness, the novel outpaces theory by presenting every presumption of such correspondence within the frame of fiction. As a consequence of this novelistic self-awareness, critical efforts to derive an objective truth about social or political reality directly from a work of fiction fall into a confusion of categories. A valid critique will be aware of the mediate character of "the reality effect" in fictional works and will try to elucidate how fiction is constructed with thematic building blocks that include portions of reality without reproducing its infinite complexity.

If imagination is fermented memory, then memory and its fermentation are the necessary objects of narrative. Saizarbitoria understands that literary images rely on a previous signification, but unlike deconstructionists, meaning for him is not permanently deferred but is ultimately supported by the objective world. Unless he is a Dadaist, the writer does not interpret the linguistic sign arbitrarily, does not fully surrender to the game of literariness, but codifies the signs of experience in the process of turning it into memory. This is the reason that in *Hamaika Pauso* (*The Countless Steps*) (1995), the composition of a dictionary proves absurd and even impossible, as the writing of Iñaki Abaitua gradually turns into the story of Daniel Zabalegi, and this into the novel in which the reader contemplates the osmosis between a text based on a closed system of retro feeding signs (the dictionary) and the novel's open system of countless steps. Countless not insofar as the referent is inexhaustible, but because it is always possible to begin all over again from any of the narrated moments by shifting the perspective. This is why, in a moment of unguarded sincerity that is wrongly interpreted as a joke, Abaitua proposes replacing the dictionary's alphabetical order with a less arbitrary order based on the enticement of what Heidegger calls "worldhood" and defines as a context of assignations (*Being and Time* 1962, 121).

But to modify the perspective, be it ever so slightly, implies altering the context in which the object is perceived. This context is the world, and first of all the world encountered as a system of uses: the city, the streets and squares with names that can be ascertained on a map, the landmarks and features of the landscape, the stores and cider bars where the old *gudaris* (Basque soldiers) meet. All of this comes together in a bundle of familiar relationships that have grown inextricable from the objects trapped in their orbit. The world that I deem external supports my memory while being integral to it. Without anchors in time and space, I cannot secure any memory. To retain anything in my memory, I need coordinates that fix the recollection of something in particular. This outside world that orients my perspective is the condition of possibility of my experience. I am not referring to the famous *lieux de mémoire*, which transpose the transcendental conditions of experience to the theory of the social construction of memory. I am referring to the fact that consciousness, which is not an object in the world, stands nonetheless in a relation of immediacy to it through a body that can only be abolished at the cost of abolishing thought at the same time. If the laws of perception delude us, for instance when we see as broken a stick that is submerged in water, we cannot alter that perception no matter how often we repeat the experience. I can only correct my vision intellectually by relying on my knowledge of the refraction of light. I realize that I suffer an illusion, but I cannot modify what my pupil registers by changing the stick or the puddle. The illusion caused by the deflection of the light rays when they pass through a liquid medium is simply invincible on the physiological plane.

Saizarbitoria approaches memory in a similar fashion. To remember is to get one's bearings from the standpoint of experience. But upon entering a certain environment, the mnemonic rays take on a life of their own and remembering loses every objective other than filling up empty time and space. By turning itself into an object, memory produces an illusion of reality, a semblance of the ontological presence of what it recalls. The protagonist of *Bihotz bi. Gerrako kronikak* (*Love and War*) (1996) can set Samuel's memory in motion by simply mentioning a key phrase, such as "orduan Carrasco hil egin zuten" [then they killed Carrasco] (36). These few words trigger Samuel's memory as surely as the stick bends upon entering the puddle:

> Samuelek lehen aldia izan balitz bezala kontatzen zuen, eta gainerako guztiek errespetuz entzuten zioten, pentsatu ere egin gabe "pasarte hori honezkero mila aldiz entzun diagu" edo antzekorik esatea, bai baikenekien ez zuela kontagai zuena jakinarazteko asmoz kontatzen, baizik eta, pertsonarik isilenak ere, noizbehinka, barrena hustu beharra izaten duelako [Samuel told it as if it were the first time, and the others listened respectfully, without even occurring to them to say: 'We have heard this story at least one thousand times' or something like that. Because we knew that, if he told it, it was not because he wanted to make known what he was saying, but because even the quietest people need now and then to let out what they have inside].
>
> (*Bihotz bi. Gerrako kronikak* 1996, 36)

What Samuel had inside is perfectly familiar to his small circle of friends but, as time passes and the distance grows between his immediate audience and the hypothetical addressee of the story, Samuel's intimacy becomes spectral and ceases to move anyone. Yet it is precisely the ability to move (to be refracted in the consciousness of others) that endows memory with consistency. Listening to Samuel, the narrator muses: "Pasadizoa kontatzen zuen bakoitzean, neronek ere garrasi haiek entzun nitzakeela iruditzen zitzaidan" [Every time he recounted that event, it seemed to me that even I could hear those cries] (*Bihotz bi. Gerrako kronikak* 1996, 37). Which proves, if proof be needed, that emotion creates its object.

Objectified through sheer repetition, remembrances become conventional. What memory gains in truth, it loses in authenticity. "Nik, gerraz hitz egingo zutenez," reflects the narrator, "hiztegi entziklopedikoetan ez datozen historiak konta zitzaten nahi nuen" [Since they were going to talk about war, I would have preferred that their stories be different from those in encyclopedias] (*Bihotz bi. Gerrako kronikak* 1996, 29–30). There is irony in the fact that the narrator, who makes a living by peddling encyclopedias, is convinced that Knowledge and Reason (capitalized in his mind) are the highest qualities, and remains of this opinion even after he murders his wife for attempting to please him sexually ((*Bihotz bi. Gerrako kronikak* 1996, 7). With his encyclopedic optimism and his ability to memorize numerous definitions, this character is a variant – or a refraction – of Iñaki Abaitua, the creator of definitions for a dictionary in *Hamaika pauso*. But whereas Abaitua finally realizes the absurdity of reducing experience to a definition, the narrator of *Love and War* believes that the two may coincide. Even so, he acknowledges that emotion is inseparable from the refraction of the past in individual memory, whereas restricting subjectivity by means of what one has learned impoverishes the narration:

Berez, kontalariak, kontakizun duen historia bizi izandako norbaiten aurrean ari denean batez ere, kontaketa objetiboa egiteko joera izaten baitu; historialari bihurtu nahi duela esango genuke, kontalari papera utzita [Normally, the narrator, especially in the presence of someone who witnessed the situation he is narrating, feels the need to present an objective account. One could say that he renounces his role as narrator, that is, that he desists from contributing subjective nuances and tries to assume the historian's function].

(*Bihotz bi. Gerrako kronikak* 1996, 24)

Thus, Samuel and his friends, convinced that they are remembering their war experiences, talk in fact about altitudes and coordinates, draw the lines of trenches with the help of the silverware and show the movements of troops shifting the glasses around the table. "Hala eta guztiz ere," the narrator observes, "batzuetan, esaten zuten gauza interesgarririk, gainerakoak artean heldu gabe zeudelako, edo alde eginak zirelako jada; alegia, haietako batekin bakarka geratuz gero, egiten zituzten bestelako aitorpenak ere" [In any case, sometimes they actually said interesting things, either because the others had not arrived yet, or because they had already left. In other words, if you were alone with one of them, they used to make other kinds of confessions] (*Bihotz bi. Gerrako kronikak* 1996, 31). Perhaps the things they dared to say in the absence of witnesses were more interesting than those they told to the group. But the problem with these monolog confessions is that they elude the proof of the community. Being a longitudinal cross-section in the collective memory, the personal narration cannot aspire to the status of truth in the absence of other testimony. Truthfulness is not an attribute intrinsic to an assertion, but a quality furnished by the distinction between what the assertion derives from the object and what the narrator brings to it. No matter how interesting they may be, individual testimonies by themselves do not suffice to establish a historical memory. Only the intersubjective creation of memory, which is after all subject to conventions, can convert the emotion to knowledge and fill the volumes of encyclopedias and history books. That is why the narrator asserts that the bars of Euskadi teem with old drunkards searching for victims on whom to foist a monolog about the war, which would fill at most "Lau folioren espazioa eskatuko luke, laurogei lerro, mila hitz baino gutxiago" [the space of four pages, less than eighty lines, about one thousand words] (*Bihotz bi. Gerrako kronikak* 1996, 23). There is therefore an idiosyncrasy of memory, and the narrator recognizes its charm:

> Nik, ordea, ez dut erabat galdu umeek ohi duten gustua, historia bera behin eta berriz entzuteko. Ez dakit zergatik, beharbada ez naizelako erabat heldua, kontua da kontakizun baten emanaldi desberdinen arteko xehetasun eta ñabardurak atzematea atsegin dudala, askotan; kontaketa, historia bera baino nahiago, esan nahi dut [For whatever reason, I have not lost completely that childish fondness for listening to the same story again and again. I don't know why, perhaps because I have not completely matured, the fact is that, often, I like to appreciate the details and nuances of different versions of the same story; that is, I prefer narration, the plot, to the tale itself].
>
> (*Bihotz bi. Gerrako kronikak* 1996, 23)

In this novel Saizarbitoria retains the metanarrative concern of his previous work, but what gives impetus to the story is the activation of memory through the accumulation of new details (Olaziregi 2008, 393).

The narrator of *Love and War* exerts his memory according to the needs of the plot, which progresses through trial and iterations, adapting remembrance to the verisimilitude of conventional fiction. Trying to reconstruct the dialogue in which his wife confessed her infidelity, he hesitates about the sequence of the exchange:

> Ez dirudi oso sinesgarria; "Ez iezadazu historia hondatu" horrek, bereziki. Oso naturala ez behintzat, batez ere nik "ez nazazu utzi" esan ondoren kokatua. [. . .] Hasierak, ordea, ez du dudarik, "banoa" esaten dit, nik ea zer duen galdetutakoan. Ziur da hori. [. . .] "Ez nazazu abandonatu" – edo "ez nazazu utzi," eta gerritik besarkatzen dut. Sinesgarriagoa dirudi [It does not seem very credible; especially that "do not spoil the story." At least not very natural, especially after my saying "do not leave me." [. . .] Regarding the beginning, however, there is no doubt; she says "I am leaving" when I ask her what's the problem with her. That much is certain. [. . .] "Do not leave me" – or "do not abandon me," and I put my arm around her waist. It looks more plausible].
>
> (*Bihotz bi. Gerrako kronikak* 1996:172–173)

Reflecting on the story's effect on memory and the impossibility of an access to the past free from narrative distortion is Saizarbitoria's main contribution to Basque literature and – through his concept of imagination as fermented memory – to a general theory of fiction. His interest in the fermenting of memory transpires in the repetition of situations around which the author builds the variations of his novels. There is always an inaccessible experience around which discourses are endlessly generated in a hopeless effort to reconstruct it. David Laraway turns to Lacanian psychoanalysis by way of Žižek to interpret the material memory in the tale about Sabino Arana's exhumation in the collection *Gorde Nazazu Lurpean*. He understands the relic as "an emblem of a particular structural lack within the discourse of Basque nationalism" (Laraway 2007, 365). This assertion is not necessarily false, to the extent that the Lacanian structural lack underlies every symbolic system, but a less politicized reading may better agree with Saizarbitoria's concern with the incommensurability between logos and experience in memory processes. I do not deny the author's political position. Regarding the story of the exhumation, Saizarbitoria has declared that he wished to betray the legacy of Basque nationalism. And the nationalist Spanish press was quick to seize upon that statement (Echeverría 2002). But perhaps not enough attention has been paid to his explanation about the inordinate weight of the ideological legacy in Basque nationalism, a legacy whose constraints are proportional to the countervailing Spanish nationalism that opposes it. Aware of the dangers of running away from the dictates of one ideology only to sacrifice one's critical autonomy to the opposite ideology, Saizarbitoria distances himself from former Basque militants converted to militant Spanish nationalism and claims for himself a sentimental space commensurable with the individual. "I do not wish the fatherland to make me unhappy, nor do I want to shoulder patriotic tasks that are not within reach of my strength" (Echeverría 2002). All in all, he urges us to regain a sense of balance between experience, which in this instance happens to be historical, and its sentimental or dogmatic extensions in time.

In his work, historical experience is generally associated with the Spanish Civil War and its projection on the present (a projection of which ETA is only one consequence). But to consider this war the only cause of the dislocation of the present may be a generational delusion, a convention accepted by the friends who gather in a cider bar every evening. The name of this establishment, "Hunger," is surely meaningful. As a space of projection or a sounding board for the collective memory, "Hunger" announces the impossibility of satisfying the essential lack. Ruminating on the past, going over the same commonplaces and familiar stories time and again does not satisfy. Yet emptiness at the core of life compels the defeated to retrace the same episodes over and over in monotonous circles, in the same way that Claudia can gobble endless servings of eggs fried with chorizo. Violence lurks in the labyrinth of words, fascinating by its invisible presence. It is a primary experience without dates or concrete memories but capable of being transmitted from grandparents to grandchildren, like the mole on Violet's throat, at once the trace of a forgotten story and the omen of a death whose anticipated terror shapes life. It may be due to the primordial, pre-logical character of violence that *Love and War* begins with its assertion. From this point of view Flora's murder would be a variation of the plot against the background of the fable's monotony, which is still the indelible pressure of a war story on the collective memory.

The group of veterans who are constantly weaving the web of memory reappears in the collection of stories *Gorde nazazu lurpean* (*Keep me under the ground*) (2000). In this book "Gudari zaharraren gerra galdua" [The Old Gudari's Lost War] stands out for its reflection on memory's fermentation. War is at once the source of remembrance and a metaphor for the effort to incorporate experience into social memory. In face of this effort, the witness's impotence to recount his knowledge amounts to losing the war a second time. As the victims of atrocities often assert, the *gudari* only wants to tell his story, to establish its truth. But his true desire is to recover his amputated leg, to restore his body's integrity, to heal his wound, to undo his lack, to work out his trauma. But who wishes to look at a festering wound that has reopened after years and oozes what Saizarbitoria calls "fermented memory"? Only the military authority, and then pro-forma, to certify the *gudari*'s status as one of the vanquished in a humiliating examination. In despair, the *gudari* hires a prostitute not to engage in sex but to turn her into a paid *voyeuse* of his wound.

The fermentation of memory centers the *gudari*'s narrative. His wound starts oozing many years after the amputation. The alleged cause is high blood sugar, but oddly the scar reopens when he is forced to show his stump to a military medical tribunal. And this event is contemporary with the first post-Franco Prime Minister, Adolfo Suárez's proclamation: "*Hay que restañar las heridas de la guerra*" [We must heal the wounds of the war] ("Gudari zaharraren gerra galdua" 2000, 27). It was paradoxically around this time, when the Francoists and the opposition tacitly subscribed to a pact on forgetting, that a court of victors had to decide on the extent and validity of the memory of the vanquished. After four decades of enforced silence, the head of the government wanted wounds to heal which no one had thought it necessary to treat. Built into his exhortation to forget was, however, the allusion to a memory that had been not so much superseded as amputated.

The basic problem of historical memory does not lie in the *what* but in the *how*, in the way the past is narrated. The old *gudari* is constrained to establish through notarization, that is, through impersonal protocol, something that he knows from personal experience. His dilemma is *how* to prove, that is, how to objectify what he has lived in the flesh. The government demands that he bring witnesses. And then his problems begin. The *gudari* decides to take Eguía and Elorza along, "Elorzaz aparte ez zegoelako beste inor batailoikorik" [because, other than Elorza, nobody from his battalion remains alive] ("Gudari zaharraren gerra galdua" 2000, 13), and although Eguía had fought in a different unit, he was stationed only a couple of miles away from where the events took place. Besides, they were instructing Eguía on the details about the battalion, and by dint of listening to the story in the Paco Bueno – the name of the cider bar in this narration – they all knew it by heart ("Gudari zaharraren gerra galdua" 2000, 13). There is also Amiano, who tells the story best, although he was not a direct witness. But he is dying and cannot appear before the notary public. In the end, the witnesses are superfluous; the notary only asks the *gudari* for the facts and checks his attempt to describe them in Balzacian detail by prompting him repeatedly to "go to the point," that is to gravitate to the fable, leaving aside the subtleties of plot. At the limit, the ideal narrative would correspond to a generic formula free from individualizing circumstances: the vision of the broken stick, here the amputated leg, corrected by the political equivalent of the refraction of light. But the *gudari* knows that the plot determines the story's value:

> Aditzera ematen ez diren arte ideia batzuk ez baitira zehatz taxutzen, eta, era berean, buru barruan itzulika interesgarriak diruditen pentsakizunek, sarritan, hitz bihurtu bezain pronto erakutsi ohi dutelako beren zentzugabekeriaren egia [he knew that ideas do not take shape until they're expressed and that they often seem interesting while we're thinking them, and yet reveal themselves stupid as soon as we put them into words].

> ("Gudari zaharraren gerra galdua" 2000, 33)

Naturally, we can ask what ideas are and whether they exist before they are embodied in language. And if they do, whether they enjoy immediate knowledge of things. Such immediacy, if it exists, would be lost as soon as ideas come under the semantic and grammatical rigor of the phrase. This theory of expression is essentially Platonic, ideas (which in Plato are the object of contemplation) playing here the part of paradise lost when the soul is reborn in the reflected world of the copy. Plato's reincarnation theory is a theory of memory in disguise, a myth concocted to support the belief in innate ideas, that is, to provide a metaphysical foundation for the human capacity for deductive reasoning or, in Kantian terms, for a priori synthetic judgments. Unaware of the philosophical implications of his quandary, the *gudari* confronts the question of the existence of memory that is independent of analytical propositions, that is, in Kantian language, propositions that are conceptually determined. He attempts to overcome the constraints of language logic by condensing truth in a discourse that tends to simultaneity and hence to silence:

> Askotan gertatzen zitzaion zerbait kontatu beharra zuenean nondik hasi ezin asmatzea. Beti, egia esan; eta gehiago, entzulea aspertu nahi ez zuelako-edo, gauzak

ahalik eta lasterren kontatzera behartuta sentitzen zenean [He often did not know where to begin a story. To be honest, it happened almost always; above all when, trying not to bore his interlocutor, he felt compelled to tell it all as fast as possible].

("Gudari zaharraren gerra galdua" 2000, 33)

How can one preserve truth in its purity, in the sense of pure intuition, when language has the power of verisimilitude? Faced with this problem, the *gudari* opts for withholding those facts that do not fit into the official discourse of memory; facts such as his having leaned out of the trench just before the explosion that tore his leg. He suppresses certain particulars in order not to compromise the pension he hopes to obtain or to avoid producing an effect that would run counter to his purpose at the moment, although "Baina hori zen egia, eta ongi asko zeukan gogoan" [it was the truth and he would never be able to get it out of his head] ("Gudari zaharraren gerra galdua" 2000, 38). He must, therefore, keep to discursive formulas and the parameters of plausibility in order to make sense. "Lasaitasuna behar zen zerbait kontatzeko; edonondik hasteko libertatea gero, kontakizuna puntu batean utzi, eta, behar izanez gero, beste bati ekiteko" [To tell anything one needed calm and the freedom to begin the story just about anywhere; to be able to break the narrative thread at any point and, if necessary, to pick it up elsewhere] ("Gudari zaharraren gerra galdua" 2000, 33). Discourse is oriented by the speech act, which organizes its elements to inspire an interest which the *gudari* seeks by "entzulea aspertu nahi ez zuelako-edo" [trying not to bore his interlocutor] ("Gudari zaharraren gerra galdua" 2000, 33). The plot – as distinguished from the fable – is responsible for the pragmatic organization of discourse. Telling has an implicit purpose, and the audience determines the form of the narrative by affecting which materials will go into the composition and which will be excluded:

> Horregatik, ideia irristakor haiek zehazki taxutzeko orduan berehala konturatzen zen, ahoskatu barik, bere golkorako esan orduko, zentzurik gabeko hitzak zirela; gehienez ere Amiano, Elorza eta besteak samintzeko baino balio ez zutenak [The truth is that he spent hours trying to give shape to those elusive ideas that he hardly ever managed to share, because he realized, as soon as he formulated them, just by saying them to himself, that they lacked sense; that they only served to hurt Amiano, Elorza, and the rest of his friends].

("Gudari zaharraren gerra galdua" 2000, 43)

In reality the important distinction is not between ideas formulated in the recesses of consciousness and ideas expressed through the voice (or the alphabet) in a specific social context. The decisive distinction is between pre-verbal experience (the truth that "he would never be able to get out of his head") and memory, understood as the symbolic organization of experience within a temporal perspective; in other words, a symbolic arrangement that *means* for the point of view sustained by the present state of signification.

The *gudari*'s drama stems from his need to prove that he was maimed in the war. But this proof is unobtainable. To fully account for his suffering, he would have to communicate the experience, and experience of the past is off limits because it has been displaced by memory. And memory is unreliable. Like the professor from the great Lagado academy, who proposed to abolish words and replace them with things, the *gudari* gives up on telling his story and goes in search of the only irrefutable witness, the lost limb. Strictly speaking, recovering his leg is the only way to restore his integrity (filling in the lack at the core of nationalism, as a Lacanian reading of the story would have it) and the sole conclusive proof of his existence as a *gudari*. But since retrieving the past is impossible, he will die in the attempt. The incongruity between memory and existence makes of the places of memory not points of access to the past but spaces for the insertion of particular mythologies. At the crossroads where he asks the cab driver to stop near the old front line, the *gudari* discovers a monolith with the following inscription in Basque and Spanish: "Euzkadi'k emen geldi-azoeban / etsaiaren jazarraldia 1936–10–4, 1937–4–20 ta 23" [Here Euzkadi halted the invader 4–10–1936, 20 and 23–4–1937] ("Gudari zaharraren gerra galdua" 2000, 45).

This is a Basque version of the Spanish *no pasarán*, transferred from the mythology of the left to that of nationalism. But the fixing of the historical flow on specific dates distorts the historical truth, and the uselessness of the sign's deictic purpose (on the date the monolith was inaugurated it no longer signaled the presence of a border) calls attention to the freezing of Basque nationalism's historical memory at the instant immediately before its constitutive trauma: the bombing of Guernica three days after the presumed victory celebrated in the monolith. The fictional transcription of this freezing of the Basque historical memory is the *gudari*'s watch, permanently stopped at four thirty, the hour when Guernica's bombing began. The airplanes flying over the area occupied by the *gudari*'s unit are the Junker and Heinkel that carried out the action in Guernica. And although this action took place six days after the facts related by the *gudari*, the incongruence may be due to his memory's imprecision: "Ez zekien memoriaren joera ote zen data zehatzik gabeko oroitzapen asko egun hartan finkatzekoa" [He did not know if grouping many memories without precise dates in the same day was due to faulty memory] ("Gudari zaharraren gerra galdua" 2000, 49). Just as imagination projects the emotions onto the outer world, when violence has been suffered the memory tends to concentrate on a traumatic instant. From this moment on the war is no longer a chain of events causally linked to each other, but a spiritual black hole where impressions melt into memories before disappearing forever:

—Gerrako abenturak gogoratzera, orduan – esan zuen txoferrak.
[—So, on your way to remember the adventures of the war – said the driver.]
"Gerra gogoratzera ez, ezin baitut burutik kendu" esatea bururatu zitzaion, baina ez zuen esan. ("Gudari zaharraren gerra galdua" 2000, 41) [He was tempted to reply "Not to remember the war, because I can't get it out of my head," but he kept quiet].

It is not by chance that the recounting of the facts, blocked by the notarial interrogation, flows during the taxi ride to Mount Ascensio. The journey in space helps temporalize memory, ordering things in a sequence equivalent to the stringing of words in the tale. When the *gudari* feels that his story is stalling because of the need to tell one thing at a time, he is in fact feeling the resistance of time to the pain accumulated in one single instant. The traumatic moment encapsulates his entire life and, for reasons that remain inscrutable, is the only time available on his watch. Although he tries to wind up the watch, it is of no avail. He cannot historicize the fixed idea that fills his consciousness. If time existed objectively – and the stopped watch suggests it does not – it might ease the pain by drawing it out over an infinity of moments. The timelessness of trauma prevents him from telling it all at once.

Telling all at once is what the protagonist of *Love and War* attempts by beginning his narration with a phrase that contains the only important fact in the story. This is so emphatically the case that the rest is an overgrown triteness, as if the novel's signifying surface were a balloon and the words so much hot air helping it take off.

The narrator of *Hamaika pauso* also reveals the end at the beginning, but he does so in full awareness of the arbitrariness of the narrative order:

Ordu gutxi barru bistaz hartzen duen eremuko punturen batean hilko dela dakienean jada: hortik has daiteke kontakizuna, edo lehenagotik, lehenagotik baitzekien alboan, badiara ematen duen etxean, leiho bat aukeratuko zuela—Juliaren salakoa—bere azken begiradarentzat euskarri [When he already knows that he's going to die in a few hours at some point in the panorama that his eyes encompass: that could be the beginning of the story. Or earlier, because long before that moment he knew that he would choose a window—the one in Julia's living room—there, in the house looking on the bay, as support for his last gaze].

(*Hamaika pauso* 1995, 7)

In effect, if death is the conclusion of everything that can be narrated, it is also the perspective that makes it possible to link up the facts leading to that horizon. To call attention to his character's existential boundary, not because of an absurd aestheticism (Izurieta 2004, 83), Saizarbitoria introduces the window right away as the frame and support for the narrative perspective. Death is the foundation of every story, not just because the threat of extinction stimulates consciousness, but because, as a definitive and irrefutable limit, it inaugurates all life possibilities by turning every action into a genuine choice. Stories are not only retrospective but retroactive as well. The anticipated interruption of the future transforms it into a field of limited possibilities, forcing consciousness to select and order the experiences that become significant in light of the unexpected:

Momentu orok du lehenago bat eta, gauzak hasieratik kontatzeko ahalegina alfer-rikakoa denez, zilegi da historiari edozein pasartetik ekitea. Eta amaieratik hobe. Amaierak bai, zehatzak baitira, erabatekoak askotan [Every moment has a previous one and, since it is useless to try to tell things from the beginning, the story can start anywhere. Better by the end, since endings, at least, are concrete, often definitive].

(*Hamaika pauso* 1995, 7)

Concreteness and finality are aspects of the same intuition. If only the ending is concrete, then everything coming before is tentative or reversible, and time is abolished. Time was often ignored in the classic novel, a genre in which diachrony is the equivalent of universal gravitation in Newtonian physics. In a classic story, time is a factor of extension: first comes one thing, which makes room for another, and so on with a rhythm that replicates the movement of the clock and the turning of pages in the calendar. That very linearity precluded time from being perceived. That is why Bergson's encounter with duration led to the discovery of the time "lost" in the novel, of time as the novel's forgotten protagonist. Saizarbitoria's narrative technique has been compared to play (Kortazar 2005) or with an aesthetic fetishism at the service of the ideology of modernism, postmodernism, and capitalism (Izurieta 2004, 84). Critics have missed the rigorous logic with which he incorporates a phenomenological intuition of time and avoids treating this essential component of narrative as an abstraction. If we take seriously the notion that Saizarbitoria's formal efforts evince technical innovation, then we have to consider his work in relation to the philosophical thought that was responsible for the displacement of abstract time through lived time in the contemporary novel. Bergson is the philosopher who most inspired the modernist experimenting with heterogeneous temporalities, circularity, and fragmentation of the narrative consciousness. I will not attempt to summarize his reflections on time and memory. Suffice it to say that Saizarbitoria's formal experimentation is a distant echo of the rigor with which Bergson replaced the abstract concepts of classical philosophy with others better adapted to the appearance of things. This revolution in the priorities elicited by the strict description of the movement of consciousness finds correspondence in the Basque novelist's handling of his materials.

Bergson asserted that a true philosopher writes one single work in the course of his life. Genuine philosophy is a complex effort to express something infinitely simple, so simple in fact that the philosopher never succeeds in expressing it. The magnitude of the challenge is what keeps him speaking or writing all his life. "All the complexity of his doctrine, which would go to infinity, is nothing but the incommensurability between his simple intuition and the means of expression at his disposal" (Bergson 1934, 137). The simplicity of the intuition that captures the total sense of life is the only referent on which the man who is about to die fixes his attention. Knowing that his death is near, Iñaki Abaitua, the protagonist of *Hamaika pauso*, thinks that "Oso objetu zehatz, mugatua, elementu bat aukeratu beharko duela bistaren euskarritzat" [he will have to fix his eyes on a single element, one single object] (*Hamaika pauso* 1995, 7–8). Apparently, he transfers to his own death, or more precisely to the anticipated imagination of his own death, the last impression of Zabalegi, who at the last moment seeks support for his gaze in "magnolia ezinezko baten hostoa" [the leaf of an impossible magnolia tree] (*Hamaika pauso* 1995, 357). In reality, Abaitua could not have known that last reflex act of someone he had seen only once and for the briefest moment, someone who in any case could not have told anyone about his last earthly impression. The transference happens in the opposite direction. Abaitua transfers to Zabalegi's death his own nostalgia for a memory that has long since pervaded the landscape Abaitua chooses to die in: the Bay of Chingudi at the mouth of the Bidasoa river, the background of the place where Julia had once offered him a magnolia flower (*Hamaika pauso* 1995, 22–23).

Saizarbitoria weaves the deaths of Zabalegi and Abaitua into a thick textual web formed by a childhood reading of *Una mañana de invierno en Inglaterra*, a popular novel about a British spy, the court martial summary against Zabalegi, inspired by the actual court record of Angel Otaegi's process, newspaper headlines, conversations with real-life characters such as José María Bandrés, and literary and critical (even metacritical) references whose purpose is to incorporate the reflection on form to the narrative content. The interpenetration of Zabalegi's and Abaitua's destinies, triggered by the fortuitous forgetting of a cigarette lighter, develops gradually, while Abaitua gathers the materials to write a book about Zabalegi's death titled *Hamaika pauso*, which is not – it cannot be, on account of reflexivity – the novel the reader is occupied with. How to explain this apparent doubling and suggested replication? Simply, through an alteration of conventional writing by inverting the point of view. In the novel, this inversion has to do with Abaitua's growing sense of futility in his philological work, as his obsession with Zabalegi's fate increases and his emotional identification with the ETA collaborator makes him the vicarious protagonist of the book he plans to write. Abaitua does not broach this project on the level of detached archival research but from the intuition of the bleeding spirit of a man who dies in the no man's land between the filthy, irrational hatred of the Spanish police and the empty patriotic hallowing of the Basque nationalist community.

The narrative's complexity, its false starts, meandering progress, and new beginnings; the narrator's countless steps, which will not reach the goal except by leaping over the external description to direct participation in duration and death – all this arises from the incommensurability between the simplicity of intuition and the expressive means available. Abaitua realizes that a definition is not a phrase sewn to a word with the thread of a stable thought. Stable relations between signs and meaning are a fiction; the dictionary is founded on it. Challenging the mirage of common sense (and common meanings), Bergson asserts: "The truth is that above the word and above the phrase there is something much simpler than a phrase and even than a word: the meaning, which is less a thing that is thought than a movement of thought; and less a movement than a direction" (1934, 152). A movement whose steps cannot be counted, only provisionally suspended in order to start all over again, progressing through the various inner planes until one reaches the plane of language, which communicates the inner and the outer, sound and sense, signifier and signified. Just as the phrase consists of preexisting words, narrative is put together with ready-made materials, in this case with narrative syntagms – hence the intertextual references to the popular novel, Gide, Proust, Robbe-Grillet, Claude Simon, Unamuno, and others. Nevertheless, as Bergson remarks, the phrase can choose its initial elements arbitrarily, provided that the others are complementary (1934, 153). That is to say, the story may start almost in any way whatsoever, which explains the hesitant beginning of *Hamaika pauso*. But once the novel has got underway, an increasing necessity and narrative coherence manifest themselves, even if the story presents the aspect of *trencadís*, that is, of a work that is at once fragmentary and unified, like the Gaudí mosaics, which Claude Simon compared to the form of memory (*Hamaika pauso* 1995, 26).

If we agree that memory is the novel's substance, we must also grant that memory is its primordial sense, the source of the inner necessity and coherence binding the phrases that the author has strung together apparently at random. But we must keep in mind that the sense of a work of art is less an object of thought than the movement of thought the work provokes, just as the Park Güell's *trencadís* is not the broken china it is made of so much as the waving movement of the benches in which the fragments of cups, saucers, and dishes are integrated. This is how Saizarbitoria conceives memory and, as a result, the art of the novel: "Oroitzapenak apetaren hegaletan etorri ohi direnez, zilegi da haien ordena ilun eta misteriotsua errespetatzea, kontakizuna konbentzionalki, kronologikoki edo linealki egokitzeaz arduratu gabe" [since memories tend to come to us rather whimsically, it is right to respect their secret and mysterious order, without being concerned to adopt a conventionally chronological layout for the narration] (*Hamaika pauso* 1995, 25). The narratological referents point again to Bergson, although he is never mentioned, and the author has declared that he has not read him (conversation with the author on July 11, 2013). The Bergsonian critique of chronology comes down through Michel Butor, who is cited in support of the idea that we rarely experience time as a continuous flow (*Hamaika pauso* 1995, 26). This, of course, refers to diachronic, abstract time, which we do not truly experience, because it exists only as a concept and a convention. It is a time, as Bergson would say, comprised of instants, which are static, juxtaposed images and can never furnish the intuition of time, the *durée*, just as we can never obtain a line by adding points or a poem by adding letters.

Abaitua is a contemplative character, hence his customary self-positioning by the window during the gatherings at Julia's house. His drama stems from this irrepressible trait in a context where everything colludes to subordinate the intellect to praxis. His opposite is Ortiz de Zárate, a terrorist whose life has become a pure survival strategy. His operative superiority is basic skill to use the circumstances on the spur of the moment, without questioning the deeper nature of things. For him, Zabalegi was merely a liaison, Abaitua a minor collaborator from whom one exacts small services with an increasing level of risk, the armed struggle a war of national liberation. Zárate, no less than the political apprentices who meet at Julia's house, confronts reality with concepts that muddle it. Abaitua realizes that concepts do not mirror reality's mobility and instability, and that they themselves are volatile. It is not by chance that precisely when Iñaki closes his eyes to protect them from the sand, the wind blows away the stack of papers on which he had written his definitions of words for years. Concepts blind and create a parallel reality, so that things become ungraspable. "Ezingo dituzu denak jaso"

[You won't be able to catch them all], shouts a boy to Abaitua, who is running after the fluttering sheets of paper along the beach (*Hamaika pauso* 1995, 346). Losing those notes would have seemed a tragedy to him just one month earlier, but now, says the narrator, "Hendaiara joan eta, sinbolikoki hizkuntzari alde egiten utzi zion puntuan, Bidasoaz bestaldera so egon, besterik ez zuen nahi" [his only wish was to go to Hendaya and remain there, staring at the other bank of the Bidasoa, from that point where, symbolically, he had lost his language] (*Hamaika pauso* 1995, 347).

That point is, as Bergson would say, not so much a movement (or the cause of a movement) as a direction, which can be intuited if, instead of apprehending life and time by means of pre-existing concepts, one rejects the juxtaposition of abstract moments and steps into the concrete flow of duration. "Paperak besterik ez dira, paperak eta hitzak" [They're nothing but papers, papers and words] (*Hamaika pauso* 1995, 347), replies Abaitua to the boy. Nonetheless, he tucks away in his pocket the only piece of paper that the boy is able to catch. It is inscribed with the word *Heriotza*, the end of the human life (*Hamaika pauso* 1995, 347). Passing from abstraction to the feeling of duration and awareness of the end, Abaitua progresses toward the intuitive understanding of things and the mystical communion with Zabalegi's unwarranted and yet ineluctable death. Before he leaves the house on his suicidal mission, Abaitua takes one sheet from the aborted dictionary project to imitate Zabalegi's posthumous gesture when the latter tried in vain to write a good-bye note just before his execution. The sheet, chosen at random, corresponds to the word "muga" [frontier], defined as "zerbait amaitzen den tokia edo unea. Zu zara guztien hasiera, iturburua, iraupena eta muga" [the moment or place where something ends. You are the beginning, the springhead, the duration and frontier of all] (*Hamaika pauso* 1995, 441). Frontier: the place toward which Abaitua moves in time and space. It is the beginning, springhead, and duration of contemporary Basque reality, and also the condition of the unity of the novel's multiple points of view, the gathering in one single duration of the constellations of memories issuing from the Big Bang of the consciousness of one's own death. It is this consciousness that sets off the narrative, the countless steps that Abitua takes inside his memory and constitute the march, the discourse of this remarkable novel.

Works cited

Bergson, Henri. 1934. *La pensé et le mouvant*. Paris: Félix Alcan.

Echeverría, Rosa María. 2002. "Saizarbitoria: 'La herencia nacionalista es una carga muy dificil de llevar'." *ABC*, March 23.

Etxeberria, Hasier. 2002. *Cinco escritores vascos*. Irun: Alberdania.

Heidegger, Martin. 1962. *Being and Time*. Translated by John Macquarrie and Edward Robinson. New York: Harper & Row.

Izurieta, Ibon. 2004. "Ramón Saizarbitoria's High Modernist Novel in Contemporary Basque Literature." *Arizona Journal of Hispanic Cultural Studies* 8: 75–86.

Kortazar, Jon. 2005. "Literatura y juego en la obra de Ramón Saizarbitoria." *Bulletin of Hispanic Studies* 82 (2): 207–231.

Laraway, David. 2007. "Nationalism in Mourning: An Epitaph for Ideology in Ramón Saizarbitoria's *Gorde Nazazu Lurpean*." *Journal of Spanish Cultural Studies* 8 (3): 357–378.

Olaziregi, Mari Jose. 2008. "Robbe-Grillet's Concept of Realism and His Influence on the Basque Novelist Ramon Saizarbitoria." *Bulletin of Hispanic Studies* 85 (3): 383–396.

Saizarbitoria, Ramon. 1995. *Hamaika pauso*. Donostia: Erein.

———. 1996. *Bihotz bi. Gerrako kronikak*. Donostia: Erein.

———. 2000. "Gudari zaharraren gerra galdua." In *Gorde nazazu lurpean*, 7–63. Donostia: Erein.

47

OF TREASURE MAPS AND DICTIONARIES

Searching for home in *Carlota Fainberg,* *Bilbao-New York-Bilbao* and *L'últim patriarca*

Laura Lonsdale

Iberian Studies is born of a frustration with what Joan Ramón Resina describes as "Hispanism's cosy monolingualism" (2013, 2), in a move at once disciplinary and political that seeks to assert the multilingual diversity of the Iberian Peninsula and of Spain in particular. This assertion of plurality and multilingualism speaks, of course, to Spain's polemical constitution (and Constitution) as a "nation of nations, or a nation of nations and regions" (Balfour and Quiroga 2007, 2), but it may also be considered a response to globalisation and the challenges and opportunities it offers to the articulation of local identities. As Daniele Conversi argues:

> On the one hand, the changed [globalised] context has provided novel opportunities for minority nations to advance differentialist claims that are no longer based on the homogeneous concept of the nation-state. On the other hand, the erosion of representative political institutions as a consequence of globalization has contributed to a potential backlash against cultural difference and a desire to revert to past notions of homogeneity – and these are inevitably bound to affect indigenous minorities as well.
>
> (2014, 36)

Iberian Studies is particularly concerned with the "indigenous minorities" of Spain and establishing greater dialogue between its cultural and linguistic traditions; but if we consider the claims of Iberian Studies as a response not just to the tension between nationalism and nation-statism (Conversi 2014, 29, 40), but as a wider manifestation of the problem of articulating local identities in a globalised context, it casts a somewhat different light on the ways in which authors choose to articulate their sense of belonging in relation to both territory and language. If our present era is defined by travel, migration and globalisation, what function does language play in our sense of who we are? How can local identities be maintained or assumed in a multilingual and transnational reality? These are evidently significant questions for writers in minority languages, though they also have broader implications in a world dominated by English and the United States.

This chapter looks at three works that explore different facets of the problem of articulating the local in the context of the global, reflecting concerns that are expressive of the globalised dimension of local identity in the Iberian context, with territory and language figured in the map and the dictionary. Antonio Muñoz Molina's *Carlota Fainberg* (1999) is a satirical, bilingual novella that considers the linguistic formulation of Spanish and North American cultural values in the context of the United States' cultural ascendancy; Kirmen Uribe's *Bilbao-New York-Bilbao* (2009) is a work of autofiction that reflects on the past and future of Basque language and culture in the age of the Internet; and Najat El Hachmi's *L'últim patriarca* (2008) is a novel of immigration in which the young Moroccan protagonist seeks emancipation in an adopted culture and language (Catalan). Muñoz Molina and Uribe employ the treasure map as a motif for discovery, where X marks the spot of home as well as the promise of the unknown, and as a means of exploring power relations between nations; while Uribe and El Hachmi use the dictionary as a motif for cultural values they hold dear, in a spirit of preservation and emancipation, respectively.

Antonio Muñoz Molina, *Carlota Fainberg*

Carlota Fainberg reflects on the cultural fortunes of Spanish and Spain in a globalised world, in which the US is the dominant force. A round satire of literary studies in the American university, the novella employs both intratextual and intertextual strategies to map one man's migration of cultural values from his home to his host nation and back again. Written bilingually, both the intratextual encounter of Spanish and English and the intertextual encounter with Borges and Robert Louis Stevenson generate an ironic perspective on the narrator's attempt to negotiate the complex and uneven pathways of cultural identity.

The novella's protagonist and narrator (Claudio, a Spaniard) is an associate professor who has lived in the US for several years and now hopes to achieve tenure in his university post. Claudio's experience of living in America has led to a gradual assimilation of American values – he does not smoke, he protects his personal space, he splits the bill – and an increasingly dismissive view of his compatriots as politically incorrect pleasure seekers. Waiting at Pittsburgh airport for a delayed flight to Buenos Aires, where he will give a conference paper on 'Narratividad e intertextualidad' in Borges's sonnet 'Blind Pew,' Claudio is accosted by the voluble Spaniard Marcelo Abengoa, a loud, expansive, and irritatingly generous man who has in abundance all the characteristics that Claudio squeamishly associates with Spanishness. He certainly shares none of Claudio's embarrassment and temerity, both of which seem to have been enhanced by his experience of being a foreigner in the US. An engaging raconteur, Abengoa tells Claudio the story of Carlota Fainberg, a red-lipped, honeysuckle-perfumed, rampantly feminine glamour puss he once met in the dilapidated Town Hall hotel in Buenos Aires. Both the pleasurable 'naivety' of Abengoa's linear narrative and the political incorrectness of his theme are deeply troubling to Claudio, who is not only hyper-correct in his politics but has also adopted all the postmodernist sophistication of his host nation, and can only speak of pleasure, beauty and value between heavily inverted commas. Yet Abengoa, whose physical and linguistic habits remind Claudio of his father and uncle, not only succeeds in fascinating him with this story of a blonde bombshell who encapsulates all the clichés of masculine fantasy, but also displays a remarkable ability to tap unintentionally into Claudio's thoughts, an ability that suggests they share a frame of cultural reference, though Claudio would hate to admit it. In this way Abengoa becomes, ironically and against the narrator's will, an embodiment of the 'wrong' kind of 'narratividad' and 'intertextualidad,' as the author parodies, subverts and caricatures the narrator's migration of values.

This migration is most clearly reflected in Claudio's use of language, a Spanish peppered with words, phrases and idioms in American English, none of which is italicised, translated or otherwise marked out within the text. Though Claudio himself clearly regards this as a mark of his successful cultural assimilation, Muñoz Molina employs it ironically, as we see in the following examples:

> Estaba Abengoa, sin saberlo, ejerciendo la digression como transgression, como ruptura del discurso narrativo canónico, al modo de ciertos textos de Juan Goytisolo.
>
> (52–53)

> Mientras escuchaba a Abengoa, yo miraba instintivamente a mi alrededor, [. . .] como si estuviera en el departamento y alguna faculty de feminismo agresivo rondara en busca de una oportunidad de acusarme de verbal harrassment o de male chauvinism.
>
> (49)

> Uno se va haciendo poco a poco a la vida de aquí, y cuando vuelve a España ya encuentra algo upsetting que las mujeres se pinten los labios y se pongan tacones y minifalda para hacer el shopping en la mantequería de la esquina, o que las chicas acudan a la junior high school maquilladas como gheisas, con corpiño, o top, según creo que llaman a esa prenda innegablemente turbadora.
>
> (48–49)

Claudio's use of English reflects his assimilation of North American cultural values to varying degrees, such that questions of acculturation are more deeply – and more ironically – embedded in some word choices than others. At the most superficial level, the words 'faculty' and 'junior high school' simply reveal something of Claudio's adaptation to the institutional structures of American society. At a deeper level, 'La digression como transgression' reveals Claudio's self-conscious adaptation to the institutionalised parlance of the North American university (as synecdoche of the culture as a whole), while also giving the phrase the distinctively ironic ring of a received idea or trendy formulation. In a similar way, the terms 'verbal harassment' and 'male chauvinism' are implicitly dismissed as artificial verbal constructs belonging to the language of political correctness; Claudio's cowardly sense of being under threat from 'alguna faculty de feminismo agresivo' suggests both a self-conscious acceptance of, and perhaps an unconscious resistance to, the values they encode. At a still deeper and seemingly more unconscious level, the word 'upsetting' has a precious quality in English that perfectly captures Claudio's prudishness, apparently absorbed from North American culture. The word 'shopping' has a pretentious ring here, but also perhaps evokes something more directly associated with consumer culture than 'ir de compras' might in Spanish; and the word 'top' is contrasted with the not quite accurate, and somehow rather old-fashioned, Spanish equivalent of *corpiño*. In each case Claudio reveals that the Anglophone culture of the US has begun to significantly shape his thoughts on cultural matters but, in addition to revealing his incomplete process of assimilation, the use of words and phrases in English attaches a certain weight of criticism to the culture from which they derive: it is modish and vacuous; precious and pretentious; prudish yet louche. This creates an ironic counterpoint to Claudio's sense that Spain is backward or outmoded in its values. Though he dismisses Spanish attitudes to women as 'igual de antiguo[s] que el abrigo echado por los hombros de mi padre' (49), the warm, textured image of his father's coat conveys a comforting nostalgia that does more to reveal the brittleness of Claudio's adopted values than to reinforce them.

The intratextual use of English as a means of exploring cultural values is an expression of a broader interest in intertextuality within the novella, an interest that deepens and enhances what might otherwise appear a rather crude satire of cultural identity. The text on which Claudio is to give his conference paper, Borges's sonnet "Blind Pew," is itself a complex intertext, not least because it evokes the cosmopolitan figure of its Argentine author, that giant of international letters who, to quote George Steiner, "moves with a cat's assurance through the sound-world of many tongues" (1972, 26). Steiner refers to Borges as a "universalist" (26), an "unhoused" writer with a "disdain of anchor" (27), and indeed his cosmopolitanism and linguistic dexterity seem to form a kind of aspirational backdrop to the novella. Despite his "unhousedness" Borges's nationality is not incidental here; the Buenos Aires hotel where Abengoa meets the beautiful and exotic Carlota Fainberg is a crumbling relic of an old Europe on a new continent, creating a network of New World–Old World relationships that Muñoz Molina ironically explores.

The intertext to Borges's sonnet is in turn Robert Louis Stevenson's adventure novel, *Treasure Island*, which itself becomes an intertext to Muñoz Molina's text by association with certain supposed taboos of contemporary academic discourse. As a story, it constitutes exactly the kind of linear, pleasurable narrative towards which Claudio shows dutiful suspicion, and which the garrulous Abengoa is so good at producing. Secondly, with its masculine swashbuckling and its appropriative adventuring, it would by all accounts constitute a guilty pleasure to the literary critic with one eye on the politics of gender and another on postcolonialism. *Treasure Island* is in many ways an allegory of the New World and the opportunities it offers rough white men to become rich and free; the colonial history implied by the ship *Hispaniola* may be secondary to the novel's adventure story, but it is nevertheless the history of imperialism and colonialism – and associated history of trade and piracy – that makes the story possible at all. It is precisely on this basis that Claudio's meekly delivered contribution to the conference in Buenos Aires is derided by the famous and terrifying Ann Gadea Simpson Mariátegui, an overwrought caricature of a feminist academic if ever there was one: ". . . de Palo Alto, California . . . exhibe los apellidos de sus ex maridos como si fueran los trofeos de un guerrero jíbaro, y . . . la . . . llaman, no sin razón, la Terminator del New Lesbian Criticism" (135). Unluckily for Claudio, Ann Gadea's keynote speech also happens to be on Borges, and in contrast to the modest subject of Claudio's paper it is entitled: 'From Aleph to Anus: Faces (and feces) in Borges. An attempt at Postcolonial Anal/ysis' (136). With aggressive derision Ann Gadea dismisses Borges as "dead white male trash" (142) and accuses Claudio of being complicit with the "fascinación europea, heterosexual y masculina por los mitos del expolio colonial" (140) represented by *Treasure Island.* Not only is Claudio complicit with this gendered Eurocentricity (Europe=Eu/rape in Gadea's own formulation), but is barred from speaking with any authority about Borges because he is from Spain, and not from Latin America (139).

It is here that we begin to see the extended ironic significance of the assimilation of North American values reflected in Claudio's use of language: he has accepted a hierarchy of progress in his mind according to which the US must show the way to retrograde Old World nations such as Spain, but in his encounter with Ann Gadea we are brought back to an observation he made earlier, that any Spaniard in America soon discovers "que ha de cargar resignadamente sobre sus hombros con todo el peso intacto de la Leyenda Negra" (24). The black legend singled out Spain for, among other things, its brutality and plunder overseas even when other European nations were engaged in aggressive imperialist campaigns of their own, and Ann Gadea's dismissal of Claudio on the basis of his nationality carries the historical weight of a long-standing demonization of Spain. The equivalence between Spain and colonialist plunder that is at the heart of the black legend begins to appear as an accepted and acceptable form of "othering," a sanctioned rejection of a particular national culture that Claudio himself has already associated in his own mind with deep-seated political incorrectness. The hypocrisy and perceived injustice of this fact is compounded by the perpetuation of the legend by academics supposedly immersed in and alert to the language of cultural relations. So contained within the satire of American academia and, especially, of its language, is an accusation of hypocrisy that comes to us partly through the intertextual allusion to *Treasure Island*.

In contrast to Ann Gadea's tortuous cultural logic and impenetrable jargon, Borges and his "recóndito tesoro" seem to stand as embodiments of something more truly authentic, cosmopolitan and open, as we learn about the value and hope encapsulated in the mystery and promise of the unknowable: the "vasta y vaga y necesaria muerte." In the elegant simplicity of its diction and form the sonnet undoubtedly forms a counterpoint to the aggressive conviction, moral righteousness and theoretical sophistry of Ann Gadea, whose wordplay appears empty, exclusive and tyrannical in comparison. But Ann Gadea is a caricature, like Claudio and Abengoa no doubt but with none of their redeeming qualities, a reductive essence of something that is both feared and despised; and together with the fantasy blonde she might well be considered the target of an angry and wounded pride, masculine and national, covered over with a dubious claim to the cosmopolitan. This undermines what is otherwise a funny, ironic and unusual text, alert to the linguistic formulation of cultural values in the context of unequal relationships of power.

Kirmen Uribe, *Bilbao-New York-Bilbao*

Bilbao-New York-Bilbao is also a work about home, globalisation and language, though unlike *Carlota Fainberg* it is written in a minor key. A work of autofiction originally written in Basque (though here read in Spanish translation), the book is narrated by an author travelling by air between Bilbao and New York, drawing an explicit contrast between seafaring and air travel, and evoking through family history the marine culture of the Basque Country and the changes wrought by modernity. The crossing of the Atlantic and the naming of many places on its shores give a sense of the global perspective of the work, despite its interest in the local and personal. Structured associatively in the manner of a "red" (Kortazar 2010, 26), perhaps evoking Barthes's "réseaux" but, more specifically, both the fisherman's net and the Internet, the text interweaves stories, reflections and experiences, "hyperlinking" themes and motifs through repetition and association. One of these motifs is the map, an image of physical space in contrast to the virtual space of the Net, which Uribe employs to reflect on the place of a minority language and culture in a globalised context. Cartography is associated ambivalently with the transition from the pre-modern to the modern, figured in terms of imperialist territorial expansion (the overwhelming of the small), though also in terms of the potential forging of new connections between small entities, thus ensuring their survival. In this way maps and map-making become figures for the problems and opportunities of globalisation for minority languages and cultures.

The narrator's father, we are told, once sailed mapless but guided by Columbus's writings from the Cantabrian coast to the Caribbean (183–184). This mention of Columbus evokes the association between cartography and imperialism, an idea reinforced by a brief but significant intertextual reference to Borges's "Del rigor en la ciencia," a microfictional and supposedly apocryphal tale about cartography and empire which begins:

> En aquel Imperio, el Arte de la Cartografía logró tal Perfección que el Mapa de una sola Provincia ocupaba toda una Ciudad, y el Mapa del Imperio, toda una Provincia. Con el tiempo, estos Mapas Desmesurados no satisficieron y los Colegios de

Cartógrafos levantaron un Mapa del Imperio, que tenía el Tamaño del Imperio y coincidía puntualmente con él.

(Borges 1975, 143)

The map is left to rot in the desert by the "Generaciones Siguientes," who understand "que ese dilatado Mapa era Inútil" (143). It is a suggestive choice of intertext, not least because Borges' labyrinthine, librarian mode (especially in "El Jardín de senderos que se bifurcan") is sometimes considered a model of the hypertext (Manovich 2003, 15). Borges's "Del rigor . . ." also highlights the association between map-making and representation, and the potentially absurd and tautological desire for exactitude. It may be a comment on scientific method, as the title indicates, but it is also surely a comment on artistic representation and verisimilitude, which entails both a claim to total knowledge (empire) and a preservationist but also domineering desire to capture things exactly (map). This is significant to the metafictional and self-referential mode in which Uribe's book is written, and underscores his choice of the net rather than the map as the structuring image of his work: the fishing net/Internet avoids the expansionist, imperialist domination of space implied by the map, evoking both the local and the global, the physical and the virtual, the past and the present, a layered and complex space rather than just its two-dimensional representation.

A concern with both maps and map-making is first introduced by the narrator in the form of an anecdote about himself and his father. Shortly after the latter's retirement from the sea, the narrator presented him with an atlas and a pen and asked him to draw a line showing the way to Rockall, a small island off the coast of Scotland where he used to fish. His father's reaction is one of suspicious surprise: "[. . .] se quedó de piedra [. . .] Mostró desconfianza, como si otro patrón de pesca le estuviera pidiendo algún secreto del mar, el camino a una cala oculta" (43). With a "mano nerviosa" his father eventually traces a line revealing a secret that, but for the map and the pen, would have died with him; and it is precisely the thought that his father will one day die that assails the narrator as he observes the line he has drawn. The father's suspicion and nervousness seem to owe themselves to the fact that "un patrón no enseña jamás sus cartas de navegación, cuando llega a puerto se lleva con él los rollos a casa" (43), but in the context of this scene between father and son it seems inexplicable. Why should the father react in this way to his son's request? The father was himself responsible for drawing the first fishing maps of the area around Rockall, as the narrator remembers from his childhood: "Ellos tuvieron que cartografiar los mapas. Yo mismo recuerdo cómo trazaba mi padre las cartas en casa; imaginaba los fondos marinos de aquella zona con rotuladores azules, rojos y negros" (171–172). This description presents cartography as an act of writing, an inscribing of knowledge much more detailed and comprehensive than the crude line the narrator asks his father to trace across the atlas; the father's suspicion perhaps concerns then to what use the knowledge will be put, as the allusion to another "patrón de pesca" indicates. Though the father's response may be pragmatic rather than philosophical, the narrator both acknowledges and extends its implications: his own preservationist instinct, the one that drives him to ask his father to mark the way to Rockall, is complicated not only by the father's sense of a loss of ownership but also by his own sudden intuition of mortality, as if in recognition of the fact that any act of preservation marks both an appropriation and an ending.

In a fine example of Uribe's networking of ideas, this becomes significant to his concern with the balance between preservation and renewal necessary to guarantee the survival and reinvigoration of a minority language and its culture. The balance is a fragile one, requiring the sensitivity and lightness of touch proper to the blowing of fine glass (180) or the cultivation of roses (194), and characteristic of Uribe's prose. The skills required for these crafts, as for fishing and good seamanship, resonate in the book for their common association with the pre-industrial (the narrator's father is himself associated with the adventurous seafaring of a romantic and artisanal age) and Uribe highlights this by associating such skills with inheritance rather than acquisition. The glass blower will excel at his craft because his forebears have taught him to know and love glass (180–181); the sailor will sail successfully because he knows and loves boats, the wind and the stars. Map-making, in this context, is an ambivalent process: it is a preservation of knowledge, but also a rationalisation of it. The graphic separation of knowledge from its source, the sense that the map makes knowledge available to others, and will last long after the man who drew it dies, breaks that chain of inherited tradition that is associated with craftsmanship, and breaks also the connection between the experience that gave rise to knowledge and the acquisition of that knowledge. Does this express an anxiety about the preservation of a language that relies on acquiring new speakers to survive, that relies, in other words, on a separation from its cultural history and tradition of inherited speech?

The narrator expresses the association between language and autochthonous culture most powerfully in his account of the compiling of the *Diccionario de los pescadores vizcaínos*, a highly conservationist enterprise that sought to capture, first in recordings and then in the dictionary itself, the vocabulary of Basque fishermen. Of course, what this emphasises is not just the conservation of a language but of a culture and craft traditionally associated with that language. One of the fishermen to be recorded, the narrator's uncle, is heard to say on tape that "antes el mar estaba llenos de peces, ahora de agua," a phrase the narrator interprets to mean, "Habrá técnica pero no hay peces, porque se ha pescado demasiado" (75). In the next paragraph the narrator reflects: "Cómo se hace un diccionario. Muchas veces me lo he preguntado. En la grabación se aprecia con claridad la técnica de Barrutia [the compiler]" (75). By means of the word *técnica*, "hyperlinked" from fishing to Barrutia's compiling of the dictionary, Uribe brings to mind again the technical knowledge associated with craftsmanship and the labour of love, and also directly unites the compiling of a dictionary of Basque fishing terms with fishing in a depleted sea. Even in translation the fisherman's vocabulary is specialised and unfamiliar: "El profesor enuncia una palabra, la mayor parte de las veces en castellano, y el tío la traduce al euskera del pueblo. Por ejemplo, cuando le pregunta 'sotavento,' el tío responde 'haixebekaldo,' y, si le dice 'barlovento,' entonces 'haixekaldi'" (75). The act of fishing, the language of fishing, and the language *of the language* of fishing are indivisible and perishing. And yet the conservation of this cultural history is both vital and precious, beyond monetary value:

> [Nerea] trabaja en un banco. [. . .] un cliente, cada vez que ella lo atiende, le entrega un papelito con palabras antiguas escritas en él. "Hace tiempo que no he oído esta palabra," le dice, y a continuación le pide a Nerea que la guarde. El marino retirado le lleva palabras, refranes, nombres de peces. En el sitio donde se guarda el dinero él pone a salvo las palabras antiguas.
>
> (154)

If the map figures a break in a community's inherited tradition and experience, in the same way that a grammar book might figure a break in the life of an autonomous linguistic community, its outward movement nonetheless presents opportunities for new kinds of connection and even reconnection. Uribe consistently evokes other minority European, especially Celtic cultures and languages in relation to his own, and notes a legend shared by the Scots and the Basques derived from the Tower of Babel. This is the legend of Tubal, grandson of Noah, who according to chronicle brought the Basque language from Babel to the Iberian Peninsula, where he remained (25). Later, on a visit to Stornoway in Scotland, the narrator discovers that "los escoceses creían que la lengua de Tubal era el gaélico, igual que los vascos" (149). This shared tradition does a number of things: it marks the Basque language as very ancient, but belonging to a family of languages rather than existing in isolation, as commonly thought; it offers a genetic "mapping" of Celtic cultures that establishes new but also ancient connections not formerly understood (as BBC Wales reported in 2001, genetically speaking "the Celtic populations turn out to be statistically indistinguishable from the Basques"); it places the history of the Basque language in the context of diversity (Babel), but also rootedness ("se quedó a vivir" [25]); and it inscribes Basque history as legend and chronicle, in keeping with its ancient roots and oral traditions.

At a conference of writers in Estonia, the narrator tells us, the Welsh writer Meredid Puw Davies argued that for minority languages to make themselves heard they must live in the present and take advantage of technology, recognising that "[a]hora no se escribía únicamente para los miembros de la misma comunidad. Ahora el mundo era más pequeño" (101). Preservation is therefore a question of renewal, of adjustment to new ways of living and communicating. At a talk given at the University of Oxford in October 2014, Uribe stressed the importance of this openness in guaranteeing the survival of a language: Basques must not be possessive of their language, but must encourage more and more people to learn it. He explained that an "Euskaldun" is not necessarily a native speaker, but rather a person who is in possession of the language; and he suggested that this democratic concept of language allowed any speaker of Basque to become, in a sense, Basque. In the book, the map is again significant to this question. On a visit to the US in 2003, the narrator tells us that "la escritora neoyorquina Phyllis Levin me regaló la definición más bella de un idioma que he escuchado en mi vida" (29). Looking at a text in Basque, she notes the frequency of the letter x:

> "Vuestra lengua parece el mapa del tesoro," me descubrió. "Si desenfocas el resto de letras y percibes sólo las *x*, parece como si te guiaran por la ruta del tesoro."
>
> Me pareció que aquello era lo más bonito que se podía decir de un idioma que no conoces, que se asemejaba a un mapa del tesoro.
>
> (29–30)

At the same talk in Oxford, the author explained that most Basque speakers are not born to the language, but have rather had to acquire it in a process of discovery, and this was for him the particular significance of the treasure map. If we return to the observations about map-making outlined previously, we could also argue that the image speaks to those questions of preservation and renewal, conservation and value, representation and communication, craftsmanship and knowledge, the passion of adventure and the labour of love, that give the novel its delicate focus.

Does this delicacy mean that the novel can bear no historical or ideological weight? Luisa Elena Delgado argues that the view from above allows it to reconcile differences too easily, smoothing over a history of violence in line with "esa cultura de consenso que asume que en una realidad compleja todo es inteligible y compatible:"

> No me parece casual, en ese sentido, que la obra de Uribe se desarrolle durante un vuelo transatlántico, esto es, literalmente suspendida en el aire, lejos de las fronteras

concretas institucionales, pero también de los vínculos que marcan la pertenencia a uno y otro lugar, ideológico y geográfico. Es quizá sólo en el aire donde, hoy por hoy, su visión integradora de la identidad vasca puede tener lugar.

(2014, Kindle loc. 3307)

But as we have seen, the map and the web evoke not the flattening out of difference but rather the complex layering of time and space, according to which the local finds expression in the connections afforded by the global, precisely allowing for the creation of new networks with alternative centres. The novel is therefore less concerned with compatibility than it is with complex association; less with integration than the fragile balance between opposing terms; and it is less indebted to a national culture of consensus than it is to a transnational imaginary.

Najat El Hachmi, *L'últim patriarca*

In Najat El Hachmi's novel the associations between language and culture established by the other two authors are shaped by a concern with female emancipation in a migratory context. Written in two parts, the novel is narrated by a young Moroccan-born girl who first tells the story of her father, Mimoun, the violent, unpredictable, authoritarian, gambling, drinking, womanising eponymous patriarch, before relating her own coming of age. Her struggle to release herself from his influence is figured in linguistic terms, as the narrator immerses herself in Catalan language and literature as a means of escape and self-expression. Despite its difficult subject matter the novel is ironic and often funny, frequently bordering on the sarcastic. This tone of detachment helps to establish some distance between the narrator and her narration, suggesting she has come a long way in the interpretation of her experience; but in the best tradition of irony, it also generates a strong sense of ambiguity. A novel whose structure and principal intertexts – the Catalan dictionary and Mercè Rodoreda's *La plaça del Diamant* (1962) – suggest a narrative of cultural assimilation and female emancipation, it is at least partly destabilised by this ironic ambiguity.

The nameless narrator-protagonist moves to Barcelona with her parents and brothers when she is a young girl. Unlike her subjugated and abused mother, who rarely leaves the house and never learns to speak Catalan, the narrator is schooled in the Catalan language and becomes acutely aware in adolescence of the conflicting demands of her "esperit de rebel·lió" (II, ch. 14) and the cultural demands of home. Subjected like the rest of her family to the whims of her father, in a moment of crisis she turns to the Catalan dictionary in an attempt to relieve and express herself:

> Per escapar del *poltergeist* [. . .] has de riure molt, fins a sentir que tens les costelles a punt de petar, o has de plorar molt, fins a sentir que t'has buidat, o has de tenir un orgasme, que, fet i fet, també és buidar-se. Jo encara no en sabia, de tenir orgasmes, al pare no li agradava que ningú plorés i a la mare no li agradava que ningú rigués. De manera que vaig començar a llegir, paraula per paraula, aquell diccionari de la llengua catalana. Tothom deia quina nena més intel·ligent, quina nena més estudiosa, però només era per buscar una de les tres coses.
>
> (Part II, ch. 4, para. 1)

This is significant because, as Kathryn Crameri notes, "neither [the narrator's] mother nor father have any real command of Catalan (her mother hardly even speaks Spanish), and it is therefore in some senses a language of her own, giving her access to a world that is hidden from them" (2013, 5). In addition, the dictionary not only represents her adoptive culture but also symbolises her education, which she achieves largely by reading. Though her reading of the dictionary – symbolic in some sense of all her other reading – can be interpreted as a feat of emancipation through education, the young narrator undertakes it almost unconsciously and with a misguided sense of what it can achieve, as her evocation of physical drives rather than conscious objectives illustrates.

The narrator first picks up the dictionary at a moment of extreme stress (II, ch 4) – her bullied and depressed mother appears to be starving herself to death – and ends, as she reaches Z, just before she embarks on her first serious romantic relationship with a man (II, ch 27). If her reading of the dictionary is an exercise in liberation, it is significant that it should end with an act of rebellion against her father and an adult assertion of control over her own life; but in fact both the rebellion and self-determination are illusory, ending in her marriage to a man no less unreliable and restrictive than her father. Though she never comments or gives up on her enterprise, her failure to find what she is looking for is reflected in her sampling of dictionary entries at the end of each chapter, where there is often more dryness than joy, more frustration than fascination, more obscurity than enlightenment: "*Daci, dàcia*, que és un adjectiu, *dació* que és una acció i *dacita* que és una roca" (II, ch. 5); "*Yperita*, iperita. *Ypressià – ana*, relatiu a l'ypressià" (II, ch. 26). Often she conveys meanings that seem to partially converge with her own feelings without giving them direct expression, as if maintaining the still repressed nature of her desires: the bitter mustard gas of the letter Y; the mysterious O of menstruation; the ironically pastoral images of R; the paternal and priestly P; the inhibiting cardiac glucose of U, the bathetic V of *va vana* and a herd of cows. The idea that a dictionary, of all texts, will provoke *in*articulate self-expression and physical or emotional climax is both comically and poignantly expressive of the narrator's desperate search for any means of escape; and to the extent that liberation is not achieved on reaching Z, the reading of the dictionary has been a failure.

The dictionary is not only emotionally sterile but sometimes also beyond comprehension: "Jo tot això no ho entenia, però ho llegia igualment, per veure com sonava" (II, ch. 4). On several occasions she fails altogether to interpret or communicate meaning: "és força difícil de definir" (II, ch. 9); "era massa complicat per llegir-me'n la definició" (II, ch. 13); "és molt complicat" (II, ch. 14); "és massa complicat" (II, ch. 18); "un terme massa complicat" (266). On other occasions she draws attention to the morphological similarity of semantically unrelated words, as if to highlight the arbitrariness of meaning: "*Taba*, astròleg. *Tabac*, que és una planta. *Tabac*, que és una cistelleta rodona; *tàbac*, que és un cop de puny" (II, ch. 21); "*Wagnerisme*, un corrent dramaticomusical. *Wagnerita*, un fluosofat de magnesi" (II, ch. 24). Of course, words are meaningless until they are articulated in context, as the apparently arbitrary listing of them implies; and they do not provide expression or release until they are meaningfully articulated. It is precisely the articulation of her cultural context, and of herself within it, that her father's own arbitrariness makes so problematic. A good example of this is the narrator's decision – having reached the letter M – to wear a Muslim headscarf, a decision initially in keeping with the impulsive devoutness of her father. Her father disapproves of the headscarf, despite the traditional modesty associated with it, and warns her not to wear it; the narrator defies him – partly because she thinks he must be joking, partly because her "esperit de rebel·lió" chooses to express itself "en les situacions menys esperades" (II, ch. 14) – and she is severely punished. How to articulate a context, and herself within in it, when it is regulated by the impossibly capricious terms of her father's dominance? The decontextualized, arbitrary, often technical and obscure words of the dictionary help her neither to express what she feels nor to understand what she experiences, so though her consciousness is beginning to develop thanks to the novels of Rodoreda and others, the symbolic power of the dictionary remains latent.

By the end of the novel the narrator has left her husband, and is living independently in a bedsit. But this has not rid her of the influence of her father, who pesters her constantly (II, ch. 38). Visited one evening by her uncle, an Islamic scholar on his way to a conference in Paris, she engages in anal sex with him and exposes their act to her father by means of the video entry system. The resonances of this are multiple: anal sex is the means by which Moroccan girls preserve their virginity for marriage, as we learn at some length in Part I; it is incestuous with an uncle, Mimoun's brother, the very one her father has always jealously suspected of an adulterous liaison with his wife; Mimoun was himself probably raped by his own uncle at the age of twelve, though this has never been openly discussed (ch. 6); and it is voyeuristic, evoking the Muslim taboo of the veiled woman, and the narrator's earlier para-doxical attempt to rebel against her father by wearing the headscarf. All these resonances are highly culturally specific; and where they cross with images of Westernised sexual behaviour, such as in the reference to the anal sex scene of *Last Tango in Paris*, they are humorously "brought home" (the narrator explains that, being Mediterranean, she and her uncle used olive oil in place of Marlon Brando's butter).

The release the narrator experiences through multiple orgasm, as she hovers between pleas-ure and pain, is nothing if not ambiguous. In its contrast with the difficult penetration and false orgasms of her previous sexual relationship, we can assume this "venjança en tota regla" (ch. 39) against her father to represent a personal triumph and a sexual liberation; but as a statement of cultural and gendered identity it is very difficult to read. For Cristián Ricci, the narrator reaffirms "una libertad que da por tierra con la tradición moral musulmana: rechazo a la monotonía del amor convencional y burla al honor. En términos foucauldianos la trasgresión deliberada propiciada por el 'discurso ilícito' que invita a deformar la realidad, consigna una clara afirmación de la sublimación concupiscente, lo demoníaco y lo prohibido" (2010, 79). But this sexual affirmation relies on a reclaiming of terms, and the reclaiming of terms is always a risky business; after all, the sexual act they perform belongs entirely to the system of patriarchal taboos and double standards it is also designed to undermine. Read positively, this act with her uncle brings together all the images of sexual hypocrisy and paranoia identified in the novel with patriarchy in the culturally specific form in which she has experienced it, and transmits them back to the patriarch in a spirit of rebellion and a bid for self-expression. Only by relaying the message to him in terms he can recognise – if not understand – will he receive its full force, and this guarantees that he will never again play the patriarch, "no pas amb mi" (II, ch. 39, final para).

For me, the image of the narrator in dubious sexual liaison with her uncle remains ironi-cally ambiguous. But what does seem evident is that the inarticulacy of expressed emotion gives way at last to the articulation of contextualised meaning, in the form of the narration. If a child's first language is the one "in which personal involvement is expressed, and the second [is] the language of distance and detachment" (Pavlenko and Dewaele 2002, cited in Crameri 2013, 4), it is significant that the emotional and physical release of orgasm should be achieved in sexual liaison with a man belonging to the intimate world of her childhood. It is only by returning to the world of her first language that she can access the emotional and physical well-spring she had hoped to find in Catalan, which becomes rather the language of ironic distance that allows her to process her emotions and experiences intellectually (Crameri 2013, 7). It is interesting in this context that the final word of the novel, "estimada," should evoke not the father's violence, but his love; a notion itself charged with irony, but which also suggests that her articulacy and rebellion come at an emotional cost. Arguably, the real winner in this novel is not the narrator but Catalonia itself; firstly, because its language and literature are conceived not in peripheral relation to the Spanish, but as emancipatory expressions of Western culture in their own right; and secondly, because the narrator's identification of herself as Catalan seems to uphold its civic model of national identity. But the ambiguity of the novel's ending also troubles and perhaps resists the rhetoric of assimilation, associating it with ambivalence and emotional loss.

Conclusion

These three works offer powerfully distinctive readings of the tensions surrounding local and linguistic identity in a globalised or migratory context, which is nevertheless highly particular to the multilingual constitution of Spain itself. In his challenge to US hegemony, Muñoz Molina posits fantasy and humour as liberating alternatives to new forms of cultural authoritarianism, but the novella protests too much, generating an uncomfortable blend of cosmopolitan ambition and nationalist nostalgia in the process. Uribe's book spins the most delicate of narrative webs around the question of local identity in a global context, finding in both craftsmanship and new technology an opportunity for survival and expansion. It is a creative response to the need, in Andreas Huyssen's words, to "focus on differential histories and deep cultural knowledge as they shape the incorporation of the global in local or regional economies and cultures" (2008, 11). El Hachmi stakes a bold claim for emancipation and inclusion in terms both gendered and cultural, while recognising the emotional cost of acculturation. All three works place a strong value on the idea of home, while recognising the complex transnational networks within which linguistic and cultural identity must operate.

Works cited

Balfour, Sebastian and Alejandro Quiroga. 2007. *The Reinvention of Spain: Nation and Identity since Democracy*. Oxford: Oxford University Press.

Borges, Jorge Luis. [1960] 1975. *El Hacedor*. Madrid: Alianza.

Conversi, Daniele. 2014. "Between the Hammer of Globalization and the Anvil of Nationalism: Is Europe's Complex Diversity under Threat?" *Ethnicities* 14 (1): 25–49.

Crameri, Kathryn. 2013. "Searching for Orgasms in the Dictionary: Language and Emotion in *L'últim patriarca* by Najat El Hachmi." Paper presented at the AHGBI conference, Oxford, March 25–27.

Delgado, Luisa Elena. 2014. *La nación singular. Fantasía de la normalidad democrática española (1996–2011)*. Madrid: Siglo XXI. Kindle edition.

El Hachmi, Najat. 2008. *L'últim patriarca*. Kindle ed.

Huyssen, Andreas. 2008. *Other Cities, Other Worlds: Urban Imaginaries in a Globalizing Age*. Durham, NC: Duke University Press.

Kortazar, P. 2010. "Entre la asimilación y la diferencia: Interview with Kirmen Uribe." *Insula* 768: 23–28.

Manovich, Lev. 2003. "New Media from Borges to HTML." In *The New Media Reader*, edited by Noah Wardrip-Fruin and Nick Montfort, 13–25. Cambridge, MA: MIT Press.

Muñoz Molina, Antonio. [1999] 2007. *Carlota Fainberg*. Madrid: Alfaguara.

Pavlenko, Aneta and Jean-Marc Dewaele. 2002. "Emotion Vocabulary in Interlanguage." *Language Learning* 52 (2): 263–322.

Resina, Joan Ramón. 2013. "Iberian Modalities: The Logic of an Intercultural Field." In *Iberian Modalities: A Relational Approach to the Study of Culture in the Iberian Peninsula*, edited by Joan Ramón Resina, 1–22. Liverpool: Liverpool University Press.

Ricci, Cristián. 2010. "*L'últim patriarca* de Najat El Hachmi y el forjamiento de una identidad amazigh-catalana." *Journal of Spanish Cultural Studies* 11 (1): 71–91.

Steiner, George. 1972. *Extra-Territorial: Papers on Literature and the Language Revolution*. London: Faber & Faber.

Uribe, Kirmen. 2009. *Bilbao-New York-Bilbao*. Translated by Ana Arregi. Barcelona: Seix Barral.

48

REWRITING THE IBERIAN FEMALE DETECTIVE

Deciphering truth, memory, and identity in the twenty-first-century novel

Antonia L. Delgado-Poust

Following the death of Francisco Franco in 1975 as well as the subsequent Transition to democracy and *desencanto* felt throughout Spain, the *novela negra* was the genre of choice for many Spanish writers who sought to expose the existing socio-political concerns of the moment. As Shelley Godsland articulates in her analysis of women's crime fiction in Spain, the *novela negra* is a sub-genre that, like its North American predecessors, features a "lone private eye very much at odds with the social environment within which he operated, investigating crimes that uncovered high-level corruption and law-breaking as well as other ills that plagued society" (2007, 6). The perceived failure of the democratic system and the (un)official compulsion to suppress any memory of a painful, inconvenient past or truth have contributed to the overwhelming popularity of crime narrative on the Peninsula. Nevertheless, Godsland reminds us that female-authored crime fiction tends to be overlooked in both national and international explorations of the genre, an oversight that she insists literary scholars must rectify. Since the turn of the millennium, various female Peninsular novelists have endeavored to give voice to marginalized individuals – women, in particular – whose stories were silenced for far too long. As a result, women writers offer a perspective that departs from the official version of the truth. By unearthing the details of, or shedding new light on, an obscure past and crime, their unconventional detectives or killers are compelled to reflect not only on the problematic concepts of truth and fabrication, but also upon their own past and identity as well.

This chapter examines the inextricable connection among the notions of truth and lie, memory, and identity in three novels by contemporary female authors from the Basque Country, Madrid, and Galicia: Dolores Redondo's *El guardián invisible* [*Zaindari Ikusezina*] (2013), Rosa Montero's *Lágrimas en la lluvia* (2011), and Marina Mayoral's *Casi perfecto* [*Case perfecto*] (2007), respectively. While these novelists infuse the local color of a particular region of Spain into their novels, their respective works underscore universal themes that transcend cultural and geographical origins. For one, all three protagonists are women who occupy positions of power (as professional detectives, police inspectors, and novelists), yet they also grapple with varying degrees of gender discrimination and existential insecurity in a patriarchal society. It is in their search for justice and in their reconstruction of the truth that these women come to better understand themselves and the cases to which they are tied. As doubly marginalized individuals (first as women, second as citizens of "peripheral" autonomous regions of

Spain or a non-human race), these female protagonists identify with and defend the interests of the Other, feeling a personal urgency to bring the(ir) truth to light. Furthermore, each novelist emphasizes the multifaceted and ambiguous nature of truth, memory, and identity, thus challenging hegemony, orthodoxy, and the conventions of detective fiction.

For Renée Craig-Odders, the Spanish crime novel serves as a barometer of socio-political change (2009, 2) and, in the same vein, I consider that these works not only make valuable contributions to the crime and detective genres, but that they also impel their reading public to reflect on the repeated discrimination of women in contemporary Spain. The protagonists of these novels are women who, on a daily basis, must confront the vestiges of sexism and xenophobia inherited from previous generations. In my analysis, I first consider these works as examples of feminist revisions of detective or crime fiction. Then, I present a brief synopsis of each novel before moving on to examine the themes of memory, identity, truth, and (in)justice, or patriarchal oppression, that not only tie these works together, but are also intrinsic to the female-authored detective genre itself. Finally, I contend that in their respective novels, Redondo, Montero, and Mayoral propose the need for more comprehensive social change that seeks to combat ignorance and inequality throughout Spain.

Feminist revisions of detective fiction

The detective genre has been associated largely with male sleuths who solve crimes by means of rational and objective deductions. This tradition is deeply entrenched not only in the values of Cartesian reasoning, the search for social justice, and the pursuit of knowledge and truth, but also in misogyny. In various contemporary novels written by women authors, female detectives – unlike their male counterparts – defy the conventional gender roles and biases that have characterized detective and crime fiction since its inception. These fictional women are so far removed from the "norm," or mainstream, that they not only represent what Godsland has described as a negation of hard-boiled masculinity (26), but they also offer new interpretations of reality and the truth, from the perspective of the Other. As in previous female-authored Peninsular detective novels, the female sleuth and the circumstances and details surrounding the crime she investigates are strongly correlated.

With the advent of democracy on the Peninsula came the desire for justice and truth as well as the need to make reparations to those who had been wronged previously, and while this tendency is manifest in much of the literature of the post-Franco era, it seems fitting that such themes be addressed in the detective novel. Within the realm of detective fiction, then, it is especially effective if the individual seeking to establish the truth is one who, at some point, has been the victim of injustice. While some characters may identify with or see themselves as the victim of violence or oppression, they all serve as advocates for justice and equality. In *El guardián invisible*, *Lágrimas en la lluvia*, and *Casi perfecto*, all three protagonists are independent, assertive career women who combat inequality and sexism in the workplace and, by extension, in their respective societies. Godsland highlights the (post-)feminist nature of the Peninsular private eye, claiming that without the democratization of Spanish society and the influence of feminism, the fictional female Spanish sleuth would not exist today (2007, 13). It is logical, then, that contemporary female-authored and feminist Peninsular detective fiction should engage with women's issues, such as gender violence, misogyny, women's rights, and the struggle for authority and respect in a still highly androcentric environment. By bringing to the forefront of their novels instances of rape, murder, and physical or psychological aggression directed against women, Redondo, Montero, and Mayoral make clear their criticism of patriarchal culture, other hierarchical systems, and the continued legacy of machismo in democratic

Spain. By raising public awareness of the pervasive victimization of women, these authors render relevant what were once silenced taboos, thereby incorporating the peripheral into a national, collective discourse in order to effect palpable socio-political change through their reading public. In what follows, I carry out a brief overview of each novel before considering in further detail the themes of identity, memory, and truth that are present in all three works.

Dolores Redondo's *El guardián invisible*

Critics of Redondo's *El guardián invisible* maintain that the story represents a distinctive combination of *noir* fiction and Basque-Navarrese mythology and traditions. Interestingly, Redondo centers much of her attention on the hostile, sinister quality of the Baztán River Valley and chooses to situate her murder mystery in the deceivingly quiet community of Elizondo, an actual town nestled in the province of Navarre. Because of its relative isolation, cold temperatures, and rural setting, Elizondo epitomizes the ideal location for a murder mystery. The omniscient narrator observes that Elizondo and the Basque Country constitute part of the protagonist's genetic makeup. By returning to the natural elements and the traditional mythology characteristic of her hometown and surrounding area, Regional Inspector Amaia Salazar comes to a deeper understanding of her own identity and origins. As indicated in the synopsis of the novel, Amaia must disentangle a series of crimes that forces her to come to terms with a traumatic childhood and adolescence. Redondo paints the picture of a tortured individual haunted by memories of a painful past whose details are revealed incrementally to us via analepsis. Upon visiting the family bakery for the first time in years, disturbing memories of her past resurface: "[u]na abrumadora oleada de recuerdos oscuros la aturdió de repente y los ecos del pasado la bloquearon por completo" (152). Early on, the reader learns that Amaia's past and family members become entwined with the investigation – something that complicates the detective's ability to remain objective. For one, when the police inspectors discover the lifeless bodies of the female victims lying in the woods, they find a *txantxigorri* – a traditional Basque pastry and specialty of her family's hundred-year-old bakery – strategically placed on the corpses at the scenes of the crime. In the end, the individual responsible for the murders of the young women turns out to be Amaia's seemingly innocuous brother-in-law.

Amaia is the counterpart to the conventional male detective, who is depicted as an alcoholic loner, pessimist, and all around difficult person. Redondo purposely portrays Amaia as a "typical" working-woman, who takes her job seriously, unlike some of her male colleagues in the field. To arrive at the truth, Salazar avails herself of what the omniscient narrator refers to as her female intuition – rooted in careful observation, reflection, and tarot readings: "[a]ún no entendía cómo funcionaba el instinto, la complicada maquinaria que se ponía en marcha dentro de un investigador, [. . .] haciendo que todo cobrase sentido, como si en su avance fuera apartando velos de niebla que hubiera tenido ante los ojos" (390). This fog metaphor will reappear in the subsequent novels, as each protagonist must either sift through or hide behind a figurative blindness and ambiguity before arriving at or concealing the truth. Aside from her presumed clairvoyance or heightened sensitivity to external or covert signs, Amaia realizes that to solve the enigma she must try to understand the criminal and his motives for wanting the young women dead.

Rosa Montero's *Lágrimas en la lluvia*

Unlike Redondo's novel, which is set at the beginning of the twenty-first century, Montero situates her story in a futuristic, albeit strangely familiar, twenty-second-century milieu. Aside from the fact that the action takes place in Madrid, we are no longer in Spain – the independent sovereign state that we currently know – but rather, in *Los Estados Unidos de la Tierra*. Nevertheless, in an effort to orient her reader, Montero's 2109 Madrid has managed to retain some of its twenty-first-century charm, as many streets and landmarks from previous eras remain intact, though slightly transformed. By creating such a foreign, yet familiar, setting for the action of her novel, the novelist challenges her reader to reflect on the problems of his or her present reality. Like many of her literary predecessors, Montero presents her audience with a dystopian world characterized by unregulated capitalism, social isolation, environmental degradation, and a society plagued by its fear of the Other. The corruption and immunity of politicians, the resurgence of supremacist groups, and the flaws in the justice system are all too evocative of the Spanish and global political climate of the late twentieth- and early twenty-first centuries. The novel's protagonist, Bruna Husky, embodies the hybrid fusion of the familiar – the human-like – and the unfamiliar – the android, or non-human. As we become acquainted with Bruna and her struggle, it becomes increasingly difficult to distinguish what is different about her from what is familiar, thus impelling us to identify with her plight and come to view the Other as an extension of the Self.

Bruna is engaged as much in her search for existential meaning as in the investigation of the case to which she has been assigned – the mysterious deaths of androids who turn psychotic before indiscriminately killing humans. As the only replicant detective officially designated to examine the homicides, it is important that Bruna solve the murders because, ironically, she, like the reps who committed the crimes, has been cast as a terrorist assassin and a threat to humanity. Moreover, to proceed with the case without being attacked on the streets of Madrid by humans, Bruna must transform herself into the Other – in this case the more socially acceptable, familiar Other – by dressing incognito as a member of a human supremacist group who is collaborating with other human supremacists to exterminate the techno-human race. Her face-to-face encounter with the enemy – a collective, obscure adversary that wants her and other androids dead – is particularly eye-opening for the android, as it exposes significant truths regarding the case, but also challenges her to step out of her comfort zone and adopt, albeit out of necessity, the position of the foe. Discerning the distinctions between good and evil, or truth and lie, is a challenge even for the experienced detective. Nevertheless, Montero highlights that, as a supposedly false, ambiguous being whose intrinsic hybridity and contradictory nature seem monstrous to the human masses, Bruna is the most appropriate individual to uncover the truth.

Marina Mayoral's *Casi perfecto*

This quest for truth and justice is also at the heart of Marina Mayoral's text. Like Clarín, Pardo Bazán, and Valle-Inclán, Mayoral situates many of her novels in the Gothic-like setting of her native Galicia. Nevertheless, it must be noted that *Casi perfecto* is actually situated in Madrid, where the narrator-protagonist lives and works. Yet the narrator makes frequent allusions to her Galician roots throughout the text and intersperses her account with various Galician terms that emphasize her sense of cultural identity. In keeping with the style she cultivates in her previous "crime" novels, Mayoral's female protagonist and first-person narrator in this epistolary novel reminiscent of the *novela negra* is a novelist by trade whose perception and representation of reality are contradictory and thus unreliable. In response to the accusation of her youngest son, Peque, that she plotted the murder of his father (her estranged husband) and modeled it on the fictional murder of one of her characters, the narrator Ana writes him a letter in which she fervently justifies her behavior through the years whilst unfalteringly maintaining her innocence. Mayoral portrays her narrator-protagonist in a psychologically complex light, in which we observe her inconsistencies and imperfections through first-person narration. Through writing, Ana unearths a series of painful memories and reflects on her past mistakes as a mother, daughter, and wife to defend her actions.

At first glance, Ana's letter appears to be written in a stream of consciousness, as she returns to past events, mistakes, and emotions by way of analepsis. Nonetheless, it soon becomes evident that she has shrewdly planned out her argument with the intention of simultaneously convincing her son (and larger audience) of her innocence and justifying her motives for his father's death. Mayoral herself has asserted that her novels rarely contain obvious, indisputable truths, and here she creates a number of conceivable interpretations that require the reader to draw conclusions on her or his own, thus behaving like a veritable detective who must make connections, question the veracity of the narrator's version of events, and fill in the blanks when necessary. Ana distorts facts and embellishes her physical deformities while stressing the interconnectedness and fluidity of reality and fiction. She strategically garners the sympathy of her reader by enumerating her experiences as a woman in a hostile patriarchal environment. Godsland contends that female writers whose protagonists are women criminals furnish "their female readership with fantasies of contesting victimization, while also articulating the extent of violence against women in contemporary Spain" (2007, 113). Although the protagonist never admits to experiencing physical violence at the hands of her husband or any other man, by delineating the times in which she felt wronged or discriminated against by men, she justifies her offenses as a response to her adverse circumstances and marginalization. In the case of Ana, her probable culpability in the death of her estranged husband is tied to her frustration with a society that she feels has ostracized her purely because of her sex.

Traumatic memory, identity, and truth

The concepts of truth and memory are essential to the resolution of a mystery and, thus, to the detective genre. Memory is fundamental in piecing together the past, while objective truth is what the detective seeks to ascertain and the criminal aims to keep impenetrable. It should be no surprise, then, that references to memory and its inextricable connection to concepts of truth and identity abound in these three texts. Some of the novels considered here are clearly retrospective in nature, as they present an adult protagonist who remembers traumatic experiences from her childhood or formative years, whereas others attempt to reconstruct the past in order to make better sense of the present. A victim of years of domestic oppression as a child, *El guardián invisible*'s Amaia suffers from abnormalities of memory that are characteristic of post-traumatic disorders, which cause her to sporadically remember too much or too little. For years she has tried to escape her past by abandoning her hometown and pursuing a career unrelated to the family business, all the while repressing her childhood memories of fear and abuse. In his seminal study, Michel de Certeau evokes the dangers of forced amnesia and notes that, inevitably, the forgotten, repressed aspects of the past always return in some form or another (1988, 4). For Amaia, it is precisely upon returning to Elizondo to investigate the puzzling murders of two young local women that the specters of her past come back to haunt her. She remarks to her husband that, like "fantasmas resucitados" (119), all of her memories and sensations of the past take shape when she returns to her hometown. As Judith Lewis Herman asserts in her insightful analysis of crime and memory, Amaia's "memories intrude when they are not wanted, in the form of nightmares, flashbacks, and behavioral re-enactments" (1996,

5). Speaking on behalf of her niece, Tía Engrasi – who is, coincidentally, a psychologist by trade – claims:

> Hay ocasiones en que el dolor es tan grande [. . .] que uno desea y cree que se quedará
> así para siempre, [. . .] sin querer afrontar el hecho de que los dolores que no han sido
> llorados y expiados en su momento regresan una y otra vez a nuestras vidas como
> restos de un naufragio [. . .] que irá[n] regresando poco a poco para esclavizarnos de
> por vida.
>
> (376)

She suspects that Amaia has (sub)consciously disremembered these memories from the night her mother tried to kill her, out of fear that they will only further distract her from the case. Ironically, however, because she has never faced these remembrances head on, they actually impede her from moving forward in both her personal life and the investigation. Therefore, her traumatic past and memories condition her worldview, her professional aspirations, and quest for justice, as well as her understanding of self. Once she publicly acknowledges the truth and her trauma to her family, she has an epiphany and soon identifies the perpetrator, solving the case.

Personal memory refers to narratives that provide meaning and order to an individual's personal biography. Salvador Cardús i Ros reminds us that memory is not rooted necessarily in precision or recollection, but it instead follows the logic of oral, written, or audio-visual narrative (2007, 23). The critic proposes that memory is "an open narrative that incorporates personal and external recollection, but also includes fiction, things forgotten and errors that are *necessary* in order to make memory coherent and significant" (23; italics in original). Therefore, memory comprises various truths and untruths, as it relies on the dual processes of erasure and reinvention. As various contemporary postmodern novelists have sought to highlight, the truth can come in many forms and depends entirely on the perspective of the individual engaging in the remembrance process. According to Michael Schmid, with the passage of time, we integrate new memories into "false" memories, thereby creating what for us comes to represent a legitimate, albeit reconstructed, past (2004, 2), so as to give our lives and identity meaning. Montero's and Mayoral's respective texts highlight the inherent artificiality of memory and human existence, and all three novels prove that memory is the foundation for identity. While investigating the case of the dying replicants, Bruna begins to research artificial memories and the illicit *memas* (that come in pill form) the androids use to acquire false memories. As a techno-human herself, Bruna's memories are both fabricated and true, for while they technically do not belong to her, they were copied from actual events, relationships, and emotions derived from her *memorista*'s – or creator's – past. The painful realization that her suffering and memories of her mother are not simply false, but rather, the simulations and reminiscences of her creator only further exacerbates her existential angst: "[n]o sólo su recuerdo era todo mentira, sino que ahora además tenía la certeza de que se trataba de la verdad de otro" (464). What disturbs Bruna is that if her memories are indeed false, then her identity or conception of self must be a sham as well.

The distinction between what is true and false is increasingly difficult to ascertain, for that which has been falsified appears even more real than the original. Baudrillard claims that imitation not only reproduces reality, but it also improves it to the point that it could be deemed more authentic than the original. This point is illustrated in a scene in which Bruna and her creator, Pablo Nopal, conduct a clandestine meeting at an art exhibition entitled "Historia de los Falsos: el fraude como arte revolucionario." According to the omniscient narrator, art critics and aestheticians "habían decretado que la impostura era la manifestación artística más pura y radical" of the twenty-second century (86). For one to be considered "un Falso," one must both counterfeit a famous painting or sculpture to perfection and convince an art expert of its authenticity. The greater the deceit, the more prestigious the forgery once it is exposed as such. Bruna disapproves of the trend of falsified art; as a simulation herself, it reminds her of her own illegitimacy. She wonders if Nopal assumes she would appreciate the exhibit because, "¿[. . .] yo también soy una copia, una imitación, una falsificación de ser humano?" (86). Instances of simulation and impostura abound throughout the novel and help to illustrate the complex nature of truth and identity and to emphasize that imitation is universal.

As is typical of *noir* fiction, moral and existential uncertainty pervade Bruna's world and are the source of great anxiety. Throughout the course of the investigation, she works on a puzzle of the Cosmos and struggles to find the necessary pieces that will complete the image and provide a sense of order and meaning to her chaotic existence. In the puzzle there was "muchísima negrura y pocos cuerpos celestes por los que orientarse. [Bruna] [m]iró [. . .] los bordes [. . .] del hueco [. . .], intentando encontrar alguna que encajara" (72). The puzzle clearly serves as a metaphor for the epistemological process of the detective figure, but also for the existential enigma Bruna has long sought to resolve. While simultaneously attempting to solve the puzzle and uncover both an objective and a personal truth, the detective must sift through the chaos, "negrura," and "jirones de niebla" (402) that envelop her and, like Amaia, allow her intuition to be her guide. Near the dénouement of the novel, the detective realizes that while in a drunken haze the night before she finally managed to complete the puzzle: "[l] a imagen del Cosmos estaba completa; y en el centro, en la zona crítica que antes le faltaba y que [. . .] se le había resistido durante meses, ahora se veía la nebulosa planetaria Hélix" (402). The Helix Nebula, more colloquially dubbed the "Eye of God," gazes back at Bruna and reminds her that what she has been searching for – whether it is a missing puzzle piece, a shred of evidence, or the "truth" – has been within reach all along. Montero ties the image of the nebula to Soulages's expression, "C'est ce que je fais qui m'apprend ce que je cherche" (Cloup 2014). As a result of Bruna's investigation into the mysterious deaths of her brethren – replicants whose memories have been manipulated – the detective makes a series of discoveries that give her the peace of mind she had desired for so long, among which are the identity of her creator – a revelation that has repercussions for her own identity – the importance of camaraderie with the Other, as well as the notion that nothing – not even her fate, identity, or the truth – is entirely certain.

In the first few pages of her letter, Ana announces that she would like to defend herself (12) and that writing is the only means she has to do so: "Por eso escribo, porque es mi manera de llegar a la verdad" (14). Yet, as a writer of fiction, Ana has limited experience with representing the truth. Near the end of her epistle, she reveals to her reader that "[e]scribiendo soy mucho más convincente" (237). If we compare these assertions and read between the lines, it appears as though the narrator insinuates that the act of writing allows her to convince the addressee of *her* truth, not necessarily an objective reproduction of events. To be compelling, one must persuade, or manipulate, the audience into believing that what one says and who one is are equally authentic. By employing the rhetorical appeal of ethos, Ana tries to make her perspective and character credible to her audience. In effect, the writing process – which allows the writer to devise a thesis, mull over her words, and edit her thoughts – grants Ana the ability to convince her addressee more effectively than if she were to defend herself verbally in real time, say, in court or when facing her accuser(s). As the rhetor of her text, Ana informs her reader of the (other) motives underlying her decision to compose the letter: "[é]sta es la única razón por la que te escribo. Sólo quiero que [. . .] vuelvas a quererme" (82). These words are an appeal to her son, but the recurring accusatory, incriminating tone she uses, as well as the conflicting reasons she claims to have for writing the letter, subsequently impel the reader to question her real intentions.

Although Ana's letter is composed of numerous family anecdotes, it is she who has complete jurisdiction over how they are remembered and documented for posterity. This is problematic, as even she alludes to her own memory's deficiencies. Although in writing her letter Ana originally sets out to establish the truth, she admits that in the end the facts and her interpretation might be distorted and fabricated (97). Moreover, the narrator's therapist observes that many of her childhood memories are in fact incidences of postmemory, or inherited remembrances passed down from her mother and grandmother that she herself never experienced. She then adds that this may be "un ejemplo de mi capacidad fabuladora más que una muestra de memoria excepcional" (125–126). Years later, when referencing a trip she took with a former male companion while Peque lay in bed with a fever, Ana confesses that she cannot recall their vacation destination: "se me ha borrado de mi memoria por completo, como si no hubiera existido [. . .] me sentí culpable por dejarte solo e intenté eliminar esa parte de mi vida" (119). Her ability to – conveniently and intentionally – forget certain details from her past because they provoke feelings of guilt is critical information for the reader who must assess her reliability and innocence in her husband's death. Consequently, relatively subtle acknowledgements such as these cause the reader to call into question the veracity of the account.

Reinterpreting the truth and the evidence of female oppression

Glenn W. Most observes that the detective and reader undertake similar endeavors, as the act of reading is a form of detection in itself. He argues that the detective is "the figure for the reader within the text, the one character whose activities most closely parallel the reader's own," as both reader and detective seek to unravel the mystery of the crime (1983, 348). In this same vein, Jorge Luis Andrade Fernandes proposes that "the detective is a master reader of signs," who "must read the world as would a criminal; he must not only be able to read the crime scene as a text authored by the criminal, but also anticipate the narrative's unfolding" (2008, 111–112). As effective investigators, Montero's Bruna and Redondo's Amaia observe and interpret the world around them, often negotiating meaning and sifting through ambiguous and misleading signs. In *El guardián invisible*, the victims of the murders are adolescent girls who are on the cusp of becoming women. Their lifeless bodies are discovered with their palms facing up in a sign of submission, their faces devoid of any makeup, their pubis shaved, and their hair parted and clothes torn open and left at their sides. Detective Salazar reads the young women's corpses as if they were corporeal texts, searching for clues and any story they can still tell. When examining the bodies, she frequently asks her subordinates, "¿Qué nos cuentan las niñas?" (181). Amaia's intuition and ability to read signs lead her to deduce that the assassin is someone who disapproves of these girls desiring to become women so prematurely and that the corpses denote the androcentric desire to control and punish women. Because the murderer is convinced that these women have consciously defied nature and tradition, he punishes them by erasing the first signs of womanhood and imposes on his victims his own conception of purity. Ironically, he disregards nature and seeks to reverse its course by returning the girls to what he believes to be a more virginal state. Redondo presents this obsession with recovering antiquated, misogynistic values and traditions as retrograde and destructive, particularly for women. While rape does not appear to have taken place in these serial killings, since it would contradict the criminal's desire for chastity and prelapsarian innocence,

Redondo emphasizes the monstrous nature of the paternalistic, heterosexual male gaze and the devastating repercussions of female objectification.

According to Mayoral's Ana, her son is a deficient reader of reality, for she alleges that he distorts meaning and frequently misinterprets facts. Perhaps for this very reason, before commencing her letter, she discloses that she will have to use "las palabras que puedas entender" (15). Nevertheless, suspecting that her son will not see through her artful narrative techniques, Ana is able to control her own story and garbles the truth, thereby confusing and manipulating her reader into sympathizing with her. The truth, in *Casi perfecto*, is relative, incomplete and, as in most postmodern literature, always ambiguous. In effect, the narrator's ability to read reality, or herself, is flawed as well. As postmodern readers, we perceive that Ana's narration and the self-portrait she paints are neither complete nor reliable. Furthermore, the fact that Ana is missing an eye is significant, for it underscores her tendency to neglect or omit certain truths and prioritize her perspective over those of others. Her corporeal incoherence and fragmentation mirror the inconsistencies and lacunae in her defense and narration. Coincidentally, the word *brétema* – or Brétema, a provincial and imaginary Galician city in Mayoral's novels – means "fog" (*niebla*) in Galician. Analogous to an opaque veil that obstructs one's view or perception of things, the Galician fog and Ana's partial blindness are metaphors for her inability, or unwillingness, to accept and represent the truth. Similarly, it seems as though the reader is left in a mental miasma after poring over the letter to distinguish the truth that lies beyond the distractions deposited throughout the text. In a related vein, Ana's daughter-in-law, Gabriela, makes a significant observation regarding her field of expertise – photography – by declaring that "la cámara recoge casi siempre lo que el ojo quiere ver, aunque a veces también recoge algo que no vemos o que no queremos ver" (211). Here, Gabriela correlates the image viewed and consciously chosen through the camera lens with the perspective of the individual, one that is inherently biased and often blind. What is more, the metaphor encapsulates the very nature of Ana's account, as well as her tendency to see and portray solely what she wants to see, thereby frequently ignoring the existence of an objective truth. We, as experienced readers, must disentangle Ana's contradictory and partial account of events in order to come to a better understanding of the bigger picture and what may have happened to her husband.

The physical traits of these women reflect their individual struggles, existential angst, and idiosyncrasies, thus inciting the reader to identify with their victimization and otherness. For instance, Montero's Bruna Husky is visibly different from her human counterparts because, as an android, she towers above and is physically stronger than most males and is unable to reproduce. Her body and physical characteristics unsettle many humans, who, upon seeing her shaved head and tattoo – "una fina línea negra que recorría verticalmente el cuerpo entero" (30) – equate her with the monstrous, indefinable Other. This line reminds us of Bruna's inherent contradictions and hybrid nature as a representative of what is simultaneously true and fabricated. As noted previously, Mayoral's Ana is both "coja y tuerta" (19), and while she at first considers herself to be a victim of nature, with the help of a family friend she eventually comes to accept her physical deficiencies for their beauty and exoticism and learns to use them to her advantage. Her ability to modify her self-perception highlights the fact that identity is a malleable construct that can be refashioned to coincide with the story one wants to believe and project to others. Ana's perception of her situation highlights her determination, not to mention her ability to turn a negative into a positive, that is, to manipulate the "truth" in order to fit her own needs. In other words, her rich imagination allows her to overcome her supposed defects and (re)invent her own reality and identity.

While the grotesque fate of the victims incites repulsion in male police officers, Amaia sympathizes with the young women because she identifies with their victimhood. Examining the bodies for clues, Amaia feels "desolada por el dolor ajeno" (67). Her ability to relate to the suffering of the Other, one that is not so different from her younger self, is quite pronounced. One might argue that her decision to become a detective is a direct result of her own traumatic experiences as a victim of her mother's cruelty and is equally rooted in her desire to seek justice for those who, like her, were unable to defend themselves. Alison Young (1996, 83) observes that in societal responses to crime, members of a social group tend to identify with the victim of violence because they consider that they, too, could become – or, in the case of Amaia, have already been – a victim of a similar crime. Much like Amaia, Montero's Bruna has a personal stake in the case of the suicidal reps, and not only for professional reasons. As a replicant herself, she identifies and is associated with the marginalized Other and, in large part, her determination to solve the case is founded on her desire to repair the abysmal reputation of her kind, which has been demonized by influential humans.

Embodying the female detective: demanding justice and subverting the archetype of the male investigator

While all three protagonists face manifestations of discrimination at one point or another, each novel features the importance of female camaraderie, either in the resolution of a mystery or by helping the protagonist to reach a deeper understanding of reality and herself. Kathleen Gregory Klein claims that feminism "values female bonding, awareness of women without continual reference to or affiliation with men, and the self-knowledge which prompts women to independent judgement on both public and personal issues" (1995, 201). Redondo's Amaia experiences various degrees of sexism as a result of her professional success, particularly because of her promotion to homicide inspector for the Elizondo murders. As the sole woman in the highly patriarchal institution of the police force, Amaia must assert herself in front of her male peers in order to be taken seriously. Nevertheless, certain colleagues undermine her efforts and make her job much more challenging. Inspectors Montes and Zabalza are threatened by Amaia's authority over them and view her as "una zorra arrogante" (263). While he never makes his negative feelings towards her public knowledge, Zabalza's subtle disrespect for his female superior exemplifies the complexities and inconspicuousness of covert sexism. Nonetheless, despite the jealousy and disrespect of her male peers, the moral support and tough love of Amaia's aunt, who understands her niece and is aware of her traumatic past, helps her in her healing process and thus, indirectly, in the case.

In *Lágrimas en la lluvia*, Bruna encounters instances of sexism and xenophobia as a female android, both in her investigation and when interacting with others. Her physical appearance incites fear in the humans who pass her on the street and her mere existence as a female android causes revulsion in human supremacists. While interrogating a cult leader about a piece of evidence found on the body of a dead android, the supremacist does not mince his words regarding his opinion of technohumans: "¿Qué nos importa a nosotros que maten o no a esas cosas? No [. . .] cuentan. No existen. No tienen más entidad que la hebilla de tu zapato" (292). Not only does this passage represent the contempt that many humans feel about the android race and the widespread denial of the androids' dignity and existence, but it also reflects a reactionary society that repeats the atrocities of the past.

By serving as authorities of truth – as either investigators or writers – the female protagonists analyzed here are endowed with agency and the ability to subvert traditional discourse.

As Thompson-Casado (2004, 137) claims in her analysis of female-authored detective fiction, the plots of the novels considered in this study are constructed around female protagonists who, despite their respective differences, are courageous, economically independent, and socially progressive professionals. Montero's Bruna and Redondo's Amaia are portrayed as agents of social justice and change who fight to defend the victims of the crimes they endeavor to solve. These victims, like the detectives who seek the truth regarding their deaths, represent the marginalized of patriarchal society. Perceiving the victims as extensions of themselves, Inspectors Husky and Salazar empathize with their suffering and, thus, have a personal interest in not only seeking justice, but also in effecting some kind of positive social change in their respective communities. For Salazar, the death of the young women represents her community's – and society's – failure to protect those who need it most. In identifying the individual responsible for the young women's deaths, Amaia feels that her own suffering as a child and adult as a result of her mother's physical and psychological cruelty can be redeemed.

Whilst addressing other allegations that Peque made against her in his childhood diary – that she confesses to reading – Ana's feelings of jealousy and injustice surface. When he compares her inadequacies as a mother to the notable competence of others – namely, his father, or other women – Ana interprets it as a personal attack and retaliates. She acrimoniously probes, "¿Y qué te dio tu padre para que a él lo adorases? [. . .] ¿[Q]ué hizo él por ti que no haya hecho yo?" (120). Ultimately, Ana's anger and frustration towards her husband and son – both supporters of Francoist ideals of femininity – stem from her feelings of inadequacy as a wife and mother living in a misogynistic domestic milieu. She feels devalued because of what Peque, her husband, and patriarchal society perceive to be her shortcomings and deems that she has been held unjustly to a lofty standard to which her husband has not. Professionally, she claims to have been denied respect and a real space in which to work. Ana channels her irritation with her son into a counterattack against him in order to paint herself as the victim of misguided criticism and adherence to outdated gender constructs. She turns the tables on Peque, attempting to prove that his complaints are not only unfounded and naïve, but hypocritical as well. In doing so, she hopes to compel him to feel just as guilty as her for his past behavior and unrealistic expectations. In one instance, she admits that "[y]o hago las cosas mal [. . .], pero suelo darme cuenta y pido perdón e intento reparar el daño, mientras que tú pocas veces has rectificado en tus actitudes" (202). The contrast Ana creates between mother and son is designed to highlight his double standards and unwillingness to engage in self-reflection, while allowing her to regain the moral high ground and present herself as an honest woman.

As marginalized individuals who seek to determine the truth on their own terms, these female protagonists subvert the traditional archetype of the male investigator or criminal and tackle problems that deal specifically with the oppression of the minority. Redondo denounces gender violence, while Montero censures the intolerance of everyone and everything that is considered different and, in turn, monstrous, subsequently compelling her reader to reexamine his or her own cultural values. What is more, Montero uses her novel to underscore the importance of action and the perils of inaction in contemporary society. Near the end of the novel, when Bruna and a friend learn of the reversal of a controversial piece of legislation, she reminds him and, by extension, us that we must not relinquish our ability to improve the status quo (475). Bruna seeks out equality, justice, and humanity in a world that is devoid of all three. Ana, who identifies as a victim of patriarchy and sexism, tries to defend herself and avenge her own perceived victimization by rewriting the truth from her perspective. Although she does not seek to exact profound social change, she demands justice for herself, by refashioning patriarchal discourse and the truth and demanding for all women who write a room of their own.

Conclusion

In these postmodern detective stories, the concepts of truth and justice are portrayed as largely imprecise and relative entities. At the end of *El guardián invisible*, certain enigmas are left unresolved and the reader is never provided with an opportunity to understand fully the motives behind the crimes, whereas in *Casi perfecto* the narrator's culpability and the (in)authenticity of her account are never officially exposed. *Lágrimas en la lluvia* underscores for its readers that as a result of the political climate of Montero's twenty-second-century dystopia, justice is not always served and the mistakes of the past are too often repeated. As Susan Elizabeth Sweeney argues, feminist detective fiction may name a single person as the guilty party, but the individual's actions reflect a broader social problem (1999, 125). Because the main causes underlying the crimes committed in these novels happen to be misogyny, xenophobia, and revenge, in light of perceived gender oppression, the three novelists stress that truly solving the crime requires making profound changes in patriarchal culture as well as identifying the individual responsible for the offense. Although justice may not be served in a manner that is entirely satisfactory to the protagonists or reader, it is the epistemological and writing processes that prove to be the most fulfilling for the three females. Much like Soulages's dictum referenced previously, it is in their attempt to discover, conceal, and create their own version of the truth that these women come to a deeper understanding of themselves and the society in which they live. By positioning resilient, feminist female investigators and (un)likely killers at the forefront of their novels, Redondo, Montero, and Mayoral challenge the conventions of detective narrative and offer a new perspective on women's experience on the Iberian Peninsula in the twenty-first century.

Works cited

Andrade Fernandes, Jorge Luis. 2008. *Challenging Euro-America's Politics of Identity: The Return of the Native*. London: Routledge.

Cardús i Ros, Salvador. 2007. "Politics and the Invention of Memory: For a Sociology of the Transition to Democracy in Spain." In *Disremembering the Dictatorship: The Politics of Memory in the Spanish Transition to Democracy*, edited by Joan Ramon Resina, 17–28. Amsterdam: Rodopi.

Cloup, Geneviève. 2014. "Pierre Soulages: 'Je rêve encore à la toile que je peindrai demain'." *Gala*, May 30. Accessed June 15, 2014. http://www.gala.fr/l_actu/culture/pierre_soulages_je_reve_encore_a_la_toile_que_je_peidrai_demain_318256.

Craig-Odders, Renée W. 2009. "Introduction." In *Crime Scene Spain: Essays on Post-Franco Crime Fiction*, edited by Renée W. Craig-Odders and Jacky Collins, 1–9. Jefferson: McFarland.

de Certeau, Michel. 1988. *The Writing of History*. New York: Columbia University Press.

Godsland, Shelley. 2007. *Killing Carmens: Women's Crime Fiction from Spain*. Cardiff: University of Wales Press.

Herman, Judith Lewis. 1996. "Crime and Memory." In *Trauma and Self*, edited by Charles B. Strozier and Michael Flynn, 3–18. Lanham, MD: Rowman and Littlefield.

Klein, Kathleen Gregory. 1995. *The Woman Detective: Gender & Genre*. Champaign, IL: University of Illinois Press.

Mayoral, Marina. 2007. *Casi perfecto*. Madrid: Alfaguara.

Montero, Rosa. 2011. *Lágrimas en la lluvia*. Madrid: Seix Barral.

Most, Glenn W. 1983. "The Hippocratic Smile: John LeCarre and the Traditions of the Detective Novel." In *The Poetics of Murder: Detective Fiction and Literary Theory*, edited by Glenn W. Most and William W. Stowe, 341–365. Ann Arbor, MI: Harcourt.

Redondo, Dolores. 2013. *El guardián invisible*. Barcelona: Destino.

Schmid, Michael. 2004. "Narrative Memory and the Impact of Trauma on Individuals with Reference to One Short Sequence from *Memento*." Term paper, University of Santa Cruz.

Sweeney, Susan Elizabeth. 1999. "Gender-Blending, Genre Bending and the Rendering of Identity in Barbara Wilson's *Gaudí Afternoon*." In *Multicultural Detective Fiction: Murder from the 'Other' Side*, edited by Adrienne Johnson Gosselin, 123–141. London: Garland.

Thompson-Casado, Kathleen. 2004. "On the Case of the Spanish Female Sleuth." In *Reading the Popular in Contemporary Spanish Texts*, edited by Shelley Godsland and Nickianne Moody, 136–149. Newark, NJ: University of Delaware Press.

Young, Alison. 1996. *Imagining Crime: Textual Outlaws and Criminal Conversations*. London: Sage.

49

REFLEXIVITY IN IBERIAN DOCUMENTARY FILM

Samuel Amago

To be reflexive is to reveal that films – all films, whether they are labeled fiction, documentary, or art – are created structured articulations of the filmmaker and not authentic truthful objective records.

(Ruby 1977, 10)

"El prestigio del documental sólo fue alcanzado gracias a la experimentación. Sin experimentación, el documental pierde sentido. Sin experimentación, el documental deja de existir."

(Cavalcanti [1948] 2003, 451)

The crucial interdependency of reality and fiction that Susan Martin-Márquez (2004, 751) highlights in her description of contemporary Spanish media has only grown stronger in the Iberian context of the twenty-first century, where the flexibility and permeability of documentary forms has transformed nonfiction film in particular into "la punta del iceberg de una nueva concepción del audiovisual tanto a nivel de producción como a nivel artístico" (Gallego and Martínez 2012, 28). Filmmakers throughout the Iberian Peninsula have used reflexive and experimental documentary modes to draw attention to local geographies and historical realities, critique dominant modes of representation, analyze global pressures on local cultures, and reflect on the audiovisual structures of history and memory. In an essay written after the 2008 Festival de Cannes, Cyril Neyrat posited that it is precisely the opening up of the border between fiction and documentary that constitutes the principal sign of "la vitalidad de todo un sector de cine" (Neyrat 2009, 15). Surveying a number of nonfiction titles emerging from China, Catalonia, Portugal, Philippines, and beyond, Neyrat remarks – echoing Bill Nichols's early assertion that "documentary film practice is the site of contestation and change" (1991, 12) – that it is the mixing of documentary and fiction that has inspired so many aesthetic innovations in the history of the cinema. Francisco Javier Ruiz del Olmo goes so far as to suggest, in an essay on "Compromiso y veracidad en el reciente cine documental español," that documentary film has achieved "un nivel creativo muy elevado, muy por encima del cine narrativo convencional" (2009, 32). He ends by asserting that films such as *El efecto Iguazú* (Pere Joan Ventura and Georgina Cisquella 2002), *La leyenda del tiempo* (Isaki Lacuesta 2006), and *En construcción* (José Luis Guerín 2001), whose committed use of a "fructífera mezcolanza audiovisual" (20) engages critically with social, political, emotional and metaphysical realities, in fact represent the "vanguardia creativa de nuestra cinematografía" (32).

While Ruiz del Olmo's assertions of quality may perhaps be taken with a grain of salt, his rhetoric is nonetheless instructive when we talk about documentary film in the Iberian context, where both the writing on documentary and the production of documentary nearly always rely on possessive determiners and national markers of identification. This is perhaps ironic given the fact that digital modes of film production and reception, reduced production costs, and new modes of exhibition have contributed to the formation of geographically dispersed communities of viewers who have enjoyed unprecedented access to what would otherwise be "invisible" forms of cinema. The more conventional and largely urban international film festivals that have always sustained independent cinema (nonfiction and fiction) have been supplemented and in many cases replaced by more innovative platforms such as the Festival Internacional de Cinema Rural Carlos Velo, the Cinema Palleiriso, and the Festival de Cans, and digital venues such as the Festival Europeo de Cine Invisible (an online film festival organized by Filmotech), mubi.com, Netflix, Amazon Prime, and so on. As Gallego and Martínez note, digitalization, self-production, and new online channels of distribution and exhibition have increased access across the board, creating "microaudiences" for new audiovisual content produced through "la hibración de géneros y formatos" (2012, 36). The same technologies and practices that have democratized cinematic creativity on the production side have made it possible for what Roberto Cueto calls a "third public" (2008, 10) to view films that likely would otherwise remain unseen.[1] Existing somewhere between the popular audience and a more elite cinephile public, the "third public" described by Cueto has taken advantage of novel modes of distribution and reception in order to seek out "cine alternativo o 'diferente'" (2008, 10). Cueto asserts that "antes que una invisibilidad, se está produciendo un desplazamiento de la visibilidad a otros espacios y hábitos de consumo" (2008, 10). Gallego and Martínez (2012, 29) argue, alongside Cueto, that rather than the death of cinema we are seeing the demise of old ways of thinking about it.

This essay examines how contemporary Iberian filmmakers have continued the tradition of innovation and rupture that has been present in the documentary form from its beginnings, and analyzes how those directors meld fictional and nonfictional modes of representation in their films in order to observe, critique, or otherwise erode traditional boundaries between reality and representation, showing and telling, narrative and testimony, realism and formalism. The essay centers on three works from three corners of the Iberian Peninsula that in one way or another question the "rhetorics of authenticity" upon which traditional documentary films have relied: from Galicia, *Todos vós sodes capitáns* (Oliver Laxe 2010), a reflexive film about globalism and social issues that also problematizes the ability of European cameras to document the social reality of non-European Others; from Portugal, *Aquele Querido Mês de Agosto* (Miguel Gomes 2008), a more observational film about Portuguese regional identity that contains within itself parallel narratives about the making of a "fictional" film-within-the-film and a romantic melodrama; and, from Catalonia, *Bicicleta, cullera, poma* (Carles Bosch 2011), an expository documentary on Pasqual Maragall's battle with Alzheimer's disease. One of this essay's central goals is to demonstrate how the aesthetics of reflexivity function within and across Iberian cultural contexts in the twenty-first century.[2]

Reflexive ethnography in *Todos vós sodes capitáns* (2010)

> Un documental tamén pode ser arte, pero sitúanos nunha disposición diferente. E a min resúltame máis intenso.
>
> (Borrazás 2007, 73)

Todos vós sodes capitáns (2010), Galician director Oliver Laxe's first feature-length film, was shot during the years he spent in Tangier organizing a filmmaking workshop for socially marginalized youths. The film opens by drawing attention to the dual practices of looking and traveling that have historically encompassed ethnographic film, as a group of children observe and comment upon an approaching airplane, exhorting their companions to "look" and "see" it as it grows larger in their view. Following a cut to a noisy classroom, a teacher tells the children that "we are all here today to help your teacher Oliver to make his movie," which in turn introduces the ostensible topic of the film, which will document, according to the teacher, "gestures used here in the Magreb" so that "the audience and foreigners can understand us." The teacher's lesson on hand gestures highlights intertwined notions of visuality and pedagogy, and functions reflexively to signal the vexed relationship between Us and Them that stands at the center of any ethnographic film.

Laxe, who appears within the film as a fictionalized version of himself, works constantly to undermine his own authorial authority by including sequences in which he appears as a European outsider ill-equipped to represent the children or their social reality. His onscreen persona is that of a culturally oblivious pedant of cinema who lacks sensitivity to the children's situation. In an early sequence, the orphans express their doubts about Laxe's concern for their welfare, complaining that the director forces them to awake at five in the morning to begin shooting. When Laxe first appears onscreen, it is to explain to the children the photographic qualities of lenses and the cinematic apparatus they will use to make their movie; the diagrams and drawings appearing on the blackboard are clearly beyond the children's (and most viewers') capacity for comprehension. A later scene shot in a marketplace depicts vendors and shopkeepers confronting the camera, forbidding the European crew from shooting their faces; finally Laxe and his film crew capitulate, and surrender their camera to a Moroccan child who returns to the alleyway, where it is assumed he will have more success at shooting this street scene than the European outsiders.[3]

These "fictional" plot complications dominate the movie's first half, and serve to problematize, from the beginning, the premise that any foreign filmmaker might document Moroccan social reality authentically. At the film's midway point the director ostensibly cedes control of his film to the children when he engages a young man named Shakib to take the kids and their cameras on an excursion into the country. At this point, the children, who are already accustomed to producing things with their hands – using the machinery of sewing, metal working, and other tasks to earn their keep in the orphanage in which they live – are allowed to appropriate the cinematic apparatus for themselves. Following this apparent transference of authorship, the film shifts from an observational or "objective" ethnographic mode to a more poetic and subjective one. Narrative development slows in the film's second half, and the movie ends with a series of long takes in which the children swim in a creek, explore ruined stone buildings, and walk together through fields and forests where the wind can be heard whipping through branches and undulating wheat fields.[4] Immediately after the credits, there appears a painterly silent montage of 16-mm footage of the children, the landscape they inhabit, some animals that live in the orphanage garden, and the architecture of the orphanage buildings.

Todos vós sodes capitáns hinges on Oliver Laxe's deployment of two interrelated fictions. The first is the notion that the onscreen Laxe might actually be exploiting the children in order to shoot his film. Laxe's fictional insensitivity to the children's plight is a method of ridiculing himself in the first half of the film, and thus allows him to critique his own status as European outsider while preparing the viewer for his later (apparent) transference of power over the cinematic apparatus from himself to the children. The second fiction, which is perhaps less apparent, is that the real Laxe actually relinquishes power over the cinematic apparatus. The director admits in an interview that even after he has given the children power over the cameras he is clearly still there ("Claro, yo estoy siempre ahí" [Pena 2010, 15]), but this conceit nonetheless functions to reflect on the problematic historical relationship between European documentary filmmakers and Third-World subjects. Laxe's onscreen surrender of the camera and subsequent disappearance from the diegesis represents a formal acknowledgement of his moral responsibility before the objects of his directorial gaze. This metacinematic gesture would seem to respond preemptively to inevitable critiques of "romantic preservationism" (Rony 1996, 102) and cinematic "taxidermy" (Gaines 1999, 8) that critics have levied historically upon ethnographic films such as Robert Flaherty's *Nanook of the North* (1921).

In the end, the viewer must determine whether Laxe's removal of himself from the film (as the director of the film within the film) represents an authentic attempt to question the power relations – institutional, discursive, narrative – that always arise when a Western filmmaker sets out to shoot a film about non-Western Others, or whether the film – despite its recognition of the problem – represents simply a disavowal of unavoidable pitfalls of ethnography. On the one hand, the film evinces a meta-awareness of some of the ideological problems that Nichols sees operating at the center of the European anthropological unconscious:

> whiteness; maleness; the body of the observer; the experiential; canonical conventions of Western narrative; narrative conventions and forms from other cultures; the full indexical particularly of the image and its emotional impact; the erotics of the gaze; textual theory and interpretation; the actual workings of the institutional procedures that determine what counts as anthropological knowledge; and the viewer or audience for ethnographic film.
>
> (1994, 65)

On the other hand, through its thoughtful contemplation of questions of authorship and authority, and through its refusal to perpetuate naively the problematic discourses of traditional ethnographic film, *Todos vós sodes capitáns* clearly seeks to position itself as a kind of *"thinking* Eurocentrism" that would respond critically and reflectively to the more "unthinking" varieties analyzed by Shohat and Stam (1994). In this regard the film's genealogy might be traced through the progressive realism of Third-Worldist films that engage with neo-colonial representations of subaltern sociality and histories. In this line, there exists a tradition of films that have sought, from Third-Worldist perspectives, to rewrite colonial history through reflexive realist lenses. While many of these kinds of films, as analyzed by Shohat and Stam, end with the reflexive topos of filmmakers deciding not to make the film (although "the audience knows the film has in fact been made" [1994, 281]), the reflexive forms comprising *Todos vós sodes capitáns* signal Laxe's ethical recognition of the ideological implications of a European filmmaker making a film about non-European Others. The aesthetics of reflexivity function in the film to acknowledge the moral obligation of Western documentary filmmakers to resist the siren song of realism and to reject ideological illusions of objectivity in documentary modes of ethnographic representation.

Landscape and reflexive melodrama in *Aquele querido mês de agosto* (2008)

No es oportuno hablar de cine de ficción o de no ficción como dos modalidades de representación totalmente autónomas, ya que el documental está constantemente traspasando esta barrera para apropiarse de las herramientas y elementos propios del cine de ficción para ponerlos a su disposición y a la de la historia.

(Gallego and Martínez 2012, 29)

Aquele Querido Mês de Agosto (2008) has been described as "at once a musical, a travelogue, a quasi-incestuous family melodrama, an ethnographic portrait of Portuguese folk traditions and an account of its own chaotic production" (Lim 2010). What links Gomes's film to Laxe's is the way in which both filmmakers work reflexively across fictional and non-fictional registers in the confection of their ethnographic portraits, all the while situating the apparatus of cinematic representation within the ideological, historical, and spatial contexts to which it responds. *Aquele Querido Mês de Agosto* takes place in the municipality of Arganil, located in the mountainous geographical center of Portugal, where a movie crew waits for the green light to shoot an elaborate screen melodrama. Conversations between the director and his producer suggest that filming of the movie is not going well. Meanwhile, extended fragments of documentary footage shot, apparently, by the same crew documents the denizens of these Portuguese mountain zones and their summertime activities. A variety of people appear onscreen to share oral accounts of their personal histories and stories: volunteer firefighters, a wild boar – hunting collective, an English anarchist expatriate, municipal music groups, the adventures of a fun-loving ne'er-do-well named Paulo "Miller," the publishers and printers of *O Comarca de Arganil* (a town newspaper), a roving band of motorcyclists, an octogenarian couple. The Portuguese film crew's efforts to shoot their film about a boy and a girl in love represent simply one activity among many. If there is one theme that brings all these people and happenings together it is the notion of spectacle, which ranges from music, carnival, moviemaking and shadow plays, to watchtowers, religious processions, and hunting lodges. Present in all the forms of human activity portrayed onscreen are the interrelated actions of looking, observing, acting, playing.

Following a playful prelude in which a fox observes a chain-link hen house, the film's opening sequence takes the viewer to a plaza in the Aldeia da Benfeita where Banda Gomape is performing a song. A power outage cuts the music and the light, and the film goes black. Contingency and accidents become minor keys or punctuations for the ensuing "narrative," which documents central Portugal social reality through the increasingly unreliable lens of Miguel Gomes, the onscreen director, who is engaged in completing his troubled film production. The appearance of Gomes's bored film crew, who passes the time by stacking dominoes, reinforces the film's ludic aims. Within the strictly realist historical mise-en-scene of small towns dispersed through Portugal's mountainous interior, these idle filmmakers function doubly as the actual documentary filmmakers and as fictional characters in the melodrama that finally begins, at the one-hour seventeen-minute mark, on the bridge over the river Alva in the town of Coja.

The real bridge across the Alva at once serves as a marker of geographical specificity and as a bridge from non-fiction into fiction. While *Todos vós sodes capitáns* ends as poetic anti-ethnography, *Aquele Querido Mês de Agosto* playfully rejects documentary realism in favor of fiction and melodrama. Neyrat has characterized Gomes's film as "un camino hacia la ficción"

(2009, 16), since it begins as an observational documentary about Portuguese life, customs, and music, only to relinquish its claims to the "real" in favor of the romantic tale that Gomes has been trying to realize. The film's reflexive structures – extreme long takes, mise-en-scene of the making-of within the film, a mysterious concluding dialogue between Gomes and his director of sound production, Vasco Pimentel – allow Gomes to move his characters back and forth between reality and fiction, from realism to make believe, from social space to the world of melodrama. These self-reflexive moments draw strategic attention to Portuguese motion picture workers, musicians, writers, radio hosts, and boar hunters as situated within concrete cultural, geographical, and historical contexts.

As the narrative concludes, the viewer becomes aware – through the film's elongated temporality and metacinematic gestures – of what Nichols calls "a thickened, denser sense of the textuality of the viewing experience" (2001, 62), that works to create a sense of mutual coexistence of historical world and the fictional world of representation. This deeper sense of layered textuality is complemented by the film's extended play with temporality, since long takes and lingering pans across Portuguese landscapes, people, and performances create in the viewer a meta-consciousness of the fact that all cinematic images necessarily require "the time of our perception" (Wahlberg 2008, ix). In *Aquele Querido Mês de Agosto*, textual, temporal, and auditory self-consciousness function to link the array of people, stories, geographical zones, into a loosely meandering, fictional documentary about Portugal's interior and the things that might happen there during an extremely slow month of summer vacation.

Pasqual Maragall as *Lloc de memòria* in *bicicleta, cullera, poma* (2011)

The cinema in Spain is, in Brad Epps' words, "inconceivable without Catalonia" (2013, 71), thanks to an industrial infrastructure and an array of practices that rendered Barcelona, especially during the early twentieth century, a crucial "capital of cinematic production in Spain" (2013, 72), home to "an established local film industry" (Colmeiro and Gabilondo 2013, 82). And yet, within the history of writing on motion picture production in Spain, Catalan language and culture have tended to be only perceptible as echoes and traces. The 2011 Goya Awards telecast may have marked a turning point: in the twenty-year history of the Goya Awards, Agustí Villaronga's *Pa negre* (2010) was the first film shot in a Spanish official language other than Castilian to win Best Picture, along with eight other awards. The televised program, which *La Vanguardia* called a "Goyas con sabor catalán" (2011), was hosted by Catalan television personality and comic Andreu Buenafuente.[5] But it was Pasqual Maragall's acceptance, with his wife, Diana Garrigosa, of the Goya award for Best Feature-Length Documentary for *Bicicleta, cullera, poma* (Carles Bosch 2011), that provided sentimental gravitas to a show that at times felt like a belated celebration of Catalonia's contributions to audiovisual culture in Spain.

Bosch's film narrates two years of Maragall's ongoing battle with Alzheimer's and documents his ongoing efforts to draw attention to the disease, control the advance of his own symptoms, and promote international research on treatments. The film opens with a close-up of Maragall, who responds to a question posed by the off-screen voice of the director, who asks, in Catalan, "What kind of movie should we do?" to which Maragall says, "divertida hòstia [. . .] divertida, interessant," then, in English, Maragall remarks, "I am fed up with the issue of 'pobrecitos, pobrecitos.' Let's kill the animal. The illness. And then we'll talk about it." This opening dialogue is followed by the title of the film and an oral account of Maragall's symptoms narrated by his wife, Diana Garrigosa. Her description of her family's experience of the disease is intercut with images of an indoor construction site where a crane is fabricating what will later become the stage where a group of global experts in Alzheimer research and treatment gather to discuss the disease. Maragall appears within these shots of the construction site, observing the work in progress.

Bicicleta, cullera, poma focuses on one man, Maragall, as he moves through the intimate and institutional spaces where he has engaged both privately and publically with his struggle to first overcome, and then to come to terms with his condition. A series of painterly dissolves connect shots of simultaneous research happening across the globe in a variety of research centers, in Barcelona and Madrid, Spain; Rochester, United States; Rotterdam, Holland; and Hyderabad, India. These images of far-flung locales are accompanied by a series of emotionally charged conversations in which Alzheimer sufferers share their experiences as they go through the same stages of the disease. Montage works throughout the film to create an effect of simultaneity, reduced geographical scale, and, thus, a sense of transnational community and interconnectedness between Maragall and his counterparts in India, the United States, and beyond. Interviews draw Maragall into real and conceptual contact with other people situated in remote parts of the planet, while also bringing to the fore the physicians, researchers, and fundraising agents who are doing their work today. Brain models, CT scans, and experts' technical explanations of the disease make visible the technologies, people and practices that comprise the worldwide battle against dementia. Bosch accompanies Maragall to an Alzheimer's Association meeting in Chicago and, following a Friends of Pasqual Maragall Foundation meeting, Maragall and Bosch visit the New York City apartment where Maragall lived with his wife while he was doing graduate study at the New School. Towards the end of the film Maragall travels to Buenos Aires for the birth of his granddaughter.

Bicicleta, cullera, poma is reflexive in the way many interactive documentary films are reflexive; these kinds of documentaries "draw their social actors into direct encounter with the filmmaker" (Nichols 1991, 47) in a way that makes clearer the constructed nature of the film while signaling the director's role as organizing agent and originator of the exposition. Bosch's voice is the first sound heard on the soundtrack, over a black screen. The improvisatory nature of the film's opening sequence ("What kind of movie should we do?"), considered alongside the images of construction that immediately follow it, serve to create a sense of present-tense temporality; these are things that are happening now, all across the planet. By placing himself within his film, Bosch further signals his partiality vis-à-vis his cinematic object, suggesting that Maragall is a co-generator of his own cinematic story. At the same time, close-ups and poignant dialogues with Maragall's children and spouse create a sense of community between Maragall and Catalan viewers familiar with the man's public persona, but ignorant perhaps of the details of his private life. *Bicicleta, cullera, poma* is thus both an expository and interactive kind of documentary in which viewers are allowed to engage more or less directly with the relation between filmmaker and his subject. Bosch works to lay bare his emotional connection to the object under observation, and positions himself as the Catalan viewer's intermediary and mode of access to the real person that is Maragall.

In this regard, *Bicicleta, cullera, poma* is an extremely touching reflection on the personal life of one of contemporary Catalonia's most visible and successful politicians. The film's wide-ranging geographical specificity is accompanied by a more sobering temporal punctuation by which Bosch signals the time elapsed since Maragall's public announcement of the disease (6 months, 9 months, 1 year, 1½ years, 2 years). Temporal markers add urgency to a film that focuses on the man, the treatment, the research, the funding, and, finally, on the time that draws that man inexorably towards a sadly foregone conclusion. These privileged views of Maragall's life are leavened by the man's sense of humor, much of which is self-referential: Maragall remarks, as he is entering a laboratory, that those were "good shots" since the cameraman filmed him trying to open the wrong door: "Ha ido muy bien porque me han filmado que me equivocaba dos veces." And later, Maragall uses his camera phone to film the cameraman, and he observes, playfully, "grabo el grabador." Queco Novell, who impersonated Maragall on TV3's satirical political program, *Polònia*, appears early in the documentary putting on the wig and costume that he used in his act, but the film ends with Novell taking off his costume and retiring the character.

The film traces Maragall's personal journey through a globally interconnected matrix of institutes, think tanks, treatment centers, and other more quotidian spaces where Maragall reflects on his loss of memory and comments on his past. The ease with which the former politician navigates a variety of global contexts makes him an appropriate representative of what Dominic Keown has described as the "refreshing outgoingness" of contemporary Catalan identity, which has tended to be "more international in orientation" (Keown 2011, 36). Indeed, Maragall appears comfortable wherever he finds himself and expresses himself adroitly in a handful of languages. At the same time, the multilingual soundtrack and wide-ranging geographical specificity of *Bicicleta, cullera, poma* work to universalize Maragall's battle with Alzheimer's. Thus, Maragall himself is represented in the film as a highly mobile, multiply coded site of memory who functions as a documentary synecdoche for a globally inflected Catalan identity, and whose persona echoes what Martí-Olivella has described as a Catalan cinematic idiom that has always been transnational and in-between (2011, 203). The film's urgency and poignancy are derived from a temporal structure that marks the relentless progression of a disease without a cure, as the viewer – alongside Bosch – contemplates the tragic loss of a human icon of contemporary Catalonia.

The politics of Iberian documentary

Like poetry, reflexive strategies remove the encrustations of habit.
(Nichols 1991, 67)

In the limited cross-section of documentaries analyzed in this essay one can see that the forms and functions of reflexive aesthetics in documentary film are as diverse as the subjects they treat. Indeed, as Colmeiro and Gabilondo note, "The historical mapping of cinema in Spain reveals a complex, fragmented picture composed of several singular cinemas marked by particular political and economic developments as well as by cultural [. . .] and linguistic diversity" (2013, 82). When we consider the Iberian Peninsula in its entirety, the picture acquires even greater intricacy. Yet, in each of the three cases outlined in this chapter we can see how a reflexive approach to documentary filmmaking allows filmmakers to draw attention to the crucial power of the cinema to shape not only representation but also ways of thinking about the relation between representation and reality. Therein lies the political importance of the reflexive mode, which allows filmmakers to be more forthcoming with their audiences about how:

> knowledge is hyper-situated, placed not only in relation to the filmmaker's physical presence, but also in relation to fundamental issues about the nature of the world, the structure and function of language, the authenticity of documentary sound and image, the difficulties of verification, and the status of empirical evidence in Western culture.
>
> (Nichols 1991, 61)

Reflexive techniques make visible the same tension between representation and reality that in other forms of documentary is perhaps less apparent, but that is nevertheless always there. In so doing, these kinds of movies refuse to perpetuate the false consciousness that a more straightforward version of documentary realism might promote. As Jay Ruby notes in his essay on reflexive approaches to visual anthropology, "documentary filmmakers have a social obligation to *not* be objective" (1977, 10).

Keeping in mind this question of objectivity and its relation to realism and representation, and in keeping with the reflexive thrust of this essay, I conclude by reflecting on how some of the very same technologies that have revolutionized production and reception are also affecting scholarly approaches to the study of audiovisual culture. Academic critics have tended to remain largely invisible to the producers and creators of global popular cultural production. Mainstream critics and journalists are perhaps slightly more perceptible in the blurbs and sound bites that circulate in the blockbuster's paracinematic orbit, and in Spain at least one newspaper critic has found himself (strategically for him) embroiled in a high profile written-word feud with Pedro Almodóvar (Cerdán and Fernández Labayen 2013, 129–30). But scholarly criticism remains, with a few notable exceptions, largely unseen by the producers of the art under analysis. But when you write about small-scale documentaries of the kind I have been describing in this essay, you become visible to that cinema's producers in ways that are sometimes disconcerting, occasionally helpful, and always theoretically interesting. I conclude with an example from Galicia: a few weeks after the description of my talk was posted on the University of Texas at Austin webpage, on March 18, 2014, I received an email from Martin Pawley, of Zeitun Films, based in A Coruña, which pointed to a misattribution appearing in that description. Pawley noted that the director of *Todos vós sodes capitáns* is not Catalan but Galician.[6] His note was corrective, but also courteous and informative. He wrote:

> Por supuesto, me interesaría mucho conocer tu análisis de la película, si pudiera ser posible. Quiero eso sí matizar que la película no es catalana sino gallega, al igual que el propio director, Oliver Laxe. De hecho en Galicia se está viviendo un momento cinematográfico muy interesante, en particular en el campo de la no ficción, con películas como *Vikingland* o *Costa da morte*.

Indeed Galician documentary filmmakers are producing very interesting work, much of it deserving of scholarly attention. But the fact that a film shot in Tangier in French and Arabic and Castilian, and featuring mostly Moroccan actors, should be defined as Galician says a lot about the high stakes involved in twenty-first-century Iberian audiovisual culture.[7] It also brings up vital questions about critics' position within the global system of documentary film production, distribution, and reception.

I have spent a lot time thinking and writing about reflexive aesthetics in film and literature, but this was the first time that I found myself drawn so directly into dialogue with the object of my study *in medias res*. My electronic interaction with the Zeitun Films producer reminded me of Claude Lévi-Strauss's introduction to the works of Marcel Mauss, in which Lévi-Strauss noted that even "the most objectively conducted analysis of [the objects of study] could not fail to reintegrate them inside the analyst's subjectivity" (49). Lévi-Strauss was principally interested in explaining the importance of Mauss's formulation of the "total social fact," or the idea of the social as system ([1950] 1997, 51–52), which not only held that *everything observed is part of the observation*, but also, and above all, that in a science in which the observer is of the same nature as the object of his study, *the observer himself is a part of his observation* [. . .]. The situation particular to the social sciences is different in nature; the difference is to do with the intrinsic character of the object of study, which is that it is object and subject both at once, or both 'thing' and 'representation'" (47, italics in original). Writing several decades later, Clifford Geertz argued that it is this awareness of and attention to the "multiplicity of complex conceptual structures, many of them superimposed upon or knotted into one another" (1973, 150) that make the social anthropologist's reflective attention to the elaboration of a "thick description" so important.

The reflexive possibilities that come with digital distribution, reception, and criticism have made the subjective relationship between scholars and their objects of study visible in novel ways, and have contributed to my new awareness of what we might call the "total documentary fact." In an era in which film producers are wont and able to Google themselves and their movies, effectively policing the reception and interpretation of their work, academic critics can find themselves drawn vitally into conversation with them. This reality is disconcerting because scholars labor so often from the solitary confines of library carrels, department offices, cafés, and home studies. But the same digital media that have facilitated our access to audiovisual artifacts produced in an array of locations also allows alert documentary producers to keep tabs on the critical fortunes of their films as they circulate throughout the world, surveying their online presence and curating the critical work on them. Skype, Twitter, Facebook, and Google's crawling algorithms allow documentary producers to put themselves into instant contact with the downstream users, viewers, analysts, and students of their movies. As I write these lines, I know that my analysis of these films will likely be read by the very people who produced them, and I know that my somewhat arbitrary and utterly formalist method of selecting these titles over others will result in the conferral of a certain kind of access to Anglophone academic audiences. Of course, this has always been the case: scholars have unavoidable roles as canonizers and promoters of the work that they would analyze objectively.

The reduced economies of scale that characterize (and that will likely always characterize) contemporary Iberian documentary (reflexive or otherwise) give the deceiving impression that this is a small world; but as Mette Hjort and Duncan Petrie (2007) note, when you are talking about the cinema of small nations, it is precisely the question of scale that makes access to global audiovisual circuits all the more crucial. Hjort and Petrie describe how the interrelated forces of globalization and internationalization have often been felt especially intensely in these smaller kinds of cultural contexts, since "small nations by definition have very limited domestic markets for all locally produced goods and services – including culture – and so have been forced by the neo-liberal economic and political pressures of globalization into a greater dependency on external markets" (2007, 15). At the same time, these same small nations "have emerged out of twentieth-century processes of decolonization and liberation struggles [with] a strong vested interest in nation-building and the maintenance of a strong sense of national identity relevant both internally and externally to the nation" (2007, 15). This is especially the case in Galicia, which provides an ideal location for exploring "conflicting trends of globalization and identity" (Hooper and Puga Moruxa 2011, 1) and which possesses a "minority cinema within a minority national film industry" (Colmeiro 2011, 215). This is why it is so important to Zeitun Films that even an entirely or apparently postnational (from the Galician perspective) reflection on Moroccan social reality should bear the mark of Galician national identity as it circulates abroad. The geographical specificity of a film like *Aquele Querido Mês de Agosto* works to activate international viewers' consciousness of (remote) Portuguese landscapes and cultural identities, even as it has some fun with the technologies and practices that make those landscapes visible onscreen and audible on the soundtrack. *Bicicleta, cullera, poma* is perhaps the least exportable film of the three, since it depends on viewers' fluency in Catalan cultural referents. Yet in all three cases we can see how Iberian documentary film has made productive use of a variety of reflexive visual strategies and audiovisual technologies to tell stories about its people's place in the world, and to make those places visible within the audiovisual structures of their moving pictures.

There exists a fundamental contradiction at the center of Iberian documentary of the twenty-first century. If, as Nichols notes, "documentary as a concept or practice occupies no fixed territory" (1991, 12), then in the contemporary Iberian context this formal fluidity is held in tension against an opposing and somewhat rigid territorial consciousness. On the one hand, as I outlined previously in the film analyses, filmmakers have worked to erode the distinctions between modes and styles of documentary practice through their strategic use of hybrid techniques whose ultimate goal is to blur the distinction between reality and fiction, showing and telling, mimesis and poiesis. Yet at the same time that they have problematized formal barriers, boundaries, and distinctions, these same directors have also drawn special attention to national and regional geographies, cultures, identities, and languages. Jay Ruby proposes, in the first epigraph to this essay, that "to be reflexive is to reveal that films – all films, whether they are labeled fiction, documentary, or art – are created structured articulations of the filmmaker and not authentic truthful objective records" (1977, 10). In the contemporary Iberian cultural context there is a crucial final distinction that must be made. For Iberian documentary filmmakers, to be reflexive is also to contest the global economic, technological, and critical processes that are always working to deterritorialize film texts. Their self-conscious representation of the spaces and practices of representation allow them to reterritorialize cultural identity and project it outwards into the global mediascape. The reflexive Iberian documentary signals the fact that, like the minor literatures theorized by Deleuze and Guattari, "everything in them is political" (1986, 17).[8]

Notes

1 Ines Vázquez notes that in the Galician cultural context new technologies "facilitaron que calquera persoa poida construír un discurso propio, facer unha película ou unha cámara barata e o difundir, isto marca unha diferenza moi grande con outros tempos" (*Cultura galega* 2014, n.p.).

2 The flexible hybrid forms operating in the field of Iberian documentary have also been observed in a variety of Iberian literatures, where novelists and writers have played with what Sara Brenneis (2014) calls "genre fusion," which works to produce a more complex representation of history, culture, and politics than might be possible to artists working exclusively within a single genre.

3 The director notes in an interview that this fictional recourse was intended as a way of "disappearing" (Pena 2010, 15) from the film, in order to avoid falling into a paternalistic orientalist trap (Pena 2010, 16). The film's reflexive visual structures can also be seen in a sequence in which the children film a group of tourists with their cameras. The European tourists are clearly uncomfortable under the gaze of the Moroccan youths, and as the tourists scurry up a city street one of them mutters, "They should ask for our permission to film us."

4 As Benavente notes in his review of the film, "Siguiendo la deriva de la tropa infantil por la geografía rural, casi al borde del ensueño o del trance, se entrega entonces a un modo contemplativo, a una película de exploración y descubrimiento de un mundo no evidente" (2011, 29).

5 Even the Catalan performance artist Jimmy Jump (Jaume Marquet) made a surprise appearance on the program, inspiring Buenafuente to say later, "Como catalán, me avergüenzo del 'imbécil' que ha salido con la barretina" (2011).

6 I am grateful to the faculty and graduate students at the University of Texas at Austin for their engaged and constructive feedback on an earlier version of this essay.

7 Despite the better efforts of the film's Galician producers to identify the film as Galician, a headline published above a review of the film in *Cahiers du Cinéma España* describes *Todos vós sodes capitáns* as "una única película íntegramente española y dirigida por un español" (Pena 2010, 14).

8 Deleuze and Guattari argue that "the three characteristics of minor literature are the deterritorialization of language, the connection of the individual to a political immediacy, and the collective

assemblage of enunciation" (1986, 18). My use of their work here was inspired in part by Joan Ramon Resina's (1987) essay on time and community in Mercè Rodoreda's *La plaça del Diamant* (1962).

Works cited

Aquele Querido Mês de Agosto. Directed by Miguel Gomes. 2008. New York: Cinema Guild, 2012. DVD.

Benavente, Fran. 2011. "Como soldados bajo un sol intenso." *Cahiers du Cinéma España* 46: 29.

Bicicleta, cullera, poma. Directed by Carles Bosch. 2010. Barcelona: Tema Distribuciones, 2011. DVD.

Borrazás, Xurxo. 2007. *Arte e parte. Dos patriarcas á arte suicida.* Vigo: Galaxia.

Brenneis, Sara J. 2014. *Genre Fusion: A New Approach to History, Fiction, and Memory in Contemporary Spain.* West Lafayette, IN: Purdue University Press.

Cavalcanti, Alberto. [1948] 2003. "Anotaciones para los jóvenes documentalistas." In *Cine documental en América Latina*, edited by Paulo Antonio Paranaguá and José Carlos Avellar, 449–451. Madrid: Cátedra.

Cerdán, Josetxo and Miguel Fernández Labayen. 2013. "Almodóvar and Spanish Patterns of Film Reception." In *A Companion to Pedro Almodóvar*, edited by Marvin D'Lugo and Kathleen Vernon, 129–152. Malden, MA: John Wiley & Sons.

Colmeiro, José. 2011. "Imagining Galician Cinema: Utopian Visions?" In *Contemporary Galician Cultural Studies: Between the Local and the Global*, edited by Kirsty Hooper and Manuel Puga Moruxa, 202–220. New York: Modern Language Association of America.

Colmeiro, José and Joseba Gabilondo. 2013. "Negotiating the Local and the Global: Andalusia, the Basque Country, and Galicia." In *A Companion to Spanish Cinema*, edited by Jo Labanyi and Tatjana Pavlović, 81–110. West Sussex: Wiley-Blackwell.

Cueto, Roberto. 2008. "Pero, ¿Existe un cine invisible?" *Cahiers du Cinéma España* 14, July–August 9–10.

Cultura Galega. "Agro e cinema: No ronsel de Cans," May 21, 2014. Accessed January 19, 2015. http://www.culturagalega.org/noticia.php?id=24279

Deleuze, Gilles and Félix Guattari. 1986. *Kafka: Toward a Minor Literature.* Minneapolis, MN: University of Minnesota Press.

Epps, Brad. 2013. "Echoes and Traces: Catalan Cinema, or Cinema in Catalonia." In *A Companion to Spanish Cinema*, edited by Jo Labanyi and Tatjana Pavlović, 50–80. West Sussex: Wiley-Blackwell.

Gaines, Jane M. 1999. "Introduction: 'The Real Returns'." In *Collecting Visible Evidence*, edited by Jane Gaines and Michael Renov, 1–18. Minneapolis, MN: University of Minnesota Press.

Gallego, María and Isabel Martínez. 2012. "La red: una aliada estratégica en el cine de no ficción." In *El documental en el entorno digital*, edited by Miquel Francés, Josep Gavaldà, Germà Llorca, and Àlvar Peris, 27–37. Barcelona: Editorial UOC.Geertz, Clifford. 1973. *The Interpretation of Cultures. Selected Essays.* New York: Basic Books.

Hjort, Mette and Duncan J. Petrie. 2007. *The Cinema of Small Nations.* Edinburgh: Edinburgh University Press.

Hooper, Kirsty and Manuel Puga Moruxa. 2011. "Introduction: Galician Geographies." In *Contemporary Galician Cultural Studies: Between the Local and the Global*, edited by Kirsty Hooper and Manuel Puga Moruxa, 1–16. New York: Modern Language Association of America.

Keown, Dominic. 2011. "Contemporary Catalan Culture." In *A Companion to Catalan Culture*, edited by Dominc Keown, 13–40. Woodbridge: Tamesis.

La Vanguardia. "*Pa negre* triunfa en los Goya," February 13, 2011. Accessed January 19, 2015. http://www.lavanguardia.com/cultura/20110213/54113771301/pa-negre-triunfa-en-los-goya.html.

Lévi-Strauss, Claude. [1950] 1997. "Introduction to the Work of Marcel Mauss." In *The Logic of the Gift: Toward and Ethic of Generosity*, edited by Alan D. Shrift, 45–69. London and New York: Routledge.

Lim, Dennis. 2010. "It's Actual Life. No, It's Drama. No, It's Both." *New York Times*, August 20. Accessed January 19, 2015. http://www.nytimes.com/2010/08/22/movies/22hybrid.html.

Martí-Olivella, Jaume. 2011. "Catalan Cinema: An Uncanny Transnational Performance." In *A Companion to Catalan Culture*, edited by Dominc Keown, 185–205. Woodbridge: Tamesis.

Martin-Márquez, Susan. 2004. "Spanish Literature and the Language of New Media." In *The Cambridge History of Spanish Literature*, edited by David T. Gies, 739–755. Cambridge: Cambridge University Press.

Neyrat, Cyril. 2009. "Sin etiquetas." *Cahiers du Cinéma España* 19: 14–17.

Nichols, Bill. 1991. *Representing Reality: Issues and Concepts in Documentary*. Bloomington, IN: Indiana University Press.

———. 1994. *Blurred Boundaries: Questions of Meaning in Contemporary Culture*. Bloomington, IN: Indiana University Press.

———. 2001. *Introduction to Documentary*. Bloomington, IN: Indiana University Press.

Pena, Jaime. 2010. "Filmar a cualquier precio." *Cahiers du Cinéma España* 34: 14–16.

Resina, Joan Ramon. 1987. "The Link in Consciousness: Time and Community in Rodoreda's *La plaça del Diamant*." *Catalan Review* 2 (2): 225–246.

Rony, Fatimah Tobing. 1996. *The Third Eye: Race, Cinema, and Ethnographic Spectacle*. Durham, NC: Duke University Press.

Ruby, Jay. 1977. "Reflexivity and the Documentary Film." *Journal of the University Film Association*. 29 (4): 3–11.

Ruiz del Olmo, Francisco Javier. 2009. "Compromiso y veracidad en el reciente cine documental español." In *Doc 21: Panorama del reciente cine documental en España*, edited by Inmaculada Sánchez and Marta Díaz, 19–33. Girona: Luces de Gálibo.

Shohat, Ella and Robert Stam. 1994. *Unthinking Eurocentrism: Multiculturalism and the Media*. London and New York: Routledge.

Todos *vós sodes capitáns*. Directed by Oliver Laxe. 2010. A Coruña: Zeitun Films, 2010. DVD.

Wahlberg, Malin. 2008. *Documentary Time: Film and Phenomenology*. Minneapolis, MN: University of Minnesota Press.

50

HUMAN MEMORY AND THE ACT OF REMEMBERING IN CONTEMPORARY IBERIAN GRAPHIC NOVELS

Javier Muñoz-Basols and Micaela Muñoz-Calvo

I closed the book, and felt this strange mixture of wistfulness and hope, and
I wondered if a memory is something you have or something you've lost.
Closing lines of Woody Allen's *Another Woman* (1988)

Following a long-standing tradition, comics and graphic novels have in the past decade attained particular prominence in the literary landscape of the Iberian Peninsula. In the early twenty-first century, graphic literature has become an intergenerational phenomenon transcending its traditional function of providing entertainment primarily for children and young adults, while expanding its reach to readers of all ages.

This study focuses on three Iberian graphic novels that have contributed to the greater visibility of the genre: *Alicia en un mundo real / Alícia en un món real* (2010), by Isabel Franc and Susanna Martín; *Ardalén* (2012) by Miguelanxo Prado; and *Arrugas* (2007) by Paco Roca. These works are linked by the theme of memory and the act of remembering, mechanisms by which we store a system of feelings that connect us to our environment and to other people. Their analysis reveals how, by means of the duality of text and image, the authors are able to transmit emotions and feelings about the human condition thereby transforming the reading experience into a journey through their characters' personal memories.

The golden age of comics and graphic novels on the Iberian Peninsula

Shortly after receiving the Spanish National Comics Prize in 2013, the Galician graphic artist, Miguelanxo Prado, declared this to be a "golden age" for comics. People are reading more and more graphic literature and "el momento que vive el cómic nacional no es 'una efervescencia juvenil'," but rather "un 'fenómeno intergeneracional' producto de una 'absoluta madurez' del género" (Europa Press 2013). Although Spain has enjoyed a long tradition of cartoonists and illustrators, the graphic genres have taken much longer to establish themselves in the Spanish marketplace and with the Spanish public than in other countries (France, Belgium, Japan, etc.), where this type of literature has always had a significant presence. Nonetheless, graphic literature has in the past decade seen a development in terms of the genre's status that has given it a prestige comparable to that of the narrative. As García points out, "Nos encontramos con lectores adultos que esperan la llegada de nuevos cómics no con la intención de aumentar una colección iniciada cuando tenían quince años, sino porque su lectura les resulta tan apetecible como la última novela de Paul Auster, Michel Houllebecq o Roberto Bolaño" (2013, 14). This boom has been reinforced by diverse events such as meetings and symposia, international shows and exhibits, prizes, grants and competitions, as well as by institutions, such as the Instituto Quevedo, devoted to bringing new readers to the world of graphic literature. The appearance of specialized journals, as well as the creation and consolidation of publishing houses that have made a commitment to this type of publication, has likewise been a factor in confirming the exuberant reception of this literary genre.[1]

Additionally, the success of this literature owes much to its relationship to multimodality, in other words, "the use of several semiotic modes in the design of a semiotic product or event, together with the particular way in which these modes are combined" (Kress and Van Leeuwen 2001, 20). The semantic duality of the binomial text-image allows authors to use an array of different stimuli to serve the narrative (Muñoz-Basols and Muñoz-Calvo 2015, 164–165). These are, so to speak, hybrid genres, whose combination of textual and visual traits enhances their multimodal value by means of different techniques (linguistic, typographical, pictographical and pictorial) (Kaindl 2004, 173). All of these modes are available to serve expression and narrative, while possessing a function related to communication as well as meaning: "comics, with their unique and powerful combination of picture and word, are multimodal texts *par excellence*. [They] are, in this new understanding of literacy and text, not only genuine texts – the experience of which constitutes genuine reading – but are also particularly interesting and important examples of this wider understanding of text" (Leber-Cook and Cook 2013, 28). Components such as the type of drawing, the style of the print, its line (size and thickness), the colours used, etc., contribute to the transmission of meaning and emotion. Indeed, the very frame of the comic (or its lack of frame) is part of its non-verbal language. Also important are the shape, size and number of cartoon strips per page as aspects determining the narrative strategy used to mark the rhythm of the reading and thus capture the reader's attention. It is the presence of this multimodality in graphic literature that allows the reader to enjoy a wide range of sensations in an immediate way (Muñoz-Basols and Muñoz-Calvo 2015, 179–184).

Yet another important aspect of graphic literature is its thematic versatility. As Miguelanxo Prado explains, "Mucha gente ha empezado a darse cuenta de que se pueden abordar muchos temas" (Constenla 2013). This characteristic allows authors to reach their readers by helping them "visualize" complex social themes that we encounter in our daily lives and which are based on human experience.

Thus, in this article we analyse three of the graphic novels that have contributed to the rise of graphic literature in the Iberian Peninsula over the past decade. As we see herein, all three employ memory and the actual act of remembering as the centrepiece of their narrative development. These themes are employed in sharing personal memories and experiences while having to battle cancer in *Alicia en un mundo real* / *Alícia en un món real* (2010), by Isabel Franc and Susanna Martín; they are used as a journey of introspection, reflection and memory in *Ardalén* (2012) by Miguelanxo Prado; and finally to show the ontological disconnectedness produced when a person suffering from Alzheimer's disease is unable to remember, which is the subject Paco Roca treats in *Arrugas* (2007). These three works signal the success of the Iberian contemporary graphic novel and its participation in this genre's "golden age," given their vivid capacity to delve into both personal and social identity to capture reality.

Sharing personal memories as therapy: battling against cancer in
Alicia en un mundo real / Alícia en un món real (2010)

Until the 1980s, female authors of graphic literature in the Iberian Península faced the challenge of "romper una a una las paredes de las muchas celdas con las que se encerraba a la mujer" (Pons 2015, 2). Nor did it help to have a well-established tradition of male writers of comics and cartoons dedicated to political satire appearing in the nation's principal newspapers during the years before and after the Transition, and well into the new democracy. However, with the new century a greater number of female authors have been able to popularize the comic, the graphic novel and the illustrated book (Constenla 2015, 1–2). So much so that there is now an association of women illustrators, the Asociación de Autoras de Cómic (AAC), as well as various published anthologies of works by women (e.g., *Enjambre* [2014], edited by Susanna Martin).[2]

Alicia en un mundo real / Alícia en un món real (Norma Editorial 2010) is an example of the visibility of women authors within today's panorama of Iberian graphic literature. The brainchild of two authors from Barcelona, Isabel Franc (writer) and Susanna Martín (illustrator), it was published simultaneously in Spanish and in Catalan. The work, whose title is a reference to Lewis Carroll's *Alice in Wonderland*, transports the reader into a reality increasingly faced by women today: the battle against breast cancer, a disease which in Spain alone affects more than 25,000 women each year (SEOM 2014, 12). This graphic novel is replete with autobiographical components that reflect experiences lived by Franc, the author, and retold through her persona: Alicia, the main character, is a journalist who is diagnosed with breast cancer. In fact, Franc adopted the format of a graphic novel in view of her own experience. As she herself states, this is a book:

> para la gente que tiene contacto con la enfermedad, de forma directa o indirecta. Me planteé qué tipo de libro me gustaría a mí leer cuando estaba con el tratamiento de la quimioterapia, ya que en esa situación tienes mucho tiempo para leer pero muy pocas energías para hacerlo. Y me pareció que el formato gráfico podría ser útil y también llegar a un público más amplio.
>
> (García Sierra 2010)

Indeed, the graphic element is the key to making this a work of highly therapeutic value, for in sharing her memories, the author takes the reader along the path of the suffering patient all the way from the diagnosis of the disease to its cure. Using this format, she brings the reader into the story of the cancer patient by means of cartoons and humour that serve to play down this dreaded disease. By allowing the reader to "visualize" the experiences she went through, she contributes to reinforcing the therapeutic effect of the novel. Humour, of course, constitutes a crucial element: in Franc's words, "una forma de resistencia y de supervivencia" (García Sierra 2010). It provides the novel with an ironic perspective on life, one that helps the reader to cope with the disease by facing the problem with optimism, hope and faith in the future.

Martín's illustrations are a combination of simple drawings in black and white, using imaginative visual resources influenced by manga drawings, mainly by Katsuhiro Otomo, as well as drawings by Hergé, combined with a fluid graphic narrative. The illustrator "explota tots els recursos de la composició de la vinyeta, la pàgina i els diferents capítols per obtenir un ritme atractiu i proper que convida a la lectura i a fer una immersió en la vida de la protagonista, per convidar el lector a viure en el món imaginari de l'Alícia" (Ojeda 2010) (see Figure 50.1). The

Figure 50.1 Alícia en un món real. Norma Editorial, 2010, 115.

script is ingenious and fun; both in Catalan and Spanish, it uses colloquial, everyday language that is natural and spontaneous, and interspersed with literary and cultural references. The authors have as their motto: "La vida después del cáncer ya nunca es igual [. . .] pero viene a ser lo mismo" (2010, 115) and consequently they assert, "Y, si viene a ser lo mismo, hay que ponerse las pilas y lanzarse a vivir" (2010, 116). As a result of this approach, the novel is full of positive references and "ansias por vivir cada momento" (2010, 120), ranging from the portrayal of Alicia as a "superwoman" fighting against the world in a boxing ring (2010, 71) to that of a phoenix rising from the ashes (2010, 94).

In a casual tone, Alicia makes the reader participate in her recollections of the different stages of her illness and recovery: diagnosis, chemotherapy, x-ray treatment, hair loss, the impact on the patient's appearance, surgery, and her mastectomy trauma (together with its repercussions on her social, emotional and romantic relationships). Needless to say, these events significantly affect the character's state of mind: she experiences doubt, fear, sadness, nervousness, anger, loneliness and a loss of self-esteem and self-confidence. Alicia reflects on what it means to be a woman in today's society, commenting that "algunas mujeres no soportan mirarse," "se duchan con la luz apagada para no verse" (2010, 97). When she is asked to write an article about feminine beauty, she questions the canon, remarking on how it has changed in the course of history (2010, 100–102). Included are references to "La maja de Goya" (2010, 114) and the "Picasso beauty" (2010, 121), together with comments regarding the meaning of beauty. The author points out that the aesthetic canon varies not only with the epoch but also with the culture (2010, 102). One of the novel's objectives is, therefore, to "reivindicar el rechazo a esta esclavitud hacia la estética que tenemos las mujeres y que la protagonista resuelve con tanto humor" (García Sierra 2010). When Alicia ponders what to do after her mastectomy, she decides to have a tattoo made over the scar on her chest, paralleling Franc's own decision.

Because Alicia is a lesbian, this graphic novel also touches on the LGBTQ theme. As a backdrop to the story, the reader is introduced to the circle of women friends who support the protagonist during her illness: "a fractured, funhouse mirror in which we LGBTQ people can view ourselves and allow others to see us as well" (Hall 2013, 7). Instead of leaning on the traditional family structure, the feisty, demanding, and positive protagonist has around her several women who give her their unconditional friendship while conforming to different models of conduct: Berta, her ex; Maite, a "friend with benefits;" Pilar, her gynaecologist; Maru, her editor; Cris, a designer confused about her own sexuality; Carna, another breast cancer sufferer; Merche, her beautician; and a plethora of friends: Nicky, Lidu, Lea, and last but not least, Farinelli, a castrated, pot-bellied cat affectionately called "el Fari." It is by means of this particular mode of framing the action that the novel gives visibility to the homosexual theme. As Justin Hall (2013, 1) indicates:

> LGBTQ comics have fought a long, uphill battle for recognition [. . .]. They have existed in a parallel universe alongside the rest of comics, appearing almost exclusively in gay newspapers and gay bookstores and published by gay publishers. Queer comics have been primarily created for their own communities, and they have been neither interested in, nor able to gain, a wider market.

Yet, regardless of the reader's gender or sexual orientation, it is easy to identify with some of the episodes that crop up in the course of the narrative and with the multiple reflections about life that they generate. The main character's memories, the accumulated knowledge and the life-lessons offered acquire a meaningful therapeutic function and value. The novel thus becomes a clear example of the communicative capacity of verbal and visual language to bring the reader face to face with a difficult experience such as the ordeal of cancer, and in the process promote and encourage empathy with people who are suffering from this illness, if not also help readers to confront their own problematic diagnosis.

From reflection to introspection: the functioning of memory in
Ardalén (2012)

Ardalén (2012) is Miguelanxo Prado's most extensive work and the winner of the Spanish National Comics Prize in 2013. Born in A Coruña, Prado, who has had a prominent career as an illustrator and author in the world of the comic, put three years of intensive work into this graphic novel and published it simultaneously in Galician and Spanish under the same title.

The novel is set in the Galician mountains, in a place where dreamlike landscapes appear superimposed upon real ones. The reader is transported to experiences lived on the sea and on land through the interwoven personal memories of various characters. By means of this poetic text the author immerses us in a story that moves around in a magical nebula, as well as in reality, and where human beings and fantastic creatures wander around in a universe of memories: a combination of reality and dream, remembering and forgetting – a combination of memories with sensations, present and past. The story analyses how personal remembrance is constituted, starting from a conglomeration of experiences. Because we are what we remember, and what others remember about us, our memories are a mixture of the experiences that we and others have lived.

The structure of the novel is as complex as the very functioning of memory, based as it is on fragments of lived experience and the reflection of a journey through different lives, places and time periods, thus allowing us to get close to the different identities of the characters. As the reader reads on, the plot gathers meaning. It is composed of different stories and discrete pieces of information that are progressively incorporated into the narrative. The language possesses great poetic depth and contributes to a development of the action, which is characteristically slow. This slow progress is created by means of the images, which allow the reader to take delight in what he or she reads and sees. It is painting rather than drawing that predominates in this graphic novel, as a palette of colours in mostly greenish and ochre tones gives the different vignettes their magical quality, even as it emphasizes the multimodal aspect of this type of literature and contributes to the reading experience (see Figure 50.2).

The main character is Sabela Rego Lamas (Sabeliña), a 42-year-old woman who has just become separated from her partner. She comes to a Galician village with the intention of looking for information about her grandfather, Francisco Lamas, who emigrated to Cuba in his youth, returned three years later and then disappeared. Sabela asks Fidel, a lonely, older man living in the village, to help her by trying to remember if he ever knew her grandfather. Nicknamed "El Náufrago" by the men of the tavern, Fidel claims to have been to Cuba and many other places, but in reality he has never been on a ship. Sabela is the only person who has paid any attention to him in many years, "tantos años que ya los he olvidado" (2012, 158). As she tries to tap into Fidel's recollections to reconstruct part of her grandfather's story, the old man's memories and experiences inevitably become mixed up with his memories of other people and other lives: "Al mismo tiempo que Fidel reconstruía la historia de mi abuelo, reconstruía la suya propia. O la de alguien que se llamó Antonio y que, por caminos extraños e inexplicables, acabó formando parte de su propia memoria" (2012, 224).

Fidel has memories that are not his, and the novel insists on the idea that to remember is also to relive experiences based on what others have lived and the appropriation of their memories. Fidel is not sure he can distinguish between what he has lived and what he has imagined: "Los recuerdos, que son muchos, van y vienen, sin que yo consiga colocarlos. Nunca estoy seguro de qué sucedió antes o después, me bailan los nombres, las caras . . . . Es como si el libro de mi vida allá se hubiese deshecho y me quedara en las manos un puñado de hojas que no consigo

Figure 50.2   Ardalén. El Patito Editorial, 2012, 37.

ordenar de nuevo. A veces, incluso, es como si esos recuerdos no fuesen míos" (2012, 37). These memories, as the fairy Xaniña tells Fidel, are like "Ese viento, el Ardalén, que viene del otro lado del océano, llega cargado de recuerdos de otras vidas . . . de otras muertes. [. . .] Hay quien, como tú, se empapa como esponja de esos recuerdos ajenos" (2012, 164).

A notable example of how visual elements can be used in graphic literature to enhance the reading experience is the sprinkling of the text with fictional facsimiles of the epoch, purporting to authenticate the story and its setting. This involved considerable research, with results such as: a travel ticket owned by Francisco Lamas Caímzo (2012, 54); a bill of exchange from the Banco de Ultramar (2012, 56); a letter from Francisco Lamas to his wife and daughters (2012, 58); a document regarding the inheritance of Doña Raimunda Taboada Rey, Fidel's aunt (2012, 117); a photograph of Mariela as a "jinetera" in Havana (2012, 122); an official report on the sinking of the cargo ship "Cienfuegos" in French Guyana waters on July 17, 1954 (2012, 139–140); a study of the "Los asombrosos peces voladores" (2012, 152–154); a forensic psychiatric report on Fidel (2012, 211–212); a letter from the Venezuelan Embassy in Spain (2012, 219); the lyrics of the bolero "Reencuentros" (2012, 220); and handwritten notes by Sabela (2012, 224). These documents help the reader to "remember" and to connect the data provided by the novel and its characters by visualizing many of the components that make up the narrative.

Lastly, many literary, anthropological and scientific comments about memory and the act of remembering make their appearance throughout the novel. For example, Mercedes Prieto Dunwald, a Chilean anthropologist (2012, 125–126), assures us that "No hay presente," given that "El tiempo pasa sin transición de ser futuro a ser pasado. Entre uno y otro no hay nada. Creo que es Henri Bergson quien dice que 'toda percepción ya es memoria.' Y la interpretación de eso que no es ni pasado ni futuro es lo que provoca las diferencias" (2012, 126). We also have the words of Eva Fontes (2012, 59–62), who writes that "Somos lo que recordamos y lo que los demás recuerdan de nosotros" and affirms that "nuestra identidad se sostiene sobre el entramado de la memoria" (2012, 59). The inclusion at the beginning of the novel of a page with quotes, including one taken from Adolfo Bioy Casares' *El sueño de los héroes* ("Siempre había afirmado que había que cuidar los recuerdos, porque eran la vida de cada uno"), demonstrates the author's intention to make the reader a participant in the singular feature of human experience that is the ability to reflect on memory and the act of remembering. It is by means of all this information that the author urges the reader to stop for a moment to enjoy the experiences he has lived: "quien no recuerda, no vive" (on the back cover).

The ontological disconnectedness of Alzheimer's disease: the impossibility of remembering in *Arrugas* (2007)

Paco Roca, winner of the Spanish National Comic Prize in 2008, is one of the internationally best-known authors and illustrators of the Iberian Peninsula. His literary production is characterized by versatility and an ability to work in a variety of genres: adventures, neorealism, magical realism, history and social critique.

Arrugas (2007) has been one of the most successful and best-selling graphic novels of the past decade and an international prize winner. It takes on themes that had never been dealt with before in Iberian comics, such as Alzheimer's disease, senility and dementia. The Valencia-based author drew his inspiration from the story of a friend's father and from research conducted by visiting care homes and listening to residents' anecdotes. This allowed him to extract the essential characteristics and ingredients for the novel. His observation of the behaviour of real people is seen in the accurate psychological portraiture of characters which include not only the patients themselves, but also their family members and caregivers.

The story takes place in an old people's home, with its main character, Emilio, an elderly man suffering from Alzheimer's, formerly a bank manager, who has been taken there by his family. As soon as he arrives he meets his roguish roommate Miguel, a bachelor with no children, whose sharp sense of irony and humour counteracts the sadness, boredom and tragedy that typify the day-to-day reality of the hermetic, hopeless universe that these characters live in, where "te conviertes en un trasto inútil para la sociedad" (2007, 35). Miguel represents the values of friendship and companionship, and his attitude during the story changes as a result of his relationship with his new friend. Showing Emilio around the facility, he introduces him to the other elderly residents and summarizes their lives in a few words, as he teaches Emilio the daily routine of that new closed and monotonous environment in which he will live, with its fixed schedule of medications, naps, meals and gym. This is a completely new life, from which there is no escape, and which is defined by the static quality which old age takes on in such a place: "Esto es el mundo al revés. El tiempo que hay entre las comidas es tiempo perdido. Duermes o te quedas vegetando mientras ves la tele esperando la próxima comida" (2007, 34).

The novel is characterized by recurrent flashbacks in which the characters share their memories with the reader, and which get mixed up with the present moment. It is with this technique that the author manages to sensitize the reader to the disconnectedness from reality that the Alzheimer's victim suffers: the loss of autobiographical memory (Mace 2010), a collection of disordered memories that also impinge on other mental faculties, as the protagonist's physician explains: "Además de la memoria reciente, con el tiempo se destruye la memoria pasada, la orientación, el lenguaje, la capacidad del enfermo para cuidarse y dirigir sus actos por sí mismo" (2007, 57). Thus, lived time, the memories lost as a result of the illness, and the impact of Alzheimer's disease on the social and familial context, constitute the central themes of the work. "La familia nos usa para hacer recados y recoger a los nietos del colegio. Y cuando ya no somos capaces de hacerlo nos dejan aquí para olvidarse de nosotros" (2007, 37). Through this graphic novel, in which the quality of the script is complemented by the graphics, Paco Roca creates a well-structured story with a profound narrative. The rhythm is slow and the various characters move around in a fictional space, one in which the reality of the dialogues and the reflections uttered in a loud voice come up in the characters' conversations, thereby gathering importance in view of their veracity with respect to the reality of the patient: "un ritmo explicativo en que la tragedia, el mundo de lo imaginario y el humor se combinan equilibradamente" (Quintanilla 2012, 57).

Paco Roca's style of drawing belongs to the so-called Franco-Belgian style, that is, one that is subordinate to the narrative, with a classic division of sequential vignettes on the page. It employs close-ups of objects and gestures to express the sensation of loss of memory and the feeling of love and complicity among the characters. Soft, solid colours serve to distinguish different time periods, day from night, or cold from heat, so as to create sensations and transmit the state of mind of the characters and to mark the rhythm of the narrative within a closed scene. For example, a chromatic gradation is used to summarize the life of the old person in two pages, in which colour marks the flow of the story, as the monotonous passing of the daylight hours appears reflected in a clock that marks time from nine o'clock in the morning to a quarter past eight at night, when one sees empty chairs and all the old people are sleeping. The vignette comes to a final end with Miguel asking Emilio: "¿Qué tal el día?" (2007, 46–47) (see Figure 50.3).

Throughout the novel, the author portrays the various characters through the feelings, values and virtues they represent: a collection of impressions, memories and experiences

Figure 50.3   *Arrugas*. Astiberri Ediciones, 2007, 46–47.

Figure 50.3 Continued.

lived as universal concepts. This is how we learn about Dolores' love, her tender qualities, and her decision to go and live in the old-age facility together with her husband Modesto who has reached an advanced stage of Alzheimer's; it is how we learn of Rosario's fantasy of travelling on the Orient Express to Istanbul; of Señora Sol's hope of calling her children to tell them that she is already well and that they should come and get her; of Carmencita's fear of being taken away by Martians; of Miguel's roguish ways of looking for any chance to take advantage of others; and of the despair of Emilio who, together with the reader, discovers his increasing disconnectedness from reality. Thus the reader is put in the position of identifying with these elderly people, with their memories and feelings, allowing himself to fear what fate has in store for him, even as he empathizes with the realism of the story so full of close, commonplace and very human experiences.

The success of the story lies in the universality of the themes broached and the author's capacity to create a reality that is both accurate and realistic, one in which the reader is immersed and made to participate in an environment to which he is not accustomed. The very reading of this graphic novel helps the reader to reflect on and understand the process of "el largo adiós" (2007, 22): the loss of memory, the inability to remember and the gradual decomposition of identity that leads to the rupture of memory, that bridge between lived experiences and the present moment.

Recalling the past: "Vivir para recordar y recordar para vivir"

The three graphic novels we have analysed develop the parallel themes of memory and the act of remembering as central to the narrative. The significance of these themes can be summarized in the popular saying: "vivir para recordar y recordar para vivir." Memory and the act of remembering constitute the very essence of our existence, of our perception of our own life and identity:

> En la memoria guardamos el complejo sistema de sentimientos que nos relacionan con nuestro entorno y con los demás, nuestras simpatías, los cariños y amores, las indiferencias y los odios; nuestros gustos y disgustos, nuestras preferencias y nuestras emociones. La constatación de que toda esa información sigue ahí, a nuestra disposición, cada mañana, al despertar, gracias a un sofisticadísimo proceso bioquímico y neuronal en nuestro cerebro, es lo que nos transmite el tranquilizador sosiego de la seguridad de seguir siendo quienes creemos que somos.
>
> (*Ardalén* 2012, 59)

The covers of these novels highlight the act of remembering as central to each of the three works. In *Alicia en un mundo real* (2010), the main character appears accompanied by her cat, pointing to herself and wearing a shirt featuring the radioactivity symbol, thus reminding us of the treatment for cancer and the ever-present and inevitable memory of having to face this illness (see Figure 50.4). On the cover of *Ardalén* (2012) we see a thoughtful Fidel at the bottom of the sea surrounded by marine life set against a landscape of mountains and palm trees, by way of indicating a journey through the different worlds constituted by the protagonist's memories and, simultaneously, those of other people (see Figure 50.5). In *Arrugas* (2007) we see Emilio looking out of a train window as photographs – some with images and some turned the other way as if they were blank – are seen coming out of his head: symbols of escaping memories that dissipate and are lost since Alzheimer's makes it impossible to remember (see Figure 50.6).

Figure 50.4   Alicia en un mundo real. Book Cover. Norma Editorial, 2010.

As we have seen, although the central theme of these novels has to do with memory and the act of remembering, each novel deals with different lives, histories, scenes, situations and human experiences, thereby fulfilling different functions. *Alicia en un mundo real* (2010) shares with the reader the inevitable act of remembering the before and the after of cancer, and the desire to have the reader share in the experiences and navigate them in a positive way, all the while metaphorically holding the main character's hand through the illness in order to witness it first-hand and thus sympathize with its victim. As a result, the journey made by the reader transforms itself into a therapeutic learning experience about the illness, its environment and its consequences. By contrast, *Ardalén* (2012) makes us see how memories dissipate with time and become mixed up with the lived experiences of other people, to such an extent that we become incapable of discerning whether what we remember is fully ours, or whether it is the shared memories and experiences of other people. As the novel tells us: "Podemos también, por propia iniciativa o inducidos por otros, crear falsos recuerdos que, pasado un cierto tiempo, resultarán indistinguibles de los verdaderos y resistirán incólumes cualquier tentativa de desenmascarami-ento" (2012, 59–60). Finally, the impossibility of distinguishing past from present in *Arrugas* (2007) brings us closer to the mentality and environment of the Alzheimer's patient, what he

Figure 50.5   Ardalén. Book Cover. El Patito Editorial, 2012.

lives and feels when unable to remember. After all, it is through reading that one becomes capable of understanding how the gradual loss of memories that one has been collecting throughout one's life brings with it an ontological disconnectedness from reality and thus the loss of
identity. Such a feeling is represented by the author in a two-page scene in which the reader,
like in many other instances throughout the novel, sees the world through the character's eyes.
This time, instead of travelling back in time in a flashback, we see how Miguel's face becomes
blurred to Emilio, fading progressively to a blank gap at the bottom of the page, akin to the mind
of the Alzheimer's sufferer (see Figure 50.7).

Starting from a desire to share the common memories and experiences of human beings, the
three graphic novels reflect a particular way of seeing and interpreting the world by means of a
process of investigation and documentation on the part of the authors of the actual experiences
they or other people have lived. Such stories evoke multiple reflections in the reader about
human relations, feelings, society, the changes experienced in the course of a lifetime and
the identity of a person. Taken together, they constitute a palimpsest of the human experience
and a journey that reflects the importance of memory. More importantly, they address a wide
public by exploring complex themes such as illness, loneliness and old age which, though less

Figure 50.6   Arrugas. Book Cover. Astiberri Ediciones, 2007.

prevalent in graphic literature, are an integral part of what it means to be human. Humour in these three novels contributes to playing down the problematic situations in which the main characters find themselves. Indeed, humour serves as an escape valve, a way to overcome some of the sadness and the pain produced by the reality of the themes being developed.

Lastly, the journey as a metaphor of life is the means by which memories and experiences are shared. Present in all three works, the journey represents a connection between travel and life, as in *Alicia en un mundo real* which opens with an explicit quote: "Cada vida es un viaje y su itinerario no es siempre el deseado" (2010, 9). In *Ardalén* (2012), we are taken on a quest for the past through the memory of the journeys made by Fidel, who travels to remote places and relives several shipwrecks – but none of them his; whereas *Arrugas* (2007) is about a coming and going between past and present, with an increasingly limited recollection of lived memories and experiences within the closed universe of the old people's home at the final stage of life, as Emilio embarks on his journey of no return.

Figure 50.7   Arrugas. Astiberri Ediciones, 2007, 95–96.

Figure 50.7 Continued.

Conclusion

Although our analysis has only focused on a small sample of some of the most successful Iberian graphic novels of the past decade, it demonstrates that this type of literature is characterized by considerable aesthetic and linguistic sensitivity and that, like any literary genre, it allows us to reflect on the reality that surrounds us. Likewise, we have shown that comics and graphic novels possess a thematic versatility that makes it possible to develop numerous themes. Because of the multimodal value provided by the binomial text-image, these novels are capable of directly transmitting to the reader a great variety of sensations. The key to the success of the three graphic novels analysed here is their ability to show the continuous dependency of human beings on memory and the act of remembering. This becomes manifest in the behaviour of the various characters, in the reach of the themes explored, and in the sensitivity with which they are developed. With this analysis, we not only testify to the popularity and the reach that graphic genres have in the Iberian Peninsula today, but we also show the vitality with which these genres claim their role and function as a literature which is becoming an important part of the literary, visual and multimodal canon of the twenty-first century.

Notes

1 For instance, Astiberri Ediciones, Ediciones B, Ediciones La Cúpula, Lumen, Norma Editorial, Reservoir Books, Sexto Piso, etc.

2 Some examples of women illustrators are: Carla Berrocal, Paula Bonet, Raquel Córcoles "Moderna de Pueblo," Cristina Durán, Ana Galvañ, Txus García, Sara Herranz, Pupi Herrera, María Herreros, Lola Lorente, Mamen Moreu, Míriam Muñoz, Elena Odriozola, Paulapé, Sonia Pulido, Emma Ríos, Srta. M, Noemí Villamuza, etc. (see Cano 2014; Pons 2015, 2).

Works cited

Cano, José. 2014. "Dibujantas." *El Mundo*, October 7. Accessed February 28, 2015. http://www.elmundo. es/cultura/2014/10/16/5437d88522601dfd668b4579.html.

Constenla, Tereixa. 2013. "Miguelanxo Prado gana el Nacional de Cómic con 'Ardalén'." *El País*, October 31. Accessed November 14, 2014. http://cultura.elpais.com/cultura/2013/10/31/actuali dad/1383212225_972461.html.

———. 2015. "Ellas pintan mucho." *El País* (Revista de verano), August 16, 1–2.

Europa Press. 2013. "Miguelanxo Prado: 'El cómic español está viviendo su Edad de Oro'." October 31. Accessed November 14, 2014. http://www.europapress.es/cultura/exposiciones-00131/noticia-miguelanxo-prado-comic-espanol-viviendo-edad-oro-20131031143514.html.

Franc, Isabel and Susanna Martín. 2010. *Alicia en un mundo real*. Barcelona: Norma Editorial.

———. 2010. *Alícia en un món real*. Barcelona: Norma Editorial.

García, Santiago. 2013. "Después del cómic: una introducción." In *Supercómic: mutaciones de la novela gráfica contemporánea*, edited by Santiago García, 7–23. Madrid: Errata Naturae.

García Sierra, Jesús. 2010. "Entrevista a Isabel Franc y Susanna Martín." *El Diario Montañés*, May 3. Accessed November 14, 2014. http://www.guiadelcomic.es/entrevistas/yexus/susanna-martin-isabel-franc-10.htm.

Hall, Justin, ed. 2013. *No Straight Lines: Four Decades of Queer Comics*. Hong Kong: Fantagrapics Books.

Kaindl, Klaus. 2004. "Multimodality in the Translation of Humour in Comics." In *Perspectives on Multimodality*, edited by Eija Ventola, Cassily Charles, and Martin Kaltenbacher, 173–192. Amsterdam: John Benjamins.

Kress, Gunther and Theo Van Leeuwen. 2001. *Multimodal Discourse. The Modes and Media of Contemporary Communication*. London: Arnold.

Mace, John H., ed. 2010. *The Act of Remembering: Toward an Understanding of How We Recall the Past*. Malden, MA: Wiley.

Martín, Susanna, ed. 2014. *Enjambre*. Barcelona: Norma Editorial.

Muñoz-Basols, Javier and Micaela Muñoz-Calvo. 2015. "La traducción de textos humorísticos multimodales." In *La traducción. Nuevos planteamientos teórico-metodológicos*, edited by María Azucena Penas Ibáñez, 159–184. Madrid: Síntesis.

Leber-Cook, Alice and Roy T. Cook. 2013. "Stigmatization, Multimodality and Metaphor: Comics in the Adult English as a Second Language Classroom." In *Graphic Novels and Comics in the Classroom: Essays on the Educational Power of Sequential Art*, edited by Carrye Kay Syma and Robert G. Weiner, 23–34. Jefferson, NC: McFarland.

Ojeda, Jordi. 2010. "Vinyetes com a teràpia." *Diari d'Andorra*, May 31, 23.

Pons, Álvaro. 2015. "Adiós a las etiquetas." *El País* (Revista de verano), August 16, 2.

Prado, Miguelanxo. 2012. *Ardalén* (Galician). Santiago de Compostela: El Patito Editorial.

———. 2012. *Ardalén* (Spanish). Santiago de Compostela: El Patito Editorial.

Quintanilla, Ismael. 2012. "Un truhán, un señor." In *Paco Roca. Dibujante ambulante*, edited by Paco Roca, 57–65. València: Museo Valenciano de la Ilustración y la Modernidad (MUVIM).

Roca, Paco. 2007. *Arrugas*. Bilbao: Astiberri Ediciones.

Sociedad Española de Oncología Médica (SEOM). 2014. "Las cifras del cáncer en España." Accessed November 18, 2014. http://www.seom.org/seomcms/images/stories/recursos/Las_cifras_del_cancer_2014.pdf.

COLOUR ILLUSTRATIONS

Figure 10.1 Hercules. The Creation Tapestry, upper border, c. 1097. Museum of the Treasury of the
Cathedral of Girona.

© Catedral de Girona.

Figure 10.2 Detail of the warriors fighting. San Esteban de Almazorre (Huesca), mural paintings, apse,
central register, c. 1131.

© Antonio García Omedes.

Figure 10.3 Patriarchal Cross of Anglesola (Lleida), anvers. Jerusalem, c. 1150–70.

© Ajuntament d'Anglesola.

Figure 10.4 Dispute and Arrest of Saint Catherine. Mural Paintings of Santa Caterina de la Seu d'Urgell, c. 1241–52.

© MNAC-Museu Nacional d'Art de Catalunya. Barcelona. Calveras/Mérida/Sagristá.

Figure 10.5 Saint James and his pilgrims. Santiago de Turégano (Segovia), apse, painted reliefs, c. 1232.

© Manuel Castiñeiras.

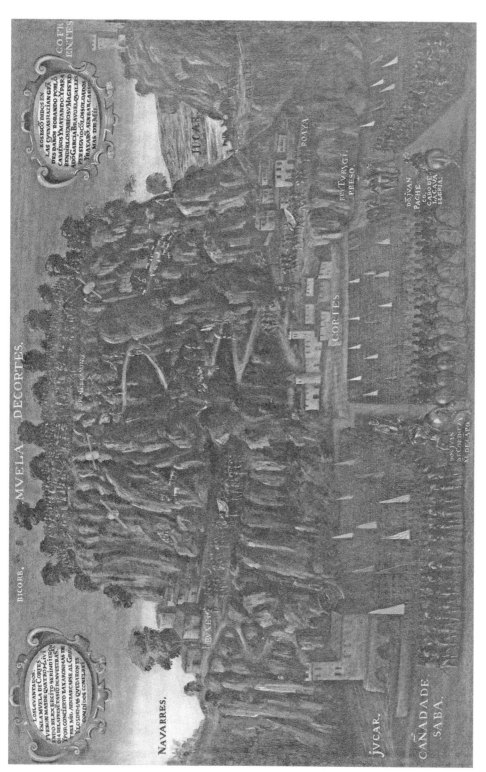

Figure 15.1 Rebelión de los moriscos en la Muela de Cortes. Vicent Mestre, 1613. València, Fundación Bancaja, Permanent Collection.

Figure 15.2 Sandro Botticelli, *The Abyss of Hell*, c. 1485. Biblioteca Apostolica, Vatican. Wikimedia Commons.

Figure 15.3 Detail, Sandro Botticelli, *The Abyss of Hell*, c. 1485. Biblioteca Apostolica, Vatican. Wikimedia Commons.

Figure 15.4   Detail, *Rebelión de los moriscos en la Sierra de Laguar*. Jerónimo Espinosa, 1612–13. Valencia, Fundación Bancaja, Permanent Collection.

Figure 15.5   Detail, *Rebelión de los moriscos en la Sierra de Laguar*. Jerónimo Espinosa, 1612–13. Valencia, Fundación Bancaja, Permanent Collection.

Figure 15.6   Detail, *Desembarco de los moriscos en el Puerto de Orán*. Vicent Mestre, 1613. Valencia, Fundación Bancaja, Permanent Collection.

Figure 15.7 Detail, *Embarque de los moriscos en el Puerto de Denia*. Vicent Mestre, 1612–13. Valencia, Fundación Bancaja, Permanent Collection.

Figure 15.8 Embarque de los moriscos en el Puerto de Alicante. Pere Oromig and Francisco Peralta, 1612–13. Valencia, Private Collection.

Figure 15.9 *Embarque de los moriscos del Grau de Valencia*. Pere Oromig, 1612–13. Valencia, Fundación Bancaja, Permanent Collection.

Figure 15.10   Detail, *Embarque de los moriscos del Grau de Valencia*. Pere Oromig, 1612–13. Valencia, Fundación Bancaja, Permanent Collection.

Figure 15.11   Detail, *Embarque de los moriscos del Grau de Valencia*. Pere Oromig, 1612–13. Valencia, Fundación Bancaja, Permanent Collection.

Figure 15.12   Detail, *Embarque de los moriscos del Grau de Valencia*. Pere Oromig, 1612–13. Valencia, Fundación Bancaja, Permanent Collection.

In astrologos.

Icare per superos qui raptus et aëra, donec
In mare praecipitem cera liquata daret,
Nunc te cera eadem, feruensque exusciat ignis,
Exemplo ut doceas dogmata certa tuo.
Astrologus caueat quicquam praedicere: praeceps
Nam cadet impostor, dum super astra uolat.

H

In temerarios.

Aspicis aurigam currus Phaëtonta paterni
Igniuomos ausum flectere solis equos.
Maxima quo postquam terris incendia sparsit,
Est temere insesso lapsus ab axe miser.
Sic plerique rotis Fortunae ad sidera Reges
Euecti, ambitio quos iuuenilis agit,
Post magnam humani generis lademque suamque,
Cunctorum poenas denique dant scelerum.

E

Figure 20.1 Andreas Alciatus, "In temerarios." In *Emblemata* (Lyons and Madison, Probonne, 1550).

Figure 20.3 Anonymous after Otto Vaenius, "In medio consistit virtus." In *Quinti Horatii Flacci Emblemata* (Antuerpiae: Philippus Lifaert, 1612).

Figure 20.4 Francisco Pacheco, *Apoteosis de Hércules*, 1604. Tempera on canvas. Casa de Pilatos, Seville.

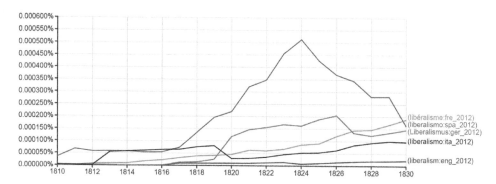

Figure 24.1 Relative frequency of the use of the term "liberalism" in five European languages, 1810–1830.

Source: Google Ngram Viewer, July 25, 2014.

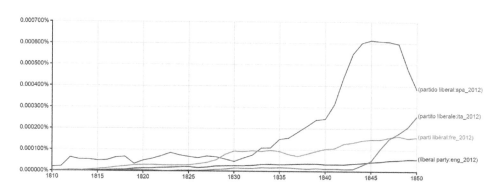

Figure 24.2 Relative frequency of the use of "liberal party" in four European languages, 1810–1850.

Source: Google Ngram Viewer, July 25, 2014.

Figure 30.1 Francisco Bayeu y Subías, *El Olimpo. Batalla de los gigantes*, 1764, oil on canvas, 68 x 123 cm.
© Museo Nacional del Prado, Madrid [P604].

Figure 30.2 Francisco de Goya y Lucientes, *El quitasol*, 1777, oil on canvas, 104 x 152 cm.
© Museo Nacional del Prado, Madrid [P773].

Figure 30.4 Francisco de Goya y Lucientes (copy), *Carlos IV*, 1799, oil on canvas, 207 x 127 cm.

© Museo Nacional del Prado, Madrid [P727].

Figure 30.3 Anton Raphael Mengs, *Carlos IV, Príncipe de Asturias*, c. 1765, oil on canvas, 152.5 x 111 cm.

© Museo Nacional del Prado, Madrid [P2188].

Figure 30.5   Francisco de Goya y Lucientes, *Corral de locos*, 1794, oil on tin-plated iron.

© Meadows Museum, Algur H. Meadows Collection, Dallas, Texas [67.01].

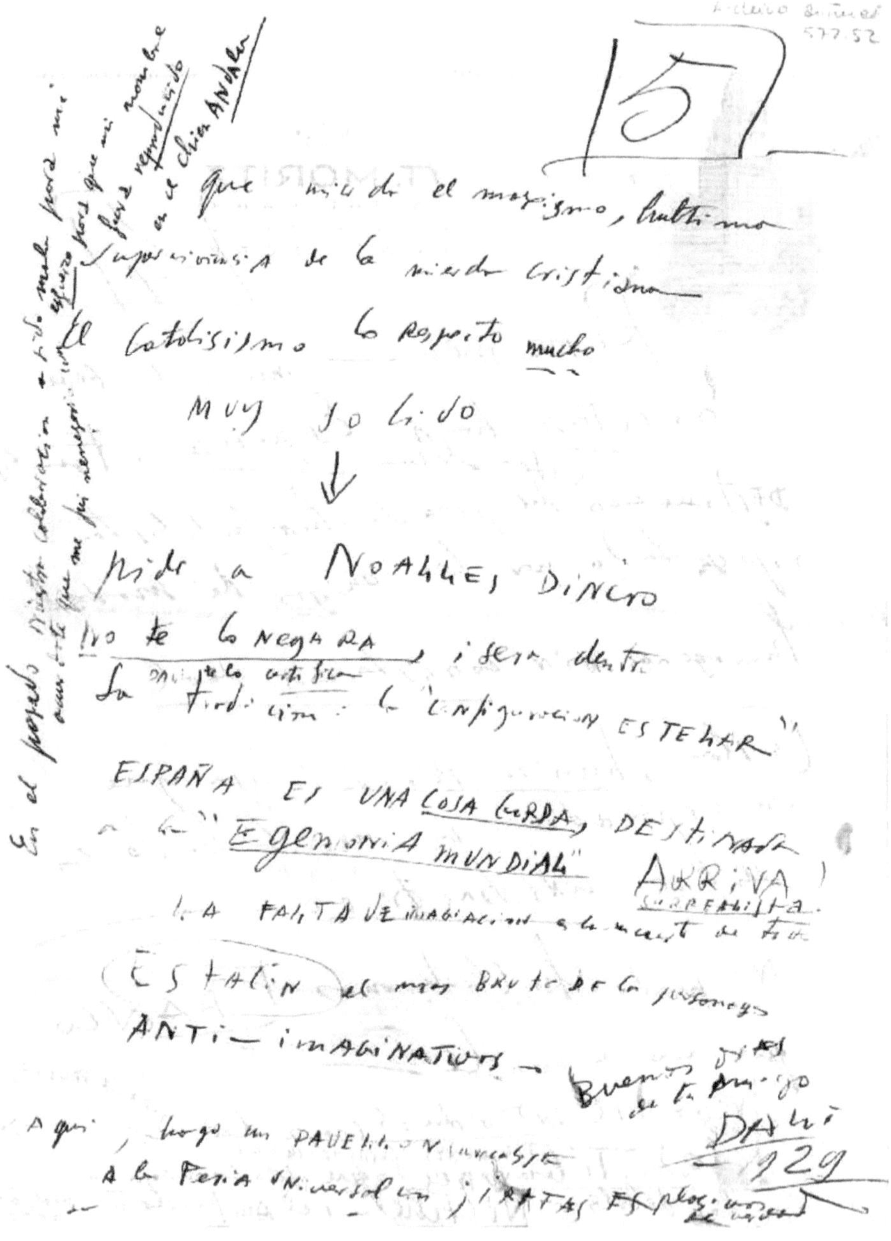

Figure 36.1 Dalí's letter to Buñuel from New York, 1939.

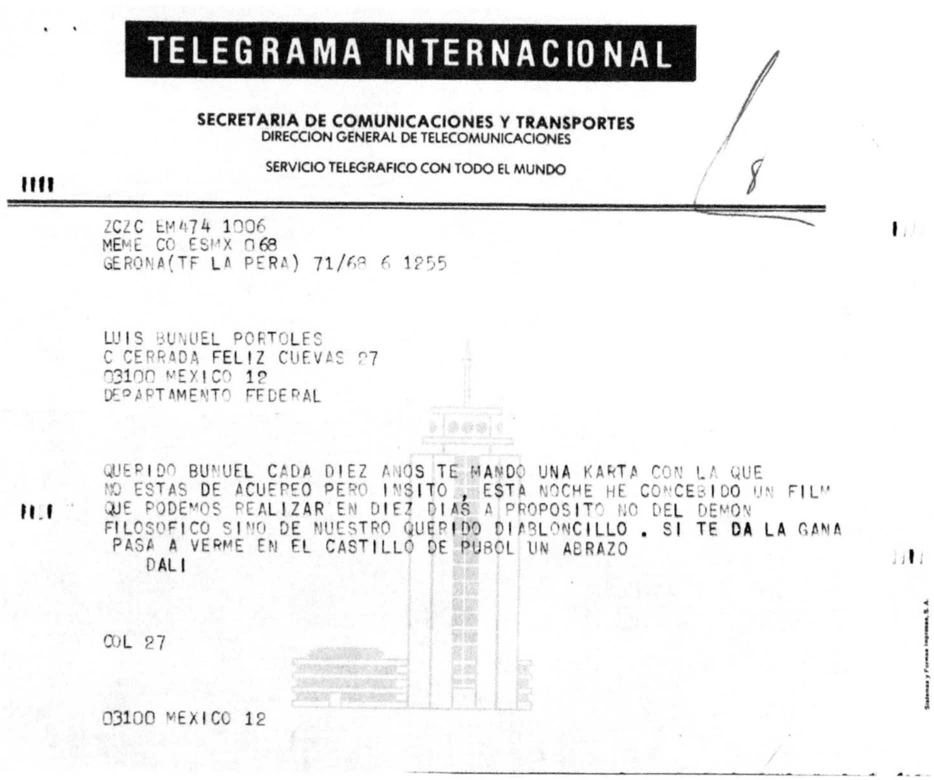

TELEGRAMA INTERNACIONAL

SECRETARIA DE COMUNICACIONES Y TRANSPORTES
DIRECCION GENERAL DE TELECOMUNICACIONES

SERVICIO TELEGRAFICO CON TODO EL MUNDO

8

ZCZC EM474 1006
MEME CO ESMX 068
GERONA(TF LA PERA) 71/68 6 1255

LUIS BUNUEL PORTOLES
C CERRADA FELIZ CUEVAS 27
03100 MEXICO 12
DEPARTAMENTO FEDERAL

QUERIDO BUNUEL CADA DIEZ ANOS TE MANDO UNA KARTA CON LA QUE
NO ESTAS DE ACUERDO PERO INSITO , ESTA NOCHE HE CONCEBIDO UN FILM
QUE PODEMOS REALIZAR EN DIEZ DIAS A PROPOSITO NO DEL DEMON
FILOSOFICO SINO DE NUESTRO QUERIDO DIABLONCILLO . SI TE DA LA GANA
PASA A VERME EN EL CASTILLO DE PUBOL UN ABRAZO
DALI

COL 27

03100 MEXICO 12

Figure 36.2 Dalí's telegram to Buñuel, November 6, 1982.

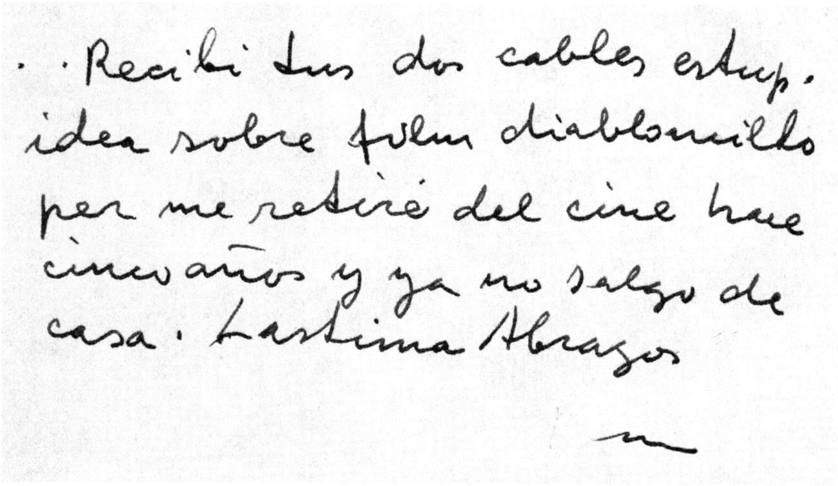

Recibí tus dos cables estup.
idea sobre film diabloncillo
pero me retiré del cine hace
cinco años y ya no salgo de
casa. Lástima Abrazos

Figure 36.3 Buñuel's reply to Dalí's telegram.

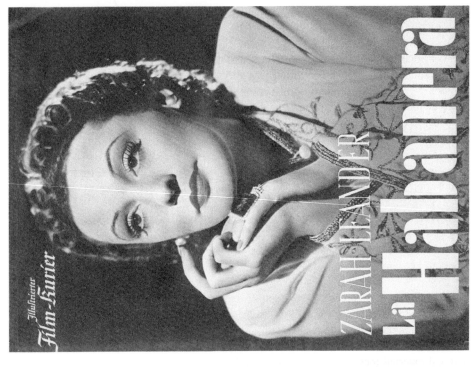

Figure 39.2 Zarah Leander in Detlev Sierck's *La Habanera*, UFA, 1937.

Figure 39.1 Poster for *Carmen la de Triana*, Hispano-Film-Produktion, 1938.

Figure 39.3   Still from José Luis Sáenz de Heredia's *Raza*. Consejo de la Hispanidad, 1942.

Figure 39.4   Jorge Brum do Canto, *João Ratão*. Tobis Portuguesa, 1940.

Figure 50.1   Alícia en un món real. Norma Editorial, 2010, 115.

Figure 50.2 Ardalén. El Patito Editorial, 2012, 37.

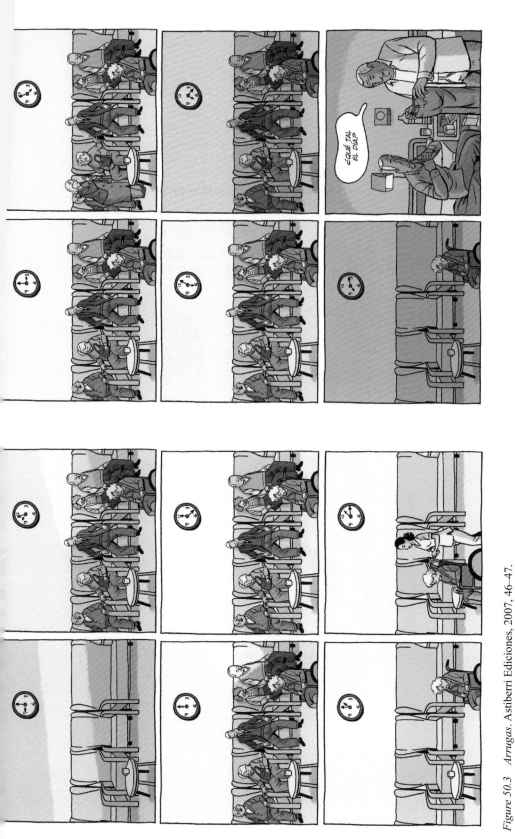

Figure 50.3 *Arrugas.* Astiberri Ediciones, 2007, 46–47.

Figure 50.4   *Alicia en un mundo real.* Book Cover. Norma Editorial, 2010.

Figure 50.5   Ardalén. Book Cover. El Patito Editorial, 2012.

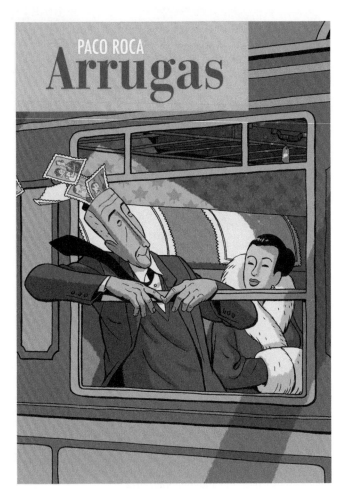

Figure 50.6 *Arrugas*. Book Cover. Astiberri Ediciones, 2007.

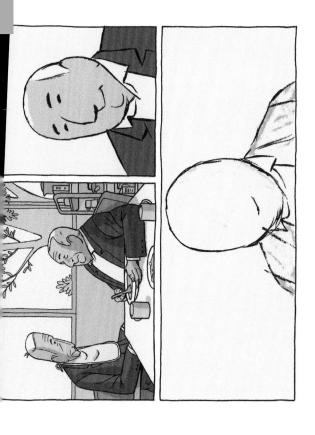

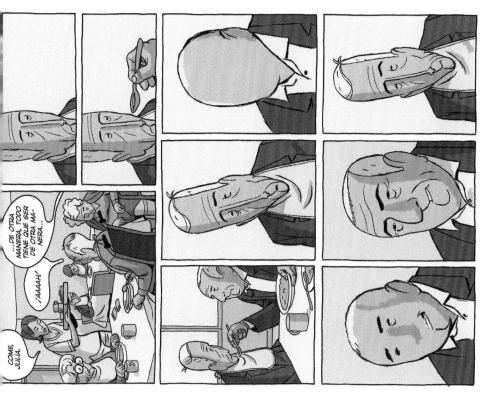

Figure 50.7 *Arrugas*. Astiberri Ediciones, 2007, 95–96.
© 2007 Guy Delcourt Productions–Paco Roca. By permission of Astiberri Ediciones.

INDEX

Note: Italicized page numbers indicate a figure on the corresponding page. Page numbers in bold indicate a table on the corresponding page.

Printed and bound by CPI Group (UK) Ltd, Croydon, CR0 4YY
08/05/2025
01864334-0001